The Founders' Constitution

The Founders' Constitution

Edited by
Philip B. Kurland
and
Ralph Lerner

VOLUME ONE
Major Themes

Liberty Fund

This book is published by Liberty Fund, Inc., a foundation established to encourage study of the ideal of a society of free and responsible individuals.

The cuneiform inscription that serves as our logo and as the design motif for our endpapers is the earliest-known written appearance of the word "freedom" (*amagi*), or "liberty." It is taken from a clay document written about 2300 B.C. in the Sumerian city-state of Lagash.

Philip B. Kurland was the William R. Kenan, Jr., Distinguished Service Professor in the College and professor in the Law School, University of Chicago.

Ralph Lerner is the Benjamin Franklin Professor in the College and professor in the Committee on Social Thought, University of Chicago.

23 24 25 26 27 P 11 10 9 8 7

Library of Congress Cataloging-in-Publication Data

The Founders' Constitution / edited by Philip B. Kurland and Ralph Lerner.
   p. cm.
  Originally published: Chicago: University of Chicago Press, 1987.
  Includes bibliographical references and index.
  Contents: v. 1. Major themes—v. 2. Preamble through Article 1, Section 8, Clause 4—v. 3. Article 1, Section 8, Clause 5, through Article 2, Section 1—v. 4. Article 2, Section 2, through Article 7—v. 5. Amendments I–XII.
   ISBN 0-86597-279-6 (set: pbk.: alk. paper)—ISBN 0-86597-302-4 (v. 1: pbk.: alk. paper)—ISBN 0-86597-303-2 (v. 2: pbk.: alk. paper)
   1. Constitutional history—United States—Sources. I. Kurland, Philip B. II. Lerner, Ralph.

KF4502 .F68 2000
342.73′029—dc21   99-052811

ISBN 0-86597-304-0 (v. 3 pbk.: alk. paper)
ISBN 0-86597-305-9 (v. 4 pbk.: alk. paper)
ISBN 0-86597-306-7 (v. 5 pbk.: alk. paper)

Liberty Fund, Inc.
11301 North Meridian Street
Carmel, Indiana 46032
libertyfund.org

Cover design by Erin Kirk New, Watkinsville, Georgia
Printed and bound by Sheridan Books, Chelsea, Michigan

To Carol

Contents

A Reader's Advisory

This collection of thoughts, opinions, and arguments of the Founders is meant to be useful to different kinds of readers, and hence useful in a variety of ways. How one uses this book will depend on the energy, time, and needs of the particular individual. Those desiring a general view of the state of the question that ultimately took the form of a specific phrase or clause in the Constitution will find materials assembled under the article, section, and clause numbers of that provision. Readers wishing to pursue their inquiries further are directed—within and at the end of each unit or chapter—to the location of other primary materials that they might find germane. Some of those materials are reprinted here under the headings of thematic chapters in volume 1 or under other, closely related, constitutional clauses, and their location will be so indicated. Many other documents will be of a kind that we could not accommodate within the already stretched confines of this collection; references to their published locations are clearly noted.

Other users may be interested less in the exact language of the Constitution's text than in the more general questions of political science and political practice that informed the making of that frame of government. Those readers may find it more useful to begin with one or more of the thematic chapters of volume 1 and then follow those leads into the appropriate clauses of the Constitution.

From these remarks it should become clear that this collection may be engaged at any number of points. The oversharp distinction between theoretical reflection and practical activity was alien to the leading members of the Founders' generation. They usually thought and acted as though theory and practice should inform each other rather than remain in separate compartments. The arrangement of this collection is meant to foster that kind of free movement and interchange. Investigators and browsers alike may trace their own paths starting from their particular points of departure. This is not to deny that the Constitution of 1787 has its own beginning, middle, and end. In urging readers to enter this collection at whatever juncture their need or curiosity suggests, we do not mean to discount the logic underlying the order of discussion in volume 1. But, again, our primary intention is that this collection be serviceable to a wide range of possible users. We have recognized that few are likely to read this book from cover to cover and have made our editorial judgments and arrangements accordingly.

We have sought to find a middle ground between needlessly duplicating texts that could with good reason have been included under more than one head, and requiring repeated search for cross-references. On the other hand, we have not hesitated to disassemble a large and many-faceted discussion and range its parts under several headings. Throughout, we have tried to anticipate the modes of inquiry of the likely readers.

References to documents follow a consistent pattern both in the cross-references (in the detailed tables of contents) and in the indexes. Where a document in volume 1 is being cited, reference is to chapter and document number: thus, for example, ch. 15, no. 23. Where the document is to be found in one of the subsequent volumes, which are organized by Constitutional article, section, and clause, or by amendment, reference is in this mode: 1.8.8, no. 12; or, Amend. I (religion), no. 66. Each document heading consists of its serial number in that particular chapter; an author and title (or letter writer and addressee, or speaker and forum); date of publication, writing, or speaking; and, where not given in the first part of the heading, an identification of the source of the text being reprinted. These sources are presented in short-title form, the author of the source volume being presumed (unless otherwise noted) to be the first proper name mentioned in the document heading. Thus, for example, in the case of a letter from Alexander Hamilton to Governor George Clinton, "Papers 1:425–28" would be understood to refer to the edition fully described under "Hamilton, Papers" in the list of short titles found at the back of each volume.

A somewhat different form has been followed in the case of the proceedings of the Constitutional Convention that met in Philadelphia from late May to mid-September of 1787. As might be expected, we have included many extracts from the various records kept by the participants while they were deliberating over the shape and character of a new charter of government. For any particular chapter or unit, those extracts have been grouped as a single document, titled "Records of the Federal Convention," and placed undated in that chapter's proper time slot. The bracketed note that precedes each segment within that selection of the "Records" lists the volume and opening page numbers in the printed source (Max Farrand's edition), the name of the participant whose notes are here being reproduced (overwhelmingly Madison, but also Mason, Yates, others, and the Convention's official Journal), and the month and day of 1787 when the reported transaction took place.

We have followed the orthography and typographical style of whatever edition of the text is being cited. Where those editions seek to preserve the irregularities of eighteenth-century manuscripts, readers may expect to encounter many misspellings. It seems that among the Founders only Franklin the printer had a sure hand in this respect. Nor ought one to be surprised by the grammatical incoherence of notes—for example, Madison's—taken in the midst of debate by men who were active participants and not mere reporters.

We are pleased to acknowledge the help that we have received from individuals and institutions in preparing this manuscript and bringing it to publication. Faithful and intelligent diligence was exercised by our editorial assistants: Dr. Gayle McKeen, Michael A. McAlister, Joshua Lerner, and Benjamin Fiedler. Unreserved and expert criticisms of the introductory essays in volume 1 were bestowed by Professors Marvin Meyers (Brandeis University), Thomas S. Schrock (University of California, Santa Barbara), Gerald Stourzh (University of Vienna), and Nathan Tarcov (University of Chicago). Needless to say, our sins of editorial omission and commission remain ours and not theirs who gladly tried to shield us from blunder.

If "money is with propriety considered as the vital principle of the body politic" (as Hamilton, and Hobbes before him, observed), no less is it the blood even of scholarly publishing. Our project to help bring the Founders' Constitution back into this generation's consciousness would have come to nought but for the confidence and support of benefactors who were pleased by the notion and equally pleased to leave all further decisions to the editors. For this we (and, we hope, our readers) owe special thanks to the Institute for Educational Affairs and its then-president, Philip N. Marcus. We have made ample use of the facilities and services afforded by The College and The Law School of The University of Chicago. And we have had the continuous unbounded assistance and loyalty of Mrs. Artie Scott even though it has proved the first publication in thirty years of one of the editors that she has not typed and retyped from beginning to end.

Introduction

This is an anthology of reasons and of the political arguments that thoughtful men and women drew from, and used to support, those reasons. We believe that those reasons and political arguments have enduring interest and significance for anyone who purports to think about constitutional government in general and the Constitution of the United States in particular. For those who know in advance that thought is at bottom reducible to interest, or who regard political argument as synonymous with ideology, such a belief is at best naive. Yet we venture to assert that that belief is not merely personal or idiosyncratic, however quaint it might appear. For our belief in the continuing relevance of the Founders' Constitution and of the arguments that centered on it is itself based on reasons.

It would, however, be foolish and obstinate to deny that many teachers, students, and practitioners who might examine these assembled writings would be disposed—indeed powerfully disposed—against the premise of this work. They too would have their reasons. Common usage and custom now casually equate thought and ideology, neither caring nor wishing to strike out the sense of tendentious, partisan argumentation implicit in the latter term. Political argument, it is asserted, is apologetics for something deeper, something material, something concealed. "What's he really after?" people ask, certain that the visible argument is only discreet drapery. One would have to have lived very little in the world not to know that political life is suffused with pleasant-sounding nonsense parading as grave argumentation. The sound rule, then, would seem to be: in case of doubt, doubt.

Beyond this fundamental skepticism lies another set of misgivings that work against taking these arguments of yesteryear seriously. By immersing ourselves in seventeenth- and eighteenth-century documents and arguments, we are in effect seeking to recover an "original understanding" of those who agitated for, proposed, argued over, and ultimately voted for or against the Constitution of 1787. Such an effort at recovery might be faulted on at least three grounds. The first and most obvious misgiving concerns the historical effort itself: we have no way of recovering the intentions of a widely scattered and long-since-dead generation of political actors. Being utterly dependent on the chance survival of arguments committed to paper, we are left in the dark concerning whatever else was thought but not said, said but not written, written but not saved, saved but not found. Needless to say, we are almost utterly in the dark about the manner in which arguments were made or received: the wink, the look of disgust, the detection of sophisms, are rarely matters of record and most often are matters of fanciful speculation by the reader. Very seldom indeed, then, can we speak with simple confidence of what this or that provision meant for eighteenth-century Americans.

Even speaking of such an aggregation as a whole may be suspect. Notwithstanding the glowing account of "one connected, fertile, wide spreading country" as the providentially designated inheritance of "a band of brethren" (John Jay, *Federalist,* no. 2), America might better be seen as a collection of highly diverse, discrete settlements, more intimately acquainted with England than with one another, more closely tied to their ancestral home (three months' sea voyage away) than to their neighbors. Under these circumstances the search for a single state of mind is unhistorical, however gratifying to the historical investigator. That diversity, moreover, characterized the individual states perhaps as much as the aggregation. And, as is usually the case, the least favored, least educated, least prominent portions of the population were the least heard and the least likely to be heard two hundred years after the fact. As a record of reasons and arguments, then, a collection of surviving paper is necessarily slanted.

Finally, the effort to recover past ways of thinking may be, in this instance, simply irrelevant, excusable perhaps in historians of a certain persuasion, but of little or no practical import. For does not the effort presuppose something like a coherent, guiding intention, and is not that given the lie by the fact that the Philadelphia Convention had to truck and barter, compromise and fudge, down to the bitter end in order to have any constitution at all to propose to the people? Were not the leading advocates of the Constitution disappointed and even disgusted by various features they were obliged to accept? Given the many concessions to expediency that marked the proceedings, is it not preposterous to look for and expect coherence, clarity, and consistency? Furthermore, even were a coherent political argument to be discovered, what great weight would it have? The fears and hopes of a generation some of whose members could still recall agitation over the Stuart Pretender can have little bearing on the fears and hopes of a generation preoccupied with ICBMs and entitlement programs. If the Constitution is to be a viable instrument of governance, then, it must (as it has to a great degree) cut itself free from its eighteenth-century moorings. The thought of the Founders, even to the extent it is discoverable, may be curious, even at times amusing or maddening, but it cannot be binding.

These are some of the reasons—by no means trivial, and certainly current and persistent—that might incline the holder of this volume to wish to conserve time and energy and read no further. Yet we think that to act on that inclination would be a mistake, if our own experience is any guide. Prompted neither by antiquarianism nor by simple piety, we have come to discover pleasures, second thoughts, and better understanding in matters that we once believed we understood tolerably well. We are loath to dangle before the reader yet another promise that the crooked will be made straight and the rough places plain; we promise, rather, complexity and complication. The simplistic truisms (clipped coinage if ever there was such) that pass for good currency today may be detected more readily for what they are by a timely recourse to the source, the reasonings of the political actors themselves. Any fair-minded reader can discover that those actors—politicians, land speculators, philosophers, village-pump orators, historians, ordinary and not-so-ordinary lawyers, common folk with little or no schooling, statesmen with analytical powers developed through long study and closely observed experience—that all those are people whose thoughts are worth knowing better. Far from being struck by their simplemindedness or paranoia, we are impressed rather by their political literacy, the vigor and the articulateness of their arguments, and the absence of condescension from their complex, even sophisticated, reasoning. The level of their public political discourse is simply remarkable.

All this, however, speaks to pleasure and the surprise of being pleased. It does not reach the core of the objections or misgivings outlined above. Can one discover what was intended? Can one trust what one does discover? Does it matter?

Some things can be discovered. There is an original understanding about a number of constitutional provisions. There is the possibility of discovering how a particular concept or institutional arrangement developed, growing clear and simple or (alternatively) unclear and complex. None of such discoveries admits of unequivocal demonstrative proof, but students of history and of the law usually have settled for probable causes, and the record assembled here affords the possibility of making quite a few such cases.

What weight to give to such nondemonstrative arguments is a harder question. It is impossible to presume that one has at hand a fair sample of all the arguments, all the considerations, that entered into a position or into the decision to adopt a position. Yet we do have more than the precipitate of unknowable private reasons and private decisions. Because the largest decisions were necessarily public—to propose, to support or oppose, to vote—and because those public occasions were repeated—in the Philadelphia Convention, in the press, in the courthouses and taverns where the politically relevant part of the people met and argued, and in the state ratifying conventions—there was a good opportunity for a broad range of arguments to be put forth and to leave some traces. Then, too, the larger issues stirred by the events leading up to the proposal and adoption of the Constitution were hardly novelties of 1787–88 and in many cases not even novelties of 1774–76. Self-government in America dates from the earliest charters of the seventeenth century. The practical and theoretical issues that vexed contemporary British political life and thought were not alien to American readers of Sidney and Locke, Cato and Montesquieu, Blackstone

and Burgh. The issues, accordingly, were familiar, the occasion pressing, the participants attentive and broadly informed, and the resulting public debate vigorous, full, and open. Twenty-two months elapsed between the Annapolis commissioners' call for a full convention and New York State's ratification of the Constitution. Just about everything that had to be aired was aired and, more often than not, aired forcefully and well.

Granting the possibility of all this leaves still unanswered the most difficult question: what difference does it make? In one sense, none. Clio's career in the courts has left her and the courts rather the worse for wear. Courts have had a hard enough time taking yesterday's legislative history seriously; it would be fatuous to expect very much direct effect from researches into a more remote and ambiguous record.

In another sense, very much might be hoped for. The duration of the eighteenth-century debates, the quality of the participants, the wide-ranging considerations that were raised, the high degree of self-consciousness that attended the proceedings: all made for a singular moment, an occasion of rare interest and value for discovering anew the foundations of a complex political and economic order. To the extent that the Constitution still matters—as a framework, as a statement of broad purposes, as a point of recurring reference, as a legitimation of further developments, as a restraint on the overbearing and the righteous—to that extent it is worthwhile to try to enter into that world of discourse. The Founders prided themselves almost never on their lineage and rarely on their wealth, but rather on their reasonableness. It is worth taking note of the candor and quiet confidence that could state matter-of-factly: "My motives must remain in the depository of my own breast: My arguments will be open to all, and may be judged of by all" (Alexander Hamilton, *Federalist*, no. 1). That self-presentation might be deemed naive, perhaps hypocritical, possibly irrelevant. But after all is said, there remain the arguments, the reasons, remaining to be examined, weighed, and judged.

Only those for whom reasons have no standing or value will casually cast these aside. But such perhaps are not to be counted among the readers of books. Those who read only to be confirmed in their views will find some, but not much, recompense in these pages; a judicious sampling here and there will do. But those who would run the risk of being vexed into further reflection will find their patience tried—and sometimes rewarded. It was a world of the leisurely essay, the hour-long sermon, a great hunger for the printed word, and a discerning appreciation for good argument. People are apt to savor slowly what they most enjoy, and the generation of the Founders had a great taste for political discourse.

Recurring, then, to these sources of the Founders' Constitution is a precondition for being able to see that Constitution whole: the reach—and limits—of their aspirations, the preoccupations of the day and of the morrow, the principles which they chose and shaped and thought worth preserving and bequeathing. By these they wished to be judged; and as if to guarantee that they would be so judged (to the extent that mortals may guarantee anything), they were assiduous record-keepers, preservers of documents, copiers of correspondence. The archivist-founder is a founder who invites his successors to scrutinize his principles and acts. It was and remains a standing invitation.

Confronted, however, with the sheer bulk of surviving materials, the successor might well regard the invitation less as an offer one cannot refuse than as an offer one dare not accept. At times it seems there is altogether too much irrelevant chaff to winnow. At other times the recurrence of nearly identical arguments tends to drain even the best of their force. One risks in turn being overcome by tedium or being cloyed. Our editorial selection has been guided by an awareness of those risks and by a clear sense of the use and limits of this collection.

We mean to present arguments of yesteryear that are worthy of reexamination and reconsideration today either because they were weighty then or because they are still telling or might yet lead to further reflection on the problems under discussion. In the finest cases, of course, all three considerations hold and the gulf of the intervening centuries disappears altogether. But whether the reader's immediate interests are historical or theoretical or practical, he is likely to find at hand a broad array of nontrivial reasons.

Here then is a sample of intelligence focused on the problems of establishing and maintaining free popular government, drawn from the two centuries between the beginnings under the early Stuarts and the end of the Marshall era. The earlier bound might not seem to require any justification: the earliest beginnings of American self-government were undertaken by Elizabethans, Jacobeans, Cavaliers, and Roundheads. The later bound is more problematic: why should the documentation of the Founders' Constitution go as far as 1835, or for that matter stop there? The short answer is that the debate did in fact continue beyond ratification, beyond the debates in the First Congress, beyond the turmoil over the Neutrality Proclamation and the Alien and Sedition Acts. The preoccupation with intentions and meanings was intense in the second generation as well—John Quincy Adams, Joseph Story, John C. Calhoun, Abraham Lincoln, come immediately to mind. But perhaps it is enough to say that some of the most extraordinary Founders were marked by extraordinary longevity. They lived long enough to observe and judge the fruits of their labors well beyond the events of '87: in the cases of John Adams and Jefferson thirty-nine years, of Jay forty-two, of Marshall forty-eight, of Madison forty-nine. Whether the same voices always spoke with the same accents is not our immediate concern. But it is a material fact that founders of this stature were in a position to supply a gloss to their earlier words and deeds. Their accounts of what they meant to do, however qualified and judged by their successors, clearly enjoy a special standing in the study of American constitutionalism.

Having said all that, however, we must own that this anthology, bulky as it is, omits much of importance and very much of interest. The complex politics of ratification can be perceived only dimly in these selections. The complex dynamics of the Philadelphia Convention—the barely averted collapse, the near-misses, the bluster and bluffing, the hard listening, the give-and-take—can barely be perceived in a nonsequential selection; for that the *Records of the Federal Convention* remain indispensable. Finally, it would take another kind of study to recover the social and economic setting in which thirteen dissimilar and distant states managed to mitigate their fears and jealousies and particular dreams, coping with diversity and distrust within their several borders even while overcoming to some measure diversity and distrust in the Union as a whole.

If these are questions and issues that are not central to this collection, it is not because we judge them trivial. Indeed, relative to the questions and issues that *are* central to this collection, these are hardly neglected by current scholarship and current curricula. What does strike us as sadly neglected is the Constitution itself, seen as the precipitate of hard thinking (and, yes, hard bargaining) by men of remarkable intelligence and seriousness. This collection is intended to make it easier for their intelligent and serious successors of today to come to see that for themselves. In the process, we hope, the Founders' reasons will be reexamined and their questions reconsidered, and their hope that among a self-governing people liberty and learning would support each other will come closer to fulfillment.

1

Fundamental Documents

Introduction

The very designation "fundamental" is in effect a claim that here one has touched bottom, reached bedrock. Relative to this, other matters are at best anticipatory, preliminary, or derivative. Where the subject is American constitutionalism and the Founders' Constitution, it takes no argument to give pride of place to the Constitution of 1787. But only a self-defeating literalism would leave it at that. American constitutionalism is embodied not only in *a* form of government but, from the outset, in a variety of modes and models—models to be followed or improved. Likewise, American constitutionalism comprehends not only the distribution of powers and organization of offices, but the declaration of rights. The most famous and influential of those forms and declarations may properly be designated fundamental and stand at the head of this collection.

The frequent reappearance of portions of these documents in the following chapters under one or another theme or constitutional provision suggests that these documents are fundamental not merely in the sense of sustaining but also in the sense of being pervasive. Beyond that, their recurrence points to the necessity of being able to see each of these documents as a whole, as the sum or more than the sum of its discrete parts. Their reproduc-

tion here in their entirety is a reminder that each of these public documents was presented to a candid (and even skeptical) world as a coherent whole. Whether ultimately persuasive or not, each has an internal logic that deserves to be seen as such.

One of the documents in this chapter might seem to be in the wrong company and hence in need of special justification. The excerpt from Edmund Burke's speech on conciliation with the American colonies (no. 2) can hardly be said to be a document of American constitutionalism, let alone a fundamental one. But constitutionalism, as the following chapters will develop at length, involves not only general forms and abstract declarations, but a particular people, a specific place, concrete circumstances. Burke's depiction of those details in the American case has never been surpassed. Whatever its shortcomings or oversimplifications, it captures the mood and situation of a people intent on defining and refining its notions of self-government. If that was the Americans' revolutionary moment, it was (as the size and contents of this collection amply testify) neither brief nor simple. In that sense the fundamental documents of the Founders' Constitution are not epilogue but prologue.

1

CONTINENTAL CONGRESS, DECLARATION
AND RESOLVES
14 Oct. 1774
Tansill 1–5

Whereas, since the close of the last war, the British parliament, claiming a power, of right, to bind the people of America by statutes in all cases whatsoever, hath, in some

acts, expressly imposed taxes on them, and in others, under various pretences, but in fact for the purpose of raising a revenue, hath imposed rates and duties payable in these colonies, established a board of commissioners, with unconstitutional powers, and extended the jurisdiction of courts of admiralty, not only for collecting the said duties, but for the trial of causes merely arising within the body of a county.

And whereas, in consequence of other statutes, judges, who before held only estates at will in their offices, have been made dependant on the crown alone for their salaries, and standing armies kept in times of peace: And whereas it has lately been resolved in parliament, that by force of a statute, made in the thirty-fifth year of the reign of King Henry the Eighth, colonists may be transported to England, and tried there upon accusations for treasons and misprisions, or concealments of treasons committed in the colonies, and by a late statute, such trials have been directed in cases therein mentioned:

And whereas, in the last session of parliament, three statutes were made; one entitled, "An act to discontinue, in such manner and for such time as are therein mentioned, the landing and discharging, lading, or shipping of goods, wares and merchandise, at the town, and within the harbour of Boston, in the province of Massachusetts-Bay in North-America;" another entitled, "An act for the better regulating the government of the province of Massachusetts-Bay in New England;" and another entitled, "An act for the impartial administration of justice, in the cases of persons questioned for any act done by them in the execution of the law, or for the suppression of riots and tumults, in the province of the Massachusetts-Bay in New England;" and another statute was then made, "for making more effectual provision for the government of the province of Quebec, etc." All which statutes are impolitic, unjust, and cruel, as well as unconstitutional, and most dangerous and destructive of American rights:

And whereas, assemblies have been frequently dissolved, contrary to the rights of the people, when they attempted to deliberate on grievances; and their dutiful, humble, loyal, and reasonable petitions to the crown for redress, have been repeatedly treated with contempt, by his Majesty's ministers of state:

The good people of the several colonies of New-Hampshire, Massachusetts-Bay, Rhode-Island and Providence Plantations, Connecticut, New-York, New-Jersey, Pennsylvania, Newcastle, Kent, and Sussex on Delaware, Maryland, Virginia, North-Carolina, and South-Carolina, justly alarmed at these arbitrary proceedings of parliament and administration, have severally elected, constituted, and appointed deputies to meet, and sit in general Congress, in the city of Philadelphia, in order to obtain such establishment, as that their religion, laws, and liberties, may not be subverted: Whereupon the deputies so appointed being now assembled, in a full and free representation of these colonies, taking into their most serious consideration, the best means of attaining the ends aforesaid, do, in the first place, as Englishmen, their ancestors in like cases have usually done, for asserting and vindicating their rights and liberties, DECLARE,

That the inhabitants of the English colonies in North-America, by the immutable laws of nature, the principles of the English constitution, and the several charters or compacts, have the following RIGHTS:

Resolved, N. C. D. 1. That they are entitled to life, liberty and property: and they have never ceded to any foreign power whatever, a right to dispose of either without their consent.

Resolved, N. C. D. 2. That our ancestors, who first settled these colonies, were at the time of their emigration from the mother country, entitled to all the rights, liberties, and immunities of free and natural-born subjects, within the realm of England.

Resolved, N. C. D. 3. That by such emigration they by no means forfeited, surrendered, or lost any of those rights, but that they were, and their descendants now are, entitled to the exercise and enjoyment of all such of them, as their local and other circumstances enable them to exercise and enjoy.

Resolved, 4. That the foundation of English liberty, and of all free government, is a right in the people to participate in their legislative council: and as the English colonists are not represented, and from their local and other circumstances, cannot properly be represented in the British parliament, they are entitled to a free and exclusive power of legislation in their several provincial legislatures, where their right of representation can alone be preserved, in all cases of taxation and internal polity, subject only to the negative of their sovereign, in such manner as has been heretofore used and accustomed: But, from the necessity of the case, and a regard to the mutual interest of both countries, we cheerfully consent to the operation of such acts of the British parliament, as are bona fide, restrained to the regulation of our external commerce, for the purpose of securing the commercial advantages of the whole empire to the mother country, and the commercial benefits of its respective members; excluding every idea of taxation internal or external, for raising a revenue on the subjects, in America, without their consent.

Resolved, N. C. D. 5. That the respective colonies are entitled to the common law of England, and more especially to the great and inestimable privilege of being tried by their peers of the vicinage, according to the course of that law.

Resolved, 6. That they are entitled to the benefit of such of the English statutes, as existed at the time of their colonization; and which they have, by experience, respectively found to be applicable to their several local and other circumstances.

Resolved, N. C. D. 7. That these, his majesty's colonies, are likewise entitled to all the immunities and privileges granted and confirmed to them by royal charters, or secured by their several codes of provincial laws.

Resolved, N. C. D. 8. That they have a right peaceably to assemble, consider of their grievances, and petition the king; and that all prosecutions, prohibitory proclamations, and commitments for the same, are illegal.

Resolved, N. C. D. 9. That the keeping a standing army in these colonies, in times of peace, without the consent of the legislature of that colony, in which such army is kept, is against law.

Resolved, N. C. D. 10. It is indispensably necessary to good government, and rendered essential by the English constitution, that the constituent branches of the legislature be independent of each other; that, therefore, the exercise of legislative power in several colonies, by a council appointed, during pleasure, by the crown, is unconstitutional, dangerous and destructive to the freedom of American legislation.

All and each of which the aforesaid deputies, in behalf of themselves, and their constituents, do claim, demand, and insist on, as their indubitable rights and liberties; which cannot be legally taken from them, altered or abridged by any power whatever, without their own consent, by their representatives in their several provincial legislatures.

In the course of our inquiry, we find many infringements and violations of the foregoing rights, which, from an ardent desire, that harmony and mutual intercourse of affection and interest may be restored, we pass over for the present, and proceed to state such acts and measures as have been adopted since the last war, which demonstrate a system formed to enslave America.

Resolved, N. C. D. That the following acts of parliament are infringements and violations of the rights of the colonists; and that the repeal of them is essentially necessary, in order to restore harmony between Great-Britain and the American colonies, viz.

The several acts of 4 Geo. III. ch. 15, and ch. 34.—5 Geo. III. ch. 25.—6 Geo. III. ch. 52.—7 Geo. III. ch. 41. and ch. 46.—8 Geo. III. ch. 22. which impose duties for the purpose of raising a revenue in America, extend the power of the admiralty courts beyond their ancient limits, deprive the American subject of trial by jury, authorise the judges certificate to indemnify the prosecutor from damages, that he might otherwise be liable to, requiring oppressive security from a claimant of ships and goods seized, before he shall be allowed to defend his property, and are subversive of American rights.

Also 12 Geo. III. ch. 24. intituled, "An act for the better securing his majesty's dockyards, magazines, ships, ammunition, and stores," which declares a new offence in America, and deprives the American subject of a constitutional trial by jury of the vicinage, by authorising the trial of any person, charged with the committing any offence described in the said act, out of the realm, to be indicted and tried for the same in any shire or county within the realm.

Also the three acts passed in the last session of parliament, for stopping the port and blocking up the harbour of Boston, for altering the charter and government of Massachusetts-Bay, and that which is entitled, "An act for the better administration of justice, etc."

Also the act passed in the same session for establishing the Roman Catholic religion, in the province of Quebec, abolishing the equitable system of English laws, and erecting a tyranny there, to the great danger (from so total a dissimilarity of religion, law and government) of the neighbouring British colonies, by the assistance of whose blood and treasure the said country was conquered from France.

Also the act passed in the same session, for the better providing suitable quarters for officers and soldiers in his majesty's service, in North-America.

Also, that the keeping a standing army in several of these colonies, in time of peace, without the consent of the legislature of that colony, in which such army is kept, is against law.

To these grievous acts and measures, Americans cannot submit, but in hopes their fellow subjects in Great-Britain will, on a revision of them, restore us to that state, in which both countries found happiness and prosperity, we have for the present, only resolved to pursue the following peaceable measures: 1. To enter into a non-importation, non-consumption, and non-exportation agreement or association. 2. To prepare an address to the people of Great-Britain, and a memorial to the inhabitants of British America: and 3. To prepare a loyal address to his majesty, agreeable to resolutions already entered into.

2

EDMUND BURKE, SPEECH ON CONCILIATION
WITH THE COLONIES
22 Mar. 1775
Works 1:464–71

In this character of the Americans, a love of freedom is the predominating feature which marks and distinguishes the whole: and as an ardent is always a jealous affection, your colonies become suspicious, restive, and untractable, whenever they see the least attempt to wrest from them by force, or shuffle from them by chicane, what they think the only advantage worth living for. This fierce spirit of liberty is stronger in the English colonies probably than in any other people of the earth; and this from a great variety of powerful causes; which, to understand the true temper of their minds, and the direction which this spirit takes, it will not be amiss to lay open somewhat more largely.

First, the people of the colonies are descendants of Englishmen. England, Sir, is a nation, which still I hope respects, and formerly adored, her freedom. The colonists emigrated from you when this part of your character was most predominant; and they took this bias and direction the moment they parted from your hands. They are therefore not only devoted to liberty, but to liberty according to English ideas, and on English principles. Abstract liberty, like other mere abstractions, is not to be found. Liberty inheres in some sensible object; and every nation has formed to itself some favourite point, which by way of eminence becomes the criterion of their happiness. It happened, you know, Sir, that the great contests for freedom in this country were from the earliest times chiefly upon the question of taxing. Most of the contests in the ancient commonwealths turned primarily on the right of election of magistrates; or on the balance among the several orders of the state. The question of money was not with them so immediate. But in England it was otherwise. On this point of taxes the ablest pens, and most eloquent tongues, have been exercised; the greatest spirits have acted and suffered. In order to give the fullest satisfaction concerning the importance of this point, it was not only necessary for those who in argument defended the excellence of the English constitution, to insist on this privilege of granting money as a dry point of fact, and to prove, that the right had been acknowledged in ancient parchments, and blind usages, to reside in a certain body called a House of Commons. They went much farther; they attempted to prove, and they succeeded, that in theory it ought to be so, from the particular nature of a House of Commons, as an immediate representative of the people; whether the old records had delivered this oracle or not. They took infinite pains to inculcate, as a fundamental principle, that in all monarchies the people must in effect themselves, mediately or immediately, possess the power of granting their own money, or no shadow of liberty could subsist. The colonies draw from you, as with their life-blood, these ideas and principles. Their love of liberty, as with you, fixed and attached on this specific point of taxing. Liberty might be safe, or might be endangered, in twenty other particulars, without their being much pleased or alarmed. Here they felt its pulse; and as they found that beat, they thought themselves sick or sound. I do not say whether they were right or wrong in applying your general arguments to their own case. It is not easy indeed to make a monopoly of theorems and corollaries. The fact is, that they did thus apply those general arguments; and your mode of governing them, whether through lenity or indolence, through wisdom or mistake, confirmed them in the imagination, that they, as well as you, had an interest in these common principles.

They were further confirmed in this pleasing error by the form of their provincial legislative assemblies. Their governments are popular in a high degree; some are merely popular; in all, the popular representative is the most weighty; and this share of the people in their ordinary government never fails to inspire them with lofty sentiments, and with a strong aversion from whatever tends to deprive them of their chief importance.

If anything were wanting to this necessary operation of the form of government, religion would have given it a complete effect. Religion, always a principle of energy, in this new people is no way worn out or impaired; and their mode of professing it is also one main cause of this free spirit. The people are Protestants; and of that kind which is the most adverse to all implicit submission of mind and opinion. This is a persuasion not only favourable to liberty, but built upon it. I do not think, Sir, that the reason of this averseness in the dissenting churches, from all that looks like absolute government, is so much to be sought in their religious tenets, as in their history. Every one knows that the Roman Catholic religion is at least coeval with most of the governments where it prevails; that it has generally gone hand in hand with them, and received great favour and every kind of support from authority. The Church of England too was formed from her cradle under the nursing care of regular government. But the dissenting interests have sprung up in direct opposition to all the ordinary powers of the world; and could justify that opposition only on a strong claim to natural liberty. Their very existence depended on the powerful and unremitted assertion of that claim. All Protestantism, even the most cold and passive, is a sort of dissent. But the religion most prevalent in our northern colonies is a refinement on the principle of resistance; it is the dissidence of dissent, and the Protestantism of the Protestant religion. This religion, under a variety of denominations agreeing in nothing but in the communion of the spirit of liberty, is predominant in most of the northern provinces; where the Church of England, notwithstanding its legal rights, is in reality no more than a sort of private sect, not composing most probably the tenth of the people. The colonists left England when this spirit was high, and in the emigrants was the highest of all; and even that stream of foreigners, which has been constantly flowing into these colonies, has, for the greatest part, been composed of dissenters from the establishments of their several countries, and have brought with them a temper and character far from alien to that of the people with whom they mixed.

Sir, I can perceive by their manner, that some gentlemen object to the latitude of this description; because in the southern colonies the Church of England forms a large body, and has a regular establishment. It is certainly true. There is, however, a circumstance attending these colonies, which, in my opinion, fully counterbalances this difference, and makes the spirit of liberty still more high and haughty than in those to the northward. It is, that in Virginia and the Carolinas they have a vast multitude of slaves. Where this is the case in any part of the world, those who are free, are by far the most proud and jealous of their freedom. Freedom is to them not only an enjoyment, but a kind of rank and privilege. Not seeing there, that freedom, as in countries where it is a common blessing, and as broad and general as the air, may be united with much abject toil, with great misery, with all the exterior of servitude, liberty looks, amongst them, like something that is more noble and liberal. I do not mean, Sir, to commend the superior morality of this sentiment, which has at least as much pride as virtue in it; but I cannot alter the nature of man. The fact is so; and these people of the southern colonies are much more strongly, and with a higher and more stubborn spirit, attached to liberty, than those to the northward. Such were all the ancient commonwealths; such were our Gothic ancestors; such in our days were the Poles; and such will be all masters of slaves, who are not slaves themselves. In such a people, the haughtiness of domination combines with the spirit of freedom, fortifies it, and renders it invincible.

Permit me, Sir, to add another circumstance in our colonies, which contributes no mean part towards the growth and effect of this untractable spirit. I mean their education. In no country perhaps in the world is the law so general a study. The profession itself is numerous and powerful; and in most provinces it takes the lead. The greater number of the deputies sent to the congress were lawyers. But all who read, and most do read, endeavour to obtain some smattering in that science. I have been told by an eminent bookseller, that in no branch of his business, after tracts of popular devotion, were so many books as those on the law exported to the plantations. The colonists have now fallen into the way of printing them for their own use. I hear that they have sold nearly as many of Blackstone's Commentaries in America as in England. General Gage marks out this disposition very particularly in a letter on your table. He states, that all the people in his government are lawyers, or smatterers in law; and that in Boston they have been enabled, by successful chicane, wholly to evade many parts of one of your capital penal constitutions. The smartness of debate will say, that this knowledge ought to teach them more clearly the rights of legislature, their obligations to obedience, and the penalties of rebellion. All this is mighty well. But my honourable and learned friend on the floor, who condescends to mark what I say for animadversion, will disdain that ground. He has heard, as well as I, that when great honours and great emoluments do not win over this knowledge to the service of the state, it is a formidable adversary to government. If the spirit be not tamed and broken by these happy methods, it is stubborn and litigious. *Abeunt studia in mores.* This study renders men acute, inquisitive, dexterous, prompt in attack, ready in defence, full of resources. In other countries, the people, more simple, and of a less mercurial cast, judge of an ill principle in government only by an actual grievance; here they anticipate the evil, and judge of the pressure of the grievance by the badness of the principle. They augur misgovernment at a distance; and snuff the approach of tyranny in every tainted breeze.

The last cause of this disobedient spirit in the colonies is hardly less powerful than the rest, as it is not merely moral, but laid deep in the natural constitution of things. Three thousand miles of ocean lie between you and them. No contrivance can prevent the effect of this distance in weakening government. Seas roll, and months pass, between the order and the execution; and the want of a speedy explanation of a single point is enough to defeat a whole system. You have, indeed, winged ministers of vengeance, who carry your bolts in their pounces to the remotest verge of the sea. But there a power steps in, that limits the arrogance of raging passions and furious elements, and says, "So far shalt thou go, and no farther." Who are you, that should fret and rage, and bite the chains of nature?—Nothing worse happens to you than does to all nations who have extensive empire; and it happens in all the forms into which empire can be thrown. In large bodies, the circulation of power must be less vigorous at the extremities. Nature has said it. The Turk cannot govern Egypt, and Arabia, and Curdistan, as he governs Thrace; nor has he the same dominion in Crimea and Algiers, which he has at Brusa and Smyrna. Despotism itself is obliged to truck and huckster. The Sultan gets such obedience as he can. He governs with a loose rein, that he may govern at all; and the whole of the force and vigour of his authority in his centre is derived from a prudent relaxation in all his borders. Spain, in her provinces, is, perhaps, not so well obeyed as you are in yours. She complies too; she submits; she watches times. This is the immutable condition, the eternal law, of extensive and detached empire.

Then, Sir, from these six capital sources; of descent; of form of government; of religion in the northern provinces; of manners in the southern; of education; of the remoteness of situation from the first mover of government; from all these causes a fierce spirit of liberty has grown up. It has grown with the growth of the people in your colonies, and increased with the increase of their wealth; a spirit, that unhappily meeting with an exercise of power in England, which, however lawful, is not reconcilable to any ideas of liberty, much less with theirs, has kindled this flame that is ready to consume us.

I do not mean to commend either the spirit in this excess, or the moral causes which produce it. Perhaps a more smooth and accommodating spirit of freedom in them would be more acceptable to us. Perhaps ideas of liberty might be desired, more reconcilable with an arbitrary and boundless authority. Perhaps we might wish the colonists to be persuaded, that their liberty is more secure when held in trust for them by us (as their guardians during a perpetual minority) than with any part of it in their own hands. The question is, not whether their spirit deserves praise or blame, but—what, in the name of God, shall we do with it? You have before you the object, such as it is, with all its glories, with all its imperfections on its head. You see the magnitude; the importance; the temper; the habits; the disorders. By all these considerations we are strongly urged to determine something concerning it. We are called upon to fix some rule and line for our future conduct, which may give a little stability to our politics, and prevent the return of such unhappy deliberations as the present. Every such return will bring the matter before us in a still more untractable form. For, what astonishing and incredible things have we not seen already! What monsters have not been generated from this unnatural contention! Whilst every principle of authority and resistance has been pushed, upon both sides, as far as it would go, there is nothing so solid and certain, either in reasoning or in practice, that has not been shaken. Until very lately, all authority in America seemed to be nothing but an emanation from yours. Even the popular part of the colony constitution derived all its activity, and its first vital movement, from the pleasure of the crown. We thought, Sir, that the utmost which the discontented colonists could do, was to disturb authority; we never dreamt they could of themselves supply it; knowing in general what an operose business it is to establish a government absolutely new. But having, for our purposes in this contention, resolved, that none but an obedient assembly should sit; the humours of the people there, finding all passage through the legal channel stopped, with great violence broke out another way. Some provinces have tried their experiment, as we have tried ours; and theirs has succeeded. They have formed a government sufficient for its purposes, without the bustle of a revolution, or the troublesome formality of an election. Evident necessity, and tacit consent, have done the business in an instant. So well they have done it, that Lord Dunmore (the account is among the fragments on your table) tells you, that the new institution is infinitely better obeyed than the ancient government ever was in its most fortunate periods. Obedience is what makes government, and not the names by which it is called; not the name of governor, as formerly, or committee, as at present. This new government has originated directly from the people; and was not transmitted through any of the ordinary artificial media of a positive constitution. It was not a manufacture ready formed, and transmitted to them in that condition from England. The evil arising from hence is this; that the colonists having once found the possibility of enjoying the advantages of order in the midst of a struggle for liberty, such struggles will not henceforward seem so terrible to the settled and sober part of mankind as they had appeared before the trial.

Pursuing the same plan of punishing by the denial of the exercise of government to still greater lengths, we wholly abrogated the ancient government of Massachusetts. We were confident that the first feeling, if not the very prospect of anarchy, would instantly enforce a complete submission. The experiment was tried. A new, strange, unexpected face of things appeared. Anarchy is found tolerable. A vast province has now subsisted, and subsisted in a considerable degree of health and vigour, for near a twelvemonth, without governor, without public council, without judges, without executive magistrates. How long it will continue in this state, or what may arise out of this unheard-of situation, how can the wisest of us conjecture? Our late experience has taught us that many of those fundamental principles, formerly believed infallible, are either not of the importance they were imagined to be; or that we have not at all adverted to some other far more important and far more powerful principles, which entirely overrule those we had considered as omnipotent. I am much against any further experiments, which tend to put to the proof any more of these allowed opinions, which contribute so much to the public tranquillity. In effect, we suffer as much at home by this loosening of all ties, and this concussion of all established opinions, as we do abroad. For, in order to prove that the Americans have no right to their liberties, we are every day endeavouring to subvert the maxims which preserve the whole spirit of our own. To prove that the Americans ought not to be free, we are obliged to depreciate the value of freedom itself; and we never seem to gain a paltry advantage over them in debate, without attacking some of those principles, or deriding some of those feelings, for which our ancestors have shed their blood.

3

VIRGINIA DECLARATION OF RIGHTS
12 June 1776
Mason Papers 1:287–89

A DECLARATION OF RIGHTS made by the Representatives of the good people of VIRGINIA, assembled in full and free Convention; which rights do pertain to them and their posterity, as the basis and foundation of Government.

1. That all men are by nature equally free and independent, and have certain inherent rights, of which, when they enter into a state of society, they cannot, by any compact, deprive or divest their posterity; namely, the enjoyment of life and liberty, with the means of acquiring and possessing property, and pursuing and obtaining happiness and safety.

2. That all power is vested in, and consequently derived from, the People; that magistrates are their trustees and servants, and at all times amenable to them.

3. That Government is, or ought to be, instituted for the common benefit, protection, and security of the people, nation, or community;—of all the various modes and forms of Government that is best which is capable of producing the greatest degree of happiness and safety, and is

most effectually secured against the danger of mal-administration;—and that, whenever any Government shall be found inadequate or contrary to these purposes, a majority of the community hath an indubitable, unalienable, and indefeasible right, to reform, alter, or abolish it, in such manner as shall be judged most conducive to the publick weal.

4. That no man, or set of men, are entitled to exclusive or separate emoluments and privileges from the community, but in consideration of publick services; which, not being descendible, neither ought the offices of Magistrate, Legislator, or Judge, to be hereditary.

5. That the Legislative and Executive powers of the State should be separate and distinct from the Judicative; and, that the members of the two first may be restrained from oppression, by feeling and participating the burdens of the people, they should, at fixed periods, be reduced to a private station, return into that body from which they were originally taken, and the vacancies be supplied by frequent, certain, and regular elections, in which all, or any part of the former members, to be again eligible, or ineligible, as the law shall direct.

6. That elections of members to serve as Representatives of the people, in Assembly, ought to be free; and that all men, having sufficient evidence of permanent common interest with, and attachment to, the community, have the right of suffrage, and cannot be taxed or deprived of their property for publick uses without their own consent or that of their Representative so elected, nor bound by any law to which they have not, in like manner, assented, for the publick good.

7. That all power of suspending laws, or the execution of laws, by any authority, without consent of the Representatives of the people, is injurious to their rights, and ought not to be exercised.

8. That in all capital or criminal prosecutions a man hath a right to demand the cause and nature of his accusation, to be confronted with the accusers and witnesses, to call for evidence in his favour, and to a speedy trial by an impartial jury of his vicinage, without whose unanimous consent he cannot be found guilty, nor can he be compelled to give evidence against himself; that no man be deprived of his liberty except by the law of the land, or the judgment of his peers.

9. That excessive bail ought not to be required, nor excessive fines imposed, nor cruel and unusual punishments inflicted.

10. That general warrants, whereby any officer or messenger may be commanded to search suspected places without evidence of a fact committed, or to seize any person or persons not named, or whose offence is not particularly described and supported by evidence, are grievous and oppressive, and ought not to be granted.

11. That in controversies respecting property, and in suits between man and man, the ancient trial by Jury is preferable to any other, and ought to be held sacred.

12. That the freedom of the Press is one of the greatest bulwarks of liberty, and can never be restrained but by despotick Governments.

13. That a well-regulated Militia, composed of the body

of the people, trained to arms, is the proper, natural, and safe defence of a free State; that Standing Armies, in time of peace, should be avoided as dangerous to liberty; and that, in all cases, the military should be under strict subordination to, and governed by, the civil power.

14. That the people have a right to uniform Government; and, therefore, that no Government separate from, or independent of, the Government of *Virginia,* ought to be erected or established within the limits thereof.

15. That no free Government, or the blessing of liberty, can be preserved to any people but by a firm adherence to justice, moderation, temperance, frugality, and virtue, and by frequent recurrence to fundamental principles.

16. That Religion, or the duty which we owe to our *Creator,* and the manner of discharging it, can be directed only by reason and conviction, not by force or violence; and, therefore, all men are equally entitled to the free exercise of religion, according to the dictates of conscience; and that it is the mutual duty of all to practise Christian forbearance, love, and charity, towards each other.

4

VIRGINIA CONSTITUTION
29 June 1776
Jefferson Papers 1:377–83

In a General Convention.

Begun and holden at the Capitol, in the City of Williamsburg, on Monday the sixth day of May, one thousand seven hundred and seventy six, and continued, by adjournments to the   day of June following:

A CONSTITUTION, OR FORM OF GOVERNMENT,

agreed to and resolved upon by the Delegates and Representatives of the several Counties and Corporations of Virginia.

Whereas George the Third, King of Great Britain and Ireland, and Elector of Hanover, heretofore intrusted with the exercise of the Kingly Office in this Government, hath endeavoured to pervert the same into a detestable and insupportable Tyranny; by putting his negative on laws the most wholesome and necessary for the publick good;

by denying his Governours permission to pass Laws of immediate and pressing importance, unless suspended in their operation for his assent, and, when so suspended, neglecting to attend to them for many Years;

by refusing to pass certain other laws, unless the persons to be benefited by them would relinquish the inestimable right of representation in the legislature;

by dissolving legislative assemblies repeatedly and continually, for opposing with manly firmness his invasions of the rights of the people;

when dissolved, by refusing to call others for a long space of time, thereby leaving the political system without any legislative head;

by endeavouring to prevent the population of our Country, and, for that purpose, obstructing the laws for the naturalization of foreigners;

by keeping among us, in times of peace, standing Armies and Ships of war;

by affecting to render the Military independent of, and superiour to, the civil power;

by combining with others to subject us to a foreign Jurisdiction, giving his assent to their pretended Acts of Legislation;

for quartering large bodies of armed troops among us;

for cutting off our Trade with all parts of the World;

for imposing Taxes on us without our Consent;

for depriving us of the Benefits of Trial by Jury;

for transporting us beyond Seas, to be tried for pretended Offences;

for suspending our own Legislatures, and declaring themselves invested with power to legislate for us in all Cases whatsoever;

by plundering our Seas, ravaging our Coasts, burning our Towns, and destroying the lives of our People;

by inciting insurrections of our fellow Subjects, with the allurements of forfeiture and confiscation;

by prompting our Negroes to rise in Arms among us, those very negroes whom, by an inhuman use of his negative, he hath refused us permission to exclude by Law;

by endeavouring to bring on the inhabitants of our Frontiers the merciless Indian savages, whose known rule of Warfare is an undistinguished Destruction of all Ages, Sexes, and Conditions of Existance;

by transporting, at this time, a large Army of foreign Mercenaries, to compleat the Works of Death, desolation, and Tyranny, already begun with circumstances of Cruelty and Perfidy unworthy the head of a civilized Nation;

by answering our repeated Petitions for Redress with a Repetition of Injuries;

and finally, by abandoning the Helm of Government, and declaring us out of his Allegiance and Protection;

By which several Acts of Misrule, the Government of this Country, as formerly exercised under the Crown of Great Britain, is totally dissolved; We therefore, the Delegates and Representatives of the good People of Virginia, having maturely considered the Premises, and viewing with great concern the deplorable condition to which this once happy Country must be reduced, unless some regular adequate Mode of civil Polity is speedily adopted, and in Compliance with a Recommendation of the General Congress, do ordain and declare the future Form of Government of Virginia to be as followeth:

The legislative, executive, and judiciary departments, shall be separate and distinct, so that neither exercise the Powers properly belonging to the other; nor shall any person exercise the powers of more than one of them at the same time, except that the Justices of the County Courts shall be eligible to either House of Assembly.

The legislative shall be formed of two distinct branches, who, together, shall be a complete Legislature. They shall meet once, or oftener, every Year, and shall be called the General Assembly of Virginia.

One of these shall be called the House of Delegates, and consist of two Representatives to be chosen for each County, and for the District of West Augusta, annually, of such Men as actually reside in and are freeholders of the same, or duly qualified according to Law, and also of one Delegate or Representative to be chosen annually for the city of Williamsburg, and one for the Borough of Norfolk, and a Representative for each of such other Cities and Boroughs, as may hereafter be allowed particular Representation by the legislature; but when any City or Borough shall so decrease as that the number of persons having right of Suffrage therein shall have been for the space of seven Years successively less than half the number of Voters in some one County in Virginia, such City or Borough thenceforward shall cease to send a Delegate or Representative to the Assembly.

The other shall be called the Senate, and consist of twenty four Members, of whom thirteen shall constitute a House to proceed on Business for whose election the different Counties shall be divided into twenty four districts, and each County of the respective District, at the time of the election of its Delegates, shall vote for one Senator, who is actually a resident and freeholder within the District, or duly qualified according to Law, and is upwards of twenty five Years of Age; And the sheriff of each County, within five days at farthest after the last County election in the District, shall meet at some convenient place, and from the Poll so taken in their respective Counties return as a Senator to the House of Senators the Man who shall have the greatest number of Votes in the whole District. To keep up this Assembly by rotation, the Districts shall be equally divided into four Classes, and numbered by Lot. At the end of one Year after the General Election, the six Members elected by the first division shall be displaced, and the vacancies thereby occasioned supplied from such Class or division, by new Election, in the manner aforesaid. This Rotation shall be applied to each division, according to its number, and continued in due order annually.

The right of Suffrage in the Election of Members for both Houses shall remain as exercised at present, and each House shall choose its own Speaker, appoint its own Officers, settle its own rules of proceding, and direct Writs of Election for supplying intermediate vacancies.

All Laws shall originate in the House of Delegates, to be approved or rejected by the Senate or to be amended with the Consent of the House of Delegates; except Money Bills, which in no instance shall be altered by the Senate but wholly approved or rejected.

A Governour, or chief Magistrate, shall be chosen annually, by joint Ballot of both Houses, (to be taken in each House respectively, deposited in the Conference room, the Boxes examined jointly by a Committee of each House, and the numbers severally reported to them, that the appointments may be entered, which shall be the mode of taking the joint Ballot of both Houses in all Cases) who shall not continue in that office longer than three Years successively, nor be eligible until the expiration of four Years after he shall have been out of that office: An adequate, but moderate Salary, shall be settled on him during his Continuance in Office; and he shall, with the advice of a Council of State, exercise the Executive powers of Government according to the laws of this Commonwealth; and shall not, under any pretence, exercise any power or prerogative by virtue of any Law, statute, or Custom, of England; But he shall, with the advice of the Council of State, have the power of granting reprieves or pardons, except where the prosecution shall have been carried on by the House of Delegates, or the Law shall otherwise particularly direct; in which Cases, no reprieve or Pardon shall be granted but by resolve of the House of Delegates.

Either House of the General Assembly may adjourn themselves respectively: The Governour shall not prorogue or adjourn the Assembly during their setting, nor dissolve them at any Time; but he shall, if necessary, either by advice of the Council of State, or on application of a Majority of the House of Delegates, call them before the time to which they shall stand prorogued or adjourned.

A Privy Council, or Council of State, consisting of eight Members, shall be chosen by joint Ballot of both Houses of Assembly, either from their own Members or the People at large, to assist in the Administration of Government. They shall annually choose out of their own Members, a President, who, in case of the death, inability, or necessary absence of the Governour from the Government, shall act as lieutenant Governour. Four Members shall be sufficient to act, and their Advice and proceedings shall be entered of Record, and signed by the Members present (to any part whereof any Member may enter his dissent) to be laid before the General Assembly, when called for by them. This Council may appoint their own Clerk, who shall have a Salary settled by Law, and take an Oath of Secrecy in such matters as he shall be directed by the Board to conceal. A sum of Money appropriated to that purpose shall be divided annually among the Members, in proportion to their attendance; and they shall be incapable, during their continuance in Office, of sitting in either House of Assembly. Two Members shall be removed, by joint Ballot of both houses of Assembly at the end of every three Years, and be ineligible for the three next years. These Vacancies, as well as those occasioned by death or incapacity, shall be supplied by new Elections, in the same manner.

The Delegates for Virginia to the Continental Congress shall be chosen annually, or superseded in the mean time by joint Ballot of both Houses of Assembly.

The present Militia Officers shall be continued, and Vacancies supplied by appointment of the Governour, with the advice of the privy Council, or recommendations from the respective County Courts; but the Governour and Council shall have a power of suspending any Officer, and ordering a Court-Martial on Complaint for misbehaviour or inability, or to supply Vacancies of Officers happening when in actual Service. The Governour may embody the Militia, with the advice of the privy Council; and, when embodied, shall alone have the direction of the Militia under the laws of the Country.

The two Houses of Assembly shall, by joint Ballot, appoint judges of the supreme Court of Appeals, and General Court, Judges in Chancery, Judges of Admiralty, Secretary, and the Attorney-General, to be commissioned by the Governour, and continue in Office during good behaviour. In case of death, incapacity, or resignation, the Governour, with the advice of the privy Council, shall appoint Persons to succeed in Office, to be approved or displaced by both Houses. These Officers shall have fixed and adequate Salaries, and, together with all others holding lucrative Offices, and all Ministers of the Gospel of every Denomination, be incapable of being elected Members of either House of Assembly, or the privy Council.

The Governour, with the Advice of the privy Council, shall appoint Justices of the Peace for the Counties; and in case of Vacancies, or a necessity of increasing the number hereafter, such appointments to be made upon the recommendation of the respective County Courts. The present acting Secretary in Virginia, and Clerks of all the County Courts, shall continue in Office. In case of Vacancies, either by death, incapacity, or resignation, a Secretary shall be appointed as before directed, and the Clerks by the respective Courts. The present and future Clerks shall hold their Offices during good behaviour, to be judged of and determined in the General Court. The Sheriffs and Coroners shall be nominated by the respective Courts, approved by the Governour with the advice of the privy Council, and commissioned by the Governour. The Justices shall appoint Constables, and all fees of the aforesaid Officers be regulated by law.

The Governour, when he is out of Office, and others offending against the State, either by Mal-administration, Corruption, or other Means, by which the safety of the State may be endangered, shall be impeachable by the House of Delegates. Such impeachment to be prosecuted by the Attorney General, or such other Person or Persons as the House may appoint in the General Court, according to the laws of the Land. If found guilty, he or they shall be either for ever disabled to hold any Office under Government, or removed from such Office *Pro tempore,* or subjected to such Pains or Penalties as the laws shall direct.

If all, or any of the Judges of the General Court, should, on good grounds (to be judged of by the House of Delegates) be accused of any of the Crimes or Offences beforementioned, such House of Delegates may, in like manner, impeach the Judge or Judges so accused, to be prosecuted in the Court of Appeals; and he or they, if found guilty, shall be punished in the same manner as is prescribed in the preceding Clause.

Commissions and Grants shall run, *In the Name of the Common Wealth of* Virginia, and bear teste by the Governour, with the Seal of the Common wealth annexed. Writs shall run in the same manner, and bear teste by the Clerks of the several Courts. Indictments shall conclude, *Against the Peace and Dignity of the Common-Wealth.*

A Treasurer shall be appointed annually, by joint Ballot of both Houses.

All escheats, penalties, and forfeitures, heretofore going to the King, shall go to the Common Wealth, save only such, as the Legislature may abolish, or otherwise provide for.

The territories contained within the Charters erecting the Colonies of Maryland, Pennsylvania, North and South Carolina, are hereby ceded, released, and forever confirmed to the People of those Colonies respectively, with all the rights of property, jurisdiction, and Government, and all other rights whatsoever which might at any time heretofore have been claimed by Virginia, except the free Navigation and use of the Rivers Potowmack and Pohomoke, with the property of the Virginia Shores or strands bordering on either of the said Rivers, and all improvements which have been or shall be made thereon. The western and northern extent of Virginia shall in all other respects stand as fixed by the Charter of King James the first, in the Year one thousand six hundred and nine, and by the publick Treaty of Peace between the Courts of Great Britain and France in the year one thousand seven hundred and sixty three; Unless by act of this legislature, one or more Territories shall hereafter be laid off, and Governments established Westward of the *Allegheny* Mountains. And no purchases of Land shall be made of the *Indian* Natives but on behalf of the Publick, by authority of the General Assembly.

In order to introduce this Government, the Representatives of the People met in Convention shall choose a Governour and privy Council, also such other Officers directed to be chosen by both Houses as may be judged necessary to be immediately appointed. The Senate, to be first chosen by the people, to continue until the last day of March next, and the other Officers until the end of the succeeding Session of Assembly. In case of Vacancies, the Speaker of either House shall issue Writs for new Elections.

5

DECLARATION OF INDEPENDENCE
4 July 1776
Tansill 22–26

In Congress, July 4, 1776
The unanimous Declaration
of the thirteen united States of America

When in the Course of human events, it becomes necessary for one people to dissolve the political bands which have connected them with another, and to assume among the powers of the earth, the separate and equal station to which the Laws of Nature and of Nature's God entitle them, a decent respect to the opinions of mankind requires that they should declare the causes which impel them to the separation.—We hold these truths to be self-evident, that all men are created equal, that they are endowed by their Creator with certain unalienable Rights, that among these are Life, Liberty and the pursuit of Happiness.—That to secure these rights, Governments are instituted among Men, deriving their just powers from the consent of the governed,—That whenever any Form of Government becomes destructive of these ends, it is the

Right of the People to alter or to abolish it, and to institute new Government, laying its foundation on such principles and organizing its powers in such form, as to them shall seem most likely to effect their Safety and Happiness. Prudence, indeed, will dictate that Governments long established should not be changed for light and transient causes; and accordingly all experience hath shown, that mankind are more disposed to suffer, while evils are sufferable, than to right themselves by abolishing the forms to which they are accustomed. But when a long train of abuses and usurpations, pursuing invariably the same Object evinces a design to reduce them under absolute Despotism, it is their right, it is their duty, to throw off such Government, and to provide new Guards for their future security.—Such has been the patient sufferance of these Colonies; and such is now the necessity which constrains them to alter their former Systems of Government. The history of the present King of Great Britain is a history of repeated injuries and usurpations, all having in direct object the establishment of an absolute Tyranny over these States. To prove this, let Facts be submitted to a candid world.—He has refused his Assent to Laws, the most wholesome and necessary for the public good.—He has forbidden his Governors to pass Laws of immediate and pressing importance, unless suspended in their operation till his Assent should be obtained; and when so suspended, he has utterly neglected to attend to them.—He has refused to pass other Laws for the accommodation of large districts of people, unless those people would relinquish the right of Representation in the Legislature, a right inestimable to them and formidable to tyrants only.—He has called together legislative bodies at places unusual, uncomfortable, and distant from the depository of their public Records, for the sole purpose of fatiguing them into compliance with his measures.—He has dissolved Representative Houses repeatedly, for opposing with manly firmness his invasions on the rights of the people.—He has refused for a long time, after such dissolutions, to cause others to be elected; whereby the Legislative powers, incapable of Annihilation, have returned to the People at large for their exercise; the State remaining in the mean time exposed to all the dangers of invasion from without, and convulsions within.—He has endeavoured to prevent the population of these States; for that purpose obstructing the Laws for Naturalization of Foreigners; refusing to pass others to encourage their migration hither, and raising the conditions of new Appropriations of Lands.—He has obstructed the Administration of Justice, by refusing his Assent to Laws for establishing Judiciary powers.—He has made Judges dependent on his Will alone, for the tenure of their offices, and the amount and payment of their salaries.—He has erected a multitude of New Offices, and sent hither swarms of Officers to harrass our people, and eat out their substance.—He has kept among us, in times of peace, Standing Armies, without the Consent of our legislatures.—He has affected to render the Military independent of and superior to the Civil power.—He has combined with others to subject us to a jurisdiction foreign to our constitution, and unacknowledged by our laws; giving his Assent to their Acts of pretended Legislation:—For

quartering large bodies of armed troops among us:—For protecting them, by a mock Trial, from punishment for any Murders which they should commit on the Inhabitants of these States:—For cutting off our Trade with all parts of the world:—For imposing Taxes on us without our Consent:—For depriving us in many cases, of the benefits of Trial by Jury:—For transporting us beyond Seas to be tried for pretended offences:—For abolishing the free System of English Laws in a neighbouring Province, establishing therein an Arbitrary government, and enlarging its Boundaries so as to render it at once an example and fit instrument for introducing the same absolute rule into these Colonies:—For taking away our Charters, abolishing our most valuable Laws, and altering fundamentally the Forms of our Governments:—For suspending our own Legislatures, and declaring themselves invested with power to legislate for us in all cases whatsoever.—He has abdicated Government here, by declaring us out of his Protection and waging War against us.—He has plundered our seas, ravaged our Coasts, burnt our towns, and destroyed the lives of our people.—He is at this time transporting large Armies of foreign Mercenaries to compleat the works of death, desolation and tyranny, already begun with circumstances of Cruelty & perfidy scarcely paralleled in the most barbarous ages, and totally unworthy the Head of a civilized nation.—He has constrained our fellow Citizens taken Captive on the high Seas to bear Arms against their Country, to become the executioners of their friends and Brethren, or to fall themselves by their Hands.—He has excited domestic insurrections amongst us, and has endeavoured to bring on the inhabitants of our frontiers, the merciless Indian Savages, whose known rule of warfare, is an undistinguished destruction of all ages, sexes and conditions. In every stage of these Oppressions We have Petitioned for Redress in the most humble terms: Our repeated Petitions have been answered only by repeated injury. A Prince, whose character is thus marked by every act which may define a Tyrant, is unfit to be the ruler of a free people. Nor have We been wanting in attentions to our Brittish brethren. We have warned them from time to time of attempts by their legislature to extend an unwarrantable jurisdiction over us. We have reminded them of the circumstances of our emigration and settlement here. We have appealed to their native justice and magnanimity, and we have conjured them by the ties of our common kindred to disavow these usurpations, which, would inevitably interrupt our connections and correspondence. They too have been deaf to the voice of justice and of consanguinity. We must, therefore, acquiesce in the necessity, which denounces our Separation, and hold them, as we hold the rest of mankind, Enemies in War, in Peace Friends.—

WE, THEREFORE, the REPRESENTATIVES of the UNITED STATES OF AMERICA, in General Congress, Assembled, appealing to the Supreme Judge of the world for the rectitude of our intentions, do, in the Name, and by Authority of the good People of these Colonies, solemnly publish and declare, That these United Colonies are, and of Right ought to be FREE AND INDEPENDENT STATES; that they are Absolved from all Allegiance to the British Crown, and that all political connection between them and the State of Great Britain, is and ought to be totally dissolved; and that as Free and Independent States, they have full Power to levy War, conclude Peace, contract Alliances, establish Commerce, and to do all other Acts and Things which Independent States may of right do.—And for the support of this Declaration, with a firm reliance on the protection of Divine Providence, we mutually pledge to each other our Lives, our Fortunes and our sacred Honor.

John Hancock

[New Hampshire]
Josiah Bartlett
Wm. Whipple
Matthew Thornton

[Massachusett Bay]
Saml. Adams
John Adams
Robt. Treat Paine
Elbridge Gerry

[Rhode Island]
Step. Hopkins
William Ellery

[Connecticut]
Roger Sherman
Sam'el Huntington
Wm. Williams
Oliver Wolcott

[New York]
Wm. Floyd
Phil. Livingston
Frans. Lewis
Lewis Morris

[New Jersey]
Richd. Stockton
Jno. Witherspoon
Fras. Hopkinson
John Hart
Abra. Clark

[Pennsylvania]
Robt. Morris
Benjamin Rush
Benja. Franklin
John Morton
Geo. Clymer
Jas. Smith
Geo. Taylor
James Wilson
Geo. Ross

[Delaware]
Caesar Rodney
Geo. Read
Tho. M'Kean

[Maryland]
Samuel Chase
Wm. Paca
Thos. Stone
Charles Carroll
of Carrollton

[Virginia]
George Wythe
Richard Henry Lee
Th. Jefferson
Benja. Harrison
Ths. Nelson, Jr.
Francis Lightfoot Lee
Carter Braxton

[North Carolina]
Wm. Hooper
Joseph Hewes
John Penn

[South Carolina]
Edward Rutledge
Thos. Heyward,
Junr.
Thomas Lynch, Junr.
Arthur Middleton

[Georgia]
Button Gwinnett
Lyman Hall
Geo. Walton

6

MASSACHUSETTS CONSTITUTION
2 Mar. 1780
Handlin 441–72

A CONSTITUTION OR FRAME OF GOVERNMENT, Agreed upon by the Delegates of the People of the STATE OF MASSACHUSETTS-BAY,—In Convention,—*Begun and held at* Cambridge, *on the First of* September, *1779, and continued by Adjournments to the Second of* March, *1780.*

Preamble.

The end of the institution, maintenance and administration of government, is to secure the existence of the body-politic; to protect it; and to furnish the individuals who compose it, with the power of enjoying, in safety and tranquillity, their natural rights, and the blessings of life: And whenever these great objects are not obtained, the people have a right to alter the government, and to take measures necessary for their safety, prosperity and happiness.

The body-politic is formed by a voluntary association of individuals: It is a social compact, by which the whole people covenants with each citizen, and each citizen with the whole people, that all shall be governed by certain laws for the common good. It is the duty of the people, therefore, in framing a Constitution of Government, to provide for an equitable mode of making laws, as well as for an impartial interpretation, and a faithful execution of them; that every man may, at all times, find his security in them.

We, therefore, the people of Massachusetts, acknowledging, with grateful hearts, the goodness of the Great Legislator of the Universe, in affording us, in the course of His providence, an opportunity, deliberately and peaceably, without fraud, violence or surprise, of entering into an original, explicit, and solemn compact with each other; and of forming a new Constitution of Civil Government, for ourselves and posterity; and devoutly imploring His direction in so interesting a design, DO agree upon, ordain and establish, the following *Declaration of Rights, and Frame of Government,* as the CONSTITUTION of the COMMONWEALTH of MASSACHUSETTS.

Part the First. A Declaration of the Rights of the Inhabitants of the Commonwealth of Massachusetts.

ART. I.—All men are born free and equal, and have certain natural, essential, and unalienable rights; among which may be reckoned the right of enjoying and defending their lives and liberties; that of acquiring, possessing, and protecting property; in fine, that of seeking and obtaining their safety and happiness.

II.—It is the right as well as the duty of all men in society, publicly, and at stated seasons, to worship the SUPREME BEING, the great creator and preserver of the universe. And no subject shall be hurt, molested, or restrained, in his person, liberty, or estate, for worshipping GOD in the manner and season most agreeable to the dictates of his own conscience; or for his religious profession or sentiments; provided he doth not disturb the public peace, or obstruct others in their religious worship.

III.—As the happiness of a people, and the good order and preservation of civil government, essentially depend upon piety, religion and morality; and as these cannot be generally diffused through a community, but by the institution of the public worship of GOD, and of public instructions in piety, religion and morality: Therefore, to promote their happiness and to secure the good order and preservation of their government, the people of this Commonwealth have a right to invest their legislature with power to authorize and require, and the legislature shall, from time to time, authorize and require, the several towns, parishes, precincts, and other bodies-politic, or religious societies, to make suitable provision, at their own expense, for the institution of the public worship of GOD, and for the support and maintenance of public protestant teachers of piety, religion and morality, in all cases where such provision shall not be made voluntarily.

And the people of this Commonwealth have also a right to, and do, invest their legislature with authority to enjoin upon all the subjects an attendance upon the instructions of the public teachers aforesaid, at stated times and seasons, if there be any on whose instructions they can conscientiously and conveniently attend.

Provided notwithstanding, that the several towns, parishes, precincts, and other bodies-politic, or religious societies, shall, at all times, have the exclusive right of electing their public teachers, and of contracting with them for their support and maintenance.

And all monies paid by the subject to the support of public worship, and of the public teachers aforesaid, shall, if he require it, be uniformly applied to the support of the public teacher or teachers of his own religious sect or denomination, provided there be any on whose instructions he attends: otherwise it may be paid towards the support of the teacher or teachers of the parish or precinct in which the said monies are raised.

And every denomination of christians, demeaning themselves peaceably, and as good subjects of the Commonwealth, shall be equally under the protection of the law: And no subordination of any one sect or denomination to another shall ever be established by law.

IV.—The people of this Commonwealth have the sole and exclusive right of governing themselves as a free, sovereign, and independent state; and do, and forever hereafter shall, exercise and enjoy every power, jurisdiction, and right, which is not, or may not hereafter, be by them expressly delegated to the United States of America, in Congress assembled.

V.—All power residing originally in the people, and being derived from them, the several magistrates and officers of government, vested with authority, whether legislative, executive, or judicial, are their substitutes and

agents, and are at all times accountable to them.

VI.—No man, nor corporation, or association of men, have any other title to obtain advantages, or particular and exclusive privileges, distinct from those of the community, than what arises from the consideration of services rendered to the public; and this title being in nature neither hereditary, nor transmissible to children, or descendants, or relations by blood, the idea of a man born a magistrate, lawgiver, or judge, is absurd and unnatural.

VII.—Government is instituted for the common good; for the protection, safety, prosperity and happiness of the people; and not for the profit, honor, or private interest of any one man, family, or class of men; Therefore the people alone have an incontestible, unalienable, and indefeasible right to institute government; and to reform, alter, or totally change the same, when their protection, safety, prosperity and happiness require it.

VIII.—In order to prevent those, who are vested with authority, from becoming oppressors, the people have a right, at such periods and in such manner as they shall establish by their frame of government, to cause their public officers to return to private life; and to fill up vacant places by certain and regular elections and appointments.

IX.—All elections ought to be free; and all the inhabitants of this Commonwealth, having such qualifications as they shall establish by their frame of government, have an equal right to elect officers, and to be elected, for public employments.

X.—Each individual of the society has a right to be protected by it in the enjoyment of his life, liberty and property, according to standing laws. He is obliged, consequently, to contribute his share to the expense of this protection; to give his personal service, or an equivalent, when necessary: But no part of the property of any individual, can, with justice, be taken from him, or applied to public uses without his own consent, or that of the representative body of the people: In fine, the people of this Commonwealth are not controlable by any other laws, than those to which their constitutional representative body have given their consent. And whenever the public exigencies require, that the property of any individual should be appropriated to public uses, he shall receive a reasonable compensation therefor.

XI.—Every subject of the Commonwealth ought to find a certain remedy, by having recourse to the laws, for all injuries or wrongs which he may receive in his person, property, or character. He ought to obtain right and justice freely, and without being obliged to purchase it; completely, and without any denial; promptly, and without delay; conformably to the laws.

XII.—No subject shall be held to answer for any crime or offence, until the same is fully and plainly, substantially and formally, described to him; or be compelled to accuse, or furnish evidence against himself. And every subject shall have a right to produce all proofs, that may be favorable to him; to meet the witnesses against him face to face, and to be fully heard in his defence by himself, or his council, at his election. And no subject shall be arrested, imprisoned, despoiled, or deprived of his property, immunities, or privileges, put out of the protection of the law, exiled, or deprived of his life, liberty, or estate; but by the judgment of his peers, or the law of the land.

And the legislature shall not make any law, that shall subject any person to a capital or infamous punishment, excepting for the government of the army and navy, without trial by jury.

XIII.—In criminal prosecutions, the verification of facts in the vicinity where they happen, is one of the greatest securities of the life, liberty, and property of the citizen.

XIV.—Every subject has a right to be secure from all unreasonable searches, and seizures of his person, his houses, his papers, and all his possessions. All warrants, therefore, are contrary to this right, if the cause or foundation of them be not previously supported by oath or affirmation; and if the order in the warrant to a civil officer, to make search in suspected places, or to arrest one or more suspected persons, or to seize their property, be not accompanied with a special designation of the persons or objects of search, arrest, or seizure: and no warrant ought to be issued but in cases, and with the formalities, prescribed by the laws.

XV.—In all controversies concerning property, and in all suits between two or more persons, except in cases in which it has heretofore been otherways used and practised, the parties have a right to a trial by jury; and this method of procedure shall be held sacred, unless, in causes arising on the high-seas, and such as relate to mariners wages, the legislature shall hereafter find it necessary to alter it.

XVI.—The liberty of the press is essential to the security of freedom in a state: it ought not, therefore, to be restrained in this Commonwealth.

XVII.—The people have a right to keep and to bear arms for the common defence. And as in time of peace armies are dangerous to liberty, they ought not to be maintained without the consent of the legislature; and the military power shall always be held in an exact subordination to the civil authority, and be governed by it.

XVIII.—A frequent recurrence to the fundamental principles of the constitution, and a constant adherence to those of piety, justice, moderation, temperance, industry, and frugality, are absolutely necessary to preserve the advantages of liberty, and to maintain a free government: The people ought, consequently, to have a particular attention to all those principles, in the choice of their officers and representatives: And they have a right to require of their law-givers and magistrates, an exact and constant observance of them, in the formation and execution of the laws necessary for the good administration of the Commonwealth.

XIX.—The people have a right, in an orderly and peaceable manner, to assemble to consult upon the common good; give instructions to their representatives; and to request of the legislative body, by the way of addresses, petitions, or remonstrances, redress of the wrongs done them, and of the grievances they suffer.

XX.—The power of suspending the laws, or the execution of the laws, ought never to be exercised but by the legislature, or by authority derived from it, to be exercised in such particular cases only as the legislature shall expressly provide for.

XXI.—The freedom of deliberation, speech and debate, in either house of the legislature, is so essential to the rights of the people, that it cannot be the foundation of any accusation or prosecution, action or complaint, in any other court or place whatsoever.

XXII.—The legislature ought frequently to assemble for the redress of grievances, for correcting, strengthening, and confirming the laws, and for making new laws, as the common good may require.

XXIII.—No subsidy, charge, tax, impost, or duties, ought to be established, fixed, laid, or levied, under any pretext whatsoever, without the consent of the people, or their representatives in the legislature.

XXIV.—Laws made to punish for actions done before the existence of such laws, and which have not been declared crimes by preceding laws, are unjust, oppressive, and inconsistent with the fundamental principles of a free government.

XXV.—No subject ought, in any case, or in any time, to be declared guilty of treason or felony by the legislature.

XXVI.—No magistrate or court of law shall demand excessive bail or sureties, impose excessive fines, or inflict cruel or unusual punishments.

XXVII.—In time of peace no soldier ought to be quartered in any house without the consent of the owner; and in time of war such quarters ought not to be made but by the civil magistrate, in a manner ordained by the legislature.

XXVIII.—No person can in any case be subjected to law-martial, or to any penalties or pains, by virtue of that law, except those employed in the army or navy, and except the militia in actual service, but by authority of the legislature.

XXIX.—It is essential to the preservation of the rights of every individual, his life, liberty, property and character, that there be an impartial interpretation of the laws, and administration of justice. It is the right of every citizen to be tried by judges as free, impartial and independent as the lot of humanity will admit. It is therefore not only the best policy, but for the security of the rights of the people, and of every citizen, that the judges of the supreme judicial court should hold their offices as long as they behave themselves well; and that they should have honorable salaries ascertained and established by standing laws.

XXX.—In the government of this Commonwealth, the legislative department shall never exercise the executive and judicial powers, or either of them: The executive shall never exercise the legislative and judicial powers, or either of them: The judicial shall never exercise the legislative and executive powers, or either of them: to the end it may be a government of laws and not of men.

Part the Second. The Frame of Government.

The people, inhabiting the territory formerly called the Province of Massachusetts-Bay, do hereby solemnly and mutually agree with each other, to form themselves into a free, sovereign, and independent body-politic or state, by the name of THE COMMONWEALTH OF MASSACHU-SETTS.

Chapter I. The Legislative Power.

Section I. The General Court.

ART. I.—The department of legislation shall be formed by two branches, *a Senate* and *House of Representatives:* each of which shall have a negative on the other.

The legislative body shall assemble every year, on the last Wednesday in May, and at such other times as they shall judge necessary; and shall dissolve and be dissolved on the day next preceding the said last Wednesday in May; and shall be styled, THE GENERAL COURT OF MASSACHU-SETTS.

II.—No bill or resolve of the Senate or House of Representatives shall become a law, and have force as such, until it shall have been laid before the Governor for his revisal: And if he, upon such revision, approve thereof, he shall signify his approbation by signing the same. But if he have any objection to the passing of such bill or resolve, he shall return the same, together with his objections thereto, in writing, to the Senate or House of Representatives, in which soever the same shall have originated; who shall enter the objections sent down by the Governor, at large, on their records, and proceed to reconsider the said bill or resolve: But if, after such reconsideration, two thirds of the said Senate or House of Representatives, shall, notwithstanding the said objections, agree to pass the same, it shall, together with the objections, be sent to the other branch of the legislature, where it shall also be reconsidered, and if approved by two thirds of the members present, shall have the force of a law: But in all such cases the votes of both houses shall be determined by yeas and nays; and the names of the persons voting for, or against, the said bill or resolve, shall be entered upon the public records of the Commonwealth.

And in order to prevent unnecessary delays, if any bill or resolve shall not be returned by the Governor within five days after it shall have been presented, the same shall have the force of a law.

III.—The General Court shall forever have full power and authority to erect and constitute judicatories and courts of record, or other courts, to be held in the name of the Commonwealth, for the hearing, trying, and determining of all manner of crimes, offences, pleas, processes, plaints, actions, matters, causes and things, whatsoever, arising or happening within the Commonwealth, or between or concerning persons inhabiting, or residing, or brought within the same; whether the same be criminal or civil, or whether the said crimes be capital or not capital, and whether the said pleas be real, personal, or mixt; and for the awarding and making out of execution thereupon: To which courts and judicatories are hereby given and granted full power and authority, from time to time, to administer oaths or affirmations, for the better discovery of truth in any matter in controversy or depending before them.

IV.—And further, full power and authority are hereby given and granted to the said General Court, from time to time, to make, ordain, and establish, all manner of wholesome and reasonable orders, laws, statutes, and ordinances, directions and instructions, either with penalties or without; so as the same be not repugnant or contrary to this Constitution, as they shall judge to be for the good and welfare of this Commonwealth, and for the government and ordering thereof, and of the subjects of the same, and for the necessary support and defence of the government thereof; and to name and settle annually, or provide by fixed laws, for the naming and settling all civil officers within the said Commonwealth, the election and constitution of whom are not hereafter in this Form of Government otherwise provided for; and to set forth the several duties, powers and limits; of the several civil and military officers of this Commonwealth, and the forms of such oaths or affirmations as shall be respectively administered unto them for the execution of their several offices and places, so as the same be not repugnant or contrary to this Constitution; and to impose and levy proportional and reasonable assessments, rates, and taxes, upon all the inhabitants of, and persons resident, and estates lying, within the said Commonwealth; and also to impose, and levy reasonable duties and excises, upon any produce, goods, wares, merchandize, and commodities whatsoever, brought into, produced, manufactured, or being within the same; to be issued and disposed of by warrant, under the hand of the Governor of this Commonwealth for the time being, with the advice and consent of the Council, for the public service, in the necessary defence and support of the government of the said Commonwealth, and the protection and preservation of the subjects thereof, according to such acts as are or shall be in force within the same.

And while the public charges of government, or any part thereof, shall be assessed on polls and estates, in the manner that has hitherto been practised, in order that such assessments may be made with equality, there shall be a valuation of estates within the Commonwealth taken anew once in every ten years at least, and as much oftener as the General Court shall order.

Chapter I.

Section II. Senate.

ART. I.—There shall be annually elected by the freeholders and other inhabitants of this Commonwealth, qualified as in this Constitution is provided, forty persons to be Counsellors and Senators for the year ensuing their election; to be chosen by the inhabitants of the districts, into which the Commonwealth may from time to time be divided by the General Court for that purpose: And the General Court, in assigning the numbers to be elected by the respective districts, shall govern themselves by the proportion of the public taxes paid by the said districts; and timely make known to the inhabitants of the Commonwealth, the limits of each district, and the number of Counsellors and Senators to be chosen therein; provided, that the number of such districts shall never be less than thirteen; and that no district be so large as to entitle the same to choose more than six Senators.

And the several counties in this Commonwealth shall, until the General Court shall determine it necessary to alter the said districts, be districts for the choice of Counsellors and Senators, (except that the counties of Dukes County and Nantucket shall form one district for that purpose) and shall elect the following number for Counsellors and Senators, viz:

Suffolk	Six
Essex	Six
Middlesex	Five
Hampshire	Four
Plymouth	Three
Barnstable	One
Bristol	Three
York	Two
Dukes County and Nantucket	One
Worcester	Five
Cumberland	One
Lincoln	One
Berkshire	Two.

II.—The Senate shall be the first branch of the legislature; and the Senators shall be chosen in the following manner, viz: There shall be a meeting on the first Monday in April annually, forever, of the inhabitants of each town in the several counties of this Commonwealth; to be called by the Selectmen, and warned in due course of law, at least seven days before the first Monday in April, for the purpose of electing persons to be Senators and Counsellors: And at such meetings every male inhabitant of twenty-one years of age and upwards, having a freehold estate within the Commonwealth, of the annual income of three pounds, or any estate of the value of sixty pounds, shall have a right to give in his vote for the Senators for the district of which he is an inhabitant. And to remove all doubts concerning the meaning of the word "inhabitant" in this constitution, every person shall be considered as an inhabitant, for the purpose of electing and being elected into any office, or place within this State, in that town, district, or plantation, where he dwelleth, or hath his home.

The Selectmen of the several towns shall preside at such meetings impartially; and shall receive the votes of all the inhabitants of such towns present and qualified to vote for Senators, and shall sort and count them in open town meeting, and in presence of the Town Clerk, who shall make a fair record in presence of the Selectmen, and in open town meeting, of the name of every person voted for, and of the number of votes against his name; and a fair copy of this record shall be attested by the Selectmen and the Town-Clerk, and shall be sealed up, directed to the Secretary of the Commonwealth for the time being, with a superscription, expressing the purport of the contents thereof, and delivered by the Town-Clerk of such towns, to the Sheriff of the county in which such town lies, thirty days at least before the last Wednesday in May annually; or it shall be delivered into the Secretary's office seventeen days at least before the said last Wednesday in May; and the Sheriff of each county shall deliver all such certificates by him received, into the Secretary's office seventeen days before the said last Wednesday in May.

And the inhabitants of plantations unincorporated, qualified as this Constitution provides, who are or shall be empowered and required to assess taxes upon themselves toward the support of government, shall have the same privilege of voting for Counsellors and Senators, in the plantations where they reside, as town inhabitants have in their respective towns; and the plantation-meetings for that purpose shall be held annually on the same first Monday in April, at such place in the plantations respectively, as the Assessors thereof shall direct; which Assessors shall have like authority for notifying the electors, collecting and returning the votes, as the Selectmen and Town-Clerks have in their several towns, by this Constitution. And all other persons living in places unincorporated (qualified as aforesaid) who shall be assessed to the support of government by the Assessors of an adjacent town, shall have the privilege of giving in their votes for Counsellors and Senators, in the town where they shall be assessed, and be notified of the place of meeting by the Selectmen of the town where they shall be assessed, for that purpose, accordingly.

III.—And that there may be a due convention of Senators on the last Wednesday in May annually, the Governor, with five of the Council, for the time being, shall, as soon as may be, examine the returned copies of such records; and fourteen days before the said day he shall issue his summons to such persons as shall appear to be chosen by a majority of voters, to attend on that day, and take their seats accordingly: Provided nevertheless, that for the first year the said returned copies shall be examined by the President and five of the Council of the former Constitution of Government; and the said President shall, in like manner, issue his summons to the persons so elected, that they may take their seats as aforesaid.

IV.—The Senate shall be the final judge of the elections, returns and qualifications of their own members, as pointed out in the Constitution; and shall, on the said last Wednesday in May annually, determine and declare who are elected by each district, to be Senators, by a majority of votes: And in case there shall not appear to be the full number of Senators returned elected by a majority of votes for any district, the deficiency shall be supplied in the following manner, viz. The members of the House of Representatives, and such Senators as shall be declared elected, shall take the names of such persons as shall be found to have the highest number of votes in such district, and not elected, amounting to twice the number of Senators wanting, if there be so many voted for; and, out of these, shall elect by ballot a number of Senators sufficient to fill up the vacancies in such district: And in this manner all such vacancies shall be filled up in every district of the Commonwealth; and in like manner all vacancies in the Senate, arising by death, removal out of the State, or otherwise, shall be supplied as soon as may be after such vacancies shall happen.

V.—Provided nevertheless, that no person shall be capable of being elected as a Senator, who is not seized in his own right of a freehold within this Commonwealth, of the value of three hundred pounds at least, or possessed of personal estate to the value of six hundred pounds at least, or of both to the amount of the same sum, and who has not been an inhabitant of this Commonwealth for the space of five years immediately preceding his election, and, at the time of his election, he shall be an inhabitant in the district, for which he shall be chosen.

VI.—The Senate shall have power to adjourn themselves, provided such adjournments do not exceed two days at a time.

VII.—The Senate shall choose its own President, appoint its own officers, and determine its own rules of proceeding.

VIII.—The Senate shall be a court with full authority to hear and determine all impeachments made by the House of Representatives, against any officer or officers of the Commonwealth, for misconduct and mal-administration in their offices. But, previous to the trial of every impeachment, the members of the Senate shall respectively be sworn, truly and impartially to try and determine the charge in question, according to evidence. Their judgment, however, shall not extend further than to removal from office and disqualification to hold or enjoy any place of honor, trust, or profit, under this Commonwealth: But the party, so convicted, shall be, nevertheless, liable to indictment, trial, judgment, and punishment, according to the laws of the land.

IX.—Not less than sixteen members of the Senate shall constitute a quorum for doing business.

Chapter I.

Section III. House of Representatives.

ART. I.—There shall be in the Legislature of this Commonwealth, a representation of the people, annually elected, and founded upon the principle of equality.

II.—And in order to provide for a representation of the citizens of this Commonwealth, founded upon the principle of equality, every corporate town, containing one hundred and fifty rateable polls, may elect one Representative: Every corporate town, containing three hundred and seventy-five rateable polls, may elect two Representa-tives: Every corporate town, containing six hundred rateable polls, may elect three Representatives; and proceeding in that manner, making two hundred and twenty-five rateable polls the mean increasing number for every additional Representative.

Provided nevertheless, that each town now incorporated, not having one hundred and fifty rateable polls, may elect one Representative: but no place shall hereafter be incorporated with the privilege of electing a Representative, unless there are within the same one hundred and fifty rateable polls.

And the House of Representatives shall have power, from time to time, to impose fines upon such towns as shall neglect to choose and return members to the same, agreeably to this Constitution.

The expenses of travelling to the General Assembly, and returning home, once in every session, and no more, shall be paid by the government, out of the public treasury, to every member who shall attend as seasonably as he can, in the judgment of the House, and does not depart without leave.

III.—Every member of the House of Representatives shall be chosen by written votes; and for one year at least next preceding his election shall have been an inhabitant of, and have been seized in his own right of a freehold of the value of one hundred pounds within the town he shall be chosen to represent, or any rateable estate to the value of two hundred pounds; and he shall cease to represent the said town immediately on his ceasing to be qualified as aforesaid.

IV.—Every male person, being twenty-one years of age, and resident in any particular town in this Commonwealth for the space of one year next preceding, having a freehold estate within the same town, of the annual income of three pounds, or any estate of the value of sixty pounds, shall have a right to vote in the choice of a Representative or Representatives for the said town.

V.—The members of the House of Representatives shall be chosen annually in the month of May, ten days at least before the last Wednesday of that month.

VI.—The House of Representatives shall be the Grand Inquest of this Commonwealth; and all impeachments made by them shall be heard and tried by the Senate.

VII.—All money-bills shall originate in the House of Representatives; but the Senate may propose or concur with amendments, as on other bills.

VIII.—The House of Representatives shall have power to adjourn themselves; provided such adjournment shall not exceed two days at a time.

IX.—Not less than sixty members of the House of Representatives shall constitute a quorum for doing business.

X.—The House of Representatives shall be the judge of the returns, elections, and qualifications of its own members, as pointed out in the constitution; shall choose their own Speaker; appoint their own officers, and settle the rules and orders of proceeding in their own house: They shall have authority to punish by imprisonment, every person, not a member, who shall be guilty of disrespect to the House, by any disorderly, or contemptuous behaviour, in its presence; or who, in the town where the General Court is sitting, and during the time of its sitting, shall threaten harm to the body or estate of any of its members, for any thing said or done in the House; or who shall assault any of them therefor; or who shall assault, or arrest, any witness, or other person, ordered to attend the House, in his way in going, or returning; or who shall rescue any person arrested by the order of the House.

And no member of the House of Representatives shall be arrested, or held to bail on mean process, during his going unto, returning from, or his attending, the General Assembly.

XI.—The Senate shall have the same powers in the like cases; and the Governor and Council shall have the same authority to punish in like cases. Provided, that no imprisonment on the warrant or order of the Governor, Council, Senate, or House of Representatives, for either of the above described offences, be for a term exceeding thirty days.

And the Senate and House of Representatives may try, and determine, all cases where their rights and privileges are concerned, and which, by the Constitution, they have authority to try and determine, by committees of their own members, or in such other way as they may respectively think best.

Chapter II. Executive Power.

Section I. Governor.

ART. I.—There shall be a Supreme Executive Magistrate, who shall be styled, THE GOVERNOR OF THE COMMONWEALTH OF MASSACHUSETTS; and whose title shall be—HIS EXCELLENCY.

II.—The Governor shall be chosen annually: And no person shall be eligible to this office, unless at the time of his election, he shall have been an inhabitant of this Commonwealth for seven years next preceding; and unless he shall, at the same time, be seized in his own right, of a freehold within the Commonwealth, of the value of one thousand pounds; and unless he shall declare himself to be of the christian religion.

III.—Those persons who shall be qualified to vote for Senators and Representatives within the several towns of this Commonwealth, shall, at a meeting, to be called for that purpose, on the first Monday of April annually, give in their votes for a Governor, to the Selectmen, who shall preside at such meetings; and the Town Clerk, in the presence and with the assistance of the Selectmen, shall, in open town meeting, sort and count the votes, and form a list of the persons voted for, with the number of votes for each person against his name; and shall make a fair record of the same in the town books, and a public declaration thereof in the said meeting; and shall, in the presence of the inhabitants, seal up copies of the said list, attested by him and the Selectmen, and transmit the same to the Sheriff of the county, thirty days at least before the last

Wednesday in May; and the Sheriff shall transmit the same to the Secretary's office seventeen days at least before the said last Wednesday in May; or the Selectmen may cause returns of the same to be made to the office of the Secretary of the Commonwealth seventeen days at least before the said day; and the Secretary shall lay the same before the Senate and the House of Representatives, on the last Wednesday in May, to be by them examined: And in case of an election by a majority of all the votes returned, the choice shall be by them declared and published: But if no person shall have a majority of votes, the House of Representatives shall, by ballot, elect two out of four persons who had the highest number of votes, if so many shall have been voted for; but, if otherwise, out of the number voted for; and make return to the Senate of the two persons so elected; on which, the Senate shall proceed, by ballot, to elect one, who shall be declared Governor.

IV.—The Governor shall have authority, from time to time, at his discretion, to assemble and call together the Counsellors of this Commonwealth for the time being; and the Governor, with the said Counsellors, or five of them at least, shall, and may, from time to time, hold and keep a Council, for the ordering and directing the affairs of the Commonwealth, agreeably to the Constitution and the laws of the land.

V.—The Governor, with advice of Council, shall have full power and authority, during the session of the General Court, to adjourn or prorogue the same to any time the two Houses shall desire; and to dissolve the same on the day next preceding the last Wednesday in May; and, in the recess of the said Court, to prorogue the same from time to time, not exceeding ninety days in any one recess; and to call it together sooner than the time to which it may be adjourned or prorogued, if the welfare of the Commonwealth shall require the same: And in case of any infectious distemper prevailing in the place where the said Court is next at any time to convene, or any other cause happening whereby danger may arise to the health or lives of the members from their attendance, he may direct the session to be held at some other the most convenient place within the State.

And the Governor shall dissolve the said General Court on the day next preceding the last Wednesday in May.

VI.—In cases of disagreement between the two Houses, with regard to the necessity, expediency or time of adjournment, or prorogation, the Governor, with advice of the Council, shall have a right to adjourn or prorogue the General Court, not exceeding ninety days, as he shall determine the public good shall require.

VII.—The Governor of this Commonwealth, for the time being, shall be the commander-in-chief of the army and navy, and of all the military forces of the State, by sea and land; and shall have full power, by himself, or by any commander, or other officer or officers, from time to time, to train, instruct, exercise and govern the militia and navy; and, for the special defence and safety of the Commonwealth, to assemble in martial array, and put in warlike posture, the inhabitants thereof, and to lead and conduct them, and with them, to encounter, repel, resist, expel and pursue, by force of arms, as well as by sea as by land, within or without the limits of this Commonwealth, and also to kill, slay and destroy, if necessary, and conquer, by all fitting ways, enterprizes and means whatsoever, all and every such person and persons as shall, at any time hereafter, in a hostile manner, attempt or enterprize the destruction, invasion, detriment, or annoyance of this Commonwealth; and to use and exercise, over the army and navy, and over the militia in actual service, the law martial, in time of war or invasion, and also in time of rebellion, declared by the legislature to exist, as occasion shall necessarily require; and to take and surprise by all ways and means whatsoever, all and every such person or persons, with their ships, arms, ammunition and other goods, as shall, in a hostile manner, invade, or attempt the invading, conquering, or annoying this Commonwealth; and that the Governor be intrusted with all these and other powers, incident to the offices of Captain-General and Commander-in-Chief, and Admiral, to be exercised agreeably to the rules and regulations of the Constitution, and the laws of the land, and not otherwise.

Provided, that the said Governor shall not, at any time hereafter, by virtue of any power by this Constitution granted, or hereafter to be granted to him by the legislature, transport any of the inhabitants of this Commonwealth, or oblige them to march out of the limits of the same, without their free and voluntary consent, or the consent of the General Court; except so far as may be necessary to march or transport them by land or water, for the defence of such part of the State, to which they cannot otherwise conveniently have access.

VIII.—The power of pardoning offences, except such as persons may be convicted of before the Senate by an impeachment of the House, shall be in the Governor, by and with the advice of Council: But no charter of pardon, granted by the Governor, with advice of the Council, before conviction, shall avail the party pleading the same, notwithstanding any general or particular expressions contained therein, descriptive of the offence, or offences intended to be pardoned.

IX.—All judicial officers, the Attorney-General, the Solicitor-General, all Sheriffs, Coroners, and Registers of Probate, shall be nominated and appointed by the Governor, by and with the advice and consent of the Council; and every such nomination shall be made by the Governor, and made at least seven days prior to such appointment.

X.—The Captains and subalterns of the militia shall be elected by the written votes of the train-band and alarm list of their respective companies, of twenty-one years of age and upwards: The field-officers of Regiments shall be elected by the written votes of the captains and subalterns of their respective regiments: The Brigadiers shall be elected in like manner, by the field officers of their respective brigades: And such officers, so elected, shall be commissioned by the Governor, who shall determine their rank.

The Legislature shall, by standing laws, direct the time and manner of convening the electors, and of collecting votes, and of certifying to the Governor the officers elected.

The Major-Generals shall be appointed by the Senate and House of Representatives, each having a negative upon the other; and be commissioned by the Governor.

And if the electors of Brigadiers, field-officers, captains or subalterns, shall neglect or refuse to make such elections, after being duly notified, according to the laws for the time being, then the Governor, with advice of Council, shall appoint suitable persons to fill such offices.

And no officer, duly commissioned to command in the militia, shall be removed from his office, but by the address of both houses to the Governor, or by fair trial in court martial, pursuant to the laws of the Commonwealth for the time being.

The commanding officers of regiments shall appoint their Adjutants and Quarter-masters; the Brigadiers their Brigade-Majors; and the Major-Generals their Aids: and the Governor shall appoint the Adjutant General.

The Governor, with advice of Council, shall appoint all officers of the continental army, whom by the confederation of the United States it is provided that this Commonwealth shall appoint,—as also all officers of forts and garrisons.

The divisions of the militia into brigades, regiments and companies, made in pursuance of the militia laws now in force, shall be considered as the proper divisions of the militia of this Commonwealth, until the same shall be altered in pursuance of some future law.

XI.—No monies shall be issued out of the treasury of this Commonwealth, and disposed of (except such sums as may be appropriated for the redemption of bills of credit or Treasurer's notes, or for the payment of interest arising thereon) but by warrant under the hand of the Governor for the time being, with the advice and consent of the Council, for the necessary defence and support of the Commonwealth; and for the protection and preservation of the inhabitants thereof, agreeably to the acts and resolves of the General Court.

XII.—All public boards, the Commissary-General, all superintending officers of public magazines and stores, belonging to this Commonwealth, and all commanding officers of forts and garrisons within the same, shall, once in every three months, officially and without requisition, and at other times, when required by the Governor, deliver to him an account of all goods, stores, provisions, ammunition, cannon with their appendages, and small arms with their accoutrements, and of all other public property whatever under their care respectively; distinguishing the quantity, number, quality and kind of each, as particularly as may be; together with the condition of such forts and garrisons: And the said commanding officer shall exhibit to the Governor, when required by him, true and exact plans of such forts, and of the land and sea, or harbour or harbours adjacent.

And the said boards, and all public officers, shall communicate to the Governor, as soon as may be after receiving the same, all letters, dispatches, and intelligences of a public nature, which shall be directed to them respectively.

XIII.—As the public good requires that the Governor should not be under the undue influence of any of the members of the General Court, by a dependence on them for his support—that he should, in all cases, act with freedom for the benefit of the public—that he should not have his attention necessarily diverted from that object to his private concerns—and that he should maintain the dignity of the Commonwealth in the character of its chief magistrate—it is necessary that he should have an honorable stated salary, of a fixed and permanent value, amply sufficient for those purposes, and established by standing laws: And it shall be among the first acts of the General Court, after the Commencement of this Constitution, to establish such salary by law accordingly.

Permanent and honorable salaries shall also be established by law for the Justices of the Supreme Judicial Court.

And if it shall be found, that any of the salaries aforesaid, so established, are insufficient, they shall, from time to time, be enlarged, as the General Court shall judge proper.

Chapter II.

Section II. Lieutenant-Governor.

ART. I.—There shall be annually elected a Lieutenant-Governor of the Commonwealth of Massachusetts, whose title shall be HIS HONOR—and who shall be qualified, in point of religion, property, and residence in the Commonwealth, in the same manner with the Governor: And the day and manner of his election, and the qualifications of the electors, shall be the same as are required in the election of a Governor. The return of the votes for this officer, and the declaration of his election, shall be in the same manner: And if no one person shall be found to have a majority of all the votes returned, the vacancy shall be filled by the Senate and House of Representatives, in the same manner as the Governor is to be elected, in case no one person shall have a majority of the votes of the people to be Governor.

II.—The Governor, and in his absence the Lieutenant-Governor, shall be President of the Council, but shall have no vote in Council: And the Lieutenant-Governor shall always be a member of the Council, except when the chair of the Governor shall be vacant.

III.—Whenever the chair of the Governor shall be vacant, by reason of his death, or absence from the Commonwealth, or otherwise, the Lieutenant-Governor, for the time being, shall, during such vacancy, perform all the duties incumbent upon the Governor, and shall have and exercise all the powers and authorities, which by this Constitution the Governor is vested with, when personally present.

Chapter II.

Section III. Council, and the Manner of Settling Elections by the Legislature.

ART. I.—There shall be a Council for advising the Governor in the executive part of government, to consist of nine persons besides the Lieutenant-Governor, whom the Governor, for the time being, shall have full power and authority, from time to time, at his discretion, to assemble and call together. And the Governor, with the said Counsellors, or five of them at least, shall and may, from time to time, hold and keep a council, for the ordering and directing the affairs of the Commonwealth, according to the laws of the land.

II.—Nine Counsellors shall be annually chosen from among the persons returned for Counsellors and Senators, on the last Wednesday in May, by the joint ballot of the Senators and Representatives assembled in one room: And in case there shall not be found, upon the first choice, the whole number of nine persons who will accept a seat in the Council, the deficiency shall be made up by the electors aforesaid from among the people at large; and the number of Senators left shall constitute the Senate for the year. The seats of the persons thus elected from the Senate, and accepting the trust, shall be vacated in the Senate.

III.—The Counsellors, in the civil arrangements of the Commonwealth, shall have rank next after the Lieutenant-Governor.

IV.—Not more than two Counsellors shall be chosen out of any one district of this Commonwealth.

V.—The resolutions and advice of the Council shall be recorded in a register, and signed by the members present; and this record may be called for at any time by either House of the Legislature; and any member of the Council may insert his opinion contrary to the resolution of the majority.

VI.—Whenever the office of the Governor and Lieutenant-Governor shall be vacant, by reason of death, absence, or otherwise, then the Council or the major part of them, shall, during such vacancy, have full power and authority, to do, and execute, all and every such acts, matters and things, as the Governor or the Lieutenant-Governor might or could, by virtue of this Constitution, do or execute, if they, or either of them, were personally present.

VII.—And whereas the elections appointed to be made by this Constitution, on the last Wednesday in May annually, by the two Houses of the Legislature, may not be completed on that day, the said elections may be adjourned from day to day until the same shall be completed. And the order of elections shall be as follows; the vacancies in the Senate, if any, shall first be filled up; the Governor and Lieutenant-Governor shall then be elected, provided there should be no choice of them by the people: And afterwards the two Houses shall proceed to the election of the Council.

Chapter II.

Section IV. Secretary, Treasurer, Commissary, etc.

ART. I.—The Secretary, Treasurer and Receiver-General, and the Commissary-General, Notaries-Public, and Naval-Officers, shall be chosen annually, by joint ballot of the Senators and Representatives in one room. And that the citizens of this Commonwealth may be assured, from time to time, that the monies remaining in the public Treasury, upon the settlement and liquidation of the public accounts, are their property, no man shall be eligible as Treasurer and Receiver-General more than five years successively.

II.—The records of Commonwealth shall be kept in the office of the Secretary, who may appoint his Deputies, for whose conduct he shall be accountable, and he shall attend the Governor and Council, the Senate and House of Representatives, in person, or by his deputies, as they shall respectively require.

Chapter III. Judiciary Power.

ART. I.—The tenure that all commission officers shall by law have in their offices, shall be expressed in their respective commissions. All judicial officers, duly appointed, commissioned and sworn, shall hold their offices during good behaviour, excepting such concerning whom there is different provision made in this Constitution: Provided, nevertheless, the Governor, with consent of the Council, may remove them upon the address of both Houses of the Legislature.

II.—Each branch of the Legislature, as well as the Governor and Council, shall have authority to require the opinions of the Justices of the Supreme Judicial Court, upon important questions of law, and upon solemn occasions.

III.—In order that the people may not suffer from the long continuance in place of any Justice of the Peace, who shall fail of discharging the important duties of his office with ability or fidelity, all commissions of Justices of the Peace shall expire and become void, in the term of seven years from their respective dates; and, upon the expiration of any commission, the same may, if necessary, be renewed, or another person appointed, as shall most conduce to the well being of the Commonwealth.

IV.—The Judges of Probate of Wills, and for granting letters of administration, shall hold their courts at such places or places, on fixed days, as the convenience of the people shall require. And the Legislature shall, from time to time, hereafter appoint such times and places; until which appointments, the said Courts shall be holden at the times and places which the respective Judges shall direct.

V.—All causes of marriage, divorce and alimony, and all appeals from the Judges of Probate, shall be heard and determined by the Governor and Council until the Legislature shall, by law, make other provisions.

Chapter IV. Delegates to Congress.

The delegates of this Commonwealth to the Congress of the United States, shall, sometime in the month of June annually, be elected by the joint ballot of the Senate and House of Representatives, assembled together in one room; to serve in Congress for one year, to commence on the first Monday in November then next ensuing. They shall have commissions under the hand of the Governor, and the great seal of the Commonwealth; but may be recalled at any time within the year, and others chosen and commissioned, in the same manner, in their stead.

Chapter V. The University at Cambridge, and Encouragement of Literature, etc.

Section I. The University.

ART. I.—Whereas our wise and pious ancestors, so early as the year one thousand six hundred and thirty six, laid the foundation of Harvard-College, in which University many persons of great eminence have, by the blessing of GOD, been initiated in those arts and sciences, which qualified them for public employments, both in Church and State: And whereas the encouragement of Arts and Sciences, and all good literature, tends to the honor of GOD, the advantage of the christian religion, and the great benefit of this, and the other United States of America—It is declared, That the PRESIDENT AND FELLOWS OF HARVARD-COLLEGE, in their corporate capacity, and their successors in that capacity, their officers and servants, shall have, hold, use, exercise and enjoy, all the powers, authorities, rights, liberties, privileges, immunities and franchises, which they now have, or are entitled to have, hold, use, exercise and enjoy: And the same are hereby ratified and confirmed unto them, the said President and Fellows of Harvard-College, and to their successors, and to their officers and servants, respectively, forever.

II.—And whereas there have been at sundry times, by divers persons, gifts, grants, devises of houses, lands, tenements, goods, chattels, legacies and conveyances, heretofore made, either to Harvard-College in Cambridge, in New-England, or to the President and Fellows of Harvard-College, or to the said College, by some other description, under several charters successively: IT IS DECLARED, That all the said gifts, grants, devises, legacies and conveyances, are hereby forever confirmed unto the President and Fellows of Harvard-College, and to their successors, in the capacity aforesaid, according to the true intent and meaning of the donor or donors, grantor or grantors, devisor or devisors.

III.—And whereas by an act of the General Court of the Colony of Massachusetts-Bay, passed in the year one thousand six hundred and forty-two, the Governor and Deputy-Governor, for the time being, and all the magistrates of that jurisdiction, were, with the President, and a number of the clergy in the said act described, constituted the Overseers of Harvard-College: And it being necessary, in this new Constitution of Government, to ascertain who shall be deemed successors to the said Governor, Deputy-Governor and Magistrates: IT IS DECLARED, That the Governor, Lieutenant-Governor, Council and Senate of this Commonwealth, are, and shall be deemed, their successors; who, with the President of Harvard-College, for the time being, together with the ministers of the congregational churches in the towns of Cambridge, Watertown, Charlestown, Boston, Roxbury, and Dorchester, mentioned in the said act, shall be, and hereby are, vested with all the powers and authority belonging, or in any way appertaining to the Overseers of Harvard-College; PROVIDED, that nothing herein shall be construed to prevent the Legislature of this Commonwealth from making such alterations in the government of the said university, as shall be conducive to its advantage, and the interest of the republic of letters, in as full a manner as might have been done by the Legislature of the late Province of the Massachusetts-Bay.

Chapter V.

Section II. The Encouragement of Literature, etc.

Wisdom, and knowledge, as well as virtue, diffused generally among the body of the people, being necessary for the preservation of their rights and liberties; and as these depend on spreading the opportunities and advantages of education in the various parts of the country, and among the different orders of the people, it shall be the duty of legislators and magistrates, in all future periods of this Commonwealth, to cherish the interests of literature and the sciences, and all seminaries of them; especially the university at Cambridge, public schools, and grammar schools in the towns; to encourage private societies and public institutions, rewards and immunities, for the promotion of agriculture, arts, sciences, commerce, trades, manufactures, and a natural history of the country; to countenance and inculcate the principles of humanity and general benevolence, public and private charity, industry and frugality, honesty and punctuality in their dealings; sincerity, good humour, and all social affections, and generous sentiments among the people.

Chapter VI. Oaths and Subscriptions; Incompatibility of and Exclusion from Offices; Pecuniary Qualifications; Commissions; Writs; Confirmation of Laws; Habeas Corpus; The Enacting Style; Continuance of Officers; Provision for a future Revisal of the Constitution, etc.

ART I.—Any person chosen Governor, Lieutenant-Governor, Counsellor, Senator, or Representative, and accepting the trust, shall, before he proceed to execute the duties of his place or office, make and subscribe the following declaration, viz.—

"I, A. B. do declare, that I believe the christian religion, and have a firm persuasion of its truth; and that I am seized and possessed, in my own right, of the property re-

quired by the Constitution as one qualification for the office or place to which I am elected."

And the Governor, Lieutenant-Governor, and Counsellors, shall make and subscribe the said declaration, in the presence of the two Houses of Assembly; and the Senators and Representatives first elected under this Constitution, before the President and five of the Council of the former Constitution, and, forever afterwards, before the Governor and Council for the time being.

And every person chosen to either of the places or offices aforesaid, as also any person appointed or commissioned to any judicial, executive, military, or other office under the government, shall, before he enters on the discharge of the business of his place or office, take and subscribe the following declaration, and oaths or affirmations, viz.—

"I, A. B. do truly and sincerely acknowledge, profess, testify and declare, that the Commonwealth of Massachusetts is, and of right ought to be, a free, sovereign and independent State; and I do swear, that I will bear true faith and allegiance to the said Commonwealth, and that I will defend the same against traitorous conspiracies and all hostile attempts whatsoever: And that I do renounce and adjure all allegiance, subjection and obedience to the King, Queen or Government of Great Britain, (as the case may be) and every other foreign power whatsoever: And that no foreign Prince, Person, Prelate, State or Potentate, hath, or ought to have, any jurisdiction, superiority, preeminence, authority, dispensing or other power, in any matter, civil, ecclesiastical or spiritual, within this Commonwealth; except the authority and power which is or may be vested by their Constituents in the Congress of the United States: And I do further testify and declare, that no man or body of men hath or can have any right to absolve or discharge me from the obligation of this oath, declaration or affirmation; and that I do make this acknowledgment, profession, testimony, declaration, denial, renunciation and abjuration, heartily and truly, according to the common meaning and acceptation of the foregoing words, without any equivocation, mental evasion, or secret reservation whatsoever. So help me GOD."

"I, A. B. do solemnly swear and affirm, that I will faithfully and impartially discharge and perform all the duties incumbent on me as   ; according to the best of my abilities and understanding, agreeably to the rules and regulations of the Constitution, and the laws of this Commonwealth." "So help me GOD."

Provided always, that when any person, chosen or appointed as aforesaid, shall be of the denomination of the people called Quakers, and shall decline taking the said oaths, he shall make his affirmation in the foregoing form, and subscribe the same, omitting the words "I do swear," "and adjure," "oath or," "and abjuration," in the first oath; and in the second oath, the words "swear and;" and in each of them the words "So help me GOD;" subjoining instead thereof, "This I do under the pains and penalties of perjury."

And the said oaths or affirmations shall be taken and subscribed by the Governor, Lieutenant Governor, and Counsellors, before the President of the Senate, in the presence of the two Houses of Assembly; and by the Senators and Representatives first elected under this Constitution, before the President and five of the Council of the former Constitution; and forever afterwards before the Governor and Council for the time being: And by the residue of the officers aforesaid, before such persons and in such manner as from time to time shall be prescribed by the Legislature.

II.—No Governor, Lieutenant Governor, or Judge of the Supreme Judicial Court, shall hold any other office or place, under the authority of this Commonwealth, except such as by this Constitution they are admitted to hold, saving that the Judges of the said Court may hold the offices of Justices of the Peace through the State; nor shall they hold any other place or office, or receive any pension or salary from any other State or Government or Power whatever.

No person shall be capable of holding or exercising at the same time, within this State, more than one of the following offices, viz:—Judge of Probate—Sheriff—Register of Probate—or Register of Deeds—and never more than any two offices which are to be held by appointment of the Governor, or the Governor and Council, or the Senate, or the House of Representatives, or by the election of the people of the State at large, or of the people of any county, military offices and the offices of Justices of the Peace excepted, shall be held by one person.

No person holding the office of Judge of the Supreme Judicial Court—Secretary—Attorney General—Solicitor General—Treasurer or Receiver General—Judge of Probate—Commissary General—President, Professor, or Instructor of Harvard College—Sheriff—Clerk of the House of Representatives—Register of Probate—Register of Deeds—Clerk of the Supreme Judicial Court—Clerk of the Inferior Court of Common Pleas—or Officer of the Customs, including in this description Naval Officers—shall at the same time have a seat in the Senate or House of Representatives; but their being chosen or appointed to, and accepting the same, shall operate as a resignation of their seat in the Senate or House of Representatives; and the place so vacated shall be filled up.

And the same rule shall take place in case any judge of the said Supreme Judicial Court, or Judge of Probate, shall accept a seat in Council; or any Counsellor shall accept of either of those offices or places.

And no person shall ever be admitted to hold a seat in the Legislature, or any office of trust or importance under the Government of this Commonwealth, who shall, in the due course of law, have been convicted of bribery or corruption in obtaining an election or appointment.

III.—In all cases where sums of money are mentioned in this Constitution, the value thereof shall be computed in silver at six shillings and eight pence per ounce: And it shall be in the power of the Legislature from time to time to increase such qualifications, as to property, of the persons to be elected to offices, as the circumstances of the Commonwealth shall require.

IV.—All commissions shall be in the name of the Commonwealth of Massachusetts, signed by the Governor, and attested by the Secretary or his Deputy, and have the great seal of the Commonwealth affixed thereto.

V.—All writs, issuing out of the clerk's office in any of the Courts of law, shall be in the name of the Commonwealth of Massachusetts: They shall be under the seal of the Court from whence they issue: They shall bear test of the first Justice of the Court to which they shall be returnable, who is not a party, and be signed by the clerk of such court.

VI.—All the laws which have heretofore been adopted, used and approved in the Province, Colony or State of Massachusetts Bay, and usually practiced on in the Courts of law, shall still remain and be in full force, until altered or repealed by the Legislature; such parts only excepted as are repugnant to the rights and liberties contained in this Constitution.

VII.—The privilege and benefit of the writ of *habeas corpus* shall be enjoyed in this Commonwealth in the most free, easy, cheap, expeditious and ample manner; and shall not be suspended by the Legislature, except upon the most urgent and pressing occasions, and for a limited time not exceeding twelve months.

VII.—The enacting style, in making and passing all acts, statutes and laws, shall be—"Be it enacted by the Senate and House of Representatives, in General Court assembled, and by the authority of the same."

IX.—To the end there may be no failure of justice or danger arise to the Commonwealth from a change of the Form of Government—all officers, civil and military, holding commissions under the government and people of Massachusetts Bay in New-England, and all other officers of the said government and people, at the time this Constitution shall take effect, shall have, hold, use, exercise and enjoy all the powers and authority to them granted or committed, until other persons shall be appointed in their stead: And all courts of law shall proceed in the execution of the business of their respective departments; and all the executive and legislative officers, bodies and powers shall continue in full force, in the enjoyment and exercise of all their trusts, employments and authority; until the General Court and the supreme and executive officers under this Constitution are designated and invested with their respective trusts, powers and authority.

X.—In order the more effectually to adhere to the principles of the Constitution, and to correct those violations which by any means may be made therein, as well as to form such alterations as from experience shall be found necessary—the General Court, which shall be in the year of our Lord one thousand seven hundred and ninety-five, shall issue precepts to the Selectmen of the several towns, and to the Assessors of the unincorporated plantations, directing them to convene the qualified voters of their respective towns and plantations for the purpose of collecting their sentiments on the necessity or expediency of revising the Constitution, in order to amendments.

And if it shall appear by the returns made, that two thirds of the qualified voters throughout the State, who shall assemble and vote in consequence of the said precepts, are in favor of such revision or amendment, the General Court shall issue precepts, or direct them to be issued from the Secretary's office to the several towns, to elect Delegates to meet in Convention for the purpose aforesaid.

The said Delegates to be chosen in the same manner and proportion as their Representatives in the second branch of the Legislature are by this Constitution to be chosen.

XI.—This form of government shall be enrolled on parchment, and deposited in the Secretary's office, and be a part of the laws of the land—and printed copies thereof shall be prefixed to the book containing the laws of this Commonwealth, in all future editions of the said laws.

JAMES BOWDOIN, *President.*
Attest. SAMUEL BARRETT, *Secretary.*

7

ARTICLES OF CONFEDERATION
1 Mar. 1781
Tansill 27–37

To all to whom these Presents shall come, we the under signed Delegates of the States affixed to our Names, send greeting.

Whereas the Delegates of the United States of America, in Congress assembled, did, on the 15th day of November, in the Year of Our Lord One thousand Seven Hundred and Seventy seven, and in the Second Year of the Independence of America, agree to certain articles of Confederation and perpetual Union between the States of Newhampshire, Massachusetts-bay, Rhodeisland and Providence Plantations, Connecticut, New York, New Jersey, Pennsylvania, Delaware, Maryland, Virginia, North-Carolina, South-Carolina, and Georgia in the words following, viz. "Articles of Confederation and perpetual Union between the states of Newhampshire, Massachusetts-bay, Rhodeisland and Providence Plantations, Connecticut, New-York, New-Jersey, Pennsylvania, Delaware, Maryland, Virginia, North-Carolina, South-Carolina and Georgia.

ARTICLE I. The Stile of this confederacy shall be "The United States of America."

ARTICLE II. Each state retains its sovereignty, freedom, and independence, and every Power, Jurisdiction and right, which is not by this confederation expressly delegated to the United States, in Congress assembled.

ARTICLE III. The said states hereby severally enter into a firm league of friendship with each other, for their common defence, the security of their Liberties, and their mutual and general welfare, binding themselves to assist each other, against all force offered to, or attacks made upon them, or any of them, on account of religion, sovereignty, trade, or any other pretence whatever.

ARTICLE IV. The better to secure and perpetuate mutual friendship and intercourse among the people of the different states in this union, the free inhabitants of each of these states, paupers, vagabonds and fugitives from justice excepted, shall be entitled to all privileges and immunities of free citizens in the several states; and the people of each state shall have free ingress and regress to and from any other state, and shall enjoy therein all the privileges of trade and commerce, subject to the same duties, impositions and restrictions as the inhabitants thereof respectively, provided that such restriction shall not extend so far as to prevent the removal of property imported into any state, to any other state, of which the Owner is an inhabitant; provided also that no imposition, duties or restriction shall be laid by any state, on the property of the united states, or either of them.

If any Person guilty of, or charged with treason, felony, or other high misdemeanor in any state, shall flee from Justice, and be found in any of the united states, he shall, upon demand of the Governor or executive power, of the state from which he fled, be delivered up and removed to the state having jurisdiction of his offence.

Full faith and credit shall be given in each of these states to the records, acts and judicial proceedings of the courts and magistrates of every other state.

ARTICLE V. For the more convenient management of the general interests of the united states, delegates shall be annually appointed in such manner as the legislature of each state shall direct, to meet in Congress on the first Monday in November, in every year, with a power reserved to each state, to recal its delegates, or any of them, at any time within the year, and to send others in their stead, for the remainder of the Year.

No state shall be represented in Congress by less than two, nor by more than seven Members; and no person shall be capable of being a delegate for more than three years in any term of six years; nor shall any person, being a delegate, be capable of holding any office under the united states, for which he, or another for his benefit receives any salary, fees or emolument of any kind.

Each state shall maintain its own delegates in a meeting of the states, and while they act as members of the committee of the states.

In determining questions in the united states in Congress assembled, each state shall have one vote.

Freedom of speech and debate in Congress shall not be impeached or questioned in any Court, or place out of Congress, and the members of congress shall be protected in their persons from arrests and imprisonments, during the time of their going to and from, and attendance on congress, except for treason, felony, or breach of the peace.

ARTICLE VI. No state, without the Consent of the united states in congress assembled, shall send any embassy to, or receive any embassy from, or enter into any conference, agreement, alliance or treaty with any King prince or state;

nor shall any person holding any office of profit or trust under the united states, or any of them, accept of any present, emolument, office or title of any kind whatever from any king, prince or foreign state; nor shall the united states in congress assembled, or any of them, grant any title of nobility.

No two or more states shall enter into any treaty, confederation or alliance whatever between them, without the consent of the united states in congress assembled, specifying accurately the purposes for which the same is to be entered into, and how long it shall continue.

No state shall lay any imposts or duties, which may interfere with any stipulations in treaties, entered into by the united states in congress assembled, with any king, prince or state, in pursuance of any treaties already proposed by congress, to the courts of France and Spain.

No vessels of war shall be kept up in time of peace by any state, except such number only, as shall be deemed necessary by the united states in congress assembled, for the defence of such state, or its trade; nor shall any body of forces be kept up by any state, in time of peace, except such number only, as in the judgment of the united states, in congress assembled, shall be deemed requisite to garrison the forts necessary for the defence of such state; but, every state shall always keep up a well regulated and disciplined militia, sufficiently armed and accoutred, and shall provide and constantly have ready for use, in public stores, a due number of field pieces and tents, and a proper quantity of arms, ammunition and camp equipage.

No state shall engage in any war without the consent of the united states in congress assembled, unless such state be actually invaded by enemies, or shall have received certain advice of a resolution being formed by some nation of Indians to invade such state, and the danger is so imminent as not to admit of a delay till the united states in congress assembled can be consulted: nor shall any state grant commissions to any ships or vessels of war, nor letters of marque or reprisal, except it be after a declaration of war by the united states in congress assembled, and then only against the kingdom or state and the subjects thereof, against which war has been so declared, and under such regulations as shall be established by the united states in congress assembled, unless such state be infested by pirates, in which case vessels of war may be fitted out for that occasion, and kept so long as the danger shall continue, or until the united states in congress assembled, shall determine otherwise.

ARTICLE VII. When land-forces are raised by any state for the common defence, all officers of or under the rank of colonel, shall be appointed by the legislature of each state respectively, by whom such forces shall be raised, or in such manner as such state shall direct, and all vacancies shall be filled up by the State which first made the appointment.

ARTICLE VIII. All charges of war, and all other expences that shall be incurred for the common defence or general welfare, and allowed by the united states in con-

gress assembled, shall be defrayed out of a common treasury, which shall be supplied by the several states in proportion to the value of all land within each state, granted to or surveyed for any Person, as such land and the buildings and improvements thereon shall be estimated according to such mode as the united states in congress assembled, shall from time to time direct and appoint.

The taxes for paying that proportion shall be laid and levied by the authority and direction of the legislatures of the several states within the time agreed upon by the united states in congress assembled.

ARTICLE IX. The united states in congress assembled, shall have the sole and exclusive right and power of determining on peace and war, except in the cases mentioned in the sixth article—of sending and receiving ambassadors—entering into treaties and alliances, provided that no treaty of commerce shall be made whereby the legislative power of the respective states shall be restrained from imposing such imposts and duties on foreigners as their own people are subjected to, or from prohibiting the exportation or importation of any species of goods or commodities, whatsoever—of establishing rules for deciding in all cases, what captures on land or water shall be legal, and in what manner prizes taken by land or naval forces in the service of the united states shall be divided or appropriated—of granting letters of marque and reprisal in times of peace—appointing courts for the trial of piracies and felonies committed on the high seas and establishing courts for receiving and determining finally appeals in all cases of captures, provided that no member of congress shall be appointed a judge of any of the said courts.

The united states in congress assembled shall also be the last resort on appeal in all disputes and differences now subsisting or that hereafter may arise between two or more states concerning boundary, jurisdiction or any other cause whatever; which authority shall always be exercised in the manner following. Whenever the legislative or executive authority or lawful agent of any state in controversy with another shall present a petition to congress stating the matter in question and praying for a hearing, notice thereof shall be given by order of congress to the legislative or executive authority of the other state in controversy, and a day assigned for the appearance of the parties by their lawful agents, who shall then be directed to appoint by joint consent, commissioners or judges to constitute a court for hearing and determining the matter in question: but if they cannot agree, congress shall name three persons out of each of the united states, and from the list of such persons each party shall alternately strike out one, the petitioners beginning, until the number shall be reduced to thirteen; and from that number not less than seven, nor more than nine names as congress shall direct, shall in the presence of congress be drawn out by lot, and the persons whose names shall be so drawn or any five of them, shall be commissioners or judges, to hear and finally determine the controversy, so always as a major part of the judges who shall hear the cause shall agree in the determination: and if either party shall neglect to attend at the day appointed, without showing reasons, which congress shall judge sufficient, or being present shall refuse to strike, the congress shall proceed to nominate three persons out of each state, and the secretary of congress shall strike in behalf of such party absent or refusing; and the judgment and sentence of the court to be appointed, in the manner before prescribed, shall be final and conclusive; and if any of the parties shall refuse to submit to the authority of such court, or to appear or defend their claim or cause, the court shall nevertheless proceed to pronounce sentence, or judgment, which shall in like manner be final and decisive, the judgment or sentence and other proceedings being in either case transmitted to congress, and lodged among the acts of congress for the security of the parties concerned: provided that every commissioner, before he sits in judgment, shall take an oath to be administered by one of the judges of the supreme or superior court of the state, where the cause shall be tried, "well and truly to hear and determine the matter in question, according to the best of his judgment, without favour, affection or hope of reward:" provided also, that no state shall be deprived of territory for the benefit of the united states.

All controversies concerning the private right of soil claimed under different grants of two or more states, whose jurisdictions as they may respect such lands, and the states which passed such grants are adjusted, the said grants or either of them being at the same time claimed to have originated antecedent to such settlement of jurisdiction, shall on the petition of either party to the congress of the united states, be finally determined as near as may be in the same manner as is before prescribed for deciding disputes respecting territorial jurisdiction between different states.

The united states in congress assembled shall also have the sole and exclusive right and power of regulating the alloy and value of coin struck by their own authority, or by that of the respective states—fixing the standard of weights and measures throughout the united states—regulating the trade and managing all affairs with the Indians, not members of any of the states, provided that the legislative right of any state within its own limits be not infringed or violated—establishing or regulating post-offices from one state to another, throughout all the united states, and exacting such postage on the papers passing thro' the same as may be requisite to defray the expences of the said office—appointing all officers of the land forces, in the service of the united states, excepting regimental officers—appointing all the officers of the naval forces, and commissioning all officers whatever in the service of the united states—making rules for the government and regulation of the said land and naval forces, and directing their operations.

The united states in congress assembled shall have authority to appoint a committee, to sit in the recess of congress, to be denominated "A Committee of the States," and to consist of one delegate from each state; and to appoint such other committees and civil officers as may be necessary for managing the general affairs of the united states under their direction—to appoint one of their number to preside, provided that no person be allowed to serve in the office of president more than one year in any term of three years; to ascertain the necessary sums of money to be raised for the service of the united states, and to appropriate and apply the same for defraying the public expences—to borrow money, or emit bills on the credit of the united states, transmitting every half year to the respective states an account of the sums of money so borrowed or emitted,—to build and equip a navy—to agree upon the number of land forces, and to make requisitions from each state for its quota, in proportion to the number of white inhabitants in such state; which requisition shall be binding, and thereupon the legislature of each state shall appoint the regimental officers, raise the men and cloath, arm and equip them in a soldier like manner, at the expence of the united states; and the officers and men so cloathed, armed and equipped shall march to the place appointed, and within the time agreed on by the united states in congress assembled: But if the united states in congress assembled shall, on consideration of circumstances judge proper that any state should not raise men, or should raise a smaller number than its quota, and that any other state should raise a greater number of men than the quota thereof, such extra number shall be raised, officered, cloathed, armed and equipped in the same manner as the quota of such state, unless the legislature of such state shall judge that such extra number cannot be safely spared out of the same, in which case they shall raise officer, cloath, arm and equip as many of such extra number as they judge can be safely spared. And the officers and men so cloathed, armed and equipped, shall march to the place appointed, and within the time agreed on by the united states in congress assembled.

The united states in congress assembled shall never engage in a war, nor grant letters of marque and reprisal in time of peace, nor enter into any treaties or alliances, nor coin money, nor regulate the value thereof, nor ascertain the sums and expences necessary for the defence and welfare of the united states, or any of them, nor emit bills, nor borrow money on the credit of the united states, nor appropriate money, nor agree upon the number of vessels of war, to be built or purchased, or the number of land or sea forces to be raised, nor appoint a commander in chief of the army or navy, unless nine states assent to the same: nor shall a question on any other point, except for adjourning from day to day be determined, unless by the votes of a majority of the united states in congress assembled.

The congress of the united states shall have power to adjourn to any time within the year, and to any place within the united states, so that no period of adjournment be for a longer duration than the space of six Months, and shall publish the Journal of their proceedings monthly, except such parts thereof relating to treaties, alliances or military operations, as in their judgment require secrecy; and the yeas and nays of the delegates of each state on any question shall be entered on the Journal, when it is desired by any delegate; and the delegates of a state, or any of them, at his or their request shall be furnished with a transcript of the said Journal, except such parts as are above excepted, to lay before the legislatures of the several states.

Article X. The committee of the states, or any nine of them, shall be authorized to execute, in the recess of congress, such of the powers of congress as the united states in congress assembled, by the consent of nine states, shall from time to time think expedient to vest them with; provided that no power be delegated to the said committee, for the exercise of which, by the articles of confederation, the voice of nine states in the congress of the united states assembled is requisite.

Article XI. Canada acceding to this confederation, and joining in the measures of the united states, shall be admitted into, and entitled to all the advantages of this union: but no other colony shall be admitted into the same, unless such admission be agreed to by nine states.

Article XII. All bills of credit emitted, monies borrowed and debts contracted by, or under the authority of congress, before the assembling of the united states, in pursuance of the present confederation, shall be deemed and considered as a charge against the united states, for payment and satisfaction whereof the said united states, and the public faith are hereby solemnly pledged.

Article XIII. Every state shall abide by the determinations of the united states in congress assembled, on all questions which by this confederation are submitted to them. And the Articles of this confederation shall be inviolably observed by every state, and the union shall be perpetual; nor shall any alteration at any time hereafter be made in any of them; unless such alteration be agreed to in a congress of the united states, and be afterwards confirmed by the legislatures of every state.

And Whereas it hath pleased the Great Governor of the World to incline the hearts of the legislatures we respectively represent in congress, to approve of, and to authorize us to ratify the said articles of confederation and perpetual union. Know Ye that we the undersigned delegates, by virtue of the power and authority to us given for that purpose, do by these presents, in the name and in behalf of our respective constituents, fully and entirely ratify and confirm each and every of the said articles of confederation and perpetual union, and all and singular the matters and things therein contained: And we do further solemnly plight and engage the faith of our respective constituents, that they shall abide by the determinations of the united states in congress assembled, on all questions, which by the said confederation are submitted to them. And that the articles thereof shall be inviolably observed by the states we respectively represent, and that the union shall be perpetual. In Witness whereof we have hereunto set our hands in Congress. Done at Philadelphia in the state of Pennsylvania the ninth day of July, in the Year of our Lord one Thousand seven Hundred and Seventy-eight, and in the third year of the independence of America.

Josiah Bartlett, John Wentworth, junr August 8th, 1778, — On the part & behalf of the State of New Hampshire.

John Hancock, Samuel Adams, Elbridge Gerry, Francis Dana, James Lovell, Samuel Holten, — On the part and behalf of the State of Massachusetts Bay.

William Ellery, Henry Marchant, John Collins, — On the part and behalf of the State of Rhode-Island and Providence Plantations.

Roger Sherman, Samuel Huntington, Oliver Wolcott, Titus Hosmer, Andrew Adams, — On the part and behalf of the State of Connecticut.

Jas Duane, Fra: Lewis, Wm Duer, Gouvr Morris, — On the part and behalf of the State of New York.

Jno Witherspoon, Nathl Scudder, — On the Part and in Behalf of the State of New Jersey, November 26th, 1778.

Robert Morris, Daniel Roberdeau, Jon. Bayard Smith, William Clingan, Joseph Reed, 22d July, 1778, — On the part and behalf of the State of Pennsylvania.

Thos McKean, Febr 22d, 1779, John Dickinson, May 5th, 1779, Nicholas Van Dyke, — On the part & behalf of the State of Delaware.

John Hanson, March 1, 1781, Daniel Carroll, do — On the part and behalf of the State of Maryland.

Richard Henry Lee, John Banister, Thomas Adams, Jno Harvie, Francis Lightfoot Lee, — On the Part and Behalf of the State of Virginia.

John Penn, July 21st, 1778, Corns Harnett, Jno Williams, — On the part and behalf of the State of North Carolina.

Henry Laurens, William Henry Drayton, Jno Mathews, Richd Hutson, Thos Heyward, junr. — On the part and on behalf of the State of South Carolina.

Jno Walton, 24th July, 1778, Edwd Telfair, Edwd Langworthy, — On the part and behalf of the State of Georgia

8

NORTHWEST ORDINANCE
13 July 1787
Tansill 47–54

An Ordinance for the government of the territory of the United States northwest of the river Ohio

SECTION 1. *Be it ordained by the United States in Congress assembled,* That the said Territory, for the purpose of temporary government, be one district, subject, however, to be divided into two districts, as future circumstances may, in the opinion of Congress, make it expedient.

SEC. 2. *Be it ordained by the authority aforesaid,* That the estates both of resident and non-resident proprietors in the said territory, dying intestate, shall descend to, and be distributed among, their children and the descendants of a deceased child in equal parts, the descendants of a deceased child or grandchild to take the share of their deceased parent in equal parts among them; and where there shall be no children or descendants, then in equal parts to the next of kin, in equal degree; and among collaterals, the children of a deceased brother or sister of the intestate shall have, in equal parts among them, their deceased parent's share; and there shall, in no case, be a distinction between kindred of the whole and half blood; saving in all cases to the widow of the intestate, her third part of the real estate for life, and one-third part of the personal estate; and this law relative to descents and dower, shall remain in full force until altered by the legislature of the district. And until the governor and judges shall adopt laws as hereinafter mentioned, estates in the said territory may be devised or bequeathed by wills in writing, signed and sealed by him or her in whom the estate may be, (being of full age,) and attested by three witnesses; and real estates may be conveyed by lease and release, or bargain and sale, signed, sealed, and delivered by the person, being of full age, in whom the estate may be, and attested by two witnesses, provided such wills be duly proved, and such conveyances be acknowledged, or the execution thereof duly proved, and be recorded within one year after proper magistrates, courts, and registers, shall be appointed for that purpose; and personal property may be transferred by delivery, saving, however, to the French and Canadian inhabitants, and other settlers of the Kaskaskies, Saint Vincents, and the neighboring villages, who have heretofore professed themselves citizens of Virginia, their laws and customs now in force among them, relative to the descent and conveyance of property.

SEC. 3. *Be it ordained by the authority aforesaid,* That there shall be appointed, from time to time, by Congress, a governor, whose commission shall continue in force for the term of three years, unless sooner revoked by Congress; he shall reside in the district, and have a freehold estate therein, in one thousand acres of land, while in the exercise of his office.

SEC. 4. There shall be appointed from time to time, by Congress, a secretary, whose commission shall continue in force for four years, unless sooner revoked; he shall reside in the district, and have a freehold estate therein, in five hundred acres of land, while in the exercise of his office. It shall be his duty to keep and preserve the acts and laws passed by the legislature, and the public records of the district, and the proceedings of the governor in his executive department, and transmit authentic copies of such acts and proceedings every six months to the Secretary of Congress. There shall also be appointed a court, to consist of three judges, any two of whom to form a court, who shall have a common-law jurisdiction and reside in the district, and have each therein a freehold estate, in five hundred acres of land, while in the exercise of their offices; and their commissions shall continue in force during good behavior.

SEC. 5. The governor and judges, or a majority of them, shall adopt and publish in the district such laws of the original States, criminal and civil, as may be necessary, and best suited to the circumstances of the district, and report them to Congress from time to time, which laws shall be in force in the district until the organization of the general assembly therein, unless disapproved of by Congress; but afterwards the legislature shall have authority to alter them as they shall think fit.

SEC. 6. The governor, for the time being, shall be commander-in-chief of the militia, appoint and commission all officers in the same below the rank of general officers; all general officers shall be appointed and commissioned by Congress.

SEC. 7. Previous to the organization of the general assembly the governor shall appoint such magistrates, and other civil officers, in each county or township, as he shall find necessary for the preservation of the peace and good order in the same. After the general assembly shall be organized the powers and duties of magistrates and other civil officers shall be regulated and defined by the said assembly; but all magistrates and other civil officers, not herein otherwise directed, shall, during the continuance of this temporary government, be appointed by the governor.

SEC. 8. For the prevention of crimes, and injuries, the laws to be adopted or made shall have force in all parts of the district, and for the execution of process, criminal and civil, the governor shall make proper divisions thereof; and he shall proceed, from time to time, as circumstances may require, to lay out the parts of the district in which the Indian titles shall have been extinguished, into counties and townships, subject, however, to such alterations as may thereafter be made by the legislature.

SEC. 9. So soon as there shall be five thousand free male inhabitants, of full age, in the district, upon giving proof thereof to the governor, they shall receive authority, with time and place, to elect representatives from their counties or townships, to represent them in the general assembly: *Provided,* That for every five hundred free male inhabitants there shall be one representative, and so on, progressively, with the number of free male inhabitants, shall the right of representation increase, until the number of representatives shall amount to twenty-five; after which the number and proportion of representatives shall be regulated by the legislature: *Provided,* That no person be eligible or qualified to act as a representative, unless he shall have been a citizen of one of the United States three years, and be a resident in the district, or unless he shall have resided in the district three years; and, in either case, shall likewise hold in his own right, in fee-simple, two hundred acres of land within the same: *Provided also,* That a freehold in fifty acres of land in the district, having been a citizen of one of the States, and being resident in the district, or the like freehold and two years' residence in the district, shall be necessary to qualify a man as an elector of a representative.

SEC. 10. The representatives thus elected shall serve for the term of two years; and in case of the death of a representative, or removal from office, the governor shall issue a writ to the county or township, for which he was a member, to elect another in his stead, to serve for the residue of the term.

SEC. 11. The general assembly, or legislature, shall consist of the governor, legislative council, and a house of representatives. The legislative council shall consist of five members, to continue in office five years, unless sooner removed by Congress; any three of whom to be a quorum; and the members of the council shall be nominated and appointed in the following manner, to wit: As soon as representatives shall be elected the governor shall appoint a time and place for them to meet together, and when met they shall nominate ten persons, resident in the district, and each possessed of a freehold in five hundred acres of land, and return their names to Congress, five of whom Congress shall appoint and commission to serve as aforesaid; and whenever a vacancy shall happen in the Council, by death or removal from office, the house of representatives shall nominate two persons, qualified as aforesaid, for each vacancy, and return their names to Congress, one of whom Congress shall appoint and commission for the residue of the term; and every five years, four months at least before the expiration of the time of service of the members of the council, the said house shall nominate ten persons, qualified as aforesaid, and return their names to Congress, five of whom Congress shall appoint and commission to serve as members of the council five years, unless sooner removed. And the governor, legislative council, and house of representatives shall have authority to make laws in all cases for the good government of the district, not repugnant to the principles and articles in this ordinance established and declared. And all bills, having passed by a majority in the house, and by a majority in the council, shall be referred to the governor for his assent; but no bill, or legislative act whatever, shall be of any force without his assent. The governor shall have power to convene, prorogue, and dissolve the general assembly when, in his opinion, it shall be expedient.

SEC. 12. The governor, judges, legislative council, secretary, and such other officers as Congress shall appoint in the district, shall take an oath or affirmation of fidelity, and of office; the governor before the President of Congress, and all other officers before the governor. As soon as a legislature shall be formed in the district, the council and house assembled, in one room, shall have authority, by joint ballot, to elect a delegate to Congress, who shall have a seat in Congress, with a right of debating, but not of voting, during this temporary government.

SEC. 13. And for extending the fundamental principles of civil and religious liberty, which form the basis whereon these republics, their laws and constitutions, are erected; to fix and establish those principles as the basis of all laws, constitutions, and governments, which forever hereafter shall be formed in the said territory; to provide, also, for the establishment of States, and permanent government therein, and for their admission to a share in the Federal councils on an equal footing with the original States, at as early periods as may be consistent with the general interest:

SEC. 14. It is hereby ordained and declared, by the authority aforesaid, that the following articles shall be considered as articles of compact, between the original States and the people and States in the said territory, and forever remain unalterable, unless by common consent, to wit:

Article I

No person, demeaning himself in a peaceable and orderly manner, shall ever be molested on account of his mode of worship, or religious sentiments, in the said territory.

Article II

The inhabitants of the said territory shall always be entitled to the benefits of the writs of *habeas corpus,* and of the trial by jury; of a proportionate representation of the people in the legislature, and of judicial proceedings according to the course of the common law. All persons shall be bailable, unless for capital offences, where the proof shall be evident, or the presumption great. All fines shall be moderate; and no cruel or unusual punishment shall be inflicted. No man shall be deprived of his liberty or property, but by the judgment of his peers, or the law of the land, and should the public exigencies make it necessary, for the common preservation, to take any person's property, or to demand his particular services, full compensation shall be made for the same. And, in the just preservation of rights and property, it is understood and declared, that no law ought ever to be made or have force in the said territory, that shall, in any manner whatever, interfere with or affect private contracts, or engagements, *bona fide,* and without fraud previously formed.

Article III

Religion, morality, and knowledge being necessary to good government and the happiness of mankind, schools and the means of education shall forever be encouraged. The utmost good faith shall always be observed towards the Indians; their lands and property shall never be taken from them without their consent; and in their property, rights, and liberty they never shall be invaded or disturbed unless in just and lawful wars authorized by Congress; but laws founded in justice and humanity shall, from time to time, be made, for preventing wrongs being done to them, and for preserving peace and friendship with them.

Article IV

The said territory, and the States which may be formed therein, shall forever remain a part of this confederacy of the United States of America, subject to the articles of Confederation, and to such alterations therein as shall be constitutionally made; and to all the acts and ordinances of the United States in Congress assembled, conformable thereto. The inhabitants and settlers in the said territory shall be subject to pay a part of the Federal debts, contracted, or to be contracted, and a proportional part of the expenses of government to be apportioned on them by Congress, according to the same common rule and measure by which apportionments thereof shall be made on the other States; and the taxes for paying their proportion shall be laid and levied by the authority and direction of the legislatures of the district, or districts, or new States, as in the original States, within the time agreed upon by the United States in Congress assembled. The legislatures of those districts, or new States, shall never interfere with the primary disposal of the soil by the United States in Congress assembled, nor with any regulations Congress may find necessary for securing the title in such soil to the *bona-fide* purchasers. No tax shall be imposed on lands the property of the United States; and in no case shall nonresident proprietors be taxed higher than residents. The navigable waters leading into the Mississippi and Saint Lawrence, and the carrying places between the same, shall be common highways, and forever free, as well to the inhabitants of the said territory as to the citizens of the United States, and those of any other States that may be admitted into the confederacy, without any tax, impost, or duty therefor.

Article V

There shall be formed in the said territory not less than three nor more than five States; and the boundaries of the States, as soon as Virginia shall alter her act of cession and consent to the same, shall become fixed and established as follows, to wit: The western State, in the said territory, shall be bounded by the Mississippi, the Ohio, and the Wabash Rivers; a direct line drawn from the Wabash and Post Vincents, due north, to the territorial line between the United States and Canada; and by the said territorial line to the Lake of the Woods and Mississippi. The middle State shall be bounded by the said direct line, the Wabash from Post Vincents to the Ohio, by the Ohio, by a direct line drawn due north from the mouth of the Great Miami to the said territorial line, and by the said territorial line. The eastern State shall be bounded by the last-mentioned direct line, the Ohio, Pennsylvania, and the said territorial line: *Provided, however,* And it is further understood and declared, that the boundaries of these three States shall be subject so far to be altered, that, if Congress shall hereafter find it expedient, they shall have authority to form one or two States in that part of the said territory which lies north of an east and west line drawn through the southerly bend or extreme of Lake Michigan. And whenever any of the said States shall have sixty thousand free inhabitants therein, such State shall be admitted by its delegates, into the Congress of the United States, on an equal footing with the original States, in all respects whatever; and shall be at liberty to form a permanent constitution and State government: *Provided,* The constitution and government, so to be formed, shall be republican, and in conformity to the principles contained in these articles, and, so far as it can be consistent with the general interest of the confederacy, such admission shall be allowed at an earlier period, and when there may be a less number of free inhabitants in the State than sixty thousand.

Article VI

There shall be neither slavery nor involuntary servitude in the said territory, otherwise than in the punishment of crimes, whereof the party shall have been duly convicted: *Provided always,* That any person escaping into the same, from whom labor or service is lawfully claimed in any one of the original States, such fugitive may be lawfully reclaimed, and conveyed to the person claiming his or her labor or service as aforesaid.

Be it ordained by the authority aforesaid, That the resolutions of the 23d of April, 1784, relative to the subject of this ordinance, be, and the same are hereby, repealed, and declared null and void.

Done by the United States, in Congress assembled, the 13th day of July, in the year of our Lord 1787, and of their sovereignty and independence the twelfth.

9

CONSTITUTION OF THE UNITED STATES AND THE FIRST TWELVE AMENDMENTS
1787–1804
Tansill 989–1002, 1066–69

We the People of the United States, in Order to form a more perfect Union, establish Justice, insure domestic Tranquility, provide for the common defence, promote the general Welfare, and secure the Blessings of Liberty to ourselves and our Posterity, do ordain and establish this Constitution for the United States of America.

Article. I.

SECTION 1. All legislative Powers herein granted shall be vested in a Congress of the United States, which shall consist of a Senate and House of Representatives.

SECTION 2. The House of Representatives shall be composed of Members chosen every second Year by the People of the several States, and the Electors in each State shall have the Qualifications requisite for Electors of the most numerous Branch of the State Legislature.

No person shall be a Representative who shall not have attained to the Age of twenty five Years, and been seven Years a Citizen of the United States, and who shall not, when elected, be an Inhabitant of that State in which he shall be chosen.

Representatives and direct Taxes shall be apportioned among the several States which may be included within this Union, according to their respective Numbers, which shall be determined by adding to the whole Number of free Persons, including those bound to Service for a Term of Years, and excluding Indians not taxed, three fifths of all other Persons. The actual Enumeration shall be made within three Years after the first Meeting of the Congress of the United States, and within every subsequent Term of ten Years, in such Manner as they shall by Law direct. The Number of Representatives shall not exceed one for every thirty Thousand, but each State shall have at Least one Representative; and until such enumeration shall be made, the State of New Hampshire shall be entitled to chuse three, Massachusetts eight, Rhode-Island and Providence Plantations one, Connecticut five, New-York six, New Jersey four, Pennsylvania eight, Delaware one, Maryland six, Virginia ten, North Carolina five, South Carolina five, and Georgia three.

When vacancies happen in the Representation from any State, the Executive Authority thereof shall issue Writs of Election to fill such Vacancies.

The House of Representatives shall chuse their Speaker and other Officers; and shall have the sole Power of Impeachment.

SECTION 3. The Senate of the United States shall be composed of two Senators from each State, chosen by the Legislature thereof, for six Years; and each Senator shall have one Vote.

Immediately after they shall be assembled in Consequence of the first Election, they shall be divided as equally as may be into three Classes. The Seats of the Senators of the first Class shall be vacated at the Expiration of the second Year, of the second Class at the Expiration of the fourth Year, and of the third Class at the Expiration of the sixth Year, so that one third may be chosen every second Year; and if Vacancies happen by Resignation, or otherwise, during the Recess of the Legislature of any State, the Executive thereof may make temporary Appointments until the next Meeting of the Legislature, which shall then fill such Vacancies.

No Person shall be a Senator who shall not have attained to the Age of thirty Years, and been nine Years a Citizen of the United States, and who shall not, when elected, be an Inhabitant of that State for which he shall be chosen.

The Vice President of the United States shall be President of the Senate, but shall have no Vote, unless they be equally divided.

The Senate shall chuse their other Officers, and also a President pro tempore, in the Absence of the Vice President, or when he shall exercise the Office of President of the United States.

The Senate shall have the sole Power to try all Impeachments. When sitting for that Purpose, they shall be on Oath or Affirmation. When the President of the United States is tried, the Chief Justice shall preside: And no Person shall be convicted without the Concurrence of two thirds of the Members present.

Judgment in Cases of Impeachment shall not extend further than to removal from Office, and disqualification to hold and enjoy any Office of honor, Trust or Profit under the United States: but the Party convicted shall nevertheless be liable and subject to Indictment, Trial, Judgment and Punishment, according to Law.

SECTION 4. The Times, Places and Manner of holding Elections for Senators and Representatives, shall be prescribed in each State by the Legislature thereof; but the Congress may at any time by Law make or alter such Regulations, except as to the Places of chusing Senators.

The Congress shall assemble at least once in every Year, and such Meeting shall be on the first Monday in December, unless they shall by Law appoint a different Day.

SECTION 5. Each House shall be the Judge of the Elections, Returns and Qualifications of its own Members, and a Majority of each shall constitute a Quorum to do Business; but a smaller Number may adjourn from day to day, and may be authorized to compel the Attendance of absent Members, in such Manner, and under such Penalties as each House may provide.

Each House may determine the Rules of its Proceedings, punish its Members for disorderly Behaviour, and, with the Concurrence of two thirds, expel a Member.

Each House shall keep a Journal of its Proceedings, and from time to time publish the same, excepting such Parts as may in their Judgment require Secrecy; and the Yeas and Nays of the Members of either House on any question shall, at the Desire of one fifth of those Present, be entered on the Journal.

Neither House, during the Session of Congress, shall, without the Consent of the other, adjourn for more than three days, nor to any other Place than that in which the two Houses shall be sitting.

SECTION 6. The Senators and Representatives shall receive a Compensation for their Services, to be ascertained by Law, and paid out of the Treasury of the United States. They shall in all Cases, except Treason, Felony and Breach of the Peace, be privileged from Arrest during their Attendance at the Session of their respective Houses, and in going to and returning from the same; and for any Speech or Debate in either House, they shall not be questioned in any other Place.

No Senator or Representative shall, during the Time for which he was elected, be appointed to any civil Office under the Authority of the United States, which shall have been created, or the Emoluments whereof shall have been encreased during such time; and no Person holding any Office under the United States, shall be a Member of either House during his Continuance in Office.

SECTION 7. All Bills for raising Revenue shall originate in the House of Representatives; but the Senate may propose or concur with Amendments as on other Bills.

Every Bill which shall have passed the House of Representatives and the Senate, shall, before it become a Law, be presented to the President of the United States; If he approve he shall sign it, but if not he shall return it, with his Objections to that House in which it shall have originated, who shall enter the Objections at large on their Journal, and proceed to reconsider it. If after such Reconsideration two thirds of that House shall agree to pass the Bill, it shall be sent, together with the Objections, to the other House, by which it shall likewise be reconsidered, and if approved by two thirds of that House, it shall become a Law. But in all such Cases the Votes of both Houses shall be determined by yeas and Nays, and the Names of the Persons voting for and against the Bill shall be entered on the Journal of each House respectively. If any Bill shall not be returned by the President within ten days (Sundays excepted) after it shall have been presented to him, the Same shall be a Law, in like Manner as if he had signed it, unless the Congress by their Adjournment prevent its Return in which Case it shall not be a Law.

Every Order, Resolution, or Vote to which the Concurrence of the Senate and House of Representatives may be necessary (except on a question of Adjournment) shall be presented to the President of the United States; and before the Same shall take Effect, shall be approved by him, or being disapproved by him, shall be repassed by two thirds of the Senate and House of Representatives, according to the Rules and Limitations prescribed in the Case of a Bill.

SECTION 8. The Congress shall have Power To lay and collect Taxes, Duties, Imposts and Excises, to pay the Debts and provide for the common Defence and general Welfare of the United States; but all Duties, Imposts and Excises shall be uniform throughout the United States;

To borrow Money on the credit of the United States;

To regulate Commerce with foreign Nations, and among the several States, and with the Indian Tribes;

To establish an uniform Rule of Naturalization, and uniform Laws on the subject of Bankruptcies throughout the United States;

To coin Money, regulate the Value thereof, and of foreign Coin, and fix the Standard of Weights and Measures;

To provide for the Punishment of counterfeiting the Securities and current Coin of the United States;

To establish Post Offices and post Roads;

To promote the progress of Science and useful Arts, by securing for limited Times to Authors and Inventors the exclusive Right to their respective Writings and Discoveries;

To constitute Tribunals inferior to the supreme Court;

To define and punish Piracies and Felonies committed on the high Seas, and Offences against the Law of Nations;

To declare War, grant Letters of Marque and Reprisal, and make Rules concerning Captures on Land and Water;

To raise and support Armies, but no Appropriation of Money to that Use shall be for a longer Term than two Years;

To provide and maintain a Navy;

To make Rules for the Government and Regulation of the land and naval Forces;

To provide for calling forth the Militia to execute the Laws of the Union, suppress Insurrections and repel Invasions;

To provide for organizing, arming, and disciplining, the Militia, and for governing such Part of them as may be employed in the Service of the United States, reserving to the States respectively, the Appointment of the Officers, and the Authority of training the Militia according to the discipline prescribed by Congress;

To exercise exclusive Legislation in all Cases whatsoever, over such District (not exceeding ten Miles square) as may, by Cession of particular States, and the Acceptance of Congress, become the Seat of the Government of the United States, and to exercise like Authority over all Places purchased by the Consent of the Legislature of the State in which the Same shall be, for the Erection of Forts, Magazines, Arsenals, dock-Yards, and other needful Buildings;—And

To make all Laws which shall be necessary and proper for carrying into Execution the foregoing Powers, and all other Powers vested by this Constitution in the Government of the United States, or in any Department or Officer thereof.

SECTION 9. The Migration or Importation of such Persons as any of the States now existing shall think proper to admit, shall not be prohibited by the Congress prior to the Year one thousand eight hundred and eight, but a Tax or duty may be imposed on such Importation, not exceeding ten dollars for each Person.

The Privilege of the Writ of Habeas Corpus shall not be suspended, unless when in Cases of Rebellion or Invasion the public Safety may require it.

No Bill of Attainder or ex post facto Law shall be passed.

No Capitation, or other direct, Tax shall be laid, unless in Proportion to the Census or Enumeration herein before directed to be taken.

No Tax or Duty shall be laid on Articles exported from any State.

No Preference shall be given by any Regulation of Commerce or Revenue to the Ports of one State over those of another: nor shall Vessels bound to, or from, one State, be obliged to enter, clear, or pay Duties in another.

No Money shall be drawn from the Treasury, but in Consequence of Appropriations made by Law; and a regular Statement and Account of the Receipts and Expenditures of all public Money shall be published from time to time.

No Title of Nobility shall be granted by the United States: And no Person holding any Office of Profit or Trust under them, shall, without the Consent of the Congress, accept of any present, Emolument, Office, or Title, of any kind whatever, from any King, Prince, or foreign State.

SECTION 10. No State shall enter into any Treaty, Alliance, or Confederation; grant Letters of Marque and Reprisal; coin Money; emit Bills of Credit; make any Thing but gold and silver Coin a Tender in Payment of Debts; pass any Bill of Attainder, ex post facto Law, or Law impairing the Obligation of Contracts, or grant any Title of Nobility.

No State shall, without the Consent of the Congress, lay any Imposts or Duties on Imports or Exports, except what may be absolutely necessary for executing it's inspection Laws: and the net Produce of all Duties and Imposts, laid by any State on Imports or Exports, shall be for the Use of the Treasury of the United States; and all such Laws shall be subject to the Revision and Controul of the Congress.

No State shall, without the Consent of Congress, lay any Duty of Tonnage, keep Troops, or Ships of War in time of Peace, enter into any Agreement or Compact with another State, or with a foreign Power, or engage in War, unless actually invaded, or in such imminent Danger as will not admit of delay.

Article. II.

SECTION 1. The executive Power shall be vested in a President of the United States of America. He shall hold his Office during the Term of four Years, and, together with the Vice President, chosen for the same Term, be elected as follows

Each State shall appoint, in such Manner as the Legislature thereof may direct, a Number of Electors, equal to the whole Number of Senators and Representatives to which the State may be entitled in the Congress: but no Senator or Representative, or Person holding an Office of Trust or Profit under the United States, shall be appointed an Elector.

The Electors shall meet in their respective States, and vote by Ballot for two Persons, of whom one at least shall not be an Inhabitant of the same State with themselves. And they shall make a List of all the Persons voted for, and of the Number of Votes for each; which List they shall sign and certify, and transmit sealed to the Seat of the Government of the United States, directed to the President of the Senate. The President of the Senate shall, in the Presence of the Senate and House of Representatives, open all the Certificates, and the Votes shall then be counted. The Person having the greatest Number of Votes shall be the President, if such Number be a Majority of the whole Number of Electors appointed; and if there be more than one who have such Majority, and have an equal Number of Votes, then the House of Representatives shall immediately chuse by Ballot one of them for President; and if no Person have a Majority, then from the five highest on the List the said House shall in like Manner chuse the President. But in chusing the President, the Votes shall be taken by States, the Representation from each State having one Vote; A quorum for this Purpose shall consist of a Member or Members from two thirds of the States, and a Majority of all the States shall be necessary to a Choice. In every Case, after the Choice of the President, the Person having the greatest Number of Votes of the Electors shall be the Vice President. But if there should remain two or more who have equal Votes, the Senate shall chuse from them by Ballot the Vice President.

The Congress may determine the Time of chusing the Electors, and the Day on which they shall give their Votes; which Day shall be the same throughout the United States.

No Person except a natural born Citizen, or a Citizen of the United States, at the time of the Adoption of this Constitution, shall be eligible to the Office of President; neither shall any Person be eligible to that Office who shall not have attained to the Age of thirty five Years, and been fourteen Years a Resident within the United States.

In Case of the Removal of the President from Office, or of his Death, Resignation, or Inability to discharge the Powers and Duties of the said Office, the Same shall devolve on the Vice President, and the Congress may by Law provide for the Case of Removal, Death, Resignation or Inability, both of the President and Vice President, declaring what Officer shall then act as President, and such Officer shall act accordingly, until the Disability be removed, or a President shall be elected.

The President shall, at stated Times, receive for his Services, a Compensation, which shall neither be encreased nor diminished during the Period for which he shall have been elected, and he shall not receive within that Period any other Emolument from the United States, or any of them.

Before he enter on the Execution of his Office, he shall take the following Oath or Affirmation:—"I do solemnly swear (or affirm) that I will faithfully execute the Office of President of the United States, and will to the best of my Ability, preserve, protect and defend the Constitution of the United States."

SECTION 2. The President shall be Commander in Chief of the Army and Navy of the United States, and of the Militia of the several States, when called into the actual Service of the United States; he may require the Opinion, in writing, of the principal Officer in each of the executive Departments, upon any Subject relating to the Duties of their respective Offices, and he shall have Power to grant Reprieves and Pardons for Offences against the United States, except in Cases of Impeachment.

He shall have Power, by and with the Advice and Consent of the Senate, to make Treaties, provided two thirds of the Senators present concur; and he shall nominate, and by and with the Advice and Consent of the Senate, shall appoint Ambassadors, other public Ministers and Consuls, Judges of the supreme Court, and all other Officers of the United States, whose Appointments are not herein otherwise provided for, and which shall be established by Law: but the Congress may by Law vest the Appointment of such inferior Officers, as they think proper, in the President alone, in the Courts of Law, or in the Heads of Departments.

The President shall have Power to fill up all Vacancies that may happen during the Recess of the Senate, by granting Commissions which shall expire at the End of their next Session.

SECTION 3. He shall from time to time give to the Congress Information of the State of the Union, and recommend to their Consideration such Measures as he shall judge necessary and expedient; he may, on extraordinary Occasions, convene both Houses, or either of them, and in

CHAPTER 1, FUNDAMENTAL DOCUMENTS, NO. 9

Case of Disagreement between them, with Respect to the Time of Adjournment, he may adjourn them to such Time as he shall think proper; he shall receive Ambassadors and other public Ministers; he shall take Care that the Laws be faithfully executed, and shall Commission all the Officers of the United States.

SECTION 4. The President, Vice President and all civil Officers of the United States, shall be removed from Office on Impeachment for, and Conviction of, Treason, Bribery, or other high Crimes and Misdemeanors.

Article. III.

SECTION 1. The judicial Power of the United States, shall be vested in one supreme Court, and in such inferior Courts as the Congress may from time to time ordain and establish. The Judges, both of the supreme and inferior Courts, shall hold their Offices during good Behaviour, and shall, at stated Times, receive for their Services, a Compensation, which shall not be diminished during their Continuance in Office.

SECTION 2. The judicial Power shall extend to all Cases, in Law and Equity, arising under this Constitution, the Laws of the United States, and Treaties made, or which shall be made, under their Authority;—to all Cases affecting Ambassadors, other public Ministers and Consuls;—to all Cases of admiralty and maritime Jurisdiction;—to Controversies to which the United States shall be a Party;—to Controversies between two or more States;—between a State and Citizens of another State;—between Citizens of different States,—between Citizens of the same State claiming Lands under Grants of different States, and between a State, or the Citizens thereof, and foreign States, Citizens or Subjects.

In all Cases affecting Ambassadors, other public Ministers and Consuls, and those in which a State shall be Party, the supreme Court shall have original Jurisdiction. In all the other Cases before mentioned, the supreme Court shall have appellate Jurisdiction, both as to Law and Fact, with such Exceptions, and under such Regulations as the Congress shall make.

The Trial of all Crimes, except in Cases of Impeachment, shall be by Jury; and such Trial shall be held in the State where the said Crimes shall have been committed; but when not committed within any State, the Trial shall be at such Place or Places as the Congress may by Law have directed.

SECTION 3. Treason against the United States, shall consist only in levying War against them, or in adhering to their Enemies, giving them Aid and Comfort. No Person shall be convicted of Treason unless on the Testimony of two Witnesses to the same overt Act, or on Confession in open Court.

The Congress shall have Power to declare the Punishment of Treason, but no Attainder of Treason shall work Corruption of Blood, or Forfeiture except during the Life of the Person attainted.

Article. IV.

SECTION 1. Full Faith and Credit shall be given in each State to the public Acts, Records, and judicial Proceedings of every other State. And the Congress may by general Laws prescribe the Manner in which such Acts, Records and Proceedings shall be proved, and the Effect thereof.

SECTION 2. The Citizens of each State shall be entitled to all Privileges and Immunities of Citizens in the several States.

A Person charged in any State with Treason, Felony, or other Crime, who shall flee from Justice, and be found in another State, shall on Demand of the executive Authority of the State from which he fled, be delivered up, to be removed to the State having Jurisdiction of the Crime.

No Person held to Service or Labour in one State, under the Laws thereof, escaping into another, shall, in Consequence of any Law or Regulation therein, be discharged from such Service or Labour, but shall be delivered up on Claim of the Party to whom such Service or Labour may be due.

SECTION 3. New States may be admitted by the Congress into this Union; but no new State shall be formed or erected within the Jurisdiction of any other State; nor any State be formed by the Junction of two or more States, or Parts of States, without the Consent of the Legislatures of the States concerned as well as of the Congress.

The Congress shall have Power to dispose of and make all needful Rules and Regulations respecting the Territory or other Property belonging to the United States; and nothing in this Constitution shall be so construed as to Prejudice any Claims of the United States, or of any particular State.

SECTION 4. The United States shall guarantee to every State in this Union a Republican Form of Government, and shall protect each of them against Invasion; and on Application of the Legislature, or of the Executive (when the Legislature cannot be convened) against domestic Violence.

Article. V.

The Congress, whenever two thirds of both Houses shall deem it necessary, shall propose Amendments to this Constitution, or, on the Application of the Legislatures of two thirds of the several States, shall call a Convention for proposing Amendments, which, in either Case, shall be valid to all Intents and Purposes, as Part of this Constitution, when ratified by the Legislatures of three fourths of the several States, or by Conventions in three fourths thereof, as the one or the other Mode of Ratification may be proposed by the Congress; Provided that no Amendment which may be made prior to the Year One thousand eight hundred and eight shall in any Manner affect the first and fourth Clauses in the Ninth Section of the first Article; and that no State, without its Consent, shall be deprived of it's equal Suffrage in the Senate.

Article. VI.

All Debts contracted and Engagements entered into, before the Adoption of this Constitution, shall be as valid against the United States under this Constitution, as under the Confederation.

This Constitution, and the Laws of the United States which shall be made in Pursuance thereof; and all Treaties made, or which shall be made, under the Authority of the United States, shall be the supreme Law of the Land; and the Judges in every State shall be bound thereby, any Thing in the Constitution or Laws of any State to the Contrary notwithstanding.

The Senators and Representatives before mentioned, and the Members of the several State Legislatures, and all executive and judicial Officers, both of the United States and of the several States, shall be bound by Oath or Affirmation, to support this Constitution; but no religious Test shall ever be required as a Qualification to any Office or public Trust under the United States.

Article. VII.

The Ratification of the Conventions of nine States, shall be sufficient for the Establishment of this Constitution between the States so ratifying the Same.

> The Word, "the," being interlined between the seventh and eighth Lines of the first Page, The Word "Thirty" being partly written on an Erazure in the fifteenth Line of the first Page, The Words "is tried" being interlined between the thirty second and thirty third Lines of the first Page and the Word "the" being interlined between the forty third and forty fourth Lines of the second Page.
> Attest WILLIAM JACKSON Secretary

done in Convention by the Unanimous Consent of the States present the Seventeenth Day of September in the Year of our Lord one thousand seven hundred and Eighty seven and of the Independance of the United States of America the Twelfth In witness whereof We have hereunto subscribed our Names,

Go: WASHINGTON—Presidt. and deputy from Virginia

New Hampshire	John Langdon Nicholas Gilman
Massachusetts	Nathaniel Gorham Rufus King
Connecticut	Wm. Saml. Johnson Roger Sherman
New York	Alexander Hamilton
New Jersey	Wil: Livingston David Brearley. Wm. Paterson. Jona: Dayton

Pensylvania	B Franklin Thomas Mifflin Robt Morris Geo. Clymer Thos. FitzSimons Jared Ingersoll James Wilson Gouv Morris
Delaware	Geo: Read Gunning Bedford jun John Dickinson Richard Bassett Jaco: Broom
Maryland	James McHenry Dan of St Thos. Jenifer Danl Carroll
Virginia	John Blair— James Madison Jr.
North Carolina	Wm. Blount Richd. Dobbs Spaight. Hu Williamson
South Carolina	J. Rutledge Charles Cotesworth Pinckney Charles Pinckney Pierce Butler.
Georgia	William Few Abr Baldwin

Amendments to the Constitution

Article I

Congress shall make no law respecting an establishment of religion, or prohibiting the free exercise thereof; or abridging the freedom of speech, or of the press; or the right of the people peaceably to assemble, and to petition the Government for a redress of grievances.

Article II

A well regulated Militia, being necessary to the security of a free State, the right of the people to keep and bear Arms, shall not be infringed.

Article III

No Soldier shall, in time of peace be quartered in any house, without the consent of the Owner, nor in time of war, but in a manner to be prescribed by law.

Article IV

The right of the people to be secure in their persons, houses, papers, and effects, against unreasonable searches and seizures, shall not be violated, and no Warrants shall issue, but upon probable cause, supported by Oath or affirmation, and particularly describing the place to be searched, and the persons or things to be seized.

Article V

No person shall be held to answer for a capital, or otherwise infamous crime, unless on a presentment or indictment of a Grand Jury, except in cases arising in the land or naval forces, or in the Militia, when in actual service in time of War or public danger; nor shall any person be subject for the same offence to be twice put in jeopardy of life or limb; nor shall be compelled in any criminal case to be a witness against himself, nor be deprived of life, liberty, or property, without due process of law; nor shall private property be taken for public use, without just compensation.

Article VI

In all criminal prosecutions, the accused shall enjoy the right to a speedy and public trial, by an impartial jury of the State and district wherein the crime shall have been committed, which district shall have been previously ascertained by law, and to be informed of the nature and cause of the accusation; to be confronted with the witnesses against him; to have compulsory process for obtaining witnesses in his favor, and to have the Assistance of Counsel for his defence.

Article VII

In Suits at common law, where the value in controversy shall exceed twenty dollars, the right of trial by jury shall be preserved, and no fact tried by a jury, shall be otherwise re-examined in any Court of the United States, than according to the rules of the common law.

Article VIII

Excessive bail shall not be required, nor excessive fines imposed, nor cruel and unusual punishments inflicted.

Article IX

The enumeration in the Constitution, of certain rights, shall not be construed to deny or disparage others retained by the people.

Article X

The powers not delegated to the United States by the Constitution, nor prohibited by it to the States, are reserved to the States respectively, or to the people.

Article XI

The Judicial power of the United States shall not be construed to extend to any suit in law or equity, commenced or prosecuted against one of the United States by Citizens of another State, or by Citizens or Subjects of any Foreign State.

Article XII

The Electors shall meet in their respective states, and vote by ballot for President and Vice-President, one of whom, at least, shall not be an inhabitant of the same state with themselves; they shall name in their ballots the person voted for as President, and in distinct ballots the person voted for as Vice-President, and they shall make distinct lists of all persons voted for as President, and of all persons voted for as Vice-President, and of the number of votes for each, which lists they shall sign and certify, and transmit sealed to the seat of the government of the United States, directed to the President of the Senate;—The President of the Senate shall, in the presence of the Senate and House of Representatives, open all the certificates and the votes shall then be counted;—The person having the greatest number of votes for President, shall be the President, if such number be a majority of the whole number of Electors appointed; and if no person have such majority, then from the persons having the highest numbers not exceeding three on the list of those voted for as President, the House of Representatives shall choose immediately, by ballot, the President. But in choosing the President, the votes shall be taken by states, the representation from each state having one vote; a quorum for this purpose shall consist of a member or members from two-thirds of the states, and a majority of all the states shall be necessary to a choice. And if the House of Representatives shall not choose a President whenever the right of choice shall devolve upon them, before the fourth day of March next following, then the Vice-President shall act as President, as in the case of the death or other constitutional disability of the President. The person having the greatest number of votes as Vice-President, shall be the Vice-President, if such number be a majority of the whole number of Electors appointed, and if no person have a majority, then from the two highest numbers on the list, the Senate shall choose the Vice-President; a quorum for the purpose shall consist of two-thirds of the whole number of Senators, and a majority of the whole number shall be necessary to a choice. But no person constitutionally ineligible to the office of President shall be eligible to that of Vice-President of the United States.

We the People of the United States, . . .

2

Popular Basis of Political Authority

Introduction

If all men are by nature perfectly free and equal, there can then be no claim grounded in nature of one to rule another. To be sure, there may be attributes of superiority—age, looks, name, connections—that endow some individuals with political influence. And, as John Locke noted, "*Excellency of Parts and Merit* may place others above the Common Level." Yet these differences among human beings cannot outweigh the politically decisive corollary of original freedom and equality: it is consent and consent alone that makes a member of any commonwealth, and accordingly no one has a right to govern another without his consent. Whether that consent is explicit or implicit, Locke explained (no. 1), does not affect the basic principle, and in either case the consent given is necessarily conditional. An individual can no more agree to eschew measures of self-help for preservation than a community can agree to forgo measures to save itself "from the attempts and designs of any Body, even of their Legislators, whenever they shall be so foolish, or so wicked, as to lay and carry on designs against the Liberties and Properties of the Subject." The powers of governors are fiduciary in char-

acter; the trustees are necessarily and properly accountable to those who have vested trust in them.

David Hume (no. 4), however, points to the obvious. "Almost all the governments which exist at present, or of which there remains any record in story, have been founded originally either on usurpation or conquest or both, without any pretense of a fair consent or voluntary subjection of the people." Similarly, subjects everywhere acknowledge their prince's rights "and suppose themselves born under obligations of obedience to a certain sovereign." Is it, then, not absurd to posit a contractual arrangement "so much unknown to all of them that over the face of the whole earth there scarcely remain any traces or memory of it?" This was an objection Locke had anticipated. He attempted to answer it by showing that his compact theory might be reconciled with the history of political origins. Hume clearly thought his the better argument, though the appeal to common practice proved less persuasive than he might have wished. Indeed, James Otis thought this no refutation at all of the consensual basis of political life (no. 5). In the last analysis, he said, it was not compact but "the necessity of our natures" that made us associate. Government might be considered an expression of the laws of nature and of nature's god. But here on earth, the indispensable "original supreme Sovereign, absolute, and uncontroulable," is the people. Those on whom they confer sovereignty hold it in trust and on condition that the trustee "shall *incessantly* consult *their* good." If practice deviates from right, so much the worse for practice: "if every prince since *Nimrod* had been a tyrant, it would not prove a *right* to tyranize."

Locke's argument sat especially well with advocates of popular government; the argument of 1689 became the premise of 1776. But the reach of the argument goes far beyond the ordinary forms of unmixed popular government, as every reader of the Declaration of Independence can recall. For it is "governments"—without restriction—that are there said to derive their just powers from the consent of the governed, and it is "any form of government" that is held accountable if it becomes destructive of the ends for which governments are instituted in the first place. As a statement of right, then, the principle is a universal: all forms of government derive their legitimacy from the consent of the governed; all forms of government claiming legitimacy are subject to the master principle of popular sovereignty and hence are accountable to the governed for the faithful performance of their charge.

Governance as Trusteeship

This statement of right was argued by Locke and by Thomas Gordon in *Cato's Letters* (no. 2), and assumed by Otis. For James Burgh (no. 6), this was the old doctrine; it was those who denied that governors are responsible to their constituents who were the innovators. For the inhabitants of Mecklenburg County, North Carolina, the right was reducible to "maxims" that no longer needed argument, only acknowledgment "in the Bills of Rights" (no. 8). And if the representatives of Berkshire County, Massachusetts, retraced this reasoning, it was principally to reach a necessary conclusion: those to whom legislative power had been entrusted could not themselves prescribe "the foundation upon which the Legislature stands" (no. 9). To suppose that the sovereign people would or could delegate their right to give life to "the fundamental Constitution of a free state" was absurd; to argue in this way imported "if not impiety, yet real popery in politicks."

Popular consent and responsibility had become a truth that dripped from everyone's lips—and yet no simple truth. Repeated crises in constitution making had disclosed some of the complexities and ambiguities inherent in the Americans' common premise. Arguing against those who doubted the legitimacy of reallocating governmental powers while living under the Articles of Confederation, James Wilson turned to the highest written authorities to support the assertion that "the supreme, absolute and uncontrollable authority, remains with the people" (no. 14). "The great and penetrating mind of Locke seems to be the only one that pointed towards even the theory of this great truth," but it was the Americans, acting on the language of the second paragraph of the Declaration of Indepen-

dence, who had and would continue to put that truth into effect. But under what circumstances, and how? American experience would refine the theory.

The People: Uncertain Guardians

John Adams (no. 12) argued that the people, far from being (as Marchamont Nedham would have it) "the best keepers of their own liberties," are in fact "the worst conceivable; they are no keepers at all." Yet Adams also held it indisputable that "the original and fountain of all power and government" is in this very people who have a clear right to erect any form of government they deem fit to secure their liberty, their happiness, and their prosperity. Being neither forgetful nor thoughtless, Adams was acknowledging what most of the Founders recognized: that the sole—the indisputable—source of legitimacy was seriously vulnerable to seduction, corruption, error, impetuosity, and worse. The principle of popular consent and responsibility was unchallenged; only its application was problematic.

To steer the argument around the shoals and snags took a sharp eye and a steady hand. Madison, in *Federalist*, no. 49 (no. 19), showed both of these (along with his usual finesse) when publicly correcting the "original, comprehensive and accurate" turn of thinking of his closest friend. In his *Notes on the State of Virginia* (1784), Thomas Jefferson had proposed recurring to a constitutional convention not only when altering the constitution, but also when countering unconstitutional exercises of power by the more domineering branches of government. To be sure, Madison agreed, "a constitutional road to the decision of the people" was a requirement of republican theory. But Jefferson's proposed resort to that original authority in order to correct breaches of the constitution promised difficulties likely to be as numerous as the breaches themselves. American successes in founding new governments argued against more of the same; "it must be confessed, that the experiments are of too ticklish a nature to be unnecessarily multiplied." Resort to the people in their authoritative capacity ought to be reserved for "certain great and extraordinary occasions." Madison's coauthor, Hamilton, pushed the matter further in, *Federalist*, no. 78 (no. 22). Even if the judges knew that public sentiment opposed some provision of the Constitution, they should be obliged to resist any departure from it, whatever the clamor, "until the people have by some solemn and authoritative act annulled or changed the established form." Again, while the right of the people to alter or abolish governments was unquestionable, the occasions of its exercise demanded the closest scrutiny.

Jefferson's commitment to popular control continued to lead him down some ways where Madison would not follow. In his remarkable essay of 6 September 1789 (no. 23), Jefferson produced what in form was a letter to his fellow Virginian, but in fact perhaps a position paper for his French friends in whose daily revolutionary activities he was then taking a barely concealed part. In it the American minister to the French court argued that it was "self evident" that "the earth belongs always to the living generation." No generation could bind its successors either to its debts or to what it might please to call a perpetual constitution. Once a generation had ceased to form the majority of the entire living population of a country—a moment calculated easily enough by means of actuarial tables—the new majority could do as it pleased. And what it pleased was to be determined by what it expressly declared, not by any presumed tacit consent. The practical applications of this principle were indeed "very extensive . . . and most especially in France." It was largely those practical applications that Madison addressed in his artful reply (no. 24). (He could have said with Hume that the case with men is not "as is the case with silkworms and butterflies" [no. 4].) Many things might be said for a constitution being up for grabs every eighteen years, eight months, or whatever, but stability was not one of them. Further, to Madison there seemed to be "a foundation in the nature of things, in the relation which one generation bears to another, for the descent of obligations from one to another." Consider the capital investments of one generation in such long-term projects as a system of roads or safe water; consider the crushing debt assumed by one generation in repelling a conqueror so that future generations might not have to live under a tyrant's heel. Indeed, was not their own situation, the situation of those who had succeeded in making a revolution, the telling case in point? Finally, could one conceive of property rights where no stable expectations were possible? Could one, indeed, even have majority rule without the assumption that every newly maturing member of the society had given his tacit assent to the principle that the voice of the majority binds the minority?

All these Madisonian objections, like those expressed in the *Federalist,* bespoke a prudential concern for the complications of popular sovereignty. Jefferson surely was not blind to these. He came to see and mourn over the fatal errors of honest French patriots—"but closet politicians merely, unpractised in the knowledge of men." He came to see how a people unprepared for liberty had fallen victim first to "the unprincipled and bloody tyranny of Robespierre" and then to "the equally unprincipled and maniac tyranny of Bonaparte" (no. 27). But the right of nations to self-government being his "pole star," Jefferson confessed in a burst of hyperbole, "my partialities are steered by it, without asking whether it is a Bonaparte or an Alexander towards whom the helm is directed" (Letter to Correa de Serra, 28 June 1815).

Although this was a late word of Jefferson's, it was not his last word. For all his singular formulations, he was not that far removed from the other Founders and their predecessors in limning the conditions and limits of popular consent. All could agree with Thomas Gordon's Cato (no. 2) that the distinguishing feature of a free nation lay principally in its magistrates having to "consult the Voice and Interest of the People." But while it was incontestable that "every Man ought to know what it concerns All to know," that did not necessarily imply direct governance by the people. Samuel Adams (no. 11) saw continued value in township democracy and acknowledged the revolutionary utility of county conventions and popular committees. But "as we now have constitutional & regular Governments

and all our Men in Authority depend upon the annual & free Elections of the People, we are safe without them." Madison agreed: it was sufficient for a government derived from the great body of the people that its administering officials be appointed directly or indirectly by the people (see ch. 4, no. 24). The "American Governments"— i.e., those organized under the state constitutions and the Articles of Confederation, as well as the proposed new federal Constitution—were distinguished by *"the total exclusion of the people in their collective capacity* from any share" in governance (see ch. 4, no. 27).

Similarly, all might agree with the mechanics of New York City (14 June 1776) that everyone has enough God-given sense to judge of his safety, advantages, and interest. This was a version of Hobbes's assertion in the *Leviathan* 125 years earlier that "a plain husbandman is more prudent in affairs of his own house, than a privy-councillor in the affairs of another man." In neither case was direct democracy the intended political conclusion. The mechanics' claim on behalf of the people's good sense was compatible with Montesquieu's distinction between what the people could know and hence do for themselves and what the people could not know and hence have to depute to their ministers. Although Montesquieu (no. 3) thought the people "extremely well qualified for choosing those whom they are to intrust with part of their authority," some American founders were impressed with how hard even that primary choice was for them. Arguing in defense of a two-level election of a senate for Virginia, Jefferson (no. 7) said he had "ever observed that a choice by the people themselves is not generally distinguished for its wisdom. The first secretion from them is usually crude and heterogeneous." That argued not only for the indirect election of senators, but more fundamentally for legislative plans "to illuminate, as far as practicable, the minds of the people at large" and to render "those persons, whom nature hath endowed with genius and virtue," worthy and effective guardians of "the sacred deposit of the rights and liberties of their fellow citizens" (see ch. 18, no. 11).

The sheer ungainliness of the whole body of a great nation meant for John Adams (no. 12) that the people could not "act, judge, think, or will, as a body politic or corporation." Even at the level of municipal self-governance, it was necessary, he thought, to "temper their authority in legislation with the maturer counsels of the one and the few." The pseudonymous Caesar, an early proponent of the Constitution, pushed the matter further (no. 13). Using confessedly "blunt and ungracious reasoning," he thought the people "very ill qualified to judge for themselves what government will best suit their peculiar situations." Where even experts disagreed, how could it be otherwise? And yet Caesar was careful not to impugn the people's *"inherent rights"* to accept or reject a proposed new form of government. Still it remained a puzzle. "How are the people to profit by this inherent right?" How could they best discover their interests? Caesar's nonhumble answer: "As I humbly conceive, by a tractable and docile disposition, and by honest men endeavoring to keep their minds easy, while others, of the same disposition, with the advantages of genius and learning, are constructing the bark that may, by the blessing of Heaven, carry them to the port of rest and happiness, if they will embark without diffidence and proceed without mutiny." But the popular case for restraints on popular sovereignty had yet to be made. Hamilton, speaking as Publius, found a way of explaining in public why the people would reject "servile pliancy" in an executive, why they would "despise the adulator, who should pretend that they always *reason right* about the *means* of promoting" the common good that they "commonly *intend*" (no. 21). The people, when they were honest with themselves, knew that sometimes they must be protected from themselves.

The People: Their Own Best Guardians

It was no less true, however, that the people could not do without protection from their governors. On this both defenders and attackers of the new Constitution agreed. The Anti-Federalists were especially exercised over what they took to be the inadequate safeguards for holding the governors to account. Vox Populi (Nov. 1787) had no apologies to make for his republican jealousy and distrust; they lay at the foundations of the very act of political association. Likewise, the minority of the Pennsylvania ratifying convention (no. 15) deplored the likelihood that only "the lordly and high-minded" would find a place in the new Congress, men remote from the concerns of ordinary people and hence neither deserving of, nor able to secure, popular confidence. Much more was needed, the Federal Farmer argued (no. 16), to establish the proper relationships of dependence upon the people. Considering that "we must, after all, trust a vast deal to a few men, who, far removed from their constituents, will administer the federal government," the odds were that they would not be "oppressed with a sense of dependance and responsibility." Legislators ought to be subject to recall. Much evil would be avoided and much good accomplished if there were a compulsory rotation of members of Congress. The Federal Farmer was at least as much interested in producing thereby "attention, activity, and a diffusion of knowledge in the community" as in countering the tendency of "even good men in office, in time, imperceptibly [to] lose sight of the people."

Some of this concern was present in James Wilson's mind as expressed in his lectures on law (no. 25). Why might not republican government, too, receive the "beautiful and solid form" of a pyramid, with broad, strong, deep foundations in "the authority, the interests, and the affections of the people at large," and with a superstructure "raised to a dignified altitude"? Wilson sought for some golden mean between utter preoccupation with private affairs and quixotic political enthusiasm: "must the bow of honest industry be always bent?" A properly directed "relaxation" would lead to citizens conversing, reading, deliberating, and so exercising their right of suffrage as to form among them "the most rational, the most improving, and the most endearing connexion." The correlative to self-government would be an informed and dignified obedience to themselves.

American experience showed that there was more to consent than the bare decision of the people to accept or reject. At its best, consent involved a rational judgment of what had been proposed, nothing less than a second debate. When the towns of Massachusetts first rejected and then accepted the proposed state constitutions of 1778 and 1780 (see the returns in ch. 4, no. 8; ch. 14, nos. 16 and 17; and ch. 15, nos. 22 and 26), and when the several state ratifying conventions of 1787–88 accepted the Philadelphia Convention's handiwork with varying degrees of enthusiasm, they gave voice to more than a shout of yea or nay. Leading up to the global vote—and informing it—was an articulated judgment of what the proposed measure meant, and (where consent was indeed obtained) a more or less explicit injunction to pursue that judgment under the new regime. Far from being the hoarse cry of an orchestrated mob, the delight of tyrants ancient and modern, consent was rather "a key" by which later generations might discover "the legitimate meaning of the Instrument" (Madison, no. 28).

In the last analysis, the effectiveness of consent and responsibility depended on the quality and vigor of public opinion—and not only in the original instance when measures were first pending. Madison's very brief, understated, newspaper essay (no. 26) touched on most of the important points: the reciprocal effects of public opinion and government; the tension between governmental authority and liberty; the effects of a large territory upon each; and the varied means available for supporting liberty. The premise of the day was not to be effected by the labor of an hour.

1

JOHN LOCKE, SECOND TREATISE,
§§ 4–15, 54, 119–22, 163
1689

---

4. To understand Political Power right, and derive it from its Original, we must consider what State all Men are naturally in, and that is, a *State of perfect Freedom* to order their Actions, and dispose of their Possessions, and Persons as they think fit, within the bounds of the Law of Nature, without asking leave, or depending upon the Will of any other Man.

A *State* also *of Equality,* wherein all the Power and Jurisdiction is reciprocal, no one having more than another: there being nothing more evident, than that Creatures of the same species and rank promiscuously born to all the same advantages of Nature, and the use of the same faculties, should also be equal one amongst another without Subordination or Subjection, unless the Lord and Master of them all, should by any manifest Declaration of his Will set one above another, and confer on him by an evident and clear appointment an undoubted Right to Dominion and Sovereignty.

5. This *equality* of Men by Nature, the Judicious *Hooker* looks upon as so evident in it self, and beyond all question, that he makes it the Foundation of that Obligation to mutual Love amongst Men, on which he Builds the Duties they owe one another, and from whence he derives the great Maxims *of Justice* and *Charity*. His words are;

The like natural inducement, hath brought Men to know that it is no less their Duty, to Love others than themselves, for seeing those things which are equal, must needs all have one measure; If I cannot but wish to receive good, even as much at every Man's hands, as any Man can wish unto his own Soul, how should I look to have any part of my desire herein satisfied, unless my self be careful to satisfie the like desire, which is undoubtedly in other Men, being of one and the same nature? to have any thing offered them repugnant to this desire, must needs in all respects grieve them as much as me, so that if I do harm, I must look to suffer, there being no reason that others should shew greater measure of love to me, than they have by me, shewed unto them: my desire therefore to be lov'd of my equals in nature, as much as possible may be, imposeth upon me a natural Duty of bearing to themward, fully the like affection; From which relation of equality between our selves and them, that are as our selves, what several Rules and Canons, natural reason hath drawn for direction of Life, no Man is ignorant. Eccl. Pol. Lib. 1.

6. But though this be a *State of Liberty*, yet it is *not a State of Licence*, though Man in that State have an uncontroleable Liberty, to dispose of his Person or Possessions, yet he has not Liberty to destroy himself, or so much as any Creature in his Possession, but where some nobler use, than its bare Preservation calls for it. The *State of Nature* has a Law of Nature to govern it, which obliges every one: And Reason, which is that Law, teaches all Mankind, who will but consult it, that being all equal and independent, no one ought to harm another in his Life, Health, Liberty, or Possessions. For Men being all the Workmanship of one Omnipotent, and infinitely wise Maker; All the Servants of one Sovereign Master, sent into the World by his order and about his business, they are his Property, whose Workmanship they are, made to last during his, not one anothers Pleasure. And being furnished with like Faculties, sharing all in one Community of Nature, there cannot be supposed any such *Subordination* among us, that may Authorize us to destroy one another, as if we were made for one anothers uses, as the inferior ranks of Creatures are for ours. Every one as he is *bound to preserve himself*, and not to quit his Station wilfully; so by the like reason when his own Preservation comes not in competition, ought he, as much as he can, *to preserve the rest of Mankind*, and may not unless it be to do Justice on an Offender, take away, or impair the life, or what tends to the Preservation of the Life, Liberty, Health, Limb or Goods of another.

7. And that all Men may be restrained from invading others Rights, and from doing hurt to one another, and the Law of Nature be observed, which willeth the Peace and *Preservation of all Mankind*, the *Execution* of the Law of Nature is in that State, put into every Mans hands, whereby everyone has a right to punish the transgressors of that Law to such a Degree, as may hinder its Violation. For the *Law of Nature* would, as all other Laws that concern Men in this World, be in vain, if there were no body that in the State of Nature, had a *Power to Execute* that Law, and thereby preserve the innocent and restrain offenders, and if any one in the State of Nature may punish another, for any evil he has done, every one may do so. For in that *State of perfect Equality*, where naturally there is no superiority or jurisdiction of one, over another, what any may do in Prosecution of that Law, every one must needs have a Right to do.

8. And thus in the State of Nature, *one Man comes by a Power over another;* but yet no Absolute or Arbitrary Power, to use a Criminal when he has got him in his hands, according to the passionate heats, or boundless extravagancy of his own Will, but only to retribute to him, so far as calm reason and conscience dictates, what is proportionate to his Transgression, which is so much as may serve for *Reparation* and *Restraint*. For these two are the only reasons, why one Man may lawfully do harm to another, which is that we call *punishment*. In transgressing the Law of Nature, the Offender declares himself to live by another Rule, than that of *reason* and common Equity, which is that measure God has set to the actions of Men, for their mutual security: and so he becomes dangerous to Mankind, the tye, which is to secure them from injury and violence, being slighted and broken by him. Which being a trespass against the whole Species, and the Peace and Safety of it, provided for by the Law of Nature, every man upon this score, by the Right he hath to preserve Mankind in general, may restrain, or where it is necessary, destroy things noxious to them, and so may bring such evil on any one, who hath transgressed that Law, as may make him repent the doing of it, and thereby deter him, and by his Example others, from doing the like mischief. And in this case, and upon this ground, every *Man hath a Right to punish the Offender, and be Executioner of the Law of Nature.*

9. I doubt not but this will seem a very strange Doctrine to some Men: but before they condemn it, I desire them to resolve me, by what Right any Prince or State can put to death, or *punish an Alien*, for any Crime he commits in their Country. 'Tis certain their Laws by vertue of any Sanction they receive from the promulgated Will of the Legislative, reach not a Stranger. They speak not to him, nor if they did, is he bound to hearken to them. The Legislative Authority, by which they are in Force over the Subjects of that Common-wealth, hath no Power over him. Those who have the Supream Power of making Laws in *England, France* or *Holland*, are to an *Indian*, but like the rest of the World, Men without Authority: And therefore if by the Law of Nature, every Man hath not a Power to punish Offences against it, as he soberly judges the Case to require, I see not how the Magistrates of any Community, can *punish an Alien* of another Country, since in reference to him, they can have no more Power, than what every Man naturally may have over another.

10. Besides the Crime which consists in violating the Law, and varying from the right Rule of Reason, whereby

a Man so far becomes degenerate, and declares himself to quit the Principles of Human Nature, and to be a noxious Creature, there is commonly *injury* done to some Person or other, and some other Man receives damage by his Transgression, in which Case he who hath received any damage, has besides the right of punishment common to him with other Men, a particular Right to seek *Reparation* from him that has done it. And any other Person who finds it just, may also joyn with him that is injur'd, and assist him in recovering from the Offender, so much as may make satisfaction for the harm he has suffer'd.

11. From these *two distinct Rights,* the one of *Punishing* the Crime *for restraint,* and preventing the like Offence, which right of punishing is in every body; the other of taking *reparation,* which belongs only to the injured party, comes it to pass that the Magistrate, who by being Magistrate, hath the common right of punishing put into his hands, can often, where the publick good demands not the execution of the Law, *remit* the punishment of Criminal Offences by his own Authority, but yet cannot *remit* the satisfaction due to any private Man, for the damage he has received. That, he who has suffered the damage has a Right to demand in his own name, and he alone can *remit:* The damnified Person has this Power of appropriating to himself, the Goods or Service of the Offender, by *Right of Self-preservation,* as every Man has a Power to punish the Crime, to prevent its being committed again, *by the Right he has of Preserving all Mankind,* and doing all reasonable things he can in order to that end: and thus it is, that every Man in the State of Nature, has a Power to kill a Murderer, both to deter others from doing the like Injury, which no Reparation can compensate, by the Example of the punishment that attends it from every body, and also *to secure* Men from the attempts of a Criminal, who having renounced Reason, the common Rule and Measure, God hath given to Mankind, hath by the unjust Violence and Slaughter he hath committed upon one, declared War against all Mankind, and therefore may be destroyed as a *Lyon* or a *Tyger,* one of those wild Savage Beasts, with whom Men can have no Society nor Security: And upon this is grounded the great Law of Nature, *Who so sheddeth Mans Blood, by Man shall his Blood be shed.* And *Cain* was so fully convinced, that every one had a Right to destroy such a Criminal, that after the Murther of his Brother, he cries out, *Every one that findeth me, shall slay me;* so plain was it writ in the Hearts of all Mankind.

12. By the same reason, may a Man in the State of Nature *punish the lesser breaches* of that Law. It will perhaps be demanded, with death? I answer, Each Transgression may be *punished* to that *degree,* and with so much *Severity* as will suffice to make it an ill bargain to the Offender, give him cause to repent, and terrifie others from doing the like. Every Offence that can be committed in the State of Nature, may in the State of Nature be also punished, equally, and as far forth as it may, in a Common-wealth; for though it would be besides my present purpose, to enter here into the particulars of the Law of Nature, or its *measures of punishment;* yet, it is certain there is such a Law, and that too, as intelligible and plain to a rational Crea-

ture, and a Studier of that Law, as the positive Laws of Common-wealths, nay possibly plainer; As much as Reason is easier to be understood, than the Phansies and intricate Contrivances of Men, following contrary and hidden interests put into Words; For so truly are a great part of the *Municipal Laws* of Countries, which are only so far right, as they are founded on the Law of Nature, by which they are to be regulated and interpreted.

13. To this strange Doctrine, *viz.* That *in the State of Nature, every one has the Executive Power* of the Law of Nature, I doubt not but it will be objected, That it is unreasonable for Men to be Judges in their own Cases, that Self-love will make Men partial to themselves and their Friends. And on the other side, that Ill Nature, Passion and Revenge will carry them too far in punishing others. And hence nothing but Confusion and Disorder will follow, and that therefore God hath certainly appointed Government to restrain the partiality and violence of Men. I easily grant, that *Civil Government* is the proper Remedy for the Inconveniences of the State of Nature, which must certainly be Great, where Men may be Judges in their own Case, since 'tis easily to be imagined, that he who was so unjust as to do his Brother an Injury, will scarce be so just as to condemn himself for it: But I shall desire those who make this Objection, to remember that *Absolute Monarchs* are but Men, and if Government is to be the Remedy of those Evils, which necessarily follow from Mens being Judges in their own Cases, and the State of Nature is therefore not to be endured, I desire to know what kind of Government that is, and how much better it is than the State of Nature, where one Man commanding a multitude, has the Liberty to be Judge in his own Case, and may do to all his Subjects whatever he pleases, without the least liberty to any one to question or controle those who Execute his Pleasure? And in whatsoever he doth, whether led by Reason, Mistake or Passion, must be submitted to? Much better it is in the State of Nature wherein Men are not bound to submit to the unjust will of another: And if he that judges, judges amiss in his own, or any other Case, he is answerable for it to the rest of Mankind.

14. 'Tis often asked as a mighty Objection, *Where are, or ever were,* there any *Men in such a State of Nature?* To which it may suffice as an answer at present; That since all *Princes* and Rulers of *Independent* Governments all through the World, are in a State of Nature, 'tis plain the World never was, nor ever will be, without Numbers of Men in that State. I have named all Governors of *Independent* Communities, whether they are, or are not, in League with others: For 'tis not every Compact that puts an end to the State of Nature between Men, but only this one of agreeing together mutually to enter into one Community, and make one Body Politick; other Promises and Compacts, Men may make one with another, and yet still be in the State of Nature. The Promises and Bargains for Truck, &c. between the two Men in the Desert Island, mentioned by *Garcilasso De la vega,* in his History of *Peru,* or between a *Swiss* and an *Indian,* in the Woods of *America,* are binding to them, though they are perfectly in a State of Nature, in reference to one another. For Truth and keeping

of Faith belongs to Men, as Men, and not as Members of Society.

15. To those that say, There were never any Men in the State of Nature; I will not only oppose the Authority of the Judicious *Hooker, Eccl. Pol. Lib.* I. *Sect.* 10. where he says, *The Laws which have been hitherto mentioned*, i.e. the Laws of Nature, *do bind Men, although they have never any settled fellowship, never any Solemn Agreement amongst themselves what to do or not to do, but for as much as we are not by our selves sufficient to furnish our selves with competent store of things, needful for such a Life, as our Nature doth desire, a Life, fit for the Dignity of Man; therefore to supply those Defects and Imperfections which are in us, as living singly and solely by our selves, we are naturally induced to seek Communion and Fellowship with others, this was the Cause of Mens uniting themselves, at first in Politick Societies.* But I moreover affirm, That all Men are naturally in that State, and remain so, till by their own Consents they make themselves Members of some Politick Society; And I doubt not in the Sequel of this Discourse, to make it very clear.

. . . . .

54. Though I have said above, Chap. II, *That all Men by Nature are equal*, I cannot be supposed to understand all sorts of *Equality: Age* or *Virtue* may give Men a just Precedency: *Excellency of Parts and Merit* may place others above the Common Level: *Birth* may subject some, and *Alliance* or *Benefits* others, to pay an Observance to those to whom Nature, Gratitude or other Respects may have made it due; and yet all this consists with the *Equality*, which all Men are in, in respect of Jurisdiction or Dominion one over another, which was the *Equality* I there spoke of, as proper to the Business in hand, being that *equal Right* that every Man hath, *to his Natural Freedom*, without being subjected to the Will or Authority of any other Man.

. . . . .

119. *Every Man* being, as has been shewed, *naturally free*, and nothing being able to put him into subjection to any Earthly Power, but only his own Consent; it is to be considered, what shall be understood to be *a sufficient Declaration of* a Mans Consent, *to make him subject* to the Laws of any Government. There is a common distinction of an express and a tacit consent, which will concern our present Case. No body doubts but an *express Consent*, of any Man, entring into any Society, makes him a perfect Member of that Society, a Subject of that Government. The difficulty is, what ought to be look'd upon as a *tacit Consent*, and how far it binds, *i.e.* how far any one shall be looked on to have consented, and thereby submitted to any Government, where he has made no Expressions of it at all. And to this I say, that every Man, that hath any Possession, or Enjoyment, of any part of the Dominions of any Government, doth thereby give his *tacit Consent*, and is as far forth obliged to Obedience to the Laws of that Government, during such Enjoyment, as any one under it; whether this his Possession be of Land, to him and his Heirs for ever, or a Lodging only for a Week; or whether it be barely travelling freely on the Highway; and in Effect, it reaches as far as the very being of any one within the Territories of that Government.

120. To understand this the better, it is fit to consider, that every Man, when he, at first, incorporates himself into any Commonwealth, he, by his uniting himself thereunto, annexed also, and submits to the Community those Possessions, which he has, or shall acquire, that do not already belong to any other Government. For it would be a direct Contradiction, for any one, to enter into Society with others for the securing and regulating of Property: And yet to suppose his Land, whose Property is to be regulated by the Laws of the Society, should be exempt from the Jurisdiction of that Government, to which he himself the Proprietor of the Land, is a Subject. By the same Act therefore, whereby any one unites his person, which was before free, to any Commonwealth; by the same he unites his Possessions, which were before free, to it also; and they become, both of them, Person and Possession, subject to the Government and Dominion of that Commonwealth, as long as it hath a being. *Whoever* therefore, from thenceforth, by Inheritance, Purchase, Permission, or otherways *enjoys any part of the Land*, so annext to, and under the Government *of that Commonwealth, must take it with the Condition* it is under; that is, *of submitting to the Government of the Commonwealth*, under whose Jurisdiction it is, as far forth, as any Subject of it.

121. But since the Government has a direct Jurisdiction only over the Land, and reaches the Possessor of it, (before he has actually incorporated himself in the Society) only as he dwells upon, and enjoys that: *The Obligation* any one is under, by Virtue of such Enjoyment, *to submit to the Government, begins and ends with the Enjoyment;* so that whenever the Owner, who has given nothing but such a *tacit Consent* to the Government, will, by Donation, Sale, or otherwise, quit the said Possession, he is at liberty to go and incorporate himself into any other Commonwealth, or to agree with others to begin a new one, *in vacuis locis*, in any part of the World, they can find free and unpossessed: Whereas he, that has once, by actual Agreement, and any *express* Declaration, given his *Consent* to be of any Commonweal, is perpetually and indispensably obliged to be and remain unalterably a Subject to it, and can never be again in the liberty of the state of Nature; unless by any Calamity, the Government, he was under, comes to be dissolved; or else by some publick Act cuts him off from being any longer a Member of it.

122. But submitting to the Laws of any Country, living quietly, and enjoying Priviledges and Protection under them, *makes not a Man a Member of that Society:* This is only a local Protection and Homage due to, and from all those, who, not being in a state of War, come within the Territories belonging to any Government, to all parts whereof the force of its Law extends. But this no more *makes a Man a Member of that Society*, a perpetual Subject of that Commonwealth, than it would make a Man a Subject to another in whose Family he found it convenient to abide for some time; though, whilst he continued in it, he were obliged to comply with the Laws, and submit to the Government he found there. And thus we see, that *Foreigners*, by living all their Lives under another Government, and enjoying the Priviledges and Protection of it, though they are bound, even in Conscience, to submit to its Adminis-

tration, as far forth as any Denison; yet do not thereby come to be *Subjects or Members of that Commonwealth*. Nothing can make any Man so, but his actually entering into it by positive Engagement, and express Promise and Compact. This is that, which I think, concerning the beginning of Political Societies, and that *Consent which makes any one a Member* of any Commonwealth.

. . . . .

163. And therefore they have a very wrong Notion of Government, who say, that the People have *incroach'd upon the Prerogative*, when they have got any part of it to be defined by positive Laws. For in so doing, they have not pulled from the Prince any thing, that of right belong'd to him, but only declared, that that Power which they indefinitely left in his, or his Ancestors, hands, to be exercised for their good, was not a thing, which they intended him, when he used it otherwise. For the end of government being the good of the Community, whatsoever alterations are made in it, tending to that end, cannot be an *incroachment* upon any body: since no body in Government can have a right tending to any other end. And those only are *incroachments* which prejudice or hinder the publick good. Those who say otherwise, speak as if the Prince had a distinct and separate Interest from the good of the Community, and was not made for it, the Root and Source, from which spring almost all those Evils, and Disorders, which happen in Kingly Governments. And indeed if that be so, the People under his Government are not a Society of Rational Creatures entred into a Community for their mutual good; they are not such as have set Rulers over themselves, to guard, and promote that good; but are to be looked on as an Herd of inferiour Creatures, under the Dominion of a Master, who keeps them, and works them for his own Pleasure or Profit. If men were so void of Reason, and brutish, as to enter into Society upon such Terms, *Prerogative* might indeed be, what some Men would have it, an Arbitrary Power to do things hurtful to the People.

2

THOMAS GORDON, CATO'S LETTERS, NO. 38
22 July 1721
Jacobson 93–95, 96, 99–101

The Right and Capacity of the People to judge of Government.

The World has, from Time to Time, been led into such a long Maze of Mistakes, by those who gained by deceiving, that whoever would instruct Mankind, must begin with removing their Errors; and if they were every where honestly apprized of Truth, and restored to their Senses, there would not remain one Nation of Bigots or Slaves under the Sun: A Happiness always to be wished, but never expected!

In most Parts of the Earth there is neither Light nor Liberty; and even in the best Parts of it they are but little encouraged, and coldly maintained; there being, in all Places, many engaged, through Interest, in a perpetual Conspiracy against them. They are the two greatest Civil Blessings, inseparable in their Interests, and the mutual Support of each other; and whoever would destroy one of them, must destroy both. Hence it is, that we every where find Tyranny and Imposture, Ignorance and Slavery, joined together; and Oppressors and Deceivers mutually aiding and paying constant Court to each other. Whereever Truth is dangerous, Liberty is precarious.

Of all the Sciences that I know in the World, that of Government concerns us most, and is the easiest to be known, and yet is the least understood. Most of those who manage it would make the lower World believe that there is I know not what Difficulty and Mystery in it, far above vulgar Understandings; which Proceeding of theirs is direct Craft and Imposture: Every Ploughman knows a good Government from a bad one, from the Effects of it: he knows whether the Fruits of his Labour be his own, and whether he enjoy them in Peace and Security: And if he do not know the Principles of Government, it is for want of Thinking and Enquiry, for they lie open to common Sense; but People are generally taught not to think of them at all, or to think wrong of them.

What is Government, but a Trust committed by All, or the Most, to One, or a Few, who are to attend upon the Affairs of All, that every one may, with the more Security, attend upon his own? A great and honourable Trust; but too seldom honourably executed; those who possess it having it often more at Heart to encrease their Power, than to make it useful; and to be terrible, rather than beneficent. It is therefore a Trust, which ought to be bounded with many and strong Restraints, because Power renders Men wanton, insolent to others, and fond of themselves. Every Violation therefore of this Trust, where such Violation is considerable, ought to meet with proportionable Punishment; and the smallest Violation of it ought to meet with some, because Indulgence to the least Faults of Magistrates may be Cruelty to a whole People.

Honesty, Diligence, and plain Sense, are the only Talents necessary for the executing of this Trust; and the public Good is its only End: As to Refinements and Finesses, they are often only the false Appearances of Wisdom and Parts, and oftener Tricks to hide Guilt and Emptiness; and they are generally mean and dishonest: they are the Arts of Jobbers in Politicks, who, playing their own Game under the publick Cover, subsist upon poor Shifts and Expedients; starved Politicians, who live from Hand to Mouth, from Day to Day, and following the little Views of Ambition, Avarice, Revenge, and the like personal Passions, are ashamed to avow them, yet want Souls great enough to forsake them; small wicked Statesmen, who make a private Market of the Publick, and deceive it, in order to sell it.

These are the poor Parts which great and good Governors scorn to play, and cannot play; their Designs, like their Stations, being purely publick, are open and undisguised. They do not consider their People as their Prey, nor lie in Ambush for their Subjects; nor dread, and treat and surprize them like Enemies, as all ill Magistrates do; who are not Governors, but Jaylors and Spunges, who chain them and squeeze them, and yet take it very ill if they do but murmur; which is yet much less than a People so abused ought to do. There have been Times and Countries, when publick Ministers and publick Enemies have been the same individual Men. What a melancholy Reflection is this, that the most terrible and mischievous Foes to a Nation should be its own Magistrates! And yet in every enslaved Country, which is almost every Country, this is their woful Case.

. . . . .

But some have said, *It is not the Business of private Men to meddle with Government.* A bold, false, and dishonest Saying; and whoever says it, either knows not what he says, or cares not, or slavishly speaks the Sense of others. It is a Cant now almost forgot in *England,* and which never prevailed but when Liberty and the Constitution were attacked, and never can prevail but upon the like Occasion.

. . . . .

What is the Publick, but the collective Body of private Men, as every private Man is a Member of the Publick? And as the Whole ought to be concerned for the Preservation of every private Individual, it is the Duty of every Individual to be concerned for the Whole, in which himself is included.

One Man, or a few Men, have often pretended the Publick, and meant themselves, and consulted their own personal Interest, in Instances essential to its Well-being; but the whole People, by consulting their own Interest, consult the Publick, and act for the Publick by acting for themselves: This is particularly the Spirit of our Constitution, in which the whole Nation is represented; and our Records afford Instances, where the House of Commons have declined entering upon a Question of Importance, till they had gone into the Country, and consulted their Principals, the People: So far were they from thinking that private Men had no Right to meddle with Government. In Truth, our whole worldly Happiness and Misery (abating for Accidents and Diseases) are owing to the Order or Mismanagement of Government; and he who says that private Men have no Concern with Government, does wisely and modestly tell us, that Men have no Concern in that which concerns them most; it is saying that People ought not to concern themselves whether they be naked or clothed, fed or starved, deceived or instructed, and whether they be protected or destroyed: What Nonsense and Servitude in a free and wise Nation!

For myself, who have thought pretty much of these Matters, I am of Opinion, that a whole Nation are like to be as much attached to themselves, as one Man or a few Men are like to be, who may by many Means be detached from the Interest of a Nation. It is certain that one Man, and several Men, may be bribed into an Interest opposite to that of the Publick; but it is as certain that a whole Country can never find an Equivalent for itself, and consequently a whole Country can never be bribed. It is the eternal Interest of every Nation, that their Government should be good; but they who direct it frequently reason a contrary Way, and find their own Account in Plunder and Oppres-

sion; and while the publick Voice is pretended to be declared, by one or a few, for vile and private Ends, the Publick know nothing of what is done, till they feel the terrible Effects of it.

By the Bill of Rights, and the Act of Settlement, at the *Revolution,* a Right is asserted to the People of applying to the King and to the Parliament, by Petition and Address, for a Redress of publick Grievances and Mismanagements, when such there are, of which They are left to judge; And the Difference between free and enslaved Countries lies principally here, that in the former, their Magistrates must consult the Voice and Interest of the People; but in the latter, the private Will, Interest, and Pleasure of the Governors, are the sole End and Motives of their Administration.

Such is the Difference between *England* and *Turkey;* which Difference they who say that private Men have no Right to concern themselves with Government, would absolutely destroy; they would convert Magistrates into Bashaws, and introduce Popery into Politicks. The late Revolution stands upon the very opposite Maxim; and that any Man dares to contradict it since the *Revolution,* would be amazing, did we not know that there are, in every Country, Hirelings who would betray it for a Sop.

3

MONTESQUIEU, SPIRIT OF LAWS, BK. 2, CH. 2
1748

2.—Of the Republican Government, and the Laws in relation to Democracy

When the body of the people is possessed of the supreme power, it is called a democracy. When the supreme power is lodged in the hands of a part of the people, it is then an aristocracy.

In a democracy the people are in some respects the sovereign, and in others the subject.

There can be no exercise of sovereignty but by their suffrages, which are their own will; now, the sovereign's will is the sovereign himself. The laws, therefore, which establish the right of suffrage are fundamental to this government. And indeed it is as important to regulate in a republic, in what manner, by whom, to whom, and concerning what suffrages are to be given, as it is in a monarchy to know who is the prince, and after what manner he ought to govern.

Libanius says that at "Athens a stranger who intermeddled in the assemblies of the people was punished with death." This is because such a man usurped the rights of sovereignty.

It is an essential point to fix the number of citizens who are to form the public assemblies; otherwise it would be uncertain whether the whole or only a part of the people had given their votes. At Sparta the number was fixed at ten thousand. But Rome, designed by Providence to rise from the weakest beginnings to the highest pitch of grandeur; Rome, doomed to experience all the vicissitudes of fortune; Rome, who had sometimes all her inhabitants without her walls, and sometimes all Italy and a considerable part of the world within them; Rome, I say, never fixed the number; and this was one of the principal causes of her ruin.

The people, in whom the supreme power resides, ought to have the management of everything within their reach: that which exceeds their abilities must be conducted by their ministers.

But they cannot properly be said to have their ministers, without the power of nominating them: it is, therefore, a fundamental maxim in this government, that the people should choose their ministers—that is, their magistrates.

They have occasion, as well as monarchs, and even more so, to be directed by a council or senate. But to have a proper confidence in these, they should have the choosing of the members; whether the election be made by themselves, as at Athens, or by some magistrate deputed for that purpose, as on certain occasions was customary at Rome.

The people are extremely well qualified for choosing those whom they are to intrust with part of their authority. They have only to be determined by things to which they cannot be strangers, and by facts that are obvious to sense. They can tell when a person has fought many battles, and been crowned with success; they are, therefore, capable of electing a general. They can tell when a judge is assiduous in his office, gives general satisfaction, and has never been charged with bribery: this is sufficient for choosing a praetor. They are struck with the magnificence or riches of a fellow-citizen; no more is requisite for electing an edile. These are facts of which they can have better information in a public forum than a monarch in his palace. But are they capable of conducting an intricate affair, of seizing and improving the opportunity and critical moment of action? No; this surpasses their abilities.

Should we doubt the people's natural capacity, in respect to the discernment of merit, we need only cast an eye on the series of surprising elections made by the Athenians and Romans; which no one surely will attribute to hazard.

We know that though the people of Rome assumed the right of raising plebeians to public offices, yet they never would exert this power; and though at Athens the magistrates were allowed, by the law of Aristides, to be elected from all the different classes of inhabitants, there never was a case, says Xenophon, when the common people petitioned for employments which could endanger either their security or their glory.

As most citizens have sufficient ability to choose, though unqualified to be chosen, so the people, though capable of calling others to an account for their administration, are incapable of conducting the administration themselves.

The public business must be carried on with a certain motion, neither too quick nor too slow. But the motion of the people is always either too remiss or too violent. Sometimes with a hundred thousand arms they overturn all before them; and sometimes with a hundred thousand feet they creep like insects.

In a popular state the inhabitants are divided into certain classes. It is in the manner of making this division that great legislators have signalized themselves; and it is on this the duration and prosperity of democracy have ever depended.

Servius Tullius followed the spirit of aristocracy in the distribution of his classes. We find in Livy and in Dionysius Halicarnassus in what manner he lodged the right of suffrage in the hands of the principal citizens. He had divided the people of Rome into 193 centuries, which formed six classes; and ranking the rich, who were in smaller numbers, in the first centuries, and those in middling circumstances, who were more numerous, in the next, he flung the indigent multitude into the last; and as each century had but one vote, it was property rather than numbers that decided the election.

Solon divided the people of Athens into four classes. In this he was directed by the spirit of democracy, his intention not being to fix those who were to choose, but such as were eligible: therefore, leaving to every citizen the right of election, he made the judges eligible from each of those four classes; but the magistrates he ordered to be chosen only out of the first three, consisting of persons of easy fortunes.

As the division of those who have a right of suffrage is a fundamental law in republics, so the manner of giving this suffrage is another fundamental.

The suffrage by lot is natural to democracy; as that by choice is to aristocracy.

The suffrage by lot is a method of electing that offends no one, but animates each citizen with the pleasing hope of serving his country.

Yet as this method is in itself defective, it has been the endeavor of the most eminent legislators to regulate and amend it.

Solon made a law at Athens that military employments should be conferred by choice; but that senators and judges should be elected by lot.

The same legislator ordained that civil magistracies, attended with great expense, should be given by choice, and the others by lot.

In order, however, to amend the suffrage by lot, he made a rule that none but those who presented themselves should be elected; that the person elected should be examined by judges, and that every one should have a right to accuse him if he were unworthy of the office; this participated at the same time of the suffrage by lot and of that by choice. When the time of their magistracy had expired, they were obliged to submit to another judgment in regard to their conduct. Persons utterly unqualified must have been extremely backward in giving in their names to be drawn by lot.

The law which determines the manner of giving suffrage is likewise fundamental in a democracy. It is a question of some importance whether the suffrages ought to be public or secret. Cicero observes that the laws which rendered them secret towards the close of the republic were the cause of its decline. But as this is differently practised in different republics, I shall offer here my thoughts concerning this subject.

The people's suffrages ought doubtless to be public; and this should be considered as a fundamental law of democracy. The lower class ought to be directed by those of higher rank, and restrained within bounds by the gravity of eminent personages. Hence, by rendering the suffrages secret in the Roman republic, all was lost; it was no longer possible to direct a populace that sought its own destruction. But when the body of the nobles are to vote in an aristocracy, or in a democracy the senate, as the business is then only to prevent intrigues, the suffrages cannot be too secret.

Intriguing in a senate is dangerous; it is dangerous also in a body of nobles; but not so among the people, whose nature is to act through passion. In countries where they have no share in the government, we often see them as much inflamed on account of an actor as ever they could be for the welfare of the state. The misfortune of a republic is when intrigues are at an end; which happens when the people are gained by bribery and corruption: in this case they grow indifferent to public affairs, and avarice becomes their predominant passion. Unconcerned about the government and everything belonging to it, they quietly wait for their hire.

It is likewise a fundamental law in democracies, that the people should have the sole power to enact laws. And yet there are a thousand occasions on which it is necessary the senate should have the power of decreeing; nay, it is frequently proper to make some trial of a law before it is established. The constitutions of Rome and Athens were excellent—the decrees of the senate had the force of laws for the space of a year, but did not become perpetual till they were ratified by the consent of the people.

4

DAVID HUME, OF THE ORIGINAL CONTRACT
1752

When we consider how nearly equal all men are in their bodily force, and even in their mental powers and faculties, till cultivated by education, we must necessarily allow that nothing but their own consent could at first associate them together and subject them to any authority. The people, if we trace government to its first origin in the woods and deserts, are the source of all power and jurisdiction, and voluntarily, for the sake of peace and order, abandoned their native liberty and received laws from their equal and companion. The conditions upon which they were willing to submit were either expressed or were so clear and obvious that it might well be esteemed superfluous to express them. If this, then, be meant by the *original contract*, it cannot be denied that all government is, at first, founded on a contract and that the most ancient rude combinations of mankind were formed chiefly by that principle. In vain are we asked in what records this charter of our liberties is registered. It was not written on parchment, nor yet on leaves or barks of trees. It preceded the use of writing and all the other civilized arts of life. But we trace it plainly in the nature of man and in the equality, or something approaching equality, which we find in all the individuals of that species. The force which now prevails, and which is founded on fleets and armies, is plainly political and derived from authority, the effect of established government. A man's natural force consists only in the vigor of his limbs and the firmness of his courage, which could never subject multitudes to the command of one. Nothing but their own consent and their sense of the advantages resulting from peace and order could have had that influence.

Yet even this consent was long very imperfect and could not be the basis of a regular administration. The chieftain, who had probably acquired his influence during the continuance of war, ruled more by persuasion than command; and till he could employ force to reduce the refractory and disobedient, the society could scarcely be said to have attained a state of civil government. No compact or agreement, it is evident, was expressly formed for general submission, an idea far beyond the comprehension of savages. Each exertion of authority in the chieftain must have been particular and called forth by the present exigencies of the case. The sensible utility resulting from his interposition made these exertions become daily more frequent; and their frequency gradually produced a habitual and, if you please to call it so, a voluntary and therefore precarious acquiescence in the people.

But philosophers who have embraced a party—if that be not a contradiction in terms—are not content with these concessions. They assert not only that government in its earliest infancy arose from consent, or rather the voluntary acquiescence of the people, but also that, even at present, when it has attained its full maturity, it rests on no other foundation. They affirm that all men are still born equal and owe allegiance to no prince or government unless bound by the obligation and sanction of a *promise*. And as no man, without some equivalent, would forego the advantages of his native liberty and subject himself to the will of another, this promise is always understood to be conditional and imposes on him no obligation, unless he meet with justice and protection from his sovereign. These advantages the sovereign promises him in return; and if he fail in the execution, he has broken on his part the articles of engagement, and has thereby freed his subject from all obligations to allegiance. Such, according to these philosophers, is the foundation of authority in every government, and such the right of resistance possessed by every subject.

But would these reasoners look abroad into the world, they would meet with nothing that in the least corresponds to their ideas or can warrant so refined and philosophical a system. On the contrary, we find everywhere princes who claim their subjects as their property and assert their independent right of sovereignty from conquest or succession. We find also everywhere subjects who acknowledge this right in their prince and suppose themselves born under obligations of obedience to a certain sovereign, as much as under the ties of reverence and duty to certain parents. These connections are always conceived to be equally independent of our consent, in Persia and China, in France and Spain, and even in Holland and England, wherever the doctrines above mentioned have not been carefully inculcated. Obedience or subjection becomes so familiar that most men never make any inquiry about its origin or cause, more than about the principle of gravity, resistance, or the most universal laws of nature. Or if curiosity ever move them, as soon as they learn that they themselves and their ancestors have, for several ages, or from time immemorial, been subject to such a form of government or such a family, they immediately acquiesce and acknowledge their obligation to allegiance. Were you to preach, in most parts of the world, that political connections are founded altogether on voluntary consent or a mutual promise, the magistrate would soon imprison you as seditious for loosening the ties of obedience, if your friends did not before shut you up as delirious for advancing such absurdities. It is strange that an act of the mind which every individual is supposed to have formed, and after he came to the use of reason too—otherwise it could have no authority—that this act, I say, should be so much unknown to all of them that over the face of the whole earth there scarcely remain any traces or memory of it.

But the contract on which government is founded is said to be the *original contract,* and consequently may be supposed too old to fall under the knowledge of the present generation. If the agreement by which savage men first associated and conjoined their force be here meant, this is acknowledged to be real; but being so ancient and being obliterated by a thousand changes of government and princes, it cannot now be supposed to retain any authority. If we would say anything to the purpose, we must assert that every particular government which is lawful and which imposes any duty of allegiance on the subject was at first founded on consent and a voluntary compact. But besides that this supposes the consent of the fathers to bind the children, even to the most remote generations—which republican writers will never allow—besides this, I say, it is not justified by history or experience in any age or country of the world.

Almost all the governments which exist at present, or of which there remains any record in story, have been founded originally either on usurpation or conquest or both, without any pretense of a fair consent or voluntary subjection of the people. When an artful and bold man is placed at the head of an army or faction, it is often easy for him, by employing sometimes violence, sometimes false pretenses, to establish his dominion over a people a hundred times more numerous than his partisans. He allows no such open communication that his enemies can know with certainty their number or force. He gives them no leisure to assemble together in a body to oppose him. Even all those who are the instruments of his usurpation may wish his fall, but their ignorance of each other's intention keeps them in awe and is the sole cause of his security. By such arts as these many governments have been established, and this is all the *original contract* which they have to boast of.

The face of the earth is continually changing by the increase of small kingdoms into great empires, by the disso-

lution of great empires into smaller kingdoms, by the planting of colonies, by the migration of tribes. Is there anything discoverable in all these events but force and violence? Where is the mutual agreement or voluntary association so much talked of?

Even the smoothest way by which a nation may receive a foreign master, by marriage or a will, is not extremely honorable for the people, but supposes them to be disposed of like a dowry or a legacy, according to the pleasure or interest of their rulers.

But where no force interposes and election takes place, what is this election so highly vaunted? It is either the combination of a few great men who decide for the whole and will allow of no opposition or it is the fury of a multitude that follow a seditious ringleader who is not known, perhaps, to a dozen among them and who owes his advancement merely to his own impudence or to the momentary caprice of his fellows.

Are these disorderly elections, which are rare too, of such mighty authority as to be the only lawful foundation of all government and allegiance?

In reality there is not a more terrible event than a total dissolution of government, which gives liberty to the multitude and makes the determination or choice of a new establishment depend upon a number which nearly approaches to that of the body of the people. For it never comes entirely to the whole body of them. Every wise man, then, wishes to see at the head of a powerful and obedient army a general who may speedily seize the prize and give to the people a master which they are so unfit to choose for themselves—so little correspondent is fact and reality to those philosophical notions.

Let not the establishment at the Revolution deceive us or make us so much in love with a philosophical origin to government as to imagine all others monstrous and irregular. Even that event was far from corresponding to these refined ideas. It was only the succession, and that only in the regal part of the government, which was then changed. And it was only the majority of seven hundred who determined that change for near ten millions. I doubt not, indeed, but the bulk of those ten millions acquiesced willingly in the determination. But was the matter left in the least to their choice? Was it not justly supposed to be from that moment decided and every man punished who refused to submit to the new sovereign? How otherwise could the matter have ever been brought to any issue or conclusion?

. . . . .

It is in vain to say that all governments are or should be at first founded on popular consent as much as the necessity of human affairs will admit. This favors entirely my pretension. I maintain that human affairs will never admit of this consent, seldom of the appearance of it; but that conquest or usurpation—that is, in plain terms, force—by dissolving the ancient governments, is the origin of almost all the new ones which were ever established in the world. And that in the few cases where consent may seem to have taken place, it was commonly so irregular, so confined, or so much intermixed either with fraud or violence that it cannot have any great authority.

My intention here is not to exclude the consent of the people from being one just foundation of government. Where it has place, it is surely the best and most sacred of any. I only contend that it has very seldom had place in any degree, and never almost in its full extent, and that, therefore, some other foundation of government must also be admitted.

Were all men possessed of so inflexible a regard to justice that of themselves they would totally abstain from the properties of others, they had forever remained in a state of absolute liberty, without subjection to any magistrate or political society. But this is a state of perfection of which human nature is justly deemed incapable. Again, were all men possessed of so perfect an understanding as always to know their own interests, no form of government had ever been submitted to but what was established on consent and was fully canvassed by every member of the society. But this state of perfection is likewise much superior to human nature. Reason, history, and experience show us that all political societies have had an origin much less accurate and regular; and were one to choose a period of time when the people's consent was the least regarded in public transactions, it would be precisely on the establishment of a new government. In a settled constitution their inclinations are often consulted, but during the fury of revolutions, conquests, and public convulsions, military force or political craft usually decides the controversy.

When a new government is established, by whatever means, the people are commonly dissatisfied with it and pay obedience more from fear and necessity than from any idea of allegiance or of moral obligation. The prince is watchful and jealous, and must carefully guard against every beginning or appearance of insurrection. Time, by degrees, removes all these difficulties and accustoms the nation to regard as their lawful or native princes that family which at first they considered as usurpers or foreign conquerors. In order to found this opinion, they have no recourse to any notion of voluntary consent or promise which, they know, never was in this case either expected or demanded. The original establishment was formed by violence and submitted to from necessity. The subsequent administration is also supported by power and acquiesced in by the people, not as a matter of choice but of obligation. They imagine not that their consent gives their prince a title. But they willingly consent because they think that, from long possession, he has acquired a title independent of their choice or inclination.

Should it be said that, by living under the dominion of a prince which one might leave, every individual has given a *tacit* consent to his authority and promised him obedience, it may be answered that such an implied consent can only have place where a man imagines that the matter depends on his choice. But where he thinks—as all mankind do who are born under established governments—that by his birth he owes allegiance to a certain prince or certain form of government, it would be absurd to infer a consent or choice which he expressly in this case renounces and disclaims.

. . . . .

Did one generation of men go off the stage at once and

another succeed, as is the case with silkworms and butterflies, the new race, if they had sense enough to choose their government, which surely is never the case with men, might voluntarily and by general consent establish their own form of civil polity without any regard to the laws or precedents which prevailed among their ancestors. But as human society is in perpetual flux, one man every hour going out of the world, another coming into it, it is necessary in order to preserve stability in government that the new brood should conform themselves to the established constitution and nearly follow the path which their fathers, treading in the footsteps of theirs, had marked out to them. Some innovations must necessarily have place in every human institution; and it is happy where the enlightened genius of the age give these a direction to the side of reason, liberty, and justice. But violent innovations no individual is entitled to make. They are even dangerous to be attempted by the legislature. More ill than good is ever to be expected from them. And if history affords examples to the contrary, they are not to be drawn into precedent and are only to be regarded as proofs that the science of politics affords few rules which will not admit of some exception and which may not sometimes be controlled by fortune and accident. The violent innovations in the reign of Henry VIII proceeded from an imperious monarch seconded by the appearance of legislative authority; those in the reign of Charles I were derived from faction and fanaticism; and both of them have proved happy in the issue. But even the former were long the source of many disorders, and still more dangers; and if the measures of allegiance were to be taken from the latter, a total anarchy must have place in human society and a final period at once be put to every government.

Suppose that a usurper, after having banished his lawful prince and royal family, should establish his dominion for ten or a dozen years in any country and should preserve so exact a discipline in his troops and so regular a disposition in his garrisons that no insurrection had ever been raised or even murmur heard against his administration. Can it be asserted that the people, who in their hearts abhor his treason, have tacitly consented to his authority and promised him allegiance merely because, from necessity, they live under his dominion? Suppose again their native prince restored by means of an army which he levies in foreign countries. They receive him with joy and exultation, and show plainly with what reluctance they had submitted to any other yoke. I may now ask upon what foundation the prince's title stands? Not on popular consent surely; for though the people willingly acquiesce in his authority, they never imagine that their consent made him sovereign. They consent because they apprehend him to be already, by birth, their lawful sovereign. And as to tacit consent, which may now be inferred from their living under his dominion, this is no more than what they formerly gave to the tyrant and usurper.

. . . . .

But would we have a more regular, at least a more philosophical, refutation of this principle of an original contract or popular consent, perhaps the following observations may suffice.

All *moral* duties may be divided into two kinds. The *first* are those to which men are impelled by a natural instinct or immediate propensity which operates on them, independent of all ideas of obligation and of all views either to public or private utility. Of this nature are love of children, gratitude to benefactors, pity to the unfortunate. When we reflect on the advantage which results to society from such humane instincts, we pay them the just tribute of moral approbation and esteem. But the person actuated by them feels their power and influence antecedent to any such reflection.

The *second* kind of moral duties are such as are not supported by any original instinct of nature, but are performed entirely from a sense of obligation, when we consider the necessities of human society and the impossibility of supporting it if these duties were neglected. It is thus *justice*, or a regard to the property of others, *fidelity*, or the observance of promises, become obligatory and acquire an authority over mankind. For as it is evident that every man loves himself better than any other person, he is naturally impelled to extend his acquisitions as much as possible; and nothing can restrain him in this propensity but reflection and experience, by which he learns the pernicious effects of that license and the total dissolution of society which must ensue from it. His original inclination, therefore, or instinct, is here checked and restrained by a subsequent judgment or observation.

The case is precisely the same with the political or civil duty of *allegiance* as with the natural duties of justice and fidelity. Our primary instincts lead us either to indulge ourselves in unlimited freedom or to seek dominion over others; and it is reflection only which engages us to sacrifice such strong passions to the interests of peace and public order. A small degree of experience and observation suffices to teach us that society cannot possibly be maintained without the authority of magistrates, and that this authority must soon fall into contempt where exact obedience is not paid to it. The observation of these general and obvious interests is the source of all allegiance and of that moral obligation which we attribute to it.

5

JAMES OTIS, THE RIGHTS OF THE BRITISH
COLONIES ASSERTED AND PROVED
1764
Political Writings 308–11

Let no Man think I am about to commence advocate for *despotism*, because I affirm that government is founded on the necessity of our natures; and that an original supreme Sovereign, absolute, and uncontroulable, *earthly* power *must* exist in and preside over every society; from whose final decisions there can be no appeal but directly to Heaven. It is therefore *originally* and *ultimately* in the peo-

ple. I say supreme absolute power is *originally* and *ultimately* in the people; and they never did in fact *freely*, nor can they *rightfully* make an absolute, unlimited renunciation of this divine right.* It is ever in the nature of the thing given in *trust*, and on a condition, the performance of which no mortal can dispence with; namely, that the person or persons on whom the sovereignty is confer'd by the people, shall *incessantly* consult *their* good. Tyranny of all kinds is to be abhor'd, whether it be in the hands of one, or of the few, or of the many.—And tho' "in the last age a generation of men sprung up that would flatter Princes with an opinion that *they* have a *divine right* to absolute power"; yet "slavery is so vile and miserable an estate of man, and so directly opposite to the generous temper and courage of our nation, that 'tis hard to be conceived that an *englishman*, much less a *gentleman*, should plead for it."† Especially at a time when the finest writers of the most polite nations on the continent of *Europe*, are enraptured with the beauties of the civil constitution of *Great-Britain;* and envy her, no less for the *freedom* of her sons, than for her immense *wealth* and *military* glory.

But let the *origin* of government be placed where it may, the *end* of it is manifestly the good of *the whole*. *Salus populi supreme lex esto*, is of the law of nature, and part of that grand charter given the human race, (tho' too many of them are afraid to assert it,) by the only monarch in the universe, who has a clear and indisputable right to *absolute* power; because he is the *only* One who is *omniscient* as well as *omnipotent*.

It is evidently contrary to the first principles of reason, that supreme *unlimited* power should be in the hands of *one* man. It is the greatest "*idolatry*, begotten by *flattery*, on the body of *pride*", that could induce one to think that a *single mortal* should be able to hold so great a power, if ever so well inclined. Hence the origin of *deifying* princes: It was from the trick of gulling the vulgar into a belief that their tryants were *omniscient*, and that it was therefore right, that they should be considered as *omnipotent*. Hence the *Dii majorum et minorum gentium;* the great, the monarchical, the little Provincial subordinate and subaltern gods, demigods, and semidemi-gods, ancient and modern. Thus deities of all kinds were multiplied and increased in *abundance;* for every devil incarnate, who could enslave a people, acquired a title to *divinity;* and thus the "rabble of the skies" was made up of locusts and caterpillars; lions, tygers and harpies; and other devourers translated from plaguing the earth!‡

The *end* of government being the *good* of mankind,

---

*The power of GOD almighty is the only power that can properly and strictly be called supreme and absolute. In the order of nature immediately under him, comes the power of a simple *democracy*, or the power of the whole over the whole. Subordinate to both these, are all other political powers, from that of the French Monarque to a petty constable.

†Mr. Locke.

‡Kingcraft and Priestcraft have fell out so often, that 'tis a wonder this grand and ancient alliance is not broken off forever. Happy for mankind will it be, when such a separation shall take place.

points out its great duties: It is above all things to provide for the security, the quiet, and happy enjoyment of life, liberty, and property. There is no one act which a government can have a *right* to make, that does not tend to the advancement of the security, tranquility and prosperity of the people. If life, liberty and property could be enjoyed in as great perfection in *solitude,* as in *society,* there would be no need of government. But the experience of ages has proved that such is the nature of man, a weak, imperfect being; that the valuable ends of live cannot be obtained without the union and assistance of many. Hence 'tis clear that men cannot live apart or independent of each other: In solitude men would perish; and yet they cannot live together without contests. These contests require some arbitrator to determine them. The necessity of a common, indifferent and impartial judge, makes all men seek one; tho' few find him in the *sovereign power,* of their respective states or any where else in *subordination* to it.

Government is founded *immediately* on the necessities of human nature, and *ultimately* on the will of God, the author of nature; who has not left it to men in general to choose, whether they will be members of society or not, but at the hazard of their senses if not of their lives. Yet it is left to every man as he comes of age to chuse *what society* he will continue to belong to. Nay if one has a mind to turn *Hermit,* and after he has been born, nursed, and brought up in the arms of society, and acquired the habits and passions of social life, is willing to run the risque of starving alone, which is generally most unavoidable in a state of hermitage, who shall hinder him? I know of no human law, founded on the law of *nature,* to restrain him from separating himself from the species, if he can find it in his heart to leave them; unless it should be said, it is against the great law of *self-preservation:* But of this every man will think himself *his own judge.*

The few *Hermits* and *Misanthropes* that have ever existed, show that those states are *unnatural.* If we were to take out from them, those who have made great *worldly* gain of their *godly* hermitage, and those who have been under the madness of *enthusiasm,* or *disappointed* hopes in their *ambitious* projects, for the detriment of mankind; perhaps there might not be left ten from *Adam* to this day.

The form of government is by *nature* and by *right* so far left to the *individuals* of each society, that they may alter it from a simple democracy or government of all over all, to any other form they please. Such alteration may and ought to be made by express compact: But how seldom this right has been asserted, history will abundantly show. For once that it has been fairly settled by compact; *fraud force or accident* have determined it an hundred times. As the people have gained upon tyrants, these have been obliged to relax, *only* till a fairer opportunity has put it in their power to encroach again.

But if every prince since *Nimrod* had been a tyrant, it would not prove a *right* to tyranize. There can be no prescription old enough to supersede the law of nature, and the grant of God almighty; who has given to all men a natural right to be *free,* and they have it ordinarily in their power to make themselves so, if they please.

Government having been proved to be necessary by the law of nature, it makes no difference in the thing to call it from a certain period, *civil.* This term can only relate to form, to additions to, or deviations from, the substance of government: This being founded in nature, the super-structures and the whole administration should be conformed to the law of universal reason. A supreme legislative and supreme executive power, must be placed *somewhere* in every common-wealth: Where there is no other positive provision or compact to the contrary, those powers remain in the *whole body of the people.* It is also evident there can be but *one* best way of depositing those powers; but what that way is, mankind have been disputing in peace and in war more than five thousand years. If we could suppose the individuals of a community met to deliberate, whether it were best to keep those powers in *their own* hands, or dispose of them in *trust,* the following questions would occur—Whether those two great powers of *Legislation* and *Execution* should remain united? If so, whether in the hands of the many, or jointly or severally in the hands of a few, or jointly in some one individual? If both those powers are retained in the hands of the many, where nature seems to have placed them originally, the government is a simple *democracy,* or a government of all over all. This can be administered, only by establishing it as a first principle, that the votes of the majority shall be taken as the voice of the whole. If those powers are lodged in the hands of a few, the government is an *Aristocracy* or *Oligarchy.* Here too the first principles of a practicable administration is that the majority rules the whole. If those great powers are both lodged in the hands of one man, the government is a *simple Monarchy,* commonly, though falsely called *absolute,* if by that term is meant a right to do as one pleases.—*Sic volo, sic jubeo, stet pro ratione voluntas,* belongs not of right to any mortal man.

The same law of nature and of reason is equally obligatory on a *democracy,* an *aristocracy,* and a *monarchy:* Whenever the administrators, in any of those forms, deviate from truth, justice and equity, they verge towards tyranny, and are to be opposed; and if they prove incorrigible, they will be *deposed* by the people, if the people are not rendered too abject. Deposing the administrators of a *simple democracy* may sound oddly, but it is done every day, and in almost every vote. A.B. & C. for example, make a *democracy.* Today A & B are for so vile a measure as a standing army. Tomorrow B & C vote it out. This is as really deposing the former administrators, as setting up and making a new king is deposing the old one. *Democracy* in the one case, and *monarchy* in the other, still remain; all that is done is to change the administration.

The first principle and great end of government being to provide for the best good of all the people, this can be done only by a supreme legislative and executive ultimately in the people, or whole community, where God has placed it; but the inconveniencies, not to say impossibility, attending the consultations and operations of a large body of people have made it necessary to transfer the power of the whole to a *few*: This necessity gave rise to deputation, proxy or a right of representation.

6

JAMES BURGH, POLITICAL DISQUISITIONS
1:3–4, 186–89, 190, 190–93, 201–2
1774

All lawful authority, legislative, and executive, originates from the *people*. Power in the *people* is like light in the sun, native, original, inherent and unlimited by any thing human. In governors, it may be compared to the reflected light of the moon; for it is only borrowed, delegated, and limited by the intention of the people, whose it is, and to whom governors are to consider themselves as responsible, while the people are answerable only to God, themselves being the losers, if they pursue a false scheme of politics. Of which more hereafter.

As the people are the fountain of power, so are they the object of government, in such manner, that where the people are safe, the ends of government are answered, and where the people are sufferers by their governors, those governors have failed of the main design of the institution, and it is of no importance what other ends they may have answered.

As the people are the fountain of power, and object of government, so are they the last resource, when governors betray their trust. And happy is that people, who have originally so principled their constitution, that they themselves can without violence to it, lay hold of its power, wield it as they please, and turn it, when necessary, against those to whom it was entrusted, and who have exerted it to the prejudice of its original proprietors. Of all which more copiously hereafter.

. . . . .

The doctrine so much preached of late, by our speech-makers and courtly writers, that members of parliament are not obliged to regard the instructions of their constituents, is a mere innovation. In former times their receiving wages supposed an obligation to do the business of those who paid them, and that they were to do it in the manner their employers chose it should be done. And their constant language in the house is, "We *dare* not grant any more subsidies. Who *sent* us hither? Whose *business* are we doing? How shall we *answer* this to the people? What will the *people* of *England* say to this? &c."

"The very nature of the house of commons is changed," (says the duke of *Buckingham* in the house of peers, A.D. 1677.) "They do not now think they are an assembly of men, that are to return to their own homes, and become *private* men again (as by the laws of the land and constitution of parliaments, they ought to be) but look upon themselves as a *standing* senate, as men picked out to be legislators for the rest of their *lives*."

Our ancestors shewed themselves to be *constituents*, by fining, imprisoning, and incapacitating their members, when they acted contrary to their intention. Absentees were fined 20 *l.* a large sum in those days. *Our* members

are our *masters*, and insist on a dictatorial independency on us for 7 years, and to give no account of their conduct at the 7 years end, nor have we any power over them, but that of not re-electing them to a new parliament, if they have betrayed us in the last. Nay, the majority of the members *command* their own election, and sit in parliament, as the peers, for life. And yet we are a *free* people. Well may the neighbouring nations admire so *mysterious* a system.

The *abbé Reynel* thinks, the antient custom of the king's giving out, in the summonses to parliament, the business, for which it was to meet, was very useful, because the constitutents could then instruct their members how to vote; whereas now, says he, "the people are obliged to give their representatives an *unlimited* power, which they use as they think proper." The knights hesitated about granting *Edw.* III. supplies, till they had the consent of their constituents. The barons agreed. There is no mention of the burgesses. They desired, that there might be a new parliament summoned, which might come prepared with *authority* from their constituents. The commons did not presume to grant *Edw.* III. any tax, till they *consulted* their constituents. The commons, in the time of *Rich.* II. being desired to grant a subsidy, soon after *Tyler's* insurrection, answered, that by reason of the "evil heats and rancour of the people throughout the whole realm, they neither durst, nor would grant any manner of tallage." Here the sense of the responsibility to the people operated properly. *Elsynge* says, "When the commons gave their answer touching the subsidy demanded for the wars, they desired leave to return into the *country* to confer with their *neighbours*, promising their endeavours for the same at next parliament."

"Some of our principal law-books tell us, that in antient times, this house has often refused to agree to propositions made by the court for this reason only, That they could not, till they went home, and *consulted* with their *constituents*." The words of Mr. *Plummer's* speech on the motion for repealing the septennial act, A.D. 1734.

"We shall have little thanks for our labour, when we go *home*," said *Wentworth*, in the debate in parliament about a saving clause in the petition of right. In those days, the members considered what thanks they were likely to have from their *constituents*. In ours they consider what thanks they are likely to have from the *treasury*.

It was enacted 1 *Hen.* V. at the petition of the commons, that none, but *residents* in the places they represented, should be chosen knights, citizens or burgesses. They had not then invented the refinements of our times, that the members are representatives for the whole kingdom, and from the moment of their election, are alike independent on their particular constituents, and on the whole body of electors, through the kingdom.

. . . . .

The style of former times was, "the commons desired certain lords to confer with them about their *charge*." In those days the commons thought they had a *charge*, for which they were *answerable*.

. . . . .

The following phrases in *Cromwel's* summonses to sheriffs for parliament elections, shew, that responsibility was in those days thought the duty of members.—"So that the said knights severally may have full and sufficient *power* for themselves, and the people of that county, to do and consent unto those things which then and there by common consent of the said parliament shall be ordered," &c.

By the strain of the *Remonstrance of the Commons of England to the house of commons*, in the republican times, we see how this matter appeared to our ancestors of last century.

"We must desire you to call to your remembrance, that *we* are still the *body* of the commons of *England, you* but the *representatives;* that we have not so *delegated* the power to you, as to make you the *governors* of us and our estates. You are in truth but our *procurators* to speak for us in the great council. That of right we ought to have *access* to those, whom we have thus chosen, and to the *house,* as there shall be cause to impart our *desires* to you, and you *ought not* to *refuse* us. That by involving *our* votes in *yours,* we had no purpose to make you perpetual *dictators.*"

Members of parliament, says the excellent *Sidney,* do not act by a power derived from *kings,* but from those who *choose* them. And those, who give power, do not give an unreserved power. Members of parliament are therefore *accountable* to their *constituents.* It is true, the constituents do not call them to an account, otherwise than by not electing them again, if they have disapproved of their conduct. [This proves in fact a very inadequate punishment, because the right of election comes so *seldom* into the hands of the people, and because (in all, but the present incorrupt times) by far the greatest part of the members have been *imposed* upon their constituents by *power* or by *bribery.*] "Many members, he says afterwards, in all ages, and sometimes the whole body of the commons, have *refused* to vote, till they *consulted* those who *sent* them. The houses have been often adjourned, to give them time to do this; and if this were done more frequently, or if towns, cities, and counties, had on some occasions, given instructions to their deputies, matters would probably have gone better in parliament than they have often done."

That stern old patriot, in his XLIVth sect. overthrows the doctrine of absolute power delegated to the members of the house of commons by their constituents. He considers members of parliament as the *servants* of the public. "I take, says he, what servant I please, and when I have taken him, I must, according to this doctrine, suffer him to do what *he* pleases. But from whence should this necessity arise? Why may I not take one to be my groom, another to be my cook, and keep them both to the offices, for which I took them? And if I am free, in my private capacity, to regulate my particular affairs according to my own discretion, and to allot to each servant his proper work, why have not I, with my associates the freemen of *England,* the like liberty of directing and *limiting* the powers of the servants we employ in our public affairs?"

Milton and *Locke* bring very substantial arguments for calling even *kings,* with all their sacred majesty, their *jure divino,* and their impeccability (kings can do no wrong) to account, if they govern in any manner inconsistent with the good of the *people.* How much more lords, or *commons,* who have never even challenged to *themselves* any divine attributes? *Jam.* I. owned himself to be the great *servant* of the state.

"Who, says *Locke,* shall be judge, whether his trustee, or his deputy" [are not members of the house of commons *trustees* and *deputies* in the strictest sense of the word?] "acts well, and according to the trust reposed in him, but he, who deputes him, and must, by having deputed him, have still power to discard him, when he fails in his trust? If this be reason in particular cases of private men, why should it be otherwise in cases of the greatest moment, where the welfare of millions is concerned!"

. . . . .

No single man, or set of men, ought to be trusted with power without account to the people, the original proprietors of power. "There is not upon earth" (says the excellent *Gordon*) "a nation, which having had unaccountable magistrates, has not felt them to be crying and consuming mischiefs. In truth, where they are most limited, it has been often as much as a whole people could do to restrain them to their trust, and to keep them from violence; and such frequently has been their propensity to be lawless, that nothing but a violent death could cure them of their violence. This evil has its root in human nature; men will never think they have enough, whilst they can take more; nor be content with a part, when they can seize the whole."

The history of mankind for two or three thousand years backwards (which is as far backwards as history goes) is a sermon upon this text, Nothing more *dangerous* than *power* without *responsibility.* But the *species* resembles an *individual.* As the *father's* experience does not make the *son* wiser, so neither does the history of the sufferings of *former* generations teach the *succeeding* to secure themselves against the mischiefs of unaccountable power.

"When we elect persons to *represent* us in parliament (says a judicious writer) we must not be supposed to depart from the smallest right which we have *deposited* with them. We make a *lodgment,* not a *gift;* we *entrust,* but *part* with nothing. And, were it possible, that they should attempt to destroy that constitution which we had appointed them to maintain, they can no more be held in the rank of representatives than a factor, turned *pirate,* can continue to be called the factor of those merchants whose goods he had plundered, and whose confidence he had betrayed. The men, whom we thus depute to parliament, are not the bare likeness or reflexion of us their constituents; they actually contain our *powers* and *privileges,* and are, as it were, the very persons of the people they represent. We are the parliament in them; we speak and act by them. We have, therefore, a *right* to *know* what they are *saying* and *doing.* And should they contradict our sense, or swerve from our interests, we have a *right* to remonstrate, inform, and direct them. By which means, we become the regulators of our *own* conduct, and the institutors of our *own* laws, and nothing material can be done but by *our* authority and consent."

7

THOMAS JEFFERSON TO EDMUND PENDLETON
26 Aug. 1776
Papers 1:503–4

You seem to have misapprehended my proposition for the choice of a Senate. I had two things in view: to get the wisest men chosen, and to make them perfectly independent when chosen. I have ever observed that a choice by the people themselves is not generally distinguished for it's wisdom. This first secretion from them is usually crude and heterogeneous. But give to those so chosen by the people a second choice themselves, and they generally will chuse wise men. For this reason it was that I proposed the representatives (and not the people) should chuse the Senate, and thought I had notwithstanding that made the Senators (when chosen) perfectly independent of their electors. However I should have no objection to the mode of election proposed in the printed plan of your committee, to wit, that the people of each county should chuse twelve electors, who should meet those of the other counties in the same district and chuse a senator. I should prefer this too for another reason, that the upper as well as lower house should have an opportunity of superintending and judging of the situation of the whole state and be not all of one neighborhood as our upper house used to be. So much for the wisdom of the Senate. To make them independent, I had proposed that they should hold their places for nine years, and then go out (one third every three years) and be incapable for ever of being re-elected to that house. My idea was that if they might be re-elected, they would be casting their eyes forward to the period of election (however distant) and be currying favor with the electors, and consequently dependent on them. My reason for fixing them in office for a term of years rather than for life, was that they might have in idea that they were at a certain period to return into the mass of the people and become the governed instead of the governors which might still keep alive that regard to the public good that otherwise they might perhaps be induced by their independance to forget. Yet I could submit, tho' not so willingly to an appointment for life, or to any thing rather than a mere creation by and dependance on the people.

one year and they have agreed to the following Instructions which you are to observe with the strictest regard viz.: You are instructed:

1. That you shall consent to and approve the Declaration of the Continental Congress declaring the thirteen United Colonies free and independent States.

2. That you shall endeavor to establish a free government under the authority of the people of the State of North Carolina and that the Government be a simple Democracy or as near it as possible.

3. That in fixing the fundamental principles of Government you shall oppose everything that leans to aristocracy or power in the hands of the rich and chief men exercised to the oppression of the poor.

4. That you shall endeavor that the form of Government shall set forth a bill of rights containing the rights of the people and of individuals which shall never be infringed in any future time by the law-making power or other derived powers in the State.

5. That you shall endeavour that the following maxims be substantially acknowledged in the Bills of Rights (viz.):

1st. Political power is of two kinds, one principal and superior, the other derived and inferior.

2d. The principal supreme power is possessed by the people at large, the derived and inferior power by the servants which they employ.

3d. Whatever persons are delegated, chosen, employed and intrusted by the people are their servants and can possess only derived inferior power.

4th. Whatever is constituted and ordained by the principal supreme power can not be altered, suspended or abrogated by any other power, but the same power that ordained may alter, suspend and abrogate its own ordinances.

5th. The rules whereby the inferior power is to be exercised are to be constituted by the principal supreme power, and can be altered, suspended and abrogated by the same and no other.

6th. No authority can exist or be exercised but what shall appear to be ordained and created by the principal supreme power or by derived inferior power which the principal supreme power hath authorized to create such authority.

7th. That the derived inferior power can by no construction or pretence assume or exercise a power to subvert the principal supreme power.

8

INSTRUCTIONS TO THE DELEGATES FROM MECKLENBURG, NORTH CAROLINA, TO THE PROVINCIAL CONGRESS AT HALIFAX
1 Nov. 1776
Colonial Records 10:870a–b

Gentlemen: You are chosen by the inhabitants of this county to serve them in Congress or General Assembly for

9

STATEMENT OF THE BERKSHIRE COUNTY, MASSACHUSETTS, REPRESENTATIVES
17 Nov. 1778
Handlin 374–78

To the Honorable Committee from the General Court of Massachusetts Bay now convened at Pittsfield—

Mr. Chairman, Sir

We whose Names are underwritten indulging some Apprehensions of the Importance of Civil and religious Liberty, the destructive Nature of Tyranny and lawless power, and the absolute necessity of legal Government, to prevent Anarchy and Confusion; have taken this method to indulge our own Feelings and Sentiments respecting the important matters that have for some Time been the Subject of debate in this present Meeting—Political Disquisitions, if managed with Decency, Moderation and Candor are a good preservative against Ignorance and Servility and such a state of perfect Quietude as would endanger the Rights of Mankind united in the Bands of Society. We wish to preserve this Character in what we have now to offer in the Defence of our Constituents in opposing, in times past, the executive Courts of Justice in this County.

We wish with the least Delay to come to the Merits of the cause, and shall now proceed to make those observations on the Nature of Government which are necessary to bring into view the Apprehensions we indulge respecting the present Condition of this state, whether we have a fundamental Constitution or not; and how far we have Government duly organized and how far not: In free States the people are to be considered as the fountain of power. And the social Tie as founded in Compact. The people at large are endowed with alienable and unalienable Rights. Those which are unalienable, are those which belong to Conscience respecting the worship of God and the practice of the Christian Religion, and that of being determined or governed by the Majority in the Institution or formation of Government. The alienable are those which may be delegated for the Common good, or those which are for the common good to be parted with. It is of the unalienable Rights, particularly that of being determined or governed by the Majority in the Institution or formation of Government of which something further is necessary to be considered at this Time. That the Majority should be governed by the Minority in the first Institution of Government is not only contrary to the common apprehensions of Mankind in general, but it contradicts the common Law of Justice and benevolence.

Mankind being in a state of nature equal, the larger Number (Caeteris paribus) is of more worth than the lesser, and the common happiness is to be preferred to that of Individuals. When Men form the social Compact, for the Majority to consent to be governed by the Minority is down right popery in politicks, as submission to him who claims Infallibility, and of being the only Judge of Right and rong, is popery in Religion. In all free Governments duly organized there is an essential Distinction to be observed between the fundamental Constitution, and Legislation. The fundamental Constitution is the Basis and ground work of Legislation, and asscertains the Rights Franchises, Immunities and Liberties of the people, Howr and how often officers Civil and military shall be elected by the people, and circumscribing and defining the powers of the Rulers, and so affoarding a sacred Barrier against Tyranny and Despotism. This in antient and corrupt Kingdoms when they have woke out of Slavery to some happy dawnings of Liberty, has been called a Bill of Rights, Magna Charta etc. which must be considered as imperfect Emblems of the Securities of the present grand period. Legislators stand on this foundation, and enact Laws agreeably to it. They cannot give Life to the Constitution: it is the approbation of the Majority of the people at large that gives Life and being to it. This is the foundation of Legislation that is agreeable to true Liberty, it is above the whole Legislature of a free state, it being the foundation upon which the Legislature stands. A Representative Body may form but cannot impose said Constitution upon a free people. The giving Existence to the fundamental Constitution of a free state is a Trust that cannot be delegated. For any rational person to give his vote for another person to aid and assist in forming said Constitution with a view of imposing it on the people without reserving to himself a Right of Inspection Approbation rejection or Amendment, imports, if not impiety, yet real popery in politicks. We could bring many Vouchers for this Doctrine sufficient for our present purpose is the following Extract from a Noted Writer. in answer to that assertion of another respectable writer that "The bare Idea of a State without a power some where vested to alter every part of its Laws is the height of political Absurdity." [Introduction to Blackstone's *Commentaries*, p. 97; note by the editor of *Acts and Resolves*] He remarks upon it, "A position, which I apprehend, ought to be, in some Measure limited and explained. For if it refers to those particular Regulations, which take place in Consequence of Immemorial Custom, or are enacted by positive Statue, and at the same Time, are subordinate to the fundamental Constitution from which the Legislature itself derives its Authority; it is admitted to be within the power or Trust vested in the Legislature to alter these, pro, Re nata, as the good of Society may require. But this power or Authority of the Legislature to make Alterations cannot be supposed to extend to the Infringement of those essentials Rights and previleges, which are reserved to the Members of a free state at large, as their undoubted Birthright and unalienable property. I say, in every free State there are some Liberties and previleges, which the Society has not given out of their own Hands to their Governors, not even to the Legislature: and to suppose the contrary would be the height of political absurdity; for it is saying that a state is free and not free at the same Time; or which is the same thing, that its Members are possessed of Liberties, of all which they may be divested at the will of the Legislature; that is, they enjoy them during pleasure, but can claim no property in them

In a word nothing is more certain than that Government in the general nature of it is a Trust in behalf of the people. And there cannot be a Maxim, in my opinion, more ill grounded, than that there must be an arbitrary power lodged somewhere in every Government. If this were true, the different kinds of Government in the world would be more alike, and on a level, than they are generally supposed to be. In our own Government in particular, tho' no one thinks with more respect of the powers which the Constitution hath vested in every branch of the Legislature; yet I must be excused in saying what is strictly true, that the whole Legislature is so far from having an absolute power, that it hath not power in several Cases that might be mentioned. For instance, their Authority does not extend to making the house of Commons perpetual, or giving that house a power to fill up their own vacancies: the house of Commons being the representatives of all the Commons of England and in that Capassity only a branch of the Legislature; and if they concur in destroying the foundation on which they themselves stand; and if they annihilate the Rights of their Constituents and claim a share in the Legislature upon any other footing than that upon which the Constitution hath given it to them; they subvert the very Trust under which alone they act, and thereby forfeit all their Authority. In short they cannot dispence with any of those essential Rights of the people which it ought to be the great object of Government as it is of our Constitution in particular to preserve."—

These reasonings tend abundantly to evince, that the whole Legislature of any state is insufficient to give Life to the fundamental Constitution of such state, it being the foundation on which they themselves stand and from which alone the Legislature derives its Authority—

May it be considered, further, that to suppose the Representative Body capable of forming and imposing this Compact or Constitution without the Inspection and Approbation Rejection or Amendment of the people at large would involve in it the greatest Absurdity. This would make them greater than the people who send them, this supposes them their own Creators, formers of the foundation upon which they themselve stand. This imports uncontroulable Dominion over their Constituents for what should hinder them from making such a Constitution as invests them and their successors in office with unlimited Authority, if it be admitted that the Representatives are the people as to forming and imposing the fundamental Constitution of the state upon them without their Approbation and perhaps in opposition to their united sense— In this the very essence of true Liberty consists, viz in every free state the Constitution is adopted by the Majority.

It is needful to be observed that we are not to Judge of true Liberty by other Nations of the Earth, darkness has overspread the Earth, Tyranny Triumps thro' the world. The Day light of Liberty, only begins to dawn upon these Ends of the Earth. To measure the freedom, the Rights and previleges of the American Empire by those enjoyed by other Nations would be folly.

It is now both easy and natural to apply these reasonings to the present State of Massachusetts Bay. We think it undeniably follows from the preceeding Reasonings that the Compact in this state is not yet formed: when did the Majority of the people at large assent to such Constitution, and what is it? if the Majority of the people of this state have adopted any such fundamental Constitution it is unknown to us and we shall submit to it as we always mean to be governed by the Majority—

Nor will any of those consequences follow on this supposition, that we have no Law, or that the Honorable Council and House of Representatives are Usurpers and Tyrants. Far from it. We consider our case as very Ex-

traordinary. We do not consider this state in all Respects as in a state of Nature tho' destitute of such fundamental Constitution. When the powers of Government were totally dissolved in this state, we esteemed the State Congress as a necessary and useful body of Men suited to our Exigencies and sufficiently authorized to levy Taxes, raise an Army and do what was necessary for our common defence and it is Sir in this Light that we view our present Honorable Court and for these and other reasons *have inculcated* a careful Adherence to their orders. Time will not permit to argue this Matter any longer, for your Honors patience must have been tryed already. These have been some of the reasons we have indulged, and Sentiments we have cultivated respecting Constitution, and for these Reasons we have been looking forward towards a new Constitution—But we must further add

That a fear of being finally deprived of a Constitution and of being thrown into confusion and divisions by delaying the formation of a new Constitution, has caused our Constituents so early and invariably to oppose the executive Courts—We have feared, we now realize those fears, that upon our submission we shall sink down into a dead Calm and never transmit to posterity a single Right nor leave them the least Knowledge of so fair an Inheritance, as we may now convey to them.—

10

THOMAS JEFFERSON, PREAMBLE TO A BILL FOR THE MORE GENERAL DIFFUSION OF KNOWLEDGE
Fall 1778

Papers 2:526–27

(See ch. 18, no. 11)

11

SAMUEL ADAMS TO NOAH WEBSTER
30 Apr. 1784

Writings 4:305–6

I hope it will not be in the Power of any designing Men, by imposing upon credulous tho' well meaning Persons long to keep this Country, who may be happy if they will, long in a State of Discord & Animosity. We may see, from the present State of Great Britain, how rapidly such a Spirit will drive a Nation to destruction. It is prudent for the People to keep a watchful Eye over the Conduct of all those who are entrusted with Publick Affairs. Such Attention is the Peoples great Security. But there is Decency & Respect due to Constitutional Authority, and those Men, who under any Pretence or by any Means whatever, would lessen the Weight of Government lawfully exercised, must be Enemies to our happy Revolution & the Common Liberty. County Conventions & popular Committees servd an excellent Purpose when they were first in Practice. No one therefore needs to regret the Share he may then have had in them. But I candidly own it is my Opinion, with Deferrence to the Opinions of other Men, that as we now have constitutional & regular Governments and all our Men in Authority depend upon the annual & free Elections of the People, we are safe without them. To say the least, they are become useless. Bodies of Men, under any Denomination whatever, who convene themselves for the Purpose of deliberating upon & adopting Measures which are cognizable by Legislatures only will, if continued, bring Legislatures to Contempt & Dissolution. If the publick Affairs are illy conducted, if dishonest or incapable Men have crept unawares into Government, it is happy for us, that under our American Constitutions the Remedy is at hand, & in the Power of the great Body of the People. Due Circumspection & Wisdom at the next Elections will set all right, without the Aid of any self Created Conventions or Societies of Men whatever. While we retain those simple Democracies in all our Towns which are the Basis of our State Constitutions, and make a good Use of them, it appears to me we cannot be enslaved or materially injured. It must however be confessd, that Imperfection attends all human affairs.

12

JOHN ADAMS, DEFENCE OF THE CONSTITUTIONS OF GOVERNMENT OF THE UNITED STATES
1787

Works 6:6–8, 114, 116–17

Marchamont Nedham lays it down as a fundamental principle and an undeniable rule, "That the people, (that is, such as shall be successively chosen to represent the people,) are the best keepers of their own liberties, and that for many reasons. First, because they never think of usurping over other men's rights, but mind which way to preserve their own."

Our first attention should be turned to the proposition itself,—"The people are the best keepers of their own liberties."

But who are the people?

"Such as shall be successively chosen to represent them."

Here is a confusion both of words and ideas, which, though it may pass with the generality of readers in a fugitive pamphlet, or with a majority of auditors in a popular harangue, ought, for that very reason, to be as carefully avoided in politics as it is in philosophy or mathematics. If by *the people* is meant the whole body of a great nation, it should never be forgotten, that they can never act, consult, or reason together, because they cannot march five hundred miles, nor spare the time, nor find a space to meet; and, therefore, the proposition, that they

are the best keepers of their own liberties, is not true. They are the worst conceivable; they are no keepers at all. They can neither act, judge, think or will, as a body politic or corporation. If by *the people* is meant all the inhabitants of a single city, they are not in a general assembly, at all times, the best keepers of their own liberties, nor perhaps at any time, unless you separate from them the executive and judicial power, and temper their authority in legislation with the maturer counsels of the one and the few. If it is meant by *the people*, as our author explains himself, a representative assembly, "such as shall be successively chosen to represent the people," still they are not the best keepers of the people's liberties or their own, if you give them all the power, legislative, executive, and judicial. They would invade the liberties of the people, at least the majority of them would invade the liberties of the minority, sooner and oftener than an absolute monarchy, such as that of France, Spain, or Russia, or than a well-checked aristocracy, like Venice, Bern, or Holland.

An excellent writer has said, somewhat incautiously, that "a people will never oppress themselves, or invade their own rights." This compliment, if applied to human nature, or to mankind, or to any nation or people in being or in memory, is more than has been merited. If it should be admitted that a people will not unanimously agree to oppress themselves, it is as much as is ever, and more than is always, true. All kinds of experience show, that great numbers of individuals do oppress great numbers of other individuals; that parties often, if not always, oppress other parties, and majorities almost universally minorities. All that this observation can mean then, consistently with any color of fact, is, that the people will never unanimously agree to oppress themselves. But if one party agrees to oppress another, or the majority the minority, the people still oppress themselves, for one part of them oppress another.

"The people never think of usurping over other men's rights."

What can this mean? Does it mean that the people never *unanimously* think of usurping over other men's rights? This would be trifling; for there would, by the supposition, be no other men's rights to usurp. But if the people never, jointly nor severally, think of usurping the rights of others, what occasion can there be for any government at all? Are there no robberies, burglaries, murders, adulteries, thefts, nor cheats? Is not every crime a usurpation over other men's rights? Is not a great part, I will not say the greatest part, of men detected every day in some disposition or other, stronger or weaker, more or less, to usurp over other men's rights? There are some few, indeed, whose whole lives and conversations show that, in every thought, word, and action, they conscientiously respect the rights of others. There is a larger body still, who, in the general tenor of their thoughts and actions, discover similar principles and feelings, yet frequently err. If we should extend our candor so far as to own, that the majority of men are generally under the dominion of benevolence and good intentions, yet, it must be confessed, that a vast majority frequently transgress; and, what is more directly to the point, not only a majority, but almost all, confine their benevolence to their families, relations, personal friends, parish, village, city, county, province, and that very few, indeed, extend it impartially to the whole community. Now, grant but this truth, and the question is decided. If a majority are capable of preferring their own private interest, or that of their families, counties, and party, to that of the nation collectively, some provision must be made in the constitution, in favor of justice, to compel all to respect the common right, the public good, the universal law, in preference to all private and partial considerations.

The proposition of our author, then, should be reversed, and it should have been said, that they mind so much their own, that they never think enough of others.

. . . . .

We concur also most sincerely in our author's conclusion, in part, namely,—"That since kings and all standing powers are so inclinable to act according to their own wills and interests, in making, expounding, and executing of laws, to the prejudice of the people's liberty and security, no laws whatsoever should be made but by the people's consent, as the only means to prevent arbitrariness." But we must carry the conclusion farther, namely,—that since all men are so inclinable to act according to their own wills and interests, in making, expounding, and executing laws, to the prejudice of the people's liberty and security, the sovereign authority, the legislative, executive, and judicial power, can never be safely lodged in one assembly, though chosen annually by the people; because the majority and their leaders, the *principes populi,* will as certainly oppress the minority, and make, expound, and execute laws for their own wealth, power, grandeur, and glory, to the prejudice of the liberty and security of the minority, as hereditary kings or standing senates.

The conclusion, therefore, that "the people, in a succession of their supreme single assemblies, are the best keepers of their liberties," must be wholly reprobated.

. . . . .

It is indeed a "most excellent maxim, that the original and fountain of all just power and government is in the people;" and if ever this maxim was fully demonstrated and exemplified among men, it was in the late American Revolution, where thirteen governments were taken down from the foundation, and new ones elected wholly by the people, as an architect would pull down an old building and erect a new one. There will be no dispute, then, with Cicero, when he says, "A mind well instructed by the light of nature, will pay obedience," willingly "to none but such as command, direct, or govern for its good or benefit;" nor will our author's inferences from these passages from that oracle of human wisdom be denied:

"1. That by the light of nature people are taught to be their own carvers and contrivers in the framing of that government under which they mean to live.

"2. That none are to preside in government, or sit at the helm, but such as shall be judged fit, and chosen by the people.

"3. That the people are the only proper judges of the convenience or inconvenience of a government when it is

erected, and of the behavior of governors after they are chosen."

But then it is insisted, that rational and regular means shall be used that the whole people may be their own carvers, that they may judge and choose who shall preside, and that they may determine on the convenience or inconvenience of government, and the behavior of governors. But then it is insisted, that the town of Berwick upon Tweed shall not carve, judge, choose, and determine for the whole kingdom of Great Britain, nor the county of Berkshire for the Massachusetts; much less that a lawless tyrannical rabble shall do all this for the state, or even for the county of Berkshire.

It may be, and is admitted, that a free government is most natural, and only suitable to the reason of mankind; but it by no means follows "that the other forms, as of a standing power in the hands of a particular person, as a king; or of a set number of great ones, as in a senate," much less that a mixture of the three simple forms "are beside the dictates of nature, and mere artificial devices of great men, squared out only to serve the ends and interests of avarice, pride, and ambition of a few, to a vassalizing of the community." If the original and fountain of all power and government is in the people, as undoubtedly it is, the people have as clear a right to erect a simple monarchy, aristocracy, or democracy, or an equal mixture, or any other mixture of all three, if they judge it for their liberty, happiness, and prosperity, as they have to erect a democracy; and infinitely greater and better men than Marchamont Nedham, and the wisest nations that ever lived, have preferred such mixtures, and even with such standing powers as ingredients in their compositions. But even those nations who choose to reserve in their own hands the periodical choice of the first magistrate, senate, and assembly, at certain stated periods, have as clear a right to appoint a first magistrate for life as for years, and for perpetuity in his descendants as for life.

When I say for perpetuity or for life, it is always meant to imply, that the same people have at all times a right to interpose, and to depose for maladministration—to appoint anew. No appointment of a king or senate, or any standing power, can be, in the nature of things, for a longer period than *quam diu se bene gesserit,* the whole nation being judge. An appointment for life or perpetuity can be no more than an appointment until further order; but further order can only be given by the nation.

13

CAESAR, NO. 2
17 Oct. 1787
Essays 287–89

I am not one of those who gain an influence by cajoling the unthinking mass (tho' I pity their delusions), and ring-ing in their ears the gracious sound of their *absolute Sovereignty.* I despise the trick of such dirty policy. I know there are Citizens, who, to gain their own private ends, enflame the minds of the well-meaning, tho' less intelligent parts of the community, by sating their vanity with that cordial and unfailing specific, that *all power is seated in the people.* For my part, I am not much attached to the *majesty of the multitude,* and therefore waive all pretensions (founded on such conduct), to their countenance. I consider them in general as very ill qualified to judge for themselves what government will best suit their peculiar situations; nor is this to be wondered at. The science of government is not easily understood. Cato will admit, I presume, that men of good education and deep reflection, only, are judges of the *form* of a government; whether it is constituted on such principles as will restrain arbitrary power, on the one hand, and equal to the exclusion of corruption and the destruction of licentiousness on the other; whether the New Constitution, if adopted, will prove adequate to such desirable ends, time, the mother of events, will show. For my own part, I sincerely esteem it a system, which, without the finger of *God,* never could have been suggested and agreed upon by such a diversity of interests. I will not presume to say that a more perfect system might not have been fabricated; but who expects perfection at once? And it may be asked, *who are judges of it?* Few, I believe, who have leisure to study the nature of Government scientifically, but will frequently disagree about the quantum of power to be delegated to Rulers, and the different modifications of it. Ingenious men will give every plausible, and, it may be, pretty substantial reasons, for the adoption of two plans of Government, which shall be fundamentally different in their construction, and not less so in their operation; yet both, if honestly administered, might operate with safety and advantage. When a new form of government is fabricated, it lies with the people at large to receive or reject it—that is, their *inherent rights.* Now, I would ask (without intending to triumph over the weaknesses or follies of any men), how are the people to profit by this inherent right? By what conduct do they discover that they are sensible of their own interests in this situation? Is it by the exercise of a well-disciplined reason, and a correspondent education? I believe not. How then? As I humbly conceive, by a tractable and docile disposition, and by honest men endeavoring to keep their minds easy, while others, of the same disposition, with the advantages of genius and learning, are constructing the bark that may, by the blessing of Heaven, carry them to the port of rest and happiness, if they will embark without diffidence and proceed without mutiny. I know this is blunt and ungracious reasoning; it is the best, however, which I am prepared to offer on this momentous business; and, since my own heart does not reproach me, I shall not be very solicitous about its reception. If truth, then, is permitted to speak, the mass of the people of America (any more than the mass of other countries) cannot judge with any degree of precision concerning the fitness of this New Constitution to the peculiar situation of America; they have, however, done wisely in delegating the power of framing a govern-

ment to those every way worthy and well-qualified; and, if this Government is snatched, untasted, from them, it may not be amiss to inquire into the causes which will probably occasion their disappointment. Out of several, which present to my mind, I shall venture to select *one,* baneful enough, in my opinion, to work this dreadful evil. There are always men in society of some talents, but more ambition, in quest of *that* which it would be impossible for them to obtain in any other way than by working on the passions and prejudices of the less discerning classes of citizens and yeomanry. It is the plan of men of this stamp to frighten the people with ideal bugbears, in order to mould them to their own purposes. The unceasing cry of these designing croakers is, My friends, your liberty is invaded! Have you thrown off the yoke of one tyrant to invest yourselves with that of another? Have you fought, bled and conquered for *such a change?* If you have—go—retire into silent obscurity, and kiss the rod that scourges you.

To be serious: These state empirics leave no species of deceit untried to convince the unthinking people that they have power to do—what? Why truly to do much mischief, and to occasion anarchy and wild uproar. And for what reason do these political jugglers incite the peaceably disposed to such extravagant commotions? Because until the people really discover that they have *power,* by some outrageous act, they never can become of any importance. The misguided people never reflect during this frenzy, that the moment they become riotous, they renounce, from that moment, their independence, and commence vassals to their ambitious leaders, who instantly, and with a high hand, rob them of their consequence, and apply it to their own present or future aggrandisement; nor will these tyrants over the people stick at sacrificing *their* good, if an advantageous compromise can be effected for *themselves.*

14

JAMES WILSON, PENNSYLVANIA
RATIFYING CONVENTION
4 Dec. 1787
McMaster 315–17

It has not been, nor, I presume, will it be denied, that somewhere there is, and of necessity must be, a supreme, absolute and uncontrollable authority. This, I believe, may justly be termed the sovereign power; for from that gentleman's (Mr. Findley) account of the matter, it cannot be sovereign, unless it is supreme; for, says he, a subordinate sovereignty is no sovereignty at all. I had the honor of observing, that if the question was asked, where the supreme power resided, different answers would be given by different writers. I mentioned that Blackstone will tell you, that in Britain it is lodged in the British parliament; and I believe there is no writer on this subject on the other side of the Atlantic, but supposes it to be vested in that body. I stated further, that if the question was asked, some politician, who had not considered the subject with sufficient accuracy, where the supreme power resided in our governments, would answer, that it was vested in the State constitutions. This opinion approaches near the truth, but does not reach it; for the truth is, that the supreme, absolute and uncontrollable authority, *remains* with the people. I mentioned also, that the practical recognition of this truth was reserved for the honor of this country. I recollect no constitution founded on this principle: but we have witnessed the improvement, and enjoy the happiness, of seeing it carried into practice. The great and penetrating mind of Locke seems to be the only one that pointed towards even the theory of this great truth.

When I made the observation, that some politicians would say the supreme power was lodged in our State constitutions, I did not suspect that the honorable gentleman from Westmoreland (Mr. Findley) was included in that description; but I find myself disappointed; for I imagined his opposition would arise from another consideration. His position is, that the supreme power resides in the States, as governments; and mine is, that it *resides* in the PEOPLE, as the fountain of government; that the people have not—that the people mean not—and that the people ought not, to part with it to any government whatsoever. In their hands it remains secure. They can delegate it in such proportions, to such bodies, on such terms, and under such limitations, as they think proper. I agree with the members in opposition, that there cannot be two sovereign powers on the same subject.

I consider the people of the United States as forming one great community, and I consider the people of the different States as forming communities again on a lesser scale. From this great division of the people into distinct communities it will be found necessary that different proportions of legislative powers should be given to the governments, according to the nature, number and magnitude of their objects.

Unless the people are considered in these two views, we shall never be able to understand the principle on which this system was constructed. I view the States as made *for* the people as well as *by* them, and not the people as made for the States. The people, therefore, have a right, whilst enjoying the undeniable powers of society, to form either a general government, or state governments, in what manner they please; or to accommodate them to one another, and by this means preserve them all. This, I say, is the inherent and unalienable right of the people, and as an illustration of it, I beg to read a few words from the Declaration of Independence, made by the representatives of the United States, and recognized by the whole Union.—

"We hold these truths to be self-evident, that all men are created equal; that they are endowed by their Creator with certain unalienable rights; that among these are life, liberty, and the pursuit of happiness. That to secure these rights, *governments* are instituted among men, *deriving their just powers from the consent of the governed;* that whenever any form of government becomes destructive of these ends, it is the RIGHT of the people to alter or to abolish it, and institute a new government, laying its foundation on such principles, and organizing its powers in such forms, as to them shall seem most likely to effect their safety and happiness."

This is the broad basis on which our independence was placed. On the same certain and solid foundation this system is erected.

15

THE ADDRESS AND REASONS OF DISSENT OF THE MINORITY OF THE CONVENTION OF PENNSYLVANIA TO THEIR CONSTITUENTS 18 Dec. 1787
Storing 3.11.48–50

For the moderate exercise of this power, there is no controul left in the state governments, whose intervention is destroyed. No relief, or redress of grievances can be extended, as heretofore by them. There is not even a declaration of RIGHTS to which the people may appeal for the vindication of their wrongs in the court of justice. They must therefore, implicitly obey the most arbitrary laws, as the worst of them will be pursuant to the principles and form of the constitution, and that strongest of all checks upon the conduct of administration, *responsibility to the people,* will not exist in this government. The permanency of the appointments of senators and representatives, and the controul the congress have over their election, will place them independent of the sentiments and resentment of the people, and the administration having a greater interest in the government than in the community, there will be no consideration to restrain them from oppression and tyranny. In the government of this state, under the old confederation, the members of the legislature are taken from among the people, and their interests and welfare are so inseparably connected with those of their constituents, that they can derive no advantage from oppressive laws and taxes, for they would suffer in common with their fellow citizens; would participate in the burthens they impose on the community, as they must return to the common level, after a short period; and notwithstanding every ex[er]tion of influence, every means of corruption, a necessary rotation excludes them from permanency in the legislature.

This large state is to have but ten members in that Congress which is to have the liberty, property and dearest concerns of every individual in this vast country at absolute command and even these ten persons, who are to be our only guardians; who are to supercede the legislature of Pennsylvania, will not be of the choice of the people, nor amenable to them. From the mode of their election and appointment they will consist of the lordly and high-minded; of men who will have no congenial feelings with the people, but a perfect indifference for, and contempt of them; they will consist of those harpies of power, that prey upon the very vitals; that riot on the miseries of the community. But we will suppose, although in all probability it may never be realized in fact, that our deputies in Congress have the welfare of their constituents at heart, and will exert themselves in their behalf, what security could even this afford; what relief could they extend to their oppressed constituents? To attain this, the majority of the deputies of the twelve other states in Congress must be alike well disposed; must alike forego the sweets of power, and relinquish the pursuits of ambition, which from the nature of things is not to be expected. If the people part with a responsible representation in the legislature, founded upon fair, certain and frequent elections, they have nothing left they can call their own. Miserable is the lot of that people whose every concern depends on the WILL and PLEASURE of their rulers. Our soldiers will become Janissaries, and our officers of government Bashaws; in short, the system of despotism will soon be compleated.

From the foregoing investigation, it appears that the Congress under this constitution will not possess the confidence of the people, which is an essential requisite in a good government; for unless the laws command the confidence and respect of the great body of the people, so as to induce them to support them, when called on by the civil magistrate, they must be executed by the aid of a numerous standing army, which would be inconsistent with every idea of liberty; for the same force that may be employed to compel obedience to good laws, might and probably would be used to wrest from the people their constitutional liberties. The framers of this constitution appear to have been aware of this great deficiency; to have been sensible that no dependence could be placed on the people for their support; but on the contrary, that the government must be executed by force. They have therefore made a provision for this purpose in a permanent STANDING ARMY, and a MILITIA that may be subjected to as strict discipline and government.

16

FEDERAL FARMER, NO. 11
10 Jan. 1788
Storing 2.8.147

When the confederation was formed, it was considered essentially necessary that the members of congress should at any time be recalled by their respective states, when the states should see fit, and others be sent in their room. I do not think it less necessary that this principle should be extended to the members of congress under the new constitution, and especially to the senators. I have had occasion

several times to observe, that let us form a federal constitution as extensively, and on the best principles in our power, we must, after all, trust a vast deal to a few men, who, far removed from their constituents, will administer the federal government; there is but little danger these men will feel too great a degree of dependance: the necessary and important object to be attended to, is to make them feel dependant enough. Men elected for several years, several hundred miles distant from their states, possessed of very extensive powers, and the means of paying themselves, will not, probably, be oppressed with a sense of dependance and responsibility.

The senators will represent sovereignties, which generally have, and always ought to retain, the power of recalling their agents; the principle of responsibility is strongly felt in men who are liable to be recalled and censured for their misconduct; and, if we may judge from experience, the latter will not abuse the power of recalling their members; to possess it, will, at least be a valuable check. It is in the nature of all delegated power, that the constituents should retain the right to judge concerning the conduct of their representatives; they must exercise the power, and their decision itself, their approving or disapproving that conduct implies a right, a power to continue in office, or to remove from it. But whenever the substitute acts under a constitution, then it becomes necessary that the power of recalling him be expressed. The reasons for lodging a power to recall are stronger, as they respect the senate, than as they respect the representatives; the latter will be more frequently elected, and changed of course, and being chosen by the people at large, it would be more difficult for the people than for the legislatures to take the necessary measures for recalling: but even the people, if the powers will be more beneficial to them than injurious, ought to possess it. The people are not apt to wrong a man who is steady and true to their interests; they may for a while be misled by party representations, and leave a good man out of office unheard; but every recall supposes a deliberate decision, and a fair hearing; and no man who believes his conduct proper, and the result of honest views, will be the less useful in his public character, on account of the examination his actions may be liable to; and a man conscious of the contrary conduct, ought clearly to be restrained by the apprehensions of a trial. I repeat it, it is interested combinations and factions we are particularly to guard against in the federal government, and all the rational means that can be put into the hands of the people to prevent them, ought to be provided and furnished for them. Where there is a power to recall, trusty centinels among the people, or in the state legislatures, will have a fair opportunity to become useful. If the members in congress from the states join in such combinations, or favour them, or pursue a pernicious line of conduct, the most attentive among the people, or in the state legislatures, may formally charge them before their constituents: the very apprehensions of such constitutional charges may prevent many of the evils mentioned, and the recalling the members of a single state, a single senator, or representative, may often prevent many more; nor do I, at present, discover any danger in such proceedings, as every man who shall move for a recall will put his reputation at stake, to shew he has reasonable grounds for his motion; and it is not probable such motions will be made unless there be good apparent grounds for succeeding; nor can the charge or motion be any thing more than the attack of an individual or individuals, unless a majority of the constituents shall see cause to go into the enquiry. Further, the circumstance of such a power being lodged in the constituents, will tend continually to keep up their watchfulness, as well as the attention and dependance of the federal senators and representatives.

By the confederation it is provided, that no delegate shall serve more than three years in any term of six years, and thus, by the forms of the government, a rotation of members is produced: a like principle has been adopted in some of the state governments, and also in some antient and modern republics. Whether this exclusion of a man for a given period, after he shall have served a given time, ought to be ingra[f]ted into a constitution or not, is a question, the proper decision materially depends upon the leading features of the government: some governments are so formed as to produce a sufficient fluctuation and change of members of course, in the ordinary course of elections, proper numbers of new members are, from time to time, brought into the legislature, and a proportionate number of old ones go out, mix, and become diffused among the people. This is the case with all numerous representative legislatures, the members of which are frequently elected, and constantly within the view of their constituents. This is the case with our state governments, and in them a constitutional rotation is unimportant. But in a government consisting of but a few members, elected for long periods, and far removed from the observation of the people, but few changes in the ordinary course of elections take place among the members; they become in some measure a fixed body, and often inattentive to the public good, callous, selfish, and the fountain of corruption. To prevent these evils, and to force a principle of pure animation into the federal government, which will be formed much in this last manner mentioned, and to produce attention, activity, and a diffusion of knowledge in the community, we ought to establish among others the principle of rotation. Even good men in office, in time, imperceptibly lose sight of the people, and gradually fall into measures prejudicial to them. It is only a rotation among the members of the federal legislature I shall contend for: judges and officers at the heads of the judicial and executive departments, are in a very different situation, their offices and duties require the information and studies of many years for performing them in a manner advantageous to the people. These judges and officers must apply their whole time to the detail business of their offices, and depend on them for their support: then they always act under masters or superiors, and may be removed from office for misconduct; they pursue a certain round of executive business: their offices must be in all societies confined to a few men, because but few can become qualified to fill them: and were they, by annual appointments, open

to the people at large, they are offices of such a nature as to be of no service to them; they must leave these offices in the possession of the few individuals qualified to fill them, or have them badly filled. In the judicial and executive departments also, the body of the people possess a large share of power and influence, as jurors and subordinate officers, among whom there are many and frequent rotations. But in every free country the legislatures are all on a level, and legislation becomes partial whenever, in practice, it rests for any considerable time in a few hands. It is the true republican principle to diffuse the power of making the laws among the people, and so to modify the forms of the government as to draw in turn the well informed of every class into the legislature.

To determine the propriety or impropriety of this rotation, we must take the inconveniencies as well as the advantages attending it into view: on the one hand, by this rotation, we may sometimes exclude good men from being elected. On the other hand, we guard against those pernicious connections, which usually grow up among men left to continue long periods in office, we increase the number of those who make the laws and return to their constituents; and thereby spread information, and preserve a spirit of activity and investigation among the people: hence a balance of interests and exertions are preserved, and the ruinous measures of factions rendered more impracticable. I would not urge the principle of rotation, if I believed the consequence would be an uninformed federal legislature; but I have no apprehension of this in this enlightened country. The members of congress, at any one time, must be but very few, compared with the respectable well informed men in the United States; and I have no idea there will be any want of such men for members of congress, though by a principle of rotation the constitution should exclude from being elected for two years those federal legislators, who may have served the four years immediately preceding, or any four years in the six preceding years. If we may judge from experience and fair calculations, this principle will never operate to exclude at any one period a fifteenth part, even of those men who have been members of congress. Though no man can sit in congress, by the confederation, more than three years in any term of six years, yet not more than three, four, or five men in any one state, have been made ineligible at any one period; and if a good man happen to be excluded by this rotation, it is only for a short time. All things considered, the inconveniencies of the principle must be very inconsiderable compared with the many advantages of it. It will generally be expedient for a man who has served four years in congress to return home, mix with the people, and reside some time with them: this will tend to reinstate him in the interests, feelings, and views similar to theirs, and thereby confirm in him the essential qualifications of a legislator. Even in point of information, it may be observed, the useful information of legislators is not acquired merely in studies in offices, and in meeting to make laws from day to day; they must learn the actual situation of the people, by being among them, and when they have made laws, return home, and observe how they operate. Thus occasionally to be among the people, is not only necessary to prevent or banish the callous habits and self interested views of office in legislators, but to afford them necessary information, and to render them useful: another valuable end is answered by it, sympathy, and the means of communication between them and their constituents, is substantially promoted; so that on every principle legislators, at certain periods, ought to live among their constituents.

Some men of science are undoubtedly necessary in every legislature; but the knowledge, generally, necessary for men who make laws, is a knowledge of the common concerns, and particular circumstances of the people. In a republican government seats in the legislature are highly honorable; I believe but few do, and surely none ought to consider them as places of profit and permanent support. Were the people always properly attentive, they would, at proper periods, call their law makers home, by sending others in their room: but this is not often the case, and therefore, in making constitutions, when the people are attentive, they ought cautiously to provide for those benefits, those advantageous changes in the administration of their affairs, which they are often apt to be inattentive to in practice. On the whole, to guard against the evils, and to secure the advantages I have mentioned, with the greatest degree of certainty, we ought clearly, in my opinion, to increase the federal representation, to secure elections on proper principles, to establish a right to recall members, and a rotation among them.

17

JAMES MADISON, FEDERALIST, NO. 39, 251
16 Jan. 1788

(See ch. 4, no. 24)

18

JAMES MADISON, FEDERALIST, NO. 46, 315
29 Jan. 1788

(See ch. 8, no. 30)

19

JAMES MADISON, FEDERALIST, NO. 49, 338–43
2 Feb. 1788

The author of the "Notes on the state of Virginia," quoted in the last paper, has subjoined to that valuable work, the draught of a constitution which had been prepared in order to be laid before a convention expected to be called in 1783 by the legislature, for the establishment of a constitution for that commonwealth. The plan, like every thing from the same pen, marks a turn of thinking original, comprehensive and accurate; and is the more worthy of attention, as it equally displays a fervent attachment to republican government, and an enlightened view of the dangerous propensities against which it ought to be guarded. One of the precautions which he proposes, and on which he appears ultimately to rely as a palladium to the weaker departments of power, against the invasions of the stronger, is perhaps altogether his own, and as it immediately relates to the subject of our present enquiry, ought not to be overlooked.

His proposition is, "that whenever any two of the three branches of government shall concur in opinion, each by the voices of two thirds of their whole number, that a convention is necessary for altering the constitution or *correcting breaches of it*, a convention shall be called for the purpose."

As the people are the only legitimate fountain of power, and it is from them that the constitutional charter, under which the several branches of government hold their power, is derived; it seems strictly consonant to the republican theory, to recur to the same original authority, not only whenever it may be necessary to enlarge, diminish, or new-model the powers of government; but also whenever any one of the departments may commit encroachments on the chartered authorities of the others. The several departments being perfectly co-ordinate by the terms of their common commission, neither of them, it is evident, can pretend to an exclusive or superior right of settling the boundaries between their respective powers; and how are the encroachments of the stronger to be prevented, or the wrongs of the weaker to be redressed, without an appeal to the people themselves; who, as the grantors of the commission, can alone declare its true meaning and enforce its observance?

There is certainly great force in this reasoning, and it must be allowed to prove, that a constitutional road to the decision of the people, ought to be marked out, and kept open, for certain great and extraordinary occasions. But there appear to be insuperable objections against the proposed recurrence to the people, as a provision in all cases for keeping the several departments of power within their constitutional limits.

In the first place, the provision does not reach the case of a combination of two of the departments against a third. If the legislative authority, which possesses so many means of operating on the motives of the other departments, should be able to gain to its interest either of the others, or even one-third of its members, the remaining department could derive no advantage from this remedial provision. I do not dwell however on this objection, because it may be thought to lie rather against the modification of the principle, than against the principle itself.

In the next place, it may be considered as an objection inherent in the principle, that as every appeal to the people would carry an implication of some defect in the government, frequent appeals would in great measure deprive the government of that veneration, which time bestows on every thing, and without which perhaps the wisest and freest governments would not possess the requisite stability. If it be true that all governments rest on opinion, it is no less true that the strength of opinion in each individual, and its practical influence on his conduct, depend much on the number which he supposes to have entertained the same opinion. The reason of man, like man himself is timid and cautious, when left alone; and acquires firmness and confidence, in proportion to the number with which it is associated. When the examples, which fortify opinion, are *antient* as well as *numerous,* they are known to have a double effect. In a nation of philosophers, this consideration ought to be disregarded. A reverence for the laws, would be sufficiently inculcated by the voice of an enlightened reason. But a nation of philosophers is as little to be expected as the philosophical race of kings wished for by Plato. And in every other nation, the most rational government will not find it a superfluous advantage, to have the prejudices of the community on its side.

The danger of disturbing the public tranquility by interesting too strongly the public passions, is a still more serious objection against a frequent reference of constitutional questions, to the decision of the whole society. Notwithstanding the success which has attended the revisions of our established forms of government, and which does so much honour to the virtue and intelligence of the people of America, it must be confessed, that the experiments are of too ticklish a nature to be unnecessarily multiplied. We are to recollect that all the existing constitutions were formed in the midst of a danger which repressed the passions most unfriendly to order and concord; of an enthusiastic confidence of the people in their patriotic leaders, which stifled the ordinary diversity of opinions on great national questions; of a universal ardor for new and opposite forms, produced by a universal resentment and indignation against the antient government; and whilst no spirit of party, connected with the changes to be made, or the abuses to be reformed, could mingle its leven in the operation. The future situations in which we must expect to be usually placed, do not present any equivalent security against the danger which is apprehended.

But the greatest objection of all is, that the decisions which would probably result from such appeals, would not answer the purpose of maintaining the constitutional equilibrium of the government. We have seen that the tendency of republican governments is to an aggrandizement of the legislative, at the expence of the other departments. The appeals to the people therefore would usually be made by the executive and judiciary departments. But whether made by one side or the other, would each side enjoy equal advantages on the trial? Let us view their different situations. The members of the executive and judiciary departments, are few in number, and can be personally known to a small part only of the people. The latter by the mode of their appointment, as well as, by the nature and permanency of it, are too far removed from the peo-

ple to share much in their prepossessions. The former are generally the objects of jealousy: And their administration is always liable to be discoloured and rendered unpopular. The members of the legislative department, on the other hand, are numerous. They are distributed and dwell among the people at large. Their connections of blood, of friendship and of acquaintance, embrace a great proportion of the most influencial part of the society. The nature of their public trust implies a personal influence among the people, and that they are more immediately the confidential guardians of the rights and liberties of the people. With these advantages, it can hardly be supposed that the adverse party would have an equal chance for a favorable issue.

But the legislative party would not only be able to plead their cause most successfully with the people. They would probably be constituted themselves the judges. The same influence which had gained them an election into the legislature, would gain them a seat in the convention. If this should not be the case with all, it would probably be the case with many, and pretty certainly with those leading characters, on whom every thing depends in such bodies. The convention in short would be composed chiefly of men, who had been, who actually were, or who expected to be, members of the department whose conduct was arraigned. They would consequently be parties to the very question to be decided by them.

It might however sometimes happen, that appeals would be made under circumstances less adverse to the executive and judiciary departments. The usurpations of the legislature might be so flagrant and so sudden, as to admit of no specious colouring. A strong party among themselves might take side with the other branches. The executive power might be in the hands of a peculiar favorite of the people. In such a posture of things, the public decision might be less swayed by prepossessions in favor of the legislative party. But still it could never be expected to turn on the true merits of the question. It would inevitably be connected with the spirit of pre-existing parties, or of parties springing out of the question itself. It would be connected with persons of distinguished character and extensive influence in the community. It would be pronounced by the very men who had been agents in, or opponents of the measure, to which the decision would relate. The *passions* therefore not *the reason,* of the public, would sit in judgment. But it is the reason of the public alone that ought to controul and regulate the government. The passions ought to be controuled and regulated by the government.

We found in the last paper that mere declarations in the written constitution, are not sufficient to restrain the several departments within their legal limits. It appears in this, that occasional appeals to the people would be neither a proper nor an effectual provision, for that purpose. How far the provisions of a different nature contained in the plan above quoted, might be adequate, I do not examine. Some of them are unquestionably founded on sound political principles, and all of them are framed with singular ingenuity and precision.

20

JAMES MADISON, FEDERALIST, NO. 63, 424–28
1 Mar. 1788

(See ch. 4, no. 27)

21

ALEXANDER HAMILTON, FEDERALIST, NO. 71,
482–83
18 Mar. 1788

There are some, who would be inclined to regard the servile pliancy of the executive to a prevailing current, either in the community, or in the Legislature, as its best recommendation. But such men entertain very crude notions, as well of the purposes for which government was instituted, as of the true means by which the public happiness may be promoted. The republican principle demands, that the deliberate sense of the community should govern the conduct of those to whom they entrust the management of their affairs; but it does not require an unqualified complaisance to every sudden breese of passion, or to every transient impulse which the people may receive from the arts of men, who flatter their prejudices to betray their interests. It is a just observation, that the people commonly *intend* the PUBLIC GOOD. This often applies to their very errors. But their good sense would despise the adulator, who should pretend that they always *reason right* about the *means* of promoting it. They know from experience, that they sometimes err; and the wonder is, that they so seldom err as they do; beset as they continually are by the wiles of parasites and sycophants, by the snares of the ambitious, the avaricious, the desperate; by the artifices of men, who possess their confidence more than they deserve it, and of those who seek to possess, rather than to deserve it. When occasions present themselves in which the interests of the people are at variance with their inclinations, it is the duty of the persons whom they have appointed to be the guardians of those interests, to withstand the temporary delusion, in order to give them time and opportunity for more cool and sedate reflection. Instances might be cited, in which a conduct of this kind has saved the people from very fatal consequences of their own mistakes, and has procured lasting monuments of their gratitude to the men, who had courage and magnanimity enough to serve them at the peril of their displeasure.

But however inclined we might be to insist upon an unbounded complaisance in the executive to the inclinations of the people, we can with no propriety contend for a like complaisance to the humors of the Legislature. The latter may sometimes stand in opposition to the former; and at other times the people may be entirely neutral. In either

supposition, it is certainly desirable that the executive should be in a situation to dare to act his own opinion with vigor and decision.

22

ALEXANDER HAMILTON, FEDERALIST, NO. 78,
527–29
28 May 1788

This independence of the judges is equally requisite to guard the constitution and the rights of individuals from the effects of those ill humours which the arts of designing men, or the influence of particular conjunctures, sometimes disseminate among the people themselves, and which, though they speedily give place to better information and more deliberate reflection, have a tendency in the mean time to occasion dangerous innovations in the government, and serious oppressions of the minor party in the community. Though I trust the friends of the proposed constitution will never concur with its enemies in questioning that fundamental principle of republican government, which admits the right of the people to alter or abolish the established constitution whenever they find it inconsistent with their happiness; yet it is not to be inferred from this principle, that the representatives of the people, whenever a momentary inclination happens to lay hold of a majority of their constituents incompatible with the provisions in the existing constitution, would on that account be justifiable in a violation of those provisions; or that the courts would be under a greater obligation to connive at infractions in this shape, than when they had proceeded wholly from the cabals of the representative body. Until the people have by some solemn and authoritative act annulled or changed the established form, it is binding upon themselves collectively, as well as individually; and no presumption, or even knowledge of their sentiments, can warrant their representatives in a departure from it, prior to such an act. But it is easy to see that it would require an uncommon portion of fortitude in the judges to do their duty as faithful guardians of the constitution, where legislative invasions of it had been instigated by the major voice of the community.

But it is not with a view to infractions of the constitution only that the independence of the judges may be an essential safeguard against the effects of occasional ill humours in the society. These sometimes extend no farther than to the injury of the private rights of particular classes of citizens, by unjust and partial laws. Here also the firmness of the judicial magistracy is of vast importance in mitigating the severity, and confining the operation of such laws. It not only serves to moderate the immediate mischiefs of those which may have been passed, but it operates as a check upon the legislative body in passing them; who, perceiving that obstacles to the success of an iniquitous intention are to be expected from the scruples of the courts, are in a manner compelled by the very motives of the injustice they meditate, to qualify their attempts. This is a circumstance calculated to have more influence upon the character of our governments, than but few may be aware of. The benefits of the integrity and moderation of the judiciary have already been felt in more states than one; and though they may have displeased those whose sinister expectations they may have disappointed, they must have commanded the esteem and applause of all the virtuous and disinterested. Considerate men of every description ought to prize whatever will tend to beget or fortify that temper in the courts; as no man can be sure that he may not be tomorrow the victim of a spirit of injustice, by which he may be a gainer to-day. And every man must now feel that the inevitable tendency of such a spirit is to sap the foundations of public and private confidence, and to introduce in its stead, universal distrust and distress.

23

THOMAS JEFFERSON TO JAMES MADISON
6 Sept. 1789
Papers 15:392–97

I sit down to write to you without knowing by what occasion I shall send my letter. I do it because a subject comes into my head which I would wish to develope a little more than is practicable in the hurry of the moment of making up general dispatches.

The question Whether one generation of men has a right to bind another, seems never to have been started either on this or our side of the water. Yet it is a question of such consequences as not only to merit decision, but place also, among the fundamental principles of every government. The course of reflection in which we are immersed here on the elementary principles of society has presented this question to my mind; and that no such obligation can be so transmitted I think very capable of proof.—I set out on this ground, which I suppose to be self evident, *"that the earth belongs in usufruct to the living"*: that the dead have neither powers nor rights over it. The portion occupied by an individual ceases to be his when himself ceases to be, and reverts to the society. If the society has formed no rules for the appropriation of it's lands in severalty, it will be taken by the first occupants. These will generally be the wife and children of the decedent. If they have formed rules of appropriation, those rules may give it to the wife and children, or to some one of them, or to the legatee of the deceased. So they may give it to his creditor. But the child, the legatee, or creditor takes it, not by any natural right, but by a law of the society of which they are members, and to which they are subject. Then no man can, by *natural right*, oblige the lands he occupied, or the persons who succeed him in that occupation, to the paiment of debts contracted by him. For if he could, he might, during his own life, eat up the usufruct of the lands for several generations to come, and then the lands would belong to the dead, and not to the living, which would be the reverse of our principle.

What is true of every member of the society individually, is true of them all collectively, since the rights of the whole can be no more than the sum of the rights of the individuals.—To keep our ideas clear when applying them to a multitude, let us suppose a whole generation of men to be born on the same day, to attain mature age on the same day, and to die on the same day, leaving a succeeding generation in the moment of attaining their mature age all together. Let the ripe age be supposed of 21. years, and their period of life 34. years more, that being the average term given by the bills of mortality to persons who have already attained 21. years of age. Each successive generation would, in this way, come on, and go off the stage at a fixed moment, as individuals do now. Then I say the earth belongs to each of these generations, during it's course, fully, and in their own right. The 2d. generation receives it clear of the debts and incumberances of the 1st. the 3d of the 2d. and so on. For if the 1st. could charge it with a debt, then the earth would belong to the dead and not the living generation. Then no generation can contract debts greater than may be paid during the course of it's own existence. At 21. years of age they may bind themselves and their lands for 34. years to come: at 22. for 33: at 23. for 32. and at 54. for one year only; because these are the terms of life which remain to them at those respective epochs.—But a material difference must be noted between the succession of an individual, and that of a whole generation. Individuals are parts only of a society, subject to the laws of the whole. These laws may appropriate the portion of land occupied by a decedent to his creditor rather than to any other, or to his child on condition he satisfies the creditor. But when a whole generation, that is, the whole society dies, as in the case we have supposed, and another generation or society succeeds, this forms a whole, and there is no superior who can give their territory to a third society, who may have lent money to their predecessors beyond their faculties of paying.

What is true of a generation all arriving to self-government on the same day, and dying all on the same day, is true of those in a constant course of decay and renewal, with this only difference. A generation coming in and going out entire, as in the first case, would have a right in the 1st. year of their self-dominion to contract a debt for 33. years, in the 10th. for 24. in the 20th. for 14. in the 30th. for 4. whereas generations, changing daily by daily deaths and births, have one constant term, beginning at the date of their contract, and ending when a majority of those of full age at that date shall be dead. The length of that term may be estimated from the tables of mortality, corrected by the circumstances of climate, occupation &c. peculiar to the country of the contractors. Take, for instance, the table of M. de Buffon wherein he states 23,994 deaths, and the ages at which they happened. Suppose a society in which 23,994 persons are born every year, and live to the ages stated in this table. The conditions of that society will be as follows. 1st. It will consist constantly of 617,703. persons of all ages. 2ly. Of those living at any one instant of time, one half will be dead in 24. years 8. months. 3dly. 1[8],675 will arrive every year at the age of 21. years complete. 4ly. It will constantly have 348,417 persons of all ages above 21. years. 5ly. And the half of those of 21. years and upwards living at any one instant of time will be dead in 18. years 8. months, or say 19. years as the nearest integral number. Then 19. years is the term beyond which neither the representatives of a nation, nor even the whole nation itself assembled, can validly extend a debt.

To render this conclusion palpable by example, suppose that Louis XIV. and XV. had contracted debts in the name of the French nation to the amount of 10,000 milliards of livres, and that the whole had been contracted in Genoa. The interest of this sum would be 500. milliards, which is said to be the whole rent roll or nett proceeds of the territory of France. Must the present generation of men have retired from the territory in which nature produced them, and ceded it to the Genoese creditors? No. They have the same rights over the soil on which they were produced, as the preceding generations had. They derive these rights not from their predecessors, but from nature. They then and their soil are by nature clear of the debts of their predecessors.

Again suppose Louis XV. and his cotemporary generation had said to the money-lenders of Genoa, give us money that we may eat, drink, and be merry in our day; and on condition you will demand no interest till the end of 19. years you shall then for ever after receive an annual interest of 12⅝ per cent. The money is lent on these conditions, is divided among the living, eaten, drank, and squandered. Would the present generation be obliged to apply the produce of the earth and of their labour to replace their dissipations? Not at all.

I suppose that the recieved opinion, that the public debts of one generation devolve on the next, has been suggested by our seeing habitually in private life that he who succeeds to lands is required to pay the debts of his ancestor or testator: without considering that this requisition is municipal only, not moral; flowing from the will of the society, which has found it convenient to appropriate lands, become vacant by the death of their occupant, on the condition of a paiment of his debts: but that between society and society, or generation and generation, there is no municipal obligation, no umpire but the law of nature. We seem not to have percieved that, by the law of nature, one generation is to another as one independant nation to another.

The interest of the national debt of France being in fact but a two thousandth part of it's rent roll, the paiment of it is practicable enough: and so becomes a question merely of honor, or of expediency. But with respect to future debts, would it not be wise and just for that nation to declare, in the constitution they are forming, that neither the legislature, nor the nation itself, can validly contract more debt than they may pay within their own age, or within the term of 19. years? And that all future contracts will be deemed void as to what shall remain unpaid at the end of 19. years from their date? This would put the lenders, and the borrowers also, on their guard. By reducing too the

faculty of borrowing within it's natural limits, it would bridle the spirit of war, to which too free a course has been procured by the inattention of money-lenders to this law of nature, that succeeding generations are not responsible for the preceding.

On similar ground it may be proved that no society can make a perpetual constitution, or even a perpetual law. The earth belongs always to the living generation. They may manage it then, and what proceeds from it, as they please, during their usufruct. They are masters too of their own persons, and consequently may govern them as they please. But persons and property make the sum of the objects of government. The constitution and the laws of their predecessors extinguished then in their natural course with those who gave them being. This could preserve that being till it ceased to be itself, and no longer. Every constitution then, and every law, naturally expires at the end of 19 years. If it be enforced longer, it is an act of force, and not of right.—It may be said that the succeeding generation exercising in fact the power of repeal, this leaves them as free as if the constitution or law has been expressly limited to 19 years only. In the first place, this objection admits the right, in proposing an equivalent. But the power of repeal is not an equivalent. It might be indeed if every form of government were so perfectly contrived that the will of the majority could always be obtained fairly and without impediment. But this is true of no form. The people cannot assemble themselves. Their representation is unequal and vicious. Various checks are opposed to every legislative proposition. Factions get possession of the public councils. Bribery corrupts them. Personal interests lead them astray from the general interests of their constituents: and other impediments arise so as to prove to every practical man that a law of limited duration is much more manageable than one which needs a repeal.

This principle that the earth belongs to the living, and not to the dead, is of very extensive application and consequences, in every country, and most especially in France. It enters into the resolution of the questions Whether the nation may change the descent of lands holden in tail? Whether they may change the appropriation of lands given antiently to the church, to hospitals, colleges, orders of chivalry, and otherwise in perpetuity? Whether they may abolish the charges and privileges attached on lands, including the whole catalogue ecclesiastical and feudal? It goes to hereditary offices, authorities and jurisdictions; to hereditary orders, distinctions and appellations; to perpetual monopolies in commerce, the arts and sciences; with a long train of et ceteras: and it renders the question of reimbursement a question of generosity and not of right. In all these cases, the legislature of the day could authorize such appropriations and establishments for their own time, but no longer; and the present holders, even where they, or their ancestors, have purchased, are in the case of bonâ fide purchasers of what the seller had no right to convey.

Turn this subject in your mind, my dear Sir, and particularly as to the power of contracting debts; and develope it with that perspicuity and cogent logic so peculiarly yours. Your station in the councils of our country gives

you an opportunity of producing it to public consideration, of forcing it into discussion. At first blush it may be
rallied, as a theoretical speculation: but examination will
prove it to be solid and salutary. It would furnish matter
for a fine preamble to our first law for appropriating the
public revenue; and it will exclude at the threshold of our
new government the contagious and ruinous errors of this
quarter of the globe, which have armed despots with
means, not sanctioned by nature, for binding in chains
their fellow men. We have already given in example one
effectual check to the Dog of war by transferring the
power of letting him loose from the Executive to the Legislative body, from those who are to spend to those who
are to pay. I should be pleased to see this second obstacle
held out by us also in the first instance. No nation can
make a declaration against the validity of long-contracted
debts so disinterestedly as we, since we do not owe a shilling which may not be paid with ease, principal and interest, within the time of our own lives.—Establish the principle also in the new law to be passed for protecting
copyrights and new inventions, by securing the exclusive
right for 19. instead of 14. years. Besides familiarising us
to this term, it will be an instance the more of our taking
reason for our guide, instead of English precedent, the
habit of which fetters us with all the political heresies of a
nation equally remarkeable for it's early excitement from
some errors, and long slumbering under others.

24

JAMES MADISON TO THOMAS JEFFERSON
4 Feb. 1790
Papers 13:18–21

Your favor of the 9th. of Jany. inclosing one of Sepr. last
did not get to hand till a few days ago. The idea which the
latter evolves is a great one, and suggests many interesting
reflections to legislators; particularly when contracting and
providing for public debts. Whether it can be received in
the extent your reasonings give it, is a question which I
ought to turn more in my thoughts than I have yet been
able to do, before I should be justified in making up a full
opinion on it. My first thoughts though coinciding with
many of yours, lead me to view the doctrine as not in *all*
respects compatible with the course of human affairs. I
will endeavor to sketch the grounds of my skepticism.

> "As the earth belongs to the living, not to the dead, a
> living generation can bind itself only: In every society
> the will of the majority binds the whole: According to
> the laws of mortality, a majority of those ripe at any mo-
> ment for the exercise of their will do not live beyond
> nineteen years: To that term then is limited the validity
> of *every* act of the Society: Nor within that limitation, can
> any declaration of the public will be valid which is not
> *express.*"

This I understand to be the outline of the argument.

The Acts of a political Society may be divided into three
classes.
1. The fundamental Constitution of the Government.
2. Laws involving stipulations which render them irrevocable at the will of the Legislature
3. Laws involving no such irrevocable quality.

However applicable in Theory the doctrine may be to a
Constitution, in [*sic*] seems liable in practice to some very
powerful objections. Would not a Government so often revised become too mutable to retain those prejudices in its
favor which antiquity inspires, and which are perhaps a
salutary aid to the most rational Government in the most
enlightened age? Would not such a periodical revision engender pernicious factions that might not otherwise come
into existence? Would not, in fine, a Government depending for its existence beyond a fixed date, on some positive
and authentic intervention of the Society itself, be too subject to the casualty and consequences of an actual inter-
regnum?

In the 2d. class, exceptions at least to the doctrine seem
to be requisite both in Theory and practice.

If the earth be the gift of nature to the living their title
can extend to the earth in its natural State only. The *improvements* made by the dead form a charge against the
living who take the benefit of them. This charge can no
otherwise be satisfyed than by executing the will of the
dead accompanying the improvements.

Debts may be incurred for purposes which interest the
unborn, as well as the living: such are debts for repelling
a conquest, the evils of which descend through many generations. Debts may even be incurred principally for the
benefit of posterity: such perhaps is the present debt of
the U. States, which far exceeds any burdens which the
present generation could well apprehend for itself. The
term of 19 years might not be sufficient for discharging
the debts in either of these cases.

There seems then to be a foundation in the nature of
things, in the relation which one generation bears to another, for the *descent* of obligations from one to another.
Equity requires it. Mutual good is promoted by it. All that
is indispensable in adjusting the account between the dead
& the living is to see that the debits against the latter do
not exceed the advances made by the former. Few of the
incumbrances entailed on Nations would bear a liquidation
even on this principle.

The objections to the doctrine as applied to the 3d. class
of acts may perhaps be merely practical. But in that view
they appear to be of great force.

Unless such laws should be kept in force by new acts
regularly anticipating the end of the term, all the rights
depending on positive laws, that is, most of the rights of
property would become absolutely defunct; and the most
violent struggles be generated between those interested in
reviving and those interested in new-modelling the former
State of property. Nor would events of this kind be improbable. The obstacles to the passage of laws which render a power to repeal inferior to an opportunity of rejecting, as a security agst. oppression, would here render an
opportunity of rejecting, an insecure provision agst. anarchy. Add, that the possibility of an event so hazardous to

the rights of property could not fail to depreciate its value; that the approach of the crisis would increase this effect; that the frequent return of periods superseding all the obligations depending on antecedent laws & usages, must by weak[en]ing the reverence for those obligations, co-operate with motives to licentiousness already too powerful; and that the uncertainty incident to such a state of things would on one side discourage the steady exertions of industry produced by permanent laws, and on the other, give a disproportionate advantage to the more, over the less, sagacious and interprizing part of the Society.

I find no relief from these consequences, but in the received doctrine that a tacit assent may be given to established Constitutions and laws, and that this assent may be inferred, where no positive dissent appears. It seems less impracticable to remedy, by wise plans of Government, the dangerous operation of this doctrine, than to find a remedy for the difficulties inseparable from the other.

May it not be questioned whether it be possible to exclude wholly the idea of tacit assent, without subverting the foundation of civil Society? On what principle does the voice of the majority bind the minority? It does not result I conceive from the law of nature, but from compact founded on conveniency. A greater proportion might be required by the fundamental constitution of a Society, if it were judged eligible. Prior then to the establishment of this principle, *unanimity* was necessary; and strict Theory at all times presupposses the assent of every member to the establishment of the rule itself. If this assent can not be given tacitly, or be not implied where no positive evidence forbids, persons born in Society would not on attaining ripe age be bound by acts of the Majority; and either a *unanimous* repetition of every law would be necessary on the accession of new members, or an express assent must be obtained from these to the rule by which the voice of the Majority is made the voice of the whole.

If the observations I have hazarded be not misapplied, it follows that a limitation of the validity of national acts to the computed life of a nation, is in some instances not required by Theory, and in others cannot be accomodated to practice. The observations are not meant however to impeach either the utility of the principle in some particular cases; or the general importance of it in the eye of the philosophical Legislator. On the contrary it would give me singular pleasure to see it first announced in the proceedings of the U. States, and always kept in their view, as a salutary curb on the living generation from imposing unjust or unnecessary burdens on their successors. But this is a pleasure which I have little hope of enjoying. The spirit of philosophical legislation has never reached some parts of the Union, and is by no means the fashion here, either within or without Congress. The evils suffered & feared from weakness in Government, and licentiousness in the people, have turned the attention more towards the means of strengthening the former, than of narrowing its extent in the minds of the latter. Besides this, it is so much easier to espy the little difficulties immediately incident to every great plan, than to comprehend its general and remote benefits, that our hemisphere must be still more enlightened before many of the sublime truths which are seen thro' the medium of Philosophy, become visible to the naked eye of the ordinary Politician.

25

JAMES WILSON, OF GOVERNMENT, THE LEGISLATIVE DEPARTMENT, OF CITIZENS AND ALIENS, LECTURES ON LAW 1791

Works 1:292–93, 403–5; 2:574–75

Habits contracted before the late revolution of the United States, operate, in the same manner, since that time, though very material alterations may have taken place in the objects of their operations.

Before that period, the executive and the judicial powers of government were placed neither in the people, nor in those, who professed to receive them under the authority of the people. They were derived from a different and a foreign source: they were regulated by foreign maxims: they were directed to foreign purposes. Need we be surprised, that they were objects of aversion and distrust? Need we be surprised, that every occasion was seized for lessening their influence, and weakening their energy? On the other hand, our assemblies were chosen by ourselves: they were the guardians of our rights, the objects of our confidence, and the anchor of our political hopes. Every power, which could be placed in them, was thought to be safely placed: every extension of that power was considered as an extension of our own security.

At the revolution, the same fond predilection, and the same jealous dislike, existed and prevailed. The executive and the judicial as well as the legislative authority was now the child of the people; but, to the two former, the people behaved like stepmothers. The legislature was still discriminated by excessive partiality; and into its lap, every good and precious gift was profusely thrown.

Even at this time, people can scarcely devest themselves of those opposite prepossessions: they still hold, when, perhaps, they perceive it not, the language, which expresses them. In observations on this subject, we hear the legislature mentioned as the *people's representatives*. The distinction, intimated by concealed implication, though probably, not avowed upon reflection, is, that the executive and judicial powers are not connected with the people by a relation so strong, or near, or dear.

But it is high time that we should chastise our prejudices; and that we should look upon the different parts of government with a just and impartial eye. The executive and judicial powers are now drawn from the same source, are now animated by the same principles, and are now directed to the same ends, with the legislative authority: they who execute, and they who administer the laws, are as much the servants, and therefore as much the friends of the people, as they who make them. The character, and interest, and glory of the two former are as intimately and as necessarily connected with the happiness and prosperity of the people, as the character, and interest, and glory of the latter are. Besides, the execution of the law, and the administration of justice under the law, bring it home to the fortunes, and farms, and houses, and business of the people. Ought the executive or the judicial magistrates, then, to be considered as foreigners? ought they to be treated with a chilling indifference?

. . . . .

The pyramid of government—and a republican government may well receive that beautiful and solid form—should be raised to a dignified altitude: but its foundations must, of consequence, be broad, and strong, and deep. The authority, the interests, and the affections of the people at large are the only foundation, on which a superstructure, proposed to be at once durable and magnificent, can be rationally erected.

Representation is the chain of communication between the people and those, to whom they have committed the exercise of the powers of government. If the materials, which form this chain, are sound and strong, it is unnecessary to be solicitous about the very high degree, to which they are polished. But in order to impart to them the true republican lustre, I know no means more effectual, than to invite and admit the freemen to the right of suffrage, and to enhance, as much as possible, the value of that right. Its value cannot, in truth, be enhanced too highly. It is a right of the greatest import, and of the most improving efficacy. It is a right to choose those, who shall be intrusted with the authority and with the confidence of the people: and who may employ that authority and that confidence for the noblest interests of the commonwealth, without the apprehension of disappointment or control.

This surely must have a powerful tendency to open, to enlighten, to enlarge, and to exalt the mind. I cannot, with sufficient energy, express my own conceptions of the value and the dignity of this right. In real majesty, an independent and unbiassed elector stands superiour to princes, addressed by the proudest titles, attended by the most magnificent retinues, and decorated with the most splendid regalia. Their sovereignty is only derivative, like the pale light of the moon: his is original, like the beaming splendour of the sun.

The benign influences, flowing from the possession and exercise of this right, deserve to be clearly and fully pointed out. I wish it was in my power to do complete justice to the important subject. Hitherto those benign influences have been little understood; they have been less valued; they have been still less experienced. This part of the knowledge and practice of government is yet, as has been observed, in its childhood. Let us, however, nurse and nourish it. In due time, it will repay our care and our labour; for, in due time, it will grow to the strength and stature of a full and perfect man.

The man, who enjoys the right of suffrage, on the extensive scale which is marked by our constitutions, will naturally turn his thoughts to the contemplation of publick men and publick measures. The inquiries he will make,

the information he will receive, and his own reflections on both, will afford a beneficial and amusing employment to his mind. I am far from insinuating, that every citizen should be an enthusiast in politicks, or that the interests of himself, his family, and those who depend on him for their comfortable situation in life, should be absorbed in Quixote speculations about the management or the reformation of the state. But there is surely a golden mean in things; and there can be no real incompatibility between the discharge of one's publick, and that of his private duty. Let private industry receive the warmest encouragement; for it is the basis of publick happiness. But must the bow of honest industry be always bent? At no moment shall a little relaxation be allowed? That relaxation, if properly directed, may prove to be instructive as well as agreeable. It may consist in reading a newspaper, or in conversing with a fellow citizen. May not the newspaper convey some interesting intelligence, or contain some useful essay? May not the conversation take a pleasing and an improving turn? Many hours, I believe, are every where spent, in talking about the unimportant occurrences of the day, or in the neighbourhood; and, perhaps, the frailties or the imperfections of a neighbour form, too often, one of the sweet but poisoned ingredients of the discourse. Would it be any great detriment to society or to individuals, if other characters, and with different views, were more frequently brought upon the carpet?

Under our constitutions, a number of important appointments must be made at every election. To make them is, indeed, the business only of a day. But it ought to be the business of much more than a day, to be prepared for making them well. When a citizen elects to office—let me repeat it—he performs an act of the first political consequence. He should be employed, on every convenient occasion, in making researches after proper persons for filling the different departments of power; in discussing, with his neighbours and fellow citizens, the qualities, which ought to be possessed by those, who enjoy places of publick trust; and in acquiring information, with the spirit of manly candour, concerning the manners and characters of those, who are likely to be candidates for the publick choice.

A habit of conversing and reflecting on these subjects, and of governing his actions by the result of his deliberations, would produce, in the mind of the citizen, a uniform, a strong, and a lively sensibility to the interests of his country. The same causes will effectuate a warm and enlightened attachment to those, who are best fitted, and best disposed, to support and promote those interests. By these means and in this manner, pure and genuine patriotism, that kind, which consists in liberal investigation and disinterested conduct, is produced, cherished, and strengthened in the mind: by these means and in this manner, the warm and generous emotion glows and is reflected from breast to breast.

Investigations of this nature are useful and improving, not to their authors only; they are so to their objects likewise. The love of honest and well earned fame is deeply rooted in honest and susceptible minds. Can there be a stronger incentive to the operations of this passion, than the hope of becoming the object of well founded and distinguishing applause? Can there be a more complete gratification of this passion, than the satisfaction of knowing that this applause is given—that it is given upon the most honourable principles, and acquired by the most honourable pursuits? To souls truly ingenuous, indiscriminate praise, misplaced praise, flattering praise, interested praise have no bewitching charms. But when publick approbation is the result of publick discernment, it must be highly pleasing to those who give, and to those who receive it.

If the foregoing remarks and deductions be just; and I believe they are so; the right of suffrage, properly understood, properly valued, and properly exercised, in a free and well constituted government, is an abundant source of the most rational, the most improving, and the most endearing connexion among the citizens.

．．．．．

When a man acts as one of the numerous party to the agreements, of which I have taken notice; it is his right, according to the tenour of his agreements, to govern; he is one of the *people*. When he acts as the single party to that agreement, which he has made with all the other members of the society; it is his duty, according to the tenour of his agreement, to obey; he is a *single citizen*. Of this agreement, indeed, it is impossible to ascertain all the articles. From the most obvious deduction of reason, however, one article may be specified, beyond all possibility of doubt. This article, of prime importance, is—that to the publick will of the society, the private will of every associated member must, in matters respecting the social union, be subordinate and submissive. The publick will of the society is declared by the laws. Obedience, therefore—civil obedience—obedience to the laws and to the administration of the laws—this is a distinguishing feature in the countenance of a citizen, when he is seen from this point of view.

That men ought to be governed, seems to have been agreed on all hands: the reason is, that, without government, they could never attain any high or permanent share of perfection or happiness. But the question has been—by whom should they be governed? And this has been made a question, by reason of two others—by whom *can* they be governed?—are they capable of governing themselves?

To this last question, Mr. Burke, in the spirit of his late creed, has answered in the negative. "Society," says he, "requires not only that the passions of individuals should be subjected, but that even in the mass and body as well as in the individuals, the inclinations of men should frequently be thwarted, their will controlled, and their passions brought into subjection. This can only be done *by a power out of themselves*." This negative answer has been, from time immemorial, the strong hold of tyranny: and if this negative answer be the true one, the strong hold of tyranny is, in fact, impregnable to all the artillery of freedom. If men should be governed; and if they cannot govern themselves; what is the consequence? They must be governed by other masters.

An opinion, however, has, by some, been entertained, that the question, which I last mentioned, may receive an answer in the affirmative. Men, it has been thought, are capable of governing themselves. In the United States, this opinion, which heretofore rested chiefly on theory, has lately been put in a train of fair practical experiment. That this experiment, to human happiness so interesting, may be crowned with abundant and glorious success, is, of all things in this world, the "consummation most devoutly to be wished."

But to its glorious and abundant success, the obedience of the citizens is of a necessity, absolute and supreme. The question, which has been proposed—the question, in the negative answer to which, tyranny has triumphed so long and so generally—the question, concerning which philosophers and patriots have indulged, and been pleased with indulging, a contrary sentiment—the question, which, in the United States, is now put upon an experiment—this all-important question is—not merely nor chiefly—are men capable of governing? Of this, even tyrants will admit the affirmative; and will point to themselves as living proofs of its truth. But the question is—are men capable of governing *themselves*? In other words; are they qualified—and are they disposed to be their *own* masters? For a moral as well as an intellectual capability is involved in the question. In still other words; are they qualified—and are they disposed to *obey themselves*? For to government, the correlative inseparable is obedience. To think, to speak, or to act, as if the former may be exercised, and, at the same time, the latter may not be performed, is to think, to speak, or to act, in a manner the most contradictory and absurd.

26

JAMES MADISON, PUBLIC OPINION
19 Dec. 1791
Papers 14:170

Public opinion sets bounds to every government, and is the real sovereign in every free one.

As there are cases where the public opinion must be obeyed by the government; so there are cases, where not being fixed, it may be influenced by the government. This distinction, if kept in view, would prevent or decide many debates on the respect due from the government to the sentiments of the people.

In proportion as government is influenced by opinion, it must be so, by whatever influences opinion. This decides the question concerning a *Constitutional Declaration of Rights*, which requires an influence on government, by becoming a part of the public opinion.

The larger a country, the less easy for its real opinion to be ascertained, and the less difficult to be counterfeited; when ascertained or presumed, the more respectable it is in the eyes of individuals. This is favorable to the authority of government. For the same reason, the more extensive a country, the more insignificant is each individual in his own eyes. This may be unfavorable to liberty.

Whatever facilitates a general intercourse of sentiments, as good roads, domestic commerce, a free press, and particularly a *circulation of newspapers through the entire body of the people,* and *Representatives going from, and returning among every part of them,* is equivalent to a contraction of territorial limits, and is favorable to liberty, where these may be too extensive.

27

THOMAS JEFFERSON TO MARQUIS DE LAFAYETTE
14 Feb. 1815

Writings 14:245–47

Your letter of August the 14th has been received, and read again and again, with extraordinary pleasure. It is the first glimpse which has been furnished me of the interior workings of the late unexpected but fortunate revolution of your country. The newspapers told us only that the great beast was fallen; but what part in this the patriots acted, and what the egotists, whether the former slept while the latter were awake to their own interests only, the hireling scribblers of the English press said little and knew less. I see now the mortifying alternative under which the patriot there is placed, of being either silent, or disgraced by an association in opposition with the remains of Bonapartism. A full measure of liberty is not now perhaps to be expected by your nation, nor am I confident they are prepared to preserve it. More than a generation will be requisite, under the administration of reasonable laws favoring the progress of knowledge in the general mass of the people, and their habituation to an independent security of person and property, before they will be capable of estimating the value of freedom, and the necessity of a sacred adherence to the principles on which it rests for preservation. Instead of that liberty which takes root and growth in the progress of reason, if recovered by mere force or accident; it becomes, with an unprepared people, a tyranny still, of the many, the few, or the one. Possibly you may remember, at the date of the *jeu de paume,* how earnestly I urged yourself and the patriots of my acquaintance, to enter then into a compact with the king, securing freedom of religion, freedom of the press, trial by jury, *habeas corpus,* and a national legislature, all of which it was known he would then yield, to go home, and let these work on the amelioration of the condition of the people, until they should have rendered them capable of more, when occasions would not fail to arise for communicating to them more. This was as much as I then thought them able to bear, soberly and usefully for themselves. You thought otherwise, and that the dose might still be larger. And I found you were right; for subsequent events proved

they were equal to the Constitution of 1791. Unfortunately, some of the most honest and enlightened of our patriotic friends, (but closet politicians merely, unpractised in the knowledge of man,) thought more could still be obtained and borne. They did not weigh the hazards of a transition from one form of government to another, the value of what they had already rescued from those hazards, and might hold in security if they pleased, nor the imprudence of giving up the certainty of such a degree of liberty, under a limited monarch, for the uncertainty of a little more under the form of a republic. You differed from them. You were for stopping there, and securing the Constitution which the National Assembly had obtained. Here, too, you were right; and from this fatal error of the republicans, from their separation from yourself and the constitutionalists, in their councils, flowed all the subsequent sufferings and crimes of the French nation. The hazards of a second change fell upon them by the way. The foreigner gained time to anarchise by gold the government he could not overthrow by arms, to crush in their own councils the genuine republicans, by the fraternal embraces of exaggerated and hired pretenders, and to turn the machine of Jacobinism from the change to the destruction of order; and, in the end, the limited monarchy they had secured was exchanged for the unprincipled and bloody tyranny of Robespierre, and the equally unprincipled and maniac tyranny of Bonaparte. You are now rid of him, and I sincerely wish you may continue so. But this may depend on the wisdom and moderation of the restored dynasty. It is for them now to read a lesson in the fatal errors of the republicans; to be contented with a certain portion of power, secured by formal compact with the nation, rather than, grasping at more, hazard all upon uncertainty, and risk meeting the fate of their predecessor, or a renewal of their own exile.

28

JAMES MADISON TO THOMAS RITCHIE
15 Sept. 1821

Writings 9:72

As a guide in expounding and applying the provisions of the Constitution, the debates and incidental decisions of the Convention can have no authoritative character. However desirable it be that they should be preserved as a gratification to the laudable curiosity felt by every people to trace the origin and progress of their political Institutions, & as a source perhaps of some lights on the Science of Govt. the legitimate meaning of the Instrument must be derived from the text itself; or if a key is to be sought elsewhere, it must be not in the opinions or intentions of the Body which planned & proposed the Constitution, but in the sense attached to it by the people in their respective State Conventions where it recd. all the Authority which it possesses.

SEE ALSO:

Samuel Adams, Valerius Poplicola, 28 Oct. 1771, Writings 2:256–61

John Adams, Autobiography, Oct. 1775, Diary 3:354–57

Address of the Mechanics of New York City, 14 June 1776, Niles 174–75

Vox Populi, Nov. 1787, Storing 4.4.10, 16

Alexander Hamilton, Federalist, no. 22, 14 Dec. 1787, 145–46

Thomas Jefferson to M. Correa de Serra, 28 June 1815, Writings 14:330

Thomas Jefferson to Major John Cartwright, 5 June 1824, Writings 16:42–44

3

Right of Revolution

Introduction

As is sufficiently illustrated by the documents assembled in chapters 2 and 17, propositions about rights form some of the basic premises of the Constitution. It is to secure these rights that governments are instituted among men. Just as an individual may take whatever actions he deems necessary to ward off his destruction or the perceived threat of his destruction, so too may a people act in their self-defense against a magistrate's lawlessness or viciousness: "Whatever is lawful against a thief, who submits to no law, is lawful against him" (Sidney, no. 1).

What others called the right of resistance or the right of revolution is at bottom the natural right of preservation. The supporting case was developed with bold thought and cautious speech by John Locke, whose *Second Treatise* (no. 2) rightly was regarded by many of the Founders as a fit and necessary text for a self-governing people. An executive's use of force without right left a suffering people with no choice: "cry up their Gouvernours, as much as you will for Sons of *Jupiter* . . . ; give them out for whom or what you please, the same will happen. *The People generally ill treated,* and contrary to right, will be ready upon any occasion to ease themselves of a burden that sits heavy upon them." Far from instigating "Civil Wars, or Intestine Broils," his doctrine (Locke insisted) would have an opposite effect. The mischiefs concocted by "a busie head, or turbulent spirit" would not succeed in the absence of a general sense of being wronged. In fact the people were, if anything, too slow to resent transgressions. Moreover, a people well instructed in their rights would reduce the likelihood of civil commotions by disabusing would-be tyrants of their wicked fancies.

The American experience shows the colonials to have been quicker learners of Locke's lessons than the ministers of George III. The complex of grievances and restless stirrings that agitated the Americans in the 1760s and beyond had sent their ablest men to their libraries and their writing desks. But by the mid-seventies events had reached a point where entreaties were futile and researches "among old parchments, or musty records" superfluous. "When the first principles of civil society are violated, and the rights of a whole people are invaded, the common forms of municipal law are not to be regarded" (Hamilton, no. 5).

With a popular government of their own in place, recourse to extraordinary remedies up to and including revolution remained a right and a problem. Jefferson's liking "a little rebellion now and then" and likening it to an atmospheric storm (Letter to Abigail Adams, 22 Feb. 1787) was said in reference to a few thousand debt-ridden farmers in postwar western Massachusetts (see ch. 18, no. 21), not to tax evaders in war-pressed Virginia (no. 6) and certainly not in reference to the tumbrils of the Terror. Yet of course it hardly behooved proud revolutionaries (Wilson, no. 13) to deny that "weighty causes of discontent given by the government" might lead to consequences beyond prediction or control (Hamilton [see ch. 8, no. 22]). An "original right of self-defence" was assumed and might be relied on to resist the grosser forms of governmental usurpation (no. 9). The "right of the people to alter or abolish the established constitution whenever they find it inconsistent with their happiness" was fundamental to republican government, according to Hamilton; and because that right was fundamental, it was not to be regarded flippantly or exercised vicariously. Nothing less would do than a "solemn and authoritative" expression of the people themselves. In the absence of that, "even knowledge of their sentiments" could not authorize the people's representatives to change what the people had once solemnly determined (Hamilton [see ch. 2, no. 22]).

Yet the Philadelphia Convention itself, and the Continental Congress before it, and the various state constitutional conventions, had all acted as the hour required undeterred by any "little ill-timed scruples." In this the Convention, at least, displayed "a manly confidence" in the people, fortified by the knowledge that if the people approved their extraordinary actions "all antecedent errors and irregularities" would be blotted out. The "transcendent and precious right of the people to 'abolish or alter their governments' " first excused and then justified others in proposing how the people might best exercise that right (Madison [see ch. 6, no. 20]). But for Madison, no less than for Hamilton, the right called for more than popular self-expression. A people on the eve of revolution was surely a vexed people, but not every vexation was justification for revolt. Just as popular government sought to express "the cool and deliberate sense of the community" (see ch. 4, no. 27), so too ought popular resistance and revolution to express the settled desperation of people in extreme cases, not the pique of those who merely cannot have things their way (no. 14).

1

ALGERNON SIDNEY, DISCOURSES CONCERNING
GOVERNMENT
1698 (posthumous)
Works 188–95, 458–62

Tumult is from the disorderly manner of those assemblies, where things can seldom be done regularly; and war is that "decertatio per vim," or trial by force, to which men come when other ways are ineffectual.

If the laws of God and men are therefore of no effect, when the magistracy is left at liberty to break them, and if the lusts of those, who are too strong for the tribunals of justice, cannot be otherwise restrained, than by sedition, tumults, and war, those seditions, tumults, and wars, are justified by the laws of God and man.

I will not take upon me to enumerate all the cases in which this may be done, but content myself with three, which have most frequently given occasion for proceedings of this kind.

The first is, when one or more men take upon them the power and name of a magistracy, to which they are not justly called.

The second, when one or more, being justly called, continue in their magistracy longer than the laws by which they are called do prescribe.

And the third, when he or they, who are rightly called, do assume a power, though within the time prescribed, that the law does not give; or turn that which the law does give, to an end different and contrary to that which is intended by it.

For the first, Filmer forbids us to examine titles. He tells us, we must submit to the power, whether acquired by usurpation or otherwise; not observing the mischievous absurdity of rewarding the most detestable villainies with the highest honours, and rendering the veneration due to the supreme magistrate, as father of the people, to one who has no other advantage above his brethren, than what he has gained by injuriously dispossessing or murdering him that was so. Hobbes, fearing the advantages that may be taken from such desperate nonsense, or not thinking it necessary to his end to carry the matter so far, has no regard at all to him who comes in without title or consent; and, denying him to be either king or tyrant, gives him no other name than "hostis et latro;" and allows all things to be lawful against him, that may be done to a public enemy or pirate: which is as much as to say, any man may destroy him how he can. Whatever he may be guilty of in other respects, he does in this follow the voice of mankind, and the dictates of common sense: for no man can make himself a magistrate for himself; and no man can have the right of a magistrate, who is not a magistrate. If he be justly accounted an enemy to all, who injures all, he above all must be the public enemy of a nation, who, by usurping a power over them, does the greatest and most public injury that a people can suffer. For which reason, by an established law among the most virtuous nations, every man might kill a tyrant; and no names are recorded in history with more honour, than of those who did it.

These are by other authors called "tyranni sine titulo." And that name is given to all those who obtain the supreme power by illegal and unjust means. The laws which they overthrow can give them no protection; and every man is a soldier against him who is a public enemy.

The same rule holds, though they are more in number; as the magi, who usurped the dominion of Persia after the death of Cambyses; the thirty tyrants at Athens overthrown by Thrasybulus; those of Thebes slain by Pelopidas; the decemviri of Rome, and others. For though the multitude of offenders may sometimes procure impunity, yet that act which is wicked in one, must be so in ten or twenty; and whatever is lawful against one usurper is so against them all.

2. If those who were rightly created continue beyond the time limited by the law, it is the same thing. That which is expired is as if it had never been. He that was created consul for a year, or dictator for six months, was after that a private man; and, if he had continued in the exercise of his magistracy, had been subject to the same punishment as if he had usurped it at the first. This was known to Epaminondas; who finding that his enterprize against Sparta could not be accomplished within the time for which he was made Boeotarchon, rather chose to trust his countrymen with his life than to desist; and was saved merely through an admiration of his virtue, assurance of his good intentions, and the glory of the action.

The Roman decemviri, though duly elected, were proceeded against as private men usurping the magistracy, when they continued beyond their time. Other magistrates had ceased; there was none that could regularly call the senate or people to an assembly. But when their ambition was manifest, and the people exasperated by the death of Virginia, they laid aside all ceremonies. The senate and people met; and, exercising their authority in the same manner, as if they had been regularly called by the magistrate appointed to that end, they abrogated the power of the decemviri, proceeded against them as enemies and tyrants, and by that means preserved themselves from utter ruin.

3. The same course is justly used against a legal magistrate, who takes upon him, though within the time prescribed by the law, to exercise a power which the law does not give; for in that respect he is a private man, "quia," as Grotius says, eatenùs non habet imperium," and may be restrained as well as any other, because he is not set up to do what he lists, but what the law appoints for the good of the people; and as he has no other power than what the law allows, so the same law limits and directs the exercise of that which he has. This right, naturally belonging to nations, is no way impaired by the name of supreme given to their magistrates; for it signifies no more, than that they do act sovereignly in the matters committed to their charge. Thus are the parliaments of France called "cours souveraines;" for they judge of life and death, determine controversies concerning estates, and there is no appeal from their decrees. But no man ever thought, that it was therefore lawful for them to do what they pleased; or that they might not be opposed, if they should attempt to do that which they ought not. And though the Roman dictators and consuls were supreme magistrates, they were subject to the people, and might be punished, as well as others, if they transgressed the law. Thuanus carries the word so far, that when Burlota, Giustiniano, and others who were but colonels, were sent as commanders in chief of three or four thousand men upon an enterprize, he always says, "summum imperium ei delatum." Grotius explains this point, by distinguishing those who have the "summum imperium summo modo," from those who have it "modo non summo." I know not where to find an example of this sovereign power, enjoyed without restriction, under a better title than "occupation;" which relates not to our purpose, who seek only that which is legal and just. Therefore, laying aside that point for the present, we may follow Grotius in examining the right of those who are certainly limited, "ubi partem imperii habet rex, partem senatus sive populus:" in which case he says, "regi in partem non suam involanti vis justa opponi potest;" inasmuch as they who have a part cannot but have a right of defending that part; "quia, datâ facultate, datur jus facultatem tuendi," without which it could be of no effect.

The particular limits of the rights belonging to each can only be judged by the precise letter, or general intention of the law. The dukes of Venice have certainly a part in the government, and could not be called magistrates, if they had not. They are said to be supreme: all laws and public acts bear their names. The embassador of the state,

speaking to pope Paul the fifth, denied that he acknowledged any other superior besides God. But they are so well known to be under the power of the law, that divers of them have been put to death for transgressing it; and a marble gallows is seen at the foot of the stairs in St. Mark's palace, upon which some of them, and no others, have been executed. But if they may be duly opposed, when they commit undue acts, no man of judgement will deny, that if one of them by an outrageous violence should endeavour to overthrow the law, he might by violence be suppressed and chastised.

Again, some magistrates are entrusted with a power of providing ships, arms, ammunition, and victuals for war, raising and disciplining soldiers, appointing officers to command in forts and garrisons, and making leagues with foreign princes and states. But if one of these should imbezzle, sell, or give to an enemy those ships, arms, ammunition, or provisions, betray the forts, employ only or principally such men as will serve him in those wicked actions, and, contrary to the trust reposed in him, make such leagues with foreigners, as tend to the advancement of his personal interests, and to the detriment of the public, he abrogates his own magistracy; and the right he had, perishes, as the lawyers say, "frustratione finis." He cannot be protected by the law which he has overthrown, nor obtain impunity for his crimes from the authority that was conferred upon him, only that he might do good with it. He was "singulis major," on account of the excellence of his office; but "universis minor," from the nature and end of his institution. The surest way of extinguishing his prerogative was by turning it to the hurt of those who gave it. When matters are brought to this posture, the author of the mischief, or the nation, must perish. A flock cannot subsist under a shepherd that seeks its ruin, nor a people under an unfaithful magistrate. Honour and riches are justly heaped upon the heads of those who rightly perform their duty, because the difficulty as well as the excellency of the work is great. It requires courage, experience, industry, fidelity, and wisdom. "The good shepherd, says our Saviour, lays down his life for his sheep." The hireling, who flies in time of danger, is represented under an ill character; but he that sets himself to destroy his flock, is a wolf. His authority is incompatible with their subsistence. And whoever disapproves tumults, seditions, or war, by which he may be removed from it, if gentler means are ineffectual, subverts the foundation of all law, exalts the fury of one man to the destruction of a nation, and giving an irresistible power to the most abominable iniquity, exposes all that are good to be destroyed, and virtue to be utterly extinguished.

Few will allow such a pre-eminence to the dukes of Venice or Genoa, the avoyers of Switzerland, or the burgomasters of Amsterdam. Many will say these are rascals if they prove false, and ought rather to be hanged, than suffered to accomplish the villainies they design. But if this be confessed in relation to the highest magistrates that are among those nations, why should not the same be in all others, by what name soever they are called? When did God confer upon those nations the extraordinary privilege of providing better for their own safety than others? Or was the gift universal, though the benefit accrue only to those who have banished great titles from among them? If this be so, it is not their felicity, but their wisdom, that we ought to admire and imitate. But why should any think their ancestors had not the same care? Have not they, who retained in themselves a power over a magistrate of one name, the like over another? Is there a charm in words, or any name of such efficacy, that he who receives it should immediately become master of those that created him; whereas all others do remain for ever subject to them? Would the Venetian government change its nature, if they should give the name of king to their prince? Are the Polanders less free since the title of king is conferred upon their dukes? Or are the Moscovites less slaves, because their chief magistrate has no other than that of duke? If we examine things but a little, it will appear, that magistrates have enjoyed large powers, who never had the name of kings; and none were ever more restrained by laws than those of Sparta, Arragon, the Goths in Spain, Hungary, Bohemia, Sweden, Denmark, Poland, and others, who had that title. There is therefore no such thing as a right universally belonging to a name; but every one enjoys that which the laws, by which he is, confer upon him. The law that gives the power, regulates it. And they, who give no more than what they please, cannot be obliged to suffer him to whom they give it, to take more than they thought fit to give, or to go unpunished if he do. The agreements made are always confirmed by oath, and the treachery of violating them is consequently aggravated by perjury. They are excellent philosophers, and able divines, who think that this can create a right to those who had none; or that the laws can be a protection to such as overthrow them, and give opportunity of doing the mischiefs they design! If not, then he that was a magistrate, by such actions returns into the condition of a private man; and whatever is lawful against a thief, who submits to no law, is lawful against him.

Men who delight in cavils may ask, who shall be the judge of these occasions? and whether I intend to give to the people the decision of their own cause? To which I answer, that when the contest is between the magistrate and the people, the party, to which the determination is referred, must be the judge of his own case; and the question is only, whether the magistrate should depend upon the judgment of the people, or the people on that of the magistrate, and which is most to be suspected of injustice? that is, whether the people of Rome should judge Tarquin, or Tarquin judge the people? He that knew all good men abhorred him for the murder of his wife, brother, father-in-law, and the best of the senate, would certainly strike off the heads of the most eminent remaining poppies; and having incurred the general hatred of the people by the wickedness of his government, he feared revenge; and endeavouring to destroy those he feared, that is the city, he might easily have accomplished his work, if the judgment had been referred to him. If the people judge Tarquin, it is hard to imagine how they should be brought to give an unjust sentence: they loved their former kings, and hated him only for his villainies: they did not fancy, but know his cruelty. When the best were slain, no man

that any way resembled them could think himself secure. Brutus did not pretend to be a fool, till, by the murder of his brother, he found how dangerous a thing it was to be thought wise. If the people, as our author says, be always lewd, foolish, mad, wicked, and desirous to put the power into the hands of such as are most like to themselves, he and his sons were such men as they fought, and he was sure to find favourable judges: if virtuous and good, no injustice was to be feared from them, and he could have no other reason to decline their judgment, than what was suggested by his own wickedness. Caligula, Nero, Domitian, and the like had probably the same considerations. But no man of common sense ever thought that the senate and people of Rome did not better deserve to judge, whether such monsters should reign over the best part of mankind to their destruction, than they to determine whether their crimes should be punished or not.

If I mention some of these known cases, every man's experience will suggest others of the like nature. And whoever condemns all seditions, tumults, and wars, raised against such princes, must say, that none are wicked, or seek the ruin of their people, which is absurd; for Caligula wished the people had but one neck, that he might cut it off at a blow. Nero set the city on fire. And we have known such as have been worse than either of them. They must either be suffered to continue in the free exercise of their rage, that is, to do all the mischief they design, or must be restrained by a legal, judicial, or extrajudicial way. They who disallow the extrajudicial, do as little like the judicial. They will not hear of bringing a supreme magistrate before a tribunal, when it may be done. "They will," says our author, "depose their kings." Why should they not be deposed, if they become enemies to their people, and set up an interest in their own persons inconsistent with public good, for the promoting of which they were erected? If they were created by the public consent, for the public good, shall they not be removed when they prove to be of public damage? If they set up themselves, may they not be thrown down? Shall it be lawful for them to usurp a power over the liberty of others, and shall it not be lawful for an injured people to resume their own? If injustice exalt itself, must it be for ever established? Shall great persons be rendered sacred by rapine, perjury, and murder? Shall the crimes, for which private men do justly suffer the most grievous punishments, exempt them from all, who commit them in the highest excess, with most power, and most to the prejudice of mankind? Shall the laws that solely aim at the prevention of crimes be made to patronize them, and become snares to the innocent, whom they ought to protect? Has every man given up into the common store his right of avenging the injuries he may receive, that the public power, which ought to protect or avenge him, should be turned to the destruction of himself, his posterity, and the society into which they enter, without any possibility of redress? Shall the ordinance of God be rendered of no effect; or the powers he has appointed to be set up, for the distribution of justice, be made subservient to the lusts of one or a few men, and by impunity encourage them to commit all manner of crimes? Is the corruption of man's nature so little known, that such as have common sense should expect justice from those, who fear no punishment if they do injustice; or that the modesty, integrity, and innocence, which is seldom found in one man, though ever so cautiously chosen, should be constantly found in all those who by any means attain to greatness, and continue for ever in their successors; or that there can be any security under their government, if they have them not? Surely if this were the condition of men living under government, forests would be more safe than cities; and it were better for every man to stand in his own defence, than to enter into societies. He that lives alone might encounter such as should assault him upon equal terms, and stand or fall according to the measure of his courage and strength; but no valour can defend him, if the malice of his enemy be upheld by a public power. There must therefore be a right of proceeding judicially or extrajudicially against all persons who transgress the laws; or else those laws, and the societies that should subsist by them, cannot stand; and the ends for which governments are constituted, together with the governments themselves, must be overthrown. Extrajudicial proceedings, by sedition, tumult, or war, must take place, when the persons concerned are of such power, that they cannot be brought under the judicial. They who deny this deny all help against an usurping tyrant, or the perfidiousness of a lawfully created magistrate, who adds the crimes of ingratitude and treachery to usurpation. These of all men are the most dangerous enemies to supreme magistrates. For as no man desires indemnity for such crimes as are never committed, he that would exempt all from punishment, supposes they will be guilty of the worst; and by concluding, that the people will depose them if they have the power, acknowledges, that they pursue an interest annexed to their persons, contrary to that of their people, which they would not bear if they could deliver themselves from it. This, shewing all those governments to be tyrannical, lays such a burden upon those who administer them, as must necessarily weigh them down to destruction.

If it be said, that the word sedition implies that which is evil, I answer, that it ought not then to be applied to those who seek nothing but that which is just; and though the ways of delivering an oppressed people from the violence of a wicked magistrate, who has armed a crew of lewd villains, and fatted them with the blood and confiscations of such as were most ready to oppose them, be extraordinary, the inward righteousness of the act does fully justify the authors. "He that has virtue and power to save a people, can never want a right of doing it." Valerius Asiaticus had no hand in the death of Caligula; but when the furious guards began tumultuously to inquire who had killed him, he appeased them with wishing he had been the man. No wise man ever asked by what authority Thrasybulus, Harmodius, Aristogiton, Pelopidas, Epaminondas, Dion, Timoleon, Lucius Brutus, Publicola, Horatius, Valerius, Marcus Brutus, Caius Cassius, and the like, delivered their countries from tyrants. Their actions carried in themselves their own justification, and their virtues will never be forgotten, while the names of Greece and Rome are remembered in the world.

If this be not enough to declare the justice inherent in, and the glory that ought to accompany these works, the examples of Moses, Aaron, Othniel, Ehud, Barak, Gideon, Samuel, Jephthah, David, Jehu, Jehoiada, the Maccabees, and other holy men raised up by God for the deliverance of his people from their oppressors, decide the question. They are perpetually renowned for having led the people by extraordinary ways (which such as our author express under the names of sedition, tumult, and war) to recover their liberties, and avenge the injuries received from foreign or domestic tyrants. The work of the apostles was not in their time to set up or pull down any civil state; but they so behaved themselves in relation to all the powers of the earth, that they gained the name of pestilent, seditious fellows, disturbers of the people; and left it as an inheritance to those, who, in succeeding ages, by following their steps, should deserve to be called their successors; whereby they were exposed to the hatred of corrupt magistrates, and brought under the necessity of perishing by them, or defending themselves against them. And he who denies them that right does at once condemn the most glorious actions of the wisest, best, and holiest men that have been in the world, together with the laws of God and man, upon which they were founded.

Nevertheless, there is a sort of sedition, tumult, and war, proceeding from malice, which is always detestable, aiming only at the satisfaction of private lust, without regard to the public good. This cannot happen in a popular government, unless it be among the rabble; or when the body of the people is so corrupted, that it cannot stand; but is most frequent in, and natural to absolute monarchies.

· · · · ·

But if the patience of a conquered people may have limits, and they, who will not bear oppression from those who had spared their lives, may deserve praise and reward from their conquerors, it would be madness to think, that any nation can be obliged to bear whatever their own magistrates think fit to do against them. This may seem strange to those who talk so much of conquests made by kings, immunities, liberties, and privileges, granted to nations, oaths of allegiance taken, and wonderful benefits conferred upon them. But, having already said as much as is needful concerning conquests, and that the magistrate, who has nothing except what is given to him, can only dispense out of the public stock such franchises and privileges as he has received for the reward of services done to the country, and encouragement of virtue, I shall at present keep myself to the two last points.

Allegiance signifies no more (as the words "ad legem" declare) than such an obedience as the law requires. But as the law can require nothing from the whole people, who are masters of it, allegiance can only relate to particulars, and not to the whole nation. No oath can bind any other than whose who take it, and that only in the true sense and meaning of it: but single men only take this oath, and therefore single men are only obliged to keep it. The body of a people neither does, nor can perform any such act. Agreements and contracts have been made; as the tribe of Judah, and the rest of Israel afterward, made a covenant with David, upon which they made him king; but no wise man can think, that the nation did thereby make themselves the creature of their own creature.

The sense also of an oath ought to be considered. No man can by an oath be obliged to any thing beyond, or contrary to the true meaning of it. Private men, who swear obedience "ad legem," swear no obedience "extra" or "contra legem." Whatever they promise or swear can detract nothing from the public liberty, which the law principally intends to preserve. Though many of them may be obliged, in their several stations and capacities, to render peculiar services to a prince, the people continue as free as the internal thoughts of a man, and cannot but have a right to preserve their liberty, or avenge the violation.

If matters are well examined, perhaps not many magistrates can pretend to much upon the title of merit, especially if they or their progenitors have continued long in office. The conveniences annexed to the exercise of the sovereign power may be thought sufficient to pay such scores, as they grow due, even to the best: and as things of that nature are handled, I think it will hardly be found, that all princes can pretend to an irresistible power upon the account of beneficence to their people. When the family of the Medici came to be masters of Tuscany, that country was, without dispute, in men, money, and arms, one of the most flourishing provinces in the world, as appears by Machiavel's account, and the relation of what happened between Charles the eighth, and the magistrates of Florence, which I have mentioned already from Guicciardini. Now, whoever shall consider the strength of that country in those days, together with what it might have been in the space of a hundred and forty years, in which they have had no war, nor any other plague, than the extortion, fraud, rapine, and cruelty of their princes, and compare it with their present desolate, wretched, and contemptible condition, may, if he please, think, that much veneration is due to the princes that govern them; but will never make any man believe, that their title can be grounded upon beneficence. The like may be said of the duke of Savoy, who, pretending, upon I know not what account, that every peasant in the dutchy ought to pay him two crowns every half-year, did in 1662 subtilly find out, that in every year there were thirteen halves; so that a poor man, who had nothing but what he gained by hard labour, was through his fatherly care and beneficence forced to pay six and twenty crowns to his royal highness, to be employed in his discreet and virtuous pleasures at Turin.

The condition of the seventeen provinces of the Netherlands (and even of Spain itself) when they fell to the house of Austria, was of the same nature: and I will confess as much as can be required, if any other marks of their government do remain, than such as are manifest evidences of their pride, avarice, luxury, and cruelty.

France, in outward appearance, makes a better shew; but nothing in this world is more miserable, than that people under the fatherly care of their triumphant monarch. The best of their condition is like asses and mastiff-dogs, to work and fight, to be oppressed and killed for him; and those among them, who have any understanding, well know, that their industry, courage, and good success, is not only unprofitable, but destructive to them; and that, by increasing the power of their master, they add weight to their own chains. And if any prince, or succession of princes, have made a more modest use of their power, or more faithfully discharged the trust reposed in them, it must be imputed peculiarly to them, as a testimony of their personal virtue, and can have no effect upon others.

The rights therefore of kings are not grounded upon conquest: the liberties of nations do not arise from the grants of their princes: the oath of allegiance binds no private man to more than the law directs, and has no influence upon the whole body of every nation. Many princes are known to their subjects only by the injuries, losses, and mischiefs, brought upon them. Such as are good and just ought to be rewarded for their personal virtue, but can confer no right upon those who no way resemble them; and whoever pretends to that merit must prove it by his actions. Rebellion, being nothing but a renewed war, can never be against a government that was not established by war, and of itself is neither good nor evil, more than any other war; but is just or unjust, according to the cause or manner of it. Besides, that rebellion, which by Samuel is compared to witchcraft, is not of private men, or a people, against the prince, but of the prince against God. The Israelites are often said to have rebelled against the law, word, or command of God; but though they frequently opposed their kings, I do not find rebellion imputed to them on that account, nor any ill character put upon such actions. We are told also of some kings who had been subdued, and afterwards rebelled against Chedorlaomer, and other kings; but their cause is not blamed, and we have some reason to believe it good, because Abraham took part with those who had rebelled. However, it can be of no prejudice to the cause I defend: for though it were true, that those subdued kings could not justly rise against the person who had subdued them, or that generally no king, being once vanquished, could have a right of rebellion against his conqueror, it could have no relation to the actions of a people vindicating their own laws and liberties against a prince who violates them; for that war which never was can never be renewed. And if it be true in any case, that hands and swords are given to men, that they only may be slaves who have no courage, it must be when liberty is overthrown by those, who of all men ought with the utmost industry and vigour to have defended it.

That this should be known, is not only necessary for the safety of nations, but advantageous to such kings as are wise and good. They who know the frailty of human nature will always distrust their own; and desiring only to do what they ought, will be glad to be restrained from that which they ought not to do. Being taught by reason and experience, that nations delight in the peace and justice of a good government, they will never fear a general insurrection, whilst they take care it be rightly administered; and finding themselves by this means to be safe will never be unwilling, that their children or successors should be obliged to tread in the same steps.

If it be said, that this may sometimes cause disorders, I acknowledge it; but no human condition being perfect, such a one is to be chosen, which carries with it the most tolerable inconveniences: and it being much better, that the irregularities and excesses of a prince should be restrained or suppressed, than that whole nations should perish by them, those constitutions that make the best provision against the greatest evils are most to be commended. If governments were instituted to gratify the lusts of one man, those could not be good that set limits to them; but all reasonable men confessing that they are instituted for the good of nations, they only can deserve praise, who above all things endeavour to procure it, and appoint means proportioned to that end. The great variety of governments, which we see in the world, is nothing but the effect of this care; and all nations have been, and are more or less happy, as they or their ancestors have had vigour of spirit, integrity of manners, and wisdom to invent and establish such orders, as have better or worse provided for this common good, which was sought by all. But as no rule can be so exact as to make provision against all contestations; and all disputes about right do naturally end in force when justice is denied (ill men never willingly submitting to any decision, that is contrary to their passions and interests) the best constitutions are of no value, if there be not a power to support them. This power first exerts itself in the execution of justice by the ordinary officers. But no nation having been so happy, as not sometimes to produce such princes as Edward the second and Richard the second, and such ministers, as Gaveston, Spencer, and Tresilian, the ordinary officers of justice often want the will, and always the power, to restrain them. So that the rights and liberties of a nation must be utterly subverted and abolished, if the power of the whole may not be employed to assert them, or punish the violation of them. But as it is the fundamental right of every nation to be governed by such laws, in such manner, and by such persons, as they think most conducing to their own good, they cannot be accountable to any but themselves for what they do in that most important affair.

2

JOHN LOCKE, SECOND TREATISE, §§ 149, 155,
168, 207–10, 220–31, 240–43
1689

---

149. Though in a Constituted Commonwealth, standing upon its own Basis, and acting according to its own Nature, that is, acting for the preservation of the Community, there can be but *one Supream Power,* which is *the Legislative,* to which all the rest are and must be subordinate, yet the Legislative being only a Fiduciary Power to act for certain ends, there remains still *in the People a Supream Power* to remove or *alter the Legislative,* when they find the *Legis-*

lative act contrary to the trust reposed in them. For all *Power given with trust* for the attaining an *end,* being limited by that end, whenever that *end* is manifestly neglected, or opposed, the *trust* must necessarily be *forfeited,* and the Power devolve into the hands of those that gave it, who may place it anew where they shall think best for their safety and security. And thus the *Community* perpetually *retains a Supream Power* of saving themselves from the attempts and designs of any Body, even of their Legislators, whenever they shall be so foolish, or so wicked, as to lay and carry on designs against the Liberties and Properties of the Subject. For no Man, or Society of Men, having a Power to deliver up their *Preservation,* or consequently the means of it, to the Absolute Will and arbitrary Dominion of another; whenever any one shall go about to bring them into such a Slavish Condition, they will always have a right to preserve what they have not a Power to part with; and to rid themselves of those who invade this Fundamental, Sacred, and unalterable Law of *Self-Preservation,* for which they enter'd into Society. And thus the *Community* may be said in this respect to be *always the Supream Power,* but not as considered under any Form of Government, because this Power of the People can never take place till the Government be dissolved.

. . . . .

155. It may be demanded here, What if the Executive Power being possessed of the Force of the Commonwealth, shall make use of that force to hinder the *meeting* and *acting of the Legislative,* when the Original Constitution, or the publick Exigencies require it? I say using Force upon the People without Authority, and contrary to the Trust put in him, that does so, is a state of War with the People, who have a right to *reinstate* their *Legislative in the Exercise* of their Power. For having erected a Legislative, with an intent they should exercise the Power of making Laws, either at certain set times, or when there is need of it; when they are hindr'd by any force from, what is so necessary to the Society, and wherein the Safety and preservation of the People consists, the People have a right to remove it by force. In all States and Conditions the true remedy of *Force* without Authority, is to oppose *Force* to it. The use of *force* without Authority, always puts him that uses it into a *state of War,* as the Aggressor, and renders him liable to be treated accordingly.

. . . . .

168. The old Question will be asked in this matter of *Prerogative,* But *who shall be Judge* when this Power is made a right use of? I Answer: Between an Executive Power in being, with such a Prerogative, and a Legislative that depends upon his will for their convening, there can be no *Judge on Earth:* As there can be none, between the Legislative, and the People, should either the Executive, or the Legislative, when they have got the Power in their hands, design, or go about to enslave, or destroy them. The People have no other remedy in this, as in all other cases where they have no Judge on Earth, but to *appeal to Heaven.* For the Rulers, in such attempts, exercising a Power the People never put into their hands (who can never be supposed to consent, that any body should rule

over them for their harm) do that, which they have not a right to do. And where the Body of the People, or any single Man, is deprived of their Right, or is under the Exercise of a power without right, and have no Appeal on Earth, there they have a liberty to appeal to Heaven, whenever they judge the Cause of sufficient moment. And therefore, tho' the *People* cannot be *Judge,* so as to have by the Constitution of that Society any Superiour power, to determine and give effective Sentence in the case; yet they have, by a Law antecedent and paramount to all positive Laws of men, reserv'd that ultimate Determination to themselves, which belongs to all Mankind, where there lies no Appeal on Earth, *viz.* to judge whether they have just Cause to make their Appeal to Heaven. And this Judgment they cannot part with, it being out of a Man's power so to submit himself to another, as to give him a liberty to destroy him; God and Nature never allowing a Man so to abandon himself, as to neglect his own preservation: And since he cannot take away his own Life, neither can he give another power to take it. Nor let any one think, this lays a perpetual foundation for Disorder: for this operates not, till the Inconvenience is so great, that the Majority feel it, and are weary of it, and find a necessity to have it amended. But this the Executive Power, or wise Princes, never need come in the danger of: And 'tis the thing of all others, they have most need to avoid, as of all others the most perilous.

. . . . .

207. *Thirdly,* Supposing a Government wherein the Person of the Chief Magistrate is not thus Sacred; yet this *Doctrine* of the lawfulness of *resisting* all unlawful exercises of his Power, *will not* upon every slight occasion indanger him, or *imbroil the Government.* For where the injured Party may be relieved, and his damages repaired by Appeal to the Law, there can be no pretence for Force, which is only to be used, where a Man is intercepted from appealing to the Law. For nothing is to be accounted Hostile Force, but where it leaves not the remedy of such an Appeal. And 'tis such *Force* alone, that *puts* him that uses it *into a state of War,* and makes it lawful to resist him. A Man with a Sword in his Hand demands my Purse in the High-way, when perhaps I have not 12 *d.* in my Pocket; This Man I may lawfully kill. To another I deliver 100 *l.* to hold only whilst I alight, which he refuses to restore me, when I am got up again, but draws his Sword to defend the possession of it by force, if I endeavour to retake it. The mischief this Man does me, is a hundred, or possibly a thousand times more, than the other perhaps intended me, (whom I killed before he really did me any) and yet I might lawfully kill the one, and cannot so much as hurt the other lawfully. The Reason whereof is plain; because the one using *force,* which threatned my Life, I could not have *time to appeal* to the Law to secure it: And when it was gone, 'twas too late to appeal. The Law could not restore Life to my dead Carcass: The Loss was irreparable; which to prevent, the Law of Nature gave me a Right to *destroy* him, who had put himself into a state of War with me, and threatned my destruction. But in the other case, my Life not being in danger, I may have the *benefit of appeal-*

ing to the Law, and have Reparation for my 100 *l.* that way.

208. *Fourthly,* But if the unlawful acts done by the Magistrate, be maintained (by the Power he has got) and the remedy which is due by Law, be by the same Power obstructed; yet the *Right of resisting,* even in such manifest Acts of Tyranny, *will not* suddenly, or on slight occasions, *disturb the Government.* For if it reach no farther than some private Mens Cases, though they have a right to defend themselves, and to recover by force, what by unlawful force is taken from them; yet the Right to do so, will not easily ingage them in a Contest, wherein they are sure to perish; it being as impossible for one or a few oppressed Men to *disturb the Government,* where the Body of the People do not think themselves concerned in it, as for a raving mad Man, or heady Male-content to overturn a well-settled State; the People being as little apt to follow the one, as the other.

209. But if either these illegal Acts have extended to the Majority of the People; or if the Mischief and Oppression has light only on some few, but in such Cases, as the Precedent, and Consequences seem to threaten all, and they are perswaded in their Consciences, that their Laws, and with them their Estates, Liberties, and Lives are in danger, and perhaps their Religion too, how they will be hindered from resisting illegal force, used against them, I cannot tell. This is an *Inconvenience,* I confess, that *attends all Governments* whatsoever, when the Governours have brought it to this pass, to be generally suspected of their People; the most dangerous state which they can possibly put themselves in: wherein they are the less to be pitied, because it is so easie to be avoided; It being as impossible for a Governor, if he really means the good of his People, and the preservation of them and their Laws together, not to make them see and feel it; as it is for the Father of a Family, not to let his Children see he loves, and takes care of them.

210. But if all the World shall observe Pretences of one kind, and Actions of another; Arts used to elude the Law, and the Trust of Prerogative (which is an Arbitrary Power in some things left in the Prince's hand to do good, not harm to the People) employed contrary to the end, for which it was given: if the People shall find the Ministers, and subordinate Magistrates chosen suitable to such ends, and favoured, or laid by proportionably, as they promote, or oppose them: If they see several Experiments made of Arbitrary Power, and that Religion underhand favoured (though publickly proclaimed against) which is readiest to introduce it, and the Operators in it supported, as much as may be; and when that cannot be done, yet approved still, and liked the better: if a *long Train of Actings shew the Councils* all tending that way, how can a Man any more hinder himself from being perswaded in his own Mind, which way things are going; or from casting about how to save himself, than he could from believing the Captain of the Ship he was in, was carrying him, and the rest of the Company to *Algiers,* when he found him always steering that Course, though cross Winds, Leaks in his Ship, and

want of Men and Provisions did often force him to turn his Course another way for some time, which he steadily returned to again, as soon as the Wind, Weather, and other Circumstances would let him?

. . . . .

220. In these and the like Cases, *when the Government is dissolved,* the People are at liberty to provide for themselves, by erecting a new Legislative, differing from the other, by the change of Persons, or Form, or both as they shall find it most for their safety and good. For the *Society* can never, by the fault of another, lose the Native and Original Right it has to preserve it self, which can only be done by a settled Legislative, and a fair and impartial execution of the Laws made by it. But the state of Mankind is not so miserable that they are not capable of using this Remedy, till it be too late to look for any. To tell *People* they *may provide for themselves,* by erecting a new Legislative, when by Oppression, Artifice, or being delivered over to a Foreign Power, their old one is gone, is only to tell them they may expect Relief, when it is too late, and the evil is past Cure. This is in effect no more than to bid them first be Slaves, and then to take care of their Liberty; and when their Chains are on, tell them, they may act like Freemen. This, if barely so, is rather Mockery than Relief; and Men can never be secure from Tyranny, if there be no means to escape it, till they are perfectly under it: And therefore it is, that they have not only a Right to get out of it, but to prevent it.

221. There is therefore, secondly, another way whereby *Governments are dissolved,* and that is; when the Legislative, or the Prince, either of them act contrary to their Trust.

First, The *Legislative acts against the Trust* reposed in them, when they endeavour to invade the Property of the Subject, and to make themselves, or any part of the Community, Masters, or Arbitrary Disposers of the Lives, Liberties, or Fortunes of the People.

222. The Reason why Men enter into Society, is the preservation of their Property; and the end why they chuse and authorize a Legislative, is, that there may be Laws made, and Rules set as Guards and Fences to the Properties of all the Members of the Society, to limit the Power, and moderate the Dominion of every Part and Member of the Society. For since it can never be supposed to be the Will of the Society, that the Legislative should have a Power to destroy that, which every one designs to secure, by entering into Society, and for which the People submitted themselves to the Legislators of their own making; whenever the *Legislators endeavour to take away, and destroy the Property of the People,* or to reduce them to Slavery under Arbitrary Power, they put themselves into a state of War with the People, who are thereupon absolved from any farther Obedience, and are left to the common Refuge, which God hath provided for all Men, against Force and Violence. Whensoever therefore the *Legislative* shall transgress this fundamental Rule of Society; and either by Ambition, Fear, Folly or Corruption, *endeavour to grasp* themselves, *or put into the hands of any other an Absolute Power* over the Lives, Liberties, and Estates of the People;

By this breach of Trust they *forfeit the Power,* the People had put into their hands, for quite contrary ends, and it devolves to the People, who have a Right to resume their original Liberty, and, by the Establishment of a new Legislative (such as they shall think fit) provide for their own Safety and Security, which is the end for which they are in Society. What I have said here, concerning the Legislative, in general, holds true also concerning the *supreame Executor,* who having a double trust put in him, both to have a part in the Legislative, and the supreme Execution of the Law, Acts against both, when he goes about to set up his own Arbitrary Will, as the Law of the Society. He *acts* also *contrary to his Trust,* when he either imploys the Force, Treasure, and Offices of the Society, to corrupt the *Representatives,* and gain them to his purposes: or openly preingages the *Electors,* and prescribes to their choice, such, whom he has by Sollicitations, Threats, Promises, or otherwise won to his designs; and imploys them to bring in such, who have promised before-hand, what to Vote, and what to Enact. Thus to regulate Candidates and *Electors,* and new model the ways of *Election,* what is it but to cut up the Government by the Roots, and poison the very Fountain of publick Security? For the People having reserved to themselves the Choice of their *Representatives,* as the Fence to their Properties, could do it for no other end, but that they might always be freely chosen, and so chosen, freely act and advise, as the necessity of the Commonwealth, and the publick Good should, upon examination, and mature debate, be judged to require. This, those who give their Votes before they hear the Debate, and have weighed the Reasons on all sides, are not capable of doing. To prepare such an Assembly as this, and endeavour to set up the declared Abettors of his own Will, for the true *Representatives* of the People, and the Law-makers of the Society, is certainly as great a *breach of trust,* and as perfect a Declaration of a design to subvert the Government, as is possible to be met with. To which, if one shall add Rewards and Punishments visibly imploy'd to the same end, and all the Arts of perverted Law made use of, to take off and destroy all that stand in the way of such a design, and will not comply and consent to betray the Liberties of their Country, 'twill be past doubt what is doing. What Power they ought to have in the Society, who thus imploy it contrary to the trust went along with it in its first Institution, is easie to determine; and one cannot but see, that he, who has once attempted any such thing as this, cannot any longer be trusted.

223. To this perhaps it will be said, that the People being ignorant, and always discontented, to lay the Foundation of Government in the unsteady Opinion, and uncertain Humour of the People, is to expose it to certain ruine; And *no Government will be able long to subsist,* if the People may set up a new Legislative, whenever they take offence at the old one. To this, I Answer: Quite the contrary. People are not so easily got out of their old Forms, as some are apt to suggest. They are hardly to be prevailed with to amend the acknowledg'd Faults, in the Frame they have been accustom'd to. And if there be any Original de-

fects, or adventitious ones introduced by time, or corruption; 'tis not an easie thing to get them changed, even when all the World sees there is an opportunity for it. This slowness and aversion in the People to quit their old Constitutions, has, in the many Revolutions which have been seen in this Kingdom, in this and former Ages, still kept us to, or, after some interval of fruitless attempts, still brought us back again to our old Legislative of King, Lords and Commons: And whatever provocations have made the Crown be taken from some of our Princes Heads, they never carried the People so far, as to place it in another Line.

224. But 'twill be said, this *Hypothesis* lays a *ferment* for frequent *Rebellion*. To which I Answer,

First, No more than any other *Hypothesis*. For when the *People* are made *miserable*, and find themselves *exposed to the ill usage of Arbitrary Power*, cry up their Governours, as much as you will for Sons of *Jupiter*, let them be Sacred and Divine, descended or authoriz'd from Heaven; give them out for whom or what you please, the same will happen. *The People generally ill treated*, and contrary to right, will be ready upon any occasion to ease themselves of a burden that sits heavy upon them. They will wish and seek for the opportunity, which, in the change, weakness, and accidents of humane affairs, seldom delays long to offer it self. He must have lived but a little while in the World, who has not seen Examples of this in his time; and he must have read very little, who cannot produce Examples of it in all sorts of Governments in the World.

225. Secondly, I Answer, such *Revolutions happen* not upon every little mismanagement in publick affairs. *Great mistakes* in the ruling part, many wrong and inconvenient Laws, and all the *slips* of humane frailty will be *born by the People*, without mutiny or murmur. But if a long train of Abuses, Prevarications, and Artifices, all tending the same way, make the design visible to the People, and they cannot but feel, what they lie under, and see, whither they are going; 'tis not to be wonder'd, that they should then rouze themselves, and endeavour to put the rule into such hands, which may secure to them the ends for which Government was at first erected; and without which, ancient Names, and specious Forms, are so far from being better, that they are much worse, than the state of Nature, or pure Anarchy; the inconveniencies being all as great and as near, but the remedy farther off and more difficult.

226. Thirdly, I Answer, That *this Doctrine* of a Power in the People of providing for their safety a-new by a new Legislative, when their Legislators have acted contrary to their trust, by invading their Property, is *the best fence against Rebellion*, and the probablest means to hinder it. For Rebellion being an Opposition, not to Persons, but Authority, which is founded only in the Constitutions and Laws of the Government; those, whoever they be, who by force break through, and by force justifie their violation of them, are truly and properly *Rebels*. For when Men by entering into Society and Civil Government, have excluded force, and introduced Laws for the preservation of Property, Peace, and Unity amongst themselves; those who set up force again in opposition to the Laws, do *Rebellare*, that is, bring back again the state of War, and are properly Rebels: Which they who are in Power (by the pretence they have to Authority, the temptation of force they have in their hands, and the Flattery of those about them) being likeliest to do; the properest way to prevent the evil, is to shew them the danger and injustice of it, who are under the greatest temptation to run into it.

227. In both the forementioned Cases, when either the Legislative is changed, or the Legislators act contrary to the end for which they were constituted; those who are guilty are *guilty of Rebellion*. For if any one by force takes away the establish'd Legislative of any Society, and the Laws by them made pursuant to their trust, he thereby takes away the Umpirage, which every one had consented to, for a peaceable decision of all their Controversies, and a bar to the state of War amongst them. They, who remove, or change the Legislative, take away this decisive power, which no Body can have, but by the appointment and consent of the People; and so destroying the Authority, which the People did, and no Body else can set up, and introducing a Power, which the People hath not authoriz'd, they actually *introduce a state of War*, which is that of Force without Authority: And thus by removing the Legislative establish'd by the Society (in whose decisions the People acquiesced and united, as to that of their own will) they unty the Knot, and *expose the People a new to the state of War*. And if those, who by force take away the Legislative, are *Rebels*, the *Legislators* themselves, as has been shewn, can be no less esteemed so; when they, who were set up for the protection, and preservation of the People, their Liberties and Properties, shall by force invade, and indeavour to take them away; and so they putting themselves into a state of War with those, who made them the Protectors and Guardians of their Peace, are properly, and with the greatest aggravation, *Rebellantes* Rebels.

228. But if they, who say it *lays a foundation for Rebellion*, mean that it may occasion Civil Wars, or Intestine Broils, to tell the People they are absolved from Obedience, when illegal attempts are made upon their Liberties or Properties, and may oppose the unlawful violence of those, who were their Magistrates, when they invade their Properties contrary to the trust put in them; and that therefore this Doctrine is not to be allow'd, being so destructive to the Peace of the World. They may as well say upon the same ground, that honest Men may not oppose Robbers or Pirates, because this may occasion disorder or bloodshed. If any *mischief* come in such Cases, it is not *to be charged* upon him, who defends his own right, but *on him*, that *invades* his Neighbours. If the innocent honest Man must quietly quit all he has for Peace sake, to him who will lay violent hands upon it, I desire it may be consider'd, what a kind of Peace there will be in the World, which consists only in Violence and Rapine; and which is to be maintain'd only for the benefit of Robbers and Oppressors. Who would not think it an admirable Peace betwixt the Mighty and the Mean, when the Lamb, without resistance, yielded his Throat to be torn by the imperious Wolf? *Polyphemus's* Den

gives us a perfect Pattern of such a Peace, and such a Government, where in *Ulysses* and his Companions had nothing to do, but quietly to suffer themselves to be devour'd. And no doubt *Ulysses,* who was a prudent Man, preach'd up *Passive Obedience,* and exhorted them to a quiet Submission, by representing to them of what concernment Peace was to Mankind; and by shewing the inconveniencies might happen, if they should offer to resist *Polyphemus,* who had now the power over them.

229. The end of Government is the good of Mankind, and which is *best for Mankind,* that the People should be always expos'd to the boundless will of Tyranny, or that the Rulers should be sometimes liable to be oppos'd, when they grow exorbitant in the use of their Power, and imploy it for the destruction, and not the preservation of the Properties of their People?

230. Nor let any one say, that mischief can arise from hence, as often as it shall please a busie head, or turbulent spirit, to desire the alteration of the Government. 'Tis true, such Men may stir, whenever they please, but it will be only to their own just ruine and perdition. For till the mischief be grown general, and the ill designs of the Rulers become visible, or their attempts sensible to the greater part, the People, who are more disposed to suffer, than right themselves by Resistance, are not apt to stir. The examples of particular Injustice, or Oppression of here and there an unfortunate Man, moves them not. But if they universally have a perswasion, grounded upon manifest evidence, that designs are carrying on against their Liberties, and the general course and tendency of things cannot but give them strong suspicions of the evil intention of their Governors, who is to be blamed for it? Who can help it, if they, who might avoid it, bring themselves into this suspicion? Are the People to be blamed, if they have the sence of rational Creatures, and can think of things no otherwise than as they find and feel them? And is it not rather *their fault,* who puts things in such a posture that they would not have them thought, to be as they are? I grant, that the Pride, Ambition, and Turbulency of private Men have sometimes caused great Disorders in Commonwealths, and Factions have been fatal to States and Kingdoms. But whether the *mischief* hath *oftner* begun *in the Peoples Wantonness,* and a Desire to cast off the lawful Authority of their Rulers; or *in the Rulers Insolence,* and Endeavours to get, and exercise an Arbitrary Power over their People; whether Opression, or Disobedience gave the first rise to the Disorder, I leave it to impartial History to determine. This I am sure, whoever, either Ruler or Subject, by force goes about to invade the Rights of either Prince or People, and lays the foundation for *overturning* the Constitution and Frame of *any Just Government,* is guilty of the greatest Crime, I think, a Man is capable of, being to answer for all those mischiefs of Blood, Rapine, and Desolation, which the breaking to pieces of Governments bring on a Countrey. And he who does it, is justly to be esteemed the common Enemy and Pest of Mankind; and is to be treated accordingly.

231. That *Subjects,* or *Foreigners* attempting by force on the Properties of any People, may be *resisted* with force, is agreed on all hands. But that *Magistrates* doing the same thing, may be *resisted,* hath of late been denied: As if those who had the greatest Priviledges and Advantages by the Law, had thereby a Power to break those Laws, by which alone they were set in a better place than their Brethren: Whereas their Offence is thereby the greater, both as being ungrateful for the greater share they have by the Law, and breaking also that Trust, which is put into their hands by their Brethren.

. . . . .

240. Here, 'tis like, the common Question will be made, *Who shall be Judge* whether the Prince or Legislative act contrary to their Trust? This, perhaps, ill affected and factious Men may spread amongst the People, when the Prince only makes use of his due Prerogative. To this I reply, *The People shall be Judge;* for who shall be *Judge* whether his Trustee or Deputy acts well, and according to the Trust reposed in him, but he who deputes him, and must, by having deputed him have still a Power to discard him, when he fails in his Trust? If this be reasonable in particular Cases of private Men, why should it be otherwise in that of the greatest moment; where the Welfare of Millions is concerned, and also where the evil, if not prevented, is greater, and the Redress very difficult, dear, and dangerous?

241. But farther, this Question, *(Who shall be Judge?)* cannot mean, that there is no Judge at all. For where there is no Judicature on Earth, to decide Controversies, amongst Men, *God* in Heaven is *Judge:* He alone, 'tis true, is Judge of the Right. But *every Man is Judge* for himself, as in all other Cases, so in this, whether another hath put himself into a State of War with him, and whether he should appeal to the Supreme Judge, as *Jephtha* did.

242. If a Controversie arise betwixt a Prince and some of the People, in a matter where the Law is silent, or doubtful, and the thing be of great Consequence, I should think the proper *Umpire,* in such a Case, should be the Body of the *People.* For in Cases where the Prince hath a Trust reposed in him, and is dispensed from the common ordinary Rules of the Law; there, if any Men find themselves aggrieved, and think the Prince acts contrary to, or beyond that Trust, who so proper to *Judge* as the Body of the *People,* (who, at first, lodg'd that Trust in him) how far they meant it should extend? But if the Prince, or whoever they be in the Administration, decline that way of Determination, the Appeal then lies no where but to Heaven. Force between either Persons, who have no known Superiour on Earth, or which permits no Appeal to a Judge on Earth, being properly a state of War, wherein the Appeal lies only to Heaven, and in that State the *injured Party must judge* for himself, when he will think fit to make use of that Appeal, and put himself upon it.

243. To conclude, The *Power that every individual gave the Society,* when he entered into it, can never revert to the Individuals again, as long as the Society lasts, but will al-

ways remain in the Community; because without this, there can be no Community, no Common-wealth, which is contrary to the original Agreement: So also when the Society hath placed the Legislative in any Assembly of Men, to continue in them and their Successors, with Direction and Authority for providing such Successors, *the Legislative can never revert to the People* whilst that Government lasts: Because having provided a Legislative with Power to continue for ever, they have given up their Political Power to the Legislative, and cannot resume it. But if they have set Limits to the Duration of their Legislative, and made this Supreme Power in any Person, or Assembly, only temporary: Or else when by the Miscarriages of those in Authority, it is forfeited; upon the Forfeiture of their Rulers, or at the Determination of the Time set, *it reverts to the Society,* and the People have a Right to act as Supreme, and continue the Legislative in themselves, or erect a new Form, or under the old form place it in new hands, as they think good.

3

WILLIAM BLACKSTONE, COMMENTARIES
1:119–23, 157, 237–38, 243–44
1765

Now the rights of persons that are commanded to be observed by the municipal law are of two sorts; first, such as are due *from* every citizen, which are usually called civil *duties;* and, secondly, such as belong *to* him, which is the more popular acceptation of *rights* or *jura.* Both may indeed be comprized in this latter division; for, as all social duties are of a relative nature, at the same time that they are due *from* one man, or set of men, they must also be due *to* another. But I apprehend it will be more clear and easy, to consider many of them as duties required from, rather than as rights belonging to, particular persons. Thus, for instance, allegiance is usually, and therefore most easily, considered as the duty of the people, and protection as the duty of the magistrate; and yet they are, reciprocally, the rights as well as duties of each other. Allegiance is the right of the magistrate, and protection the right of the people.

Persons also are divided by the law into either natural persons, or artificial. Natural persons are such as the God of nature formed us: artificial are such as created and devised by human laws for the purposes of society and government; which are called corporations or bodies politic.

The rights of persons considered in their natural capacities are also of two sorts, absolute, and relative. Absolute, which are such as appertain and belong to particular men, merely as individuals or single persons: relative, which are incident to them as members of society, and standing in various relations to each other. The first, that is, absolute rights, will be the subject of the present chapter.

By the absolute *rights* of individuals we mean those which are so in their primary and strictest sense; such as would belong to their persons merely in a state of nature, and which every man is intitled to enjoy whether out of society or in it. But with regard to the absolute *duties,* which man is bound to perform considered as a mere individual, it is not to be expected that any human municipal laws should at all explain or enforce them. For the end and intent of such laws being only to regulate the behaviour of mankind, as they are members of society, and stand in various relations to each other, they have consequently no business or concern with any but social or relative duties. Let a man therefore be ever so abandoned in his principles, or vitious in his practice, provided he keeps his wickedness to himself, and does not offend against the rules of public decency, he is out of the reach of human laws. But if he makes his vices public, though they be such as seem principally to affect himself, (as drunkenness, or the like) they then become, by the bad example they set, of pernicious effects to society; and therefore it is then the business of human laws to correct them. Here the circumstance of publication is what alters the nature of the case. *Public* sobriety is a relative duty, and therefore enjoined by our laws: *private* sobriety is an absolute duty, which, whether it be performed or not, human tribunals can never know; and therefore they can never enforce it by any civil sanction. But, with respect to *rights,* the case is different. Human laws define and enforce as well those rights which belong to a man considered as an individual, as those which belong to him considered as related to others.

For the principal aim of society is to protect individuals in the enjoyment of those absolute rights, which were vested in them by the immutable laws of nature; but which could not be preserved in peace without that mutual assistance and intercourse, which is gained by the institution of friendly and social communities. Hence it follows, that the first and primary end of human laws is to maintain and regulate these *absolute* rights of individuals. Such rights as are social and *relative* result from, and are posterior to, the formation of states and societies: so that to maintain and regulate these, is clearly a subsequent consideration. And therefore the principal view of human laws is, or ought always to be, to explain, protect, and enforce such rights as are absolute, which in themselves are few and simple; and, then, such rights as are relative, which arising from a variety of connexions, will be far more numerous and more complicated. These will take up a greater space in any code of laws, and hence may appear to be more attended to, though in reality they are not, than the rights of the former kind. Let us therefore proceed to examine how far all laws ought, and how far the laws of England actually do, take notice of these absolute rights, and provide for their lasting security.

The absolute rights of man, considered as a free agent, endowed with discernment to know good from evil, and with power of choosing those measures which appear to him to be most desirable, are usually summed up in one general appellation, and denominated the natural liberty of mankind. This natural liberty consists properly in a power of acting as one thinks fit, without any restraint or control, unless by the law of nature: being a right inherent in us by birth, and one of the gifts of God to man at his creation, when he endued him with the faculty of free-will. But every man, when he enters into society, gives up a part of his natural liberty, as the price of so valuable a purchase; and, in consideration of receiving the advantages of mutual commerce, obliges himself to conform to those laws, which the community has thought proper to establish. And this species of legal obedience and conformity is infinitely more desirable, than that wild and savage liberty which is sacrificed to obtain it. For no man, that considers a moment, would wish to retain the absolute and uncontroled power of doing whatever he pleases; the consequence of which is, that every other man would also have the same power; and then there would be no security to individuals in any of the enjoyments of life. Political therefore, or civil, liberty, which is that of a member of society, is no other than natural liberty so far restrained by human laws (and no farther) as is necessary and expedient for the general advantage of the publick. Hence we may collect that the law, which restrains a man from doing mischief to his fellow citizens, though it diminishes the natural, increases the civil liberty of mankind: but every wanton and causeless restraint of the will of the subject, whether practiced by a monarch, a nobility, or a popular assembly, is a degree of tyranny. Nay, that even laws themselves, whether made with or without our consent, if they regulate and constrain our conduct in matters of mere indifference, without any good end in view, are laws destructive of liberty: whereas if any public advantage can arise from observing such precepts, the control of our private inclinations, in one or two particular points, will conduce to preserve our general freedom in others of more importance; by supporting that state, of society, which alone can secure our independence. Thus the statute of king Edward IV, which forbad the fine gentlemen of those times (under the degree of a lord) to wear pikes upon their shoes or boots of more than two inches in length, was a law that savoured of oppression; because, however ridiculous the fashion then in use might appear, the restraining it by pecuniary penalties could serve no purpose of common utility. But the statute of king Charles II, which prescribes a thing seemingly as indifferent; viz. a dress for the dead, who are all ordered to be buried in woollen; is a law consistent with public liberty, for it encourages the staple trade, on which in great measure depends the universal good of the nation. So that laws, when prudently framed, are by no means subversive but rather introductive of liberty; for (as Mr Locke has well observed) where there is no law, there is no freedom. But then, on the other hand, that constitution or frame of government, that system of laws, is alone calculated to maintain civil liberty, which leaves the subject entire master of his own conduct, except in those points wherein the public good requires some direction or restraint.

The idea and practice of this political or civil liberty flourish in their highest vigour in these kingdoms, where it falls little short of perfection, and can only be lost or destroyed by the folly or demerits of it's owner: the legislature, and of course the laws of England, being peculiarly adapted to the preservation of this inestimable blessing even in the meanest subject. Very different from the modern constitutions of other states, on the continent of Europe, and from the genius of the imperial law; which in general are calculated to vest an arbitrary and despotic power of controlling the actions of the subject in the prince, or in a few grandees. And this spirit of liberty is so deeply implanted in our constitution, and rooted even in our very soil, that a slave or a negro, the moment he lands in England, falls under the protection of the laws, and with regard to all natural rights becomes *eo instanti* a freeman.

The absolute rights of every Englishman (which, taken in a political and extensive sense, are usually called their liberties) as they are founded on nature and reason, so they are coeval with our form of government; though subject at times to fluctuate and change: their establishment (excellent as it is) being still human. At some times we have seen them depressed by overbearing and tyrannical princes; at others so luxuriant as even to tend to anarchy, a worse state than tyranny itself, as any government is better than none at all. But the vigour of our free constitution has always delivered the nation from these embarassments, and, as soon as the convulsions consequent on the struggle have been over, the ballance of our rights and liberties has settled to it's proper level; and their fundamental articles have been from time to time asserted in parliament, as often as they were thought to be in danger.

. . . . .

It must be owned that Mr Locke, and other theoretical writers, have held, that "there remains still inherent in the people a supreme power to remove or alter the legislative, when they find the legislative act contrary to the trust reposed in them: for when such trust is abused, it is thereby forfeited, and devolves to those who gave it." But however just this conclusion may be in theory, we cannot adopt it, nor argue from it, under any dispensation of government at present actually existing. For this devolution of power, to the people at large, includes in it a dissolution of the whole form of government established by that people, reduces all the members to their original state of equality, and by annihilating the sovereign power repeals all positive laws whatsoever before enacted. No human laws will therefore suppose a case, which at once must destroy all law, and compel men to build afresh upon a new foundation; nor will they make provision for so desperate an event, as must render all legal provisions ineffectual. So long therefore as the English constitution lasts, we may venture to affirm, that the power of parliament is absolute and without control.

. . . . .

Next, as to cases of ordinary public oppression, where the vitals of the constitution are not attacked, the law hath also assigned a remedy. For, as a king cannot misuse his power, without the advice of evil counsellors, and the assistance of wicked ministers, these men may be examined and punished. The constitution has therefore provided, by means of indictments, and parliamentary impeachments, that no man shall dare to assist the crown in contradiction to the laws of the land. But it is at the same time a maxim in those laws, that the king himself can do no wrong; since it would be a great weakness and absurdity in any system of positive law, to define any possible wrong, without any possible redress.

For, as to such public oppressions as tend to dissolve the constitution, and subvert the fundamentals of government, they are cases which the law will not, out of decency, suppose; being incapable of distrusting those, whom it has invested with any part of the supreme power; since such distrust would render the exercise of that power precarious and impracticable. For, where-ever the law expresses it's distrust of abuse of power, it always vests a superior coercive authority in some other hand to correct it; the very notion of which destroys the idea of sovereignty. If therefore (for example) the two houses of parliament, or either of them, had avowedly a right to animadvert on the king, or each other, or if the king had a right to animadvert on either of the houses, that branch of the legislature, so subject to animadversion, would instantly cease to be part of the supreme power; the ballance of the constitution would be overturned; and that branch or branches, in which this jurisdiction resided, would be completely sovereign. The supposition of *law* therefore is, that neither the king nor either house of parliament (collectively taken) is capable of doing any wrong; since in such cases the law feels itself incapable of furnishing any adequate remedy. For which reason all oppressions, which may happen to spring from any branch of the sovereign power, must necessarily be out of the reach of any *stated rule*, or *express legal* provision: but, if ever they unfortunately happen, the prudence of the times must provide new remedies upon new emergencies.

Indeed, it is found by experience, that whenever the unconstitutional oppressions, even of the sovereign power, advance with gigantic strides and threaten desolation to a state, mankind will not be reasoned out of the feelings of humanity; nor will sacrifice their liberty by a scrupulous adherence to those political maxims, which were originally established to preserve it. And therefore, though the positive laws are silent, experience will furnish us with a very remarkable case, wherein nature and reason prevailed. When king James the second invaded the fundamental constitution of the realm, the convention declared an abdication, whereby the throne was rendered vacant, which induced a new settlement of the crown. And so far as this precedent leads, and no farther, we may now be allowed to lay down the *law* of redress against public oppression. If therefore any future prince should endeavour to subvert the constitution by breaking the original contract between king and people, should violate the fundamental laws, and should withdraw himself out of the kingdom; we are now authorized to declare that this conjunction of circumstances would amount to an abdication, and the throne would be thereby vacant. But it is not for us to say, that any one, or two, of these ingredients would amount

to such a situation; for there our precedent would fail us. In these therefore, or other circumstances, which a fertile imagination may furnish, since both law and history are silent, it becomes us to be silent too; leaving to future generations, whenever necessity and the safety of the whole shall require it, the exertion of those inherent (though latent) powers of society, which no climate, no time, no constitution, no contract, can ever destroy or diminish.

. . . . .

After what has been premised in this chapter, I shall not (I trust) be considered as an advocate for arbitrary power, when I lay it down as a principle, that in the exertion of lawful prerogative, the king is and ought to be absolute; that is, so far absolute, that there is no legal authority that can either delay or resist him. He may reject what bills, may make what treaties, may coin what money, may create what peers, may pardon what offences he pleases: unless where the constitution hath expressly, or by evident consequence, laid down some exception or boundary; declaring, that thus far the prerogative shall go and no farther. For otherwise the power of the crown would indeed be but a name and a shadow, insufficient for the ends of government, if, where it's jurisdiction is clearly established and allowed, any man or body of men were permitted to disobey it, in the ordinary course of law: I say, in the *ordinary* course of law; for I do not now speak of those *extraordinary* recourses to first principles, which are necessary when the contracts of society are in danger of dissolution, and the law proves too weak a defence against the violence of fraud or oppression. And yet the want of attending to this obvious distinction has occasioned these doctrines, of absolute power in the prince and of national resistance by the people, to be much misunderstood and perverted by the advocates for slavery on the one hand, and the demagogues of faction on the other. The former, observing the absolute sovereignty and transcendent dominion of the crown laid down (as it certainly is) most strongly and emphatically in our lawbooks, as well as our homilies, have denied that any case can be excepted from so general and positive a rule; forgetting how impossible it is, in any practical system of laws, to point out beforehand those eccentrical remedies, which the sudden emergence of national distress may dictate, and which that alone can justify. On the other hand, over-zealous republicans, feeling the absurdity of unlimited passive obedience, have fancifully (or sometimes factiously) gone over to the other extreme: and, because resistance is justifiable to the person of the prince when the being of the state is endangered, and the public voice proclaims such resistance necessary, they have therefore allowed to every individual the right of determining this expedience, and of employing private force to resist even private oppression. A doctrine productive of anarchy, and (in consequence) equally fatal to civil liberty as tyranny itself. For civil liberty, rightly understood, consists in protecting the rights of individuals by the united force of society: society cannot be maintained, and of course can exert no protection, without obedience to some sovereign power: and obedience is an empty name, if every individual has a right to decide how far he himself shall obey.

4

SAMUEL ADAMS, BOSTON GAZETTE
27 Feb. 1769
Writings 1:316–19

In the days of the STUARTS, it was look'd upon by some men as a high degree of prophaness, for any subject to enquire into what was called the *mysteries of government*: *James* the first thundered his anathema against Dr. *Cowel,* for his daring presumption in treating of—those *mysteries;* and forbad his subjects to read his books, or even to keep them in their houses. In those days *passive obedience, non-resistance,* the *divine hereditary right* of kings, and their being accountable to God *alone,* were doctrines generally taught, believ'd and practiced: But behold the sudden transition of human affairs! In the very next reign the people assum'd the right of *free enquiry,* into the nature and end of government, and the conduct of those who were entrusted with it: *Laud* and *Strafford* were bro't to the block; and after the horrors of a civil war, in which some of the best blood of the nation was spilt as water upon the ground, they finally called to account, arraign'd, adjudg'd, condemn'd and even executed the monarch himself! and for a time held his son and heir in exile. The two sons of *Charles* the first, after the death of *Oliver Cromwell,* reigned in their turns; but by copying after their father, their administration of government was *grievous* to their subjects, and *infamous* abroad. *Charles* the second indeed reign'd till he died; but his brother *James* was oblig'd to abdicate the throne, which made room for *William* the third, and his royal consort *Mary,* the daughter of the unfortunate *James*—This was the fate of a race of Kings, bigotted to the greatest degree to the doctrines of *slavery* and regardless of the *natural, inherent, divinely hereditary* and *indefeasible* rights of their subjects.—At the revolution, the British constitution was again restor'd to its original principles, declared in the bill of rights; which was afterwards pass'd into a law, and stands as a bulwark to the natural rights of subjects. "To vindicate these rights, says Mr. *Blackstone,* when actually violated or attack'd, the subjects of England are entitled first to the regular administration and *free course of justice* in the courts of law—next to the right of *petitioning the King* and parliament for redress of grievances—and lastly, to the right of *having and using arms for self-preservation and defence.*" These he calls "auxiliary subordinate rights, which serve principally as *barriers* to protect and maintain inviolate the three great and primary rights of *personal security, personal liberty* and *private property*": And that of *having arms for their defence* he tells us is "a public allowance, under due restrictions, of the *natural right of resistance and self preservation,* when the sanctions of society and laws are found *insufficient* to restrain the *violence of oppression.*"—How little do those persons attend to the rights of the constitution, if they know anything about them, who find fault with a late vote of this town, calling upon the inhabitants to *provide themselves with arms for their defence* at any time; but more especially, when they had reason to fear, there would be a necessity of the means of self preservation against the *violence of oppression.*—Every one knows that the exercise of the military power is forever *dangerous* to civil rights; and we have had recent instances of *violences* that have been offer'd to *private subjects,* and the last week, even *to a magistrate in the execution of his office!*—Such violences are no more than might have been expected from *military troops:* A power, which is apt enough at all times to take a wanton lead, even when in the midst of civil society; but more especially so, when they are led to believe that *they* are become *necessary,* to awe a spirit of *rebellion,* and *preserve peace and good order.* But there are some persons, who would, if possibly they could, perswade the people *never to make use* of their *constitutional* rights or terrify them from doing it. No wonder that a resolution of this town to *keep arms* for its own defence, should be represented as having at bottom a *secret intention* to oppose the landing of the King's troops: when those very persons, who gave it this colouring, had before represented the peoples petitioning their Sovereign, as proceeding from a *factious* and *rebellious* spirit; and would now insinuate that there is an *impropriety* in their addressing even a *plantation Governor* upon public business—Such are the times we are fallen into!

5

ALEXANDER HAMILTON, THE FARMER REFUTED
23 Feb. 1775
Papers 1:86–89, 121–22, 135–36

I shall, for the present, pass over to that part of your pamphlet, in which you endeavour to establish the supremacy of the British Parliament over America. After a proper eclaircissement of this point, I shall draw such inferences, as will sap the foundation of every thing you have offered.

The first thing that presents itself is a wish, that "*I* had, explicitly, declared to the public my ideas of the *natural rights* of mankind. Man, in a state of nature (you say) may be considered, as perfectly free from all restraints of *law* and *government,* and, then, the weak must submit to the strong."

I shall, henceforth, begin to make some allowance for that enmity, you have discovered to the *natural rights* of mankind. For, though ignorance of them in this enlightened age cannot be admitted, as a sufficient excuse for you; yet, it ought, in some measure, to extenuate your guilt. If you will follow my advice, there still may be hopes of your reformation. Apply yourself, without delay, to the study of the law of nature. I would recommend to your perusal, Grotius, Puffendorf, Locke, Montesquieu, and Burlemaqui. I might mention other excellent writers on this subject; but if you attend, diligently, to these, you will not require any others.

There is so strong a similitude between your political

principles and those maintained by Mr. Hobb[e]s, that, in judging from them, a person might very easily *mistake* you for a disciple of his. His opinion was, exactly, coincident with yours, relative to man in a state of nature. He held, as you do, that he was, then, perfectly free from all restraint of *law* and *government*. Moral obligation, according to him, is derived from the introduction of civil society; and there is no virtue, but what is purely artificial, the mere contrivance of politicians, for the maintenance of social intercourse. But the reason he run into this absurd and impious doctrine, was, that he disbelieved the existence of an intelligent superintending principle, who is the governor, and will be the final judge of the universe.

As you, sometimes, swear *by him that made you,* I conclude, your sentiment does not correspond with his, in that which is the basis of the doctrine, you both agree in; and this makes it impossible to imagine whence this congruity between you arises. To grant, that there is a supreme intelligence, who rules the world, and has established laws to regulate the actions of his creatures; and, still, to assert, that man, in a state of nature, may be considered as perfectly free from all restraints of *law* and *government,* appear to a common understanding, altogether irreconcileable.

Good and wise men, in all ages, have embraced a very dissimilar theory. They have supposed, that the deity, from the relations, we stand in, to himself and to each other, has constituted an eternal and immutable law, which is, indispensibly, obligatory upon all mankind, prior to any human institution whatever.

This is what is called the law of nature, "which, being coeval with mankind, and dictated by God himself, is, of course, superior in obligation to any other. It is binding over all the globe, in all countries, and at all times. No human laws are of any validity, if contrary to this; and such of them as are valid, derive all their authority, mediately, or immediately, from this original." BLACKSTONE.

Upon this law, depend the natural rights of mankind, the supreme being gave existence to man, together with the means of preserving and beatifying that existence. He endowed him with rational faculties, by the help of which, to discern and pursue such things, as were consistent with his duty and interest, and invested him with an inviolable right to personal liberty, and personal safety.

Hence, in a state of nature, no man had any *moral* power to deprive another of his life, limbs, property or liberty; nor the least authority to command, or exact obedience from him; except that which arose from the ties of consanguinity.

Hence also, the origin of all civil government, justly established, must be a voluntary compact, between the rulers and the ruled; and must be liable to such limitations, as are necessary for the security of the *absolute rights* of the latter; for what original title can any man or set of men have, to govern others, except their own consent? To usurp dominion over a people, in their own despite, or to grasp at a more extensive power than they are willing to entrust, is to violate that law of nature, which gives every man a right to his personal liberty; and can, therefore, confer no obligation to obedience.

"The principal aim of society is to protect individuals, in the enjoyment of those absolute rights, which were vested in them by the immutable laws of nature; but which could not be preserved, in peace, without that mutual assistance, and intercourse, which is gained by the institution of friendly and social communities. Hence it follows, that the first and primary end of human laws, is to maintain and regulate these *absolute rights* of individuals." BLACKSTONE.

If we examine the pretensions of parliament, by this criterion, which is evidently, a good one, we shall, presently detect their injustice. First, they are subversive of our natural liberty, because an authority is assumed over us, which we by no means assent to. And secondly, they divest us of that moral security, for our lives and properties, which we are intitled to, and which it is the primary end of society to bestow. For such security can never exist, while we have no part in making the laws, that are to bind us; and while it may be the interest of our uncontroled legislators to oppress us as much as possible.

To deny these principles will be not less absurd, than to deny the plainest axioms: I shall not, therefore, attempt any further illustration of them.

. . . . .

Thus Sir, I have taken a pretty general survey of the American Charters; and proved to the satisfaction of every unbiassed person, that they are intirely, discordant with that sovereignty of parliament, for which you are an advocate. The disingenuity of your extracts (to give it no harsher name) merits the severest censure; and will no doubt serve to discredit all your former, as well as future labours, in your favourite cause of despotism.

It is true, that New-York has no Charter. But, if it could support it's claim to liberty in no other way, it might, with justice, plead the common principles of colonization: for, it would be unreasonable, to seclude one colony, from the enjoyment of the most important privileges of the rest. There is no need, however, of this plea: The sacred rights of mankind are not to be rummaged for, among old parchments, or musty records. They are written, as with a sun beam, in the whole *volume* of human nature, by the hand of the divinity itself; and can never be erased or obscured by mortal power.

The nations of Turkey, Russia, France, Spain, and all other despotic kingdoms, in the world, have an inherent right, when ever they please, to shake off the yoke of servitude, (though sanctified by the immemorial usage of their ancestors;) and to model their government, upon the principles of civil liberty.

. . . . .

Had the rest of America passively looked on, while a sister colony was subjugated, the same fate would gradually have overtaken all. The safety of the whole depends upon the mutual protection of every part. If the sword of oppression be permitted to lop off one limb without opposition, reiterated strokes will soon dismember the whole body. Hence it was the duty and interest of all the colonies to succour and support the one which was suffering. It is sometimes sagaciously urged, that we ought to commisserate the distresses of the people of Massachusetts; but not intermeddle in their affairs, so far, as perhaps to bring ourselves into like circumstances with them. This might be good reasoning, if our neutrality would not be more dangerous, than our participation: But I am unable to conceive how the colonies in general would have any security against oppression, if they were once to content themselves, with barely *pitying* each other, while parliament was prosecuting and enforcing its demands. Unless they continually protect and assist each other, they must all inevitably fall a prey to their enemies.

Extraordinary emergencies, require extraordinary expedients. The best mode of opposition was that in which there might be an union of councils. This was necessary to ascertain the boundaries of our rights; and to give weight and dignity to our measures, both in Britain and America. A Congress was accordingly proposed, and universally agreed to.

You, Sir, triumph in the supposed *illegality* of this body; but, granting your supposition were true, it would be a matter of no real importance. When the first principles of civil society are violated, and the rights of a whole people are invaded, the common forms of municipal law are not to be regarded. Men may then betake themselves to the law of nature; and, if they but conform their actions, to that standard, all cavils against them, betray either ignorance or dishonesty. There are some events in society, to which human laws cannot extend; but when applied to them lose all their force and efficacy. In short, when human laws contradict or discountenance the means, which are necessary to preserve the essential rights of any society, they defeat the proper end of all laws, and so become null and void.

6

THOMAS JEFFERSON TO GARRET VAN METER
27 Apr. 1781

Papers 5:566

I am sorry such a Spirit of Disobedience has shewn itself in your County; it must be subdued. Laws made by common Consent must not be trampled on by Individuals. It is very much the Interest of the good to force the unworthy into their due Share of Contributions to the Public Support, otherwise the burthen on them will become oppressive indeed. We have no power by the law of raising Cavalry in the Counties generally, but on some similar Occasions we have recommended to the County Lieutenants, who have the power of forming their Militia Companies as they please, to form into one Company such Individuals of their Militia as will engage to mount and equip themselves and to serve as mounted Infantry and we give Commissions to the Officers in the ordinary Stile. These may be used as effectually as Cavalry, and men on horseback have been found the most certain Instrument of public punishment.

Their best way too perhaps is not to go against the mutineers when embodied which would bring on perhaps an open Rebellion or Bloodshed most certainly, but when they shall have dispersed to go and take them out of their Beds, singly and without Noise, or if they be not found the first time to go again and again so that they may never be able to remain in quiet at home. This is what I must recommend to you and therefore furnish the Bearers with the Commissions as you desire.

If you find this Service considerable you will of Course give the Individuals Credit for it as a Tour of Duty.

7

ALEXANDER HAMILTON, FEDERALIST, NO. 16,
103–5
4 Dec. 1787

(See ch. 8, no. 22)

8

THOMAS JEFFERSON TO JAMES MADISON
20 Dec. 1787

Papers 12:442

(See ch. 18, no. 21)

9

ALEXANDER HAMILTON, FEDERALIST, NO. 28,
178–79
26 Dec. 1787

Independent of all other reasonings upon the subject, it is a full answer to those who require a more peremptory provision against military establishments in time of peace, that the whole power of the proposed government is to be in the hands of the representatives of the people. This is the essential, and after all the only efficacious security for the rights and privileges of the people which is attainable in civil society.

If the representatives of the people betray their constituents, there is then no resource left but in the exertion of that original right of self-defence, which is paramount to all positive forms of government; and which, against the usurpations of the national rulers, may be exerted with infinitely better prospect of success, than against those of the rulers of an individual State. In a single State, if the persons entrusted with supreme power became usurpers, the different parcels, subdivisions or districts, of which it consists, having no distinct government in each, can take no regular measures for defence. The citizens must rush tumultuously to arms, without concert, without system, without resource; except in their courage and despair. The usurpers, cloathed with the forms of legal authority, can too often crush the opposition in embryo. The smaller the extent of territory, the more difficult will it be for the people to form a regular or systematic plan of opposition; and the more easy will it be to defeat their early efforts. Intelligence can be more speedily obtained of their preparations and movements; and the military force in the possession of the usurpers, can be more rapidly directed against the part where the opposition has begun. In this situation, there must be a peculiar coincidence of circumstances to ensure success to the popular resistance.

The obstacles to usurpation and the facilities of resistance increase with the increased extent of the state; provided the citizens understand their rights and are disposed to defend them. The natural strength of the people in a large community, in proportion to the artificial strength of the government, is greater than in a small; and of course more competent to a struggle with the attempts of the government to establish a tyranny. But in a confederacy the people, without exaggeration, may be said to be entirely the masters of their own fate. Power being almost always the rival of power; the General Government will at all times stand ready to check the usurpations of the state governments; and these will have the same disposition towards the General Government. The people, by throwing themselves into either scale, will infallibly make it preponderate. If their rights are invaded by either, they can make use of the other, as the instrument of redress. How wise will it be in them by cherishing the Union to preserve to themselves an advantage which can never be too highly prised!

10

JAMES MADISON, FEDERALIST, NO. 40, 264–67
18 Jan. 1788

(See ch. 6, no. 20)

11

JAMES MADISON, FEDERALIST, NO. 46, 320–22
29 Jan. 1788

(See ch. 8, no. 30)

12

BRUTUS, NO. 15
20 Mar. 1788
Storing 2.9.196

(See ch. 8, no. 34)

13

JAMES WILSON, OF THE STUDY OF THE LAW IN
THE UNITED STATES, LECTURES ON LAW
1791
Works 1:76–79

A question deeply interesting to the American States now presents itself. Should the elements of a law education, particularly as it respects publick law, be drawn entirely from another country—or should they be drawn, in part, at least, from the constitutions and governments and laws of the United States, and of the several States composing the Union?

The subject, to one standing where I stand, is not without its delicacy: let me, however, treat it with the decent but firm freedom, which befits an independent citizen, and a professor in independent states.

Surely I am justified in saying, that the principles of the constitutions and governments and laws of the United States, and the republicks, of which they are formed, are materially different from the principles of the constitution and government and laws of England; for that is the only country, from the principles of whose constitution and government and laws, it will be contended, that the elements of a law education ought to be drawn. I presume to go further: the principles of our constitutions and governments and laws are materially *better* than the principles of the constitution and government and laws of England.

Permit me to mention one great principle, the *vital* principle I may well call it, which diffuses animation and vigour through all the others. The principle I mean is this, that the supreme or sovereign power of the society resides in the citizens at large; and that, therefore, they always retain the right of abolishing, altering, or amending their constitution, at whatever time, and in whatever manner, they shall deem it expedient.

By Sir William Blackstone, from whose Commentaries, a performance in many respects highly valuable, the elements of a foreign law education would probably be borrowed—by Sir William Blackstone, this great and fundamental principle is treated as a political chimera, existing only in the minds of some theorists; but, in practice, inconsistent with the dispensation of any government upon earth.

. . . . .

And yet, even in England, there have been revolutions of government: there has been one within very little more than a century ago. The learned Author of the Commentaries admits the fact; but denies it to be a ground on which any constitutional principle can be established.

If the same precise "conjunction of circumstances" should happen a second time; the revolution of one thousand six hundred and eighty eight would form a precedent: but were only one or two of the circumstances, forming that conjunction, to happen again; "the precedent would fail us."

The three circumstances, which formed that conjunction, were these: 1. An endeavour to subvert the constitution, by breaking the original contract between the king and people. 2. Violation of the fundamental laws. 3. Withdrawing out of the kingdom.

Now, on this state of things, let us make a supposition—not a very foreign one—and see the consequences, which would unquestionably follow from the principles of Sir William Blackstone. Let us suppose, that, on some occasion, a prince should form a conjunction of only two of the circumstances; for instance, that he should only violate the fundamental laws, and endeavour to subvert the constitution: let us suppose, that, instead of completing the conjunction, by withdrawing out of his government, he should only employ some forty or fifty thousand troops to give full efficacy to the two first circumstances: let us suppose all this—and it is surely not unnatural to suppose, that a prince, who shall form the two first parts of the conjunction, will not, like James the second, run away from the execution of them—let us, I say, suppose all this; and what, on the principles of Sir William Blackstone, would be the undeniable consequence? In the language of the Commentaries, "our precedent would fail us."

But we have thought, and we have acted upon revolution principles, without offering them up as sacrifices at the shrine of revolution precedents.

Why should we not teach our children those principles, upon which we ourselves have thought and acted? Ought we to instil into their tender minds a theory, especially if unfounded, which is contradictory to our own practice, built on the most solid foundation? Why should we reduce them to the cruel dilemma of condemning, either those principles which they have been taught to believe, or those persons whom they have been taught to revere?

It is true, that the learned Author of the Commentaries concludes this very passage, by telling us, that "there are inherent, though latent powers of society, which no climate, no time, no constitution, no contract can ever destroy or diminish." But what does this prove? not that revolution principles are, in his opinion, recognized by the English constitution; but that the English constitution, whether considered as a law, or as a contract, cannot destroy or diminish those principles.

It is the opinion of many, that the revolution of one thousand six hundred and eighty eight did more than set a mere precedent, even in England. But be that as it may:

a revolution principle certainly is, and certainly should be taught as a principle of the constitution of the United States, and of every State in the Union.

This revolution principle—that, the sovereign power residing in the people, they may change their constitution and government whenever they please—is not a principle of discord, rancour, or war: it is a principle of melioration, contentment, and peace. It is a principle not recommended merely by a flattering theory: it is a principle recommended by happy experience. To the testimony of Pennsylvania—to the testimony of the United States I appeal for the truth of what I say.

14

JAMES MADISON TO DANIEL WEBSTER
15 Mar. 1833
Writings 9:604–5

I return my thanks for the copy of your late very powerful Speech in the Senate of the United S. It crushes "nullification" and must hasten the abandonment of "Secession." But *this* dodges the blow by confounding the claim to secede at will, with the right of seceding from intolerable oppression. The former answers itself, being a violation, without cause, of a faith solemnly pledged. The latter is another name only for revolution, about which there is no theoretic controversy. Its double aspect, nevertheless, with the countenance recd from certain quarters, is giving it a popular currency here which may influence the approaching elections both for Congress & for the State Legislature. It has gained some advantage also, by mixing itself with the question whether the Constitution of the U.S. was formed by the people or by the States, now under a theoretic discussion by animated partizans.

It is fortunate when disputed theories, can be decided by undisputed facts. And here the undisputed fact is, that the Constitution was made by the people, but as imbodied into the several states, who were parties to it and therefore made by the States in their highest authoritative capacity. They might, by the same authority & by the same process have converted the Confederacy into a mere league or treaty; or continued it with enlarged or abridged powers; or have imbodied the people of their respective States into one people, nation or sovereignty; or as they did by a mixed form make them one people, nation, or sovereignty, for certain purposes, and not so for others.

The Constitution of the U.S. being established by a Competent authority, by that of the sovereign people of the several States who were the parties to it, it remains only to inquire what the Constitution is; and here it speaks for itself. It organizes a Government into the usual Legislative Executive & Judiciary Departments; invests it with specified powers, leaving others to the parties to the Constitution; it makes the Government like other Governments to operate directly on the people; places at its Command the needful Physical means of executing its powers; and finally proclaims its supremacy, and that of the laws made in pursuance of it, over the Constitutions & laws of the States; the powers of the Government being exercised, as in other elective & responsible Governments, under the controul of its Constituents, the people & legislatures of the States, and subject to the Revolutionary *Rights* of the people in extreme cases.

It might have been added, that whilst the Constitution, therefore, is admitted to be in force, its *operation,* in *every respect* must be precisely the *same,* whether its authority be derived from that of the *people,* in the one or the other of the modes, in question; the authority being equally Competent in both; and that, without an annulment of the Constitution itself its supremacy must be submitted to.

The only distinctive effect, between the two modes of forming a Constitution by the authority of the people, is that if formed by them as imbodied into separate communities, as in the case of the Constitution of the U.S. a dissolution of the Constitutional Compact would replace them in the condition of separate communities, that being the Condition in which they entered into the compact; whereas if formed by the people as one community, acting as such by a numerical majority, a dissolution of the compact would reduce them to a state of nature, as so many individual persons. But whilst the Constitutional compact remains undissolved, it must be executed according to the forms and provisions specified in the compact. It must not be forgotten, that compact, express or implied is the vital principle of free Governments as contradistinguished from Governments not free; and that a revolt against this principle leaves no choice but between anarchy and despotism.

SEE ALSO:

Generally ch. 14

Daniel Defoe, The Original Power of the Collective Body of the People of England, Examined and Asserted 5–6, 8–13, 19 (1702)

John Trenchard, Cato's Letters, no. 59, 30 Dec. 1721, Jacobson 106–15

Alexander Hamilton, A Full Vindication of the Measures of Congress, 15 Dec. 1774, Papers 1:50–51

Thomas Jefferson to Abigail Adams, 22 Feb. 1787, Cappon 1:172–73

Brutus, no. 6, 27 Dec. 1787, Storing 2.9.69

Brutus, no. 10, 24 Jan. 1788, Storing 2.9.128

4

Republican Government

Introduction

The republicanism of the Founders' Constitution might seem to be a matter of course. According to Article 4, section 4, the United States shall guarantee to every state in the Union a republican form of government, but nothing is said to add specificity and clarification to the critical term. If that clause evoked little alarm or comment when the Constitution was being drafted, debated, and ratified, that was owing more to general agreement about the clause's intent than to any general agreement about the meaning of republicanism. In fact the usage of the word "republican" was as amorphous as it was common.

At the core of the notion of republican government appears to be the principle that the many should rule, and that the body politic "should move that way whither the greater force carries it, which is the consent of the majority" (Locke, no. 1). Which way that greater force moved was for the people to determine, consulting their interests and their better second thoughts. In that sense a variety of forms of institutional arrangements might all deserve the name "republican," with the greater fitness of one or the other form turning on the particular, even peculiar, cir-

cumstances of people, time, and place. What was critical, John Adams insisted (Novanglus, no. 7, 6 Mar. 1775), was that the government be "bound by fixed laws, which the people have a voice in making, and a right to defend."

Throughout his long lifetime Adams was to refine and enlarge and qualify this early effort at defining republicanism, but even at this stage he was sharply at odds with others for whom republic meant minimally and irreducibly, no king. Thus, for his friend and fellow revolutionary Benjamin Rush, there were hard-and-fast lines between "absolute republicanism and absolute monarchy." Titles of nobility were suspect (Art. 1, sec. 9, cl. 8; Art. 1, sec. 10, cl. 1), and the study of the classical languages as well. Rush detected in them devices whereby some contrived to separate themselves from their fellow creatures, the better to abuse and enslave them (no. 30). And thus, too, for Adams's bête noire and fellow revolutionary Tom Paine, it was a travesty to honor England with the name "republic" (no. 4). Its freedom depended on "the virtue of the House of Commons (the republican part in the Constitution)," and with that part corrupted and "eaten out," nothing was left but the remains of monarchical and aristocratical tyranny. Moreover, the hereditary principle, with which the English were so infatuated, provided a basis of power independent of the people and hence "in a *constitutional* sense" contributed nothing toward the freedom of the state. In rejecting both monarchy and hereditary rule, Americans would be rejecting an otherwise endless legacy of "blood and ashes."

Thomas Jefferson's republicanism was less flamboyant than Paine's, but not less radically opposed to monarchical and hereditary rule. It was evident to him in 1776 (he recollected in 1821) that independence demanded a consistent republicanism, and hence a sloughing off of monarchic, aristocratic, and other incompatible vestiges of prerepublican rule. To some extent his collaborators in the revision of Virginia's laws shared his belief, though none would match his devotion and assiduity in that project. With no royal negatives "to restrain us from doing right, it should be corrected, in all it's parts, with a single eye to reason, & the good of those for whose government it was framed" (no. 7). Jefferson considered four of 126 proposed bills "as forming a system by which every fibre would be eradicated of antient or future aristocracy; and a foundation laid for a government truly republican." His singling out of bills repealing entail and abolishing primogeniture helps cast some light on the otherwise incongruous inclusion of a law of inheritance in the Northwest Ordinance (see ch. 1, no. 8). The third bill would relieve the people from "taxation for the support of a religion not theirs." The fourth would provide for a general education of the people so as to qualify them for self-government by teaching them how to understand and maintain their rights. Among Jefferson's many fine epitomes of his republicanism, this autobiographical passage may stand first.

The Problem of Balance

Reading from Jefferson's *Autobiography* it is easy to forget that the case for republicanism had still to be made. Yet according to John Adams's account, a large body of contemporary opinion expressed itself in "the sneers of modern Englishmen" who contemned the principles, reasoning, and very memories and names of those whom they dismissed as regicides, commonwealthmen, and radical Whigs. "No small fortitude is necessary to confess that one has read them." In so confessing, Adams meant also to prepare "any candid mind" for a pro-republican argument in the form of a definition: "there is no good government but what is Republican . . . because the very definition of a Republic, is 'an Empire of Laws, and not of men.'" (no. 5). On these Harringtonian foundations Adams proceeded to develop his thoughts, culminating in 1787 with the "true and only true definition of a republic": "a government, in which all men, rich and poor, magistrates and subjects, officers and people, masters and servants, the first citizen and the last, are equally subject to the laws" (no. 10). The implications were liberty for all, not only for a majority; the protection of persons as well as of the acquisition, use, and transfer of property at the individual's discretion; and the contrivance of devices to engage the political interests of "the real middling people" and to secure their predominance in the state.

Principled republican that he was, Adams resisted the simplistic dichotomies adopted by both friends and foes of republican government. That seeker of royal and republican loans was "no king-killer, king-hater, or king-despiser" (Letter to Marquis de Lafayette, 21 May 1782). In an advanced stage of popular corruption and civil conflict, a desperate people might well be driven to institute hereditary offices, the very lineaments of Paine's detested British polity. So prudence might dictate muffling the antimonarchical and antiaristocratical drums for the present, even while laboring to contrive popular elective embodiments of monarchical and aristocratical principles. The truly challenging problem for Adams was to embed in republican institutions and procedures the self-sustaining elements of his cherished notion of a balanced government. From that point of view he thought he could already discern a major weakness in the new American Constitution: the monarchical element in it required enlargement and bolstering against the all-engrossing aristocratical power (no. 29).

It was, however, reserved for the two principal authors of the *Federalist* to recast the terms of the public discussion of republicanism by insisting on treating a republic as a species of popular government and distinguishing it from the other species, democracy, by the use of representation. Rule by popular majorities was not enough. The good name of popular self-government would be redeemed by a republic properly constructed (no. 12; see also ch. 17, no. 22). Among other things this entailed rejecting in the name of majority rule the right of equal suffrage in the national legislature enjoyed by the small states under the Articles of Confederation (see ch. 5, no. 23), and reconsidering how much dependence and popular derivation were necessary to proclaim a constitution in conformity with the true principles of republican government (nos. 24, 26).

The Problem of Size

The *Federalist*'s great vindication of republicanism called forth Hamilton's intense efforts and Madison's truly original contribution to political thought. No small part of their task was to convert a widely held objection to the proposed Constitution into a matter of rightful relief and pride. Montesquieu had taught moderns an ancient lesson (but for modern purposes), that republics would thrive only in fairly compact territories. The contiguity of private and public good would be more visible, more intelligible, more attainable, more actual, in a small state of relatively homogeneous free men. The Anti-Federalist dread of consolidated government turned largely on this Montesquieuan premise (nos. 14, 16). Hamilton's riposte was to claim that the dread was ill placed. Not largeness but smallness lay at the root of the domestic turmoil and sedition that made "the petty Republics of Greece and Italy" horrible and disgusting to contemplate, and the recent doings in western Massachusetts and Rhode Island even more vivid. A literal reading of Montesquieu would bode ill for America, for when Montesquieu said "small" he meant small, not a Virginia of 125,525 square miles (according to Jefferson's calculation in *Notes on the State of Virginia*). By this token Americans would be reduced to the alternative "either of taking refuge at once in the arms of monarchy, or of splitting ourselves into an infinity of little jealous, clashing, tumultuous commonwealths, the wretched nurseries of unceasing discord and the miserable objects of universal pity or contempt." Happily, modern improvements now made it possible for "the enlightened friends to liberty" to stand forth as republicans (no. 18). Of those progressive developments in political science, none was more critical than the discovery that "the enlargement of the sphere is found to lessen the insecurity of private rights" (see Madison, ch. 5, no. 16). In part this lessening would come about in a large republic almost as a matter of course thanks to the barriers to easy collusion posed by distance, time, and heterogeneity. In part it might come about through a properly devised "process of elections as will most certainly extract from the mass of the Society the purest and noblest characters which it contains." In and of itself, however, the extended republic might well favor protracted misrepresentation rather than the refinement and enlargement of popular views (nos. 19, 27). Nature had still to be perfected by political art. With cool self-assurance the proponents of the Constitution would point to that document as an unparalleled exemplar of the art that was needed.

The Problem of Commerce

Even with the extended republic temporarily secure and orthodox republican leaders in office, there still was cause for concern. Would the Americans' zeal for a commercial republic prove the undoing of both republic and republicans? It is tempting, but unhistorical, to treat this concern as a quaint or irrelevant atavism in a people as zealously commercial as the Americans. It was one thing to recognize the inevitable prominence of commerce in American life, as did Jefferson (Letter to George Washington, 15 Mar. 1784), Adams (Letter to John Jay, 6 Dec. 1785), and Hamilton (see ch. 7, nos. 13, 14). It was another matter to assess accurately the benefits and costs of that development. Following Montesquieu (no. 2) and Hume (no. 3), some Americans could recognize and welcome the ways in which commerce would soften men's harshness and hatred, creating bonds within and among states (no. 32; see also Agrippa, no. 1, 23 Nov. 1787, and ch. 18, no. 30). Hamilton was loath to credit such pacific expectations (see ch. 7, no. 10), though of course this in no way diminished his ardor for the promotion of commerce and manufacturing (no. 31).

Much more vexing were the probable effects of those developments upon the habits, tastes, and concerns of a self-governing people. Republicanism presupposes a people who care about the *res publica*, the public thing. Commerce changes the focus of individuals' vision; manufacturing permits, while encouraging, the indulgence of private gratifications; and a life cut off from the soil is, to that extent, a life of increased dependency on the wills of other men. Could one still speak of republican citizens when contemplating merchants, for which the "mere spot they stand on does not constitute so strong an attachment as that from which they draw their gains"? (Jefferson to Horatio Gates Spafford, 17 Mar. 1817, cited in Papers 14:221). Would the avarice that set men in motion leave them the taste or energy for pursuing the public's concerns? Recognizing those problems was a first step toward trying to cope with them, and there were, among the American founders of republican government, those who were intent on facing that challenge (see ch. 18).

1

JOHN LOCKE, *SECOND TREATISE*, §§ 95–99
1689

95. Men being, as has been said, by Nature, all free, equal and independent, no one can be put out of this Estate, and subjected to the Political Power of another, without his own *Consent*. The only way whereby any one devests himself of his Natural Liberty, and *puts on the bonds of Civil Society* is by agreeing with other Men to joyn and unite into a Community, for their comfortable, safe, and peaceable living one amongst another, in a secure Enjoyment of their Properties, and a greater Security against any that are not of it. This any number of Men may do, because it injures not the Freedom of the rest; they are left as they were in the Liberty of the State of Nature. When any number of Men have so *consented to make one Community* or Government, they are thereby presently incorporated, and make *one Body Politick*, wherein the *Majority* have a Right to act and conclude the rest.

96. For when any number of Men have, by the consent of every individual, made a *Community*, they have thereby made that *Community* one Body, with a Power to Act as one Body, which is only by the will and determination of the *majority*. For that which acts any Community, being only the consent of the individuals of it, and it being necessary to that which is one body to move one way; it is necessary the Body should move that way whither the greater force carries it, which is the *consent of the majority:* or else it is impossible it should act or continue one Body, *one Community*, which the consent of every individual that united into it, agreed that it should; and so every one is bound by that consent to be concluded by the *majority*. And therefore we see that in Assemblies impowered to act by positive Laws where no number is set by that positive Law which impowers them, the *act of the Majority* passes for the act of the whole, and of course determines, as having by the Law of Nature and Reason, the power of the whole.

97. And thus every Man, by consenting with others to make one Body Politick under one Government, puts himself under an Obligation to every one of that Society, to submit to the determination of the *majority*, and to be concluded by it; or else this *original Compact*, whereby he with others incorporates into *one Society*, would signifie nothing, and be no Compact, if he be left free, and under no other ties, than he was in before in the state of Nature. For what appearance would there be of any Compact? What new Engagement if he were no farther tied by any Decrees of the Society, than he himself thought fit, and did actually consent to? This would be still as great a liberty, as he himself had before his Compact, or any one else in the State of Nature hath, who may submit himself and consent to any acts of it if he thinks fit.

98. For if *the consent of the majority* shall not in reason, be received, *as the act of the whole*, and conclude every individual; nothing but the consent of every individual can make any thing to be the act of the whole: But such a consent is next impossible ever to be had, if we consider the Infirmities of Health, and Avocations of Business, which in a number, though much less than that of a Common-wealth, will necessarily keep many away from the publick Assembly. To which if we add the variety of Opinions, and contrariety of Interests, which unavoidably happen in all Collections of Men, the coming into Society upon such terms, would be only like *Cato*'s coming into the Theatre, only to go out again. Such a Constitution as this would make the mighty *Leviathan* of a shorter duration, than the feeblest Creatures; and not let it outlast the day it was born in: which cannot be suppos'd till we can think, that Rational Creatures should desire and constitute Societies only to be dissolved. For where the *majority* cannot conclude the rest, there they cannot act as one Body, and consequently will be immediately dissolved again.

99. Whosoever therefore out of a state of Nature unite into a *Community*, must be understood to give up all the power, necessary to the ends for which they unite into Society, to the *majority* of the Community, unless they expressly agreed in any number greater than the majority. And this is done by barely agreeing to *unite into one Political Society*, which is *all the Compact that* is, or needs be, between the Individuals, that enter into, or make up a *Commonwealth*. And thus that, which begins and actually *constitutes any Political Society*, is nothing but the consent of any number of Freemen capable of a majority to unite and incorporate into such a Society. And this is that, and that only, which did, or could give *beginning* to any *lawful Government* in the World.

2

MONTESQUIEU, SPIRIT OF LAWS, BK. 20, CHS. 1–8
1748

1.—Of Commerce

The following subjects deserve to be treated in a more extensive manner than the nature of this work will permit. Fain would I glide down a gentle river, but I am carried away by a torrent.

Commerce is a cure for the most destructive prejudices; for it is almost a general rule, that wherever we find agreeable manners, there commerce flourishes; and that wherever there is commerce, there we meet with agreeable manners.

Let us not be astonished, then, if our manners are now less savage than formerly. Commerce has everywhere diffused a knowledge of the manners of all nations: these are compared one with another, and from this comparison arise the greatest advantages.

Commercial laws, it may be said, improve manners for the same reason that they destroy them. They corrupt the purest morals. This was the subject of Plato's complaints; and we every day see that they polish and refine the most barbarous.

2.—Of the Spirit of Commerce

Peace is the natural effect of trade. Two nations who traffic with each other become reciprocally dependent; for if one has an interest in buying, the other has an interest in selling; and thus their union is founded on their mutual necessities.

But if the spirit of commerce unites nations, it does not in the same manner unite individuals. We see that in countries [Holland] where the people move only by the spirit of commerce, they make a traffic of all the humane, all the moral virtues; the most trifling things, those which humanity would demand, are there done, or there given, only for money.

The spirit of trade produces in the mind of a man a certain sense of exact justice, opposite, on the one hand, to robbery, and on the other to those moral virtues which forbid our always adhering rigidly to the rules of private interest, and suffer us to neglect this for the advantage of others.

The total privation of trade, on the contrary, produces robbery, which Aristotle ranks in the number of means of acquiring; yet it is not at all inconsistent with certain moral virtues. Hospitality, for instance, is most rare in trading countries, while it is found in the most admirable perfection among nations of vagabonds.

It is a sacrilege, says Tacitus, for a German to shut his door against any man whomsoever, whether known or unknown. He who has behaved with hospitality to a stranger goes to show him another house where this hospitality is also practised; and he is there received with the same humanity. But when the Germans had founded kingdoms, hospitality had become burdensome. This appears by two laws of the code of the Burgundians; one of which inflicted a penalty on every barbarian who presumed to show a stranger the house of a Roman; and the other decreed, that whoever received a stranger should be indemnified by the inhabitants, every one being obliged to pay his proper proportion.

3.—Of the Poverty of the People

There are two sorts of poor; those who are rendered such by the severity of government: these are, indeed, incapable of performing almost any great action, because their indigence is a consequence of their slavery. Others are poor, only because they either despise or know not the conveniences of life; and these are capable of accomplishing great things, because their poverty constitutes a part of their liberty.

4.—Of Commerce in different Governments

Trade has some relation to forms of government. In a monarchy, it is generally founded on luxury; and though it be also founded on real wants, yet the principal view with which it is carried on is to procure everything that can contribute to the pride, the pleasure, and the capricious whims of the nation. In republics, it is commonly founded on economy. Their merchants, having an eye to all the nations of the earth, bring from one what is wanted by another. It is thus that the republics of Tyre, Carthage, Athens, Marseilles, Florence, Venice, and Holland engaged in commerce.

This kind of traffic has a natural relation to a republican government: to monarchies it is only occasional. For as it is founded on the practice of gaining little, and even less than other nations, and of remedying this by gaining incessantly, it can hardly be carried on by a people swallowed up in luxury, who spend much, and see nothing but objects of grandeur.

Cicero was of this opinion, when he so justly said, "that he did not like that the same people should be at once both the lords and factors of the whole earth." For this would, indeed, be to suppose that every individual in the state, and the whole state collectively, had their heads constantly filled with grand views, and at the same time with small ones; which is a contradiction.

Not but that the most noble enterprises are completed also in those states which subsist by economical commerce: they have even an intrepidity not to be found in monarchies. And the reason is this:

One branch of commerce leads to another, the small to the moderate, the moderate to the great; thus he who has gratified his desire of gaining a little raises himself to a situation in which he is not less desirous of gaining a great deal.

Besides, the grand enterprises of merchants are always necessarily connected with the affairs of the public. But, in monarchies, these public affairs give as much distrust to the merchants as in free states they appear to give safety.

Great enterprises, therefore, in commerce are not for monarchical, but for republican, governments.

In short, an opinion of greater certainty, as to the possession of property in these states, makes them undertake everything. They flatter themselves with the hopes of receiving great advantages from the smiles of fortune; and thinking themselves sure of what they have already acquired, they boldly expose it in order to acquire more; risking nothing, but as the means of obtaining.

I do not pretend to say that any monarchy is entirely excluded from an economical commerce; but of its own nature it has less tendency towards it: neither do I mean that the republics with which we are acquainted are absolutely deprived of the commerce of luxury; but it is less connected with their constitution.

With regard to a despotic state, there is no occasion to mention it. A general rule: A nation in slavery labors more to preserve than to acquire; a free nation, more to acquire than to preserve.

5.—Of Nations that have entered into an economical Commerce

Marseilles, a necessary retreat in the midst of a tempestuous sea; Marseilles, a harbor which all the winds, the shelves of the sea, the disposition of the coasts, point out for a landing-place, became frequented by mariners; while the sterility of the adjacent country determined the citizens to an economical commerce. It was necessary that they should be laborious to supply what nature had refused; that they should be just, in order to live among barbarous nations, from whom they were to derive their prosperity; that they should be moderate, to the end that they might always taste the sweets of a tranquil government; in fine, that they should be frugal in their manners, to enable them to subsist by trade—a trade the more certain as it was less advantageous.

We everywhere see violence and oppression give birth to a commerce founded on economy, while men are constrained to take refuge in marshes, in isles, in the shallows of the sea, and even on rocks themselves. Thus it was that Tyre, Venice, and the cities of Holland were founded. Fugitives found there a place of safety. It was necessary that they should subsist; they drew, therefore, their subsistence from all parts of the world.

6.—Some Effects of an extensive Navigation

It sometimes happens that a nation, when engaged in an economical commerce, having need of the merchandise of one country, which serves as a capital or stock for procuring the commodities of another, is satisfied with making very little profit, and frequently none at all, in trading with the former, in expectation of gaining greatly by the latter. Thus, when the Dutch were almost the only nation that carried on the trade from the south to the north of Europe, the French wines which they imported to the north were in some measure only a capital or stock for conducting their commerce in that part of the world.

It is a known fact that there are some kinds of merchandise in Holland which, though imported from afar, sell for very little more than they cost upon the spot. They account for it thus: a captain who has occasion to ballast his ship will load it with marble; if he wants wood for stowage, he will buy it; and, provided he loses nothing by the bargain, he will think himself a gainer. Thus it is that Holland has its quarries and its forests.

Further, it may happen so that not only a commerce which brings in nothing shall be useful, but even a losing trade shall be beneficial. I have heard it affirmed in Holland that the whale fishery in general does not answer the expense; but it must be observed that the persons employed in building the ships, as also those who furnish the rigging and provisions, are jointly concerned in the fishery. Should they happen to lose in the voyage, they have had a profit in fitting out the vessel. This commerce, in short, is a kind of lottery, and every one is allured with the hopes of a prize. Mankind are generally fond of gaming; and even the most prudent have no aversion to it, when the disagreeable circumstances attending it, such as dissipation, anxiety, passion, loss of time, and even of life and fortune, are concealed from their view.

7.—*The Spirit of England with respect to Commerce*

The tariff or customs of England are very unsettled with respect to other nations; they are changed, in some measure, with every parliament, either by taking off particular duties, or by imposing new ones. They endeavor by these means still to preserve their independence. Supremely jealous with respect to trade, they bind themselves but little by treaties, and depend only on their own laws.

Other nations have made the interests of commerce yield to those of politics; the English, on the contrary, have ever made their political interests give way to those of commerce.

They know better than any other people upon earth how to value, at the same time, these three great advantages—religion, commerce, and liberty.

8.—*In what Manner economical Commerce has been sometimes restrained*

In several kingdoms laws have been made extremely proper to humble the states that have entered into economical commerce. They have forbidden their importing any merchandise, except the product of their respective countries; and have permitted them to traffic only in vessels built in the kingdom to which they brought their commodities.

It is necessary that the kingdom which imposes these laws should itself be able easily to engage in commerce; otherwise it will, at least, be an equal sufferer. It is much more advantageous to trade with a commercial nation, whose profits are moderate, and who are rendered in some sort dependent by the affairs of commerce; with a nation whose larger views and whose extended trade enable them to dispose of their superfluous merchandise; with a wealthy nation, who can take off many of their commodities, and make them a quicker return in specie; with

a nation under a kind of necessity to be faithful, pacific from principle, and that seeks to gain, and not to conquer: it is much better, I say, to trade with such a nation than with others, their constant rivals, who will never grant such great advantages.

3

DAVID HUME, OF COMMERCE
1752

The greatness of a state and the happiness of its subjects, how independent soever they may be supposed in some respects, are commonly allowed to be inseparable with regard to commerce; and as private men receive greater security in the possession of their trade and riches from the power of the public, so the public becomes powerful in proportion to the opulence and extensive commerce of private men. This maxim is true in general, though I cannot forbear thinking that it may possibly admit of exceptions, and that we often establish it with too little reserve and limitation. There may be some circumstances where the commerce and riches and luxury of individuals, instead of adding strength to the public, will serve only to thin its armies and diminish its authority among the neighboring nations. Man is a very variable being and susceptible of many different opinions, principles, and rules of conduct. What may be true while he adheres to one way of thinking will be found false when he has embraced an opposite set of manners and opinions.

The bulk of every state may be divided into *husbandmen* and *manufacturers*. The former are employed in the culture of the land; the latter works up the materials furnished by the former into all the commodities which are necessary or ornamental to human life. As soon as men quit their savage state, where they live chiefly by hunting and fishing, they must fall into these two classes, though the arts of agriculture employ, *at first*, the most numerous part of the society. Time and experience improve so much these arts that the land may easily maintain a much greater number of men than those who are immediately employed in its culture or who furnish the more necessary manufactures to such as are so employed.

If these superfluous hands apply themselves to the finer arts, which are commonly denominated the arts of *luxury*, they add to the happiness of the state, since they afford to many the opportunity of receiving enjoyments with which they would otherwise have been unacquainted. But may not another scheme be proposed for the employment of these superfluous hands? May not the sovereign lay claim to them and employ them in fleets and armies, to increase the dominions of the state abroad and spread its fame over distant nations? It is certain that the fewer desires and wants are found in the proprietors and laborers of land, the fewer hands do they employ; and consequently the superfluities of the land, instead of maintaining tradesmen and manufacturers, may support fleets and armies to a much greater extent than where a great many arts are required to minister to the luxury of particular persons. Here, therefore, seems to be a kind of opposition between the greatness of the state and the happiness of the subject. A state is never greater than when all its superfluous hands are employed in the service of the public. The ease and convenience of private persons require that these hands should be employed in their service. The one can never be satisfied but at the expense of the other. As the ambition of the sovereign must entrench on the luxury of individuals, so the luxury of individuals must diminish the force and check the ambition of the sovereign.

Nor is this reasoning merely chimerical, but is founded on history and experience. The republic of Sparta was certainly more powerful than any state now in the world consisting of an equal number of people, and this was owing entirely to the want of commerce and luxury. The Helotes were the laborers, the Spartans were the soldiers or gentlemen. It is evident that the labor of the Helotes could not have maintained so great a number of Spartans had these latter lived in ease and delicacy, and given employment to a great variety of trades and manufactures. The like policy may be remarked in Rome. And, indeed, throughout all ancient history it is observable that the smallest republics raised and maintained greater armies than states consisting of triple the number of inhabitants are able to support at present. It is computed that, in all European nations, the proportion between soldiers and people does not exceed one to a hundred. But we read that the city of Rome alone, with its small territory, raised and maintained in early times ten legions against the Latins. Athens, the whole of whose dominions was not larger than Yorkshire, sent to the expedition against Sicily near forty thousand men. Dionysius the elder, it is said, maintained a standing army of a hundred thousand foot and ten thousand horse, besides a large fleet of four hundred sail, though his territories extended no further than the city of Syracuse—about a third of the island of Sicily, and some seaport towns and garrisons on the coast of Italy and Illyricum. It is true the ancient armies, in time of war, subsisted much upon plunder; but did not the enemy plunder in their turn?—which was a more ruinous way of levying a tax than any other that could be devised. In short, no probable reason can be assigned for the great power of the more ancient states above the modern but their want of commerce and luxury. Few artisans were maintained by the labor of the farmers, and therefore more soldiers might live upon it. Livy says that Rome, in his time, would find it difficult to raise as large an army as that which, in her early days, she sent out against the Gauls and Latins. Instead of those soldiers who fought for liberty and empire in Camillus' time, there were in Augustus' days musicians, painters, cooks, players, and tailors; and if the land was equally cultivated at both periods, it could certainly maintain equal numbers in the one profession as in the other. They added nothing to the mere necessaries of life in the latter period more than in the former.

It is natural on this occasion to ask whether sovereigns may not return to the maxims of ancient policy and consult their own interest in this respect more than the happiness of their subjects? I answer that it appears to me almost impossible, and that because ancient policy was violent and contrary to the more natural and usual course of things. It is well known with what peculiar laws Sparta was governed and what a prodigy that republic is justly esteemed by everyone who has considered human nature as it has displayed itself in other nations and other ages. Were the testimony of history less positive and circumstantial, such a government would appear a mere philosophical whim or fiction and impossible ever to be reduced to practice. And though the Roman and other ancient republics were supported on principles somewhat more natural, yet was there an extraordinary concurrence of circumstances to make them submit to such grievous burdens. They were free states; they were small ones; and the age being martial, all their neighbors were continually in arms. Freedom naturally begets public spirit, especially in small states, and this public spirit, this *amor patriae*, must increase when the public is almost in continual alarm and men are obliged every moment to expose themselves to the greatest dangers for its defense. A continual succession of wars makes every citizen a soldier; he takes the field in his turn, and during his service he is chiefly maintained by himself. This service is indeed equivalent to a heavy tax, yet is it less felt by a people addicted to arms who fight for honor and revenge more than pay, and are unacquainted with gain and industry as well as pleasure. Not to mention the great equality of fortunes among the inhabitants of the ancient republics, where every field belonging to a different proprietor was able to maintain a family and rendered the numbers of citizens very considerable, even without trade and manufactures.

But though the want of trade and manufactures among a free and very martial people may sometimes have no other effect than to render the public more powerful, it is certain that in the common course of human affairs it will have a quite contrary tendency. Sovereigns must take mankind as they find them, and cannot pretend to introduce any violent change in their principles and ways of thinking. A long course of time with a variety of accidents and circumstances are requisite to produce those great revolutions which so much diversify the face of human affairs. And the less natural any set of principles are which support a particular society, the more difficulty will a legislator meet with in raising and cultivating them. It is his best policy to comply with the common bent of mankind and give it all the improvements of which it is susceptible. Now according to the most natural course of things, industry and arts and trade increase the power of the sovereign as well as the happiness of the subjects, and that policy is violent which aggrandizes the public by the poverty of individuals. This will easily appear from a few considerations which will present to us the consequences of sloth and barbarity.

Where manufactures and mechanic arts are not cultivated, the bulk of the people must apply themselves to agriculture; and if their skill and industry increase, there must arise a great superfluity from their labor beyond what suffices to maintain them. They have no temptation, therefore, to increase their skill and industry, since they cannot exchange that superfluity for any commodities which may serve either to their pleasure or vanity. A habit of indolence naturally prevails. The greater part of the land lies uncultivated. What is cultivated yields not its utmost, for want of skill and assiduity in the farmers. If at any time the public exigencies require that great numbers should be employed in the public service, the labor of the people furnishes now no superfluities by which these numbers can be maintained. The laborers cannot increase their skill and industry on a sudden. Lands uncultivated cannot be brought into tillage for some years. The armies, meanwhile, must either make sudden and violent conquests or disband for want of subsistence. A regular attack or defense, therefore, is not to be expected from such a people, and their soldiers must be as ignorant and unskillful as their farmers and manufacturers.

Everything in the world is purchased by labor, and our passions are the only causes of labor. When a nation abounds in manufactures and mechanic arts, the proprietors of land, as well as the farmers, study agriculture as a science and redouble their industry and attention. The superfluity which arises from their labor is not lost, but is exchanged with manufactures for those commodities which men's luxury now makes them covet. By this means, land furnishes a great deal more of the necessaries of life than what suffices for those who cultivate it. In times of peace and tranquillity, this superfluity goes to the maintenance of manufacturers and the improvers of liberal arts. But it is easy for the public to convert many of these manufacturers into soldiers and maintain them by that superfluity which arises from the labor of the farmers. Accordingly we find that this is the case in all civilized governments. When the sovereign raises an army, what is the consequence? He imposes a tax. This tax obliges all the people to retrench what is least necessary to their subsistence. Those who labor in such commodities must either enlist in the troops or turn themselves to agriculture, and thereby oblige some laborers to enlist for want of business. And to consider the matter abstractly, manufactures increase the power of the state only as they store up so much labor, and that of a kind to which the public may lay claim without depriving anyone of the necessaries of life. The more labor, therefore, that is employed beyond mere necessaries, the more powerful is any state; since the persons engaged in that labor may easily be converted to the public service. In a state without manufactures, there may be the same number of hands; but there is not the same quantity of labor nor of the same kind. All the labor is there bestowed upon necessaries, which can admit of little or no abatement.

Thus the greatness of the sovereign and the happiness of the state are in a great measure united with regard to trade and manufactures. It is a violent method, and in most cases impracticable, to oblige the laborer to toil in order to raise from the land more than what subsists himself and family. Furnish him with manufactures and commodities, and he will do it of himself; afterward you will find it easy to seize some part of his superfluous labor and employ it in the public service without giving him his wonted return. Being accustomed to industry, he will think this less grievous than if at once you obliged him to an augmentation of labor without any reward. The case is the same with regard to the other members of the state. The greater is the stock of labor of all kinds, the greater quantity may be taken from the heap without making any sensible alteration in it.

A public granary of corn, a storehouse of cloth, a magazine of arms—all these must be allowed real riches and strength in any state. Trade and industry are really nothing but a stock of labor which, in times of peace and tranquillity, is employed for the ease and satisfaction of individuals, but in the exigencies of state may in part be turned to public advantage. Could we convert a city into a kind of fortified camp and infuse into each breast so martial a genius and such a passion for public good as to make everyone willing to undergo the greatest hardships for the sake of the public, these affections might now, as in ancient times, prove alone a sufficient spur to industry and support the community. It would then be advantageous, as in camps, to banish all arts and luxury, and by restrictions on equipage and tables make the provisions and forage last longer than if the army were loaded with a number of superfluous retainers. But as these principles are too disinterested and too difficult to support, it is requisite to govern men by other passions and animate them with a spirit of avarice and industry, art and luxury. The camp is, in this case, loaded with a superfluous retinue, but the provisions flow in proportionately larger. The harmony of the whole is still supported, and the natural bent of the mind being more complied with, individuals as well as the public find their account in the observance of those maxims.

4

Thomas Paine, Common Sense
10 Jan. 1776
Life 2:97–110, 114–20, 120–22

On the Origin and Design of Government in General,
With Concise Remarks on the English Constitution

Some writers have so confounded society with government, as to leave little or no distinction between them; whereas they are not only different, but have different origins. Society is produced by our wants and government by our wickedness; the former promotes our happiness *positively* by uniting our affections, the latter *negatively* by restraining our vices. The one encourages intercourse, the other creates distinctions. The first is a patron, the last a punisher.

Society in every state is a blessing, but government, even in its best state, is but a necessary evil; in its worst state an intolerable one: for when we suffer, or are exposed to the same miseries *by a government,* which we might expect in a country *without government,* our calamity is heightened by reflecting that we furnish the means by which we suffer. Government, like dress, is the badge of lost innocence; the palaces of kings are built upon the ruins of the bowers of paradise. For were the impulses of conscience clear, uniform and irresistibly obeyed, man would need no other law-giver; but that not being the case, he finds it necessary to surrender up a part of his property to furnish means for the protection of the rest; and this he is induced to do by the same prudence which in every other case advises him, out of two evils to choose the least. Wherefore, security being the true design and end of government, it unanswerably follows that whatever form thereof appears most likely to ensure it to us, with the least expence and greatest benefit, is preferable to all others.

In order to gain a clear and just idea of the design and end of government, let us suppose a small number of persons settled in some sequestered part of the earth, unconnected with the rest; they will then represent the first peopling of any country, or of the world. In this state of natural liberty, society will be their first thought. A thousand motives will excite them thereto; the strength of one man is so unequal to his wants, and his mind so unfitted for perpetual solitude, that he is soon obliged to seek assistance and relief of another, who in his turn requires the same. Four or five united would be able to raise a tolerable dwelling in the midst of a wilderness, but one man might labor out the common period of life without accomplishing any thing; when he had felled his timber he could not remove it, nor erect it after it was removed; hunger in the mean time would urge him to quit his work, and every different want would call him a different way. Disease, nay even misfortune, would be death; for though neither might be mortal, yet either would disable him from living, and reduce him to a state in which he might rather be said to perish than to die.

Thus necessity, like a gravitating power, would soon form our newly arrived emigrants into society, the reciprocal blessings of which would supercede, and render the obligations of law and government unnecessary while they remained perfectly just to each other; but as nothing but Heaven is impregnable to vice, it will unavoidably happen that in proportion as they surmount the first difficulties of emigration, which bound them together in a common cause, they will begin to relax in their duty and attachment to each other: and this remissness will point out the necessity of establishing some form of government to supply the defect of moral virtue.

Some convenient tree will afford them a State House, under the branches of which the whole colony may assemble to deliberate on public matters. It is more than probable that their first laws will have the title only of regulations and be enforced by no other penalty than public disesteem. In this first parliament every man by natural right will have a seat.

But as the colony increases, the public concerns will increase likewise, and the distance at which the members may be separated, will render it too inconvenient for all of them to meet on every occasion as at first, when their number was small, their habitations near, and the public concerns few and trifling. This will point out the convenience of their consenting to leave the legislative part to be managed by a select number chosen from the whole body, who are supposed to have the same concerns at stake which those have who appointed them, and who will act in the same manner as the whole body would act were they present. If the colony continue increasing, it will become necessary to augment the number of representatives, and that the interest of every part of the colony may be attended to, it will be found best to divide the whole into convenient parts, each part sending its proper number: and that the *elected* might never form to themselves an interest separate from the *electors,* prudence will point out the propriety of having elections often: because as the *elected* might by that means return and mix again with the general body of the *electors* in a few months, their fidelity to the public will be secured by the prudent reflection of not making a rod for themselves. And as this frequent interchange will establish a common interest with every part of the community, they will mutually and naturally support each other, and on this, (not on the unmeaning name of king,) depends the *strength of government, and the happiness of the governed.*

Here then is the origin and rise of government; namely, a mode rendered necessary by the inability of moral virtue to govern the world; here too is the design and end of government, viz. freedom and security. And however our eyes may be dazzled with show, or our ears deceived by sound; however prejudice may warp our wills, or interest darken our understanding, the simple voice of nature and reason will say, 'tis right.

I draw my idea of the form of government from a principle in nature which no art can overturn, viz. that the more simple any thing is, the less liable it is to be disordered, and the easier repaired when disordered; and with this maxim in view I offer a few remarks on the so much boasted Constitution of England. That it was noble for the dark and slavish times in which it was erected, is granted. When the world was overrun with tyranny the least remove therefrom was a glorious rescue. But that it is imperfect, subject to convulsions, and incapable of producing what it seems to promise, is easily demonstrated.

Absolute governments, (though the disgrace of human nature) have this advantage with them, they are simple; if the people suffer, they know the head from which their suffering springs; know likewise the remedy; and are not bewildered by a variety of causes and cures. But the Constitution of England is so exceedingly complex, that the nation may suffer for years together without being able to discover in which part the fault lies; some will say in one and some in another, and every political physician will advise a different medicine.

I know it is difficult to get over local or long standing prejudices, yet if we will suffer ourselves to examine the component parts of the English Constitution, we shall find them to be the base remains of two ancient tyrannies, compounded with some new Republican materials.

First.—The remains of monarchical tyranny in the person of the king.

Secondly.—The remains of aristocratical tyranny in the persons of the peers.

Thirdly.—The new Republican materials, in the persons of the Commons, on whose virtue depends the freedom of England.

The two first, by being hereditary, are independent of the people; wherefore in a *constitutional sense* they contribute nothing towards the freedom of the State.

To say that the Constitution of England is an *union* of three powers, reciprocally *checking* each other, is farcical; either the words have no meaning, or they are flat contradictions.

To say that the Commons is a check upon the king, presupposes two things.

First.—That the king is not to be trusted without being looked after; or in other words, that a thirst for absolute power is the natural disease of monarchy.

Secondly.—That the Commons, by being appointed for that purpose, are either wiser or more worthy of confidence than the crown.

But as the same constitution which gives the Commons a power to check the king by withholding the supplies, gives afterwards the king a power to check the Commons, by empowering him to reject their other bills; it again supposes that the king is wiser than those whom it has already supposed to be wiser than him. A mere absurdity!

There is something exceedingly ridiculous in the composition of monarchy; it first excludes a man from the means of information, yet empowers him to act in cases where the highest judgment is required. The state of a king shuts him from the world, yet the business of a king requires him to know it thoroughly; wherefore the different parts, by unnaturally opposing and destroying each other, prove the whole character to be absurd and useless.

Some writers have explained the English Constitution thus: the king, say they, is one, the people another; the peers are a house in behalf of the king, the Commons in behalf of the people; but this hath all the distinctions of a house divided against itself; and though the expressions be pleasantly arranged, yet when examined they appear idle and ambiguous; and it will always happen, that the nicest construction that words are capable of, when applied to the description of something which either cannot exist, or is too incomprehensible to be within the compass of description, will be words of sound only, and though they may amuse the ear, they cannot inform the mind: for this explanation includes a previous question, viz. *how came the king by a power which the people are afraid to trust, and always obliged to check?* Such a power could not be the gift of a wise people, neither can any power, *which needs checking,* be from God; yet the provision which the Constitution makes supposes such a power to exist.

But the provision is unequal to the task; the means either cannot or will not accomplish the end, and the whole affair is a *Felo de se:* for as the greater weight will always carry up the less, and as all the wheels of a machine are put in motion by one, it only remains to know which power in the constitution has the most weight, for that will govern: and though the others, or a part of them, may clog, or, as the phrase is, check the rapidity of its motion, yet so long as they cannot stop it, their endeavours will be ineffectual: The first moving power will at last have its way, and what it wants in speed is supplied by time.

That the crown is this overbearing part in the English Constitution needs not be mentioned, and that it derives its whole consequence merely from being the giver of places and pensions is self-evident; wherefore, though we have been wise enough to shut and lock a door against absolute Monarchy, we at the same time have been foolish enough to put the crown in possession of the key.

The prejudice of Englishmen, in favor of their own government, by king, lords and Commons, arises as much or more from national pride than reason. Individuals are undoubtedly safer in England than in some other countries: but the will of the king is as much the law of the land in Britain as in France, with this difference, that instead of proceeding directly from his mouth, it is handed to the people under the formidable shape of an act of Parliament. For the fate of Charles the First hath only made kings more subtle—not more just.

Wherefore, laying aside all national pride and prejudice in favor of modes and forms, the plain truth is that *it is wholly owing to the constitution of the people, and not to the constitution of the government* that the crown is not as oppressive in England as in Turkey.

An inquiry into the *constitutional errors* in the English form of government, is at this time highly necessary; for as we are never in a proper condition of doing justice to others, while we continue under the influence of some leading partiality, so neither are we capable of doing it to ourselves while we remain fettered by any obstinate prejudice. And as a man who is attached to a prostitute is unfitted to choose or judge of a wife, so any prepossession in favor of a rotten constitution of government will disable us from discerning a good one.

Of Monarchy and Hereditary Succession

Mankind being originally equals in the order of creation, the equality could only be destroyed by some subsequent circumstance: the distinctions of rich and poor may in a great measure be accounted for, and that without having recourse to the harsh ill-sounding names of oppression and avarice. Oppression is often the *consequence,* but seldom or never the *means* of riches; and though avarice will preserve a man from being necessitously poor, it generally makes him too timorous to be wealthy.

But there is another and greater distinction for which no truly natural or religious reason can be assigned, and that is the distinction of men into KINGS and SUBJECTS. Male and female are the distinctions of nature, good and bad the distinctions of heaven; but how a race of men came into the world so exalted above the rest, and distinguished like some new species, is worth inquiring into, and whether they are the means of happiness or of misery to mankind.

In the early ages of the world, according to the scripture chronology there were no kings; the consequence of which was, there were no wars; it is the pride of kings which throws mankind into confusion. Holland, without a king hath enjoyed more peace for this last century than any of the monarchical governments in Europe. Antiquity favors the same remark; for the quiet and rural lives of the first Patriarchs have a happy something in them, which vanishes when we come to the history of Jewish royalty.

Government by kings was first introduced into the world by the heathens, from whom the children of Israel copied the custom. It was the most prosperous invention the devil ever set on foot for the promotion of idolatry. The heathens paid divine honors to their deceased kings, and the Christian world has improved on the plan by doing the same to their living ones. How impious is the title of sacred majesty applied to a worm, who in the midst of his splendor is crumbling into dust!

As the exalting one man so greatly above the rest cannot be justified on the equal rights of nature, so neither can it be defended on the authority of scripture; for the will of the Almighty as declared by Gideon, and the prophet Samuel, expressly disapproves of government by kings. All anti-monarchical parts of scripture, have been very smoothly glossed over in monarchical governments, but they undoubtedly merit the attention of countries which have their governments yet to form. *Render unto Cesar the things which are Cesar's,* is the scripture doctrine of courts, yet it is no support of monarchical government, for the Jews at that time were without a king, and in a state of vassalage to the Romans.

Near three thousand years passed away, from the Mosaic account of the creation, till the Jews under a national delusion requested a king. Till then their form of government (except in extraordinary cases where the Almighty interposed) was a kind of Republic, administered by a judge and the elders of the tribes. Kings they had none, and it was held sinful to acknowledge any being under that title but the Lord of Hosts. And when a man seriously reflects on the idolatrous homage which is paid to the persons of kings, he need not wonder that the Almighty, ever jealous of his honor, should disapprove a form of government which so impiously invades the prerogative of heaven.

. . . . .

These portions of scripture are direct and positive. They admit of no equivocal construction. That the Almighty hath here entered his protest against monarchical government is true, or the scripture is false. And a man hath good reason to believe that there is as much of kingcraft as priestcraft in withholding the scripture from the public in popish countries. For monarchy in every instance is the popery of government.

To the evil of monarchy we have added that of hereditary succession; and as the first is a degradation and lessening of ourselves, so the second, claimed as a matter of right, is an insult and imposition on posterity. For all men being originally equals, no one by birth could have a right to set up his own family in perpetual preference to all others for ever, and though himself might deserve some decent degree of honors of his cotemporaries, yet his descendants might be far too unworthy to inherit them. One of the strongest natural proofs of the folly of hereditary right in kings, is that nature disapproves it, otherwise she would not so frequently turn it into ridicule, by giving mankind an *ass for a lion.*

Secondly, as no man at first could possess any other public honors than were bestowed upon him, so the givers of those honors could have no power to give away the right of posterity, and though they might say "We choose you for our head," they could not without manifest injustice to their children say "that your children and your children's children shall reign over ours forever." Because such an unwise, unjust, unnatural compact might (perhaps) in the next succession put them under the government of a rogue or a fool. Most wise men in their private sentiments have ever treated hereditary right with contempt; yet it is one of those evils which when once established is not easily removed: many submit from fear, others from superstition, and the more powerful part shares with the king the plunder of the rest.

This is supposing the present race of kings in the world to have had an honorable origin: whereas it is more than probable, that, could we take off the dark covering of antiquity and trace them to their first rise, we should find the first of them nothing better than the principal ruffian of some restless gang; whose savage manners or pre-eminence in subtilty obtained him the title of chief among plunderers; and who by increasing in power and extending his depredations, overawed the quiet and defenceless to purchase their safety by frequent contributions. Yet his electors could have no idea of giving hereditary right to his descendants, because such a perpetual exclusion of themselves was incompatible with the free and unrestrained principles they professed to live by. Wherefore, hereditary succession in the early ages of monarchy could not take place as a matter of claim, but as something casual or complemental; but as few or no records were extant in those days, and traditionary history stuff'd with fables, it was very easy, after the lapse of a few generations, to trump up some superstitious tale conveniently timed, Mahomet-like, to cram hereditary right down the throats of the vulgar. Perhaps the disorders which threatened, or seemed to threaten, on the decease of a leader and the choice of a new one (for elections among ruffians could not be very orderly) induced many at first to favour hereditary pretensions; by which means it happened, as it hath happened since, that what at first was submitted to as a convenience was afterwards claimed as a right.

England since the conquest hath known some few good monarchs, but groaned beneath a much larger number of bad ones; yet no man in his senses can say that their claim under William the Conqueror is a very honorable one. A French bastard landing with an armed banditti and establishing himself king of England against the consent of the natives, is in plain terms a very paltry rascally original. It certainly hath no divinity in it. However it is needless to spend much time in exposing the folly of hereditary right; if there are any so weak as to believe it, let them promiscuously worship the ass and the lion, and welcome. I shall neither copy their humility, nor disturb their devotion.

Yet I should be glad to ask how they suppose kings came at first? The question admits but of three answers, viz. either by lot, by election, or by usurpation. If the first king was taken by lot, it establishes a precedent for the next, which excludes hereditary succession. Saul was by lot, yet the succession was not hereditary, neither does it appear from that transaction that there was any intention it ever should. If the first king of any country was by election, that likewise establishes a precedent for the next; for to say, that the right of all future generations is taken away, by the act of the first electors, in their choice not only of a king but of a family of kings for ever, hath no parallel in or out of scripture but the doctrine of original sin, which supposes the free will of all men lost in Adam; and from such comparison, and it will admit of no other, hereditary succession can derive no glory. For as in Adam all sinned, and as in the first electors all men obeyed; as in the one all mankind were subjected to Satan, and in the other to sovereignty; as our innocence was lost in the first, and our authority in the last; and as both disable us from reassuming some former state and privilege, it unanswerably follows that original sin and hereditary succession are parallels. Dishonorable rank! inglorious connection! yet the most subtle sophist cannot produce a juster simile.

As to usurpation, no man will be so hardy as to defend it; and that William the Conqueror was an usurper is a fact not to be contradicted. The plain truth is, that the antiquity of English monarchy will not bear looking into.

But it is not so much the absurdity as the evil of hereditary succession which concerns mankind. Did it insure a race of good and wise men it would have the seal of divine authority, but as it opens a door to the *foolish,* the *wicked,* and the *improper,* it has in it the nature of oppression. Men who look upon themselves born to reign, and others to obey, soon grow insolent. Selected from the rest of mankind, their minds are early poisoned by importance; and the world they act in differs so materially from the world at large, that they have but little opportunity of knowing its true interests, and when they succeed to the government are frequently the most ignorant and unfit of any throughout the dominions.

Another evil which attends hereditary succession is, that the throne is subject to be possessed by a minor at any age; all which time the regency acting under the cover of a king have every opportunity and inducement to betray their trust. The same national misfortune happens when a king worn out with age and infirmity enters the last stage of human weakness. In both these cases the public becomes a prey to every miscreant who can tamper successfully with the follies either of age or infancy.

The most plausible plea which hath ever been offered in favor of hereditary succession is, that it preserves a nation from civil wars; and were this true, it would be weighty; whereas it is the most barefaced falsity ever imposed upon mankind. The whole history of England disowns the fact. Thirty kings and two minors have reigned in that distracted kingdom since the conquest, in which time there has been (including the revolution) no less than eight civil wars and nineteen rebellions. Wherefore instead of making for peace, it makes against it, and destroys the very foundation it seems to stand upon.

. . . . .

In short, monarchy and succession have laid (not this or that kingdom only) but the world in blood and ashes. 'Tis a form of government which the word of God bears testimony against, and blood will attend it.

If we inquire into the business of a king, we shall find that in some countries they may have none; and after sauntering away their lives without pleasure to themselves or advantage to the nation, withdraw from the scene, and leave their successors to tread the same idle round. In absolute monarchies the whole weight of business civil and military lies on the king; the children of Israel in their request for a king urged this plea, "that he may judge us, and go out before us and fight our battles." But in countries where he is neither a judge nor a general, as in England, a man would be puzzled to know what *is* his business.

The nearer any government approaches to a Republic, the less business there is for a king. It is somewhat difficult to find a proper name for the government of England. Sir William Meredith calls it a Republic; but in its present state it is unworthy of the name, because the corrupt influence of the crown, by having all the places in its disposal, hath so effectually swallowed up the power, and eaten out the virtue of the House of Commons (the republican part in the Constitution) that the government of England is nearly as monarchical as that of France or Spain. Men fall out with names without understanding them. For 'tis the republican and not the monarchical part of the Constitution of England which Englishmen glory in, viz. the liberty of choosing an House of Commons from out of their own body—and it is easy to see that when republican virtues fail, slavery ensues. Why is the Constitution of England sickly, but because monarchy hath poisoned the Republic; the crown has engrossed the Commons?

In England a king hath little more to do than to make war and give away places; which, in plain terms, is to empoverish the nation and set it together by the ears. A pretty business indeed for a man to be allowed eight hundred thousand sterling a year for, and worshipped into the bargain! Of more worth is one honest man to society, and in the sight of God, than all the crowned ruffians that ever lived.

5

JOHN ADAMS, THOUGHTS ON GOVERNMENT
Apr. 1776
Papers 4:86–93

If I was equal to the task of forming a plan for the government of a colony, I should be flattered with your request, and very happy to comply with it; because as the divine science of politicks is the science of social happiness, and the blessings of society depend entirely on the constitutions of government, which are generally institutions that last for many generations, there can be no employment more agreeable to a benevolent mind, than a re-search after the best.

Pope flattered tyrants too much when he said,

> "For forms of government let fools contest,
> That which is best administered is best."

Nothing can be more fallacious than this: But poets read history to collect flowers not fruits—they attend to fanciful images, not the effects of social institutions. Nothing is more certain from the history of nations, and the nature of man, than that some forms of government are better fitted for being well administered than others.

We ought to consider, what is the end of government, before we determine which is the best form. Upon this point all speculative politicians will agree, that the happiness of society is the end of government, as all Divines and moral Philosophers will agree that the happiness of the individual is the end of man. From this principle it will follow, that the form of government, which communicates ease, comfort, security, or in one word happiness to the greatest number of persons, and in the greatest degree, is the best.

All sober enquiries after truth, ancient and modern, Pagan and Christian, have declared that the happiness of man, as well as his dignity consists in virtue. Confucius, Zoroaster, Socrates, Mahomet, not to mention authorities really sacred, have agreed in this.

If there is a form of government then, whose principle and foundation is virtue, will not every sober man acknowledge it better calculated to promote the general happiness than any other form?

Fear is the foundation of most governments; but is so sordid and brutal a passion, and renders men, in whose breasts it predominates, so stupid, and miserable, that Americans will not be likely to approve of any political institution which is founded on it.

Honor is truly sacred, but holds a lower rank in the scale of moral excellence than virtue. Indeed the former is but a part of the latter, and consequently has not equal pretensions to support a frame of government productive of human happiness.

The foundation of every government is some principle or passion in the minds of the people. The noblest principles and most generous affections in our nature then, have the fairest chance to support the noblest and most generous models of government.

A man must be indifferent to the sneers of modern Englishmen to mention in their company the names of Sidney, Harrington, Locke, Milton, Nedham, Neville, Burnet, and Hoadley. No small fortitude is necessary to confess that one has read them. The wretched condition of this country, however, for ten or fifteen years past, has frequently reminded me of their principles and reasonings. They will convince any candid mind, that there is no good government but what is Republican. That the only valuable part of the British constitution is so; because the very definition of a Republic, is "an Empire of Laws, and not of men." That, as a Republic is the best of governments, so that par-ticular arrangement of the powers of society, or in other words that form of government, which is best contrived to secure an impartial and exact execution of the laws, is the best of Republics.

Of Republics, there is an inexhaustable variety, because the possible combinations of the powers of society, are capable of innumerable variations.

As good government, is an empire of laws, how shall your laws be made? In a large society, inhabiting an extensive country, it is impossible that the whole should assemble, to make laws: The first necessary step then, is, to depute power from the many, to a few of the most wise and good. But by what rules shall you chuse your Representatives? Agree upon the number and qualifications of persons, who shall have the benefit of choosing, or annex this priviledge to the inhabitants of a certain extent of ground.

The principal difficulty lies, and the greatest care should be employed in constituting this Representative Assembly. It should be in miniature, an exact portrait of the people at large. It should think, feel, reason, and act like them. That it may be the interest of this Assembly to do strict justice at all times, it should be an equal representation, or in other words equal interest among the people should have equal interest in it. Great care should be taken to effect this, and to prevent unfair, partial, and corrupt elections. Such regulations, however, may be better made in times of greater tranquility than the present, and they will spring up of themselves naturally, when all the powers of government come to be in the hands of the people's friends. At present it will be safest to proceed in all established modes to which the people have been familiarised by habit.

A representation of the people in one assembly being obtained, a question arises whether all the powers of government, legislative, executive, and judicial, shall be left in this body? I think a people cannot be long free, nor ever happy, whose government is in one Assembly. My reasons for this opinion are as follow.

1. A single Assembly is liable to all the vices, follies and frailties of an individual. Subject to fits of humour, starts of passion, flights of enthusiasm, partialities of prejudice, and consequently productive of hasty results and absurd judgments: And all these errors ought to be corrected and defects supplied by some controuling power.

2. A single Assembly is apt to be avaricious, and in time will not scruple to exempt itself from burthens which it will lay, without compunction, on its constituents.

3. A single Assembly is apt to grow ambitious, and after a time will not hesitate to vote itself perpetual. This was one fault of the long parliament, but more remarkably of Holland, whose Assembly first voted themselves from annual to septennial, then for life, and after a course of years, that all vacancies happening by death, or otherwise, should be filled by themselves, without any application to constituents at all.

4. A Representative Assembly, altho' extremely well qualified, and absolutely necessary as a branch of the legislature, is unfit to exercise the executive power, for want of two essential properties, secrecy and dispatch.

5. A Representative Assembly is still less qualified for the judicial power; because it is too numerous, too slow, and too little skilled in the laws.

6. Because a single Assembly, possessed of all the powers of government, would make arbitrary laws for their own interest, execute all laws arbitrarily for their own interest, and adjudge all controversies in their own favour.

But shall the whole power of legislation rest in one Assembly? Most of the foregoing reasons apply equally to prove that the legislative power ought to be more complex—to which we may add, that if the legislative power is wholly in one Assembly, and the executive in another, or in a single person, these two powers will oppose and enervate upon each other, until the contest shall end in war, and the whole power, legislative and executive, be usurped by the strongest.

The judicial power, in such case, could not mediate, or hold the balance between the two contending powers, because the legislative would undermine it. And this shews the necessity too, of giving the executive power a negative upon the legislative, otherwise this will be continually encroaching upon that.

To avoid these dangers let a [distinct] Assembly be constituted, as a mediator between the two extreme branches of the legislature, that which represents the people and that which is vested with the executive power.

Let the Representative Assembly then elect by ballot, from among themselves or their constituents, or both, a distinct Assembly, which for the sake of perspicuity we will call a Council. It may consist of any number you please, say twenty or thirty, and should have a free and independent exercise of its judgment, and consequently a negative voice in the legislature.

These two bodies thus constituted, and made integral parts of the legislature, let them unite, and by joint ballot choose a Governor, who, after being stripped of most of those badges of domination called prerogatives, should have a free and independent exercise of his judgment, and be made also an integral part of the legislature. This I know is liable to objections, and if you please you may make him only President of the Council, as in Connecticut: But as the Governor is to be invested with the executive power, with consent of Council, I think he ought to have a negative upon the legislative. If he is annually elective, as he ought to be, he will always have so much reverence and affection for the People, their Representatives and Councillors, that although you give him an independent exercise of his judgment, he will seldom use it in opposition to the two Houses, except in cases the public utility of which would be conspicuous, and some such cases would happen.

In the present exigency of American affairs, when by an act of Parliament we are put out of the royal protection, and consequently discharged from our allegiance; and it has become necessary to assume government for our immediate security, the Governor, Lieutenant-Governor, Secretary, Treasurer, Commissary, Attorney-General, should be chosen by joint Ballot, of both Houses. And these and all other elections, especially of Representatives, and Councillors, should be annual, there not being in the whole circle of the sciences, a maxim more infallible than this, "Where annual elections end, there slavery begins."

These great men, in this respect, should be, once a year

"Like bubbles on the sea of matter borne,
They rise, they break, and to that sea return."

This will teach them the great political virtues of humility, patience, and moderation, without which every man in power becomes a ravenous beast of prey.

This mode of constituting the great offices of state will answer very well for the present, but if, by experiment, it should be found inconvenient, the legislature may at its leisure devise other methods of creating them, by elections of the people at large, as in Connecticut, or it may enlarge the term for which they shall be chosen to seven years, or three years, or for life, or make any other alterations which the society shall find productive of its ease, its safety, its freedom, or in one word, its happiness.

A rotation of all offices, as well as of Representatives and Councillors, has many advocates, and is contended for with many plausible arguments. It would be attended no doubt with many advantages, and if the society has a sufficient number of suitable characters to supply the great number of vacancies which would be made by such a rotation, I can see no objection to it. These persons may be allowed to serve for three years, and then excluded three years, or for any longer or shorter term.

Any seven or nine of the legislative Council may be made a Quorum, for doing business as a Privy Council, to advise the Governor in the exercise of the executive branch of power, and in all acts of state.

The Governor should have the command of the militia, and of all your armies. The power of pardons should be with the Governor and Council.

Judges, Justices and all other officers, civil and military, should be nominated and appointed by the Governor, with the advice and consent of Council, unless you choose to have a government more popular; if you do, all officers, civil and military, may be chosen by joint ballot of both Houses, or in order to preserve the independence and importance of each House, by ballot of one House, concurred by the other. Sheriffs should be chosen by the freeholders of counties—so should Registers of Deeds and Clerks of Counties.

All officers should have commissions, under the hand of the Governor and seal of the Colony.

The dignity and stability of government in all its branches, the morals of the people and every blessing of society, depends so much upon an upright and skillful administration of justice, that the judicial power ought to be distinct from both the legislative and executive, and independent upon both, that so it may be a check upon both, as both should be checks upon that. The Judges therefore should always be men of learning and experience in the laws, of exemplary morals, great patience, calmness, coolness and attention. Their minds should not be distracted with jarring interests; they should not be dependant upon any man or body of men. To these ends they should hold estates for life in their offices, or in other words their commissions should be during good behaviour, and their salaries ascertained and established by law. For misbehaviour the grand inquest of the Colony, the House of Representatives, should impeach them before the Governor and Council, where they should have time and opportunity to make their defence, but if convicted should be removed from their offices, and subjected to such other punishment as shall be thought proper.

A Militia Law requiring all men, or with very few exceptions, besides cases of conscience, to be provided with arms and ammunition, to be trained at certain seasons, and requiring counties, towns, or other small districts to be provided with public stocks of ammunition and entrenching utensils, and with some settled plans for transporting provisions after the militia, when marched to defend their country against sudden invasions, and requiring certain districts to be provided with field-pieces, companies of matrosses and perhaps some regiments of light horse, is always a wise institution, and in the present circumstances of our country indispensable.

Laws for the liberal education of youth, especially of the lower class of people, are so extremely wise and useful, that to a humane and generous mind, no expence for this purpose would be thought extravagant.

The very mention of sumptuary laws will excite a smile. Whether our countrymen have wisdom and virtue enough to submit to them I know not. But the happiness of the people might be greatly promoted by them, and a revenue saved sufficient to carry on this war forever. Frugality is a great revenue, besides curing us of vanities, levities and fopperies which are real antidotes to all great, manly and warlike virtues.

But must not all commissions run in the name of a king? No. Why may they not as well run thus, "The Colony of   to A. B. greeting," and be tested by the Governor?

Why may not writs, instead of running in the name of a King, run thus, "The Colony of   to the Sheriff, &c." and be tested by the Chief Justice.

Why may not indictments conclude, "against the peace of the Colony of   and the dignity of the same?"

A Constitution, founded on these principles, introduces knowledge among the People, and inspires them with a conscious dignity, becoming Freemen. A general emulation takes place, which causes good humour, sociability, good manners, and good morals to be general. That elevation of sentiment, inspired by such a government, makes the common people brave and enterprizing. That ambition which is inspired by it makes them sober, industrious and frugal. You will find among them some elegance, perhaps, but more solidity; a little pleasure, but a great deal of business—some politeness, but more civility. If you compare such a country with the regions of domination, whether Monarchial or Aristocratical, you will fancy yourself in Arcadia or Elisium.

If the Colonies should assume governments separately, they should be left entirely to their own choice of the forms, and if a Continental Constitution should be formed, it should be a Congress, containing a fair and adequate Representation of the Colonies, and its authority should sacredly be confined to these cases, viz. war, trade, disputes between Colony and Colony, the Post-Office, and the unappropriated lands of the Crown, as they used to be called.

These Colonies, under such forms of government, and in such a union, would be unconquerable by all the Monarchies of Europe.

You and I, my dear Friend, have been sent into life, at a time when the greatest law-givers of antiquity would have wished to have lived. How few of the human race have ever enjoyed an opportunity of making an election of government more than of air, soil, or climate, for themselves or their children. When! Before the present epocha, had three millions of people full power and a fair opportunity to form and establish the wisest and happiest government that human wisdom can contrive? I hope you will avail yourself and your country of that extensive learning and indefatigable industry which you possess, to assist her in the formations of the happiest governments, and the best character of a great People. For myself, I must beg you to keep my name out of sight, for this feeble attempt, if it should be known to be mine, would oblige me to apply to myself those lines of the immortal John Milton, in one of his sonnets,

> "I did but teach the age to quit their cloggs
> By the plain rules of ancient Liberty,
> When lo! a barbarous noise surrounded me,
> Of owls and cuckoos, asses, apes and dogs."

6

GOUVERNEUR MORRIS, POLITICAL ENQUIRIES
1776
Amerikastudien 21:329 (1978)

Of Political Liberty

Political Liberty is defined, the Right of assenting to or dissenting from every Public Act by which a Man is to be bound. Hence, the perfect Enjoyment of it presupposes a Society in which unanimous Consent is required to every public Act. It is less perfect where the Majority governs. Still less where the Power is in a representative Body. Still less where either the executive or judicial is not elected. Still less where only the legislative is elected. Still less where a Part of the Representatives can decide. Still less where such Part is not a Majority of the whole. Still less where the Decisions of such Majority may be delayed or overruled. Thus the Shades grow weaker and weaker, till no Trace remains. But is it not destroyed by the first Restriction?

In England, a Majority of Citizens does not elect the Majority of Representatives. A certain Part of those Representatives being met, a Majority of them can bind the Electors. The Decisions of these Representatives are confined to the legislative Department. And the Dissent of the Lords or of the King sets aside what the Commons had determined. The Englishman therefore does not, in any Degree, possess the Right of dissenting from Acts by which he is affected, so far as those Acts relate to the Executive or judicial Departments. And in Respect to the legislative, his political Liberty consists in the Chance that certain Persons will not consent to Acts which he would not have approved. And is that a Right which, depending on a Complication of Chances, gives one thousand against him for one in his favor? Right is not only independent of, but excludes the Idea of Chance.

7

THOMAS JEFFERSON, AUTOBIOGRAPHY
1821
Works 1:66–71, 77–78

So far we were proceeding in the details of reformation only; selecting points of legislation prominent in character & principle, urgent, and indicative of the strength of the general pulse of reformation. When I left Congress, in 76. it was in the persuasion that our whole code must be reviewed, adapted to our republican form of government, and, now that we had no negatives of Councils, Governors & Kings to restrain us from doing right, that it should be corrected, in all it's parts, with a single eye to reason, & the good of those for whose government it was framed. Early therefore in the session of 76. to which I returned, I moved and presented a bill for the revision of the laws; which was passed on the 24th. of October, and on the 5th. of November Mr. Pendleton, Mr. Wythe, George Mason, Thomas L. Lee and myself were appointed a committee to execute the work. We agreed to meet at Fredericksburg to settle the plan of operation and to distribute the work. We met there accordingly, on the 13th. of January 1777. The first question was whether we should propose to abolish the whole existing system of laws, and prepare a new and complete Institute, or preserve the general system, and only modify it to the present state of things. Mr. Pendleton, contrary to his usual disposition in favor of antient things, was for the former proposition, in which he was joined by Mr. Lee. To this it was objected that to abrogate our whole system would be a bold measure, and probably far beyond the views of the legislature; that they had been in the practice of revising from time to time the laws of the colony, omitting the expired, the repealed and the obsolete, amending only those retained, and probably meant we should now do the same, only including the British statutes as well as our own: that to compose a new Institute like those of Justinian and Bracton, or that of Blackstone, which was the model proposed by Mr. Pendleton, would be an arduous undertaking, of vast research, of great consideration & judgment; and when reduced to a text, every word of that text, from the imperfection of human lan-

guage, and it's incompetence to express distinctly every shade of idea, would become a subject of question & chicanery until settled by repeated adjudications; that this would involve us for ages in litigation, and render property uncertain until, like the statutes of old, every word had been tried, and settled by numerous decisions, and by new volumes of reports & commentaries; and that no one of us probably would undertake such a work, which, to be systematical, must be the work of one hand. This last was the opinion of Mr. Wythe, Mr. Mason & myself. When we proceeded to the distribution of the work, Mr. Mason excused himself as, being no lawyer, he felt himself unqualified for the work, and he resigned soon after. Mr. Lee excused himself on the same ground, and died indeed in a short time. The other two gentlemen therefore and myself divided the work among us. The common law and statutes to the 4. James I. (when our separate legislature was established) were assigned to me; the British statutes from that period to the present day to Mr. Wythe, and the Virginia laws to Mr. Pendleton. As the law of Descents, & the criminal law fell of course within my portion, I wished the commee to settle the leading principles of these, as a guide for me in framing them. And with respect to the first, I proposed to abolish the law of primogeniture, and to make real estate descendible in parcenary to the next of kin, as personal property is by the statute of distribution. Mr. Pendleton wished to preserve the right of primogeniture, but seeing at once that that could not prevail, he proposed we should adopt the Hebrew principle, and give a double portion to the elder son. I observed that if the eldest son could eat twice as much, or do double work, it might be a natural evidence of his right to a double portion; but being on a par in his powers & wants, with his brothers and sisters, he should be on a par also in the partition of the patrimony, and such was the decision of the other members.

On the subject of the Criminal law, all were agreed that the punishment of death should be abolished, except for treason and murder; and that, for other felonies should be substituted hard labor in the public works, and in some cases, the Lex talionis. How this last revolting principle came to obtain our approbation, I do not remember. There remained indeed in our laws a vestige of it in a single case of a slave. it was the English law in the time of the Anglo-Saxons, copied probably from the Hebrew law of "an eye for an eye, a tooth for a tooth," and it was the law of several antient people. But the modern mind had left it far in the rear of it's advances. These points however being settled, we repaired to our respective homes for the preparation of the work.

Feb. 6. In the execution of my part I thought it material not to vary the diction of the antient statutes by modernizing it, nor to give rise to new questions by new expressions. The text of these statutes had been so fully explained and defined by numerous adjudications, as scarcely ever now to produce a question in our courts. I thought it would be useful also, in all new draughts, to reform the style of the later British statutes, and of our own acts of assembly, which from their verbosity, their endless tautologies, their involutions of case within case, and parenthesis within parenthesis, and their multiplied efforts at certainty by *saids* and *aforesaids,* by *ors* and by *ands,* to make them more plain, do really render them more perplexed and incomprehensible, not only to common readers, but to the lawyers themselves. We were employed in this work from that time to Feb. 1779, when we met at Williamsburg, that is to say, Mr. Pendleton, Mr. Wythe & myself, and meeting day by day, we examined critically our several parts, sentence by sentence, scrutinizing and amending until we had agreed on the whole. We then returned home, had fair copies made of our several parts, which were reported to the General Assembly June 18. 1779. by Mr. Wythe and myself, Mr. Pendleton's residence being distant, and he having authorized us by letter to declare his approbation. We had in this work brought so much of the Common law as it was thought necessary to alter, all the British statutes from Magna Charta to the present day, and all the laws of Virginia, from the establishment of our legislature, in the 4th. Jac. I. to the present time, which we thought should be retained, within the compass of 126 bills, making a printed folio of 90 pages only. Some bills were taken out occasionally, from time to time, and passed; but the main body of the work was not entered on by the legislature until after the general peace, in 1785. when by the unwearied exertions of Mr. Madison, in opposition to the endless quibbles, chicaneries, perversions, vexations and delays of lawyers and demi-lawyers, most of the bills were passed by the legislature, with little alteration.

. . . . .

I considered 4 of these bills, passed or reported, as forming a system by which every fibre would be eradicated of antient or future aristocracy; and a foundation laid for a government truly republican. The repeal of the laws of entail would prevent the accumulation and perpetuation of wealth in select families, and preserve the soil of the country from being daily more & more absorbed in Mortmain. The abolition of primogeniture, and equal partition of inheritances removed the feudal and unnatural distinctions which made one member of every family rich, and all the rest poor, substituting equal partition, the best of all Agrarian laws. The restoration of the rights of conscience relieved the people from taxation for the support of a religion not theirs; for the establishment was truly of the religion of the rich, the dissenting sects being entirely composed of the less wealthy people; and these, by the bill for a general education, would be qualified to understand their rights, to maintain them, and to exercise with intelligence their parts in self-government: and all this would be effected without the violation of a single natural right of any one individual citizen. To these too might be added, as a further security, the introduction of the trial by jury, into the Chancery courts, which have already ingulfed and continue to ingulf, so great a proportion of the jurisdiction over our property.

8

THE ESSEX RESULT
29 Apr. 1778
Handlin 324–40

In Convention of Delegates from the several towns of Lynn, Salem, Danvers, Wenham, Manchester, Gloucester, Ipswich, Newbury-Port, Salisbury, Methuen, Boxford, and Topsfield, holden by adjournment at Ipswich, on the twenty-ninth day of April, one thousand seven hundred and seventy-eight.

PETER COFFIN ESQ; in the Chair.

The Constitution and form of Government framed by the Convention of this State, was read paragraph by paragraph, and after debate, the following votes were passed.

1. That the present situation of this State renders it best, that the framing of a Constitution therefor, should be postponed 'till the public affairs are in a more peaceable and settled condition.

2. That a bill of rights, clearly ascertaining and defining the rights of conscience, and that security of person and property, which every member in the State hath a right to expect from the supreme power thereof, ought to be settled and established, previous to the ratification of any constitution for the State.

3. That the executive power in any State, ought not to have any share or voice in the legislative power in framing the laws, and therefore, that the second article of the Constitution is liable to exception.

4. That any man who is chosen Governor, ought to be properly qualified in point of property—that the qualification therefor, mentioned in the third article of the Constitution, is not sufficient—nor is the same qualification directed to be ascertained on fixed principles, as it ought to be, on account of the fluctuation of the nominal value of money, and of property.

5. That in every free Republican Government, where the legislative power is rested in an house or houses of representatives, all the members of the State ought to be equally represented.

6. That the mode of representation proposed in the sixth article of the constitution, is not so equal a representation as can reasonably be devised.

7. That therefore the mode of representation in said sixth article is exceptionable.

8. That the representation proposed in said article is also exceptionable, as it will produce an unwieldy assembly.

9. That the mode of election of Senators pointed out in the Constitution is exceptionable.

10. That the rights of conscience, and the security of person and property each member of the State is entitled to, are not ascertained and defined in the Constitution, with a precision sufficient to limit the legislative power—and therefore, that the thirteenth article of the constitution is exceptionable.

11. That the fifteenth article is exceptionable, because the numbers that constitute a quorum in the House of Representatives and Senate, are too small.

12. That the seventeenth article of the constitution is exceptionable, because the supreme executive officer is not vested with proper authority—and because an independence between the executive and legislative body is not preserved.

13. That the nineteenth article is exceptionable, because a due independence is not kept up between the supreme legislative, judicial, and executive powers, nor between any two of them.

14. That the twentieth article is exceptionable, because the supreme executive officer hath a voice, and must be present in that Court, which alone hath authority to try impeachments.

15. That the twenty second article is exceptionable, because the supreme executive power is not preserved distinct from, and independent of, the supreme legislative power.

16. That the twenty third article is exceptionable, because the power of granting pardons is not solely vested in the supreme executive power of the State.

17. That the twenty eighth article is exceptionable, because the delegates for the Continental Congress may be elected by the House of Representatives, when all the Senators may vote against the election of those who are delegated.

18. That the thirty fourth article is exceptionable, because the rights of conscience are not therein clearly defined and ascertained; and further, because the free exercise and enjoyment of religious worship is there said to be *allowed* to all the protestants in the State, when in fact, that free exercise and enjoyment is the natural and uncontroulable right of every member of the State.

A committee was then appointed to attempt the ascertaining of the true principles of government, applicable to the territory of the Massachusetts-Bay; to state the nonconformity of the constitution proposed by the Convention of this State to those principles, and to delineate the general outlines of a constitution conformable thereto; and to report the same to this Body.

This Convention was then adjourned to the twelfth day of May next, to be holden at Ipswich.

The Convention met pursuant to adjournment, and their committee presented the following report.

The committee appointed by this Convention at their last adjournment, have proceeded upon the service assigned them. With diffidence have they undertaken the several parts of their duty, and the manner in which they have executed them, they submit to the candor of this Body. When they considered of what vast consequence, the forming of a Constitution is to the members of this State, the length of time that is necessary to canvass and digest any proposed plan of government, before the establishment of it, and the consummate coolness, and solemn deliberation which should attend, not only those gentlemen who have, reposed in them, the important trust of delineating the several lines in which the various powers of government are to move, but also all those, who are to

form an opinion of the execution of that trust, your committee must be excused when they express a surprise and regret, that so short a time is allowed the freemen inhabiting the territory of the Massachusetts-Bay, to revise and comprehend the form of government proposed to them by the convention of this State, to compare it with those principles on which every free government ought to be founded, and to ascertain it's conformity or non-conformity thereto. All this is necessary to be done, before a true opinion of it's merit or demerit can be formed. This opinion is to be certified within a time which, in our apprehension, is much too short for this purpose, and to be certified by a people, who, during that time, have had and will have their minds perplexed and oppressed with a variety of public cares. The committee also beg leave to observe, that the constitution proposed for public approbation, was formed by gentlemen, who, at the same time, had a large share in conducting an important war, and who were employed in carrying into execution almost all the various powers of government.

The committee however proceeded in attempting the task assigned them, and the success of that attempt is now reported.

The reason and understanding of mankind, as well as the experience of all ages, confirm the truth of this proposition, that the benefits resulting to individuals from a free government, conduce much more to their happiness, than the retaining of all their natural rights in a state of nature. These benefits are greater or less, as the form of government, and the mode of exercising the supreme power of the State, are more or less conformable to those principles of equal impartial liberty, which is the property of all men from their birth as the gift of their Creator, compared with the manners and genius of the people, their occupations, customs, modes of thinking, situation, extent of country, and numbers. If the constitution and form of government are wholly repugnant to those principles, wretched are the subjects of that State. They have surrendered a portion of their natural rights, the enjoyment of which was in some degree a blessing, and the consequence is, they find themselves stripped of the remainder. As an anodyne to compose the spirits of these slaves, and to lull them into a passively obedient state, they are told, that tyranny is preferable to no government at all; a proposition which is to be doubted, unless considered under some limitation. Surely a state of nature is more excellent than that, in which men are meanly submissive to the haughty will of an imperious tyrant, whose savage passions are not bounded by the laws of reason, religion, honor, or a regard to his subjects, and the point to which all his movements center, is the gratification of a brutal appetite. As in a state of nature much happiness cannot be enjoyed by individuals, so it has been conformable to the inclinations of almost all men, to enter into a political society so constituted, as to remove the inconveniences they were obliged to submit to in their former state, and, at the same time, to retain all those natural rights, the enjoyment of which would be consistent with the nature of a free government, and the necessary subordination to the supreme power of the state.

To determine what form of government, in any given case, will produce the greatest possible happiness to the subject, is an arduous task, not to be compassed perhaps by any human powers. Some of the greatest geniuses and most learned philosophers of all ages, impelled by their sollicitude to promote the happiness of mankind, have nobly dared to attempt it: and their labours have crowned them with immortality. A Solon, a Lycurgus of Greece, a Numa of Rome are remembered with honor, when the wide extended empires of succeeding tyrants, are hardly important enough to be faintly sketched out on the map, while their superb thrones have long since crumbled into dust. The man who alone undertakes to form a constitution, ought to be an unimpassioned being; one enlightened mind; biassed neither by the lust of power, the allurements of pleasure, nor the glitter of wealth; perfectly acquainted with all the alienable and unalienable rights of mankind; possessed of this grand truth, that all men are born equally free, and that no man ought to surrender any part of his natural rights, without receiving the greatest possible equivalent; and influenced by the impartial principles of rectitude and justice, without partiality for, or prejudice against the interest or professions of any individuals or class of men. He ought also to be master of the histories of all the empires and states which are now existing, and all those which have figured in antiquity, and thereby able to collect and blend their respective excellencies, and avoid those defects which experience hath pointed out. Rousseau, a learned foreigner, a citizen of Geneva, sensible of the importance and difficulty of the subject, thought it impossible for any body of people, to form a free and equal constitution for themselves, in which, every individual should have equal justice done him, and be permitted to enjoy a share of power in the state, equal to what should be enjoyed by any other. Each individual, said he, will struggle, not only to retain all his own natural rights, but to acquire a controul over those of others. Fraud, circumvention, and an union of interest of some classes of people, combined with an inattention to the rights of posterity, will prevail over the principles of equity, justice, and good policy. The Genevans, perhaps the most virtuous republicans now existing, thought like Rousseau. They called the celebrated Calvin to their assistance. He came, and, by their gratitude, have they embalmed his memory.

The freemen inhabiting the territory of the Massachusetts-Bay are now forming a political society for themselves. Perhaps their situation is more favorable in some respects, for erecting a free government, than any other people were ever favored with. That attachment to old forms, which usually embarrasses, has not place amongst them. They have the history and experience of all States before them. Mankind have been toiling through ages for their information; and the philosophers and learned men of antiquity have trimmed their midnight lamps, to transmit to them instruction. We live also in an age, when the principles of political liberty, and the foundation of governments, have been freely canvassed, and fairly settled. Yet some difficulties we have to encounter. Not content with removing our attachment to the old government, per-

haps we have contracted a prejudice against some part of it without foundation. The idea of liberty has been held up in so dazzling colours, that some of us may not be willing to submit to that subordination necessary in the freest States. Perhaps we may say further, that we do not consider ourselves united as brothers, with an united interest, but have fancied a clashing of interests amongst the various classes of men, and have acquired a thirst of power, and a wish of domination, over some of the community. We are contending for freedom—Let us all be equally free—It is possible, and it is just. Our interests when candidly considered are one. Let us have a constitution founded, not upon party or prejudice—not one for to-day or to-morrow—but for posterity. Let *Esto perpetua* be it's motto. If it is founded in good policy; it will be founded in justice and honesty. Let all ambitious and interested views be discarded, and let regard be had only to the good of the whole, in which the situation and rights of posterity must be considered: and let equal justice be done to all the members of the community; and we thereby imitate our common father, who at our births, dispersed his favors, not only with a liberal, but with an equal hand.

Was it asked, what is the best form of government for the people of the Massachusetts-Bay? we confess it would be a question of infinite importance: and the man who could truly answer it, would merit a statue of gold to his memory, and his fame would be recorded in the annals of late posterity, with unrivalled lustre. The question, however, must be answered, and let it have the best answer we can possibly give it. Was a man to mention a despotic government, his life would be a just forfeit to the resentments of an affronted people. Was he to hint monarchy, he would deservedly be hissed off the stage, and consigned to infamy. A republican form is the only one consonant to the feelings of the generous and brave Americans. Let us now attend to those principles, upon which all republican governments, who boast any degree of political liberty, are founded, and which must enter into the spirit of a FREE republican constitution. For all republics are not FREE.

All men are born equally free. The rights they possess at their births are equal, and of the same kind. Some of those rights are alienable, and may be parted with for an equivalent. Others are unalienable and inherent, and of that importance, that no equivalent can be received in exchange. Sometimes we shall mention the surrendering of a power to controul our natural rights, which perhaps is speaking with more precision, than when we use the expression of parting with natural rights—but the same thing is intended. Those rights which are unalienable, and of that importance, are called the rights of conscience. We have duties, for the discharge of which we are accountable to our Creator and benefactor, which no human power can cancel. What those duties are, is determinable by right reason, which may be, and is called, a well informed conscience. What this conscience dictates as our duty, is so; and that power which assumes a controul over it, is an usurper; for no consent can be pleaded to justify the controul, as any consent in this case is void. The alienation of some rights, in themselves alienable, may be also void, if the bargain is of that nature, that no equivalent can be received. Thus, if a man surrender all his alienable rights, without reserving a controul over the supreme power, or a right to resume in certain cases, the surrender is void, for he becomes a slave; and a slave can receive no equivalent. Common equity would set aside this bargain.

When men form themselves into society, and erect a body politic or State, they are to be considered as one moral whole, which is in possession of the supreme power of the State. This supreme power is composed of the powers of each individual collected together, and VOLUNTARILY parted with by him. No individual, in this case, parts with his unalienable rights, the supreme power therefore cannot controul them. Each individual also surrenders the power of controuling his natural alienable rights, ONLY WHEN THE GOOD OF THE WHOLE REQUIRES it. The supreme power therefore can do nothing but what is for the good of the whole; and when it goes beyond this line, it is a power usurped. If the individual receives an equivalent for the right of controul he has parted with, the surrender of that right is valid; if he receives no equivalent, the surrender is void, and the supreme power as it respects him is an usurper. If the supreme power is so directed and executed that he does not enjoy political liberty, it is an illegal power, and he is not bound to obey. Political liberty is by some defined, a liberty of doing whatever is not prohibited by law. The definition is erroneous. A tyrant may govern by laws. The republic's of Venice and Holland govern by laws, yet those republic's have degenerated into insupportable tyrannies. Let it be thus defined; political liberty is the right every man in the state has, to do whatever is not prohibited by laws, TO WHICH HE HAS GIVEN HIS CONSENT. This definition is in unison with the feelings of a free people. But to return—If a fundamental principle on which each individual enters into society is, that he shall be bound by no laws but those to which he has consented, he cannot be considered as consenting to any law enacted by a minority: for he parts with the power of controuling his natural rights, only when the good of the whole requires it; and of this there can be but one absolute judge in the State. If the minority can assume the right of judging, there may then be two judges; for however large the minority may be, there must be another body still larger, who have the same claim, if not a better, to the right of absolute determination. If therefore the supreme power should be so modelled and exerted, that a law may be enacted by a minority, the inforcing of that law upon an individual who is opposed to it, is an act of tyranny. Further, as every individual, in entering into the society, parted with a power of controuling his natural rights equal to that parted with by any other, or in other words, as all the members of the society contributed an equal portion of their natural rights, towards the forming of the supreme power, so every member ought to receive equal benefit from, have equal influence in forming, and retain an equal controul over, the supreme power.

It has been observed, that each individual parts with the power of controuling his natural alienable rights, only when the good of the whole requires it, he therefore has remaining, after entering into political society, all his unalienable natural rights, and a part also of his alienable natural rights, provided the good of the whole does not require the sacrifice of them. Over the class of unalienable rights the supreme power hath no controul, and they ought to be clearly defined and ascertained in a BILL OF RIGHTS, previous to the ratification of any constitution. The bill of rights should also contain the equivalent every man receives, as a consideration for the rights he has surrendered. This equivalent consists principally in the security of his person and property, and is also unassailable by the supreme power: for if the equivalent is taken back, those natural rights which were parted with to purchase it, return to the original proprietor, as nothing is more true, than that ALLEGIANCE AND PROTECTION ARE RECIPROCAL.

The committee also proceeded to consider upon what principles, and in what manner, the supreme power of the state thus composed of the powers of the several individuals thereof, may be formed, modelled, and exerted in a republic, so that every member of the state may enjoy political liberty. This is called by some, *the ascertaining of the political law of the state*. Let it now be called *the forming of a constitution*.

The reason why the supreme governor of the world is a rightful and just governor, and entitled to the allegiance of the universe is, because he is infinitely good, wise, and powerful. His goodness prompts him to the best measures, his wisdom qualifies him to discern them, and his power to effect them. In a state likewise, the supreme power is best disposed of, when it is so modelled and balanced, and rested in such hands, that it has the greatest share of goodness, wisdom, and power, which is consistent with the lot of humanity.

That state, (other things being equal) which has reposed the supreme power in the hands of one or a small number of persons, is the most powerful state. An union, expedition, secrecy and dispatch are to be found only here. Where power is to be executed by a large number, there will not probably be either of the requisites just mentioned. Many men have various opinions: and each one will be tenacious of his own, as he thinks it preferable to any other; for when he thinks otherwise, it will cease to be his opinion. From this diversity of opinions results disunion; from disunion, a want of expedition and dispatch. And the larger the number to whom a secret is entrusted, the greater is the probability of it's disclosure. This inconvenience more fully strikes us when we consider that want of secrecy may prevent the successful execution of any measures, however excellently formed and digested.

But from a single person, or a very small number, we are not to expect that political honesty, and upright regard to the interest of the body of the people, and the civil rights of each individual, which are essential to a good and free constitution. For these qualities we are to go to the body of the people. The voice of the people is said to be the voice of God. No man will be so hardy and presumptuous, as to affirm the truth of that proposition in it's fullest extent. But if this is considered as the intent of it, that the people have always a disposition to promote their own happiness, and that when they have time to be informed, and the necessary means of information given them, they will be able to determine upon the necessary measures therefor, no man, of a tolerable acquaintance with mankind, will deny the truth of it. The inconvenience and difficulty in forming any free permanent constitution are, that such is the lot of humanity, the bulk of the people, whose happiness is principally to be consulted in forming a constitution, and in legislation, (as they include the majority) are so situated in life, and such are their laudable occupations, that they cannot have time for, nor the means of furnishing themselves with proper information, but must be indebted to some of their fellow subjects for the communication. Happy is the man, and blessings will attend his memory, who shall improve his leisure, and those abilities which heaven has indulged him with, in communicating that true information, and impartial knowledge, to his fellow subjects, which will insure their happiness. But the artful demagogue, who to gratify his ambition or avarice, shall, with the gloss of false patriotism, mislead his countrymen, and meanly snatch from them the golden glorious opportunity of forming a system of political and civil liberty, fraught with blessings for themselves, and remote posterity, what language can paint his demerit? The execrations of ages will be a punishment inadequate; and his name, though ever blackening as it rolls down the stream of time, will not catch its proper hue.

Yet, when we are forming a Constitution, by deductions that follow from established principles, (which is the only good method of forming one for futurity,) we are to look further than to the bulk of the people, for the greatest wisdom, firmness, consistency, and perseverance. These qualities will most probably be found amongst men of education and fortune. From such men we are to expect genius cultivated by reading, and all the various advantages and assistances, which art, and a liberal education aided by wealth, can furnish. From these result learning, a thorough knowledge of the interests of their country, when considered abstractedly, when compared with the neighbouring States, and when with those more remote, and an acquaintance with it's produce and manufacture, and it's exports and imports. All these are necessary to be known, in order to determine what is the true interest of any state; and without that interest is ascertained, impossible will it be to discover, whether a variety of certain laws may be beneficial or hurtful. From gentlemen whose private affairs compel them to take care of their own household, and deprive them of leisure, these qualifications are not to be generally expected, whatever class of men they are enrolled in.

Let all these respective excellencies be united. Let the supreme power be so disposed and ballanced, that the laws may have in view the interest of the whole; let them be wisely and consistently framed for that end, and firmly adhered to; and let them be executed with vigour and dispatch.

Before we proceed further, it must be again considered, and kept always in view, that we are not attempting to form a temporary constitution, one adjusted only to our present circumstances. We wish for one founded upon such principles as will secure to us freedom and happiness, however our circumstances may vary. One that will smile amidst the declensions of European and Asiatic empires,

and survive the rude storms of time. It is not therefore to be understood, that all the men of fortune of the present day, are men of wisdom and learning, or that they are not. Nor that the bulk of the people, the farmers, the merchants, the tradesmen, and labourers, are all honest and upright, with single views to the public good, or that they are not. In each of the classes there are undoubtedly exceptions, as the rules laid down are general. The proposition is only this. That among gentlemen of education, fortune and leisure, we shall find the largest number of men, possessed of wisdom, learning, and a firmness and consistency of character. That among the bulk of the people, we shall find the greatest share of political honesty, probity, and a regard to the interest of the whole, of which they compose the majority. That wisdom and firmness are not sufficient without good intentions, nor the latter without the former. The conclusion is, let the legislative body unite them all. The former are called the excellencies that result from an aristocracy; the latter, those that result from a democracy.

The supreme power is considered as including the legislative, judicial, and executive powers. The nature and employment of these several powers deserve a distinct attention.

The legislative power is employed in making laws, or prescribing such rules of action to every individual in the state, as the good of the whole requires, to be conformed to by him in his conduct to the governors and governed, with respect both to their persons and property, according to the several relations he stands in. What rules of action the good of the whole requires, can be ascertained only by the majority, for a reason formerly mentioned. Therefore the legislative power must be so formed and exerted, that in prescribing any rule of action, or, in other words, enacting any law, the majority must consent. This may be more evident, when the fundamental condition on which every man enters into society, is considered. No man consented that his natural alienable rights should be wantonly controuled: they were controulable, only when that controul should be subservient to the good of the whole; and that subserviency, from the very nature of government, can be determined but by one absolute judge. The minority cannot be that judge, because then there may be two judges opposed to each other, so that this subserviency remains undetermined. Now the enacting of a law, is only the exercise of this controul over the natural alienable rights of each member of the state; and therefore this law must have the consent of the majority, or be invalid, as being contrary to the fundamental condition of the original social contract. In a state of nature, every man had the sovereign controul over his own person. He might also have, in that state, a qualified property. Whatever lands or chattels he had acquired the peaceable possession of, were exclusively his, by right of occupancy or possession. For while they were unpossessed he had a right to them equally with any other man, and therefore could not be disturbed in his possession, without being injured; for no man could lawfully dispossess him, without having a better right, which no man had. Over this qualified property every man in a state of nature had also a sovereign controul.

And in entering into political society, he surrendered this right of controul over his person and property, (with an exception to the rights of conscience) to the supreme legislative power, to be exercised by that power, *when the good of the whole demanded it.* This was all the right he could surrender, being all the alienable right of which he was possessed. The only objects of legislation therefore, are the person and property of the individuals which compose the state. If the law affects only the persons of the members, the consent of a majority of any members is sufficient. If the law affects the property only, the consent of those who hold a majority of the property is enough. If it affects, (as it will very frequently, if not always,) both the person and property, the consent of a majority of the members, and of those members also, who hold a majority of the property is necessary. If the consent of the latter is not obtained, their interest is taken from them against their consent, and their boasted security of property is vanished. Those who make the law, in this case give and grant what is not theirs. The law, in it's principles, becomes a second stamp act. Lord Chatham very finely ridiculed the British house of commons upon that principle. "You can give and grant, said he, only your own. Here you give and grant, what? The property of the Americans." The people of the Masssachusetts-Bay then thought his Lordship's ridicule well pointed. And would they be willing to merit the same? Certainly they will agree in the principle, should they mistake the application. The laws of the province of Massachusetts-Bay adopted the same principle, and very happily applied it. As the votes of proprietors of common and undivided lands in their meetings, can affect only their property, therefore it is enacted, that in ascertaining the majority, the votes shall be collected according to the respective interests of the proprietors. If each member, without regard to his property, has equal influence in legislation with any other, it follows, that some members enjoy greater benefits and powers in legislation than others, when these benefits and powers are compared with the rights parted with to purchase them. For the property-holder parts with the controul over his person, as well as he who hath no property, and the former also parts with the controul over his property, of which the latter is destitute. Therefore to constitute a perfect law in a free state, affecting the persons and property of the members, it is necessary that the law be for the good of the whole, which is to be determined by a majority of the members, and that majority should include those, who possess a major part of the property in the state.

The judicial power follows next after the legislative power; for it cannot act, until after laws are prescribed. Every wise legislator annexes a sanction to his laws, which is most commonly penal, (that is) a punishment either corporal or pecuniary, to be inflicted on the member who shall infringe them. It is the part of the judicial power (which in this territory has always been, and always ought to be, a court and jury) to ascertain the member who hath broken the law. Every man is to be presumed innocent, until the judicial power hath determined him guilty. When that decision is known, the law annexes the punishment, and the offender is turned over to the executive arm, by whom it is inflicted on him. The judicial power hath also to determine what legal contracts have been broken, and what member hath been injured by a violation of the law, to consider the damages that have been sustained, and to ascertain the recompense. The executive power takes care that this recompense is paid.

The executive power is sometimes divided into the external executive, and internal executive. The former comprehends war, peace, the sending and receiving ambassadors, and whatever concerns the transactions of the state with any other independent state. The confederation of the United States of America hath lopped off this branch of the executive, and placed it in Congress. We have therefore only to consider the internal executive power, which is employed in the peace, security and protection of the subject and his property, and in the defence of the state. The executive power is to marshal and command her militia and armies for her defence, to enforce the law, and to carry into execution all the orders of the legislative powers.

A little attention to the subject will convince us, that these three powers ought to be in different hands, and independent of one another, and so ballanced, and each having that check upon the other, that their independence shall be preserved—If the three powers are united, the government will be absolute, *whether these powers are in the hands of one or a large number.* The same party will be the legislator, accuser, judge and executioner; and what probability will an accused person have of an acquittal, however innocent he may be, when his judge will be also a party.

If the legislative and judicial powers are united, the maker of the law will also interpret it; and the law may then speak a language, dictated by the whims, the caprice, or the prejudice of the judge, with impunity to him—And what people are so unhappy as those, whose laws are uncertain. It will also be in the breast of the judge, when grasping after his prey, to make a retrospective law, which shall bring the unhappy offender within it; and this also he can do with impunity—The subject can have no peaceable remedy—The judge will try himself, and an acquittal is the certain consequence. He has it also in his power to enact any law, which may shelter him from deserved vengeance.

Should the executive and legislative powers be united, mischiefs the most terrible would follow. The executive would enact those laws it pleased to execute, and no others—The judicial power would be set aside as inconvenient and tardy—The security and protection of the subject would be a shadow—The executive power would make itself absolute, and the government end in a tyranny—Lewis the eleventh of France, by cunning and treachery compleated the union of the executive and legislative powers of that kingdom, and upon that union established a system of tyranny. France was formerly under a free government.

The assembly or representatives of the united states of Holland, exercise the executive and legislative powers, and the government there is absolute.

Should the executive and judicial powers be united, the subject would then have no permanent security of his person and property. The executive power would interpret the laws and bend them to his will; and, as he is the judge, he may leap over them by artful constructions, and gratify, with impunity, the most rapacious passions. Perhaps no cause in any state has contributed more to promote internal convulsions, and to stain the scaffold with it's best blood, than this unhappy union. And it is an union which the executive power in all states, hath attempted to form: if that could not be compassed, to make the judicial power dependent upon it. Indeed the dependence of any of these powers upon either of the others, which in all states has always been attempted by one or the other of them, has so often been productive of such calamities, and of the shedding of such oceans of blood, that the page of history seems to be one continued tale of human wretchedness.

The following principles now seem to be established.

1. That the supreme power is limited, and cannot controul the unalienable rights of mankind, nor resume the equivalent (that is, the security of person and property) which each individual receives, as a consideration for the alienable rights he parted with in entering into political society.

2. That these unalienable rights, and this equivalent, are to be clearly defined and ascertained in a BILL OF RIGHTS, previous to the ratification of any constitution.

3. That the supreme power should be so formed and modelled, as to exert the greatest possible power, wisdom, and goodness.

4. That the legislative, judicial, and executive powers, are to be lodged in different hands, that each branch is to be independent, and further, to be so ballanced, and be able to exert such checks upon the others, as will preserve it from a dependence on, or an union with them.

5. That government can exert the greatest power when it's supreme authority is vested in the hands of one or a few.

6. That the laws will be made with the greatest wisdom, and best intentions, when men, of all the several classes in the state concur in the enacting of them.

7. That a government which is so constituted, that it cannot afford a degree of political liberty nearly equal to all it's members, is not founded upon principles of freedom and justice, and where any member enjoys no degree of political liberty, the government, so far as it respects him, is a tyranny, for he is controuled by laws to which he has never consented.

8. That the legislative power of a state hath no authority to controul the natural rights of any of it's members, unless the good of the whole requires it.

9. That a majority of the state is the only judge when the general good does require it.

10. That where the legislative power of the state is so formed, that a law may be enacted by the minority, each member of the state does not enjoy political liberty. And

11. That in a free government, a law affecting the person and property of it's members, is not valid, unless it has the consent of a majority of the members, which majority should include those, who hold a major part of the property in the state.

9

THOMAS JEFFERSON, NOTES ON THE STATE OF VIRGINIA, QUERY 19, 164–65
1784

We never had an interior trade of any importance. Our exterior commerce has suffered very much from the beginning of the present contest. During this time we have manufactured within our families the most necessary articles of cloathing. Those of cotton will bear some comparison with the same kinds of manufacture in Europe; but those of wool, flax and hemp are very coarse, unsightly, and unpleasant: and such is our attachment to agriculture, and such our preference for foreign manufactures, that be it wise or unwise, our people will certainly return as soon as they can, to the raising raw materials, and exchanging them for finer manufactures than they are able to execute themselves.

The political oeconomists of Europe have established it as a principle that every state should endeavour to manufacture for itself: and this principle, like many others, we transfer to America, without calculating the difference of circumstance which should often produce a difference of result. In Europe the lands are either cultivated, or locked up against the cultivator. Manufacture must therefore be resorted to of necessity not of choice, to support the surplus of their people. But we have an immensity of land courting the industry of the husbandman. Is it best then that all our citizens should be employed in its improvement, or that one half should be called off from that to exercise manufactures and handicraft arts for the other? Those who labour in the earth are the chosen people of God, if ever he had a chosen people, whose breasts he has made his peculiar deposit for substantial and genuine virtue. It is the focus in which he keeps alive that sacred fire, which otherwise might escape from the face of the earth. Corruption of morals in the mass of cultivators is a phaenomenon of which no age nor nation has furnished an example. It is the mark set on those, who not looking up to heaven, to their own soil and industry, as does the husbandman, for their subsistance, depend for it on the casualties and caprice of customers. Dependance begets subservience and venality, suffocates the germ of virtue, and prepares fit tools for the designs of ambition. This, the natural progress and consequence of the arts, has sometimes perhaps been retarded by accidental circumstances: but, generally speaking, the proportion which the aggregate of the other classes of citizens bears in any state to that of its husbandmen, is the proportion of its unsound to its healthy parts, and is a good-enough barometer whereby to measure its degree of corruption. While we have land to labour then, let us never wish to see our citizens occupied at a work-bench, or twirling a distaff. Carpenters, masons, smiths, are wanting in husbandry: but, for the general operations of manufacture, let our workshops remain in Europe. It is better to carry provisions and materials to workmen there, than bring them to the provisions and materials, and with them their manners and principles. The loss by the transportation of commodities across the Atlantic will be made up in happiness and permanence of government. The mobs of great cities add just so much to the support of pure government, as sores do to the strength of the human body. It is the manners and spirit of a people which preserve a republic in vigour. A degeneracy in these is a canker which soon eats to the heart of its laws and constitution.

10

JOHN ADAMS, DEFENCE OF THE CONSTITUTIONS
OF GOVERNMENT OF THE UNITED STATES
1787
Works 5:453–59

But of all the words in all languages, perhaps there has been none so much abused in this way as the words *republic, commonwealth,* and *popular state.* In the *Rerum-Publicarum Collectio,* of which there are fifty and odd volumes, and many of them very incorrect, France, Spain, and Portugal, the four great empires, the Babylonian, Persian, Greek, and Roman, and even the Ottoman, are all denominated republics. If, indeed, a republic signifies nothing but public affairs, it is equally applicable to all nations; and every kind of government, despotisms, monarchies, aristocracies, democracies, and every possible or imaginable composition of them are all republics. There is, no doubt, a public good and evil, a commonwealth and a common impoverishment in all of them. Others define a republic to be a government of more than one. This will exclude only the despotisms; for a monarchy administered by laws, requires at least magistrates to register them, and consequently more than one person in the government. Some comprehend under the term only aristocracies and democracies, and mixtures of these, without any distinct executive power. Others, again, more rationally, define a republic to signify only a government, in which all men, rich and poor, magistrates and subjects, officers and people, masters and servants, the first citizen and the last, are equally subject to the laws. This, indeed, appears to be the true and only true definition of a republic. The word *res,* every one knows, signified in the Roman language wealth, riches, property; the word *publicus,* quasi populicus, and per syncope pôplicus, signified public, common, belonging to the people; *res publica,* therefore, was publica res, the wealth, riches, or property of the people. *Res populi,* and the original meaning of the word *republic* could be no other than a government in which the property of the people predominated and governed; and it had more relation to property than liberty. It signified a government, in which the property of the public, or people, and of

every one of them, was secured and protected by law. This idea, indeed, implies liberty; because property cannot be secure unless the man be at liberty to acquire, use, or part with it, at his discretion, and unless he have his personal liberty of life and limb, motion and rest, for that purpose. It implies, moreover, that the property and liberty of all men, not merely of a majority, should be safe; for the people, or public, comprehends more than a majority, it comprehends all and every individual; and the property of every citizen is a part of the public property, as each citizen is a part of the public, people, or community. The property, therefore, of every man has a share in government, and is more powerful than any citizen, or party of citizens; it is governed only by the law. There is, however, a peculiar sense in which the words *republic, commonwealth, popular state,* are used by English and French writers; who mean by them a democracy, or rather a representative democracy; a "government in one centre, and that centre the nation;" that is to say, that centre a single assembly, chosen at stated periods by the people, and invested with the whole sovereignty; the whole legislative, executive, and judicial power, to be exercised in a body, or by committees, as they shall think proper. This is the sense in which it was used by Marchamont Nedham, and in this sense it has been constantly used from his time to ours, even by writers of the most mathematical precision, the most classical purity, and extensive learning. What other authority there may be for this use of those words is not known; none has been found, except in the following observations of Portenari, in which there are several other inaccuracies; but they are here inserted, chiefly because they employ the words *republic, commonwealth,* and *popular state,* in the same sense with the English and French writers.

"We may say with the philosopher [Aristotle, in the *Politics*], that six things are so necessary to a city, that without them it cannot stand. 1. The first is provisions, without which its inhabitants cannot live. 2. The second is clothes, habitations, houses, and other things, which depend upon the arts, without which civil and political life cannot subsist. 3. The third is arms, which are necessary to defend the city from its enemies, and to repress the boldness of those who rebel against the laws. 4. The fourth is money, most necessary to a city in peace and in war. 5. The fifth is the care of divine worship. 6. The sixth is the administration of justice, and the government of the people. For the first are necessary, cultivators of the land; for the second, artificers; for the third, soldiers; for the fourth, merchants and capitalists; for the fifth, priests; for the sixth, judges and magistrates. Seven sorts of men, therefore, are necessary to a city: husbandmen, artificers, soldiers, merchants, rich men, priests, and judges.

"But, according to the same philosopher, as in the body natural not all those things, without which it is never found, are parts of it, but only instruments subservient to some uses, as in animals, the horns, the nails, the hair, so not all those seven sorts of men are parts of the city; but some of them, namely, the husbandmen, the artificers, and the merchants, are only instruments useful to civil life, as is thus demonstrated. A city is constituted for felicity, as to its ultimate end; and human felicity, here below, is reposed, according to the same philosopher, in the operations of virtue, and chiefly in the exertions of wisdom and prudence; those men, therefore, are not parts of a city, the operations of whom are not directed to those virtues; such are the husbandmen who are occupied, not in wisdom and prudence, but in laboring the earth; such are the artisans, who fatigue themselves night and day to gain a livelihood for themselves and their poor families; such, finally, are the merchants, who watch and labor continually, not in wisdom and prudence, but in the acquisition of gold. It is therefore clear, that neither husbandmen, artificers, nor merchants, are parts of a city, nor ought to be numbered among the citizens, but only as instruments which subserve certain uses and conveniences of the city."

We must pause here and admire! The foregoing are not only the grave sentiments of Portenari and of Aristotle, but form the doctrine almost of the whole earth, and of all mankind; not only every despotism, empire, and monarchy, in Asia, Africa, and Europe, but every aristocratical republic, has adopted it in all its latitude. There are only two or three of the smallest cantons in Switzerland, besides England, who allow husbandmen, artificers, and merchants, to be citizens, or to have any voice or share in the government of the state, or in the choice or appointment of any who have. There is no doctrine, and no fact, which goes so far as this towards forfeiting to the human species the character of rational creatures. Is it not amazing, that nations should have thus tamely surrendered themselves, like so many flocks of sheep, into the hands of shepherds, whose great solicitude to devour the lambs, the wool, and the flesh, scarcely leave them time to provide water or pasture for the animals, or even shelter against the weather and the wolves?

It is, indeed, impossible that the several descriptions of men, last enumerated, should, in a great nation and extensive territory, ever assemble in a body to act in concert; and the ancient method of taking the sense of an assembly of citizens in the capital, as in Rome for example, for the sense of all the citizens of a whole republic, or a large empire, was very imperfect, and extremely exposed to corruption; but, since the invention of representative assemblies, much of that objection is removed, though even that was no sufficient reason for excluding farmers, merchants, and artificers, from the rights of citizens. At present a husbandman, merchant, or artificer, provided he has any small property, by which he may be supposed to have a judgment and will of his own, instead of depending for his daily bread on some patron or master, is a sufficient judge of the qualifications of a person to represent him in the legislature. A representative assembly, fairly constituted, and made an integral part of the sovereignty, has power forever to control the rich and illustrious in another assembly, and a court and king, where there is a king. This, too, is the only instrument by which the body of the people can act; the only way in which their opinions can be known and collected; the only means by which their wills can be united, and their strength exerted, according to any principle or continued system.

It is sometimes said, that mobs are a good mode of expressing the sense, the resentments, and feelings of the people. Whig mobs to be sure are meant! But if the principle is once admitted, liberty and the rights of mankind will infallibly be betrayed; for it is giving liberty to tories and courtiers to excite mobs as well as to patriots; and all history and experience shows, that mobs are more easily excited by courtiers and princes, than by more virtuous men, and more honest friends of liberty.

It is often said, too, that farmers, merchants, and mechanics, are too inattentive to public affairs, and too patient under oppression. This is undoubtedly true, and will forever be so; and, what is worse, the most sober, industrious, and peaceable of them, will forever be the least attentive, and the least disposed to exert themselves in hazardous and disagreeable efforts of resistance. The only practicable method, therefore, of giving to farmers, &c. the equal right of citizens, and their proper weight and influence in society, is by elections, frequently repeated, of a house of commons, an assembly which shall be an essential part of the sovereignty. The meanest understanding is equal to the duty of saying who is the man in his neighborhood whom he most esteems, and loves best, for his knowledge, integrity, and benevolence. The understandings, however, of husbandmen, merchants, and mechanics, are not always the meanest; there arise, in the course of human life, many among them of the most splendid geniuses, the most active and benevolent dispositions, and most undaunted bravery. The moral equality that nature has unalterably established among men, gives these an undoubted right to have every road opened to them for advancement in life and in power that is open to any others. These are the characters which will be discovered in popular elections, and brought forward upon the stage, where they may exert all their faculties, and enjoy all the honors, offices, and commands, both in peace and war, of which they are capable. The dogma of Aristotle, and the practice of the world, is the most unphilosophical, the most inhuman and cruel that can be conceived. Until this wicked position, which is worse than the slavery of the ancient republics, or modern West Indies, shall be held up to the derision and contempt, the execration and horror, of mankind, it will be to little purpose to talk or write about liberty. This doctrine of Aristotle is the more extraordinary, as it seems to be inconsistent with his great and common principles, "that a happy life must arise from a course of virtue; that virtue consists in a medium; and that the middle life is the happiest.

"In every city the people are divided into three sorts, the very rich, the very poor, and the middle sort. If it is admitted that the medium is the best, it follows that, even in point of fortune, a mediocrity is preferable. The middle state is most compliant to reason. Those who are very beautiful, or strong, or noble, or rich, or, on the contrary, those who are very poor, weak, or mean, with difficulty obey reason. The former are capricious and flagitious; the latter, rascally and mean; the crimes of each arising from their different excesses. Those who excel in riches, friends, and influence, are not willing to submit to command or law; this begins at home, where they are brought up too delicately, when boys, to obey their preceptors. The constant want of what the rich enjoy makes the poor too mean; the poor know not how to command, but are in the habit of being commanded, too often as slaves. The rich know not how to submit to any command; nor do they know how to rule over freemen, or to command others, but despotically. A city composed only of the rich and the poor, consists but of masters and slaves, not freemen; where one party despise, and the other hate; where there is no possibility of friendship, or political community, which supposes affection. It is the genius of a free city to be composed, as much as possible, of equals; and equality will be best preserved when the greatest part of the inhabitants are in the middle state. These will be best assured of safety as well as equality; they will not covet nor steal, as the poor do, what belongs to the rich; nor will what they have be coveted or stolen; without plotting against any one, or having any one plot against them, they will live free from danger. For which reason, Phocylides wisely wishes for the middle state, as being most productive of happiness. It is plain then that the most perfect community must be among those who are in the middle rank; and those states are best instituted, wherein these are a larger and more respectable part, if possible, than both the other; or, if that cannot be, at least than either of them separate; so that, being thrown into the balance, it may prevent either scale from preponderating. It is, therefore, the greatest happiness which the citizen can enjoy, to possess a moderate and convenient fortune. When some possess too much, and others nothing at all, the government must either be in the hands of the meanest rabble, or else a pure oligarchy. The middle state is best, as being least liable to those seditions and insurrections which disturb the community; and for the same reason extensive governments are least liable to these inconveniences; for there those in the middle state are very numerous; whereas, in small ones, it is easy to pass to the two extremes, so as hardly to have any medium remaining, but the one half rich, and the other poor. We ought to consider, as a proof of this, that the best lawgivers were those in the middle rank of life, among whom was Solon, as is evident from his poems, and Lycurgus, for he was not a king; and Charondas, and, indeed, most others. Hence, so many free states have changed either to democracies or oligarchies; for whenever the number of those in the middle state has been too small, those who were the more numerous, whether the rich or the poor, always overpowered them, and assumed to themselves the administration. When, in consequence of their disputes and quarrels with each other, either the rich get the better of the poor, or the poor of the rich, neither of them will establish a free state, but, as a record of their victory, will form one which inclines to their own principles, either a democracy or an oligarchy. It is, indeed, an established custom of cities, not to desire an equality, but either to aspire to govern, or, when they are conquered, to submit."

These are some of the wisest sentiments of Aristotle; but can you reconcile them with his other arbitrary doctrine, and tyrannical exclusion of husbandmen, merchants, and tradesmen, from the rank and rights of citizens? These, or

at least, those of them who have acquired property enough to be exempt from daily dependence on others, are the real middling people, and generally as honest and independent as any; these, however, it must be confessed, are too inattentive to public and national affairs, and too apt to submit to oppression. When they have been provoked beyond all bearing, they have aimed at demolishing the government, and when they have done that, they have sunk into their usual inattention, and left others to erect a new one as rude and ill-modelled as the former. A representative assembly, elected by them, is the only way in which they can act in concert; but they have always allowed themselves to be cheated by false, imperfect, partial, and inadequate representations of themselves, and have never had their full and proper share of power in a state.

11

JAMES MADISON, VICES OF THE POLITICAL SYSTEM OF THE UNITED STATES
Apr. 1787
Papers 9:350–51

(See ch. 5, no. 16)

12

RECORDS OF THE FEDERAL CONVENTION

[1:134; Madison, 6 June]

Mr. Madison considered an election of one branch at least of the Legislature by the people immediately, as a clear principle of free Govt. and that this mode under proper regulations had the additional advantage of securing better representatives, as well as of avoiding too great an agency of the State Governments in the General one.— He differed from the member from Connecticut (Mr. Sherman) in thinking the objects mentioned to be all the principal ones that required a National Govt. Those were certainly important and necessary objects; but he combined with them the necessity, of providing more effectually for the security of private rights, and the steady dispensation of Justice. Interferences with these were evils which had more perhaps than any thing else, produced this convention. Was it to be supposed that republican liberty could long exist under the abuses of it practiced in some of the States. The gentleman (Mr. Sherman) had admitted that in a very small State, faction & oppression wd. prevail. It was to be inferred then that wherever these prevailed the State was too small. Had they not prevailed in the largest as well as the smallest tho' less than in the smallest; and were we not thence admonished to enlarge the sphere as far as the nature of the Govt. would admit. This was the only defence agst. the inconveniences of democracy consistent with the democratic form of Govt. All civilized Societies would be divided into different Sects, Factions, & interests, as they happened to consist of rich & poor, debtors & creditors, the landed the manufacturing, the commercial interests, the inhabitants of this district, or that district, the followers of this political leader or that political leader, the disciples of this religious sect or that religious sect. In all cases where a majority are united by a common interest or passion, the rights of the minority are in danger. What motives are to restrain them? A prudent regard to the maxim that honesty is the best policy is found by experience to be as little regarded by bodies of men as by individuals. Respect for character is always diminished in proportion to the number among whom the blame or praise is to be divided. Conscience, the only remaining tie is known to be inadequate in individuals: In large numbers, little is to be expected from it. Besides, Religion itself may become a motive to persecution & oppression.—These observations are verified by the Histories of every Country antient & modern. In Greece & Rome the rich & poor, the creditors & debtors, as well as the patricians & plebeians alternately oppressed each other with equal unmercifulness. What a source of oppression was the relation between the parent Cities of Rome, Athens & Carthage, & their respective provinces: the former possessing the power & the latter being sufficiently distinguished to be separate objects of it? Why was America so justly apprehensive of Parliamentary injustice? Because G. Britain had a separate interest real or supposed, & if her authority had been admitted, could have pursued that interest at our expense. We have seen the mere distinction of colour made in the most enlightened period of time, a ground of the most oppressive dominion ever exercised by man over man. What has been the source of those unjust laws complained of among ourselves? Has it not been the real or supposed interest of the major number? Debtors have defrauded their creditors. The landed interest has borne hard on the mercantile interest. The Holders of one species of property have thrown a disproportion of taxes on the holders of another species. The lesson we are to draw from the whole is that where a majority are united by a common sentiment and have an opportunity, the rights of the minor party become insecure. In a Republican Govt. the Majority if united have always an opportunity. The only remedy is to enlarge the sphere, & thereby divide the community into so great a number of interests & parties, that in the 1st. place a majority will not be likely at the same moment to have a common interest separate from that of the whole or of the minority; and in the 2d. place, that in case they shd. have such an interest, they may not be apt to unite in the pursuit of it. It was incumbent on us then to try this remedy, and with that view to frame a republican system on such a scale & in such a form as will controul all the evils wch. have been experienced.

[1:288; Madison, 18 June]

[Mr. Hamilton.] This view of the subject almost led him to despair that a Republican Govt. could be established over so great an extent. He was sensible at the same time that it would be unwise to propose one of any other form.

In his private opinion he had no scruple in declaring, supported as he was by the opinions of so many of the wise & good, that the British Govt. was the best in the world: and that he doubted much whether any thing short of it would do in America. He hoped Gentlemen of different opinions would bear with him in this, and begged them to recollect the change of opinion on this subject which had taken place and was still going on. It was once thought that the power of Congs was amply sufficient to secure the end of their institution. The error was now seen by every one. The members most tenacious of republicanism, he observed, were as loud as any in declaiming agst. the vice of democracy. This progress of the public mind led him to anticipate the time, when others as well as himself would join in the praise bestowed by Mr. Neckar on the British Constitution, namely, that it is the only Govt. in the world "which unites public strength with individual security."— In every community where industry is encouraged, there will be a division of it into the few & the many. Hence separate interests will arise There will be debtors & Creditors &c. Give all power to the many, they will oppress the few. Give all power to the few they will oppress the many. Both therefore ought to have power, that each may defend itself agst. the other. To the want of this check we owe our paper money—instalment laws &c To the proper adjustment of it the British owe the excellence of their Constitution. Their house of Lords is a most noble institution. Having nothing to hope for by a change, and a sufficient interest by means of their property, in being faithful to the National interest, they form a permanent barrier agst. every pernicious innovation, whether attempted on the part of the Crown or of the Commons. No temporary Senate will have firmness en'o' to answer the purpose. The Senate (of Maryland) which seems to be so much appealed to, has not yet been sufficiently tried. Had the people been unanimous & eager, in the late appeal to them on the subject of a paper emission they would would have yielded to the torrent. Their acquiescing in such an appeal is a proof of it.—Gentlemen differ in their opinions concerning the necessary checks, from the different estimates they form of the human passions. They suppose Seven years a sufficient period to give the Senate an adequate firmness, from not duly considering the amazing violence & turbulence of the democratic spirit. When a great object of Govt. is pursued, which seizes the popular passions, they spread like wild fire, and become irresistable. He appealed to the gentlemen from the N. England States whether experience had not there verified the remark. As to the Executive, it seemed to be admitted that no good one could be established on Republican principles. Was not this giving up the merits of the question; for can there be a good Govt. without a good Executive. The English model was the only good one on this subject. The Hereditary interest of the King was so interwoven with that of the Nation, and his personal emoluments so great, that he was placed above the danger of being corrupted from abroad—and at the same time was both sufficiently independent and sufficiently controuled, to answer the purpose of the institution at home. one of the weak sides of Republics was their being liable to foreign influence & corruption. Men of little character, acquiring great power become easily the tools of intermedling neibours. Sweeden was a striking instance. The French & English had each their parties during the late Revolution which was effected by the predominant influence of the former. What is the inference from all these observations? That we ought to go as far in order to attain stability and permanency, as republican principles will admit. Let one branch of the Legislature hold their places for life or at least during good-behaviour. Let the Executive also be for life. He appealed to the feelings of the members present whether a term of seven years, would induce the sacrifices of private affairs which an acceptance of public trust would require, so so as to ensure the services of the best Citizens. On this plan we should have in the Senate a permanent will, a weighty interest, which would answer essential purposes. But is this a Republican Govt. it will be asked? Yes, if all the Magistrates are appointed, and vacancies are filled, by the people, or a process of election originating with the people.

[1:421; Madison, 26 June]

Mr. Madison. In order to judge of the form to be given to this institution [the second branch of the legislature], it will be proper to take a view of the ends to be served by it. These were first to protect the people agst. their rulers: secondly to protect the people agst. the transient impressions into which they themselves might be led. A people deliberating in a temperate moment, and with the experience of other nations before them, on the plan of Govt. most likely to secure their happiness, would first be aware, that those chargd. with the public happiness, might betray their trust. An obvious precaution agst. this danger wd. be to divide the trust between different bodies of men, who might watch & check each other. In this they wd. be governed by the same prudence which has prevailed in organizing the subordinate departments of Govt. where all business liable to abuses is made to pass thro' separate hands, the one being a check on the other. It wd. next occur to such a people, that they themselves were liable to temporary errors, thro' want of information as to their true interest, and that men chosen for a short term, & employed but a small portion of that in public affairs, might err from the same cause. This reflection wd. naturally suggest that the Govt. be so constituted, as that one of its branches might have an oppy. of acquiring a competent knowledge of the public interests. Another reflection equally becoming a people on such an occasion, wd. be that they themselves, as well as a numerous body of Representatives, were liable to err also, from fickleness and passion. A necessary fence agst. this danger would be to select a portion of enlightened citizens, whose limited number, and firmness might seasonably interpose agst. impetuous counsels. It ought finally to occur to a people deliberating on a Govt. for themselves, that as different interests necessarily result from the liberty meant to be secured, the major interest might under sudden impulses be tempted to commit injustice on the minority. In all civilized Countries the people fall into different classes havg. a real or supposed difference of interests. There will be creditors & debtors, farmers, merchts. & manufacturers. There will be particularly the distinction of rich & poor. It was true as had been observed. (by Mr Pinkney) we had not among us those hereditary distinctions, of rank which were a great source of the contests in the ancient Govts. as well as the modern States of Europe, nor those extremes of wealth or poverty which characterize the latter. We cannot however be regarded even at this time, as one homogeneous mass, in which every thing that affects a part will affect in the same manner the whole. In framing a system which we wish to last for ages, we shd. not lose sight of the changes which ages will produce. An increase of population will of necessity increase the proportion of those who will labour under all the hardships of life, & secretly sigh for a more equal distribution of its blessings. These may in time outnumber those who are placed above the feelings of indigence. According to the equal laws of suffrage, the power will slide into the hands of the former. No agrarian attempts have yet been made in this Country, but symptoms of a leveling spirit, as we have understood, have sufficiently appeared in a certain quarters to give notice of the future danger. How is this danger to be guarded agst. on republican principles? How is the danger in all cases of interested co-alitions to oppress the minority to be guarded agst.? Among other means by the establishment of a body in the Govt. sufficiently respectable for its wisdom & virtue, to aid on such emergencies, the preponderance of justice by throwing its weight into that scale. Such being the objects of the second branch in the proposed Govt. he thought a considerable duration ought to be given to it. He did not conceive that the term of nine years could threaten any real danger; but in pursuing his particular ideas on the subject, he should require that the long term allowed to the 2d. branch should not commence till such a period of life as would render a perpetual disqualification to be re-elected little inconvenient either in a public or private view. He observed that as it was more than probable we were now digesting a plan which in its operation wd. decide forever the fate of Republican Govt we ought not only to provide every guard to liberty that its preservation cd. require, but be equally careful to supply the defects which our own experience had particularly pointed out.

13

NORTHWEST ORDINANCE
13 July 1787
Tansill 47–54
(See ch. 1, no. 8)

14

BRUTUS, NO. 1
18 Oct. 1787
Storing 2.9.10–21

Let us now proceed to enquire, as I at first proposed, whether it be best the thirteen United States should be reduced to one great republic, or not? It is here taken for granted, that all agree in this, that whatever government we adopt, it ought to be a free one; that it should be so framed as to secure the liberty of the citizens of America, and such an one as to admit of a full, fair, and equal representation of the people. The question then will be, whether a government thus constituted, and founded on such principles, is practicable, and can be exercised over the whole United States, reduced into one state?

If respect is to be paid to the opinion of the greatest and wisest men who have ever thought or wrote on the science of government, we shall be constrained to conclude, that a free republic cannot succeed over a country of such immense extent, containing such a number of inhabitants, and these encreasing in such rapid progression as that of the whole United States. Among the many illustrious authorities which might be produced to this point, I shall content myself with quoting only two. The one is the baron de Montesquieu, spirit of laws, chap. xvi. vol. I [book VIII]. "It is natural to a republic to have only a small territory, otherwise it cannot long subsist. In a large republic there are men of large fortunes, and consequently of less moderation; there are trusts too great to be placed in any single subject; he has interest of his own; he soon begins to think that he may be happy, great and glorious, by oppressing his fellow citizens; and that he may raise himself to grandeur on the ruins of his country. In a large republic, the public good is sacrificed to a thousand views; it is subordinate to exceptions, and depends on accidents. In a small one, the interest of the public is easier perceived, better understood, and more within the reach of every citizen; abuses are of less extent, and of course are less protected." Of the same opinion is the marquis Beccarari.

History furnishes no example of a free republic, any thing like the extent of the United States. The Grecian republics were of small extent; so also was that of the Romans. Both of these, it is true, in process of time, extended their conquests over large territories of country; and the consequence was, that their governments were changed from that of free governments to those of the most tyrannical that ever existed in the world.

Not only the opinion of the greatest men, and the experience of mankind, are against the idea of an extensive republic, but a variety of reasons may be drawn from the reason and nature of things, against it. In every government, the will of the sovereign is the law. In despotic governments the supreme authority being lodged in one, his will is law, and can be as easily expressed to a large extensive territory as to a small one. In a pure democracy the people are the sovereign, and their will is declared by themselves; for this purpose they must all come together to deliberate, and decide. This kind of government cannot be exercised, therefore, over a country of any considerable extent; it must be confined to a single city, or at least limited to such bounds as that the people can conveniently assemble, be able to debate, understand the subject submitted to them, and declare their opinion concerning it.

In a free republic, although all laws are derived from the consent of the people, yet the people do not declare their consent by themselves in person, but by representatives, chosen by them, who are supposed to know the minds of their constituents, and to be possessed of integrity to declare this mind.

In every free government, the people must give their assent to the laws by which they are governed. This is the true criterion between a free government and an arbitrary one. The former are ruled by the will of the whole, expressed in any manner they may agree upon; the latter by the will of one, or a few. If the people are to give their assent to the laws, by persons chosen and appointed by them, the manner of the choice and the number chosen, must be such, as to possess, be disposed, and consequently qualified to declare the sentiments of the people; for if they do not know, or are not disposed to speak the sentiments of the people, the people do not govern, but the sovereignty is in a few. Now, in a large extended country, it is impossible to have a representation, possessing the sentiments, and of integrity, to declare the minds of the people, without having it so numerous and unwieldly, as to be subject in great measure to the inconveniency of a democratic government.

The territory of the United States is of vast extent; it now contains near three millions of souls, and is capable of containing much more than ten times that number. Is it practicable for a country, so large and so numerous as they will soon become, to elect a representation, that will speak their sentiments, without their becoming so numerous as to be incapable of transacting public business? It certainly is not.

In a republic, the manners, sentiments, and interests of the people should be similar. If this be not the case, there will be a constant clashing of opinions; and the representatives of one part will be continually striving, against those of the other. This will retard the operations of government, and prevent such conclusions as will promote the public good. If we apply this remark to the condition of the United States, we shall be convinced that it forbids that we should be one government. The United States includes a variety of climates. The productions of the different parts of the union are very variant, and their interests, of consequence, diverse. Their manners and habits differ as much as their climates and productions; and their sentiments are by no means coincident. The laws and customs of the several states are, in many respects, very diverse, and in some opposite; each would be in favor of its own interests and customs, and, of consequence, a legislature, formed of representatives from the respective parts, would not only be too numerous to act with any care or decision, but would be composed of such heterogenous and discordant principles, as would constantly be contending with each other.

The laws cannot be executed in a republic, of an extent equal to that of the United States, with promptitude.

The magistrates in every government must be supported in the execution of the laws, either by an armed force, maintained at the public expence for that purpose; or by the people turning out to aid the magistrate upon his command, in case of resistance.

In despotic governments, as well as in all the monarchies of Europe, standing armies are kept up to execute the commands of the prince or the magistrate, and are employed for this purpose when occasion requires: But they have always proved the destruction of liberty, and [are] abhorrent to the spirit of a free republic. In England, where they depend upon the parliament for their annual support, they have always been complained of as oppressive and unconstitutional, and are seldom employed in executing of the laws; never except on extraordinary occasions, and then under the direction of a civil magistrate.

A free republic will never keep a standing army to execute its laws. It must depend upon the support of its citizens. But when a government is to receive its support from the aid of the citizens, it must be so constructed as to have the confidence, respect, and affection of the people. Men who, upon the call of the magistrate, offer themselves to execute the laws, are influenced to do it either by affection to the government, or from fear; where a standing army is at hand to punish offenders, every man is actuated by the latter principle, and therefore, when the magistrate calls, will obey: but, where this is not the case, the government must rest for its support upon the confidence and respect which the people have for their government and laws. The body of the people being attached, the government will always be sufficient to support and execute its laws, and to operate upon the fears of any faction which may be opposed to it, not only to prevent an opposition to the execution of the laws themselves, but also to compel the most of them to aid the magistrate; but the people will not be likely to have such confidence in their rulers, in a republic so extensive as the United States, as necessary for these purposes. The confidence which the people have in their rulers, in a free republic, arises from their knowing them, from their being responsible to them for their conduct, and from the power they have of displacing them when they misbehave: but in a republic of the extent of this continent, the people in general would be acquainted with very few of their rulers; the people at large would know little of their proceedings, and it would be extremely difficult to change them. The people in Georgia and New-Hampshire would not know one another's mind, and therefore could not act in concert to enable them to effect a general change of representatives. The different parts of so extensive a country could not possibly be made acquainted with the conduct of their representatives, nor be informed of the reasons upon which measures were founded. The consequence will be, they will have no confidence in their legislature, suspect them of ambitious

views, be jealous of every measure they adopt, and will not support the laws they pass. Hence the government will be nerveless and inefficient, and no way will be left to render it otherwise, but by establishing an armed force to execute the laws at the point of the bayonet—a government of all others the most to be dreaded.

In a republic of such vast extent as the United-States, the legislature cannot attend to the various concerns and wants of its different parts. It cannot be sufficiently numerous to be acquainted with the local condition and wants of the different districts, and if it could, it is impossible it should have sufficient time to attend to and provide for all the variety of cases of this nature, that would be continually arising.

In so extensive a republic, the great officers of government would soon become above the controul of the people, and abuse their power to the purpose of aggrandizing themselves, and oppressing them. The trust committed to the executive offices, in a country of the extent of the United-States, must be various and of magnitude. The command of all the troops and navy of the republic, the appointment of officers, the power of pardoning offences, the collecting of all the public revenues, and the power of expending them, with a number of other powers, must be lodged and exercised in every state, in the hands of a few. When these are attended with great honor and emolument, as they always will be in large states, so as greatly to interest men to pursue them, and to be proper objects for ambitious and designing men, such men will be ever restless in their pursuit after them. They will use the power, when they have acquired it, to the purposes of gratifying their own interest and ambition, and it is scarcely possible, in a very large republic, to call them to account for their misconduct, or to prevent their abuse of power.

These are some of the reasons by which it appears, that a free republic cannot long subsist over a country of the great extent of these states. If then this new constitution is calculated to consolidate the thirteen states into one, as it evidently is, it ought not to be adopted.

15

JAMES MADISON TO THOMAS JEFFERSON
24 Oct. 1787
Papers 10:212–14
(See ch. 17, no. 22)

16

CATO, NO. 3
Fall 1787
Storing 2.6.12–20

The recital, or premises on which this new form of government is erected, declares a consolidation or union of all the thirteen parts, or states, into one great whole, under the firm [form?] of the United States, for all the various and important purposes therein set forth.—But whoever seriously considers the immense extent of territory comprehended within the limits of the United States, together with the variety of its climates, productions, and commerce, the difference of extent, and number of inhabitants in all; the dissimilitude of interest, morals, and policies, in almost every one, will receive it as an intuitive truth, that a consolidated republican form of government therein, can never *form a perfect union, establish justice, insure domestic tranquility, promote the general welfare, and secure the blessings of liberty to you and your posterity,* for to these objects it must be directed: this unkindred legislature therefore, composed of interests opposite and dissimilar in their nature, will in its exercise, emphatically be, like a house divided against itself.

The governments of Europe have taken their limits and form from adventitious circumstances, and nothing can be argued on the motive of agreement from them; but these adventitious political principles, have nevertheless produced effects that have attracted the attention of philosophy, which has established axioms in the science of politics therefrom, as irrefragable as any in Euclid. It is natural, says Montesquieu, *to a republic to have only a small territory, otherwise it cannot long subsist: in a large one, there are men of large fortunes, and consequently of less moderation; there are too great deposits to intrust in the hands of a single subject, an ambitious person soon becomes sensible that he may be happy, great, and glorious by oppressing his fellow citizens, and that he might raise himself to grandeur, on the ruins of his country. In large republics, the public good is sacrificed to a thousand views; in a small one the interest of the public is easily perceived, better understood, and more within the reach of every citizen; abuses have a less extent, and of course are less protected*—he also shews you, that the duration of the republic of Sparta, was owing to its having continued with the same extent of territory after all its wars; and that the ambition of Athens and Lacedemon to command and direct the union, lost them their liberties, and gave them a monarchy.

From this picture, what can you promise yourselves, on the score of consolidation of the United States, into one government—impracticability in the just exercise of it—your freedom insecure—even this form of government limited in its continuance—the employments of your country disposed of to the opulent, to whose contumely you will continually be an object—you must risque much, by indispensably placing trusts of the greatest magnitude, into the hands of individuals, whose ambition for power, and aggrandizement, will oppress and grind you—where, from the vast extent of your territory, and the complication of interests, the science of government will become intricate and perplexed, and too misterious for you to understand, and observe; and by which you are to be conducted into a monarchy, either limited or despotic; the latter, Mr. Locke remarks, *is a government derived from neither nature, nor compact.*

Political liberty, the great Montesquieu again observes, *consists in security, or at least in the opinion we have of security;* and this *security* therefore, or the *opinion,* is best obtained in moderate governments, where the mildness of the laws, and the equality of the manners, beget a confidence in the people, which produces this security, or the opinion. This moderation in governments, depends in a great measure on their limits, connected with their political distribution.

The extent of many of the states in the Union, is at this time, almost too great for the superintendence of a republican form of government, and must one day or other, revolve into more vigorous ones, or by separation be reduced into smaller, and more useful, as well as moderate ones. You have already observed the feeble efforts of Massachusetts against their insurgents; with what difficulty did they quell that insurrection; and is not the province of Main at this moment, on the eve of separation from her. The reason of these things is, that for the security of the *property* of the community, in which expressive term Mr. Locke makes life, liberty, and estate, to consist—the wheels of a free republic are necessarily slow in their operation; hence in large free republics, the evil sometimes is not only begun, but almost completed, before they are in a situation to turn the current into a contrary progression: the extremes are also too remote from the usual seat of government, and the laws therefore too feeble to afford protection to all its parts, and insure *domestic tranquility* without the aid of another principle. If, therefore, this state [New York], and that of N. Carolina, had an army under their controul, they never would have lost Vermont, and Frankland, nor the state of Massachusetts suffer an insurrection, or the dismemberment of her fairest district, but the exercise of a principle which would have prevented these things, if we may believe the experience of ages, would have ended in the destruction of their liberties.

Will this consolidated republic, if established, in its exercise beget such confidence and compliance, among the citizens of these states, as to do without the aid of a standing army—I deny that it will.—The mal-contents in each state, who will not be a few, nor the least important, will be exciting factions against it—the fear of a dismemberment of some of its parts, and the necessity to enforce the execution of revenue laws (a fruitful source of oppression) on the extremes and in the other districts of the government, will incidentally, and necessarily require a permanent force, to be kept on foot—will not political security, and even the opinion of it, be extinguished? can mildness and moderation exist in a government, where the primary incident in its exercise must be force? will not violence destroy confidence, and can equality subsist, where the extent, policy, and practice of it, will naturally lead to make odious distinctions among citizens?

The people, who may compose this national legislature from the southern states, in which, from the mildness of the climate, the fertility of the soil, and the value of its productions, wealth is rapidly acquired, and where the same causes naturally lead to luxury, dissipation, and a passion for aristocratic distinctions; where slavery is encouraged, and liberty of course, less respected, and protected; who know not what it is to acquire property by their own toil, nor to oeconomise with the savings of industry—will these men therefore be as tenacious of the liberties and interests of the more northern states, where freedom, independence, industry, equality, and frugality, are natural to the climate and soil, as men who are your own citizens, legislating in your own state, under your inspection, and whose manners, and fortunes, bear a more equal resemblance to your own?

It may be suggested, in answer to this, that whoever is a citizen of one state, is a citizen of each, and that therefore he will be as interested in the happiness and interest of all, as the one he is delegated from; but the argument is fallacious, and, whoever has attended to the history of mankind, and the principles which bind them together as parents, citizens, or men, will readily perceive it. These principles are, in their exercise, like a pebble cast on the calm surface of a river, the circles begin in the center, and are small, active, and forcible, but as they depart from that point, they lose their force, and vanish into calmness.

The strongest principle of union resides within our domestic walls. The ties of the parent exceed that of any other; as we depart from home, the next general principle of union is amongst citizens of the same state, where acquaintance, habits, and fortunes, nourish affection, and attachment; enlarge the circle still further, and, as citizens of different states, though we acknowledge the same national denomination, we lose the ties of acquaintance, habits, and fortunes, and thus, by degrees, we lessen in our attachments, till, at length, we no more than acknowledge a sameness of species. Is it therefore, from certainty like this, reasonable to believe, that inhabitants of Georgia, or New-Hampshire, will have the same obligations towards you as your own, and preside over your lives, liberties, and property, with the same care and attachment? Intuitive reason, answers in the negative.

17

ALEXANDER HAMILTON, FEDERALIST, NO. 6, 31–35
14 Nov. 1787

(See ch. 7, no. 10)

18

ALEXANDER HAMILTON, FEDERALIST, NO. 9, 50–53
21 Nov. 1787

A Firm Union will be of the utmost moment to the peace and liberty of the States as a barrier against domestic faction and insurrection. It is impossible to read the history of the petty Republics of Greece and Italy, without feeling sensations of horror and disgust at the distractions with which they were continually agitated, and at the rapid succession of revolutions, by which they were kept in a state of perpetual vibration, between the extremes of tyranny and anarchy. If they exhibit occasional calms, these only serve as short-lived contrasts to the furious storms that are to succeed. If now and then intervals of felicity open themselves to view, we behold them with a mixture of regret arising from the reflection that the pleasing scenes before us are soon to be overwhelmed by the tempestuous waves of sedition and party-rage. If momentary rays of glory break forth from the gloom, while they dazzle us with a transient and fleeting brilliancy, they at the same time admonish us to lament that the vices of government should pervert the direction and tarnish the lustre of those bright talents and exalted indowments, for which the favoured soils, that produced them, have been so justly celebrated.

From the disorders that disfigure the annals of those republics, the advocates of despotism have drawn arguments, not only against the forms of republican government, but against the very principles of civil liberty. They have decried all free government, as inconsistent with the order of society, and have indulged themselves in malicious exultation over its friends and partizans. Happily for mankind, stupendous fabrics reared on the basis of liberty, which have flourished for ages, have in a few glorious instances refuted their gloomy sophisms. And, I trust, America will be the broad and solid foundation of other edifices not less magnificent, which will be equally permanent monuments of their errors.

But it is not to be denied that the portraits, they have sketched of republican government, were too just copies of the originals from which they were taken. If it had been found impracticable, to have devised models of a more perfect structure, the enlightened friends to liberty would have been obliged to abandon the cause of that species of government as indefensible. The science of politics, however, like most other sciences has received great improvement. The efficacy of various principles is now well understood, which were either not known at all, or imperfectly known to the ancients. The regular distribution of power into distinct departments—the introduction of legislative ballances and checks—the institution of courts composed of judges, holding their offices during good behaviour—the representation of the people in the legislature by deputies of their own election—these are either wholly new discoveries or have made their principal progress towards perfection in modern times. They are means, and powerful means, by which the excellencies of republican government may be retained and its imperfections lessened or avoided. To this catalogue of circumstances, that tend to the amelioration of popular systems of civil government, I shall venture, however novel it may appear to some, to add one more on a principle, which has been made the foundation of an objection to the New Constitution, I mean the ENLARGEMENT of the ORBIT within which such systems are to revolve either in respect to the dimensions of a single State, or to the consolidation of several smaller States into one great confederacy. The latter is that which immediately concerns the object under consideration. It will however be of use to examine the principle in its application to a single State which shall be attended to in another place.

The utility of a confederacy, as well to suppress faction and to guard the internal tranquillity of States, as to increase their external force and security, is in reality not a new idea. It has been practiced upon in different countries and ages, and has received the sanction of the most applauded writers, on the subjects of politics. The opponents of the PLAN proposed have with great assiduity cited and circulated the observations of Montesquieu on the necessity of a contracted territory for a republican government. But they seem not to have been apprised of the sentiments of that great man expressed in another part of his work, nor to have adverted to the consequences of the principle to which they subscribe, with such ready acquiescence.

When Montesquieu recommends a small extent for republics, the standards he had in view were of dimensions, far short of the limits of almost every one of these States. Neither Virginia, Massachusetts, Pennsylvania, New-York, North-Carolina, nor Georgia, can by any means be compared with the models, from which he reasoned and to which the terms of his description apply. If we therefore take his ideas on this point, as the criterion of truth, we shall be driven to the alternative, either of taking refuge at once in the arms of monarchy, or of splitting ourselves into an infinity of little jealous, clashing, tumultuous commonwealths, the wretched nurseries of unceasing discord and the miserable objects of universal pity or contempt. Some of the writers, who have come forward on the other side of the question, seem to have been aware of the dilemma; and have even been bold enough to hint at the division of the larger States, as a desirable thing. Such an infatuated policy, such a desperate expedient, might, by the multiplication of petty offices, answer the views of men, who possess not qualifications to extend their influence beyond the narrow circles of personal intrigue, but it could never promote the greatness or happiness of the people of America.

19

JAMES MADISON, FEDERALIST, NO. 10, 56–65
22 Nov. 1787

Among the numerous advantages promised by a well constructed Union, none deserves to be more accurately developed than its tendency to break and control the violence of faction. The friend of popular governments, never finds himself so much alarmed for their character and fate, as when he contemplates their propensity to this dangerous vice. He will not fail therefore to set a due value on any plan which, without violating the principles to which he is attached, provides a proper cure for it. The instability, injustice and confusion introduced into the public councils, have in truth been the mortal diseases under which popular governments have every where perished; as they continue to be the favorite and fruitful topics from which the adversaries to liberty derive their most specious declamations. The valuable improvements made by the American Constitutions on the popular models, both ancient and modern, cannot certainly be too much admired; but it would be an unwarrantable partiality, to contend that they have as effectually obviated the danger on this side as was wished and expected. Complaints are every where heard from our most considerate and virtuous citizens, equally the friends of public and private faith, and of public and personal liberty; that our governments are too unstable; that the public good is disregarded in the conflicts of rival parties; and that measures are too often decided, not according to the rules of justice, and the rights of the minor party; but by the superior force of an interested and over-bearing majority. However anxiously we may wish that these complaints had no foundation, the evidence of known facts will not permit us to deny that they are in some degree true. It will be found indeed, on a candid review of our situation, that some of the distresses under which we labor, have been erroneously charged on the operation of our governments; but it will be found, at the same time, that other causes will not alone account for many of our heaviest misfortunes; and particularly, for that prevailing and increasing distrust of public engagements, and alarm for private rights, which are echoed from one end of the continent to the other. These must be chiefly, if not wholly, effects of the unsteadiness and injustice, with which a factious spirit has tainted our public administrations.

By a faction I understand a number of citizens, whether amounting to a majority or minority of the whole, who are united and actuated by some common impulse of passion, or of interest, adverse to the rights of other citizens, or to the permanent and aggregate interests of the community.

There are two methods of curing the mischiefs of faction: the one, by removing its causes; the other, by controling its effects.

There are again two methods of removing the causes of faction: the one by destroying the liberty which is essential to its existence; the other, by giving to every citizen the same opinions, the same passions, and the same interests.

It could never be more truly said than of the first remedy, that it is worse than the disease. Liberty is to faction, what air is to fire, an aliment without which it instantly expires. But it could not be a less folly to abolish liberty, which is essential to political life, because it nourishes faction, than it would be to wish the annihilation of air, which is essential to animal life, because it imparts to fire its destructive agency.

The second expedient is as impracticable, as the first would be unwise. As long as the reason of man continues fallible, and he is at liberty to exercise it, different opinions will be formed. As long as the connection subsists between his reason and his self-love, his opinions and his passions will have a reciprocal influence on each other; and the former will be objects to which the latter will attach themselves. The diversity in the faculties of men from which the rights of property originate, is not less an insuperable obstacle to a uniformity of interests. The protection of these faculties is the first object of Government. From the protection of different and unequal faculties of acquiring property, the possession of different degrees and kinds of property immediately results: and from the influence of these on the sentiments and views of the respective proprietors, ensues a division of the society into different interests and parties.

The latent causes of faction are thus sown in the nature of man; and we see them every where brought into different degrees of activity, according to the different circumstances of civil society. A zeal for different opinions concerning religion, concerning Government and many other points, as well of speculation as of practice; an attachment to different leaders ambitiously contending for pre-eminence and power; or to persons of other descriptions whose fortunes have been interesting to the human passions, have in turn divided mankind into parties, inflamed them with mutual animosity, and rendered them much more disposed to vex and oppress each other, than to co-operate for their common good. So strong is this propensity of mankind to fall into mutual animosities, that where no substantial occasion presents itself, the most frivolous and fanciful distinctions have been sufficient to kindle their unfriendly passions, and excite their most violent conflicts. But the most common and durable source of factions, has been the various and unequal distribution of property. Those who hold, and those who are without property, have ever formed distinct interests in society. Those who are creditors, and those who are debtors, fall under a like discrimination. A landed interest, a manufacturing interest, a mercantile interest, a monied interest, with many lesser interests, grow up of necessity in civilized nations, and divide them into different classes, actuated by different sentiments and views. The regulation of these various and interfering interests forms the principal task of modern Legislation, and involves the spirit of party and faction in the necessary and ordinary operations of Government.

No man is allowed to be a judge in his own cause; because his interest would certainly bias his judgment, and, not improbably, corrupt his integrity. With equal, nay with greater reason, a body of men, are unfit to be both judges and parties, at the same time; yet, what are many of the most important acts of legislation, but so many judicial determinations, not indeed concerning the rights of single persons, but concerning the rights of large bodies of citizens; and what are the different classes of legislators, but advocates and parties to the causes which they determine? Is a law proposed concerning private debts? It is a question to which the creditors are parties on one side, and the debtors on the other. Justice ought to hold the balance between them. Yet the parties are and must be themselves the judges; and the most numerous party, or, in other words, the most powerful faction must be expected to prevail. Shall domestic manufactures be encouraged, and in what degree, by restrictions on foreign manufacturers? are questions which would be differently decided by the landed and the manufacturing classes; and probably by neither, with a sole regard to justice and the public good. The apportionment of taxes on the various descriptions of property, is an act which seems to require the most exact impartiality; yet, there is perhaps no legislative act in which greater opportunity and temptation are given to a predominant party, to trample on the rules of justice.

Every shilling with which they over-burden the inferior number, is a shilling saved to their own pockets.

It is in vain to say, that enlightened statesmen will be able to adjust these clashing interests, and render them all subservient to the public good. Enlightened statesmen will not always be at the helm: Nor, in many cases, can such an adjustment be made at all, without taking into view indirect and remote considerations, which will rarely prevail over the immediate interest which one party may find in disregarding the rights of another, or the good of the whole.

The inference to which we are brought, is, that the *causes* of faction cannot be removed; and that relief is only to be sought in the means of controling its *effects*.

If a faction consists of less than a majority, relief is supplied by the republican principle, which enables the majority to defeat its sinister views by regular vote: It may clog the administration, it may convulse the society; but it will be unable to execute and mask its violence under the forms of the Constitution. When a majority is included in a faction, the form of popular government on the other hand enables it to sacrifice to its ruling passion or interest, both the public good and the rights of other citizens. To secure the public good, and private rights, against the danger of such a faction, and at the same time to preserve the spirit and the form of popular government, is then the great object to which our enquiries are directed: Let me add that it is the great desideratum, by which alone this form of government can be rescued from the opprobrium under which it has so long labored, and be recommended to the esteem and adoption of mankind.

By what means is this object attainable? Evidently by one of two only. Either the existence of the same passion or interest in a majority at the same time, must be prevented; or the majority, having such co-existent passion or interest, must be rendered, by their number and local situation, unable to concert and carry into effect schemes of oppression. If the impulse and the opportunity be suffered to coincide, we well know that neither moral nor religious motives can be relied on as an adequate control. They are not found to be such on the injustice and violence of individuals, and lose their efficacy in proportion to the number combined together; that is, in proportion as their efficacy becomes needful.

From this view of the subject, it may be concluded, that a pure Democracy, by which I mean, a Society, consisting of a small number of citizens, who assemble and administer the Government in person, can admit of no cure for the mischiefs of faction. A common passion or interest will, in almost every case, be felt by a majority of the whole; a communication and concert results from the form of Government itself; and there is nothing to check the inducements to sacrifice the weaker party, or an obnoxious individual. Hence it is, that such Democracies have ever been spectacles of turbulence and contention; have ever been found incompatible with personal security, or the rights of property; and have in general been as short in their lives, as they have been violent in their deaths. Theoretic politicans, who have patronized this species of Government, have erroneously supposed, that by reducing mankind to a perfect equality in their political rights, they would, at the same time, be perfectly equalized and assimilated in their possessions, their opinions, and their passions.

A Republic, by which I mean a Government in which the scheme of representation takes place, opens a different prospect, and promises the cure for which we are seeking. Let us examine the points in which it varies from pure Democracy, and we shall comprehend both the nature of the cure, and the efficacy which it must derive from the Union.

The two great points of difference between a Democracy and a Republic are, first, the delegation of the Government, in the latter, to a small number of citizens elected by the rest: secondly, the greater number of citizens, and greater sphere of country, over which the latter may be extended.

The effect of the first difference is, on the one hand to refine and enlarge the public views, by passing them through the medium of a chosen body of citizens, whose wisdom may best discern the true interest of their country, and whose patriotism and love of justice, will be least likely to sacrifice it to temporary or partial considerations. Under such a regulation, it may well happen that the public voice pronounced by the representatives of the people, will be more consonant to the public good, than if pronounced by the people themselves convened for the purpose. On the other hand, the effect may be inverted. Men of factious tempers, of local prejudices, or of sinister designs, may by intrigue, by corruption or by other means, first obtain the suffrages, and then betray the interests of the people. The question resulting is, whether small or extensive Republics are most favorable to the election of proper guardians of the public weal: and it is clearly decided in favor of the latter by two obvious considerations.

In the first place it is to be remarked that however small the Republic may be, the Representatives must be raised to a certain number, in order to guard against the cabals of a few; and that however large it may be, they must be limited to a certain number, in order to guard against the confusion of a multitude. Hence the number of Representatives in the two cases, not being in proportion to that of the Constituents, and being proportionally greatest in the small Republic, it follows, that if the proportion of fit characters, be not less, in the large than in the small Republic, the former will present a greater option, and consequently a greater probability of a fit choice.

In the next place, as each Representative will be chosen by a greater number of citizens in the large than in the small Republic, it will be more difficult for unworthy candidates to practise with success the vicious arts, by which elections are too often carried; and the suffrages of the people being more free, will be more likely to centre on men who possess the most attractive merit, and the most diffusive and established characters.

It must be confessed, that in this, as in most other cases, there is a mean, on both sides of which inconveniencies will be found to lie. By enlarging too much the number of electors, you render the representative too little acquainted with all their local circumstances and lesser inter-ests; as by reducing it too much, you render him unduly attached to these, and too little fit to comprehend and pursue great and national objects. The Federal Constitution forms a happy combination in this respect; the great and aggregate interests being referred to the national, the local and particular, to the state legislatures.

The other point of difference is, the greater number of citizens and extent of territory which may be brought within the compass of Republican, than of Democratic Government; and it is this circumstance principally which renders factious combinations less to be dreaded in the former, than in the latter. The smaller the society, the fewer probably will be the distinct parties and interests composing it; the fewer the distinct parties and interests, the more frequently will a majority be found of the same party; and the smaller the number of individuals composing a majority, and the smaller the compass within which they are placed, the more easily will they concert and execute their plans of oppression. Extend the sphere, and you take in a greater variety of parties and interests; you make it less probable that a majority of the whole will have a common motive to invade the rights of other citizens; or if such a common motive exists, it will be more difficult for all who feel it to discover their own strength, and to act in unison with each other. Besides other impediments, it may be remarked, that where there is a consciousness of unjust or dishonorable purposes, communication is always checked by distrust, in proportion to the number whose concurrence is necessary.

Hence it clearly appears, that the same advantage, which a Republic has over a Democracy, in controling the effects of faction, is enjoyed by a large over a small Republic—is enjoyed by the Union over the States composing it. Does this advantage consist in the substitution of Representatives, whose enlightened views and virtuous sentiments render them superior to local prejudices, and to schemes of injustice? It will not be denied, that the Representation of the Union will be most likely to possess these requisite endowments. Does it consist in the greater security afforded by a greater variety of parties, against the event of any one party being able to outnumber and oppress the rest? In an equal degree does the encreased variety of parties, comprised within the Union, encrease this security. Does it, in fine, consist in the greater obstacles opposed to the concert and accomplishment of the secret wishes of an unjust and interested majority? Here, again, the extent of the Union gives it the most palpable advantage.

The influence of factious leaders may kindle a flame within their particular States, but will be unable to spread a general conflagration through the other States: a religious sect, may degenerate into a political faction in a part of the Confederacy: but the variety of sects dispersed over the entire face of it, must secure the national Councils against any danger from that source: a rage for paper money, for an abolition of debts, for an equal division of property, or for any other improper or wicked project, will be less apt to pervade the whole body of the Union, than a particular member of it; in the same proportion as such a malady is more likely to taint a particular county or district, than an entire State.

In the extent and proper structure of the Union, therefore, we behold a Republican remedy for the diseases most incident to Republican Government. And according to the degree of pleasure and pride, we feel in being Republicans, ought to be our zeal in cherishing the spirit, and supporting the character of Federalists.

20

ALEXANDER HAMILTON, FEDERALIST, NO. 11,
65–73
24 Nov. 1787

(See ch. 7, no. 13)

21

ALEXANDER HAMILTON, FEDERALIST, NO. 12,
73–74
27 Nov. 1787

(See ch. 7, no. 14)

22

JAMES MADISON, FEDERALIST, NO. 14, 88–89
30 Nov. 1787

Hearken not to the unnatural voice which tells you that the people of America, knit together as they are by so many chords of affection, can no longer live together as members of the same family; can no longer continue the mutual guardians of their mutual happiness; can no longer be fellow citizens of one great respectable and flourishing empire. Hearken not to the voice which petulantly tells you that the form of government recommended for your adoption is a novelty in the political world; that it has never yet had a place in the theories of the wildest projectors; that it rashly attempts what it is impossible to accomplish. No my countrymen, shut your ears against this unhallowed language. Shut your hearts against the poison which it conveys; the kindred blood which flows in the veins of American citizens, the mingled blood which they have shed in defence of their sacred rights, consecrate their union, and excite horror at the idea of their becoming aliens, rivals, enemies. And if novelties are to be shunned, believe me the most alarming of all novelties, the most wild of all projects, the most rash of all attempts, is that of rending us in pieces, in order to preserve our liberties and promote our happiness. But why is the experiment of an extended republic to be rejected merely because it may comprise what is new? Is it not the glory of the people of America, that whilst they have paid a decent regard to the opinions of former times and other nations, they have not suffered a blind veneration for antiquity, for custom, or for names, to overrule the suggestions of their own good sense, the knowledge of their own situation, and the lessons of their own experience? To this manly spirit, posterity will be indebted for the possession, and the world for the example of the numerous innovations displayed on the American theatre, in favor of private rights and public happiness. Had no important step been taken by the leaders of the revolution for which a precedent could not be discovered, no government established of which an exact model did not present itself, the people of the United States might, at this moment, have been numbered among the melancholy victims of misguided councils, must at best have been labouring under the weight of some of those forms which have crushed the liberties of the rest of mankind. Happily for America, happily we trust for the whole human race, they pursued a new and more noble course. They accomplished a revolution which has no parallel in the annals of human society: They reared the fabrics of governments which have no model on the face of the globe. They formed the design of a great confederacy, which it is incumbent on their successors to improve and perpetuate. If their works betray imperfections, we wonder at the fewness of them. If they erred most in the structure of the union; this was the work most difficult to be executed; this is the work which has been new modelled by the act of your Convention, and it is that act on which you are now to deliberate and to decide.

23

ALEXANDER HAMILTON, FEDERALIST, NO. 22,
138–39
14 Dec. 1787

(See ch. 5, no. 23)

24

JAMES MADISON, FEDERALIST, NO. 39, 250–53
16 Jan. 1788

The first question that offers itself is, whether the general form and aspect of the government be strictly republican? It is evident that no other form would be reconcileable with the genius of the people of America; with the fundamental principles of the revolution; or with that honorable determination, which animates every votary of freedom, to rest all our political experiments on the capacity of mankind for self-government. If the plan of the Convention therefore be found to depart from the republican character, its advocates must abandon it as no longer defensible.

What then are the distinctive characters of the republican form? Were an answer to this question to be sought, not by recurring to principles, but in the application of the term by political writers, to the constitutions of different States, no satisfactory one would ever be found. Holland, in which no particle of the supreme authority is derived from the people, has passed almost universally under the denomination of a republic. The same title has been bestowed on Venice, where absolute power over the great body of the people, is exercised in the most absolute manner, by a small body of hereditary nobles. Poland, which is a mixture of aristocracy and of monarchy in their worst forms, has been dignified with the same appellation. The government of England, which has one republican branch only, combined with a hereditery aristocracy and monarchy, has with equal impropriety been frequently placed on the list of republics. These examples, which are nearly as dissimilar to each other as to a genuine republic, shew the extreme inaccuracy with which the term has been used in political disquisitions.

If we resort for a criterion, to the different principles on which different forms of government are established, we may define a republic to be, or at least may bestow that name on, a government which derives all its powers directly or indirectly from the great body of the people; and is administered by persons holding their offices during pleasure, for a limited period, or during good behaviour. It is *essential* to such a government, that it be derived from the great body of the society, not from an inconsiderable proportion, or a favored class of it; otherwise a handful of tyrannical nobles, exercising their oppressions by a delegation of their powers, might aspire to the rank of republicans, and claim for their government the honorable title of republic. It is *sufficient* for such a government, that the persons administering it be appointed, either directly or indirectly, by the people; and that they hold their appointments by either of the tenures just specified; otherwise every government in the United States, as well as every other popular government that has been or can be well organized or well executed, would be degraded from the republican character. According to the Constitution of every State in the Union, some or other of the officers of government are appointed indirectly only by the people. According to most of them the chief magistrate himself is so appointed. And according to one, this mode of appointment is extended to one of the coordinate branches of the legislature. According to all the Constitutions also, the tenure of the highest offices is extended to a definite period, and in many instances, both within the legislative and executive departments, to a period of years. According to the provisions of most of the constitutions, again, as well as according to the most respectable and received opinions on the subject, the members of the judiciary department are to retain their offices by the firm tenure of good behaviour.

On comparing the Constitution planned by the Convention, with the standard here fixed, we perceive at once that it is in the most rigid sense conformable to it. The House of Representatives, like that of one branch at least of all the State Legislatures, is elected immediately by the great body of the people. The Senate, like the present Congress, and the Senate of Maryland, derives its appointment indirectly from the people. The President is indirectly derived from the choice of the people, according to the example in most of the States. Even the judges, with all other officers of the Union, will, as in the several States, be the choice, though a remote choice, of the people themselves. The duration of the appointments is equally conformable to the republican standard, and to the model of the State Constitutions. The House of Representatives is periodically elective as in all the States: and for the period of two years as in the State of South-Carolina. The Senate is elective for the period of six years; which is but one year more than the period of the Senate of Maryland; and but two more than that of the Senates of New-York and Virginia. The President is to continue in office for the period of four years; as in New-York and Delaware, the chief magistrate is elected for three years, and in South-Carolina for two years. In the other States the election is annual. In several of the States however, no constitutional provision is made for the impeachment of the Chief Magistrate. And in Delaware and Virginia, he is not impeachable till out of office. The President of the United States is impeachable at any time during his continuance in office. The tenure by which the Judges are to hold their places, is, as it unquestionably ought to be, that of good behaviour. The tenure of the ministerial offices generally will be a subject of legal regulation, conformably to the reason of the case, and the example of the State Constitutions.

Could any further proof be required of the republican complextion of this system, the most decisive one might be found in its absolute prohibition of titles of nobility, both under the Federal and the State Governments; and in its express guarantee of the republican form to each of the latter.

25

FEDERAL FARMER, NO. 18
25 Jan. 1788
Storing 2.8.226–27

We must observe, that the citizens of a state will be subject to state as well as federal taxes, and the inhabitants of the federal city and districts, only to such taxes as congress may lay—We are not to suppose all our people are attached to free government, and the principles of the common law, but that many thousands of them will prefer a city governed, not on republican principles—This city, and the government of it, must indubitably take their tone from the characters of the men, who from the nature of its situation and institution, must collect there. This city will not be established for productive labour, for mercantile, or mechanic industry; but for the residence of government, its officers and attendants. If hereafter it should ever become a place of trade and industry, in the early periods of its existence, when its laws and government must receive their fixed tone, it must be a mere court, with its appendages, the executive, congress, the law courts, gentlemen of fortune and pleasure, with all the officers, attendants, suitors, expectants and dependants on the whole, however brilliant and honourable this collection may be, if we expect it will have any sincere attachments to simple and frugal republicanism, to that liberty and mild government, which is dear to the laborious part of a free people, we most assuredly deceive ourselves. This early collection will draw to it men from all parts of the country, of a like political description: we see them looking towards the place already.

Such a city, or town, containing a hundred square miles, must soon be the great, the visible, and dazzling centre, the mistress of fashions, and the fountain of politics. There may be a free or shackled press in this city, and the streams which may issue from it may overflow the country, and they will be poisonous or pure, as the fountain may be corrupt or not. But not to dwell on a subject that must give pain to the virtuous friends of freedom, I will only add, can a free and enlightened people create a common head so extensive, so prone to corruption and slavery, as this city probably will be, when they have it in their power to form one pure and chaste, frugal and republican.

26

James Madison, Federalist, no. 57, 384–85
19 Feb. 1788

The *third* charge against the House of Representatives is, that it will be taken from that class of citizens which will have least sympathy with the mass of the people, and be most likely to aim at an ambitious sacrifice of the many to the aggrandizement of the few.

Of all the objections which have been framed against the Foederal Constitution, this is perhaps the most extraordinary. Whilst the objection itself is levelled against a pretended oligarchy, the principle of it strikes at the very root of republican government.

The aim of every political Constitution is or ought to be first to obtain for rulers, men who possess most wisdom to discern, and most virtue to pursue the common good of the society; and in the next place, to take the most effectual precautions for keeping them virtuous, whilst they continue to hold their public trust. The elective mode of obtaining rulers is the characteristic policy of republican government. The means relied on in this form of government for preventing their degeneracy are numerous and various. The most effectual one is such a limitation of the term of appointments, as will maintain a proper responsibility to the people.

Let me now ask what circumstance there is in the Constitution of the House of Representatives, that violates the principles of republican government; or favors the elevation of the few on the ruins of the many? Let me ask whether every circumstance is not, on the contrary, strictly conformable to these principles; and scrupulously impar-

tial to the rights and pretensions of every class and description of citizens?

Who are to be the electors of the Foederal Representatives? Not the rich more than the poor; not the learned more than the ignorant; not the haughty heirs of distinguished names, more than the humble sons of obscure and unpropitious fortune. The electors are to be the great body of the people of the United States. They are to be the same who exercise the right in every State of electing the correspondent branch of the Legislature of the State.

Who are to be the objects of popular choice? Every citizen whose merit may recommend him to the esteem and confidence of his country. No qualification of wealth, of birth, of religious faith, or of civil profession, is permitted to fetter the judgment or disappoint the inclination of the people.

27

James Madison, Federalist, no. 63, 422–29
1 Mar. 1788

A fifth desideratum illustrating the utility of a Senate, is the want of a due sense of national character. Without a select and stable member of the government, the esteem of foreign powers will not only be forfeited by an unenlightened and variable policy, proceeding from the causes already mentioned; but the national councils will not possess that sensibility to the opinion of the world, which is perhaps not less necessary in order to merit, than it is to obtain, its respect and confidence.

An attention to the judgment of other nations is important to every government for two reasons: The one is, that independently of the merits of any particular plan or measure, it is desireable on various accounts, that it should appear to other nations as the offspring of a wise and honorable policy: The second is, that in doubtful cases, particularly where the national councils may be warped by some strong passion, or momentary interest, the presumed or known opinion of the impartial world, may be the best guide that can be followed. What has not America lost by her want of character with foreign nations? And how many errors and follies would she not have avoided, if the justice and propriety of her measures had in every instance been previously tried by the light in which they would probably appear to the unbiassed part of mankind?

Yet however requisite a sense of national character may be, it is evident that it can never be sufficiently possessed by a numerous and changeable body. It can only be found in a number so small, that a sensible degree of the praise and blame of public measures may be the portion of each individual; or in an assembly so durably invested with public trust, that the pride and consequence of its members may be sensibly incorporated with the reputation and prosperity of the community. The half-yearly representatives of Rhode-Island, would probably have been little affected in their deliberations on the iniquitous measures of that state, by arguments drawn from the light in which such measures would be viewed by foreign nations, or even by the sister states; whilst it can scarcely be doubted, that if the concurrence of a select and stable body had been necessary, a regard to national character alone, would have prevented the calamities under which that misguided people is now labouring.

I add as a *sixth* defect, the want in some important cases of a due responsibility in the government to the people, arising from that frequency of elections, which in other cases produces this responsibility. This remark will perhaps appear not only new but paradoxical. It must nevertheless be acknowledged, when explained, to be as undeniable as it is important.

Responsibility in order to be reasonable must be limited to objects within the power of the responsible party; and in order to be effectual, must relate to operations of that power, of which a ready and proper judgment can be formed by the constituents. The objects of government may be divided into two general classes; the one depending on measures which have singly an immediate and sensible operation; the other depending on a succession of well chosen and well connected measures, which have a gradual and perhaps unobserved operation. The importance of the latter description to the collective and permanent welfare of every country needs no explanation. And yet it is evident, that an assembly elected for so short a term as to be unable to provide more than one or two links in a chain of measures, on which the general welfare may essentially depend, ought not to be answerable for the final result, any more than a steward or tenant, engaged for one year, could be justly made to answer for places or improvements, which could not be accomplished in less than half a dozen years. Nor is it possible for the people to estimate the *share* of influence which their annual assemblies may respectively have on events resulting from the mixed transactions of several years. It is sufficiently difficult at any rate to preserve a personal responsibility in the members of a *numerous* body, for such acts on the body as have an immediate, detached and palpable operation on its constituents.

The proper remedy for this defect must be an additional body in the legislative department, which, having sufficient permanency to provide for such objects as require a continued attention, and a train of measures, may be justly and effectually answerable for the attainment of those objects.

Thus far I have considered the circumstances which point out the necessity of a well constructed senate, only as they relate to the representatives of the people. To a people as little blinded by prejudice, or corrupted by flattery, as those whom I address, I shall not scruple to add, that such an institution may be sometimes necessary, as a defence to the people against their own temporary errors and delusions. As the cool and deliberate sense of the community ought in all governments, and actually will in all free governments ultimately prevail over the views of its rulers; so there are particular moments in public affairs, when the people stimulated by some irregular pas-

sion, or some illicit advantage, or misled by the artful misrepresentations of interested men, may call for measures which they themselves will afterwards be the most ready to lament and condemn. In these critical moments, how salutary will be the interference of some temperate and respectable body of citizens, in order to check the misguided career, and to suspend the blow mediated by the people against themselves, until reason, justice and truth, can regain their authority over the public mind? What bitter anguish would not the people of Athens have often escaped, if their government had contained so provident a safeguard against the tyranny of their own passions? Popular liberty might then have escaped the indelible reproach of decreeing to the same citizens, the hemlock on one day, and statues on the next.

It may be suggested that a people spread over an extensive region, cannot like the crouded inhabitants of a small district, be subject to the infection of violent passions; or to the danger of combining in the pursuit of unjust measures. I am far from denying that this is a distinction of peculiar importance. I have on the contrary endeavoured in a former paper, to shew that it is one of the principal recommendations of a confederated republic. At the same time this advantage ought not to be considered as superseding the use of auxiliary precautions. It may even be remarked that the same extended situation which will exempt the people of America from some of the dangers incident to lesser republics, will expose them to the inconveniency of remaining for a longer time, under the influence of those misrepresentations which the combined industry of interested men may succeed in distributing among them.

It adds no small weight to all these considerations, to recollect, that history informs us of no long lived republic which had not a senate. Sparta, Rome and Carthage are in fact the only states to whom that character can be applied. In each of the two first there was a senate for life. The constitution of the senate in the last, is less known. Circumstantial evidence makes it probable that it was not different in this particular from the two others. It is at least certain that it had some quality or other which rendered it an anchor against popular fluctuations; and that a smaller council drawn out of the senate was appointed not only for life; but filled up vacancies itself. These examples, though as unfit for the imitation, as they are repugnant to the genius of America, are notwithstanding, when compared with the fugitive and turbulent existence of other antient republics, very instructive proofs of the necessity of some institution that will blend stability with liberty. I am not unaware of the circumstances which distinguish the American from other popular governments, as well antient as modern; and which render extreme circumspection necessary in reasoning from the one case to the other. But after allowing due weight to this consideration, it may still be maintained that there are many points of similitude which render these examples not unworthy of our attention. Many of the defects as we have seen, which can only be supplied by a senatorial institution, are common to a numerous assembly frequently elected by the people, and to the people themselves. There are others peculiar to the former, which require the controul of such an institution. The people can never wilfully betray their own interests: But they may possibly be betrayed by the representatives of the people; and the danger will be evidently greater where the whole legislative trust is lodged in the hands of one body of men, than where the concurrence of separate and dissimilar bodies is required in every public act.

The difference most relied on between the American and other republics, consists in the principle of representation, which is the pivot on which the former move, and which is supposed to have been unknown to the latter, or at least to the antient part of them. The use which has been made of this difference, in reasonings contained in former papers, will have shewn that I am disposed neither to deny its existence nor to undervalue its importance. I feel the less restraint therefore in observing that the position concerning the ignorance of the antient government on the subject of representation is by no means precisely true in the latitude commonly given to it. Without entering into a disquisition which here would be misplaced, I will refer to a few known facts in support of what I advance.

In the most pure democracies of Greece, many of the executive functions were performed not by the people themselves, but by officers elected by the people, and *representing* the people in their *executive* capacity.

Prior to the reform of Solon, Athens was governed by nine Archons, annually *elected by the people at large*. The degree of power delegated to them seems to be left in great obscurity. Subsequent to that period, we find an assembly first of four and afterwards of six hundred members, annually *elected by the people;* and *partially* representing them in their *legislative* capacity; since they were not only associated with the people in the function of making laws; but had the exclusive right of originating legislative propositions to the people. The senate of Carthage also, whatever might be its power or the duration of its appointment, appears to have been *elective* by the suffrages of the people. Similar instances might be traced in most if not all the popular governments of antiquity.

Lastly in Sparta, we meet with the Ephori, and in Rome with the Tribunes; two bodies, small indeed in number, but annually *elected by the whole body of the people,* and considered as the *representatives* of the people, almost in their *plenipotentiary* capacity. The Cosmi of Crete were also annually *elected by the people;* and have been considered by some authors as an institution analogous to those of Sparta and Rome; with this difference only that in the election of that representative body, the right of suffrage was communicated to a part only of the people.

From these facts, to which many others might be added, it is clear that the principle of representation was neither unknown to the antients, nor wholly overlooked in their political constitutions. The true distinction between these and the American Governments lies *in the total exclusion of the people in their collective capacity* from any share in the *latter,* and not in the *total exclusion of representatives of the people,* from the administration of the *former.* The distinction however thus qualified must be admitted to leave a most advantageous superiority in favor of the United States. But to ensure to this advantage its full effect, we must be careful not to separate it from the other advantage, of an extensive territory. For it cannot be believed that any form of representative government, could have succeeded within the narrow limits occupied by the democracies of Greece.

In answer to all these arguments, suggested by reason, illustrated by examples, and enforced by our own experience, the jealous adversary of the constitution will probably content himself with repeating, that a senate appointed not immediately by the people, and for the term of six years, must gradually acquire a dangerous preeminence in the government, and finally transform it into a tyrannical aristocracy.

To this general answer the general reply ought to be sufficient; that liberty may be endangered by the abuses of liberty, as well as by the abuses of power; that there are numerous instances of the former as well as of the latter; and that the former rather than the latter is apparently most to be apprehended by the United States.

28

CHARLES PINCKNEY, SOUTH CAROLINA
RATIFYING CONVENTION
14 May 1788
Elliot 4:320–23

The first knowledge necessary for us to acquire, was a knowledge of the people for whom this system was to be formed; for unless we were acquainted with their situation, their habits, opinions, and resources, it would be impossible to form a government upon adequate or practicable principles.

If we examine the reasons which have given rise to the distinctions of rank that at present prevail in Europe, we shall find that none of them do, or in all probability ever will, exist in the Union.

The only distinction that may take place is that of wealth. Riches, no doubt, will ever have their influence; and where they are suffered to increase to large amounts in a few hands, there they may become dangerous to the public—particularly when, from the cheapness of labor and the scarcity of money, a great proportion of the people are poor. These, however, are dangers that I think we have very little to apprehend, for these reasons: One is from the destruction of the right of primogeniture; by which means, the estates of intestates are equally to be divided among all their children—a provision no less consonant to the principles of a republican government, than it is to those of general equity and parental affection. To endeavor to raise a name by accumulating property in one branch of a family, at the expense of others equally related and deserving, is a vanity no less unjust and cruel than dangerous to the interests of liberty; it is a practice no wise state will ever encourage or tolerate. In the Northern and Eastern States, such distinctions among children are seldom heard of. Laws have been long since passed in all of them, destroying the right of primogeniture, and as laws never fail to have a powerful influence upon the manners of a people, we may suppose that, in future, an equal division of property among children will, in general, take place in all the states, and one means of amassing inordinate wealth in the hands of individuals be, as it ought, forever removed.

Another reason is that, in the Eastern and Northern States, the landed property is nearly equally divided: very few have large bodies, and there are few that have not small tracts.

The greater part of the people are employed in cultivating their own lands; the rest in handicraft and commerce. They are frugal in their manner of living. Plain tables, clothing, and furniture, prevail in their houses, and expensive appearances are avoided. Among the landed interest, it may be truly said there are few of them rich, and few of them very poor; nor, while the states are capable of supporting so many more inhabitants that they contain at present—while so vast a territory on our frontier remains uncultivated and unexplored—while the means of subsistence are so much within every man's power—are those dangerous distinctions of fortune to be expected which at present prevail in other countries.

The people of the Union may be classed as follows: Commercial men, who will be of consequence or not, in the political scale, as commerce may be made an object of the attention of government. As far as I am able to judge, and presuming that proper sentiments will ultimately prevail upon this subject, it does not appear to me that the commercial line will ever have much influence in the politics of the Union. Foreign trade is one of the enemies against which we must be extremely guarded—more so than against any other, as none will ever have a more unfavorable operation. I consider it as the root of our present public distress—as the plentiful source from which our future national calamities will flow, unless great care is taken to prevent it. Divided as we are from the old world, we should have nothing to do with their politics, and as little as possible with their commerce: they can never improve, but must inevitably corrupt us.

Another class is that of professional men, who, from their education and pursuits, must ever have a considerable influence, while your government retains the republican principle, and its affairs are agitated in assemblies of the people.

The third, with whom I will connect the mechanical, as generally attached to them, are the landed interest—the owners and cultivators of the soil—the men attached to the truest interests of their country from those motives which always bind and secure the affections of the nation. In these consists the great body of the people; and here rests, and I hope ever will continue, all the authority of the government.

I remember once to have seen, in the writings of a very celebrated author upon national wealth, the following remarks: "Finally," says he, "there are but three ways for a nation to acquire wealth. The first is by war, as the Romans did in plundering their conquered neighbors: this is

robbery. The second is by commerce, which is generally cheating. The third is by agriculture, the only honest way, wherein a man receives a real increase of the seed thrown into the ground, in a kind of continual miracle wrought by the hand of God in his favor, as a reward for his innocent life and virtuous industry."

I do not agree with him so far as to suppose that commerce is generally cheating. I think there are some kinds of commerce not only fair and valuable, but such as ought to be encouraged by government. I agree with him in this general principle—that all the great objects of government should be subservient to the increase of agriculture and the support of the landed interest, and that commerce should only be so far attended to, as it may serve to improve and strengthen them; that the object of a republic is to render its citizens virtuous and happy; and that an unlimited foreign commerce can seldom fail to have a contrary tendency.

These classes compose the people of the Union; and, fortunately for their harmony, they may be said in a great measure to be connected with and dependent upon each other.

The merchant is dependent upon the planter, as the purchaser of his imports, and as furnishing him with the means of his remittances. The professional men depend upon both for employment in their respective pursuits, and are, in their turn, useful to both. The landholder, though the most independent of the three, is still, in some measure, obliged to the merchant for furnishing him at home with a ready sale for his productions.

From this mutual dependence, and the statement I have made respecting the situation of the people of the Union, I am led to conclude that mediocrity of fortune is a leading feature in our national character; that most of the causes which lead to destructions of fortune among other nations being removed, and causes of equality existing with us which are not to be found among them, we may with safety assert that the great body of national wealth is nearly equally in the hands of the people, among whom there are few dangerously rich or few miserably poor; that we may congratulate ourselves with living under the blessings of a mild and equal government, which knows no distinctions but those of merits or talents—under a government whose honors and offices are equally open to the exertions of all her citizens, and which adopts virtue and worth for her own, wheresoever she can find them.

29

JOHN ADAMS TO ROGER SHERMAN
18 July 1789
Works 6:429–31

In my letter of yesterday I think it was demonstrated that the English government is a republic, and that the regal negative upon the laws is essential to that republic. Because, without it, that government would not be what it is, a monarchical republic; and, consequently, could not preserve the balance of power between the executive and legislative powers, nor that other balance which is in the legislature,—between the one, the few, and the many; in which two balances the excellence of that form of government must consist.

Let us now inquire, whether the new constitution of the United States is or is not a monarchical republic, like that of Great Britain. The monarchical and the aristocratical power in our constitution, it is true, are not hereditary; but this makes no difference in the nature of the power, in the nature of the balance, or in the name of the species of government. It would make no difference in the power of a judge or justice, or general or admiral, whether his commission were for life or years. His authority during the time it lasted, would be the same whether it were for one year or twenty, or for life, or descendible to his eldest son. The people, the nation, in whom all power resides originally, may delegate their power for one year or for ten years; for years, or for life; or may delegate it in fee simple or fee tail, if I may so express myself; or during good behavior, or at will, or till further orders.

A nation might unanimously create a dictator or a despot, for one year or more, or for life, or for perpetuity with hereditary descent. In such a case, the dictator for one year would as really be a dictator for the time his power lasted, as the other would be whose power was perpetual and descendible. A nation in the same manner might create a simple monarchy for years, life, or perpetuity, and in either case the creature would be equally a simple monarch during the continuance of his power. So the people of England might create king, lords, and commons, for a year, or for several years, or for life, and in any of these cases, their government would be a monarchical republic, or, if you will, a limited monarchy, during its continuance, as much as it is now, when the king and nobles are hereditary. They might make their house of commons hereditary too. What the consequence of this would be it is easy to foresee; but it would not in the first moment make any change in the legal power, nor in the name of the government.

Let us now consider what our constitution is, and see whether any other name can with propriety be given it, than that of a monarchical republic, or if you will, a limited monarchy. The duration of our president is neither perpetual nor for life; it is only for four years; but his power during those four years is much greater than that of an avoyer, a consul, a podestà, a doge, a stadtholder; nay, than a king of Poland; nay, than a king of Sparta. I know of no first magistrate in any republican government, excepting England and Neuchatel, who possesses a constitutional dignity, authority, and power comparable to his. The power of sending and receiving ambassadors, of raising and commanding armies and navies, of nominating and appointing and commissioning all officers, of managing the treasures, the internal and external affairs of the nation; nay, the whole executive power, coextensive with the legislative power, is vested in him, and he has the right, and his is the duty, to take care that the laws be faithfully executed. These rights and duties, these prerogatives and dignities, are so transcendent that they must naturally and necessarily excite in the nation all the jealousy, envy, fears, apprehensions, and opposition, that are so constantly observed in England against the crown.

That these powers are necessary, I readily admit. That the laws cannot be executed without them; that the lives, liberties, properties and characters of the citizens cannot be secure without their protection, is most clear. But it is equally certain, I think, they they ought to have been still greater, or much less. The limitations upon them in the cases of war, treaties, and appointments to office, and especially the limitation on the president's independence as a branch of the legislative, will be the destruction of this constitution, and involve us in anarchy, if not amended. I shall pass over all particulars for the present, except the last; because that is now the point in dispute between you and me. Longitude, and the philosopher's stone, have not been sought with more earnestness by philosophers than a guardian of the laws has been studied by legislators from Plato to Montesquieu; but every project has been found to be no better than committing the lamb to the custody of the wolf, except that one which is called a *balance of power*. A simple sovereignty in one, a few, or many, has no balance, and therefore no laws. A divided sovereignty without a balance, or in other words, where the division is unequal, is always at war, and consequently has no laws. In our constitution the sovereignty,—that is, the legislative power,— is divided into three branches. The house and senate are equal, but the third branch, though essential, is not equal. The president must pass judgment upon every law; but in some cases his judgment may be overruled. These cases will be such as attack his constitutional power; it is, therefore, certain he has not equal power to defend himself, or the constitution, or the judicial power, as the senate and house have.

Power naturally grows. Why? Because human passions are insatiable. But that power alone can grow which already is too great; that which is unchecked; that which has no equal power to control it. The legislative power, in our constitution, is greater than the executive; it will, therefore, encroach, because both aristocratical and democratical passions are insatiable. The legislative power will increase, the executive will diminish. In the legislature, the monarchical power is not equal either to the aristocratical or democratical; it will, therefore, decrease, while the other will increase. Indeed, I think the aristocratical power is greater than either the monarchical or democratical. That will, therefore, swallow up the other two.

30

BENJAMIN RUSH TO JOHN ADAMS
21 July 1789
Letters 1:522–24

From an unfortunate concurrence of circumstances, I find myself under the influence of the same difficult command in corresponding with the Vice-President of the United States which the King of Syria gave to the captains of his chariots: "Fight ye not with small or great, save only with the KING of Israel."

The subjects upon which we differ are *monarchy, titles,* and the *Latin* and *Greek* languages.

I repeat again that republicanism has never yet had a fair trial in the world. It is now likely to be tried in the United States. Had our government been more completely balanced, that is, had the President possessed more power, I believe it would have realized all the wishes of the most sanguine friends to republican liberty. Licentiousness, factions, seditions, and rebellions have not been restrained by monarchy even in Great Britain. They have been more numerous in that country than in any of the *less* free monarchies or *more* free republics of Europe. The factions, seditions, and rebellions of republics arose wholly from the want of checks or balances and from a defect of equal representation. The wisdom of modern times has discovered and in part remedied these evils. We may hope therefore that our republican forms of government will be more safe and durable than formerly. When we reject a republic, I wish we may adopt an absolute monarchy, for governments (like women, among whom it is said no one between a virtuous woman and a prostitute ought ever to please) should know no medium between absolute republicanism and absolute monarchy. There cannot be a greater absurdity than to connect together in one government the *living* principle of liberty in the people with the *deadly* principle of tyranny in an hereditary monarch. They must in time, with the best balance in the world, overset each other. They are created with implements of war in their hands. Fighting will be natural and necessary to each of them to preserve an existence. From a variety of circumstances, the victory 99 times in an 100 will be in favor of the monarch, and hence will arise the annihilation of liberty.

An hundred years hence, absolute monarchy will probably be rendered necessary in our country by the corruption of our people. But why should we precipitate an event for which we are not yet prepared? Shall I at five-and-twenty years of age, because I expect to be an old man, draw my teeth, put on artificial gray hairs, and bend my back over a short cane? No, I will enjoy the health and vigor of youth and manhood, and leave old age to take care of itself. I will do more. I will husband my health and vigor, and try to keep off old age as long as I can by temperance, proper clothing, simple manners, and the practice of domestic virtues.

The characters you so much admire among the ancients were formed wholly by republican forms of governments.

Republican forms of government are more calculated to promote Christianity than monarchies. The precepts of the Gospel and the maxims of republics in many instances agree with each other.

Please to take notice that when I speak of a republic I mean a government consisting of *three* branches, and each derived at different times and for different periods from the PEOPLE. Where this circulation is wanting between rulers and the ruled, there will be an obstruction to genuine government. A king or a senate not chosen by the people at certain periods becomes a sebimus, a bubo, or an abscess in the body politic which must sooner or later destroy the healthiest state.

A simple democracy, or an unbalanced republic, is one of the greatest of evils. I think with Dr. Zubly that "a democracy (with only one branch) is the Tivil's own government." Those words he uttered at my table in the spring of 1776, upon my giving as a toast the "Commonwealth of America." At the same instant that he spoke the words, he turned his glass upside downwards and refused to drink the toast.

I have no objection to men being accosted by the titles which they derive from their offices. Mr. President, Mr. Vice-President, Senator, Councilor, Judge, or even Constable may all be used with propriety, but why should we prefix *noble, honorable,* or *elective* to them? Such epithets are a transgression of a rule in composition which forbids us to use unnecessary adjectives, inasmuch as they always enfeeble the sense of a sentence. I cannot think with you that titles overawe or restrain the profligate part of a community. The very atmosphere of London is impregnated with the sounds of "my Lord," "my Lady," "Right honorable," "your Honor," "Sir John and Sir James"—and yet where will you find more profligate manners than among the citizens of London? The use of titles begets pride in rulers and baseness among the common people. Among the Romans, whom you so much admire, Caesar was Caesar, and Scipio was Scipio in all companies. The conquered provinces I believe first introduced titles. Among the Quakers the highest degrees of order are preserved without titles. But if we begin with titles in the United States, where will they end? A new vocabulary must be formed to provide for all the officers of the federal and state governments, for the states still retain the power of creating titles. If titles are given to men, must not their women be permitted to share in them? By what rule shall we settle precedency? Shall a law or a title office be necessary for this purpose? In a word, my friend, I see no end to the difficulties, disputes, and absurdities of admitting titles into our country. They are equally contrary to reason and religion, and in my opinion are no more necessary to give dignity or energy to a government than swearing is to govern a ship's crew, or spirituous liquors to gather in the fruits of the earth.

31

ALEXANDER HAMILTON, REPORT ON MANUFACTURES
5 Dec. 1791

Papers 10:252–56

III. As to the additional employment of classes of the community, not ordinarily engaged in the particular business.

This is not among the least valuable of the means, by which manufacturing institutions contribute to augment the general stock of industry and production. In places where those institutions prevail, besides the persons regularly engaged in them, they afford occasional and extra employment to industrious individuals and families, who are willing to devote the leisure resulting from the intermissions of their ordinary pursuits to collateral labours, as a resource of multiplying their acquisitions or [their] enjoyments. The husbandman himself experiences a new source of profit and support from the encreased industry of his wife and daughters; invited and stimulated by the demands of the neighboring manufactories.

Besides this advantage of occasional employment to classes having different occupations, there is another of a nature allied to it [and] of a similar tendency. This is—the employment of persons who would otherwise be idle (and in many cases a burthen on the community), either from the byass of temper, habit, infirmity of body, or some other cause, indisposing, or disqualifying them for the toils of the Country. It is worthy of particular remark, that, in general, women and Children are rendered more useful and the latter more early useful by manufacturing establishments, than they would otherwise be. Of the number of persons employed in the Cotton Manufactories of Great Britain, it is computed that $\frac{4}{7}$ nearly are women and children; of whom the greatest proportion are children and many of them of a very tender age.

And thus it appears to be one of the attributes to manufactures, and one of no small consequence, to give occasion to the exertion of a greater quantity of Industry, even by the *same number* of persons, where they happen to prevail, than would exist, if there were no such establishments.

IV. As to the promoting of emigration from foreign Countries.

Men reluctantly quit one course of occupation and livelihood for another, unless invited to it by very apparent and proximate advantages. Many, who would go from one country to another, if they had a prospect of continuing with more benefit the callings, to which they have been educated, will often not be tempted to change their situation, by the hope of doing better, in some other way. Manufacturers, who listening to the powerful invitations of a better price for their fabrics, or their labour, of greater cheapness of provisions and raw materials, of an exemption from the chief part of the taxes burthens and restraints, which they endure in the old world, of greater personal independence and consequence, under the operation of a more equal government, and of what is far more precious than mere religious toleration—a perfect equality of religious privileges; would probably flock from Europe to the United States to pursue their own trades or professions, if they were once made sensible of the advantages they would enjoy, and were inspired with an assurance of encouragement and employment, will, with difficulty, be induced to transplant themselves, with a view to becoming Cultivators of Land.

If it be true then, that it is the interest of the United States to open every possible [avenue to] emigration from abroad, it affords a weighty argument for the encouragement of manufactures; which for the reasons just assigned, will have the strongest tendency to multiply the inducements to it.

Here is perceived an important resource, not only for extending the population, and with it the useful and productive labour of the country, but likewise for the prosecution of manufactures, without deducting from the number of hands, which might otherwise be drawn to tillage; and even for the indemnification of Agriculture for such as might happen to be diverted from it. Many, whom Manufacturing views would induce to emigrate, would afterwards yield to the temptations, which the particular situation of this Country holds out to Agricultural pursuits. And while Agriculture would in other respects derive many signal and unmingled advantages, from the growth of manufactures, it is a problem whether it would gain or lose, as to the article of the number of persons employed in carrying it on.

V. As to the furnishing greater scope for the diversity of talents and dispositions, which discriminate men from each other.

This is a much more powerful mean of augmenting the fund of national Industry than may at first sight appear. It is a just observation, that minds of the strongest and most active powers for their proper objects fall below mediocrity and labour without effect, if confined to uncongenial pursuits. And it is thence to be inferred, that the results of human exertion may be immensely increased by diversifying its objects. When all the different kinds of industry obtain in a community, each individual can find his proper element, and can call into activity the whole vigour of his nature. And the community is benefitted by the services of its respective members, in the manner, in which each can serve it with most effect.

If there be anything in a remark often to be met with—namely that there is, in the genius of the people of this country, a peculiar aptitude for mechanic improvements, it would operate as a forcible reason for giving opportunities to the exercise of that species of talent by the propagation of manufactures.

VI. As to the affording a more ample and various field for enterprise.

This also is of greater consequence in the general scale of national exertion, than might perhaps on a superficial view be supposed, and has effects not altogether dissimilar from those of the circumstance last noticed. To cherish and stimulate the activity of the human mind, by multiplying the objects of enterprise, is not among the least considerable of the expedients, by which the wealth of a nation may be promoted. Even things in themselves not positively advantageous, sometimes become so, by their tendency to provoke exertion. Every new scene, which is opened to the busy nature of man to rouse and exert itself, is the addition of a new energy to the general stock of effort.

The spirit of enterprise, useful and prolific as it is, must necessarily be contracted or expanded in proportion to the simplicity or variety of the occupations and productions, which are to be found in a Society. It must be less in a nation of mere cultivators, than in a nation of cultivators and merchants; less in a nation of cultivators and merchants, than in a nation of cultivators, artificers and merchants.

32

THOMAS PAINE, RIGHTS OF MAN, PART 2
1792
Life 7:6–7

In contemplating the whole of this subject, I extend my views into the department of commerce. In all my publications, where the matter would admit, I have been an advocate for commerce, because I am a friend to its effects. It is a pacific system, operating to unite mankind by rendering nations, as well as individuals, useful to each other. As to the mere theoretical reformation, I have never preached it up. The most effectual process is that of improving the condition of man by means of his interest; and it is on this ground that I take my stand.

If commerce were permitted to act to the universal extent it is capable of, it would extirpate the system of war, and produce a revolution in the uncivilized state of governments. The invention of commerce has arisen since those governments began, and is the greatest approach toward universal civilization, that has yet been made by any means not immediately flowing from moral principles.

Whatever has a tendency to promote the civil intercourse of nations by an exchange of benefits is a subject as worthy of philosophy as of politics. Commerce is no other than the traffic of two individuals, multiplied on a scale of numbers; and by the same rule that nature intended the intercourse of two, she intended that of all. For this purpose she has distributed the materials of manufacturers and commerce in various and distant parts of a nation and of the world; and as they cannot be procured by war so cheaply or so commodiously as by commerce, she has rendered the latter the means of extirpating the former.

As the two are nearly the opposites of each other, consequently the uncivilized state of European governments is injurious to commerce. Every kind of destruction or embarrassment serves to lessen the quantity, and it matters but little in what part of the commercial world the reduction begins. Like blood, it cannot be taken from any of the parts without being taken from the whole mass in circulation, and all partake of the loss. When the ability in any nation to buy is destroyed, it equally involves the seller. Could the government of England destroy the commerce of all other nations, she would most effectually ruin her own.

33

THOMAS JEFFERSON, FIRST INAUGURAL ADDRESS
4 Mar. 1801
Richardson 1:321–24

Friends and Fellow-Citizens:

Called upon to undertake the duties of the first executive office of our country, I avail myself of the presence of that portion of my fellow-citizens which is here assembled to express my grateful thanks for the favor with which they have been pleased to look toward me, to declare a sincere consciousness that the task is above my talents, and that I approach it with those anxious and awful presentiments which the greatness of the charge and the weakness of my powers so justly inspire. A rising nation, spread over a wide and fruitful land, traversing all the seas with the rich productions of their industry, engaged in commerce with nations who feel power and forget right, advancing rapidly to destinies beyond the reach of mortal eye—when I contemplate these transcendent objects, and see the honor, the happiness, and the hopes of this beloved country committed to the issue and the auspices of this day, I shrink from the contemplation, and humble myself before the magnitude of the undertaking. Utterly, indeed, should I despair did not the presence of many whom I here see remind me that in the other high authorities provided by our Constitution I shall find resources of wisdom, of virtue, and of zeal on which to rely under all difficulties. To you, then, gentlemen, who are charged with the sovereign functions of legislation, and to those associated with you, I look with encouragement for that guidance and support which may enable us to steer with safety the vessel in which we are all embarked amidst the conflicting elements of a troubled world.

During the contest of opinion through which we have passed the animation of discussions and of exertions has sometimes worn an aspect which might impose on strangers unused to think freely and to speak and to write what they think; but this being now decided by the voice of the nation, announced according to the rules of the Constitution, all will, of course, arrange themselves under the will of the law, and unite in common efforts for the common good. All, too, will bear in mind this sacred principle, that though the will of the majority is in all cases to prevail, that will to be rightful must be reasonable; that the minority possess their equal rights, which equal law must protect, and to violate would be oppression. Let us, then, fellow-citizens, unite with one heart and one mind. Let us restore to social intercourse that harmony and affection without which liberty and even life itself are but dreary things. And let us reflect that, having banished from our land that religious intolerance under which mankind so long bled and suffered, we have yet gained little if we countenance a political intolerance as despotic, as wicked, and capable of as bitter and bloody persecutions. During the throes and convulsions of the ancient world, during the agonizing spasms of infuriated man, seeking through blood and slaughter his long-lost liberty, it was not wonderful that the agitation of the billows should reach even this distant and peaceful shore; that this should be more felt and feared by some and less by others, and should divide opinions as to measures of safety. But every difference of opinion is not a difference of principle. We have called by different names brethren of the same principle. We are all Republicans, we are all Federalists. If there be any among us who would wish to dissolve this Union or to change its republican form, let them stand undisturbed as monuments of the safety with which error of opinion may be tolerated where reason is left free to combat it. I know, indeed, that some honest men fear that a republican government can not be strong, that this Government is not strong enough; but would the honest patriot, in the full tide of successful experiment, abandon a government which has so far kept us free and firm on the theoretic and visionary fear that this Government, the world's best hope, may by possibility want energy to preserve itself? I trust not. I believe this, on the contrary, the strongest Government on earth. I believe it the only one where every man, at the call of the law, would fly to the standard of the law, and would meet invasions of the public order as his own personal concern. Sometimes it is said that man can not be trusted with the government of himself. Can he, then, be trusted with the government of others? Or have we found angels in the forms of kings to govern him? Let history answer this question.

Let us, then, with courage and confidence pursue our own Federal and Republican principles, our attachment to union and representative government. Kindly separated by nature and a wide ocean from the exterminating havoc of one quarter of the globe; too high-minded to endure the degradations of the others; possessing a chosen country, with room enough for our descendants to the thousandth and thousandth generation; entertaining a due sense of our equal right to the use of our own faculties, to the acquisitions of our own industry, to honor and confidence from our fellow-citizens, resulting not from birth, but from our actions and their sense of them; enlightened by a benign religion, professed, indeed, and practiced in various forms, yet all of them inculcating honesty, truth, temperance, gratitude, and the love of man; acknowledg-

ing and adoring an overruling Providence, which by all its dispensations proves that it delights in the happiness of man here and his greater happiness hereafter—with all these blessings, what more is necessary to make us a happy and a prosperous people? Still one thing more, fellow-citizens—a wise and frugal Government, which shall restrain men from injuring one another, shall leave them otherwise free to regulate their own pursuits of industry and improvement, and shall not take from the mouth of labor the bread it has earned. This is the sum of good government, and this is necessary to close the circle of our felicities.

About to enter, fellow-citizens, on the exercise of duties which comprehend everything dear and valuable to you, it is proper you should understand what I deem the essential principles of our Government, and consequently those which ought to shape its Administration. I will compress them within the narrowest compass they will bear, stating the general principle, but not all its limitations. Equal and exact justice to all men, of whatever state or persuasion, religious or political; peace, commerce, and honest friendship with all nations, entangling alliances with none; the support of the State governments in all their rights as the most competent administrations for our domestic concerns and the surest bulwarks against antirepublican tendencies; the preservation of the General Government in its whole constitutional vigor, as the sheet anchor of our peace at home and safety abroad; a jealous care of the right of election by the people—a mild and safe corrective of abuses which are lopped by the sword of revolution where peaceable remedies are unprovided; absolute acquiescence in the decisions of the majority, the vital principle of republics, from which is no appeal but to force, the vital principle and immediate parent of despotism; a well-disciplined militia, our best reliance in peace and for the first moments of war, till regulars may relieve them; the supremacy of the civil over the military authority; economy in the public expense, that labor may be lightly burthened; the honest payment of our debts and sacred preservation of the public faith; encouragement of agriculture, and of commerce as its handmaid; the diffusion of information and arraignment of all abuses at the bar of the public reason; freedom of religion; freedom of the press, and freedom of person under the protection of the habeas corpus, and trial by juries impartially selected. These principles form the bright constellation which has gone before us and guided our steps through an age of revolution and reformation. The wisdom of our sages and blood of our heroes have been devoted to their attainment. They should be the creed of our political faith, the text of civic instruction, the touchstone by which to try the services of those we trust; and should we wander from them in moments of error or of alarm, let us hasten to retrace our steps and to regain the road which alone leads to peace, liberty, and safety.

I repair, then, fellow-citizens, to the post you have assigned me. With experience enough in subordinate offices to have seen the difficulties of this the greatest of all, I have learnt to expect that it will rarely fall to the lot of imperfect man to retire from this station with the reputation and the favor which bring him into it. Without pretensions to that high confidence you reposed in our first and greatest revolutionary character, whose preeminent services had entitled him to the first place in his country's love and destined for him the fairest page in the volume of faithful history, I ask so much confidence only as may give firmness and effect to the legal administration of your affairs. I shall often go wrong through defect of judgment. When right, I shall often be thought wrong by those whose positions will not command a view of the whole ground. I ask your indulgence for my own errors, which will never be intentional, and your support against the errors of others, who may condemn what they would not if seen in all its parts. The approbation implied by your suffrage is a great consolation to me for the past, and my future solicitude will be to retain the good opinion of those who have bestowed it in advance, to conciliate that of others by doing them all the good in my power, and to be instrumental to the happiness and freedom of all.

Relying, then, on the patronage of your good will, I advance with obedience to the work, ready to retire from it whenever you become sensible how much better choice it is in your power to make. And may that Infinite Power which rules the destinies of the universe lead our councils to what is best, and give them a favorable issue for your peace and prosperity.

34

THOMAS JEFFERSON TO JOSEPH C. CABELL
2 Feb. 1816
Writings 14:421–23

No, my friend, the way to have good and safe government, is not to trust it all to one, but to divide it among the many, distributing to every one exactly the functions he is competent to. Let the national government be entrusted with the defence of the nation, and its foreign and federal relations; the State governments with the civil rights, laws, police, and administration of what concerns the State generally; the counties with the local concerns of the counties, and each ward direct the interests within itself. It is by dividing and subdividing these republics from the great national one down through all its subordinations, until it ends in the administration of every man's farm by himself; by placing under every one what his own eye may superintend, that all will be done for the best. What has destroyed liberty and the rights of man in every government which has ever existed under the sun? The generalizing and concentrating all cares and power into one body, no matter whether of the autocrats of Russia or France, or of the aristocrats of a Venetian senate. And I do believe that if the Almighty has not decreed that man shall never be free, (and it is a blasphemy to believe it,) that the secret will be found to be in the making himself the depository of the powers respecting himself, so far as he is competent to them, and delegating only what is beyond his compe-

tence by a synthetical process, to higher and higher orders of functionaries, so as to trust fewer and fewer powers in proportion as the trustees become more and more oligarchical. The elementary republics of the wards, the county republics, the State republics, and the republic of the Union, would form a gradation of authorities, standing each on the basis of law, holding every one its delegated share of powers, and constituting truly a system of fundamental balances and checks for the government. Where every man is a sharer in the direction of his ward-republic, or of some of the higher ones, and feels that he is a participator in the government of affairs, not merely at an election one day in the year, but every day; when there shall not be a man in the State who will not be a member of some one of its councils, great or small, he will let the heart be torn out of his body sooner than his power be wrested from him by a Caesar or a Bonaparte. How powerfully did we feel the energy of this organization in the case of embargo? I felt the foundations of the government shaken under my feet by the New England townships. There was not an individual in their States whose body was not thrown with all its momentum into action; and although the whole of the other States were known to be in favor of the measure, yet the organization of this little selfish minority enabled it to overrule the Union. What would the unwieldy counties of the Middle, the South, and the West do? Call a county meeting, and the drunken loungers at and about the courthouses would have collected, the distances being too great for the good people and the industrious generally to attend. The character of those who really met would have been the measure of the weight they would have had in the scale of public opinion. As Cato, then, concluded every speech with the words, *"Carthago delenda est,"* so do I every opinion, with the injunction, "divide the counties into wards." Begin them only for a single purpose; they will soon show for what others they are the best instruments. God bless you, and all our rulers, and give them the wisdom, as I am sure they have the will, to fortify us against the degeneracy of our government, and the concentration of all its powers in the hands of the one, the few, the well-born or the many.

SEE ALSO:

Generally ch. 18; 1.9.8; 1.10.1; 4.4

Thomas Jefferson, Commonplace Book, § 320, The Commonplace Book of Thomas Jefferson: A Repertory of His Ideas on Government 83 (Chinard ed., 1926)

John Adams, Novanglus, no. 7, 6 Mar. 1775, Papers 2:314–15

Pittsfield, Massachusetts, Memorial, 26 Dec. 1775, Handlin 61–64

Instructions of Stoughton, Massachusetts, 1779, Handlin 422–27

Alexander Hamilton to Robert Morris, 30 Apr. 1781, Papers 2:617–18

John Jay to Robert Morris, 25 Apr. 1782, Correspondence 2:196–97

John Adams to Marquis de Lafayette, 21 May 1782, Works 7:593

Thomas Jefferson to George Washington, 15 Mar. 1784, Papers 7:25–27

John Adams to John Jay, 6 Dec. 1785, Works 8:357

James Madison to James Monroe, 5 Oct. 1786, Papers 9:140–41

George Mason, Protest against the Port Bill, Nov.–Dec. 1786, Papers 2:862–63

John Adams, Defence of the Constitutions of Government of the United States, 1787, Works 4:309–10

Hugh Williamson, Letters of Sylvius, no. 3, Aug. 1787, Historical Papers of the Trinity College Historical Society 11:16–21 (1915)

Agrippa, no. 1, 23 Nov. 1787, Storing 4.6.6

James Madison, Virginia Ratifying Convention, 20 June 1788, Elliot 3:536–37

John Adams to Benjamin Rush, 9 June 1789, Old Family Letters 1:37–38

John Adams to Roger Sherman, 17 July 1789, Works 6:427–29

Roger Sherman to John Adams, 20 July 1789, Adams Works 6:437–38

Henry Lee to James Madison, 4 Mar. 1790, Madison Papers 13:87–90

John Adams to Samuel Adams, 18 Oct. 1790, Works 6:414–16

Thomas Jefferson to M. D'Ivernois, 6 Feb. 1795, Works 8:165–66

Benjamin Rush, Of the Mode of Education Proper in a Republic, 1798, Selected Writings 94

Thomas Jefferson to Mr. Lithson, 4 Jan. 1805, Writings 11:55–56

John Adams to Benjamin Rush, 20 June 1808, Old Family Letters 1:186–87

John Adams to Benjamin Rush, 25 July 1808, Old Family Letters 1:191

John Adams to Benjamin Rush, 27 Sept. 1808, Old Family Letters 1:200–201

Thomas Jefferson to John Adams, 28 Oct. 1813, Cappon 2:390

Thomas Jefferson to Samuel Kercheval, 12 July 1816, Works 12:3–15

Thomas Jefferson to Major John Cartwright, 5 June 1824, Writings 16:44–46

. . . in Order to form a more perfect Union, . . .

5

Deficiencies of the Confederation

Introduction

Prominent among the problems of postrevolutionary America were the deficiencies of its fundamental charter, the Articles of Confederation. And yet, many of the problems of the day would have been acute no matter what the government, given the situation of the United States: a new nation, possessed of a vast but sparsely populated territory, burdened with foreign and domestic debt, its commerce disrupted by a protracted war. The population stretched over a long, thin littoral, surrounded on three sides by resentful neighbors or suspicious powers, separated within its borders by physical barriers to travel and easy communication as well as by long-standing feelings of localism and deeply different ways of life. All this boded weakness and disunion. Some might dream of America cutting a figure in world affairs, but the immediate realities pointed in quite another direction.

Beyond these difficulties inherent in the situation loomed a further range of problems attributable to, or at least exacerbated by, the government of the Confederation. There seemed to be no prospect of coping with the war debts that were overwhelming both nation and states; the British could not be compelled to honor their agreement under the Treaty of Paris to vacate the western forts; the western settlers increasingly felt they owed little to a government that could guarantee the security neither of their person nor of their trade routes. Ultimately a new government, formed on different principles than those of the Articles of Confederation, would come to cope with these problems.

In stressing the defects of the Confederation and in ignoring its substantial achievements (carrying the war for independence through to victory, forming a diplomatic corps of genuine distinction, providing for the orderly organization and incorporation of a vast public domain), we notice those sources of discontent that contemporaries traced to the Articles themselves. The movement to amend and finally to replace the Articles grew out of a clear conviction that the fault lay not in the stars but in themselves. The political undertaking consisted in making that realization prevalent and, above all, in not letting people evade the imperatives for action implicit in it. The managers of the movement for a new government thus had to contend with every passion and cause that might make men loath to overturn existing structures: familiarity, caution, timidity, indifference, mistaken confidence, present interest, future hope. Further, they had both to convince a nationally distributed majority that the distempers of the time were indeed systemic disorders and to keep that majority energized with the bracing thought that they were living through not merely awkward or bad times but critical ones. The pressing question, they argued, concerned not the daily balance sheet—how good or bad are things at the moment?—but rather the whole movement or tendency of political affairs. There is a cumulative momentum in bad governance: things go from bad to worse to worst, from Shaysite disorders and the disregard of Congressional requisitions to recourse ultimately to antirepublican measures and disunion. The proper remedy, once adopted, would develop its own cumulative momentum, restoring tranquility and prosperity at home and honor to the republican cause.

The materials drawn from a decade of complaint, politicking, and agitation do not purport to be a full account of even the major forces at work. Thus the deep divisions over the national assumption of state debts, the bitter rivalry over claims to western lands and their development, the mutual suspicions and fears entertained by the staple-producing South and the mercantile Northeast, are barely hinted at though they carried certain implications for the organization and powers of government. The debate focused on larger and more general questions: How much of a central government was needed for the United States of America? Supposing the Confederation fell short of that need, how much of a change was required to render it "adequate to the exigencies of the Union"?

The most energetic and unremitting critic of the Articles was Alexander Hamilton. His letter to Governor Clinton (no. 1), written while he was still in his early twenties, was part of a sustained effort to raise the Confederation's tone, vigor, and powers. His early criticism of the quality of representation in Congress conceded, while lamenting, the precedence of state over nation. Hamilton might view it as "a most pernicious mistake," but each state did in fact prefer "to promote its own internal government and prosperity" and, to do so, "selected the best members to fill the offices within itself, and conduct its own affairs." When Jefferson—no provincial—spoke of "my country," he referred as a matter of course to Virginia, and in this he was hardly alone. Constitution-making, revisal of laws, governance—all at the state level—called forth the energies and concerns of the ablest, and at times left Congress (as Washington all but said out loud) trivial and contemptible (Letter to George Mason, 27 Mar. 1779). By 1780 Hamilton's criticism took in the very premises of the Articles (no. 2). The problems of the Confederation were owing not merely to small men thinking small thoughts. The defects were radical, and effective remedies could not be less so. In this context the pleas of the man responsible for the financial affairs of the nation bespoke utter desperation and pathos: Robert Morris was equally short of indispensable information and of money, and could barely believe that even the plainest talk would get him either (no. 3). Two years later he could write, without satisfaction, of exhausted American credit: *The thing has happened which was expected* (no. 7).

Meanwhile, Congress wrestled with contending anxieties, its sense of urgency quickened by the audible stirrings of an armed, unpaid, and under-occupied officer corps. (See the Newburgh Resolves and the matters leading up to them in *Journals* 24:295–314.) How far ought the federal principles underlying the Confederation to be altered to secure a more adequate and reliable revenue? Could it be done without subverting "the fundamental principles of liberty" (nos. 5, 6)? Congress's inability to cope with large matters and small persuaded nationalists that change was overdue, and even those with the deepest misgivings concerning nationalist intentions acknowledged something should be done. Yet Richard Henry Lee feared being hastened into ill-considered measures more dangerous than the distempers they were to cure (no. 8). Similar misgivings were detailed in letters written by Massachusetts' delegates to the Continental Congress in response to the resolutions of the state legislature calling for a convention to recommend revision of the Articles. Prudence dictated making enlargement of Congressional power only temporary especially in view of the difficulty of amending the Articles. Then, too, a general convention might well be the occasion for frustrated aristocrats to do their worst. Caution was the byword. (Massachusetts Delegates to Gov. James Bowdoin, 3 Sept. 1785; Nathan Dane to Rufus King, 8 Oct. 1785.)

Such hesitation and misgiving struck Washington as inexplicable. America's dependence on commerce with foreign nations was by now hardly a matter for speculative inquiry. The urgent business at hand was to set that commerce right with a single, just national policy. Anything hindering that development betrayed America's fondest hopes and brightest prospects (nos. 9, 11). William Grayson of the Virginia delegation saw part of the problem, but was less sure than Washington of the appropriate remedy (Letter to James Madison, 22 Mar. 1786); Rufus King, writing to his partner in the previous year's rejection of the Massachusetts resolutions, saw the deteriorating situation with a new urgency (no. 10). Yet when Congress attempted to address directly the problems of nonuniform commercial policies, nonpayment of state quotas, insufficient sources of national revenue, and nonattendance by state delegates, its proposed amendments to the Articles could never even be brought to a vote (no. 12). Five weeks later the Annapolis convention set in motion the campaign for a fuller and more ambitious convention.

That campaign was much helped by the agitation over paper money in New Jersey and Rhode Island and especially by the fright occasioned by Shays's rebellion in western Massachusetts (nos. 13, 14). But it still was easier to see that something had to be done than to know what to do (no. 15). The partition of the country into separate confederacies was bruited about, and even monarchy was hinted at. Madison found "men of reflection much less sanguine as to a new than despondent as to the present System" (Letter to Edmund Pendleton, 24 Feb. 1787). But being the kind of man he was, Madison addressed in his mind the subject of the forthcoming convention and tried to think clearly, calmly, and as he confessed to Washington (see ch. 8, no. 6) radically about the "Vices of the Political system of the U. States." His memorandum bearing that name (no. 16) is a distillation of close observation and trenchant analysis. By the time Madison was sitting in Philadelphia waiting for the other Convention delegates to assemble, he had done his homework well.

Those on the outside looking on (although unable to look in) were of divided minds about what the Convention might do and about what needed remedying. Richard Henry Lee still worried about flying from one extreme to the next in undertaking reforms. Moreover, it seemed to him, impatience had come to attribute to failures of governmental structure what really was owing to "vicious manners" (no. 18). It was unrealistic to expect those neglectful of their duties under one form of government to be scrupulous about them under another. But at the same time Lee saw fit to propose some structural reforms—an exclusive power in Congress over paper money, a general supremacy over state legislation—which "would be a great step towards correcting morals." Edward Carrington traced the "nefarious Acts of State Governments" to something other than "the natural dispositions of the people." A profoundly faulty system had produced "disgust and apathy throughout"; seducers of the people and traducers of the facts worked upon a credulous public, unchallenged by men of integrity (no. 19). Jefferson responded cautiously from Paris; in general, he thought, the defects of the Confederation being limited and specific, the remedial changes ought to be commensurate (no. 20).

These fundamentally different orientations persisted when the handiwork of the Convention came under public scrutiny and debate. The Federal Farmer deplored the skewed vision and exaggerated expectations that had led people to magnify "extravagantly" the Confederation's defects and attribute to the system what were "merely the consequences of a severe and tedious war" (no. 25). Centinel, too, saw no reason to charge the natural consequences of private extravagance to a lack of energy in government (no. 24). All in all, the Anti-Federalist critics were willing to concede weaknesses in parts of the existing structure, but not a fundamental viciousness in the entire system (no. 27). The depictions of crisis were overwrought, a "gilded bait" (as Centinel put it), given the lie by the actual condition of the people (Plebeian, no. 26). There can be no doubt that the *Federalist*'s famous characterization of life under the Articles—"almost the last stage of national humiliation"—was "high-wrought" if not overwrought. Hamilton's decade of frustration had exploded in an attack marked by audacity, persistence, overwhelming rhetorical power, and a ready command of every weapon at hand (nos. 21, 22, 23). Next to this bravura performance, John Jay's Address to the people of New York might seem like tepid stuff. His condemnation of the vices of the Confederation, however, was no less damning, though subdued in tone. Inexperience—"an amiable mistake"—and a general preoccupation with private and local matters had led to a "new and wonderful system of government" that now (Spring 1788) had left "almost every national object of every kind . . . unprovided for." Americans needed only to take note of their painfully acquired experience. And that, apparently, was what they did (no. 28).

1

ALEXANDER HAMILTON TO GOV. GEORGE CLINTON
13 Feb. 1778
Papers 1:425–28

There is a matter, which often obtrudes itself upon my mind, and which requires the attention of every person of sense and influence, among us. I mean a degeneracy of representation in the great council of America. It is a melancholy truth Sir, and the effects of which we dayly see and feel, that there is not so much wisdom in a certain body, as there ought to be, and as the success of our affairs absolutely demands. Many members of it are no doubt men in every respect, fit for the trust, but this cannot be said of it as a body. Folly, caprice a want of foresight, comprehension and dignity, characterise the general tenor of their actions. Of this I dare say, you are sensible, though you have not perhaps so many opportunities of knowing it as I have. Their conduct with respect to the army especially is feeble indecisive and improvident—insomuch, that we are reduced to a more terrible situation than you can conceive. False and contracted views of economy have prevented them, though repeatedly urged to it, from making that provision for officers which was requisite to interest them in the service; which has produced such carelessness and indifference to the service, as is subversive of every officer-like quality. They have disgusted the army by repeated instances of the most whimsical favouritism in their promotions; and by an absurd prodigality of rank to foreigners and to the meanest staff of the army. They have not been able to summon resolution enough to withstand the impudent importunity and vain boasting of foreign pretenders; but have manifested such a ductility and inconstancy in their proceedings, as will warrant the charge of suffering themselves to be bullied, by every petty rascal, who comes armed with ostentatious pretensions of military merit and experience. Would you believe it Sir, it is become almost proverbial in the mouths of the French officers and other foreigners, that they have nothing more to do, to obtain whatever they please, than to assume a high tone and assert their own merit with confidence and perserverance? These things wound my feelings as a republican more than I can express; and in some degree make me contemptible in my own eyes.

By injudicious changes and arrangements in the Commissary's department, in the middle of a campaign, they have exposed the army frequently to temporary want, and to the danger of a dissolution, from absolute famine. At this very day there are complaints from the whole line, of having been three or four days without provisions; desertions have been immense, and strong features of mutiny begin to show themselves. It is indeed to be wondered at, that the soldiery have manifested so unparallelled a degree of patience, as they have. If effectual measures are not speedily adopted, I know not how we shall keep the army together or make another campaign.

I omit saying any thing of the want of Cloathing for the army. It may be disputed whether more could have been done than has been done.

If you look into their conduct in the civil line, you will equally discover a deficiency of energy dignity and extensiveness of views; but of this you can better judge than myself, and it is unnecessary to particularise.

America once had a representation, that would do honor to any age or nation. The present falling off is very alarming and dangerous. What is the cause? or how is it to be remedied? are questions that the welfare of these states requires should be well attended to. The great men who composed our first council; are they dead, have they deserted the cause, or what has become of them? Very few are dead and still fewer have deserted the cause;—they are all except the few who still remain in Congress either in the field, or in the civil offices of their respective states; far the greater part are engaged in the latter. The only remedy then is to take them out of these employments and return them to the place, where their presence is infinitely more important.

Each State in order to promote its own internal government and prosperity, has selected its best members to fill the offices within itself, and conduct its own affairs. Men have been fonder of the emoluments and conveniences, of being employed at home, and local attachment, falsely operating, has made them more provident for the particular interests of the states to which they belonged, than for the common interests of the confederacy. This is a most pernicious mistake, and must be corrected. However important it is to give form and efficiency to your interior constitutions and police; it is infinitely more important to have a wise general council; otherwise a failure of the measures of the union will overturn all your labours for the advancement of your particular good and ruin the common cause. You should not beggar the councils of the United States to enrich the administration of the several members. Realize to yourself the consequences of having a Congress despised at home and abroad. How can the common force be exerted, if the power of collecting it be put in weak foolish and unsteady hands? How can we hope for success in our European negociations, if the nations of Europe have no confidence in the wisdom and vigor, of the great Continental Government? This is the object on which their eyes are fixed, hence it is America will derive its importance or insignificance, in their estimation.

Arguments to you Sir, need not be multiplied to enforce the necessity of having a good general council, neither do I think we shall very widely differ as to the fact that the present is very far from being such.

The sentiments I have advanced are not fit for the vulgar ear; and circumstanced as I am, I should with caution utter them except to those in whom I may place an entire confidence. But it is time that men of weight and understanding should take the alarm, and excite each other to a proper remedy.

2

ALEXANDER HAMILTON TO JAMES DUANE
3 Sept. 1780

Papers 2:400–403, 404–8, 409, 417

Agreeably to your request and my promise I sit down to give you my ideas of the defects of our present system, and the changes necessary to save us from ruin. They may perhaps be the reveries of a projector rather than the sober views of a politician. You will judge of them, and make what use you please of them.

The fundamental defect is a want of power in Congress. It is hardly worth while to show in what this consists, as it seems to be universally acknowleged, or to point out how it has happened, as the only question is how to remedy it. It may however be said that it has originated from three causes—an excess of the spirit of liberty which has made the particular states show a jealousy of all power not in their own hands; and this jealousy has led them to exercise a right of judging in the last resort of the measures recommended by Congress, and of acting according to their own opinions of their propriety or necessity, a diffidence in Congress of their own powers, by which they have been timid and indecisive in their resolutions, constantly making concessions to the states, till they have scarcely left themselves the shadow of power; a want of sufficient means at their disposal to answer the public exigencies and of vigor to draw forth those means; which have occasioned them to depend on the states individually to fulfil their engagements with the army, and the consequence of which has been to ruin their influence and credit with the army, to establish its dependence on each state separately rather than *on them,* that is rather than on the whole collectively.

It may be pleaded, that Congress had never any definitive powers granted them and of course could exercise none—could do nothing more than recommend. The manner in which Congress was appointed would warrant, and the public good required, that they should have considered themselves as vested with full power *to preserve the republic from harm.* They have done many of the highest acts of sovereignty, which were always chearfully submitted to—the declaration of independence, the declaration of war, the levying an army, creating a navy, emitting money, making alliances with foreign powers, appointing a dictator &c. &c.—all these implications of a complete sovereignty were never disputed, and ought to have been a standard for the whole conduct of Administration. Undefined powers are discretionary powers, limited only by the object for which they were given—in the present case, the independence and freedom of America. The confederation made no difference; for as it has not been generally adopted, it had no operation. But from what I recollect of it, Congress have even descended from the authority which the spirit of that act gives them, while the particular states have no further attended to it than as it suited their pretensions and convenience. It would take too much time to enter into particular instances, each of which separately might appear inconsiderable; but united are of serious import. I only mean to remark, not to censure.

But the confederation itself is defective and requires to be altered; it is neither fit for war, nor peace. The idea of an uncontrolable sovereignty in each state, over its internal police, will defeat the other powers given to Congress, and make our union feeble and precarious. There are instances without number, where acts necessary for the general good, and which rise out of the powers given to Congress must interfere with the internal police of the states, and there are as many instances in which the particular states by arrangements of internal police can effectually though indirectly counteract the arrangements of Congress. You have already had examples of this for which I refer you to your own memory.

The confederation gives the states individually too much influence in the affairs of the army; they should have nothing to do with it. The entire formation and disposal of our military forces ought to belong to Congress. It is an essential cement of the union; and it ought to be the policy of Congress to destroy all ideas of state attachments in the army and make it look up wholly to them. For this purpose all appointments promotions and provisions whatsoever ought to be made by them. It may be apprehended that this may be dangerous to liberty. But nothing appears more evident to me, than that we run much greater risk of having a weak and disunited federal government, than one which will be able to usurp upon the rights of the people. Already some of the lines of the army would obey their states in opposition to Congress notwithstanding the pains we have taken to preserve the unity of the army—if any thing would hinder this it would be the personal influence of the General, a melancholy and mortifying consideration.

The forms of our state constitutions must always give them great weight in our affairs and will make it too difficult to bend them to the persuit of a common interest, too easy to oppose whatever they do not like and to form partial combinations subversive of the general one. There is a wide difference between our situation and that of an empire under one simple form of government, distributed into counties provinces or districts, which have no legislatures but merely magistratical bodies to execute the laws of a common sovereign. Here the danger is that the sovereign will have too much power to oppress the parts of which it is composed. In our case, that of an empire composed of confederated states each with a government completely organised within itself, having all the means to draw its subjects to a close dependence on itself—the danger is directly the reverse. It is that the common sovereign will not have power sufficient to unite the different members together, and direct the common forces to the interest and happiness of the whole.

The leagues among the old Grecian republics are a proof of this. They were continually at war with each other, and for want of union fell a prey to their neighbours. They frequently held general councils, but their resolutions were no further observed than as they suited the interests and inclinations of all the parties and at length, they sunk intirely into contempt.

. . . . .

Our own experience should satisfy us. We have felt the difficulty of drawing out the resources of the country and inducing the states to combine in equal exertions for the common cause. The ill success of our last attempt is striking. Some have done a great deal, others little or scarcely any thing. The disputes about boundaries &c. testify how flattering a prospect we have of future tranquillity, if we do not frame in time a confederacy capable of deciding the differences and compelling the obedience of the respective members.

The confederation too gives the power of the purse too intirely to the state legislatures. It should provide perpetual funds in the disposal of Congress—by a land tax, poll tax, or the like. All imposts upon commerce ought to be laid by Congress and appropriated to their use, for without certain revenues, a government can have no power; that power, which holds the purse strings absolutely, must rule. This seems to be a medium, which without making Congress altogether independent will tend to give reality to its authority.

Another defect in our system is want of method and energy in the administration. This has partly resulted from the other defect, but in a great degree from prejudice and the want of a proper executive. Congress have kept the power too much into their own hands and have meddled too much with details of every sort. Congress is properly a deliberative corps and it forgets itself when it attempts to play the executive. It is impossible such a body, numerous as it is, constantly fluctuating, can ever act with sufficient decision, or with system. Two thirds of the members, one half the time, cannot know what has gone before them or what connection the subject in hand has to what has been transacted on former occasions. The members, who have been more permanent, will only give information, that promotes the side they espouse, in the present case, and will as often mislead as enlighten. The variety of business must distract, and the proneness of every assembly to debate must at all times delay.

Lately Congress, convinced of these inconveniences, have gone into the measure of appointing boards. But this is in my opinion a bad plan. A single man, in each department of the administration, would be greatly preferable. It would give us a chance of more knowlege, more activity, more responsibility and of course more zeal and attention. Boards partake of a part of the inconveniencies of larger assemblies. Their decisions are slower their energy less their responsibility more diffused. They will not have the same abilities and knowlege as an administration by single men. Men of the first pretensions will not so readily engage in them, because they will be less cospicuous, of less importance, have less opportunity of distinguishing themselves. The members of boards will take less pains to inform themselves and arrive to eminence, because they have fewer motives to do it. All these reasons conspire to give a preference to the plan of vesting the great executive departments of the state in the hands of individuals. As these men will be of course at all times under the direction of Congress, we shall blend the advantages of a monarchy and republic in our constitution.

A question has been made, whether single men could be found to undertake these offices. I think they could, because there would be then every thing to excite the ambition of candidates. But in order to this Congress by their manner of appointing them and the line of duty marked out must show that they are in earnest in making these offices, offices of real trust and importance.

I fear a little vanity has stood in the way of these arrangements, as though they would lessen the importance of Congress and leave them nothing to do. But they would have precisely the same rights and powers as heretofore, happily disencumbered of the detail. They would have to inspect the conduct of their ministers, deliberate upon their plans, originate others for the public good—only observing this rule that they ought to consult their ministers, and get all the information and advice they could from them, before they entered into any new measures or made changes in the old.

A third defect is the fluctuating constitution of our army. This has been a pregnant source of evil; all our military misfortunes, three fourths of our civil embarrassments are to be ascribed to it. The General has so fully enumerated the mischief of it in a late letter of the [20th August] to Congress that I could only repeat what he has said, and will therefore refer you to that letter.

The imperfect and unequal provision made for the army is a fourth defect which you will find delineated in the same letter. Without a speedy change the army must dissolve; it is now a mob, rather than an army, without cloathing, without pay, without provision, without morals, without discipline. We begin to hate the country for its neglect of us; the country begins to hate us for our oppressions of them. Congress have long been jealous of us; we have now lost all confidence in them, and give the worst construction to all they do. Held together by the slenderest ties we are ripening for a dissolution.

The present mode of supplying the army—by state purchases—is not one of the least considerable defects of our system. It is too precarious a dependence, because the states will never be sufficiently impressed with our necessities. Each will make its own ease a primary object, the supply of the army a secondary one. The variety of channels through which the business is transacted will multiply the number of persons employed and the opportunities of embezzling public money. From the popular spirit on which most of the governments turn, the state agents, will be men of less character and ability, nor will there be so rigid a responsibility among them as there might easily be among those in the employ of the continent, of course not so much diligence care or economy. Very little of the money raised in the several states will go into the Continental treasury, on pretence, that it is all exhausted in pro-

viding the quotas of supplies, and the public will be without funds for the other demands of governments. The expence will be ultimately much greater and the advantages much smaller. We actually feel the insufficiency of this plan and have reason to dread under it a ruinous extremity of want.

These are the principal defects in the present system that now occur to me. There are many inferior ones in the organization of particular departments and many errors of administration which might be pointed out; but the task would be troublesome and tedious, and if we had once remedied those I have mentioned the others would not be attended with much difficulty.

I shall now propose the remedies, which appear to me applicable to our circumstances, and necessary to extricate our affairs from their present deplorable situation.

The first step must be to give Congress powers competent to the public exigencies. This may happen in two ways, one by resuming and exercising the discretionary powers I suppose to have been originally vested in them for the safety of the states and resting their conduct on the candor of their country men and the necessity of the conjuncture: the other by calling immediately a convention of all the states with full authority to conclude finally upon a general confederation, stating to them beforehand explicity the evils arising from a want of power in Congress, and the impossibily of supporting the contest on its present footing, that the delegates may come possessed of proper sentiments as well as proper authority to give to the meeting. Their commission should include a right of vesting Congress with the whole or a proportion of the unoccupied lands, to be employed for the purpose of raising a revenue, reserving the jurisdiction to the states by whom they are granted.

The first plan, I expect will be thought too bold an expedient by the generality of Congress; and indeed their practice hitherto has so rivetted the opinion of their want of power, that the success of this experiment may very well be doubted.

I see no objection to the other mode, that has any weight in competition with the reasons for it. The Convention should assemble the 1st of November next, the sooner, the better; our disorders are too violent to admit of a common or lingering remedy. The reasons for which I require them to be vested with plenipotentiary authority are that the business may suffer no delay in the execution, and may in reality come to effect. A convention may agree upon a confederation; the states individually hardly ever will. We must have one at all events, and a vigorous one if we mean to succeed in the contest and be happy hereafter. As I said before, to engage the states to comply with this mode, Congress ought to confess to them plainly and unanimously the impracticability of supporting our affairs on the present footing and without a solid coercive union. I ask that the Convention should have a power of vesting the whole or a part of the unoccupied land in Congress, because it is necessary that body should have some property as a fund for the arrangements of finance; and I know of no other kind that can be given them.

The confederation in my opinion should give Congress

complete sovereignty; except as to that part of internal police, which relates to the rights of property and life among individuals and to raising money by internal taxes. It is necessary, that every thing, belonging to this, should be regulated by the state legislatures. Congress should have complete sovereignty in all that relates to war, peace, trade, finance, and to the management of foreign affairs, the right of declaring war of raising armies, officering, paying them, directing their motions in every respect, of equipping fleets and doing the same with them, of building fortifications arsenals magazines &c. &c., of making peace on such conditions as they think proper, of regulating trade, determining with what countries it shall be carried on, granting indulgencies laying prohibitions on all the articles of export or import, imposing duties granting bounties & premiums for raising exporting importing and applying to their own use the product of these duties, only giving credit to the states on whom they are raised in the general account of revenues and expences, instituting Admiralty courts &c., of coining money, establishing banks on such terms, and with such privileges as they think proper, appropriating funds and doing whatever else relates to the operations of finance, transacting every thing with foreign nations, making alliances offensive and defensive, treaties of commerce, &c. &c.

The confederation should provide certain perpetual revenues, productive and easy of collection, a land tax, poll tax or the like, which together with the duties on trade and the unlocated lands would give Congress a substantial existence, and a stable foundation for their schemes of finance. What more supplies were necessary should be occasionally demanded of the states, in the present mode of quotas.

The second step I would recommend is that Congress should instantly appoint the following great officers of state—A secretary for foreign affairs—a President of war—A President of Marine—A Financier—A President of trade; instead of this last a board of Trade may be preferable as the regulations of trade are slow and gradual and require prudence and experience (more than other qualities), for which boards are very well adapted.

Congress should choose for these offices, men of the first abilities, property and character in the continent—and such as have had the best opportunities of being acquainted with the several branches.

. . . . .

These offices should have nearly the same powers and functions as those in France analogous to them, and each should be chief in his department, with subordinate boards composed of assistant clerks &c. to execute his orders.

In my opinion a plan of this kind would be of inconceivable utility to our affairs; its benefits would be very speedily felt. It would give new life and energy to the operations of government. Business would be conducted with dispatch method and system. A million of abuses now existing would be corrected, and judicious plans would be formed and executed for the public good.

. . . . .

And, in future, My Dear Sir, two things let me recommend, as fundamental rules for the conduct of Congress— to attach the army to them by every motive, to maintain an air of authority (not domineering) in all their measures with the states. The manner in which a thing is done has more influence than is commonly imagined. Men are governed by opinion; this opinion is as much influenced by appearances as by realities; if a Government appears to be confident of its own powers, it is the surest way to inspire the same confidence in others; if it is diffident, it may be certain, there will be a still greater diffidence in others, and that its authority will not only be distrusted, controverted, but contemned.

I wish too Congress would always consider that a kindness consists as much in the manner as in the thing: the best things done hesitatingly and with an ill grace lose their effect, and produce disgust rather than satisfaction or gratitude. In what Congress have at any time done for the army, they have commonly been too late: They have seemed to yield to importunity rather than to sentiments of justice or to a regard to the accomodation of their troops. An attention to this idea is of more importance than it may be thought. I who have seen all the workings and progress of the present discontents, am convinced, that a want of this has not been among the most inconsiderable causes.

3

ROBERT MORRIS, CIRCULAR TO THE GOVERNORS
OF THE STATES
25 July 1781
Papers 1:380–83

I had the honor to write you the 16th Instant enclosing A certified copy of the account of your State as it stands in the Treasury Books of the United States; I now pray leave to recall your attention to it. It gives me very great pain to learn that there is A pernicious Idea prevalent among some of the States that their accounts are not to be adjusted with the Continent; such an Idea cannot fail to spread A listless languor over all our operations. To suppose this expensive War can be carryed on without joint and strenuous efforts is beneath the wisdom of those who are called to the high Offices of Legislation. Those who inculcate maxims which tend to relax these efforts, most certainly injure the comon cause whatever may be the motives which inspire their conduct. If once an opinion is admitted that those States who do least and charge most will derive the greatest benefit and endure the smallest Evils, Your Excellency must perceive that shameless inactivity must take place of that noble emulation which ought to pervade and animate the whole Union. It is my particular Duty Sir while I remind my fellow Citizens of those tasks which it is incumbent on them to perform to remove if I can every impediment which lies in the way or which may have been raised by disaffection, Self Interest, or mistake.

I take therefore this early opportunity to assure you that all the accounts of the United States shall be speedily liquidated If I can possibly effect it and my efforts for that purpose shall be unceasing. I make this assurance in the most solemn manner and I entreat the consequences of A contrary assertion may be most seriously weighed and considered before it is made or beleived. These accounts naturally divide themselves into two considerable branches vizt. Those which are previous and those which are subsequent to the resolutions of Congress of the 18th March 1780. The former must be adjusted as soon as proper Officers can be found and appointed for the purpose and proper principles established so as that they may be liquidated in an equitable manner for I am determined Justice shall be the rule of my conduct as farr as the measure of abilities which the Almighty has been pleased to bestow shall enable me to distinguish between right and wrong. I shall never permit A doubt that the States will do what is right; neither will I ever believe that any one of them can expect to derive any advantage from doing what is wrong. It is by being just to Individuals, to each other, to the Union, to all; by generous grants of solid Revenue, and by adopting energetic measures to collect that Revenue; and not by complainings, vauntings, or recriminations that these States must expect to establish their Independance and rise into Power, Consequence, and Grandeur. I speak to your Excellency with freedom because it is my duty so to speak and because I am convinced that the language of plain sincerity is the only proper language to the first Magistrate of A free Community. The accounts I have mentioned as subsequent to the Resolutions of the 18th March 1780 admit of an imediate settlement; the several States have all the necessary materials; One side of the account consists of demands made by the Resolutions of Congress long since forwarded. The other must consist of compliances with those demands; this latter part I am not in capacity to state and for that reason I am to request the earliest information which the nature of things will permit of the Moneys, Supplies, Transportation &ca which have been paid, advanced, or furnished by your State in order that I may know what remains due; the sooner full information can be obtained the sooner shall we know what to rely on and how to do equal Justice to those who have contributed and those who have not, to those who have contributed at one period and to those who have contributed at another.

I enclose you an account of the specific supplies demanded of your State as extracted from the Journals of Congress tho without any mention of what has been done in consequence of those Resolutions because as I have already observed your Excellcy. will be able to discern the Ballance much better than I can. I am further to entreat Sir that I may be favored with copies of the several acts passed in your State since the 18th March 1780 for the collection of Taxes and furnishing supplies or other aids to the United States, the manner in which such acts have been executed, the time which may have been necessary for them to operate, and the consequences of their operation. I must also pray to be informed of so much of the internal Police of your State as relates to the laying, Assessing, Levying and collecting of Taxes. I beg leave to assure your Excellency that I am not prompted by an idle curiosity or by any wish to discover what prudence wou'd dictate to conceal. It is necessary I shou'd be informed of these things and I take the plain, open, candid method of acquiring information. To paliate or conceal any evils or disorders in our situation can answer no good purpose; they must be known before they can be cured; we must also know what resources can be brought forth that we may proportion our efforts to our means and our demands to both. It is necessary we shoud be in A condition to carry on the War with ease before we can expect to lay down our Arms with security, before we can treat of peace honorably, and before we can conclude it to advantage. I feel myself fettered at every moment and embarassed in every operation from my ignorance of our actual state and what is reasonably to be asked or expected, yet when I consider our real wealth and numbers and when I compare them with other Countrys I feel A thorough conviction that we may do much more than we have yet done and with more ease to ourselves than we have yet felt provided we adopt the proper mode of Revenue and Expenditure. Your Excellencys good sense will anticipate my observation on the necessity of being informed what Moneys are in your Treasury and what sums you expect to have there as also of the times they must probably be brought in. In addition to this, I must pray you to communicate the several appropriations.

A misfortune peculiar to America requires that I entreat your Excellency to undertake one more task which perhaps is farr from being the least difficult. It is Sir that you write very fully as to the amount of the several paper Currencys now circulating in your State, the probable Increase or decrease of each and the respective rates of depreciation; having now stated the several communications which are most indispensable let me entreat of your Excellencys goodness that they may be made as speedily as possible to the end I may be early prepared with those propositions which from A view of all circumstances may be most likely to extricate us from our present difficultys. I am also to entreat that you will inform me when your Legislature is to meet; my reason for making this request is that any proposals to be made to them may arrive in season for their attentive deliberation.

I know that I give you A great deal of trouble but I also know it will be pleasing to you because the time and the labour will be expended in the service of your Country. If Sir my feeble but honest efforts shou'd open to us the prospect of American glory, if we shou'd be able to look forward to A period when supported by solid Revenue and Resource, this War shou'd have no other duration or extent than the wisdom of Congress might allow when its object shoud be the honor not the Independance of our Country, If with these fair views the States shou'd be rouzed, excited, animated in the pursuit and unitedly determining to be in that happy situation find themselves placed there by the very determination.

If Sir these things should happen soon the reflection

that your Industry has principally contributed to effect them woud be the rich reward of your Toils and give to your best feelings their amplest gratification. I have the honor to be Your Excellency's Most Obedient and humble servant.

4

GOUVERNEUR MORRIS TO JOHN JAY
1 Jan. 1783
Jay Unpublished Papers 2:485–86

Gen. McDougall, Col. Brooks of the Massachusetts and Col. Ogden of the Jersey Line are now here with a Petition to Congress from the Army for Pay. The Army are now disciplined and their wants as to food and Cloathing are relieved but they are not paid. Their back Accounts are not settled. If settled the Ballances are not secured by competent funds. No Provision is made for the Half-Pay promised them. Some Persons and indeed some States pretend to dispute their Claim to it. (THE ARMY HAVE SWORDS IN THEIR HANDS.* YOU KNOW ENOUGH OF THE HISTORY OF MANKIND TO KNOW MUCH MORE THAN I HAVE SAID AND POSSIBLY MUCH MORE THAN THEY THEMSELVES YET THINK OF.) I will add however that I am glad to see Things in their present Train. Depend on it good will arise from the Situation to which we are hastening. And this you may rely on that my Efforts will not be wanting. I pledge myself to you on the present occasion and ALTHOUGH I THINK IT PROBABLE THAT MUCH OF CONVULSION WILL ENSUE, YET IT MUST TERMINATE IN GIVING TO GOVERNMENT THAT POWER WITHOUT WHICH GOVERNMENT IS BUT A NAME. GOVERNMENT IN AMERICA IS NOT POSSESSED OF IT (BUT THE PEOPLE ARE WELL PREPARED. WEARIED WITH THE WAR, THEIR ACQUIESCENCE MAY BE DEPENDED ON WITH ABSOLUTE CERTAINTY AND YOU AND I, MY FRIEND, KNOW BY EXPERIENCE THAT WHEN A FEW MEN OF SENSE AND SPIRIT GET TOGETHER AND DECLARE THAT THEY ARE THE AUTHORITY, SUCH FEW AS ARE OF A DIFFERENT OPINION MAY EASILY BE CONVINCED OF THEIR MISTAKE BY THAT POWERFUL ARGUMENT THE HALTER. IT IS, HOWEVER, A MOST MELANCHOLY CONSIDERATION THAT A PEOPLE SHOULD REQUIRE SO MUCH OF EXPERIENCE BEFORE THEY WILL BE WISE. IT IS STILL MORE PAINFUL TO THINK THAT THIS EXPERIENCE IS ALWAYS BOUGHT SO DEAR. ON THE WISDOM OF THE PRESENT MOMENT DEPENDS MORE THAN IS EASILY IMAGINED, AND WHEN I LOOK ROUND FOR THE ACTORS—LET US CHANGE THE SUBJECT.)

*Capitalized matter was in cipher.

5

JAMES MADISON, NOTES ON DEBATES IN CONGRESS
28 Jan. 1783
Papers 6:142–49

On the motion of Mr. Madison the whole proposition was new-modelled as follows;

"That it is the opinion of Congress that the establishment of permanent & adequate funds to operate generally throughout the U. States is indispensibly necessary for doing complete justice to the Creditors of the U. S., for restoring public credit, & for providing for the future exigencies of the war." The words "to be collected under the authority of Congress" were as a seperate question left to be added afterwards.

Mr. Rutlidge objected to the term "generally", as implying a degree of uniformity in the tax which would render it unequal. He had in view particularly a land tax according to quantity as had been proposed by the office of finance. He thought the prejudices of the people opposed to the idea of a general tax & seemed on the whole to be disinclined to it himself, at least if extended beyond an impost on trade; urging the necessity of pursuing a valuation of land, and requisitions grounded thereon.

Mr. Lee 2ded. the opposition to the term "general." he contended that the States wd. never consent to a uniform tax because it wd. be unequal; that it was moreover repugnant to the articles of confederation; and by placing the purse in the same hands with the sword, was subversive of the fundamental principles of liberty. He mentioned the repeal of the impost by Virga. himself alone opposing it & that too on the inexpediency in point of time, as proof of the aversion to a general revenue. He reasoned upon the subject finally as if it was proposed that Congress sd. assume & exercise a power immediately & without the previous Sanction of the States, of levying money on them. In consequence.

Mr. Wilson rose & explained the import of the motion to be that Congress should recommend to the States the investing them with power. He observed that the confederation was so far from precluding, that it expressly provided for future alterations; that the power given to Congress by that Act was too little not too formidable, that there was more of a centrifugal than centripetal force in the States & that the funding of a common debt in the manner proposed would produce a salutary invigoration & cement of the Union.

Mr. Elseworth acknowledged himself to be undecided in his opinion: that on the one side he felt the necessity of continental funds for making good the continental engagements but on the other desponded of a unanimous concurrence of the States in such an establishment. He observed that it was a question of great importance how far the federal govt. can or ought to exert coercion against delinquent members of the confederacy; & that without such coercion no certainty could attend the constitutional mode which referred every thing to the unanimous punctuality of thirteen different councils. Considering therefore a continental revenue as unattainable, and periodical requisitions from Congress as inadequate, he was inclined to make trial of the middle mode of permanent State funds, to be provided at the recommendation of Congs. and appropriated to the discharge of the common debt.

Mr. Hamilton in reply to Mr. Elseworth dwelt long on the inefficacy of State funds, He supposed too that greater obstacles would arise to the execution of the plan than to that of a general revenue. As an additional reason for the latter to be collected by officers under the appointment of Congress, he signified that as the energy of the federal Govt. was evidently short of the degree necessary for pervading & uniting the States it was expedient to introduce the influence of officers deriving their emoluments from & consequently interested in supporting the power of, Congress.*

Mr. Williamson was of opinion that continental funds altho' desirable, were unattainable at least to the full amount of the public exigences. He thought if they could be obtained for the foreign debt, it would be as much as could be expected, and that they would also be less essential for the domestic debt.

Mr. Madison observed that it was needless to go into proofs of the necessity of payg. the public debts; that the idea of erecting our national independence on the ruins of public faith and national honor must be horrid to every mind which retained either honesty or pride; that the motion before Congress contained a simple proposition with respect to the truth of which every member was called upon to give his opinion. That this opinion must necessarily be in the affirmative, unless the several objects; of doing justice to the public Creditors, &c &c. could be compassed by some other plan than the one proposed, that the 2 last objects depended essentially on the first; since the doing justice to the Creditors alone wd. restore public credit, & the restoration of this alone could provide for the future exigencies of the war. Is then a continl revenue indispensibly necessary for doing complete justice &? This is the question. To answer it the other plans proposed must first be reviewed.

In order to do complete justice to the public Creditors, either the principal must be paid off, or the interest paid punctually. The 1st. is admitted to be impossible on any plan. The only plans opposed to the continl one for the latter purpose; are 1st. periodical requisitions according to the foederal articles: 2dly. permanent funds established by each State within itself & the proceeds consigned to the discharge of public debts.

---

*This remark was imprudent & injurious to the cause wch. it was meant to serve. This influence was the very source of jealousy which rendered the States averse to a revenue under the collection as well as appropriation of Congress. All the members of Congress who concurred in any degree with the States in this jealousy smiled at the disclosure. Mr. Bland & still more Mr. L. who were of this number took notice in private conversation that Mr. Hamilton had let out the secret.

Will the 1st. be adequate to the object? The contrary seems to be maintained by no one. If reason did not sufficiently premonish, experience has sufficiently demonstrated that a punctual & unfailing compliance by 13 separate & independent Govts. with periodical demands of money from Congress, can never be reckoned upon with the certainty requisite to satisfy our present creditors, or to tempt others to become our creditors in future.

2dly. Will funds separately established within each State & the amount submitted to the appropriation of Congress be adequate to the object? The only advantage which is thought to recommend this plan, is that the States will be with less difficulty prevailed upon to adopt it. Its imperfections are 1st. that it must be preceded by a final & satisfactory adjustment of all accts. between the U. S. and individual States; and by an apportionment founded on a valuation of all the lands throughout each of the States in pursuance of the law of the confederation: for although the States do not as yet insist on these prerequisites in the case of annual demands on them with wch. they very little comply & that only in the way of an open acct.; yet these conditions wd. certainly be exacted in case of a permanent cession of revenue; and the difficulties & delays to say the least incident to these conditions, can escape no one. 2dly. the produce of the funds being always in the first instance in the hands & under the controul of the States separately, might at any time & on various pretences, be diverted to State-objects. 3dly. That jealousy which is as natural to the States as to individuals & of which so many proofs have appeared, that *others* will not fulfil their respective portions of the common obligations, will be continually & mutually suspending remittances to the common treasury, until it finally stops them altogether. These imperfections are too radical to be admitted into any plan intended for the purposes in question.

It remains to examine the merits of the plan of a general revenue operating throughout the U. S. under the superintendence of Congress.

One obvious advantage is suggested by the last objection to separate revenues in the different States; that is, it will exclude all jealousy among them on that head, since each will know whilst it is submitting to the tax, that all the others are necessaryly at the same instant bearing their respective portions of the burden.

Again it will take from the States the opportunity as well as the temptation to divert their incomes from the general to internal purposes since these incomes will pass *directly* into the treasury of the U. S.

Another advantage attending a general revenue is that in case of the concurrence of the States in establishing it, it would become soonest productive; and would consequently soonest obtain the objects in view. Nay so assured a prospect would give instantaneous confidence & content to the public creditors at home & abroad, and place our affairs in the most happy train.

The consequences with respect to the Union, of omitting such a provision for the debts of the Union also claims particular attention. The tenor of the memorial from Penna. and of the information just given on the floor by one of its delegates (Mr Fitzimmons) renders it extremely probable that that State would as soon as it sd. be known that Congress had declined such provision or the States rejected it, appropriate the revenue required by Congress, to the payment of its own Citizens & troops, creditors of the U. S. The irregular conduct of other States on this subject enforced by such an example could not fail to spread the evil throughout the whole continent. What then wd become of the confederation? What wd. be the authority of Congress? wt. the tie by which the States cd. be held together? what the source by which the army could be subsisted & cloathed? What the mode of dividing & discharging our foreign debts? What the rule of settling the internal accts? What the tribunal by which controversies amg the States could be adjudicated?

It ought to be carefully remembered that this subject was brought before Congress by a very solemn appeal from the army to the justice & gratitude of their Country. Besides immediate pay, they ask for permanent security for arrears. Is not this request a reasonable one? will it be just or politic to pass over the only adequate security that can be devised, & instead of fulfilling the stipulations of the U. S. to them, to leave them to seek their rewards separately from the States to which they respectively belong? The patience of the army has been equal to their bravery, but that patience must have its limits; and the result of despair can not be foreseen, nor ought it to be risked.

It has been objected agst. a general revenue that it contravenes the articles of confederation. These Articles as has been observed have presupposed the necessity of alterations in the foederal system & have left a door open for them: They moreover authorize Congress to borrow money. Now in order to borrow money permanent & certain provision is necessary, & if this provision cannot be made in any other way as has been shewn, a general revenue is within the spirit of the confederation.

It has been objected that such a revenue is subversive of the soverignty & liberty of the States. If it were to be assumed without the free gift of the States this objection might be of force, but no assumption is proposed. In fact Congress are already invested by the States with the constitutional authority over the purse as well as the sword. A general revenue would only give this authority a more certain & equal efficacy. They have a right to fix the *quantum* of money necessary for the common purposes. The right of the States is limited to the *mode* of supply. A requisition of Congress on the States for money is as much a law to them; as their revenue acts when passed are laws to their respective Citizens. If for want of the faculty or means of enforcing a requisition, the law of Congress proves inefficient; does it not follow that in order to fullfil the views of the foederal constitution, such a change sd. be made as will render it efficient? Without such efficiency the end of this Constitution which is to preserve order & justice among the members of the Union, must fail; as without a like efficiency would the end of State constitutions wch. is to preserve like order & justice among its members.

It has been objected that the States have manifested such aversion to the impost on trade as renders any recommendations of a general revenue hopeless & imprudent. It must be admitted that the conduct of the States

on that subject is less encouraging than were to be wished. A review of it however does not excite despondence. The impost was adopted immediately & in its utmost latitude by several of the States. Several also which complied partially with it at first, have since complied more liberally. One of them after long refusal has complied substantially. Two States only have failed altogether & as to one of them it is not known that its failure has proceeded from a decided opposition to it. On the whole it appears that the necessity & reasonableness of the scheme have been gaining ground among the States. He was aware that one exception ought to be made to this inference: an exception too wch peculiarly concerned him to advert to. The State of Virga as appears by an Act yesterday laid before Congress, has withdrawn its assent once given to the scheme. This circumstance cd. not but produce some embarrassment in a representative of that State advocating the scheme; one too whose principles were extremely unfavorable to a disregd. of the sense of Constitnts. But it ought not to deter him from listening to considerations which in the present case ought to prevail over it. One of these considerations was that altho' the delegates who compose Congress, more immediately represented & were amenable to the States from which they respectively come, yet in another view they owed a fidelity to the collective interests of the whole. 2dly. Altho' not only the express instructions, but even the declared sense of constituents as in the present case, were to be a law in general to these representatives, still there were occasions on which the latter ought to hazard personal consequences from a respect to what his clear conviction determines to be the true interest of the former; and the present he conceived to fall under this exception. Lastly the part he took on the present occasion was the more fully justified to his own mind by his thorough persuasion, that with the same knowledge of public affairs which his station commanded, the Legislature of Va would not have repealed the law in favor of the impost & would even now rescind the repeal.

The result of these observations was that it was the duty of Congress under whose authority the public debts had been contracted to aim at a general revenue as the only means of discharging them; & that this dictate of justice & gratitude was enforced by a regard to the preservation of the confederacy, to our reputation abroad & to our internal tranquility.

Mr. Rutledge complained that those who so strenuously urged the necessity & competency of a general revenue operating throughout all the States at the same time, declined specifying any general objects from which such a revenue could be drawn He was thought to insinuate that these objects were kept back intentionally untill the general principle cd. be irrevocably fixed when Congs. wd. be bound at all events to go on with the project, whereupon Mr. Fitzimmons expressed some concern at the turn wch. the discussion seemed to be taking. He said that unless mutual confidence prevailed no progress could be made towards the attainment of those ends wch. all in some way or other aimed at. It was a mistake to suppose that any specific plan had been preconcerted among the patrons of a general revenue.

Mr. Wilson with whom the motion originated gave his assurances that it was neither the effect of preconcert with others, nor of any determinate plan matured by himself, that he had been led into it, by the declaration on Saturday last by Congs. that substantial funds ought to be provided; by the memorial of the army from which that declaration had resulted, by the memorials from the State of Pa. holding out the idea of separate appropriations of her revenue unless provision were made for the public creditors, by the deplorable & dishonorable situation of public affairs which had compelled Congress to draw bills on the unpromised & contingent bounty of their ally, and which was likely to banish the Superintdt. of Finance whose place cd not be supplied, from his department. He observed that he had not introduced details into the debate because he thought them premature, until a general principle should be fixed; and that as soon as the principle sd. be fixed he would altho' not furnished with any digested plan, contribute all in his power to the forming such a one.

Mr. Rutledge moved that the proposition might be committed in order that some practicable plan might be reported, before Congress sd. declare that it ought to be adopted.

Mr. Izard 2ded. the motion from a conciliating view.

Mr. Madison thought the commitment unnecessary: and would have the appearance of delay; that too much delay had already taken place, that the deputation of the army had a right to expect an answer to their memorial as soon as it could be decided by Congress. He differed from Mr. Wilson in thinking that a specification of the objects of a general revenue would be improper, and thought that those who doubted of its practicability had a right to expect proof of it from details before they cd. be expected to assent to the general principle; but he differed also from Mr. Rutledge who thought a commitment necessary for the purpose; since his views would be answered by leaving the motion before the house and giving the debate a greater latitude. He suggested as practicable objects of a general revenue. 1st an impost on trade 2dly. a poll tax under certain qualifications 3dly. a land tax under do.

Mr. Hamilton suggested a house & window tax. he was in favor of the mode of conducting the discussion urged by Mr. Madison

On the motion for the commt. 6 States were in favor of it, & five agst. it. so it was lost—in this vote the merits of the main proposition very little entered.

Mr. Lee said that it was a waste of time to be forming resolutions & settling principles on this subject. He asked whether these wd. ever bring any money into the public treasury. His opinion was that Congress ought in order to guard agst. the inconveniency of meetings of the different Legislatures at different & even distant periods, to call upon the Executives to convoke them all at one period, & to lay before them a full state of our public affairs. He said the States would never agree to those plans which tended to aggrandize Congress; that they were jealous of the power of Congress; & that he acknowledged himself to be one of those who thought this jealousy not an unreasonable one; that no one who had ever opened a page or read a line on the subject of liberty, could be insensible to the

danger of surrendering the purse into the same hand which held the sword.

The debate was suspended by an adjournment.

6

JAMES MADISON, NOTES ON DEBATES IN CONGRESS
21 Feb. 1783
Papers 6:270–73

Mr. Mercer made some remarks tending to a reconsideration of the act declaring general funds to be necessary, which revived the discussion of that subject.

Mr Madison said that he had observed throughout the proceedings of Congress relative to the establishmt. of such funds that the power delegated to Congress by the confederation had been very differently construed by different members & that this difference of construction had materially affected their reasonings & opinions on the several propositions which had been made; that in particular it had been represented by sundry members that Congress was merely an Executive body; and therefore that it was inconsistent with the principles of liberty & the spirit of the Constitution, to submit to them a permanent revenue which wd. be placing the purse & the sword in the same hands; that he wished the true doctrine of the confederation to be ascertained as it might perhaps remove some embarrassments; and towards that end would offer his ideas on the subject.

He said that he did not conceive in the first place that the opinion was sound that the power of Congress in cases of revenue was in no respect Legislative, but merely Executive: and in the second place that admitting the power to be Executive a permanent revenue collected & dispensed by them in the discharge of the debts to wch. it sd. be appropriated, would be inconsistent with the nature of an Executive body, or dangerous to the liberties of the republic.

As to the first opinion he observed that by the articles of Confederation Congs. had clearly & expressly the right to fix the quantum of revenue necessary for the public exigences, & to require the same from the States respectively in proportion to the value of their land; that the requisitions thus made were a law to the States, as much as the acts of the latter for complying with them were a law to their individual members: that the foederal constitution was as sacred & obligatory as the internal constitutions of the several States; and that nothing could justify the States in disobeying acts warranted by it, but some previous abuse or infraction on the part of Congs.; that as a proof that the power of fixing the quantum & making requisitions of money, was considered as a legislative power over the purse, he would appeal to the proposition made by the British Minister of giving this power to the B. Parliamt. & leaving to the American assemblies the privilege of complying in their own modes; & to the reasonings of Congress & the several States on that proposition. He observed further that by the articles of Confederation was delegated to Congs. a right to borrow money indefinitely, and emit bills of Credit which was a species of borrowing, for repayment & redemption of which the faith of the States was pledged & their legislatures constitutionally bound. He asked whether these powers were reconcileable with the idea that Congress was a body merely Executive? He asked what would be thought in G. B. from whose constitution our Political reasonings were so much drawn, of an attempt to prove that a power of making requisitions of money on the Parliament, & of borrowing money for discharge of which the Parlt sd. be bound, might be annexed to the Crown without changing its quality of an Executive branch; and that the leaving to the Parliamt. the mode only of complying with the requisitions of the Crown, would be leaving to it its supreme & exclusive power of Legislation?

As to the second point he referred again to the British Constitution & the mode in which provision was made for the public debts; observing that although the Executive had no authority to contract a debt; yet that when a debt had been authorized or admitted by the parliament a permanent & irrevocable revenue was granted by the Legislature, to be collected & dispensed by the Executive; and that this practice had never been deemed a subversion of the Constitution or a dangerous association of a power over the purse with the power of the Sword.

If these observations were just as he concieved them to be, the establishment of a permanent revenue not by any assumed authority of Congress, but by the authority of the States at the recommendation of Congs: to be collected & applied by the latter to the discharge of the public debts, could not be deemed inconsistent with the spirit of the foederal constitution, or subversive of the principles of liberty; and that all objections drawn from such a supposition ought [to] be withdrawn. Whether other objections of sufficient weight might not lie agst. such an establishmt. was another question. For his part altho' for various reasons*

*Among other reasons privately weighing with him, he had observed that many of the most respectable people of America supposed the preservation of the Confederacy, essential to secure the blessings of the revolution; and permant funds essential for discharging debts essential to the preservation of Union. A disappointmt to this class wd. certainly abate their ardor & in a critical emergence might incline them to prefer some political connection with G. B. as a necessary cure for our internal instability, again Without permanent & general funds he did not concieve that the danger of convulsions from the army could be effectually obviated, lastly he did not think that any thing wd. be so likely to prevent disputes among the States with the calamities consequent on them. The States were jealous of each other, each supposing itself to be on the whole a creditor to the others: The Eastern States in particular thought themselves so with regard to the S. States (see Mr. Ghorum in the debates of this day). If general funds were not introduced it was not likely the balances wd. be ever be discharged, even if they sd. be liquidated. The consequence wd. be a rupture of the confederacy. The E. States wd. at sea be powerful & rapacious, the S. opulent & weak. This wd. be a temptation. the demands on the S. Sts would be an occasion. Reprisals wd. be instituted. Foreign aid would be called in by first the weaker, then the stronger side; & finally both be made subservient to the wars & politics of Europe.

he had wished for such a plan as most eligible, he had never been sanguine that it was practicable & the discussions which had taken place had finally satisfied him that it would be necessary to limit the call for a general revenue to duties on commerce & to call for the deficiency in the most permanent way that could be reconciled with a revenue established within each State separately & appropriated to the Common Treasury. He said the rule which he had laid down to himself in this business was to concur in every arrangemt. that sd. appear necessary for an honorable & just fulfilment of the public engagements; & in no measure tending to augment the power of Congress which sd appear to be unnecessary; and particularly disclaimed the idea of perpetuating a public debt.

Mr. Lee in answer to Mr. Madison said the doctrine maintained by him was pregnant with dangerous consequences to the liberties of the confederated States; that notwithstanding the specious arguments that had been employed it was an established truth that the purse ought not to be put into the same hands with the Sword; that like arguments had been used in favor of Ship money in the reign of Charles I it being then represented as essential to the support of the Govt., that the Executive should be assured of the means of fulfilling its engagements for the public service: He said it had been urged by several in behalf of such an establishment for public credit that without it Congress was nothing more than a rope of sand. on this head he would be explicit; he had rather see Congress a rope of sand than a rod of Iron. He urged finally as a reason why some States would not & ought not to concur in granting to Congress a permanent revenue, that some States as Virga, would receive back a small part by paymt. from the U. S. to its Citizens; whilst others as Pena. wd. receive a vast surplus; & consequently be enriched by draining the former of its wealth.

Mr. Mercer said if he conceived the foederal compact to be such as it had been represented he would immediately withdraw from Congress & do every thing in his power to destroy its existence: that if Congs. had a right to borrow money as they pleased and to make requisitions on the States that wd. be binding on them, the liberties of the States were ideal; that requisitions ought to be consonant to the Spirit of liberty; that they should go frequently & accompanied with full information. that the States must be left to judge of the nature of them, of their abilities to comply with them & to regulate their compliance accordingly; he laid great stress on the omission of Congs. to transmit half yearly to the States an acct. of the monies borrowed by them &c. and even insinuated that this omission had absolved the States in some degree from the engagements.

7

ROBERT MORRIS TO THE PRESIDENT OF CONGRESS
17 Mar. 1783
Wharton 6:309–11

I have gone into these few details merely to elucidate one position, viz., that *all the money now at our command, and which we may expect from the States for this two months to come, will not do more than satisfy the various engagements which will by that time have fallen due.*

It is of importance that Congress should know their true situation, and therefore I could wish that a committee were appointed to confer with the minister of France. My reason for that wish is, that every member of Congress may have the same conviction which I feel of one important fact—*that there is no hope of any further pecuniary aid from Europe.* The conduct of the French court on the subject has been decisive. Some persons have indeed flattered themselves that her positive declarations were merely calculated to restrain our rashness and moderate our excess, but these ideas can no longer have place in any sound and discerning mind. Her conduct has been consistent with her declarations, and if she had ever so much inclination to assist us with money, *it is not in her power.*

But whatever may be the ability of nations or individuals, we can have no right to hope, much less to expect the aid of others, while we show so much unwillingness to help ourselves. It can no longer be a doubt to Congress *that our public credit is gone.* It was very easy to foresee that this would be the case, and it was my particular duty to predict it. This has been done repeatedly. I claim no merit from the prediction, because a man must be naturally or wilfully blind who could not see *that credit can not long be supported without funds.*

From what has already been said, Congress will clearly perceive the necessity of further resources. What means they shall adopt it is their wisdom to consider. They can not borrow, and the States will not pay. *The thing has happened which was expected.* I can not presume to advise. Congress well know that I never pretended to any extraordinary knowledge of finance, and that my deficiences on this subject were a principal reason for declining the office. I have since had reason to be still more convinced of my incompetency, because the plans which I did suggest have not met with approbation. I hope, therefore, that some abler mind will point out the means to save our country from ruin.

I do assure you, sir, that it is extremely painful to me to be obliged to address Congress on this subject. I wish most sincerely that I could look at our future prospects with the same indifference that others have brought themselves to regard them. Perhaps I am not sufficiently sanguine. It is common for age to listen more to the voice of experience than youth is inclined. The voice of experience foretold

these evils long since. There was a time when we might have obviated them, but I fear that precious moment is passed.

Before I conclude this letter, I must observe on the misconstructions which men totally ignorant of our affairs have put on that conduct which severe necessity compelled me to pursue. Such men, affecting an intimate knowledge of things, have charged the destruction of public credit to me, and interpreted the terms of my resignation into reflections upon Congress. I hope, sir, that so long as I have the honor to serve the United States I shall feel a proper contempt for all such scurrility. I shall confidently repose myself on the candor of Congress. It is for them to judge of my conduct on full and intimate knowledge. Writers for a newspaper may, indeed, through the medium of misrepresentation, pervert the public opinion, but the official conduct of your servants is not amenable to that tribunal. I hope, however, to be excused for observing that, on the day in which I was publicly charged with ruining your credit, those despatches arrived from Europe which tell you it was already at an end. The circumstances which I alluded to in my letter of resignation were not yet known in Europe. It was not yet known that Rhode Island had unanimously refused to pass the impost law, and that Virginia had repealed it. The very delays which the measures of Congress had met with were sufficient to sap the foundations of their credit; and we now know that they have had that effect. When those circumstances, therefore, shall be known, it must be overturned. I saw this clearly, and I knew that, until some plain and rational system should be adopted and acceded to, the business of this office would be a business of expedient and chicane. I have neither the talents nor the disposition to engage in such business, and therefore I pray to be dismissed.

8

RICHARD HENRY LEE TO SAMUEL ADAMS
14 Mar. 1785
Letters 2:343–45

The selfishness and corruption of Europe I have no doubt about, and therefore wish most sincerely that our free Republics may not suffer themselves to be changed and wrongly wrought upon by the corrupt maxims of policy that pervade European Councils—where artful and refined plausibility is forever called in to aid the most pernicious designs. It would seem as if there were a general jealousy beyond the water, of the powerful effects to be derived from Republican virtue here, and so we hear a constant cry from thence, echoed & reechoed here by all Expectants from the Treasury of the United States—That Congress must have more power—That we cannot be secure & happy until Congress command implicitly both purse & sword. So that our confederation must be perpetually changing to answer sinister views in the greater part, until every fence is thrown down that was designed to protect & cover the rights of Mankind. It is a melancholy consideration that many wise & good men have, some how or other, fallen in with these ruinous opinions. I think Sir that the first maxim of a man who loves liberty should be, never to grant to Rulers an atom of power that is not most clearly & indispensably necessary for the safety and well being of Society. To say that these Rulers are revocable, and holding their places during pleasure may not be supposed to design evil for self-aggrandizement, is affirming what I cannot easily admit. Look to history and see how often the liberties of mankind have been opressed & ruined by the same delusive hopes & fallacious reasoning. The fact is, that power poisons the mind of its possessor and aids him to remove the shackles that restrain itself. To be sure, all things human must partake of human infirmity, and therefore the Confederation should not be presumptuously called an infallible system for all times and all situations—but tho' this is true, yet as it is a great and fundamental system of Union & Security, no change should be admitted until proved to be necessary by the fairest fullest & most mature experience. Upon these principles I have ever been opposed to the 5 P Cent imposts, My idea is still that of the Confederation, Fix the sum, apportion it & let every State by its own means, and in its own way faithfully & honestly make its payment. That the now federal mode of apportionment is productive of delay, of great expence, and still liable to frequent change, is certain. And therefore I see no inconvenience in so far altering the Confederation as to make the Rule of Apportionment lie upon the numbers as stated in the recommendation of Congress upon that Subject. But I can never agree that this Body shall dictate the mode of Taxation, or that the collection shall in any manner be subject to Congressional controul. It is said that this will more effectually secure the Revenue—But how so? if a spirit prevails to neglect a duty imposed by the Confederation, may not the same spirit render abortive at any time Acts passed for granting the Impost? Besides that we are depending for the payment of our debts upon uncertainty, when the most certain revenues of the State ought to be appropriated for that purpose. Whilst every good man wishes great punctuality to prevail in the payment of debts, he must at the same time condemn and discourage large importations which impoverish by increasing the balance of trade against us. So that from this system we are to expect our greatest good from our greatest evil. A good physician will tell you that contrary indications of cure threaten danger to human life, and by a just parity of reason, contrary indications threaten danger to the Political body. But happily for us, our political disease admits of simple remedies for its cure, if rightly judged of, and wisely practised upon. Let it be therefore the effort of every Patriot to encourage a punctual payment of each State's quota of the foederal demand, and let the money be found in ways most agreable to the circumstances of every State. This is the plan of the Confederation, and this I own will be mine, until more satisfactory experience has proved its inefficacy.

9

The war, as you have very justly observed, has terminated most advantageously for America, and a fair field is presented to our view; but I confess to you freely, My Dr. Sir, that I do not think we possess wisdom or Justice enough to cultivate it properly. Illiberality, Jealousy, and local policy mix too much in all our public councils for the good government of the Union. In a word, the confederation appears to me to be little more than a shadow without the substance; and Congress a nugatory body, their ordinances being little attended to. To *me*, it is a solecism in politics; indeed it is one of the most extraordinary things in nature, that we should confederate as a Nation, and yet be afraid to give the rulers of that nation, who are the creatures of our making, appointed for a limited and short duration, and who are amenable for every action, and recallable at any moment, and are subject to all the evils which they may be instrumental in producing, sufficient powers to order and direct the affairs of the same. By such policy as this the wheels of Government are clogged, and our brightest prospects, and that high expectation which was entertained of us by the wondering world, are turned into astonishment; and from the high ground on which we stood, we are descending into the vale of confusion and darkness.

That we have it in our power to become one of the most respectable Nations upon Earth, admits, in my humble opinion, of no doubt; if we would but pursue a wise, just, and liberal policy towards one another, and would keep good faith with the rest of the World: that our resources are ample and encreasing, none can deny; but while they are grudgingly applyed, or not applyed at all, we give a vital stab to public faith, and shall sink, in the eyes of Europe, into contempt.

It has long been a speculative question among Philosophers and wise men, whether foreign Commerce is of real advantage to any Country; that is, whether the luxury, effeminacy, and corruptions which are introduced along with it; are counterbalanced by the convenience and wealth which it brings with it; but the decision of this question is of very little importance to us: we have abundant reason to be convinced, that the spirit for Trade which pervades these States is not to be restrained; it behooves us then to establish just principles; and this, any more than other matters of national concern, cannot be done by thirteen heads differently constructed and organized. The necessity, therefore, of a controuling power is obvious; and why it should be withheld is beyond my comprehension.

. . . . .

The great works of improving and extending the inland

navigations of the two large rivers Potomac and James, which interlock with the waters of the Western Territory, are already begun, and I have little doubt of their success. The consequences to the Union, in my judgment are immense: more so in a political, than in a commercial view; for unless we can connect the new States which are rising to our view in those regions, with those on the Atlantic by *interest,* (the only binding cement, and no otherwise to be effected but by opening such communications as will make it easier and cheaper for them to bring the product of their labour to our markets, instead of going to the Spaniards southerly, or the British northerly), they will be quite a distinct people; and ultimately may be very troublesome neighbours to us. In themselves considered merely as a hardy race, this *may* happen; how much more so, if linked with either of those powers in politics and commerce.

10

RUFUS KING TO ELBRIDGE GERRY
30 Apr. 1786
Life 1:133–34

We go on in Congress as when you left us. Three days since October only have nine States been on the Floor. Eight are now here, when we shall have nine is a melancholy uncertainty. I proposed a few days since that Congress should resolve, that provided on a certain day, sufficiently distant for information to reach all the States in season, the States were not so represented as to give power to administer the Government, Congress would adjourn without day. Something of this kind must be done. It is a mere farce to remain here as we have done since last October. Foreigners know our situation and the friends of free Governments through the world must regret it.

Resolves have been passed upon Resolves—and letter after letter has been sent to the deficient States, and all without the desired effect. We are without money or the prospect of it in the Federal Treasury; and the States, many of them, care so little about the Union, that they take no measures to keep a representation in Congress. The civil list begin to clamour—there is not money to pay them: they are now unpaid for a longer period than since the circulation of Paper Money. The handful of troops over the Ohio are mutinous and desert because they are unpaid. The money borrowed in Europe is exhausted and this very day our Foreign Ministers have it not in their power to receive their salaries for their support.

Where, my dear friend, will the evils consequent to this inattention in the States terminate? The people of the States do not know their dangerous situation; this torpor and inactivity should alarm the Guardians of the People; but indeed the Legislatures seem the least attentive. Pray think of our situation *and advise me.* I can open my heart with freedom to you; you are now at home, and will be concerned in the Government of the State. Can there be

no means devised whereby Massachusetts can yield something to the common Treasury? Since the organization of the Board of Treasury, the State has paid *nothing.* We are told of it in Congress—we justify by declaring that past exertions have exhausted us; but that we should revive, when the States would accede to such commercial Regulations as would place the American Navigation on *an equal footing* with that of Foreigners.

This is ostensible—but poor as we are I hope we could do more than we now accomplish—indeed the State neither pays anything to the federal Treasury, nor supports her Delegates.

11

GEORGE WASHINGTON TO JOHN JAY
1 Aug. 1786
Writings 28:502–3

Your sentiments, that our affairs are drawing rapidly to a crisis, accord with my own. What the event will be, is also beyond the reach of my foresight. We have errors to correct; we have probably had too good an opinion of human nature in forming our confederation. Experience has taught us, that men will not adopt and carry into execution measures the best calculated for their own good, without the intervention of a coercive power. I do not conceive we can exist long as a nation without having lodged some where a power, which will pervade the whole Union in as energetic a manner, as the authority of the State Governments extends over the several States.

To be fearful of investing Congress, constituted as that body is, with ample authorities for national purposes, appears to me the very climax of popular absurdity and madness. Could Congress exert them for the detriment of the public, without injuring themselves in an equal or greater proportion? Are not their interests inseparably connected with those of their constituents? By the rotation of appointment, must they not mingle frequently with the mass of Citizens? Is it not rather to be apprehended, if they were possessed of the powers before described, that the individual members would be induced to use them, on many occasions, very timidly and inefficaciously for fear of losing their popularity and future election? We must take human nature as we find it: perfection falls not to the share of mortals. Many are of opinion that Congress have too frequently made use of the suppliant humble tone of requisition, in applications to the States, when they had a right to assert their imperial dignity and command obedience. Be that as it may, requisitions are a perfect nihility where thirteen sovereign independent disunited States are in the habit of discussing and refusing compliance with them at their option. Requisitions are actually little better than a jest and a bye word throughout the land. If you tell the Legislatures they have violated the Treaty of Peace, and invaded the prerogatives of the confederacy, they will laugh in your face. What then is to be done? Things cannot go on in the same train forever. It is much to be feared, as you observe, that the better kind of people, being disgusted with the circumstances, will have their minds prepared for any revolution whatever. We are apt to run from one extreme into another. To anticipate and prevent disastrous contingencies, would be the part of wisdom and patriotism.

What astonishing changes a few years are capable of producing. I am told that even respectable characters speak of a monarchical form of Government without horror. From thinking proceeds speaking, thence to acting is often but a single step. But how irrevocable and tremendous! what a triumph for our enemies to verify their predictions! what a triumph for the advocates of despotism to find that we are incapable of governing ourselves, and that systems founded on the basis of equal liberty are merely ideal and fallacious! Would to God that wise measures may be taken in time to avert the consequences we have but too much reason to apprehend.

12

CONTINENTAL CONGRESS, REPORT ON PROPOSED AMENDMENTS
7 Aug. 1786
Journals 31:494–98

The Grand Committee consisting of Mr. [Samuel] Livermore, Mr. [Nathan] Dane, Mr. [James] Manning, Mr. [William Samuel] Johnson, Mr. [Melancton] Smith, Mr. [John Cleves] Symmes, Mr. [Charles] Pettit, Mr. [William] Henry, Mr. [Henry] Lee, Mr. [Timothy] Bloodworth, Mr. [Charles] Pinckney and Mr. [William] Houstoun appointed to report such amendments to the confederation, and such resolutions as it may be necessary to recommend to the several states for the purpose of obtaining from them such powers as will render the federal government adequate to the ends for which it was instituted.

Beg leave to submit the following Report to the consideration of Congress:

Resolved, That it be recommended to the Legislatures of the several States to adopt the following Articles as Articles of the Confederation, and to authorise their Delegates in Congress to sign and ratify the same severally as they shall be adopted, to wit:

ART. 14. The United States in Congress Assembled shall have the sole and exclusive power of regulating the trade of the States as well with foreign Nations as with each other and of laying such prohibitions and such Imposts and duties upon imports and exports as may be Necessary for the purpose; provided the Citizens of the States shall in no instance be subjected to pay higher duties and Imposts that those imposed on the subjects of foreign powers, provided also, that all such duties as may be imposed shall be collected under such regulations as the united States in

Congress Assembled shall establish consistent with the Constitutions of the States Respectively and to accrue to the use of the State in which the same shall be payable; provided also, that the Legislative power of the several States shall not be restrained from laying embargoes in time of Scarcity and provided lastly that every Act of Congress for the above purpose shall have the assent of Nine States in Congress Assembled, and in that proportion when there shall be more than thirteen in the Union.

ART. 15. That the respective States may be induced to perform the several duties mutually and solemnly agreed to be performed by their federal Compact, and to prevent unreasonable delays in any State in furnishing her just proportion of the common Charges of the Union when called upon, and those essential evils which have heretofore often arisen to the Confederacy from such delays, it is agreed that whenever a requisition shall be made by Congress upon the several States on the principles of the Confederation for their quotas of the common charges or land forces of the Union Congress shall fix the proper periods when the States shall pass Legislative Acts complying therewith and give full and compleat effect to the same and if any State shall neglect, seasonably to pass such Acts such State shall be charged with an additional sum to her quota called for from the time she may be required to pay or furnish the same, which additional sum or charge shall be at the rate of ten per Cent pr. annum on her said Quota, and if the requisition shall be for Land forces, and any State shall neglect to furnish her quota in time the average expence of such quota shall be ascertained by Congress, and such State shall be charged therewith, or with the average expence of what she may be deficient and in addition thereto from the time her forces were required to be ready to act in the field with a farther sum which sum shall be at the rate of twelve per Cent per Annum on the amount of such expences.

ART. 16. And that the resources of any State which may be negligent in furnishing her just proportion of the Common expence of the Union may in a reasonable time be applied, it is further agreed that if any State shall so Neglect as aforesaid to pass laws in compliance with the said Requisition and to adopt measures to give the same full effect for the space of Ten months, and it shall then or afterwards be found that a Majority of the States have passed such laws and adopted such measures the United States in Congress Assembled shall have full power and authority to levy, assess, and collect all sums and duties with which any such state so neglecting to comply with the requisition may stand charged on the same by the Laws and Rules by which the last State tax next preceeding such requisition in such State was levied, assessed and Collected, to apportion the sum so required on the Towns or Counties in such State to order the sums so apportioned to be assessed by the assessors of such last State tax and the said assessments to be committed to the Collector of the same last State tax to collect and to make returns of such assessments and Commitments to the Treasurer of the United States who by himself or his deputy, when directed by Congress shall have power to recover the monies of such Collectors for the use of the United States in the same manner and under the same penalties as State taxes are recovered and collected by the Treasurers of the respective States and the several Towns or Counties respectively shall be responsible for the conduct of said Assessors and Collectors and in case there shall be any vacancy in any of said Offices of Assessors or Collectors by death, removal, refusal to serve, resignation or otherwise, then other fit persons shall be chosen to fill such Vacancies in the usual manner in such Town or County within Twenty days after Notice of the assessment, and in case any Towns or Counties, any assessor, Collectors or Sheriffs shall Neglect or refuse to do their duty Congress shall have the same rights and powers to compel them that the State may have in assessing and collecting State Taxes.

And if any state by any Legislative Act shall prevent or delay the due Collection of said sums as aforesaid, Congress shall have full power and authority to appoint assessors and Collectors thereof and Sheriffs to enforce the Collections under the warrants of distress issued by the Treasurer of the United States, and if any further opposition shall be made to such Collections by the State or the Citizens thereof, and their conduct not disapproved of by the State, such conduct on the part of the State shall be considered as an open Violation of the federal compact.

ART. 17. And any State which from time to time shall be found in her payments on any Requisition in advance on an average of the payments made by the State shall be allowed an interest of six —— per Cent pr. annum on her said advanced sums or expences and the State which from time to time shall be found in arrear on the principles aforesaid shall be charged with an Interest of six —— per Cent pr. annum on the sums in which she may be so in arrear.

ART. 18. In case it shall hereafter be found Necessary by Congress to establish any new Systems of Revenue and to make any new regulations in the finances of the U.S. for a limited term not exceeding fifteen years in their operation for supplying the common Treasury with monies for defraying all charges of war, and all other expences that shall be incurred for the common defence or general welfare, and such new Systems or regulations shall be agreed to and adopted by the United States in Congress Assembled and afterwards be confirmed by the Legislatures of eleven States and in that proportion when there shall be more than thirteen States in the Union, the same shall become binding on all the States, as fully as if the Legislatures of all the States should confirm the same.

ART. 19. The United States in Congress Assembled shall have the sole and exclusive power of declaring what offences against the United States shall be deemed treason, and what Offences against the same Mis-prison of treason, and what Offences shall be deemed piracy or felony on the high Seas and to annex suitable punishments to all the Offences aforesaid respectively, and power to institute a federal Judicial Court for trying and punishing all officers appointed by Congress for all crimes, offences, and misbehaviour in their Offices and to which Court an Appeal shall be allowed from the Judicial Courts of the several States in all Causes wherein questions shall arise on the meaning and construction of Treaties entered into by the United States with any foreign power, or on the Law of Nations, or wherein any question shall arise respecting any regulations that may hereafter be made by Congress relative to trade and Commerce, or the Collection of federal Revenues pursuant to powers that shall be vested in that body or wherein questions of importance may arise and the United States shall be a party—provided that the trial of the fact by Jury shall ever be held sacred, and also the benefits of the writ of *Habeas Corpus;* provided also that no member of Congress or officer holding any other office under the United States shall be a Judge of said Court, and the said Court shall consist of Seven Judges, to be appointed from the different parts of the Union to wit, one from New Hampshire, Rhode Island, and Connecticut, one from Massachusetts, one from New York and New Jersey, one from Pennsylvania, one from Delaware and Maryland, one from Virginia, and one from North Carolina, South Carolina and Georgia, and four of whom shall be a quorum to do business.

ART. 20. That due attention may be given to the affairs of the Union early in the federal year, and the sessions of Congress made as short as conveniently may be each State shall elect her Delegates annually before the first of July and make it their duty to give an Answer before the first of September in every year, whether they accept their appointments or not, and make effectual provision for filling the places of those who may decline, before the first of October yearly, and to transmit to Congress by the tenth of the same month, the names of the Delegates who shall be appointed and accept their appointments, and it shall be the indispensable duty of Delegates to make a representation of their State in Congress on the first Monday in November annually, and if any Delegate or Delegates, when required by Congress to attend so far as may be Necessary to keep up a Reprsentation of each State in Congress, or having taken his or their Seat, shall withdraw without leave of Congress, unless recalled by the State, he or they shall be proceeded against as Congress shall direct, provided no punishment shall be further extended than to disqualifications any longer to be members of Congress, or to hold any Office of trust or profit under the United States or any individual State, and the several States shall adopt regulations effectual to the attainment of the ends of this Article.

13

JOHN JAY TO THOMAS JEFFERSON
27 Oct. 1786
Correspondence 3:212–13

The inefficacy of our government becomes daily more and more apparent. Our treasury and our credit are in a sad situation; and it is probable that either the wisdom or the passions of the people will produce changes. A spirit of licentiousness has infected Massachusetts, which appears more formidable than some at first apprehended. Whether similar symptoms will not soon mark a like disease in several other States is very problematical.

The public papers herewith sent contain everything generally known about these matters. A reluctance to taxes, an impatience of government, a rage for property and little regard to the means of acquiring it, together with a desire of equality in all things, seem to actuate the mass of those who are uneasy in their circumstances. To these may be added the influence of ambitious adventurers, and the speculations of the many characters who prefer private to public good, and of others who expect to gain more from wrecks made by tempests than from the produce of patient and honest industry. As the knaves and fools of this world are forever in alliance, it is easy to perceive how much vigour and wisdom a government, from its construction and administration, should possess, in order to repress the evils which naturally flow from such copious sources of injustice and evil.

Much, I think, is to be feared from the sentiments which such a state of things is calculated to infuse into the minds of the rational and well-intended. In their eyes, the charms of liberty will daily fade; and in seeking for peace and security, they will too naturally turn towards systems in direct opposition to those which oppress and disquiet them.

If faction should long bear down law and government, tyranny may raise its head, or the more sober part of the people may even think of a king.

In short, my dear sir, we are in a very unpleasant situation. Changes are necessary; but, what they ought to be, what they will be, and how and when to be produced, are arduous questions. I feel for the cause of liberty, and for the honour of my countrymen who have so nobly asserted it, and who, at present, so abuse its blessings. If it should not take root in this soil, little pains will be taken to cultivate it in any other.

14

SAMUEL OSGOOD TO JOHN ADAMS
14 Nov. 1786
Adams Works 8:419–21

. . . in a government where expedients only keep up its existence, it is impossible to foresee what sudden and unexpected changes may take place. The federal government seems to be as near a crisis as it is possible for it to be. The State governments are weak and selfish enough, and they will of course annihilate the first. Their stubborn dignity will never permit a federal government to exist. There are, however, a few men in every state, who are very seriously impressed with the idea that, without a proper federal head, the individual states must fall a prey to themselves, or any power that is disposed to injure them. With this idea, they are thinking, very seriously, in what manner to effect the most easy and natural change of the present

form of the federal government to one more energetic, that will, at the same time, create respect, and secure properly life, liberty, and property. It is, therefore, not uncommon to hear the principles of government stated in common conversation. Emperors, kings, stadtholders, governors-general, with a senate or house of lords, and house of commons, are frequently the topics of conversation. Many are for abolishing all the state governments, and for establishing some kind of general government; but I believe very few agree in the general principles, much less in the details, of such a government.

How to effect a change, is the difficulty. The confederation provides that congress shall make the alterations, and that they shall be adopted by the several legislatures. Yet the idea of a special convention, appointed by the states, to agree upon and propose such alterations as may appear necessary, seems to gain ground. But the danger is, that neither congress nor a convention will do the business. For the situation of the United States, and of some of the particular states, is such, that an army must be kept up, and the probability is, at present, that this army will be seriously employed; and, in case of a civil war, the men of property will certainly attach themselves very closely to that army, the final issue of which, it is feared, will be, that the army will make the government of the United States. Many say, already, any change will be for the better, and are ready to risk any thing to effect it. The disturbances in Massachusetts seem most likely to produce some very important event. It is a little surprising to some, how they come to break out in such a manner there. It is said that the insurgents have two objects in view; one, to reduce their state debt and those securities given by the United States to citizens of that state for their services or moneys loaned, to their current value in the market; the other, to annihilate private debts. Perhaps this may be in part true, and the greater number may have nothing further in view but to remedy some supposed grievances; yet, as it affords a fine opportunity for the restless enemies of this country to sow dissensions, we have too much reason to believe, that they are not only looking on as spectators, but that they are industriously employed in disseminating disaffection to the present forms of government. If these enemies are British, or their old adherents among us, which seems to be the case, because they are traced from Hampshire and Berkshire to Vermont, and from thence to Canada, if they are British, their object must be something further than mere revenge; and that object can be nothing short of establishing a monarchical government in this country, and placing some one of George's sons on the throne. If this object is worth to the British from five to ten millions sterling, and they can advance the money, they can and will effect it; not by force of arms, for, if they should come out openly against us, we should fight again; but, be assured, this country is extremely poor, as well as extravagant, and I have no doubt that ten millions, artfully applied, would secure nearly the whole country. That the British will and do cherish all their old adherents, is not to be doubted; and that those adherents never will be Americans, is a principle founded in nature.

That the French will not be silent, unoperative spectators in these negotiations, if they should happen, is most certainly to be expected. They wish to keep us just where we are, or, if a little more insignificant, quite as well; they will, therefore, view without emotion any civil commotions that tend to weaken us. But if there should be any danger of the scales preponderating in favor of any other foreign power, they will act with their usual address.

The British party is and will be great; the French party also; the genuine Americans, few; the speculators numerous, who care not what the government is, so that they can speculate upon and spunge it.

Mr. Jay will probably have furnished you with the newspapers of this country, which will contain much with respect to the hostile disposition of the Indians. That the British instigate them to make depredations on us, is very natural; but why they are reënforcing Canada, which by the public papers appears to be the case, is not so easy to determine.

All things are operating here to bring the Cincinnati into vogue. I cannot say I think they are all for supporting government, but they are for having government.

The leader of the insurgents in Massachusetts is entitled to the ribbon and eagle. He left the army in the fall of 1780, being then a captain of good reputation; his name is Shays, a man without education, but not without abilities. He is privately involved, which may be the reason why he has adopted such violent measures. It is generally supposed that he cannot retreat.

As to the situation of the finances of the United States, they can scarcely be in a worse condition. As to making any further attempt to discharge any part of the principal or interest of our foreign debt, it is in vain. The thirteen states do not pay enough to keep the civil list together, which does not require more than one hundred thousand dollars a year. I have inclosed you a schedule, which will give you a full view of the requisitions of congress, the payments, and balances due.

15

JOHN JAY TO GEORGE WASHINGTON
7 Jan. 1787
MS Columbia Univ.

They who regard the public good with more attention and attachment than they do mere personal Concerns must feel and confess the Force of such Sentiments as are expressed in your Letter to me by Col. Humphreys last Fall. The Situation of our affairs calls not only for Reflection and Prudence but for Exertion. What is to be done? is a common Question, but it is a Question not easy to answer.

Would the giving *any* further degree of power to congress, do the Business? I am much inclined to think it would not for among other Reasons it is natural to suppose there will always be members who will find it convenient to make their Seats subservient to partial and personal purposes—and they who may be able and willing to

concert and promote useful and national measures, will seldom be unembarrassed by the Ignorance, Prejudices, Fears or interested views of others.

In so large a Body secrecy and Dispatch will be too uncommon and foreign as well as local Influence will frequently oppose and sometimes frustrate the wisest measures. Large Assemblies often misunderstand or neglect the Obligations of Character, Honor and Dignity, and will collectively do or omit things which individual Gentlemen in private Capacities would not approve as the many divide blame and also divide Credit, too little a portion of either falls to each Mans Share to affect him strongly, even in Cases where the whole blame or the whole Credit must be national. It is not easy for those to think and feel as Sovereigns who have been always accustomed to think and feel as Subjects.

The executive Business of Sovereignty depending on so many Wills, and those wills moved by such a Variety of Contradictory motives and Enducements, will in general be but feebly done.

Such a Sovereign however theoretically responsible, cannot be effectually so [in] its Departments and Officers, without adequate judicatories.

I therefore promise myself nothing very desireable from any change which does not divide the Sovereignty into its proper Departments. Let Congress legislate—let others execute—let others judge.

Shall we have a King? Not in my opinion while other Expedients remain untried. Might we not have a Governor General limited in his Prerogatives and Duration? Might not Congress be divided into an upper and lower House—the former appointed for Life, the latter annually, and let the Governor general (to preserve the Ballance) with the Advice of a Council formed for that *only* purpose of the great judicial officers, have a Negative on their Acts? Our Government should in some Degree be suited to our Manners and Circumstances, and They you know are not strictly democratical.

What Powers should be granted to the Gov[ernmen]t so constituted is a Question which deserves much Thought. I think the more, the better—the States retaining only so much as may be necessary for domestic purposes and all their principal officers civil and military being commissioned and removable by the national Gov[ernmen]t.

These are short Hints. Details would exceed the Limits of a Letter and to you be superfluous.

16

JAMES MADISON, VICES OF THE POLITICAL SYSTEM
OF THE UNITED STATES
Apr. 1787
Papers 9:348–57

---

1. Failure of the States to comply with the Constitutional requisitions.

This evil has been so fully experienced both during the war and since the peace, results so naturally from the number and independent authority of the States and has been so uniformly examplified in every similar Confederacy, that it may be considered as not less radically and permanently inherent in, than it is fatal to the object of, the present System.

2. Encroachments by the States on the federal authority.

Examples of this are numerous and repetitions may be foreseen in almost every case where any favorite object of a State shall present a temptation. Among these examples are the wars and Treaties of Georgia with the Indians—The unlicensed compacts between Virginia and Maryland, and between Pena. & N. Jersey—the troops raised and to be kept up by Massts.

3. Violations of the law of nations and of treaties.

From the number of Legislatures, the sphere of life from which most of their members are taken, and the circumstances under which their legislative business is carried on, irregularities of this kind must frequently happen. Accordingly not a year has passed without instances of them in some one or other of the States. The Treaty of peace—the treaty with France—the treaty with Holland have each been violated. The causes of these irregularities must necessarily produce frequent violations of the law of nations in other respects.

As yet foreign powers have not been rigorous in animadverting on us. This moderation however cannot be mistaken for a permanent partiality to our faults, or a permanent security agst. those disputes with other nations, which being among the greatest of public calamities, it ought to be least in the power of any part of the Community to bring on the whole.

4. Trespasses of the States on the rights of each other.

These are alarming symptoms, and may be daily apprehended as we are admonished by daily experience. See the law of Virginia restricting foreign vessels to certain ports—of Maryland in favor of vessels belonging to her own citizens—of N. York in favor of the same.

Paper money, instalments of debts, occlusion of Courts, making property a legal tender, may likewise be deemed aggressions on the rights of other States. As the Citizens of every State aggregately taken stand more or less in the relation of Creditors or debtors, to the Citizens of every other States, Acts of the debtor State in favor of debtors, affect the Creditor State, in the same manner, as they do its own citizens who are relatively creditors towards other citizens. This remark may be extended to foreign nations. If the exclusive regulation of the value and alloy of coin was properly delegated to the federal authority, the policy of it equally requires a controul on the States in the cases above mentioned. It must have been meant 1. to preserve uniformity in the circulating medium throughout the nation. 2. to prevent those frauds on the citizens of other

States, and the subjects of foreign powers, which might disturb the tranquility at home, or involve the Union in foreign contests.

The practice of many States in restricting the commercial intercourse with other States, and putting their productions and manufactures on the same footing with those of foreign nations, though not contrary to the federal articles, is certainly adverse to the spirit of the Union, and tends to beget retaliating regulations, not less expensive & vexatious in themselves, than they are destructive of the general harmony.

5. want of concert in matters where common interest requires it.

This defect is strongly illustrated in the state of our commercial affairs. How much has the national dignity, interest, and revenue suffered from this cause? Instances of inferior moment are the want of uniformity in the laws concerning naturalization & literary property; of provision for national seminaries, for grants of incorporation for national purposes, for canals and other works of general utility, wch. may at present be defeated by the perverseness of particular States whose concurrence is necessary.

6. want of guaranty to the States of their Constitutions & laws against internal violence.

The confederation is silent on this point and therefore by the second article the hands of the federal authority are tied. According to Republican Theory, Right and power being both vested in the majority, are held to be synonimous. According to fact and experience a minority may in an appeal to force, be an overmatch for the majority. 1. If the minority happen to include all such as possess the skill and habits of military life, & such as possess the great pecuniary resources, one third only may conquer the remaining two thirds. 2. One third of those who participate in the choice of the rulers, may be rendered a majority by the accession of those whose poverty excludes them from a right of suffrage, and who for obvious reasons will be more likely to join the standard of sedition than that of the established Government. 3. Where slavery exists the republican Theory becomes still more fallacious.

7. want of sanction to the laws, and of coercion in the Government of the Confederacy.

A sanction is essential to the idea of law, as coercion is to that of Government. The federal system being destitute of both, wants the great vital principles of a Political Cons[ti]tution. Under the form of such a Constitution, it is in fact nothing more than a treaty of amity of commerce and of alliance, between so many independent and Sovereign States. From what cause could so fatal an omission have happened in the articles of Confederation? from a mistaken confidence that the justice, the good faith, the honor, the sound policy, of the several legislative assemblies would render superfluous any appeal to the ordinary motives by which the laws secure the obedience of individuals: a confidence which does honor to the enthusiastic virtue of the compilers, as much as the inexperience of the crisis apologizes for their errors. The time which has since elapsed has had the double effect, of increasing the light, and tempering the warmth, with which the arduous work may be revised. It is no longer doubted that a unanimous and punctual obedience of 13 independent bodies, to the acts of the federal Government, ought not be calculated on. Even during the war, when external danger supplied in some degree the defect of legal & coercive sanctions, how imperfectly did the States fulfil their obligations to the Union? In time of peace, we see already what is to be expected. How indeed could it be otherwise? In the first place, Every general act of the Union must necessarily bear unequally hard on some particular member or members of it. Secondly the partiality of the members to their own interests and rights, a partiality which will be fostered by the Courtiers of popularity, will naturally exaggerate the inequality where it exists, and even suspect it where it has no existence. Thirdly a distrust of the voluntary compliance of each other may prevent the compliance of any, although it should be the latent disposition of all. Here are causes & pretexts which will never fail to render federal measures abortive. If the laws of the States, were merely recommendatory to their citizens, or if they were to be rejudged by County authorities, what security, what probability would exist, that they would be carried into execution? Is the security or probability greater in favor of the acts of Congs. which depending for their execution on the will of the state legislatures, wch. are tho' nominally authoritative, in fact recommendatory only.

8. Want of ratification by the people of the articles of Confederation.

In some of the States the Confederation is recognized by, and forms a part of the constitution. In others however it has received no other sanction than that of the Legislative authority. From this defect two evils result: 1. Whenever a law of a State happens to be repugnant to an act of Congress, particularly when the latter is of posterior date to the former, it will be at least questionable whether the latter must not prevail; and as the question must be decided by the Tribunals of the State, they will be most likely to lean on the side of the State. 2. As far as the Union of the States is to be regarded as a league of sovereign powers, and not as a political Constitution by virtue of which they are become one sovereign power, so far it seems to follow from the doctrine of compacts, that a breach of any of the articles of the confederation by any of the parties to it, absolves the other parties from their respective obligations, and gives them a right if they chuse to exert it, of dissolving the Union altogether.

9. Multiplicity of laws in the several States.

In developing the evils which viciate the political system of the U. S. it is proper to include those which are found within the States individually, as well as those which directly affect the States collectively, since the former class

have an indirect influence on the general malady and must not be overlooked in forming a compleat remedy. Among the evils then of our situation may well be ranked the multiplicity of laws from which no State is exempt. As far as laws are necessary, to mark with precision the duties of those who are to obey them, and to take from those who are to administer them a discretion, which might be abused, their number is the price of liberty. As far as the laws exceed this limit, they are a nusance: a nusance of the most pestilent kind. Try the Codes of the several States by this test, and what a luxuriancy of legislation do they present. The short period of independency has filled as many pages as the century which preceded it. Every year, almost every session, adds a new volume. This may be the effect in part, but it can only be in part, of the situation in which the revolution has placed us. A review of the several codes will shew that every necessary and useful part of the least voluminous of them might be compressed into one tenth of the compass, and at the same time be rendered tenfold as perspicuous.

10. mutability of the laws of the States.

This evil is intimately connected with the former yet deserves a distinct notice as it emphatically denotes a vicious legislation. We daily see laws repealed or superseded, before any trial can have been made of their merits: and even before a knowledge of them can have reached the remoter districts within which they were to operate. In the regulations of trade this instability becomes a snare not only to our citizens but to foreigners also.

11. Injustice of the laws of States.

If the multiplicity and mutability of laws prove a want of wisdom, their injustice betrays a defect still more alarming: more alarming not merely because it is a greater evil in itself, but because it brings more into question the fundamental principle of republican Government, that the majority who rule in such Governments, are the safest Guardians both of public Good and of private rights. To what causes is this evil to be ascribed?

These causes lie 1. in the Representative bodies.

2. in the people themselves.

1. Representative appointments are sought from 3 motives. 1. ambition 2. personal interest. 3. public good. Unhappily the two first are proved by experience to be most prevalent. Hence the candidates who feel them, particularly, the second, are most industrious, and most successful in pursuing their object: and forming often a majority in the legislative Councils, with interested views, contrary to the interest, and views, of their Constituents, join in a perfidious sacrifice of the latter to the former. A succeeding election it might be supposed, would displace the offenders, and repair the mischief. But how easily are base and selfish measures, masked by pretexts of public good and apparent expediency? How frequently will a repetition of the same arts and industry which succeeded in the first instance, again prevail on the unwary to misplace their confidence?

How frequently too will the honest but unenlightened representative be the dupe of a favorite leader, veiling his selfish views under the professions of public good, and varnishing his sophistical arguments with the glowing colours of popular eloquence?

2. A still more fatal if not more frequent cause lies among the people themselves. All civilized societies are divided into different interests and factions, as they happen to be creditors or debtors—Rich or poor—husbandmen, merchants or manufacturers—members of different religious sects—followers of different political leaders—inhabitants of different districts—owners of different kinds of property &c &c. In republican Government the majority however composed, ultimately give the law. Whenever therefore an apparent interest or common passion unites a majority what is to restrain them from unjust violations of the rights and interests of the minority, or of individuals? Three motives only 1. a prudent regard to their own good as involved in the general and permanent good of the Community. This consideration although of decisive weight in itself, is found by experience to be too often unheeded. It is too often forgotten, by nations as well as by individuals that honesty is the best policy. 2dly. respect for character. However strong this motive may be in individuals, it is considered as very insufficient to restrain them from injustice. In a multitude its efficacy is diminished in proportion to the number which is to share the praise or the blame. Besides, as it has reference to public opinion, which within a particular Society, is the opinion of the majority, the standard is fixed by those whose conduct is to be measured by it. The public opinion without the Society, will be little respected by the people at large of any Country. Individuals of extended views, and of national pride, may bring the public proceedings to this standard, but the example will never be followed by the multitude. Is it to be imagined that an ordinary citizen or even an assemblyman of R. Island in estimating the policy of paper money, ever considered or cared in what light the measure would be viewed in France or Holland; or even in Massts or Connect.? It was a sufficient temptation to both that it was for their interest: it was a sufficient sanction to the latter that it was popular in the State; to the former that it was so in the neighbourhood. 3dly. will Religion the only remaining motive be a sufficient restraint? It is not pretended to be such on men individually considered. Will its effect be greater on them considered in an aggregate view? quite the reverse. The conduct of every popular assembly acting on oath, the strongest of religious Ties, proves that individuals join without remorse in acts, against which their consciences would revolt if proposed to them under the like sanction, separately in their closets. When indeed Religion is kindled into enthusiasm, its force like that of other passions, is increased by the sympathy of a multitude. But enthusiasm is only a temporary state of religion, and while it lasts will hardly be seen with pleasure at the helm of Government. Besides as religion in its coolest state, is not infallible, it may become a motive to oppression as well as a restraint from injustice. Place three individuals in a situation wherein the interest of each depends on the voice of the others, and give to two of them an interest opposed to the rights of the third? Will the latter be secure? The prudence of every man would shun the danger. The rules & forms of justice suppose & guard against it. Will two thousand in a like situation be less likely to encroach on the rights of one thousand? The contrary is witnessed by the notorious factions & oppressions which take place in corporate towns limited as the opportunities are, and in little republics when uncontrouled by apprehensions of external danger. If an enlargement of the sphere is found to lessen the insecurity of private rights, it is not because the impulse of a common interest or passion is less predominant in this case with the majority; but because a common interest or passion is less apt to be felt and the requisite combinations less easy to be formed by a great than by a small number. The Society becomes broken into a greater variety of interests, of pursuits, of passions, which check each other, whilst those who may feel a common sentiment have less opportunity of communication and concert. It may be inferred that the inconveniences of popular States contrary to the prevailing Theory, are in proportion not to the extent, but to the narrowness of their limits.

The great desideratum in Government is such a modification of the Sovereignty as will render it sufficiently neutral between the different interests and factions, to controul one part of the Society from invading the rights of another, and at the same time sufficiently controuled itself, from setting up an interest adverse to that of the whole Society. In absolute Monarchies, the prince is sufficiently, neutral towards his subjects, but frequently sacrifices their happiness to his ambition or his avarice. In small Republics, the sovereign will is sufficiently controuled from such a Sacrifice of the entire Society, but is not sufficiently neutral towards the parts composing it. As a limited Monarchy tempers the evils of an absolute one; so an extensive Republic meliorates the administration of a small Republic.

An auxiliary desideratum for the melioration of the Republican form is such a process of elections as will most certainly extract from the mass of the Society the purest and noblest characters which it contains; such as will at once feel most strongly the proper motives to pursue the end of their appointment, and be most capable to devise the proper means of attaining it.

12. Impotence of the laws of the States

17

JAMES MADISON TO GEORGE WASHINGTON
16 Apr. 1787
Papers 9:382–85

(See ch. 8, no. 6)

18

RICHARD HENRY LEE TO GEORGE MASON
15 May 1787
Mason Papers 3:876–79

It has given me much pleasure to be informed that General Washington and yourself have gone to the Convention. We may hope, from such efforts, that alterations beneficial will take place in our Federal Constitution, if it shall be found, on deliberate inquiry, that the evils now felt do flow from errors in that constitution; but, alas! sir, I fear it is more in vicious manners, than mistakes in form, that we must seek for the causes of the present discontent. The present causes of complaint seem to be, that Congress cannot command the money necessary for the just purposes of paying debts, or for supporting the federal government; and that they cannot make treaties of commerce, unless power unlimited, of regulating trade be given. The Confederation now gives right to name the sums necessary, and to apportion the quotas by a rule established. This rule is, unfortunately, very difficult of execution, and, therefore the recommendations of Congress on this subject have not been made in federal mode; so that States have thought themselves justified in non-compliance. If the rule were plain and easy, and refusal were then to follow demand, I see clearly, that no form of government whatever, short of force, will answer; for the same want of principle that produces neglect now, will do so under any change not supported by power compulsory; the difficulty certainly is, how to give this power in such manner as that it may only be used to good, and not abused to bad, purposes. Whoever shall solve this difficulty will receive the thanks of this and future generations. With respect to the want of power to make treaties of trade, for want of legislation, to regulate the general commerce, it appears to me, that the right of making treaties, and the legislative power contended for are essentially different things; the former may be given and executed without the danger attending upon the States parting with their legislative authority, in the instance contended for. If the third paragraph of the sixth article were altered, by striking out the words, in pursuance of any treaties already proposed by Congress, to the courts of France and Spain; and the proviso stricken out of the first section in the ninth article, Congress would then have a complete and unlimited right of making treaties of all kinds, and, so far, I really think it both right and necessary; but this is very different from, and in danger far short of, giving an exclusive power of regulating trade. A minister of Congress may go to a foreign court with full power to make a commercial treaty; but if he were to propose to such court that the eight northern States in this Union, should have the exclusive right of carrying the products of the five southern States, or of supplying these States with foreign articles, such a proposition of monopoly would be rejected; and, there-

fore, no danger here from the power of making treaty; but a legislative right to regulate trade through the States may, in a thousand artful modes, be so abused as to produce the monopoly aforesaid, to the extreme oppression of the staple States, as they are called. I do not say that this would be done, but I contend that it might be done; and, where interest powerfully prompts, it is greatly to be feared that it would be done. Whoever has served long in Congress, knows that the restraint of making the consent of nine States necessary, is feeble and incompetent. Some will sometimes sleep, and some will be negligent, but it is certain that improper power not given cannot be improperly used.

The human mind is too apt to rush from one extreme to another; it appears, by the objections that came from the different States, when the Confederation was submitted for consideration, that the universal apprehension was, of the too great, not the defective powers of Congress. Whence this immense change of sentiment, in a few years? For now the cry is power, give Congress power. Without reflecting that every free nation, that hath ever existed, has lost its liberty by the same rash impatience, and want of necessary caution. I am glad, however, to find, on this occasion, that so many gentlemen, of competent years, are sent to the Convention, for, certainly, "youth is the season of credulity, and confidence a plant of slow growth in an aged bosom." The States have been so unpardonably remiss, in furnishing their federal quotas, as to make impost necessary, for a term of time, with a provisional security, that the money arising shall be unchangeably applied to the payment of their public debts; that accounts of the application, shall be annually sent to each State; and the collecting officers appointed by, and be amenable to the States: or, if not so, very strong preventives and correctives of official abuse and misconduct, interpose, to shield the people from oppression. Give me leave, sir, to detain you a moment longer, with a proposition that I have not heard mentioned. It is that the right of making paper money shall be exclusively vested in Congress; such a right will be clearly within the spirit of the fourth section of the ninth article of the present confederation. This appears to me, to be a restraint of the last importance to the peace and happiness of the Union, and of every part of it. Knaves assure, and fools believe, that calling paper money, and making it tender, is the way to be rich and happy; thus the national mind is kept in constant ferment; and the public councils in continual disturbance by the intrigues of wicked men, for fraudulent purposes, for speculating designs. This would be a great step towards correcting morals, and suppressing legislative frauds, which, of all frauds, is the most hateful to society. Do you not think, sir, that it ought to be declared, by the new system, that any State act of legislation that shall contravene, or oppose, the authorized acts of Congress, or interfere with the expressed rights of that body, shall be *ipso facto* void, and of no force whatsoever?

My respects, if you please, to your brethren of the Convention, from this State, and pardon me for the liberty I have taken of troubling you with my sentiments on the interesting business that calls you to Philadelphia.

19

EDWARD CARRINGTON TO THOMAS JEFFERSON
9 June 1787
Jefferson Papers 11:408–9

The importance of this event [the assembling of the Philadelphia Convention] is every day growing in the public mind, and it will, in all probability, produce an happy era in our political existence; taking a view of the circumstances which have occasioned our calamities, and the present state of things and opinions, I am flattered with this prospect. Public events in the United States since the peace have given a cast to the American character, which is by no means its true countenance. Delinquencies of the States in their foederal obligations; acts of their legislatures violating public Treaties and private Contracts, and an universal imbecility in the public administrations, it is true, form the great features of our political conduct; but these have resulted rather from constitutional defects, and accidental causes than the natural dispositions of the people. Destitute as the foederal sovereignty is of coercive principle, backwardness in the component parts to comply with its recommendations, is natural and inevitable. Coercion in Government produces a double effect—while it compels the obedience of the refractory, it redoubles the alertness of the virtuous by inspiring a confidence in the impartiality of its burthens. From defect of penalty, ideas of delinquency are inseparable. States, as well as individuals, will contemplate both together, and apprehensions of unequal performance, produce disgust and apathy throughout.

The nefarious Acts of State Governments have proceeded not from the will of the people. Peace once obtained, men whose abilities and integrity had gained the intire popular confidence, whose zeal or indolence in the public affairs alike moved or lulled the people, retired from the busy scene, or at least acted with indifference. The news papers ceased to circulate with public information. Demagogues of desperate fortunes, mere adventurers in fraud, were left to act unopposed. Their measures, of course, either obtained the consent of the multitude by misrepresentation, or assumed the countenance of popularity because none said nay. Hence have proceeded paper money, breaches of Treaty &c. The ductility of the Multitude is fully evidenced in the case of the late tumults in Massachusetts. Men who were of good property and owed not a shilling, were involved in the train of desperado's to suppress the courts. A full representation of the public affairs from the General Court through the Clergy has reclaimed so great a proportion of the deluded, that a Rebellion which a few months ago threatened the subversion of the Government is, by measures scarcely deserving the name of exertion, suppressed, and one decided act of authority would eradicate it forever. In this experiment it is proved that full intelligence of the public affairs not only would keep the people right, but will set them so after they have got wrong.

Civil Liberty, in my opinion, never before took up her residence in a country so likely to afford her a long and grateful protection as the United States.—A people more generally enlightened than any other under the sun, and in the habits of owning, instead of being mere tenants in, the Soil, must be proportionably alive to her sacred rights, and qualified to guard them; and I am persuaded that the time is fast approaching when all these advantages will have their fullest influence. Our tendency to anarchy and consequent despotism is felt, and the alarm is spreading. Men are brought into action who had consigned themselves to an eve of rest, and the Convention, as a Beacon, is rousing the attention of the Empire.

20

THOMAS JEFFERSON TO EDWARD CARRINGTON
4 Aug. 1787
Papers 11:678–79

I am happy to find that the states have come so generally into the scheme of the Federal Convention, from which I am sure we shall see wise propositions. I confess I do not go as far in the reforms thought necessary as some of my correspondents in America; but if the Convention should adopt such propositions I shall suppose them necessary. My general plan would be to make the states one as to every thing connected with foreign nations, and several as to every thing purely domestic. But with all the imperfections of our present government, it is without comparison the best existing or that ever did exist. It's greatest defect is the imperfect manner in which matters of commerce have been provided for. It has been so often said, as to be generally believed, that Congress have no power by the confederation to enforce any thing, e.g. contributions of money. It was not necessary to give them that power expressly; they have it by the law of nature. When two nations make a compact, there results to each a power of compelling the other to execute it. Compulsion was never so easy as in our case, where a single frigate would soon levy on the commerce of any state the deficiency of it's contributions; nor more safe than in the hands of Congress which has always shewn that it would wait, as it ought to do, to the last extremities before it would execute any of it's powers which are disagreeable.—I think it very material to separate in the hands of Congress the Executive and Legislative powers, as the Judiciary already are in some degree. This I hope will be done. The want of it has been the source of more evil than we have ever experienced from any other cause. Nothing is so embarrassing nor so mischievous in a great assembly as the details of execution. The smallest trifle of that kind occupies as long as the most important act of legislation, and takes place of every thing else. Let any man recollect, or look over the files of Congress, he will observe the most important propositions hanging over from week to week and month to month, till the occasions have past them, and the thing never done. I have ever viewed the executive details as the greatest cause of evil to us, because they in fact place us as if we had no federal head, by diverting the attention of that head from great to small objects; and should this division of power not be recommended by the Convention, it is my opinion Congress should make it itself by establishing an Executive committee.

21

ALEXANDER HAMILTON, FEDERALIST, NO. 15,
90–98
1 Dec. 1787

In pursuance of the plan, which I have laid down, for the discussion of the subject, the point next in order to be examined is the "insufficiency of the present confederation to the preservation of the Union." It may perhaps be asked, what need is there of reasoning or proof to illustrate a position, which is not either controverted or doubted; to which the understandings and feelings of all classes of men assent; and which in substance is admitted by the opponents as well as by the friends of the New Constitution? It must in truth be acknowleged that however these may differ in other respects, they in general appear to harmonise in this sentiment at least, that there are material imperfections in our national system, and that something is necessary to be done to rescue us from impending anarchy. The facts that support this opinion are no longer objects of speculation. They have forced themselves upon the sensibility of the people at large, and have at length extorted from those, whose mistaken policy has had the principal share in precipitating the extremity, at which we are arrived, a reluctant confession of the reality of those defects in the scheme of our Foederal Government, which have been long pointed out and regretted by the intelligent friends of the Union.

We may indeed with propriety be said to have reached almost the last stage of national humiliation. There is scarcely any thing that can wound the pride, or degrade the character of an independent nation, which we do not experience. Are there engagements to the performance of which we are held by every tie respectable among men? These are the subjects of constant and unblushing violation. Do we owe debts to foreigners and to our own citizens contracted in a time of imminent peril, for the preservation of our political existence? These remain without any proper or satisfactory provision for their discharge. Have we valuable territories and important posts in the possession of a foreign power, which by express stipulations ought long since to have been surrendered? These are still retained, to the prejudice of our interests not less than of our rights. Are we in a condition to resent, or to repel the aggression? We have neither troops nor treasury nor government.* Are we even in a condition to remonstrate with dignity? The just imputations on our own faith, in respect to the same treaty, ought first to be removed. Are we entitled by nature and compact to a free participation in the navigation of the Mississippi? Spain excludes us from it. Is public credit an indispensable resource in time of public danger? We seem to have abandoned its cause as desperate and irretrievable. Is commerce of importance to national wealth? Ours is at the lowest point of declension. Is respectability in the eyes of foreign powers a safeguard against foreign encroachments? The imbecility of our Government even forbids them to treat with us: Our ambassadors abroad are the mere pageants of mimic sovereignty. Is a violent and unnatural decrease in the value of land a symptom of national distress? The price of improved land in most parts of the country is much lower than can be accounted for by the quantity of waste land at market, and can only be fully explained by that want of private and public confidence, which are so alarmingly prevalent among all ranks and which have a direct tendency to depreciate property of every kind. Is private credit the friend and patron of industry? That most useful kind which relates to borrowing and lending is reduced within the narrowest limits, and this still more from an opinion of insecurity than from the scarcity of money. To shorten an enumeration of particulars which can afford neither pleasure nor instruction it may in general be demanded, what indication is there of national disorder, poverty and insignificance that could befal a community so peculiarly blessed with natural advantages as we are, which does not form a part of the dark catalogue of our public misfortunes?

This is the melancholy situation, to which we have been brought by those very maxims and councils, which would now deter us from adopting the proposed constitution; and which not content with having conducted us to the brink of a precipice, seem resolved to plunge us into the abyss, that awaits us below. Here, my Countrymen, impelled by every motive that ought to influence an enlightened people, let us make a firm stand for our safety, our tranquillity, our dignity, our reputation. Let us at last break the fatal charm which has too long seduced us from the paths of felicity and prosperity.

It is true, as has been before observed, that facts too stubborn to be resisted have produced a species of general assent to the abstract proposition that there exist material defects in our national system; but the usefulness of the concession, on the part of the old adversaries of foederal measures, is destroyed by a strenuous opposition to a remedy, upon the only principles, that can give it a chance of success. While they admit that the Government of the United States is destitute of energy; they contend against conferring upon it those powers which are requisite to supply that energy: They seem still to aim at things repugnant and irreconcilable—at an augmentation of Foederal authority without a diminution of State authority—at sovereignty in the Union and complete independence in the

*I mean for the Union.

members. They still in fine seem to cherish with blind devotion the political monster of an *imperium in imperio*. This renders a full display of the principal defects of the confederation necessary, in order to shew, that the evils we experience do not proceed from minute or partial imperfections, but from fundamental errors in the structure of the building which cannot be amended otherwise than by an alteration in the first principles and main pillars of the fabric.

The great and radical vice in the construction of the existing Confederation is in the principle of LEGISLATION for STATES or GOVERNMENTS, in their CORPORATE or COLLECTIVE CAPACITIES and as contradistinguished from the INDIVIDUALS of whom they consist. Though this principle does not run through all the powers delegated to the Union; yet it pervades and governs those, on which the efficacy of the rest depends. Except as to the rule of apportionment, the United States have an indefinite discretion to make requisitions for men and money; but they have no authority to raise either by regulations extending to the individual citizens of America. The consequence of this is, that though in theory their resolutions concerning those objects are laws, constitutionally binding on the members of the Union, yet in practice they are mere recommendations, which the States observe or disregard at their option.

It is a singular instance of the capriciousness of the human mind, that after all the admonitions we have had from experience on this head, there should still be found men, who object to the New Constitution for deviating from a principle which has been found the bane of the old; and which is in itself evidently incompatible with the idea of GOVERNMENT; a principle in short which if it is to be executed at all must substitute the violent and sanguinary agency of the sword to the mild influence of the Magistracy.

There is nothing absurd or impracticable in the idea of a league or alliance between independent nations, for certain defined purposes precisely stated in a treaty; regulating all the details of time, place, circumstance and quantity; leaving nothing to future discretion; and depending for its execution on the good faith of the parties. Compacts of this kind exist among all civilized nations subject to the usual vicissitudes of peace and war, of observance and non observance, as the interests or passions of the contracting powers dictate. In the early part of the present century, there was an epidemical rage in Europe for this species of compacts; from which the politicians of the times fondly hoped for benefits which were never realised. With a view to establishing the equilibrium of power and the peace of that part of the world, all the resources of negotiation were exhausted, and triple and quadruple alliances were formed; but they were scarcely formed before they were broken, giving an instructive but afflicting lesson to mankind how little dependence is to be placed on treaties which have no other sanction than the obligations of good faith; and which oppose general considerations of peace and justice to the impulse of any immediate interest and passion.

If the particular States in this country are disposed to stand in a similar relation to each other, and to drop the project of a general DISCRETIONARY SUPERINTENDENCE, the scheme would indeed be pernicious, and would entail upon us all the mischiefs that have been enumerated under the first head; but it would have the merit of being at least consistent and practicable. Abandoning all views towards a confederate Government, this would bring us to a simple alliance offensive and defensive; and would place us in a situation to be alternately friends and enemies of each other as our mutual jealousies and rivalships nourished by the intrigues of foreign nations should prescribe to us.

But if we are unwilling to be placed in this perilous situation; if we will still adhere to the design of a national government, or which is the same thing of a superintending power under the direction of a common Council, we must resolve to incorporate into our plan those ingredients which may be considered as forming the characteristic difference between a league and a government; we must extend the authority of the union to the persons of the citizens,—the only proper objects of government.

Government implies the power of making laws. It is essential to the idea of a law, that it be attended with a sanction; or, in other words, a penalty or punishment for disobedience. If there be no penalty annexed to disobedience, the resolutions or commands which pretend to be laws will in fact amount to nothing more than advice or recommendation. This penalty, whatever it may be, can only be inflicted in two ways; by the agency of the Courts and Ministers of Justice, or by military force; by the COERTION of the magistracy, or by the COERTION of arms. The first kind can evidently apply only to men—the last kind must of necessity be employed against bodies politic, or communities or States. It is evident, that there is no process of a court by which their observance of the laws can in the last resort be enforced. Sentences may be denounced against them for violations of their duty; but these sentences can only be carried into execution by the sword. In an association where the general authority is confined to the collective bodies of the communities that compose it, every breach of the laws must involve a state of war, and military execution must become the only instrument of civil obedience. Such a state of things can certainly not deserve the name of government, nor would any prudent man choose to commit his happiness to it.

There was a time when we were told that breaches, by the States, of the regulations of the foederal authority were not to be expected—that a sense of common interest would preside over the conduct of the respective members, and would beget a full compliance with all the constitutional requisitions of the Union. This language at the present day would appear as wild as a great part of what we now hear from the same quarter will be thought, when we shall have received further lessons from that best oracle of wisdom, experience. It at all times betrayed an ignorance of the true springs by which human conduct is actuated, and belied the original inducements to the establishment of civil power. Why has government been instituted at all? Because the passions of men will not conform to the dictates of reason and justice, without constraint. Has it been found that bodies of men act with more rectitude or greater disinterestedness than individuals? The contrary of this has been inferred by all accurate observers of the conduct of mankind; and the inference is founded upon obvious reasons. Regard to reputation has a less active influence, when the infamy of a bad action is to be divided among a number, than when it is to fall singly upon one. A spirit of faction which is apt to mingle its poison in the deliberations of all bodies of men, will often hurry the persons of whom they are composed into improprieties and excesses, for which they would blush in a private capacity.

In addition to all this, there is in the nature of sovereign power an impatience of controul, that disposes those who are invested with the exercise of it, to look with an evil eye upon all external attempts to restrain or direct its operations. From this spirit it happens that in every political association which is formed upon the principle of uniting in a common interest a number of lesser sovereignties, there will be found a kind of excentric tendency in the subordinate or inferior orbs, by the operation of which there will be a perpetual effort in each to fly off from the common center. This tendency is not difficult to be accounted for. It has its origin in the love of power. Power controuled or abridged is almost always the rival and enemy of that power by which it is controuled or abriged. This simple proposition will teach us how little reason there is to expect, that the persons, entrusted with the administration of the affairs of the particular members of a confederacy, will at all times be ready, with perfect good humour, and an unbiassed regard to the public weal, to execute the resolutions or decrees of the general authority. The reverse of this results from the constitution of human nature.

If therefore the measures of the confederacy cannot be executed, without the intervention of the particular administrations, there will be little prospect of their being executed at all. The rulers of the respective members, whether they have a constitutional right to do it or not, will undertake to judge of the propriety of the measures themselves. They will consider the conformity of the thing proposed or required to their immediate interests or aims, the momentary conveniences or inconveniences that would attend its adoption. All this will be done, and in a spirit of interested and suspicious scrutiny, without that knowledge of national circumstances and reasons of state, which is essential to a right judgment, and with that strong predilection in favour of local objects, which can hardly fail to mislead the decision. The same process must be repeated in every member of which the body is constituted; and the execution of the plans, framed by the councils of the whole, will always fluctuate on the discretion of the ill-informed and prejudiced opinion of every part. Those who have been conversant in the proceedings of popular assemblies; who have seen how difficult it often is, when there is no exterior pressure of circumstances, to bring them to harmonious resolutions on important points, will readily conceive how impossible it must be to induce a number of such assemblies, deliberating at a distance from each other, at different times, and under different impressions, long to cooperate in the same views and pursuits.

In our case, the concurrence of thirteen distinct sovereign wills is requisite under the confederation to the complete execution of every important measure, that proceeds from the Union. It has happened as was to have been foreseen. The measures of the Union have not been executed; and the delinquencies of the States have step by step matured themselves to an extreme; which has at length arrested all the wheels of the national government, and brought them to an awful stand. Congress at this time scarcely possess the means of keeping up the forms of administration; 'till the States can have time to agree upon a more substantial substitute for the present shadow of a foederal government. Things did not come to this desperate extremity at once. The causes which have been specified produced at first only unequal and disproportionate degrees of compliance with the requisitions of the Union. The greater deficiencies of some States furnished the pretext of example and the temptation of interest to the complying, or to the least delinquent States. Why should we do more in proportion than those who are embarked with us in the same political voyage? Why should we consent to bear more than our proper share of the common burthen? These were suggestions which human selfishness could not withstand, and which even speculative men, who looked forward to remote consequences, could not, without hesitation, combat. Each State yielding to the persuasive voice of immediate interest and convenience has successively withdrawn its support, 'till the frail and tottering edifice seems ready to fall upon our heads and to crush us beneath its ruins.

22

ALEXANDER HAMILTON, FEDERALIST, NO. 21,
129–33
12 Dec. 1787

The next most palpable defect of the subsisting confederation is the total want of a SANCTION to its laws. The United States as now composed, have no power to exact obedience, or punish disobedience to their resolutions, either by pecuniary mulcts, by a suspension or divestiture of privileges, or in any other constitutional mode. There is no express delegation of authority to them to use force against delinquent members; and if such a right should be ascribed to the foederal head, as resulting from the nature of the social compact between the States, it must be by inference and construction, in the face of that part of the second article, by which it is declared, "each State shall retain every power, jurisdiction and right, not *expressly* delegated to the United States in Congress assembled." There is doubtless, a striking absurdity in supposing that a right of this kind does not exist, but we are reduced to the dilemma either of embracing that supposition, preposterous as it may seem, or of contravening or explaining away a provision, which has been of late a repeated theme of the eulogies of those, who oppose the new constitution; and the want of which in that plan, has been the subject of much plausible animadversions and severe criticism. If we are unwilling to impair the force of this applauded provision, we shall be obliged to conclude, that the United States afford the extraordinary spectacle of a government, destitute even of the shadow of constitutional power to enforce the execution of its own laws. It will appear from the specimens which have been cited, that the American confederacy in this particular, stands discriminated from every other institution of a similar kind, and exhibits a new and unexampled phenomenon in the political world.

The want of a mutual guarantee of the State governments is another capital imperfection in the foederal plan. There is nothing of this kind declared in the articles that compose it; and to imply a tacit guarantee from considerations of utility, would be a still more flagrant departure from the clause which has been mentioned, than to imply a tacit power of coertion, from the like consideration. The want of a guarantee, though it might in its consequences endanger the Union, does not so immediately attack its existence as the want of a constitutional sanction to its laws.

Without a guarantee, the assistance to be derived from the Union in repelling those domestic dangers, which may sometimes threaten the existence of the State constitutions, must be renounced. Usurpation may rear its crest in each State, and trample upon the liberties of the people; while the national government could legally do nothing more than behold its encroachments with indignation and regret. A successful faction may erect a tyranny on the ruins of order and law, while no succour could constitutionally be afforded by the Union to the friends and supporters of the government. The tempestuous situation, from which Massachusetts has scarcely emerged, evinces that dangers of this kind are not merely speculative. Who can determine what might have been the issue of her late convulsions, if the mal-contents had been headed by a Caesar or by a Cromwell? Who can predict what effect a despotism established in Massachusetts, would have upon the liberties of New-Hampshire or Rhode-Island; of Connecticut or New-York?

The inordinate pride of State importance has suggested to some minds an objection to the principle of a guarantee in the foederal Government; as involving an officious interference in the domestic concerns of the members. A scruple of this kind would deprive us of one of the principal advantages to be expected from Union; and can only flow from a misapprehension of the nature of the provision itself. It could be no impediment to reforms of the State Constitutions by a majority of the people in a legal and peaceable mode. This right would remain undiminished. The guarantee could only operate against changes to be effected by violence. Towards the prevention of calamities of this kind too many checks cannot be provided. The peace of society, and the stability of government, depend absolutely on the efficacy of the precautions adopted on this head. Where the whole power of the government is in the hands of the people, there is less pretence for the use of violent remedies, in partial or occasional distempers of the State. The natural cure for an ill administration, in a popular or representative constitution, is a change of men. A guarantee by the national authority would be as much levelled against the usurpations of rulers, as against the ferments and outrages of faction and sedition in the community.

The principle of regulating the contributions of the States to the common treasury by QUOTAS is another fundamental error in the confederation. Its repugnancy to an adequate supply of the national exigencies has been already pointed out, and has sufficiently appeared from the trial which has been made of it. I speak of it now solely with a view to equality among the States. Those who have been accustomed to contemplate the circumstances, which produce and constitute natural wealth, must be satisfied that there is no common standard, or barometer, by which the degrees of it can be ascertained. Neither the value of lands nor the numbers of the people, which have been successively proposed as the rule of State contributions, has any pretension to being a just representative. If we compare the wealth of the United Netherlands with that of Russia or Germany or even of France; and if we at the same time compare the total value of the lands, and the aggregate population of that contracted district, with the total value of the lands, and the aggregate population of the immense regions of either of the three last mentioned countries, we shall at once discover that there is no comparison between the proportion of either of these two objects and that of the relative wealth of those nations. If the like parallel were to be run between several of the American States; it would furnish a like result. Let Virginia be contrasted with North-Carolina, Pennsylvania with Connecticut, or Maryland with New-Jersey, and we shall be convinced that the respective abilities of those States, in relation to revenue, bear little or no analogy to their comparative stock in lands or to their comparative population. The position may be equally illustrated by a similar process between the counties of the same State. No man who is acquainted with the State of New-York will doubt, that the active wealth of Kings County bears a much greater proportion to that of Montgomery, than it would appear to do, if we should take either the total value of the lands or the total numbers of the people as a criterion!

The wealth of nations depends upon an infinite variety of causes. Situation, soil, climate, the nature of the productions, the nature of the government, the genius of the citizens—the degree of information they possess—the state of commerce, of arts, of industry—these circumstances and many much too complex, minute, or adventitious, to admit of a particular specification, occasion differences hardly conceivable in the relative opulence and riches of different countries. The consequence clearly is, that there can be no common measure of national wealth; and of course, no general or stationary rule, by which the ability of a State to pay taxes can be determined. The attempt therefore to regulate the contributions of the members of a confederacy, by any such rule, cannot fail to be productive of glaring inequality and extreme oppression.

This inequality would of itself be sufficient in America to work the eventual destruction of the Union, if any mode of inforcing a compliance with its requisitions could be devised. The suffering States would not long consent to remain associated upon a principle which distributed the public burthens with so unequal a hand; and which was calculated to impoverish and oppress the citizens of some States, while those of others would scarcely be conscious of the small proportion of the weight they were required to sustain. This however is an evil inseparable from the principle of quotas and requisitions.

23

ALEXANDER HAMILTON, FEDERALIST, NO. 22, 135–41, 143–46
14 Dec. 1787

In addition to the defects already enumerated in the existing Foederal system, there are others of not less importance, which concur in rendering it altogether unfit for the administration of the affairs of the Union.

The want of a power to regulate commerce is by all parties allowed to be of the number. The utility of such a power has been anticipated under the first head of our inquiries; and for this reason as well as from the universal conviction entertained upon the subject, little need be added in this place. It is indeed evident, on the most superficial view, that there is no object, either as it respects the interests of trade or finance that more strongly demands a Foederal superintendence. The want of it has already operated as a bar to the formation of beneficial treaties with foreign powers; and has given occasions of dissatisfaction between the States. No nation acquainted with the nature of our political association would be unwise enough to enter into stipulations with the United States, by which they conceded privileges of any importance to them, while they were apprised that the engagements on the part of the Union, might at any moment be violated by its members; and while they found from experience that they might enjoy every advantage they desired in our markets, without granting us any return, but such as their momentary convenience might suggest. It is not therefore to be wondered at, that Mr. Jenkinson in ushering into the House of Commons a bill for regulating the temporary intercourse between the two countries, should preface its introduction by a declaration that similar provisions in former bills had been found to answer every purpose to the commerce of Great Britain, & that it would be prudent to persist in the plan until it should appear whether the American government was likely or not to acquire greater consistency.

Several States have endeavoured by separate prohibitions, restrictions and exclusions, to influence the conduct of that kingdom in this particular; but the want of concert, arising from the want of a general authority, and from clashing, and dissimilar views in the States, has hitherto frustrated every experiment of the kind; and will continue

to do so as long as the same obstacles to an uniformity of measures continue to exist.

The interfering and unneighbourly regulations of some states contrary to the true spirit of the Union, have in different instances given just cause of umbrage and complaint to others; and it is to be feared that examples of this nature, if not restrained by a national controul, would be multiplied and extended till they became not less serious sources of animosity and discord, than injurious impediments to the intercourse between the different parts of the confederacy. "The commerce of the German empire,* is in continual trammels from the multiplicity of the duties which the several Princes and States exact upon the merchandizes passing through their territories; by means of which the fine streams and navigable rivers with which Germany is so happily watered, are rendered almost useless." Though the genius of the people of this country might never permit this description to be strictly applicable to us, yet we may reasonably expect, from the gradual conflicts of State regulations, that the citizens of each, would at length come to be considered and treated by the others in no better light than that of foreigners and aliens.

The power of raising armies, by the most obvious construction of the articles of the confederation, is merely a power of making requisitions upon the States for quotas of men. This practice, in the course of the late war, was found replete with obstructions to a vigorous and to an oeconomical system of defence. It gave birth to a competition between the States, which created a kind of auction for men. In order to furnish the quotas required of them, they outbid each other, till bounties grew to an enormous and insupportable size. The hope of a still further increase afforded an inducement to those who were disposed to serve to procrastinate their inlistment; and disinclined them to engaging for any considerable periods. Hence slow and scanty levies of men in the most critical emergencies of our affairs—short inlistments at an unparalleled expence—continual fluctuations in the troops, ruinous to their discipline, and subjecting the public safety frequently to the perilous crisis of a disbanded army. Hence also those oppressive expedients for raising men which were upon several occasions practised, and which nothing but the enthusiasm of liberty would have induced the people to endure.

This method of raising troops is not more unfriendly to oeconomy and vigor, than it is to an equal distribution of the burthen. The States near the seat of war, influenced by motives of self preservation, made efforts to furnish their quotas, which even exceeded their abilities, while those at a distance from danger were for the most part as remiss as the others were diligent in their exertions. The immediate pressure of this inequality was not in this case, as in that of the contributions of money, alleviated by the hope of a final liquidation. The States which did not pay their proportions of money, might at least be charged with their deficiencies; but no account could be formed of the deficiencies in the supplies of men. We shall not, however, see much reason to regret the want of this hope, when we

Encyclopedie article *empire*.

consider how little prospect there is, that the most delinquent States will ever be able to make compensation for their pecuniary failures. The system of quotas and requisitions, whether it be applied to men or money, is in every view a system of imbecility in the union, and of inequality and injustice among the members.

The right of equal suffrage among the States is another exceptionable part of the confederation. Every idea of proportion, and every rule of fair representation conspire to condemn a principle, which gives to Rhode-Island an equal weight in the scale of power with Massachusetts, or Connecticut, or New-York; and to Delaware, an equal voice in the national deliberations with Pennsylvania or Virginia, or North-Carolina. Its operation contradicts that fundamental maxim of republican government, which requires that the sense of the majority should prevail. Sophistry may reply, that sovereigns are equal, and that a majority of the votes of the States will be a majority of confederated America. But this kind of logical legerdemain will never counteract the plain suggestions of justice and common sense. It may happen that this majority of States is a small minority of the people of America;* and two thirds of the people of America, could not long be persuaded, upon the credit of artificial distinctions and syllogistic subtleties, to submit their interests to the management and disposal of one third. The larger States would after a while revolt from the idea of receiving the law from the smaller. To acquiesce in such a privation of their due importance in the political scale, would be not merely to be insensible to the love of power, but even to sacrifice the desire of equality. It is neither rational to expect the first, nor just to require the last—the smaller States considering how peculiarly their safety and welfare depend on union, ought readily to renounce a pretension; which, if not relinquished would prove fatal to its duration.

It may be objected to this, that not seven but nine States, or two thirds of the whole number must consent to the most important resolutions; and it may be thence inferred, that nine States would always comprehend a majority of the inhabitants of the Union. But this does not obviate the impropriety of an equal vote between States of the most unequal dimensions and populousness; nor is the inference accurate in point of fact; for we can enumerate nine States which contain less than a majority of the people;† and it is constitutionally possible, that these nine may give the vote. Besides there are matters of considerable moment determinable by a bare majority; and there are others, concerning which doubts have been entertained, which if interpreted in favor of the sufficiency of a vote of seven States, would extend its operation to interests of the first magnitude. In addition to this, it is to be observed, that there is a probability of an increase in the number of States, and no provision for a proportional augmentation of the ratio of votes.

*New-Hampshire, Rhode-Island, New-Jersey, Delaware, Georgia, South-Carolina and Maryland, are a majority of the whole number of the States, but they do not contain one third of the people.

†Add New-York and Connecticut, to the foregoing seven, and they will still be less than a majority.

But this is not all; what at first sight may seem a remedy, is in reality a poison. To give a minority a negative upon the majority (which is always the case where more than a majority is requisite to a decision) is in its tendency to subject the sense of the greater number to that of the lesser number. Congress from the non-attendance of a few States have been frequently in the situation of a Polish Diet, where a single veto has been sufficient to put a stop to all their movements. A sixtieth part of the Union, which is about the proportion of Delaware and Rhode-Island, has several times been able to oppose an intire bar to its operations. This is one of those refinements which in practice has an effect, the reverse of what is expected from it in theory. The necessity of unanimity in public bodies, or of something approaching towards it, has been founded upon a supposition that it would contribute to security. But its real operation is to embarrass the administration, to destroy the energy of government, and to substitute the pleasure, caprice or artifices of an insignificant, turbulent or corrupt junto, to the regular deliberations and decisions of a respectable majority. In those emergencies of a nation, in which the goodness or badness, the weakness or strength of its government, is of the greatest importance, there is commonly a necessity for action. The public business must in some way or other go forward. If a pertinacious minority can controul the opinion of a majority respecting the best mode of conducting it; the majority in order that something may be done, must conform to the views of the minority; and thus the sense of the smaller number will over-rule that of the greater, and give a tone to the national proceedings. Hence tedious delays—continual negotiation and intrigue—contemptible compromises of the public good. And yet in such a system, it is even happy when such compromises can take place: For upon some occasions, things will not admit of accommodation; and then the measures of government must be injuriously suspended or fatally defeated. It is often, by the impracticability of obtaining the concurrence of the necessary number of votes, kept in a state of inaction. Its situation must always savour of weakness—sometimes border upon anarchy.

It is not difficult to discover that a principle of this kind gives greater scope to foreign corruption as well as to domestic faction, than that which permits the sense of the majority to decide; though the contrary of this has been presumed. The mistake has proceeded from not attending with due care to the mischiefs that may be occasioned by obstructing the progress of government at certain critical seasons. When the concurrence of a large number is required by the constitution to the doing of any national act, we are apt to rest satisfied that all is safe, because nothing improper will be likely *to be done;* but we forget how much good may be prevented, and how much ill may be produced, by the power of hindering the doing what may be necessary, and of keeping affairs in the same unfavorable posture in which they may happen to stand at particular periods.

. . . . .

A circumstance, which crowns the defects of the confederation, remains yet to be mentioned—the want of a judiciary power. Laws are a dead letter without courts to expound and define their true meaning and operation. The treaties of the United States to have any force at all, must be considered as part of the law of the land. Their true import as far as respects individuals, must, like all other laws, be ascertained by judicial determinations. To produce uniformity in these determinations, they ought to be submitted in the last resort, to one SUPREME TRIBUNAL. And this tribunal ought to be instituted under the same authority which forms the treaties themselves. These ingredients are both indispensable. If there is in each State, a court of final jurisdiction, there may be as many different final determinations on the same point, as there are courts. There are endless diversities in the opinions of men. We often see not only different courts, but the Judges of the same court differing from each other. To avoid the confusion which would unavoidably result from the contradictory decisions of a number of independent judicatories, all nations have found it necessary to establish one court paramount to the rest—possessing a general superintendance, and authorised to settle and declare in the last resort, an uniform rule of civil justice.

This is the more necessary where the frame of the government is so compounded, that the laws of the whole are in danger of being contravened by the laws of the parts. In this case if the particular tribunals are invested with a right of ultimate jurisdiction, besides the contradictions to be expected from difference of opinion, there will be much to fear from the bias of local views and prejudices, and from the interference of local regulations. As often as such an interference was to happen, there would be reason to apprehend, that the provisions of the particular laws might be preferred to those of the general laws; for nothing is more natural to men in office, than to look with peculiar deference towards that authority to which they owe their official existence.

The treaties of the United States, under the present constitution, are liable to the infractions of thirteen different Legislatures, and as many different courts of final jurisdiction, acting under the authority of those Legislatures. The faith, the reputation, the peace of the whole union, are thus continually at the mercy of the prejudices, the passions, and the interests of every member of which it is composed. Is it possible that foreign nations can either respect or confide in such a government? Is it possible that the People of America will longer consent to trust their honor, their happiness, their safety, on so precarious a foundation?

In this review of the Confederation, I have confined myself to the exhibition of its most material defects; passing over those imperfections in its details, by which even a great part of the power intended to be conferred upon it has been in a great measure rendered abortive. It must be by this time evident to all men of reflection, who can divest themselves of the prepossessions of preconceived opinions, that it is a system so radically vicious and unsound, as to admit not of amendment but by an entire change in its leading features and characters.

The organization of Congress, is itself utterly improper for the exercise of those powers which are necessary to be deposited in the Union. A single Assembly may be a proper receptacle of those slender, or rather fettered authorities, which have been heretofore delegated to the foederal head; but it would be inconsistent with all the principles of good government, to intrust it with those additional powers which even the moderate and more rational adversaries of the proposed constitution admit ought to reside in the United States. If that plan should not be adopted; and if the necessity of union should be able to withstand the ambitious aims of those men, who may indulge magnificent schemes of personal aggrandizement from its dissolution; the probability would be, that we should run into the project of conferring supplementary powers upon Congress as they are now constituted; and either the machine, from the intrinsic feebleness of its structure, will moulder into pieces in spite of our ill-judged efforts to prop it; or by successive augmentations of its force and energy, as necessity might prompt, we shall finally accumulate in a single body, all the most important prerogatives of sovereignty; and thus entail upon our posterity, one of the most execrable forms of government that human infatuation ever contrived. Thus we should create in reality that very tyranny, which the adversaries of the new constitution either are, or affect to be solicitous to avert.

It has not a little contributed to the infirmities of the existing foederal system, that it never had a ratification by the PEOPLE. Resting on no better foundation than the consent of the several Legislatures; it has been exposed to frequent and intricate questions concerning the validity of its powers; and has in some instances given birth to the enormous doctrine of a right of legislative repeal. Owing its ratification to the law of a State, it has been contended, that the same authority might repeal the law by which it was ratified. However gross a heresy it may be, to maintain that *a party* to *a compact* has a right to revoke that *compact,* the doctrine itself has had respectable advocates. The possibility of a question of this nature, proves the necessity of laying the foundations of our national government deeper than in the mere sanction of delegated authority. The fabric of American Empire ought to rest on the solid basis of THE CONSENT OF THE PEOPLE. The streams of national power ought to flow immediately from that pure original fountain of all legitimate authority.

24

CENTINEL, NO. 6
22 Dec. 1787
Storing 2.7.102–3

Man is the glory, jest, and riddle of the world.—Pope.

Incredible transition! the people who, seven years ago, deemed every earthly good, every other consideration, as worthless, when placed in competition with liberty, that heaven-born blessing, that zest of all others; the people, who, actuated by this noble ardor of patriotism, rose superior to every weakness of humanity, and shone with such dazzling lustre amidst the greatest difficulties; who, emulous of eclipsing each other in the glorious assertion of the dignity of human nature, courted every danger, and were ever ready, when necessary, to lay down their lives at the altar of liberty: I say the people, who exhibited so lately a spectacle, that commanded the admiration, and drew the plaudits of the most distant nations, are now reversing the picture, are now lost to every noble principle, are about to sacrifice that inestimable jewel liberty, to the genius of despotism. A *golden phantom* held out to them, by the crafty and aspiring despots among themselves, is alluring them into the fangs of arbitrary power; and so great is their infatuation, that it seems, as if nothing short of the reality of misery necessarily attendant on slavery, will rouse them from their false confidence, or convince them of the direful deception: but then alas! it will be too late, the chains of despotism will be fast rivetted and all escape precluded.

For years past, the harpies of power have been industriously inculcating the idea that all our difficulties proceed from the impotency of Congress, and have at length succeeded to give to this sentiment almost universal currency and belief: the devastations, losses and burthens occasioned by the late war; the excessive importations of foreign merchandise and luxuries, which have drained the country of its specie and involved it in debt, are all overlooked, and the inadequacy of the powers of the present confederation is erroneously supposed to be the only cause of our difficulties; hence persons of every description are revelling in the anticipation of the halcyon days, consequent on the establishment of the new constitution.—What gross deception and fatal delusion! Although very considerable benefit might be derived from strengthening the hands of Congress, so as to enable them to regulate commerce, and counteract the adverse restrictions of other nations, which would meet with the concurrence of all persons; yet this benefit, is accompanied in the new constitution with the scourge of despotic power, that will render the citizens of America tenants at will of every species of property, of every enjoyment, and make them the meer drudges of government. The gilded bait conceals corrosives that will eat up their whole substance.

25

FEDERAL FARMER, NO. 17
23 Jan. 1788
Storing 2.8.205–7

I am not about to defend the confederation, or to charge the proposed constitution with imperfections not in it; but we ought to examine facts, and strip them of the false colourings often given them by incautious observations, by unthinking or designing men. We ought to premise, that laws for raising men and monies, even in consolidated

governments, are not often punctually complied with. Historians, except in extraordinary cases, but very seldom take notice of the detail collection of taxes: but these facts we have fully proved, and well attested; that the most energetic governments have relinquished taxes frequently, which were of many years standing. These facts amply prove, that taxes assessed, have remained many years uncollected. I agree there have been instances in the republics of Greece, Holland &c. in the course of several centuries, of states neglecting to pay their quotas of requisitions; but it is a circumstance certainly deserving of attention, whether these nations which have depended on requisitions principally for their defence, have not raised men and monies nearly as punctually as entire governments, which have taxed directly; whether we have not found the latter as often distressed for the want of troops and monies as the former. It has been said that the Amphictionic council, and the Germanic head, have not possessed sufficient powers to controul the members of the republic in a proper manner. Is this, if true, to be imputed to requisitions? Is it not principally to be imputed to the unequal powers of those members, connected with this important circumstance, that each member possessed power to league itself with foreign powers, and powerful neighbours, without the consent of the head. After all, has not the Germanic body a government as good as its neighbours in general? and did not the Grecian republic remain united several centuries, and form the theatre of human greatness? No government in Europe has commanded monies more plentifully than the government of Holland. As to the United States, the separate states lay taxes directly, and the union calls for taxes by way of requisitions; and is it a fact, that more monies are due in proportion on requisitions in the United States, than on the state taxes directly laid?—It is but about ten years since congress begun to make requisitions, and in that time, the monies, &c. required, and the bounties given for men required of the states, have amounted, specie value, to about 36 million dollars, about 24 millions of dollars of which have been actually paid; and a very considerable part of the 12 millions not paid, remains so not so much from the neglect of the states, as from the sudden changes in paper money, &c. which in a great measure rendered payments of no service, and which often induced the union indirectly to relinquish one demand, by making another in a different form. Before we totally condemn requisitions, we ought to consider what immense bounties the states gave, and what prodigious exertions they made in the war, in order to comply with the requisitions of congress; and if since the peace they have been delinquent, ought we not carefully to enquire, whether that delinquency is to be imputed solely to the nature of requisitions? ought it not in part to be imputed to two other causes? I mean first, an opinion, that has extensively prevailed, that the requisitions for domestic interest have not been founded on just principles; and secondly, the circumstance, that the government itself, by proposing imposts, &c. has departed virtually from the constitutional system; which proposed changes, like all changes proposed in government, produce an inattention and negligence in the execution of the government in being.

I am not for depending wholly on requisitions; but I mention these few facts to shew they are not so totally futile as many pretend. For the truth of many of these facts I appeal to the public records; and for the truth of the others, I appeal to many republican characters, who are best informed in the affairs of the United States. Since the peace, and till the convention reported, the wisest men in the United States generally supposed, that certain limited funds would answer the purposes of the union: and though the states are by no means in so good a condition as I wish they were, yet, I think, I may very safely affirm, they are in a better condition than they would be had congress always possessed the powers of taxation now contended for. The fact is admitted, that our federal government does not possess sufficient powers to give life and vigor to the political system; and that we experience disappointments, and several inconveniences; but we ought carefully to distinguish those which are merely the consequences of a severe and tedious war, from those which arise from defects in the federal system. There has been an entire revolution in the United States within thirteen years, and the least we can compute the waste of labour and property at, during that period, by the war, is three hundred million of dollars. Our people are like a man just recovering from a severe fit of sickness. It was the war that disturbed the course of commerce, introduced floods of paper money, the stagnation of credit, and threw many valuable men out of steady business. From these sources our greatest evils arise; men of knowledge and reflection must perceive it;—but then, have we not done more in three or four years past, in repairing the injuries of the war, by repairing houses and estates, restoring industry, frugality, the fisheries, manufactures, &c. and thereby laying the foundation of good government, and of individual and political happiness, than any people ever did in a like time; we must judge from a view of the country and facts, and not from foreign newspapers, or our own, which are printed chiefly in the commercial towns, where imprudent living, imprudent importations, and many unexpected disappointments, have produced a despondency, and a disposition to view every thing on the dark side. Some of the evils we feel, all will agree, ought to be imputed to the defective administration of the governments. From these and various considerations, I am very clearly of opinion, that the evils we sustain, merely on account of the defects of the confederation, are but as a feather in the balance against a mountain, compared with those which would, infallibly, be the result of the loss of general liberty, and that happiness men enjoy under a frugal, free, and mild government.

Heretofore we do not seem to have seen danger any where, but in giving power to congress, and now no where but in congress wanting powers; and, without examining the extent of the evils to be remedied, by one step, we are for giving up to congress almost all powers of any importance without limitation. The defects of the confederation are extravagantly magnified, and every species of pain we feel imputed to them: and hence it is inferred, there must be a total change of the principles, as well as forms of government: and in the main point, touching the federal powers, we rest all on a logical inference, totally inconsistent with experience and sound political reasoning.

26

A PLEBEIAN, AN ADDRESS TO THE PEOPLE OF THE STATE OF NEW-YORK
Spring 1788
Storing 6.11.5–7, 22

It is insisted, that the present situation of our country is such, as not to admit of a delay in forming a new government, or of time sufficient to deliberate and agree upon the amendments which are proper, without involving ourselves in a state of anarchy and confusion.

On this head, all the powers of rhetoric, and arts of description, are employed to paint the condition of this country, in the most hideous and frightful colours. We are told, that agriculture is without encouragement; trade is languishing; private faith and credit are disregarded, and public credit is prostrate; that the laws and magistrates are contemned and set at nought; that a spirit of licentiousness is rampant, and ready to break over every bound set to it by the government; that private embarrassments and distresses invade the house of every man of middling property, and insecurity threatens every man in affluent circumstances: in short, that we are in a state of the most grievous calamity at home, and that we are contemptible abroad, the scorn of foreign nations, and the ridicule of the world. From this high-wrought picture, one would suppose, that we were in a condition the most deplorable of any people upon earth. But suffer me, my countrymen, to call your attention to a serious and sober estimate of the situation in which you are placed, while I trace the embarrassments under which you labour, to their true sources. What is your condition? Does not every man sit under his own vine and under his own fig-tree, having none to make him afraid? Does not every one follow his calling without impediments and receive the reward of his well-earned industry? The farmer cultivates his land, and reaps the fruit which the bounty of heaven bestows on his honest toil. The mechanic is exercised in his art, and receives the reward of his labour. The merchant drives his commerce, and none can deprive him of the gain he honestly acquires; all classes and callings of men amongst us are protected in their various pursuits, and secured by the laws in the possession and enjoyment of the property obtained in those pursuits. The laws are as well executed as they ever were, in this or any other country. Neither the hand of private violence, nor the more to be dreaded hand of legal oppression, are reached out to distress us.

It is true, many individuals labour under embarrassments, but these are to be imputed to the unavoidable circumstances of things, rather than to any defect in our governments. We have just emerged from a long and expensive war. During its existence few people were in a situation to encrease their fortunes, but many to diminish them. Debts contracted before the war were left unpaid while it existed, and these were left a burden too heavy to be borne at the commencement of peace. Add to these, that when the war was over, too many of us, instead of reassuming our old habits of frugality and industry, by which alone every country must be placed in a prosperous condition, took up the profuse use of foreign commodities. The country was deluged with articles imported from abroad, and the cash of the country has been sent out to pay for them, and still left us labouring under the weight of a huge debt to persons abroad. These are the true sources to which we are to trace all the private difficulties of individuals: But will a new government relieve you from these? The advocates for it have not yet told you how it will do it—And I will venture to pronounce, that there is but one way in which it can be effected, and that is by industry and oeconomy; limit your expences within your earnings; sell more than you buy, and every thing will be well on this score. Your present condition is such as is common to take place after the conclusion of a war. Those who can remember our situation after the termination of the war preceding the last, will recollect that our condition was similar to the present, but time and industry soon recovered us from it. Money was scarce, the produce of the country much lower than it has been since the peace, and many individuals were extremely embarrassed with debts; and this happened, although we did not experience the ravages, desolations, and loss of property, that were suffered during the late war.

With regard to our public and national concerns, what is there in our condition that threatens us with any immediate danger? We are at peace with all the world; no nation menaces us with war; Nor are we called upon by any cause of sufficient importance to attack any nation. The state governments answer the purposes of preserving the peace, and providing for present exigencies. Our condition as a nation is in no respect worse than it has been for several years past. Our public debt has been lessened in various ways, and the western territory, which has always been relied upon as a productive fund to discharge the national debt, has at length been brought to market, and a considerable part actually applied to its reduction. I mention these things to shew, that there is nothing special, in our present situation, as it respects our national affairs, that should induce us to accept the proffered system, without taking sufficient time to consider and amend it. I do not mean by this, to insinuate, that our government does not stand in need of a reform. It is admitted by all parties, that alterations are necessary in our federal constitution, but the circumstances of our case do by no means oblige us to precipitate this business, or require that we should adopt a system materially defective. We may safely take time to deliberate and amend, without in the mean time hazarding a condition, in any considerable degree, worse than the present.

. . . . .

Far be it from me to object to granting the general government the power of regulating trade, and of laying imposts and duties for that purpose, as well as for raising a

revenue: But it is as far from me to flatter people with hopes of benefits to be derived from such a change in our government, which can never be realized. Some advantages may accrue from vesting in one general government, the right to regulate commerce, but it is a vain delusion to expect any thing like what is promised. The truth is, this country buys more than it sells: It imports more than it exports. There are too many merchants in proportion to the farmers and manufacturers. Until these defects are remedied, no government can relieve us. Common sense dictates, that if a man buys more than he sells, he will remain in debt; the same is true of a country.—And as long as this country imports more goods than she exports—the overplus must be paid for in money or not paid at all. These few remarks may convince us, that the radical remedy for the scarcity of cash is frugality and industry. Earn much and spend little, and you will be enabled to pay your debts, and have money in your pockets; and if you do not follow this advice, no government that can be framed, will relieve you.

27

IMPARTIAL EXAMINER, NO. 5
18 June 1788
Storing 5.14.41–49

When a change, so momentous in it's nature, as that of new modelling a *plan* of government, becomes the object of any people's meditation, every citizen, whose mind is duly impressed with a regard for the welfare of his country, will consider himself under an indispensible obligation to make some such enquiries, as the following.—Whence flows the necessity of a change?—Does it proceed from certain *vicious properties*, which reside in the old system and form the essential parts of it?—Or will such a measure become eligible, because *evils* have arisen from the feeble texture of the plan, or a loose exercise of government, which could not well be avoided?—What are the *evils* complained of? and what will be their correspondent remedies?—Are the evils *radical*, and not be removed but by a *general* reform throughout the constitution?—Or do they result from a defect in some particular branch only? and may an adequate remedy be effected by introducing a new regulation merely as to *that* branch?

If investigations like these are seriously and dispassionately pursued, and it should be found that the present confederation of the American states contains *vicious properties*, which are inherent, fundamental, and tending to produce a general corruption, the *necessity of a change* must then be manifest. This discovery will lead to another enquiry; and that is—Do such properties pervade the whole system and contaminate all the parts of it? If so—then a *thorough change* will appear to be expedient, and it may be necessary to new model the system.

If, on the other hand, *evils* are found existing, which

proceed, not so much from any internal corrupt *qualities,* as from the *feeble texture* of any parts of the system, or a *laxity* in the exercise of it's powers, it should seem advise-able to make alterations so far as to add a due degree of strength to the *weak parts,* and thereby insure *efficacy* in the government.

Should it appear, after a proper enquiry into the nature of the evils, that they are *radical,* and strike at the *vital principles* of the constitution—then to apply a *correspondent remedy,* an institution, which would produce a *general reform,* might with great propriety be deemed requisite.

If the defects are of a trivial nature, and subsist merely in some particular department or branch of the system— then amendments in the *defective branch,* tending to give energy where it had hitherto been wanting, would be am-ply sufficient for removing the *evils* and forming a com-petent remedy.

In order to discover how far the present system is vi-cious, or inadequate to the purposes of *this* great confed-erated society, for which it was established, a retrospect of the *original design* of the confederacy *itself* may afford no small degree of assistance.—Let it be recollected, then, that the *primary* object was to *form a perfect union.* This is mani-fested by the very "stile of the confederacy."—That it was intended to promote *justice* equally between all the states cannot be doubted; because it is an institution, calculated to unite a number of *independent republics* under a *firm league* of amity, and to provide that contributions of every kind, which had been, or might be, necessary towards sup-porting their *general* government, should be furnished in due proportions—whilst it was stipulated that a *mutual in-tercourse* and *reciprocal privileges* and *immunities* should sub-sist between the citizens of *all* the several states. Again, to *ensure domestic tranquility* must have been another impor-tant object with the framers of this confederation: for union, harmony and justice cannot fail to promote tran-quility; and whenever a contract is formed for the purpose of procuring the *three first,* it follows, as a regular conse-quence, that the *other* should partake of the intention.— This great association is expressly declared to be entered into between the states "for their common defence, the se-curity of their liberties, and their mutual and general wel-fare, binding themselves to assist each other against all force offered to, or attacks made upon, them, or any of them, on account of religion, sovereignty, trade, or any other pretence whatever."

The objects herein recited do certainly form the chief design of the present confederation; and the same are de-clared to be the great *ends* of the *proposed* plan of govern-ment. So far then do they agree. A subject of much con-tention, however, and with which the minds of different citizens are variously agitated, has arose.

It has been said that some of *these advantages,* and of high import too, cannot be obtained under the present system. It is the opinion of some citizens that the consti-tution proposed to us will secure all *these objects* and form a complete remedy for every *evil* now subsisting; whilst it is asserted by others that amendments might be intro-duced in the former, which would be competent to every *good* purpose, and promote *some* of very great conse-

quence, that might be endangered by an adoption of the latter. Thus it is inferred that *this* system extends too far— and, like many human institutions, flits by a rapid progress from *one* extreme to *another.*

Those, who cannot approve of this plan, have very strong objections to it, because they apprehend that no *se-curity for their liberties* will remain after it's adoption: and although some of the *ends* proposed might be obtained thereby; yet they think the sacrifice will be too great for the benefit to be received. To enjoy a competent degree of *liberty* they consider as the greatest of human blessings— for the loss of which no acquisitions whatsoever can com-pensate. They esteem this (and deservedly too) as the *soul* of *all* political happiness.

It seems to be agreed on all sides that in the present system of union the Congress are not invested with suffi-cient powers for *regulating commerce,* and procuring the *requisite contributions* for all expences, that may be incurred for the *common defence* or *general welfare.* Hence arise the *principal* defects;—and it is presumed that the *evils* result-ing from *these weak* branches in the foederal government might be adequately remedied by making due amend-ments merely *therein.*

It is thought by some that the powers of making and enforcing the observance of treaties are not ample enough at present. If so—cannot these be enlarged so as to answer every desirable purpose of *that branch* in the foederal insti-tution? Thus, while many citizens cannot think that the confederation is *fundamentally vicious,* but that all the *evils* now complained of do rather proceed from a weakness in some of its parts, they apprehend no necessity for an in-novation further than strengthening *those parts.* If such measures were effectually established, they conceive that all the great ends of the *general* government might be pro-moted.—No contention, therefore, subsists about support-ing a *union,* but only concerning the *mode;* and as well those, who disapprove of the proposed plan, as those, who approve of it, consider the existence of a *union* as essential to their happiness.

28

DAVID HUMPHREYS TO THOMAS JEFFERSON
29 Nov. 1788
Jefferson Papers 14:300–301

There has been an extraordinary revolution in the senti-ments of men, respecting political affairs, since I came to America; and much more favorable in the result than could then have been reasonably expected. At the close of the war, after the little season of unlimited credit was passed, the people in moderate circumstances found themselves very much embarrassed by the scarcity of money, by debts and taxes. They affected to think that the part of Society composed of men in the liberal professions and those who had considerable property were in combination to distress them, and to establish an Aristocracy. Demagogues made use of these impressions to procure their own elections and to carry their own schemes into execution. Lawyers, in some States, by these artifices, became indiscriminately odious. In others men of the strongest local prejudices and narrowest principles had the whole direction of the affairs of their States. You will feel the force of this assertion the more readily, when you shall have been informed that the same Genl. Wadsworth, who was in Congress with you at Annapolis became, in conjunction with two or three of his Subalterns the director of every political measure in Connecticut; and prevented, in almost every instance, a compliance with the Requisitions of Congress. On the other part, great numbers of those who wished to see an efficient foederal government prevail, began to fear that the bulk of the people would never submit to it. In short some of them, who had been utterly averse to Royalty, began to imagine that hardly anything but a king could cure the evil. It was truly astonishing to have been witness to some conversations, which I have heard. Still all the more reasonable men saw that the remedy would be infinitely worse than the disease. In this fluctuating and irritable situation the public mind continued, for some time. The insurrection in Massachusetts was not without its benefits. From a view of the impotence of the general government, of the contempt in which we were held abroad and of the want of happiness at home, the Public was thus gradually wrought to a disposition for receiving a government possessed of sufficient energy to prevent the calamities of Anarchy and civil war; and yet guarded, as well as the nature of circumstances will admit, so as to prevent it from degenerating into Aristocracy, Oligarchy or Monarchy. True it is, that honest and wise men have differed in sentiment about the kind of checks and balances which are necessary for this purpose: but equally true it is that there is not an honest and wise man who does not see and feel the indispensable necessity of preserving the Union.

SEE ALSO:

George Washington to George Mason, 27 Mar. 1779, Mason Papers 2:493–94

Alexander Hamilton to George Washington, 13 Feb. 1783, Papers 3:253–55

Gouverneur Morris to Gen. Nathanael Greene, 15 Feb. 1783, Life 1:250–51

Hugh Williamson to James Iredell, 17 Feb. 1783, Iredell Papers 2:377

Gen. Henry Knox to Gouverneur Morris, 21 Feb. 1783, Morris Life 1:256

Gen. Nathanael Greene to Gouverneur Morris, 3 Apr. 1783, Morris Life 1:251–52

John Jay to Alexander Hamilton, 28 Sept. 1783, Wharton 6:705–6

Richard Henry Lee to James Monroe, 5 Jan. 1784, Letters 2:289

Resolutions of the General Court of Massachusetts, 1 July 1785, King Life 1:58

Delegates of Massachusetts in Congress to Gov. James Bowdoin, 18 Aug. 1785, King Life 1:59

Delegates of Massachusetts in Congress to Gov. James Bowdoin, 3 Sept. 1785, King Life 1:60–66

Nathan Dane to Rufus King, 8 Oct. 1785, King Life 1:67–70

William Grayson to James Madison, 22 Mar. 1786, Madison Papers 8:509–10

James Madison to Edmund Pendleton, 24 Feb. 1787, Papers 9:294–95

Henry Knox to Mercy Warren, 30 May 1787, Warren-Adams Letters 2:294–95

Candidus, no. 1, 6 Dec. 1787, Storing 4.9.18

John Jay, An Address to the People of the State of New York, Spring 1788, Correspondence 3:296–301

Impartial Examiner, no. 1, 20 Feb. 1788, Storing 5.14.1

6

Convention

Introduction

Whatever its defects, the Continental Congress created by the Articles of Confederation was indeed the government of the United States. It was the government the British had come to recognize, to which the Dutch bankers had lent money, and which the Algerine pirates continued to treat with contempt. It was the government the moving spirits behind the Philadelphia Convention would continue to acknowledge until it was replaced by their own creature. The fact that there already was a federal government naturally raised questions about the status of the 1787 Convention and its handiwork.

At the outset, though, not much was made of the irregularities attending the business since all that seemed in prospect was a conference of sorts that might recommend some amendments to the Articles. When the proposed reforms turned out to be nothing less than a revolutionary reconstruction of government, harder questions were asked. And when, finally, the plan was forwarded to the several state ratifying conventions for the consent of the people on terms that directly violated the Articles' provision for amendment, there was no blinking the fact that the Philadelphia Convention had acted beyond its authority.

Constitution making by convention was certainly known to Americans, who had the respectable example of Massachusetts before them, but it was by no means the inevitable course. Indeed, in some regards it was the least eligible mode of proceeding "to render the constitution of the Federal Government adequate to the exigencies of the Union." For, to begin with, the Articles provided for their own amendment—and not by convention. Then too, the adoption of extraordinary, extraconstitutional means implied an immediate denigration of the authority of the Continental Congress. It might be argued that in recommending the convening at Philadelphia and in transmitting the Convention's plan to the states (albeit without endorsement), the Congress had been guilty of a striking act of self-denigration. Finally, the proposed mode of ratification was a most radical departure in law and principle from the rule of unanimity that lay at the heart of the Articles.

Notwithstanding these difficulties, the convention proved to be the preferred mode for the very reason that made major revision or replacement of the Articles necessary in the first place: the government constituted by the Articles seemed as incapable of self-rectification as it was of energetic governance. The impatience and unwillingness to stick at fine points, illustrated by the letters of Washington (nos. 5, 8) and Madison (no. 9), show that there were indeed reasons for Patrick Henry and others to have "smelt a Rat." Anti-Federalists were correct in suspecting a hidden agenda among those who had so rapidly enlarged the objectives of the earlier Annapolis Convention (see ch. 8, no. 12). Congress, following the leads of New York and Massachusetts, reflected this suspicion by trying to narrow the terms of the proposed federal convention (even while avoiding any mention of the Annapolis proposers). Delaware gave full expression to these misgivings. Its legislature hoped to avert the unspeakable by sending delegates to Philadelphia with a most confining commission, so confining, in fact, that those terms subsequently had to be enlarged before the Delaware delegation could feel free to participate in the Convention's developing business.

Still the hard questions posed by those who challenged

the legitimacy of the Philadelphia Convention's actions could not be entirely ignored by those striving to establish a new constitution. For all the rhetoric about dictation, no party in fact was in a position to dictate anything. Accordingly, arguments (both good and bad) figured prominently. What, then, could be said in response to the charges that the whole business was a series of escalating usurpations ending in the subversion of a duly constituted government (nos. 17, 19)? The pseudonymous Republican Federalist in Massachusetts could rightly ask (9 Jan. 1788), what precedent did such behavior set for the observance of future solemn covenants? By exceeding their instructions and the provisions of state and federal constitutions, had the delegates to the Philadelphia Convention not undermined their own product?

The initial Federalist response was to declaim against petty quibbling—while engaging in some of their own. After trying to show that the Convention had left standing "good and valid" every article of the old constitution not otherwise amended or annulled (Pelatiah Webster, Oct. 1787), or that the Convention had not exceeded its powers because strictly speaking it had only recommended, much as any private individual or group might do (Wilson, no. 18), or that "the great principles of the Constitution proposed by the Convention, may be considered less as abso-lutely new, than as the expansion of principles which are found in the articles of Confederation" (Madison, no. 20)—disingenuous argument finally was put aside. Such sops to the timid sat ill with a defense that rested openly and boldly on the assertion of the radical defects of the old charter and the radical remedies of the new.

The real question, proponents of the new had to insist, was whether the Constitution was good, whether it was better than the existing arrangement. If the Convention's proposal was indeed good, then the work of those who cast aside "little ill-timed scruples," saw their duty clearly, and acted on it, would secure the approval of the people. And with that seal of popular ratification, "all antecedent errors and irregularities" would be eradicated. The procedural issues, then, ought to be subsumed under the basic principle of popular consent as the source of political authority. If the Philadelphia Convention could only propose (as was in fact the case), it remained for the people, acting through their elected delegates in state conventions, to dispose, to make or to unmake political arrangements. In exercising their incontestable right, the people should direct their attention to matters of substance, to the merits of the Constitution itself. And it was to those alleged merits that proponents and opponents alike turned their thoughts.

1

VIRGINIA GENERAL ASSEMBLY
21 Jan. 1786
Tansill 38

A motion was made, that the House do come to the following resolution:

Resolved, That Edmund Randolph, James Madison, jun. Walter Jones, Saint George Tucker and Meriwether Smith, Esquires, be appointed commissioners, who, or any three of whom, shall meet such commissioners as may be appointed by the other States in the Union, at a time and place to be agreed on, to take into consideration the trade of the United States; to examine the relative situations and trade of the said States; to consider how far a uniform system in their commercial regulations may be necessary to their common interest and their permanent harmony; and to report to the several States, such an act relative to this great object, as, when unanimously ratified by them, will enable the United States in Congress, effectually to provide for the same.

2

ANNAPOLIS CONVENTION
11–14 Sept. 1786
Tansill 39–43

Proceedings of Commissioners to Remedy Defects of the Federal Government

Annapolis in the State of Maryland
September 11th. 1786

At a meeting of Commissioners, from the States of New York, New Jersey, Pennsylvania, Delaware and Virginia—

Present

Alexander Hamilton Egbert Benson	New York
Abraham Clarke William C. Houston James Schuarman	New Jersey
Tench Coxe	Pennsylvania
George Read John Dickinson Richard Bassett	Delaware
Edmund Randolph James Madison, Junior Saint George Tucker	Virginia

Mr. Dickinson was unanimously elected Chairman.

The Commissioners produced their Credentials from their respective States; which were read.

After a full communication of Sentiments, and deliberate consideration of what would be proper to be done by the Commissioners now assembled, it was unanimously agreed: that a Committee be appointed to prepare a draft of a Report to be made to the States having Commissioners attending at this meeting—Adjourned 'till Wednesday Morning.

Wednesday September 13th. 1786

Met agreeable to Adjournment.

The Committee, appointed for that purpose, reported the draft of the report; which being read, the meeting proceeded to the consideration thereof, and after some time spent therein, Adjourned 'till tomorrow Morning.

Thursday Septr. 14th. 1786

Met agreeable to Adjournment.

The meeting resumed the consideration of the draft of the Report, and after some time spent therein, and amendments made, the same was unanimously agreed to, and is as follows, to wit.

To the Honorable, the Legislatures of Virginia, Delaware, Pennsylvania, New Jersey, and New York—
The Commissioners from the said States, respectively assembled at Annapolis, humbly beg leave to report.

That, pursuant to their several appointments, they met, at Annapolis in the State of Maryland, on the eleventh day of September Instant, and having proceeded to a Communication of their powers; they found that the States of New York, Pennsylvania, and Virginia, had, in substance, and nearly in the same terms, authorised their respective Commissioners "to meet such Commissioners as were, or might be, appointed by the other States in the Union, at such time and place, as should be agreed upon by the said Commissioners to take into consideration the trade and Commerce of the United States, to consider how far an uniform system in their commercial intercourse and regulations might be necessary to their common interest and permanent harmony, and to report to the several States such an Act, relative to this great object, as when unanimously ratified by them would enable the United States in Congress assembled effectually to provide for the same."

That the State of Delaware, had given similar powers to their Commissioners, with this difference only, that the Act to be framed in virtue of those powers, is required to be reported "to the United States in Congress assembled, to be agreed to by them, and confirmed by the Legislatures of every State."

That the State of New Jersey had enlarged the object of their appointment, empowering their Commissioners, "to consider how far an uniform system in their commercial regulations and *other important matters*, might be necessary to the common interest and permanent harmony of the several States," and to report such an Act on the subject, as when ratified by them "would enable the United States in Congress assembled, effectually to provide for the exigencies of the Union."

That appointments of Commissioners have also been made by the States of New Hampshire, Massachusetts, Rhode Island, and North Carolina, none of whom however have attended; but that no information has been received by your Commissioners, of any appointment having been made by the States of Connecticut, Maryland, South Carolina or Georgia.

That the express terms of the powers to your Commissioners supposing a deputation from all the States, and having for object the Trade and Commerce of the United States, Your Commissioners did not conceive it advisable to proceed on the business of their mission, under the Circumstance of so partial and defective a representation.

Deeply impressed however with the magnitude and importance of the object confided to them on this occasion, your Commissioners cannot forbear to indulge an expression of their earnest and unanimous wish, that speedy measures may be taken, to effect a general meeting, of the States, in a future Convention, for the same, and such other purposes, as the situation of public affairs, may be found to require.

If in expressing this wish, or in intimating any other sentiment, your Commissioners should seem to exceed the strict bounds of their appointment, they entertain a full confidence, that a conduct, dictated by an anxiety for the welfare, of the United States, will not fail to receive an indulgent construction.

In this persuasion, your Commissioners submit an opinion, that the Idea of extending the powers of their Deputies, to other objects, than those of Commerce, which has been adopted by the State of New Jersey, was an improvement on the original plan, and will deserve to be incorporated into that of a future Convention; they are the more naturally led to this conclusion, as in the course of their reflections on the subject, they have been induced to think, that the power of regulating trade is of such comprehensive extent, and will enter so far into the general System of the foederal government, that to give it efficacy, and to obviate questions and doubts concerning its precise nature and limits, may require a correspondent adjustment of other parts of the Foederal System.

That there are important defects in the system of the Foederal Government is acknowledged by the Acts of all those States, which have concurred in the present Meeting; That the defects, upon a closer examination, may be found greater and more numerous, than even these acts imply, is at least so far probable, from the embarrassments which characterise the present State of our national affairs, foreign and domestic, as may reasonably be supposed to merit a deliberate and candid discussion, in some mode, which will unite the Sentiments and Councils of all the States. In the choice of the mode, your Commissioners are of opinion, that a Convention of Deputies from the different States, for the special and sole purpose of entering into this investigation, and digesting a plan for supplying such defects as may be discovered to exist, will be entitled to a preference from considerations, which will occur, without being particularised.

Your Commissioners decline an enumeration of those national circumstances on which their opinion respecting the propriety of a future Convention, with more enlarged powers, is founded; as it would be an useless intrusion of facts and observations, most of which have been frequently the subject of public discussion, and none of which can have escaped the penetration of those to whom they would in this instance be addressed. They are however of a nature so serious, as, in the view of your Commissioners to render the situation of the United States delicate and critical, calling for an exertion of the united virtue and wisdom of all the members of the Confederacy.

Under this impression, Your Commissioners, with the most respectful deference, beg leave to suggest their unanimous conviction, that it may essentially tend to advance the interests of the union, if the States, by whom they have been respectively delegated, would themselves concur, and use their endeavours to procure the concurrence of the other States, in the appointment of Commissioners, to meet at Philadelphia on the second Monday in May next, to take into consideration the situation of the United States, to devise such further provisions as shall appear to them necessary to render the constitution of the Foederal Government adequate to the exigencies of the Union; and to report such an Act for that purpose to the United States in Congress assembled, as when agreed to, by them, and afterwards confirmed by the Legislatures of every State, will effectually provide for the same.

Though your Commissioners could not with propriety address these observations and sentiments to any but the States they have the honor to Represent, they have nevertheless concluded from motives of respect, to transmit Copies of this Report to the United States in Congress assembled, and to the executives of the other States.

By order of the Commissioners.

Dated at Annapolis }
September 14th, 1786 }

Resolved, that the Chairman sign the aforegoing Report in behalf of the Commissioners.

Then adjourned without day—

Egbt. Benson Alexander Hamilton }	New York
Abra: Clark Wm Chll. Houston Js. Schureman }	New Jersey
Tench Coxe	Pennsylvania
Geo: Read John Dickinson Richard Bassett }	Delaware
Edmund Randolph Js. Madison Jr. St. George Tucker }	Virginia

3

VIRGINIA GENERAL ASSEMBLY
1 Dec. 1786
Farrand 3:559–61

AN ACT for appointing Deputies from this Commonwealth to a Convention proposed to be held in the City of Philadelphia in May next for the purpose of revising the federal Constitution.

WHEREAS the Commissioners who assembled at Annapolis on the fourteenth day of September last for the purpose of devising and reporting the means of enabling Congress to provide effectually for the Commercial Interests of the United States have represented the necessity of extending the revision of the foederal System to all it's defects and have recommended that Deputies for that purpose be appointed by the several Legislatures to meet in Convention in the City of Philadelphia on the second day of May next a provision which was preferable to a discussion of the subject in Congress where it might be too much interrupted by the ordinary business before them and where it would besides be deprived of the valuable Counsels of sundry Individuals who are disqualified by the Constitution or Laws of particular States or restrained by peculiar circumstances from a Seat in that Assembly: AND WHEREAS the General Assembly of this Commonwealth taking into view the actual situation of the Confederacy as well as reflecting on the alarming representations made from time to time by the United States in Congress particularly in their Act of the fifteenth day of February last can no longer doubt that the Crisis is arrived at which the good People of America are to decide the solemn question whether they will by wise and magnanimous Efforts reap the just fruits of that Independence which they have so gloriously acquired and of that Union which they have cemented with so much of their common Blood, or whether by giving way to unmanly Jealousies and Prejudices or to partial and transitory Interests they will renounce the auspicious blessings prepared for them by the Revolution, and furnish to its Enemies an eventual Triumph over those by whose virtue and valor it has been accomplished: AND WHEREAS the same noble and extended policy and the same fraternal and affectionate Sentiments which originally determined the Citizens of this Commonwealth to unite with their Brethren of the other States in establishing a Foederal Government cannot but be Felt with equal force now as motives to lay aside every inferior consideration and to concur in such farther concessions and Provisions as may be necessary to secure the great Objects for which that Government was instituted and to render the *United States* as happy in peace as they have been glorious in War BE IT THEREFORE ENACTED by the General Assembly of the Commonwealth of Virginia that seven Commissioners be appointed by joint Ballot of both Houses of Assembly who or any three of them are hereby authorized as Deputies from this Commonwealth to meet such Deputies as may be appointed and authorized by other States to assemble in Convention at Philadelphia as above recommended and to join with them in devising and discussing all such Alterations and farther Provisions as may be necessary to render the Foederal Constitution adequate to the Exigencies of the Union and in reporting such an Act for that purpose to the United States in Congress as when agreed to by them and duly confirmed by the several States will effectually provide for the same. AND BE IT FURTHER ENACTED that in case of the death of any of the said Deputies or of their declining their appointments the Executive are hereby authorized to supply such Vacancies. AND the Governor is requested to transmit forthwith a Copy of this Act to the United States in Congress and to the Executives of each of the States in the Union.

4

JOHN JAY TO GEORGE WASHINGTON
7 Jan. 1787
MS Columbia Univ.

A convention is in Contemplation, and I am glad to find your name among those of its intended members.

To me the policy of *such* a Convention appears questionable. Their authority is to be derived from Acts of the State Legislatures. Are the State Legislatures authorized, either by Themselves or others, to alter constitutions[?] I think not. They who hold commissions, can by virtue of them neither retrench nor Extend the Powers conveyed by them.

Perhaps it is intended that this Convention shall not ordain, but only recommend. If so, there is Danger that their Recommendations will produce endless Discussion, and perhaps Jealousies and party Heats.

Would it not be better for Congress plainly and in strong Terms to declare that the present federal Government is inadequate to the purposes for which it was instituted. That they forbear to point out its particular Defects or to ask for an Extension of any particular powers, lest improper Jealousies should thence arise; but that in their opinion it would be expedient for the people of the States without Delay to appoint State Conventions (in the way they chuse the general assemblies) with the sole and express power of appointing Deputies to a general Convention who or the majority of whom should take into Consideration the Articles of Confederation, and make such Alterations, amendments and additions Thereto, as to them should appear necessary and proper and which being by them ordained and published should have the same force and Obligation which all or any of the present Articles now have.

No alteration in the Government should I think be made, nor if attempted will easily take place, unless deduceable from the only Source of just authority, *The People*.

5

GEORGE WASHINGTON TO HENRY KNOX
3 Feb. 1787
Writings 29:152–53

The legality of this Convention I do not mean to discuss, nor how problematical the issue of it may be. That powers are wanting, none can deny. Through what medium they are to be derived, will, like other matters, engage public attention. That which takes the shortest course to obtain them, will, in my opinion, under present circumstances, be found best. Otherwise, like a house on fire, whilst the most regular mode of extinguishing it is contended for, the building is reduced to ashes. My opinion of the energetic wants of the federal government are well known; publickly and privately I have declared it; and however constitutionally it may be for Congress to point out the defects of the foederal System, I am strongly inclined to believe that it would not be found the most efficatious channel for the recommendation, more especially the alterations, to flow, for reasons too obvious to enumerate.

6

CONTINENTAL CONGRESS
21 Feb. 1787
Tansill 44–46

The report of a grand comee. consisting of Mr. Dane Mr. Varnum Mr. S. M. Mitchell Mr. Smith Mr. Cadwallader Mr. Irwine Mr. N. Mitchell Mr. Forrest Mr. Grayson Mr. Blount Mr. Bull & Mr. Few, to whom was referred a letter of 14 Septr. 1786 from J. Dickinson written at the request of Commissioners from the States of Virginia Delaware Pensylvania New Jersey & New York assembled at the City of Annapolis together with a copy of the report of the said commissioners to the legislatures of the States by whom they were appointed, being an order of the day was called up & which is contained in the following resolution viz

"Congress having had under consideration the letter of John Dickinson esqr. chairman of the Commissioners who assembled at Annapolis during the last year also the proceedings of the said commissioners and entirely coinciding with them as to the inefficiency of the federal government and the necessity of devising such farther provisions as shall render the same adequate to the exigencies of the Union do strongly recommend to the different legislatures to send forward delegates to meet the proposed convention on the second Monday in May next at the city of Philadelphia"

The delegates for the state of New York thereupon laid

before Congress Instructions which they had received from their constituents, & in pursuance of the said instructions moved to postpone the farther consideration of the report in order to take up the following proposition to wit

"That it be recommended to the States composing the Union that a convention of representatives from the said States respectively be held at ——— on ——— for the purpose of revising the Articles of Confederation and perpetual Union between the United States of America and reporting to the United States in Congress assembled and to the States respectively such alterations and amendments of the said Articles of Confederation as the representatives met in such convention shall judge proper and necessary to render them adequate to the preservation and support of the Union"

On the question to postpone for the purpose above mentioned the yeas & nays being required by the delegates for New York.

Massachusetts	Mr. King	ay	} ay	
	Mr. Dane	ay		
Connecticut	Mr. Johnson	ay	} d	
	Mr. S. M. Mitchell	no		
New York	Mr. Smith	ay	} ay	•
	Mr. Benson	ay		
New Jersey	Mr. Cadwallader	ay	} no	
	Mr. Clarke	no		
	Mr. Schurman	no		
Pensylvania	Mr. Irwine	no	} no	
	Mr. Meredith	ay		
	Mr. Bingham	no		
Delaware	Mr. N. Mitchell	no	x	
Maryland	Mr. Forest	no	x	
Virginia	Mr. Grayson	ay	} ay	
	Mr. Madison	ay		
North Carolina	Mr. Blount	no	} no	
	Mr. Hawkins	no		
South Carolina	Mr. Bull	no	} no	
	Mr. Kean	no		
	Mr. Huger	no		
	Mr. Parker	no		
Georgia	Mr. Few	ay	} d	
	Mr. Pierce	no		

So the question was lost.

A motion was then made by the delegates for Massachusetts to postpone the farther consideration of the report in order to take into consideration a motion which they read in their place, this being agreed to, the motion of the delegates for Massachusetts was taken up and being amended was agreed to as follows

Whereas there is provision in the Articles of Confederation & perpetual Union for making alterations therein by the assent of a Congress of the United States and of the legislatures of the several States; And whereas experience hath evinced that there are defects in the present Confederation, as a mean to remedy which several of the States and particularly the State of New York by express instructions to their delegates in Congress have suggested a convention for the purposes expressed in the following resolution and such convention appearing to be the most probable mean of establishing in these states a firm national government.

Resolved that in the opinion of Congress it is expedient that on the second Monday in May next a Convention of delegates who shall have been appointed by the several states be held at Philadelphia for the sole and express purpose of revising the Articles of Confederation and reporting to Congress and the several legislatures such alterations and provisions therein as shall when agreed to in Congress and confirmed by the states render the federal constitution adequate to the exigencies of Government & the preservation of the Union.

7

EDMUND RANDOLPH TO JAMES MADISON
27 Mar. 1787
Madison Papers 9:335

I have turned my mind somewhat to the business of may next: but am hourly interrupted. At present I conceive
  1. that the alterations shd. be grafted on the old confederation
  2. that what is best in itself, not merely what can be obtained from the assemblies, be adopted.
  3. that the points of power to be granted be so detached from each other, as to permit a state to reject one part, without mutilating the whole.

With these objects, ought not some general propositions to be prepared for feeling the pulse of the convention on the subject at large? Ought not an address to accompany the new constitution?

8

GEORGE WASHINGTON TO JAMES MADISON
31 Mar. 1787
Writings 29:191–92

It gives me great pleasure to hear that there is a probability of a full representation of the States in Convention; but if the delegates come to it under fetters, the salutary ends proposed will in my opinion be greatly embarrassed and retarded, if not altogether defeated. I am anxious to know how this matter really is, as my wish is, that the Convention may adopt no temporizing expedient, but probe the defects of the Constitution to the bottom, and provide radical cures; whether they are agreed to or not; a conduct like this, will stamp wisdom and dignity on the proceedings, and be looked to as a luminary, which sooner or later will shed its influence.

9

JAMES MADISON TO EDMUND RANDOLPH
8 Apr. 1787
Papers 9:369–71

I am glad to find that you are turning your thoughts towards the business of May next. My despair of your finding the necessary leisure as signified in one of your letters, with the probability that some leading propositions at least would be expected from Virga. had engaged me in a closer attention to the subject than I should otherwise have given. I will just hint the ideas which have occurred, leaving explanations for our interview.

I think with you that it will be well to retain as much as possible of the old Confederation, tho' I doubt whether it may not be best to work the valuable articles into the new System, instead of engrafting the latter on the former. I am also perfectly of your opinion that in framing a system, no material sacrifices ought to be made to local or temporary prejudices. An explanatory address must of necessity accompany the result of the Convention on the main object. I am not sure that it will be practicable to present the several parts of the reform in so detached a manner to the States as that a partial adoption will be binding. Particular States may view the different articles as conditions of each other, and would only ratify them as such. Others might ratify them as independent propositions. The consequence would be that the ratification of both would go for nothing. I have not however examined this point thoroughly. In truth my ideas of a reform strike so deeply at the old Confederation, and lead to such a systematic change, that they scarcely admit of the expedient.

I hold it for a fundamental point that an individual independence of the States, is utterly irreconcileable with the idea of an aggregate sovereignty. I think at the same time that a consolidation of the States into one simple republic is not less unattainable than it would be inexpedient. Let it be tried then whether any middle ground can be taken which will at once support a due supremacy of the national authority, and leave in force the local authorities so far as they can be subordinately useful.

The first step to be taken is I think a change in the principle of representation. According to the present form of the Union, an equality of suffrage if not just towards the larger members of it, is at least safe to them, as the liberty they exercise of rejecting or executing the acts of Congress, is uncontroulable by the nominal sovereignty of Congress. Under a system which would operate without the intervention of the States, the case would be materially altered. A vote from Delaware would have the same effect as one from Massts. or Virga.

Let the national Government be armed with a positive & compleat authority in all cases where uniform measures are necessary. As in trade &c. &c. Let it also retain the powers which it now possesses.

Let it have a negative in all cases whatsoever on the Legislative Acts of the States as the K. of G. B. heretofore had. This I conceive to be essential and the least possible abridgement of the State Soveriegnties. Without such a defensive power, every positive power that can be given on paper will be unavailing. It will also give internal stability to the States. There has been no moment since the peace at which the federal assent wd have been given to paper money &c. &c.

Let this national supremacy be extended also to the Judiciary departmt. If the judges in the last resort depend on the States & are bound by their oaths to them and not to the Union, the intention of the law and the interests of the nation may be defeated by the obsequiousness of the Tribunals to the policy or prejudices of the States. It seems at least essential that an appeal should lie to some national tribunals in all cases which concern foreigners, or inhabitants of other States. The admiralty jurisdiction may be fully submitted to the national Government.

The supremacy of the whole in the Executive department seems liable to some difficulty. Perhaps an extension of it to the case of the Militia may be necessary & sufficient.

A Government formed of such extensive powers ought to be well organized. The Legislative department may be divided into two branches: One of them to be chosen every   years by the Legislatures or the people at large; the other to consist of a more select number, holding their appointments for a longer term and going out in rotation. Perhaps the negative on the State laws may be most conveniently lodged in this branch. A Council of Revision may be superadded, including the great ministerial officers.

A National Executive will also be necessary. I have scarcly venturd to form my own opinion yet either of the manner in which it ought to be constituted or of the authorities with which it ought [to be] cloathed.

An article ought to be inserted expressly guarantying the tranquility of the States agst. internal as well as external dangers.

To give the new system its proper energy it will be desirable to have it ratified by the authority of the people, and not merely by that of the Legislatures.

I am afraid you will think this project, if not extravagant, absolutely unattainable and unworthy of being attempted. Conceiving it my self to go no further than is essential, The objections drawn from this source are to be laid aside. I flatter myself however that they may be less formidable on trial than in contemplation. The change in the principle of representation will be relished by a majority of the States, and those too of most influence. The Northern States will be reconciled to it by the *actual* superiority of their populousness: the Southern by their *expected* superiority in this point. This principle established, the repugnance of the large States to part with power will in a great degree subside, and the smaller States must ultimately yield to the predominant Will. It is also already seen by many & must by degrees be seen by all that unless the Union be organized efficiently & on Republican Principles, innovations of a much more objectionable form may be obtruded, or in the most favorable event, the partition of the Empire into rival & hostile confederacies, will ensue.

10

RECORDS OF THE FEDERAL CONVENTION

[1:41; McHenry, 30 May]

1st resolution from Mr. Randol.

Mr. R. wishes to have that resol. dissented to. The resol. postponed to take up the following:

1st. That a union of the States merely foederal will not accomplish the object proposed by the articles of confederation, namely, "common defence, security of liberty, and general welfare".

Mr. C. Pinkney wishes to know whether the establishment of this Resolution is intended as a ground for a consolidation of the several States into one.

Mr. Randol has nothing further in contemplation than what the propositions he has submitted yesterday has expressed.

2. Resolved that no treaty or treaties between the whole or a less number of the States in their sovereign capacities will accomplish their common defence, liberty or welfare.

3. Resolved therefore that a national governmen ought to be established consisting of a supreme legislature, judiciary and executive.

Mr. Whythe presumes from the silence of the house that they gentn. are prepared to pass on the resolution and proposes its being put.

Mr. Butler—does not think the house prepared, that he is not. Wishes Mr. Randolph to shew that the existence of the States cannot be preserved by any other mode than a national government.

Gen. Pinkney—Thinks agreeing to the resolve is declaring that the convention does not act under the authority of the recommendation of Congress.

The first resolution postponed to take up the 3d. viz—Resolved that a national government ought to be established consisting of a supreme legislature, judiciary and executive.

1787, 21 Febry. Resolution of Congress.

Resolved that in the opinion of Congress it is expedient that on the 2d Monday of May next a convention of delegates who shall have been appointed by the several States to be held at Philada. for the sole and expres purpose of *revising the articles of confederation,* and reporting to Congress and the several legislatures, such alterations and provisions therein as shall when agreed to in Congress, and confirmed by the States, render the *foederal constitution,* adequate to the exigencies of government and the preservation of the union."

Mr. Randolph explains the intention of the 3d Resolution. Repeats the substance of his yesterdays observations. It is only meant to give the national government a power

to defend and protect itself. To take therefore from the respective legislatures or States, no more soverignty than is competent to this end.

Mr. Dickinson. Under obligations to the gentlemen who brought forward the systems laid before the house yesterday. Yet differs from the mode of proceeding to which the resolutions or propositions before the Committee lead. Would propose a more simple mode. All agree that the confederation is defective all agree that it ought to be amended. We are a nation altho' consisting of parts or States—we are also confederated, and he hopes we shall always remain confederated. The enquiry should be—

1. What are the legislative powers which we should vest in Congress.

2. What judiciary powers.

3 What executive powers.

We may resolve therefore, in order to let us into the business. That the confederation is defective; and then proceed to the definition of such powers as may be thought adequate to the objects for which it was instituted.

Mr. E. Gerry. Does not rise to speak to the *merits* of the question before the Committee but to the *mode.*

A distinction has been made between a *federal* and *national* government. We ought not to determine that there is this distinction for if we do, it is questionable not only whether this convention can propose an government totally different or whether Congress itself would have a right to pass such a resolution as that before the house. The commission from Massachusetts empowers the deputies to proceed agreeably to the recommendation of Congress. This the foundation of the convention. If we have a right to pass this resolution we have a right to annihilate the confederation.

Proposes—In the opinion of this convention, provision should be made for the establishment of a foederal legislative, judiciary, and executive.

Governeur Morris. Not yet ripe for a decision, because men seem to have affixed different explanations to the terms before the house. 1. We are not now under a foederal government. 2. There is no such thing. A foederal government is that which has a right to compel every part to do its duty. The foederal gov. has no such compelling capacities, whether considered in their legislative, judicial or Executive qualities.

The States in their appointments Congress in their recommendations point directly to the establishment of a *supreme* government capable of "the common defence, security of liberty and general welfare.

Cannot conceive of a government in which there can exist two *supremes.* A federal agreement which each party may violate at pleasure cannot answer the purpose. One government better calculated to prevent wars or render them less expensive or bloody than many.

We had better take a supreme government now, than a despot twenty years hence—for come he must.

Mr. Reed, Genl. Pky [Pinckney] 2dng. proposes—In order to carry into execution the design of the States in

this meeting and to accomplish the *objects* proposed by the confederation resolved that A more effective government consisting of a legislative judiciary and executive ought to be established.

In order to carry into execution

Mr. R. King—The object of the motion from Virginia, an establishment of a government that is to act upon the whole people of the U.S.

The object of the motion from Delaware seems to have application merely to the strenghtening the confederation by some additional powers—

Mr. Maddison—The motion does go to bring out the sense of the house—whether the States shall be governed by one power. If agreed to it will decide nothing. The meaning of the States that the confed. is defect. and ought to be amended.

[1:177; Madison, 9 June]

Mr. Patterson considered the proposition for a proportional representation as striking at the existence of the lesser States. He wd. premise however to an investigation of this question some remarks on the nature structure and powers of the Convention. The Convention he said was formed in pursuance of an Act of Congs. that this act was recited in several of the Commissions, particularly that of Massts. which he required to be read: That the amendment of the confederacy was the object of all the laws and commissions on the subject; that the articles of the confederation were therefore the proper basis of all the proceedings of the Convention. We ought to keep within its limits, or we should be charged by our constituents with usurpation. that the people of America were sharpsighted and not to be deceived. But the Commissions under which we acted were not only the measure of our power. they denoted also the sentiments of the States on the subject of our deliberation. The idea of a national Govt. as contradistinguished from a federal one, never entered into the mind of any of them, and to the public mind we must accommodate ourselves. We have no power to go beyond the federal scheme, and if we had the people are not ripe for any other. We must follow the people; the people will not follow us.

[1:249, 253, 255; Madison, 16 June]

Mr. Lansing called for the reading of the 1st. resolution of each plan, which he considered as involving principles directly in contrast; that of Mr. Patterson says he sustains the sovereignty of the respective States, that of Mr. Randolph distroys it: the latter requires a negative on all the laws of the particular States; the former, only certain general powers for the general good. The plan of Mr. R. in short absorbs all power except what may be exercised in the little local matters of the States which are not objects worthy of the supreme cognizance. He grounded his preference of Mr. P'.s plan, chiefly on two objections agst that of Mr. R. 1. want of power in the Convention to discuss & propose it. 2 the improbability of its being adopted. 1. He was decidedly of opinion that the power of the Convention was restrained to amendments of a federal nature, and having for their basis the Confederacy in being. The Act of Congress The tenor of the Acts of the States, the commissions produced by the several deputations all proved this. and this limitation of the power to an amendment of the Confederacy, marked the opinion of the States, that it

was unnecessary & improper to go farther. He was sure that this was the case with his State. N. York would never have concurred in sending deputies to the convention, if she had supposed the deliberations were to turn on a consolidation of the States, and a National Government. 2. was it probable that the States would adopt & ratify a scheme, which they had never authorized us to propose? and which so far exceeded what they regarded as sufficient? We see by their several acts particularly in relation to the plan of revenue proposed by Congs. in 1783 not authorized by the articles of Confederation, what were the ideas they then entertained. Can so great a change be supposed to have already taken place. To rely on any change which is hereafter to take place in the sentiments of the people would be trusting to too great an uncertainty. We know only what their present sentiments are, and it is in vain to propose what will not accord with these. The States will never feel a sufficient confidence in a general Government to give it a negative on their laws. The Scheme is itself totally novel. There is no parallel to it to be found. The authority of Congress is familiar to the people, and an augmentation of the powers of Congress will be readily approved by them.

Mr. Patterson. said as he had on a former occasion given his sentiments on the plan proposed by Mr. R. he would now avoiding repetition as much as possible give his reasons in favor of that proposed by himself. He preferred it because it accorded 1. with the powers of the Convention. 2 with the sentiments of the people. If the confederacy was radically wrong, let us return to our States, and obtain larger powers, not assume them of ourselves. I came here not to speak my own sentiments, but the sentiments of those who sent me. Our object is not such a Governmt. as may be best in itself, but such a one as our Constituents have authorized us to prepare, and as they will approve. If we argue the matter on the supposition that no Confederacy at present exists, it can not be denied that all the States stand on the footing of equal sovereignty. All therefore must concur before any can be bound. If a proportional representation be right, why do we not vote so here? If we argue on the fact that a federal compact actually exists, and consult the articles of it we still find an equal Sovereignty to be the basis of it. He reads the 5th. art: of Confederation giving each State a vote—& the 13th. declaring that no alteration shall be made without unanimous consent. This is the nature of all treaties. What is unanimously done, must be unanimously undone. It was observed (by Mr. Wilson) that the larger State[s] gave up the point, not because it was right, but because the circumstances of the moment urged the concession. Be it so. Are they for that reason at liberty to take it back. Can the donor resume his gift Without the consent of the donee. This doctrine may be convenient, but it is a doctrine that will sacrifice the lesser States.

. . . . .

[Mr. Wilson:] With regard to the *power of the Convention*, he conceived himself authorized to *conclude nothing*, but to be at liberty to *propose any thing*. In this particular he felt himself perfectly indifferent to the two plans.

. . . . .

Mr. Randolph. was not scrupulous on the point of power. When the salvation of the Republic was at stake, it would be treason to our trust, not to propose what we found necessary. He painted in strong colours, the imbecility of the existing confederacy, & the danger of delaying a substantial reform. In answer to the objection drawn from the sense of our Constituents as denoted by their acts relating to the Convention and the objects of their deliberation, he observed that as each State acted separately in the case, it would have been indecent for it to have charged the existing Constitution with all the vices which it might have perceived in it. The first State that set on foot this experiment would not have been justified in going so far, ignorant as it was of the opinion of others, and sensible as it must have been of the uncertainty of a successful issue to the experiment. There are certainly reasons of a peculiar nature where the ordinary cautions must be dispensed with; and this is certainly one of them. He wd. not as far as depended on him leave any thing that seemed necessary, undone. The present moment is favorable, and is probably the last that will offer.

[1:283; Madison, 18 June]

[Mr. Hamilton:] As to the powers of the Convention, he thought the doubts started on that subject had arisen from distinctions & reasonings too subtle. A *federal* Govt. he conceived to mean an association of independent Communities into one. Different Confederacies have different powers, and exercise them in different ways. In some instances the powers are exercised over collective bodies; in others over individuals. as in the German Diet—& among ourselves in cases of piracy. Great latitude therefore must be given to the signification of the term. The plan last proposed departs itself from the *federal* idea, as understood by some, since it is to operate eventually on individuals. He agreed moreover with the Honble. gentleman from Va. (Mr. R.) that we owed it to our Country, to do on this emergency whatever we should deem essential to its happiness. The States sent us here to provide for the exigences of the Union. To reply on & propose any plan not adequate to these exigences, merely because it was not clearly within our powers, would be to sacrifice the means to the end. It may be said that the *States* can not *ratify* a plan not within the purview of the article of Confederation providing for alterations & amendments. But may not the States themselves in which no constitutional authority equal to this purpose exists in the Legislatures, have had in view a reference to the people at large. In the Senate of N. York, a proviso was moved, that no act of the Convention should be binding untill it should be referred to the people & ratified; and the motion was lost by a single voice only, the reason assigned agst. it, being that it might possibly be found an inconvenient shackle.

The great question is what provision shall we make for the happiness of our Country?

[1:314, 323; Madison, 19 June]

Mr. Madison. Much stress had been laid by some gentlemen on the want of power in the Convention to propose any other than a *federal* plan. To what had been answered by others, he would only add, that neither of the characteristics attached to a *federal* plan would support this objection. One characteristic, was that in a *federal* Government, the power was exercised not on the people individually; but on the people *collectively,* on the *States.* Yet in some instances as in piracies, captures &c. the existing Confederacy, and in many instances, the amendments to it proposed by Mr. Patterson must operate immediately on individuals. The other characteristic was, that a *federal* Govt. derived its appointments not immediately from the people, but from the States which they respectively composed. Here too were facts on the other side. In two of the States, Connect. and Rh. Island, the delegates to Congs. were chosen, not by the Legislatures, but by the people at large; and the plan of Mr. P. intended no change in this particular.

It had been alledged (by Mr. Patterson) that the Confederation having been formed by unanimous consent, could be dissolved by unanimous Consent only Does this doctrine result from the nature of compacts? does it arise from any particular stipulation in the articles of Confederation? If we consider the federal union as analogous to the fundamental compact by which individuals compose one Society, and which must in its theoretic origin at least, have been the unanimous act of the component members, it cannot be said that no dissolution of the compact can be effected without unanimous consent. a breach of the fundamental principles of the compact by a part of the Society would certainly absolve the other part from their obligations to it. If the breach of *any* article by *any* of the parties, does not set the others at liberty, it is because, the contrary is *implied* in the compact itself, and particularly by that law of it, which gives an indefinite authority to the majority to bind the whole in all cases. This latter circumstance shews that we are not to consider the federal Union as analogous to the social compact of individuals: for if it were so, a Majority would have a right to bind the rest, and even to form a new Constitution for the whole, which the Gentn: from N. Jersey would be among the last to admit. If we consider the federal union as analogous not to the social compacts among individual men: but to the conventions among individual States. What is the doctrine resulting from these conventions? Clearly, according to the Expositors of the law of Nations, that a breach of any one article, by any one party, leaves all the other parties at liberty, to consider the whole convention as dissolved, unless they choose rather to compel the delinquent party to repair the breach. In some treaties indeed it is expressly stipulated that a violation of particular articles shall not have this consequence, and even that particular articles shall remain in force during war, which in general is understood to dissolve all susbsisting Treaties. But are there any exceptions of this sort to the Articles of confederation? So far from it that there is not even an express stipulation that force shall be used to compel an offending member of the Union to discharge its duty. He observed that the violations of the federal articles had been numerous & notorious. Among the most notorious was an Act of N. Jersey herself; by which she *expressly refused* to comply with a constitutional requisition of Congs.—and yielded no farther to the expostulations of their deputies, than barely to rescind her vote of refusal without passing any positive act of compliance. He did not wish to draw any rigid inferences from these observations. He thought it proper however that the true nature of the existing confederacy should be investigated, and he was not anxious to strengthen the foundations on which it now stands

. . . . .

[Mr. King:] He conceived that the import of the terms "States" "Sovereignty" *"national"* "federal," had been often used & applied in the discussion inaccurately & delusively. The States were not "sovereigns" in the sense contended for by some. They did not possess the peculiar features of sovereignty. They could not make war, nor peace, nor alliances, nor treaties. Considering them as political Beings, they were dumb, for they could not speak to any forign Sovereign whatever. They were deaf, for they could not hear any propositions from such Sovereign. They had not even the organs or faculties of defence or offence, for they could not of themselves raise troops, or equip vessels, for war. On the other side, if the Union of the States comprises the idea of a confederation, it comprises that also of consolidation. A Union of the States is a union of the men composing them, from whence a *national* character results to the whole. Congs. can act alone without the States—they can act & their acts will be binding agst. the Instructions of the States. If they declare war, war is de jure declared, captures made in pursuance of it are lawful. No acts of the States can vary the situation, or prevent the judicial consequences. If the States therefore retained some portion of their sovereignty, they had certainly divested themselves of essential portions of it. If they formed a confederacy in some respects—they formed a Nation in others. The Convention could clearly deliberate on & propose any alterations that Congs. could have done under ye. federal articles. and could not Congs. propose by virtue of the last article, a change in any article whatever: And as well that relating to the equality of suffrage, as any other. He made these remarks to obviate some scruples which had been expressed. He doubted much the practicability of annihilating the States; but thought that much of their power ought to be taken from them.

Mr. Martin, said he considered that the separation from G. B. placed the 13 States in a state of nature towards each other; that they would have remained in that state till this time, but for the confederation; that they entered into the confederation on the footing of equality; that they met now to to amend it on the same footing, and that he could never accede to a plan that would introduce an inequality and lay 10 States at the mercy of Va. Massts. and Penna.

Mr. Wilson, could not admit the doctrine that when the Colonies became independent of G. Britain, they became independent also of each other. He read the declaration of Independence, observing thereon that the *United Colonies* were declared to be free & independent States; and inferring that they were independent, not *Individually* but *Unitedly* and that they were confederated as they were independent, States.

Col. Hamilton, assented to the doctrine of Mr. Wilson. He denied the doctrine that the States were thrown into a State of nature He was not yet prepared to admit the doctrine that the Confederacy, could be dissolved by partial infractions of it. He admitted that the States met now on an equal footing but could see no inference from that against concerting a change of the system in this particular.

11

FEDERAL CONVENTION, RESOLUTION AND LETTER TO THE CONTINENTAL CONGRESS
17 Sept. 1787
Farrand 2:665–67

In Convention Monday September 17th. 1787

Present

The States of

New Hampshire, Massachusetts, Connecticut, Mr. Hamilton from New York, New Jersey, Pennsylvania, Delaware, Maryland, Virginia, North Carolina, South Carolina and Georgia.

Resolved,

That the preceding Constitution be laid before the United States in Congress assembled, and that it is the Opinion of this Convention, that it should afterwards be submitted to a Convention of Delegates, chosen in each State by the People thereof, under the Recommendation of its Legislature, for their Assent and Ratification; and that each Convention assenting to, and ratifying the Same, should give Notice thereof to the United States in Congress assembled.

Resolved, That it is the Opinion of this Convention, that as soon as the Conventions of nine States shall have ratified this Constitution, the United States in Congress assembled should fix a Day on which Electors should be appointed by the States which shall have ratified the same, and a Day on which the Electors should assemble to vote for the President, and the Time and place for commencing Proceedings under this Constitution. That after such Publication the Electors should be appointed, and the Senators and Representatives elected: That the Electors should meet on the Day fixed for the Election of the President, and should transmit their votes certified signed, sealed and directed, as the Constitution requires, to the Secretary of the United States in Congress assembled, that the Senators and Representatives should convene at the Time and Place asigned; that the Senators should appoint a President of the Senate, for the sole Purpose of receiving, opening and counting the Votes for President; and, that after he shall be chosen, the Congress, together with the President, should, without Delay, proceed to execute this Constitution.

By the Unanimous Order of the Convention
Go: Washington Presidt.
W. Jackson Secretary

[LETTER TO THE PRESIDENT OF CONGRESS]

In Convention, September 17, 1787.

Sir,

We have now the honor to submit to the consideration of the United States in Congress assembled, that Constitution which has appeared to us the most adviseable.

The friends of our country have long seen and desired, that the power of making war, peace and treaties, that of levying money and regulating commerce, and the correspondent executive and judicial authorities should be fully and effectually vested in the general government of the Union: but the impropriety of delegating such extensive trust to one body of men is evident—Hence results the necessity of a different organization.

It is obviously impracticable in the foederal government of these States, to secure all rights of independent sovereignty to each, and yet provide for the interest and safety of all—Individuals entering into society, must give up a share of liberty to preserve the rest. The magnitude of the sacrifice must depend as well on situation and circumstance, as on the object to be obtained. It is at all times difficult to draw with precision the line between those rights which must be surrendered, and those which may be reserved; and on the present occasion this difficulty was encreased by a difference among the several States as to their situation, extent, habits, and particular interests.

In all our deliberations on this subject we kept steadily in our view, that which appears to us the greatest interest of every true American, the consolidation of our Union, in which is involved our prosperity, felicity, safety, perhaps our national existence. This important consideration, seriously and deeply impressed on our minds, led each State in the Convention to be less rigid on points of inferior magnitude, than might have been otherwise expected; and thus the Constitution, which we now present, is the result of a spirit of amity, and of that mutual deference and concession which the peculiarity of our political situation rendered indispensable.

That it will meet the full and entire approbation of every State is not perhaps to be expected; but each will doubtless consider, that had her interest alone been consulted, the consequences might have been particularly disagreeable or injurious to others; that it is liable to as few exceptions as could reasonably have been expected, we hope and believe; that it may promote the lasting welfare of that country so dear to us all, and secure her freedom and happiness, is our most ardent wish.

With great respect,
We have the honor to be.
SIR,
Your EXCELLENCY'S most
Obedient and humble Servants,
GEORGE WASHINGTON, PRESIDENT.

By unanimous Order of the CONVENTION.

12

CONTINENTAL CONGRESS
26–28 Sept. 1787
Jensen 1:327–37, 339–40

[Nathan Dane's Motion, 26 Sept.]

Whereas Congress Sensible that there were defects in the present Confederation; and that several of the States were desirous that a Convention of Delegates should be formed to consider the same, and to propose necessary alterations in the federal Constitution; in February last resolved that it was expedient that a Convention of the States should be held for the Sole and express purpose of revising the articles of Confederation and reporting to Congress and the several legislatures such alterations and provisions therein, as Should when agreed to in Congress, and be confirmed by the States, render the federal Constitution adequate to the exigencies of Government, and the preservation of the union—

And whereas it appears by Credentials laid before Congress, that twelve States appointed Delegates who assembled in Convention accordingly, and who did on the 17th. instant, by the unanimous consent of the States then present in convention agree upon, and afterwards lay before Congress, a Constitution for the United States, to be submitted to a convention of Delegates, chosen in each State by the people thereof, under the recommendation of its legislature, for their assent and ratification which constitution appears to be intended as an entire system in itself, and not as any part of, or alteration in the Articles of Confederation;—to alterations in which articles, the deliberations and powers of Congress are, in this Case, constitutionally confined—and whereas Congress cannot with propriety proceed to examine and alter the said Constitution proposed, unless it be with a view so essentially to change the principles and forms of it, as to make it an additional part in the said Confederation and the members of Congress not feeling themselves authorised by the forms of Government under which they are assembled, to express an opinion respecting a system of Government no way connected with those forms; but conceiving that the respect they owe their constituents and the importance of the subject require, that the report of the Convention should, with all convenient dispatch, be transmitted to the Several States to be laid before the respective legislatures ther[eof,] therefore

Resolved that there be transmitted to the Supreme executive of each State a copy of the report of the Convention of the States lately Assembled in the City of Philadelphia signed by their deputies the seventeenth instant including their resolutions and their letter directed to the president of Congress—

[*Melancton Smith's Notes, 26 Sept.*]

Pierce Butler: Wishes to know the motives that produced the motion. He thinks it is calculated to disapprove [the Constitution].

Nathan Dane: Asks to know what words are objectionable.

1. The consolidation [is] imperfect and will not work.

2. If it does, it will not work on free principles. It must be supported by a standing army. It will oppress the honest and industrious, [and] it will advantage a few. Is not averse to examination, is open to conviction, and, if convinced, will support it. Is willing the present motion should be amended so as to be neutral. If it [the Constitution] is to be approved, it will be moved to take it up by paragraphs, objections stated, [and] amendments moved. Congress [has] no constitutional right to consider [the Constitution].

[*Melancton Smith's Notes, 27 Sept.*]

Richard Henry Lee: Every man to see with his own eyes; to judge for themselves. Congress, acting under the present Constitution definitely limiting their powers, have no right to recommend a plan subverting the government. This remark felt, as a gentleman yesterday justify, by the necessity of the case. This [is] dangerous because this principle has been abused to bad 100 times [to one] where it is used for good. The Impost [of 1781] referred [to] as an instance to justify; that [was] within the powers [of Congress; it was] sent to [receive?] the approval of 13 states; and within this line this [Constitution] by [the approval of] nine [states]. This plan proposes [to] destroy the Confederation of 13 and [to] establish a new one of 9. Yet it would be indecent not to send it to the states for 12 states sent delegates [to the Federal Convention], as he understands, to amend the present government. Men of respected characters have agreed upon this. It [the Constitution] should be forwarded. A gentleman yesterday said the Confederation says nothing of [a] convention. It is true it does not point [to] a convention, but it does not forbid [this?] to be proposed by one, or any other way. Congress is only to agree. If this was not destructive, but an amendment, Congress might consider [the Constitution]. Proposes a resolution, stating that as Congress have no right under the Confederation to recommend alterations of the Confederation unless agreed to by 13 states, and this [Constitution] proposes an amendment by 9.

[*Richard Henry Lee's Motion, Journals of Congress, 27 Sept.*]

And a motion being made by Richard Henry Lee, seconded by Melancton Smith in the words following: "Resolved, That Congress after due attention to the Constitution under which this body exists and acts find that the said Constitution in the thirteenth article thereof limits the power of Congress to the amendment of the present Confederacy of thirteen states, but does not extend it to the creation of a new confederacy of nine states; and the late Convention having been constituted under the authority of twelve states in this Union it is deemed respectful to transmit, and it is accordingly ordered, that the plan of a new Federal Constitution laid before Congress by the said Convention be sent to the executive of every state in this Union to be laid before their respective legislatures."

[*Melancton Smith's Notes, 27 Sept.*]

William Grayson: . . . Is in favor of the new Constitution. This [Confederation] proposes a mode of altering. If we depart from the mode in this case, it will form a precedent from doing it in the old one—[in] the [way the] 13th Article [found?]. 9 states may agree to the new [Constitution]; the other 4 ought to be left in possession of this [Confederation] if they choose and not [be] forced to come in. Does not think there has yet been any departure from the Confederation. Congress had a right to refer to any body to report. Keep the present [Confederation] until you get a better.

. . . . .

James Madison: Can't accede to it [Lee's motion]. [It] is not respectful to the Convention. After what has been done, if Congress does not agree, [it] implies a disagreement. Congress from former acts do not object to a national government. . . . The question is, whether on the whole it is best to adopt it, and [we] ought to say so. The powers of [the] Convention [are] the same as of Congress. The reason of Convention [was] that they might not be interrupted; and that persons might be admitted [to the Convention] whether or not [they] be in Congress, and to prevent jealousies. If this House can't approve [the Constitution], it says the crisis is not yet arrived and implies a disapp[robation]. [In] a great many instances, Congress have recommended what they have no right [to recommend].

Richard Henry Lee: The Convention have not proceeded as this House were bound [by the Articles of Confederation]. It is to be agreed to by the states and means the 13 [states]. But this [Constitution] recommends a new confederacy of 9 [states]. The Convention [had] no more powers than Congress, yet if 9 states agree [the Constitution] becomes supreme law. Knows no instance on the Journals, as he remembers, opposing the Confederacy. The Impost [of 1781] was to be adopted by 13 [states]. The resolution from [New] Jersey approves [the Constitution] for Congress don't send out anything but such as they approve.

Abraham Clark: Unhappy to differ from [Richard Henry] Lee. He reveres his judgment. If his objection [is] good, his own proposal [is] liable to the like objection.

William Samuel Johnson: Hardly possible to send it out without approving or disapproving. For this reason, Mr. Lee's motion [ought to be postponed]. Congress ought to approve or disapprove. They may do it. It is their duty to do it. The people will see [that] we, that Congress, act without power in the case of 9 or 13 [states]. They will see, that the act of [21] February [calling the Convention] was departing from the Constitution. [The] Confederation says Congress was to make alterations. Congress appoint a Convention to do it. He saw it so at the time and opposed it. The argument then was salus populi. Nothing from Congress would do. The proposal from [the] Convention [is] not a proposal to 9 [states] but to all. It is hoped all will [agree]. Mr. Lee says, if 9 agree to alter by the people; this says, if 9 do in this case, we will set it going on the principle of majority. On the principle of Congress referring to the Convention, they are a committee and have made report. Congress then must approve or disapprove. It don't imply an approbation of all its parts, but the best upon the whole, a matter of accommodation. We say it is better than the present [constitution], better than running the risk of another.

James Madison: Did not say the Convention moved exactly in the line of their appointment. Congress did depart from the idea of [a] federal and recommend a national government in February 1781. Congress did [so] from the principle [of] *salus populi.* The western country, its sale and government, [is] an instance of exceeding powers, as Congress have in many instances exceeded their power. If it does not in this instance approve, it will imply disapproval.

[*Journals of Congress, 27 Sept.*]

On the question to postpone [Lee's motion] for the purpose above mentioned [for considering Abraham Clark's motion] the yeas and nays being required by Richard Henry Lee: . . . .

So it was resolved in the affirmative.

On motion of Edward Carrington seconded by William Bingham, the motion of Abraham Clarke was postponed to take into consideration the following motion, viz.: "Congress proceeded to the consideration of the Constitution for the United States by the late Convention held in the city of Philadelphia and thereupon resolved that Congress do agree thereto and that it be recommended to the legislatures of the several states to cause conventions to be held as speedily as may be to the end that the same may be adopted, ratified and confirmed."

[*Melancton Smith's Notes, 27 Sept.*]

The motion from Richard Henry Lee was postponed, and then a motion was made by Edward Carrington.

Henry Lee: Thinks the matter [the Constitution] was to be taken up [by Congress] in its parts, but cannot agree to it in all its parts, without [an] examination by paragraphs and propose [such?] amendments [as] are necessary. Congress will subject themselves to disgrace by voting on a matter which they have not examined. Moves to postpone [Carrington's motion] and [have the Constitution] taken up by paragraphs.

Nathaniel Gorham: Thinks not necessary to take up [the Constitution] by paragraphs. Every gentleman may propose amendments. No necessity of a bill of rights, because a bill of rights in state governments was intended to retain certain powers [in the people] as the legislatures had unlimited powers.

James Madison: The business is open to consideration. Should feel delicacy if he had not assented in Convention though he did not approve it. Gentlemen have said this is in the situation of a bill agreed to by one house. This principle will oppose amendments because the act if altered will not be the act of both. It must be altered in all stages. It may be, but it cannot succeed, nor any other alteration if all are to agree in this manner. [The] Confederation was proposed without alteration. No probability of Congress

agreeing in alterations. Those who disagree, differ in their opinions. A bill of rights [is] unnecessary because the powers are enumerated and only extend to certain cases, and the people who are to agree to it are to establish this.

Richard Henry Lee: It is admitted and [a] fact that this [Constitution] was to be sent to Congress, but surely it was to be considered and altered, and not to be sent forward without. The bill of rights will be brought forward. [A bill of rights] not necessary in [the] Confederation because it is expressly declared [that] no power should be exercised, but such as is expressly given, and therefore no constructive power can be exercised. To prevent this [is] the great use of a bill of rights.

Rufus King: The House cannot constitutionally make alterations. The idea of [the] Convention originated in the states, and this led the House to agree. They proposed the Convention should propose alterations, which when agreed to here and confirmed by the states [should be adopted], and therefore [Congress] are to agree or disagree to the alterations and cannot alter [the Constitution] consistently with their own act. Congress have taken their line, but in consequence of that [decision they are put?]. The majority of the people, it is said [by Richard Henry Lee], may alter, and if they have manifested a desire to change, this House may advise it, as it is not obligatory. We may advise as any other body of men. To satisfy forms it was ordered to pass this House. They may agree or disagree. If they do disagree it will not prevent them [the states] to accept. If they [Congress] agree it will give weight.

Richard Henry Lee: Strangest doctrine he ever heard, that [in] referring a matter of report, that no alterations should be made. The idea the common sense of man. The states and Congress, he thinks, had the idea that Congress was to amend if they thought proper. He wishes to give it a candid inquiry, and proposes such alterations as are necessary. If the gentleman [King] wishes it should go forth without amendments, let it go with all its imperfections on its head, and the amendments by themselves. To insist that it should go as it is without amendments is like presenting a hungry man 50 dishes and insisting he should eat all or none.

James Madison: A circumstance distinguishes this report from others. The Convention was not appointed by Congress, but by the people from whom Congress derive their power. Congress only to concur. Admits Congress may alter, but if they do alter, it is not the act of Convention but of Congress; and excludes [the] Convention entirely and confines the House in the trammels of the Confederation. Not unusual to propose things in the lump. So the Confederation was presented.

Richard Henry Lee: A report implies a right to consider on the whole or part. The Confederation went in such way as to admit of objections, and most states proposed them. If it is amended, he thinks it will be more likely to succeed, as capital objections will probably be removed. The idea seems to be, this must be agreed to or nothing else. Why this idea? This supposes all wisdom centers in the Convention.

Nathaniel Gorham: Why does not the gentleman propose

his amendments? Then the question of the expediency of the amendments will be considered.

William Samuel Johnson: The term of report: a general expression, not meant as in cases where [a] report is made to Congress. The people and Congress agree the alterations shall be made by Convention, and the nature of things forbids any alteration as it will make it no act of Convention. Congress are not to judge in the last resort, but the people; and therefore it must be approved or disapproved in the whole.

Richard Henry Lee: Is it the idea of Convention that not only Congress but the states must agree in the whole, or else to reject it? And it seems all idea of amendments are precluded.

James Madison: The proper question is whether any amendments shall be made, and that the House should decide. Suppose alterations sent to the states. The Arts. [Articles of Confederation] requires the delegates [in Congress] to report [alterations] to them [i.e., the state legislatures]. There will be two plans. Some will accept one and some another. That will create confusion and proves it was not the intent of the state.

Richard Henry Lee: Some admit the right but doubt the expediency and proposes amendments.

. . . . .

Nathan Dane: The gentlemen from the Convention are pushing the business by refinements. [Is] that the common sense of the country? If the House mean to preclude amendments, the gentleman [i.e., Dane] will stand excused to vote in the negative.

Edward Carrington: When he made the motion, supposed every man had a right to examine [the Constitution]. He had considered and made up his mind. If any gentleman has not made up his mind, he ought to have a liberty of amending. For though he thinks it inexpedient to amend, as he fears it would defeat the whole. Important amendments are offered by a member. He ought to have a right to support them.

Abraham Clark: The motion by Mr. Lee for amendments will do injury by coming on the Journal, and therefore the House, upon cool reflection, will think it best to agree to send it [the Constitution] out without agreeing.

William Grayson: It is a curious situation. It is urged all alterations are precluded. Has not made up his mind, and thinks it precipitant to urge a decision in two days on a subject [which] took 4 months. If we have no right to amend, then we ought to give a silent passage, for if we cannot alter, why should we deliberate. His opinion [is that] they should stand solely upon the opinion of [the] Convention. The salus populi much talked of. This Constitution will not remove our difficulties—the great defects a disinclination to pay money. That removed, our great difficulty would be over. No necessity to urge a hasty decision. In 2 or 3 years we should get a good government.

[*Journals of Congress, Friday, 28 Sept.*]

Congress having received the report of the Convention lately assembled in Philadelphia.

"Resolved unanimously, That the said report with the resolutions and letter accompanying the same be transmitted to the several legislatures in order to be submitted to a convention of delegates chosen in each state by the people thereof in conformity to the resolves of the Convention made and provided in that case."

13

WILLIAM FINDLEY, PENNSYLVANIA HOUSE OF
ASSEMBLY
28 Sept. 1787
Storing 3.1.1–3

I have, no doubt, *but a Convention might be called, and will be called. That it ought to be called, and will be called,* is seen so clearly, that I shall add nothing to enforce it—therefore, I take it—that the propriety of calling a convention is not the question before us. After declaring my sentiments so far, I shall proceed—Sir, now to examine the ground on which we stand—I believe we stand on foederal ground; therefore, we are not in a state of nature. If we were in a state of nature, all the arguments produced, for hastening this business, would apply—but as we are not, I would observe, that the most deliberate manner of proceeding, is the best manner—But the manner in which this subject has been introduced, is an indeliberate manner, and seems to argue, that we are not on foederal ground. The design of carrying this through, I say, Sir, is a presumption, that we are in a state of nature: if that is the case, then it can only be proper to use this expedition. What I mean, Sir, by a state of nature, is with respect to the confederation, or union of the states, and not any wise alluding to our particular state government. Now my opinion is, Sir, that we are on foederal ground—that the foederal convention was a foederal convention—that it had the powers of a foederal convention, and that they were limited to act foederally—that they have acted agreeable to the limitation, and have acted foederally. I know by some of the arguments which have been used, that some gentlemen suppose otherwise. Well then, Sir, we will have recourse to the confederation itself, and then to the law which appointed delegates to the convention, and let them decide whether we are on foederal ground or not.

The sixth article of the confederation says, "No two or more states shall enter into any treaty, confederation, or alliance whatever between them, without the consent of the United States in Congress assembled, specifying, accurately, the purposes for which the same is to be entered into, and how long it shall continue." It may be said this don't apply—Well let us examine what it says further in the thirteenth article—"The articles of confederation shall be inviolably observed by every state, and the union shall be perpetual; nor shall any alteration at any time hereafter be made in any of them, unless such alteration be agreed to in a congress of the United States, and be afterwards confirmed by the legislatures of every state." Now did we act in conformity with these articles by passing the law appointing delegates to the convention, or did we not? I say we did. I know the contrary has been said, but let us have recourse to our own act. I don't mean, as I said before, to reply particularly to any arguments, but to establish the point that we have all along acted upon foederal principles, and that we ought to continue foederal, and I have no doubt but we shall. But what says the preamble of the law—Hear our own words, Sir,— "Whereas the general assembly of this commonwealth, taking into their serious consideration the representations heretofore made to the legislatures of the several states in the union, by the United States in Congress assembled," &c. It has been mentioned that we took it up in consequence of Virginia's having engaged in the measure; and as the reasons are only mentioned in the preamble, they may not deserve much attention, but the second section of the law decides this point. The words are, after enumerating the persons, that they are hereby constituted and appointed deputies from this state, with powers to meet such deputies as may be appointed and authorized by the other states to assemble in the said convention at the city aforesaid, and to join with them in devising, deliberating on, and discussing all such alterations and further provisions as may be necessary to render the foederal constitution fully adequate to the exigencies of the Union; and in reporting such act or acts for that purpose, to the United States in Congress assembled, as when agreed to by them, and duly confirmed by the several states, will effectually provide for the same.

Now I consider it as a question of importance, whether we are to take up the new constitution, as being in a state of nature, or acting on federal ground, whether we stand unconnected or subordinate to the present confederation; if we are bound by that, it obliges us to continue on federal ground. I should conceive, that we are still bound by the confederation, and that the conduct of the House has hitherto been federal; that the convention was federal as appears by their appointment, and their report to Congress. Did they, Sir, address their report to this House? No, Sir, they did not. It is true, Sir, we were honored with a report from our own delegates. No, Sir, I retract the word—the delegates were honored; they did themselves the honour of communicating the result of their deliberations. But did the convention address this House? No, Sir, they did not. They addressed Congress, as they were ordered to do.—Hitherto the business has been in a federal channel, and this, Sir, is the first step that places us upon unfederal ground. The report is before Congress, and it is to be presumed Congress will agree to it—but has such a length of time elapsed, as to induce us to suspect they will not concur, or to justify our going into it without their recommendation? We may act, Sir, without due deliberation, and hurry on without consideration, but Congress will not. I know the propriety of waiting to hear from them must have weight with every Member, and I ask every gentleman in this House, will they take upon themselves to doubt of the acquiescence of Congress, in order to furnish an argument for dispatch? If any will, let him say so, and take the consequences upon his character. No doubt can be entertained, but Congress will recommend,

as the acquisition of power is a desirable object with them. Their disposition must be to promote the present plan, but they must wish to preserve the appearance of decency on such a subject. I ask, can any gentleman suppose but what Congress will come readily into it? They who have been many years recommending and requiring, nay I may say, begging for such powers as are now proposed to be given them, cannot change their disposition, and decline receiving an increase. Well, what does all this tend to prove; have we not all along been a federal state, remarkably so? And shall we be the first to step out of our way wantonly, and without any reason? Certainly we will not.

14

HUGH BRACKENRIDGE, PENNSYLVANIA HOUSE OF ASSEMBLY
28 Sept. 1787
McMaster 58–59

All efforts to restore energy to the federal government have proved ineffectual, when exerted in the mode directed by the 13th article of the confederation, and it is in consequence of this that recourse is once more had to the *authority of the people.* The first step toward obtaining this was anti-federal; the acquiescence of Congress was anti-federal; the whole process has been anti-federal so far as it was not conducted in the manner prescribed by the articles of union. But the first and every step was *federal,* inasmuch as it was sanctioned by the PEOPLE OF THE UNITED STATES. The member from Westmoreland [William Findley] pleases his fancy with being on federal ground, pursuing federal measures, and being a very federal sort of person; he concludes we are not in a state of nature, because we are on federal ground. But, Sir, we are not on federal ground, but on the wild and extended field of nature, unrestrained by any former compact, bound by no peculiar tie; at least so far are we disengaged, as to be capable of forming a constitution which shall be the wonder of the universe. It is on the principle of self-conservation that we act. The former articles of confederation have received sentence of death, and though they may be on earth, yet are inactive, and have no efficacy. But the gentleman would still have us to be bound by them, and tells you your acts must correspond with their doctrine. This he proves, Sir, from the 13th article: but in this he is like some over-studious divines, who in commenting on their text, turn it to different shapes, and force it to prove what it never meant, or in the words of the poet,

> As critics, learned critics view,
> In Homer, more than Homer knew.

He will not suffer the old to be dissolved until the new is adopted; he will not quit his old cabin, till the new house is furnished, not if it crumbles about his ears. But, Sir, we are not now forsaking our tenement, it has already been forsaken: and I conceive we have the power to proceed independent of Congress or Confederation.

15

JAMES MADISON TO GEORGE WASHINGTON
30 Sept. 1787
Papers 10:179–81

I found on my arrival here that certain ideas unfavorable to the Act of the Convention which had created difficulties in that body, had made their way into Congress. They were patronised cheifly by Mr. R. H. L. and Mr. Dane of Massts. It was first urged that as the new Constitution was more than an Alteration of the Articles of Confederation under which Congress acted, and even subverted these articles altogether, there was a Constitutional impropriety in their taking any positive agency in the work. The answer given was that the Resolution of Congress in Feby. had recommended the Convention as the best mean of obtaining a firm *national Government;* that as the powers of the Convention were defined by their Commissions in nearly the same terms with the powers of Congress given by the Confederation on the subject of alterations, Congress were not more restrained from acceding to the new plan, than the Convention were from proposing it. If the plan was within the powers of the Convention it was within those of Congress; if beyond those powers, the same necessity which justified the Convention would justify Congress; and a failure of Congress to Concur in what was done, would imply either that the Convention had done wrong in exceeding their powers, or that the Government proposed was in itself liable to insuperable objections; that such an inference would be the more natural, as Congress had never scrupled to recommend measures foreign to their Constitutional functions, whenever the Public good seemed to require it; and had in several instances, particularly in the establishment of the new Western Governments, exercised assumed powers of a very high & delicate nature, under motives infinitely less urgent than the present state of our affairs, if any faith were due to the representations made by Congress themselves, ecchoed by 12 States in the Union, and confirmed by the general voice of the People. An attempt was made in the next place by R. H. L. to amend the Act of the Convention before it should go forth from Congress. He proposed a bill of Rights—provision for juries in civil cases & several other things corresponding with the ideas of Col. M. He was supported by Mr. Me— Smith of this State. It was contended that Congress had an undoubted right to insert amendments, and that it was their duty to make use of it in a case where the essential guards of liberty had been omitted. On the other side the right of Congress was not denied, but the inexpediency of exerting it was urged on the following grounds. 1. that every circumstance indi-

cated that the introduction of Congress as a party to the reform, was intended by the States merely as a matter of form and respect. 2. that it was evident from the contradictory objections which had been expressed by the different members who had animadverted on the plan, that a discussion of its merits would consume much time, without producing agreement even among its adversaries. 3. that it was clearly the intention of the States that the plan to be proposed should be the act of the Convention with the assent of Congress, which could not be the case, if alterations were made, the Convention being no longer in existence to adopt them. 4. that as the Act of the Convention, when altered would instantly become the mere act of Congress, and must be proposed by them as such, and of course be addressed to the Legislatures, not conventions of the States, and require the ratification of thirteen instead of nine States, and as the unaltered act would go forth to the States directly from the Convention under the auspices of that Body—Some States might ratify one & some the other of the plans, and confusion & disappointment be the least evils that could ensue. These difficulties which at one time threatened a serious division in Congs. and popular alterations with the yeas & nays on the journals, were at length fortunately terminated by the following Resolution—"Congress having recd. the Report of the Convention lately assembled in Philada., Resold. *unanimously* that the said Report, with the Resolutions & letter accompanying the same, be transmitted to the several Legislatures, in order to be submitted to a Convention of Delegates chosen in each State by the people thereof, in conformity to the Resolves of the Convention made & provided in that case." Eleven States were present, the absent ones R.I. & Maryland. A more direct approbation would have been of advantage in this & some other States, where stress will be laid on the agency of Congress in the matter, and a handle taken by adversaries of any ambiguity on the subject. With regard to Virginia & some other States, reserve on the part of Congress will do no injury. The circumstance of unaninimity must be favorable every where.

16

RICHARD HENRY LEE TO GEORGE MASON
1 Oct. 1787
Mason Papers 3:996–97

I have waited until now to answer your favor of Septr. 18th from Philadelphia, that I might inform you how the Convention plan of Government was entertained by Congress. Your prediction of what would happen in Congress was exactly verified. It was with us, as with you, this or nothing; & this urged with a most extreme intemperance. The greatness of the powers given, & the multitude of Places to be created, produces a coalition of Monarchy men, Military Men, Aristocrats, and Drones whose noise, imprudence & zeal exceeds all belief—Whilst the Commercial plunder of the South stimulates the rapacious Trader. In this state of things the Patriot voice is raised in vain for such changes and securities as Reason and Experience prove to be necessary against the encroachments of power upon the indispensable rights of human nature. Upon due consideration of the Constitution under which we now Act, some of us were clearly of opinion that the 13th article of the Confederation precluded us from giving an opinion concerning a plan subversive of the present system and eventually forming a New Confederacy of Nine instead of 13 States. The contrary doctrine was asserted with great violence in expectation of the strong majority with which they might send it forward under terms of much approbation. Having procured an opinion that Congress was qualified to consider, to amend, to approve or disapprove—the next game was to determine that tho a right to amend existed, it would be highly inexpedient to exercise that right; but merely to transmit it with respectful marks of approbation. In this state of things I availed myself of the Right to amend, & moved the Amendments copy of which I send herewith & called the ayes & nays to fix them on the journal. This greatly alarmed the Majority & vexed them extremely—for the plan is, to push the business on with great dispatch, & with as little opposition as possible: that it may be adopted before it has stood the test of Reflection & due examination. They found it most eligible at last to transmit it merely, without approving or disapproving; provided nothing but the transmission should appear on the Journal. This compromise was settled and they took the opportunity of inserting the word *Unanimously,* which applied only to simple transmission, hoping to have it mistaken for an Unanimous approbation of the thing. It states that Congress having Received the Constitution unanimously transmit it &c. It is certain that no Approbation was given. This constitution has a great many excellent Regulations in it and if it could be reasonably amended would be a fine System. As it is, I think 'tis past doubt, that if it should be established, either a tyranny will result from it, or it will be prevented by a Civil war. I am clearly of opinion with you that it should be sent back with amendments Reasonable and Assent to it with held until such amendments are admitted. You are well acquainted with Thos. Stone & others of influence in Maryland—I think it will be a great point to get Maryld. & Virginia to join in the plan of Amendments & return it with them. If you are in correspondence with our Chancelor Pendelton it will be of much use to furnish him with the objections, and if he approves our plan, his opinion will have great weight with our Convention and I am told that his relation Judge Pendleton of South Carolina has decided weight in the State & that he is sensible & independent. How important will it be then to procure his union with our plan, which might probably be the case, if our Chancelor was to write largely and pressingly to him on the subject; that if possible it may be amended there also. It is certainly the most rash and violent proceeding in the world to cram thus suddenly into Men a business of such infinite Moment to the happiness of Millions.

. . . . .

Suppose when the Assembly recommended a Convention to consider this new Constitution they were to use some words like these—It is earnestly recommended to the good people of Virginia to send their most wise & honest Men to this Convention that it may undergo the most intense consideration before a plan shall be without amendments adopted that admits of abuses being practised by which the best interests of this Country may be injured and Civil Liberty greatly endanger'd. This might perhaps give a decided Tone to the business.

17

ROBERT WHITEHILL, PENNSYLVANIA
RATIFYING CONVENTION
28 Nov. 1787
McMaster 257–59

It will be proper, perhaps, to review the origin of this business. It was certainly, Mr. President, acknowledged on all hands, that an additional share of power for federal purposes ought to be delegated to Congress; and with a view to enquire how far it was necessary to strengthen and enlarge the jurisdiction of that body, the late convention was appointed under the authority, and by legislative acts of the several states. But how, Sir, did the convention act upon this occasion? Did they pursue the authority which was given to them? By the State of Pennsylvania that authority was strictly defined in the following words:

"And the said Thomas Mifflin, Robert Morris, George Clymer, Jared Ingersoll, Thomas Fitzsimons, James Wilson and Gouverneur Morris, Esqrs., or any four of them, are hereby constituted and appointed deputies from this state, with powers to meet such deputies as may be appointed and authorized by the other states to assemble in the said convention at the city aforesaid, and to join with them in devising, deliberating on and discussing all such alterations and further provisions as may be necessary to render the federal constitution fully adequate to the exigencies of the union; and in reporting such act or acts for that purpose to the United States in Congress assembled, as when agreed to by them, and duly confirmed by the several states, will effectually provide for the same."

Thus, Sir, it appears that no other power was given to the delegates from this state (and I believe the power given by the other states was of the same nature and extent) than to increase in a certain degree the strength and energy of Congress; but it never was in the contemplation of any man that they were authorized to dissolve the present union, to abrogate the state sovereignties, and to establish one comprehensive government, novel in its structure, and in its probable operation oppressive and despotic. Can it then be said that the late convention did not assume powers to which they had no legal title? On the contrary, Sir, it is clear that they set aside the laws under which they were appointed, and under which alone they could derive any legitimate authority, they arrogantly exercised any powers that they found convenient to their object, and in the end they have overthrown that government which they were called upon to amend, in order to introduce one of their own fabrication.

True it is, Mr. President, that if the people intended to engage in one comprehensive system of continental government, the power to frame that system must have been conferred by them; for the legislatures of the states are sworn to preserve the independence of their respective constitutions, and therefore they could not, consistently with their most sacred obligations, authorize an act which sacrificed the individual to the aggregate sovereignty of the states. But it appears from the origin and nature of the commission under which the late convention assembled, that a more perfect confederation was the only object submitted to their wisdom, and not, as it is attempted by this plan, the total destruction of the government of Pennsylvania, and of every other state. So far, Sir, the interference of the legislatures was proper and efficient; but the moment the convention went beyond that object, they ceased to act under any legitimate authority, for the assemblies could give them none, and it cannot be pretended that they were called together by the people; for, till the preamble was produced, it never was understood that the people at large had been consulted upon the occasion, or that otherwise than through their representatives in the several states, they had given a sanction to the proceedings of that body. If, indeed, the federal convention, finding that the old system was incapable of repair, had represented the incurable defects to Congress, and advised that the original and inherent power of the people might be called into exercise for the institution of a new government, then, Sir, the subject would have come fairly into view, and we should have known upon what principles we proceeded. At present we find a convention appointed by one authority, but acting under the arbitrary assumption of another; and instead of transacting the business which was assigned to them, behold! they have produced a work of supererogation, after a mysterious labor of three months.

18

JAMES WILSON, PENNSYLVANIA
RATIFYING CONVENTION
4 Dec. 1787

McMaster 331–32

I come now to consider the last set of objections that are offered against this constitution. It is urged, that this is not such a system as was within the powers of the convention; they assumed the *power of proposing.* I believe they might have made proposals without going beyond their powers. I never heard before, that to make a proposal was an exercise of power. But if it is an exercise of power, they certainly did assume it; yet they did not act as that body who framed the present constitution of Pennsylvania acted; they did not by an ordinance attempt to rivet the constitution on the people, before they could vote for members of assembly under it. Yet such was the effect of the ordinance that attended the constitution of this commonwealth. I think the late convention have done nothing beyond their powers. The fact is, they have exercised no power at all. And in point of validity, this constitution proposed by them for the government of the United States, claims no more than a production of the same nature would claim, flowing from a private pen. It is laid before the citizens of the United States, unfettered by restraint; it is laid before them, to be judged by the natural, civil and political rights of men. By their FIAT, it will become of value and authority; without it, it will never receive the character of authenticity and power. The business, we are told, which was entrusted to the late convention, was merely to amend the present articles of confederation. This observation has been frequently made, and has often brought to my mind a story that is related of Mr. Pope, who it is well known, was not a little deformed. It was customary with him, to use this phrase, "God mend me," when any little incident happened. One evening a link boy was lighting him along, and coming to a gutter, the boy jumped nimbly over it—Mr. Pope called to him to turn, adding, "God mend me:" The arch rogue turned to light him—looked at him, and repeated, "God mend you! he would sooner make a half-a-dozen new ones." This would apply to the present confederation; for it would be easier to make another than to mend this. The gentlemen urge, that this is such a government as was not expected by the people, the legislatures, nor by the honorable gentlemen who mentioned it. Perhaps it was not such as was expected, *but it may be* BETTER; and is that a reason why it should not be adopted? It is not worse, I trust, than the former. So that the argument of its being a system not expected, is an argument more strong in its favor than against it. The letter which accompanies this constitution, must strike every person with the utmost force. "The friends of our country have long seen and desired the power of war, peace and treaties, that of levying money and regulating commerce, and the corresponding executive and judicial authorities, should be fully and effectually vested in the general government of the union; but the impropriety of delegating such extensive trust to one body of men, is evident. *Hence results the necessity of a different organization.*" I therefore do not think it can be urged as an objection against this system, that it was not expected by the people.

19

LUTHER MARTIN, GENUINE INFORMATION
1788

Storing 2.4.111–14

By our original articles of confederation any alterations proposed, are in the first place to be *approved* by Congress.—Accordingly as the resolutions were originally adopted by the convention, and as they were reported by the committee of detail, it was proposed that this system should be laid before Congress *for their approbation;* but, Sir, the warm advocates of this system fearing it would not meet with the approbation of Congress, and determined, even though Congress and the respective State legislatures should disapprove the same, to force it upon them, if possible, through the intervention of the people at large, moved to strike out the words "for their approbation" and succeeded in their motion; to which, it being directly in violation of the mode prescribed by the articles of confederation for the alteration of our federal government, a part of the convention, and myself in the number, thought it a duty to give a decided negative.

Agreeable to the articles of confederation entered into in the most *solemn manner,* and for the *observance* of which the States *pledged* themselves to each other, and called upon the *Supreme Being* as a *witness* and *avenger* between them, *no alterations* are to be made in those articles unless after they are approved by Congress, they are agreed to and ratified by the *legislature* of *every* State; but by the resolve of the convention this constitution is not to be ratified by the legislatures of the respective States, but is to be submitted to conventions chosen by the people, and if ratified by them is to be binding.

This resolve was opposed among others by the delegation of Maryland;—your delegates were of opinion, that as the form of government proposed was, if adopted, most essentially to *alter* the *constitution* of *this State,* and as our constitution had pointed out a mode by which, and by which *only,* alterations were to be made therein, a convention of the people could not be called to agree to and ratify the said form of government without a *direct violation* of our constitution, which it is the duty of every individual in this State to protect and support;—In this opinion all your delegates who were attending were unanimous; I, Sir, opposed it also upon a more extensive ground, as being directly *contrary* to the mode of altering our federal government *established* in our original compact, and as such being a *direct violation* of the mutual faith plighted by the States to each other, I gave it my negative.

I also was of opinion, that the States considered as States, in their political capacity, are the members of a federal government; that the States in their political capacity, or as Sovereignties, are entitled, and *only entitled* originally to agree upon the form of, and submit themselves to, a federal government, and afterwards by mutual consent to dissolve or alter it—That every thing which relates to the formation, the dissolution or the alteration of a *federal government* over States equally free, sovereign and independent is the *peculiar* province of the *States* in their *sovereign* or *political* capacity, in the same manner as what relates to forming alliance or treaties of peace, amity or commerce, and that the people at large in their individual capacity, have no more right to interfere in the one case than in the other: That according to these principles we originally acted in forming our confederation; it was the States as States, by their representatives in Congress, that formed the articles of confederation; it was the States as States, by

their legislatures, ratified those articles, and it was there established and provided that the States as States, that is by their legislatures, should agree to any alterations that should hereafter be proposed in the federal government, before they should be binding—and any alterations agreed to in any other manner cannot release the States from the obligation they are under to each other by virtue of the original articles of confederation. The people of the different States never made any objection to the manner the articles of confederation were formed or ratified, or to the mode by which alterations were to be made in that government—with the rights of their respective States they wished not to interfere—Nor do I believe the people in their individual capacity, would ever have expected or desired to have been appealed to on the present occasion, in violation of the rights of their respective States, if the favourers of the proposed constitution, imagining they had a better chance of forcing it to be adopted by a *hasty* appeal to the people at large, who could not be so good judges of the dangerous consequence, had not insisted upon this mode—nor do these positions in the least interfere with the principle, that all power originates from the people, because when once the people have *exercised their power* in *establishing* and *forming* themselves into a *State government,* it never devolves *back* to them, nor have they a *right* to *resume* or *again to exercise that power* until such events takes place as will amount to a *dissolution* of their *State government:*—And it is an established principle that a dissolution or alteration of a *federal* government doth not dissolve the *State* governments which compose it. It was also my opinion, that upon *principles of sound policy,* the agreement or disagreement to the proposed system ought to have been by the State legislatures, in which case, let the event have been what it would, there would have been but little prospects of the *public peace* being *disturbed* thereby—Whereas the attempt to force down this system, although Congress and the respective State legislatures should disapprove, by appealing to the people, and to procure its establishment in a manner totally unconstitutional, has a tendency to set the *State governments* and their *subjects* at *variance* with each other—to *lessen* the *obligations* of *government*—to *weaken* the *bands* of *society*—to introduce *anarchy* and *confusion*—And to *light* the *torch* of *discord* and *civil war* throughout this continent. All these considerations weighed with me most forcibly against giving my assent to the mode by which it is resolved this system is to be ratified, and were urged by me in opposition to the measure.

20

JAMES MADISON, FEDERALIST, NO. 40, 258–67
18 Jan. 1788

The *second* point to be examined is, whether the Convention were authorised to frame and propose this mixed Constitution.

The powers of the Convention ought in strictness to be determined, by an inspection of the commissions given to the members by their respective constituents. As all of these however had reference, either to the recommendation from the meeting at Annapolis in September, 1786, or to that from Congress in February, 1787, it will be sufficient to recur to these particular acts.

The act from Annapolis recommends the "appointment of commissioners to take into consideration, the situation of the United States, to devise *such further provisions* as shall appear to them necessary to render the Constitution of the Foederal Government *adequate to the exigencies of the Union;* and to report such an act for that purpose, to the United States in Congress assembled, as when agreed to by them, and afterwards confirmed by the Legislature of every State, will effectually provide for the same."

The recommendatory act of Congress is in the words following: "Whereas there is provision in the articles of confederation and perpetual Union, for making alterations therein, by the assent of a Congress of the United States, and of the Legislatures of the several States: And whereas experience hath evinced, that there are defects in the present confederation, as a mean to remedy which, several of the States, and *particularly the State of New-York,* by express instructions to their delegates in Congress, have suggested a Convention for the purposes expressed in the following resolution; and such Convention appearing to be the most probable mean of establishing in these States, *a firm national government.*

"Resolved, That in the opinion of Congress, it is expedient, that on the 2d Monday in May next, a Convention of delegates, who shall have been appointed by the several States, be held at Philadelphia for the sole and express purpose *of revising the articles of confederation,* and reporting to Congress and the several Legislatures, such *alterations and provisions therein,* as shall, when agreed to in Congress, and confirmed by the States, render the Foederal Constitution *adequate to the exigencies of government and the preservation of the Union.*"

From these two acts it appears, 1st. that the object of the Convention was to establish in these States, *a firm national government;* 2d. that this Government was to be such as would be *adequate to the exigencies of government* and *the preservation of the Union;* 3d. that these purposes were to be effected by *alterations and provisions in the articles of confederation,* as it is expressed in the act of Congress, or by *such further provisions as should appear necessary,* as it stands in the recommendatory act from Annapolis; 4th. that the alterations and provisions were to be reported to Congress, and to the States, in order to be agreed to by the former, and confirmed by the latter.

From a comparison and fair construction of these several modes of expression, is to be deduced the authority, under which the Convention acted. They were to frame a *national government,* adequate to the *exigencies of government* and *of the Union,* and to reduce the articles of confederation into such form as to accomplish these purposes.

There are two rules of construction dictated by plain reason, as well as founded on legal axioms. The one is, that every part of the expression ought, if possible, to be allowed some meaning, and be made to conspire to some common end. The other is, that where the several parts cannot be made to coincide, the less important should give way to the more important part; the means should be sacrificed to the end, rather than the end to the means.

Suppose then that the expressions defining the authority of the Convention, were irreconcileably at variance with each other; that a *national* and *adequate government* could not possibly, in the judgment of the Convention, be effected by *alterations* and *provisions* in the *articles of confederation,* which part of the definition ought to have been embraced, and which rejected? Which was the more important, which the less important part? Which the end, which the means? Let the most scrupulous expositors of delegated powers: Let the most inveterate objectors against those exercised by the Convention, answer these questions. Let them declare, whether it was of most importance to the happiness of the people of America, that the articles of confederation should be disregarded, and an adequate government be provided, and the Union preserved; or that an adequate government should be omitted, and the articles of confederation preserved. Let them declare, whether the preservation of these articles was the end for securing which a reform of the government was to be introduced as the means; or whether the establishment of a government, adequate to the national happiness, was the end at which these articles themselves originally aimed, and to which they ought, as insufficient means, to have been sacrificed.

But is it necessary to suppose that these expressions are absolutely irreconcileable to each other; that no *alterations* or *provisions* in *the articles of the confederation,* could possibly mould them into a national and adequate government; into such a government as has been proposed by the Convention?

No stress it is presumed will in this case be laid on the *title,* a change of that could never be deemed an exercise of ungranted power. *Alterations* in the body of the instrument, are expressly authorised. *New provisions* therein are also expressly authorised. Here then is a power to change the title; to insert new articles; to alter old ones. Must it of necessity be admitted that this power is infringed, so long as a part of the old articles remain? Those who maintain the affirmative, ought at least to mark the boundary between authorised and usurped innovations, between that degree of change, which lies within the compass of *alterations and further provisions;* and that which amounts to a *transmutation* of the government. Will it be said that the alterations ought not to have touched the substance of the confederation? The States would never have appointed a Convention with so much solemnity, nor described its objects with so much latitude, if some *substantial* reform had not been in contemplation. Will it be said that the *fundamental principles* of the confederation were not within the purview of the Convention, and ought not to have been varied? I ask what are these principles? do they require that in the establishment of the Constitution, the States should be regarded as distinct and independent sovereigns? They are so regarded by the Constitution proposed. Do they require that the members of the government should derive their appointment from the Legislatures, not from the people of the State? One branch of the new government is to be appointed by these Legislatures; and under the confederation the delegates to Congress *may all* be appointed immediately by the people, and in two States* are actually so appointed. Do they require that the powers of the Government should act on the States, and not immediately on individuals? In some instances, as has been shewn, the powers of the new Government will act on the States in their collective characters. In some instances also those of the existing Government act immediately on individuals. In cases of capture, of piracy, of the post-office, of coins, weights and measures, of trade with the Indians, of claims under grants of land by different States, and above all, in the case of trials by Courts-martial in the army and navy, by which death may be inflicted without the intervention of a jury, or even of a civil Magistrate; in all these cases the powers of the confederation operate immediately on the persons and interests of individual citizens. Do these fundamental principles require particularly, that no tax should be levied without the intermediate agency of the States! The confederation itself authorises a direct tax to a certain extent on the post-office. The power of coinage has been so construed by Congress, as to levy a tribute immediately from that source also. But pretermitting these instances, was it not an acknowledged object of the Convention, and the universal expectation of the people, that the regulation of trade should be submitted to the general government in such a form as would render it an immediate source of general revenue? Had not Congress repeatedly recommended this measure as not inconsistent with the fundamental principles of the confederation? Had not every State but one, had not New-York herself, so far complied with the plan of Congress, as to recognize the *principle* of the innovation? Do these principles in fine require that the powers of the general government should be limited, and that beyond this limit, the States should be left in possession of their sovereignty and independence? We have seen that in the new government as in the old, the general powers are limited, and that the States in all unenumerated cases, are left in the enjoyment of their sovereign and independent jurisdiction.

The truth is, that the great principles of the Constitution proposed by the Convention, may be considered less as absolutely new, than as the expansion of principles which are found in the articles of Confederation. The misfortune under the latter system has been, that these principles are so feeble and confined as to justify all the charges of inefficiency which have been urged against it; and to require a degree of enlargement which gives to the new system, the aspect of an entire transformation of the old.

In one particular it is admitted that the Convention have departed from the tenor of their commission. Instead of reporting a plan requiring the confirmation *of the Legislatures of all the States,* they have reported a plan which is to be confirmed by the *people,* and may be carried into effect

by *nine States only.* It is worthy of remark, that this objection, though the most plausible, has been the least urged in the publications which have swarmed against the Convention. The forbearance can only have proceeded from an irresistible conviction of the absurdity of subjecting the fate of 12 States, to the perverseness or corruption of a thirteenth; from the example of inflexible opposition given by *a majority* of 1-60th of the people of America, to a measure approved and called for by the voice of twelve States comprising 59-60ths of the people; an example still fresh in the memory and indignation of every citizen who has felt for the wounded honor and prosperity of his country. As this objection, therefore, has been in a manner waved by those who have criticised the powers of the Convention, I dismiss it without further observation.

The *third* point to be enquired into is, how far considerations of duty arising out of the case itself, could have supplied any defect of regular authority.

In the preceding enquiries, the powers of the Convention have been analised and tried with the same rigour, and by the same rules, as if they had been real and final powers, for the establishment of a Constitution for the United States. We have seen, in what manner they have borne the trial, even on that supposition. It is time now to recollect, that the powers were merely advisory and recommendatory; that they were so meant by the States, and so understood by the Convention; and that the latter have accordingly planned and proposed a Constitution, which is to be of no more consequence than the paper on which it is written, unless it be stamped with the approbation of those to whom it is addressed. This reflection places the subject in a point of view altogether different, and will enable us to judge with propriety of the course taken by the Convention.

Let us view the ground on which the Convention stood. It may be collected from their proceedings, that they were deeply and unanimously impressed with the crisis which had led their country almost with one voice to make so singular and solemn an experiment, for correcting the errors of a system by which this crisis had been produced; that they were no less deeply and unanimously convinced, that such a reform as they have proposed, was absolutely necessary to effect the purposes of their appointment. It could not be unknown to them, that the hopes and expectations of the great body of citizens, throughout this great empire, were turned with the keenest anxiety, to the event of their deliberations. They had every reason to believe that the contrary sentiments agitated the minds and bosoms of every external and internal foe to the liberty and prosperity of the United States. They had seen in the origin and progress of the experiment, the alacrity with which the *proposition* made by a single State (Virginia) towards a partial amendment of the confederation, had been attended to and promoted. They had seen the *liberty assumed* by a *very few* deputies, from a *very few* States, convened at Annapolis, of recommending a great and critical object, wholly foreign to their commission, not only justified by the public opinion, but actually carried into effect, by twelve out of the thirteen States. They had seen in a variety of instances, assumptions by Congress, not only of

---

*Connecticut and Rhode-island.

recommendatory, but of operative powers, warranted in the public estimation, by occasions and objects infinitely less urgent than those by which their conduct was to be governed. They must have reflected, that in all great changes of established governments, forms ought to give way to substance; that a rigid adherence in such cases to the former, would render nominal and nugatory, the transcendent and precious right of the people to "abolish or alter their governments as to them shall seem most likely to effect their safety and happiness;"* since it is impossible for the people spontaneously and universally, to move in concert towards their object; and it is therefore essential, that such changes be instituted by some *informal and unauthorised propositions,* made by some patriotic and respectable citizen or number of citizens. They must have recollected that it was by this irregular and assumed privilege of proposing to the people plans for their safety and happiness, that the States were first united against the danger with which they were threatened by their antient government; that Committees and Congresses, were formed for concentrating their efforts, and defending their rights; and that *Conventions* were *elected* in *the several States,* for establishing the constitutions under which they are now governed; nor could it have been forgotten that no little ill-timed scruples, no zeal for adhering to ordinary forms, were any where seen, except in those who wished to indulge under these masks, their secret enmity to the substance contended for. They must have borne in mind, that as the plan to be framed and proposed, was to be submitted *to the people themselves,* the disapprobation of this supreme authority would destroy it for ever; its approbation blot out all antecedent errors and irregularities. It might even have occurred to them, that where a disposition to cavil prevailed, their neglect to execute the degree of power vested in them, and still more their recommendation of any measure whatever not warranted by their commission, would not less excite animadversion, than a recommendation at once of a measure fully commensurate to the national exigencies.

Had the Convention under all these impressions, and in the midst of all these considerations, instead of exercising a manly confidence in their country, by whose confidence they had been so peculiarly distinguished, and of pointing out a system capable in their judgment of securing its happiness, taken the cold and sullen resolution of disappointing its ardent hopes of sacrificing substance to forms, of commiting the dearest interests of their country to the uncertainties of delay, and the hazard of events; let me ask the man, who can raise his mind to one elevated conception; who can awaken in his bosom, one patriotic emotion, what judgment ought to have been pronounced by the impartial world, by the friends of mankind, by every virtuous citizen, on the conduct and character of this assembly, or if there be a man whose propensity to condemn, is susceptible of no controul, let me then ask what sentence he has in reserve for the twelve States, who *usurped the power* of sending deputies to the Convention, a body utterly unknown to their constitutions; for Congress, who recommended the appointment of this body, equally unknown to the confederation; and for the State of New-York in particular, who first urged and then complied with this authorised interposition.

But that the objectors may be disarmed of every pretext, it shall be granted for a moment, that the Convention were neither authorised by their commission, nor justified by circumstances, in proposing a Constitution for their country: Does it follow that the Constitution ought for that reason alone to be rejected? If according to the noble precept it be lawful to accept good advice even from an enemy, shall we set the ignoble example of refusing such advice even when it is offered by our friends? The prudent enquiry in all cases, ought surely to be not so much *from whom* the advice comes, as whether the advice be *good.*

The sum of what has been here advanced and proved, is that the charge against the Convention of exceeding their powers, except in one instance little urged by the objectors, has no foundation to support it; that if they had exceeded their powers, they were not only warranted but required, as the confidential servants of their country, by the circumstances in which they were placed, to exercise the liberty which they assumed, and that finally, if they had violated both their powers, and their obligations in proposing a Constitution, this ought nevertheless to be embraced, if it be calculated to accomplish the views and happiness of the people of America. How far this character is due to the Constitution, is the subject under investigation.

*Declaration of Independence.

SEE ALSO:

Credentials of the Delaware Delegation to the Federal
    Convention, 3 Feb. 1787, Farrand 3:574–75
Federal Farmer, no. 1, 8 Oct. 1787, Storing 2.8.7
Pelataiah Webster, Remarks on the Address of Sixteen Members
    of the Assembly of Pennsylvania to Their Constituents, Dated
    September 29, 1787, Oct. 1787, McMaster 94
A Republican Federalist, no. 3, 9 Jan. 1788, Storing 4.13.15
The Fallacies of the Freeman Detected by a Farmer,
    23 Apr. 1788, Storing 3.14.22

7

Union

Introduction

Union may not have been quite the simple good old cause that proponents of the new Constitution made it out to be. But however separate and distinct the American colonies were in their foundations, temper, and internal self-government, they had shared a long history under a common imperial authority. For over a century and a half that central authority in Britain had set policy on war and peace, commerce, westward expansion, and the like. Hence the crisis that issued in a revolutionary declaration of independence not only involved colonial resistance to an old central authority, but also almost necessarily entailed the burden of creating a new continental authority. In that concrete sense the problems of union were rooted deep in the colonial past, in the nature of the British empire, and in the central conflicts of the Revolution. So while many abstractions figured in the debate over union, they were abstractions grounded in persistent historical and geographical facts.

The first halting efforts by Americans to make "out of many, one" were beset by much the same difficulties and considerations that vexed the United States down to the eve of civil war. Union, indispensable for the survival of the parts, threatened to engulf and devour them. The considerations of self-preservation and political effectiveness that argued for a union of all the colonies or states militated by the same token against a partial union or several confederacies; yet the heterogeneity of the colonies or states made some less comprehensive grouping appear the surer and safer project. Further, in seeking as they did a union that would legislate for its parts, the Americans resigned themselves to the kind of tension that attends complex solutions. Theirs was to be neither alliance nor amalgam. The parts as parts would continue; but the parts would not and could not be more than parts of a greater whole.

One great constitutional manifestation of this effort to combine goals that do not sit easily together will be examined in ch. 8 under the heading Federal v. Consolidated Government. But that formulation already presupposes some kind of union, and it is with that first step that one leaves the world of simple solutions and simple troubles.

The tentative early proposals of the Albany Commissioners (no. 1) for a union with certain limited but significant purposes and powers of legislation already contain the germ of much that was to follow. Franklin's explanatory "reasons and motives" (no. 2) lay bare the inherent difficulties, complicated by the need to accommodate the great third party, the imperial government, through its crown representative. Though the plan tries to avoid uncertainty and controversy by eschewing any legislative prerogatives beyond "*such only* as shall be necessary" for enumerated purposes, and denies any intention that the general government "interfere with the constitution and government of the particular colonies," it nevertheless leaves unsettled the boundary between the general and particular governments. In truth, the subject admits of no mathematical exactness or finality. Patrick Henry, ever wary and sniffing consolidation from a distance, accordingly could later trace the Americans' success in resisting British tyranny to the failure of the Albany plan: American liberty had flourished in the absence of concentered governmental strength and energy (see Elliot 3:172–73). Therein, he thought, lay a great cautionary lesson.

With growing colonial protest and resistance to intrusive central authority, Americans were led to create their own institutions for common action. And as independence became their more or less openly avowed object, they were led to give their ad hoc union constitutional form. The tension between the whole and parts persists in Franklin's 21 July 1775 draft of the Articles of Confederation (see *Journals* 2:195–99). Under that plan Congress may "Make such General Ordinances as tho' necessary to the General Welfare, particular Assemblies cannot be competent to," yet at the same time each of *"The United Colonies of North America"* continues to "enjoy and retain as much as it may think fit of its own present Laws, Customs, Rights, Privileges, and peculiar Jurisdictions within its own Limits." The proposal moves a long way toward national union by permitting the delegates to vote as individuals rather than as a single colonial delegation; in this sense it partakes less of the character of a mere league than either John Dickinson's subsequent draft of 12 July 1776 (see *Journals* 5:546–54) or the final version of the Articles of Confederation (see ch. 1, no. 7).

Most or all adherents of the revolutionary cause understood, at some level, that henceforth they were no longer simply Virginians or New Yorkers, but Americans. The Continental Congress's letter transmitting the proposed Articles to the state legislatures for ratification (no. 4) drew upon this awareness even while trying desperately to augment it. Stressing simultaneously the many elements that divided the Americans and the considerations that made those diverse folk "brethren and fellow-citizens," Congress seemed to be confessing in one breath the greatness of the task and the modesty of their proffered means. As the event proved, their urgent appeal to feelings of union was neither superfluous nor especially effective: the Articles finally were ratified only after a delay of more than three years and only after one of those divisive elements (conflicting state claims to Western lands) had been resolved.

The shortcomings of the Articles were widely remarked on, not least by those who came to be called Anti-Federalists. But those deficiencies did not point ineluctably to a single remedy. Here lies the core of the debate over the Constitution, for not all could accept the explicit premise of those who agitated for a change and led the fight for the Constitution's ratification: that "a more perfect Union" required a government differently constituted (nos. 5, 6). Even among some later self-styled Federalists it was a question whether union on republican principles was possible, whether general laws, equitable to all, were within the reach of a legislature elected by a highly diverse people. Perhaps a more perfect union might better be approached through disunion, followed by reunion of the more neighborly and kindred states (Rush, no. 7; see also Benjamin Lincoln to Rufus King, 11 Feb. 1786, and J. T. Main, *The Antifederalists: Critics of the Constitution* 283–84 [1961]). Madison would soon rebut this misgiving by turning it on its head. Union on republican principles is not only possible but essential to a just and lasting republic (see ch. 4, no. 22). As for the Anti-Federalists, a more perfect union on national grounds threatened rather to suffocate the states or reduce them to nonentities (see ch. 8). In the extreme case, a most thoughtful Anti-Federalist was prepared to accept division as the lesser evil (Centinel, no. 18). A more moderate alternative would be to recognize the diversity of state interests in the very structure of government. But here again there were deep differences. Madison relied on the competition of interests both within and outside the national legislature (see ch. 4, no. 19, and ch. 10, no. 16), anticipating that heterogeneity among and within the states would temper political extremes and make for a firmer union. Similarly, Hamilton sought to show how the very diversity of circumstances in the country might promote a useful economic complementarity (no. 23). The Impartial Examiner (27 Feb. 1788), in contrast, thought to reconcile or unite those interests by accommodating the states in the critical respect—by leaving the power of the purse in their several hands.

With suggestions such as this latter being bruited about, Publius held it far from "superfluous to offer arguments to prove the utility of the UNION" (no. 9). The "proof" consisted, as is characteristic of the *Federalist Papers,* in an adroit appeal to fears and hopes, to calculation and sentiment. It was either union on the terms of the proposed Constitution, or "dismemberment" of the already existing union. (See also C. C. Pinckney, no. 19; Jay, no. 22.) Union was the old cause, the source of much of the greatness that America already had achieved (see ch. 4, no. 22). Those who advocated, or failed to forfend, separation were the true innovators and would unwittingly deprive America of its due influence for good in the world. Their heedlessness might have even more perilous consequences, for they seemed oblivious of a lesson attested by "the accumulated experience of ages": fences make bad neighbors. Wars were not merely a royal disease; and commerce, far from pacifying men, had only changed the objects of war. In this sense America was like unto all the nations. But more particularly (Hamilton went on with obvious relish), America fairly bristled with peculiar circumstances that made even more likely its becoming a bloody theater for hostile pretensions and legitimately differing interests. Unless, that is, an effective superintending power could hold all these in check (nos. 10, 11).

Beyond these urgent concerns lay another case for union, at once self-serving and philanthropic. Union was the precondition for America's becoming a nation, forming a national character "adapted to the principles and genius of our system of government" (Wilson, no. 17). Union under the Constitution promised to help "diffuse those generous *federal* sentiments, without which, we never can be a happy and flourishing people." As used here by A [Massachusetts] Federalist, "federal" is contrasted with the crabbed, parochial sentiments fostered by the existing state constitutions (no. 16). A united America would somehow be greater and finer than the sum of its parts.

Again, one man's dream was another's nightmare. A firmer union might open the way to America's becoming a great nation whose growing territory, population, resources, and wealth would enable it to exert its power—and the power of republican example for the world. Alternatively, a firmer union might tempt a people to a career of national splendor, glory, and domination at the sacrifice of liberty and quiet domestic happiness. (See chs. 8 and 9.)

Such promises or anticipations bent under the weight of earthier concerns. When a state or region felt its interests slighted or threatened, its rightful influence waning or denied, its very necessities jeopardized, visions of a grand collective future were small solace. These resentments and alarms were given voice in turn by each of the great parts out of which union was so painfully being formed: the Mississippi Valley (George Nicholas to James Madison, 31 Dec. 1790), New England (Pickering, no. 24), and the South. The last, being the keenest and most fearsome challenge to the principles of union, elicited the most profound restatements of the Founders' understanding of what they had wrought. (See also James Madison to Edward Everett, 28 Aug. 1830; and Joseph Story, *Commentaries on the Constitution of the United States* 1:§§ 321–40, 361–72 [1833].) "The happy Union of the States" might indeed be "a wonder; their Constn. a miracle" (as Madison exclaimed in 1829), but the record of surviving documents points unequivocally to the tireless efforts of politically adroit men who knew what they wanted and why.

1

ALBANY PLAN OF UNION
10 July 1754
Franklin Papers 5:387–92

PLAN of a Proposed Union of the Several Colonies of Masachusets-bay, New Hampshire, Coneticut, Rhode Island, New York, New Jerseys, Pensilvania, Maryland, Virginia, North Carolina, and South Carolina, For their Mutual Defence and Security, and for Extending the British Settlements in North America.

THAT humble Application be made for an Act of the Parliament of Great Britain, by Virtue of which, one General Government may be formed in America, including all the said Colonies, within and under which Government, each Colony may retain its present Constitution, except in the Particulars wherein a Change may be directed by the said Act, as hereafter follows.

That the said General Government be administred by a President General, To be appointed and Supported by the Crown, and a Grand Council to be Chosen by the Representatives of the People of the Several Colonies, met in their respective Assemblies.

That within   Months after the passing of such Act, The House of Representatives in the Several Assemblies, that Happen to be Sitting within that time or that shall be Specially for that purpose Convened, may and Shall Choose Members for the Grand Council in the following Proportions, that is to say.

Masachusets-Bay....................7.
New Hampshire...................2.
Coneticut.........................5.
Rhode-Island......................2.
New-York.........................4.
New-Jerseys......................3.
Pensilvania.......................6.
Maryland.........................4.
Virginia.........................7.
North-Carolina...................4.
South-Carolina...................4.
                                 ___
                                 48.

Who shall meet for the first time at the City of Philadelphia, in Pensilvania, being called by the President General as soon as conveniently may be, after his Appointment.

That there shall be a New Election of Members for the Grand Council every three years; And on the Death or Resignation of any Member his Place shall be Supplied by a New Choice at the next Sitting of the Assembly of the Colony he represented.

That after the first three years, when the Proportion of Money arising out of each Colony to the General Treasury can be known, The Number of Members to be Chosen, for each Colony shall from time to time in all ensuing Elections be regulated by that proportion (yet so as that the Number to be Chosen by any one Province be not more than Seven nor less than Two).

That the Grand Council shall meet once in every Year, and oftner if Occasion require, at such Time and place as they shall adjourn to at the last preceeding meeting, or as they shall be called to meet at by the President General, on any Emergency, he having first obtained in Writing the Consent of seven of the Members to such call, and sent due and timely Notice to the whole.

That the Grand Council have Power to Chuse their Speaker, and shall neither be Dissolved, prorogued nor Continue Sitting longer than Six Weeks at one Time without their own Consent, or the Special Command of the Crown.

That the Members of the Grand Council shall be Allowed for their Service ten shillings Sterling per Diem, during their Sessions or Journey to and from the Place of Meeting; Twenty miles to be reckoned a days Journey.

That the Assent of the President General be requisite, to all Acts of the Grand Council, and that it be His Office, and Duty to cause them to be carried into Execution.

That the President General with the Advice of the Grand Council, hold or Direct all Indian Treaties in which the General Interest or Welfare of the Colony's may be Concerned; And make Peace or Declare War with the Indian Nations. That they make such Laws as they Judge Necessary for regulating all Indian Trade. That they make all Purchases from Indians for the Crown, of Lands not within the Bounds of Particular Colonies, or that shall not be within their Bounds when some of them are reduced to more Convenient Dimensions. That they make New Settlements on such Purchases, by Granting Lands in the Kings Name, reserving a Quit Rent to the Crown, for the use of the General Treasury. That they make Laws for regulating and Governing such new Settlements, till the Crown shall think fit to form them into Particular Governments.

That they raise and pay Soldiers, and build Forts for the Defence of any of the Colonies, and equip Vessels of Force to Guard the Coasts and Protect the Trade on the Ocean, Lakes, or Great Rivers; But they shall not Impress Men in any Colonies, without the Consent of its Legislature. That for these purposes they have Power to make Laws And lay and Levy such General Duties, Imposts, or Taxes, as to them shall appear most equal and Just, Considering the Ability and other Circumstances of the Inhabitants in the Several Colonies, and such as may be Collected with the least Inconvenience to the People, rather discouraging Luxury, than Loading Industry with unnecessary Burthens. That they may Appoint a General Treasurer and a Particular Treasurer in each Government, when Necessary, And from Time to Time may Order the Sums in the Treasuries of each Government, into the General Treasury, or draw on them for Special payments as they find most Convenient; Yet no money to Issue, but by joint Orders of the President General and Grand Council Except where Sums have been Appropriated to particular Purposes, And the President General is previously impowered By an Act to draw for such Sums.

That the General Accounts shall be yearly Settled and Reported to the Several Assembly's.

That a Quorum of the Grand Council impower'd to Act with the President General, do consist of Twenty-five Members, among whom there shall be one, or more from a Majority of the Colonies. That the Laws made by them for the Purposes aforesaid, shall not be repugnant but as near as may be agreeable to the Laws of England, and Shall be transmitted to the King in Council for Approbation, as Soon as may be after their Passing and if not disapproved within Three years after Presentation to remain in Force.

That in case of the Death of the President General The Speaker of the Grand Council for the Time Being shall Succeed, and be Vested with the Same Powers, and Authority, to Continue until the King's Pleasure be known.

That all Military Commission Officers Whether for Land or Sea Service, to Act under this General Constitution, shall be Nominated by the President General But the Approbation of the Grand Council, is to be Obtained before they receive their Commissions, And all Civil Officers are to be Nominated, by the Grand Council, and to receive the President General's Approbation, before they Officiate; But in Case of Vacancy by Death or removal of any Officer Civil or Military under this Constitution, The Governor of the Province, in which such Vacancy happens, may Appoint till the Pleasure of the President General and Grand Council can be known. That the Particular Military as well as Civil Establishments in each Colony remain in their present State, this General Constitution Notwithstanding. And that on Sudden Emergencies any Colony may Defend itself, and lay the Accounts of Expence thence Arisen, before the President General and Grand Council, who may allow and order payment of the same As far as they Judge such Accounts Just and reasonable.

2

BENJAMIN FRANKLIN, REASONS AND MOTIVES FOR THE ALBANY PLAN OF UNION
July 1754
Papers 5:399–417

I. Reasons and Motives on which the Plan of Union was formed.

The Commissioners from a number of the northern colonies being met at Albany, and considering the difficulties that have always attended the most necessary general measures for the common defence, or for the annoyance of the enemy, when they were to be carried through the several particular assemblies of all the colonies; some assemblies being before at variance with their governors or councils, and the several branches of the government not on terms of doing business with each other; others taking the opportunity, when their concurrence is wanted, to push for favourite laws, powers, or points that they think could not at other times be obtained, and so *creating* disputes and quarrels; one assembly waiting to see what another will do, being afraid of doing more than its share, or desirous of doing less; or refusing to do any thing, because its country is not at present so much exposed as others, or because another will reap more immediate advantage; from one or other of which causes, the assemblies of six (out of seven) colonies applied to, had granted no assistance to Virginia, when lately invaded by the French, though purposely convened, and the importance of the occasion earnestly urged upon them: Considering moreover, that one principal encouragement to the French, in invading and insulting the British American dominions, was their knowledge of our disunited state, and of our weakness arising from such want of union; and that from hence different colonies were, at different times, extremely harassed, and put to great expence both of blood and treasure, who would have remained in peace, if the enemy had had cause to fear the drawing on themselves the resentment and power of the whole; the said Commissioners, considering also the present incroachments of the French, and the mischievous consequences that may be expected from them, if not opposed with our force, came to an unanimous resolution, *That an union of the colonies is absolutely necessary for their preservation.*

The *manner* of forming and establishing this union was the next point. When it was considered that the colonies were seldom all in equal danger at the same time, or equally near the danger, or equally sensible of it; that some of them had particular interests to manage, with which an union might interfere; and that they were extremely jealous of each other; it was thought impracticable to obtain a joint agreement of all the colonies to an union, in which the expence and burthen of defending any of them should be divided among them all; and if ever acts of assembly in all the colonies could be obtained for that purpose, yet as any colony, on the least dissatisfaction, might repeal its own act and thereby withdraw itself from the union, it would not be a stable one, or such as could be depended on: for if only one colony should, on any disgust withdraw itself, others might think it unjust and unequal that they, by continuing in the union, should be at the expence of defending a colony which refused to bear its proportionable part, and would therefore one after another, withdraw, till the whole crumbled into its original parts. Therefore the commissioners came to another previous resolution, viz. *That it was necessary the union should be established by act of parliament.*

They then proceeded to sketch out a *plan of union,* which they did in a plain and concise manner, just sufficient to shew their sentiments of the kind of union that would best suit the circumstances of the colonies, be most agreeable to the people, and most effectually promote his Majesty's service and the general interest of the British empire. This was respectfully sent to the assemblies of the several colonies for their consideration, and to receive such alterations and improvements as they should think fit and necessary; after which it was proposed to be transmitted to England to be perfected, and the establishment of it there humbly solicited.

This was as much as the commissioners could do.

II. Reasons against partial Unions.

It was proposed by some of the Commissioners to form the colonies into two or three distinct unions; but for these reasons that proposal was dropped even by those that made it; [viz.]

1. In all cases where the strength of the whole was necessary to be used against the enemy, there would be the same difficulty in degree, to bring the several unions to unite together, as now the several colonies; and consequently the same delays on our part and advantage to the enemy.

2. Each union would separately be weaker than when joined by the whole, obliged to exert more force, be more oppressed by the expence, and the enemy less deterred from attacking it.

3. Where particular colonies have *selfish views,* as New York with regard to Indian trade and lands; or are *less exposed,* being covered by others, as New Jersey, Rhode Island, Connecticut, Maryland; or have *particular whims and prejudices* against warlike measures in general, as Pensylvania, where the Quakers predominate; such colonies would have more weight in a partial union, and be better able to oppose and obstruct the measures necessary for the general good, than where they are swallowed up in the general union.

4. The Indian trade would be better regulated by the union of the whole than by partial unions. And as Canada is chiefly supported by that trade, if it could be drawn into the hands of the English, (as it might be if the Indians were supplied on moderate terms, and by honest traders appointed by and acting for the public) that alone would contribute greatly to the weakening of our enemies.

5. The establishing of new colonies westward on the Ohio and the lakes, (a matter of considerable importance to the increase of British trade and power, to the breaking that of the French, and to the protection and security of our present colonies,) would best be carried on by a joint union.

6. It was also thought, that by the frequent meetings-together of commissioners or representatives from all the colonies, the circumstances of the whole would be better known, and the good of the whole better provided for; and that the colonies would by this connection learn to consider themselves, not as so many independent states, but as members of the same body; and thence be more ready to afford assistance and support to each other, and to make diversions in favour even of the most distant, and to join cordially in any expedition for the benefit of all against the common enemy.

These were the principal reasons and motives for forming the plan of union as it stands. To which may be added this that as the union of the

The remainder of this article is lost.

III. Plan of a proposed Union of the several Colonies of Massachusett's Bay, New Hampshire, Connecticut, Rhode Island, New York, New Jersey, Pennsylvania, Maryland, Virginia, North Carolina, and South Carolina for their mutual Defence and Security, and for extending the British Settlements in North America, with the Reasons and Motives for each Article of the Plan [as far as could be remembered.]

It is proposed. That humble application be made for an act of parliament of Great Britain, by virtue of which one general government may be formed in America including all the said colonies, within and under which government each colony may retain its present constitution, except in the particulars wherein a change may be directed by the said act as hereafter follows.

President General, and Grand Council.

That the said general government be administered by a President General to be appointed and supported by the crown; and a Grand Council to be chosen by the representatives of the people of the several colonies met in their respective assemblies.

It was thought that it would be best the President General should be supported as well as appointed by the crown; that so all disputes between him and the Grand Council concerning his salary might be prevented; as such disputes have been frequently of mischievous consequence in particular colonies, especially in time of public danger. The quit-rents of crown-lands in America, might in a short time be sufficient for this purpose. The choice of members for the grand council is placed in the house of representatives of each government, in order to give the people a share in this new general government, as the crown has its share by the appointment of the President General.

But it being proposed by the gentlemen of the council of New York, and some other counsellors among the commissioners, to alter the plan in this particular, and to give the governors and council of the several provinces a share in the choice of the grand council, or at least a power of approving and confirming or of disallowing the choice made by the house of representatives, it was said:

"That the government or constitution proposed to be formed by the plan, consists of two branches; a President General appointed by the crown, and a council chosen by the people, or by the people's representatives, which is the same thing.

"That by a subsequent article, the council chosen by the people can effect nothing without the consent of the President General appointed by the crown; the crown possesses therefore full one half of the power of this constitution.

"That in the British constitution, the crown is supposed to possess but one third, the Lords having their share.

"That this constitution seemed rather more favourable for the crown.

"That it is essential to English liberty, [that] the subject should not be taxed but by his own consent or the consent of his elected representatives.

"That taxes to be laid and levied by this proposed constitution will be proposed and agreed to by the representatives of the people, if the plan in this particular be preserved:

"But if the proposed alteration should take place, it seemed as if matters may be so managed as that the crown shall finally have the appointment not only of the President General, but of a majority of the grand council; for, seven out of eleven governors and councils are appointed by the crown:

"And so the people in all the colonies would in effect be taxed by their governors.

"It was therefore apprehended that such alterations of the plan would give great dissatisfaction, and that the colonies could not be easy under such a power in governors, and such an infringement of what they take to be English liberty.

"Besides, the giving a share in the choice of the grand council would not be equal with respect to all the colonies, as their constitutions differ. In some, both governor and council are appointed by the crown. In others, they are both appointed by the proprietors. In some, the people have a share in the choice of the council; in others, both government and council are wholly chosen by the people. But the house of representatives is every where chosen by the people; and therefore placing the right of choosing the grand council in the representatives, is equal with respect to all.

"That the grand council is intended to represent all the several houses of representatives of the colonies, as a house of representatives doth the several towns or counties of a colony. Could all the people of a colony be consulted and unite in public measures, a house of representatives would be needless: and could all the assemblies conveniently consult and unite in general measures, the grand council would be unnecessary.

"That a house of commons or the house of representatives, and the grand council, are thus alike in their nature and intention. And as it would seem improper that the King or house of Lords should have a power of disallowing or appointing members of the house of commons; so likewise that a governor and council appointed by the crown should have a power of disallowing or appointing members of the grand council, (who, in this constitution, are to be the representatives of the people.)

"If the governors and councils therefore were to have a share in the choice of any that are to conduct this general government, it should seem more proper that they chose the President General. But this being an office of great trust and importance to the nation, it was thought better to be filled by the immediate appointment of the crown.

"The power proposed to be given by the plan to the grand council is only a concentration of the powers of the several assemblies in certain points for the general welfare; as the power of the President General is of the powers of the several governors in the same points.

"And as the choice therefore of the grand council by the representatives of the people, neither gives the people any new powers, nor diminishes the power of the crown, it was thought and hoped the crown would not disapprove of it."

Upon the whole, the commissioners were of opinion, that the choice was most properly placed in the representatives of the people.

Election of Members.

That within   months after the passing such act, the house of representatives that happen to be sitting within that time, or that shall be especially for that purpose convened, may and shall choose members for the grand council, in the following proportion, that is to say,

Massachussett's Bay	*7*
New Hampshire	*2*
Connecticut	*5*
Rhode Island	*2*
New York	*4*
New Jerseys	*3*
Pensylvania	*6*
Maryland	*4*

Virginia 7
North Carolina.................. 4
South Carolina................. 4
                              ——
                               48

It was thought that if the least colony was allowed two, and the others in proportion, the number would be very great and the expence heavy; and that less than two would not be convenient, as a single person, being by any accident prevented appearing at the meeting, the colony he ought to appear for would not be represented. That as the choice was not immediately popular, they would be generally men of good abilities for business, and men of reputation for integrity; and that forty-eight such men might be a number sufficient. But, though it was thought reasonable that each colony should have a share in the representative body in some degree, according to the proportion it contributed to the general treasury; yet the proportion of wealth or power of the colonies is not to be judged by the proportion here fixed; because it was at first agreed that the greatest colony should not have more than seven members, nor the least less than two: and the settling these proportions between these two extremes was not nicely attended to, as it would find itself, after the first election from the sums brought into the treasury, as by a subsequent article.

Place of first Meeting.

—who shall meet for the first time at the city of Philadelphia in Pensylvania, being called by the President General as soon as conveniently may be after his appointment.

Philadelphia was named as being the nearer the center of the colonies where the Commissioners would be well and cheaply accommodated. The high-roads through the whole extent, are for the most part very good, in which forty or fifty miles a day may very well be and frequently are travelled. Great part of the way may likewise be gone by water. In summer-time the passages are frequently performed in a week from Charles Town to Philadelphia and New York; and from Rhode Island to New York through the Sound in two or three days; and from New York to Philadelphia by water and land in two days, by stage-boats and wheel-carriages that set out every other day. The journey from Charles Town to Philadelphia may likewise be facilitated by boats running up Chesapeak Bay three hundred miles. But if the whole journey be performed on horseback, the most distant members, (viz. the two from New Hampshire and from South Carolina) may probably render themselves at Philadelphia in fifteen or twenty-two days; the majority may be there in much less time.

New Election.

That there shall be a new election of the members of the Grand Council every three years; and on the death or resignation of any member, his place shall be supplied by a new choice at the next sitting of the assembly of the colony he represented.

Some colonies have annual assemblies, some continue during a governor's pleasure; three years was thought a reasonable medium, as affording a new member time to improve himself in the business, and to act after such

improvement; and yet giving opportunities, frequent enough, to change him if he has misbehaved.

Proportion of Members after the first three Years.

That after the first three years, when the proportion of money arising out of each colony to the general treasury can be known, the number of members to be chosen for each colony shall from time to time, in all ensuing elections, be regulated by that proportion (yet so as that the number to be chosen by any one province be not more than seven, nor less than two).

By a subsequent article it is proposed, that the general council shall lay and levy such general duties as to them may appear most equal and least burthensome, &c. Suppose, for instance, they lay a small duty or excise on some commodity imported into or made in the colonies, and pretty generally and equally used in all of them; as rum perhaps, or wine: the yearly produce of this duty or excise, if fairly collected, would be in some colonies greater, in others less, as the colonies are greater or smaller. When the collectors accounts are brought in, the proportions will appear; and from them it is proposed to regulate the proportion of representatives to be chosen at the next general election, within the limits however of seven and two. These numbers may therefore vary in course of years, as the colonies may in the growth and increase of people. And thus the quota of tax from each colony would naturally vary with its circumstances; thereby preventing all disputes and dissatisfactions about the just proportions due from each; which might otherwise produce pernicious consequences, and destroy the harmony and good agreement that ought to subsist between the several parts of the union.

Meetings of the Grand Council, and Call.

That the Grand Council shall meet once in every year and oftener if occasion require, at such time and place as they shall adjourn to at the last preceding meeting, or as they shall be called to meet at by the President General on any emergency; he having first obtained in writing the consent of seven of the members to such call, and sent due and timely notice to the whole.

It was thought, in establishing and governing new colonies or settlements, regulating Indian trade, Indian treaties, &c. there would be every year sufficient business arise to require at least one meeting, and at such meeting many things might be suggested for the benefit of all the colonies. This annual meeting may either be at a time or place certain, to be fixed by the President General and grand council at their first meeting; or left at liberty, to be at such time and place as they shall adjourn to, or be called to meet at by the President General.

In *time of war* it seems convenient, that the meeting should be in that colony, which is nearest the seat of action.

The power of calling them on any emergency seemed necessary to be vested in the President General; but that such power might not be wantonly used to harass the members, and oblige them to make frequent long journies to little purpose, the consent of seven at least to such call was supposed a convenient guard.

Continuance.

That the Grand Council have power to choose their speaker; and shall neither be dissolved, prorogued, nor continued sitting longer than six weeks at one time; without their own consent or the special command of the crown.

The speaker should be presented for approbation; it being convenient, to prevent misunderstandings and disgusts, that the mouth of the council should be a person agreeable, if possible, both to the council and the President General.

Governors have sometimes wantonly exercised the power of proroguing or continuing the sessions of assemblies, merely to harass the members and compel a compliance; and sometimes dissolve them on slight disgusts. This it was feared might be done by the President General, if not provided against: and the inconvenience and hardship would be greater in the general government than in particular colonies, in proportion to the distance the members must be from home, during sittings, and the long journies some of them must necessarily take.

Members' Allowance.

That the members of the Grand Council shall be allowed for their service ten shillings sterling per diem, during their session and journey to and from the place of meeting; twenty miles to be reckoned a day's journey.

It was thought proper to allow *some* wages, lest the expence might deter some suitable persons from the service; and not to allow *too great* wages, lest unsuitable persons should be tempted to cabal for the employment for the sake of gain. Twenty miles was set down as a day's journey to allow for accidental hinderances on the road, and the greater expences of travelling than residing at the place of meeting.

Assent of President General and his Duty.

That the assent of the President General be requisite to all acts of the Grand Council; and that it be his office and duty to cause them to be carried into execution.

The assent of the President General to all acts of the grand council was made necessary, in order to give the crown its due share of influence in this government, and connect it with that of Great Britain. The President General, besides one half of the legislative power, hath in his hands the whole executive power.

Power of President General and Grand Council. Treaties of Peace and War.

That the President General, with the advice of the Grand Council, hold or direct all Indian treaties in which the general interest of the colonies may be concerned; and make peace or declare war with Indian nations.

The power of making peace or war with Indian nations is at present supposed to be in every colony, and is expressly granted to some by charter, so that no new power is hereby intended to be granted to the colonies. But as, in consequence of this power, one colony might make peace with a nation that another was justly engaged in war with; or make war on slight occasions without the concurrence or approbation of neighbouring colonies, greatly endangered by it; or make particular treaties of neutrality in case of a general war, to their own private advantage in trade, by supplying the common enemy; of all which there have been instances—it was thought better to have all treaties of a general nature under a general direction; that so the good of the whole may be consulted and provided for.

Indian Trade.

That they make such laws as they judge necessary for regulating all Indian trade.

Many quarrels and wars have arisen between the colonies and Indian nations, through the bad conduct of traders; who cheat the Indians after making them drunk, &c. to the great expence of the colonies both in blood and treasure. Particular colonies are so interested in the trade as not to be willing to admit such a regulation as might be best for the whole; and therefore it was thought best under a general direction.

Indian Purchases.

That they make all purchases from Indians for the crown, of lands not now within the bounds of particular colonies or that shall not be within their bounds when some of them are reduced to more convenient dimensions.

Purchases from the Indians made by private persons, have been attended with many inconveniences. They have frequently interfered, and occasioned uncertainty of titles, many disputes and expensive law-suits, and hindered the settlement of the land so disputed. Then the Indians have been cheated by such private purchases, and discontent and wars have been the consequence. These would be prevented by public fair purchases.

Several of the colony charters in America extend their bounds to the South Sea, which may be perhaps three or four thousand miles in length to one or two hundred miles in breadth. It is supposed they must in time be reduced to dimensions more convenient for the common purposes of government.

Very little of the land in those grants is yet purchased of the Indians.

It is much cheaper to purchase of them, than to take and maintain the possession by force: for they are generally very reasonable in their demands for land; and the expence of guarding a large frontier against their incursions is vastly great; because all must be guarded and always guarded, as we know not where or when *to expect them*.

New Settlements.

That they make new settlements on such purchases by granting lands in the King's name, reserving a quit-rent to the crown for the use of the general treasury.

It is supposed better that there should be one purchaser than many; and that the crown should be that purchaser, or the union in the name of the crown. By this means the bargains may be more easily made, the price not inhanced by numerous bidders, future disputes about private Indian purchases, and monopolies of vast tracts to particular persons (which are prejudicial to the settlement and peopling of a country) prevented; and the land being again granted in small tracts to the settlers, the quit-rents reserved may in time become a fund for support of government, for defence of the country, ease of taxes, &c.

Strong forts on the lakes, the Ohio, &c. may at the same time they secure our present frontiers, serve to defend new colonies settled under their protection; and such colonies would also mutually defend and support such forts, and better secure the friendship of the far Indians.

A particular colony has scarce strength enough to extend itself by new settlements, at so great a distance from the old: but the joint force of the union might suddenly establish a new colony or two in those parts, or extend an old colony to particular passes, greatly to the security of our present frontiers, increase of trade and people, breaking off the French communication between Canada and Louisiana, and speedy settlement of the intermediate lands.

The power of settling new colonies is therefore thought a valuable part of the plan; and what cannot so well be executed by two unions as by one.

Laws to govern them.

That they make laws for regulating and governing such new settlements, till the crown shall think fit to form them into particular governments.

The making of laws suitable for the new colonies, it was thought would be properly vested in the President General and grand council; under whose protection they will at first necessarily be, and who would be well acquainted with their circumstances, as having settled them. When they are become sufficiently populous, they may by the crown, be formed into compleat and distinct governments.

The appointment of a Sub-president by the crown, to take place in case of the death or absence of the President General, would perhaps be an improvement of the plan; and if all the governors of particular provinces were to be formed into a standing council of state, for the advice and assistance of the President General, it might be another considerable improvement.

Raise Soldiers and equip Vessels, &c.

That they raise and pay soldiers and build forts for the defence of any of the colonies, and equip vessels of force to guard the coasts and protect the trade on the ocean, lakes, or great rivers; but they shall not impress men in any colony without the consent of the legislature.

It was thought, that quotas of men to be raised and paid by the several colonies, and joined for any public service, could not always be got together with the necessary expedition. For instance, suppose one thousand men should be wanted in New Hampshire on any emergency; to fetch them by fifties and hundreds out of every colony as far as South Carolina, would be inconvenient, the transportation chargeable, and the occasion perhaps passed before they could be assembled; and therefore that it would be best to

raise them (by offering bounty-money and pay) near the place where they would be wanted, to be discharged again when the service should be over.

Particular colonies are at present backward to build forts at their own expence, which they say will be equally useful to their neighbouring colonies; who refuse to join, on a presumption that such forts *will* be built and kept up, though they contribute nothing. This unjust conduct weakens the whole; but the forts being for the good of the whole, it was thought best they should be built and maintained by the whole, out of the common treasury.

In the time of war, small vessels of force are sometimes necessary in the colonies to scour the coast of small privateers. These being provided by the Union, will be an advantage in turn to the colonies which are situated on the sea, and whose frontiers on the land-side, being covered by other colonies, reap but little immediate benefit from the advanced forts.

Power to make Laws, lay Duties, &c.

That for these purposes they have power to make laws, and lay and levy such general duties, imports, or taxes, as to them shall appear most equal and just, (considering the ability and other circumstances of the inhabitants in the several colonies,) and such as may be collected with the least inconvenience to the people; rather discouraging luxury, than loading industry with unnecessary burthens.

The laws which the President General and grand council are impowered to make, *are such only* as shall be necessary for the government of the settlements; the raising, regulating and paying soldiers for the general service; the regulating of Indian trade; and laying and collecting the general duties and taxes. (They should also have a power to restrain the exportation of provisions to the enemy from any of the colonies, on particular occasions, in time of war.) But it is not intended that they may interfere with the constitution and government of the particular colonies; who are to be left to their own laws, and to lay, levy, and apply their own taxes as before.

General Treasurer and Particular Treasurer.

That they may appoint a General Treasurer and Particular Treasurer in each government when necessary; and from time to time may order the sums in the treasuries of each government into the general treasury; or draw on them for special payments, as they find most convenient.

The treasurers here meant are only for the general funds; and not for the particular funds of each colony, which remain in the hands of their own treasurers at their own disposal.

Money how to issue.

Yet no money to issue but by joint orders of the President General and Grand Council; except where sums have been appropriated to particular purposes, and the President General is previously impowered by an act to draw for such sums.

To prevent misapplication of the money, or even application that might be dissatisfactory to the crown or the people, it was thought necessary to join the President General and grand council in all issues of money.

Accounts.

That the general Accounts shall be yearly settled and reported to the several assemblies.

By communicating the accounts yearly to each assembly, they will be satisfied of the prudent and honest conduct of their representatives in the grand council.

Quorum.

That a quorum of the Grand Council impowered to act with the President General, do consist of twenty-five members; among whom there shall be one or more from a majority of the colonies.

The quorum seems large, but it was thought it would not be satisfactory to the colonies in general, to have matters of importance to the whole transacted by a smaller number, or even by this number of twenty-five, unless there were among them one at least from a majority of the colonies; because otherwise the whole quorum being made up of members from three or four colonies at one end of the union, something might be done that would not be equal with respect to the rest, and thence dissatisfactions and discords might rise to the prejudice of the whole.

Laws to be transmitted.

That the laws made by them for the purposes aforesaid shall not be repugnant, but, as near as may be, agreeable to the laws of England, and shall be transmitted to the King in council for approbation as soon as may be after their passing; and if not disapproved within three years after presentation, to remain in force.

This was thought necessary for the satisfaction of the crown, to preserve the connection of the parts of the British empire with the whole, of the members with the head, and to induce greater care and circumspection in making of the laws, that they be good in themselves and for the general benefit.

Death of the President General.

That in case of the death of the President General, the speaker of the Grand Council for the time being shall succeed, and be vested with the same powers and authorities, to continue till the King's pleasure be known.

It might be better, perhaps, as was said before, if the crown appointed a Vice President, to take place on the death or absence of the President General; for so we should be more sure of a suitable person at the head of the colonies. On the death or absence of both, the speaker to take place (or rather the eldest King's-governor) till his Majesty's pleasure be known.

Officers how appointed.

That all military commission officers, whether for land or sea service, to act under this general constitution, shall be nominated by the President General; but the approbation of the Grand Council is to be obtained, before they receive their commissions. And all civil officers are to be nominated by the Grand Council, and to receive the President General's approbation before they officiate.

It was thought it might be very prejudicial to the service, to have officers appointed unknown to the people, or unacceptable; the generality of Americans serving willingly under officers they know; and not caring to engage in the service under strangers, or such as are often appointed by governors through favour or interest. The service here meant, is not the stated settled service in standing troops; but any sudden and short service, either for defence of our own colonies, or invading the enemies country; (such as, the expedition to Cape Breton in the last war; in which many substantial farmers and tradesmen engaged as common soldiers under officers of their own country, for whom they had an esteem and affection; who would not have engaged in a standing army, or under officers from England.) It was therefore thought best to give the council the power of approving the officers, which the people will look upon as a great security of their being good men. And without some such provision as this, it was thought the expence of engaging men in the service on any emergency would be much greater, and the number who could be induced to engage much less; and that therefore it would be most for the King's service and general benefit of the nation, that the prerogative should relax a little in this particular throughout all the colonies in America; as it had already done much more in the charters of some particular colonies, viz. Connecticut and Rhode Island.

The civil officers will be chiefly treasurers and collectors of taxes; and the suitable persons are most likely to be known by the council.

Vacancies how supplied.

But in case of vacancy by death, or removal of any officer civil or military under this constitution, the governor of the province in which such vacancy happens, may appoint till the pleasure of the President General and Grand Council can be known.

The vacancies were thought best supplied by the governors in each province, till a new appointment can be regularly made; otherwise the service might suffer before the meeting of the President General and grand council.

Each Colony may defend itself on Emergency, &c.

That the particular military as well as civil establishments in each colony remain in their present state, the general constitution notwithstanding; and that on sudden emergencies any colony may defend itself and lay the accounts of expence thence arising before the President General and general council, who may allow and order payment of the same as far as they judge such accounts just and reasonable.

Otherwise the Union of the whole would weaken the parts, contrary to the design of the union. The accounts are to be judged of by the President General and grand council, and allowed if found reasonable: this was thought necessary to encourage colonies to defend themselves, as the expence would be light when borne by the whole; and also to check imprudent and lavish expence in such defences.

Remark, Feb. 9. 1789.

On Reflection it now seems probable, that if the foregoing Plan or some thing like it, had been adopted and carried into Execution, the subsequent Separation of the Colonies from the Mother Country might not so soon have happened, nor the Mischiefs suffered on both sides have occurred, perhaps during another Century. For the Colonies, if so united, would have really been, as they then thought themselves, sufficient to their own Defence, and being trusted with it, as by the Plan, an Army from Britain, for that purpose would have been unnecessary: The Pretences for framing the Stamp-Act would then not have existed, nor the other Projects for drawing a Revenue from America to Britain by Acts of Parliament, which were the Cause of the Breach, and attended with such terrible Expence of Blood and Treasure: so that the different Parts of the Empire might still have remained in Peace and Union. But the Fate of this Plan was singular. For tho' after many Days thorough Discussion of all its Parts in Congress it was unanimously agreed to, and Copies ordered to be sent to the Assembly of each Province for Concurrence, and one to the Ministry in England for the Approbation of the Crown. The Crown disapprov'd it, as having plac'd too much Weight in the democratic Part of the Constitution; and every Assembly as having allow'd too much to Prerogative. So it was totally rejected.

Endorsed: Feb. 9, 1789. Dr. Franklin.

3

JOSEPH GALLOWAY, PLAN OF UNION
28 Sept. 1774
Journals 1:49–51

Resolution submitted by Joseph Galloway:

Resolved, That the Congress will apply to his Majesty for a redress of grievances under which his faithful subjects in America labour; and assure him, that the Colonies hold in abhorrence the idea of being considered independent communities on the British government, and most ardently desire the establishment of a Political Union, not only among themselves, but with the Mother State, upon those principles of safety and freedom which are essential in the constitution of all free governments, and particularly that of the British Legislature; and as the Colonies from their local circumstances, cannot be represented in the Parliament of Great-Britain, they will humbly propose to his Majesty and his two Houses of Parliament, the following plan, under which the strength of the whole Empire may be drawn together on any emergency, the interest of both countries advanced, and the rights and liberties of America secured.

A Plan of a proposed Union between Great Britain and the Colonies.

That a British and American legislature, for regulating the administration of the general affairs of America, be proposed and established in America, including all the said colonies; within, and under which government, each colony shall retain its present constitution, and powers of regulating and governing its own internal police, in all cases whatsoever.

That the said government be administered by a President General, to be appointed by the King, and a grand Council, to be chosen by the Representatives of the people of the several colonies, in their respective assemblies, once in every three years.

That the several assemblies shall choose members for the grand council in the following proportions, viz.

New Hampshire.	Delaware Counties.
Massachusetts-Bay.	Maryland.
Rhode Island.	Virginia.
Connecticut.	North Carolina.
New-York.	South-Carolina.
New-Jersey.	Georgia.
Pennsylvania.	

Who shall meet at the city of   for the first time, being called by the President-General, as soon as conveniently may be after his appointment.

That there shall be a new election of members for the Grand Council every three years; and on the death, removal or resignation of any member, his place shall be supplied by a new choice, at the next sitting of Assembly of the Colony he represented.

That the Grand Council shall meet once in every year, if they shall think it necessary, and oftener, if occasions shall require, at such time and place as they shall adjourn to, at the last preceding meeting, or as they shall be called to meet at, by the President-General, on any emergency.

That the grand Council shall have power to choose their Speaker, and shall hold and exercise all the like rights, liberties and privileges, as are held and exercised by and in the House of Commons of Great-Britain.

That the President-General shall hold his office during the pleasure of the King, and his assent shall be requisite to all acts of the Grand Council, and it shall be his office and duty to cause them to be carried into execution.

That the President-General, by and with the advice and consent of the Grand-Council, hold and exercise all the legislative rights, powers, and authorities, necessary for regulating and administering all the general police and affairs of the colonies, in which Great-Britain and the colonies, or any of them, the colonies in general, or more than one colony, are in any manner concerned, as well civil and criminal as commercial.

That the said President-General and the Grand Council, be an inferior and distinct branch of the British legislature, united and incorporated with it, for the aforesaid general purposes; and that any of the said general regulations may originate and be formed and digested, either in the Parliament of Great Britain, or in the said Grand Council, and being prepared, transmitted to the other for their approbation or dissent; and that the assent of both shall be requisite to the validity of all such general acts or statutes.

That in time of war, all bills for granting aid to the crown, prepared by the Grand Council, and approved by the President General, shall be valid and passed into a law, without the assent of the British Parliament.

4

CONTINENTAL CONGRESS, LETTER TRANSMITTING PROPOSED ARTICLES OF CONFEDERATION
17 Nov. 1777
Elliot 1:69–70

Congress having agreed upon a plan of confederacy for securing the freedom, sovereignty, and independence of the United States, authentic copies are now transmitted for the consideration of the respective legislatures.

This business, equally intricate and important, has, in its progress, been attended with uncommon embarrassment and delay, which the most anxious solicitude and persevering diligence could not prevent. To form a permanent union, accommodated to the opinion and wishes of the delegates of so many states, differing in habits, produce, commerce, and internal police, was found to be a work which nothing but time and reflection, conspiring with a disposition to conciliate, could mature and accomplish.

Hardly is it to be expected that any plan, in the variety of provisions essential to our union, should exactly correspond with the maxims and political views of every particular state. Let it be remarked, that, after the most careful inquiry, and the fullest information, this is proposed as the best which could be adapted to the circumstances of all, and as that alone which affords any tolerable prospect of general ratification.

Permit us, then, earnestly to recommend these Articles to the immediate and dispassionate attention of the legislatures of the respective states. Let them be candidly reviewed under a sense of the difficulty of combining in one general system the various sentiments and interests of a continent divided into so many sovereign and independent communities; under a conviction of the absolute necessity of uniting all our councils, and all our strength, to maintain and defend our common liberties; let them be examined with a liberality becoming brethren and fellow-citizens surrounded by the same imminent dangers, contending for the same illustrious prize, and deeply interested in being forever bound and connected together by ties the most intimate and indissoluble; and, finally, let them be adjusted with the temper and magnanimity of wise and patriotic legislators, who, while they are concerned for the prosperity of their own more immediate

circle, are capable of rising superior to local attachments, when they may be incompatible with the safety, happiness, and glory, of the general confederacy.

We have reason to regret the time which has elapsed in preparing this plan for consideration: with additional solicitude we look forward to that which must be necessarily spent before it can be ratified. Every motive loudly calls upon us to hasten its conclusion.

More than any other consideration, it will confound our foreign enemies, defeat the flagitious practices of the disaffected, strengthen and confirm our friends, support our public credit, restore the value of our money, enable us to maintain our fleets and armies, and add weight and respect to our councils at home and to our treaties abroad.

In short, this salutary measure can no longer be deferred. It seems essential to our very existence as a free people; and, without it, we may soon be constrained to bid adieu to independence, to liberty, and safety—blessings which, from the justice of our cause, and the favor of our Almighty Creator, visibly manifested in our protection, we have reason to expect, if, in an humble dependence on his divine providence, we strenuously exert the means which are placed in our power.

To conclude: If the legislature of any state shall not be assembled, Congress recommend to the executive authority to convene it without delay; and to each respective legislature it is recommended to invest its delegates with competent powers, ultimately, in the name and behalf of the state, to subscribe Articles of Confederation and Perpetual Union of the United States, and to attend Congress for that purpose on or before the 10th day of March next.

5

GEORGE WASHINGTON, CIRCULAR TO THE STATES
8 June 1783
Writings 26:484–89

When we consider the magnitude of the prize we contended for, the doubtful nature of the contest, and the favorable manner in which it has terminated, we shall find the greatest possible reason for gratitude and rejoicing; this is a theme that will afford infinite delight to every benevolent and liberal mind, whether the event in contemplation, be considered as the source of present enjoyment or the parent of future happiness; and we shall have equal occasion to felicitate ourselves on the lot which Providence has assigned us, whether we view it in a natural, a political or moral point of light.

The Citizens of America, placed in the most enviable condition, as the sole Lords and Proprietors of a vast Tract of Continent, comprehending all the various soils and climates of the World, and abounding with all the necessaries and conveniencies of life, are now by the late satisfactory pacification, acknowledged to be possessed of absolute freedom and Independency; They are, from this period, to be considered as the Actors on a most conspicuous Theatre, which seems to be peculiarly designated by Providence for the display of human greatness and felicity; Here, they are not only surrounded with every thing which can contribute to the completion of private and domestic enjoyment, but Heaven has crowned all its other blessings, by giving a fairer oppertunity for political happiness, than any other Nation has ever been favored with. Nothing can illustrate these observations more forcibly, than a recollection of the happy conjuncture of times and circumstances, under which our Republic assumed its rank among the Nations; The foundation of our Empire was not laid in the gloomy age of Ignorance and Superstition, but at an Epocha when the rights of mankind were better understood and more clearly defined, than at any former period, the researches of the human mind, after social happiness, have been carried to a great extent, the Treasures of knowledge, acquired by the labours of Philosophers, Sages and Legislatures, through a long succession of years, are laid open for our use, and their collected wisdom may be happily applied in the Establishment of our forms of Government; the free cultivation of Letters, the unbounded extension of Commerce, the progressive refinement of Manners, the growing liberality of sentiment, and above all, the pure and benign light of Revelation, have had a meliorating influence on mankind and increased the blessings of Society. At this auspicious period, the United States came into existence as a Nation, and if their Citizens should not be completely free and happy, the fault will be intirely their own.

Such is our situation, and such are our prospects: but notwithstanding the cup of blessing is thus reached out to us, notwithstanding happiness is ours, if we have a disposition to seize the occasion and make it our own; yet, it appears to me there is an option still left to the United States of America, that it is in their choice, and depends upon their conduct, whether they will be respectable and prosperous, or contemptable and miserable as a Nation; This is the time of their political probation, this is the moment when the eyes of the whole World are turned upon them, this is the moment to establish or ruin their national Character forever, this is the favorable moment to give such a tone to our Federal Government, as will enable it to answer the ends of its institution, or this may be the ill-fated moment for relaxing the powers of the Union, annihilating the cement of the Confederation, and exposing us to become the sport of European politics, which may play one State against another to prevent their growing importance, and to serve their own interested purposes. For, according to the system of Policy the States shall adopt at this moment, they will stand or fall, and by their confirmation or lapse, it is yet to be decided, whether the Revolution must ultimately be considered as a blessing or a curse: a blessing or a curse, not to the present age alone, for with our fate will the destiny of unborn Millions be involved.

With this conviction of the importance of the present Crisis, silence in me would be a crime; I will therefore speak to your Excellency, the language of freedom and of sincerity, without disguise; I am aware, however, that those who differ from me in political sentiment, may perhaps remark, I am stepping out of the proper line of my duty, and they may possibly ascribe to arrogance or ostentation, what I know is alone the result of the purest intention, but the rectitude of my own heart, which disdains such unworthy motives, the part I have hitherto acted in life, the determination I have formed, of not taking any share in public business hereafter, the ardent desire I feel, and shall continue to manifest, of quietly enjoying in private life, after all the toils of War, the benefits of a wise and liberal Government, will, I flatter myself, sooner or later convince my Countrymen, that I could have no sinister views in delivering with so little reserve, the opinions contained in this Address.

There are four things, which I humbly conceive, are essential to the well being, I may even venture to say, to the existence of the United States as an Independent Power:

1st. An indissoluble Union of the States under one Federal Head.

2dly. A Sacred regard to Public Justice.

3dly. The adoption of a proper Peace Establishment, and

4thly. The prevalence of that pacific and friendly Disposition, among the People of the United States, which will induce them to forget their local prejudices and policies, to make those mutual concessions which are requisite to the general prosperity, and in some instances, to sacrifice their individual advantages to the interest of the Community.

These are the Pillars on which the glorious Fabrick of our Independency and National Character must be supported; Liberty is the Basis, and whoever would dare to sap the foundation, or overturn the Structure, under whatever specious pretexts he may attempt it, will merit the bitterest execration, and the severest punishment which can be inflicted by his injured Country.

On the three first Articles I will make a few observations, leaving the last to the good sense and serious consideration of those immediately concerned.

Under the first head, altho' it may not be necessary or proper for me in this place to enter into a particular disquisition of the principles of the Union, and to take up the great question which has been frequently agitated, whether it be expedient and requisite for the States to delegate a larger proportion of Power to Congress, or not, Yet it will be a part of my duty, and that of every true Patriot, to assert without reserve, and to insist upon the following positions, That unless the States will suffer Congress to exercise those prerogatives, they are undoubtedly invested with by the Constitution, every thing must very rapidly tend to Anarchy and confusion, That it is indispensable to the happiness of the individual States, that there should be lodged somewhere, a Supreme Power to regulate and govern the general concerns of the Confederated Republic, without which the Union cannot be of long duration. That there must be a faithfull and pointed compliance on the part of every State, with the late proposals and demands of Congress, or the most fatal consequences will ensue, That whatever measures have a tendency to dissolve the Union, or contribute to violate or lessen the Sovereign Authority, ought to be considered as hostile to the Liberty and Independency of America, and the Authors of them treated accordingly, and lastly, that unless we can be enabled by the concurrence of the States, to participate of the fruits of the Revolution, and enjoy the essential benefits of Civil Society, under a form of Government so free and uncorrupted, so happily guarded against the danger of oppression, as has been devised and adopted by the Articles of Confederation, it will be a subject of regret, that so much blood and treasure have been lavished for no purpose, that so many sufferings have been encountered without a compensation, and that so many sacrifices have been made in vain. Many other considerations might here be adduced to prove, that without an entire conformity to the Spirit of the Union, we cannot exist as an Independent Power; it will be sufficient for my purpose to mention but one or two which seem to me of the greatest importance. It is only in our united Character as an Empire, that our Independence is acknowledged, that our power can be regarded, or our Credit supported among Foreign Nations. The Treaties of the European Powers with the United States of America, will have no validity on a dissolution of the Union. We shall be left nearly in a state of Nature, or we may find by our own unhappy experience, that there is a natural and necessary progression, from the extreme of anarchy to the extreme of Tyranny; and that arbitrary power is most easily established on the ruins of Liberty abused to licentiousness.

6

GEORGE WASHINGTON TO REV. WILLIAM GORDON
8 July 1783
Writings 27:49–52

It now rests with the Confederated Powers, by the line of conduct they mean to adopt, to make this Country great, happy, and respectable; or to sink it into littleness; worse perhaps, into Anarchy and Confusion; for certain I am, that unless adequate Powers are given to Congress for the *general* purposes of the Federal Union that we shall soon moulder into dust and become contemptable in the Eyes of Europe, if we are not made the sport of their Politicks; to suppose that the general concern of this Country can be directed by thirteen heads, or one head without competent powers, is a solecism, the bad effects of which every Man who has had the practical knowledge to judge from, that I have, is fully convinced of; tho' none perhaps has felt them in so forcible, and distressing a degree. The People at large, and at a distance from the theatre of Action, who only know that the Machine was kept in motion, and that they are at last arrived at the first object of their Wishes are satisfied with the event, without investigating the causes of the slow progress to it, or of the Expences which have accrued and which they now seem unwilling to pay; great part of which has arisen from that want of en-

ergy in the Federal Constitution which I am complaining of, and which I wish to see given to it by a Convention of the People, instead of hearing it remarked that as we have worked through an arduous Contest with the Powers Congress already have (but which, by the by, have been gradually diminishing) why should they be invested with more?

To say nothing of the invisible workings of Providence, which has conducted us through difficulties where no human foresight could point the way; it will appear evident to a close Examiner, that there has been a concatenation of causes to produce this Event; which in all probability at no time, or under any Circumstances, will combine again. We deceive ourselves therefore by this mode of reasoning, and what would be much worse, we may bring ruin upon ourselves by attempting to carry it into practice.

We are known by no other character among Nations than as the United States; Massachusetts or Virginia is no better defined, nor any more thought of by Foreign Powers than the County of Worcester in Massachusetts is by Virginia, or Glouster County in Virginia is by Massachusetts (respectable as they are); and yet these Counties, with as much propriety might oppose themselves to the Laws of the State in wch. they are, as an Individual State can oppose itself to the Federal Government, by which it is, or ought to be bound. Each of these Counties has, no doubt, its local polity and Interests. these should be attended to, and brought before their respective legislatures with all the force their importance merits; but when they come in contact with the general Interest of the State; when superior considerations preponderate in favor of the whole, their Voices should be heard no more; so should it be with individual States when compared to the Union. Otherwise I think it may properly be asked for what purpose do we farcically pretend to be United? Why do Congress spend Months together in deliberating upon, debating, and digesting plans, which are made as palatable, and as wholesome to the Constitution of this Country as the nature of things will admit of, when some States will pay no attention to them, and others regard them but partially; by which means all those evils which proceed from delay, are felt by the whole; while the compliant States are not only suffering by these neglects, but in many instances are injured most capitally by their own exertions; which are wasted for want of the United effort. A hundd. thousand men coming one after another cannot move a Ton weight; but the united strength of 50 would transport it with ease. so has it been with great part of the expence which has been incurred this War. In a Word, I think the blood and treasure which has been spent in it has been lavished to little purpose, unless we can be better Cemented; and that is not to be effected while so little attention is paid to the recommendations of the Sovereign Power.

To me it would seem not more absurd, to hear a traveller, who was setting out on a long journey, declare he would take no Money in his pocket to defray the Expences of it but rather depend upon chance and charity lest he should misapply it, than are the expressions of so much fear of the powers and means of Congress. For Heavens sake who are Congress? are they not the Creatures of the People, amenable to them for their Conduct, and dependant from day to day on their breath? Where then can be the danger of giving them such Powers as are adequate to the great ends of Government, and to all the general purposes of the Confederation (I repeat the word *genl*, because I am no advocate for their having to do with the particular policy of any State, further than it concerns the Union at large). What may be the consequences if they have not these Powers I am at no loss to guess; and deprecate the worst; for sure I am, we shall, in a little time, become as contemptable in the great Scale of Politicks as we now have it in our power to be respectable; and that, when the band of Union gets once broken, every thing ruinous to our future prospects is to be apprehended; the best that can come of it, in my humble opinion is, that we shall sink into obscurity, unless our Civil broils should keep us in remembrance and fill the page of history with the direful consequences of them.

7

BENJAMIN RUSH TO RICHARD PRICE
27 Oct. 1786
Letters 1:408

Some of our enlightened men who begin to despair of a more complete union of the States in Congress have secretly proposed an Eastern, Middle, and Southern Confederacy, to be united by an alliance offensive and defensive. These confederacies they say will be united by nature, by interest, and by manners, and consequently they will be safe, agreeable and durable. The first will include the four New England states and New York. The second will include New Jersey, Pennsylvania, Delaware, and Maryland; and the last Virginia, North and South Carolina, and Georgia. The foreign and domestic debt of the United States they say shall be divided justly between each of the new confederations. This plan of a new continental government is at present a mere speculation. Perhaps necessity, or rather divine providence, may drive us to it. Whatever form of political existence may be before us, I am fully satisfied that our independence rests upon a firm basis and that Great Britain will never recover from any of our changes in opinion or government her former dominion or influence in this country.

8

RECORDS OF THE FEDERAL CONVENTION

[1:323; Madison, 19 June]

Mr. King, wished as everything depended on this proposition, that no objections might be improperly indulged

agst. the phraseology of it. He conceived that the import of the terms "States" "Sovereignty" "*national*" "federal," had been often used & applied in the discussion inaccurately & delusively. The States were not "sovereigns" in the sense contended for by some. They did not possess the peculiar features of sovereignty. They could not make war, nor peace, nor alliances, nor treaties. Considering them as political Beings, they were dumb, for they could not speak to any forign Sovereign whatever. They were deaf, for they could not hear any propositions from such Sovereign. They had not even the organs or faculties of defence or offence, for they could not of themselves raise troops, or equip vessels, for war. On the other side, if the Union of the States comprises the idea of a confederation, it comprises that also of consolidation. A Union of the States is a union of the men composing them, from whence a *national* character results to the whole. Congs. can act alone without the States—they can act & their acts will be binding agst. the Instructions of the States. If they declare war, war is de jure declared, captures made in pursuance of it are lawful. No acts of the States can vary the situation, or prevent the judicial consequences. If the States therefore retained some portion of their sovereignty, they had certainly divested themselves of essential portions of it. If they formed a confederacy in some respects—they formed a Nation in others. The Convention could clearly deliberate on & propose any alterations that Congs. could have done under ye. federal articles. and could not Congs. propose by virtue of the last article, a change in any article whatever: And as well that relating to the equality of suffrage, as any other. He made these remarks to obviate some scruples which had been expressed. He doubted much the practicability of annihilating the States; but thought that much of their power ought to be taken from them.

Mr. Martin, said he considered that the separation from G. B. placed the 13 States in a state of nature towards each other; that they would have remained in that state till this time, but for the confederation; that they entered into the confederation on the footing of equality; that they met now to to amend it on the same footing, and that he could never accede to a plan that would introduce an inequality and lay 10 States at the mercy of Va. Massts. and Penna.

Mr. Wilson, could not admit the doctrine that when the Colonies became independent of G. Britain, they became independent also of each other. He read the declaration of Independence, observing thereon that the *United Colonies* were declared to be free & independent States; and inferring that they were independent, not *Individually* but *Unitedly* and that they were confederated as they were independent, States.

Col. Hamilton, assented to the doctrine of Mr. Wilson. He denied the doctrine that the States were thrown into a State of nature He was not yet prepared to admit the doctrine that the Confederacy, could be dissolved by partial infractions of it. He admitted that the States met now on an equal footing but could see no inference from that against concerting a change of the system in this particular. He took this occasion of observing for the purpose of appeesing the fears of the small States, that two circumstances would render them secure under a national Govt.

in which they might lose the equality of rank they now hold: one was the local situation of the 3 largest States Virga. Masts. & Pa. They were separated from each other by distance of place, and equally so by all the peculiarities which distinguish the interests of one State from those of another. No combination therefore could be dreaded. In the second place, as there was a gradation in the States from Va. the largest down to Delaware the smallest, it would always happen that ambitious combinations among a few States might & wd. be counteracted by defensive combinations of greater extent among the rest. No combination has been seen among large Counties merely as such, agst. lesser Counties. The more close the Union of the States, and the more compleat the authority of the whole; the less opportunity will be allowed the stronger States to injure the weaker.

9

ALEXANDER HAMILTON, FEDERALIST, NO. 1, 7
27 Oct. 1787

It may perhaps be thought superfluous to offer arguments to prove the utility of the UNION, a point, no doubt, deeply engraved on the hearts of the great body of the people in every state, and one, which it may be imagined has no adversaries. But the fact is, that we already hear it whispered in the private circles of those who oppose the new constitution, that the Thirteen States are of too great extent for any general system, and that we must of necessity resort to separate confederacies of distinct portions of the whole.* This doctrine will, in all probability, be gradually propagated, till it has votaries enough to countenance an open avowal of it. For nothing can be more evident, to those who are able to take an enlarged view of the subject, than the alternative of an adoption of the new Constitution, or a dismemberment of the Union. It will therefore be of use to begin by examining the advantages of that Union, the certain evils and the probable dangers, to which every State will be exposed from its dissolution.

*The same idea, tracing the arguments to their consequences, is held out in several of the late publications against the New Constitution.

10

ALEXANDER HAMILTON, FEDERALIST, NO. 6, 28–36
14 Nov. 1787

The three last numbers of this Paper have been dedicated to an enumeration of the dangers to which we should be exposed, in a state of disunion, from the arms and arts of foreign nations. I shall now proceed to delineate dangers of a different, and, perhaps, still more alarming kind, those which will in all probability flow from dissentions between the States themselves, and from domestic factions and convulsions. These have been already in some instances slightly anticipated, but they deserve a more particular and more full investigation.

A man must be far gone in Utopian speculations who can seriously doubt, that if these States should either be wholly disunited, or only united in partial confederacies, the subdivisions into which they might be thrown would have frequent and violent contests with each other. To presume a want of motives for such contests, as an argument against their existence, would be to forget that men are ambitious, vindictive and rapacious. To look for a continuation of harmony between a number of independent unconnected sovereignties, situated in the same neighbourhood, would be to disregard the uniform course of human events, and to set at defiance the accumulated experience of ages.

The causes of hostility among nations are innumerable. There are some which have a general and almost constant operation upon the collective bodies of society: Of this description are the love of power or the desire of preeminence and dominion—the jealousy of power, or the desire of equality and safety. There are others which have a more circumscribed, though an equally operative influence, within their spheres: Such are the rivalships and competitions of commerce between commercial nations. And there are others, not less numerous than either of the former, which take their origin intirely in private passions; in the attachments, enmities, interests, hopes and fears of leading individuals in the communities of which they are members. Men of this class, whether the favourites of a king or of a people, have in too many instances abused the confidence they possessed; and assuming the pretext of some public motive, have not scrupled to sacrifice the national tranquility to personal advantage, or personal gratification.

The celebrated Pericles, in compliance with the resentments of a prostitute,* at the expence of much of the blood and treasure of his countrymen, attacked, vanquished and destroyed, the city of the *Samnians.* The same man, stimulated by private pique against the *Megarensians,*† another nation of Greece, or to avoid a prosecution with which he was threatened as an accomplice in a supposed theft of the statuary *Phidias,*‡ or to get rid of the accusations prepared to be brought against him for dissipating the funds of the State in the purchase of popularity,§ or from a combination of all these causes, was the primitive author of that famous and fatal war, distinguished in the Grecian annals by the name of the *Pelopponesian* war; which, after various vicissitudes, intermis-

*ASPASIA, vide PLUTARCH's life of Pericles.
†—Idem.
‡—Idem. Phidias was supposed to have stolen some public gold with the connivance of Pericles for the embelishment of the statue of Minerva.
§Idem.

sions and renewals, terminated in the ruin of the Athenian commonwealth.

The ambitious Cardinal, who was Prime Minister to Henry VIIIth. permitting his vanity to aspire to the Tripple-Crown,* entertained hopes of succeeding in the acquisition of that splendid prize by the influence of the Emperor Charles Vth. To secure the favour and interest of this enterprising and powerful Monarch, he precipitated England into a war with France, contrary to the plainest dictates of Policy, and at the hazard of the safety and independence, as well of the Kingdom over which he presided by his councils, as of Europe in general. For if there ever was a Sovereign who bid fair to realise the project of universal monarchy it was the Emperor Charles Vth, of whose intrigues Wolsey was at once the instrument and the dupe.

The influence which the bigottry of one female,† the petulancies of another,‡ and the cabals of a third,§ had in the co[n]temporary policy, ferments and pacifications of a considerable part of Europe are topics that have been too often descanted upon not to be generally known.

To multiply examples of the agency of personal considerations in the production of great national events, either foreign or domestic, according to their direction would be an unnecessary waste of time. Those who have but a superficial acquaintance with the sources from which they are to be drawn will themselves recollect a variety of instances; and those who have a tolerable knowledge of human nature will not stand in need of such lights, to form their opinion either of the reality or extent of that agency. Perhaps however a reference, tending to illustrate the general principle, may with propriety be made to a case which has lately happened among ourselves. If SHAYS had not been a *desperate debtor* it is much to be doubted whether Massachusetts would have been plunged into a civil war.

But notwithstanding the concurring testimony of experience, in this particular, there are still to be found visionary, or designing men, who stand ready to advocate the paradox of perpetual peace between the States, though dismembered and alienated from each other. The genius of republics (say they) is pacific; the spirit of commerce has a tendency to soften the manners of men and to extinguish those inflammable humours which have so often kindled into wars. Commercial republics, like ours, will never be disposed to waste themselves in ruinous contentions with each other. They will be governed by mutual interest, and will cultivate a spirit of mutual amity and concord.

Is it not (we may ask these projectors in politics) the true interest of all nations to cultivate the same benevolent and philosophic spirit? If this be their true interest, have they in fact pursued it? Has it not, on the contrary, invariably been found, that momentary passions and immediate interests have a more active and imperious controul over human conduct than general or remote considerations of

policy, utility or justice? Have republics in practice been less addicted to war than monarchies? Are not the former administered by *men* as well as the latter? Are there not aversions, predilections, rivalships and desires of unjust acquisition that affect nations as well as kings? Are not popular assemblies frequently subject to the impulses of rage, resentment, jealousy, avarice, and of other irregular and violent propensities? Is it not well known that their determinations are often governed by a few individuals, in whom they place confidence, and are of course liable to be tinctured by the passions and views of those individuals? Has commerce hitherto done any thing more than change the objects of war? Is not the love of wealth as domineering and enterprising a passion as that of power or glory? Have there not been as many wars founded upon commercial motives, since that has become the prevailing system of nations, as were before occasioned by the cupidity of territory or dominion? Has not the spirit of commerce in many instances administered new incentives to the appetite both for the one and for the other? Let experience the least fallible guide of human opinions be appealed to for an answer to these inquiries.

Sparta, Athens, Rome and Carthage were all Republics; two of them, Athens and Carthage, of the commercial kind. Yet were they as often engaged in wars, offensive and defensive, as the neighbouring Monarchies of the same times. Sparta was little better than a well regulated camp; and Rome was never sated of carnage and conquest.

Carthage, though a commercial Republic, was the aggressor in the very war that ended in her destruction. Hannibal had carried her arms into the heart of Italy and to the gates of Rome, before Scipio, in turn, gave him an overthrow in the territories of Carthage and made a conquest of the Commonwealth.

Venice in latter times figured more than once in wars of ambition; 'till becoming an object of terror to the other Italian States, Pope Julius the Second found means to accomplish that formidable league,‖ which gave a deadly blow to the power and pride of this haughty Republic.

The Provinces of Holland, 'till they were overwhelmed in debts and taxes, took a leading and conspicuous part in the wars of Europe. They had furious contests with England for the dominion of the sea; and were among the most persevering and most implacable of the opponents of Lewis XIV.

In the government of Britain the representatives of the people compose one branch of the national legislature. Commerce has been for ages the predominant pursuit of that country. Few nations, nevertheless, have been more frequently engaged in war; and the wars, in which that kingdom has been engaged, have in numerous instances proceeded from the people.

There have been, if I may so express it, almost as many popular as royal wars. The cries of the nation and the importunities of their representatives have, upon various occasions, dragged their monarchs into war, or continued them in it contrary to their inclinations, and, sometimes,

---

*Worn by the Popes.
†Madame De Maintenon.
‡Dutchess of Marlborough.
§Madame De Pompadoure.

‖The LEAGUE OF CAMBRAY, comprehending the Emperor, the King of France, the King of Arragon, and most of the Italian Princes and States.

contrary to the real interests of the State. In that memorable struggle for superiority, between the rival Houses of *Austria* and *Bourbon* which so long kept Europe in a flame, it is well known that the antipathies of the English against the French, seconding the ambition, or rather the avarice of a favourite leader,* protracted the war beyond the limits marked out by sound policy and for a considerable time in opposition to the views of the Court.

The wars of these two last mentioned nations have in a great measure grown out of commercial considerations—The desire of supplanting and the fear of being supplanted either in particular branches of traffic or in the general advantages of trade and navigation; and sometimes even the more culpable desire of sharing in the commerce of other nations, without their consent.

The last war but two between Britain and Spain sprang from the attempts of the English merchants, to prosecute an illicit trade with the Spanish main. These unjustifiable practices on their part produced severities on the part of the Spaniards, towards the subjects of Great Britain, which were not more justifiable; because they exceeded the bounds of a just retaliation, and were chargeable with inhumanity and cruelty. Many of the English who were taken on the Spanish coasts were sent to dig in the mines of Potosi; and by the usual progress of a spirit of resentment, the innocent were after a while confounded with the guilty in indiscriminate punishment. The complaints of the merchants kindled a violent flame throughout the nation, which soon after broke out in the house of commons, and was communicated from that body to the ministry. Letters of reprisal were granted and a war ensued, which in its consequences overthrew all the alliances that but twenty years before had been formed, with sanguine expectations of the most beneficial fruits.

From this summary of what has taken place in other countries, whose situations have borne the nearest resemblance to our own, what reason can we have to confide in those reveries, which would seduce us into an expectation of peace and cordiality between the members of the present confederacy, in a state of separation? Have we not already seen enough of the fallacy and extravagance of those idle theories which have amused us with promises of an exemption from the imperfections, weaknesses and evils incident to society in every shape? Is it not time to awake from the deceitful dream of a golden age, and to adopt as a practical maxim for the direction of our political conduct, that we, as well as the other inhabitants of the globe, are yet remote from the happy empire of perfect wisdom and perfect virtue?

Let the point of extreme depression to which our national dignity and credit have sunk—let the inconveniences felt every where from a lax and ill administration of government—let the revolt of a part of the State of North-Carolina—the late menacing disturbances in Pennsylvania and the actual insurrections and rebellions in Massachusetts declare!

So far is the general sense of mankind from corresponding with the tenets of those, who endeavour to lull asleep

*The Duke of Marlborough.

our apprehensions of discord and hostility between the States, in the event of disunion, that it has from long observation of the progress of society become a sort of axiom in politics, that vicinity, or nearness of situation, constitutes nations natural enemies. An intelligent writer expresses himself on this subject to this effect—"NEIGHBOURING NATIONS (says he) are naturally ENEMIES of each other, unless their common weakness forces them to league in a CONFEDERATE REPUBLIC, and their constitution prevents the differences that neighbourhood occasions, extinguishing that secret jealousy, which disposes all States to aggrandise themselves at the expence of their neighbours."† This passage, at the same time points out the EVIL and suggests the REMEDY.

†Vide Principes des Negotiations par L'Abbe de Mably.

11

ALEXANDER HAMILTON, FEDERALIST, NO. 7, 36–43
17 Nov. 1787

It is sometimes asked, with an air of seeming triumph, what inducements could the States have, if disunited, to make war upon each other? It would be a full answer to this question to say—precisely the same inducements, which have, at different times, deluged in blood all the nations in the world. But unfortunately for us, the question admits of a more particular answer. There are causes of difference within our immediate contemplation, of the tendency of which, even under the restraints of a Foederal Constitution, we have had sufficient experience, to enable us to form a judgment of what might be expected, if those restraints were removed.

Territorial disputes have at all times been found one of the most fertile sources of hostility among nations. Perhaps the greatest proportion of the wars that have desolated the earth have sprung from this origin. This cause would exist, among us, in full force. We have a vast tract of unsettled territory within the boundaries of the United States. There still are discordant and undecided claims between several of them; and the dissolution of the Union would lay a foundation for similar claims between them all. It is well known, that they have heretofore had serious and animated discussions concerning the right to the lands which were ungranted at the time of the revolution, and which usually went under the name of crown-lands. The States within the limits of whose colonial governments they were comprised have claimed them as their property; the others have contended that the rights of the crown in this article devolved upon the Union; especially as to all that part of the Western territory which either by actual possession or through the submission of the Indian proprietors was subjected to the jurisdiction of the King of Great Britain, till it was relinquished in the treaty of peace. This, it has been said, was at all events an acquisition to the confederacy by compact with a foreign power. It has been the prudent policy of Congress to appease this controversy, by prevailing upon the States to make cessions to the United States for the benefit of the whole. This has been so far accomplished, as under a continuation of the Union, to afford a decided prospect of an amicable termination of the dispute. A dismemberment of the confederacy however would revive this dispute, and would create others on the same subject. At present, a large part of the vacant Western territory is by cession at least, if not by any anterior right, the common property of the Union. If that were at an end, the States which made the cession on a principle of Foederal compromise, would be apt, when the motive of the grant had ceased, to reclaim the lands as a reversion. The other States would no doubt insist on a proportion, by right of representation. Their argument would be that a grant, once made, could not be revoked, and that the justice of their participating in territory acquired, or secured by the joint efforts of the confederacy remained undiminished. If contrary to probability it should be admitted by all the States, that each had a right to a share of this common stock, there would still be a difficulty to be surmounted, as to a proper rule of apportionment. Different principles would be set up by different States for this purpose; and as they would affect the opposite interests of the parties, they might not easily be susceptible of a pacific adjustment.

In the wide field of Western territory, therefore, we perceive an ample theatre for hostile pretensions, without any umpire or common judge to interpose between the contending parties. To reason from the past to the future we shall have good ground to apprehend, that the sword would sometimes be appealed to as the arbiter of their differences. The circumstances of the dispute between Connecticut and Pennsylvania, respecting the lands at Wyoming admonish us, not to be sanguine in expecting an easy accommodation of such differences. The articles of confederation obliged the parties to submit the matter to the decision of a Foederal Court. The submission was made, and the Court decided in favour of Pennsylvania. But Connecticut gave strong indications of dissatisfaction with that determination; nor did she appear to be intirely resigned to it, till by negotiation and management something like an equivalent was found for the loss she supposed herself to have sustained. Nothing here said is intended to convey the slightest censure on the conduct of that State. She no doubt sincerely believed herself to have been injured by the decision; and States like individuals acquiesce with great reluctance in determinations to their disadvantage.

Those, who had an opportunity of seeing the inside of the transactions, which attended the progress of the controversy between this State and the district of Vermont, can vouch the opposition we experienced, as well from States not interested as from those which were interested in the claim; and can attest the danger, to which the peace of the Confederacy might have been exposed, had this State attempted to assert its rights by force. Two motives preponderated in that opposition—one a jealousy enter-

tained of our future power—and the other, the interest of certain individuals of influence in the neighbouring States, who had obtained grants of lands under the actual government of that district. Even the States which brought forward claims, in contradiction to ours, seemed more solicitous to dismember this State, than to establish their own pretentions. These were New-Hampshire, Massachussets and Connecticut. New-Jersey and Rhode-Island upon all occasions discovered a warm zeal for the independence of Vermont; and Maryland, 'till alarmed by the appearance of a connection between Canada and that place, entered deeply into the same views. These being small States, saw with an unfriendly eye the perspective of our growing greatness. In a review of these transactions we may trace some of the causes, which would be likely to embroil the States with each other, if it should be their unpropitious destiny to become disunited.

The competitions of commerce would be another fruitful source of contention. The States less favourably circumstanced would be desirous of escaping from the disadvantages of local situation, and of sharing in the advantages of their more fortunate neighbours. Each State, or separate confederacy, would pursue a system of commercial polity peculiar to itself. This would occasion distinctions, preferences and exclusions, which would beget discontent. The habits of intercourse, on the basis of equal privileges, to which we have been accustomed from the earliest settlement of the country, would give a keener edge to those causes of discontent, than they would naturally have, independent of this circumstance. *We should be ready to denominate injuries those things which were in reality the justifiable acts of independent sovereignties consulting a distinct interest.* The spirit of enterprise, which characterises the commercial part of America, has left no occasion of displaying itself unimproved. It is not at all probable that this unbridled spirit would pay much respect to those regulations of trade, by which particular States might endeavour to secure exclusive benefits to their own citizens. The infractions of these regulations on one side, the efforts to prevent and repel them on the other, would naturally lead to outrages, and these to reprisals and wars.

The opportunities, which some States would have of rendering others tributary to them, by commercial regulations, would be impatiently submitted to by the tributary States. The relative situation of New-York, Connecticut and New-Jersey, would afford an example of this kind. New-York, from the necessities of revenue, must lay duties on her importations. A great part of these duties must be paid by the inhabitants of the two other States in the capacity of consumers of what we import. New York would neither be willing nor able to forego this advantage. Her citizens would not consent that a duty paid by them should be remitted in favour of the citizens of her neighbours; nor would it be practicable, if there were not this impediment in the way, to distinguish the customers in our own markets. Would Connecticut and New-Jersey long submit to be taxed by New-York for her exclusive benefit? Should we be long permitted to remain in the quiet and undisturbed enjoyment of a metropolis, from the possession of which we derived an advantage so odious to our neighbours, and, in their opinion, so oppressive? Should we be able to preserve it against the incumbent weight of Connecticut on the one side, and the co-operating pressure of New-Jersey on the other? These are questions that temerity alone will answer in the affirmative.

The public debt of the Union would be a further cause of collision between the separate States or confederacies. The apportionment, in the first instance, and the progressive extinguishment, afterwards, would be alike productive of ill humour and animosity. How would it be possible to agree upon a rule of apportionment satisfactory to all? There is scarcely any, that can be proposed, which is entirely free from real objections. These, as usual, would be exaggerated by the adverse interests of the parties. There are even dissimilar views among the States, as to the general principle of discharging the public debt. Some of them, either less impressed with the importance of national credit, or because their citizens have little, if any, immediate interest in the question, feel an indifference, if not a repugnance to the payment of the domestic debt, at any rate. These would be inclined to magnify the difficulties of a distribution. Others of them, a numerous body of whose citizens are creditors to the public, beyond the proportion of the State in the total amount of the national debt, would be strenuous for some equitable and effectual provision. The procrastinations of the former would excite the resentments of the latter. The settlement of a rule would in the mean time be postponed, by real differences of opinion and affected delays. The citizens of the States interested, would clamour, foreign powers would urge, for the satisfaction of their just demands; and the peace of the States would be hazarded to the double contingency of external invasion and internal contention.

Suppose the difficulties of agreeing upon a rule surmounted, and the apportionment made. Still there is great room to suppose, that the rule agreed upon would, upon experiment, be found to bear harder upon some States than upon others. Those which were sufferers by it would naturally seek for a mitigation of the burthen. The others would as naturally be disinclined to a revision, which was likely to end in an increase of their own incumbrances. Their refusal would be too plausible a pretext to the complaining States to withhold their contributions, not to be embraced with avidity; and the non compliance of these States with their engagements would be a ground of bitter dissention and altercation. If even the rule adopted should in practice justify the equality of its principle, still delinquencies in payment, on the part of some of the States, would result from a diversity of other causes—the real deficiency of resources—the mismanagement of their finances, accidental disorders in the administration of the government—and in addition to the rest the reluctance with which men commonly part with money for purposes, that have outlived the exigencies which produced them, and interfere with the supply of immediate wants. Delinquencies from whatever causes would be productive of complaints, recriminations and quarrels. There is perhaps nothing more likely to disturb the tranquility of nations, than their being bound to mutual contributions for any common object, which does not yield an equal and coinci-

dent benefit. For it is an observation as true, as it is trite, that there is nothing men differ so readily about as the payment of money.

Laws in violation of private contracts as they amount to aggressions on the rights of those States, whose citizens are injured by them, may be considered as another probable source of hostility. We are not authorised to expect, that a more liberal or more equitable spirit would preside over the legislations of the individual States hereafter, if unrestrained by any additional checks, than we have heretofore seen, in too many instances, disgracing their several codes. We have observed the disposition to retaliation excited in Connecticut, in consequence of the enormities perpetrated by the legislature of Rhode-Island; and we may reasonably infer, that in similar cases, under other circumstances, a war not of *parchment* but of the sword would chastise such atrocious breaches of moral obligation and social justice.

The probability of incompatible alliances between the different States, or confederacies, and different foreign nations, and the effects of this situation upon the peace of the whole, have been sufficiently unfolded in some preceding papers. From the view they have exhibited, of this part of the subject, this conclusion is to be drawn, that America, if not connected at all, or only by the feeble tie of a simple league offensive and defensive, would by the operation of such opposite and jarring alliances be gradually entangled in all the pernicious labyrinths of European politics and wars; and by the destructive contentions of the parts, into which she was divided would be likely to become a prey to the artifices and machinations of powers equally the enemies of them all. *Divide et impera** must be the motto of every nation, that either hates, or fears us.

*Divide and command.

12

JAMES MADISON, FEDERALIST, NO. 10, 56–65
22 Nov. 1787

(See ch. 4, no. 19)

13

ALEXANDER HAMILTON, FEDERALIST, NO. 11, 65–73
24 Nov. 1787

The importance of the Union, in a commercial light, is one of those points, about which there is least room to entertain a difference of opinion, and which has in fact commanded the most general assent of men, who have any acquaintance with the subject. This applies as well to our intercourse with foreign countries, as with each other.

There are appearances to authorise a supposition, that the adventurous spirit, which distinguishes the commercial character of America, has already excited uneasy sensations in several of the maritime powers of Europe. They seem to be apprehensive of our too great interference in that carrying trade, which is the support of their navigation and the foundation of their naval strength. Those of them, which have colonies in America, look forward, to what this country is capable of becoming, with painful solicitude. They foresee the dangers, that may threaten their American dominions from the neighbourhood of States, which have all the dispositions, and would possess all the means, requisite to the creation of a powerful marine. Impressions of this kind will naturally indicate the policy of fostering divisions among us, and of depriving us as far as possible of an ACTIVE COMMERCE in our own bottoms. This would answer the threefold purpose of preventing our interference in their navigation, of monopolising the profits of our trade, and of clipping the wings, by which we might soar to a dangerous greatness. Did not prudence forbid the detail, it would not be difficult to trace by facts the workings of this policy to the cabinets of Ministers.

If we continue united, we may counteract a policy so unfriendly to our prosperity in a variety of ways. By prohibitory regulations, extending at the same time throughout the States, we may oblige foreign countries to bid against each other, for the privileges of our markets. This assertion will not appear chimerical to those who are able to appreciate the importance of the markets of three millions of people—increasing in rapid progression, for the most part exclusively addicted to agriculture, and likely from local circumstances to remain so—to any manufacturing nation; and the immense difference there would be to the trade and navigation of such a nation, between a direct communication in its own ships, and an indirect conveyance of its products and returns, to and from America, in the ships of another country. Suppose, for instance, we had a government in America, capable of excluding Great-Britain (with whom we have at present no treaty of commerce) from all our ports, what would be the probable operation of this step upon her politics? Would it not enable us to negotiate with the fairest prospect of success for commercial privileges of the most valuable and extensive kind in the dominions of that kingdom? When these questions have been asked, upon other occasions, they have received a plausible but not a solid or satisfactory answer. It has been said, that prohibitions on our part would produce no change in the system of Britain; because she could prosecute her trade with us, through the medium of the Dutch, who would be her immediate customers and paymasters for those articles which were wanted for the supply of our markets. But would not her navigation be materially injured, by the loss of the important advantage of being her own carrier in that trade? Would not the principal part of its profits be intercepted by the Dutch, as a compensation for their agency and risk? Would not the mere circumstance of freight occasion a considerable deduction? Would not so circuitous an intercourse facilitate the competitions of other nations, by enhancing the price of British commodities in our markets,

and by transferring to other hands the management of this interesting branch of the British commerce?

A mature consideration of the objects, suggested by these questions, will justify a belief, that the real disadvantages to Britain, from such a state of things, conspiring with the prepossessions of a great part of the nation in favour of the American trade, and with the importunities of the West-India islands, would produce a relaxation in her present system, and would let us into the enjoyment of privileges in the markets of those islands and elsewhere, from which our trade would derive the most substantial benefits. Such a point gained from the British government, and which could not be expected without an equivalent in exemptions and immunities in our markets, would be likely to have a correspondent effect on the conduct of other nations, who would not be inclined to see themselves, altogether supplanted in our trade.

A further resource for influencing the conduct of European nations towards us, in this respect would arise from the establishment of a foederal navy. There can be no doubt, that the continuance of the Union, under an efficient government, would put it in our power, at a period not very distant, to create a navy, which, if it could not vie with those of the great maritime powers, would at least be of respectable weight, if thrown into the scale of either of two contending parties. This would be more particularly the case in relation to operations in the West-Indies. A few ships of the line sent opportunely to the reinforcement of either side, would often be sufficient to decide the fate of a campaign, on the event of which interests of the greatest magnitude were suspended. Our position is in this respect a very commanding one. And if to this consideration we add that of the usefulness of supplies from this country, in the prosecution of military operations in the West-Indies, it will readily be perceived, that a situation so favourable would enable us to bargain with great advantage for commercial privileges. A price would be set not only upon our friendship, but upon our neutrality. By a steady adherance to the Union we may hope ere long to become the Arbiter of Europe in America; and to be able to incline the ballance of European competitions in this part of the world as our interest may dictate.

But in the reverse of this elegible situation we shall discover, that the rivalships of the parts would make them checks upon each other, and would frustrate all the tempting advantages, which nature has kindly placed within our reach. In a state so insignificant, our commerce would be a prey to the wanton intermeddlings of all nations at war with each other; who, having nothing to fear from us, would with little scruple or remorse supply their wants by depredations on our property, as often as it fell in their way. The rights of neutrality will only be respected, when they are defended by an adequate power. A nation, despicable by its weakness, forfeits even the privilege of being neutral.

Under a vigorous national government, the natural strength and resources of the country, directed to a common interest, would baffle all the combinations of European jealousy to restrain our growth. This situation would even take away the motive to such combinations, by inducing an impracticability of success. An active commerce, an extensive navigation, and a flourishing marine would then be the inevitable offspring of moral and physical necessity. We might defy the little arts of little politicians to controul, or vary, the irresistible and unchangeable course of nature.

But in a state of disunion these combinations might exist, and might operate with success. It would be in the power of the maritime nations, availing themselves of our universal impotence, to prescribe the conditions of our political existence; and as they have a common interest in being our carriers, and still more in preventing our being theirs, they would in all probability combine to embarrass our navigation in such a manner, as would in effect destroy it, and confine us to a PASSIVE COMMERCE. We should thus be compelled to content ourselves with the first price of our commodities, and to see the profits of our trade snatched from us to enrich our enemies and persecutors. That unequalled spirit of enterprise, which signalises the genius of the American Merchants and Navigators, and which is in itself an inexhaustible mine of national wealth, would be stifled and lost; and poverty and disgrace would overspread a country, which with wisdom might make herself the admiration and envy of the world.

There are rights of great moment to the trade of America, which are rights of the Union. I allude to the fisheries, to the navigation of the Western lakes and to that of the Mississippi. The dissolution of the confederacy would give room for delicate questions, concerning the future existence of these rights; which the interest of more powerful partners would hardly fail to solve to our disadvantage. The disposition of Spain with regard to the Mississippi needs no comment. France and Britain are concerned with us in the fisheries; and view them as of the utmost moment to their navigation. They, of course, would hardly remain long indifferent to that decided mastery of which experience has shewn us to be possessed in this valuable branch of traffic; and by which we are able to undersell those nations in their own markets. What more natural, than that they should be disposed to exclude, from the lists, such dangerous competitors?

This branch of trade ought not to be considered as a partial benefit. All the navigating States may in different degrees advantageously participate in it and under circumstances of a greater extension of mercantile capital would not be unlikely to do it. As a nursery of seamen it now is, or when time shall have more nearly assimilated the principles of navigation in the several States, will become an universal resource. To the establishment of a navy it must be indispensible.

To this great national object a NAVY, Union will contribute in various ways. Every institution will grow and flourish in proportion to the quantity and extent of the means concentered towards its formation and support. A navy of the United States, as it would embrace the resources of all, is an object far less remote than a navy of any single State, or partial confederacy, which would only embrace the resources of a part. It happens indeed that different portions of confederated America possess each some peculiar

advantage for this essential establishment. The more Southern States furnish in greater abundance certain kinds of naval stores—tar, pitch and turpentine. Their wood for the construction of ships is also of a more solid and lasting texture. The difference in the duration of the ships of which the navy might be composed, if chiefly constructed of Southern wood would be of signal importance either in the view of naval strength or of national oeconomy. Some of the Southern and of the middle States yield a greater plenty of iron and of better quality. Seamen must chiefly be drawn from the Northern hive. The necessity of naval protection to external or maritime commerce, does not require a particular elucidation, no more than the conduciveness of that species of commerce to the prosperity of a navy. They, by a kind of reaction, mutually beneficial, promote each other.

An unrestrained intercourse between the States themselves will advance the trade of each, by an interchange of their respective productions, not only for the supply of reciprocal wants at home, but for exportation to foreign markets. The veins of commerce in every part will be replenished, and will acquire additional motion and vigour from a free circulation of the commodities of every part. Commercial enterprise will have much greater scope, from the diversity in the productions of different States. When the staple of one fails, from a bad harvest or unproductive crop, it can call to its aid the staple of another. The variety not less than the value of products for exportation, contributes to the activity of foreign commerce. It can be conducted upon much better terms, with a large number of materials of a given value, than with a small number of materials of the same value; arising from the competitions of trade and from the fluctuations of markets. Particular articles may be in great demand, at certain periods, and unsaleable at others; but if there be a variety of articles it can scarcely happen that they should all be at one time in the latter predicament; and on this account the operations of the merchant would be less liable to any considerable obstruction, or stagnation. The speculative trader will at once perceive the force of these observations; and will acknowledge that the aggregate ballance of the commerce of the United States would bid fair to be much more favorable, than that of the thirteen States, without union, or with partial unions.

It may perhaps be replied to this, that whether the States are united, or disunited, there would still be an intimate intercourse between them which would answer the same ends: But this intercourse would be fettered, interrupted and narrowed by a multiplicity of causes; which in the course of these Papers have been amply detailed. An unity of commercial, as well as political interests, can only result from an unity of government.

There are other points of view, in which this subject might be placed, of a striking and animating kind. But they would lead us too far into the regions of futurity, and would involve topics not proper for a Newspaper discussion. I shall briefly observe, that our situation invites, and our interests prompt us, to aim at an ascendant in the system of American affairs. The world may politically, as well as geographically, be divided into four parts, each having a distinct set of interests. Unhappily for the other three, Europe by her arms and by her negociations, by force and by fraud, has, in different degrees, extended her dominion over them all. Africa, Asia, and America have successively felt her domination. The superiority, she has long maintained, has tempted her to plume herself as the Mistress of the World, and to consider the rest of mankind as created for her benefit. Men admired as profound philosophers have, in direct terms, attributed to her inhabitants a physical superiority; and have gravely asserted that all animals, and with them the human species, degenerate in America—that even dogs cease to bark after having breathed a while in our atmosphere.* Facts have too long supported these arrogant pretensions of the European. It belongs to us to vindicate the honor of the human race, and to teach that assuming brother moderation. Union will enable us to do it. Disunion will add another victim to his triumphs. Let Americans disdain to be the instruments of European greatness! Let the thirteen States, bound together in a strict and indissoluble union, concur in erecting one great American system, superior to the controul of all trans-atlantic force or influence, and able to dictate the terms of the connection between the old and the new world!

*Recherches philosophiques sur les Américains.

14

ALEXANDER HAMILTON, FEDERALIST, NO. 12,
73–74
27 Nov. 1787

The effects of union upon the commercial prosperity of the States have been sufficiently delineated. Its tendency to promote the interests of revenue will be the subject of our present enquiry.

The prosperity of commerce is now perceived and acknowledged, by all enlightened statesmen, to be the most useful as well as the most productive source of national wealth; and has accordingly become a primary object of their political cares. By multiplying the means of gratification, by promoting the introduction and circulation of the precious metals, those darling objects of human avarice and enterprise, it serves to vivify and invigorate the channels of industry, and to make them flow with greater activity and copiousness. The assiduous merchant, the laborious husbandman, the active mechanic, and the industrious manufacturer, all orders of men look forward with eager expectation and growing alacrity to this pleasing reward of their toils. The often-agitated question, between agriculture and commerce, has from indubitable experience received a decision, which has silenced the rivalships, that once subsisted between them, and has proved to the

satisfaction of their friends, that their interests are intimately blended and interwoven. It has been found, in various countries, that in proportion as commerce has flourished, land has risen in value. And how could it have happened otherwise? Could that which procures a freer vent for the products of the earth—which furnishes new incitements to the cultivators of land—which is the most powerful instrument in encreasing the quantity of money in a state—could that, in fine, which is the faithful handmaid of labor and industry in every shape, fail to augment the value of that article, which is the prolific parent of far the greatest part of the objects upon which they are exerted? It is astonishing, that so simple a truth should ever have had an adversary; and it is one among a multitude of proofs, how apt a spirit of ill-informed jealousy, or of too great abstraction and refinement is to lead men astray from the plainest paths of reason and conviction.

15

JAMES MADISON, FEDERALIST, NO. 14, 88–89
30 Nov. 1787

(See ch. 4, no. 22)

16

A [MASSACHUSETTS] FEDERALIST
3 Dec. 1787
Storing 4:119 n. 1

I would ask this writer, if civil *habits* are antecedent, and prior to civil institutions? Would a wise legislator who was about to form a system of government, for a nation, in a state of nature, adapt his plan to the prevailing habits of such a people? No; his object would be, to introduce a code of laws that would *induce* those habits of civilization and order, which must result *from* good government. The truth of the case is, that as a people, we are destitute of FEDERAL FEATURES, and HABITS—the several *State Constitutions* are *local, partial,* and *selfish;* they are not calculated in their construction, to form *national views;* this great object is beyond their limits—and *dear bought* experience proves that the *unbounded* sovereignty of the individual governments, is incompatible with a *national* system.

For want of those HABITS OF NATIONALITY, we have been brought into our present contemptible and deplorable situation. The proposed *Federal Constitution* is happily calculated to form us to a *national spirit,* and to diffuse those generous *federal* sentiments, without which, we never can be a happy and flourishing people.

17

JAMES WILSON, PENNSYLVANIA
RATIFYING CONVENTION
11 Dec. 1787
McMaster 414–18

I stated on a former occasion one important advantage: by adopting this system we become a NATION; at present we are not one. Can we perform a single national act? can we do anything to procure us dignity, or to preserve peace and tranquility? can we relieve the distress of our citizens? can we provide for their welfare or happiness? The powers of our government are mere sound. If we offer to treat with a nation, we receive this humiliating answer, "You cannot in propriety of language make a treaty—because you have no power to execute it." Can we borrow money? There are too many examples of unfortunate creditors existing, both on this and the other side of the Atlantic, to expect success from this expedient. But could we borrow money, we cannot command a fund to enable us to pay either the principal or interest; for in instances where our friends have advanced the principal, they have been obliged to advance the interest also in order to prevent the principal from being annihilated in their hands by depreciation. Can we raise an army? The prospect of a war is highly probable. The accounts we receive by every vessel from Europe mention that the highest exertions are making in the ports and arsenals of the greatest maritime powers; but whatever the consequence may be, are we to lay supine? We know we are unable under the articles of confederation to exert ourselves; and shall we continue so until a stroke be made on our commerce, or we see the debarkation of an hostile army on our unprotected shores? Who will guarantee that our property will not be laid waste, that our towns will not be put under contribution, by a small naval force, and subjected to all the horror and devastation of war? May not this be done without opposition, at least effectual opposition, in the present situation of our country? There may be safety over the Appalachian mountains, but there can be none on our sea coast. With what propriety can we hope our flag will be respected while we have not a single gun to fire in its defence?

Can we expect to make internal improvement, or accomplish any of those great national objects which I formerly alluded to, when we cannot find money to remove a single rock out of a river?

This system, Sir, will at least make us a nation, and put it in the power of the Union to act as such. We will be considered as such by every nation in the world. We will regain the confidence of our own citizens, and command the respect of others.

As we shall become a nation, I trust that we shall also form a national character; and that this character will be adapted to the principles and genius of our system of government: as yet we possess none—our language, manners, customs, habits and dress, depend too much upon those of other countries. Every nation in these respects should possess originality. There are not on any part of the globe finer qualities, for forming a national character, than those possessed by the children of America. Activity, perseverance, industry, laudable emulation, docility in acquiring information, firmness in adversity, and patience and magnanimity under the greatest hardships; from these materials, what a respectable national character may be raised! In addition to this character, I think there is strong reason to believe that America may take the lead in literary improvements and national importance. This is a subject which I confess I have spent much pleasing time in considering. That language, Sir, which shall become most generally known in the civilized world, will impart great importance over the nation that shall use it. The language of the United States will in future times be diffused over a greater extent of country than any other that we now know. The French, indeed, have made laudable attempts toward establishing an universal language; but beyond the boundaries of France, even the French language is not spoken by one in a thousand. Besides the freedom of our country, the great improvements she has made and will make in the science of government will induce the patriots and literati of every nation, to read and understand our writings on that subject, and hence it is not improbable that she will take the lead in political knowledge.

If we adopt this system of government, I think we may promise security, stability and tranquility to the governments of the different States. They will not be exposed to the danger of competition on questions of territory, or any other that have heretofore disturbed them. A tribunal is here founded to decide, justly and quietly, any interfering claim; and now is accomplished, what the great mind of Henry the IV. of France had in contemplation, a system of government, for large and respectable dominions, united and bound together in peace, under a superintending head, by which all their differences may be accommodated, without the destruction of the human race! We are told by Sully, that this was the favorite pursuit of that good king during the last years of his life, and he would probably have carried it into execution, had not the dagger of an assassin deprived the world of his valuable life. I have, with pleasing emotion, seen the wisdom and beneficence of a less efficient power under the articles of confederation, in the determination of the controversy between the States of Pennsylvania and Connecticut; but, I have lamented that the authority of Congress did not extend to extinguish, entirely, the spark which has kindled a dangerous flame in the district of Wyoming.

Let gentlemen turn their attention to the amazing consequences which this principle will have in this extended country—the several States cannot war with each other; the general government is the great arbiter in contentions between them; the whole force of the Union can be called forth to reduce an aggressor to reason. What a happy exchange for the disjointed, contentious State sovereignties!

The adoption of this system will also secure us from danger, and procure us advantage from foreign nations. This, in our situation, is of great consequence. We are still an inviting object to one European power at least, and, if we cannot defend ourselves, the temptation may become too alluring to be resisted. I do not mean, that, with an efficient government, we should mix with the commotions of Europe. No, Sir, we are happily removed from them, and are not obliged to throw ourselves into the scale with any. This system will not hurry us into war; it is calculated to guard against it. It will not be in the power of a single man, or a single body of men, to involve us in such distress, for the important power of declaring war is vested in the legislature at large;—this declaration must be made with the concurrence of the House of Representatives; from this circumstance we may draw a certain conclusion, that nothing but our national interest can draw us into a war. I cannot forbear, on this occasion, the pleasure of mentioning to you the sentiments of the great and benevolent man whose works I have already quoted on another subject; Mr. Neckar has addressed this country, in language important and applicable in the strictest degree to its situation and to the present subject. Speaking of war, and the great caution that all nations ought to use in order to avoid its calamities, "And you, rising nation," says he, "whom generous efforts have freed from the yoke of Europe! let the universe be struck with still greater reverence at the sight of the privileges you have acquired, by seeing you continually employed for the public felicity: do not offer it as a sacrifice at the unsettled shrine of political ideas, and of the deceitful combinations of warlike ambition; avoid, or at least delay participating in the passions of our hemisphere; make your own advantage of the knowledge which experience alone has given to our old age, and preserve for a long time, the simplicity of childhood: in short, honor human nature, by shewing that when lost to its own feelings, it is still capable of those virtues that maintain public order, and of that prudence which insures public tranquillity."

Permit me to offer one consideration more that ought to induce our acceptance of this system. I feel myself lost in the contemplation of its magnitude. By adopting this system, we shall probably lay a foundation for erecting temples of liberty in every part of the earth. It has been thought by many, that on the success of the struggle America has made for freedom, will depend the exertions of the brave and enlightened of other nations. The advantages resulting from this system will not be confined to the United States; it will draw from Europe, many worthy characters, who pant for the enjoyment of freedom. It will induce princes, in order to preserve their subject, to restore to them a portion of that liberty of which they have for so many ages been deprived. It will be subservient to the great designs of providence, with regard to this globe; the multiplication of mankind, their improvement in knowledge, and their advancement in happiness.

18

CENTINEL, NO. 11
12 Jan. 1788
Storing 2.7.142

The other spectre that has been raised to terrify and alarm the people out of the exercise of their judgement on this great occasion, is the dread of our splitting into separate confederacies or republics, that might become rival powers and consequently liable to mutual wars from the usual motives of contention. This is an event still more improbable than the foregoing; it is a presumption unwarrantable, either by the situation of affairs, or the sentiments of the people; no disposition leading to it exists; the advocates of the new constitution seem to view such a separation with horror, and its opponents are strenuously contending for a confederation that shall embrace all America under its comprehensive and salutary protection. This hobgoblin appears to have sprung from the deranged brain of *Publius*, a New-York writer, who, mistaking sound for argument, has with Herculean labour accumulated myriads of unmeaning sentences, and *mechanically* endeavored to force conviction by a torrent of misplaced words; he might have spared his readers the fatigue of wading through his long-winded disquisitions on the direful effects of the contentions of inimical states, as totally inapplicable to the subject he was *professedly* treating; this writer has devoted much time, and wasted more paper in combating chimeras of his own creation: However, for the sake of argument, I will admit, that the necessary consequence of rejecting, or delaying the establishment of the new constitution, would be the dissolution of the union, and the institution of even rival and inimical republics; yet ought such an apprehension, if well founded, to drive us into the fangs of despotism: Infinitely preferable would be occasional wars to such an event; the former, although a severe scourge, is transient in its continuance, and in its operation partial, but a small proportion of the community are exposed to its greatest horrors, and yet fewer experience its greatest evils; the latter is permanent and universal misery, without remission or exemption: as passing clouds obscure for a time the splendour of the sun, so do wars interrupt the welfare of mankind; but despotism is a settled gloom that total extinguishes happiness, not a ray of comfort can penetrate to cheer the dejected mind; the goad of power with unabating rigor insists upon the utmost exaction, like a merciless task master, is continually inflicting the task, and is never satiated with the feast of unfeeling domination, or the most abject servility.

19

CHARLES COTESWORTH PINCKNEY, SOUTH CAROLINA
HOUSE OF REPRESENTATIVES
18 Jan. 1788
Elliot 4:300–302

Gen. CHARLES COTESWORTH PINCKNEY, in answer to Mr. Lowndes, observed, that, though ready to pay every tribute of applause to the great characters whose names were subscribed to the old Confederation, yet his respect for them could not prevent him from being thoroughly sensible of the defects of the system they had established; sad experience had convinced him that it was weak, inefficient, and inadequate to the purposes of good government; and he understood that most of the framers of it were so thoroughly convinced of this truth, that they were eager to adopt the present Constitution. The friends of the new system do not mean to shelter it under the respectability of mere names; they wish every part of it may be examined with critical minuteness, convinced that the more thoroughly it is investigated, the better it will appear. The honorable gentleman, in the warmth of his encomiums on the old plan, had said that it had carried us with success through the war. In this it has been shown that he is mistaken, as it was not finally ratified till March, 1781, and, anterior to that ratification, Congress never acted under it, or considered it as binding. Our success, therefore, ought not to be imputed to the old Confederation; but to the vast abilities of a Washington, to the valor and enthusiasm of our people, to the cruelty of our enemies, and to the assistance of our friends. The gentleman had mentioned the treaty of peace in a manner as if our independence had been granted us by the king of Great Britain. But that was not the case; we were independent before the treaty, which does not in fact grant, but acknowledges, our independence. We ought to date that invaluable blessing from a much older charter than the treaty of peace—from a charter which our babes should be taught to lisp in their cradles; which our youth should learn as a *carmen necessarium*, or indispensable lesson; which our young men should regard as their compact of freedom; and which our old should repeat with ejaculations of gratitude for the bounties it is about to bestow on their posterity: I mean the Declaration of Independence, made in Congress the 4th of July, 1776. This admirable manifesto, which, for importance of matter and elegance of composition, stands unrivalled, sufficiently confutes the honorable gentleman's doctrine of the individual sovereignty and independence of the several states.

In that Declaration the several states are not even enumerated; but after reciting, in nervous language, and with convincing arguments, our right to independence, and the tyranny which compelled us to assert it, the declaration is made in the following words: "We, therefore, the representatives of the United States of America in General Con-

gress assembled, appealing to the Supreme Judge of the world for the rectitude of our intentions, do, in the name and by the authority of the good people of these colonies, solemnly publish and declare, that these United Colonies are, and of right ought to be, FREE AND INDEPENDENT STATES." The separate independence and individual sovereignty of the several states were never thought of by the enlightened band of patriots who framed this Declaration; the several states are not even mentioned by name in any part of it,—as if it was intended to impress this maxim on America, that our freedom and independence arose from our union, and that without it we could neither be free nor independent. Let us, then, consider all attempts to weaken this Union, by maintaining that each state is separately and individually independent, as a species of political heresy, which can never benefit us, but may bring on us the most serious distresses.

20

A FREEMAN TO THE MINORITY OF THE CONVENTION
OF PENNSYLVANIA, NO. 1
23 Jan. 1788
Pennsylvania Gazette

When the people of America dissolved their connexion with the crown of Britain, they found themselves separated from all the world, but a few powerless colonies, the principal of which indeed they expected to induce into their measures. The crown having been merely a centre of *union*, the act of independence dissolved the political ties that had formerly existed among the states, and it was attended with no absolute confederacy; but many circumstances conspired to render some new form of connexion desirable and necessary. We wished not to continue distinct bodies of people, but to form a respectable nation. The remains of our ancient governments kept us in the form of thirteen political bodies, and from a variety of just and prudent considerations, we determined to enter into an indissoluble and perpetual *union*. Though a confederacy of sovereign states was the mode of connexion which was wisely desired and actually adopted, yet in that feeble and inadequate bond of union to which we assented, articles strongly partaking of the nature of consolidation are observable.

We see, for example, that the free inhabitants of each state were rendered, to all intents and purposes, *free citizens of all the rest*. Persons fleeing from justice in one state were to be *delivered up* by any other in which they might take *refuge*, contrary to the laws prevailing among *distinct* sovereignties, whereby the jurisdiction of one state pervaded the territories of all the rest, to the effectual length of trial, condemnation and punishment. The right to judge of *the sums that should be expended for the use of the nation* lies, even under the old confederation, *solely* with Congress, and after the demand is fixed by them, and formally made, the states are *bound*, as far as they can be bound by any compact, to pay their respective quotas into the foederal treasury, by which the power of the purse is fully given to them; nor can the states *constitutionally* refuse to comply. It is very certain that there is not in the present foederal government vigor enough to carry this *actually delegated* power into execution; yet, if Congress had possessed energy sufficient to have done it, there is no doubt but they would have been justifiable in the measure, though the season of invasion was unfavorable for internal contests.

We shall also find, that *the right to raise armies and build navies* is also vested in Congress by the present confederation, and they are to be the sole judges of the occasion, and the force required. The state, therefore, that refuses to fulfil the requisitions of Congress on either of these articles, acts *unconstitutionally*. It appears, then, that it was thought necessary at the time of forming the old foederal constitution, that Congress should have what is termed *"the powers of the purse and the sword."* That constitution contained a delegation of them, because the framers of it saw that those powers were necessary to *the perpetuity and efficiency* of the union, and to obtain the desirable ends of it. It is certainly very true, that the means provided to enable Congress to apply those powers, which the constitution vested in them, were so liable to opposition, interruption and delay, that the clauses containing them became a mere dead letter. This however was not expected or desired by any of the states at the time, and their subsequent defaults are *infringements* of the letter and spirit of the confederation. On these circumstances I entreat your most dispassionate and candid consideration. I beg leave to remark, however, that as in the present constitution they are only *appearances* of consolidation, irrefragably contradicted by other facts and circumstances, so also are the facts and observations in your address *merely appearances* of a consolidation, which I hope to demonstrate does not exist. The matter will be better understood by proceeding to those points which shew, that, as under the old so under the new foederal constitution, the thirteen United States were *not intended* to be, and really *are not consolidated*, in such manner as to *absorb or destroy* the sovereignties of the several states. In order to a perfect understanding of each other, it may be proper to observe here, that by your term *consolidation* I understand you mean *the final annihilation of separate state government or sovereignty, by the nature and operations of the proposed constitution.* Among the proofs you adduce of such consolidation being the *intention* of the late convention, is the expression of—"We the People."—Tho' this is a mere form of words, it will be well to see what expressions are to be found in the constitution in opposition to this, and indicative of the intentions of the convention, before we consider those things, which, as I conceive, secure the states from a possibility of losing their respective sovereignties.

First, then, tho' the convention propose that it should be the act of the people, yet it is in their capacities as citizens of *the several members of our confederacy*—for they are expresly declared to be the people of *the United States"* — to which idea the expression is *strictly* confined, and the

general term of *America,* which is constantly used in speaking of us *as a nation,* is carefully omitted: a pointed view was evidently had to our *existing union.* But we must see at once, that the reason of *"the People"* being mentioned was, that alterations of several constitutions were to be effected, which the convention well knew could be done by no authority but that of *"the people,"* either determining themselves *in their several states,* or delegating adequate powers to their *state conventions.* Had the foederal convention meant to exclude the idea of *"union,"* that is, of *several and separate* sovereignties joining in a confederacy, they would have said, we *the people of America;* for union necessarily involves the idea of component states, which complete consolidations exclude.

21

JAMES MADISON, FEDERALIST, NO. 51, 347–53
6 Feb. 1788

(See ch. 10, no. 16)

22

JOHN JAY, AN ADDRESS TO THE PEOPLE
OF THE STATE OF NEW YORK
Spring 1788
Correspondence 3:314–19

Let those who are sanguine in their expectations of a better plan from a new Convention, also reflect on the delays and risks to which it would expose us. Let them consider whether we ought, by continuing much longer in our present humiliating condition, to give other nations further time to perfect their restrictive systems of commerce, reconcile their own people to them, and to fence, and guard, and strengthen them by all those regulations and contrivances in which a jealous policy is ever fruitful. Let them consider whether we ought to give further opportunities to discord to alienate the hearts of our citizens from one another, and thereby encourage new Cromwells to bold exploits. Are we certain that our foreign creditors will continue patient, and ready to proportion their forbearance to our delays? Are we sure that our distresses, dissensions, and weakness will neither invite hostility nor insult? If they should, how ill prepared shall we be for defence, without union, without government, without money, and without credit!

It seems necessary to remind you that some time must yet elapse before all the States will have decided on the present plan. If they reject it, some time must also pass before the measure of a new Convention can be brought about and generally agreed to. A further space of time will then be requisite to elect their deputies, and send them on to Convention. What time they may expend, when met, cannot be divined; and it is equally uncertain how much time the several States may take to deliberate and decide on any plan they may recommend. If adopted, still a further space of time will be necessary to organize and set it in motion. In the meantime, our affairs are daily going from bad to worse; and it is not rash to say that our distresses are accumulating like compound interest.

But if, for reasons already mentioned, and others that we cannot now perceive, the new Convention, instead of producing a better plan, should give us only a history of our disputes, or should offer us one still less pleasing than the present, where should we be? Then the old Confederation has done its best, and cannot help us; and is now so relaxed and feeble, that, in all probability, it would not survive so violent a shock.

Then "To your tents, O Israel!" would be the word. Then every band of union would be severed. Then every State would be a little nation, jealous of its neighbour, and anxious to strengthen itself, by foreign alliances, against its former friends. Then farewell to fraternal affection, unsuspecting intercourse, and mutual participation in commerce, navigation, and citizenship. Then would rise mutual restrictions and fears, mutual garrisons and standing armies, and all those dreadful evils which for so many ages plagued England, Scotland, Wales, and Ireland, while they continued disunited, and were played off against each other.

Consider, my fellow-citizens, what you are about before it is too late; consider what in such an event would be your particular case. You know the geography of your State, and the consequences of your local position. Jersey and Connecticut, to whom your impost laws have been unkind—Jersey and Connecticut, who have adopted the present plan and expect much good from it, will impute its miscarriage and all the consequent evils to you. They now consider your opposition as dictated more by your fondness for your impost, than for those rights to which they have never been behind you in attachment. They cannot, they will not, love you; they border upon you and are your neighbours, but you will soon cease to regard their neighbourhood as a blessing. You have but one port or outlet to your commerce, and how you are to keep that outlet free and uninterrupted merits consideration. What advantages Vermont, in combination with others, might take of you, may easily be conjectured; nor will you be at a loss to perceive how much reason the people of Long Island, whom you cannot protect, have to deprecate being constantly exposed to the depredations of every invader.

These are short hints; they ought not to be more developed; you can easily in your own minds dilate and trace them through all their relative circumstances and connections. Pause then for a moment and reflect whether the matters you are disputing about are of sufficient moment to justify your running such extravagant risks. Reflect that the present plan comes recommended to you by men and fellow-citizens who have given you the highest proofs that men can give, of their justice, their love of liberty and their country, of their prudence, of their application, and of their talents. They tell you it is the best that they could form, and that in their opinion, it is necessary to redeem

you from those calamities which already begin to be heavy upon us all. You find that not only those men, but others of similar characters, and of whom you have also had very ample experience, advise you to adopt it. You find that whole States concur in the sentiment, and among them are your next neighbours, both of whom have shed much blood in the cause of liberty, and have manifested as strong and constant a predilection for a free republican government as any States in the Union, and perhaps in the world. They perceive not those latent mischiefs in it with which some double-sighted politicians endeavour to alarm you. You cannot but be sensible that this plan or Constitution will always be in the hands and power of the people, and that if on experiment it should be found defective or incompetent, they may either remedy its defects, or substitute another in its room. The objectionable parts of it are certainly very questionable, for otherwise there would not be such a contrariety of opinions about them. Experience will better determine such questions than theoretical arguments, and so far as the danger of abuses is urged against the institution of a government, remember that a power to do good always involves a power to do harm. We must, in the business of government as well as in all other business, have some degree of confidence, as well as a great degree of caution. Who, on a sick-bed, would refuse medicines from a physician merely because it is as much in his power to administer deadly poisons as salutary remedies?

You cannot be certain that by rejecting the proposed plan you would not place yourselves in a very awkward situation. Suppose nine States should nevertheless adopt it, would you not in that case be obliged either to separate from the Union or rescind your dissent? The first would not be eligible, nor could the latter be pleasant. A mere hint is sufficient on this topic. You cannot but be aware of the consequences.

Consider, then, how weighty and how many considerations advise and persuade the people of America to remain in the safe and easy path of union; to continue to move and act, as they hitherto have done, as a band of brothers; and to have confidence in themselves and in one another; and, since all cannot see with the same eyes, at least to give the proposed Constitution a fair trial, and to mend it as time, occasion, and experience may dictate. It would little become us to verify the predictions of those who ventured to prophesy that peace, instead of blessing us with happiness and tranquillity, would serve only as the signal for factions, discord, and civil contentions to rage in our land, and overwhelm it with misery and distress.

Let us all be mindful that the cause of freedom depends on the use we make of the singular opportunities we enjoy of governing ourselves wisely; for, if the event should prove that the people of this country either cannot or will not govern themselves, who will hereafter be advocates for systems which, however charming in theory and prospect, are not reducible to practice? If the people of our nation, instead of consenting to be governed by laws of their own making and rulers of their own choosing, should let licentiousness, disorder, and confusion reign over them, the minds of men everywhere will insensibly become alienated from republican forms, and prepared to prefer and acquiesce in governments which, though less friendly to liberty, afford more peace and security.

Receive this address with the same candour with which it is written; and may the spirit of wisdom and patriotism direct and distinguish your councils and your conduct.

A CITIZEN OF NEW YORK.

23

ALEXANDER HAMILTON, REPORT
ON MANUFACTURES
Dec. 1791
Papers 10:293–95

It is not uncommon to meet with an opinion that though the promoting of manufactures may be the interest of a part of the Union, it is contrary to that of another part. The Northern & southern regions are sometimes represented as having adverse interests in this respect. Those are called Manufacturing, these Agricultural states; and a species of opposition is imagined to subsist between the Manufacturing and Agricultural interests.

This idea of an opposition between those two interests is the common error of the early periods of every country, but experience gradually dissipates it. Indeed they are perceived so often to succour and to befriend each other, that they come at length to be considered as one: a supposition which has been frequently abused and is not universally true. Particular encouragements of particular manufactures may be of a Nature to sacrifice the interests of landholders to those of manufacturers; But it is nevertheless a maxim well established by experience, and generally acknowledged, where there has been sufficient experience, that the *aggregate* prosperity of manufactures, and the *aggregate* prosperity of Agriculture are intimately connected. In the Course of the discussion which has had place, various weighty considerations have been adduced operating in support of that maxim. Perhaps the superior steadiness of the demand of a domestic market for the surplus produce of the soil, is alone a convincing argument of its truth.

Ideas of a contrariety of interests between the Northern and southern regions of the Union, are in the Main as unfounded as they are mischievous. The diversity of Circumstances on which such contrariety is usually predicated, authorises a directly contrary conclusion. Mutual wants constitute one of the strongest links of political connection, and the extent of these bears a natural proportion to the diversity in the means of mutual supply.

Suggestions of an opposite complexion are ever to be deplored, as unfriendly to the steady pursuit of one great common cause, and to the perfect harmony of all the parts.

In proportion as the mind is accustomed to trace the intimate connexion of interest, which subsists between all the parts of a Society united under the *same* government—the infinite variety of channels which serve to Circulate the prosperity of each to and through the rest—in that proportion will it be little apt to be disturbed by solicitudes and Apprehensions which originate in local discriminations. It is a truth as important as it is agreeable, and one to which it is not easy to imagine exceptions, that every thing tending to establish *substantial* and *permanent order*, in the affairs of a Country, to increase the total mass of industry and opulence, is ultimately beneficial to every part of it. On the Credit of this great truth, an acquiescence may safely be accorded, from every quarter, to all institutions & arrangements, which promise a confirmation of public order, and an augmentation of National Resource.

But there are more particular considerations which serve to fortify the idea, that the encouragement of manufactures is the interest of all parts of the Union. If the Northern and middle states should be the principal scenes of such establishments, they would immediately benefit the more southern, by creating a demand for productions; some of which they have in common with the other states, and others of which are either peculiar to them, or more abundant, or of better quality, than elsewhere. These productions, principally are Timber, flax, Hemp, Cotton, Wool, raw silk, Indigo, iron, lead, furs, hides, skins and coals. Of these articles Cotton & Indigo are peculiar to the southern states; as are hitherto *Lead & Coal.* Flax and Hemp are or may be raised in greater abundance there, than in the More Northern states; and the Wool of Virginia is said to be of better quality than that of any other state: a Circumstance rendered the more probable by the reflection that Virginia embraces the same latitudes with the finest Wool Countries of Europe. The Climate of the south is also better adapted to the production of silk.

The extensive cultivation of Cotton can perhaps hardly be expected, but from the previous establishment of domestic Manufactories of the Article; and the surest encouragement and vent, for the others, would result from similar establishments in respect to them.

24

TIMOTHY PICKERING TO GEORGE CABOT
29 Jan. 1804
New-England Federalism 338–41

A friend of mine in Pennsylvania, in answering a letter, lately asked me, "Is not a great deal of our chagrin founded on personal dislikes, the pride of opinion, and the mortification of disappointment?" I replied, or, to speak correctly, I prepared the following reply. But when I had finished, perceiving the sentiments too strong for the latitude of Pennsylvania, and perhaps for the nerves of my friend, I changed the form, and now address them to you.

To those questions, perhaps to a certain degree, an affirmative answer may be given. I have more than once asked myself, For what are we struggling? Our lands yield their increase, our commerce flourishes, we are building houses, "are marrying and given in marriage," yet we are dissatisfied: not because we envy the men in office,—to most of us a private life is most desirable. The Federalists are dissatisfied, because they see the public morals debased by the corrupt and corrupting system of our rulers. Men are tempted to become apostates, not to Federalism merely, but to virtue and to religion and to good government. Apostasy and original depravity are the qualifications for official honors and emoluments, while men of sterling worth are displaced and held up to popular contempt and scorn. And shall we sit still, until this system shall universally triumph? until even in the Eastern States the principles of genuine Federalism shall be overwhelmed? Mr. Jefferson's plan of destruction has been gradually advancing. If at once he had removed from office all the Federalists, and given to the people such substitutes as we generally see, even his followers (I mean the mass) would have been shocked. He is still making progress in the same course; and he has the credit of being the real source of all the innovations which threaten the subversion of the Constitution, and the prostration of every barrier erected by it for the protection of the *best*, and therefore to him the most obnoxious, part of the community. His instruments manifest tempers so malignant, so inexorable, as convince observing Federalists that the mild manners and habits of our countrymen are the only security against their extreme vengeance. How long we shall enjoy even this security, God only knows. And must we with folded hands wait the result, or timely think of other protection? This is a delicate subject. The principles of our Revolution point to the remedy,—a separation. That this can be accomplished, and without spilling one drop of blood, I have little doubt. One thing I know, that the rapid progress of innovation, of corruption, of oppression, forces the idea upon many a reflecting mind. *Indeed,* we are not uneasy because "unplaced." But we look with dread on the ultimate issue,—an issue not remote, unless some new and extraordinary obstacle be opposed, and that speedily; for paper constitutions are become as clay in the hands of the potter. The people of the East cannot reconcile their habits, views, and interests with those of the South and West. The latter are beginning to rule with a rod of iron. When not convenient to violate the Constitution, it must be altered; and it will be made to assume any shape as an instrument to crush the Federalists. The independence of the judges is now directly assailed, and the majority are either so blind or so well trained that it will most undoubtedly be destroyed. Independently of specific charges, as ground of impeachment, John Randolph, I am informed, avows this doctrine: that the clause in the Constitution granting to the judges their offices during *good behavior* was intended merely to guard them against *Executive removals,* and not at all to restrain the two Houses of Congress, on whose representation the President ought to remove them! We should really be safer without any constitution, for then oppressive acts might excite public attention; but while the popular tyrants shelter themselves under the forms or the name of the Constitution, tortured and interpreted to suit their views, the people will not be alarmed.

By the Philadelphia papers, I see that the Supreme Court judges of Pennsylvania are to be hurled from their seats, on the pretence that, in punishing one Thomas Passmore for a contempt, they acted illegally and tyrannically. I presume that Shippen, Yates, and Smith are to be removed by the Governor, on the representation of the legislature. And when such grounds are taken, in the national and State legislatures, to destroy the rights of the judges, whose rights can be safe? Why destroy *them,* unless as the prelude to the destruction of every influential Federalist, and of every man of considerable property, who is not of the reigning sect? New judges, of characters and tempers suited to the object, will be the selected ministers of vengeance. I am not willing to be sacrificed by such popular tyrants. My life is not worth much; but, if it must be offered up, let it rather be in the hope of obtaining a more stable government, under which my children, at least, may enjoy freedom with security. Some Connecticut gentlemen (and they are all well-informed and discreet) assure me that, if the leading Democrats in that State were to get the upper hand (which would be followed by a radical change in their *unwritten* constitution), they should not think themselves safe, either in person or property, and would therefore immediately quit the State. I do not believe in the practicability of a long-continued union. A Northern confederacy would unite congenial characters, and present a fairer prospect of public happiness; while the Southern States, having a similarity of habits, might be left "to manage their own affairs in their own way." If a separation were to take place, our mutual wants would render a friendly and commercial intercourse inevitable. The Southern States would require the naval protection of the Northern Union, and the products of the former would be important to the navigation and commerce of the latter. I believe, indeed, that, if a Northern confederacy were forming, our Southern brethren would be seriously alarmed, and probably abandon their virulent measures. But I greatly doubt whether prudence should suffer the connection to continue much longer. They are so devoted to their chief, and he is so necessary to accomplish their plans of misrule and oppression, that as they have projected an alteration of the Constitution to secure his next election, with a continued preponderance of their party, so it would not surprise me, were they, soon after his next election, to choose him President for life. I am assured that some of his blind worshippers in South Carolina have started the idea.

But *when* and *how* is a separation to be effected? If, as many think, Federalism (by which I mean the solid principles of government applied to a federate republic,— principles which are founded in justice, in sound morals, and religion, and whose object is the security of life, liberty, and property, against popular delusion, injustice, and tyranny),—if, I say, Federalism is crumbling away in New England, there is no time to be lost, lest it should be overwhelmed, and become unable to attempt its own relief. Its last refuge is New England; and immediate exertion, per-haps, its only hope. It must begin in Massachusetts. The proposition would be welcomed in Connecticut; and could we doubt of New Hampshire? But New York must be as-sociated; and how is her concurrence to be obtained? She must be made the centre of the confederacy. Vermont and New Jersey would follow of course, and Rhode Island of necessity. Who can be consulted, and who will take the lead? The legislatures of Massachusetts and Connecticut meet in May, and of New Hampshire in the same month or in June. The subject has engaged the contemplation of many. The Connecticut gentlemen have seriously medi-tated upon it. We suppose the British Provinces in Canada and Nova Scotia, at no remote period, perhaps without delay, and with the assent of Great Britain, may become members of the Northern league. Certainly, that govern-ment can feel only disgust at our present rulers. She will be pleased to see them crestfallen. She will not regret the proposed division of empire. If with their own consent she relinquishes her provinces, she will be rid of the charge of maintaining them; while she will derive from *them*, as she does from *us*, all the commercial returns which her mer-chants now receive. A liberal treaty of amity and com-merce will form a bond of union between Great Britain and the Northern confederacy highly useful to both.

25

JOHN QUINCY ADAMS TO WILLIAM PLUMER
16 Aug. 1809
Writings 3:339–42

The spirit of party has become so inveterate and so viru-lent in our country, it has so totally absorbed the under-standing and the heart of almost all the distinguished men among us, that I, who cannot cease to consider all the indi-viduals of both parties as my countrymen, who can neither approve nor disapprove in a lump either of the men or the measures of either party, who see both sides claiming an exclusive privilege of patriotism, and using against each other weapons of political warfare which I never can handle, cannot but cherish that congenial spirit, which has always preserved itself pure from the infectious vapors of faction, which considers temperance as one of the first political du-ties, and which can perceive a very distinct shade of differ-ence between political candor and political hypocrisy.

It affords me constant pleasure to recollect that the his-tory of our country has fallen into the hands of such a man. For as impartiality lies at the bottom of all historical truth, I have often been not without my apprehensions, that no true history of our times would appear at least in the course of our age; that we should have nothing but federal histories, or republican histories, New England his-tories, or Virginia histories. We are indeed not over-stocked with men capable even of this, who have acted a part in the public affairs of our nation. But of men who

unite both qualifications, that of having had a practical knowledge of our affairs, and that of possessing a mind capable of impartiality in summing up the merits of our government, administrations, oppositions and people, I know not another man with whom I have ever had the opportunity of forming an acquaintance, on the correct-ness of whose narrative I should so implicitly rely.

Such a historian, and I take delight in the belief, will be a legislator without reading constituents. You have so long meditated on your plan, and so much longer upon the du-ties of man in society, as they apply to the transactions of your own life, that I am well assured your work will carry a profound political moral with it. And I hope, though upon this subject I have had no hint from you, which can ascertain that your view of the subject is the same as mine, but I hope, that the *moral* of your history will be the indis-soluble union of the North American continent. The plan of a New England combination more closely cemented than by the general ties of the federal government, a com-bination first to rule the whole, and if that should prove impracticable, to separate from the rest, has been so far matured, and has engaged the studies, the intrigues and the ambitions of so many leading men in our part of the country, that I think it will eventually produce mischievous consequences, unless seasonably and effectually discounte-nanced, by men of more influence and of more compre-hensive views. To rise upon a division system is, unfor-tunately, one of the most obvious and apparently easy courses, which plays before the eyes of individual ambition in every section of the Union. It is the natural resource of all the small statesmen who, feeling like Caesar, and find-ing that Rome is too large an object for their grasp, would strike off a village where they might aspire to the first sta-tion, without exposing themselves to derision. This has been the most powerful operative impulse upon all the *di-visionists,* from the first Kentucky conspiracy, down to the negotiations between Massachusetts, Connecticut, and New Hampshire, of the last winter and spring. Considered merely as a purpose of ambition, the great objection against this scheme is its littleness. Instead of adding all the tribes of Israel to Judah and Benjamin, like David, it is walking in the ways of Jeroboam, the son of Nabat, who made Israel to sin by breaking off Samaria from Jerusa-lem. Looking at it in reference to moral considerations, it is detestable, as it certainly cannot be accomplished by open and honorable means. The abettors are obliged to discover their real designs, to affect others, to practice continual deception, and to work upon the basest materials the selfish and dissocial passions of their instruments. Po-litically speaking, it is as injudicious, as it is contracted and dishonorable. The American people are not prepared for disunion, far less so than these people imagine. They will continue to resist and defeat every attempt of that char-acter, as they uniformly have done, and such projects will still terminate in the ruin of their projectors. But the ill consequences of this turbulent spirit will be to keep the country in a state of constant agitation, to embitter the lo-cal prejudices of fellow-citizens against each other, and *to diminish the influence which we ought to have, and might have, in the general councils of the Union.*

To counteract the tendency of these partial and foolish combinations, I know nothing so likely to have a decisive influence as historical works, honestly and judiciously executed. For if the doctrine of union were a new one, now first to be inculcated, our history would furnish the most decisive arguments in its favor. It is no longer the great lesson to be learnt, but the fundamental maxim to be confirmed, and every species of influence should be exerted by all genuine American patriots, to make its importance more highly estimated and more unquestionably established. I should have been glad to see a little more of this *tendency* in Marshall's *Life of Washington,* than I did find. For Washington was emphatically the man of the whole Union, and I see a little too much of the Virginian in Marshall. Perhaps it was unavoidable, and perhaps you will find it equally impossible to avoid disclosing the New England man. I have enough of that feeling myself most ardently to wish, that the brightest examples of a truly liberal and comprehensive American political system may be exhibited by New England men.

26

WILLIAM PINKNEY, ARGUMENT IN McCULLOCH V. MARYLAND
1819

Pinkney 550–51 (1826)

. . . the change intended to be produced by the new constitution consisted much less in the addition of new powers to the Union, than in the invigoration of the original powers. The power of regulating commerce was, indeed, a new power. But the powers relating to war and peace, fleets and armies, treaties and finance, with the other more considerable powers, were all vested in Congress by the articles of confederation. The proposed change only substituted a more effectual mode of administering them.

Under the constitution, the powers belonging to the federal government, whatever may be their extent, are just as sovereign as those of the States. The State governments are not the authors and creators of the national constitution. It does not derive its powers from them. They are preceding in point of time to the national sovereignty, but are postponed to it in point of supremacy by the will of the people. The powers of the national government are the great imperial powers by which nations are known to one another. It acts upon the people as the State governments act upon them. Its powers are given by the people, as those of the State governments are given. The national constitution was framed in the name of the people, and was ratified by the people as the State constitutions were. If the respective powers of these two governments interfere, those of the States must yield.

But it is said that the powers of the national government are limited in number and extent, and that this want of universality shows that they are not sovereign powers. But

the State governments are not unlimited in the number, or unrestrained in the exercise of their powers. They are limited by the declarations of rights contained in the State constitutions; by the nature and ends of all government; and by the restraints upon state legislation contained in the constitution of the United States.

It is said, too, that the powers of the State governments are original, and therefore more emphatically sovereign than those of the national government. But the State powers are no more original than those belonging to the Union. There is no original power but in the people, who are the fountain and source of all political power.

27

JAMES MADISON, OUTLINE
Sept. 1829

Writings 9:351–57

The compound Govt of the U. S. is without a model, and to be explained by itself, not by similitudes or analogies. The terms Union, Federal, National not to be applied to it without the qualifications peculiar to the system. The English Govt is in a great measure sui generis, and the terms Monarchy used by those who look at the executive head only, and Commonwealth, by those looking at the representative member chiefly, are inapplicable in a strict sense.

A fundamental error lies in supposing the State Governments to be the parties to the Constitutional compact from which the Govt. of the U. S. results.

It is a like error that makes the General Govt and the State governments the parties to the compact, as stated in the 4th. letter of "Algernon Sidney," [Judge Roane]. They may be parties in a judicial controversy, but are not so in relation to the original constitutional compact.

In No. XI of "Retrospects," [by Govr. Giles], in the Richmond Enquirer of Sept. 8, 1829, Mr. Jefferson is misconstrued, or rather *mistated,* as making the State Govts. & the Govt of the U. S. *foreign* to each other; the evident meaning, or rather the express language of Mr. J, being "the *States* are foreign to each other, in the portions of sovereignty not granted, as they were in the entire sovereignty before the grant," and not that the State Govts. and the Govt. of the U. S. are foreign to each other. As the State Govts. participate in appointing the Functionaries of the Genl. Govt. it can no more be said that they are altogether foreign to each other, than that the people of a State & its Govt. are foreign.

The real parties to the constl. compact of the U. S. are the *States*—that is, the people thereof respectively in their sovereign character, and they *alone,* so declared in the Resolutions of 98, and so explained in the Report of 99. In these Resolutions as originally proposed, the word *alone,* wch. guarded agst. error on this point, was struck out, [see printed debates of 98] and led to misconceptions & misreasonings concerning the true character of the pol:

system, and to the idea that it was a compact between the Govts. of the States and the Govt. of the U. S. an idea promoted by the familiar one applied to Govts. independent of the people, particularly the British, of [?] a compact between the monarch & his subjects, pledging protection on one side & allegiance on the other.

The plain fact of the case is that the Constitution of the U. S. was created by the people composing the respective States, who alone had the right; that they organized the Govt. into Legis. Ex. & Judicy. departs. delegating thereto certain portions of power to be exercised over the whole, and reserving the other portions to themselves respectively. As these distinct portions of power were to be exercised by the General Govt. & by the State Govts; by each within limited spheres; and as of course controversies concerning the boundaries of their power wd. happen, it was provided that they should be decided by the Supreme Court of the U. S. so constituted as to be as impartial as it could be made by the mode of appointment & responsibility for the Judges.

Is there then no remedy for usurpations in which the Supreme Ct. of the U. S. concur? Yes: constitutional remedies such as have been found effectual; particularly in the case of alien & sedition laws, and such as will in all cases be effectual, whilst the responsibility of the Genl. Govt to its constituents continues:—Remonstrances & instructions—recurring elections & impeachments; amendt. of Const. as provided by itself & exemplified in the 11th article limiting the suability of the States.

These are resources of the States agst. the Genl. Govt.: resulting from the relations of the States to that Govt.: whilst no corresponding controul exists in the relations of the Genl. to the individual Govts. all of whose functionaries are independent of the United States in their appt. and responsibility.

Finally should all the constitutional remedies fail, and the usurpations of the Genl. Govt. become so intolerable as absolutely to forbid a longer passive obedience & non-resistance, a resort to the original rights of the parties becomes justifiable; and redress may be sought by shaking off the yoke, as of right, might be done by part of an individual State in a like case; or even by a single citizen, could he effect it, if deprived of rights absolutely essential to his safety & happiness. In the defect of their ability to resist, the individual citizen may seek relief in expatriation or voluntary exile[1] a resort not within the reach of large portions of the community.

In all the views that may be taken of questions between the State Govts. & the Genl. Govt. the awful consequences of a final rupture & dissolution of the Union shd. never for a moment be lost sight of. Such a prospect must be deprecated, must be shuddered at by every friend to his country, to liberty, to the happiness of man. For, in the event of a dissolution of the Union, an impossibility of ever renewing it is brought home to every mind by the

difficulties encountered in establishing it. The propensity of all communities to divide when not pressed into a unity by external danger, is a truth well understood. *There is no instance of a people inhabiting even a small island, if remote from foreign danger, and sometimes in spite of that pressure, who are not divided into alien, rival, hostile tribes.* The happy Union of these States is a wonder; their Constn. a miracle; their example the hope of Liberty throughout the world. Woe to the ambition that would meditate the destruction of either!

28

JAMES MADISON TO NICHOLAS P. TRIST
15 Feb. 1830
Writings 9:354–58

It has been too much the case in expounding the Constitution of the U. S. that its meaning has been sought not in its peculiar and unprecedented modifications of Power; but by viewing it, some through the medium of a simple Govt. others thro' that of a mere League of Govts. It is neither the one nor the other; but essentially different from both. It must consequently be its own interpreter. No other Government can furnish a key to its true character. Other Governments present an individual & indivisible sovereignty. The Constitution of the U. S. divides the sovereignty; the portions surrendered by the States, composing the Federal sovereignty over specified subjects; the portions retained forming the sovereignty of each over the residuary subjects within its sphere. If sovereignty cannot be thus divided, the Political System of the United States is a chimaera, mocking the vain pretensions of human wisdom. If it can be so divided, the system ought to have a fair opportunity of fulfilling the wishes & expectations which cling to the experiment.

Nothing can be more clear than that the Constitution of the U. S. has created a Government, in as strict a sense of the term, as the Governments of the States created by their respective Constitutions. The Federal Govt. has like the State govts. its Legislative, its Executive & its Judiciary Departments. It has, like them, acknowledged cases in which the powers of these departments are to operate. And the operation is to be directly on persons & things in the one Govt. as in the others. If in some cases, the jurisdiction is concurrent as it is in others exclusive, this is one of the features constituting the peculiarity of the system.

In forming this compound scheme of Government it was impossible to lose sight of the question, what was to be done in the event of controversies which could not fail to occur, concerning the partition line, between the powers belonging to the Federal and to the State Govts. That some provision ought to be made, was as obvious and as essential, as the task itself was difficult and delicate.

That the final decision of such controversies, if left to each of the 13 now 24 members of the Union, must pro-

[1]See letter to N. P. Trist; and see also the distinction between an expatriating individual withdrawing only his person and moveable effects, and the withdrawal of a State mutilating the domain of the Union. [Madison's note.]

duce a different Constitution & different laws in the States was certain; and that such differences must be destructive of the common Govt. & of the Union itself, was equally certain. The decision of questions between the common agents of the whole & of the parts, could only proceed from the whole, that is from a collective not a separate authority of the parts.

The question then presenting itself could only relate to the least objectionable mode of providing for such occurrences, under the collective authority.

The provision immediately and ordinarily relied on, is manifestly the Supreme Court of the U. S., clothed as it is, with a Jurisdiction "in controversies to which the U. S. shall be a party;" the Court itself being so constituted as to render it independent & impartial in its decisions; [see *Federalist*, no. 39] whilst other and ulterior resorts would remain in the elective process, in the hands of the people themselves the joint constituents of the parties; and in the provision made by the Constitution for amending itself. All other resorts are extra & ultra constitutional, corresponding to the Ultima Ratio of nations renouncing the ordinary relations of peace.

If the Supreme Court of the U. S. be found or deemed not sufficiently independent and impartial for the trust committed to it, a better Tribunal is a desideratum: But whatever this may be, it must necessarily derive its authority from the whole not from the parts, from the States in some collective not individual capacity. And as some such Tribunal is a vital element, a sine qua non, in an efficient & permanent Govt. the Tribunal existing must be acquiesced in, until a better or more satisfactory one can be substituted.

Altho' the old idea of a compact between the Govt. & the people be justly exploded, the idea of a compact among those who are parties to a Govt. is a fundamental principle of free Govt.

The original compact is the one implied or presumed, but nowhere reduced to writing, by which a people agree to form one society. The next is a compact, here for the first time reduced to writing, by which the people in their social state agree to a Govt. over them. These two compacts may be considered as blended in the Constitution of the U. S., which recognises a union or society of States, and makes it the basis of the Govt. formed by the parties to it.

It is the nature & essence of a compact that it is equally obligatory on the parties to it, and of course that no one of them can be liberated therefrom without the consent of the others, or such a violation or abuse of it by the others, as will amount to a dissolution of the compact.

Applying this view of the subject to a single community, it results, that the compact being between the individuals composing it, no individual or set of individuals can at pleasure, break off and set up for themselves, without such a violation of the compact as absolves them from its obligations. It follows at the same time that, in the event of such a violation, the suffering party rather than longer yield a passive obedience may justly shake off the yoke, and can only be restrained from the attempt by a want of physical strength for the purpose. The case of individuals

expatriating themselves, that is leaving their country in its *territorial* as well as its social & political sense, may well be deemed a reasonable privilege, or rather as a right impliedly reserved. And even in this case equitable conditions have been annexed to the right which qualify the exercise of it.

Applying a like view of the subject to the case of the U. S. it results, that the compact being among individuals as imbodied into States, no State can at pleasure release itself therefrom, and set up for itself. The compact can only be dissolved by the consent of the other parties, or by usurpations or abuses of power justly having that effect. It will hardly be contended that there is anything in the terms or nature of the compact, authorizing a party to dissolve it at pleasure.

It is indeed inseparable from the nature of a compact, that there is as much right on one side to expound it & to insist on its fulfilment according to that exposition, as there is on the other so to expound it as to furnish a release from it; and that an attempt to annul it by one of the parties, may present to the other, an option of acquiescing in the annulment, or of preventing it as the one or the other course may be deemed the lesser evil. This is a consideration which ought deeply to impress itself on every patriotic mind, as the strongest dissuasion from unnecessary approaches to such a crisis. What would be the condition of the States attached to the Union & its Govt. and regarding both as essential to their well-being, if a State placed in the midst of them were to renounce its Federal obligations, and erect itself into an independent and alien nation? Could the States N. & S. of Virginia, Pennsyla. or N. York, or of some other States however small, remain associated and enjoy their present happiness, if geographically politically and practically thrown apart by such a breach in the chain which unites their interests and binds them together as neighbours & fellow citizens. It could not be. The innovation would be fatal to the Federal Governt. fatal to the Union, and fatal to the hopes of liberty and humanity; and presents a catastrophe at which all ought to shudder.

Without identifying the case of the U. S. with that of individual States, there is at least an instructive analogy between them. What would be the condition of the State of N. Y. of Massts. or of Pena. for example, if portions containing their great commercial cities, invoking original rights as paramount to social & constitutional compacts, should erect themselves into distinct & absolute sovereignties? In so doing they would do no more, unless justified by an intolerable oppression, than would be done by an individual State as a portion of the Union, in separating itself, without a like cause, from the other portions. Nor would greater evils be inflicted by such a mutilation of a State of some of its parts, than might be felt by some of the States from a separation of its neighbours into absolute and alien sovereignties.

Even in the case of a mere League between nations absolutely independent of each other, neither party has a right to dissolve it at pleasure; each having an equal right to expound its obligations, and neither, consequently a greater right to pronounce the compact void than the other has to insist on the mutual execution of it. [See, in Mr. Jefferson's volumes, his letters to J. M. Mr. Monroe & Col. Carrington]

Having suffered my pen to take this ramble over a subject engaging so much of your attention, I will not withhold the notes made by it from your persual. But being aware that without more development & precision, they may in some instances be liable to misapprehension or misconstruction, I will ask the favour of you to return the letter after it has passed under your partial & confidential eye.

I have made no secret of my surprize and sorrow at the proceedings in S. Carolina, which are understood to assert a right to annul the Acts of Congress within the State, & even to secede from the Union itself. But I am unwilling to enter the political field with the "telum imbelle" which alone I could wield. The task of combating such unhappy aberrations belongs to other hands. A man whose years have but reached the canonical three-score-&-ten (and mine are much beyond the number) should distrust himself, whether distrusted by his friends or not, and should never forget that his arguments, whatever they may be will be answered by allusions to the date of his birth.

SEE ALSO:

Benjamin Franklin, Draft of Articles of Confederation and Perpetual Union, 21 July 1775, Journals 2:195–99

John Dickinson, Draft of Articles of Confederation and Perpetual Union, 12 July 1776, Journals 5:546–54

Pelatiah Webster, A Dissertation on the Political Union and Constitution of the Thirteen United States of North-America Which Is Necessary to Their Preservation and Happiness, 16 Feb. 1783, Old South Leaflets 8:189–216 (1922)

Gen. Benjamin Lincoln to Rufus King, 11 Feb. 1786, King Life 1:156–60

Alexander Hamilton, Conjectures about the New Constitution, late Sept. 1787, Papers 4:275–77

John Jay, Federalist, no. 2, 31 Oct. 1787, 12–13

Charles Pinckney, South Carolina Ratifying Convention, 16 Jan. 1788, Elliot 4:261–63

James Madison to Edmund Pendleton, 21 Feb. 1788, Papers 10:532–33

Impartial Examiner, no. 1, 27 Feb. 1788, Storing 5.14.6

James Innes, Virginia Ratifying Convention, 25 June 1788, Elliot 3:633–34

George Nicholas to James Madison, 31 Dec. 1790, Madison Papers 13:337–40

Timothy Pickering to Richard Peters, 24 Dec. 1803, New-England Federalism 338

Timothy Pickering to Edward Pennington, 12 July 1812, New-England Federalism 388–90

James Madison to Edward Everett, 28 Aug. 1830, Writings 9:383–403

Joseph Story, Commentaries on the Constitution of the United States 1:§§ 321–40, 361–72 (1833)

Abraham Lincoln, Message to Congress in Special Session, 4 July 1861, Collected Works 4:432–37

8

Federal v. Consolidated Government

Introduction

Beset on all sides by practical problems demanding solution or at least mitigation, compelled to think through theoretical issues whose terms required redefinition or at least clarification, the Founders of necessity were driven back to the theme of federalism. All roads, it seemed, passed through this junction. And no wonder, considering the quite distinct, different, and insular communities that had developed in British North America over almost 170 years of imperial rule. The history of many of those communities was marked by protracted struggles in which local colonial authorities tried to find a voice and a place for their opposition to the policies or indifference of central British authority. This long history constituted a body of common recollection of which few could be ignorant in 1776. At the same time it reinforced the traditional view that federalism was the proper form of large republics. Compared to this deeply rooted experience, the political awareness of a single American people and of a common American authority were late Revolutionary creations. Hence republicanism, representation, and constitutionalism itself were understood in a context of federal union.

It was to be expected, accordingly, that the character

and degree of the federalism of the proposed new Constitution should be a most important, visible, and persistent point of contention. Its importance is underscored by the fact that those who had the gravest doubts about some of the implications of the federal principle nonetheless felt the need and had the wit to preempt the name "Federalists" for themselves. Its visibility is sufficiently attested by the documents assembled here. Its persistence is demonstrated by the continuing controversy and litigation over the balance of the federal system, beginning with the Sedition Act of 1798 and *Cohens* v. *Virginia* (6 Wheat. 264 [1821]). Certainly Chief Justice Marshall's early prediction in *McCulloch* v. *Maryland* has been fulfilled: questions of this sort are "perpetually arising, and will probably continue to arise" under the Constitution (4 Wheat. 316, at 405 [1819]).

The causes of this protracted controversy are complicated, and for much the same reason that other key concepts and terms such as constitutionalism, republicanism, and representation do not admit of simple explanations. A second look at the documents discloses that the thinking and language of political life were undergoing significant change, more often than not a deliberate refinement or rejection of earlier thought and speech. The developing language of political discourse was frequently a political decision by those who had the determination and skill to shape it to their ends.

How Close a Union?

Any federation is necessarily a compromise between the unity of a single central authority and the variety of separate local authorities. It thus implies and expresses a diversity of ends and an ambivalence toward the very act of federation itself as well as toward the preceding political condition. Hitherto independent units choose to federate because they have to, or because they cannot otherwise secure the good they seek (typically, security against those who would do them harm). But in federating rather than consolidating themselves into a new unit, the contracting parties express the desire not to give up the good they have hitherto enjoyed (typically, independence in pursuing the good as they see it). Like most other attempts to have one's cake and to eat it too, federation is fraught with frustration.

The anxieties centering on whether the government erected on the proposed Constitution would be a federal or consolidated union stem directly from uneasy compromise and its conflicting tendencies. The fact that even the most artful proponents of the Constitution could not give a simple answer to that question did little to calm those who feared to lose the good they had more than they hoped to gain the good they lacked. If, in the course of the discussions and debates, each side held fast to what it thought desirable, each nonetheless modified what it thought possible. A new vocabulary had to be devised to bring that accommodation about.

But all this took place against a history of federations extending for more than two millenia from ancient Greece to the Netherlands. James Madison had studied that long history assiduously at least a year before the Philadelphia Convention and came to summarize it in *Federalist,* nos. 18–20. Earlier usage had understood by "federal" or "confederal" government a league of formally equal and independent sovereign cities or states. The principal business of the federation was directed outwards—peace and war, foreign relations, and relations among the member cities or states. In general the whole was not expected to govern, let alone override, the distinctive ways of life of its parts. In reality, however (Madison and Hamilton argued), a community of sovereigns is no community at all; "a government over governments . . . is a solecism in theory" and a wretched absurdity in practice. The jealousies that kept the central authority of earlier confederacies weak and dependent upon its parts led necessarily to those parts being deprived of the strength that only union could give them. Unbridled rival ambitions, fears of being reduced to a common and inferior mode of life, hopes of achieving particular gains at the general expense: all these condemned a fatally flawed system to vibrate between anarchy and despotism.

With such melancholy examples before them, the Americans might be more amenable to a clearer and more rational understanding of federation. Indeed, precisely because their reluctance to merge stemmed, at its best, from a proper fear of despotic power, they might be reached by arguments designed to show that a more perfect union would better secure their liberties. Since those who opposed the Constitution were not intransigent in their federalism, they could be brought to accept—however reluctantly and with whatever misgivings—a Constitution that by older standards was hardly federal at all. Indeed, by accepting Hamilton's antonymy of federation or "league," on the one hand, and "government," on the other (see ch. 5, no. 21), and by granting the need for effective government at a level above that of the component units, modern defenders of federalism (as hitherto understood) had undercut themselves. Both the case for federalism and the character of federalism would come to take on a novel nature. No longer ought the question to be whether the proposed union deprived the states of the full sovereignty befitting members of a federal system, but whether the proposed union threatened to deprive them of their independence.

From the outset it appears to have been understood generally that "the good people of these colonies" had to act, in some respects at least, as one and not as many. Thus, in declaring the causes that had impelled them to separation from Britain, they adopted the form of a unanimous declaration of thirteen *united* states of America. In due succession came not thirteen separate negotiations for foreign loans or thirteen treaties of commerce and amity, but one. From this vantage the states owed their independence and very existence as states to the union, a union older than any of the states. (See Lincoln, Message to Congress in Special Session, 4 July 1861.) But at the same time the declaration of American independence had not precluded all forms of dual action: military campaigns, for instance, were undertaken by separately controlled state militias and a Continental Army. And indeed, from 1775 until the Articles of Confederation finally were ratified in 1781, the Continental Congress presided over an ad hoc confederation lacking any formal terms. Even so, there appears to have been concern from the outset that in acting as one, the distinctions of the parts not be obliterated (no. 2). Even the carefully delimited terms of the Articles of Confederation were not proof against an expansive interpretation, and hence worrisome (no. 3).

Against those who feared that enlarged powers in the center would subvert liberties in the states, were arrayed those who feared that a want of power in the center would leave the independence of all in jeopardy. James Wilson (no. 4) thought it mistaken to imagine that all powers of the Confederation were derived from the states. As "one undivided, independent nation," the government of the United States by the very act of union could be presumed to have powers that were beyond the competence of a state to grant or withhold. But for John Jay the United States had yet to take on the character of a single nation, for that presupposed reducing the several states to the rank of mere counties within a single state (Letters to J. Lowell, 10 May 1785, and John Adams, 4 May 1786). Jay's is the consolidationist position, plain and unadorned. It is deeply at odds with the concerns that led Jefferson (no. 5) to advocate a federation limited to what Locke had called the "federative" power, one having to do with all persons and communities outside the commonwealth. In the same breath, though, Jefferson could urge the internal use of federal power to shape the character and direction of the new commonwealths aborning in the West. The Western territory, he thought, ought to be carved into many small states so that government on the frontier be visible, close, and familiar. The less tractable a people were, the more important was it that they see that their government is intimately involved in their interests. Self-government implied a republic small enough to make that union of interests credible and effective. The necessary implication of Jefferson's "proper division of powers" (or graded "partition of cares" [no. 44]) was that the main business of governing those matters that touched men's daily lives most closely was to remain in the hands of distinctively diverse states. Such states, however, would already be inclined in a properly republican direction, having been bent (while still supple territories) by the conditions set by the general government.

Madison's thoughts before the Philadelphia Convention were running in quite another way (no. 6). His "middle ground" between individually independent states and a consolidation of those states into one simple republic was "a due supremacy of the national authority" with room for "the local authorities wherever they can be subordinately useful." A national veto *in all cases whatsoever* on the legislative acts of the States, as heretofore exercised by the Kingly prerogative" was, in Madison's eyes, "the least possible encroachment on the State jurisdictions." Again, the ends being sought are revealing: the veto would protect the national government from state incursions on national authority and from state evasions of their obligations. But beyond that, "the national prerogative" would curb the unjust consequences of the states' fluctuating, passionate

policies whereby local majorities were able to further their interests at the expense of the rights of local minorities and individuals. Both the survival and good name of republican government required significant inroads on the authority of the states. (See ch. 17, no. 22.) As it turned out, Madison had to settle, however reluctantly, for a combination of restraints and restrictions (Art. 1, secs. 9–10; Art. 6) that only came close to being a national veto.

Edward Carrington was thinking along the same lines, calling a "foederal sovereignty [with] a compleat controul over the state Governments" the only plan worth discussing, indeed the "most moderate of any which obtain in any general form amongst reflective and intelligent Men" (no. 8). He rightly divined that his addressee, Jefferson, would be taken by surprise at the rapid change in public sentiment (no. 11; see also Thomas Jefferson to Richard Price, 8 Jan. 1789). That change can be traced as well in the shifting usage of a leading Anti-Federalist. After detecting in the proposed Constitution an unholy alliance of "young visionary men, and the consolidating aristocracy," the Federal Farmer went on to lay out the alternative forms of free government available to a united America (no. 12). He rejected alike a purely federal form ("Distinct republics connected under a federal head" that was merely advisory or recommendatory rather than coercive), and a simple consolidated government. The one would not suffice to "answer the purposes of government"; the other was impracticable, quite out of the question. The only eligible form was a "partial consolidation," that is, "a complete consolidation, *quoad* certain objects only." Eleven weeks later, the Federal Farmer was calling those who wanted a federal government "merely advisory" not federalists, but "pretended federalists" (no. 25). There were, he thought, men in both camps who had misappropriated the name. "The honest federalists" among the supporters of the Constitution and "the true federalists" among its critics were of one mind, he thought, as regarded preserving a significant place for the state governments "united under an efficient federal head." The partial consolidationists of October had become the true federalists of December. The Federal Farmer held that the true line of demarcation between the contending parties was their respective political stance toward the rights of the people. In general those who opposed the proposals of the Philadelphia Convention were "men who support the rights of the body of the people"; in general those who advocated the adoption of the Constitution without further amendments were "not very friendly to those rights." Thus the deeper ground of division was over republicanism, and it was in that context that the issue of federal v. consolidated government had to be considered. (See also Henry, no. 38.)

Republican Limits on Union

The bulk of the Anti-Federalist criticism of consolidation supported the Federal Farmer's analysis. The Constitution was held defective especially in that it would set up a government whose natural, perhaps inevitable tendency would be to annihilate the state governments or reduce them to insignificance. (Brutus, nos. 13, 31; Smilie, no. 16;

Findley, no. 17; Henry, no. 38; Clinton, no. 39.) And that outcome would put an end to "the *free* internal Government" of a diverse people and so would be a profound rejection of the American revolutionary "Struggle for the natural Rights of Men" (S. Adams, no. 20). After events had run their course, would there be any remedy short of another revolution (Brutus, no. 34)? What, after all, was the great object in view? If the principal care of government was preserving internal peace, good order, and the due administration of law and justice, then the level of government entrusted with that care ought not be left defenseless against an aggrandizing national judiciary and legislature. Brutus acknowledged that the responsibility of the general government for protection against external dangers entailed granting that general government "authority sufficient to effect this, so far as is consistent with the providing for our internal protection and defence" (no. 26). The primacy of domestic policy was clearly a premise of Anti-Federalist thinking; not glory, but domestic happiness; not foreign adventures, but the peaceful enjoyment of liberty. (See also Federal Farmer, no. 28; Henry, no. 38.)

The response of the supporters of the Constitution was to stress, again and again, the inseparability of strength against external dangers and the enjoyment of internal peace, and the common concern of the state and general governments as related to "the great objects of life, liberty and property" (Wilson, no. 18). Hamilton in the *Federalist* attacked in turn the validity of the sharp distinction between confederation and consolidation, the viability of the federal principle as such, and even the presumption that state governmental concerns might tempt a national government to overstep its bounds ("slender allurements to ambition," he sneered in passing). He also argued that the people would be more jealous of national power; hence potentially dangerous power was better placed in hands where it would be watched. At the same time he predicted that the people were likely to proportion their confidence in a government according to the quality of its administration, a contest he openly expected the national government to win. The end in view was "ONE WHOLE."

The differences between the proponents and opponents of the Constitution often turned on questions of degree (e.g., how much ought the general government's powers to be extended?), and form (e.g., how might a national revenue best be secured?). But for both parties questions of degree and form were crucial to the survival of the union and the character of the republic. It made a great difference whether the general government could address citizens directly or largely through the intermediation of state governments. It made a great difference whether the general government could command its own means of securing money and men or had to resort to the good offices of the several states. It made a great difference whether the states had a constitutionally secured leverage in the national council that left them able to protect their notions of diversity and requisite independence. On the whole, Madison's contributions to the *Federalist* muted the threat to the states even while carefully delineating the ways in which the states would indeed find themselves in a system

that could not properly be termed "federal." It was, he maintained, "a composition" of national and federal elements, leaving the careful reader of *Federalist*, no. 39, to calculate where the center of gravity of that composition would be located. Besides, he asked in a rare flash of rhetorical indignation, had the exploded and "impious" doctrine of the divine right of kings now been converted in America to the notion that the people were made for the states, not the states for the people? The great end for whose sake Americans had fought and bled was hardly so that "particular municipal establishments, might enjoy a certain extent of power, and be arrayed with certain dignities and attributes of sovereignty." To be sure, the claims for state authority were grounded on right and principle. In confronting those claims, Madison and other advocates of the Constitution relied on a still more fundamental right: the right of the people to locate political authority where they judged it to be most likely to secure the great ends of the Revolution. Thus the division and allocation of governmental powers was an open question for a deliberating people to consider. If they found Madison's evidence and reasoning persuasive, they too would conclude that public happiness and internal justice and external security could not be isolated from one another and could not readily be achieved under a government less national than the one proposed.

In all this the Anti-Federalists saw a willful indifference to the extent to which liberty, happiness, justice, and security required not only some enhanced national powers but an array of smaller governments whose vitality would still matter. Had the allurements of splendid achievements blinded the advocates of the Constitution to a more genuine and more beautiful species of national grandeur? (Nos. 33, 38; see Richard Henry Lee to Samuel Adams, 28 Apr. 1788.) Could this unprecedented mixture of federal and national elements—"a strange hotch-potch of both" (Luther Martin, 21 Mar. 1788)—end up other than entirely national (no. 38)? By what abuse of language could this still be called "federalism" (None of the Well-Born Conspirators, 23 Apr. 1788)? Further, some Anti-Federalists continued to assert what Hamilton and Madison, in the single voice of Publius, had denied: the compatibility of sovereignty in the union and sovereignty in the states. Unless this were the case, a [Pennsylvania] Farmer rejoined in a tightly reasoned essay (no. 35), a federal republic itself would be an impossibility, a conclusion no one was prepared to concede. The objects of sovereignty could be allocated between the general government and the states; indeed, the latter "ought to be fit to keep house alone if necessary."

Madison rejected both the possibility and the desirability of individual American states being sufficient unto themselves. Even in the midst of partisan heat and clamor (no. 40), union remained for him the indispensable condition for all that Americans cherished. There were sound, practical, republican reasons for resisting tendencies toward a consolidation of governments. There were equally sound, practical, republican reasons for seeking a consolidation of the country's diverse interests and affections. In the more intense partisan heat and clamor of 1798–1800 attending passage of the Alien and Sedition Acts, it was easier to overlook his measured statements and nuanced arguments. Very much has been and might still be written of Jefferson's Kentucky Resolutions (no. 41) and of Madison's defense of the Virginia Resolutions (no. 42)—of their similarities and of their even more interesting differences in assertion, language, and tone. All the more striking is it considering that Madison had criticized Jefferson's proposal for popular conventions out of a fear that frequent recurrence to the people would weaken the stability of government (see ch. 2, no. 19). But in the Adams administration's selective enforcement of the Sedition Act, both Madison and Jefferson saw an extraordinary danger to cherished liberties and the balance of the federal system.

In this context it is worth noting that the "recurrence to fundamental principles" (of which the third Virginia Resolution is said to be an example), was defended by Madison both on grounds of sound republican practice and as a fulfillment of the Federalist response to Anti-Federalist anxieties of 1787.

If one took literally the notion that the Constitution was a compact between sovereign parties, it was a nice question whether a governor of a sovereign state should correspond with any official in Washington below the level of the President of the United States (no. 43). But such matters of protocol are appropriate only to a light-hearted intermezzo in the unfolding drama of federal versus consolidated government. Nullification—and worse—still lay ahead.

1

MONTESQUIEU, SPIRIT OF LAWS, BK. 8, CHS. 16, 17, 19, 20; BK. 9, CHS. 1–3
1748

[Book 8]

16.—Distinctive Properties of a Republic

It is natural for a republic to have only a small territory; otherwise it cannot long subsist. In an extensive republic there are men of large fortunes, and consequently of less moderation; there are trusts too considerable to be placed in any single subject; he has interests of his own; he soon begins to think that he may be happy and glorious, by oppressing his fellow-citizens; and that he may raise himself to grandeur on the ruins of his country.

In an extensive republic the public good is sacrificed to a thousand private views; it is subordinate to exceptions, and depends on accidents. In a small one, the interest of the public is more obvious, better understood, and more within the reach of every citizen; abuses have less extent, and, of course, are less protected.

The long duration of the republic of Sparta was owing to her having continued in the same extent of territory after all her wars. The sole aim of Sparta was liberty; and the sole advantage of her liberty, glory.

It was the spirit of the Greek republics to be as contented with their territories as with their laws. Athens was first fired with ambition and gave it to Lacedaemon; but it was an ambition rather of commanding a free people than of governing slaves; rather of directing than of breaking the union. All was lost upon the starting up of monarchy—a government whose spirit is more turned to increase of dominion. . . .

17.—Distinctive Properties of a Monarchy

A monarchical state ought to be of moderate extent. Were it small, it would form itself into a republic; were it

very large, the nobility, possessed of great estates, far from the eye of the prince, with a private court of their own, and secure, moreover, from sudden executions by the laws and manners of the country—such a nobility, I say, might throw off their allegiance, having nothing to fear from too slow and too distant a punishment.

Thus Charlemagne had scarcely founded his empire when he was obliged to divide it; whether the governors of the provinces refused to obey; or whether, in order to keep them more under subjection, there was a necessity of parcelling the empire into several kingdoms.

After the decease of Alexander his empire was divided. How was it possible for those Greek and Macedonian chiefs, who were each of them free and independent, or commanders at least of the victorious bands dispersed throughout that vast extent of conquered land—how was it possible, I say, for them to obey?

Attila's empire was dissolved soon after his death; such a number of kings, who were no longer under restraint, could not resume their fetters.

The sudden establishment of unlimited power is a remedy which in those cases may prevent a dissolution: but how dreadful the remedy, which after the enlargement of dominion opens a new scene of misery!

The rivers hasten to mingle their waters with the sea; and monarchies lose themselves in despotic power.

19.—Distinctive Properties of a despotic Government

A large empire supposes a despotic authority in the person who governs. It is necessary that the quickness of the prince's resolutions should supply the distance of the places they are sent to; that fear should prevent the remissness of the distant governor or magistrate; that the law should be derived from a single person, and should shift continually, according to the accidents which incessantly multiply in a state in proportion to its extent.

20.—Consequence of the preceding Chapters

If it be, therefore, the natural property of small states to be governed as a republic, of middling ones to be subject to a monarch, and of large empires to be swayed by a despotic prince; the consequence is, that in order to preserve the principles of the established government, the state must be supported in the extent it has acquired, and that the spirit of this state will alter in proportion as it contracts or extends its limits.

[Book 9]

1.—In what Manner Republics provide for their Safety

If a republic be small, it is destroyed by a foreign force; if it be large, it is ruined by an internal imperfection.

To this twofold inconvenience democracies and aristocracies are equally liable, whether they be good or bad. The evil is in the very thing itself, and no form can redress it.

It is, therefore, very probable that mankind would have been, at length, obliged to live constantly under the government of a single person, had they not contrived a kind of constitution that has all the internal advantages of a republican, together with the external force of a monarchical, government. I mean a confederate republic.

This form of government is a convention by which several petty states agree to become members of a larger one, which they intend to establish. It is a kind of assemblage of societies, that constitute a new one, capable of increasing by means of further associations, till they arrive at such a degree of power as to be able to provide for the security of the whole body.

It was these associations that so long contributed to the prosperity of Greece. By these the Romans attacked the whole globe, and by these alone the whole globe withstood them; for when Rome had arrived at her highest pitch of grandeur, it was the associations beyond the Danube and the Rhine—associations formed by the terror of her arms—that enabled the barbarians to resist her.

Hence it proceeds that Holland, Germany, and the Swiss cantons are considered in Europe as perpetual republics.

The associations of cities were formerly more necessary than in our times. A weak, defenceless town was exposed to greater danger. By conquest it was deprived not only of the executive and legislative power, as at present, but, moreover, of all human property.*

A republic of this kind, able to withstand an external force, may support itself without any internal corruption; the form of this society prevents all manner of inconveniences.

If a single member should attempt to usurp the supreme power, he could not be supposed to have an equal authority and credit in all the confederate states. Were he to have too great an influence over one, this would alarm the rest; were he to subdue a part, that which would still remain free might oppose him with forces independent of those which he had usurped, and overpower him before he could be settled in his usurpation.

Should a popular insurrection happen in one of the confederate states, the others are able to quell it. Should abuses creep into one part, they are reformed by those that remain sound. The state may be destroyed on one side, and not on the other; the confederacy may be dis-

*Civil liberty, goods, wives, children, temples, and even burying-places.

solved, and the confederates preserve their sovereignty.

As this government is composed of petty republics, it enjoys the internal happiness of each; and with regard to its external situation, by means of the association, it possesses all the advantages of large monarchies.

2.—That a confederate Government ought to be composed of States of the same Nature, especially of the republican Kind

The Canaanites were destroyed by reason that they were petty monarchies that had no union or confederacy for their common defence; and, indeed, a confederacy is not agreeable to the nature of petty monarchies.

As the confederate republic of Germany consists of free cities, and of petty states subject to different princes, experience shows us that it is much more imperfect than that of Holland and Switzerland.

The spirit of monarchy is war and enlargement of dominion: peace and moderation are the spirit of a republic. These two kinds of government cannot naturally subsist in a confederate republic.

Thus we observe, in the Roman history, that when the Veientes had chosen a king, they were immediately abandoned by all the other petty republics of Tuscany. Greece was undone as soon as the kings of Macedon obtained a seat among the Amphictyons.

The confederate republic of Germany, composed of princes and free towns, subsists by means of a chief, who is, in some respects, the magistrate of the union, in others the monarch.

3.—Other Requisites in a confederate Republic

In the republic of Holland one province cannot conclude an alliance without the consent of the others. This law, which is an excellent one, and even necessary in a confederate republic, is wanting in the Germanic constitution, where it would prevent the misfortunes that may happen to the whole confederacy, through the imprudence, ambition, or avarice of a single member. A republic united by a political confederacy has given itself entirely up, and has nothing more to resign.

It is difficult for the united states to be all of equal power and extent. The Lycian republic was an association of twenty-three towns; the large ones had three votes in the common council, the middling ones two, and the small towns one. The Dutch republic consists of seven provinces of different extent of territory, which have each one voice.

The cities of Lycia contributed to the expenses of the state, according to the proportion of suffrages. The provinces of the United Netherlands cannot follow this proportion; they must be directed by that of their power.

In Lycia the judges and town magistrates were elected by the common council, and according to the proportion already mentioned. In the republic of Holland they are not chosen by the common council, but each town names its magistrates. Were I to give a model of an excellent confederate republic, I should pitch upon that of Lycia.

2

EDWARD RUTLEDGE TO JOHN JAY
29 June 1776

Jay Unpublished Papers 1:280–81

I have been much engaged lately upon a plan of a Confederation which Dickenson has drawn. It has the Vice of all his Productions to a considerable Degree; I mean the Vice of Refining too much. Unless it is greatly curtailed it never can pass, as it is to be submitted to Men in the respective Provinces who will not be led or rather driven into Measures which may lay the Foundation of their Ruin. If the Plan now proposed should be adopted nothing less than Ruin to some Colonies will be the Consequence of it. The Idea of destroying all Provincial Distinctions and making every thing of the most minute kind bend to what they call the good of the whole, is in other Terms to say that these Colonies must be subject to the Government of the Eastern Provinces. The Force of their Arms I hold exceeding Cheap, but I confess I dread their over-ruling Influence in Council, I dread their low Cunning, and those levelling Principles which Men without Character and without Fortune in general Possess, which are so captivating to the lower Class of Mankind, and which will occasion such a fluctuation of Property as to introduce the greatest disorder. I am resolved to vest the Congress with no more Power than what is absolutely necessary, and to use a familiar Expression to keep the Staff in our own Hands, for I am confident if surrendered into the Hands of others a most pernicious use will be made of it.

3

GEORGE MASON TO THOMAS JEFFERSON
27 Sept. 1781

Papers 2:697–99

You have, no Doubt, been informed of the factious, illegal, & dangerous Schemes now in Contemplation in Congress. for dismembering the Commonwealth of Virgina, & erecting a new State or States to the Westward of the Alleghany Mountains. This power, directly contrary to the Articles of Confederation, is assumed upon the Doctrine now industriously propagated "that the late Revolution has transferred the Sovereignty formerly possessed by Great Britain, to the United States, that is to the American Congress" A Doctrine which, if not immediately arrested in it's progress, will be productive of every Evil; and the Revolution, instead of securing, as was intended, our Rights & Libertys, will only change the Name & place of Residence of our Tyrants. This that Congress who drew the Articles of

Union were sensible of & have provided against it, by expressly declaring in Article the 2d that "Each State retains it's Sovereignty, freedom, & Independence, & every Power, Jurisdiction, & right, which is not by this Confederation *expressly delegated* to the United States in Congress assembled"—& in article the 13th. that "the Articles of this Confederation shall be inviolably observed by every State, & the Union shall be perpetual; nor shall any Alteration at any time hereafter be made in any of them; unless such Alteration be agreed to in a Congress of the United States, and be afterwards confirmed by the Legislatures of every State." In the 9th Article defining the Powers of Congress; least the Power of deciding Disputes, concerning Territory between any of the States, shou'd be attended with dangerous Consequences; it is "provided that no State shall be deprived of Territory for the Benefit of the United States" and the 11th. Article declares that "Canada, acceding to this Confederation, & joining in the measures of the United States, shall be admitted into, & entitled to all the Advantages of this Union: but *no other Colony* shall be Admitted into the same, unless such Admission be agreed to by nine States." This article holds out an immediate Offer to Canada; and the words *no other Colony* plainly relate to the other British Colonys of Nova Scotia, & East & West Floridas, & clearly exclude the Idea of any absolute Power in Congress to erect new States. I had almost forgot to mention the Beginning of the 13th. Article, declaring that "Every State shall abide by the Determinations of the United States in Congress assembled, on all Questions which *by this Confederation* are submitted to them." From whence arises, by the strongest Implication, a negation & Disclaimer of any other Powers, & a Declaration that no State is bound by them if they shou'd at any time be assumed. I shou'd not have troubled you with these Quotations, but that I apprehended in the late Confusions, & sudden Removals of public, as well as private Papers, the Articles of Confederation may have been sent to some distant Place. I think they will prove that Congress are now arrogating to themselves an unwarrantable & dangerous Power; which is in its Nature subversive of American Liberty; for if they can stride over the Lines of the Confederation, & assume Rights not delegated to them by the Legislatures of the different States, in one Instance, they can in every other that the Lust of Power may suggest. I hope our Assembly will take this Subject up with the Coolness and Attention which it's Importance merits, & with proper Firmness endeavour immediately to put a Stop to such Proceedings, by positive Instructions to the Virginia Delegates in Congress. And as much will depend upon the Disposition of the Inhabitants in the western Parts, it will be prudent to secure their Affections by giving them all the advantages of Government; which will require that the executive and judiciary Powers shall be exercised among them; this may be a difficult plan, but it is an absolutely necessary one; permit me Sir to recommend it to your particular Attention. I do it, because I really know no Man whom I think so capable of digesting a proper Plan, & I know, from some former Conversation, that you have heretofore turn'd your Thoughts to this Subject.

4

JAMES WILSON, CONSIDERATIONS ON THE BANK
1785
Works 2:829–30

Though the United States in Congress assembled derive *from the particular states* no power, jurisdiction, or right, which is not expressly delegated by the confederation, it does not thence follow, that the United States in congress have *no other* powers, jurisdiction, or rights, than those delegated by the particular states.

The United States have general rights, general powers, and general obligations, not derived from any particular states, nor from all the particular states, taken separately; but resulting from the union of the whole: and, therefore, it is provided, in the fifth article of the confederation, "that for the more convenient management of the *general interests* of the United States, delegates shall be annually appointed to meet in congress."

To many purposes, the United States are to be considered as one undivided, independent nation; and as possessed of all the rights, and powers, and properties, by the law of nations incident to such.

Whenever an object occurs, to the direction of which no particular state is competent, the management of it must, of necessity, belong to the United States in congress assembled. There are many objects of this extended nature. The purchase, the sale, the defence, and the government of lands and countries, not within any state, are all included under this description. An institution for circulating paper, and establishing its credit over the whole United States, is naturally ranged in the same class.

The act of independence was made before the articles of confederation. This act declares, that *"these United colonies,"* (not enumerating them separately) "are free and independent states; and that, as free and independent states, *they* have full power to do *all* acts and things which independent states may, of right, do."

The confederation was not intended to weaken or abridge the powers and rights, to which the United States were previously entitled. It was not intended to transfer any of those powers or rights to the particular states, or any of them. If, therefore, the power now in question was vested in the United States before the confederation; it continues vested in them still. The confederation clothed the United States with many though, perhaps, not with sufficient powers: but of none did it disrobe them.

It is no new position, that rights may be vested in a political body, which did not previously reside in any or in all the members of that body. They may be derived solely from the union of those members. "The case," says the celebrated Burlamaqui, "is here very near the same as in that of several voices collected together, which, by their union, produce a harmony, that was not to be found separately in each."

A number of unconnected inhabitants are settled on each side of a navigable river; it belongs to none of them; it belongs not to them all, for they have nothing in common: let them unite; the river is the property of the united body.

The arguments drawn from the political associations of individuals into a state will apply, with equal force and propriety, to a number of states united by a confederacy.

New states must be formed and established: their extent and boundaries must be regulated and ascertained. How can this be done, unless by the United States in congress assembled?

5

THOMAS JEFFERSON TO JAMES MADISON
16 Dec. 1786
Papers 10:603

I find by the public papers that your Commercial Convention failed in point of representation. If it should produce a full meeting in May, and a broader reformation, it will still be well. To make us one nation as to foreign concerns, and keep us distinct in Domestic ones, gives the outline of the proper division of powers between the general and particular governments. But to enable the Federal head to exercise the powers given it, to best advantage, it should be organised, as the particular ones are, into Legislative, Executive and Judiciary. The 1st. and last are already separated. The 2d should also be. When last with Congress, I often proposed to members to do this by making of the Committee of the states, an Executive committee during the recess of Congress, and during it's sessions to appoint a Committee to receive and dispatch all executive business, so that Congress itself should meddle only with what should be legislative. But I question if any Congress (much less all successively) can have self-denial enough to go through with this distribution. The distribution should be imposed on them then. I find Congress have reversed their division of the Western states, and proposed to make them fewer and larger. This is reversing the natural order of things. A tractable people may be governed in large bodies; but in proportion as they depart from this character, the extent of their government must be less. We see into what small divisions the Indians are obliged to reduce their societies. This measure, with the disposition to shut up the Missisipi give me serious apprehensions of the severance of the Eastern and Western parts of our confederacy. It might have been made the interests of the Western states to remain united with us, by managing their interests honestly and for their own good. But the moment we sacrifice their interests to our own, they will see it better to govern themselves. The moment they resolve to do this, the point is settled. A forced connection is neither our interest nor within our power.

6

JAMES MADISON TO GEORGE WASHINGTON
16 Apr. 1787
Papers 9:382–85

I have been honoured with your letter of the 31 of March, and find with much pleasure that your views of the reform which ought to be pursued by the Convention, give a sanction to those which I have entertained. Temporising applications will dishonor the Councils which propose them, and may foment the internal malignity of the disease, at the same time that they produce an ostensible palliation of it. Radical attempts, although unsuccessful, will at least justify the authors of them.

Having been lately led to revolve the subject which is to undergo the discussion of the Convention, and formed in my mind *some* outlines of a new system, I take the liberty of submitting them without apology, to your eye.

Conceiving that an individual independence of the States is utterly irreconcileable with their aggregate sovereignty; and that a consolidation of the whole into one simple republic would be as inexpedient as it is unattainable, I have sought for some middle ground, which may at once support a due supremacy of the national authority, and not exclude the local authorities wherever they can be subordinately useful.

I would propose as the ground-work that a change be made in the principle of representation. According to the present form of the Union in which the intervention of the States is in all great cases necessary to effectuate the measures of Congress, an equality of suffrage, does not destroy the inequality of importance, in the several members. No one will deny that Virginia and Massts. have more weight and influence both within & without Congress than Delaware or Rho. Island. Under a system which would operate in many essential points without the intervention of the State legislatures, the case would be materially altered. A vote in the national Councils from Delaware, would then have the same effect and value as one from the largest State in the Union. I am ready to believe that such a change would not be attended with much difficulty. A majority of the States, and those of greatest influence, will regard it as favorable to them. To the Northern States it will be recommended by their present populousness; to the Southern by their expected advantage in this respect. The lesser States must in every event yield to the predominant will. But the consideration which particularly urges a change in the representation is that it will obviate the principal objections of the larger States to the necessary concessions of power.

I would propose next that in addition to the present federal powers, the national Government should be armed with positive and compleat authority in all cases which require uniformity; such as the regulation of trade, including the right of taxing both exports & imports, the fixing the terms and forms of naturalization, &c &c.

Over and above this positive power, a negative *in all cases whatsoever* on the legislative acts of the States, as heretofore exercised by the Kingly prerogative, appears to me to be absolutely necessary, and to be the least possible encroachment on the State jurisdictions. Without this defensive power, every positive power that can be given on paper will be evaded & defeated. The States will continue to invade the national jurisdiction, to violate treaties and the law of nations & to harrass each other with rival and spiteful measures dictated by mistaken views of interest. Another happy effect of this prerogative would be its controul on the internal vicisitudes of State policy; and the aggressions of interested majorities on the rights of minorities and of individuals. The great desideratum which has not yet been found for Republican Governments, seems to be some disinterested & dispassionate umpire in disputes between different passions & interests in the State. The majority who alone have the right of decision, have frequently an interest real or supposed in abusing it. In Monarchies the sovereign is more neutral to the interests and views of different parties; but unfortunately he too often forms interests of his own repugnant to those of the whole. Might not the national prerogative here suggested be found sufficiently disinterested for the decision of local questions of policy, whilst it would itself be sufficiently restrained from the pursuit of interests adverse to those of the whole Society? There has not been any moment since the peace at which the representatives of the union would have given an assent to paper money or any other measure of a kindred nature.

The national supremacy ought also to be extended as I conceive to the Judiciary departments. If those who are to expound & apply the laws, are connected by their interests & their oaths with the particular States wholly, and not with the Union, the participation of the Union in the making of the laws may be possibly rendered unavailing. It seems at least necessary that the oaths of the Judges should include a fidelity to the general as well as local constitution, and that an appeal should lie to some national tribunals in all cases to which foreigners or inhabitants of other States may be parties. The admiralty jurisdiction seems to fall entirely within the purview of the national Government.

The national supremacy in the Executive departments is liable to some difficulty, unless the officers administering them could be made appointable by the supreme Government. The Militia ought certainly to be placed in some form or other under the authority which is entrusted with the general protection and defence.

A Government composed of such extensive powers should be well organized and balanced. The Legislative department might be divided into two branches; one of them chosen every   years by the people at large, or by the legislatures; the other to consist of fewer members, to hold their places for a longer term, and to go out in such a rotation as always to leave in office a large majority of old members. Perhaps the negative on the laws might be most conveniently exercised by this branch. As a further check, a council of revision including the great ministerial officers might be superadded.

A national Executive must also be provided. I have scarcely ventured as yet to form my own opinion either of the manner in which it ought to be constituted or of the authorities with which it ought to be cloathed.

An article should be inserted expressly guarantying the tranquillity of the States against internal as well as external dangers.

In like manner the right of coercion should be expressly declared. With the resources of Commerce in hand, the national administration might always find means of exerting it either by sea or land; But the difficulty & awkwardness of operating by force on the collective will of a State, render it particularly desirable that the necessity of it might be precluded. Perhaps the negative on the laws might create such a mutuality of dependence between the General and particular authorities, as to answer this purpose. Or perhaps some defined objects of taxation might be submitted along with commerce, to the general authority.

To give a new System its proper validity and energy, a ratification must be obtained from the people, and not merely from the ordinary authority of the Legislatures. This will be the more essential as inroads on the *existing Constitutions* of the States will be unavoidable.

7

VIRGINIA PLAN
29 May 1787
Farrand 1:20–22

---

1. Resolved that the articles of Confederation ought to be so corrected & enlarged as to accomplish the objects proposed by their institution; namely. "common defence, security of liberty and general welfare."

2. Resd. therefore that the rights of suffrage in the National Legislature ought to be proportioned to the Quotas of contribution, or to the number of free inhabitants, as the one or the other rule may seem best in different cases.

3. Resd. that the National Legislature ought to consist of two branches.

4. Resd. that the members of the first branch of the National Legislature ought to be elected by the people of the several States every   for the term of   ; to be of the age of   years at least, to receive liberal stipends by which they may be compensated for the devotion of their time to public service; to be ineligible to any office established by a particular State, or under the authority of the United States, except those peculiarly belonging to the functions of the first branch, during the term of service, and for the space of   after its expiration; to be incapable of re-election for the space of   after the expiration of their term of service, and to be subject to recall.

5. Resold. that the members of the second branch of the National Legislature ought to be elected by those of the first, out of a proper number of persons nominated by the individual Legislatures, to be of the age of   years at least; to hold their offices for a term sufficient to ensure their independency, to receive liberal stipends, by which they may be compensated for the devotion of their time to public service; and to be ineligible to any office established by a particular State, or under the authority of the United States, except those peculiarly belonging to the functions of the second branch, during the term of service, and for the space of   after the expiration thereof.

6. Resolved that each branch ought to possess the right of originating Acts; that the National Legislature ought to be impowered to enjoy the Legislative Rights vested in Congress by the Confederation & moreover to legislate in all cases to which the separate States are incompetent, or in which the harmony of the United States may be interrupted by the exercise of individual Legislation; to negative all laws passed by the several States, contravening in the opinion of the National Legislature the articles of Union; and to call forth the force of the Union agst. any member of the Union failing to fulfill its duty under the articles thereof.

7. Resd. that a National Executive be instituted; to be chosen by the National Legislature for the term of   years, to receive punctually at stated times, a fixed compensation for the services rendered, in which no increase or diminution shall be made so as to affect the Magistracy, existing at the time of increase or diminution, and to be ineligible a second time; and that besides a general authority to execute the National laws, it ought to enjoy the Executive rights vested in Congress by the Confederation.

8. Resd. that the Executive and a convenient number of the National Judiciary, ought to compose a council of revision with authority to examine every act of the National Legislature before it shall operate, & every act of a particular Legislature before a Negative thereon shall be final; and that the dissent of the said Council shall amount to a rejection, unless the Act of the National Legislature be again passed, or that of a particular Legislature be again negatived by   of the members of each branch.

9. Resd. that a National Judiciary be established to consist of one or more supreme tribunals, and of inferior tribunals to be chosen by the National Legislature, to hold their offices during good behaviour; and to receive punctually at stated times fixed compensation for their services, in which no increase or diminution shall be made so as to affect the persons actually in office at the time of such increase or diminution. that the jurisdiction of the inferior tribunals shall be to hear & determine in the first instance, and of the supreme tribunal to hear and determine in the dernier resort, all piracies & felonies on the high seas, captures from an enemy; cases in which foreigners or citizens of other States applying to such jurisdictions may be interested, or which respect the collection of the National revenue; impeachments of

any National officers, and questions which may involve the national peace and harmony.

10. Resolvd. that provision ought to be made for the admission of States lawfully arising within the limits of the United States, whether from a voluntary junction of Government & Territory or otherwise, with the consent of a number of voices in the National legislature less than the whole.

11. Resd. that a Republican Government & the territory of each State, except in the instance of a voluntary junction of Government & territory, ought to be guaranteed by the United States to each State

12. Resd. that provision ought to be made for the continuance of Congress and their authorities and privileges, until a given day after the reform of the articles of Union shall be adopted, and for the completion of all their engagements.

13. Resd. that provision ought to be made for the amendment of the Articles of Union whensoever it shall seem necessary, and that the assent of the National Legislature ought not to be required thereto.

14. Resd. that the Legislative Executive & Judiciary powers within the several States ought to be bound by oath to support the articles of Union

15. Resd. that the amendments which shall be offered to the Confederation, by the Convention ought at a proper time, or times, after the approbation of Congress to be submitted to an assembly or assemblies of Representatives, recommended by the Several Legislatures to be expressly chosen by the people, to consider & decide thereon.

8

EDWARD CARRINGTON TO THOMAS JEFFERSON
9 June 1787
Jefferson Papers 11:409–10

The prevailing impression as well in as out of Convention is that a foederal Government adapted to the permanent circumstances of the Country, without respect to the habits of the day, be formed, whose efficiency shall pervade the whole Empire: it may, and probably will, at first be viewed with hesitation, but derived and patronised as it will be, its influence must extend into a general adoption as the present fabric gives way. That the people are disposed to be governed is evinced in their turning out to support the shadows under which they now live, and if a work of wisdom is prepared for them, they will not reject it to commit themselves to the dubious issue of anarchy.

The debates and proceedings of the Convention are kept in profound secrecy. Opinions of the probable result of their deliberations can only be formed from the prevailing impressions of men of reflection and understanding.—These are reducible to two schemes—the first, a con-

solidation of the whole Empire into one republic, leaving in the states nothing more than subordinate courts for facilitating the administration of the Laws.—The second an investiture of a foederal sovereignty with full and independant authority as to the Trade, Revenues, and forces of the Union, and the rights of peace and War, together with a Negative upon all the Acts of the State legislatures. The first idea, I apprehend, would be impracticable, and therefore do not suppose it can be adopted. General Laws through a Country embracing so many climates, productions, and manners as the United States would operate many oppressions, and a general legislature would be found incompetent to the formation of local ones, as a majority would in every instance be ignorant of, and unaffected by, the objects of legislation. The essential rights as well as advantages of representation would be lost, and obedience to the public decrees could only be ensured by the exercise of powers different from those derivable from a free constitution. Such an experiment must therefore terminate in a despotism, or the same inconveniencies we are now deliberating to remove. Something like the second will probably be formed; indeed I am certain that nothing less than what will give the foederal sovereignty a compleat controul over the state Governments will be thought worthy of discussion. Such a scheme constructed upon well adjusted principles would certainly give us stability and importance as a nation, and if the Executive powers can be sufficiently checked, must be eligible. Unless the whole has a decided influence over the parts, the constant effort will be to resume the delegated powers, and these cannot be an inducement in the foederal sovereignty to refuse its assent to an innocent act of a State. The negative which the King of England had upon our Laws was never found to be materially inconvenient.

The Ideas here suggested are far removed from those which prevailed when you was amongst us, and as they have arisen with the most able, from an actual view of events, it is probable you may not be prepared to expect them. They are however the most moderate of any which obtain in any general form amongst reflective and intelligent Men. The Eastern opinions are for a total surrender of the state sovereignties, and indeed some amongst them go to a monarchy at once. They have verged to anarchy, while to the southward we have only felt an inconvenience, and their proportionate disposition to an opposite extreme is a natural consequence.

9

NEW JERSEY PLAN
15 June 1787
Farrand 1:242–45

---

1. Resd. that the articles of Confederation ought to be so revised, corrected & enlarged, as to render the federal

Constitution adequate to the exigences of Government, & the preservation of the Union.*

2. Resd. that in addition to the powers vested in the U. States in Congress, by the present existing articles of Confederation, they be authorized to pass acts for raising a revenue, by levying a duty or duties on all goods or merchandizes of foreign growth or manufacture, imported into any part of the U. States, by Stamps on paper, vellum or parchment, and by a postage on all letters or packages passing through the general post-Office, to be applied to such federal purposes as they shall deem proper & expedient; to make rules & regulations for the collection thereof; and the same from time to time, to alter & amend in such manner as they shall think proper: to pass Acts for the regulation of trade & commerce as well with foreign nations as with each other: provided that all punishments, fines, forfeitures & penalties to be incurred for contravening such acts rules and regulations shall be adjudged by the Common law Judiciarys of the State in which any offence contrary to the true intent & meaning of such Acts rules & regulations shall have been committed or perpetrated, with liberty of commencing in the first instance all suits & prosecutions for that purpose in the superior Common law Judiciary in such State, subject nevertheless, for the correction of all errors, both in law & fact in rendering judgment, to an appeal to the Judiciary of the U. States

3. Resd. that whenever requisitions shall be necessary, instead of the rule for making requisitions mentioned in the articles of Confederation, the United States in Congs. be authorized to make such requisitions in proportion to the whole number of white & other free citizens & inhabitants of every age sex and condition including those bound to servitude for a term of years & three fifths of all other persons not comprehended in the foregoing description, except Indians not paying taxes; that if such requisitions be not complied with, in the time specified therein, to direct the collection thereof in the non complying States & for that purpose to devise and pass acts directing & authorizing the same; provided that none of the powers hereby vested in the U. States in Congs. shall be exercised without the consent of at least   States, and in that proportion if the number of Confederated States should hereafter be increased or diminished.

*(this plan had been concerted among the deputations or members thereof, from Cont. N. Y. N. J. Del. and perhaps Mr Martin from Maryd. who made with them a common cause on different principles. Cont. and N. Y. were agst. a departure from the principle of the Confederation, wishing rather to add a few new powers to Congs. than to substitute, a National Govt. The States of N. J. and Del. were opposed to a National Govt. because its patrons considered a proportional representation of the States as the basis of it. The eagourness displayed by the Members opposed to a Natl. Govt. from these different motives began now to produce serious anxiety for the result of the Convention.—Mr. Dickenson said to Mr. Madison you see the consequence of pushing things too far. Some of the members from the small States wish for two branches in the General Legislature, and are friends to a good National Government; but we would sooner submit to a foreign power, than submit to be deprived of an equality of suffrage, in both branches of the legislature, and thereby be thrown under the domination of the large States.) [Note by Madison.]

4. Resd. that the U. States in Congs. be authorized to elect a federal Executive to consist of   persons, to continue in office for the term of   years, to receive punctually at stated times a fixed compensation for their services, in which no increase or diminution shall be made so as to affect the persons composing the Executive at the time of such increase or diminution, to be paid out of the federal treasury; to be incapable of holding any other office or appointment during their time of service and for   years thereafter; to be ineligible a second time, & removeable by Congs. on application by a majority of the Executives of the several States; that the Executives besides their general authority to execute the federal acts ought to appoint all federal officers not otherwise provided for, & to direct all military operations; provided that none of the persons composing the federal Executive shall on any occasion take command of any troops, so as personally to conduct any enterprise as General, or in other capacity.

5. Resd. that a federal Judiciary be established to consist of a supreme Tribunal the Judges of which to be appointed by the Executive, & to hold their offices during good behaviour, to receive punctually at stated times a fixed compensation for their services in which no increase or diminution shall be made, so as to affect the persons actually in office at the time of such increase or diminution; that the Judiciary so established shall have authority to hear & determine in the first instance on all impeachments of federal officers, & by way of appeal in the dernier resort in all cases touching the rights of Ambassadors, in all cases of captures from an enemy, in all cases of piracies & felonies on the high seas, in all cases in which foreigners may be interested, in the construction of any treaty or treaties, or which may arise on any of the Acts for regulation of trade, or the collection of the federal Revenue: that none of the Judiciary shall during the time they remain in Office be capable of receiving or holding any other office or appointment during their time of service, or for   thereafter.

6. Resd. that all Acts of the U. States in Congs. made by virtue & in pursuance of the powers hereby & by the articles of confederation vested in them, and all Treaties made & ratified under the authority of the U. States shall be the supreme law of the respective States so far forth as those Acts or Treaties shall relate to the said States or their Citizens, and that the Judiciary of the several States shall be bound thereby in their decisions, any thing in the respective laws of the Individual States to the contrary notwithstanding; and that if any State, or any body of men in any State shall oppose or prevent ye. carrying into execution such acts or treaties, the federal Executive shall be authorized to call forth ye power of the Confederated States, or so much thereof as may be necessary to enforce and compel an obedience to such Acts, or an Observance of such Treaties.

7. Resd. that provision be made for the admission of new States into the Union.

8. Resd. the rule for naturalization ought to be the same in every State

9. Resd. that a Citizen of one State committing an of-

fence in another State of the Union, shall be deemed guilty of the same offence as if it had been committed by a Citizen of the State in which the Offence was committed.

10

ALEXANDER HAMILTON, FEDERAL CONVENTION
18 June 1787
Farrand 1:282–93

Mr. Hamilton, had been hitherto silent on the business before the Convention, partly from respect to others whose superior abilities age & experience rendered him unwilling to bring forward ideas dissimilar to theirs, and partly from his delicate situation with respect to his own State, to whose sentiments as expressed by his Colleagues, he could by no means accede. The crisis however which now marked our affairs, was too serious to permit any scruples whatever to prevail over the duty imposed on every man to contribute his efforts for the public safety & happiness. He was obliged therefore to declare himself unfriendly to both plans. He was particularly opposed to that from N. Jersey, being fully convinced, that no amendment of the confederation, leaving the States in possession of their sovereignty could possibly answer the purpose. On the other hand he confessed he was much discouraged by the amazing extent of Country in expecting the desired blessings from any general sovereignty that could be substituted.— As to the powers of the Convention, he thought the doubts started on that subject had arisen from distinctions & reasonings too subtle. A *federal* Govt. he conceived to mean an association of independent Communities into one. Different Confederacies have different powers, and exercise them in different ways. In some instances the powers are exercised over collective bodies; in others over individuals. as in the German Diet—& among ourselves in cases of piracy. Great latitude therefore must be given to the signification of the term. The plan last proposed departs itself from the *federal* idea, as understood by some, since it is to operate eventually on individuals. He agreed moreover with the Honbl. gentleman from Va. (Mr. R.) that we owed it to our Country, to do on this emergency whatever we should deem essential to its happiness. The States sent us here to provide for the exigences of the Union. To rely on & propose any plan not adequate to these exigences, merely because it was not clearly within our powers, would be to sacrifice the means to the end. It may be said that the *States* can not *ratify* a plan not within the purview of the article of Confederation providing for alterations & amendments. But may not the States themselves in which no constitutional authority equal to this purpose exists in the Legislatures, have had in view a reference to the people at large. In the Senate of N. York, a proviso was moved, that no act of the Convention should be binding until it should be referred to the people & ratified; and

the motion was lost by a single voice only, the reason assigned agst. it, being that it might possibly be found an inconvenient shackle.

The great question is what provision shall we make for the happiness of our Country? He would first make a comparative examination of the two plans—prove that there were essential defects in both—and point out such changes as might render a *national one,* efficacious.—The great & essential principles necessary for the support of Government. are 1. an active & constant interest in supporting it. This principle does not exist in the States in favor of the federal Govt. They have evidently in a high degree, the esprit de corps. They constantly pursue internal interests adverse to those of the whole. They have their particular debts—their partcular plans of finance &c. all these when opposed to, invariably prevail over the requisitions & plans of Congress. 2. the love of power, Men love power. The same remarks are applicable to this principle. The States have constantly shewn a disposition rather to regain the powers delegated by them than to part with more, or to give effect to what they had parted with. The ambition of their demagogues is known to hate the controul of the Genl. Government. It may be remarked too that the Citizens have not that anxiety to prevent a dissolution of the Genl. Govt as of the particular Govts. A dissolution of the latter would be fatal: of the former would still leave the purposes of Govt. attainable to a considerable degree. Consider what such a State as Virga. will be in a few years, a few compared with the life of nations. How strongly will it feel its importance & self-sufficiency? 3. an habitual attachment of the people. The whole force of this tie is on the side of the State Govt. Its sovereignty is immediately before the eyes of the people: its protection is immediately enjoyed by them. From its hand distributive justice, and all those acts which familiarize & endear Govt. to a people, are dispensed to them. 4. *Force* by which may be understood a *coertion of laws* or *coertion of arms.* Congs. have not the former except in few cases. In particular States, this coercion is nearly sufficient; tho' he held it in most cases, not entirely so. A certain portion of military force is absolutely necessary in large communities. Massts. is now feeling this necessity & making provision for it. But how can this force be exerted on the States collectively. It is impossible. It amounts to a war between the parties. Foreign powers also will not be idle spectators. They will interpose, the confusion will increase, and a dissolution of the Union ensue. 5. *influence.* he did not mean corruption, but a dispensation of those regular honors & emoluments, which produce an attachment to the Govt. almost all the weight of these is on the side of the States; and must continue so as long as the States continue to exist. All the passions then we see, of avarice, ambition, interest, which govern most individuals, and all public bodies, fall into the current of the States, and do not flow in the stream of the Genl. Govt. the former therefore will generally be an overmatch for the Genl. Govt. and render any confederacy, in its very nature precarious. Theory is in this case fully confirmed by experience. The Amphyctionic Council had it would seem ample powers for general purposes. It had in particular the power of fining and using force agst. delinquent members. What was the consequence. Their decrees were mere signals of war. The Phocian war is a striking example of it. Philip at length taking advantage of their disunion, and insinuating himself into their Councils, made himself master of their fortunes. The German Confederacy affords another lesson. The authority of Charlemagne seemed to be as great as could be necessary. The great feudal chiefs however, exercising their local sovereignties, soon felt the spirit & found the means of, encroachments, which reduced the imperial authority to a nominal sovereignty. The Diet has succeeded, which tho' aided by a Prince at its head, of great authority independently of his imperial attributes, is a striking illustration of the weakness of Confederated Governments. Other examples instruct us in the same truth. The Swiss cantons have scarce any Union at all, and have been more than once at war with one another—How then are all these evils to be avoided? only by such a compleat sovereignty in the general Govermt. as will turn all the strong principles & passions above mentioned on its side. Does the scheme of N. Jersey produce this effect? does it afford any substantial remedy whatever? On the contrary it labors under great defects, and the defect of some of its provisions will destroy the efficacy of others. It gives a direct revenue to Congs. but this will not be sufficient. The balance can only be supplied by requisitions; which experience proves can not be relied on. If States are to deliberate on the mode, they will also deliberate on the object of the supplies, and will grant or not grant as they approve or disapprove of it. The delinquency of one will invite and countenance it in others. Quotas too must in the nature of things be so unequal as to produce the same evil. To what standard will you resort? Land is a fallacious one. Compare Holland with Russia: France or Engd. with other countries of Europe. Pena. with N. Carolia. will the relative pecuniary abilities in those instances, correspond with the relative value of land. Take numbers of inhabitants for the rule and make like comparison of different countries, and you will find it to be equally unjust. The different degrees of industry and improvement in different Countries render the first object a precarious measure of wealth. Much depends too on *situation*. Cont. N. Jersey & N. Carolina, not being commercial States & contributing to the wealth of the commercial ones, can never bear quotas assessed by the ordinary rules of proportion. They will & must fail in their duty. their example will be followed, and the Union itself be dissolved. Whence then is the national revenue to be drawn? from Commerce, even from exports which notwithstanding the common opinion are fit objects of moderate taxation, from excise, &c &c. These tho' not equal, are less unequal than quotas. Another destructive ingredient in the plan, is that equality of suffrage which is so much desired by the small States. It is not in human nature that Va. & the large States should consent to it, or if they did that they shd. long abide by it. It shocks too much the ideas of Justice, and every human feeling. Bad principles in a Govt. tho slow are sure in their operation, and will gradually destroy it. A doubt has been raised whether

Congs. at present have a right to keep Ships or troops in time of peace. He leans to the negative. Mr. P.s plan provides no remedy.—If the powers proposed were adequate, the organization of Congs. is such that they could never be properly & effectually exercised. The members of Congs. being chosen by the States & subject to recall, represent all the local prejudices. Should the powers be found effectual, they will from time to time be heaped on them, till a tyrannic sway shall be established. The general power whatever be its form if it preserves itself, must swallow up the State powers. otherwise it will be swallowed up by them. It is agst. all the principles of a good Government to vest the requisite powers in such a body as Congs. Two Sovereignties can not co-exist within the same limits. Giving powers to Congs. must eventuate in a bad Govt. or in no Govt. The plan of N. Jersey therefore will not do. What then is to be done? Here he was embarrassed. The extent of the Country to be governed, discouraged him. The expence of a general Govt. was also formidable; unless there were such a diminution of expence on the side of the State Govts. as the case would admit. If they were extinguished, he was persuaded that great oeconomy might be obtained by substituting a general Govt. He did not mean however to shock the public opinion by proposing such a measure. On the other hand he saw no *other* necessity for declining it. They are not necessary for any of the great purposes of commerce, revenue, or agriculture. Subordinate authorities he was aware would be necessary. There must be district tribunals: corporations for local purposes. But cui bono, the vast & expensive apparatus now appertaining to the States. The only difficulty of a serious nature which occurred to him, was that of drawing representatives from the extremes to the center of the Community. What inducements can be offered that will suffice? The moderate wages for the 1st. branch, would only be a bait to little demagogues. Three dollars or thereabouts he supposed would be the Utmost. The Senate he feared from a similar cause, would be filled by certain undertakers who wish for particular offices under the Govt. This view of the subject almost led him to despair that a Republican Govt. could be established over so great an extent. He was sensible at the same time that it would be unwise to propose one of any other form. In his private opinion he had no scruple in declaring, supported as he was by the opinions of so many of the wise & good, that the British Govt. was the best in the world: and that he doubted much whether any thing short of it would do in America. He hoped Gentlemen of different opinions would bear with him in this, and begged them to recollect the change of opinion on this subject which had taken place and was still going on. It was once thought that the power of Congs was amply sufficient to secure the end of their institution. The error was now seen by every one. The members most tenacious of republicanism, he observed, were as loud as any in declaiming agst. the vices of democracy. This progress of the public mind led him to anticipate the time, when others as well as himself would join in the praise bestowed by Mr. Neckar on the British Constitution, namely, that it is the only Govt. in the world "which unites public strength with individual security."—In every community where industry is encouraged, there will be a division of it into the few & the many. Hence separate interests will arise There will be debtors & Creditors &c. Give all power to the many, they will oppress the few. Give all power to the few they will oppress the many. Both therefore ought to have power, that each may defend itself agst. the other. To the want of this check we owe our paper money—instalment laws &c To the proper adjustment of it the British owe the excellence of their Constitution. Their house of Lords is a most noble institution. Having nothing to hope for by a change, and a sufficient interest by means of their property, in being faithful to the National interest, they form a permanent barrier agst. every pernicious innovation, whether attempted on the part of the Crown or of the Commons. No temporary Senate will have firmness en'o' to answer the purpose. The Senate (of Maryland) which seems to be so much appealed to, has not yet been sufficiently tried. Had the people been unanimous & eager, in the late appeal to them on the subject of a paper emission they would would have yielded to the torrent. Their acquiescing in such an appeal is a proof of it.—Gentlemen differ in their opinions concerning the necessary checks, from the different estimates they form of the human passions. They suppose Seven years a sufficient period to give the Senate an adequate firmness, from not duly considering the amazing violence & turbulence of the democratic spirit. When a great object of Govt. is pursued, which seizes the popular passions, they spread like wild fire, and become irresistable. He appealed to the gentlemen from the N. England States whether experience had not there verified the remark. As to the Executive, it seemed to be admitted that no good one could be established on Republican principles. Was not this giving up the merits of the question; for can there be a good Govt. without a good Executive. The English model was the only good one on this subject. The Hereditary interest of the King was so interwoven with that of the Nation, and his personal emoluments so great, that he was placed above the danger of being corrupted from abroad—and at the same time was both sufficiently independent and sufficiently controuled, to answer the purpose of the institution at home. one of the weak sides of Republics was their being liable to foreign influence & corruption. Men of little character, acquiring great power become easily the tools of intermedling neibours. Sweeden was a striking instance. The French & English had each their parties during the late Revolution which was effected by the predominant influence of the former. What is the inference from all these observations? That we ought to go as far in order to attain stability and permanency, as republican principles will admit. Let one branch of the Legislature hold their places for life or at least during good-behaviour. Let the Executive also be for life. He appealed to the feelings of the members present whether a term of seven years, would induce the sacrifices of private affairs which an acceptance of public trust would require, so so as to ensure the services of the best Citizens. On this plan we should have in the Senate a permanent will, a weighty interest, which would answer essential purposes. But is this a Republican Govt. it will be asked? Yes, if all

the Magistrates are appointed, and vacancies are filled, by the people, or a process of election originating with the people. He was sensible that an Executive constituted as he proposed would have in fact but little of the power and independence that might be necessary. On the other plan of appointing him for 7 years, he thought the Executive ought to have but little power. He would be ambitious, with the means of making creatures; and as the object of his ambition wd. be to *prolong* his power, it is probable that in case of a war, he would avail himself of the emergence, to evade or refuse a degradation from his place. An Executive for life has not this motive for forgetting his fidelity, and will therefore be a safer depositary of power. It will be objected probably, that such an Executive will be an *elective Monarch,* and will give birth to the tumults which characterise that form of Govt. He wd. reply that *Monarch* is an indefinite term. It marks not either the degree or duration of power. If this Executive Magistrate wd. be a monarch for life—the other propd. by the Report from the Committee of the whole, wd. be a monarch for seven years. The circumstance of being elective was also applicable to both. It had been observed by judicious writers that elective monarchies wd. be the best if they could be guarded agst. the *tumults* excited by the ambition and intrigues of competitors. He was not sure that tumults were an inseparable evil. He rather thought this character of Elective Monarchies had been taken rather from particular cases than from general principles. The election of Roman Emperors was made by the *Army.* In *Poland* the election is made by great rival *princes* with independent power, and ample means, of raising commotions. In the German Empire, The appointment is made by the Electors & Princes, who have equal motives & means, for exciting cabals & parties. Might not such a mode of election be devised among ourselves as will defend the community agst. these effects in any dangerous degree? Having made these observations he would read to the Committee a sketch of a plan which he shd. prefer to either of those under consideration. He was aware that it went beyond the ideas of most members. But will such a plan be adopted out of doors? In return he would ask will the people adopt the other plan? At present they will adopt neither. But he sees the Union dissolving or already dissolved—he sees evils operating in the States which must soon cure the people of their fondness for democracies—he sees that a great progress has been already made & is still going on in the public mind. He thinks therefore that the people will in time be unshackled from their prejudices; and whenever that happens, they will themselves not be satisfied at stopping where the plan of Mr. R. wd. place them, but be ready to go as far at least as he proposes. He did not mean to offer the paper he had sketched as a proposition to the Committee. It was meant only to give a more correct view of his ideas, and to suggest the amendments which he should probably propose to the plan of Mr. R. in the proper stages of its future discussion. He read his sketch in the words following: towit

I "The Supreme Legislative power of the United States of America to be vested in two different bodies of men; the one to be called the Assembly, the other the Senate who together shall form the Legislature of the United States with power to pass all laws whatsoever subject to the Negative hereafter mentioned.

II The Assembly to consist of persons elected by the people to serve for three years.

III. The Senate to consist of persons elected to serve during good behaviour; their election to be made by electors chosen for that purpose by the people: in order to this the States to be divided into election districts. On the death, removal or resignation of any Senator his place to be filled out of the district from which he came.

IV. The supreme Executive authority of the United States to be vested in a Governour to be elected to serve during good behaviour—the election to be made by Electors chosen by the people in the Election Districts aforesaid—The authorities & functions of the Executive to be as follows: to have a negative on all laws about to be passed, and the execution of all laws passed, to have the direction of war when authorized or begun; to have with the advice and approbation of the Senate the power of making all treaties; to have the sole appointment of the heads or chief officers of the departments of Finance, War and Foreign Affairs; to have the nomination of all other officers (Ambassadors to foreign Nations included) subject to the approbation or rejection of the Senate; to have the power of pardoning all offences except Treason; which he shall not pardon without the approbation of the Senate.

V. On the death resignation or removal of the Governour his authorities to be exercised by the President of the Senate till a Successor be appointed.

VI The Senate to have the sole power of declaring war, the power of advising and approving all Treaties, the power of approving or rejecting all appointments of officers except the heads or chiefs of the departments of Finance War and foreign affairs.

VII. The Supreme Judicial authority to be vested in Judges to hold their offices during good behaviour with adequate and permanent salaries. This Court to have original jurisdiction in all causes of capture, and an appellative jurisdiction in all causes in which the revenues of the general Government or the citizens of foreign nations are concerned.

VIII. The Legislature of the United States to have power to institute Courts in each State for the determination of all matters of general concern.

IX. The Governour Senators and all officers of the United States to be liable to impeachment for mal—and corrupt conduct; and upon conviction to be removed from office, & disqualified for holding any place of trust or profit—all impeachments to be tried by a Court to consist of the Chief   or Judge of the Superior Court of Law of each State, provided such Judge shall hold his place during good behavior, and have a permanent salary.

X All laws of the particular States contrary to the Constitution or laws of the United States to be utterly void; and the better to prevent such laws being passed, the Governour or president of each state shall be appointed by the General Government and shall have a negative upon the laws about to be passed in the State of which he is Governour or President

XI No State to have any forces land or Naval; and the Militia of all the States to be under the sole and exclusive direction of the United States, the officers of which to be appointed and commissioned by them

On these several articles he entered into explanatory observations corresponding with the principles of his introductory reasoning

Comittee rose & the House adjourned.

11

THOMAS JEFFERSON TO JAMES MADISON
20 June 1787
Papers 11:480–81

The idea of separating the executive business of the confederacy from Congress, as the judiciary is already in some degree, is just and necessary. I had frequently pressed on the members individually, while in Congress, the doing this by a resolution of Congress for appointing an Executive committee to act during the sessions of Congress, as the Committee of the states was to act during their vacations. But the referring to this Committee all executive business as it should present itself, would require a more persevering self-denial than I supposed Congress to possess. It will be much better to make that separation by a federal act. The negative proposed to be given them on all the acts of the several legislatures is now for the first time suggested to my mind. Primâ facie I do not like it. It fails in an essential character, that the hole and the patch should be commensurate. But this proposes to mend a small hole by covering the whole garment. Not more than 1. out of 100. state-acts concern the confederacy. This proposition then, in order to give them 1. degree of power which they ought to have, gives them 99. more which they ought not to have, upon a presumption that they will not exercise the 99. But upon every act there will be a preliminary question. Does this act concern the confederacy? And was there ever a proposition so plain as to pass Congress without a debate? Their decisions are almost always wise: they are like pure metal. But you know of how much dross this is the result. Would not an appeal from the state judicatures to a federal court, in all cases where the act of Confederation controuled the question, be as effectual a remedy, and exactly commensurate to the defect. A British creditor, e.g. sues for his debt in Virginia; the defendant pleads an act of the state excluding him from their courts; the plaintiff urges the Confederation and the treaty made under that, as controuling the state law; the judges are weak enough to decide according to the views of their legislature. An appeal to a federal court sets all to rights. It will be said that this court may encroach on the jurisdiction of the state courts. It may. But there will be a power, to wit Congress, to watch and restrain them. But place the same authority in Congress itself, and there will be no power above them to perform the same office. They will restrain within due bounds a jurisdiction exercised by others much more rigorously than if exercised by themselves.

12

FEDERAL FARMER, NO. 1
8 Oct. 1787
Storing 2.8.4–14

The present moment discovers a new face in our affairs. Our object has been all along, to reform our federal system, and to strengthen our governments—to establish peace, order and justice in the community—but a new object now presents. The plan of government now proposed is evidently calculated totally to change, in time, our condition as a people. Instead of being thirteen republics, under a federal head, it is clearly designed to make us one consolidated government. Of this, I think, I shall fully convince you, in my following letters on this subject. This consolidation of the states has been the object of several men in this country for some time past. Whether such a change can ever be effected in any manner; whether it can be effected without convulsions and civil wars; whether such a change will not totally destroy the liberties of this country—time only can determine.

To have a just idea of the government before us, and to shew that a consolidated one is the object in view, it is necessary not only to examine the plan, but also its history, and the politics of its particular friends.

The confederation was formed when great confidence was placed in the voluntary exertions of individuals, and of the respective states; and the framers of it, to guard against usurpation, so limited and checked the powers, that, in many respects, they are inadequate to the exigencies of the union. We find, therefore, members of congress urging alterations in the federal system almost as soon as it was adopted. It was early proposed to vest congress with powers to levy an impost, to regulate trade, etc. but such was known to be the caution of the states in parting with power, that the vestment, even of these, was proposed to be under several checks and limitations. During the war, the general confusion, and the introduction of paper money, infused in the minds of people vague ideas respecting government and credit. We expected too much from the return of peace, and of course we have been disappointed. Our governments have been new and unsettled; and several legislatures, by making tender, suspension, and paper money laws, have given just cause of uneasiness to creditors. By these and other causes, several orders of men in the community have been prepared, by degrees, for a change of government; and this very abuse of power in the legislatures, which, in some cases, has been charged upon the democratic part of the community, has furnished aristocratical men with those very weapons, and those very means, with which, in great measure, they are rapidly effecting their favourite object. And should an op-

pressive government be the consequence of the proposed change, posterity may reproach not only a few overbearing unprincipled men, but those parties in the states which have misused their powers.

The conduct of several legislatures, touching paper money, and tender laws, has prepared many honest men for changes in government, which otherwise they would not have thought of—when by the evils, on the one hand, and by the secret instigations of artful men, on the other, the minds of men were become sufficiently uneasy, a bold step was taken, which is usually followed by a revolution, or a civil war. A general convention for mere commercial purposes was moved for—the authors of this measure saw that the people's attention was turned solely to the amendment of the federal system; and that, had the idea of a total change been started, probably no state would have appointed members to the convention. The idea of destroying, ultimately, the state government, and forming one consolidated system, could not have been admitted—a convention, therefore, merely for vesting in congress power to regulate trade was proposed. This was pleasing to the commercial towns; and the landed people had little or no concern about it. September, 1786, a few men from the middle states met at Annapolis, and hastily proposed a convention to be held in May, 1787, for the purpose, generally, of amending the confederation—this was done before the delegates of Massachusetts, and of the other states arrived—still not a word was said about destroying the old constitution, and making a new one—The states still unsuspecting, and not aware that they were passing the Rubicon, appointed members to the new convention, for the sole and express purpose of revising and amending the confederation—and, probably, not one man in ten thousand in the United States, till within these ten or twelve days, had an idea that the old ship was to be destroyed, and he put to the alternative of embarking in the new ship presented, or of being left in danger of sinking—The States, I believe, universally supposed the convention would report alterations in the confederation, which would pass an examination in congress, and after being agreed to there, would be confirmed by all the legislatures, or be rejected. Virginia made a very respectable appointment, and placed at the head of it the first man in America: In this appointment there was a mixture of political characters: but Pennsylvania appointed principally those men who are esteemed aristocratical. Here the favourite moment for changing the government was evidently discerned by a few men, who seized it with address. Ten other states appointed, and tho' they chose men principally connected with commerce and the judicial department yet they appointed many good republican characters—had they all attended we should now see, I am persuaded a better system presented. The non-attendance of eight or nine men, who were appointed members of the convention, I shall ever consider as a very unfortunate event to the United States.—Had they attended, I am pretty clear, that the result of the convention would not have had that strong tendency to aristocracy now discernable in every part of the plan. There would not have been so great an accumulation of powers, especially as to the internal police of the country, in a few hands, as the constitution reported proposes to vest in them—the young visionary men, and the consolidating aristocracy, would have been more restrained than they have been. Eleven states met in the convention, and after four months close attention presented the new constitution, to be adopted or rejected by the people. The uneasy and fickle part of the community may be prepared to receive any form of government; but, I presume, the enlightened and substantial part will give any constitution presented for their adoption, a candid and thorough examination; and silence those designing or empty men, who weakly and rashly attempt to precipitate the adoption of a system of so much importance—We shall view the convention with proper respect—and, at the same time, that we reflect there were men of abilities and integrity in it, we must recollect how disproportionably the democratic and aristocratic parts of the community were represented—Perhaps the judicious friends and opposers of the new constitution will agree, that it is best to let it rest solely on its own merits, or be condemned for its own defects.

In the first place, I shall premise, that the plan proposed is a plan of accommodation—and that it is in this way only, and by giving up a part of our opinions, that we can ever expect to obtain a government founded in freedom and compact. This circumstance candid men will always keep in view, in the discussion of this subject.

The plan proposed appears to be partly federal, but principally however, calculated ultimately to make the states one consolidated government.

The first interesting question, therefore suggested, is, how far the states can be consolidated into one entire government on free principles. In considering this question extensive objects are to be taken into view, and important changes in the forms of government to be carefully attended to in all their consequences. The happiness of the people at large must be the great object with every honest statesman, and he will direct every movement to this point. If we are so situated as a people, as not to be able to enjoy equal happiness and advantages under one government, the consolidation of the states cannot be admitted.

There are three different forms of free government under which the United States may exist as one nation; and now is, perhaps, the time to determine to which we will direct our views. 1. Distinct republics connected under a federal head. In this case the respective state governments must be the principal guardians of the peoples rights, and exclusively regulate their internal police; in them must rest the balance of government. The congress of the states, or federal head, must consist of delegates amenable to, and removeable by the respective states: The congress must have general directing powers; powers to require men and monies of the states; to make treaties, peace and war; to direct the operations of armies, etc. Under this federal modification of government, the powers of congress would be rather advisory or recommendatory than coercive. 2. We may do away the several state governments, and form or consolidate all the states into one entire government, with one executive, one judiciary, and one legislature, consisting of senators and representatives collected from all

parts of the union: In this case there would be a compleat consolidation of the states. 3. We may consolidate the states as to certain national objects, and leave them severally distinct independent republics, as to internal police generally. Let the general government consist of an executive, a judiciary, and balanced legislature, and its powers extend exclusively to all foreign concerns, causes arising on the seas to commerce, imports, armies, navies, Indian affairs, peace and war, and to a few internal concerns of the community; to the coin, post-offices, weights and measures, a general plan for the militia, to naturalization, *and, perhaps to bankruptcies*, leaving the internal police of the community, in other respects, exclusively to the state governments; as the administration of justice in all causes arising internally, the laying and collecting of internal taxes, and the forming of the militia according to a general plan prescribed. In this case there would be a compleat consolidation, *quoad* certain objects only.

Touching the first, or federal plan, I do not think much can be said in its favor: The sovereignty of the nation, without coercive and efficient powers to collect the strength of it, cannot always be depended on to answer the purposes of government; and in a congress of representatives of sovereign states, there must necessarily be an unreasonable mixture of powers in the same hands.

As to the second, or compleat consolidating plan, it deserves to be carefully considered at this time, by every American: If it be impracticable, it is a fatal error to model our governments, directing our views ultimately to it.

The third plan, or partial consolidation, is, in my opinion, the only one that can secure the freedom and happiness of this people. I once had some general ideas that the second plan was practicable, but from long attention, and the proceedings of the convention, I am fully satisfied, that this third plan is the only one we can with safety and propriety proceed upon. Making this the standard to point out, with candor and fairness, the parts of the new constitution which appear to be improper, is my object. The convention appears to have proposed the partial consolidation evidently with a view to collect all powers ultimately, in the United States into one entire government; and from its views in this respect, and from the tenacity of the small states to have an equal vote in the senate, probably originated the greatest defects in the proposed plan.

Independant of the opinions of many great authors, that a free elective government cannot be extended over large territories, a few reflections must evince, that one government and general legislation alone, never can extend equal benefits to all parts of the United States: Different laws, customs, and opinions exist in the different states, which by a uniform system of laws would be unreasonably invaded. The United States contain about a million of square miles, and in half a century will, probably, contain ten millions of people; and from the center to the extremes is about 800 miles.

Before we do away the state governments, or adopt measures that will tend to abolish them, and to consolidate the states into one entire government, several principles should be considered and facts ascertained:—These, and my examination into the essential parts of the proposed plan, I shall pursue in my next.

13

BRUTUS, NO. 1
18 Oct. 1787
Storing 2.9.4–9

The first question that presents itself on the subject is, whether a confederated government be the best for the United States or not? Or in other words, whether the thirteen United States should be reduced to one great republic, governed by one legislature, and under the direction of one executive and judicial; or whether they should continue thirteen confederated republics, under the direction and controul of a supreme federal head for certain defined national purposes only?

This enquiry is important, because, although the government reported by the convention does not go to a perfect and entire consolidation, yet it approaches so near to it, that it must, if executed, certainly and infallibly terminate in it.

This government is to possess absolute and uncontroulable power, legislative, executive and judicial, with respect to every object to which it extends, for by the last clause of section 8th, article 1st, it is declared "that the Congress shall have power to make all laws which shall be necessary and proper for carrying into execution the foregoing powers, and all other powers vested by this constitution, in the government of the United States; or in any department or office thereof." And by the 6th article, it is declared "that this constitution, and the laws of the United States, which shall be made in pursuance thereof, and the treaties made, or which shall be made, under the authority of the United States, shall be the supreme law of the land; and the judges in every state shall be bound thereby, any thing in the constitution, or law of any state to the contrary notwithstanding." It appears from these articles that there is no need of any intervention of the state governments, between the Congress and the people, to execute any one power vested in the general government, and that the constitution and laws of every state are nullified and declared void, so far as they are or shall be inconsistent with this constitution, or the laws made in pursuance of it, or with treaties made under the authority of the United States.—The government then, so far as it extends, is a complete one, and not a confederation. It is as much one complete government as that of New-York or Massachusetts, has as absolute and perfect powers to make and execute all laws, to appoint officers, institute courts, declare offences, and annex penalties, with respect to every object to which it extends, as any other in the world. So far therefore as its powers reach, all ideas of confederation are given up and lost. It is true this government is limited to certain objects, or to speak more properly, some small degree of power is still left to the states, but a little attention to the powers vested in the general government, will convince every candid man, that if it is capable of being executed, all that is reserved for the individual states must very soon be annihilated, except so far as they are barely necessary to the organization of the general government. The powers of the general legislature extend to every case that is of the least importance—there is nothing valuable to human nature, nothing dear to freemen, but what is within its power. It has authority to make laws which will affect the lives, the liberty, and property of every man in the United States; nor can the constitution or laws of any state, in any way prevent or impede the full and complete execution of every power given. The legislative power is competent to lay taxes, duties, imposts, and excises;—there is no limitation to this power, unless it be said that the clause which directs the use to which those taxes, and duties shall be applied, may be said to be a limitation: but this is no restriction of the power at all, for by this clause they are to be applied to pay the debts and provide for the common defence and general welfare of the United States; but the legislature have authority to contract debts at their discretion; they are the sole judges of what is necessary to provide for the common defence, and they only are to determine what is for the general welfare; this power therefore is neither more nor less, than a power to lay and collect taxes, imposts, and excises, at their pleasure; not only [is] the power to lay taxes unlimited, as to the amount they may require, but it is perfect and absolute to raise them in any mode they please. No state legislature, or any power in the state governments, have any more to do in carrying this into effect, than the authority of one state has to do with that of another. In the business therefore of laying and collecting taxes, the idea of confederation is totally lost, and that of one entire republic is embraced. It is proper here to remark, that the authority to lay and collect taxes is the most important of any power that can be granted; it connects with it almost all other powers, or at least will in process of time draw all other after it; it is the great mean of protection, security, and defence, in a good government, and the great engine of oppression and tyranny in a bad one. This cannot fail of being the case, if we consider the contracted limits which are set by this constitution, to the late [state?] governments, on this article of raising money. No state can emit paper money—lay any duties, or imposts, on imports, or exports, but by consent of the Congress; and then the net produce shall be for the benefit of the United States: the only mean therefore left, for any state to support its government and discharge its debts, is by direct taxation; and the United States have also power to lay and collect taxes, in any way they please. Every one who has thought on the subject, must be convinced that but small sums of money can be collected in any country, by direct taxe[s], when the foederal government begins to exercise the right of taxation in all its parts, the legislatures of the several states will find it impossible to raise monies to support their governments. Without money they cannot be supported, and they must dwindle away, and, as before observed, their powers absorbed in that of the general government.

It might be here shewn, that the power in the federal legislative, to raise and support armies at pleasure, as well in peace as in war, and their controul over the militia, tend, not only to a consolidation of the government, but the destruction of liberty.—I shall not, however, dwell upon these, as a few observations upon the judicial power of this government, in addition to the preceding, will fully evince the truth of the position.

The judicial power of the United States is to be vested in a supreme court, and in such inferior courts as Congress may from time to time ordain and establish. The powers of these courts are very extensive; their jurisdiction comprehends all civil causes, except such as arise between citizens of the same state; and it extends to all cases in law and equity arising under the constitution. One inferior court must be established, I presume, in each state, at least, with the necessary executive officers appendant thereto. It is easy to see, that in the common course of things, these courts will eclipse the dignity, and take away from the respectability, of the state courts. These courts will be, in themselves, totally independent of the states, deriving their authority from the United States, and receiving from them fixed salaries; and in the course of human events it is to be expected, that they will swallow up all the powers of the courts in the respective states.

How far the clause in the 8th section of the 1st article may operate to do away all idea of confederated states, and to effect an entire consolidation of the whole into one general government, it is impossible to say. The powers given by this article are very general and comprehensive, and it may receive a construction to justify the passing almost any law. A power to make all laws, which shall be *necessary and proper,* for carrying into execution, all powers vested by the constitution in the government of the United States, or any department or officer thereof, is a power very comprehensive and definite [indefinite?], and may, for ought I know, be exercised in a such manner as entirely to abolish the state legislatures. Suppose the legislature of a state should pass a law to raise money to support their government and pay the state debt, may the Congress repeal this law, because it may prevent the collection of a tax which they may think proper and necessary to lay, to provide for the general welfare of the United States? For all laws made, in pursuance of this constitution, are the supreme law of the land, and the judges in every state shall be bound thereby, any thing in the constitution or laws of the different states to the contrary notwithstanding.—By such a law, the government of a particular state might be overturned at one stroke, and thereby be deprived of every means of its support.

It is not meant, by stating this case, to insinuate that the constitution would warrant a law of this kind; or unnecessarily to alarm the fears of the people, by suggesting, that the federal legislature would be more likely to pass the limits assigned them by the constitution, than that of an individual state, further than they are less responsible to the people. But what is meant is, that the legislature of the United States are vested with the great and uncontroulable powers, of laying and collecting taxes, duties, imposts, and excises: of regulating trade, raising and supporting armies,

organizing, arming, and disciplining the militia, instituting courts, and other general powers. And are by this clause invested with the power of making all laws, *proper and necessary,* for carrying all these into execution; and they may so exercise this power as entirely to annihilate all the state governments, and reduce this country to one single government. And if they may do it, it is pretty certain they will; for it will be found that the power retained by individual states, small as it is, will be a clog upon the wheels of the government of the United States; the latter therefore will be naturally inclined to remove it out of the way. Besides, it is a truth confirmed by the unerring experience of ages, that every man, and every body of men, invested with power, are ever disposed to increase it, and to acquire a superiority over every thing that stands in their way. This disposition, which is implanted in human nature, will operate in the federal legislature to lessen and ultimately to subvert the state authority, and having such advantages, will most certainly succeed, if the federal government succeeds at all. It must be very evident then, that what this constitution wants of being a complete consolidation of the several parts of the union into one complete government, possessed of perfect legislative, judicial, and executive powers, to all intents and purposes, it will necessarily acquire in its exercise and operation.

14

JAMES MADISON TO THOMAS JEFFERSON
24 Oct. 1787
Papers 10:207–15

(See ch. 17, no. 22)

15

ALEXANDER HAMILTON, FEDERALIST, NO. 9, 52–55
21 Nov. 1787

The utility of a confederacy, as well to suppress faction and to guard the internal tranquillity of States, as to increase their external force and security, is in reality not a new idea. It has been practiced upon in different countries and ages, and has received the sanction of the most applauded writers, on the subjects of politics. The opponents of the PLAN proposed have with great assiduity cited and circulated the observations of Montesquieu on the necessity of a contracted territory for a republican government. But they seem not to have been apprised of the sentiments of that great man expressed in another part of his work, nor to have adverted to the consequences of the principle to which they subscribe, with such ready acquiescence.

When Montesquieu recommends a small extent for republics, the standards he had in view were of dimensions, far short of the limits of almost every one of these States. Neither Virginia, Massachusetts, Pennsylvania, New-York, North-Carolina, nor Georgia, can by any means be compared with the models, from which he reasoned and to which the terms of his description apply. If we therefore take his ideas on this point, as the criterion of truth, we shall be driven to the alternative, either of taking refuge at once in the arms of monarchy, or of spliting ourselves into an infinity of little jealous, clashing, tumultuous commonwealths, the wretched nurseries of unceasing discord and the miserable objects of universal pity or contempt. Some of the writers, who have come forward on the other side of the question, seem to have been aware of the dilemma; and have even been bold enough to hint at the division of the larger States, as a desirable thing. Such an infatuated policy, such a desperate expedient, might, by the multiplication of petty offices, answer the views of men, who possess not qualifications to extend their influence beyond the narrow circles of personal intrigue, but it could never promote the greatness or happiness of the people of America.

Referring the examination of the principle itself to another place, as has been already mentioned, it will be sufficient to remark here, that in the sense of the author who has been most emphatically quoted upon the occasion, it would only dictate a reduction of the SIZE of the more considerable MEMBERS of the Union; but would not militate against their being all comprehended in one Confederate Government. And this is the true question, in the discussion of which we are at present interested.

So far are the suggestions of Montesquieu from standing in opposition to a general Union of the States, that he explicitly treats of a CONFEDERATE REPUBLIC as the expedient for extending the sphere of popular government and reconciling the advantages of monarchy with those of republicanism.

"It is very probable (says he*) that mankind would have been obliged, at length, to live constantly under the government of a SINGLE PERSON, had they not contrived a kind of constitution, that has all the internal advantages of a republican, together with the external force of a monarchial government. I mean a CONFEDERATE REPUBLIC.

"This form of Government is a Convention, by which several smaller *States* agree to become members of a larger *one*, which they intend to form. It is a kind of assemblage of societies, that constitute a new one, capable of encreasing by means of new associations, till they arrive to such a degree of power as to be able to provide for the security of the united body.

"A republic of this kind, able to withstand an external force, may support itself without any internal corruption. The form of this society prevents all manner of inconveniencies.

"If a single member should attempt to usurp the supreme authority, he could not be supposed to have an

Spirit of Laws, Vol. I. Book IX. Chap. I.

equal authority and credit, in all the confederate states. Were he to have too great influence over one, this would alarm the rest. Were he to subdue a part, that which would still remain free might oppose him with forces, independent of those which he had usurped, and overpower him before he could be settled in his usurpation.

"Should a popular insurrection happen, in one of the confederate States, the others are able to quell it. Should abuses creep into one part, they are reformed by those that remain sound. The State may be destroyed on one side, and not on the other; the confederacy may be dissolved, and the confederates preserve their sovereignty.

"As this government is composed of small republics it enjoys the internal happiness of each, and with respect to its external situation it is possessed, by means of the association of all the advantages of large monarchies."

I have thought it proper to quote at length these interesting passages, because they contain a luminous abrigement of the principal arguments in favour of the Union, and must effectually remove the false impressions, which a misapplication of other parts of the work was calculated to produce. They have at the same time an intimate connection with the more immediate design of this Paper; which is to illustrate the tendency of the Union to repress domestic faction and insurrection.

A distinction, more subtle than accurate has been raised between a *confederacy* and a *consolidation* of the States. The essential characteristic of the first is said to be, the restriction of its authority to the members in their collective capacities, without reaching to the individuals of whom they are composed. It is contended that the national council ought to have no concern with any object of internal administration. An exact equality of suffrage between the members has also been insisted upon as a leading feature of a Confederate Government. These positions are in the main arbitrary; they are supported neither by principle nor precedent. It has indeed happened that governments of this kind have generally operated in the manner, which the distinction, taken notice of, supposes to be inherent in their nature—but there have been in most of them extensive exceptions to the practice, which serve to prove as far as example will go, that there is no absolute rule on the subject. And it will be clearly shewn, in the course of this investigation, that as far as the principle contended for has prevailed, it has been the cause of incurable disorder and imbecility in the government.

The definition of a *Confederate Republic* seems simply to be, an "assemblage of societies" or an association of two or more States into one State. The extent, modifications and objects of the Foederal authority are mere matters of discretion. So long as the separate organisation of the members be not abolished, so long as it exists by a constitutional necessity for local purposes, though it should be in perfect subordination to the general authority of the Union, it would still be, in fact and in theory, an association of States, or a confederacy. The proposed Constitution, so far from implying an abolition of the State Governments, makes them constituent parts of the national sovereignty by allowing them a direct representation in the Senate, and leaves in their possession certain exclusive and very important portions of sovereign power. This fully corresponds, in every rational import of the terms, with the idea of a Foederal Government.

16

JOHN SMILIE, PENNSYLVANIA
RATIFYING CONVENTION
28 Nov. 1787
McMaster 267–71

I am happy, Mr. President, to find the argument placed upon the proper ground, and that the honorable member from the city has so fully spoken on the question, whether this system proposes a consolidation or a confederation of the states, as that is, in my humble opinion, the source of the greatest objection, which can be made to its adoption. I agree likewise with him, Sir, that it is, or ought to be, the object of all governments, to fix upon the intermediate point between tyranny and licentiousness; and therefore, it will be one of the great objects of our enquiry, to ascertain how far the proposed system deviates from that point of political happiness. For my part, I will readily confess, that it appears to be well guarded against licentiousness, but I am apprehensive it has deviated a little on the left hand, and rather invites than guards against the approaches of tyranny. I think however, Mr. President, it has been clearly argued, that the proposed system does not directly abolish, the governments of the several States, because its organization, and, for some time, perhaps, its operations, naturally pre-suppose their existence. But, Sir, it is not said, nor is thought, that the words of this instrument expressly announce that the sovereignty of the several States, their independency, jurisdiction, and power, are at once absorbed and annihilated by the general government. To this position and to this alone, the arguments of the honorable gentlemen can effectually apply, and there they must undoubtedly hold as long as the forms of State Government remain, at least, till a change takes place in the federal constitution. It is, however, upon other principles that the final destruction of the individual governments is asserted to be a necessary consequence of their association under this general form,—for, Sir, it is the silent but certain operation of the powers, and not the cautious, but artful tenor of the expressions contained in this system, that can excite terror, or generate oppression. The flattery of language was indeed necessary to disguise the baneful purpose, but it is like the dazzling polish bestowed upon an instrument of death; and the visionary prospect of a magnificent, yet popular government, was the most specious mode of rendering the people accessory to the ruin of those systems which they have so recently and so ardently labored to establish. Hence, Sir, we may trace that passage which has been pronounced by the honorable delegate to the late convention with exultation and applause; but when it is declared that "We the people of the United States do ordain and establish this constitution," is not the very foundation a proof of a consolidated government, by the manifest subversion of the principle that constitutes a union of States, which are sovereign and independent, except in the specific objects of confederation? These words have a plain and positive meaning, which could not be misunderstood by those who employed them; and therefore, Sir, it is fair and reasonable to infer, that it was in contemplation of the framers of this system, to absorb and abolish the efficient sovereignty and independent powers of the several States, in order to invigorate and aggrandize the general government. The plan before us, then, explicitly proposes the formation of a new constitution upon the original authority of the people, and not an association of States upon the authority of their respective governments. On that ground, we perceive that it contains all the necessary parts of a complete system of government, the executive, legislative and judicial establishments; and when two separate governments are at the same time in operation, over the same people, it will be difficult indeed to provide for each the means of safety and defence against the other; but if those means are not provided, it will be easily foreseen, that the stronger must eventually subdue and annihilate the weaker institution. Let us then examine the force and influence of the new system, and enquire whether the small remnant of power left to the States can be adequate even to the trifling charge of its own preservation. Here, Sir, we find the right of making laws for every purpose is invested in the future governors of America, and in this is included the uncontrolled jurisdiction over the purses of the people. The power of raising money is indeed the soul, the vital prop of legislation, without which legislation itself cannot for a moment exist. It will, however, be remarked that the power of taxation, though extended to the general government, is not taken from the States individually. Yes, Sir!—but it will be remembered that the national government may take from the people just what they please, and if anything should afterwards remain, then indeed the exigencies of the State governments may be supplied from the scanty gleanings of the harvest. Permit me now, Sir, to call your attention to the powers enumerated in the 8th section of the first article, and particularly to that clause which authorizes the proposed Congress, "to lay and collect taxes, duties, imposts and excises, to pay the debts and provide for the common defence and general welfare of the United States." With such powers, Mr. President, what cannot the future governors accomplish? It will be said, perhaps, that the treasure, thus accumulated, is raised and appropriated for the general welfare and the common defence of the States; but may not this pretext be easily perverted to other purposes, since those very men who raise and appropriate the taxes, are the only judges of what shall be deemed the general welfare and common defence of the national government? If then, Mr. President, they have unlimited power to drain the wealth of the people in every channel of taxation, whether by imposts on our commercial intercourse with foreign nations, or by direct levies on the people, I repeat it, that this system must be too formidable for any single State, or even for a combination of the States, should an attempt be made to break and destroy the yoke of domination and tyranny which it will hereafter set up. If, indeed, the spirit of men, once inflamed with the knowledge of freedom, should occasionally blaze out in remonstrance, opposition and force, these symptoms would naturally excite the jealousy of their rulers, and tempt them to proceed in the career of usurpation, till the total destruction of every principle of liberty should furnish a fit security for the exercise of arbitrary power. The money which has been raised from the people, may then be effectually employed to keep them in a state of slavish subjection: the militia, regulated and commanded by the officers of the general government, will be warped from the patriotic nature of their institution, and a standing army, that most prevailing instrument of despotism, will be ever ready to enforce obedience to a government by which it is raised, supported and enriched. If, under such circumstances, the several States should presume to assert their undelegated rights, I ask again what balance remains with them to counteract the encroachments of so potent a superior? To assemble a military force would be impracticable; for the general government, foreseeing the attempt would anticipate the means, by the exercise of its indefinite control over the purses of the people; and, in order to act upon the consciences as well as the persons of men, we find it is expressly stipulated, that every officer of the State government shall be sworn to support the constitution of the United States. Hence likewise, Sir, I conclude that in every point of rivalship, in every contention for power on the one hand and for freedom on the other, the event must be favorable to the views and pretensions of a government gifted with so decisive a pre-eminence. Let us, however, regard this subject in another light. What, Mr. President, will be the feelings and ideas of the people, when by the operation of the proposed system, they are exposed to such accumulated expense, for the maintenance of the general government? Is it not easy to foresee, that however the States may be disposed individually to preserve the parade of independence and sovereignty, the people themselves will become indifferent, and at last, averse to the continuance of an expensive form, from which they derive no advantage? For, Sir, the attachment of citizens to their government and its laws is founded upon the benefits which they derive from them, and it will last no longer than the duration of the power to confer those benefits. When, therefore, the people of the respective States shall find their governments grown torpid, and divested of the means to promote their welfare and interests, they will not, Sir, vainly idolize a shadow, nor disburse their hard earned wealth without the prospect of a compensation. The constitution of the States having become weak and useless to every beneficial purpose, will be suffered to dwindle and decay, and thus if the governors of the Union are not too impatient for the accomplishment of unrivalled and absolute dominion, the destruction of State jurisdiction will be produced by its own insignificance.

17

WILLIAM FINDLEY, PENNSYLVANIA
RATIFYING CONVENTION
1 Dec. 1787
McMaster 300–301

On Saturday [Dec. 1st] Mr. Findley delivered an eloquent and powerful speech, to prove that the proposed plan of government amounted to a consolidation, and not a confederation of the states. Mr. Wilson had before admitted that if this was a just objection, it would be strongly against the system; and it seems from the subsequent silence of all its advocates upon that subject (except Doctor Rush, who on Monday insinuated that he saw and rejoiced at the eventual annihilation of the state sovereignties) Mr. Findley has established his position. Previous to an investigation of the plan, that gentleman animadverted upon the argument of necessity, which had been so much insisted upon, and showed that we were in an eligible situation to attempt the improvement of the Federal Government, but not so desperately circumstanced as to be obliged to adopt any system, however destructive to the liberties of the people, and the sovereign rights of the states. He then argued that the proposed constitution established a general government and destroyed the individual governments, from the following evidence taken from the system itself: 1st. In the preamble, it is said, *We the People*, and not *We the States*, which therefore is a compact between individuals entering into society, and not between separate states enjoying independent power, and delegating a portion of that power for their common benefit. 2d. That in the legislature each member has a vote, whereas in a confederation, as we have hitherto practised it, and from the very nature of the thing, a state can only have one voice, and therefore all the delegates of any state can only give one vote. 3d. The powers given to the Federal body for imposing internal taxation will necessarily destroy the state sovereignties, for there cannot exist two independent sovereign taxing powers in the same community, and the strongest will of course annihilate the weaker. 4th. The power given to regulate and judge of elections is a proof of a consolidation, for there cannot be two powers employed at the same time in regulating the same elections, and if they were a confederated body, the individual states would judge of the elections, and the general Congress would judge of the credentials which proved the election of its members. 5th. The judiciary power, which is coextensive with the legislative, is another evidence of a consolidation. 6th. The manner in which the wages of the members is paid, makes another proof; and lastly, The oath of allegiance directed to be taken establishes it incontrovertibly; for would it not be absurd, that the members of the legislative and executive branches of a sovereign state should take a test of allegiance to another sovereign or independent body?

18

JAMES WILSON, PENNSYLVANIA
RATIFYING CONVENTION
1–11 Dec. 1787
McMaster 301–3, 322–25, 389–91

[*1 Dec.*]

The secret is now disclosed, and it is discovered to be a dread that the boasted state sovereignties will, under this system, be disrobed of part of their power. Before I go into the examination of this point, let me ask one important question: Upon what principle is it contended that the sovereign power resides in the state governments? The honorable gentleman has said truly, that there can be no subordinate sovereignty. Now if there can not, my position is, that the sovereignty resides in the people. They have not parted with it; they have only dispensed such portions of power as were conceived necessary for the public welfare. This constitution stands upon this broad principle. I know very well, Sir, that the people have hitherto been shut out of the federal government, but it is not meant that they should any longer be dispossessed of their rights. In order to recognize this leading principle, the proposed system sets out with a declaration that its existence depends upon the supreme authority of the people alone. We have heard much about a consolidated government. I wish the honorable gentleman would condescend to give us a definition of what he meant by it. I think this the more necessary, because I apprehend that the term, in the numerous times it has been used, has not always been used in the same sense. It may be said, and I believe it has been said, that a consolidated government is such as will absorb and destroy the governments of the several States. If it is taken in this view, the plan before us is not a consolidated government, as I showed on a former day, and may, if necessary, show further on some future occasion. On the other hand, if it is meant that the general government will take from the state governments their power in some particulars, it is confessed and evident that this will be its operation and effect.

When the principle is once settled that the people are the source of authority, the consequence is that they may take from the subordinate governments powers with which they have hitherto trusted them, and place those powers in the general government, if it is thought that there they will be productive of more good. They can distribute one portion of power to the more contracted circle called State governments: they can also furnish another proportion to the government of the United States. Who will undertake to say as a state officer that the people may not give to the general government what powers and for what purposes they please? how comes it, Sir, that these State governments dictate to their superiors?—to the majesty of the people? When I say the majesty of the people, I mean the thing, and not a mere compliment to them. The honorable

gentleman went a step further and said that the State governments were kept out of this government altogether. The truth is, and it is a leading principle in this system, that not the States only but the people also shall be here represented. And if this is a crime, I confess the general government is chargeable with it; but I have no idea that a safe system of power in the government, sufficient to manage the general interest of the United States, could be drawn from any other source or rested in any other authority than that of the people at large, and I consider this authority as the rock on which this structure will stand. If this principle is unfounded, the system must fall. If honorable gentlemen, before they undertake to oppose this principle, will show that the people have parted with their power to the State governments, then I confess I cannot support this constitution.

[*4 Dec.*]

It is repeated, with confidence, "that this is not a *federal* government, but a complete one, with legislative, executive and judicial powers: it is a *consolidating* government." I have already mentioned the misuse of the term; I wish the gentleman would indulge us with his definition of the word. If, when he says it is a consolidation, he means so far as relates to the general objects of the union—so far it was intended to be a consolidation, and on such a consolidation, perhaps, our very existence, as a nation, depends. If, on the other hand (as something which has been said seems to indicate) he (Mr. Findley) means that it will absorb the governments of the individual States, so far is this position from being admitted, that it is unanswerably controverted. The existence of the State government, is one of the most prominent features of this system. With regard to those purposes which are allowed to be for the general welfare of the union, I think it no objection to this plan, that we are told it is a complete government. I think it no objection, that it is alleged the government will possess legislative, executive and judicial powers. Should it have only legislative authority? We have had examples enough of such a government, to deter us from continuing it. Shall Congress any longer continue to make requisitions from the several States, to be treated sometimes with silent, and sometimes with declared contempt? For what purpose give the power to make laws, unless they are to be executed? and if they are to be executed, the executive and judicial powers will necessarily be engaged in the business.

Do we wish a return of those insurrections and tumults to which a sister State was lately exposed? or a government of such insufficiency as the present is found to be? Let me, Sir, mention one circumstance in the recollection of every honorable gentleman who hears me. To the determination of Congress are submitted all disputes between States, concerning boundary, jurisdiction, or right of soil. In consequence of this power, after much altercation, expense of time, and considerable expense of money, this State was successful enough to obtain a decree in her favor, in a difference then subsisting between her and Connecticut; but what was the consequence? the Congress had no power to carry the decree into execution. Hence the distraction and animosity, which have ever since prevailed, and still continue in that part of the country. Ought the government then to remain any longer incomplete? I hope not; no person can be so insensible to the lessons of experience as to desire it.

It is brought as an objection "that there will be a rivalship between the State governments and the general government; on each side endeavors will be made to increase power."

Let us examine a little into this subject. The gentlemen tell you, Sir, that they expect the States will not possess any power. But I think there is reason to draw a different conclusion. Under this system their respectability and power will increase with that of the general government. I believe their happiness and security will increase in a still greater proportion. Let us attend a moment to the situation of this country: it is a maxim of every government, and it ought to be a maxim with us, that the increase of numbers increases the dignity, the security, and the respectability of all governments; it is the first command given by the Deity to man, increase and multiply; this applies with peculiar force to this country, the smaller part of whose territory is yet inhabited. We are representatives, Sir, not merely of the present age, but of future times; nor merely of the territory along the sea coast, but of regions immensely extended westward. We should fill, as fast as possible, this extensive country, with men who shall live happy, free and secure. To accomplish this great end ought to be the leading view of all our patriots and statesmen. But how is it to be accomplished, but by establishing peace and harmony among ourselves, and dignity and respectability among foreign nations? By these means, we may draw numbers from the other side of the Atlantic, in addition to the natural sources of population. Can either of these objects be attained without a protecting head? When we examine history, we shall find an important fact, and almost the only fact, which will apply to all confederacies.

They have all fallen to pieces, and have not absorbed the subordinate governments.

In order to keep republics together they must have a strong binding force, which must be either external or internal. The situation of this country shows, that no foreign force can press us together; the bonds of our union ought therefore to be indissolubly strong.

The power of the States, I apprehend, will increase with the population, and the happiness of their inhabitants. Unless we can establish a character abroad, we shall be unhappy from foreign restraints, or internal violence. These reasons, I think, prove sufficiently the necessity of having a federal head. Under it the advantages enjoyed by the whole union would be participated by every State. I wish honorable gentlemen would think not only of themselves, not only of the present age, but of others, and of future times.

It has been said, "that the State governments will not be able to make head against the general government;" but it might be said with more propriety, that the general government will not be able to maintain the powers given it against the encroachments and combined attacks of the State governments. They possess some particular advantages, from which the general government is restrained. By this system, there is a provision made in the constitution, that no senator or representative shall be appointed to any civil office under the authority of the United States, which shall have been created, or the emoluments whereof shall have been increased, during the time for which he was elected; and no person holding any office under the United States can be a member of either house; but there is no similar security against State influence, as a representative may enjoy places and even sinecures under the State governments. On which side is the door most open to corruption? If a person in the legislature is to be influenced by an office, the general government can give him none unless he vacate his seat. When the influence of office comes from the State government, he can retain his seat and salary too. But it is added, under this head, "that State governments will lose the attachment of the people, by losing the power of conferring advantages, and that the people will not be at the expense of keeping them up." Perhaps the State governments have already become so expensive as to alarm the gentlemen on that head. I am told that the civil list of this State amounted to £40,000, in one year. Under the proposed government, I think it would be possible to obtain in Pennsylvania every advantage we now possess, with a civil list that shall not exceed one-third of that sum.

How differently the same thing is talked of, if it be a favorite or otherwise! When advantages to an officer are to be derived from the general government, we hear them mentioned by the name of *bribery*, but when we are told of the State governments losing the power of conferring advantages, by the disposal of offices, it is said they will lose the *attachment* of the people. What is in one instance corruption and bribery, is in another the power of conferring advantages.

We are informed that "the State elections will be ill attended, and that the State governments will become mere boards of electors." Those who have a due regard for their country, will discharge their duty, and attend; but those who are brought only from interest or persuasion had better stay away; the public will not suffer any disadvantage from their absence. But the honest citizen, who knows the value of the privilege, will undoubtedly attend, to secure the man of his choice. The power and business of the State legislatures relates to the great objects of life, liberty and property; the same are also objects of the general government.

Certainly the citizens of America will be as tenacious in the one instance as in the other. They will be interested, and I hope will exert themselves, to secure their rights not only from being injured by the State governments, but also from being injured by the general government.

[11 Dec.]

We are next told, by the honorable gentlemen in opposition (as indeed we have been from the beginning of the debates in this convention, to the conclusion of their speeches yesterday) that this is a consolidated government, and will abolish the State governments. Definitions of a consolidated government have been called for; the gentle-men gave us what they termed definitions, but it does not seem, to me at least, that they have as yet expressed clear ideas upon that subject. I will endeavor to state their different ideas upon this point.

The gentlemen from Westmoreland (Mr. Findley) when speaking on this subject, says, that he means by a consolidation, that government which puts the thirteen States into one.

The honorable gentleman from Fayette (Mr. Smilie) gives you this definition: "What I mean by a consolidated government, is one that will transfer the sovereignty from the State governments to the general government."

The honorable member from Cumberland (Mr. White-hill) instead of giving you a definition, sir, tells you again, that "it is consolidated government, and we have proved it so."

These, I think, sir, are the different descriptions given us of a consolidated government. As to the first, that it is a consolidated government, that puts the thirteen United States into one; if it is meant, that the general government will destroy the governments of the States, I will admit that such a government would not suit the people of America: It would be improper for *this* country, because it could not be proportioned to *its extent* on the principles of freedom. But that description does not apply to the system before you. This, instead of placing the State governments in jeopardy, is founded on their existence. On this principle, its organization depends; it must stand or fall, as the State governments are secured or ruined. Therefore, though this may be a very proper description of a consolidating government, yet it must be disregarded as inapplicable to the proposed constitution. It is not treated with decency, when such insinuations are offered against it.

The honorable gentleman (Mr. Smilie) tells you, that a consolidating government "is one that will transfer the sovereignty from the State governments to the general government." Under this system, the sovereignty is not in the possession of the State governments, therefore it cannot be transferred from them to the general government. So that in no point of view of this definition, can we discover that it applies to the present system.

In the exercise of its powers will be insured the exercise of their powers to the State government; it will insure peace and stability to them; their strength will increase with its strength, their growth will extend with its growth.

Indeed, narrow minds, and some such there are in every government—narrow minds, and intriguing spirits—will be active in sowing dissentions and promoting discord between them. But those whose understandings and whose hearts are good enough to pursue the general welfare, will find, that what is the interest of the whole, must, on the great scale, be the interest of every part. It will be the duty of a State, as of an individual, to sacrifice her own convenience to the general good of the Union.

19

ALEXANDER HAMILTON, FEDERALIST, NO. 15, 90–98
1 Dec. 1787

(See ch. 5, no. 21)

20

SAMUEL ADAMS TO RICHARD HENRY LEE
3 Dec. 1787
Writings 4:324–25

I confess, as I enter the Building I stumble at the Threshold. I meet with a National Government, instead of a Federal Union of Sovereign States. I am not able to conceive why the Wisdom of the Convention led them to give the Preference to the former before the latter. If the several States in the Union are to become one entire Nation, under one Legislature, the Powers of which shall extend to every Subject of Legislation, and its Laws be supreme & controul the whole, the Idea of Sovereignty in these States must be lost. Indeed I think, upon such a Supposition, those Sovereignties ought to be eradicated from the Mind; for they would be Imperia in Imperio justly deemd a Solecism in Politicks, & they would be highly dangerous, and destructive of the Peace Union and Safety of the Nation. And can this National Legislature be competent to make Laws for the *free* internal Government of one People, living in Climates so remote and whose "Habits & particular Interests" are and probably always will be so different. Is it to be expected that General Laws can be adapted to the Feelings of the more Eastern and the more Southern Parts of so extensive a Nation? It appears to me difficult if practicable. Hence then may we not look for Discontent, Mistrust, Disaffection to Government and frequent Insurrections, which will require standing Armies to suppress them in one Place & another where they may happen to arise. Or if Laws could be made, adapted to the local Habits, Feelings, Views & Interests of those distant Parts, would they not cause Jealousies of Partiality in Government which would excite Envy and other malignant Passions productive of Wars and fighting. But should we continue distinct sovereign States, confederated for the Purposes of mutual Safety and Happiness, each contributing to the federal Head such a Part of its Sovereignty as would render the Government fully adequate to those Purposes and *no more*, the People would govern themselves more easily, the Laws of each State being well adapted to its own Genius & Circumstances, and the Liberties of the United States would be more secure than they can be, as I humbly conceive, under the proposed new Constitution. You are sensible, Sir, that the Seeds of Aristocracy began to spring even before the Conclusion of our Struggle for the natural Rights of Men, Seeds which like a Canker Worm lie at the

Root of free Governments. So great is the Wickedness of some Men, & the stupid Servility of others, that one would be almost inclined to conclude that Communities cannot be free. The few haughty Families, think *They* must govern. The Body of the People tamely consent & submit to be their Slaves. This unravels the Mystery of Millions being enslaved by the few!

21

AGRIPPA, NO. 4
3 Dec. 1787
Storing 4.6.15–17

We find, then, that after the experience of near two centuries our separate governments are in full vigour. They discover, for all the purposes of internal regulation, every symptom of strength, and none of decay. The new system is, therefore, for such purposes, useless and burdensome.

Let us now consider how far it is practicable consistent with the happiness of the people and their freedom. It is the opinion of the ablest writers on the subject, that no extensive empire can be governed upon republican principles, and that such a government will degenerate to a despotism, unless it be made up of a confederacy of smaller states, each having the full powers of internal regulation. This is precisely the principle which has hitherto preserved our freedom. No instance can be found of any free government of considerable extent which has been supported upon any other plan. Large and consolidated empires may indeed dazzle the eyes of a distant spectator with their splendour, but if examined more nearly are always found to be full of misery. The reason is obvious. In large states the same principles of legislation will not apply to all the parts. The inhabitants of warmer climates are more dissolute in their manners, and less industrious, than in colder countries. A degree of severity is, therefore, necessary with one which would cramp the spirit of the other. We accordingly find that the very great empires have always been despotick. They have indeed tried to remedy the inconveniences to which the people were exposed by local regulations; but these contrivances have never answered the end. The laws not being made by the people, who felt the inconveniences, did not suit their circumstances. It is under such tyranny that the Spanish provinces languish, and such would be our misfortune and degradation, if we should submit to have the concerns of the whole empire managed by one legislature. To promote the happiness of the people it is necessary that there should be local laws; and it is necessary that those laws should be made by the representatives of those who are immediately subject to the want of them. By endeavouring to suit both extremes, both are injured.

It is impossible for one code of laws to suit Georgia and Massachusetts. They must, therefore, legislate for themselves. Yet there is, I believe, not one point of legislation that is not surrendered in the proposed plan. Questions of every kind respecting property are determinable in a continental court, and so are all kinds of criminal causes. The continental legislature has, therefore, a right to make rules *in all cases* by which their judicial courts shall proceed and decide causes. No rights are reserved to the citizens. The laws of Congress are in all cases to be the supreme law of the land, and paramount to the constitutions of the individual states. The Congress may institute what modes of trial they please, and no plea drawn from the constitution of any state can avail. This new system is, therefore, a consolidation of all the states into one large mass, however diverse the parts may be of which it is to be composed. The idea of an uncompounded republick, on an average, one thousand miles in length, and eight hundred in breadth, and containing six millions of white inhabitants all reduced to the same standard of morals, or habits, and of laws, is in itself an absurdity, and contrary to the whole experience of mankind. The attempt made by Great-Britain to introduce such a system, struck us with horrour, and when it was proposed by some theorist that we should be represented in parliament, we uniformly declared that one legislature could not represent so many different interests for the purposes of legislation and taxation. This was the leading principle of the revolution, and makes an essential article in our creed. All that part, therefore, of the new system, which relates to the internal government of the states, ought at once to be rejected.

22

ALEXANDER HAMILTON, FEDERALIST, NO. 16,
99–105
4 Dec. 1787

The tendency of the principle of legislation for States, or communities, in their political capacities, as it has been exemplified by the experiment we have made of it, is equally attested by the events which have befallen all other governments of the confederate kind, of which we have any account, in exact proportion to its prevalence in those systems. The confirmations of this fact will be worthy of a distinct and particular examination. I shall content myself with barely observing here, that of all the confederacies of antiquity, which history has handed down to us, the Lycian and Achaean leagues, as far as there remain vestiges of them, appear to have been most free from the fetters of that mistaken principle, and were accordingly those which have best deserved, and have most liberally received the applauding suffrages of political writers.

This exceptionable principle may as truly as emphatically be stiled the parent of anarchy: It has been seen that delinquencies in the members of the Union are its natural and necessary offspring; and that whenever they happen, the only constitutional remedy is force, and the immediate effect of the use of it, civil war.

It remains to enquire how far so odious an engine of government, in its application to us, would even be capable of answering its end. If there should not be a large army, constantly at the disposal of the national government, it would either not be able to employ force at all, or when this could be done, it would amount to a war between different parts of the confederacy, concerning the infractions of a league; in which the strongest combination would be most likely to prevail, whether it consisted of those who supported, or of those who resisted the general authority. It would rarely happen that the delinquency to be redressed would be confined to a single member, and if there were more than one, who had neglected their duty, similarity of situation would induce them to unite for common defence. Independent of this motive of sympathy, if a large and influential State should happen to be the aggressing member, it would commonly have weight enough with its neighbours, to win over some of them as associates to its cause. Specious arguments of danger to the common liberty could easily be contrived; plausible excuses for the deficiencies of the party, could, without difficulty be invented, to alarm the apprehensions, inflame the passions, and conciliate the good will even of those States which were not chargeable with any violation, or omission of duty. This would be the more likely to take place, as the delinquencies of the larger members might be expected sometimes to proceed from an ambitious premeditation in their rulers, with a view to getting rid of all external controul upon their designs of personal aggrandizement; the better to effect which, it is presumable they would tamper beforehand with leading individuals in the adjacent States. If associates could not be found at home, recourse would be had to the aid of foreign powers, who would seldom be disinclined to encouraging the dissentions of a confederacy, from the firm Union of which they had so much to fear. When the sword is once drawn, the passions of men observe no bounds of moderation. The suggestions of wounded pride, the instigations of irritated resentment, would be apt to carry the States, against which the arms of the Union were exerted to any extremes necessary to revenge the affront, or to avoid the disgrace of submission. The first war of this kind would probably terminate in a dissolution of the Union.

This may be considered as the violent death of the confederacy. Its more natural death is what we now seem to be on the point of experiencing, if the foederal system be not speedily renovated in a more substantial form. It is not probable, considering the genius of this country, that the complying States would often be inclined to support the authority of the Union by engaging in a war against the non-complying States. They would always be more ready to pursue the milder course of putting themselves upon an equal footing with the delinquent members, by an imitation of their example. And the guilt of all would thus become the security of all. Our past experience has exhibited the operation of this spirit in its full light. There would in fact be an insuperable difficulty in ascertaining when force could with propriety be employed. In the article of pecuniary contribution, which would be the most usual source of delinquency, it would often be impossible

to decide whether it had proceeded from disinclination, or inability. The pretence of the latter would always be at hand. And the case must be very flagrant in which its fallacy could be detected with sufficient certainty to justify the harsh expedient of compulsion. It is easy to see that this problem alone, as often as it should occur, would open a wide field for the exercise of factious views, of partiality and of oppression, in the majority that happened to prevail in the national council.

It seems to require no pains to prove that the States ought not to prefer a national constitution, which could only be kept in motion by the instrumentality of a large army, continually on foot to execute the ordinary requisitions or decrees of the government. And yet this is the plain alternative involved by those who wish to deny it the power of extending its operations to individuals. Such a scheme, if practicable at all, would instantly degenerate into a military despotism; but it will be found in every light impracticable. The resources of the Union would not be equal to the maintenance of an army considerable enough to confine the larger States within the limits of their duty; nor would the means ever be furnished of forming such an army in the first instance. Whoever considers the populousness and strength of several of these States singly at the present juncture, and looks forward to what they will become, even at the distance of half a century, will at once dismiss as idle and visionary any scheme, which aims at regulating their movements by laws, to operate upon them in their collective capacities, and to be executed by a coertion applicable to them in the same capacities. A project of this kind is little less romantic than that monster-taming spirit, which is attributed to the fabulous heroes and demi-gods of antiquity.

Even in those confederacies, which have been composed of members smaller than many of our counties, the principle of legislation for sovereign States, supported by military coertion, has never been found effectual. It has rarely been attempted to be employed, but against the weaker members: And in most instances attempts to coerce the refractory and disobedient, have been the signals of bloody wars; in which one half of the confederacy has displayed its banners against the other half.

The result of these observations to an intelligent mind must be clearly this, that if it be possible at any rate to construct a Foederal Government capable of regulating the common concerns and preserving the general tranquility, it must be founded, as to the objects committed to its care, upon the reverse of the principle contended for by the opponents of the proposed constitution. It must carry its agency to the persons of the citizens. It must stand in need of no intermediate legislations; but must itself be empowered to employ the arm of the ordinary magistrate to execute its own resolutions. The majesty of the national authority must be manifested through the medium of the Courts of Justice. The government of the Union, like that of each State, must be able to address itself immediately to the hopes and fears of individuals; and to attract to its support, those passions, which have the strongest influence upon the human heart. It must in short, possess all the means and have a right to resort to all the methods of executing the powers, with which it is entrusted, that are possessed and exercised by the governments of the particular States.

To this reasoning it may perhaps be objected, that if any State should be disaffected to the authority of the Union, it could at any time obstruct the execution of its laws, and bring the matter to the same issue of force, with the necessity of which the opposite scheme is reproached.

The plausibility of this objection will vanish the moment we advert to the essential difference between a mere NON COMPLIANCE and a DIRECT and ACTIVE RESISTANCE. If the interposition of the State-Legislatures be necessary to give effect to a measure of the Union, they have only NOT TO ACT or TO ACT EVASIVELY, and the measure is defeated. This neglect of duty may be disguised under affected but unsubstantial provisions, so as not to appear, and of course not to excite any alarm in the people for the safety of the constitution. The State leaders may even make a merit of their surreptitious invasions of it, on the ground of some temporary convenience, exemption, or advantage.

But if the execution of the laws of the national government, should not require the intervention of the State Legislatures; if they were to pass into immediate operation upon the citizens themselves, the particular governments could not interrupt their progress without an open and violent exertion of an unconstitutional power. No omissions, nor evasions would answer the end. They would be obliged to act, and in such a manner, as would leave no doubt that they had encroached on the national rights. An experiment of this nature would always be hazardous—in the face of a constitution in any degree competent to its own defence, and of a people enlightened enough to distinguish between a legal exercise and an illegal usurpation of authority. The success of it would require not merely a factious majority in the Legislature, but the concurrence of the courts of justice, and of the body of the people. If the Judges were not embarked in a conspiracy with the Legislature they would pronounce the resolutions of such a majority to be contrary to the supreme law of the land, unconstitutional and void. If the people were not tainted with the spirit of their State representatives, they, as the natural guardians of the constitution, would throw their weight into the national scale, and give it a decided preponderancy in the contest. Attempts of this kind would not often be made with levity or rashness; because they could seldom be made without danger to the authors; unless in cases of a tyrannical exercise of the Foederal authority.

If opposition to the national government should arise from the disorderly conduct of refractory, or seditious individuals, it could be overcome by the same means which are daily employed against the same evil, under the State governments. The Magistracy, being equally the Ministers of the law of the land, from whatever source it might emanate, would doubtless be as ready to guard the national as the local regulations from the inroads of private licentiousness. As to those partial commotions and insurrections which sometimes disquiet society, from the intrigues of an inconsiderable faction, or from sudden or occasional ill humours that do not infect the great body of the community, the general government could command more extensive resources for the suppression of disturbances of that kind, than would be in the power of any single member. And as to those mortal feuds, which in certain conjunctures spread a conflagration through a whole nation, or through a very large proportion of it, proceeding either from weighty causes of discontent given by the government, or from the contagion of some violent popular paroxism, they do not fall within any ordinary rules of calculation. When they happen, they commonly amount to revolutions and dismemberments of empire. No form of government can always either avoid or controul them. It is in vain to hope to guard against events too mighty for human foresight or precaution, and it would be idle to object to a government because it could not perform impossibilities.

23

ALEXANDER HAMILTON, FEDERALIST, NO. 17,
105–8
5 Dec. 1787

An objection of a nature different from that which has been stated and answered, in my last address, may perhaps be likewise urged against the principle of legislation for the individual citizens of America. It may be said, that it would tend to render the government of the Union too powerful, and to enable it to absorb in itself those residuary authorities, which it might be judged proper to leave with the States for local purposes. Allowing the utmost latitude to the love of power, which any reasonable man can require, I confess I am at a loss to discover what temptation the persons entrusted with the administration of the general government could ever feel to divest the States of the authorities of that description. The regulation of the mere domestic police of a State appears to me to hold out slender allurements to ambition. Commerce, finance, negociation and war seem to comprehend all the objects, which have charms for minds governed by that passion; and all the powers necessary to these objects ought in the first instance to be lodged in the national depository. The administration of private justice between the citizens of the same State, the supervision of agriculture and of other concerns of a similar nature, all those things in short which are proper to be provided for by local legislation, can never be desirable cares of a general jurisdiction. It is therefore improbable that there should exist a disposition in the Foederal councils to usurp the powers with which they are connected; because the attempt to exercise those powers would be as troublesome as it would be nugatory; and the possession of them, for that reason, would contribute nothing to the dignity, to the importance, or to the splendour of the national government.

But let it be admitted for argument sake, that mere wantonness and lust of domination would be sufficient to beget that disposition, still it may be safely affirmed, that the sense of the constituent body of the national representatives, or in other words of the people of the several States would controul the indulgence of so extravagant an appetite. It will always be far more easy for the State governments to encroach upon the national authorities, than for the national government to encroach upon the State authorities. The proof of this proposition turns upon the greater degree of influence, which the State governments, if they administer their affairs with uprightness and prudence, will generally possess over the people; a circumstance which at the same time teaches us, that there is an inherent and intrinsic weakness in all Foederal Constitutions; and that too much pains cannot be taken in their organization, to give them all the force which is compatible with the principles of liberty.

The superiority of influence in favour of the particular governments would result partly from the diffusive construction of the national government; but chiefly from the nature of the objects to which the attention of the State administrations would be directed.

It is a known fact in human nature that its affections are commonly weak in proportion to the distance or diffusiveness of the object. Upon the same principle that a man is more attached to his family than to his neighbourhood, to his neighbourhood than to the community at large, the people of each State would be apt to feel a stronger byass towards their local governments than towards the government of the Union; unless the force of that principle should be destroyed by a much better administration of the latter.

This strong propensity of the human heart would find powerful auxiliaries in the objects of State regulation.

The variety of more minute interests, which will necessarily fall under the superintendence of the local administrations, and which will form so many rivulets of influence running through every part of the society, cannot be particularised without involving a detail too tedious and uninteresting to compensate for the instruction it might afford.

There is one transcendent advantage belonging to the province of the State governments which alone suffices to place the matter in a clear and satisfactory light. I mean the ordinary administration of criminal and civil justice. This of all others is the most powerful, most universal and most attractive source of popular obedience and attachment. It is that, which—being the immediate and visible guardian of life and property—having its benefits and its terrors in constant activity before the public eye—regulating all those personal interests and familiar concerns to which the sensibility of individuals is more immediately awake—contributes more than any other circumstance to impressing upon the minds of the people affection, esteem and reverence towards the government. This great cement of society which will diffuse itself almost wholly through the channels of the particular governments, independent of all other causes of influence, would ensure them so decided an empire over their respective citizens, as to render them at all times a complete counterpoise and not unfrequently dangerous rivals to the power of the Union.

The operations of the national government on the other hand falling less immediately under the observation of the mass of the citizens the benefits derived from it will chiefly be perceived and attended to by speculative men. Relating to more general interests, they will be less apt to come home to the feelings of the people; and, in proportion, less likely to inspire a habitual sense of obligation and an active sentiment of attachment.

The reasoning on this head has been abundantly exemplified by the experience of all Foederal constitutions, with which we are acquainted, and of all others, which have borne the least analogy to them.

24

ALEXANDER HAMILTON, FEDERALIST, NO. 27,
171–75
25 Dec. 1787

It has been urged in different shapes that a constitution of the kind proposed by the Convention, cannot operate without the aid of a military force to execute its laws. This however, like most other things that have been alledged on that side, rests on mere general assertion; unsupported by any precise or intelligible designation of the reasons upon which it is founded. As far as I have been able to divine the latent meaning of the objectors, it seems to originate in a pre-supposition that the people will be disinclined to the exercise of foederal authority in any matter of an internal nature. Waving any exception that might be taken to the inaccuracy or inexplicitness of the distinction between internal and external, let us enquire what ground there is to presuppose that disinclination in the people? Unless we presume, at the same time, that the powers of the General Government will be worse administered than those of the State governments, there seems to be no room for the presumption of ill-will, disaffection or opposition in the people. I believe it may be laid down as a general rule, that their confidence in and obedience to a government, will commonly be proportioned to the goodness or badness of its administration. It must be admitted that there are exceptions to this rule; but these exceptions depend so entirely on accidental causes, that they cannot be considered as having any relation to the intrinsic merits or demerits of a constitution. These can only be judged of by general principles and maxims.

Various reasons have been suggested in the course of these papers, to induce a probability that the General Government will be better administered than the particular governments: The principal of which reasons are that the extension of the spheres of election will present a greater option, or latitude of choice to the people, that through the medium of the State Legislatures, which are select bodies of men, and who are to appoint the members of the national Senate,—there is reason to expect that this branch will generally be composed with peculiar care and judgment: That these circumstances promise greater knowledge and more extensive information in the national councils: And that they will be less apt to be tainted by the spirit of faction, and more out of the reach of those occasional ill humors or temporary prejudices and propensities, which in smaller societies frequently contaminate the public councils, beget injustice and oppression of a part of the community, and engender schemes, which though they gratify a momentary inclination or desire, terminate in general distress, dissatisfaction and disgust. Several additional reasons of considerable force, to fortify that probability, will occur when we come to survey with a more critic[al] eye, the interior structure of the edifice, which we are invited to erect. It will be sufficient here to remark, that until satisfactory reasons can be assigned to justify an opinion, that the foederal government is likely to be administered in such a manner as to render it odious or contemptible to the people, there can be no reasonable foundation for the supposition, that the laws of the Union will meet with any greater obstruction from them, or will stand in need of any other methods to enforce their execution, than the laws of the particular members.

The hope of impunity is a strong incitement to sedition—the dread of punishment—a proportionately strong discouragement to it. Will not the government of the Union, which, if possessed of a due degree of power, can call to its aid the collective resources of the whole confederacy, be more likely to repress the *former* sentiment, and to inspire the *latter,* than that of a single State, which can only command the resources within itself? A turbulent faction in a State may easily suppose itself able to contend with the friends to the government in that State; but it can hardly be so infatuated as to imagine itself a match for the combined efforts of the Union. If this reflection be just, there is less danger of resistance from irregular combinations of individuals, to the authority of the confederacy, than to that of a single member.

I will in this place hazard an observation which will not be the less just, because to some it may appear new; which is, that the more the operations of the national authority are intermingled in the ordinary exercise of government; the more the citizens are accustomed to meet with it in the common occurrences of their political life; the more it is familiarised to their sight and to their feelings; the further it enters into those objects which touch the most sensible cords, and put in motion the most active springs of the human heart; the greater will be the probability that it will conciliate the respect and attachment of the community. Man is very much a creature of habit. A thing that rarely strikes his senses will generally have but little influence upon his mind. A government continually at a distance and out of sight, can hardly be expected to interest the sensations of the people. The inference is, that the authority of the Union, and the affections of the citizens towards it, will be strengthened rather than weakened by its extension to what are called matters of internal concern; and will have less occasion to recur to force in proportion to the familiarity and comprehensiveness of its agency. The more it circulates through those channels and currents, in which the passions of mankind naturally flow, the less will it require the aid of the violent and perilous expedients of compulsion.

One thing at all events, must be evident, that a government like the one proposed, would bid much fairer to avoid the necessity of using force, than that species of league contended for by most of its opponents; the authority of which should only operate upon the States in their political or collective capacities. It has been shewn, that in such a confederacy, there can be no sanction for the laws but force; that frequent delinquencies in the members, are the natural offspring of the very frame of the government; and that as often as these happen they can only be redressed, if at all, by war and violence.

The plan reported by the Convention, by extending the authority of the foederal head to the individual citizens of the several States, will enable the government to employ the ordinary magistracy of each in the execution of its laws. It is easy to perceive that this will tend to destroy, in the common apprehension, all distinction between the sources from which they might proceed; and will give the Foederal Government the same advantage for securing a due obedience to its authority, which is enjoyed by the government of each State; in addition to the influence on public opinion, which will result from the important consideration of its having power to call to its assistance and support the resources of the whole Union. It merits particular attention in this place, that the laws of the confederacy, as to the *enumerated* and *legitimate* objects of its jurisdiction, will become the SUPREME LAW of the land; to the observance of which, all officers legislative, executive and judicial in each State, will be bound by the sanctity of an oath. Thus the Legislatures, Courts and Magistrates of the respective members will be incorporated into the operations of the national government, *as far as its just and constitutional authority extends;* and will be rendered auxiliary to the enforcement of its laws. Any man, who will pursue by his own reflections the consequences of this situation, will perceive that there is good ground to calculate upon a regular and peaceable execution of the laws of the Union; if its powers are administered with a common share of prudence. If we will arbitrarily suppose the contrary, we may deduce any inferences we please from the supposition; for it is certainly possible, by an injudicious exercise of the authorities of the best government, that ever was or ever can be instituted, to provoke and precipitate the people into the wildest excesses. But though the adversaries of the proposed constitution should presume that the national rulers would be insensible to the motives of public good, or to the obligations of duty; I would still ask them, how the interests of ambition, or the views of encroachment, can be promoted by such a conduct?

25

FEDERAL FARMER, NO. 6
25 Dec. 1787
Storing 2.8.71–72

26

BRUTUS, NO. 7
3 Jan. 1788
Storing 2.9.83–87

Some of the advocates, I believe, will agree to recommend *good* amendments; but some of them will only consent to recommend indefinite, specious, but unimportant ones; and this only with a view to keep the door open for obtaining, in some favourable moment, their main object, a complete consolidation of the states, and a government much higher toned, less republican and free than the one proposed. If necessity, therefore, should ever oblige us to adopt the system, and recommend amendments, the true friends of a federal republic must see they are well defined, and well calculated, not only to prevent our system of government moving further from republican principles and equality, but to bring it back nearer to them—they must be constantly on their guard against the address, flattery, and manoeuvres of their adversaries.

The gentlemen who oppose the constitution, or contend for amendments in it, are frequently, and with much bitterness, charged with wantonly attacking the men who framed it. The unjustness of this charge leads me to make one observation upon the conduct of parties, &c. Some of the advocates are only pretended federalists; in fact they wish for an abolition of the state governments. Some of them I believe to be honest federalists, who wish to preserve *substantially* the state governments united under an efficient federal head; and many of them are blind tools without any object. Some of the opposers also are only pretended federalists, who want no federal government, or one merely advisory. Some of them are the true federalists, their object, perhaps, more clearly seen, is the same with that of the honest federalists; and some of them, probably, have no distinct object. We might as well call the advocates and opposers tories and whigs, or any thing else, as federalists and anti-federalists. To be for or against the constitution, as it stands, is not much evidence of a federal disposition; if any names are applicable to the parties, on account of their general politics, they are those of republicans and anti-republicans. The opposers are generally men who support the rights of the body of the people, and are properly republicans. The advocates are generally men not very friendly to those rights, and properly anti republicans.

The result of our reasoning in the two preceeding numbers is this, that in a confederated government, where the powers are divided between the general and the state government, it is essential to its existence, that the revenues of the country, without which no government can exist, should be divided between them, and so apportioned to each, as to answer their respective exigencies, as far as human wisdom can effect such a division and apportionment.

It has been shewn, that no such allotment is made in this constitution, but that every source of revenue is under the controul of the Congress; it therefore follows, that if this system is intended to be a complex and not a simple, a confederate and not an entire consolidated government, it contains in it the sure seeds of its own dissolution.—One of two things must happen—Either the new constitution will become a mere *nudum pactum*, and all the authority of the rulers under it be cried down, as has happened to the present confederation—Or the authority of the individual states will be totally supplanted, and they will retain the mere form without any of the powers of government.—To one or the other of these issues, I think, this new government, if it is adopted, will advance with great celerity.

It is said, I know, that such a separation of the sources of revenue, cannot be made without endangering the public safety—"unless (says a writer) it can be shewn that the circumstances which may affect the public safety are reducible within certain determinate limits; unless the contrary of this position can be fairly and rationally disputed; it must be admitted as a necessary consequence, that there can be no limitation of that authority which is to provide for the defence and protection of the community, &c." [*Federalist*, no. 23]

The pretended demonstration of this writer will instantly vanish, when it is considered, that the *protection and defence* of the community is not intended to be entrusted *solely* into the hands of the general government, and by his own confession it ought not to be. It is true this system commits to the general government the protection and defence of the community against foreign force and invasion, against piracies and felonies on the high seas, and against insurrections among ourselves. They are also authorised to provide for the administration of justice in certain matters of a general concern, and in some that I think are not so. But it ought to be left to the state governments to provide for the protection and defence of the citizen against the hand of private violence, and the wrongs done or attempted by individuals to each other—Protection and defence against the murderer, the robber, the thief, the cheat, and the unjust person, is to be derived from the respective state governments.—The just way of reasoning therefore on this subject is this, the general government is to provide for the protection and defence of the community against foreign attacks, &c., they therefore ought to have authority sufficient to effect this, so far as is consistent with the providing for our internal protection and defence. The state governments are entrusted with the care of administring justice among its citizens, and the management of other internal concerns, they ought therefore to retain power adequate to the end. The preservation of internal peace and good order, and the due administration of law and justice, ought to be the first care of every government.—The happiness of a people depends infinitely more on this than it does upon all that glory and respect which nations acquire by the most brilliant martial achievements—and I believe history will furnish but few examples of nations who have duly attended to these, who have been subdued by foreign invaders. If a proper respect and submission to the laws prevailed over all orders of men in our country; and if a spirit of public and private justice, oeconomy and industry influenced the people, we need not be under any apprehensions but what they would be ready to repel any invasion that might be made on the country. And more than this, I would not wish from them—A defensive war is the only one I think justifiable—I do not make these observations to prove, that a government ought not to be authorised to provide for the protection and defence of a country against external enemies, but to shew that this is not the most important, much less the only object of their care.

The European governments are almost all of them framed, and administered with a view to arms, and war, as that in which their chief glory consists; they mistake the end of government—it was designed to save men[']s lives, not to destroy them. We ought to furnish the world with an example of a great people, who in their civil institutions hold chiefly in view, the attainment of virtue, and happiness among ourselves. Let the monarchs in Europe, share among them the glory of depopulating countries, and butchering thousands of their innocent citizens, to revenge private quarrels, or to punish an insult offered to a wife, a mistress, or a favorite: I envy them not the honor, and I pray heaven this country may never be ambitious of it. The czar Peter the great, acquired great glory by his arms; but all this was nothing, compared with the true glory which he obtained, by civilizing his rude and barbarous subjects, diffusing among them knowledge, and establishing, and cultivating the arts of life: by the former he desolated countries, and drenched the earth with human blood: by the latter he softened the ferocious nature of his people, and pointed them to the means of human happiness. The most important end of government then, is the proper direction of its internal policy, and oeconomy; this is the province of the state governments, and it is evident, and is indeed admitted, that these ought to be under their controul. Is it not then preposterous, and in the highest degree absurd, when the state governments are vested with powers so essential to the peace and good order of society, to take from them the means of their own preservation?

27

JAMES MADISON, FEDERALIST, NO. 39, 253–57
16 Jan. 1788

But it was not sufficient, say the adversaries of the proposed Constitution, for the Convention to adhere to the republican form. They ought, with equal care, to have preserved the *federal* form, which regards the union as a *confederacy* of sovereign States; instead of which, they have framed a *national* government, which regards the union as a *consolidation* of the States. And it is asked by what authority this bold and radical innovation was undertaken. The handle which has been made of this objection requires, that it should be examined with some precision.

Without enquiring into the accuracy of the distinction on which the objection is founded, it will be necessary to a just estimate of its force, first to ascertain the real character of the government in question; secondly, to enquire how far the Convention were authorised to propose such a government; and thirdly, how far the duty they owed to their country, could supply any defect of regular authority.

First. In order to ascertain the real character of the government it may be considered in relation to the foundation on which it is to be established; to the sources from which its ordinary powers are to be drawn; to the operation of those powers; to the extent of them; and to the authority by which future changes in the government are to be introduced.

On examining the first relation, it appears on one hand that the Constitution is to be founded on the assent and ratification of the people of America, given by deputies elected for the special purpose; but on the other, that this assent and ratification is to be given by the people, not as individuals composing one entire nation; but as composing the distinct and independent States to which they respectively belong. It is to be the assent and ratification of the several States, derived from the supreme authority in each State, the authority of the people themselves. The act therefore establishing the Constitution, will not be a *national* but a *federal* act.

That it will be a federal and not a national act, as these terms are understood by the objectors, the act of the people as forming so many independent States, not as forming one aggregate nation, is obvious from this single consideration that it is to result neither from the decision of a *majority* of the people of the Union, nor from that of a *majority* of the States. It must result from the *unanimous* assent of the several States that are parties to it, differing no other wise from their ordinary assent than in its being expressed, not by the legislative authority, but by that of the people themselves. Were the people regarded in this transaction as forming one nation, the will of the majority of the whole people of the United States, would bind the minority; in the same manner as the majority in each State must bind the minority; and the will of the majority must be determined either by a comparison of the individual votes; or by considering the will of a majority of the States, as evidence of the will of a majority of the people of the United States. Neither of these rules has been adopted. Each State in ratifying the Constitution, is considered as a sovereign body independent of all others, and only to be bound by its own voluntary act. In this relation then the new Constitution will, if established, be a *federal* and not a *national* Constitution.

The next relation is to the sources from which the ordinary powers of government are to be derived. The house of representatives will derive its powers from the people of America, and the people will be represented in the same proportion, and on the same principle, as they are in the Legislature of a particular State. So far the Government is *national* not *federal*. The Senate on the other hand will derive its powers from the States, as political and co-equal societies; and these will be represented on the principle of equality in the Senate, as they now are in the existing Congress. So far the government is *federal*, not *national*. The executive power will be derived from a very compound source. The immediate election of the President is to be made by the States in their political characters. The votes allotted to them, are in a compound ratio, which considers them partly as distinct and co-equal societies; partly as unequal members of the same society. The eventual election, again is to be made by that branch of the Legislature which consists of the national representatives; but in this particular act, they are to be thrown into the form of individual delegations from so many distinct and co-equal bodies politic. From this aspect of the Government, it appears to be of a mixed character presenting at least as many *federal* as *national* features.

The difference between a federal and national Government as it relates to the *operation of the Government* is supposed to consist in this, that in the former, the powers operate on the political bodies composing the confederacy, in their political capacities: In the latter, on the individual citizens, composing the nation, in their individual capacities. On trying the Constitution by this criterion, it falls under the *national*, not the *federal* character; though perhaps not so compleatly, as has been understood. In several cases and particularly in the trial of controversies to which States may be parties, they must be viewed and proceeded against in their collective and political capacities only. So far the national countenance of the Government on this side seems to be disfigured by a few federal features. But this blemish is perhaps unavoidable in any plan; and the operation of the Government on the people in their individual capacities, in its ordinary and most essential proceedings, may on the whole designate it in this relation a *national* Government.

But if the Government be national with regard to the *operation* of its powers, it changes its aspect again when we contemplate it in relation to the *extent* of its powers. The idea of a national Government involves in it, not only an authority over the individual citizens; but an indefinite supremacy over all persons and things, so far as they are objects of lawful Government. Among a people consolidated into one nation, this supremacy is compleatly vested in the national Legislature. Among communities united for particular purposes, it is vested partly in the general, and partly in the municipal Legislatures. In the former case, all local authorities are subordinate to the supreme; and may be controuled, directed or abolished by it at pleasure. In the latter the local or municipal authorities form distinct and independent portions of the supremacy, no more subject within their respective spheres to the general authority, than the general authority is subject to them, within its own sphere. In this relation then the proposed Government cannot be deemed a *national* one; since its jurisdiction extends to certain enumerated objects only, and leaves to the several States a residuary and inviolable sovereignty over all other objects. It is true that in controversies relating to the boundary between the two jurisdictions, the tribunal which is ultimately to decide, is to be established under the general Government. But this does not change the principle of the case. The decision is to be impartially made, according to the rules of the Constitution; and all the usual and most effectual precautions are taken to secure this impartiality. Some such tribunal is clearly essential to prevent an appeal to the sword, and a dissolution of the compact; and that it ought to be established under the general, rather than under the local Governments; or to speak more properly, that it could be safely established under the first alone, is a position not likely to be combated.

If we try the Constitution by its last relation, to the authority by which amendments are to be made, we find it neither wholly *national*, nor wholly *federal*. Were it wholly national, the supreme and ultimate authority would reside in the *majority* of the people of the Union; and this authority would be competent at all times, like that of a majority of every national society, to alter or abolish its established Government. Were it wholly federal on the other hand, the concurrence of each State in the Union would be essential to every alteration that would be binding on all. The mode provided by the plan of the Convention is not founded on either of these principles. In requiring more than a majority, and particularly, in computing the proportion by *States*, not by *citizens*, it departs from the *national*, and advances towards the *federal* character: In rendering the concurrence of less than the whole number of States sufficient, it loses again the *federal*, and partakes of the *national* character.

The proposed Constitution therefore is in strictness neither a national nor a federal constitution; but a composition of both. In its foundation, it is federal, not national; in the sources from which the ordinary powers of the Government are drawn, it is partly federal, and partly national: in the operation of these powers, it is national, not federal: In the extent of them again, it is federal, not national: And finally, in the authoritative mode of introducing amendments, it is neither wholly federal, nor wholly national.

28

FEDERAL FARMER, NO. 17
23 Jan. 1788
Storing 2.8.204–5, 210, 213

I believe the people of the United States are full in the opinion, that a free and mild government can be preserved in their extensive territories, only under the substantial forms of a federal republic. As several of the ablest advocates for the system proposed, have acknowledged this (and I hope the confessions they have published will be preserved and remembered) I shall not take up time to establish this point. A question then arises, how far that system partakes of a federal republic.—I observed in a former letter, that it appears to be the first important step to a consolidation of the states; that its strong tendency is to that point.

But what do we mean by a federal republic? and what by a consolidated government? To erect a federal republic, we must first make a number of states on republican principles; each state with a government organized for the internal management of its affairs: The states, as such, must unite under a federal head, and delegate to it powers to make and execute laws in certain enumerated cases, under certain restrictions; this head may be a single assembly, like the present congress, or the Amphictionic council; or it may consist of a legislature, with one or more branches; of an executive, and of a judiciary. To form a consolidated, or one entire government, there must be no state, or local governments, but all things, persons and property, must be subject to the laws of one legislature alone; to one executive, and one judiciary. Each state government, as the government of New Jersey, &c. is a consolidated, or one entire government, as it respects the counties, towns, citizens and property within the limits of the state.—The state governments are the basis, the pillar on which the federal head is placed, and the whole together, when formed on elective principles, constitute a federal republic. A federal republic in itself supposes state or local governments to exist, as the body or props, on which the federal head rests, and that it cannot remain a moment after they cease. In erecting the federal government, and always in its councils, each state must be known as a sovereign body; but in erecting this government, I conceive, the legislature of the state, by the expressed or implied assent of the people, or the people of the state, under the direction of the government of it, may accede to the federal compact: Nor do I conceive it to be necessarily a part of a confederacy of states, that each have an equal voice in the general councils. A confederated republic being organized, each state must retain powers for managing its internal police, and all delegate to the union power to manage general concerns: The quantity of power the union must possess is one thing, the mode of exercising the powers given, is quite a different consideration; and it is the mode of exercising them, that makes one of the essential distinctions between one entire or consolidated government, and a federal republic; that is, however the government may be organized, if the laws of the union, in most important concerns, as in levying and collecting taxes, raising troops, &c. operate immediately upon the persons and property of individuals, and not on states, extend to organizing the militia, &c. the government, as to its administration, as to making and executing laws, is not federal, but consolidated. To illustrate my idea—the union makes a requisition, and assigns to each state its quota of men or monies wanted; each state, by its own laws and officers, in its own way, furnishes its quota: here the state governments stand between the union and individuals; the laws of the union operate only on states, as such, and federally: Here nothing can be done without the meetings of the state legislatures—but in the other case the union, though the state legislatures should not meet for years together, proceeds immediately, by its own laws and officers, to levy and collect monies of individuals, to inlist men, form armies, &c. [H]ere the laws of the union operate immediately on the body of the people, on persons and property; in the same manner the laws of one entire consolidated government operate.—These two modes are very distinct, and in their operation and consequences have directly opposite tendencies: The first makes the existence of the state governments indispensable, and throws all the detail business of levying and collecting the taxes, &c. into the hands of those governments, and into the hands, of course, of many thousand officers solely created by, and dependent on the state. The last entirely excludes the agency of the respective states, and throws the whole business of levying and collecting taxes, &c. into the hands of many thousand officers solely created by, and dependent upon the union, and makes the existence of the state government of no consequence in the case. It is true, congress in raising any given sum in direct taxes, must by the constitution, raise so much of it in one state, and so much in another, by a fixed rule, which most of the states some time since agreed to: But this does not effect the principle in question, it only secures each state against any arbitrary proportions. The federal mode is perfectly safe and eligible, founded in the true spirit of a confederated republic; there could be no possible exception to it, did we not find by experience, that the states will sometimes neglect to comply with the reasonable requisitions of the union. It being according to the fundamental principles of federal republics, to raise men and monies by requisitions, and for the states individually to organize and train the militia, I conceive, there can be no reason whatever for departing from them, except this, that the states sometimes neglect to comply with reasonable requisitions, and that it is dangerous to attempt to compel a delinquent state by force, as it may often produce a war. We ought, therefore, to enquire attentively, how extensive the evils to be guarded against are, and cautiously limit the remedies to the extent of the evils.

. . . . .

There are two ways further of raising checks, and guarding against undue combinations and influence in a federal system. The first is, in levying taxes, raising and keeping up armies, in building navies, in forming plans for the militia, and in appropriating monies for the support of the military, to require the attendance of a large proportion of the federal representatives, as two-thirds or three-fourths of them; and in passing laws, in these important cases, to require the consent of two-thirds or three-fourths of the members present. The second is, by requiring that certain important laws of the federal head, as a requisition or a law for raising monies by excise shall be laid before the state legislatures, and if disapproved of by a given number of them, say by as many of them as represent a majority of the people, the law shall have no effect. Whether it would be adviseable to adopt both, or either of these checks, I will not undertake to determine. We have seen them both exist in confederated republics. The first exists substantially in the confederation, and will exist in some measure in the plan proposed, as in chusing a president by the house, in expelling members; in the senate, in making treaties, and in deciding on impeachments, and in the whole in altering the constitution. The last exists in the United Netherlands, but in a much greater extent. The first is founded on this principle, that these important measures may, sometimes, be adopted by a bare quorum of members, perhaps, from a few states, and that a bare majority of the federal representatives may frequently be of the aristocracy, or some particular interests, connections, or parties in the community, and governed by motives, views, and inclinations not compatible with the general interest.—The last is founded on this principle, that the people will be substantially represented, only in their state or local assemblies; that their principal security must be found in them; and that, therefore, they ought to have ultimately a constitutional controul over such interesting measures.

. . . . .

It has been asserted, that the confederate head of a republic at best, is in general weak and dependent;—that the people will attach themselves to, and support their local governments, in all disputes with the union. Admit the fact: is it any way to remove the inconvenience by accumulating powers upon a weak organization? The fact is, that the detail administration of affairs, in this mixed republics, depends principally on the local governments; and the people would be wretched without them: and a great proportion of social happiness depends on the internal administration of justice, and on internal police. The splendor of the monarch, and the power of the government are one thing. The happiness of the subject depends on very different causes: but it is to the latter, that the best men, the greatest ornaments of human nature, have most carefully attended: it is to the former tyrants and oppressors have always aimed.

29

JAMES MADISON, FEDERALIST, NO. 45, 308–14
26 Jan. 1788

Having shewn that no one of the powers transferred to the federal Government is unnecessary or improper, the next question to be considered is whether the whole mass of them will be dangerous to the portion of authority left in the several States.

The adversaries to the plan of the Convention instead of considering in the first place what degree of power was absolutely necessary for the purposes of the federal Government, have exhausted themselves in a secondary enquiry into the possible consequences of the proposed degree of power, to the Governments of the particular States. But if the Union, as has been shewn, be essential, to the security of the people of America against foreign danger; if it be essential to their security against contentions and wars among the different States; if it be essential to guard them against those violent and oppressive factions which embitter the blessing of liberty, and against those military establishments which must gradually poison its very fountain; if, in a word the Union be essential to the happiness of the people of America, is it not preposterous, to urge as an objection to a government without which the objects of the Union cannot be attained, that such a Government may derogate from the importance of the Governments of the individual States? Was then the American revolution effected, was the American confederacy formed, was the precious blood of thousands spilt, and the hard earned substance of millions lavished, not that the people of America should enjoy peace, liberty and safety; but that the Governments of the individual States, that particular municipal establishments, might enjoy a certain extent of power, and be arrayed with certain dignities and attributes of sovereignty? We have heard of the impious doctrine in the old world that the people were made for kings, not kings for the people. Is the same doctrine to be revived in the new, in another shape, that the solid happiness of the people is to be sacrificed to the views of political institutions of a different form? It is too early for politicians to presume on our forgetting that the public good, the real welfare of the great body of the people is the supreme object to be pursued; and that no form of Government whatever, has any other value, than as it may be fitted for the attainment of this object. Were the plan of the Convention adverse to the public happiness, my voice would be, reject the plan. Were the Union itself inconsistent with the public happiness, it would be, abolish the Union. In like manner as far as the sovereignty of the States cannot be reconciled to the happiness of the people, the voice of every good citizen must be, let the former be sacrificed to the latter. How far the sacrifice is necessary, has been shewn. How far the unsacrificed residue will be endangered, is the question before us.

Several important considerations have been touched in

the course of these papers, which discountenance the supposition that the operation of the federal Government will by degrees prove fatal to the State Governments. The more I revolve the subject the more fully I am persuaded that the balance is much more likely to be disturbed by the preponderancy of the last than of the first scale.

We have seen in all the examples of antient and modern confederacies, the strongest tendency continually betraying itself in the members to despoil the general Government of its authorities, with a very ineffectual capacity in the latter to defend itself against the encroachments. Although in most of these examples, the system has been so dissimilar from that under consideration, as greatly to weaken any inference concerning the latter from the fate of the former; yet as the States will retain under the proposed Constitution a very extensive portion of active sovereignty, the inference ought not to be wholly disregarded. In the Achaean league, it is probable that the federal head had a degree and species of power, which gave it considerable likeness to the government framed by the Convention. The Lycian confederacy, as far as its principles and form are transmitted, must have borne a still greater analogy to it. Yet history does not inform us that either of them ever degenerated or tended to degenerate into one consolidated government. On the contrary, we know that the ruin of one of them proceeded from the incapacity of the federal authority to prevent the dissentions, and finally the disunion of the subordinate authorities. These cases are the more worthy of our attention, as the external causes by which the component parts were pressed together, were much more numerous and powerful than in our case; and consequently, less powerful ligaments within, would be sufficient to bind the members to the head, and to each other.

In the feudal system we have seen a similar propensity exemplified. Notwithstanding the want of proper sympathy in every instance between the local sovereigns and the people, and the sympathy in some instances between the general sovereign and the latter; it usually happened that the local sovereigns prevailed in the rivalship for encroachments. Had no external dangers, enforced internal harmony and subordination; and particularly had the local sovereigns possessed the affections of the people, the great kingdoms in Europe, would at this time consist of as many independent princes as there were formerly feudatory barons.

The State Governments will have the advantage of the federal Government, whether we compare them in respect to the immediate dependence of the one or the other; to the weight of personal influence which each side will possess; to the powers respectively vested in them; to the predilection and probable support of the people; to the disposition and faculty of resisting and frustrating the measures of each other.

The State Governments may be regarded as constituent and essential parts of the federal Government; whilst the latter is nowise essential to the operation or organisation of the former. Without the intervention of the State Legislatures, the President of the United States cannot be elected at all. They must in all cases have a great share in his appointment, and will perhaps in most cases of themselves determine it. The Senate will be elected absolutely and exclusively by the State Legislatures. Even the House of Representatives, though drawn immediately from the people, will be chosen very much under the influence of that class of men, whose influence over the people obtains for themselves an election into the State Legislatures. Thus each of the principal branches of the federal Government will owe its existence more or less to the favor of the State Governments, and must consequently feel a dependence, which is much more likely to beget a disposition too obsequious, than too overbearing towards them. On the other side, the component parts of the State Governments will in no instance be indebted for their appointment to the direct agency of the federal government, and very little if at all, to the local influence of its members.

The number of individuals employed under the Constitution of the United States, will be much smaller, than the number employed under the particular States. There will consequently be less of personal influence on the side of the former, than of the latter. The members of the legislative, executive and judiciary departments of thirteen and more States; the justices of peace, officers of militia, ministerial officers of justice, with all the county corporation and town-officers, for three millions and more of people, intermixed and having particular acquaintance with every class and circle of people, must exceed beyond all proportion, both in number and influence, those of every description who will be employed in the administration of the federal system. Compare the members of the three great departments, of the thirteen States, excluding from the judiciary department the justices of peace, with the members of the corresponding departments of the single Government of the Union; compare the militia officers of three millions of people, with the military and marine officers of any establishment which is within the compass of probability, or I may add, of possibility, and in this view alone, we may pronounce the advantage of the States to be decisive. If the federal Government is to have collectors of revenue, the State Governments will have theirs also. And as those of the former will be principally on the sea-coast, and not very numerous; whilst those of the latter will be spread over the face of the country, and will be very numerous, the advantage in this view also lies on the same side. It is true that the confederacy is to possess, and may exercise, the power of collecting internal as well as external taxes throughout the States: But it is probable that this power will not be resorted to, except for supplemental purposes of revenue; that an option will then be given to the States to supply their quotas by previous collections of their own; and that the eventual collection under the immediate authority of the Union, will generally be made by the officers, and according to the rules, appointed by the several States. Indeed it is extremely probable that in other instances, particularly in the organisation of the judicial power, the officers of the States will be cloathed with the correspondent authority of the Union. Should it happen however that separate collectors of internal revenue should be appointed under the federal Government, the influence of the whole number would not be a comparison with that of the multitude of State officers in the opposite scale. Within every district, to which a federal collector would be allotted, there would not be less than thirty or forty or even more officers of different descriptions and many of them persons of character and weight, whose influence would lie on the side of the State.

The powers delegated by the proposed Constitution to the Federal Government, are few and defined. Those which are to remain in the State Governments are numerous and indefinite. The former will be exercised principally on external objects, as war, peace, negociation, and foreign commerce; with which last the power of taxation will for the most part be connected. The powers reserved to the several States will extend to all the objects, which, in the ordinary course of affairs, concern the lives, liberties and properties of the people; and the internal order, improvement, and prosperity of the State.

The operations of the Federal Government will be most extensive and important in times of war and danger; those of the State Governments, in times of peace and security. As the former periods will probably bear a small proportion to the latter, the State Governments will here enjoy another advantage over the Federal Government. The more adequate indeed the federal powers may be rendered to the national defence, the less frequent will be those scenes of danger which might favour their ascendency over the governments of the particular States.

If the new Constitution be examined with accuracy and candour, it will be found that the change which it proposes, consists much less in the addition of NEW POWERS to the Union, than in the invigoration of its ORIGINAL POWERS. The regulation of commerce, it is true, is a new power; but that seems to be an addition which few oppose, and from which no apprehensions are entertained. The powers relating to war and peace, armies and fleets, treaties and finance, with the other more considerable powers, are all vested in the existing Congress by the articles of Confederation. The proposed change does not enlarge these powers; it only substitutes a more effectual mode of administering them. The change relating to taxation, may be regarded as the most important: And yet the present Congress have as compleat authority to REQUIRE of the States indefinite supplies of money for the common defence and general welfare, as the future Congress will have to require them of individual citizens; and the latter will be no more bound than the States themselves have been, to pay the quotas respectively taxed on them. Had the States complied punctually with the articles of confederation, or could their compliance have been enforced by as peaceable means as may be used with success towards single persons, our past experience is very far from countenancing an opinion that the State Governments would have lost their constitutional powers, and have gradually undergone an entire consolidation. To maintain that such an event would have ensued, would be to say at once, that the existence of the State Governments is incompatible with any system whatever that accomplishes the essential purposes of the Union.

30

JAMES MADISON, FEDERALIST, NO. 46, 315–23
29 Jan. 1788

Resuming the subject of the last paper, I proceed to enquire whether the Foederal Government or the State Governments will have the advantage with regard to the predilection and support of the people. Notwithstanding the different modes in which they are appointed, we must consider both of them, as substantially dependent on the great body of the citizens of the United States. I assume this position here as it respects the first, reserving the proofs for another place. The Foederal and State Governments are in fact but different agents and trustees of the people, instituted with different powers, and designated for different purposes. The adversaries of the Constitution seem to have lost sight of the people altogether in their reasonings on this subject; and to have viewed these different establishments, not only as mutual rivals and enemies, but as uncontrouled by any common superior in their efforts to usurp the authorities of each other. These gentlemen must here be reminded of their error. They must be told that the ultimate authority, wherever the derivative may be found, resides in the people alone; and that it will not depend merely on the comparative ambition or address of the different governments, whether either, or which of them, will be able to enlarge its sphere of jurisdiction at the expence of the other. Truth no less than decency requires, that the event in every case, should be supposed to depend on the sentiments and sanction of their common constituents.

Many considerations, besides those suggested on a former occasion, seem to place it beyond doubt, that the first and most natural attachment of the people will be to the governments of their respective States. Into the administration of these, a greater number of individuals will expect to rise. From the gift of these a greater number of offices and emoluments will flow. By the superintending care of these, all the more domestic, and personal interests of the people will be regulated and provided for. With the affairs of these, the people will be more familiarly and minutely conversant. And with the members of these, will a greater proportion of the people have the ties of personal acquaintance and friendship, and of family and party attachments; on the side of these therefore the popular bias, may well be expected most strongly to incline.

Experience speaks the same language in this case. The foederal administration, though hitherto very defective, in comparison with what may be hoped under a better system, had during the war, and particularly, whilst the independent fund of paper emissions was in credit, an activity and importance as great as it can well have, in any future circumstances whatever. It was engaged too in a course of measures, which had for their object, the protection of every thing that was dear, and the acquisition of every thing that could be desireable to the people at large.

It was nevertheless, invariably found, after the transient enthusiasm for the early Congresses was over, that the attention and attachment of the people were turned anew to their own particular government; that the Foederal Council, was at no time the idol of popular favor; and that opposition to proposed enlargements of its powers and importance, was the side usually taken by the men who wished to build their political consequence on the prepossessions of their fellow citizens.

If therefore, as has been elsewhere remarked, the people should in future become more partial to the foederal than to the State governments, the change can only result, from such manifest and irresistible proofs of a better administration, as will overcome all their antecedent propensities. And in that case, the people ought not surely to be precluded from giving most of their confidence where they may discover it to be most due: But even in that case, the State governments could have little to apprehend, because it is only within a certain sphere, that the foederal power can, in the nature of things, be advantageously administered.

The remaining points on which I proposed to compare the foederal and State governments, are the disposition, and the faculty they may respectively possess, to resist and frustrate the measures of each other.

It has been already proved, that the members of the foederal will be more dependent on the members of the State governments, than the latter will be on the former. It has appeared also, that the prepossessions of the people on whom both will depend, will be more on the side of the State governments, than of the Foederal Government. So far as the disposition of each, towards the other, may be influenced by these causes, the State governments must clearly have the advantage. But in a distinct and very important point of view, the advantage will lie on the same side. The prepossessions which the members themselves will carry into the Foederal Government, will generally be favorable to the States; whilst it will rarely happen, that the members of the State governments will carry into the public councils, a bias in favor of the general government. A local spirit will infallibly prevail much more in the members of the Congress, than a national spirit will prevail in the Legislatures of the particular States. Every one knows that a great proportion of the errors committed by the State Legislatures proceeds from the disposition of the members to sacrifice the comprehensive and permanent interest of the State, to the particular and separate views of the counties or districts in which they reside. And if they do not sufficiently enlarge their policy to embrace the collective welfare of their particular State, how can it be imagined, that they will make the aggregate prosperity of the Union, and the dignity and respectability of its government, the objects of their affections and consultations? For the same reason, that the members of the State Legislatures, will be unlikely to attach themselves sufficiently to national objects, the members of the Foederal Legislature will be likely to attach themselves too much to local objects. The States will be to the latter, what counties and towns are to the former. Measures will too often be decided according to their probable effect, not on the national pros-

perity and happiness, but on the prejudices, interests and pursuits of the governments and people of the individual States. What is the spirit that has in general characterized the proceedings of Congress? A perusal of their journals as well as the candid acknowledgments of such as have had a seat in that assembly, will inform us, that the members have but too frequently displayed the character, rather of partizans of their respective States, than of impartial guardians of a common interest; that whereon one occasion improper sacrifices have been made of local considerations to the aggrandizement of the Foederal Government; the great interests of the nation have suffered on an hundred, from an undue attention to the local prejudices, interests and views of the particular States. I mean not by these reflections to insinuate, that the new Foederal Government will not embrace a more enlarged plan of policy than the existing government may have pursued, much less that its views will be as confined as those of the State Legislatures; but only that it will partake sufficiently of the spirit of both, to be disinclined to invade the rights of the individual States, or the prerogatives of their governments. The motives on the part of the State governments, to augment their prerogatives by defalcations from the Foederal Government, will be overruled by no reciprocal predispositions in the members.

Were it admitted however that the Foederal Government may feel an equal disposition with the State governments to extend its power beyond the due limits, the latter would still have the advantage in the means of defeating such encroachments. If an act of a particular State, though unfriendly to the national government, be generally popular in that State, and should not too grossly violate the oaths of the State officers, it is executed immediately and of course, by means on the spot, and depending on the State alone. The opposition of the Foederal Government, or the interposition of Foederal officers, would but inflame the zeal of all parties on the side of the State, and the evil could not be prevented or repaired, if at all, without the employment of means which must always be resorted to with reluctance and difficulty. On the other hand, should an unwarrantable measure of the Foederal Government be unpopular in particular States, which would seldom fail to be the case, or even a warrantable measure be so, which may sometimes be the case, the means of opposition to it are powerful and at hand. The disquietude of the people, their repugnance and perhaps refusal to co-operate with the officers of the Union, the frowns of the executive magistracy of the State, the embarrassments created by legislative devices, which would often be added on such occasions, would oppose in any State difficulties not to be despised; would form in a large State very serious impediments, and where the sentiments of several adjoining States happened to be in unison, would present obstructions which the Foederal Government would hardly be willing to encounter.

But ambitious encroachments of the Foederal Government, on the authority of the State governments, would not excite the opposition of a single State or of a few States only. They would be signals of general alarm. Every Government would espouse the common cause. A correspondence would be opened. Plans of resistance would be concerted. One spirit would animate and conduct the whole. The same combination in short would result from an apprehension of the foederal, as was produced by the dread of a foreign yoke; and unless the projected innovations should be voluntarily renounced, the same appeal to a trial of force would be made in the one case, as was made in the other. But what degree of madness could ever drive the Foederal Government to such an extremity? In the contest with Great Britain, one part of the empire was employed against the other. The more numerous part invaded the rights of the less numerous part. The attempt was unjust and unwise; but it was not in speculation absolutely chimerical. But what would be the contest in the case we are supposing? Who would be the parties? A few representatives of the people, would be opposed to the people themselves; or rather one set of representatives would be contending against thirteen sets of representatives, with the whole body of their common constituents on the side of the latter.

The only refuge left for those who prophecy the downfall of the State Governments, is the visionary supposition that the Foederal Government may previously accumulate a military force for the projects of ambition. The reasonings contained in these papers must have been employed to little purpose indeed, if it could be necessary now to disprove the reality of this danger. That the people and the States should for a sufficient period of time elect an uninterrupted succession of men ready to betray both; that the traitors should throughout this period, uniformly and systematically pursue some fixed plan for the extension of the military establishment; that the governments and the people of the States should silently and patiently behold the gathering storm, and continue to supply the materials, until it should be prepared to burst on their own heads, must appear to every one more like the incoherent dreams of a delirious jealousy, or the misjudged exaggerations of a counterfeit zeal, than like the sober apprehensions of genuine patriotism. Extravagant as the supposition is, let it however be made. Let a regular army, fully equal to the resources of the country be formed; and let it be entirely at the devotion of the Foederal Government; still it would not be going too far to say, that the State Governments with the people on their side would be able to repel the danger. The highest number to which, according to the best computation, a standing army can be carried in any country, does not exceed one hundredth part of the whole number of souls; or one twenty-fifth part of the number able to bear arms. This proportion would not yield in the United States an army of more than twenty-five or thirty thousand men. To these would be opposed a militia amounting to near half a million of citizens with arms in their hands, officered by men chosen from among themselves, fighting for their common liberties, and united and conducted by governments possessing their affections and confidence. It may well be doubted whether a militia thus circumstanced could ever be conquered by such a proportion of regular troops. Those who are best acquainted with the late successful resistance of this country against the British arms will be most inclined to deny the possibility of it. Besides the advantage of being armed, which the Americans possess over the people of almost every other nation, the existence of subordinate governments to which the people are attached, and by which the militia officers are appointed, forms a barrier against the enterprizes of ambition, more insurmountable than any which a simple government of any form can admit of. Notwithstanding the military establishments in the several kingdoms of Europe, which are carried as far as the public resources will bear, the governments are afraid to trust the people with arms. And it is not certain that with this aid alone, they would not be able to shake off their yokes. But were the people to possess the additional advantages of local governments chosen by themselves, who could collect the national will, and direct the national force; and of officers appointed out of the militia, by these governments and attached both to them and to the militia, it may be affirmed with the greatest assurance, that the throne of every tyranny in Europe would be speedily overturned, in spite of the legions which surround it. Let us not insult the free and gallant citizens of America with the suspicion that they would be less able to defend the rights of which they would be in actual possession, than the debased subjects of arbitrary power would be to rescue theirs from the hands of their oppressors. Let us rather no longer insult them with the supposition, that they can ever reduce themselves to the necessity of making the experiment, by a blind and tame submission to the long train of insidious measures, which must precede and produce it.

The argument under the present head may be put into a very concise form, which appears altogether conclusive. Either the mode in which the Foederal Government is to be constructed will render it sufficiently dependant on the people, or it will not. On the first supposition, it will be restrained by that dependence from forming schemes obnoxious to their constituents. On the other supposition it will not possess the confidence of the people, and its schemes of usurpation will be easily defeated by the State Governments; who will be supported by the people.

On summing up the considerations stated in this and the last paper, they seem to amount to the most convincing evidence, that the powers proposed to be lodged in the Foederal Government, are as little formidable to those reserved to the individual States, as they are indispensibly necessary to accomplish the purposes of the Union; and that all those alarms which have been sounded, of a meditated or consequential annihilation of the State Governments, must, on the most favorable interpretation, be ascribed to the chimerical fears of the authors of them.

31

BRUTUS, NO. 11
31 Jan. 1788
Storing 2.9.139–42

The judicial power will operate to effect, in the most certain, but yet silent and imperceptible manner, what is evidently the tendency of the constitution:—I mean, an entire subversion of the legislative, executive and judicial powers of the individual states. Every adjudication of the supreme court, on any question that may arise upon the nature and extent of the general government, will affect the limits of the state jurisdiction. In proportion as the former enlarge the exercise of their powers, will that of the latter be restricted.

That the judicial power of the United States, will lean strongly in favour of the general government, and will give such an explanation to the constitution, as will favour an extension of its jurisdiction, is very evident from a variety of considerations.

1st. The constitution itself strongly countenances such a mode of construction. Most of the articles in this system, which convey powers of any considerable importance, are conceived in general and indefinite terms, which are either equivocal, ambiguous, or which require long definitions to unfold the extent of their meaning. The two most important powers committed to any government, those of raising money, and of raising and keeping up troops, have already been considered, and shewn to be unlimitted by any thing but the discretion of the legislature. The clause which vests the power to pass all laws which are proper and necessary, to carry the powers given into execution, it has been shewn, leaves the legislature at liberty, to do every thing, which in their judgment is best. It is said, I know, that this clause confers no power on the legislature, which they would not have had without it—though I believe this is not the fact, yet, admitting it to be, it implies that the constitution is not to receive an explanation strictly, according to its letter; but more power is implied than is expressed. And this clause, if it is to be considered, as explanatory of the extent of the powers given, rather than giving a new power, is to be understood as declaring, that in construing any of the articles conveying power, the spirit, intent and design of the clause, should be attended to, as well as the words in their common acceptation.

This constitution gives sufficient colour for adopting an equitable construction, if we consider the great end and design it professedly has in view—these appear from its preamble to be, "to form a more perfect union, establish justice, insure domestic tranquility, provide for the common defence, promote the general welfare, and secure the blessings of liberty to ourselves and posterity." The design of this system is here expressed, and it is proper to give such a meaning to the various parts, as will best promote the accomplishment of the end; this idea suggests itself naturally upon reading the preamble, and will countenance the court in giving the several articles such a sense, as will the most effectually promote the ends the constitution had in view—how this manner of explaining the constitution will operate in practice, shall be the subject of future enquiry.

2d. Not only will the constitution justify the courts in inclining to this mode of explaining it, but they will be interested in using this latitude of interpretation. Every body of men invested with office are tenacious of power; they feel interested, and hence it has become a kind of maxim, to hand down their offices, with all its rights and privileges, unimpared to their successors; the same principle will influence them to extend their power, and increase their rights; this of itself will operate strongly upon the courts to give such a meaning to the constitution in all cases where it can possibly be done, as will enlarge the sphere of their own authority. Every extension of the power of the general legislature, as well as of the judicial powers, will increase the powers of the courts; and the dignity and importance of the judges, will be in proportion to the extent and magnitude of the powers they exercise. I add, it is highly probable the emolument of the judges will be increased, with the increase of the business they will have to transact and its importance. From these considerations the judges will be interested to extend the powers of the courts, and to construe the constitution as much as possible, in such a way as to favour it; and that they will do it, appears probable.

32

LUTHER MARTIN, GENUINE INFORMATION
1788
Storing 2.4.39–41

It was urged, that the government we were forming was not in reality a *federal* but a *national* government, not founded on the principles of the *preservation*, but the *abolition* or *consolidation* of all *State governments*—That we appeared *totally to have forgot* the business for which we were sent, and the situation of the country for which we were preparing our system—That we had not been sent to form a government over the *inhabitants* of America, considered as *individuals*, that as individuals they were all subject to their respective State governments, which governments would still remain, tho' the federal government should be dissolved—That the *system of government* we were *entrusted* to prepare, was a government over *these thirteen States;* but that in our proceedings, we adopted principles which would be right and proper, *only* on the supposition that there were *no State governments at all*, but that *all the inhabitants* of this *extensive continent* were in their *individual ca-*

pacity, without government, and in a *state of nature*—That accordingly the system proposes the legislature to consist of *two branches,* the *one* to be drawn from the *people at large,* immediately in their *individual capacity;* the *other* to be chose in a *more select manner,* as a *check* upon the *first*—It is in its very *introduction* declared to be a compact between the *people* of the United States *as individuals,* and it is to be *ratified* by the *people* at large in their capacity *as individuals;* all which it was said, would be quite right and proper, if there were *no State governments,* if *all the people* of this continent were in a *state of nature,* and we were forming one *national* government *for them as individuals,* and is nearly the same as was done in most of the *States,* when they formed their governments *over the people* who compose them.

Whereas it was urged, that the principles on which a *federal* government over *States* ought to be *constructed* and *ratified* are the *reverse;* that instead of the legislature consisting of *two branches, one* branch was sufficient, whether examined by the *dictates* of *reason,* or the *experience* of *ages*—That the representation instead of being drawn from the *people at large* as *individuals,* ought to be drawn from the *States* as *States* in their *sovereign* capacity—That in a *federal* government, the *parties* to the compact are not the *people* as *individuals,* but the *States* as *States,* and that it is by the *States* as *States* in their *sovereign* capacity, that the system of government ought to be *ratified,* and not by the *people* as *individuals.*

It was further said, that in a *federal* government over States *equally* free, sovereign, and independent, *every State* ought to have an equal share in *making* the *federal laws* or *regulations;* in *deciding* upon them, and in *carrying them into execution, neither* of which was the case in *this* system, but the *reverse,* the States not having an *equal voice* in the *legislature,* nor in the *appointment* of the *executive,* the *judges,* and the *other officers of government:* it was insisted, that in the *whole* system there was but *one federal* feature, the appointment of the senators by the States in their sovereign capacity, that is by their legislatures, and the equality of suffrage in that branch; but it was said that *this feature* was only *federal in appearance.*

33

IMPARTIAL EXAMINER, NO. 1
5 Mar. 1788
Storing 5.14.13

I know it is a favorite topic with the advocates for the new government—that it will advance the dignity of Congress; and that the energy, which is now wanting in the foederal system, will be hereby rendered efficient. Nobody doubts, but the government of the union is susceptible of amendment. But can any one think that there is no medium between want of power, and the possession of it in

an unlimited degree? Between the imbecility of mere recommendatory propositions, and the sweeping jurisdiction of exercising every branch of government over the United States to the greatest extent? Between the present feeble texture of the confoederation, and the proposed nervous ligaments? Is it not possible to strengthen the hands of Congress so far as to enable them to comply with all the exigencies of the union—to regulate the great commercial concerns of the continent,—to superintend all affairs, which relate to the United States in their aggregate capacity, without devolving upon that body the supreme powers of government in all its branches? The original institution of Congressional business,—the nature, the end of that institution evince the practicability of such a reform; and shew that it is more honorable, more glorious—and will be more happy for each American state to retain its independent sovereignty. For what can be more truly great in any country than a number of different states in the full enjoyment of liberty—exercising distinct powers of government; yet associated by *one general head,* and under the influence of a mild, just and well-organized confederation duly held in *equilibrio;*—whilst all derive those external advantages, which are the great purposes of the union? This separate independency existing in each—this harmony pervading the whole—this due degree of energy in the foederal department, all together, will form a beautiful *species* of national grandeur. These will add lustre to every member, and spread a glory all around. These will command the admiration of mankind. These will exhibit a bright *specimen* of real dignity, far superior to that immense devolution of power, under which the sovereignty of each state shall shrink to nothing.

34

BRUTUS, NO. 15
20 Mar. 1788
Storing 2.9.194–96

I have, in the course of my observation on this constitution, affirmed and endeavored to shew, that it was calculated to abolish entirely the state governments, and to melt down the states into one entire government, for every purpose as well internal and local, as external and national. In this opinion the opposers of the system have generally agreed—and this has been uniformly denied by its advocates in public. Some individuals, indeed, among them, will confess, that it has this tendency, and scruple not to say, it is what they wish; and I will venture to predict, without the spirit of prophecy, that if it is adopted without amendments, or some such precautions as will ensure amendments immediately after its adoption, that the same gentlemen who have employed their talents and abilities with such success to influence the public mind to adopt this plan, will employ the same to persuade the people, that it will be for their good to abolish the state governments as useless and burdensome.

Perhaps nothing could have been better conceived to facilitate the abolition of the state governments than the constitution of the judicial. They will be able to extend the limits of the general government gradually, and by insensible degrees, and to accommodate themselves to the temper of the people. Their decisions on the meaning of the constitution will commonly take place in cases which arise between individuals, with which the public will not be generally acquainted; one adjudication will form a precedent to the next, and this to a following one. These cases will immediately affect individuals only; so that a series of determinations will probably take place before even the people will be informed of them. In the mean time all the art and address of those who wish for the change will be employed to make converts to their opinion. The people will be told, that their state officers, and state legislatures are a burden and expence without affording any solid advantage, for that all the laws passed by them, might be equally well made by the general legislature. If to those who will be interested in the change, be added, those who will be under their influence, and such who will submit to almost any change of government, which they can be persuaded to believe will ease them of taxes, it is easy to see, the party who will favor the abolition of the state governments would be far from being inconsiderable.—In this situation, the general legislature, might pass one law after another, extending the general and abridging the state jurisdictions, and to sanction their proceedings would have a course of decisions of the judicial to whom the constitution has committed the power of explaining the constitution.— If the states remonstrated, the constitutional mode of deciding upon the validity of the law, is with the supreme court, and neither people, nor state legislatures, nor the general legislature can remove them or reverse their decrees.

Had the construction of the constitution been left with the legislature, they would have explained it at their peril; if they exceed their powers, or sought to find, in the spirit of the constitution, more than was expressed in the letter, the people from whom they derived their power could remove them, and do themselves right; and indeed I can see no other remedy that the people can have against their rulers for encroachments of this nature. A constitution is a compact of a people with their rulers; if the rulers break the compact, the people have a right and ought to remove them and do themselves justice; but in order to enable them to do this with the greater facility, those whom the people chuse at stated periods, should have the power in the last resort to determine the sense of the compact; if they determine contrary to the understanding of the people, an appeal will lie to the people at the period when the rulers are to be elected, and they will have it in their power to remedy the evil; but when this power is lodged in the hands of men independent of the people, and of their representatives, and who are not, constitutionally, accountable for their opinions, no way is left to controul them but *with a high hand and an outstretched arm.*

35

THE FALLACIES OF THE FREEMAN DETECTED BY A [PENNSYLVANIA] FARMER
23 Apr. 1788
Storing 3.14.6–21

I shall proceed to define a FEDERAL REPUBLIC:—A Federal Republic is formed by two or more single or consolidated republics, uniting together by a perpetual confederacy, and without ceasing to be distinct states or sovereignties; they form together a federal republic or an empire of states. As individuals in a state of nature surrender a portion of their natural liberty to the society of which they become members, in order to receive in lieu thereof protection and conveniency; so in forming a federal republic the individual states surrender a part of their separate sovereignty to the general government or federal head, in order that, whilst they respectively enjoy internally the freedom and happiness peculiar to free republics, they may possess all that external protection, security, and weight by their confederated resources, that can possibly be obtained in the most extended, absolute monarchies.

The peculiar advantages and distinctive properties of a federal republic are, that each state or member of the confederation may be fully adequate for every local purpose, that it may subsist in a small territory, that the people may have a common interest, possess a competent knowledge of the resources and expenditures of their own particular government, that their immediate representatives in the state governments will know and be known by the citizens, will have a common interest with them, and must bear a part of all the burdens which they may lay upon the people, that they will be responsible to the people, and may be dismissed by them at pleasure; that therefore the government would be a government of confidence and possess sufficient energy without the aid of standing armies, that the collectors of the revenue would at least have the bowels of citizens, and not be the offscourings of Europe, or other states who have no interest in, or attachment to the people; that if one or more of the states should become the prey of internal despotism, or foreign foes, the other states may remain secure under the protection of their own state government; that if some popular and wealthy citizen should have influence enough to attempt the liberties of one state, he might be stopped in his career by the interposition of the others, for his influence could not be equally great in all the states; that if the general government should fail, or be revised or changed, yet the several state governments may remain entire to secure the happiness of the citizens; and that the members of a confederated republic may be encreased to any amount, and consequently its external strength without altering the nature of the government, or endangering the liberty of the citizens.

The perfection of a federal republic consists in drawing the proper line between those objects of sovereignty which are of a general nature, and which ought to be vested in the federal government, and those which are of a more local nature and ought to remain with the particular governments; any rule that can be laid down for this must vary according to the situation and circumstances of the confederating states; yet still this general rule will hold good, viz. that all that portion of sovereignty which involve the common interest of all the confederating states, and which cannot be exercised by the states in their individual capacity without endangering the liberty and welfare of the whole, ought to be vested in the general government, reserving such a proportion of sovereignty in the state governments as would enable them to exist alone, if the general government should fail either by violence or with the common consent of the confederates; the states should respectively have laws, courts, force, and revenues of their own sufficient for their own security; they ought to be fit to keep house alone if necessary; if this be not the case, or so far as it ceases to be so, it is a departure from a federal to a consolidated government; and this brings me to the next particular, which is to shew what is meant by a consolidated government.

Thirdly. The idea of a CONSOLIDATED GOVERNMENT is easily understood, where a single society or nation forms one entire separate government, and possess the whole sovereign power; this is a consolidated or national government. Whether a government be of a monarchical, aristocratical or democratical nature, it doth not alter the case, it is either a federal or a consolidated government, there being no medium as to kind.—The absoluteness of a despotic sovereignty is often restricted by corporate bodies, who are vested with peculiar privileges and franchises— and by a just distribution of the executive and ministerial powers; but although these may contribute to the happiness of the people, yet they do not change the nature of the government. Indeed, monarchies can never form a federal government; they may enter into alliances with each other; for monarchy cannot be divested of a competent proportion of sovereignty to form a general government without changing its nature. It is only free republics that can completely and safely form a federal republic; I say free republics, for there are republics who are not free, such as Venice, where a citizen carrying arms is punished with instant death, and where even the nobles dare not converse with strangers, and scarcely with their friends, and are liable by law to be put to death secretly without trial—or Poland which, in much the same words that are expressed in the new system, is by a league with the neighbouring powers guaranteed to be forever independent and of a republican form; yet a writer of their own says, that the body of the people are scarcely to be distinguished from brutes; and again he says, we have reduced the people of our kingdom by misery to a state of brutes; they drag out their days in stupidity, &c. Free republics are congenial to a federal republic. In order that a republic may preserve its liberty, it must not only have a good form of government, but it must be of small extent; for if it

possess extensive territory, it would be ruined by internal imperfection. The authority of government in a large republic does not equally pervade all the parts; nor are the political advantages equally enjoyed by the citizens remote from the capital as by those in the vicinity; combinations consequently prevail among the members of the legislature, and this introduces corruption and is destructive of that confidence in government, without which a free republic cannot be supported; besides, the high influential trusts which must be vested in the great officers of state, would at particular times endanger the government, and are necessarily destructive of that equality among the citizens, which is the only permanent basis of a republic; in short, the diversity of the situation, habits, manners, and interests of the people in an extensive dominion, subjects the government to a thousand accidents, which would embarrass a republican government. The experience of nations and the nature of things, sufficiently prove, that the government of a single person, aided by armies and controuling influence, is necessary to govern a large consolidated empire.

And on the other hand, if the territory be small, the republic is liable to be destroyed by external force, therefore, reason and observation points out a confederation of republics, as the only method to preserve internal freedom, together with external strength and respectability.— Small republics forming a federal republic on these principles, may be resembled to divers small ropes plaited together to make a large and strong one, if the latter is untwisted, the small ropes are still useful as such, but if the former are untwisted, they are reduced to hemp, the original state.

To apply these principles to our present situation without respect to the proposed plan of government; in order to render the federal government adequate to the exigencies of the confederating states, it is necessary not only that the general government should be properly constructed in its forms, but that it should be vested with powers relative to all the federal objects of government, these objects are not only the powers of making peace and war, &c. but also with the power of making treaties respecting commerce, regulating and raising revenues therefrom, &c. to make requisitions of money when necessity requires it, from each of the states, and a certain well described power of compelling delinquent states to pay up their quota of such requisitions. Perhaps if each state had its own share of the domestic debt quotaed, so as they might each pay their own citizens, the general revenues would be sufficient for the other demands of the union in times of peace, if the government itself be not made too expensive by too great a number of officers being created. Congress ought, however, to have all powers which cannot be exercised by one state, without endangering the other states, such as the power of raising troops, treating with foreign nations, &c.—The power of levying imposts, will, by the particular states, be irregularly exercised, and the revenue in a great degree lost or misapplied, therefore, it ought not to be left with the states, but under proper checks, vested in the general government. All these the minority were amongst the foremost willing to have vested in the federal head, and more than this, had never been asked by Congress, nor proposed by the greatest advocates for congressional power, nor is more than this consistent with the nature of a federal republic. When the existing confederation was adopted, powers were given with a sparing hand, and per-haps, not improperly at that period, until experience should point out the discriminating line with sufficient ex-perience, well knowing that it is easy for a government to obtain an encrease of power when common utility points out the propriety, but that powers once vested in a govern-ment, however dangerous they may prove, are rarely re-covered without bloodshed, and even that awful method of regaining lost liberty is seldom effectual. It is now how-ever evident that the power of regulating commerce, being of a general nature, ought to belong to the general gov-ernment, and the burthen of debt incurred by the revolu-tion hath rendered a general revenue necessary, for this purpose imposts upon articles of importation present themselves, not only as a productive source of revenue, but as a revenue for which the governments of the partic-ular states are for well known reasons, incompetent.—The danger of entrusting a government so far out of the peo-ple's reach as Congress must necessarily be, strongly im-pressed the public mind about four or five years since, but now a conviction of the advantage and probable safety of such a measure, pervades almost every mind, and none are more willing for putting it in operation, under proper guards, than the opposers of the new system; they are also willing to admit what the majority of the states may judge proper checks in the *form* of the general government, as far as those checks, or the distribution of powers and re-sponsibility of those who be vested with those powers, may be consistent with the security of the essential sovereignty of the respective states. The minority of the convention (who I really believe, in their address, express the serious sentiments of the majority of this state) opposed vesting such powers in Congress as can be most effectually exer-cised by the state governments in a full consistency with the general interests of the confederating states, and which, not being of a general nature, are not upon federal principles, objects of the federal government, I mean the power of capitation, or poll tax, by which the head, or in other words, the existence of every person is put in their power by the new system as a property, subject to any price or tax that may be judged proper; I do not mean to say that this implies the power of life and death, although it certainly implies the power of selling the property, or if none is to be had, of imprisoning or selling the person for a servant, who doth not chuse, or is not able to pay the poll tax; the minority also objected to vesting Congress with power to tax the property, real and personal of the citizens of the several states, to what amount, and in what manner it may please, without any check or controul upon its discretion; also to the unlimitted power over the excise; if this could extend only to spirituous liquors as is usual with us, the danger would be less, but the power of excise extends to every thing we eat, drink, or wear, and in Eu-rope it is thus extensively put in practice. Under the term duties, every species of indirect taxes is included, but it

especially means the power of levying money upon printed books, and written instruments.

The Congress, by the proposed system, have the power of borrowing money to what amount they may judge proper, consequently to mortgage all our estates, and all our sources of revenue. The exclusive power of emmitting bills of credit is also reserved to Congress. They have, moreover, the power of instituting courts of justice with-out tryal by jury, except in criminal cases, and under such regulations as Congress may think proper to decide, not only in such cases as arise out of all the foregoing powers, but in the other cases which are enumerated in the system.

The absolute sovereignty in all the foregoing instances, as well as several others not here enumerated, are vested in the general government, without being subject to any constitutional check or controul from the state govern-ments.

It remains to examine the nature of the powers which are left with the states, and on this subject it is not neces-sary to follow *Freeman* through the numerous detail of particulars with which he confuses the reader. I shall ex-amine only a few of the more considerable. The *Freeman* in his 2d Number, after mentioning in a very delusory manner divers powers which remain with the states, he says we shall find many other instances under the consti-tution which require or imply the existence or continuance of the sovereignty and severalty of the states; he as well as all the advocates of the new system, take as their strong ground the election of senators by the state legislatures, and the special representation of the states in the federal senate, to prove that internal sovereignty still remains with the states; therefore they say that the new system is so far from annihilating the state governments, that it secures them, that it cannot exist without them, that the existence of the one is essential to the existence of the other. It is true that this particular partakes strongly of that mystery which is characteristic of the system itself; but if I demon-strate that this particular, so far from implying the contin-uance of the state sovereignties, proves in the clearest manner the want of it, I hope the other particular powers will not be necessary to dwell upon.

The state legislatures do not chuse senators by legislative or sovereign authority, but by a power of ministerial agency as mere electors or boards of appointment; they have no power to direct the senators how or what duties they shall perform; they have neither power to censure the senators, nor to supercede them for misconduct. It is not the power of chusing to office merely that designates sov-ereignty, or else corporations who appoint their own offi-cers and make their own bye-laws, or the heads of depart-ment who chuse the officers under them, such as commanders of armies, &c. may be called sovereigns, be-cause they can name men to office whom they cannot dis-miss therefrom. The exercise of sovereignty does not con-sist in chusing masters, such as the senators would be, who, when chosen, would be beyond controul, but in the power of dismissing, impeaching, or the like, those to whom au-thority is delegated. The power of instructing or superced-ing of delegates to Congress under the existing confeder-ation, hath never been complained of, altho' the necessary rotation of members of Congress hath often been censured for restraining the state sovereignties too much in the objects of their choice. As well may the electors who are to vote for the president under the new constitution, be said to be vested with the sovereignty, as the state legislatures in the act of chusing senators. The senators are not even dependent on the states for their wages, but in conjunction with the federal representatives establish their own wages. The senators do not vote by states, but as individuals. The representatives also vote as individuals, representing people in a consolidated or national government; they judge upon their own elections, and, with the senate, have the power of regulating elections in time, place and manner, which is in other words to say, that they have the power of elections absolutely vested in them.

That the state governments have certain ministerial and convenient powers continued to them is not denied, and in the exercise of which they may support, but cannot controul the general government, nor protect their own citizens from the exertions of civil or military tyranny, and this ministerial power will continue with the states as long as two-thirds of Congress shall think their agency necessary; but even this will be no longer than two-thirds of Congress shall think proper to propose, and use the influence of which they would be so largely possessed to remove it.

But these powers, of which the *Freeman* gives us such a profuse detail, and in describing which he repeats the same powers with only varying the terms, such as the powers of officering and training the militia, appointing state officers, and governing in a number of internal cases, do not any of them separately, nor all taken together, amount to independent sovereignty; they are powers of mere ministerial agency, which may, and in many nations of Europe, are or have been vested, as before observed, in heads of departments, hereditary vassals of the crown, or in corporations; but not that kind of independent sovereignty which can constitute a member of a federal republic, which can enable a state to exist within itself if the general government should cease.

I have often wondered how any writer of sense could have the confidence to avow, or could suppose the people to be ignorant enough to believe, that, when a state is deprived of the power not only of standing armies (this the members of a confederacy ought to be) but of commanding its own militia, regulating its elections, directing or superceding its representatives or paying them their wages; who is, moreover, deprived of the command of any property, I mean source of revenue or taxation, or what amounts to the same thing, who may enact laws for raising revenue, but who may have these laws rendered nugatory, and the execution thereof superceded by the laws of Congress. This is not a strained construction, but the natural operation of the powers of Congress under the new constitution; for every object of revenue, every source of taxation, is vested in the general government. Even the power of making inspection laws, which, for obvious conveniency, is left with the several states, will be unproductive of the smallest revenue to the state governments; for, if any should arise, it is to be paid over to the coffers of Congress;—besides, the words "to make all laws necessary and proper for carrying into execution the foregoing powers, &c." give, without doubt, the power of repelling or forbidding the execution of any tax law whatever that may interfere with or impede the exercise of the general taxing power, and it would not be possible that two taxing powers should be exercised on the same sources of taxation without interfering with each other. May not the exercise of this power of Congress, when they think proper, operate not only to destroy those ministerial powers which are left with the states, but even the very forms? May they not forbid the state legislatures to levy a shilling to pay themselves, or those whom they employ, days wages? The state governments may contract for making roads (except postroads) erecting bridges, cutting canals, or any other object of public importance; but when the contract is performed or the work done, may not Congress constitutionally prevent the payment? Certainly they may do all this and much more, and no man would have a right to charge them with breaking the law of their appointment. It is an established maxim, that wherever the whole power of the revenue or taxation is vested, there virtually is the whole effective, influential, sovereign power, let the forms be what they may: By this armies are procured, by this every other controuling guard is defeated. Every balance or check in government is only so far effective as it hath a controul over the revenue.

The state governments are not only destitute of all sovereign command of, or controul over, the revenue or any part of it, but they are divested of the power of commanding, or prescribing the duties, wages, or punishments of their own militia, or of protecting their life, property or characters from the rigours of martial law. The power of making treason laws is both a flower and an important defence of sovereignty; it is relative to and inseparable from it; to convince the states that they are consolidated into one national government, this power is wholly to be assumed by the general government. All the prerogatives, all the essential characteristics of sovereignty, both of the internal and external kind, are vested in the general government, and consequently the several states would not be possessed of any essential power, or effective guard of sovereignty.

Thus I apprehend, it is evident that the consolidation of the states, into one national government (in contradistinction from a confederacy) would be the necessary consequence of the establishment of the new constitution, and the intention of its framers—and that consequently the state sovereignties would be eventually annihilated, though the forms may long remain as expensive and burthensome remembrances, of what they were in the days when (although labouring under many disadvantages) they emancipated this country from foreign tyranny, humbled the pride, and tarnished the glory of royalty, and erected a triumphant standard to liberty and independence.

It it not my present object to decide, whether the government is a good or a bad one, it is only to prove in support of the minority, that the new system does not in reality, whatever its appearances may be, constitute a federal but a consolidated government.—From the distinguishing characteristics of these two kinds of government which I have stated, some assistance perhaps may be derived in judging which of them would be most suitable to our circumstances, and the best calculated to promote and secure the liberty and welfare of these United States.

36

IMPARTIAL EXAMINER, NO. 2
28 May 1788
Storing 5.14.25–26

These writers [in favor of the proposed Constitution] seem not to regard any fundamentals in government, provided they can procure a plan, in which they fancy some prospects of immediate benefit are to be discovered. In conformity with the stile of the *proposed constitution,* the favorers of it have, with a peculiarity of self-applause, ascribed to themselves the distinction of foederalists; while those, who oppose the plan are marked with the epithet of anti-foederal.

The strong desire, which has been manifested, for a union between the American states, since the revolution, affords an opportunity of making the distinction, as they imagine, to their advantage.—As *foederalists,* in their opinion, they must be deemed friendly to the *union:*—as *anti-foederal,* the opposers must, in their opinion too, be considered unfriendly. Thus on the sound of names they build their fame.

For those gentlemen, however, let it be observed that the opponents seem to act on the broader scale of true *foederal principles.* The advocates for the new code wi[s]h all sovereignty to be lodged in the hands of Congress. This is not to connect thirteen independent states—but to form one extended empire by compounding the whole, and thus destroying the sovereignty of each. The other party desire a continuance of each distinct sovereignty—and are anxious for such a degree of energy in the general government, as will cement the union in the strongest manner. This they consider as one of the greatest blessings, which can attend their country.

37

GEORGE MASON, VIRGINIA RATIFYING CONVENTION
4 June 1788
Storing 5.17.1

Mr. Chairman—Whether the Constitution be good or bad, the present clause clearly discovers, that it is a National Government, and no longer a confederation. I mean that clause which gives the first hint of the General Government laying direct taxes. The assumption of this power of laying direct taxes, does of itself, entirely change the confederation of the States into one consolidated Government. This power being at discretion, unconfined, and without any kind of controul, must carry every thing before it. The very idea of converting what was formerly a confederation, to a consolidated Government, is totally subversive of every principle which has hitherto governed us. This power is calculated to annihilate totally the State Governments. Will the people of this great community submit to be individually taxed by two different and distinct powers? Will they suffer themselves to be doubly harrassed? These two concurrent powers cannot exist long together; the one will destroy the other: The General Government being paramount to, and in every respect more powerful than, the State governments, the latter must give way to the former. Is it to be supposed that one National Government will suit so extensive a country, embracing so many climates, and containing inhabitants so very different in manners, habits, and customs? It is ascertained by history, that there never was a Government, over a very extensive country, without destroying the liberties of the people: History also, supported by the opinions of the best writers, shew us, that monarchy may suit a large territory, and despotic Governments over so extensive a country; but that popular Governments can only exist in small territories. Is there a single example, on the face of the earth, to support a contrary opinion? Where is there one exception to this general rule? Was there ever an instance of a general National Government extending over so extensive a country, abounding in such a variety of climates, &c. where the people retained their liberty? I solemnly declare, that no man is a greater friend to a firm Union of the American States than I am: But, Sir, if this great end can be obtained without hazarding the rights of the people, why should we recur to such dangerous principles?

38

PATRICK HENRY, VIRGINIA RATIFYING CONVENTION
4–12 June 1788
Storing 5.16.1–2, 22–23, 27

[*4 June*]

And here I would make this enquiry of those worthy characters who composed a part of the late Federal Convention. I am sure they were fully impressed with the necessity of forming a great consolidated Government, instead of a confederation. That this is a consolidated Government is demonstrably clear, and the danger of such a Government, is, to my mind, very striking. I have the highest veneration of those Gentlemen,—but, Sir, give me leave to demand, what right had they to say, *We, the People.* My political curiosity, exclusive of my anxious solicitude for the public welfare, leads me to ask who authorised them to speak the language of, *We, the People,* instead of *We, the States?* States are the characteristics, and the soul of a confederation. If the States be not the agents of this compact, it must be one great consolidated National Government of the people of all the States.

[5 June]

I am not free from suspicion: I am apt to entertain doubts: I rose yesterday to ask a question, which arose in my own mind. When I asked the question, I thought the meaning of my interrogation was obvious: The fate of this question and America may depend on this: Have they said, we the States? Have they made a proposal of a compact between States? If they had, this would be a confederation: It is otherwise most clearly a consolidated government. The question turns, Sir, on that poor little thing—the expression, *We, the people,* instead of the States of America. I need not take much pains to show, that the principles of this system, are extremely pernicious, impolitic, and dangerous. Is this a Monarchy, like England—a compact between Prince and people; with checks on the former, to secure the liberty of the latter? Is this a Confederacy, like Holland—an association of a number of independent States, each of which retain its individual sovereignty? It is not a democracy, wherein the people retain all their rights securely. Had these principles been adhered to, we should not have been brought to this alarming transition, from a Confederacy to a consolidated government. We have no detail of those great considerations which, in my opinion, ought to have abounded before we should recur to a government of this kind. Here is a revolution as radical as that which separated us from Great Britain. It is as radical, if in this transition our rights and privileges are endangered, and the sovereignty of the States be relinquished: And cannot we plainly see, that this is actually the case? The rights of conscience, trial by jury, liberty of the press, all your immunities and franchises, all pretensions to human rights and privileges, are rendered insecure, if not lost, by this change so loudly talked of by some, and inconsiderately by others. Is this same relinquishment of rights worthy of freemen? Is it worthy of that manly fortitude that ought to characterize republicans: It is said eight States have adopted this plan. I declare that if twelve States and an half had adopted it, I would with manly firmness, and in spite of an erring world, reject it. You are not to inquire how your trade may be increased, nor how you are to become a great and powerful people, but how your liberties can be secured; for liberty ought to be the direct end of your Government.

. . . . .

The distinction between a National Government and a Confederacy is not sufficiently discerned. Had the delegates who were sent to Philadelphia a power to propose a Consolidated Government instead of a Confederacy? Were they not deputed by States, and not by the people? The assent of the people in their collective capacity is not necessary to the formation of a Federal Government. The people have no right to enter into leagues, alliances, or confederations: They are not the proper agents for this purpose: States and sovereign powers are the only proper agents for this kind of Government: Shew me an instance where the people have exercised this business: Has it not always gone through the Legislatures? I refer you to the treaties with France, Holland, and other nations: How were they made? Were they not made by the States? Are the people therefore in their aggregate capacity, the proper persons to form a Confederacy? This, therefore, ought to depend on the consent of the Legislatures; the people having never sent delegates to make any proposition of changing the Government. Yet I must say, at the same time, that it was made on grounds the most pure, and perhaps I might have been brought to consent to it so far as to the change of Government; but there is one thing in it which I never would acquiesce in. I mean the changing it into a Consolidated Government; which is so abhorrent to my mind. The Honorable Gentleman then went on to the figure we make with foreign nations; the contemptible one we make in France and Holland; which, according to the system of my notes, he attributes to the present feeble Government. An opinion has gone forth, we find, that we are a contemptible people: The time has been when we were thought otherwise: Under this same despised Government, we commanded the respect of all Europe: Wherefore are we now reckoned otherwise? The American spirit has fled from hence: It has gone to regions, where it has never been expected: It has gone to the people of France in search of a splendid Government—a strong energetic Government. Shall we imitate the example of those nations who have gone from a simple to a splendid Government. Are those nations more worthy of our imitation? What can make an adequate satisfaction to them for the loss they suffered in attaining such a Government for the loss of their liberty? If we admit this Consolidated Government it will be because we like a great splendid one. Some way or other we must be a great and mighty empire; we must have an army, and a navy, and a number of things: When the American spirit was in its youth, the language of America was different: Liberty, Sir, was then the primary object. We are descended from a people whose Government was founded on liberty: Our glorious forefathers of Great-Britain, made liberty the foundation of every thing. That country is become a great, mighty, and splendid nation; not because their Government is strong and energetic; but, Sir, because liberty is its direct end and foundation: We drew the spirit of liberty from our British ancestors; by that spirit we have triumphed over every difficulty: But now, Sir, the American spirit, assisted by the ropes and chains of consolidation, is about to convert this country to a powerful and mighty empire: If you make the citizens of this country agree to become the subjects of one great consolidated empire of America, your Government will not have sufficient energy to keep them together: Such a Government is incompatible with the genius of republicanism: There will be no checks, no real balances, in this Government: What can avail your specious imaginary balances, your rope-dancing, chain-rattling, ridiculous ideal checks and contrivances? But, Sir, we are not feared by foreigners: we do not make nations tremble: Would this, Sir, constitute happiness, or secure liberty? I trust, Sir, our political hemisphere will ever direct their operations to the security of those objects. Consider our situation, Sir: Go to the poor man, ask him what he does; he will inform you, that he enjoys the fruits of his labour, under his own fig-tree, with his wife and children around him, in peace and security. Go to every other member of the society, you will find the same tranquil ease and content; you will find no alarms or disturbances: Why then tell us of dangers to terrify us into an adoption of this new Government? and yet who knows the dangers that this new system may produce; they are out of the sight of the common people: They cannot foresee latent consequences: I dread the operation of it on the middling and lower class of people: It is for them I fear the adoption of this system.

[9 June]

We are told that this Government collectively taken, is without an example—That it is national in this part, and federal in that part, &c. We may be amused if we please, by a treatise of political anatomy. In the brain it is national: The stamina are federal—some limbs are federal—others national. The Senators are voted for by the State Legislatures, so far it is federal.—Individuals choose the members of the first branch; here it is national. It is federal in conferring general powers; but national in retaining them. It is not to be supported by the States—The pockets of individuals are to be searched for its maintenance. What signifies it to me, that you have the most curious anatomical description of it in its creation? To all the common purposes of Legislation it is a great consolidation of Government. You are not to have a right to legislate in any but trivial cases: You are not to touch private contracts: You are not to have the right of having arms in your own defence: You cannot be trusted with dealing out justice between man and man. What shall the States have to do? Take care of the poor—repair and make highways—erect bridges, and so on, and so on. Abolish the State Legislatures at once. What purposes should they be continued for? Our Legislature will indeed be a ludicrous spectacle—180 men marching in solemn farcical procession, exhibiting a mournful proof of the lost liberty of their country—without the power of restoring it. But, Sir, we have the consolation that it is a mixed Government: That is, it may work sorely on your neck; but you will have some comfort by saying, that it was a Federal Government in its origin.

I beg Gentlemen to consider—lay aside your prejudices—Is this a Federal Government? Is it not a Consolidated Government for every purpose almost? Is the Government of Virginia a State Government after this Government is adopted? I grant that it is a Republican Government—but for what purposes? For such trivial domestic considerations, as render it unworthy the name of a Legislature.

[12 June]

The State Governments, says he, will possess greater advantages than the General Government, and will consequently prevail. His opinion and mine are diametrically opposite. Bring forth the Federal allurements, and compare them with the poor contemptible things that the State Legislatures can bring forth. On the part of the State Legislatures, there are Justices of Peace and militia officers—And even these Justices and officers, are bound by oath in favour of the Constitution. A constable is the only man who is not obliged to swear paramount allegiance to this beloved Congress. On the other hand, there are rich, fat Federal emoluments—your rich, snug, fine, fat Federal offices—The number of collectors of taxes and excises will outnumber any thing from the States. Who can cope with the excisemen and taxmen? There are none in this country, that can cope with this class of men alone. But, Sir, is this the only danger? Would to Heaven that it were. If we are to ask which will last the longest—the State or the General Government, you must take an army and a navy into the account. Lay these things together, and add to the enumeration the superior abilities of those who manage the General Government. Can then the State Governments look it in the face? You dare not look it in the face now, when it is but an *embryo*. The influence of this Government will be such, that you never can get amendments; for if you propose alterations, you will affront them. Let the Honorable Gentleman consider all these things and say, whether the State Governments will last as long as the Federal Government.

39

GEORGE CLINTON, NEW YORK
RATIFYING CONVENTION
11 July 1788
Storing 6.13.25–27

The objects of this government as expressed in the preface to it, are "to form a more perfect union, establish justice, insure domestic tranquility, provide for the common defence, promote the general welfare, and secure the blessings of liberty"—These include every object for which government was established amongst man, and in every dispute about the powers granted, it is fair to infer that the means are commensurate with the end—and I believe we may venture to assert, that a good judge would not hesitate to draw this inference, especially when supported by the undefined powers granted by the 8th. section of the 1st. article and the construction that naturally arises from the prohibition against the creation of a nobility, a power which would otherwise appear to be neither expressly or impliedly granted.

I am sensible, it may be said, that the state governments are component parts of the general government and therefore that of necessity their existence must be preserved and that the Constitution has guaranteed to them a republican form[;] but this, on the least reflection, will appear to be too feeble a security to be relied on, when they are divested of every resource for their own support and the terms too indefinite to afford any security to the liberties of the people, as it includes in it the idea of an arbitrary aristocracy as well as of a free government—The form may exist without the substance. It will be remembered that this was the case in Rome when under a despotism—The Senate existed as formerly—Consuls, Tribunes etc. were chosen by the people—but their powers were merely nominal, as they were ruled by the will of the reigning Tyrant—and the most arbitrary ministers and judges generally preserve the forms of law, while they disregard its precepts and pervert them to the purposes of oppression.

From these observations, it is evident, that the general government is not constructed upon federal principles, and that its operations will terminate in a dissolution of the States—That even if this should not be the case, they will be so enfeebled as not to afford that effectual security to the rights and liberties of the people, against the undue and extensive powers vested in the general government, as its advocates have led them to expect. This being the case, the objections which have been stated against the system, must appear to well founded—and it therefore becomes our indispensable duty to obviate them by suitable amendments calculated to abridge and limit the powers to general objects. The evils pointed out in the system are now within our power to remedy—but if we suffer ourselves to be influenced by specious reasoning unsupported by example to an unconditional adoption of an imperfect government, the opportunity will be forever lost, for history does not furnish a single instance of a government once established, voluntarily yielding up its powers to secure the rights and liberties of the people.

40

JAMES MADISON, CONSOLIDATION
5 Dec. 1791
Papers 14:137–39

Much has been said, and not without reason, against a consolidation of the States into one government. Omitting lesser objections, two consequences would probably flow from such a change in our political system, which justify the cautions used against it. *First,* it would be impossible to avoid the dilemma, of either relinquishing the present energy and responsibility of a *single* executive magistrate, for some *plural* substitute, which by dividing so great a trust might lessen the danger of it; or suffering so great an accumulation of powers in the hands of that officer, as might by degrees transform him into a monarch. The incompetency of one Legislature to regulate all the various objects belonging to the local governments, would evidently force a transfer of many of them to the executive department; whilst the encreasing splendour and number

of its prerogatives supplied by this source, might prove excitements to ambition too powerful for a sober execution of the elective plan, and consequently strengthen the pretexts for an hereditary designation of the magistrate. *Second,* were the state governments abolished, the same space of country that would produce an undue growth of the executive power, would prevent that controul on the Legislative body, which is essential to a faithful discharge of its trust, neither the voice nor the sense of ten or twenty millions of people, spread through so many latitudes as are comprehended within the United States, could ever be combined or called into effect, if deprived of those local organs, through which both can now be conveyed. In such a state of things, the impossibility of acting together, might be succeeded by the inefficacy of partial expressions of the public mind, and this at length, by a universal silence and insensibility, leaving the whole government to that *self directed course,* which, it must be owned, is the natural propensity of every government.

But if a consolidation of the states into one government be an event so justly to be avoided, it is not less to be desired, on the other hand, that a consolidation should prevail in their interests and affections; and this too, as it fortunately happens, for the very reasons, among others, which lie against a governmental consolidation. For, in the first place, in proportion as uniformity is found to prevail in the interests and sentiments of the several states, will be the practicability of accommodating *Legislative* regulations to them, and thereby of withholding new and dangerous prerogatives from the executive. Again, the greater the mutual confidence and affection of all parts of the Union, the more likely they will be to concur amicably, or to differ with moderation, in the elective designation of the chief magistrate; and by such examples, to guard and adorn the vital principle of our republican constitution. Lastly, the less the supposed difference of interests, and the greater the concord and confidence throughout the great body of the people, the more readily must they sympathize with each other, the more seasonably can they interpose a common manifestation of their sentiments, the more certainly will they take the alarm at usurpation or oppression, and the more effectually will they *consolidate* their defence of the public liberty.

Here then is a proper object presented, both to those who are most jealously attached to the separate authority reserved to the states, and to those who may be more inclined to contemplate the people of America in the light of one nation. Let the former continue to watch against every encroachment, which might lead to a gradual consolidation of the states into one government. Let the latter employ their utmost zeal, by eradicating local prejudices and mistaken rivalships, to consolidate the affairs of the states into one harmonious interest; and let it be the patriotic study of all, to maintain the various authorities established by our complicated system, each in its respective constitutional sphere; and to erect over the whole, one paramount Empire of reason, benevolence and brotherly affection.

41

THOMAS JEFFERSON, RESOLUTIONS RELATIVE TO
THE ALIEN AND SEDITION ACTS
10 Nov. 1798
Writings 17:379–80, 385–91

1. *Resolved,* That the several States composing the United States of America, are not united on the principle of unlimited submission to their General Government; but that, by a compact under the style and title of a Constitution for the United States, and of amendments thereto, they constituted a General Government for special purposes,—delegated to that government certain definite powers, reserving, each State to itself, the residuary mass of right to their own self-government; and that whensoever the General Government assumes undelegated powers, its acts are unauthoritative, void, and of no force: that to this compact each State acceded as a State, and is an integral party, its co-States forming, as to itself, the other party: that the government created by this compact was not made the exclusive or final judge of the extent of the powers delegated to itself; since that would have made its discretion, and not the Constitution, the measure of its powers; but that, as in all other cases of compact among powers having no common judge, each party has an equal right to judge for itself, as well of infractions as of the mode and measure of redress.

. . . . .

8th. *Resolved,* That a committee of conference and correspondence be appointed, who shall have in charge to communicate the preceding resolutions to the legislatures of the several States; to assure them that this commonwealth continues in the same esteem of their friendship and union which it has manifested from that moment at which a common danger first suggested a common union: that it considers union, for specifed national purposes, and particularly to those specified in their late federal compact, to be friendly to the peace, happiness and prosperity of all the States: that faithful to that compact, according to the plain intent and meaning in which it was understood and acceded to by the several parties, it is sincerely anxious for its preservation: that it does also believe, that to take from the States all the powers of self-government and transfer them to a general and consolidated government, without regard to the special delegations and reservations solemnly agreed to in that compact, is not for the peace, happiness or prosperity of these States; and that therefore this commonwealth is determined, as it doubts not its co-States are, to submit to. undelegated, and consequently unlimited powers in no man, or body of men on earth: that in cases of an abuse of the delegated powers, the members of the General Government, being chosen by the people, a change by the people would be the constitutional remedy; but, where powers are assumed which have not been del-

egated, a nullification of the act is the rightful remedy: that every State has a natural right in cases not within the compact, (casus non foederis,) to nullify of their own authority all assumptions of power by others within their limits: that without this right, they would be under the dominion, absolute and unlimited, of whosoever might exercise this right of judgment for them: that nevertheless, this commonwealth, from motives of regard and respect for its co-States, has wished to communicate with them on the subject: that with them alone it is proper to communicate, they alone being parties to the compact, and solely authorized to judge in the last resort of the powers exercised under it, Congress being not a party, but merely the creature of the compact, and subject as to its assumptions of power to the final judgment of those by whom, and for whose use itself and its powers were all created and modified: that if the acts before specified should stand, these conclusions would flow from them; that the General Government may place any act they think proper on the list of crimes, and punish it themselves whether enumerated or not enumerated by the Constitution as cognizable by them: that they may transfer its cognizance to the President, or any other person, who may himself be the accuser, counsel, judge and jury, whose *suspicions* may be the evidence, his *order* the sentence, his *officer* the executioner, and his breast the sole record of the transaction: that a very numerous and valuable description of the inhabitants of these States being, by this precedent, reduced, as outlaws, to the absolute dominion of one man, and the barrier of the Constitution thus swept away from us all, no rampart now remains against the passions and the powers of a majority in Congress to protect from a like exportation, or other more grievous punishment, the minority of the same body, the legislatures, judges, governors, and counsellors of the States, nor their other peaceable inhabitants, who may venture to reclaim the constitutional rights and liberties of the States and people, or who for other causes, good or bad, may be obnoxious to the views, or marked by the suspicions of the President, or be thought dangerous to his or their election, or other interests, public or personal: that the friendless alien has indeed been selected as the safest subject of a first experiment; but the citizen will soon follow, or rather, has already followed, for already has a sedition act marked him as its prey: that these and successive acts of the same character, unless arrested at the threshold, necessarily drive these States into revolution and blood, and will furnish new calumnies against republican government, and new pretexts for those who wish it to be believed that man cannot be governed but by a rod of iron: that it would be a dangerous delusion were a confidence in the men of our choice to silence our fears for the safety of our rights: that confidence is everywhere the parent of despotism—free government is founded in jealousy, and not in confidence; it is jealousy and not confidence which prescribes limited constitutions, to bind down those whom we are obliged to trust with power: that our Constitution has accordingly fixed the limits to which, and no further, our confidence may go; and let the honest advocate of confidence read the alien and sedition acts, and say if the Constitution has not been wise in fixing limits to the government it created, and whether we should be wise in destroying those limits. Let him say what the government is, if it be not a tyranny, which the men of our choice have conferred on our President, and the President of our choice has assented to, and accepted over the friendly strangers to whom the mild spirit of our country and its laws have pledged hospitality and protection: that the men of our choice have more respected the bare *suspicions* of the President, than the solid right of innocence, the claims of justification, the sacred force of truth, and the forms and substance of law and justice. In questions of power, then, let no more be heard of confidence in man, but bind him down from mischief by the chains of the Constitution. That this commonwealth does therefore call on its co-States for an expression of their sentiments on the acts concerning aliens, and for the punishment of certain crimes herein before specified, plainly declaring whether these acts are or are not authorized by the federal compact. And it doubts not that their sense will be so announced as to prove their attachment unaltered to limited government, whether general or particular. And that the rights and liberties of their co-States will be exposed to no dangers by remaining embarked in a common bottom with their own. That they will concur with this commonwealth in considering the said acts as so palpably against the Constitution as to amount to an undisguised declaration that that compact is not meant to be the measure of the powers of the General Government, but that it will proceed in the exercise over these States, of all powers whatsoever: that they will view this as seizing the rights of the States, and consolidating them in the hands of the General Government, with a power assumed to bind the States, (not merely as the cases made federal, (casus foederis,) but in all cases whatsoever, by laws made, not with their consent, but by others against their consent: that this would be to surrender the form of government we have chosen, and live under one deriving its powers from its own will, and not from our authority; and that the co-States, recurring to their natural right in cases not made federal, will concur in declaring these acts void, and of no force, and will each take measures of its own for providing that neither these acts, nor any others of the General Government not plainly and intentionally authorized by the Constitution, shall be exercised within their respective territories.

9th. *Resolved*, That the said committee be authorized to communicate by writing or personal conferences, at any times or places whatever, with any person or persons who may be appointed by any one or more co-States to correspond or confer with them; and that they lay their proceedings before the next session of Assembly.

42

JAMES MADISON, REPORT ON THE VIRGINIA RESOLUTIONS
Jan. 1800
Elliot 4:546–50, 579

HOUSE OF DELEGATES, Session of 1799—1800.

Report of the Committee to whom were referred the Communications of various State, relative to the Resolutions of the last General Assembly of this State, concerning the Alien and Sedition Laws.

Whatever room might be found in the proceedings of some of the states, who have disapproved of the resolutions of the General Assembly of this commonwealth, passed on the 21st day of December, 1798, for painful remarks on the spirit and manner of those proceedings, it appears to the committee most consistent with the duty, as well as dignity, of the General Assembly, to hasten an oblivion of every circumstance which might be construed into a diminution of mutual respect, confidence, and affection, among the members of the Union.

The committee have deemed it a more useful task to revise, with a critical eye, the resolutions which have met with their disapprobation; to examine fully the several objections and arguments which have appeared against them; and to inquire whether there can be any errors of fact, of principle, or of reasoning, which the candor of the General Assembly ought to acknowledge and correct.

The *first* of the resolutions is in the words following:—

"*Resolved*, That the General Assembly of Virginia doth unequivocally express a firm resolution to maintain and defend the Constitution of the United States, and the Constitution of this state, against every aggression, either foreign or domestic; and that they will support the government of the United States in all measures warranted by the former."

No unfavorable comment can have been made on the sentiments here expressed. To maintain and defend the Constitution of the United States, and of their own state, against every aggression, both foreign and domestic, and to support the government of the United States in all measures warranted by their Constitution, are duties which the General Assembly ought always to feel, and to which, on such an occasion, it was evidently proper to express their sincere and firm adherence.

In their *next* resolution—

"The General Assembly most solemnly declares a warm attachment to the union of the states, to maintain which it pledges all its powers; and that, for this end, it is their duty to watch over and oppose every infraction of those principles which constitute the only basis of that Union, because a faithful observance of them can alone secure its existence and the public happiness."

The observation just made is equally applicable to this solemn declaration of warm attachment to the Union, and this solemn pledge to maintain it; nor can any question arise among enlightened friends of the Union, as to the duty of watching over and opposing every infraction of those principles which constitute its basis, and a faithful observance of which can alone secure its existence, and the public happiness thereon depending.

The *third* resolution is in the words following:—

> "That this Assembly doth explicitly and peremptorily declare, that it views the powers of the federal government, as resulting from the compact to which the states are parties, as limited by the plain sense and intention of the instrument constituting that compact—as no further valid than they are authorized by the grants enumerated in that compact; and that, in case of a deliberate, palpable, and dangerous exercise of other powers, not granted by the said compact, the states who are parties thereto have the right, and are in duty bound, to interpose, for arresting the progress of the evil and for maintaining, within their respective limits, the authorities, rights, and liberties, appertaining to them."

On this resolution the committee have bestowed all the attention which its importance merits. They have *scanned* it not merely with a strict, but with a severe eye; and they feel confidence in pronouncing that, in its just and fair construction, it is unexceptionably true in its several positions, as well as constitutional and conclusive in its inferences.

The resolution declares, *first,* that "it views the powers of the federal government as resulting from the compact to which the states are parties;" in other words, that the federal powers are derived from the Constitution; and that the Constitution is a compact to which the states are parties.

Clear as the position must seem, that the federal powers are derived from the Constitution, and from that alone, the committee are not unapprized of a late doctrine which opens another source of federal powers, not less extensive and important than it is new and unexpected. The examination of this doctrine will be most conveniently connected with a review of a succeeding resolution. The committee satisfy themselves here with briefly remarking that, in all the contemporary discussions and comments which the Constitution underwent, it was constantly justified and recommended on the ground that the powers not given to the government were withheld from it; and that, if any doubt could have existed on this subject, under the original text of the Constitution, it is removed, as far as words could remove it, by the 12th amendment, now a part of the Constitution, which expressly declares, "that the powers not delegated to the United States by the Constitution, nor prohibited by it to the states, are reserved to the states respectively, or to the people."

The other position involved in this branch of the resolution, namely, "that the states are parties to the Constitution," or compact, is, in the judgment of the committee, equally free from objection. It is indeed true that the term "states" is sometimes used in a vague sense, and sometimes in different senses, according to the subject to which it is applied. Thus it sometimes means the separate sections of territory occupied by the political societies within each; sometimes the particular governments established by those societies; sometimes those societies as organized into those particular governments; and lastly, it means the people composing those political societies, in their highest sovereign capacity. Although it might be wished that the perfection of language admitted less diversity in the signification of the same words, yet little inconvenience is produced by it, where the true sense can be collected with certainty from the different applications. In the present instance, whatever different construction of the term "states," in the resolution, may have been entertained, all will at least concur in that last mentioned; because in that sense the Constitution was submitted to the "states;" in that sense the "states" ratified it; and in that sense of the term "states," they are consequently parties to the compact from which the powers of the federal government result.

The next position is, that the General Assembly views the powers of the federal government "as limited by the plain sense and intention of the instrument constituting that compact," and "as no further valid than they are authorized by the grants therein enumerated." It does not seem possible that any just objection can lie against either of these clauses. The first amounts merely to a declaration that the compact ought to have the interpretation plainly intended by the parties to it; the other, to a declaration that it ought to have the execution and effect intended by them. If the powers granted be valid, it is solely because they are granted; and if the granted powers are valid because granted, all other powers not granted must not be valid.

The resolution, having taken this view of the federal compact, proceeds to infer, "That, in case of a deliberate, palpable, and dangerous exercise of other powers, not granted by the said compact, the states, who are parties thereto, have the right, and are in duty bound, to interpose for arresting the progress of the evil, and for maintaining, within their respective limits, the authorities, rights, and liberties, appertaining to them."

It appears to your committee to be a plain principle, founded in common sense, illustrated by common practice, and essential to the nature of compacts, that, where resort can be had to no tribunal superior to the authority of the parties, the parties themselves must be the rightful judges, in the last resort, whether the bargain made has been pursued or violated. The Constitution of the United States was formed by the sanction of the states, given by each in its sovereign capacity. It adds to the stability and dignity, as well as to the authority, of the Constitution, that it rests on this legitimate and solid foundation. The states, then, being the parties to the constitutional compact, and in their sovereign capacity, it follows of necessity that there can be no tribunal, above their authority, to decide, in the last resort, whether the compact made by them be violated; and consequently, that, as the parties to it, they must themselves decide, in the last resort, such questions as may be of sufficient magnitude to require their interposition.

It does not follow, however, because the states, as sovereign parties to their constitutional compact, must ultimately decide whether it has been violated, that such a decision ought to be interposed either in a hasty manner or on doubtful and inferior occasions. Even in the case of ordinary conventions between different nations, where, by the strict rule of interpretation, a breach of a part may be deemed a breach of the whole,—every part being deemed a condition of every other part, and of the whole,—it is always laid down that the breach must be both wilful and material, to justify an application of the rule. But in the case of an intimate and constitutional union, like that of the United States, it is evident that the interposition of the parties, in their sovereign capacity, can be called for by occasions only deeply and essentially affecting the vital principles of their political system.

The resolution has, accordingly guarded against any misapprehension of its object, by expressly requiring, for such an interposition, "the case of a deliberate, palpable, and dangerous breach of the Constitution, by the exercise of powers not granted by it." It must be a case not of a light and transient nature, but of a nature dangerous to the great purposes for which the Constitution was established. It must be a case, moreover, not obscure or doubtful in its construction, but plain and palpable. Lastly, it must be a case not resulting from a partial consideration or hasty determination, but a case stamped with a final consideration and deliberate adherence. It is not necessary, because the resolution does not require, that the question should be discussed, how far the exercise of any particular power, ungranted by the Constitution, would justify the interposition of the parties to it. As cases might easily be stated, which none would contend ought to fall within that description,—cases, on the other hand, might, with equal ease, be stated, so flagrant and so fatal as to unite every opinion in placing them within the description.

But the resolution has done more than guard against misconstruction, by expressly referring to cases of a deliberate, palpable, and dangerous nature. It specifies the object of the interposition, which it contemplates to be solely that of arresting the progress of the evil of usurpation, and of maintaining the authorities, rights, and liberties, appertaining to the states as parties to the Constitution.

From this view of the resolution, it would seem inconceivable that it can incur any just disapprobation from those who, laying aside all momentary impressions, and recollecting the genuine source and object of the Federal Constitution, shall candidly and accurately interpret the meaning of the General Assembly. If the deliberate exercise of dangerous powers, palpably withheld by the Constitution, could not justify the parties to it in interposing even so far as to arrest the progress of the evil, and thereby to preserve the Constitution itself, as well as to provide for the safety of the parties to it, there would be an end to all relief from usurped power, and a direct subversion of the rights specified or recognized under all the state constitutions, as well as a plain denial of the fundamental principle on which our independence itself was declared.

But it is objected, that the judicial authority is to be regarded as the sole expositor of the Constitution in the last resort; and it may be asked for what reason the declaration by the General Assembly, supposing it to be theoretically true, could be required at the present day, and in so solemn a manner.

On this objection it might be observed, first, that there may be instances of usurped power, which the forms of the Constitution would never draw within the control of the judicial department; secondly, that, if the decision of the judiciary be raised above the authority of the sovereign parties to the Constitution, the decisions of the other departments, not carried by the forms of the Constitution before the judiciary, must be equally authoritative and final with the decisions of that department. But the proper answer to the objection is, that the resolution of the General Assembly relates to those great and extraordinary cases, in which all the forms of the Constitution may prove ineffectual against infractions dangerous to the essential rights of the parties to it. The resolution supposes that dangerous powers, not delegated, may not only be usurped and executed by the other departments, but that the judicial department, also, may exercise or sanction dangerous powers beyond the grant of the Constitution; and, consequently, that the ultimate right of the parties to the Constitution, to judge whether the compact has been dangerously violated, must extend to violations by one delegated authority as well as by another—by the judiciary as well as by the executive, or the legislature.

However true, therefore, it may be, that the judicial department is, in all questions submitted to it by the forms of the Constitution, to decide in the last resort, this resort must necessarily be deemed the last in relation to the authorities of the other departments of the government; not in relation to the rights of the parties to the constitutional compact, from which the judicial, as well as the other departments, hold their delegated trusts. On any other hypothesis, the delegation of judicial power would annul the authority delegating it; and the concurrence of this department with the others in usurped powers, might subvert forever, and beyond the possible reach of any rightful remedy, the very Constitution which all were instituted to preserve.

The truth declared in the resolution being established, the expediency of making the declaration at the present day may safely be left to the temperate consideration and candid judgment of the American public. It will be remembered, that a frequent recurrence to fundamental principles is solemnly enjoined by most of the state constitutions, and particularly by our own, as a necessary safeguard against the danger of degeneracy, to which republics are liable, as well as other governments, though in a less degree than others. And a fair comparison of the political doctrines not unfrequent at the present day, with those which characterized the epoch of our revolution, and which form the basis of our republican constitutions, will best determine whether the declaratory recurrence here made to those principles ought to be viewed as unseasonable and improper, or as a vigilant discharge of an important duty. The authority of constitutions over governments, and of the sovereignty of the people over constitutions, are truths which are at all times necessary to be kept in mind; and at no time, perhaps, more necessary than at present.

. . . . .

These observations appear to form a satisfactory reply to every objection which is not founded on a misconception of the terms employed in the resolutions. There is one other, however, which may be of too much importance not to be added. It cannot be forgotten that, among the arguments addressed to those who apprehended danger to liberty from the establishment of the general government over so great a country, the appeal was emphatically made to the intermediate existence of the state governments between the people and that government, to the vigilance with which they would descry the first symptoms of usurpation, and to the promptitude with which they would sound the alarm to the public. This argument was probably not without its effect; and if it was a proper one then to recommend the establishment of a constitution, it must be a proper one now to assist in its interpretation.

43

JAMES MONROE TO THOMAS JEFFERSON
4 May 1801
Writings 3:282–84

There is a subject to which I wish to engage yr. particular attention. Before I came into this office I was of opinion that the correspondence between the Executive of the Genl. Govt. and a State shod. be conducted as between parties that were mutually respectful but equally independent of each other. My idea appeared to me to be sound; indeed incontrovertable in principle, and it was matter of surprise how a contrary practice had been adopted. Each govt. is in its sphere sovereign, so far as the term is applicable in a country where the people alone are so, the State govts. do not derive their authorities from the general govt.; they are not established by its ordinances, or accountable to it for their admn. like the frontier govts., or the revenue or other officers of the U. States. Their Executive, legislative and judicial departments, are constituted on the same principles and alike form the governmental sovereignty of each govt. The officers under each constitute no part of its sovereignty; they are agents employed by it to assist in their respective admns. I consider the chief magistrate of the Union in reference to a like character in each State as first among equals, and admit the same priority in the legislative and judicial departments, and the departments under them, where the individual States have correspondent institutions. If this idea is just, it follows that the communication between the two

govts. when carried on by the govr. of a State, shod. be with the President of the U. States. To subject the State govrs. to the necessity of corresponding with the officers appointed by the President, seems to place them in the same grade, to deny the right of sovereignty in the individual States, and to consider them as subaltern inferior establishments, emanating from and dependent on the general government. The laws of Congress which establish the departments under the President have no reference to the case in question. They restrict foreign ministers &c. in their correspondence to the heads of departments, and wisely, because they are the agents of their govts.; but that restriction does not comprise the govts. they represent, whether free or despotic. It wod. be extry. if the govt. of a foreign country, by which I mean President, King or Prince, shod. write on publick business to the Secy. of one of our departments, and equally so if our President shod. write such a letter to a Secy. of any foreign government. If the question of right is settled on the principle I contend for, would it not be proper for you to recognize it in some formal manner, since by so doing you wod. recognize, cherish and support the State governments? It wod. be giving them a Station in the Union to which they are entitled by the constitution but of wch. they have been in a great measure deprived by the proud imperious tone of former admns. It wod. conciliate their govts. towards yr. admn. and introduce a spirit of harmony in our system hitherto unknown to it. In the practice there wod. be no difficulty. Where letters were addressed to the President they might be referred to the heads of departments and replies drawn by them to be signed by him, tho' very probably the present practice wod. prevail, for as soon as the question was established on just and conciliatory principles, the bias of all liberal minds wod. be to dispense with an etiquette which wod. then be no more, the observance of wch. especially with characters more distinguished for their talents and merit than themselves, as wod. generally be the case, cod. not otherwise than injure them. You will be sensible that to me personally this is an affr. of the utmost indifference; indeed in the present state of things that it is peculiarly irksome.

44

THOMAS JEFFERSON, AUTOBIOGRAPHY
1821
Works 1:120–23

But there was another amendment of which none of us thought at the time and in the omission of which lurks the germ that is to destroy this happy combination of National powers in the General government for matters of National concern, and independent powers in the states for what concerns the states severally. In England it was a great point gained at the Revolution, that the commissions of the judges, which had hitherto been during pleasure, should thenceforth be made during good behavior. A Judiciary dependent on the will of the King had proved itself the most oppressive of all tools in the hands of that Magistrate. Nothing then could be more salutary than a change there to the tenure of good behavior; and the question of good behavior left to the vote of a simple majority in the two houses of parliament. Before the revolution we were all good English Whigs, cordial in their free principles, and in their jealousies of their executive Magistrate. These jealousies are very apparent in all our state constitutions; and, in the general government in this instance, we have gone even beyond the English caution, by requiring a vote of two thirds in one of the Houses for removing a judge; a vote so impossible where any defence is made, before men of ordinary prejudices & passions, that our judges are effectually independent of the nation. But this ought not to be. I would not indeed make them dependant on the Executive authority, as they formerly were in England; but I deem it indispensable to the continuance of this government that they should be submitted to some practical & impartial controul: and that this, to be imparted, must be compounded of a mixture of state and federal authorities. It is not enough that honest men are appointed judges. All know the influence of interest on the mind of man, and how unconsciously his judgment is warped by that influence. To this bias add that of the esprit de corps, of their peculiar maxim and creed that "it is the office of a good judge to enlarge his jurisdiction," and the absence of responsibility, and how can we expect impartial decision between the General government, of which they are themselves so eminent a part, and an individual state from which they have nothing to hope or fear. We have seen too that, contrary to all correct example, they are in the habit of going out of the question before them, to throw an anchor ahead and grapple further hold for future advances of power. They are then in fact the corps of sappers & miners, steadily working to undermine the independant rights of the States, & to consolidate all power in the hands of that government in which they have so important a freehold estate. But it is not by the consolidation, or concentration of powers, but by their distribution, that good government is effected. Were not this great country already divided into states, that division must be made, that each might do for itself what concerns itself

directly, and what it can so much better do than a distant authority. Every state again is divided into counties, each to take care of what lies within it's local bounds; each county again into townships or wards, to manage minuter details; and every ward into farms, to be governed each by it's individual proprietor. Were we directed from Washington when to sow, & when to reap, we should soon want bread. It is by this partition of cares, descending in gradation from general to particular, that the mass of human affairs may be best managed for the good and prosperity of all. I repeat that I do not charge the judges with wilful and ill-intentioned error; but honest error must be arrested where it's toleration leads to public ruin. As, for the safety of society, we commit honest maniacs to Bedlam, so judges should be withdrawn from their bench, whose erroneous biases are leading us to dissolution. It may indeed injure them in fame or in fortune; but it saves the republic, which is the first and supreme law.

SEE ALSO:

Generally 1.8.18; 3.2.1; Amend. XI
John Jay to J. Lowell, 10 May 1785, W. Jay, The Life of John Jay 1:190 (1833)
James Madison, Notes on Ancient and Modern Confederacies, Apr.–June 1786, Papers 9:4–22
John Jay to John Adams, 4 May 1786, Correspondence 3:194–95
James Madison, Federalist, no. 20, 11 Dec. 1787, 128–29
Alexander Hamilton, Federalist, no. 25, 21 Dec. 1787, 159
Robert Yates and John Lansing, Reasons of Dissent, 14 Jan. 1788, Storing 2.3.7–8
Luther Martin, Letter, 21 Mar. 1788, Essays 367–68
None of the Well-born Conspirators, 23 Apr. 1788, Storing 3.15.1–2
Richard Henry Lee to Samuel Adams, 28 Apr. 1788, Letters 2:464
Thomas Jefferson to Richard Price, 8 Jan. 1789, Papers 14:420
James Madison to Thomas Jefferson, 29 Dec. 1798, Writings 6:328–29n.
Alexander Hamilton to Jonathan Dayton, Oct.–Nov. 1799, Papers 23:599–604
James Madison to Peter S. DuPonceau, May 1821, Writings 9:63–65
Abraham Lincoln, Message to Congress in Special Session, 4 July 1861, Collected Works 4:432–37

. . . establish Justice, insure domestic Tranquility, provide for the common defence, promote the general Welfare, . . .

9

Energetic Government

Introduction

Just as disagreements and divisions lay beneath the general consensus that there should be a federal union, so too was it with the great substantive ends of liberal government. One could hardly fault a political order dedicated to establish justice, insure domestic tranquility, provide for the common defence, promote the general welfare, and secure the blessings of liberty. But the means for achieving or promoting those ends were matters of great controversy. Even if one agreed with the maxim that the means ought to be proportioned to the end, that did not settle the question whether the end, common defence excepted, was altogether or even largely the responsibility of the national government. In fact the controversy embraced more than this "federal" aspect; not only the institutional arrangements of the proposed Constitution but its very tone or spirit were at issue. There is little doubt that in this respect, at least, proponents and opponents understood one another's intentions very well.

No matter to what level of government the people might ultimately turn in order to help secure those great ends, it was certain that their attainment lay beyond rational expectation unless and until the principal defects of the Confederation were remedied. Proponents of the Constitution insisted on this. In the plainest terms, there could be no grounds for expecting justice, tranquility, and the rest to prevail in America until there was a national government with energy enough to secure the preconditions for justice, tranquility, and the rest. If one had to err, Pelatiah Webster argued (no. 2), it was better—indeed safer—to err on the side of sufficient energy rather than too little. In the absence of a government capable of acting on the understanding that the "public business must in some way or other go forward," public business would languish and so-

ciety itself totter on the edge of anarchy (Hamilton; see ch. 5, no. 23).

For Hamilton, of course, that public business was no crabbed or neatly contained affair. Its exact dimensions defied prediction, partly because *the extent and variety of national exigencies*" exceeded any one country's ability to define. Where the potential dangers were infinitely variable, how could one think of precisely confined governmental powers (no. 5)? There was as well a domestic impetus for energetic government: "I believe it may be regarded as a position, warranted by the history of mankind, that *in the usual progress of things, the necessities of a nation in every stage of its existence will be found at least equal to its resources*" (no. 7). In a world of ever-receding horizons, political demands stood in no danger of withering away or of being sated.

All this argued for a government well mounted, a government able and willing to undertake enlarged plans for the public good. Yet energy was but one part of the definition of good government and arguably was in some tension with the requirements posed by the "genius of Republican liberty" (Madison, no. 9). To keep that tension within safe bounds, even while benefitting from the dynamism it imparts to the whole society, was among the greater challenges encountered by the Philadelphia Convention.

Critics of the Constitution were less certain that the Convention's response to that challenge was as safe as Oliver Ellsworth made it out to be (no. 3). Their starting point might well be put in Jefferson's terms (no. 1): it is better to err on the side of insufficient energy than to risk having a sovereign's bayonet pointed at every citizen's breast. Those critics were not moved by Federalist warnings that weak government leads to poverty, disdain, and finally acts of violence by a desperate and disheartened citizenry. Such accounts Anti-Federalists pronounced highly colored fictions, in no way descriptive of the Americans' present or likely future situation. The more credible and imminent danger was that the Federalists' impatience and contempt for the Confederation would persuade the people to abandon the means of home-bred happiness in pursuit of grander, but fatal, goals. In place of government that eschewed imperial glory—but could not harm its own people—the Federalists would instead erect a powerful, efficient, but all-devouring master (nos. 11, 12). The siren song of becoming a great and powerful nation was leading the people to jeopardize their most precious liberties. Thus the controversies over the need for greater energy in government and over the adequacy of the Constitution's safeguards for liberty stirred conflicting notions of what America might yet become. Ratification of the Constitution did not put that conflict to rest.

1

THOMAS JEFFERSON, ANSWERS TO DEMEUNIER'S FIRST QUERIES
24 Jan. 1786
Papers 10:19–20

It has been often said that the decisions of Congress are impotent, because the Confederation provides no compulsory power. But when two or more nations enter into a compact, it is not usual for them to say what shall be done to the party who infringes it. Decency forbids this. And it is as unnecessary as indecent, because the right of compulsion naturally results to the party injured. by the breach. When any one state in the American Union refuses obedience to the Confederation by which they have bound themselves, the rest have a natural right to compel them to obedience. Congress would probably exercise long patience before they would recur to force; but if the case ultimately required it, they would use that recurrence. Should this case ever arise, they will probably coerce by a naval force, as being more easy, less dangerous to liberty, and less likely to produce much bloodshed.

It has been said too that our governments both federal and particular want energy; that it is difficult to restrain both individuals and states from committing wrongs. This is true, and it is an inconvenience. On the other hand that energy which absolute governments derive from an armed force, which is the effect of the bayonet constantly held at the breast of every citizen, and which resembles very much the stillness of the grave, must be admitted also to have it's inconveniences. We weigh the two together, and like best to submit to the former. Compare the number of wrongs committed with impunity by citizens among us, with those committed by the sovereigns in other countries, and the last will be found most numerous, most oppressive on the mind, and most degrading of the dignity of man.

2

PELATIAH WEBSTER, REMARKS ON THE ADDRESS OF SIXTEEN MEMBERS OF THE ASSEMBLY OF PENNSYLVANIA
12 Oct. 1787
McMaster 103–6

Upon the whole matter, I think the sixteen members have employed an address-writer of great dexterity, who has given us a strong sample of ingenious malignity and ill-nature—a master-piece of high coloring in the scare-crow way; in his account of the conduct of the sixteen members, by an unexpected openness and candor, he avows facts which he certainly cannot expect to justify, or even hope that their constituents will patronize or even approve; but he seems to lose all candor when he deals in sentiments; when he comes to point out the nature and operation of the new constitution, he appears to mistake the spirit and true principles of it very much; or which is worse, takes pleasure in showing it in the worst light he can paint it in. I however agree with him in this, that this is the time for consideration and minute examination: and I think the great subject, when viewed seriously, without passion or prejudice, will bear and brighten under the severest examination of the rational inquirer. If the provisions of the law or constitution do not exceed the occasions, if the remedies are not extended beyond the mischiefs, the government cannot be justly charged with severity; on the other hand, if the provisions are not adequate to the occasions, and the remedies not equal to the mischiefs, the government must be too lax, and not sufficiently operative to give the necessary security to the subject; to form a right judgment, we must compare these two things well together, and not suffer our minds to dwell on one of them alone, without considering them in connexion with the other; by this means we shall easily see that the one makes the other necessary.

Were we to view only the gaols and dungeons, the gallows and pillories, the chains and wheel-barrows, of any state, we might be induced to think the government severe; but when we turn our attention to the murders and parricides, and robberies and burglaries, the piracies and thefts, which merit these punishments, our idea of cruelty vanishes at once, and we admire the justice, and perhaps clemency, of that government which before shocked us as too severe. So when we fix our attention only on the superlative authority and energetic force vested in congress and our federal executive powers by the new constitution, we may at first sight be induced to think that we yield more of the sovereignty of the states and of personal liberty, than is requisite to maintain the federal government; but when on the other hand we consider with full survey the vast supports which the union requires, and the immense consequence of that union to us all, we shall probably soon be convinced that the powers aforesaid, extensive as they are, are not greater than is necessary for our benefit; for, 1. *No laws of any state, which do not carry in them a force which extends to their effectual and final execution, can afford a certain and sufficient security to the subject;* for, 2. *Laws of any kind, which fail of execution, are worse than none,* because they weaken the government, expose it to contempt, destroy the confidence of all men, both subjects and strangers, in it, and disappoint all men who have confided in it; in fine, our union can never be supported without definite and effectual laws which are coextensive with their occasions, and which are supported by authorities and powers which can give them execution with energy; if admitting such powers into our constitution can be called a sacrifice, it is a sacrifice to safety, and the only question is whether our union or federal government is worth this sacrifice. Our union, I say, *under the protection of which* every individual rests secure against foreign and domestic insult and oppression; but *without it* we can have no security against invasions, insults, and oppressions of foreign powers, or against the inroads and wars of one state on another, or even against insurrections and rebellions arising within particular states, by which our wealth and strength, as well as ease, comfort and safety, will be devoured and destroyed by enemies growing out of our own bowels. It is *our union alone* which can give us respectability abroad in the eyes of foreign nations; and secure to us all the advantages both of trade and safety, which can be derived from treaties with them.

The Thirteen States all united and well cemented together, are a strong, rich and formidable body, not of stationary, maturated power, but increasing every day in riches, strength, and numbers; thus circumstanced, we can demand the attention and respect of all foreign nations, but they will give us both in exact proportion to the solidity of our union. For if they observe our union to be lax, from insufficient principles of cement in our constitution, or mutinies and insurrections of our own people (which are the direct consequence of an insufficient cement of union); I say, when foreign nations see either of these, they will immediately abate of their attention and respect to us and confidence in us.

And, as it appears to me, that the new constitution does not vest congress with more or greater powers than are necessary to support this important union, I wish it may be admitted in the most cordial and unanimous manner by all the states.

It is a human composition, and may have errors which future experience will enable us to discover and correct; but I think it is pretty plain, if it has faults, that the ad-dress-writer of the sixteen members has not been able to find them; for he has all along either hunted down phantoms of error, that have no real existence, or which is worse, tarnished real excellencies into blemishes.

I have dwelt the longer on these remarks on this writer, because I observe that all the scribblers in our papers against the new constitution, have taken their cue principally from him, all their lucubrations contain little more than his ideas dressed out in a great variety of forms; one of which colors so high as to make the new constitution strongly resemble the Turkish government (*vide Gazetteer* of the 10th instant), which, I think, comes about as near the truth as any of the rest, and brings to my mind a sentiment in polemical divinity, which I have somewhere read, that there were once great disputes and different opinions among divines about the mark which was set on Cain, when one of them very gravely thought it was a horn fully grown out on his forehead. It is probable he could not think of a worse mark than that.

On the whole matter there is no end of the extravagancies of the human fancy, which are commonly dictated by poignant feelings, disordered passions, or affecting interests; but I could wish my fellow-citizens, in the matter of vast importance before us, would divest themselves of bias, passion, and little personal or local interests, and consider the great subject with that dignity of reason and independence of sentiment, which national interests ever require. I have here given my sentiments with the most unbiased freedom, and hope they will be received with the most candid attention and unbiased discussion, by the states in which I live, and in which I expect to leave my children.

I will conclude with one observation, which I take to be very capital, viz: that the distresses and oppressions both of nations and individuals often arise from the powers of government being too limited in their principle, too indeterminate in their definition, or too lax in their execution, and of course the safety of the citizens depends much on full and definite powers of government, and an effectual execution of them.

3

OLIVER ELLSWORTH, LANDHOLDER, NO. 3
19 Nov. 1787
Essays 146–49

TO THE HOLDERS AND TILLERS OF LAND.
Gentlemen,

When we rushed to arms for preventing British usurpation, liberty was the argument of every tongue.

This word would open all the resources of the country and draw out a brigade of militia rapidly as the most decisive orders of a despotic government. Liberty is a word which, according as it is used, comprehends the most good and the most evil of any in the world. Justly understood it is sacred next to those which we appropiate in divine adoration; but in the mouths of some it means anything, which enervate a necessary government; excite a jealousy of the rulers who are our own choice, and keep society in confusion for want of a power sufficiently concentered to promote its good. It is not strange that the licentious should tell us a government of energy is inconsistent with liberty, for being inconsistent with their wishes and their vices, they would have us think it contrary to human happiness. In the state this country was left by the war, with want of experience in sovereignty, and the feelings which the people then had; nothing but the scene we had passed thro' could give a general conviction that an internal government of strength is the only means of repressing external violence, and preserving the national [natural?] rights of the people against the injustice of their own brethren. Even the common duties of humanity will gradually go out of use, when the constitution and laws of a country do not insure justice from the public and between individuals. American experience, in our present deranged state, hath again proved these great truths, which have been verified in every age since men were made and became sufficiently numerous to form into public bodies. A government capable of controling the whole, and bringing its force to a point, is one of the prerequisites for national liberty. We combine in society, with an expectation to have our persons and properties defended against unreasonable exactions either at home or abroad. If the public are unable to protest against the unjust impositions of foreigners, in this case we do not enjoy our natural rights, and a weakness of government is the cause. If we mean to have our natural rights and properties protected, we must first create a power which is able to do it, and in our case there is no want of resources, but a civil constitution which may draw them out and point their force.

The present question is, shall we have such a constitution or not? We allow it to be a creation of power; but power when necessary for our good is as much to be desired as the food we eat or the air we breathe. Some men are mightily afraid of giving power lest it should be improved for oppression; this is doubtless possible, but where is the probability. The same objection may be made against the constitution of every state in the union, and against every possible mode of government; because a power of doing good always implies a power to do evil if the person or party be disposed.

The right of the legislature to ordain laws binding on the people, gives them a power to make bad laws.

The right of the judge to inflict punishment, gives him both power and opportunity to oppress the innocent; yet none but crazy men will from thence determine that it is best to have neither a legislature nor judges.

If a power to promote the best interest of the people, necessarily implies a power to do evil, we must never expect such a constitution in theory as will not be open in some respects to the objections of carping and jealous men. The new Constitution is perhaps more cautiously guarded than any other in the world, and at the same time creates a power which will be able to protect the subject; yet doubtless objections may be raised, and so they may

against the constitution of each state in the union. In Connecticut the laws are the constitution by which the people are governed, and it is generally allowed to be the most free and popular in the thirteen states. As this is the state in which I live and write, I will instance several things which with a proper coloring and a spice of jealousy appear most dangerous to the natural rights of the people, yet they have never been dangerous in practice, and are absolutely necessary at some times to prevent much greater evil.

The right of taxation or of assessing and collecting money out of the people, is one of those powers which may prove dangerous in the exercise, and which by the new constitution is vested solely in representatives chosen for that purpose. But by the laws of Connecticut, this power called so dangerous may be exercised by selectmen of each town, and this not only without their consent but against their express will, where they have considered the matter, and judge it improper. This power they may exercise when and so often as they judge necessary! Three justices of the quorum may tax a whole county in such sums as they think meet, against the express will of all the inhabitants. Here we see the dangerous power of taxation vested in the justices of the quorum and even in selectmen, men whom we should suppose as likely to err and tyrannize as the representatives of three millions of people in solemn deliberation, and amenable to the vengeance of their constitutents, for every act of injustice. The same town officers have equal authority where personal liberty is concerned, in a matter more sacred than all the property in the world, the disposal of your children. When they judge fit, with the advice of one justice of the peace, they may tear them from the parent's embrace, and place them under the absolute control of such masters as they please; and if the parent's reluctance excites their resentment, they may place him and his property under overseers. Fifty other instances fearfull as these might be collected from the laws of the state, but I will not repeat them lest my readers should be alarmed where there is no danger. These regulations are doubtless best; we have seen much good and no evil come from them. I adduce these instances to shew, that the most free constitution when made the subject of criticism may be exhibited in frightful colors, and such attempts we must expect against that now proposed. If, my countrymen, you wait for a constitution which absolutely bars a power of doing evil, you must wait long, and when obtained it will have no power of doing good. I allow you are oppressed, but not from the quarter that jealous and wrongheaded men would insinuate. You are oppressed by the men, who to serve their own purposes would prefer the shadow of government to the reality. You are oppressed for the want of power which can protect commerce, encourage business, and create a ready demand for the productions of your farms. You are become poor; oppression continued will make wise men mad. The landholders and farmers have long borne this oppression, we have been patient and groaned in secret, but can promise for ourselves no longer; unless relieved, madness may excite us to actions we now dread.

4

ALEXANDER HAMILTON, FEDERALIST, NO. 22,
140–41
14 Dec. 1787

(See ch. 5, no. 23)

5

ALEXANDER HAMILTON, FEDERALIST, NO. 23,
146–51
18 Dec. 1787

The necessity of a Constitution, at least equally energetic with the one proposed, to the preservation of the Union, is the point, at the examination of which we are now arrived.

This enquiry will naturally divide itself into three branches—the objects to be provided for by a Foederal Government—the quantity of power necessary to the accomplishment of those objects—the persons upon whom that power ought to operate. Its distribution and organization will more properly claim our attention under the succeeding head.

The principal purposes to be answered by Union are these—The common defence of the members—the preservation of the public peace as well against internal convulsions as external attacks—the regulation of commerce with other nations and between the States—the superintendence of our intercourse, political and commercial, with foreign countries.

The authorities essential to the care of the common defence are these—to raise armies—to build and equip fleets—to prescribe rules for the government of both—to direct their operations—to provide for their support. These powers ought to exist without limitation: *Because it is impossible to foresee or define the extent and variety of national exigencies, or the correspondent extent & variety of the means which may be necessary to satisfy them.* The circumstances that endanger the safety of nations are infinite; and for this reason no constitutional shackles can wisely be imposed on the power to which the care of it is committed. This power ought to be co-extensive with all the possible combinations of such circumstances; and ought to be under the direction of the same councils, which are appointed to preside over the common defence.

This is one of those truths, which to a correct and unprejudiced mind, carries its own evidence along with it; and may be obscured, but cannot be made plainer by argument or reasoning. It rests upon axioms as simple as they are universal. The *means* ought to be proportioned to the *end;* the persons, from whose agency the attainment of any *end* is expected, ought to possess the *means* by which it is to be attained.

Whether there ought to be a Foederal Government intrusted with the care of the common defence, is a question in the first instance open to discussion; but the moment it is decided in the affirmative, it will follow, that that government ought to be cloathed with all the powers requisite to the complete execution of its trust. And unless it can be shewn, that the circumstances which may affect the public safety are reducible within certain determinate limits; unless the contrary of this position can be fairly and rationally disputed, it must be admitted, as a necessary consequence, that there can be no limitation of that authority, which is to provide for the defence and protection of the community, in any matter essential to its efficacy; that is, in any matter essential to the *formation, direction* or *support* of the NATIONAL FORCES.

Defective as the present Confederation has been proved to be, this principle appears to have been fully recognized by the framers of it; though they have not made proper or adequate provision for its exercise. Congress have an unlimited discretion to make requisitions of men and money—to govern the army and navy—to direct their operations. As their requisitions were made constitutionally binding upon the States, who are in fact under the most solemn obligations to furnish the supplies required of them, the intention evidently was, that the United States should command whatever resources were by them judged requisite to "the common defence and general welfare." It was presumed that a sense of their true interests, and a regard to the dictates of good faith, would be found sufficient pledges for the punctual performance of the duty of the members to the Foederal Head.

The experiment has, however demonstrated, that this expectation was ill founded and illusory; and the observations made under the last head, will, I imagine, have sufficed to convince the impartial and discerning, that there is an absolute necessity for an entire change in the first principles of the system: That if we are in earnest about giving the Union energy and duration, we must abandon the vain project of legislating upon the States in their collective capacities: We must extend the laws of the Foederal Government to the individual citizens of America: We must discard the fallacious scheme of quotas and requisitions, as equally impracticable and unjust. The result from all this is, that the Union ought to be invested with full power to levy troops; to build and equip fleets, and to raise the revenues, which will be required for the formation and support of an army and navy, in the customary and ordinary modes practiced in other governments.

If the circumstances of our country are such, as to demand a compound instead of a simple, a confederate instead of a sole government, the essential point which will remain to be adjusted, will be to discriminate the OBJECTS, as far as it can be done, which shall appertain to the different provinces or departments of power; allowing to each the most ample authority for fulfilling the objects committed to its charge. Shall the Union be constituted the guardian of the common safety? Are fleets and armies and revenues necessary to this purpose? The government of the Union must be empowered to pass all laws, and to make all regulations which have relation to them. The same must be the case, in respect to commerce, and to every other matter to which its jurisdiction is permitted to extend. Is the administration of justice between the citizens of the same State, the proper department of the local governments? These must possess all the authorities which are connected with this object, and with every other that may be allotted to their particular cognizance and direction. Not to confer in each case a degree of power, commensurate to the end, would be to violate the most obvious rules of prudence and propriety, and improvidently to trust the great interests of the nation to hands, which are disabled from managing them with vigour and success.

Who so likely to make suitable provisions for the public defence, as that body to which the guardianship of the public safety is confided—which, as the center of information, will best understand the extent and urgency of the dangers that threaten—as the representative of the WHOLE will feel itself most deeply interested in the preservation of every part—which, from the responsibility implied in the duty assigned to it, will be most sensibly impressed with the necessity of proper exertions—and which, by the extension of its authority throughout the States, can alone establish uniformity and concert in the plans and measures, by which the common safety is to be secured? Is there not a manifest inconsistency in devolving upon the Foederal Government the care of the general defence, and leaving in the State governments the *effective* powers, by which it is to be provided for? Is not a want of co-operation the infallible consequence of such a system? And will not weakness, disorder, an undue distribution of the burthens and calamities of war, an unnecessary and intolerable increase of expence, be its natural and inevitable concomitants? Have we not had unequivocal experience of its effects in the course of the revolution, which we have just accomplished?

Every view we may take of the subject, as candid enquirers after truth, will serve to convince us, that it is both unwise and dangerous to deny the Foederal Government an unconfined authority, as to all those objects which are intrusted to its management. It will indeed deserve the most vigilant and careful attention of the people, to see that it be modelled in such a manner, as to admit of its being safely vested with the requisite powers. If any plan which has been, or may be offered to our consideration, should not, upon a dispassionate inspection, be found to answer this description, it ought to be rejected. A government, the Constitution of which renders it unfit to be trusted with all the powers, which a free people *ought to delegate to any government,* would be an unsafe and improper depository of the NATIONAL INTERESTS, wherever THESE can with propriety be confided, the co-incident powers may safely accompany them. This is the true result of all just reasoning upon the subject. And the adversaries of the plan, promulgated by the Convention, ought to have confined themselves to showing that the internal structure of the proposed government, was such as to render it unworthy of the confidence of the people. They ought not to have wandered into inflammatory declamations, and unmeaning cavils about the extent of the powers. The POWERS are not too extensive for the OBJECTS of Foederal administration, or in other words, for the management of our NATIONAL INTERESTS; nor can any satisfactory argument be framed to shew that they are chargeable with such an excess. If it be true, as has been insinuated by some of the writers on the other side, that the difficulty arises from the nature of the thing, and that the extent of the country will not permit us to form a government, in which such ample powers can safely be reposed, it would prove that we ought to contract our views, and resort to the expedient of separate Confederacies, which will move within more practicable spheres. For the absurdity must continually stare us in the face of confiding to a government, the direction of the most essential national interests, without daring to trust it with the authorities which are indispensable to their proper and efficient management. Let us not attempt to reconcile contradictions, but firmly embrace a rational alternative.

I trust, however, that the impracticability of one general system cannot be shewn. I am greatly mistaken, if any thing of weight, has yet been advanced of this tendency; and I flatter myself, that the observations which have been made in the course of these papers, have sufficed to place the reverse of that position in as clear a light as any matter still in the womb of time and experience can be susceptible of. This at all events must be evident, that the very difficulty itself drawn from the extent of the country, is the strongest argument in favor of an energetic government; for any other can certainly never preserve the Union of so large an empire. If we embrace the tenets of those, who oppose the adoption of the proposed Constitution, as the standard of our political creed, we cannot fail to verify the gloomy doctrines, which predict the impracticability of a national system, pervading the entire limits of the present Confederacy.

6

THOMAS JEFFERSON TO JAMES MADISON
20 Dec. 1787

Papers 12:442

(See ch. 18, no. 21)

7

ALEXANDER HAMILTON, FEDERALIST, NO. 30, 188–91
28 Dec. 1787

Money is with propriety considered as the vital principle of the body politic; as that which sustains its life and motion, and enables it to perform its most essential functions. A complete power therefore to procure a regular and adequate supply of it, as far as the resources of the community will permit, may be regarded as an indispensable ingredient in every constitution. From a deficiency in this particular, one of two evils must ensue; either the people must be subjected to continual plunder as a substitute for a more eligible mode of supplying the public wants, or the government must sink into a fatal atrophy, and in a short course of time perish.

In the Ottoman or Turkish empire, the sovereign, though in other respects absolute master of the lives and fortunes of his subjects, has no right to impose a new tax. The consequence is, that he permits the Bashaws or Governors of provinces to pillage the people without mercy; and in turn squeezes out of them the sums of which he stands in need to satisfy his own exigencies and those of the State. In America, from a like cause, the government of the Union has gradually dwindled into a state of decay, approaching nearly to annihilation. Who can doubt that the happiness of the people in both countries would be promoted by competent authorities in the proper hands, to provide the revenues which the necessities of the public might require?

The present confederation, feeble as it is, intended to repose in the United States, an unlimited power of providing for the pecuniary wants of the Union. But proceeding upon an erroneous principle, it has been done in such a manner as entirely to have frustrated the intention. Congress by the articles which compose that compact (as has been already stated) are authorised to ascertain and call for any sums of money necessary, in their judgment, to the service of the United States; and their requisitions, if conformable to the rule of apportionment, are in every constitutional sense obligatory upon the States. These have no right to question the propriety of the demand—no discretion beyond that of devising the ways and means of furnishing the sums demanded. But though this be strictly and truly the case; though the assumption of such a right be an infringement of the articles of Union; though it may seldom or never have been avowedly claimed; yet in practice it has been constantly exercised; and would continue to be so, as long as the revenues of the confederacy should remain dependant on the intermediate agency of its members. What the consequences of this system have been, is within the knowledge of every man, the least conversant in our public affairs, and has been amply unfolded in different parts of these inquiries. It is this which has chiefly contributed to reduce us to a situation which affords ample cause, both of mortification to ourselves, and of triumph to our enemies.

What remedy can there be for this situation but, in a change of the system, which has produced it? In a change of the fallacious and delusive system of quotas and requisitions? What substitute can there be imagined for this *ignis fatuus* in finance, but that of permitting the national government to raise its own revenues by the ordinary methods of taxation, authorised in every well ordered constitution of civil government? Ingenious men may declaim with plausibility on any subject; but no human ingenuity can point out any other expedient to rescue us from the inconveniences and embarrassments, naturally resulting from defective supplies of the public treasury.

The more intelligent adversaries of the new constitution admit the force of this reasoning; but they qualify their admission by a distinction between what they call *internal* and *external* taxation. The former they would reserve to the State governments; the latter, which they explain into commercial imposts, or rather duties on imported articles, they declare themselves willing to concede to the Foederal Head. This distinction, however, would violate that fundamental maxim of good sense and sound policy, which dictates that every POWER ought to be proportionate to its OBJECT; and would still leave the General Government in a kind of tutelage to the State governments, inconsistent with every idea of vigor or efficiency. Who can pretend that commercial imposts are or would be alone equal to the present and future exigencies of the Union? Taking into the account the existing debt, foreign and domestic, upon any plan of extinguishment, which a man moderately impressed with the importance of public justice and public credit could approve, in addition to the establishments, which all parties will acknowledge to be necessary, we could not reasonably flatter ourselves, that this resource alone, upon the most improved scale, would even suffice for its present necessities. Its future necessities admit not of calculation or limitation; and upon the principle, more than once adverted to, the power of making provision for them as they arise, ought to be equally unconfined. I believe it may be regarded as a position, warranted by the history of mankind, that *in the usual progress of things, the necessities of a nation in every stage of its existence will be found at least equal to its resources.*

To say that deficiencies may be provided for by requisitions upon the States, is on the one hand, to acknowledge that this system cannot be depended upon; and on the other hand, to depend upon it for every thing beyond a certain limit. Those who have carefully attended to its vices and deformities as they have been exhibited by experience, or delineated in the course of these papers, must feel an invincible repugnancy to trusting the national interests, in any degree, to its operation. Its inevitable tendency, whenever it is brought into activity, must be to enfeeble the Union and sow the seeds of discord and contention between the Foederal Head and its members, and between the members themselves. Can it be expected that the deficiencies would be better supplied in this mode, than the total wants of the Union have heretofore been supplied, in the same mode? It ought to be recollected, that if less will be required from the States, they will have proportionably less means to answer the demand. If the opinions of those who contend for the distinction which has been mentioned, were to be received as evidence of truth, one would be led to conclude that there was some known point in the oeconomy of national affairs, at which it would be safe to stop, and say, thus far the ends of public happiness will be promoted by supplying the wants of government, and all beyond this is unworthy of our care or anxiety. How is it possible that a government half supplied and always necessitous, can fulfil the purposes of its institution—can provide for the security of—advance the prosperity—or support the reputation of the commonwealth? How can it ever possess either energy or stability, dignity or credit, confidence at home or respectability abroad? How can its administration be any thing else than a succession of expedients temporising, impotent, disgraceful? How will it be able to avoid a frequent sacrifice of its engagements to immediate necessity? How can it undertake or execute any liberal or enlarged plans of public good?

8

ALEXANDER HAMILTON, FEDERALIST, NO. 31, 193–96
1 Jan. 1788

In disquisitions of every kind there are certain primary truths or first principles upon which all subsequent reasonings must depend. These contain an internal evidence, which antecedent to all reflection or combination commands the assent of the mind. Where it produces not this effect, it must proceed either from some defect or disorder in the organs of perception, or from the influence of some strong interest, or passion, or prejudice. Of this nature are the maxims in geometry, that "The whole is greater than its part; that things equal to the same are equal to one another; that two straight lines cannot inclose a space; and that all right angles are equal to each other." Of the same nature are these other maxims in ethics and politics, that there cannot be an effect without a cause; that the means ought to be proportioned to the end; that every power ought to be commensurate with its object; that there ought to be no limitation of a power destined to effect a purpose, which is itself incapable of limitation. And there are other truths in the two latter sciences, which if they cannot pretend to rank in the class of axioms, are yet such direct inferences from them, and so obvious in themselves, and so agreeable to the natural and unsophisticated dictates of common sense, that they challenge the assent of a sound and unbiassed mind, with a degree of force and conviction almost equally irresistable.

The objects of geometrical enquiry are so intirely abstracted from those pursuits which stir up and put in motion the unruly passions of the human heart, that mankind without difficulty adopt not only the more simple theorems of the science, but even those abstruse paradoxes, which however they may appear susceptible of demonstration, are at variance with the natural conceptions which the mind, without the aid of philosophy, would be led to entertain upon the subject. The INFINITE DIVISIBILITY of matter, or in other words, the INFINITE divisibility of a FINITE thing, extending even to the minutest atom, is a point agreed among geometricians; though not less incomprehensible to common sense, than any of those mysteries in religion, against which the batteries of infidelity have been so industriously levelled.

But in the sciences of morals and politics men are found far less tractable. To a certain degree it is right and useful, that this should be the case. Caution and investigation are a necessary armour against error and imposition. But this untractableness may be carried too far, and may degenerate into obstinacy, perverseness or disingenuity. Though it cannot be pretended that the principles of moral and political knowledge have in general the same degree of certainty with those of the mathematics; yet they have much better claims in this respect, than to judge from the conduct of men in particular situations, we should be disposed to allow them. The obscurity is much oftener in the passions and prejudices of the reasoner than in the subject. Men upon too many occasions do not give their own understandings fair play; but yielding to some untoward bias they entangle themselves in words and confound themselves in subtleties.

How else could it happen (if we admit the objectors to be sincere in their opposition) that positions so clear as those which manifest the necessity of a general power of taxation in the government of the union, should have to encounter any adversaries among men of discernment? Though these positions have been elsewhere fully stated, they will perhaps not be improperly recapitulated in this place, as introductory to an examination of what may have been offered by way of objection to them. They are in substance as follow:

A government ought to contain in itself every power requisite to the full accomplishment of the objects committed to its care, and to the complete execution of the trusts for which it is responsible; free from every other control, but a regard to the public good and to the sense of the people.

As the duties of superintending the national defence and of securing the public peace against foreign or domestic violence, involve a provision for casualties and dangers, to which no possible limits can be assigned, the power of making that provision ought to know no other bounds than the exigencies of the nation and the resources of the community.

As revenue is the essential engine by which the means of answering the national exigencies must be procured, the power of procuring that article in its full extent, must necessarily be comprehended in that of providing for those exigencies.

As theory and practice conspire to prove that the power of procuring revenue is unavailing, when exercised over the States in their collective capacities, the Federal government must of necessity be invested with an unqualified power of taxation in the ordinary modes.

9

JAMES MADISON, FEDERALIST, NO. 37, 233–34
11 Jan. 1788

Among the difficulties encountered by the Convention, a very important one must have lain, in combining the requisite stability and energy in Government, with the inviolable attention due to liberty, and to the Republican form. Without substantially accomplishing this part of their undertaking, they would have very imperfectly fulfilled the object of their appointment, or the expectation of the public: Yet, that it could not be easily accomplished, will be denied by no one, who is unwilling to betray his ignorance of the subject. Energy in Government is essential to that security against external and internal danger, and to that prompt and salutary execution of the laws, which enter into the very definition of good Government. Stability in Government, is essential to national character, and to the advantages annexed to it, as well as to that repose and confidence in the minds of the people, which are among the chief blessings of civil society. An irregular and mutable legislation, is not more an evil in itself, than it is odious to the people; and it may be pronounced with assurance, that the people of this country, enlightened as they are, with regard to the nature, and interested, as the great body of them are, in the effects of good Government, will never be satisfied, till some remedy be applied to the vicissitudes and uncertainties, which characterize the State administrations. On comparing, however, these valuable ingredients with the vital principles of liberty, we must perceive at once, the difficulty of mingling them together in their due proportions. The genius of Republican liberty, seems to demand on one side, not only that all power should be derived from the people; but, that those entrusted with it should be kept in dependence on the people, by a short duration of their appointments; and, that, even during this short period, the trust should be placed not in a few, but in a number of hands. Stability, on the contrary, requires, that the hands, in which power is lodged, should continue for a length of time, the same. A frequent change of men will result from a frequent return of electors, and a frequent change of measures, from a frequent change of men: whilst energy in Government requires not only a certain duration of power, but the execution of it by a single hand. How far the Convention may have succeeded in this part of their work, will better appear on a more accurate view of it. From the cursory view, here taken, it must clearly appear to have been an arduous part.

10

ALEXANDER HAMILTON, FEDERALIST, NO. 70, 471–72
15 Mar. 1788

There is an idea, which is not without its advocates, that a vigorous executive is inconsistent with the genius of republican government. The enlightened well wishers to this species of government must at least hope that the supposition is destitute of foundation; since they can never admit its truth, without at the same time admitting the con-

demnation of their own principles. Energy in the executive is a leading character in the definition of good government. It is essential to the protection of the community against foreign attacks: It is not less essential to the steady administration of the laws, to the protection of property against those irregular and high handed combinations, which sometimes interrupt the ordinary course of justice, to the security of liberty against the enterprises and assaults of ambition, of faction and of anarchy. Every man the least conversant in Roman story knows how often that republic was obliged to take refuge in the absolute power of a single man, under the formidable title of dictator, as well against the intrigues of ambitious individuals, who aspired to the tyranny, and the seditions of whole classes of the community, whose conduct threatened the existence of all government, as against the invasions of external enemies, who menaced the conquest and destruction of Rome.

There can be no need however to multiply arguments or examples on this head. A feeble executive implies a feeble execution of the government. A feeble execution is but another phrase for a bad execution: And a government ill executed, whatever it may be in theory, must be in practice a bad government.

11

LUTHER MARTIN, LETTER
4 Apr. 1788
Essays 381–83

. . . there are also persons who pretend that your situation is at present so bad that it cannot be worse, and urge that as an argument why we should embrace any remedy proposed, however desperate it may appear. Thus do the poor erring children of mortality, suffering under the presence of real or imaginary evils, have recourse to a pistol or halter for relief, and rashly launch into the untried regions of eternity—nor wake from this delusion, until they wake in endless woe. Should the citizens of America, in a fit desperation, be induced to commit this fatal act of political suicide, to which by such arguments they are stimulated, the day will come when laboring under more than Egyptian bondage; compelled to finish their quota of brick, though destitute of straw and of mortar; galled with your chains, and worn down by oppression, you will, by sad experience, be convinced (when that conviction shall be too late), that there is a difference in evils, and that the buzzing of gnats is more supportable than the sting of a serpent. From the wisdom of antiquity we might obtain excellent instruction, if we were not too proud to profit by it. Aesop has furnished us with a history of a nation of frogs, between which and our own there is a striking resemblance—whether the catastrophe be the same, rests with ourselves. Jupiter out of pure good nature, wishing to do them as little injury as possible, on being asked for a king, had thrown down into their pond a log to rule over them;—under whose government, had they been wise enough to know their own interest and to pursue it, they might to this day, have remained happy and prosperous. Terrified with the noise, and affrighted by the violent undulations of the water, they for some time kept an awful distance, and regarded their monarch with reverence; but the first impression being in some measure worn off, and perceiving him to be of a tame and peaceable disposition, they approached him with familiarity, and soon entertained for him the utmost contempt. In a little time were seen the leaders of the frogs croaking to their respective circles on the weakness and feebleness of the government at home, and of its want of dignity and respect abroad, till the sentiment being caught by their auditors, the whole pond resounded with "Oh Jupiter, good Jupiter, hear our prayers! take away from us this vile log, and give us a ruler who shall know how to support the dignity and splendor of government! give us any government you please, only let it be energetic and efficient." The Thunderer, in his wrath, sent them a crane. With what delight did they gaze on their monarch, as he came majestically floating on the wings of the wind. They admired his uncommon shape—it was such as they had never before seen—his deformities were, in their eyes, the greatest of beauties, and they were heard like Aristides to declare that, were they on the verge of eternity, they would not wish a single alteration in his form. His monstrous beak, his long neck, and his enormous poke, even these, the future means of their destruction, were subjects of their warm approbation. He took possession of his new dominions, and instantly began to swallow down his subjects, and it is said that those who had been the warmest zealots for crane administration, fared no better than the rest. The poor wretches were now much more dissatisfied than before, and with all possible humility applied to Jupiter again for his aid, but in vain—he dismissed them with this reproof, "that the evil of which they complained they had foolishly brought upon themselves, and that they had no other remedy now, but to submit with patience." Thus forsaken by the god, and left to the mercy of the crane, they sought to escape his cruelty by flight; but pursuing them to every place of retreat, and thrusting his long neck through the water to the bottom, he drew them out with his beak from their most secret hiding-places, and served them up as a regale for his ravenous appetite. The present federal government is, my fellow citizens, the log of the fable—the crane is the system now offered to your acceptance—I wish you not to remain under the government of the one, nor to become subjected to the tyranny of the other. If either of these events take place, it must arise from your being greatly deficient to yourselves—from your being, like the nation of Frogs, "a discontented, variable race, weary of liberty and fond of change." At the same time I have no hesitation in declaring, that if the one or the other must be our fate, I think the harmless, inoffensive, though contemptible Log, infinitely to be preferred to the powerful, the efficient, but all-devouring Crane.

12

JOHN TYLER, VIRGINIA RATIFYING CONVENTION
25 June 1788
Elliot 3:640–41

But much is said of the propriety of our becoming a great and powerful nation. There is a great difference between offensive and defensive war. If we can defend ourselves, it is sufficient. Shall we sacrifice the peace and happiness of this country, to enable us to make wanton war?

My conduct throughout the revolution will justify me. I have invariably wished to oppose oppressions. It is true that I have now a paltry office. I am willing to give it up—away with it! It has no influence on my present conduct. I wish Congress to have the regulation of trade. I was of opinion that a partial regulation alone would not suffice. I was among those members who, a few years ago, proposed that regulation. I have lamented that I have put my hand to it, since this measure may have grown out of it. It was the hopes of our people to have their trade on a respectable footing. But it never entered into my head that we should quit liberty, and throw ourselves into the hands of an energetic government. Do you want men to be more free, or less free, than they are? Gentlemen have been called upon to show the causes of this measure. None have been shown. Gentlemen say we shall be ruined unless we adopt it. We must give up our opinions. We cannot judge for ourselves. I hope gentlemen, before this, have been satisfied that such language is improper. All states which have heretofore been lavish in the concession of power and relinquishment of privileges have lost their liberty. It has been often observed (and it cannot be too often observed) that liberty ought not to be given up without knowing the terms. The gentlemen themselves cannot agree in the construction of various clauses of it; and so long as this is the case, so long shall liberty be in danger.

Gentlemen say we are jealous. I am not jealous of this house. I could trust my life with them. If this Constitution were safer, I should not be afraid. But its defects warrant my suspicions and fears. We are not passing laws now, but laying the foundation on which laws are to be made. We ought, therefore, to be cautious how we decide. When I consider the Constitution in all its parts, I cannot but dread its operation. It contains a variety of powers too dangerous to be vested in any set of men whatsoever.

13

THOMAS JEFFERSON, FIRST INAUGURAL ADDRESS
4 Mar. 1801
Richardson 1:321–24

(See ch. 4, no. 33)

10

Separation of Powers

Introduction

Of the doctrine of the separation of powers, so familiar to readers of Supreme Court opinions, the Constitution says not a word. In this it sets itself apart from the constitutions of Virginia, Massachusetts, and New Hampshire (1784), whose pointed and unqualified language testifies to a general acceptance of "this invaluable precept in the science of politics" (*Federalist,* no. 47). Yet the framework of government outlined in the Constitution of 1787 presupposes the separation of powers, gives expression to it, and in so doing further refines the meaning of the doctrine. Much of the controversy over drafting and ratification turned on this question of meaning. At issue was not whether the proposed Constitution embodies the separation of powers to some extent (few denied that), but whether its separation is adequate, whether the purposes for the sake of which separation of powers is indispensable are indeed well served by the peculiar manner in which the Constitution effects and compromises that separation. By the time the new government was established, the terms in which much of the debate had been conducted had themselves been redefined and clarified. The Constitution, far from being a dubious exemplar of the separation of powers, became a classic instance of the doctrine it never mentions.

The materials assembled here may appear at odds with one another, or even hopelessly confused. But such hasty judgment overlooks the very different concerns that prompt the several authors to seek a remedy in "separa-

tion." The precursors of the Constitution were not groping in the dark in search of the full-fledged doctrine. Rather, each had a more or less clear notion of the kind of separation that would overcome a perceived evil or secure a specific good.

Why Separation?

Thus Clement Walker, a member of the Long Parliament in 1648, saw distinctly enough the kind of arbitrary, tyrannical rule against which the governed had to be protected. The remedy, he thought (no. 1), lay in a separation of governmental functions cast in terms of "the Governing power," "the Legislative power," and "the Judicative power."

For Marchamont Nedham, writing under Cromwell's Protectorate in 1656 (no. 2), the required separation is that of legislative and executive powers into different "hands and persons." As used by him, the distinction resembles the sharp dichotomy between the formation of policy and its administration favored by mid-twentieth-century American administrative theorists. Separation, for Nedham, is an indispensable means for locating responsibility and fixing accountability. An executive, unambiguously charged with executing a policy set by the "Law-makers," can be held liable for its performance or nonperformance. Let that clear line of distinction and responsibility be blurred, and liberty and the people's interest are alike in jeopardy.

John Trenchard's argument of 1698 carries Nedham's separation of persons even further (no. 4). One might say that without separation of persons there cannot be a meaningful separation of powers. Here, more than accountability is sought. The freedom of England depends on a truly representative—i.e., an uncorrupt—House of Commons serving as a check on an executive which already has the power of the sword. Given the premise that "it is certain that every Man will act for his own Interest," the only safeguard against "continual Heartburnings between King and People" consists in so interweaving the representatives' interest with that of the people that in acting for themselves, the representatives must likewise act for the common interest. As is true of many eighteenth-century writers, Trenchard here drew on arguments for separation of powers and for mixed or balanced government without sharply distinguishing the two.

Among Americans reflecting on new political arrangements in the latter half of the eighteenth century, no political authority was invoked more often than "the celebrated Montesquieu." Thanks in some measure to those Americans themselves, the name of Montesquieu is firmly attached to the doctrine of the separation of powers. But like most teachings of that subtle mind, this one has its ambiguities and invites differing interpretations. Everyone agrees that the *locus classicus* of the separation of powers doctrine is the seemingly rambling, discursive chapter on the constitution of England in the *Spirit of Laws* (see ch. 17, no. 9). The book of which this chapter forms a part is entitled, "Of the Laws which Establish Political Liberty with Regard to the Constitution"; it is with a view to political liberty that separation of powers is necessary. By political liberty Montesquieu meant "a tranquillity of mind arising from the opinion each person has of his safety." Men's minds cannot be at rest if two or three of the kinds of governmental power are held in the same hands. Montesquieu's tripartite division appears to be based on a separation of functions—legislative, executive (having largely to do with foreign affairs—Locke's "federative" power), and judicial. Montesquieu's judicial power is not, however, Hamilton's or Marshall's; nor is it the Law Lords sitting as a court of last resort. It appears, rather, in the form of ad hoc tribunals, juries of one's peers who judge of both fact and law without need for the guiding intelligence of a professional judge.

Although Montesquieu separated governmental functions and separated governmental powers, there is no clear one-to-one correspondence between the two because he did not insist on an absolute separation. Thus, although the executive is a separate branch, it properly partakes (through the veto, for example) in a legislative function. This blending or overlapping of functions is in part necessitated by Montesquieu's intention that separation check the excesses of one or the other branch. Separation of powers here reinforces or even merges into balanced government. Excesses may come from all or almost all sides. Thanks to bicameralism, the licentiousness of the many and the encroachments of the few are alike checked. The nobility mediate between a potentially overbearing lower house and the executive. The executive's power to convene and prorogue the legislature and to veto its enactments are forms of self-defense, while the legislature's power to impeach and try the agents or ministers of the executive is necessary and sufficient to hold the executive accountable to examination without holding him hostage.

If the goal is liberty—that is to say, individual safety—the model to follow (Montesquieu suggested) is that of the English constitution portrayed in his pages. But one might pursue an alternative goal with more or less separation of powers and more or less happiness—like "the monarchies we are acquainted with."

Although maintaining that sovereignty resides in the king in Parliament, Blackstone draws heavily on elements of Montesquieu's argument and adapts them to his peculiar purpose (no. 6). For all his insistence on three distinct powers—and they are now the familiar executive, legislative, and judicial powers, with the latter a recognizable judiciary with independent tenure of office—and for all his insistence on separation for the sake of warding off oppressive government, Blackstone seems less interested in separation than he is in balance. His mechanical image fits his point; balance is to be sought not in total separation but in the artful involvement and mutual interactions of the several branches of the civil polity: executive, nobility, and people. The separation of powers and balance of social orders are inextricably interwoven.

If the instructions of the Bostonians to their representatives in the Massachusetts provincial congress are any sign (no. 8), the reasons of Montesquieu and the others had become commonplace by 1776. No less effective in directing American thoughts to the separation of powers would have been the protracted, painful controversies between royal governors, councils, and colonial assemblies. The colonists' experiences with what they saw as executive usurpations, corruption of elected officials, and manipulation of electoral processes focused their minds on suitable remedies. For the Bostonians the tripartite separation of powers, functions, and persons is a sine qua non if arbitrary power is to be checked and liberty secured. A correlative of the separation of persons is the prohibition of plural office-holding; and in the democratic context that entails adequate salaries so that officials are "above the necessity of stooping."

John Adams's early *Thoughts on Government* (see ch. 4, no. 5) similarly confirms the high expectations held for the separation of powers and the broad spectrum of ills that it would guard against: passionate partiality, absurd judgments, avaricious and ambitious self-serving behavior by governors, and the inefficient performance of functions.

The experiences under the early state constitutions and the Articles of Confederation reinforced the belief in separation. Jefferson's critique of the Virginia Constitution (no. 9) raised the familiar concerns with safety and efficiency; both to establish free principles and to preserve them once established required a division and balance that went beyond those embodied in existing arrangements. Despotism is no less despotic because "elective."

The Philadelphia Convention usually discussed the adequacy and proper degree of the separation of powers in terms of the ends to be achieved: stability (Dickinson), defense (Gerry, Madison, G. Morris, Wilson), independence (King), and proper function (Gerry). No less worrisome, however, was whether the means available to the several branches of government to defend themselves against the others might not be excessive (Franklin).

Madisonian Separation

Those who opposed the unqualified ratification of the Constitution thought that not enough had been done to secure the proper degree of separation or that the means of defense would be ineffectual. Against these Anti-Federalist contentions Madison launched the most extensive and theoretically coherent discussion of the doctrine of the separation of powers. Appealing from a literal reading of Montesquieu to the practice of Montesquieu's model, England, and appealing from the categorical injunctions of some of the state constitutions to the actual practices of those very states, Madison succeeded in developing a sophisticated line of reasoning that never cuts loose from the world of affairs. He admonished his readers to cease worrying about the dangers of yesteryear—the overbearing abuses of a hereditary king in collusion with a hereditary nobility—and guard instead against the dangers of today and tomorrow—the enterprising ambition of an assembly flush with a confidence derived from its base of popular support.

The theory of separation seems to presuppose the notion that the powers of government consist largely in making laws, executing laws, and applying them to particular cases through the rule of law. (The awkwardness of accounting for foreign and defense policy under this simple view is another matter.) From this point of view legislative supremacy appears to be a foregone conclusion, "and all other Powers in any Members or parts of the Society [are] derived from and subordinate to it" (Locke, no. 3). But good government requires that this tendency be countered, that the legislative department be prevented from "drawing all power into its impetuous vortex" (Madison, no. 15; also no. 17). All the more is this urgent if, as Hamilton maintained, "Energy in the executive is a leading character in the definition of good government," or if, as Madison maintained, "Energy in Government is essential" (see ch. 9, nos. 9, 10). Thus, looking beyond the preoccupation with still vivid examples of domineering royal governors and plural office-holding, the authors of *The Federalist* saw in the separation of powers an effective means of serving the need for energy as well as of securing liberty.

The solution offered in the well-known *Federalist*, no. 51, builds on the separation of powers but goes well beyond it. At bottom, of course, the primary control on an aggrandizing government must be the people themselves. But, Madison noted candidly (no. 16), "experience has taught mankind the necessity of auxiliary precautions." If parchment barriers are indeed insufficient to forfend an ominous concentration of powers, and if absolute separation is neither possible nor desirable, the end in view requires a more complex and intricate institutional arrange-

ment. Personal motives are to be enlisted in the service of a public good; relations among the parts are to be contrived to keep one another in their proper place. Going beyond his precursors and drawing on peculiar American circumstances, Madison showed the way to a double security against the usurpations of oppressive rulers—a separation of power between two distinct levels of government, and a separation of powers within each level of government. Further, he developed a theoretical case for "the extended republic of the United States," a republican safeguard against the oppression of one part of the society by "interested combinations of the majority," thereby preventing the popular guardians themselves from becoming a source of usurpation and injustice (see also Madison, ch. 4, no. 19). Thirty years later (no. 22), "the great questions" remained just that for Madison, "the experiment" of 1787 still an experiment, and the Federalist solution worthy of continued support and reinforcement.

The immediate sequel to Madison's defense and the Constitution's ratification was not silence, but continued debate. James Wilson and Nathaniel Chipman illustrate contending juristic interpretations. For Wilson separation entails a clear discrimination of powers, an independence whereby each power conducts its deliberations free of external influence, and a dependence whereby the actions of each are subject to scrutiny and control by the others. The outcome would not be deadlock, Wilson thought, but a line of movement prompted by necessity and, though (or because?) a vector of forces, closer to the requirements of public liberty and happiness. (See Lectures on Law, pt. 1, ch. 10, 1791.)

Of this Chipman (no. 18) was quite doubtful. The legislature stands, in a sense, in a privileged position. Unlike the executive or the judiciary, its members have no need of a constitutional tribunal to call them to account; as legislators they are properly and solely amenable to the tribunal of "public sentiment." What the legislature does require of the other branches is information—objections arising out of their several experiences in executing or interpreting the laws—but of the value and relevance of that information in furthering the common interest "the legislature must be the sole judges."

But what is information? And when does legislative deliberation cease to be that and come to be something more—a trespass upon the proper functions of another branch, a transgression of constitutional separation, and a threat to liberty? The materials centering on the efforts of the House of Representatives to obtain papers relating to the Jay Treaty (nos. 19, 20, 21) display the intense partisanship and the close reasoning elicited by this controversy. However clear the theory, its practical application was and would remain a matter of principled and unprincipled dispute. The resolution of disputes over constitutional separation could not be left to the parties themselves and would not be left to popular conventions, as Jefferson would have preferred (see Madison's critique and rejection, ch. 2, no. 19). Instead, another forum presented itself for resolving such disputes in the name of the settled constitutional will of a sovereign people. *Marbury* v. *Madison* (1 Cranch 137 [1803]) was just around the corner.

1

CLEMENT WALKER, RELATIONS AND
OBSERVATIONS, HISTORICALL AND POLITICK UPON
THE PARLIAMENT BEGUN ANNO DOM. 1640
1648

U. Pa. L. Rev. 86:855–56 (1938)

The KING is the only supreme Governour of this Realme of England, to regulate and protect the people by commanding the Laws to be observed and executed; and to this end He (and He alone) beareth not the Sword in vaine; yet the KING by himselfe can neither make, repeal, or alter any one law, without the concurrence of both Houses of Parliament, the Legislative power residing in all three, and not in any one. . . . Nor can the King by Himselfe, or joyntly with the Lords and Commons judge what the Law is, this is the office of the sworne Judges of the two Benches and Exchequer, who are the known Expositors, and Dispensers of Law and Justice in all Causes brought before them; yea, they do declare by what Law the King Governs, thereby keeping the KING from Governing Arbitrarily and enslaving the people. . . . Now for any one man, or any Assembly, Court, or Corporation of men (be it the two Houses of Parliament) to usurpe these three powers: 1. The Governing power. 2. The Legislative power. 3. And the Judicative power, into themselves, is to make themselves the highest Tyrants, and the people the basest slaves in the world; for to govern supremely by a Law made, and interpreted by themselves according to their own pleasure, what can be more boundlesse and arbitrary?

1. For the Governing power. 1. They coyne, enhaunce, and abate money. 2. They make War and Peace, and continue an extraordinary Militia of an Army upon us. 3. They declare who are Enemies to the Realm. 4. They maintaine forraine negotiacions. 5. They regulate matter of Trade, and exercise other Regalities: whereas all Iura Regalia belong only to the King as Supreme Governour.

2. For the Legislative power. They exclude the King from His Negative voice, and the two Houses obtrude their Ordinances (things so new, that they are not pleadable in any Court of Iustice) as Laws upon the people; laying on Excise, Assessments, and Taxes upon the people: They Vote and declare new Treasons, not known by the statute 25. Edw. 3 nor by any other known Law; yea even to make or receive any addresse to, or from the King; and they account it a Breach of Privilege, if men do not believe it to be Treason, being once declared. They out men of their free-holds, and imprison their Persons, contrary to Magna Charta, by Ordinances of Sequestration, &c.

3. For the Iudicative power. They erect Infinite many of new Iudicatories under them, as their Committees of Complaints, of secret Examinations, of Indempnities; their Country Committees, where businesses are examined, heard, and determined without, nay against Magna Charta, and the known Lawes: nay even in capitall crimes they wave the Courts of Law, and all Legall proceedings by Outlawry, Indictment, or Tryall by Peers, and Bill of Attainder; (which is the only way of Tryall in Parliament: For the Parliament cannot judicially determine any thing, but by Act of Parliament). . . .

2

MARCHAMONT NEDHAM, THE EXCELLENCIE
OF A FREE-STATE
1656

Gwyn 131–33

A fifth Errour in Policy hath been this, *viz.* a permitting of the Legislative and Executive Powers of a State, to rest in one and the same hands and persons. By the Legislative Power, we understand the Power of making, altering, or repealing Laws, which in all well-ordered Governments, hath ever been lodged in a succession of the supreme Councels of Assemblies of a Nation.

By the Executive Power, we mean that Power which is derived from the other, and by their Authority transfer'd into the hand or hands of one Person, (called a Prince) or into the hands of many (called States) for the administration of Government, in the Execution of those Laws. In the keeping of these two Powers distinct, flowing in distinct Channels, so that they may never meet in one, save upon some short extraordinary occasion consists the safety of a state.

The Reason is evident; because if the Law-makers (who ever have the Supream Power) should be also the constant Administrators and Dispencers of Law and Justice, then (by consequence) the People would be left without Remedy, in case of Injustice, since no Appeal can lie under Heaven against such as have the Supremacy; which, if once admitted, were inconsistent with the very intent and natural import of true Policy: which ever supposeth, that men in Power may be unrighteous; and therefore (presuming the worst) points always, in all determinations, at the Enormities and Remedies of Government, on the behalf of the People.

For the clearing of this, it is worthy your observation; that in all Kingdomes and States whatsoever, where they have had any thing of Freedom among them, the Legislative and Executive Powers have been managed in distinct hands: That is to say, the Law-makers have set down Laws, as Rules of Government; and then put Power into the hands of others (not their own) to govern by those Rules: by which means the people were happy having no Governours, but such as were liable to give an account of Government to the supream Councel of Law-makers. And on the other side, it is no less worthy of a very serious observation; That Kings and standing States never became absolute over the People, till they brought both the making and execution of Lawes into their own hands: and as this Usurpation of theirs took place by degrees, so unlimited Arbitrary Power crept up into the Throne, there to domineer o're the World, and defie the Liberties of the People.

Cicero, in his second Book *de Offic.* and his third, *de Legibus*, speaking of the first institution of Kings, tells us, how they were at first left to govern at their own discretion without Laws. Then their Wills, and their Words, were Law, the making and execution of Lawes was in one and the same hands.

But what was the consequence? Nothing but Injustice, and Injustice without Remedy, till the People were taught by necessity to ordain Lawes, as Rules whereby they ought to govern. Then began the meeting of the People successively in their supream Assemblies, to make Laws, whereby Kings (in such places as continued under the Kingly Form) were limited and restrained, so that they could do nothing in Government, but what was agreeable to Law; for which they were accountable, as well as other Officers were in other Forms of Government, to those supreme Councels and Assemblies: Witness all the old stories of *Athens*, *Sparta*, and other Countries of *Greece*, where you shall find, that the Law-making, and the Law-executing Powers, were placed in distinct hands under every Form of Government: For, so much of Freedom they retained still under every Form, till they were both swallowed up (as they were several times) by an absolute Domination.

In old *Rome*, we find *Romulus* their first King cut in pieces by the Senate, for taking upon him to make and execute Laws at his own pleasure. And *Livy* tells us, that the reason why they expel'd *Tarquin* their last King, was, because he took the Executive and Legislative Powers both into his own hands, making himself both Legislator, and Officer, *inconsulto Senatus* without advice, and in defiance of the Senate.

Kings being cashier'd, then their Standing-Senates came in play, who making and executing Laws, by Decrees of their own, soon grew intolerable, and put the people upon divers desperate Adventures, to get the Legislative Power out of their hands, and place it in their own; that is in a succession of their Supream Assemblies: But the Executive Power they left, part in the hands of Officers of their own, and part in the Senate; in which State it continued some hundreds of years, to the great happiness and content of all, till the Senate by sleights and subtilties got both Power into their own possession again, and turned all into confusion.

Afterwards, their Emperors (though Usurpers) durst not at first turn both these Powers into the Channel of their own unbounded Will; but did it by degrees, that they might the more insensibly deprive the people of their Liberty, till at length they openly made and executed Laws at their own pleasures, being both Legislators and Officers, without giving an account to any: and so there was an end of the Roman Liberty.

To come nearer home, let us look into the old Constitution of the Commonwealths, and Kingdomes of Europe. We find in the *Italian States; Venice*, which having the Legislative and Executive Power, confined within the narrow Pale of its Nobility in the Senate, is not so free as once *Florence* was with *Siena, Millan*, and the rest; before their Dukes, by arrogating both those Powers to themselves, worm'd them out of their Liberty.

Of all those States there, onely *Genoa* remains in a free posture, by keeping the Power of Legislation onely in their Supream Assemblies, and leaving the Execution of Law in a titular Duke, and a Councel, the keeping of these Powers asunder within their proper Sphere, is one principal Reason why they have been able to exclude Tyranny out of their own State, while it hath run the Round in *Italy*.

What made the Grand Seignior absolute of old, but his ingrossing both these Powers? and of late the Kings of *Spain* and *France*? In ancient time the case stood for otherwise; for in *Ambrosio Morales* his Chronicle you will finde, that in *Spain* the Legislative power was lodged onely in their Supreme Councel, and their King was no more but an elective Officer, to execute such Laws as they made, and in case of failing, to give them an accompt, and submit to their judgements, which was the common practice; as you may see also in *Mariana*: It was so also in *Aragon* till it was united to *Castile*, by the Mariage of *Ferdimand* and *Isabel;* and then both States soon lost their liberty, by the projects of Ferdimand and his successors, who drew the powers of Legislation and Execution of Law, within the verge and influence of the Prerogative Royall: whilest these two powers were kept distinct, then these States were free; but the ingrossing of them in one and the same hands, was the losse of their Freedom.

France likewise was once as free as any Nation under Heaven, though the King of late hath done all, and been all in all, till the time of *Lewis* the eleventh: he was no more but an Officer of State, regulated by Law, to see the Laws put in execution; and the Legislative Power (that) rested in the Assembly of the 3. States; but *Lewis*, by snatching both these Powers into the single hands of himself, and his successors, rookt them of their Liberty; which they may now recover again, if they have but so much manhood, as to reduce the two Powers into their ancient, or into better Channels.

This pattern of *Lewis* was followed close by the late King of England, who by our ancient Laws, was the same here, that *Lewis* ought to have been in *France*, an Officer in trust, to see to the execution of the Lawes: but by aiming at the same ends which *Lewis* attained, and straining, by the ruine of Parliaments, to reduce the Legislative Power, as well as the Executive into his own hands, he instead of an absolute Tyranny, which might have followed his project, brought a swift destruction upon himself and Family.

Thus you see it appears, that the keeping of these two Powers distinct, hath been a ground preservative of the peoples Interest, whereas their uniting hath been its ruine all along in so many Ages and Nations.

3

JOHN LOCKE, *SECOND TREATISE*,
§§ 143, 144, 150, 159
1689

143. The *Legislative* Power is that which has a right *to direct* how *the Force of the Commonwealth* shall be imploy'd for preserving the Community and the Members of it. But because those Laws which are constantly to be Executed, and whose force is always to continue, may be made in a little time; therefore there is no need, that the *Legislative* should be always in being, not having always business to do. And because it may be too great a temptation to humane frailty apt to grasp at Power, for the same Persons who have the Power of making Laws, to have also in their hands the power to execute them, whereby they may exempt themselves from Obedience to the Laws they make, and suit the Law, both in its making and execution, to their own private advantage, and thereby come to have a distinct interest from the rest of the Community, contrary to the end of Society and Government: Therefore in well order'd Commonwealths, where the good of the whole is so considered, as it ought, the *Legislative* Power is put into the hands of divers Persons who duly Assembled, have by themselves, or jointly with others, a Power to make Laws, which when they have done, being separated again, they are themselves subject to the Laws, they have made; which is a new and near tie upon them, to take care, that they make them for the publick good.

144. But because the Laws, that are at once, and in a short time made, have a constant and lasting force, and need a *perpetual Execution,* or an attendance thereunto: Therefore 'tis necessary there should be a *Power always in being,* which should see to the *Execution* of the Laws that are made, and remain in force. And thus the *Legislative* and *Executive Power* come often to be separated.

. . . . .

150. In all Cases, whilst the Government subsists, the *Legislative is the Supream Power.* For what can give Laws to another, must needs be superiour to him: and since the Legislative is no otherwise Legislative of the Society, but by the right it has to make Laws for all the parts and for every Member of the Society, prescribing Rules to their actions, and giving power of Execution, where they are transgressed, the *Legislative* must needs be the *Supream,* and all other Powers in any Members or parts of the Society, derived from and subordinate to it.

. . . . .

159. Where the Legislative and Executive Power are in distinct hands, (as they are in all moderated Monarchies, and well-framed Governments) there the good of the Society requires, that several things should be left to the discretion of him, that has the Executive Power. For the Legislators not being able to foresee, and provide, by Laws, for all, that may be useful to the Community, the Executor of the Laws, having the power in his hands, has by the common Law of Nature, a right to make use of it, for the good of the Society, in many Cases, where the municipal Law has given no direction, till the Legislative can conveniently be Assembled to provide for it. Many things there are, which the Law can by no means provide for, and those must necessarily be left to the discretion of him, that has the Executive Power in his hands, to be ordered by him, as the publick good and advantage shall require: nay, 'tis fit that the Laws themselves should in some Cases give way to the Executive Power, or rather to this Fundamental Law of Nature and Government, *viz.* That as much as may be, *all* the Members of the Society are to be *preserved.*

4

JOHN TRENCHARD, A SHORT HISTORIE OF
STANDING ARMIES IN ENGLAND
1698

Gwyn 138–41

There is nothing in which the generality of Mankind are so much mistaken as when they talk of Government. The different Effects of it are obvious to every one, but few can trace its Causes. Most Men having indigested Ideas of the Nature of it, attribute all publick Miscarriages to the Corruption of Mankind. They think the whole Mass is infected, that it's impossible to make any Reformation, and so submit patiently to their Country's Calamities, or else share in the Spoil: whereas Complaints of this kind are as old as the World, and every Age has thought their own the worst. We have not only our own Experience, but the Example of all times, to prove that Men in the same Circumstances will do the same things, call them by what Names of distinction you please. A Government is a mere piece of Clockwork; and having such Springs and Wheels, must act after such a manner: and there the Art is to constitute it so that it must move to the publick Advantage. It is certain that every Man will act for his own Interest; and all wise Governments are founded upon that Principle: So that this whole Mystery is only to make the Interest of the Governors and Governed the same. In an absolute Monarchy, where the whole Power is in one Man, his Interest will be only regarded: In an Aristocracy the Interest of a few; and in a free Government the Interest of every one. This would be the Case of England if some Abuses that have lately crept into our Constitution were remov'd. The Freedom of this Kingdom depends upon the Peoples chusing the House of Commons, who are a part of the Legislature, and have the sole Power of giving Mony. Were this a true Representative, and free from external Force or private Bribery, nothing could pass there but what they thought was for the publick Advantage. For their own Interest is so interwoven with the Peoples, that if they act for themselves (which every one of them will do as near as he can) they must act for the common Interest of England. And if a few among them should find it their Interest to abuse their Power, it will be the Interest of all the rest to punish them for it: and then our Government would act mechanically, and a Rogue will as naturally be hang'd as a Clock strike twelve when the hour is come. This is the Fountain-Head from whence the People expect all their Happiness, and the Redress of their Grievances; and if we can preserve them free from Corruption, they will take care to keep every body else so. Our Constitution seems to have provided for it, by never suffering the King (till Charles the Second's Reign) to have a mercenary Army to frighten them into a Compliance, nor Places or Revenues great enough to bribe them into it. The Places in the King's Gift were but few, and most of them Patent Places for Life, and the rest great Offices of State enjoy'd by single Persons, which seldom fell to the Share of the Commons, such as the Lord Chancellor, Lord Treasurer, Privy-Seal, Lord High Admiral, Exc. and when these Offices were possess'd by the Lords, the Commons were severe Inquisitors into their Actions. Thus the Government of England continu'd from the time that the Romans quitted the Island, to the time of Charles the First, who was the first I have read of that made an Opposition to himself in the House of Commons the road to Perferment; of which the Earl of Stafford and Noy were the most remarkable Instances, who from great Patriots became the chief Assertors of despotick Power. But this serv'd only to exasperate the rest; for he had not Places enough for all that expected them, nor Mony enough to bribe them. 'Tis true, he rais'd great Sums of Mony upon the People; but it being without Authority of Parliament, and having no Army to back him, it met with such Difficulties in the raising, that it did him little good, and ended at last in his Ruin, tho by the means of a long and miserable War, which brought us from one Tyranny to another; for the Army had got all things into their Power, and govern'd the Nation by a Council of War, which made all Parties join in calling in Charles the Second: So that he came in with the general applause of the People, who in a kind fit gave him a vast Revenue for Life. By this he was enabl'd to raise an Army, and bribe the Parliament, which he did to the purpose: but being a luxurious Prince, he could not part with great Sums at once. He only fed them from Hand to Mouth: So that they found it as necessary to keep him in a constant Dependance upon them, as they had upon him. They knew he would give them ready Mony no longer than he had absolute Necessity for them, and he had not Places enough in his Disposal to secure a Majority in the House: for in those early days the Art was not found out of splitting and multiplying Places; as instead of a Lord Treasurer to have five Lords of the Treasury; instead of a Lord Admiral to have seven Lords of the Admiralty; to have seven Commissioners of the Customs, nine of the Excize, fourteen of the Navy Office, ten of the Stamp Office, eight of the Prize Office, sixteen of the Commissioners of Trade, two of the Post Office, four of the Transports, four for Hackny Coaches, four for Wine-Licences, four for the Victualling Office, and Multitudes of other Offices which are endless to enumerate. I believe the Gentlemen who have the good Fortune to be in some of these Imployments, will think I complement them, if I should say they have not been better executed since they were in so many Hands, than when in fewer: and I must confess, I see no reason why they may not be made twice as many, and so *ad infinitum*, (unless the number be ascertain'd by Parliament) and what Danger this may be to our Constitution, I think of with Horror. For if in Ages to come they should be all given to Parliament Men, what will become of our so much boasted Liberty? What shall be done when the Criminal becomes the Judg, and the Malefactors are left to try themselves? We may be sure their common Danger will unite them, and they will all stand by one another. I do not speak this by guess; for I have read of a Country where there was a constant series of Mismanagement for many Years together, and yet no Body was punish'd: and even in our own Country I believe, some Men now alive can remember the time, when if the King had but twenty more Places in his Disposal, or dispos'd of those he had to the best Advantage, the Liberty of England had been at an end. I would not be understood quite to exclude Parliament-men from having Places; for a Man may serve his Country in two Capacities: but I would not have it to be a Qualification for a Place; because a poor Borough thinks a Man fit to represent them, that therefore he must be a Statesman, a Lawyer, a Soldier, an Admiral, and what not? If this Method should be taken in a future Reign, the People must not expect to see Men of Ability or Integrity in any Places, while they hold them by no other Tenure than the Disservice they do their Country in the House of Commons, and are sure to be turn'd out upon every prevalent Faction on the other side. They must then never expect to see the House of Commons act vigorously for the Interest either of King or People; but some will servilely comply with the Court to keep their Places, others will oppose it as unreasonably to get them: and those Gentlemen whose Designs are for their Countries Interest, will grow weary of the best Form of Government in the World, thinking by mistake the Fault is in our Constitution. I have heard of a Country, where the Disputes about Offices to the value of thirty thousand Pounds *per annum*, have made six Millions ineffectual; what by some Mens prostitute Compliance, and others openly clogging the Wheels, it has caus'd Want and Necessity in all kinds of Men, Bribery, Treachery, Profaneness, Atheism, Prodigality, Luxury and all the Vices that attend a remiss and corrupt Administration, and a universal Neglect of the Publick. It is natural to run from one extreme to another; and this Policy will at last turn upon any Court that uses it: for if they should be resolv'd to give all Offices to Parliament-men, the People will think themselves under a Necessity to obtain a Law that they shall give none, which has been more than once attempted in our own time. Indeed, tho there may be no great inconvenience to suffering a few Men that have Places to be in that House, such as come in naturally, without any indirect means, yet it will be fatal to us to have many: for all wise Governments endeavour as much as possible to keep the Legislative and Executive Parts asunder, that they may be a check upon one another. Our Government trusts the King with no part of the Legislative but a Negative Voice, which is absolutely necessary to preserve the Executive. One part of the Duty of the House of Commons is to punish Offenders, and redress the Grievances occasion'd by the Executive Part of the Government; and how can that be done if they should happen to be the same Persons, unless they would be publick-spirited enough to hang or drown themselves?

But in my Opinion, in another thing of no less Importance, we deviated in Charles the Second's time from our Constitution: for tho we were in a Capacity of punishing Offenders, yet we did not know legally who they were. The Law has been always very tender of the Person of the King, and therefore has dispos'd the Executive Part of the Government in such proper Channels, that whatsoever lesser Excesses are committed, they are not imputed to him, but his Ministers are accountable for them: his great Seal is kept by his Chancellor, his Revenue by his Treasurer, his Laws are executed by his Judges, his Fleet is manag'd by his Lord High Admiral, who are all accountable for their Misbehaviour. Formerly all Matters of State and Discretion was debated and resolv'd in the Privy Council, where every Man subscrib'd his Opinion, and was answerable for it. The late King Charles was the first who broke this most excellent part of our Constitution, by settling a Cabal or Cabinet Council, where all Matters of Consequence were debated and resolv'd, and then brought to the Privy Council to be confirm'd. The first footsteps we have of this Council in any European Government were in Charles the Ninth's time of France, when resolving to massacre the Protestants, he durst not trust his Council with it, but chose a few Men who he call'd his Cabinet Council: and considering what a Genealogy it had, 'tis no wonder it has been so fatal both to King and People. To the King: for whereas our Constitution has provided Ministers in the several parts of the Government to answer for Miscarriages, and to skreen him from the hatred of the People; this on the contrary protects the Ministers, and exposes the King to all the Complaints of his Subjects. And 'tis as dangerous to the People: for whatever Miscarriages there are, no body can be punish'd for them; for they justify themselves by a Sign Manual, or perhaps a private Direction from the King: and then we have run it so far, that we can't follow it. The Consequence of this must be continual Heartburnings between King and People: and no one can see the Event.

5

MONTESQUIEU, SPIRIT OF LAWS,
BK. 11, CHS. 6–7
1748

(See ch. 17, no. 9)

6

WILLIAM BLACKSTONE, COMMENTARIES
1:149–51, 259–60
1765

It is highly necessary for preserving the ballance of the constitution, that the executive power should be a branch, though not the whole, of the legislature. The total union of them, we have seen, would be productive of tyranny; the total disjunction of them for the present, would in the end produce the same effects, by causing that union, against which it seems to provide. The legislature would soon become tyrannical, by making continual encroachments, and gradually assuming to itself the rights of the executive power. Thus the long parliament of Charles the first, while it acted in a constitutional manner, with the royal concurrence, redressed many heavy grievances and established many salutary laws. But when the two houses assumed the power of legislation, in exclusion of the royal authority, they soon after assumed likewise the reins of administration; and, in consequence of these united powers, overturned both church and state, and established a worse oppression than any they pretended to remedy. To hinder therefore any such encroachments, the king is himself a part of the parliament: and, as this is the reason of his being so, very properly therefore the share of legislation, which the constitution has placed in the crown, consists in the power of *rejecting*, rather than *resolving;* this being sufficient to answer the end proposed. For we may apply to the royal negative, in this instance, what Cicero observes of the negative of the Roman tribunes, that the crown has not any power of *doing* wrong, but merely of *preventing* wrong from being done. The crown cannot begin of itself any alterations in the present established law; but it may approve or disapprove of the alterations suggested and consented to by the two houses. The legislative therefore cannot abridge the executive power of any rights which it now has by law, without it's own consent; since the law must perpetually stand as it now does, unless all the powers will agree to alter it. And herein indeed consists the true excellence of the English government, that all the parts of it form a mutual check upon each other. In the legislature, the people are a check upon the nobility, and the nobility a check upon the people; by the mutual privilege of rejecting what the other has resolved: while the king is a check upon both, which preserves the executive power from encroachments. And this very executive power is again checked, and kept within due bounds by the two houses through the privilege they have of enquiring into, impeaching, and punishing the conduct (not indeed of the king, which would destroy his constitutional independence; but, which is more beneficial to the public) of his evil and pernicious counsellors. Thus every branch of our civil polity supports and is supported, regulates and is regulated, by the rest; for the two houses naturally drawing in two directions of opposite interest, and the prerogative in another still different from them both, they mutually keep each other from exceeding their proper limits; while the whole is prevented from separation, and artificially connected together by the mixed nature of the crown, which is a part of the legislative, and the sole executive magistrate. Like three distinct powers in mechanics, they jointly impel the machine of government in a direction different from what either, acting by themselves, would have done; but at the same time in a direction partaking of each, and formed out of all; a direction which constitutes the true line of the liberty and happiness of the community.

. . . . .

In this distinct and separate existence of the judicial power, in a peculiar body of men, nominated indeed, but not removeable at pleasure, by the crown, consists one main preservative of the public liberty; which cannot subsist long in any state, unless the administration of common justice be in some degree separated both from the legislative and also from the executive power. Were it joined with the legislative, the life, liberty, and property, of the subject would be in the hands of arbitrary judges, whose decisions would be then regulated only by their own opinions, and not by any fundamental principles of law; which, though legislators may depart from, yet judges are bound to observe. Were it joined with the executive, this union might soon be an over ballance for the legislative. For which reason, by the statute of 16 Car. I. c. 10. which abolished the court of star chamber. effectual care is taken to remove all judicial power out of the hands of the king's privy council; who, as then was evident from recent instances, might soon be inclined to pronounce that for law, which was most agreeable to the prince or his officers. Nothing therefore is more to be avoided, in a free constitution, than uniting the provinces of a judge and a minister of state. And indeed, that the absolute power, claimed and exercised in a neighbouring nation, is more tolerable than that of the eastern empires, is in great measure owing to their having vested the judicial power in their parliaments, a body separate and distinct from both the legislative and executive: and, if ever that nation recovers it's former liberty, it will owe it to the efforts of those assemblies. In Turkey, where every thing is centered in the sultan or his ministers, despotic power is in it's meridian, and wears a more dreadful aspect.

7

JOHN ADAMS, THOUGHTS ON GOVERNMENT
Apr. 1776

Papers 4:88–90

(See ch. 4, no. 5)

8

INSTRUCTIONS OF THE INHABITANTS OF THE TOWN
OF BOSTON TO THEIR REPRESENTATIVES
IN CONGRESS
1776

Niles 133

It is essential to liberty, that the legislative, judicial, and executive powers of government be, as nearly as possible, independent of, and separate from each other; for where they are united in the same persons, or number of persons, there would be wanting that mutual check which is the principal security against the making of arbitrary laws, and a wanton exercise of power in the execution of them. It is also of the highest importance, that every person in a judiciary department employ the greatest part of his time and attention in the duties of his office; we therefore further instruct you, to procure the enacting such law or laws, as shall make it incompatible for the same person to hold a seat in the legislative and executive departments of government, at one and the same time: that shall render the judges, in every judicatory through the colony, dependent, not on the uncertain tenure of caprice or pleasure, but on an unimpeachable deportment in the important duties of their station, for their continuance in office: and to prevent the multiplicity of offices in the same person, that such salaries be settled upon them as will place them above the necessity of stooping to any indirect or collateral means for subsistence. We wish to avoid a profusion of the public moneys on the one hand, and the danger of sacrificing our liberties to a spirit of parsimony on the other.

9

THOMAS JEFFERSON, NOTES ON THE STATE OF
VIRGINIA, QUERY 13, 120–21
1784

---

4. All the powers of government, legislative, executive, and judiciary, result to the legislative body [in the Virginia Constitution of 1776]. The concentrating these in the same hands is precisely the definition of despotic government. It will be no alleviation that these powers will be exercised by a plurality of hands, and not by a single one. 173 despots would surely be as oppressive as one. Let those who doubt it turn their eyes on the republic of Venice. As little will it avail us that they are chosen by ourselves. An *elective despotism* was not the government we fought for; but one which should not only be founded on free principles, but in which the powers of government should be so divided and balanced among several bodies of magistracy, as that no one could transcend their legal limits, without being

effectually checked and restrained by the others. For this reason that convention, which passed the ordinance of government, laid its foundation on this basis, that the legislative, executive and judiciary department should be separate and distinct, so that no person should exercise the powers of more than one of them at the same time. But no barrier was provided between these several powers. The judiciary and executive members were left dependant on the legislative, for their subsistence in office, and some of them for their continuance in it. If therefore the legislature assumes executive and judiciary powers, no opposition is likely to be made; nor, if made, can it be effectual; because in that case they may put their proceedings into the form of an act of assembly, which will render them obligatory on the other branches. They have accordingly, in many instances, decided rights which should have been left to judiciary controversy: and the direction of the executive, during the whole time of their session, is becoming habitual and familiar. And this is done with no ill intention. The views of the present members are perfectly upright. When they are led out of their regular province, it is by art in others, and inadvertence in themselves. And this will probably be the case for some time to come. But it will not be a very long time. Mankind soon learn to make interested uses of every right and power which they possess, or may assume. The public money and public liberty, intended to have been deposited with three branches of magistracy, but found inadvertently to be in the hands of one only, will soon be discovered to be sources of wealth and dominion to those who hold them; distinguished too by this tempting circumstance, that they are the instrument, as well as the object of acquisition. With money we will get men, said Caesar, and with men we will get money. Nor should our assembly be deluded by the integrity of their own purposes, and conclude that these unlimited powers will never be abused, because themselves are not disposed to abuse them. They should look forward to a time, and that not a distant one, when corruption in this, as in the country from which we derive our origin, will have seized the heads of government, and be spread by them through the body of the people; when they will purchase the voices of the people, and make them pay the price. Human nature is the same on every side of the Atlantic, and will be alike influenced by the same causes. The time to guard against corruption and tyranny, is before they shall have gotten hold on us. It is better to keep the wolf out of the fold, than to trust to drawing his teeth and talons after he shall have entered.

10

RECORDS OF THE FEDERAL CONVENTION

[1:86; Madison, 2 June]

Mr. Dickenson considered the business as so important that no man ought to be silent or reserved. He went into a discourse of some length, the sum of which was, that the Legislative, Executive, & Judiciary departments ought to be made as independt. as possible; but that such an Executive as some seemed to have in contemplation was not consistant with a republic; that a firm Executive could only exist in a limited monarchy. In the British Govt. itself the weight of the Executive arises from the attachments which the Crown draws to itself, & not merely from the force of its prerogatives. In place of these attachments we must look out for something else. One source of stability is the double branch of the Legislature. The division of the Country into distinct States formed the other principal source of stability. This division ought therefore to be maintained, and considerable powers to be left with the States. This was the ground of his consolation for the future fate of his Country. Without this, and in case of a consolidation of the States into one great Republic we might read its fate in the history of smaller ones. A limited Monarchy he considered as *one* of the best Governments in the world. It was not *certain* that the same blessings were derivable from any other form. It was certain that equal blessings had never yet been derived from any of the republican form. A limited monarchy however was out of the question. The spirit of the times—the state of our affairs, forbade the experiment, if it were desireable. Was it possible moreover in the nature of things to introduce it even if these obstacles were less insuperable. A House of Nobles was essential to such a Govt. Could these be created by a breath, or by a stroke of the pen? No. They were the growth of ages, and could only arise under a complication of circumstances none of which existed in this Country. But though a form the most perfect *perhaps* in itself be unattainable, we must not despair. If antient republics have been found to flourish for a moment only & then vanish forever, it only proves that they were badly constituted; and that we ought to seek for every remedy for their diseases. One of these remedies he conceived to be the accidental lucky division of this country into distinct States; a division which some seemed desirous to abolish altogether.

[1:97; Madison, 4 June]

First Clause of Proposition 8th relating *to a Council of Revision* taken into consideration.

Mr. Gerry doubts whether the Judiciary ought to form a part of it, as they will have a sufficient check agst. encroachments on their own department by their exposition of the laws, which involved a power of deciding on their Constitutionality. In some States the Judges had actually set aside laws as being agst. the Constitution. This was done too with general approbation. It was quite foreign from the nature of ye. office to make them judges of the policy of public measures. He moves to postpone the clause in order to propose "that the National Executive shall have a right to negative any Legislative act which shall not be afterwards passed by   parts of each branch of the national Legislature."

Mr. King seconds the motion, observing that the Judges ought to be able to expound the law as it should come before them, free from the bias of having participated in its formation.

Mr. Wilson thinks neither the original proposition nor the amendment go far enough. If the Legislative Exetiv & Judiciary ought to be distinct & independent, The Executive ought to have an absolute negative. Without such a Self-defence the Legislature can at any moment sink it into non-existence. He was for varying the proposition in such a manner as to give the Executive & Judiciary jointly an absolute negative

On the question to postpone in order to take Mr. Gerry's proposition into consideration it was agreed to Massts. ay. Cont. no. N. Y. ay. Pa. ay. Del. no. Maryd. no. Virga. no. N. C. ay. S. C. ay. Ga. ay. [Ayes—6; noes—4.]

Mr. Gerry's proposition being now before Committee, Mr. Wilson & Mr. Hamilton move that the last part of it (viz wch. sl. not be afterwds. passed" unless by   parts of each branch of the National legislature) be struck out, so as to give the Executive an absolute negative on the laws. There was no danger they thought of such a power being too much exercised. It was mentioned (by Col: Hamilton) that the King of G. B. had not exerted his negative since the Revolution.

Mr. Gerry sees no necessity for so great a controul over the legislature as the best men in the Community would be comprised in the two branches of it.

Docr. Franklin, said he was sorry to differ from his colleague for whom he had a very great respect, on any occasion, but he could not help it on this. He had had some experience of this check in the Executive on the Legislature, under the proprietary Government of Pena. The negative of the Governor was constantly made use of to extort money. No good law whatever could be passed without a private bargain with him. An increase of his salary, or some donation, was always made a condition; till at last it became the regular practice, to have orders in his favor on the Treasury, presented along with the bills to be signed, so that he might actually receive the former before he should sign the latter. When the Indians were scalping the western people, and notice of it arrived, the concurrence of the Governor in the means of self-defence could not be got, till it was agreed that his Estate should be exempted from taxation. so that the people were to fight for the security of his property, whilst he was to bear no share of the burden. This was a mischievous sort of check. If the Executive was to have a Council, such a power would be less objectionable. It was true the King of G. B. had not, As was said, exerted his negative since the Revolution: but that matter was easily explained. The bribes and emoluments now given to the members of parliament rendered it unnecessary, everything being done according to the will of the Ministers. He was afraid, if a negative should be given as proposed, that more power and money would be demanded, till at last eno' would be gotten to influence & bribe the Legislature into a compleat subjection to the will of the Executive.

Mr. Sherman was agst. enabling any one man to stop the will of the whole. No one man could be found so far above all the rest in wisdom. He thought we ought to avail ourselves of his wisdom in revising the laws, but not permit him to overrule the decided and cool opinions of the Legislature.

[1:110; Pierce, 4 June]
Mr. Maddison in a very able and ingenious Speech, ran through the whole Scheme of the Government,—pointed out all the beauties and defects of ancient Republics; compared their situation with ours wherever it appeared to bear any anology, and proved that the only way to make a Government answer all the end of its institution was to collect the wisdom of its several parts in aid of each other whenever it was necessary. Hence the propriety of incorporating the Judicial with the Executive in the revision of the Laws. He was of opinion that by joining the Judges with the Supreme Executive Magistrate would be strictly proper, and would by no means interfere with that indepence so much to be approved and distinguished in the several departments.

Mr. Dickinson could not agree with Gentlemen in blending the national Judicial with the Executive, because the one is the expounder, and the other the Executor of the Laws.

[1:138; Madison, 6 June]
Mr. Wilson moved to reconsider the vote excluding the Judiciary from a share in the revision of the laws, and to add after "National Executive" the words "with a convenient number of the national Judiciary"; remarking the expediency of reinforcing the Executive with the influence of that Department.

Mr. Madison 2ded. the motion. He observed that the great difficulty in rendering the Executive competent to its own defence arose from the nature of Republican Govt. which could not give to an individual citizen that settled pre-eminence in the eyes of the rest, that weight of property, that personal interest agst. betraying the National interest, which appertain to an hereditary magistrate. In a Republic personal merit alone could be the ground of political exaltation, but it would rarely happen that this merit would be so preeminent as to produce universal acquiescence. The Executive Magistrate would be envied & assailed by disappointed competitors: His firmness therefore wd. need support. He would not possess those great emoluments from his station, nor that permanent stake in the public interest which wd. place him out of the reach of foreign corruption: He would stand in need therefore of being controuled as well as supported. An association of the Judges in his revisionary function wd both double the advantage and diminish the danger. It wd. also enable the Judiciary Department the better to defend itself agst. Legislative encroachments. Two objections had been made 1st. that the Judges ought not to be subject to the bias which a participation in the making of laws might give in the exposition of them. 2dly. that the Judiciary Departmt. ought to be separate & distinct from the other great Departments. The 1st. objection had some weight; but it was much diminished by reflecting that a small proportion of the laws coming in question before a Judge wd. be such wherein he had been consulted; that a small part of this proportion wd. be so ambiguous as to leave room for his prepossessions; and that but a few cases wd. probably arise in the life of a Judge under such ambiguous passages. How much good on the other hand wd. proceed from the perspicuity, the conciseness, and the systematic character wch. the Code of laws wd. receive from the Judiciary talents. As to the 2d. objection, it either had no weight, or it applied with equal weight to the Executive & to the Judiciary revision of the laws. The maxim on which the objection was founded required a separation of the Executive as well as of the Judiciary from the Legislature & from each other. There wd. in truth however be no improper mixture of these distinct powers in the present case. In England, whence the maxim itself had been drawn, the Executive had an absolute negative on the laws; and the supreme tribunal of Justice (the House of Lords) formed one of the other branches of the Legislature. In short, whether the object of the revisionary power was to restrain the Legislature from encroaching on the other co-ordinate Departments, or on the rights of the people at large; or from passing laws unwise in their principle, or incorrect in their form, the utility of annexing the wisdom and weight of the Judiciary to the Executive seemed incontestable.

Mr. Gerry thought the Executive, whilst standing alone wd. be more impartial than when he cd. be covered by the sanction & seduced by the sophistry of the Judges

Mr. King. If the Unity of the Executive was preferred for the sake of responsibility, the policy of it is as applicable to the revisionary as to the Executive power.

Mr. Pinkney had been at first in favor of joining the heads of the principal departmts. the Secretary at War, of foreign affairs &—in the council of revision. He had however relinquished the idea from a consideration that these could be called on by the Executive Magistrate whenever he pleased to consult them. He was opposed to an introduction of the Judges into the business.

[2:66; Madison, 20 July]

Mr. King expressed his apprehensions that an extreme caution in favor of liberty might enervate the Government we were forming. He wished the House to recur to the primitive axiom that the three great departments of Govts. should be separate & independent: that the Executive & Judiciary should be so as well as the Legislative: that the Executive should be so equally with the Judiciary. Would this be the case if the Executive should be impeachable? It had been said that the Judiciary would be impeachable. But it should have been remembered at the same time that the Judiciary hold their places not for a limited time, but during good behaviour. It is necessary therefore that a forum should be established for trying misbehaviour. Was the Executive to hold his place during good behaviour?—The Executive was to hold his place for a limited term like the members of the Legislature; Like them particularly the Senate whose members would continue in appointmt the same term of 6 years. he would periodically be tried for his behaviour by his electors, who would continue or discontinue him in trust according to the manner in which he had discharged it. Like them therefore, he ought to be subject to no intermediate trial, by impeachment. He ought not to be impeachable unless he hold his office during good behavior, a tenure which would be most agreeable to him; provided an independent and effectual forum could be devised; But under no circumstances ought he to

be impeachable by the Legislature. This would be destructive of his independence and of the principles of the Constitution. He relied on the vigor of the Executive as a great security for the public liberties.

[2:74, 78; Madison, 21 July]

Mr. Madison—considered the object of the motion as of great importance to the meditated Constitution. It would be useful to the Judiciary departmt. by giving it an additional opportunity of defending itself agst: Legislative encroachments; It would be useful to the Executive, by inspiring additional confidence & firmness in exerting the revisionary power: It would be useful to the Legislature by the valuable assistance it would give in preserving a consistency, conciseness, perspicuity & technical propriety in the laws, qualities peculiarly necessary; & yet shamefully wanting in our republican Codes. It would moreover be useful to the Community at large as an additional check agst. a pursuit of those unwise & unjust measures which constituted so great a portion of our calamities. If any solid objection could be urged agst. the motion, it must be on the supposition that it tended to give too much strength either to the Executive or Judiciary. He did not think there was the least ground for this apprehension. It was much more to be apprehended that notwithstanding this co-operation of the two departments, the Legislature would still be an overmatch for them. Experience in all the States had evinced a powerful tendency in the Legislature to absorb all power into its vortex. This was the real source of danger to the American Constitutions; & suggested the necessity of giving every defensive authority to the other departments that was consistent with republican principles.

Mr. Mason said he had always been a friend to this provision. It would give a confidence to the Executive, which he would not otherwise have, and without which the Revisionary power would be of little avail.

Mr. Gerry did not expect to see this point which had undergone full discussion, again revived. The object he conceived of the Revisionary power was merely to secure the Executive department agst. legislative encroachment. The Executive therefore who will best know and be ready to defend his rights ought alone to have the defence of them. The motion was liable to strong objections. It was combining & mixing together the Legislative & the other departments. It was establishing an improper coalition between the Executive & Judiciary departments. It was making Statesmen of the Judges; and setting them up as the guardians of the Rights of the people. He relied for his part on the Representatives of the people as the guardians of their Rights & interests. It was making the Expositors of the Laws, the Legislators which ought never to be done. A better expedient for correcting the laws, would be to appoint as had been done in Pena. a person or persons of proper skill, to draw bills for the Legislature.

. . . . .

Col Mason Observed that the defence of the Executive was not the sole object of the Revisionary power. He expected even greater advantages from it. Notwithstanding the precautions taken in the Constitution of the Legislature, it would so much resemble that of the individual States, that it must be expected frequently to pass unjust and pernicious laws. This restraining power was therefore essentially necessary. It would have the effect not only of hindering the final passage of such laws; but would discourage demagogues from attempting to get them passed. It had been said (by Mr. L. Martin) that if the Judges were joined in this check on the laws, they would have a double negative, since in their expository capacity of Judges they would have one negative. He would reply that in this capacity they could impede in one case only, the operation of laws. They could declare an unconstitutional law void. But with regard to every law however unjust oppressive or pernicious, which did not come plainly under this description, they would be under the necessity as Judges to give it a free course. He wished the further use to be made of the Judges, of giving aid in preventing every improper law. Their aid will be the more valuable as they are in the habit and practice of considering laws in their true principles, and in all their consequences.

Mr. Wilson. The separation of the departments does not require that they should have separate objects but that they should act separately tho' on the same objects. It is necessary that the two branches of the Legislature should be separate and distinct, yet they are both to act precisely on the same object.

Mr. Gerry had rather give the Executive an absolute negative for its own defence than thus to blend together the Judiciary & Executive departments. It will bind them together in an offensive and defensive alliance agst. the Legislature, and render the latter unwilling to enter into a contest with them.

Mr. Govr. Morris was surprised that any defensive provision for securing the effectual separation of the departments should be considered as an improper mixture of them. Suppose that the three powers, were to be vested in three persons, by compact among themselves; that one was to have the power of making—another of executing, and a third of judging, the laws. Would it not be very natural for the two latter after having settled the partition on paper, to observe, and would not candor oblige the former to admit, that as a security agst. legislative acts of the former which might easily be so framed as to undermine the powers of the two others, the two others ought to be armed with a veto for their own defence, or at least to have an opportunity of stating their objections agst. acts of encroachment? And would any one pretend that such a right tended to blend & confound powers that ought to be separately exercised? As well might it be said that If three neighbours had three distinct farms, a right in each to defend his farm agst. his neighbours, tended to blend the farms together.

[2:299; Madison, 15 Aug.]

Mr. Govr. Morris, suggested the expedient of an absolute negative in the Executive. He could not agree that the Judiciary which was part of the Executive, should be bound to say that a direct violation of the Constitution was law. A controul over the legislature might have its inconveniences. But view the danger on the other side. The

most virtuous citizens will often as members of a legislative body concur in measures which afterwards in their private capacity they will be ashamed of. Encroachments of the popular branch of the Government ought to be guarded agst. The Ephori at Sparta became in the end absolute. The Report of the Council of Censors in Pennsylva points out the many invasions of the legislative department on the Executive numerous as the latter* is, within the short term of seven years, and in a State where a strong party is opposed to the Constitution, and watching every occasion of turning the public resentments agst. it. If the Executive be overturned by the popular branch, as happened in England, the tyranny of one man will ensue—In Rome where the Aristocracy overturned the throne, the consequence was different. He enlarged on the tendency of the legislative Authority to usurp on the Executive and wished the section to be postponed, in order to consider of some more effectual check than requiring ⅔ only to overrule the negative of the Executive.

Mr. Sherman. Can one man be trusted better than all the others if they all agree? This was neither wise nor safe. He disapproved of Judges meddling in politics and parties. We have gone far enough in forming the negative as it now stands.

Mr. Carrol—when the negative to be overruled by ⅔ only was agreed to, the *quorum* was not fixed. He remarked that as a majority was now to be the quorum, 17, in the larger, and 8 in the smaller house might carry points. The Advantage that might be taken of this seemed to call for greater impediments to improper laws. He thought the controuling power however of the Executive could not be well decided, till it was seen how the formation of that department would be finally regulated. He wished the consideration of the matter to be postponed.

Mr. Ghorum saw no end to these difficulties and postponements. Some could not agree to the form of Government before the powers were defined. Others could not agree to the powers till it was seen how the Government was to be formed. He thought a majority as large a quorum as was necessary. It was the quorum almost every where fixt in the U. States.

Mr. Wilson; after viewing the subject with all the coolness and attention possible was most apprehensive of a dissolution of the Govt from the legislature swallowing up all the other powers. He remarked that the prejudices agst the Executive resulted from a misapplication of the adage that the parliament was the palladium of liberty. Where the Executive was really formidable, *King* and *Tyrant*, were naturally associated in the minds of people; not *legislature* and *tyranny*. But where the Executive was not formidable, the two last were most properly associated. After the destruction of the King in Great Britain, a more pure and unmixed tyranny sprang up in the parliament than had been exercised by the monarch. He insisted that we had not guarded agst. the danger on this side by a sufficient self-defensive power either to the Executive or Judiciary department—

*The Executive consists at this time of abt. 20 members.

11

CENTINEL, NO. 2
Oct. 1787
Storing 2.7.49–50

Mr. *Wilson* says, "the senate branches into two characters; the one legislative and the other executive. In its legislative character it can effect no purpose, without the co-operation of the house of representatives, and in its executive character it can accomplish no object without the concurrence of the president. Thus fettered, I do not know any act which the senate can of itself perform, and such dependence necessarily precludes every idea of influence and superiority." This I confess is very specious, but experience demonstrates, that checks in government, unless accompanied with *adequate* power and *independently* placed, prove *merely nominal*, and will be *inoperative*. Is it probable, that the president of the United States, limited as he is in power, and dependent on the will of the senate, in appointments to office, will either have the *firmness* or *inclination* to exercise his prerogative of a conditional controul upon the proceedings of that body, however injurious they may be to the public welfare: it will be his interest to coincide with the views of the senate, and thus become the head of the aristocratic junto. The king of England is a constituent part in the legislature, but although an hereditary monarch, in possession of the whole executive power, including the unrestrained appointment to offices, and an immense revenue, enjoys but in *name* the prerogative of a negative upon the parliament. Even the king of England, circumstanced as he is, has not dared to exercise it for near a century past. The check of the house of representatives upon the senate will likewise be rendered nugatory for want of due weight in the democratic branch, and from their constitution *they* may become so *independent* of the *people* as to be indifferent of its interests: nay as Congress would have the controul over the mode and place of their election, by ordering the representatives of a *whole* state to be elected at *one* place, and that too the most *inconvenient*, the ruling power may govern the *choice*, and thus the house of representatives may be composed of the *creatures* of the senate. Still the *semblance* of checks, may remain but without *operation*.

This mixture of the legislative and executive moreover highly tends to corruption. The chief improvement in government, in modern times, has been the compleat separation of the great distinctions of power; placing the *legislative* in different hands from those which hold the *executive;* and again severing the *judicial* part from the ordinary *administrative*. "When the legislative and executive powers (says Montesquieu) are united in the same person, or in the same body of magistrates, there can be no liberty."

12

"WILLIAM PENN," NO. 2
3 Jan. 1788
Storing 3.12.13–17

The next principle, without which it must be clear that no free government can ever subsist, is the DIVISION OF POWER among those who are charged with the execution of it. It has always been the favorite maxim of princes, to *divide* the people, in order to *govern* them; it is now time that the people should avail themselves of the same maxim, and *divide* power among their rulers, in order to prevent their abusing it—The application of this great political truth, has long been unknown to the world, and yet it is grounded upon a very plain natural principle,—If, says Montesquieu, the same man, or body of men, is possessed both of the legislative and executive power, there is NO LIBERTY, because it may be feared that the same monarch, or the same *senate*, will enact tyrannical laws, in order to execute them in a tyrannical manner—nothing can be clearer, and the natural disposition of man, to ambition and power, makes it probable that such would be the consequence—suppose for instance, that the same body, which has the power of raising money by taxes, is also entrusted with the application of that money, they will very probably raise large sums, and apply them to their own private uses; if they are empowered to create offices, and appoint the officers, they will take that opportunity of providing for themselves, and their friends, and if they have the power of inflicting penalties for offences, and of trying the offenders, there will be no bounds to their tyranny. Liberty therefore can only subsist, where the powers of government are properly *divided*, and where the different jurisdictions are inviolably kept distinct and separate.

The first and most natural division of the powers of government are into the legislative and executive branches. These two should never be suffered to have the least share of each others jurisdiction, or to intermeddle with it in any manner. For which ever of the two divides its power with the other, will certainly be subordinate to it, and if they both have a share of each others authority, they will be in fact but one body; their interest as well as their powers will be the same, and they will combine together against the people.

It is therefore a political error of the greatest magnitude, to allow the executive power a negative, or in fact any kind of control over the proceedings of the legislature. The people of Great Britain have been so sensible of this truth, that since the days of William III, no king of England has dared to exercise the negative over the acts of the two houses of parliament, to which he is clearly entitled by his prerogative.

This doctrine is not novel in America, it seems on the contrary to be every where well understood and admitted beyond controversy; in the bills of rights or constitutions of *New-Hampshire, Massachusetts, Maryland, Virginia, North-Carolina and Georgia,* it is expressly declared. *"That the legislative, executive and judicial departments, shall be forever separate and distinct from each other."* In *Pennsylvania* and *Delaware,* they are effectually separated without any particular declaration of the principle. In the other states indeed, the executive branch possesses more or less of the executive [legislative?] power—And here it must appear singular that the state of Massachusetts, where the doctrine of a separate jurisdiction is most positively established, and in whose bill of rights these remarkable words are to be found: "The executive shall never exercise the legislative and judicial powers, or either of them, to the end it may be a government of laws and not of men." (§30) Yet in that commonwealth and New-Hampshire, the executive branch, which consists of a *single magistrate,* has more controul over the legislature than in any other state; for there, if the governor refuses his assent to a bill, it cannot be passed into a law, unless two-thirds of the house afterwards concur. In New-York the same power is given to a Council of Revision, consisting of the Governor, the Chancellor and Judges of the Supreme Court, or any three of them, of which the Governor is to be one. In Rhode-Island and Connecticut, whose governments were established before the revolution, the Governor has a single vote as a member of the upper house, and New-Jersey has adopted this part of their constitution. In Georgia the laws are to be revised by the Governor and Council, but they can do no more than give their opinion upon them. In Maryland the bills are to be signed by the governor before they can be enacted, and in South-Carolina they are to be sealed with the great seal, which is in the governor's custody. But in the first of these states, the constitution prescribes, that the governor *shall* sign the bills, and in the latter, a joint committee of both houses of legislature is to wait upon chief magistrate to receive and return the great seal, which implies that he is bound to deliver it to them, for the special purpose of affixing it to the laws of the state. Pennsylvania has proceeded upon a much more rational ground, their legislature having a particular *seal* of their own, and their laws requiring only to be signed by the speaker. If in Maryland or South-Carolina a difference should ever arise between the legislature and the governor, and the latter should refuse to sign the laws, or to deliver the great seal, the most fatal consequences might ensue.

Here then we see the great leading principle of the *absolute division of the legislative from the executive jurisdiction,* admitted in almost every one of the American states as a fundamental maxim in the politics of a free country. The *theory* of this general doctrine is every where established, though a few states have somewhat swerved from it in the *practice.* From whence we must conclude, that even the knowledge and full conviction of a new political truth will not always immediately conquer inveterate habits and prejudices. The idea of the negative, which the constitution of England gives to the monarch over the proceedings of the other branches of parliament, although it has so long become obsolete, has had an effect upon timid minds, and upon the minds of those who could not distinguish between the *form* and *spirit* of the *British* constitution. They would not grant to the executive branch an absolute negative over the legislature, but yet they tried every method to introduce something similar to it. They reprobated the doctrine in the most express words, and yet they could not bear to part entirely with it. It is curious to observe how many different ways they have endeavored to conciliate truth with prejudice. Of those states who have allowed the executive branch to intermeddle with the proceedings of the legislature, no two (New-Hampshire and Massachusetts excepted) have done it exactly in the same manner. They have tried every possible medium, but having lost sight of the original principle which they had already established, and which alone could have been their safest guide, they groped about in the dark, and could not find any solid ground on which to establish a general rule. Like Noah's dove, being once out of the ark of truth, they could not find elsewhere a place to rest their feet.

13

JAMES MADISON, FEDERALIST, NO. 37, 233–34
11 Jan. 1788

(See ch. 9, no. 9)

14

JAMES MADISON, FEDERALIST, NO. 47, 323–31
30 Jan. 1788

One of the principal objections inculcated by the more respectable adversaries to the constitution, is its supposed violation of the political maxim, that the legislative, executive and judiciary departments ought to be separate and distinct. In the structure of the federal government, no regard, it is said, seems to have been paid to this essential precaution in favor of liberty. The several departments of power are distributed and blended in such a manner, as at once to destroy all symmetry and beauty of form; and to expose some of the essential parts of the edifice to the danger of being crushed by the disproportionate weight of other parts.

No political truth is certainly of greater intrinsic value or is stamped with the authority of more enlightened patrons of liberty than that on which the objection is founded. The accumulation of all powers legislative, executive and judiciary in the same hands, whether of one, a few or many, and whether hereditary, self appointed, or elective, may justly be pronounced the very definition of tyranny. Were the federal constitution therefore really chargeable with this accumulation of power or with a mixture of powers having a dangerous tendency to such an accumulation, no further arguments would be necessary to inspire a universal reprobation of the system. I persuade myself however, that it will be made apparent to every one, that the charge cannot be supported, and that the maxim on which it relies, has been totally misconceived and misapplied. In order to form correct ideas on this important subject, it will be proper to investigate the sense, in which the preservation of liberty requires, that the three great departments of power should be separate and distinct.

The oracle who is always consulted and cited on this subject, is the celebrated Montesquieu. If he be not the author of this invaluable precept in the science of politics, he has the merit at least of displaying, and recommending it most effectually to the attention of mankind. Let us endeavour in the first place to ascertain his meaning on this point.

The British constitution was to Montesquieu, what Homer has been to the didactic writers on epic poetry. As the latter have considered the work of the immortal Bard, as the perfect model from which the principles and rules of the epic art were to be drawn, and by which all similar works were to be judged; so this great political critic appears to have viewed the constitution of England, as the standard, or to use his own expression, as the mirrour of political liberty; and to have delivered in the form of elementary truths, the several characteristic principles of that particular system. That we may be sure then not to mistake his meaning in this case, let us recur to the source from which the maxim was drawn.

On the slightest view of the British constitution we must perceive, that the legislative, executive and judiciary departments are by no means totally separate and distinct from each other. The executive magistrate forms an integral part of the legislative authority. He alone has the prerogative of making treaties with foreign sovereigns, which when made have, under certain limitations, the force of legislative acts. All the members of the judiciary department are appointed by him; can be removed by him on the address of the two Houses of Parliament, and form, when he pleases to consult them, one of his constitutional councils. One branch of the legislative department forms also, a great constitutional council to the executive chief; as on another hand, it is the sole depositary of judicial power in cases of impeachment, and is invested with the supreme appellate jurisdiction, in all other cases. The judges again are so far connected with the legislative department, as often to attend and participate in its deliberations, though not admitted to a legislative vote.

From these facts by which Montesquieu was guided it may clearly be inferred, that in saying "there can be no liberty where the legislative and executive powers are united in the same person, or body of magistrates," or "if the power of judging be not separated from the legislative and executive powers," he did not mean that these departments ought to have no *partial agency* in, or no *controul* over the acts of each other. His meaning, as his own words import, and still more conclusively as illustrated by the example in his eye, can amount to no more than this, that

where the *whole* power of one department is exercised by the same hands which possess the *whole* power of another department, the fundamental principles of a free constitution, are subverted. This would have been the case in the constitution examined by him, if the King who is the sole executive magistrate, had possessed also the compleat legislative power, or the supreme administration of justice; or if the entire legislative body, had possessed the supreme judiciary, or the supreme executive authority. This however is not among the vices of that constitution. The magistrate in whom the whole executive power resides cannot of himself make a law, though he can put a negative on every law, nor administer justice in person, though he has the appointment of those who do administer it. The judges can exercise no executive prerogative, though they are shoots from the executive stock, nor any legislative function, though they may be advised with by the legislative councils. The entire legislature, can perform no judiciary act, though by the joint act of two of its branches, the judges may be removed from their offices; and though one of its branches is possessed of the judicial power in the last resort. The entire legislature again can exercise no executive prerogative, though one of its branches constitutes the supreme executive magistracy; and another, on the empeachment of a third, can try and condemn all the subordinate officers in the executive department.

The reasons on which Montesquieu grounds his maxim are a further demonstration of his meaning. "When the legislative and executive powers are united in the same person or body" says he, "there can be no liberty, because apprehensions may arise lest *the same* monarch or senate should *enact* tyrannical laws, to *execute* them in a tyrannical manner." Again "Were the power of judging joined with the legislative, the life and liberty of the subject would be exposed to arbitrary controul, for *the judge* would then be *the legislator.* Were it joined to the executive power, *the judge* might behave with all the violence of *an oppressor.*" Some of these reasons are more fully explained in other passages; but briefly stated as they are here, they sufficiently establish the meaning which we have put on this celebrated maxim of this celebrated author.

If we look into the constitutions of the several states we find that notwithstanding the emphatical, and in some instances, the unqualified terms in which this axiom has been laid down, there is not a single instance in which the several departments of power have been kept absolutely separate and distinct. New-Hampshire, whose constitution was the last formed, seems to have been fully aware of the impossibility and inexpediency of avoiding any mixture whatever of these departments; and has qualified the doctrine by declaring "that the legislative, executive and judiciary powers ought to be kept as separate from, and independent of each other *as the nature of a free government will admit; or as is consistent with that chain of connection, that binds the whole fabric of the constitution in one indissoluble bond of unity and amity.*" Her constitution accordingly mixes these departments in several respects. The senate which is a branch of the legislative department is also a judicial tribunal for the trial of empeachments. The president who is the head of the executive department, is the presiding member also of the senate; and besides an equal vote in all cases, has a casting vote in case of a tie. The executive head is himself eventually elective every year by the legislative department; and his council is every year chosen by and from the members of the same department. Several of the officers of state are also appointed by the legislature. And the members of the judiciary department are appointed by the executive department.

The constitution of Massachusetts has observed a sufficient though less pointed caution in expressing this fundamental article of liberty. It declares "that the legislative department shall never exercise the executive and judicial powers, or either of them: The executive shall never exercise the legislative and judicial powers, or either of them: The judicial shall never exercise the legislative and executive powers, or either of them." This declaration corresponds precisely with the doctrine of Montesquieu as it has been explained, and is not in a single point violated by the plan of the Convention. It goes no farther than to prohibit any one of the entire departments from exercising the powers of another department. In the very constitution to which it is prefixed, a partial mixture of powers has been admitted. The Executive Magistrate has a qualified negative on the Legislative body; and the Senate, which is a part of the Legislature, is a court of impeachment for members both of the executive and judiciary departments. The members of the judiciary department again are appointable by the executive department, and removeable by the same authority, on the address of the two legislative branches. Lastly, a number of the officers of government are annually appointed by the legislative department. As the appointment to offices, particularly executive offices, is in its nature an executive function, the compilers of the Constitution have in this last point at least, violated the rule established by themselves.

I pass over the constitutions of Rhode-Island and Connecticut, because they were formed prior to the revolution; and even before the principle under examination had become an object of political attention.

The constitution of New-York contains no declaration on this subject; but appears very clearly to have been framed with an eye to the danger of improperly blending the different departments. It gives nevertheless to the executive magistrate a partial controul over the legislative department; and what is more, gives a like controul to the judiciary department, and even blends the executive and judiciary departments in the exercise of this controul. In its council of appointment, members of the legislative are associated with the executive authority in the appointment of officers both executive and judiciary. And its court for the trial of impeachments and correction of errors, is to consist of one branch of the legislature and the principal members of the judiciary department.

The constitution of New-Jersey has blended the different powers of government more than any of the preceding. The governor, who is the executive magistrate, is appointed by the legislature; is chancellor and ordinary or surrogate of the state; is a member of the supreme court of appeals, and president with a casting vote, of one of the legislative branches. The same legislative branch acts again

as executive council to the governor, and with him constitutes the court of appeals. The members of the judiciary department are appointed by the legislative department, and removeable by one branch of it, on the impeachment of the other.

According to the constitution of Pennsylvania, the president, who is head of the executive department, is annually elected by a vote in which the legislative department predominates. In conjunction with an executive council, he appoints the members of the judiciary department, and forms a court of impeachments for trial of all officers, judiciary as well as executive. The judges of the supreme court, and justices of the peace, seem also to be removeable by the legislature; and the executive power of pardoning in certain cases to be referred to the same department. The members of the executive council are made EX OFFICIO justices of peace throughout the state.

In Delaware, the chief executive magistrate is annually elected by the legislative department. The speakers of the two legislative branches are vice-presidents in the executive department. The executive chief, with six others, appointed three by each of the legislative branches, constitute the supreme court of appeals: He is joined with the legislative department in the appointment of the other judges. Throughout the states it appears that the members of the legislature may at the same time be justices of the peace. In this state, the members of one branch of it are EX OFFICIO justices of peace; as are also the members of the executive council. The principal officers of the executive department are appointed by the legislative; and one branch of the latter forms a court of impeachments. All officers may be removed on address of the legislature.

Maryland has adopted the maxim in the most unqualified terms; declaring that the legislative, executive and judicial powers of government, ought to be forever separate and distinct from each other. Her constitution, notwithstanding makes the executive magistrate appointable by the legislative department; and the members of the judiciary, by the executive department.

The language of Virginia is still more pointed on this subject. Her constitution declares, "that the legislative, executive and judiciary departments, shall be separate and distinct; so that neither exercise the powers properly belonging to the other; nor shall any person exercise the powers of more than one of them at the same time; except that the justices of the county courts shall be eligible to either house of assembly." Yet we find not only this express exception, with respect to the members of the inferior courts; but that the chief magistrate with his executive council are appointable by the legislature; that two members of the latter are triennially displaced at the pleasure of the legislature; and that all the principal offices, both executive and judiciary, are filled by the same department. The executive prerogative of pardon, also is in one case vested in the legislative department.

The constitution of North-Carolina, which declares, "that the legislative, executive and supreme judicial powers of government, ought to be forever separate and distinct from each other," refers at the same time to the legislative department, the appointment not only of the executive chief, but all the principal officers within both that and the judiciary department.

In South-Carolina, the constitution makes the executive magistracy eligible by the legislative department. It gives to the latter also the appointment of the members of the judiciary department, including even justices of the peace and sheriffs; and the appointment of officers in the executive department, down to captains in the army and navy of the state.

In the constitution of Georgia, where it is declared, "that the legislative, executive and judiciary departments shall be separate and distinct, so that neither exercise the powers properly belonging to the other." We find that the executive department is to be filled by appointments of the legislature; and the executive prerogative of pardon, to be finally exercised by the same authority. Even justices of the peace are to be appointed by the legislature.

In citing these cases in which the legislative, executive and judiciary departments, have not been kept totally separate and distinct, I wish not to be regarded as an advocate for the particular organizations of the several state governments. I am fully aware that among the many excellent principles which they exemplify, they carry strong marks of the haste, and still stronger of the inexperience, under which they were framed. It is but too obvious that in some instances, the fundamental principle under consideration has been violated by too great a mixture, and even an actual consolidation of the different powers; and that in no instance has a competent provision been made for maintaining in practice the separation delineated on paper. What I have wished to evince is, that the charge brought against the proposed constitution, of violating a sacred maxim of free government, is warranted neither by the real meaning annexed to that maxim by its author; nor by the sense in which it has hitherto been understood in America. This interesting subject will be resumed in the ensuing paper.

15

JAMES MADISON, FEDERALIST, NO. 48, 332–38
1 Feb. 1788

It was shewn in the last paper, that the political apothegm there examined, does not require that the legislative, executive and judiciary departments should be wholly unconnected with each other. I shall undertake in the next place, to shew that unless these departments be so far connected and blended, as to give to each a constitutional controul over the others, the degree of separation which the maxim requires as essential to a free government, can never in practice, be duly maintained.

It is agreed on all sides, that the powers properly belonging to one of the departments, ought not to be directly and compleatly administered by either of the other departments. It is equally evident, that neither of them ought to possess directly or indirectly, an overruling influence over the others in the administration of their respective powers. It will not be denied, that power is of an encroaching nature, and that it ought to be effectually restrained from passing the limits assigned to it. After discriminating therefore in theory, the several classes of power, as they may in their nature be legislative, executive, or judiciary; the next and most difficult task, is to provide some practical security for each against the invasion of the others. What this security ought to be, is the great problem to be solved.

Will it be suffcient to mark with precision the boundaries of these departments in the Constitution of the government, and to trust to these parchment barriers against the encroaching spirit of power? This is the security which appears to have been principally relied on by the compilers of most of the American Constitutions. But experience assures us, that the efficacy of the provision has been greatly over-rated; and that some more adequate defence is indispensibly necessary for the more feeble, against the more powerful members of the government. The legislative department is every where extending the sphere of its activity, and drawing all power into its impetuous vortex.

The founders of our republics have so much merit for the wisdom which they have displayed, that no task can be less pleasing than that of pointing out the errors into which they have fallen. A respect for truth however obliges us to remark, that they seem never for a moment to have turned their eyes from the danger to liberty from the overgrown and all-grasping prerogative of an hereditary magistrate, supported and fortified by an hereditary branch of the legislative authority. They seem never to have recollected the danger from legislative usurpations; which by assembling all power in the same hands, must lead to the same tyranny as is threatened by executive usurpations.

In a government, where numerous and extensive prerogatives are placed in the hands of a hereditary monarch, the executive department is very justly regarded as the source of danger, and watched with all the jealousy which a zeal for liberty ought to inspire. In a democracy, where a multitude of people exercise in person the legislative functions, and are continually exposed by their incapacity for regular deliberation and concerted measures, to the ambitious intrigues of their executive magistrates, tyranny may well be apprehended on some favorable emergency, to start up in the same quarter. But in a representative republic, where the executive magistracy is carefully limited both in the extent and the duration of its power; and where the legislative power is exercised by an assembly, which is inspired by a supposed influence over the people with an intrepid confidence in its own strength; which is sufficiently numerous to feel all the passions which actuate a multitude; yet not so numerous as to be incapable of pursuing the objects of its passions, by means which reason prescribes; it is against the enterprising ambition of this department, that the people ought to indulge all their jealousy and exhaust all their precautions.

The legislative department derives a superiority in our governments from other circumstances. Its constitutional powers being at once more extensive and less susceptible of precise limits, it can with the greater facility, mask under complicated and indirect measures, the encroachments which it makes on the co-ordinate departments. It is not unfrequently a question of real-nicety in legislative bodies, whether the operation of a particular measure, will, or will not extend beyond the legislative sphere. On the other side, the executive power being restrained within a narrower compass, and being more simple in its nature; and the judiciary being described by land marks, still less uncertain, projects of usurpation by either of these departments, would immediately betray and defeat themselves. Nor is this all: As the legislative department alone has access to the pockets of the people, and has in some Constitutions full discretion, and in all, a prevailing influence over the pecuniary rewards of those who fill the other departments, a dependence is thus created in the latter, which gives still greater facility to encroachments of the former.

I have appealed to our own experience for the truth of what I advance on this subject. Were it necessary to verify this experience by particular proofs, they might be multiplied without end. I might find a witness in every citizen who has shared in, or been attentive to, the course of public administrations. I might collect vouchers in abundance from the records and archieves of every State in the Union. But as a more concise and at the same time, equally satisfactory evidence, I will refer to the example of two States, attested by two unexceptionable authorities.

The first example is that of Virginia, a State which, as we have seen, has expressly declared in its Constitution, that the three great departments ought not to be intermixed. The authority in support of it is Mr. Jefferson, who, besides his other advantages for remarking the operation of the government, was himself the chief magistrate of it. In order to convey fully the ideas with which his experience had impressed him on this subject, it will be necessary to quote a passage of some length from his very interesting "Notes on the State of Virginia." (P. 195.) "All the powers of government, legislative, executive and judiciary, result to the legislative body. The concentrating these in the same hands is precisely the definition of despotic government. It will be no alleviation that these powers will be exercised by a plurality of hands, and not by a single one, 173 despots would surely be as oppressive as one. Let those who doubt it turn their eyes on the republic of Venice. As little will it avail us that they are chosen by ourselves. An *elective despotism*, was not the government we fought for; but one which should not only be founded on free principles, but in which the powers of government should be so divided and balanced among several bodies of magistracy, as that no one could transcend their legal limits, without being effectually checked and restrained by the others. For this reason that Convention which passed the ordinance of government, laid its foundation on this basis, that the legislative, executive and judiciary departments should be separate and distinct, so that no person should exercise the powers of more than one of them at the same time. *But no barrier was provided between these several powers.* The judiciary and executive members were left dependent on the legislative for their subsistence in office,

and some of them for their continuance in it. If therefore the Legislature assumes executive and judiciary powers, no opposition is likely to be made; nor if made can it be effectual; because in that case, they may put their proceeding into the form of an act of Assembly, which will render them obligatory on the other branches. They have accordingly *in many* instances *decided rights* which should have been left to *judiciary controversy; and the direction of the executive during the whole time of their session, is becoming habitual and familiar."

The other State which I shall take for an example, is Pennsylvania; and the other authority the council of censors which assembled in the years 1783 and 1784. A part of the duty of this body, as marked out by the Constitution was, "to enquire whether the Constitution had been preserved inviolate in every part; and whether the legislative and executive branches of government had performed their duty as guardians of the people, or assumed to themselves, or exercised other or greater powers than they are entitled to by the Constitution." In the execution of this trust, the council were necessarily led to a comparison, of both the legislative and executive proceedings, with the constitutional powers of these departments; and from the facts enumerated, and to the truth of most of which, both sides in the council subscribed, it appears that the Constitution had been flagrantly violated by the Legislature in a variety of important instances.

A great number of laws had been passed violating without any apparent necessity, the rule requiring that all bills of a public nature, shall be previously printed for the consideration of the people; altho' this is one of the precautions chiefly relied on by the Constitution, against improper acts of the Legislature.

The constitutional trial by jury had been violated; and powers assumed, which had not been delegated by the Constitution.

Executive powers had been usurped.

The salaries of the Judges, which the Constitution expressly requires to be fixed, had been occasionally varied; and cases belonging to the judiciary department, frequently drawn within legislative cognizance and determination.

Those who wish to see the several particulars falling under each of these heads, may consult the Journals of the council which are in print. Some of them, it will be found may be imputable to peculiar circumstances connected with the war: But the greater part of them may be considered as the spontaneous shoots of an ill-constituted government.

It appears also, that the executive department had not been innocent of frequent breaches of the Constitution. There are three observations however, which ought to be made on this head. *First.* A great proportion of the instances, were either immediately produced by the necessities of the war, or recommended by Congress or the Commander in Chief. *Secondly.* In most of the other instances, they conformed either to the declared or the known sentiments of the legislative department. *Thirdly.* The executive department of Pennsylvania is distinguished from that of the other States, by the number of members composing it. In this respect it has as much affinity to a legislative assembly, as to an executive council. And being at once exempt from the restraint of an individual responsibility for the acts of the body, and deriving confidence from mutual example and joint influence; unauthorized measures would of course be more freely hazarded, than where the executive department is administered by a single hand or by a few hands.

The conclusion which I am warranted in drawing from these observations is, that a mere demarkation on parchment of the constitutional limits of the several departments, is not a sufficient guard against those encroachments which lead to a tyrannical concentration of all the powers of government in the same hands.

16

JAMES MADISON, FEDERALIST, NO. 51, 347–53
6 Feb. 1788

To what expedient then shall we finally resort for maintaining in practice the necessary partition of power among the several departments, as laid down in the constitution? The only answer that can be given is, that as all these exterior provisions are found to be inadequate, the defect must be supplied, by so contriving the interior structure of the government, as that its several constituent parts may, by their mutual relations, be the means of keeping each other in their proper places. Without presuming to undertake a full developement of this important idea, I will hazard a few general observations, which may perhaps place it in a clearer light, and enable us to form a more correct judgment of the principles and structure of the government planned by the convention.

In order to lay a due foundation for that separate and distinct exercise of the different powers of government, which to a certain extent, is admitted on all hands to be essential to the preservation of liberty, it is evident that each department should have a will of its own; and consequently should be so constituted, that the members of each should have as little agency as possible in the appointment of the members of the others. Were this principle rigorously adhered to, it would require that all the appointments for the supreme executive, legislative, and judiciary magistracies, should be drawn from the same fountain of authority, the people, through channels, having no communication whatever with one another. Perhaps such a plan of constructing the several departments would be less difficult in practice than it may in contemplation appear. Some difficulties however, and some additional expence, would attend the execution of it. Some deviations therefore from the principle must be admitted. In the constitution of the judiciary department in particular, it might be inexpedient to insist rigorously on the principle; first, because peculiar qualifications being essential in the members, the primary consideration ought to be to select that mode of choice, which best secures these qualifications;

secondly, because the permanent tenure by which the appointments are held in that department, must soon destroy all sense of dependence on the authority conferring them.

It is equally evident that the members of each department should be as little dependent as possible on those of the others, for the emoluments annexed to their offices. Were the executive magistrate, or the judges, not independent of the legislature in this particular, their independence in every other would be merely nominal.

But the great security against a gradual concentration of the several powers in the same department, consists in giving to those who administer each department, the necessary constitutional means, and personal motives, to resist encroachments of the others. The provision for defence must in this, as in all other cases, be made commensurate to the danger of attack. Ambition must be made to counteract ambition. The interest of the man must be connected with the constitutional rights of the place. It may be a reflection on human nature, that such devices should be necessary to controul the abuses of government. But what is government itself but the greatest of all reflections on human nature? If men were angels, no government would be necessary. If angels were to govern men, neither external nor internal controuls on government would be necessary. In framing a government which is to be administered by men over men, the great difficulty lies in this: You must first enable the government to controul the governed; and in the next place, oblige it to controul itself. A dependence on the people is no doubt the primary controul on the government; but experience has taught mankind the necessity of auxiliary precautions.

This policy of supplying by opposite and rival interests, the defect of better motives, might be traced through the whole system of human affairs, private as well as public. We see it particularly displayed in all the subordinate distributions of power; where the constant aim is to divide and arrange the several offices in such a manner as that each may be a check on the other; that the private interest of every individual, may be a centinel over the public rights. These inventions of prudence cannot be less requisite in the distribution of the supreme powers of the state.

But it is not possible to give to each department an equal power of self defence. In republican government the legislative authority, necessarily, predominates. The remedy for this inconveniency is, to divide the legislature into different branches; and to render them by different modes of election, and different principles of action, as little connected with each other, as the nature of their common functions, and their common dependence on the society, will admit. It may even be necessary to guard against dangerous encroachments by still further precautions. As the weight of the legislative authority requires that it should be thus divided, the weakness of the executive may require, on the other hand, that it should be fortified. An absolute negative, on the legislature, appears at first view to be the natural defence with which the executive magistrate should be armed. But perhaps it would be neither altogether safe, nor alone sufficient. On ordinary occasions, it might not be exerted with the requisite firmness; and on extraordinary occasions, it might be perfidiously abused. May not this defect of an absolute negative be supplied, by some qualified connection between this weaker department, and the weaker branch of the stronger department, by which the latter may be led to support the constitutional rights of the former, without being too much detached from the rights of its own department?

If the principles on which these observations are founded be just, as I persuade myself they are, and they be applied as a criterion, to the several state constitutions, and to the federal constitution, it will be found, that if the latter does not perfectly correspond with them, the former are infinitely less able to bear such a test.

There are moreover two considerations particularly applicable to the federal system of America, which place that system in a very interesting point of view.

First. In a single republic, all the power surrendered by the people, is submitted to the administration of a single government; and usurpations are guarded against by a division of the government into distinct and separate departments. In the compound republic of America, the power surrendered by the people, is first divided between two distinct governments, and then the portion allotted to each, subdivided among distinct and separate departments. Hence a double security arises to the rights of the people. The different governments will controul each other; at the same time that each will be controuled by itself.

Second. It is of great importance in a republic, not only to guard the society against the oppression of its rulers; but to guard one part of the society against the injustice of the other part. Different interests necessarily exist in different classes of citizens. If a majority be united by a common interest, the rights of the minority will be insecure. There are but two methods of providing against this evil: The one by creating a will in the community independent of the majority, that is, of the society itself; the other by comprehending in the society so many separate descriptions of citizens, as will render an unjust combination of a majority of the whole, very improbable, if not impracticable. The first method prevails in all governments possessing an hereditary or self appointed authority. This at best is but a precarious security; because a power independent of the society may as well espouse the unjust views of the major, as the rightful interests, of the minor party, and may possibly be turned against both parties. The second method will be exemplified in the federal republic of the United States. Whilst all authority in it will be derived from and dependent on the society, the society itself will be broken into so many parts, interests and classes of citizens, that the rights of individuals or of the minority, will be in little danger from interested combinations of the majority. In a free government, the security for civil rights must be the same as for religious rights. It consists in the one case in the multiplicity of interests, and in the other, in the multiplicity of sects. The degree of security in both cases will depend on the number of interests and sects; and this may be presumed to depend on the extent of country and number of people comprehended under the same government. This view of the subject must particu-

larly recommend a proper federal system to all the sincere and considerate friends of republican government: Since it shews that in exact proportion as the territory of the union may be formed into more circumscribed confederacies or states, oppressive combinations of a majority will be facilitated, the best security under the republican form, for the rights of every class of citizens, will be diminished; and consequently, the stability and independence of some member of the government, the only other security, must be proportionally increased. Justice is the end of government. It is the end of civil society. It ever has been, and ever will be pursued, until it be obtained, or until liberty be lost in the pursuit. In a society under the forms of which the stronger faction can readily unite and oppress the weaker, anarchy may as truly be said to reign, as in a state of nature where the weaker individual is not secured against the violence of the stronger: And as in the latter state even the stronger individuals are prompted by the uncertainty of their condition, to submit to a government which may protect the weak as well as themselves: So in the former state, will the more powerful factions or parties be gradually induced by a like motive, to wish for a government which will protect all parties, the weaker as well as the more powerful. It can be little doubted, that if the state of Rhode Island was separated from the confederacy, and left to itself, the insecurity of rights under the popular form of government within such narrow limits, would be displayed by such reiterated oppressions of factious majorities, that some power altogether independent of the people would soon be called for by the voice of the very factions whose misrule had proved the necessity of it. In the extended republic of the United States, and among the great variety of interests, parties and sects which it embraces, a coalition of a majority of the whole society could seldom take place on any other principles than those of justice and the general good; and there being thus less danger to a minor from the will of the major party, there must be less pretext also, to provide for the security of the former, by introducing into the government a will not dependent on the latter; or in other words, a will independent of the society itself. It is no less certain than it is important, notwithstanding the contrary opinions which have been entertained, that the larger the society, provided it lie within a practicable sphere, the more duly capable it will be of self government. And happily for the *republican cause,* the practicable sphere may be carried to a very great extent, by a judicious modification and mixture of the *federal principle.*

17

ALEXANDER HAMILTON, FEDERALIST, NO. 71,
483–84
18 Mar. 1788

The same rule, which teaches the propriety of a partition between the various branches of power, teaches us likewise that this partition ought to be so contrived as to render the one independent of the other. To what purpose separate the executive, or the judiciary, from the legislative, if both the executive and the judiciary are so constituted as to be at the absolute devotion of the legislative? Such a separation must be merely nominal and incapable of producing the ends for which it was established. It is one thing to be subordinate to the laws, and another to be dependent on the legislative body. The first comports with, the last violates, the fundamental principles of good government; and whatever may be the forms of the Constitution, unites all power in the same hands. The tendency of the legislative authority to absorb every other, has been fully displayed and illustrated by examples, in some preceding numbers. In governments purely republican, this tendency is almost irresistable. The representatives of the people, in a popular assembly, seem sometimes to fancy that they are the people themselves; and betray strong symptoms of impatience and disgust at the least sign of opposition from any other quarter; as if the exercise of its rights by either the executive or judiciary, were a breach of their privilege and an outrage to their dignity. They often appear disposed to exert an imperious controul over the other departments; and as they commonly have the people on their side, they always act with such momentum as to make it very difficult for the other members of the government to maintain the balance of the Constitution.

18

NATHANIEL CHIPMAN, SKETCHES OF THE
PRINCIPLES OF GOVERNMENT 120–27
1793

There are very obvious reasons, why these powers should be committed to separate departments in the state, and not be entrusted unitedly to one man, or body of men. Different abilities are necessary for the making, judging, and executing of laws. They require the exercise of different powers, faculties, and knowlege. No one man ever had a sufficient extent of abilities, or versatility of genius, to attend to the duties of all, at one time, or in a quick succession. Such a union must frequently occasion a confusion of principles, and remediless violation of rights. To commit their exercise to a single man, or body of men, essentially constitutes a monarchy, or aristocracy, for the time being. By giving them the power of avoiding all constitutional enquiry, it places them above a sense of accountability for their conduct. They have it in their power, either in the enacting, the interpretation, or the execution of the laws, to skreen themselves, and every member of their body, from account or punishment. The situation itself suggests to them, views and interests, different from those of the people, and leaves no common judge between them. It places them, in respect to the people, in that state of independence, which is often called a state of nature. In such case, the people, hopeless under oppression, sink into

a state of abject slavery, or roused to a sense of their injuries, assume their natural right, in such situation, oppose violence to violence, and take exemplary vengeance of their oppressors. In a government so constituted, the frequency of elections, can only aggravate the evil. The rulers, with all the powers of government in their hands, will find every instrument of corruption and factious violence devoted to their service. They will always have a hope of continuing themselves in administration. Should there happen a change of men, a change of measures, if attempted, would be of short continuance; the same situation, and the same motives, would, sooner or later, produce the same fatal effects.

To enter on a public investigation of the conduct of their predecessors, would be to set an example against themselves.* In such a confusion of powers, should any regular attempt be made to call the rulers to account, the immediate agents, and the immediate causes of the evils, would prove of difficult investigation. Mutual recriminations and powerful intrigues, would generally divert the enquiry from the proper objects, and devote only the innocent or the feeble to the vengeance of the law.

A separation and precise limitation of the legislative, judiciary, and executive powers, with frequent, free, and uncorrupted elections, is the only remedy for these evils. Those who exercise the legislative power, must be subjected to their own laws, and amenable for a violation, equally with the plainest citizen. They must, by the express provision of the constitution, be confined to the consideration of general laws, and forever excluded the right of enacting particular penalties, privileges, or exemptions. Such partial laws are the first beginnings of an attack on the equal rights of man, and a violation of the laws of nature. This provision, however, should not extend to prevent the establishment of companies, by act of legislation, for the purpose of transacting certain business, or of prosecuting certain enterprises, to which the powers of individuals, from the nature of the thing, are incompetent. In the establishment of companies for such purposes only, a new power is created, but the right of no individual is infringed. Neither should it extend to a prohibition of forming laws for the encouragement of useful knowlege. Authors of books, by which useful knowlege is disseminated, and of those inventions, which facilitate the labors of life, are entitled to the fruit of their own industry, and of the application of their powers, equally, with other citizens. But such is the nature of their productions, that, without a legislative interference in their favor, they must remain wholly at the mercy of others.

The legislature may proceed to the declaration of tyrannical laws; the judiciary to the pronouncing of unjust decisions; the executive furnishes the immediate instruments of tyranny and injustice. The executive is, in all cases, the ultimately efficient power. It is, therefore, very necessary, that the executive should be limited, with as much precision, as the nature of the power will permit, and the acts

*The history of the revolutions in the British Ministry, who, in this respect, are in nearly the same situation, confirms the truth of these remarks.

of all its ministers, rendered as conspicuous, as may possibly be, or, at least, of easy investigation, and the ministers themselves made amenable to the ordinary, or constitutional tribunals, for every abuse.

To prevent both legislative and executive abuses, the intervention of an independent judiciary is of no small importance. To the judges, the ministers of this power, it belongs to interpret all acts of the legislature, agreeably to the true principles of the constitution, as founded in the principles of natural law, and to make an impartial application, in all cases of disputed right. By this provision, the rights and interests of the legislative and executive branches will be kept in union with the rights and interests of the individual citizens. All will be equally exposed by the same unjust laws, or amenable for an arbitrary execution. The members of the legislature, cannot, from the nature of their functions, be amenable, in their legislative character, to any tribunal, but that of public sentiment. The case is different with the members of the executive and judiciary. They may, with propriety, be subjected to trial, for a violation of their trust, at the bar of a constitutional tribunal.

It may be observed, that a separation, and precise limitation of the powers of government simplifies the duties of its ministers. All their acts are, thereby, rendered distinct. Enquiry is facilitated, and abuses readily traced to their criminal causes, the particular agents. In addition to this, it gives a degree of energy to the public sentiment. Public approbation and censure, when directed to a number of men, of whom some are known to have acted well, or ill, but the particular agents are concealed, lose much of their force. The guilty hide their blushes in the crowd. Guilt, or rather the sense of guilt, is diminished in proportion to the number of associates.

The better to secure the accountability of the individuals in the great departments of the government, not only ought the powers of the several departments to be, precisely, and distinctly, limited; but the several members ought to be incapable of holding a place in more than one of the departments, at the same time. The members of one department may be eligible to a place in another; but the acceptance of the latter ought to vacate the former. A separation into distinct bodies, will be of little avail, if those bodies may be composed, principally, of the same individual members. The division and limitation of powers, will, in this case, be merely matter of form. They will remain, substantially, united.

If the above observations are well founded, the executive branch ought not to have a negative, or any directing power, in the act of passing laws. The executive may, however, within certain limits, well have a deliberative voice. Those, who are conversant in the execution of the laws, will be the centre of information upon that subject. They will, more readily than others, foresee any difficulty, which may arise in the execution. Of such information the legislature ought to be availed.

The same observations, nearly, will hold true of the judiciary. The judges, from the nature of their official employment, are informed of the difficulties, which arise in the interpretation of the laws, and of those cases, in which they prove deficient, unequal, or unjust in their operation. Such information is highly necessary to the legislative body. The principal members of the judiciary, may, when the particular duties of their office will permit, be, with propriety, united with the head of the executive department, to form a council of revision upon all laws proposed to be passed by the legislature. The business of this council should be confined, solely, to objections. It should be their duty to give information of all difficulties, which they foresee will arise, either in the interpretation, the application, or the execution of the law; and to notice all inconsistencies, either in the laws themselves, or as they relate to the principles of the constitution. They should be allowed, in no instance, to propose any amendments, or to make any leading propositions, in the enacting of laws; but simply to state to the legislature, such objections, as they find to any law, with their reasons in writing.

The information to be derived from this source, may enable the legislature to give a regular consistence to the laws, and a facility to their administration, not otherwise to be expected. Still, the legislature must be the sole judges, whether the information given coincides with the general interest of the community, and the principles of the government, or is dictated by particular views, or particular interests.

19

ALEXANDER HAMILTON TO GEORGE WASHINGTON
7 Mar. 1796
Papers 20:68–69

Mr. Livingston's motion in the House of Representatives, concerning the production of papers has attracted much attention. The opinion of those who think here is, that if the motion succeeds, it ought not to be complied with. Besides that in a matter of such a nature the production of the papers cannot fail to start [a] new and unpleasant Game—it will be fatal to the Negotiating Power of the Government if it is to be a matter of course for a call of either House of Congress to bring forth all the communication however confidential.

It seems to me that something like the following answer by the President will be advisable.

"A right in the House of Representatives, to demand and have as a matter of course, and without specification of any object all communications respecting a negotiation with a foreign power cannot be admitted without danger of much inconvenience. A discretion in the Executive Department how far and where to comply in such cases is essential to the due conduct of foreign negotiations and is essential to preserve the limits between the Legislative and Executive Departments. The present call is altogether indefinite and without any declared purpose. The Executive has no cases on which to judge of the propriety of a compliance with it and cannot therefore without forming a very dangerous precedent comply.

It does not occur that the view of the papers asked for can be relative to any purpose of the competency of the House of Representatives but that of an impeachment. In every case of a foreign Treaty the grounds for an impeachment must primarily be deduced from the nature of the Instrument itself and from nothing extrinsic. If at any time a Treaty should present such grounds and it shall have been so pronounced by the House of Representatives and a further inquiry shall be necessary to ascertain the culpable person, there being then a declared and ascertained object the President would attend with due respect to any application for necessary information."

This is but a hasty and crude outline of what has struck me as an eligible course. For while a too easy compliance will be mischievous, a too peremptory and unqualified refusal might be liable to just criticism.

20

ALEXANDER HAMILTON TO WILLIAM LOUGHTON SMITH
10 Mar. 1796
Papers 20:72–73

I observe Madison brings the power of the House of Representatives in the case of the Treaty to this Question Is the Agency of the House of Representatives on this subject *deliberative* or *Executive*? On the sophism that this Legislature and each Branch of it is *essentially deliberative* & consequently must have discretion will he, I presume, maintain the freedom of the House to concur or not.

But this sophism is easily refuted. The Legislature & each branch of it is *deliberative* but with *various* restrictions not with *unlimited discretion*. All the injunctions & restrictions in the constitution for instance abrige its *deliberative* faculty & leave it *quoad hoc* merely *executive*. Thus the Constitution enjoins that there shall be a fixed allowance for the Judges which shall not be diminished. The Legislature cannot therefore deliberate whether they will make a permanent provision & when the allowance is fixed they cannot deliberate whether they will appropriate & pay the money. So far their deliberative faculty is abrged. The *mode* of raising & appropriating the money only remains matter of deliberation.

So likewise the Constitution says that the President & Senate shall make Treaties & that these Treaties shall be supreme laws. It is a contradiction to call a thing a law which is not binding. It follows that by constitutional injunction the House of Representatives *quoad* the stipulations of Treaties, as in the case cited respecting the Judges are not deliberative, but merely executive *except* as to the *means of executing*.

Any other Doctrine would vest the Legislature & each House with *unlimited discretion* & destroy the very idea of a

Constitution limiting its discretion. The Constitution would at once vanish!

Besides the *legal* power to refuse the execution of a law is a *power to repeal* it. Thus the House of Representatives must as to Treaties concenter in itself the whole legislative power & undertake without the senate to repeal a law. For the law is *complete* by the action of the President & Senate.

Again a Treaty which is a contract between nation & nation abriges even the legislative discretion of the whole legislature by the moral obligation of keeping its faith; a fortiori that of one branch. In theory there is no method by which the obligations of a Treaty can be annulled but by mutual consent of the contracting parties—by ill faith in one of them or by a revolution of Government which is of a nature so to change the condition of parties as to render the Treaty inapplicable.

21

JAMES MADISON, HOUSE OF REPRESENTATIVES
10 Mar. 1796
Annals 5:493

The Constitution of the United States is a Constitution of limitations and checks. The powers given up by the people for the purposes of Government, had been divided into two great classes. One of these formed the State Governments; the other, the Federal Government. The powers of the Government had been further divided into three great departments; and the Legislative department again subdivided into two independent branches. Around each of these portions of power were seen also exceptions and qualifications, as additional guards against the abuses to which power is liable. With a view to this policy of the Constitution, it could not be unreasonable, if the clauses under discussion were thought doubtful, to lean towards a construction that would limit and control the Treaty-making power, rather than towards one that would make it omnipotent.

He came next to the fifth construction, which left with the PRESIDENT and Senate the power of making Treaties, but required at the same time the Legislative sanction and co operation, in those cases where the Constitution had given express and specific powers to the Legislature. It was to be presumed, that in all such cases the Legislature would exercise its authority with discretion, allowing due weight to the reasons which led to the Treaty, and to the circumstances of the existence of the Treaty. Still, however, this House, in its Legislative capacity, must exercise its reason; it must deliberate; for deliberation is implied in legislation. If it must carry all Treaties into effect, it would no longer exercise a Legislative power; it would be the mere instrument of the will of another department, and would have no will of its own. Where the Constitution contains a specific and peremptory injunction on Congress to do a particular act, Congress must, of course, do the act, because the Constitution, which is paramount over all the departments, has expressly taken away the Legislative discretion of Congress. The case is essentially different where the act of one department of Government interferes with a power expressly vested in another, and no where expressly taken away: here the latter power must be exercised according to its nature; and if it be a Legislative power, it must be exercised with that deliberation and discretion which is essential to the nature of Legislative power.

22

JAMES MADISON TO JOHN ADAMS
22 May 1817
Writings 8:390–92

I have received your favor of April 22d, with the two volumes bearing the name of Condorcet. If the length of time they remained in your hands had been in the least inconvenient to me, which was not the case, the debt would have been overpaid by the interesting observations into which you were led by your return of them.

The idea of a Government "in one centre," as expressed and espoused by this Philosopher and his theoretic associates, seems now to be every where exploded. And the views which you have given of its fallacy will be a powerful obstacle to its revival anywhere. It is remarkable that in each of our States which approached nearest to the theory changes were soon made, assimilating their constitution to the examples of the other States, which had placed the powers of Government in different depositories, as means of controlling the impulse and sympathy of the passions, and affording to reason better opportunities of asserting its prerogatives.

The great question now to be decided, and it is one in which humanity is more deeply interested than in any po-litical experiment yet made, is, whether checks and balances sufficient for the purposes of order, justice, and the general good, may not be created by a proper division and distribution of power among different bodies, differently constituted, but all deriving their existence from the elective principle, and bound by a responsible tenure of their trusts. The experiment is favored by the extent of our Country, which prevents the contagion of evil passions; and by the combination of the federal with the local systems of Government, which multiplies the divisions of power, and the mutual checks by which it is to be kept within its proper limits and direction. In aid of these considerations much is to be hoped from the force of opinion and habit, as these ally themselves with our political institutions. I am running, however, into reflections, without recollecting that all such must have fallen within the comprehensive reviews which your mind has taken of the principles of our Government, and the prospects of our Country.

SEE ALSO:

Generally chs. 11, 17
John Jay to Thomas Jefferson, 18 Aug. 1786, Jefferson Papers 10:272
Thomas Jefferson to James Madison, 16 Dec. 1786, Papers 10:603
John Jay to Thomas Jefferson, 9 Feb. 1787, Jefferson Papers 11:129
Thomas Jefferson to Edward Carrington, 4 Aug. 1787, Papers 11:679
Richard Henry Lee to Edmund Randolph, 16 Oct. 1787, Letters 2:451–52
James Wilson, Lectures on Law, pt. 1, ch. 10, 1791, Works 1:298–300
James Madison, House of Representatives, 7 Mar. 1796, Annals 5:437–38
Alexander Hamilton to Rufus King, 16 Mar. 1796, Papers 20:76–77
Alexander Hamilton, Draft of Presidential Message to the House of Representatives, Mar. 1796, Papers 20:86–103
George Washington to Alexander Hamilton, 31 Mar. 1796, Hamilton Papers 20:103–5

11

Balanced Government

Introduction

Balanced or mixed government implies simultaneously a distinction from its frequent associate, the separation of powers, and a rejection of its opposite, simple government. The case for the one involves, then, a consideration of the cases for the other two. Montesquieu's frequent recourse to arguments for a balanced government without making any sharp distinction from separation of powers suggests that the two have similar ends, that one may reinforce the other, or that one may act to mitigate the extremes implicit in the other. An examination of some of the political arguments that preceded the writing of the Constitution discloses the extent to which each of these explanations carried weight. Similarly, an examination of the case for simple government—a case that the proponents of the Constitution rejected outright and with which even most critics of the Constitution were not comfortable—discloses contemporary reasoning about both the character of the American people and the general requirements of popular government.

James Harrington (no. 2) surely was not the originator of the notion that a well-ordered commonwealth requires some kind of internal balance of its heterogeneous parts. That notion was well known in classical antiquity and given vivid restatement by Machiavelli (no. 1). But Harrington's formulation of the problem—"how a commonwealth comes to be an empire of laws and not of men"—won the minds of the Americans and shaped their political discourse. For Harrington it was a clear and simple conclusion that popular government is both the most reasonable form and the one most conducive to furthering the interest of mankind. And yet it was no less clear and true that

each individual is most moved by "the nearness of that which sticks to every man in private." Given the primacy of private interest and the rightness and indeed urgency of the public interest, the task is to secure the latter without futilely or tyrannically trying to extirpate the former. To prevent factious scrambling, Harrington proposed a system whereby one part debates and divides, yet another part resolves or chooses, and still another executes. The first two orders constitute the legislative: a senate whose claim to divide "the cake" is based on being made up of a "natural aristocracy diffused by God through the whole body of mankind" and the assembled representatives of the people as a whole whose self-interest exercised in choosing the portions is coterminous with the interest of the commonwealth. The third is the chief magistrate.

This aspect of Harrington's complex scheme of balanced government was altered, developed, and reworked by his successors. Joseph Addison found reason to congratulate his countrymen on having a legislative power that mirrored the differing "Ranks and Interests" of the society at large. Accordingly, each part of the people had its corresponding part in the legislative to care for their shared interest. Nothing less would do to guard against the despotic use of power. (See *Spectator,* no. 287, 29 Jan. 1712.)

For Hume (no. 3) the very possibility of a science of politics turned on the possibility of transcending or overcoming "the casual humors and characters of particular men." How a "republican and free government" is constituted matters much more than the idiosyncrasies of the governors. Very much, then, turns on the constitutional checks and controls that make it "the interest, even of bad men, to act for the public good." Not least important is the role of a chief magistrate powerful enough to "form a proper balance or counterpoise to the other parts of the legislature." For Hume, in contrast to Harrington, the executive's share in the legislative function seemed to make him a part of the legislative branch; balance, not separation, was intended. And yet, it was as an executive that the king truly balanced or restrained the Commons, an executive who cajoled and dangled gifts before the avaricious and, with the support of "the honest and disinterested part of the House," had so far at least been able to keep the system on an even keel. It was the joinder of the crown and the ministry through corruption that unbalanced the British government under George III.

The colonials in British North America on the whole took Hume's self-celebratory account as offering little by way of solution to their problems. Some, like Richard Henry Lee (no. 6), admired the theory but not its British execution. Others, like the anonymous author of *The People the Best Governors* (no. 8), denied the very premise of the theory of mixed or balanced government: the mutual checking of different social orders. The more the control of the people's business is in their own hands, the better; the more immediately governmental authority is dependent on the people, the safer will be the people's liberties. Similarly, the Pennsylvania author of *Four Letters on Interesting Subjects* (see ch. 17, no. 19) doubted whether the benefits of a balanced government outweighed its costs. Was the quality of deliberation enhanced, or the dispatch of public business, or the promotion of the common interest? Still others, like Tom Paine in *Common Sense* (see ch. 4, no. 4), rejected British pretensions on grounds of both theory and practice. "I draw my idea of the form of government from a principle in nature, which no art can overturn, viz. that the more simple any thing is, the less liable it is to be disordered, and the easier repaired when disordered." Viewing the practice of the day, Paine saw a crown which had succeeded only in "eat[ing] out the virtue of the house of commons" through its corrupting influence, thereby poisoning the republican part of the British constitution. Here was no model for a people with freedom to choose the form their government should take.

And yet, Farmer asserted (no. 9), a simple republic was quite out of the question. To be sure, all political authority in America now had to derive from the sovereign people, but that people neither wished nor was fit for "a simple Republick." In part their taste had been formed by the habits of living under the British monarchy: "the genius of the *Americans* . . . is of a monarchical spirit." But beyond that, the Americans were not simple republicans; there were among them a "great distinction of persons, and differences in their estates or property." Still, these were not the hereditary orders of an England. To balance the powers of American orders in a context of popular sovereignty would be the great task at hand.

Balance American Style

To this problem John Adams (no. 10) devoted his thought, his energies, and his pen. The result—a three-volume explosion triggered by Turgot's proposal that Americans abandon British models for a unicameral assembly—made the case for a balanced or mixed government based not on social orders but on natural orders. To ignore "the utility and necessity of different *orders* of men" was to ignore what the keenest minds and closest observers had found to be universally true. Adams, like Harrington, saw a natural aristocracy arising out of the natural differences among men; both asked how that aristocracy might be rendered useful and safe. Rejecting as insufficient the classical reliance upon habituation through education and discipline as the way to devoted citizenship (he saw this as too "great an end" for a large nation), Adams turned instead to institutional checks and balances. The choice is either the jealous counterpoise of constitutional parties, or a recourse to simple monarchy and a standing army to put an end to factious turmoil and to liberty itself.

Balanced government in America, then, would resemble earlier examples in some respects, yet have its own distinctive character as well. Although contemporaries might disagree over the degree of homogeneity and equality in the new United States, it was clear enough that the country had no permanent social orders. For the near future, at least, America could supply no analogues to the patricians and plebeians of Rome, the nobility and common folk of Britain or France. And yet, for all that, America too had its few and its many, its haves and its have-nots. In America too could be heard the conflicting claims of great interests of East and West, North and South, as they pressed against one another in the political forum. To contain these mighty forces—at least to the point where they could not capture the authority and power of government for their particular purposes, or bring down the entire political system in the attempt—would require all the ingenuity of the age. In the mind of an Adams or a Madison the need for balancing great and greatly diverse forces led to a search for every sort of useful institutional device and auxiliary support. Among other things Adams looked to a second legislative chamber where the able and ambitious few might be quarantined, so to speak (see ch. 12); to a monarchical principle in the shape of a unitary executive who might hold the balance between the many and the few. Madison sought to mitigate the destructive ferocity of contending interests and enthusiasms through the checks of a complicated governmental structure (see ch. 10), and by making use of the sheer size and diversity of the new country. Others, too, sought to have the two branches of the legislature mirror, respectively, the persons and the property of the nation, in recognition of the belief that each must have its voice but neither could unqualifiedly have its way (see ch. 13).

But critics of the proposed Constitution remained unpersuaded of either the analysis or the solution, or both. Had there been, could there ever be, a government such as Adams held forth as a model? Further, Centinel wondered (no. 11), "how is the welfare and happiness of the community to be the result of such jarring adverse interests?" Rely, rather, on the governors' sense of accountability to the people; and that can best be secured through "a simple structure of government" where the people easily can pinpoint the culprits who would ignore or betray their good. The Federal Farmer (no. 12) doubted that any real balance was possible in a bicameral legislature composed—as it necessarily would be in America—of "the same kind of men." Without further alterations and support, "the partitions between the two branches will be merely those of the building in which they sit." Patrick Henry took up this theme in the Virginia Ratifying Convention (no. 13): "Tell me not of checks on paper; but tell me of checks founded on self-love." The people's liberties were less safe under the proposed Constitution, this ardent republican exclaimed, than under the British monarchy, for there at least the hereditary nobility have a stake in maintaining a balance between king and Commons; their continued existence depends on it. What corresponding incentives did the American analogues possess? James Monroe, too, contrasted the balance in the Roman and English constitutions, based as they were on social orders, "each of which had a repellent quality which enabled it to preserve itself from being destroyed by the other two." The American division of power had no such basis and, indeed, no such intention: "a more faithful and regular administration" was the end in view. Like Henry, Monroe could "see no real checks" in the Constitution that would prevent a coalition of the branches of government and encroachments on the rights of the people (no. 15).

John Marshall's response in the same convention trod a narrow line (no. 14). To be sure, "In this country, there is no exclusive personal stock of interest." But that did not mean that there were no checks in the Constitution, or that reliance was placed totally upon the public-spiritedness of a few luminous characters. There were in fact powerful checks. To begin with, there would be interweaving of interests so that when the individual "promotes his own, he promotes that of the community." There is little reason to doubt that Marshall saw this blending of interests taking place as much within the society as a whole as within the several constitutional orders called for by the new framework of government. Further, there was the check of "the American spirit," the jealousy of a republican people, heedful of its powers and rights and inclined to keep its agents on a short tether.

From the point of view of Madison's presidential years, Gouverneur Morris and John Adams reached different conclusions about the effectiveness of the Constitution's balance. The issue, Adams insisted (Letter to John Taylor, Apr. 1814), was not "whether an exact balance has been hit," but whether the Constitution with its "refinements upon refinements" did in fact form "a complication of checks and balances." He thought the evidence that it had incontestable. Morris (no. 17), while denying despair, found little to please and still less to look forward to. The dilemma, presented to the Philadelphia Convention and noted subtly by Monroe at the Virginia Ratifying Convention, had remained unresolved. The balance of the system turned among other things on the Senate's being an effective counterpoise; that in turn required that the Senate be distinctive; the distinctiveness of the Senate depended ultimately on the influence of the states; and yet "a more perfect union" could be achieved only by reducing the weight and prominence of the states. For want of an independent pair of hands to hold the scales between national sovereignty and state independence, the very balance of the national government itself remained in jeopardy. There was little expectation that the federal judiciary would afford that independent judgment.

1

NICCOLÒ MACHIAVELLI, DISCOURSES ON THE FIRST TEN BOOKS OF TITUS LIVIUS, BK. 1, CH. 2
1531 (posthumous)

Of the Different Kinds of Republics, and of What Kind the Roman Republic Was

I will leave aside what might be said of cities which from their very birth have been subject to a foreign power, and will speak only of those whose origin has been independent, and which from the first governed themselves by their own laws, whether as republics or as principalities, and whose constitution and laws have differed as their origin. Some have had at the very beginning, or soon after, a legislator, who, like Lycurgus with the Lacedaemonians, gave them by a single act all the laws they needed. Others have owed theirs to chance and to events, and have received their laws at different times, as Rome did. It is a great good fortune for a republic to have a legislator sufficiently wise to give her laws so regulated that, without the necessity of correcting them, they afford security to those who live under them. Sparta observed her laws for more than eight hundred years without altering them and without experiencing a single dangerous disturbance. Unhappy, on the contrary, is that republic which, not having at the beginning fallen into the hands of a sagacious and skilful legislator, is herself obliged to reform her laws. More unhappy still is that republic which from the first has diverged from a good constitution. And that republic is furthest from it whose vicious institutions impede her progress, and make her leave the right path that leads to a good end; for those who are in that condition can hardly ever be brought into the right road. Those republics, on the other hand, that started without having even a perfect constitution, but made a fair beginning, and are capable of improvement,—such republics, I say, may perfect themselves by the aid of events. It is very true, however, that such reforms are never effected without danger, for the majority of men never willingly adopt any new law tending to change the constitution of the state, unless the necessity of the change is clearly demonstrated; and as such a necessity cannot make itself felt without being accompanied with danger, the republic may easily be destroyed before having perfected its constitution. That of Florence is a complete proof of this: reorganized after the revolt of Arezzo, in 1502, it was overthrown after the taking of Prato, in 1512.

Having proposed to myself to treat of the kind of government established at Rome, and of the events that led to its perfection, I must at the beginning observe that some of the writers on politics distinguished three kinds of government, viz. the monarchical, the aristocratic, and the democratic; and maintain that the legislators of a people must choose from these three the one that seems to them most suitable. Other authors, wiser according to the opinion of many, count six kinds of governments, three of which are very bad, and three good in themselves, but so liable to be corrupted that they become absolutely bad. The three good ones are those which we have just named; the three bad ones result from the degradation of the other three, and each of them resembles its corresponding original, so that the transition from the one to the other is very easy. Thus monarchy becomes tyranny; aristocracy degenerates into oligarchy; and the popular government lapses readily into licentiousness. So that a legislator who gives to a state which he founds, either of these three forms of government, constitutes it but for a brief time; for no precautions can prevent either one of the three that are reputed good, from degenerating into its opposite kind; so great are in these the attractions and resemblances between the good and the evil.

Chance has given birth to these different kinds of governments amongst men; for at the beginning of the world the inhabitants were few in number, and lived for a time dispersed, like beasts. As the human race increased, the necessity for uniting themselves for defence made itself felt; the better to attain this object, they chose the strongest and most courageous from amongst themselves and placed him at their head, promising to obey him. Thence they began to know the good and the honest, and to distinguish them from the bad and vicious; for seeing a man injure his benefactor aroused at once two sentiments in every heart, hatred against the ingrate and love for the benefactor. They blamed the first, and on the contrary honored those the more who showed themselves grateful, for each felt that he in turn might be subject to a like wrong; and to prevent similar evils, they set to work to make laws, and to institute punishments for those who contravened them. Such was the origin of justice. This caused them, when they had afterwards to choose a prince, neither to look to the strongest nor bravest, but to the wisest and most just. But when they began to make sovereignty hereditary and non-elective, the children quickly degenerated from their fathers; and, so far from trying to equal their virtues, they considered that a prince had nothing else to do than to excel all the rest in luxury, indulgence, and every other variety of pleasure. The prince consequently soon drew upon himself the general hatred. An object of hatred, he naturally felt fear; fear in turn dictated to him precautions and wrongs, and thus tyranny quickly developed itself. Such were the beginning and causes of disorders, conspiracies, and plots against the sovereigns, set on foot, not by the feeble and timid, but by those citizens who, surpassing the others in grandeur of soul, in wealth, and in courage, could not submit to the outrages and excesses of their princes.

Under such powerful leaders the masses armed themselves against the tyrant, and, after having rid themselves of him, submitted to these chiefs as their liberators. These, abhorring the very name of prince, constituted themselves a new government; and at first, bearing in mind the past tyranny, they governed in strict accordance with the laws which they had established themselves; preferring public interests to their own, and to administer and protect with greatest care both public and private affairs. The children succeeded their fathers, and ignorant of the changes of fortune, having never experienced its reverses, and indisposed to remain content with this civil equality, they in turn gave themselves up to cupidity, ambition, libertinage, and violence, and soon caused the aristocratic government to degenerate into an oligarchic tyranny, regardless of all civil rights. They soon, however, experienced the same fate as the first tyrant; the people, disgusted with their government, placed themselves at the command of whoever was willing to attack them, and this disposition soon produced an avenger, who was sufficiently well seconded to destroy them. The memory of the prince and the wrongs committed by him being still fresh in their minds, and having overthrown the oligarchy, the people were not willing to return to the government of a prince. A popular government was therefore resolved upon, and it was so organized that the authority should not again fall into the hands of a prince or a small number of nobles. And as all governments are at first looked up to with some degree of reverence, the popular state also maintained itself for a time, but which was never of long duration, and lasted generally only about as long as the generation that had established it; for it soon ran into that kind of license which inflicts injury upon public as well as private interests. Each individual only consulted his own passions, and a thousand acts of injustice were daily committed, so that, constrained by necessity, or directed by the counsels of some good man, or for the purpose of escaping from this anarchy, they returned anew to the government of a prince, and from this they generally lapsed again into anarchy, step by step, in the same manner and from the same causes as we have indicated.

Such is the circle which all republics are destined to run through. Seldom, however, do they come back to the original form of government, which results from the fact that their duration is not sufficiently long to be able to undergo these repeated changes and preserve their existence. But it may well happen that a republic lacking strength and good counsel in its difficulties becomes subject after a while to some neighboring state, that is better organized than itself; and if such is not the case, then they will be apt to revolve indefinitely in the circle of revolutions. I say, then, that all kinds of government are defective; those three which we have qualified as good because they are too short-lived, and the three bad ones because of their inherent viciousness. Thus sagacious legislators, knowing the vices of each of these systems of government by themselves, have chosen one that should partake of all of them, judging that to be the most stable and solid. In fact, when there is combined under the same constitution a prince, a nobility, and the power of the people, then these three powers will watch and keep each other reciprocally in check.

Amongst those justly celebrated for having established such a constitution, Lycurgus beyond doubt merits the highest praise. He organized the government of Sparta in such manner that, in giving to the king, the nobles, and the people each their portion of authority and duties, he created a government which maintained itself for over eight hundred years in the most perfect tranquillity, and reflected infinite glory upon this legislator. On the other hand, the constitution given by Solon to the Athenians, by which he established only a popular government, was of such short duration that before his death he saw the tyranny of Pisistratus arise. And although forty years afterwards the heirs of the tyrant were expelled, so that Athens recovered her liberties and restored the popular government according to the laws of Solon, yet it did not last over a hundred years; although a number of laws that had been overlooked by Solon were adopted, to maintain the government against the insolence of the nobles and the license of the populace. The fault he had committed in not tempering the power of the people and that of the prince and his nobles, made the duration of the government of Athens very short, as compared with that of Sparta.

But let us come to Rome. Although she had no legislator like Lycurgus, who constituted her government, at her very origin, in a manner to secure her liberty for a length of time, yet the disunion which existed between the Senate and the people produced such extraordinary events, that chance did for her what the laws had failed to do. Thus, if Rome did not attain the first degree of happiness, she at least had the second. Her first institutions were doubtless defective, but they were not in conflict with the principles that might bring her to perfection. For Romulus and all the other kings gave her many and good laws, well suited even to a free people; but as the object of these princes was to found a monarchy, and not a republic, Rome, upon becoming free, found herself lacking all those institutions that are most essential to liberty, and which her kings had not established. And although these kings lost their empire, for the reasons and in the manner which we have explained, yet those who expelled them appointed immediately two consuls in place of the king; and thus it was found that they had banished the title of king from Rome, but not the regal power. The government, composed of Consuls and a Senate, had but two of the three elements of which we have spoken, the monarchical and the aristocratic; the popular power was wanting. In the course of time, however, the insolence of the nobles, produced by the causes which we shall see further on, induced the people to rise against the others. The nobility, to save a portion of their power, were forced to yield a share of it to the people; but the Senate and the Consuls retained sufficient to maintain their rank in the state. It was then that the Tribunes of the people were created, which strengthened and confirmed the republic, being now composed of

the three elements of which we have spoken above. Fortune favored her, so that, although the authority passed successively from the kings and nobles to the people, by the same degrees and for the same reasons that we have spoken of, yet the royal authority was never entirely abolished to bestow it upon the nobles; and these were never entirely deprived of their authority to give it to the people; but a combination was formed of the three powers, which rendered the constitution perfect, and this perfection was attained by the disunion of the Senate and the people.

2

JAMES HARRINGTON, COMMONWEALTH OF OCEANA 56–61
1656

But seeing they that make the laws in commonwealths are but men, the main question seems to be how a commonwealth comes to be an empire of laws and not of men; or how the debate or result of a commonwealth is so sure to be according unto reason, seeing they who debate and they who resolve be but men. "And as often as reason is against a man, so often will a man be against reason."

This is thought to be a shrewd saying, but will do no harm. For be it so that reason is nothing but interest, there be divers interests and so divers reasons.

As first, there is *private reason*, which is the interest of a private man.

Secondly, there is *reason of state*, which is the interest (or "error," as was said by Solomon) of the ruler or rulers; that is to say, of the prince, of the nobility, or of the people.

Thirdly, there is that reason which is *the interest of mankind* or of the whole. [Says Richard Hooker:]

> Now if we see even in those natural agents that want sense, that as in themselves they have a law which directs them in the means whereby they tend to their own perfection, so likewise that another law there is which touches them as they are sociable parts united into one body, a law which binds them each to serve unto others' good and all to prefer the good of the whole before whatsoever their own particular, as when stones or heavy things forsake their ordinary wont or center and fly upwards as if they heard themselves commanded to let go the good they privately wish and to relieve the present distress of nature in common.

There is a common right, law of nature, or interest of the whole which is more excellent, and so acknowledged to be by the agents themselves, than the right or interest of the parts only. "Wherefore, though it may be truly said that the creatures are naturally carried forth to their proper utility or profit, that ought not to be taken in too general a sense, seeing divers of them abstain from their own profit either in regard of those of the same kind or at least of their young."

Mankind, then, must either be less just than the creature[s] or acknowledge also his common interest to be common right. And if reason be nothing else but interest, and the interest of mankind be the right interest, then the reason of mankind must be right reason. Now compute well, for if the *interest of popular government* come the nearest unto the *interest of mankind*, then the *reason of popular government* must come the nearest unto *right reason*.

But it may be said that the difficulty remains yet. For be the interest of popular government right reason, a man does not look upon reason as it is right or wrong in itself, but as it makes for him or against him. Wherefore, unless you can show such orders of a government as, like those of God in nature, shall be able to constrain this or that creature to shake off that inclination which is more peculiar to it and take up that which regards the common good or interest, all this is to no more end than to persuade every man in a popular government not to carve himself of that which he desires most, but to be mannerly at the public table and give the best from himself to decency and the common interest. But that such orders may be established as may, nay must, give the upper hand in all cases to the common right or interest, notwithstanding the nearness of that which sticks to every man in private, and this in a way of equal certainty and facility is known even to girls, being no other than those that are of common practice with them in divers cases. For example, two of them have a cake yet undivided which was given between them that each of them therefore may have that which is due. "Divide," says one to the other, "and I will choose, or let me divide, and you shall choose." If this be but once agreed upon, it is enough, for the divider dividing unequally loses in regard that the other takes the better half. Wherefore, she divides equally and so both have right. "O the depth of the wisdom of God!" and yet "by the mouths of babes and sucklings hath he set forth his strength." That which great philosophers are disputing upon in vain is brought unto light by two silly girls, even the whole mystery of a commonwealth, which lies only in dividing and choosing. Nor has God (if his works in nature be understood) left so much to mankind to dispute upon, as who shall divide and who choose, but distributed them forever into two orders, whereof the one has the natural right of dividing and the other of choosing. For example:

A commonwealth is but a civil society of men. Let us take any number of men (as twenty) and forthwith make a commonwealth. Twenty men (if they be not all idiots, perhaps if they be) can never come so together but there will be such difference in them that about a third will be wiser, or at least less foolish than all the rest. These upon acquaintance, though it be but small, will be discovered and (as stags that have the largest heads) lead the herd. For while the six discoursing and arguing one with another show the eminence of their parts, the fourteen discover things that they never thought on or are cleared in divers truths which had formerly perplexed them. Wherefore in matter of common concernment, difficulty, or danger, they hang upon their lips as children upon their fathers'

and the influence thus acquired by the six, the eminence of whose parts is found to be a stay and comfort to the fourteen, is *Authoritas Patrum*, the authority of the fathers. Wherefore this can be no other than a *natural aristocracy* diffused by God throughout the whole body of mankind to this end and purpose. And, therefore, such as the people have not only a natural, but a positive, obligation to make use of as their guides, as where the people of Israel are commanded to "take wise men and understanding and known among their tribes, to be made rulers over them." The six then approved of, as in the present case, are the senate, not by hereditary right or in regard of the greatness of their estates only, which would tend to such power as might force or draw the people, but by election for their excellent parts which tend to the advancement of the influence of their *virtue* or *authority* that leads the people. Wherefore the office of the senate is not to be commanders, but counselors of the people. And that which is proper unto counselors is, first, to debate the business whereupon they are to give advice and, afterward, to give advice in the business whereupon they have debated. Whence the decrees of the senate are never laws, nor so called, but *Senatus Consulta*, and these being maturely framed, it is their duty, *Ferre ad Populum*, to propose in the case to the people. Wherefore the senate is no more than the debate of the commonwealth. But to debate is to discern or put a difference between things that being alike are not the same, or it is separating and weighing this reason against that, and that reason against this, which is dividing.

The senate then having divided, who shall choose? Ask the girls. For if she that divided must have chosen also, it had been little worse for the other in case she had not divided at all but kept the whole cake to herself, in regard that, being to choose too, she divided accordingly. Wherefore if the senate have any further power than to divide, the commonwealth can never be equal. But in a commonwealth consisting of a single council, there is no other to choose than that which divided. Whence it is that such a council fails not to scramble, that is, to be factious, there being no other dividing of the cake in that case but among themselves.

Nor is there any remedy but to have another council to choose. The *wisdom* of the few may be the *light* of mankind, but the *interest* of the few is not the *profit* of mankind, nor of a commonwealth. Wherefore, seeing we have granted interest to be reason, they must not choose, lest it put out their light. But as the council dividing consists of the *wisdom* of the commonwealth, so the assembly or council choosing should consist of the *interest* of the commonwealth. As the wisdom of the commonwealth is in the aristocracy, so the interest of the commonwealth is in the whole body of the people. And whereas this, in case the commonwealth consist of a whole nation, is too unwieldy a body to be assembled, this council is to consist of such a representative as may be equal, and so constituted as can never contract any other interest than that of the whole people. The manner whereof being such as is best shown by exemplification, I remit to the model [presented in the second part of the work]. But in the present case, the six dividing and the fourteen choosing, must of necessity take in the whole interest of the twenty.

Dividing and choosing in the language of a commonwealth is debating and resolving, and whatsoever upon debate of the senate is proposed unto the people and resolved by them is enacted *Auctoritate Patrum Et Jussu Populi*, by the authority of the fathers and the power of the people, which concurring make a law.

But the law being made, says Hobbes, "is but words and paper without the hands and swords of men." Wherefore as those two orders of a commonwealth, namely the senate and the people, are *legislative*, so of necessity there must be a third to be *executive* of the laws made, and this is the magistracy; in which order with the rest being wrought up by art, the commonwealth consists of the senate proposing, the people resolving, and the magistracy executing. Whereby, partaking of the aristocracy as in the senate, of the democracy as in the people, and of monarchy as in the magistracy, it is complete. Now there being no other commonwealth but this in art or nature, it is no wonder if Machiavelli has showed us that the ancients held this only to be good. But it seems strange to me that they should hold that there could be any other; for if there be such a thing as pure monarchy, yet that there should be such a one as pure aristocracy or pure democracy is not in my understanding. But the magistracy both in number and function is different in different commonwealths; nevertheless, there is one condition of it that must be the same in every one or it dissolves the commonwealth where it is wanting. And this is no less than that as the hand of the magistrate is the executive power of the law, so the head of the magistrate is answerable to the people that his execution be according to the law, by which Hobbes may see that the hand or sword that executes the law is *in* it and *not above* it.

3

DAVID HUME, THAT POLITICS MAY BE REDUCED TO A SCIENCE
1742

It is a question with several whether there be any essential difference between one form of government and another, and whether every form may not become good or bad, according as it is well or ill administered? Were it once admitted that all governments are alike and that the only difference consists in the character and conduct of the governors, most political disputes would be at an end, and all *zeal* for one constitution above another must be esteemed mere bigotry and folly. But, though a friend to moderation, I cannot forbear condemning this sentiment and should be sorry to think that human affairs admit of no greater stability than what they receive from the casual humors and characters of particular men.

It is true, those who maintain that the goodness of all government consists in the goodness of the administration may cite many particular instances in history where the very same government, in different hands, has varied suddenly into the two opposite extremes of good and bad. Compare the French government under Henry III and under Henry IV. Oppression, levity, artifice on the part of the rulers, faction, sedition, treachery, rebellion, disloyalty on the part of the subjects—these compose the character of the former miserable era. But when the patriot and heroic prince who succeeded was once firmly seated on the throne, the government, the people, everything seemed to be totally changed; and all from the difference of the temper and conduct of these two sovereigns. Instances of this kind may be multiplied, almost without number, from ancient as well as modern history, foreign as well as domestic.

But here it may be proper to make a distinction. All absolute governments must very much depend on the administration, and this is one of the great inconveniences attending that form of government. But a republican and free government would be an obvious absurdity if the particular checks and controls provided by the constitution had really no influence and made it not the interest, even of bad men, to act for the public good. Such is the intention of these forms of government, and such is their real effect where they are wisely constituted; as, on the other hand, they are the source of all disorder and of the blackest crimes where either skill or honesty has been wanting in their original frame and institution.

So great is the force of laws and of particular forms of government, and so little dependence have they on the humors and tempers of men, that consequences almost as general and certain may sometimes be deduced from them as any which the mathematical sciences afford us.

The constitution of the Roman republic gave the whole legislative power to the people, without allowing a negative voice either to the nobility or consuls. This unbounded power they possessed in a collective, not in a representative body. The consequences were: when the people, by success and conquest, had become very numerous and had spread themselves to a great distance from the capital, the city tribes, though the most contemptible, carried almost every vote; they were, therefore, most cajoled by everyone that affected popularity; they were supported in idleness by the general distribution of corn and by particular bribes which they received from almost every candidate. By this means they became every day more licentious, and the Campus Martius was a perpetual scene of tumult and sedition; armed slaves were introduced among these rascally citizens, so that the whole government fell into anarchy, and the greatest happiness which the Romans could look for was the despotic power of the Caesars. Such are the effects of democracy without a representative.

A nobility may possess the whole or any part of the legislative power of a state in two different ways. Either every nobleman shares the power as a part of the whole body or the whole body enjoys the power as composed of parts which have each a distinct power and authority. The Venetian aristocracy is an instance of the first kind of gov-

342

ernment, the Polish of the second. In the Venetian government the whole body of nobility possesses the whole power, and no nobleman has any authority which he receives not from the whole. In the Polish government every nobleman, by means of his fiefs, has a distinct hereditary authority over his vassals, and the whole body has no authority but what it receives from the concurrence of its parts. The different operations and tendencies of these two species of government might be made apparent even a priori. A Venetian nobility is preferable to a Polish, let the humors and education of men be ever so much varied. A nobility who possess their power in common will preserve peace and order both among themselves and their subjects, and no member can have authority enough to control the laws for a moment. The nobles will preserve their authority over the people, but without any grievous tyranny or any breach of private property, because such a tyrannical government promotes not the interests of the whole body, however it may that of some individuals. There will be a distinction of rank between the nobility and people, but this will be the only distinction in the state. The whole nobility will form one body and the whole people another, without any of those private feuds and animosities which spread ruin and desolation everywhere. It is easy to see the disadvantages of a Polish nobility in every one of these particulars.

It is possible so to constitute a free government as that a single person, call him a doge, prince, or king, shall possess a large share of power and shall form a proper balance or counterpoise to the other parts of the legislature. This chief magistrate may be either *elective* or *hereditary;* and though the former institution may to a superficial view appear the most advantageous, yet a more accurate inspection will discover in it greater inconveniences than in the latter, and such as are founded on causes and principles eternal and immutable. The filling of the throne in such a government is a point of too great and too general interest not to divide the whole people into factions. Whence a civil war, the greatest of ills, may be apprehended almost with certainty upon every vacancy. The prince elected must be either a *foreigner* or a *native.* The former will be ignorant of the people whom he is to govern, suspicious of his new subjects and suspected by them, giving his confidence entirely to strangers who will have no other care but of enriching themselves in the quickest manner, while their master's favor and authority are able to support them. A native will carry into the throne all his private animosities and friendships and will never be viewed in his elevation without exciting the sentiment of envy in those who formerly considered him as their equal. Not to mention that a crown is too high a reward ever to be given to merit alone, and will always induce the candidates to employ force or money or intrigue to procure the votes of the electors, so that such an election will give no better chance for superior merit in the prince than if the state had trusted to birth alone for determining the sovereign.

It may, therefore, be pronounced as a universal axiom in politics *that a hereditary prince, a nobility without vassals,* *and a people voting by their representatives form the best monarchy, aristocracy, and democracy.*

4

DAVID HUME, OF THE INDEPENDENCE OF PARLIAMENT
1742

Political writers have established it as a maxim that, in contriving any system of government and fixing the several checks and controls of the constitution, every man ought to be supposed a *knave* and to have no other end, in all his actions, than private interest. By this interest we must govern him and, by means of it, make him, notwithstanding his insatiable avarice and ambition, cooperate to public good. Without this, say they, we shall in vain boast of the advantages of any constitution and shall find in the end that we have no security for our liberties or possessions except the good will of our rulers; that is, we shall have no security at all.

It is, therefore, a just *political* maxim *that every man must be supposed a knave,* though at the same time it appears somewhat strange that a maxim should be true in *politics* which is false in *fact.* But to satisfy us on this head we may consider that men are generally more honest in their private than in their public capacity, and will go greater lengths to serve a party than when their own private interest is alone concerned. Honor is a great check upon mankind; but where a considerable body of men act together, this check is in a great measure removed, since a man is sure to be approved of by his own party for what promotes the common interest, and he soon learns to despise the clamors of adversaries. To which we may add that every court or senate is determined by the greater number of voices, so that, if self-interest influences only the majority (as it will always do), the whole senate follows the allurements of this separate interest and acts as if it contained not one member who had any regard to public interest and liberty.

When there offers, therefore, to our censure and examination any plan of government, real or imaginary, where the power is distributed among several courts and several orders of men, we should always consider the separate interest of each court and each order; and if we find that, by the skillful division of power, this interest must necessarily in its operation concur with the public, we may pronounce that government to be wise and happy. If, on the contrary, separate interest be not checked and be not directed to the public, we ought to look for nothing but faction, disorder, and tyranny from such a government. In this opinion I am justified by experience, as well as by the authority of all philosophers and politicians, both ancient and modern.

How much, therefore, would it have surprised such a genius as Cicero or Tacitus to have been told that, in a future age, there should arise a very regular system of *mixed* government, where the authority was so distributed that one rank, whenever it pleased, might swallow up all the rest and engross the whole power of the constitution! Such a government, they would say, will not be a mixed government. For so great is the natural ambition of men that they are never satisfied with power; and if one order of men, by pursuing its own interest, can usurp upon every other order, it will certainly do so and render itself, as far as possible, absolute and uncontrollable.

But in this opinion experience shows they would have been mistaken. For this is actually the case with the British constitution. The share of power allotted by our constitution to the House of Commons is so great that it absolutely commands all the other parts of the government. The king's legislative power is plainly no proper check to it. For though the king has a negative in framing laws, yet this in fact is esteemed of so little moment that whatever is voted by the two houses is always sure to pass into a law, and the royal assent is little better than a form. The principal weight of the crown lies in the executive power. But besides that the executive power in every government is altogether subordinate to the legislative, besides this I say, the exercise of this power requires an immense expense, and the Commons have assumed to themselves the sole right of granting money. How easy, therefore, would it be for that house to wrest from the crown all these powers, one after another, by making every grant conditional and choosing their time so well that their refusal of supply should only distress the government, without giving foreign powers any advantage over us! Did the House of Commons depend in the same manner upon the king and had none of the members any property but from his gift, would not he command all their resolutions and be from that moment absolute? As to the House of Lords, they are a very powerful support to the crown so long as they are, in their turn, supported by it; but both experience and reason show that they have no force or authority sufficient to maintain themselves alone without such support.

How, therefore, shall we solve this paradox? And by what means is this member of our constitution confined within the proper limits, since, from our very constitution, it must necessarily have as much power as it demands and can only be confined by itself? How is this consistent with our experience of human nature? I answer that the interest of the body is here restrained by that of the individuals, and that the House of Commons stretches not its power, because such a usurpation would be contrary to the interest of the majority of its members. The crown has so many offices at its disposal that, when assisted by the honest and disinterested part of the House, it will always command the resolutions of the whole, so far, at least, as to preserve the ancient constitution from danger. We may therefore give to this influence what name we please; we may call it by the invidious appellations of *corruption* and *dependence;* but some degree and some kind of it are inseparable from the very nature of the constitution and necessary to the preservation of our mixed government.

5

THOMAS PAINE, COMMON SENSE
10 Jan. 1776
Life 2:97–107, 121–22

(See ch. 4, no. 4)

6

RICHARD HENRY LEE TO EDMUND PENDLETON
12 May 1776
Letters 1:190–91

Before this reaches you I hope much progress will have been made towards the establishment of a wise and free government, without which neith— public or private happness or security can be long expected. I make no doubt but you have seen a small pamphlet published here, with the Title of an "Address to the convention of the Colony and ancient Dominion of Virga. on the Subject of Government &c." [See ch. 18, no. 10.] This Contemptible little Tract, betrays the little Knot or Junto from whence it proceeded. Confusion of ideas, aristocratic pride, contradictory reasoning, with evident ill design, put it out of danger of doing harm, and therefore I quit it. The difficulty we have to encounter in constructing this fabric from whence so great good or evil may result, consists certainly in a blending the three simple forms of Government in such manner as to prevent the inordinate views of either from unduly affecting the others, which has never been the case in Engld., altho' it was the professed aim of that System. But there, a fine design, was spoiled in the execution. The perogative of making Peers and Boroughs effectually destroyed the equipoise, and prevented an opportunity of applying that corruption which has now swallowed up every thing but the forms of freedom in Great Britain. However imperfect the English plan was, yet our late Government in Virginia was infinitely worse. With us 2 thirds of the Legislature, and all the executive and judiciary Powers were in the same hands—In truth it was very near a Tyrany, altho' the mildness with which it was executed under Whig direction, made the evil little felt. Abridged duration, temperate revenue, and every unnecessary power withheld, are potent means of preserving integrity in public men and for securing the Community from the dangerous ambition of that too often governs the human mind.

7

FOUR LETTERS ON INTERESTING SUBJECTS 19–20
1776

(See ch. 17, no. 19)

8

THE PEOPLE THE BEST GOVERNORS
1776
Chase 1:655, 656

The just power of a free people respects first the making and secondly the executing of laws. The liberties of a people are chiefly, I may say entirely guarded by having the controul of these two branches in their own hands.

. . . . .

But it seems there is another objection started by some: That the common people are not under so good advantages to choose judges, sheriffs, and other executive officers as their representatives are. This is a mere delusion, which many have taken in, and, if I may be allowed a vulgar expression, the objectors in this instance put the cart before the horse. For they say that the people have wisdom and knowledge enough to appoint proper persons through a State to make laws, but not to execute them. It is much easier to execute, than to make and regulate the system of laws, and upon this single consideration the force of the objection fails: The more simple, and the more immediately dependent (*exteris* [*ceteris*] *paribus*), the authority is upon the people the better, because it must be granted that they themselves are the best guardians of their own liberties.

9

FARMER, ON THE PRESENT STATE OF AFFAIRS IN AMERICA
5 Nov. 1776
American Archives, 5th ser., 3:518

It should be constantly in mind that the government of these States are founded on the authority of the people only; and therefore, that there should be sufficient power left in their hands always to prevent the delegated power from becoming dangerous to their liberty. At the same time particular attention ought to be paid to the genius, manners, and customs of the people, as it is well known that innovations upon these things have often been fatal. If I may be permitted, then, to deliver my opinion of the genius of the *Americans,* I shall say it is of a monarchical spirit; this is natural from the government they have ever lived under. It is therefore impossible to found a simple Republick in *America*. Another reason that operates very strongly against such a government is the great distinction of persons, and difference in their estates or property, which cooperates strongly with the genius of the people in favour of monarchy. For these reasons I am induced to think that a mixed government is the best that can be adopted in the respective Colonies; and most of them have adopted such; but in some of them too much power is delegated from the people. One only has attempted to establish a simple Republick on the strictest principles, and this has met with the disapprobation of all parties, which is a further proof of the disposition of the people in favour of a mixed government.

And of mixed governments, the people will naturally be inclined to that which is most like what they have always been used to, viz: a supreme executive magistrate (with a necessary check) and two orders in the body of legislation. But these orders now are to derive their authority from the people only, and in a different manner from what has been usual; it therefore requires the utmost wisdom of the legislature which is to constitute them, so to balance their powers as effectually to secure the liberty and happiness of the people forever, the sole end and purpose of their appointment.

10

JOHN ADAMS, DEFENCE OF THE CONSTITUTIONS OF GOVERNMENT OF THE UNITED STATES
1787
Works 4:440, 444–45, 462–63, 556–58, 587–88; 5:90; 6:65, 118, 185–87

As we advance, we may see cause to differ widely from the judgment of Polybius, "*that it is impossible to invent a more perfect system of government* [than the Roman]." We may be convinced that the constitution of England, if its balance is seen to play, in practice, according to the principles of its theory; that is to say, if the people are fairly and fully represented, so as to have the power of *dividing or choosing,* of *drawing up hill or down,* instead of being disposed of by a few lords, is a system much more perfect. The constitutions of several of the United States, it is hoped, will prove themselves improvements both upon the Roman, the Spartan, and the English commonwealths.

The generation and corruption of governments, which may, in other words, be called the progress and course of human passions in society, are subjects which have engaged the attention of the greatest writers; and whether the essays they have left us were copied from history, or wrought out of their own conjectures and reasonings, they are very much to our purpose, to show the utility and necessity of different *orders* of men, and of an *equilibrium* of powers and privileges. They demonstrate the corruptibility of every species of simple government, by which I mean a power without a check, whether in one, a few, or many.

. . . . .

But perhaps it might be more exactly true and natural to say, that the king, the aristocracy, and the people, as soon as ever they felt themselves secure in the possession of their power, would begin to abuse it.

In M. Turgot's single assembly, those who should think themselves most distinguished by blood and education, as well as fortune, would be most ambitious; and if they found an opposition among their constituents to their elections, would immediately have recourse to entertainments, secret intrigues, and every popular art, and even to bribes, to increase their parties. This would oblige their competitors, though they might be infinitely better men, either to give up their pretensions, or to imitate these dangerous practices. There is a natural and unchangeable inconvenience in all popular elections. There are always competitions, and the candidates have often merits nearly equal. The virtuous and independent electors are often divided; this naturally causes too much attention to the most profligate and unprincipled, who will sell or give away their votes for other considerations than wisdom and virtue. So that he who has the deepest purse, or the fewest scruples about using it, will generally prevail.

It is from the natural aristocracy in a single assembly that the first danger is to be apprehended in the present state of manners in America; and with a balance of landed property in the hands of the people, so decided in their favor, the progress to degeneracy, corruption, rage, and violence, might not be very rapid; nevertheless it would begin with the first elections, and grow faster or slower every year.

Rage and violence would soon appear in the assembly, and from thence be communicated among the people at large.

The only remedy is to throw the rich and the proud into one group, in a separate assembly, and there tie their hands; if you give them scope with the people at large or their representatives, they will destroy *all equality and liberty, with the consent and acclamations of the people themselves.* They will have much more power, mixed with the representatives, than separated from them. In the first case, if they unite, they will give the law and govern all; if they differ, they will divide the state, and go to a decision by force. But placing them alone by themselves, the society avails itself of all their abilities and virtues; they become a solid check to the representatives themselves, as well as to the executive power, and you disarm them entirely of the power to do mischief.

. . . . .

Let me proceed then to make a few observations upon the Discourses of Plato and Polybius, and show how forcibly they prove the necessity of permanent laws, to restrain the passions and vices of men, and to secure to the citizens the blessings of society, in the peaceable enjoyment of their lives, liberties, and properties; and the necessity of different orders of men, with various and opposite powers, prerogatives, and privileges, to watch over one another, to balance each other, and to compel each other at all times to be real guardians of the laws.

Every citizen must look up to the laws, as his master, his guardian, and his friend; and whenever any of his fellow-citizens, whether magistrates or subjects, attempt to deprive him of his right, he must appeal to the laws; if the aristocracy encroach, he must appeal to the democracy; if they are divided, he must appeal to the monarchical power to decide between them, by appeal to the monarchical power to decide between them, by joining with that which adheres to the laws; if the democracy is on the scramble for power, he must appeal to the aristocracy and the monarchy, which by uniting may restrain it. If the regal authority presumes too far, he must appeal to the other two. Without three divisions of power, stationed to watch each other, and compare each other's conduct with the laws, it will be impossible that the laws should at all times preserve their authority and govern all men.

Plato has sufficiently asserted the honor of the laws and the necessity of proper guardians of them; but has nowhere delineated the various orders of guardians, and the necessity of a balance between them. He has, nevertheless, given us premises from whence the absolute necessity of such orders and equipoises may be inferred; he has shown how naturally every simple species of government degenerates. The aristocracy, or ambitious republic, becomes immediately an oligarchy. What shall be done to prevent it? Place two guardians of the laws to watch the aristocracy,— one, in the shape of a king, on one side of it; another, in the shape of a democratical assembly, on the other side. The aristocracy become an oligarchy, changes into a democracy. How shall it be prevented? By giving the natural aristocracy in society its rational and just weight, and by giving it a regal power to appeal to, against the madness of the people. Democracy becomes a tyranny. How shall this be prevented? By giving it an able, independent ally, in an aristocratical assembly, with whom it may unite against the unjust and illegal designs of any one man.

. . . . .

Pythagoras, as well as Socrates, Plato, and Xenophon, was persuaded that the happiness of nations depended chiefly on the form of their government. They were fully sensible of the real misery, as well as dangerous tendency, both of democratical licentiousness and monarchical tyranny; they preferred a well-tempered aristocracy to all other governments. Pythagoras and Socrates, having no idea of three independent branches in the legislature, both thought, that the laws could neither prevent the arbitrary oppressions of magistrates, nor turbulent insolence of the people, until mankind were habituated, by education and discipline, to regard the great duties of life, and to consider a reverence of themselves, and the esteem of their fellow-citizens, as the principal source of their enjoyment. In small communities, especially where the slaves were many, and the citizens few, this might be plausible; but the education of a great nation can never accomplish so great an end. Millions must be brought up, whom no principles, no sentiments derived from education, can restrain from trampling on the laws. Orders of men, watching and balancing each other, are the only security; power must be opposed to power, and interest to interest. Pythagoras found this by experience at Crotona, where the inferior ranks, elated with the destruction of Sybaris, and instigated by an artful, ambitious leader, Cylon, clamored for an equal partition of the conquered territory. This was denied them, as inconsistent with an aristocratical government; a conspiracy ensued against the magistrates, who were surprised in the senate-house, many put to death, and the rest driven from their country. Pythagoras was one of the banished, and died soon afterwards, in extreme old age, at Metapentum. The Crotonians had soon cause to repent their insurrection; for they were defeated, with all their forces, by the Locrians and Rhegians, with smaller numbers.

The other Greek cities of Italy, which had imitated the example of Crotona, in deposing their magistrates, were harassed with wars against each other, and against their neighbors. In consequence of these distresses, the disciples of Pythagoras again recovered their reputation and influence; and about sixty years afterwards, Zaleucus and Charondas, the one in Locris, and the other in Thurium, revived the Pythagorean institutions. In forty years more, a new revolution drove the Pythagoreans entirely from Italy, and completed the misery of that beautiful country. Thus, experience has ever shown, that education, as well as religion, aristocracy, as well as democracy and monarchy, are, singly, totally inadequate to the business of restraining the passions of men, of preserving a steady government, and protecting the lives, liberties, and properties of the people. Nothing has ever effected it but three different orders of men, bound by their interests to watch over each other, and stand the guardians of the laws. Religion, superstition, oaths, education, laws, all give way before passions, interest, and power, which can be resisted only by passions, interest, and power.

. . . . .

But shall the people at large elect a governor and council annually to manage the executive power, and a single assembly to have the whole legislative? In this case, the executive power, instead of being independent, will be the instrument of a few leading members of the house; because the executive power, being an object of jealousy and envy to the people, and the legislative an object of their confidence and affection, the latter will always be able to render the former unpopular, and undermine its influence. But if the people for a time support an executive disagreeable to the leaders in the legislative, the constitution will be disregarded, and the nation will be divided between the two bodies, and each must at last have an army to decide the question. A constitution consisting of an executive in one single assembly, and a legislative in another, is already composed of two armies in battle array; and nothing is wanting but the word of command to begin the combat.

In the present state of society and manners in America, with a people living chiefly by agriculture, in small numbers, sprinkled over large tracts of land, they are not subject to those panics and transports, those contagions of madness and folly, which are seen in countries where large numbers live in small places, in daily fear of perishing for want. We know, therefore, that the people can live and increase under almost any kind of government, or without any government at all. But it is of great importance to begin well; misarrangements now made, will have great, extensive, and distant consequences; and we are now employed, how little soever we may think of it, in making establishments which will affect the happiness of a hundred millions of inhabitants at a time, in a period not

very distant. All nations, under all governments, must have parties; the great secret is to control them. There are but two ways, either by a monarchy and standing army, or by a balance in the constitution. Where the people have a voice, and there is no balance, there will be everlasting fluctuations, revolutions, and horrors, until a standing army, with a general at its head, commands the peace, or the necessity of an equilibrium is made appear to all, and is adopted by all.

. . . . .

In truth, it is impossible that divisions, in any form of simple government, should ever end in the public good, or in any thing but faction. The government itself is a faction, and an absolute power in a party, which, being without fear and restraint, is as giddy in one of these forms as in any other. "De l'absolu pouvoir, vous ignorez l'ivresse." It must, therefore, divide, if it is not restrained by another faction; when that is the case, as soon as the other faction prevails, they divide, and so on; but when the three natural orders in society, the high, the middle, and the low, are all represented in the government, and constitutionally placed to watch each other, and restrain each other mutually by the laws, it is then only, that an emulation takes place for the public good, and divisions turn to the advantage of the nation.

. . . . .

It is agreed that "the end of all government is the good and ease of the people, in a secure enjoyment of their rights, without oppression;" but it must be remembered, that the rich are *people* as well as the poor; that they have rights as well as others; that they have as clear and as *sacred* a right to their large property as others have to theirs which is smaller; that oppression to them is as possible and as wicked as to others; that stealing, robbing, cheating, are the same crimes and sins, whether committed against them or others. The rich, therefore, ought to have an effectual barrier in the constitution against being robbed, plundered, and murdered, as well as the poor; and this can never be without an independent senate. The poor should have a bulwark against the same dangers and oppressions; and this can never be without a house of representatives of the people. But neither the rich nor the poor can be defended by their respective guardians in the constitution, without an executive power, vested with a negative, equal to either, to hold the balance even between them, and decide when they cannot agree. If it is asked, When will this negative be used? it may be answered, Perhaps never. The known existence of it will prevent all occasion to exercise it; but if it has not a being, the want of it will be felt every day. If it has not been used in England for a long time past, it by no means follows that there have not been occasions when it might have been employed with propriety. But one thing is very certain, that there have been many occasions since the Revolution, when the constitution would have been overturned if the negative had not been an indubitable prerogative of the crown.

. . . . .

The people are the fountain and original of the power of kings and lords, governors and senates, as well as the house of commons, or assembly of representatives. And if the people are sufficiently enlightened to see all the dangers that surround them, they will always be represented by a distinct personage to manage the whole executive power; a distinct senate, to be guardians of property against levellers for the purposes of plunder, to be a repository of the national tradition of public maxims, customs, and manners, and to be controllers, in turn, both of kings and their ministers on one side, and the representatives of the people on the other, when either discover a disposition to do wrong; and a distinct house of representatives, to be the guardians of the public purse, and to protect the people, in their turn, against both kings and nobles.

. . . . .

I am not without apprehensions that I have not made myself fully understood. The people, in all nations, are naturally divided into two sorts, the gentlemen and the simplemen, a word which is here chosen to signify the common people. By gentlemen are not meant the rich or the poor, the high-born or the low-born, the industrious or the idle; but all those who have received a liberal education, an ordinary degree of erudition in liberal arts and sciences, whether by birth they be descended from magistrates and officers of government, or from husbandmen, merchants, mechanics, or laborers; or whether they be rich or poor. We must, nevertheless, remember, that *generally* those who are rich, and descended from families in public life, will have the best education in arts and sciences, and therefore the gentlemen will ordinarily, notwithstanding some exceptions to the rule, be the richer, and born of more noted families. By the common people we mean laborers, husbandmen, mechanics, and merchants in general, who pursue their occupations and industry without any knowledge in liberal arts or sciences, or in any thing but their own trades or pursuits; though there may be exceptions to this rule, and individuals may be found in each of these classes who may really be gentlemen.

Now it seems to be clear, that the gentlemen in every country are, and ever must be, few in number, in comparison of the simplemen. If you please, then, by the democratical portion of society we will understand the common people, as before explained; by the aristocratical part of the community we will understand the gentlemen. The distinctions which have been introduced among the gentlemen, into nobility greater or lesser, are perfectly immaterial to our present purpose; knights, barons, earls, viscounts, marquises, dukes, and even princes and kings, are still but gentlemen, and the word noble signifies no more than knowable, or conspicuous. But the gentlemen are more intelligent and skilful, as well as generally richer and better connected, and therefore have more influence and power than an equal number of the common people. There is a constant energy and effort in the minds of the former to increase the advantages they possess over the latter, and to augment their wealth and influence at their expense. This effort produces resentments and jealousies, contempt, hatred, and fear, between the one sort and the other. Individuals among the common people endeavor to make friends, patrons, and protectors among the gentlemen. This produces parties, divisions, tumults, and war.

But as the former have most address and capacity, they gain more and more continually, until they become exorbitantly rich, and the others miserably poor. In this progress, the common people are continually looking up for a protector among the gentlemen, and he who is most able and willing to protect them acquires their confidence. They unite together by their feelings, more than their reflections, in augmenting his power, because the more power he has, and the less the gentlemen have, the safer they are. This is a short sketch of the history of that progress of passions and feelings which has produced every simple monarchy in the world; and, if nature and its feelings have their course without reflection, they will produce a simple monarchy forever. It has been the common people, then, and not the gentlemen, who have established simple monarchies all over the world. The common people, against the gentlemen, established a simple monarchy in Caesar at Rome, in the Medici at Florence, &c., and are now in danger of doing the same thing in Holland; and if the British constitution should have its euthanasia in simple monarchy, according to the prophecy of Mr. Hume, it will be effected by the common people, to avoid the increasing oppressions of the gentlemen.

If this is the progress and course of things (and who does not know that it is?) it follows, that it is the true interest and best policy of the common people to take away from the body of the gentlemen all share in the distribution of offices and management of the executive power. Why? Because if any body of gentlemen have the gift of offices, they will dispose of them among their own families, friends, and connections; they will also make use of their votes in disposing of offices, to procure themselves votes in popular elections to the senate or other council, or to procure themselves appointments in the executive department. It is the true policy of the common people to place the whole executive power in one man, to make him a distinct order in the state, from whence arises an inevitable jealousy between him and the gentlemen; this forces him to become a father and protector of the common people, and to endeavor always to humble every proud, aspiring senator, or other officer in the state, who is in danger of acquiring an influence too great for the law or the spirit of the constitution. This influences him to look for merit among the common people, and to promote from among them such as are capable of public employments; so that the road to preferment is open to the common people much more generally and equitably in such a government than in an aristocracy, or one in which the gentlemen have any share in appointments to office.

From this deduction it follows, that the precept of our author [Marchamont Nedham], "to educate children (of the common people) in principles of dislike and enmity against kingly government, and enter into an oath of abjuration to abjure a toleration of kings and kingly powers," is a most iniquitous and infamous aristocratical artifice, a most formal conspiracy against the rights of mankind, and against that equality between the gentlemen and the common people which nature has established as a moral right, and law should ordain as a political right, for the preservation of liberty.

By kings and kingly power is meant, both by our author and me, the executive power in a single person. American common people are too enlightened, it is hoped, ever to fall into such a hypocritical snare; the gentlemen, too, it is hoped, are too enlightened, as well as too equitable, ever to attempt such a measure; because they must know that the consequence will be, that, after suffering all the evils of contests and dissensions, cruelty and oppression, from the aristocratics, the common people will perjure themselves, and set up an unlimited monarchy instead of a regal republic.

11

CENTINEL, NO. 1
5 Oct. 1787
Storing 2.7.7–9

I have been anxiously expecting that some enlightened patriot would, ere this, have taken up the pen to expose the futility, and counteract the baneful tendency of such principles. Mr. Adams's *sine qua non* of a good government is three balancing powers, whose repelling qualities are to produce an equilibrium of interests, and thereby promote the happiness of the whole community. He asserts that the administrators of every government, will ever be actuated by views of private interest and ambition, to the prejudice of the public good; that therefore the only effectual method to secure the rights of the people and promote their welfare, is to create an opposition of interests between the members of two distinct bodies, in the exercise of the powers of government, and balanced by those of a third. This hypothesis supposes human wisdom competent to the task of instituting three co-equal orders in government, and a corresponding weight in the community to enable them respectively to exercise their several parts, and whose views and interests should be so distinct as to prevent a coalition of any two of them for the destruction of the third. Mr. Adams, although he has traced the constitution of every form of government that ever existed, as far as history affords materials, has not been able to adduce a single instance of such a government; he indeed says that the British constitution is such in theory, but this is rather a confirmation that his principles are chimerical and not to be reduced to practice. If such an organization of power were practicable, how•long would it continue? not a day—for there is so great a disparity in the talents, wisdom and industry of mankind, that the scale would presently preponderate to one or the other body, and with every accession of power the means of further increase would be greatly extended. The state of society in England is much more favorable to such a scheme of government than that of America. There they have a powerful hereditary nobility, and real distinctions of rank and interests; but even there, for want of that perfect equality of power and distinction of interests, in the three orders of government, they exist but in name; the only operative and efficient check, upon the conduct of administration, is the sense of the people at large.

Suppose a government could be formed and supported on such principles, would it answer the great purposes of civil society; if the administrators of every government are actuated by views of private interest and ambition, how is the welfare and happiness of the community to be the result of such jarring adverse interests?

Therefore, as different orders in government will not produce the good of the whole, we must recur to other principles. I believe it will be found that the form of government, which holds those entrusted with power, in the greatest responsibility to their constituents, the best calculated for freemen. A republican, or free government, can only exist where the body of the people are virtuous, and where property is pretty equally divided[;] in such a government the people are the sovereign and their sense or opinion is the criterion of every public measure; for when this ceases to be the case, the nature of the government is changed, and an aristocracy, monarchy or despotism will rise on its ruin. The highest responsibility is to be attained, in a simple structure of government, for the great body of the people never steadily attend to the operations of government, and for want of due information are liable to be imposed on—If you complicate the plan by various orders, the people will be perplexed and divided in their sentiments about the source of abuses or misconduct, some will impute it to the senate, others to the house of representatives, and so on, that the interposition of the people may be rendered imperfect or perhaps wholly abortive. But if, imitating the constitution of Pennsylvania, you vest all the legislative power in one body of men (separating the executive and judicial) elected for a short period, and necessarily excluded by rotation from permanency, and guarded from precipitancy and surprise by delays imposed on its proceedings, you will create the most perfect responsibility for then, whenever the people feel a grievance they cannot mistake the authors, and will apply the remedy with certainty and effect, discarding them at the next election. This tie of responsibility will obviate all the dangers apprehended from a single legislature, and will the best secure the rights of the people.

12

FEDERAL FARMER, NO. 11
10 Jan. 1788
Storing 2.8.145–46

The senate, as a legislative branch, is not large, but as an executive branch quite too numerous. It is not to be presumed that we can form a genuine senatorial branch in the United States, a real representation of the aristocracy and balance in the legislature, any more than we can form a genuine representation of the people. Could we separate the aristocratical and democratical interests; compose the senate of the former, and the house of assembly of the latter, they are too unequal in the United States to produce a balance. Form them on pure principles, and leave each to be supported by its real weight and connections, the senate would be feeble, and the house powerful:—I say, on pure principles; because I make a distinction between a senate that derives its weight and influence from a pure source, its numbers and wisdom, its extensive property, its extensive and permanent connections; and a senate composed of a few men, possessing small property, small and unstable connections, that derives its weight and influence from a corrupt or pernicious source; that is, merely from the power given it by the constitution and laws, to dispose of the public offices, and the annexed emoluments, and by those means to interest officers, and the hungry expectants of offices, in support of its measures. I wish the proposed senate may not partake too much of the latter description.

To produce a balance and checks, the constitution proposes two branches in the legislature; but they are so formed, that the members of both must generally be the same kind of men—men having similar interests and views, feelings and connections—men of the same grade in society, and who associate on all occasions (probably, if there be any difference, the senators will be the most democratic.) Senators and representatives thus circumstanced, as men, though convened in two rooms, to make laws, must be governed generally by the same motives and views, and therefore pursue the same system of politics; the partitions between the two branches will be merely those of the building in which they sit: there will not be found in them any of those genuine balances and checks, among the real different interests, and efforts of the several classes of men in the community we aim at; nor can any such balances and checks be formed in the present condition of the United States in any considerable degree of perfection: but to give them the greatest degree of perfection practicable, we ought to make the senate respectable as to numbers, the qualifications of the electors and of the elected; to increase the numbers of the representatives, and so to model the elections of them, as always to draw a majority of them substantially from the body of the people. Though I conclude the senators and representatives will not form in the legislature those balances and checks which correspond with the actual state of the people; yet I approve of two branches, because we may notwithstanding derive several advantages from them. The senate, from the mode of its appointment, will probably be influenced to support the state governments, and, from its periods of service will produce stability in legislation, while frequent elections may take place in the other branch. There is generally a degree of competition between two assemblies even composed of the same kind of men; and by this, and by means of every law's passing a revision in the second branch, caution, coolness, and deliberation are produced in the business of making laws. By means of a democratic branch we may particularly secure personal liberty; and by means of a senatorial branch we may particularly protect property. By the division, the house becomes the proper body to impeach all officers for misconduct in office, and the senate the proper court to try them; and in a country where limited powers must be lodged in the first magistrate, the senate, perhaps, may be the most proper body to be found to have a negative upon him in making treaties, and in managing foreign affairs.

13

PATRICK HENRY, VIRGINIA
RATIFYING CONVENTION
9 June 1788
Storing 5.16.14

. . . I cannot help taking notice of what the Honorable Gentleman said. To me it appears that there is no check in that Government. The President, Senators, and Representatives all immediately, or mediately, are the choice of the people. Tell me not of checks on paper; but tell me of checks founded on self-love. The English Government is founded on self-love. This powerful irresistible stimulous of self-love has saved that Government. It has interposed that hereditary nobility between the King and Commons. If the House of Lords assists or permits the King to overturn the liberties of the people, the same tyranny will destroy them; they will therefore keep the balance in the democratic branch. Suppose they see the Commons incroach upon the King; self-love, that great energetic check, will call upon them to interpose: For, if the King be destroyed, their destruction must speedily follow. Here is a consideration which prevails, in my mind, to pronounce the British Government, superior in this respect to any Government that ever was in any country. Compare this with your Congressional checks. I beseech Gentlemen to consider, whether they can say, when trusting power, that a mere patriotic profession will be equally operative and efficatious, as the check of self-love. In considering the experience of ages, is it not seen, that fair disinterested patriotism, and professed attachment to rectitude have never been solely trusted to by an enlightened free people?—If you depend on your President's and Senators patriotism, you are gone. Have you a resting place like the British Government? Where is the rock of your salvation? The real rock of political salvation is *self-love* perpetuated from age to age in every human breast, and manifested in every action. If they can stand the temptations of human nature, you are safe. If you have a good President, Senators and Representatives, there is no danger.—But can this be expected from human nature? Without real checks it will not suffice, that some of them are good. A good President, or Senator, or Representative, will have a natural weakness.—Virtue will slumber. The wicked will be continually watching: Consequently you will be undone. Where are your checks? You have no hereditary Nobility—An order of men, to whom human eyes can be cast up for relief: For, says the Constitution, there is no title of nobility to be granted; which, by the bye, would not have been so dangerous, as the perilous cession of powers contained in that paper: Because, as Montesquieu says, when you give titles of Nobility, you know what you give; but *when you give power, you know not what you give.*—If you say, that out of this depraved mass, you can collect luminous characters, it will not avail, unless this luminous breed will be propagated from generation to generation; and even then, if the number of vicious characters will preponderate, you are undone. And that this will certainly be the case, is, to my mind, perfectly clear.—In the British Government there are real balances and checks—In this system, there are only ideal balances. Till I am convinced that there are actual efficient checks, I will not give my assent to its establishment. The President and Senators have nothing to lose. They have not that interest in the preservation of the Government, that the King and Lords have in England. They will therefore be regardless of the interests of the people. The Constitution will be as safe with one body, as with two. It will answer every purpose of human legislation. How was the Constitution of England when only the Commons had the power? I need only remark, that it was the most unfortunate aera when that country returned to King, Lords and Commons, without sufficient responsibility in the King. When the Commons of England, in the manly language which became freemen, said to their King, *you are our servant,* then the temple of liberty was complete. From that noble source, have we derived our liberty:—That spirit of patriotic attachment to one's country:—That zeal for liberty, and that enmity to tyranny which signalized the then champions of liberty, we inherit from our British ancestors. And I am free to own, that if you cannot love a Republican Government, you may love the British Monarchy; for, although the King is not sufficiently responsible, the responsibility of his agents, and the efficient checks interposed by the British Constitution, render it less dangerous than other Monarchies, or oppressive tyrannical Aristocracies.

14

JOHN MARSHALL, VIRGINIA
RATIFYING CONVENTION
10 June 1788
Papers 1:266–67

The Gentleman tells us, there are no checks in this plan. What has become of his enthusiastic eulogium on the American spirit? We should find a check and controul when oppressed, from that source. In this country, there is no exclusive personal stock of interest. The interest of the community is blended and inseparably connected with that of the individual.—When he promotes his own, he promotes that of the community. When we consult the common good, we consult our own. When he desires such checks as these, he will find them abundantly here. They

are the best checks. What has become of his eulogium on the Virginia Constitution? Do the checks in this plan appear less excellent than those of the Constitution of Virginia? If the checks in the Constitution be compared to the checks in the Virginian Constitution, he will find the best security in the former.

The temple of liberty was complete, said he, when the people of England said to their King, that he was their servant. What are we to learn from this? Shall we embrace such a system as that? Is not liberty secure with us, where the people hold all powers in their own hands, and delegate them cautiously, for short periods, to their servants, who are accountable for the smallest mal-administration? Where is the nation that can boast greater security than we do? We want only a system like the paper before you, to strengthen and perpetuate this security.

15

JAMES MONROE, VIRGINIA
RATIFYING CONVENTION
10 June 1788
Elliot 3:218–19

There is a distinction between this government and ancient and modern ones. The division of power in ancient governments, or in any government at present in the world, was founded on different principles from those of this government. What was the object of the distribution of power in Rome? It will not be controverted, that there was a composition or mixture of aristocracy, democracy, and monarchy, each of which had a repellent quality which enabled it to preserve itself from being destroyed by the other two; so that the balance was continually maintained. This is the case in the English government, which has the most similitude to our own. There they have distinct orders in the government, which possess real, efficient repellent qualities. Let us illustrate it. If the commons prevail, may they not vote the king useless? If the king prevails, will not the commons lose their liberties? Without the interposition of a check, without a balance, the one would destroy the other. The lords, the third branch, keep up this balance. The wisdom of the English constitution has given a share of legislation to each of the three branches, which enables it effectually to defend itself, and which preserves the liberty of the people of that country.

What is the object of the division of power in America? Why is the government divided into different branches? For a more faithful and regular administration. Where is there a check? We have more to apprehend from the union of these branches than from the subversion of any; and this union will destroy the rights of the people. There is nothing to prevent this coalition; but the contest which will probably subsist between the general government and the individual governments will tend to produce it. There is a division of sovereignty between the national and state governments. How far, then, will they coalesce together? Is it not to be supposed that there will be a conflict between them? If so, will not the members of the former combine together? Where, then, will be the check to prevent encroachments on the rights of the people? There is not a third essentially distinct branch, to preserve a just equilibrium, or to prevent such encroachments. In developing this plan of government, we ought to attend to the necessity of having checks. I can see no real checks in it.

16

JOHN ADAMS TO SAMUEL ADAMS
18 Oct. 1790
Works 6:416–20

With you, I have also the honor most perfectly to harmonize in your sentiments of the humanity and wisdom of promoting education in knowledge, virtue, and benevolence. But I think that these will confirm mankind in the opinion of the necessity of preserving and strengthening the dikes against the ocean, its tides and storms. Human appetites, passions, prejudices, and self-love will never be conquered by benevolence and knowledge alone, introduced by human means. The millennium itself neither supposes nor implies it. All civil government is then to cease, and the Messiah is to reign. That happy and holy state is therefore wholly out of this question. You and I agree in the utility of universal education; but will nations agree in it as fully and extensively as we do, and be at the expense of it? We know, with as much certainty as attends any human knowledge, that they will not. We cannot, therefore, advise the people to depend for their safety, liberty, and security, upon hopes and blessings which we know will not fall to their lot. If we do our duty then to the people, we shall not deceive them, but advise them to depend upon what is in their power and will relieve them.

Philosophers, ancient and modern, do not appear to me to have studied nature, the whole of nature, and nothing but nature. Lycurgus's principle was war and family pride; Solon's was what the people would bear, &c. The best writings of antiquity upon government, those, I mean, of Aristotle, Zeno, and Cicero, are lost. We have human nature, society, and universal history to observe and study, and from these we may draw all the real principles which ought to be regarded. Disciples will follow their masters, and interested partisans their chieftains; let us like it or not, we cannot help it. But if the true principles can be discovered, and fairly, fully, and impartially laid before the people, the more light increases, the more the reason of them will be seen, and the more disciples they will have. Prejudice, passion, and private interest, which will always mingle in human inquiries, one would think might be enlisted on the side of truth, at least in the greatest number; for certainly the majority are interested in the truth, if they could see to the end of all its consequences. "Kings

have been deposed by aspiring nobles." True, and never by any other. "These" (the nobles, I suppose,) "have waged everlasting war against the common rights of men." True, when they have been possessed of the *summa imperii* in one body, without a check. So have the plebeians; so have the people; so have kings; so has human nature, in every shape and combination, and so it ever will. But, on the other hand, the nobles have been essential parties in the preservation of liberty, whenever and wherever it has existed. In Europe, they alone have preserved it against kings and people, wherever it has been preserved; or, at least, with very little assistance from the people. One hideous despotism, as horrid as that of Turkey, would have been the lot of every nation of Europe, if the nobles had not made stands. By nobles, I mean not peculiarly an hereditary nobility, or any particular modification, but the natural and actual aristocracy among mankind. The existence of this you will not deny. You and I have seen four noble families rise up in Boston,—the CRAFTS, GORES, DAWES, and AUSTINS. These are as really a nobility in our town, as the Howards, Somersets, Berties, &c., in England. Blind, undistinguishing reproaches against the aristocratical part of mankind, a division which nature has made, and we cannot abolish, are neither pious nor benevolent. They are as pernicious as they are false. They serve only to foment prejudice, jealousy, envy, animosity, and malevolence. They serve no ends but those of sophistry, fraud, and the spirit of party. It would not be true, but it would not be more egregiously false, to say that the people have waged everlasting war against the rights of men.

"The love of liberty," you say, "is interwoven in the soul of man." So it is, according to La Fontaine, in that of a wolf; and I doubt whether it be much more rational, generous, or social, in one than in the other, until in man it is enlightened by experience, reflection, education, and civil and political institutions, which are at first produced, and constantly supported and improved by a few; that is, by the nobility. The wolf, in the fable, who preferred running in the forest, lean and hungry, to the sleek, plump, and round sides of the dog, because he found the latter was sometimes restrained, had more love of liberty than most men. The numbers of men in all ages have preferred ease, slumber, and good cheer to liberty, when they have been in competition. We must not then depend alone upon the love of liberty in the soul of man for its preservation. Some political institutions must be prepared, to assist this love against its enemies. Without these, the struggle will ever end only in a change of impostors. When the people, who have no property, feel the power in their own hands to determine all questions by a majority, they ever attack those who have property, till the injured men of property lose all patience, and recur to finesse, trick, and stratagem, to outwit those who have too much strength, because they have too many hands to be resisted any other way. Let us be impartial, then, and speak the whole truth. Till we do, we shall never discover all the true principles that are necessary. The multitude, therefore, as well as the nobles, must have a check. This is one principle.

"Were the people of England free, after they had obliged King John to concede to them their ancient rights?" The people never did this. There was no people who pretended to any thing. It was the nobles alone. The people pretended to nothing but to be villains, vassals, and retainers to the king or the nobles. The nobles, I agree, were not free, because all was determined by a majority of their votes, or by arms, not by law. Their feuds deposed their "Henrys, Edwards, and Richards," to gratify lordly ambition, patrician rivalry, and "family pride." But, if they had not been deposed, those kings would have become despots, because the people would not and could not join the nobles in any regular and constitutional opposition to them. They would have become despots, I repeat it, and that by means of the villains, vassals, and retainers aforesaid. It is not family pride, my friend, but family popularity, that does the great mischief, as well as the great good. Pride, in the heart of man, is an evil fruit and concomitant of every advantage; of riches, of knowledge, of genius, of talents, of beauty, of strength, of virtue, and even of piety. It is sometimes ridiculous, and often pernicious. But it is even sometimes, and in some degree, useful. But the pride of families would be always and only ridiculous, if it had not family popularity to work with. The attachment and devotion of the people to some families inspires them with pride. As long as gratitude or interest, ambition or avarice, love, hope, or fear, shall be human motives of action, so long will numbers attach themselves to particular families. When the people will, in spite of all that can be said or done, cry a man or a family up to the skies, exaggerate all his talents and virtues, not hear a word of his weakness or faults, follow implicitly his advice, detest every man he hates, adore every man he loves, and knock down all who will not swim down the stream with them, where is your remedy? When a man or family are thus popular, how can you prevent them from being proud? You and I know of instances in which popularity has been a wind, a tide, a whirlwind. The history of all ages and nations is full of such examples.

Popularity, that has great fortune to dazzle; splendid largesses, to excite warm gratitude; sublime, beautiful, and uncommon genius or talents, to produce deep admiration; or any thing to support high hopes and strong fears, will be proud; and its power will be employed to mortify enemies, gratify friends, procure votes, emoluments, and power. Such family popularity ever did, and ever will govern in every nation, in every climate, hot and cold, wet and dry, among civilized and savage people, Christians and Mahometans, Jews and Heathens. Declamation against family pride is a pretty, juvenile exercise, but unworthy of statesmen. They know the evil and danger is too serious to be sported with. The only way, God knows, is to put these families into a hole by themselves, and set two watches upon them; a superior to them all on one side, and the people on the other.

There are a few popular men in the Massachusetts, my friend, who have, I fear, less honor, sincerity, and virtue, than they ought to have. These, if they are not guarded against, may do another mischief. They may excite a party spirit and a mobbish spirit, instead of the spirit of liberty, and produce another Wat Tyler's rebellion. They can do no more. But I really think their party language ought not

to be countenanced, nor their shibboleths pronounced. The miserable stuff that they utter about the *well-born* is as despicable as themselves. The εὐγενεῖς of the Greeks, the *bien nées* of the French, the *welgebohren* of the Germans and Dutch, the *beloved families* of the Creeks, are but a few samples of national expressions of the same thing, for which every nation on earth has a similar expression. One would think that our scribblers were all the sons of redemptioners or transported convicts. They think with Tarquin, *"In novo populo, ubi omnis repentina atque ex virtute nobilitas fit, futurum locum forti ac strenuo viro."*

Let us be impartial. There is not more of family pride on one side, than of vulgar malignity and popular envy on the other. Popularity in one family raises envy in others. But the popularity of the least deserving will triumph over envy and malignity; while that which is acquired by real merit, will very often be overborne and oppressed by it.

Let us do justice to the people and to the nobles; for nobles there are, as I have before proved, in Boston as well as in Madrid. But to do justice to both, you must establish an arbitrator between them. This is another principle.

17

GOUVERNEUR MORRIS TO ROBERT WALSH
5 Feb. 1811
Life 3:264–66

Perhaps there is still in my old bosom too much of the youthful ardor of hope, but I do not despair of our country. True it is, that the present state of things has approached with unlooked for rapidity. But in that very circumstance there is a source of comfort. In spite of the power of corruption, there is still, perhaps, enough of public sentiment left to sanctify the approaching misfortunes. Let not good men despair, because the people were not awakened by what has passed. It should be considered, that, in proportion to the size and strength of the patient, and to the dulness of his organs, the dose must be large to operate with effect. The embargo produced so much of nausea, that our State Doctors perceived the necessity of an opiate. Thus, the incipient spasm was lulled, but causes must eventually produce their effects.

This digression leads us, however, from the point of your inquiry. "How far has the Senate answered the end of its creation?" I answer, farther than was expected, but by no means so far as was wished. It is necessary here to anticipate one of your subsequent questions, "What has been, and what is now the influence of the State governments on the Federal system?" To obtain anything like a check on the rashness of democracy, it was necessary not only to organize the legislature into different bodies, (for that alone is a poor expedient,) but to endeavor that these bodies should be animated by a different spirit. To this end the States in their corporate capacity were made electors of the Senate; and so long as the State governments had considerable influence, and the consciousness of dignity, which that influence imparts, the Senate felt something of the desired sentiment, and answered in some degree the end of its institution. But that day is past.

This opens to our view a dilemma, which was not unperceived when the Constitution was formed. If the State influence should continue, the union could not last; and, if it did not, the utility of the Senate would cease. It was observed in the Convention at an early day, by one who had afterwards a considerable share of the business, when the necessity of drawing a line between national sovereignty and State independence was insisted on, "that, if Aaron's rod could not swallow the rods of the Magicians, their rods would swallow his." But it is one thing to perceive a dilemma, and another thing to get out of it. In the option between two evils, that which appeared to be the least was preferred, and the power of the union provided for. At present the influence of the general government has so thoroughly pervaded every State, that all the little wheels are obliged to turn according to the great one. Factious leaders sometimes snarl and growl, but the curs cannot bite, and are easily lashed into order by the great executive thong. It is pleasant enough to see them drop their tails, and run yelping to the kennel.

A factious spirit prevails from one end of our country to the other. And by that spirit both Senators and Representatives are chosen. By that spirit the government acts; and, as to the provisions of the Constitution, however they may fill up the space of a speech to round of[f] a period, or perfume a flower of rhetoric, they cannot restrain men heated in the chase of party game. Mr Poindexter lately observed with no little truth, that it would be vain to op-

pose what should be enjoined under the form of law, because it was forbidden by the Constitution. The Senate, in my poor opinion, is little if any check, either on the President or the House of Representatives. It has not the disposition. The members of both Houses are creatures, which, though differently born, are begotten in the same way and by the same sire. They have of course the same temper. But their opposition, were they disposed to make any, would be feeble. They would easily be borne down by the other House, in which the power resides. The President can indeed do what he pleases, provided always it shall please him to please those, who lead a majority of the Representatives. This matter is understood among the parties concerned. The Representatives, however, do not yet know, that their power has no bound except their discretion; but a pleasant lesson is easily learnt, and the more they feel their power, the less will be their discretion. Authority so placed is liable as well to excess as to abuse, and this country, unless I am much mistaken, will experience not a little of both.

SEE ALSO:

Generally chs. 10, 12, 13

Joseph Addison, Spectator, no. 287, 29 Jan. 1712

John Adams to Benjamin Rush, 19 June 1789, Old Family Letters 1:39–40

John Adams to Benjamin Rush, 4 Apr. 1790, Old Family Letters 1:56–57

John Adams to Benjamin Rush, 18 Apr. 1790, Old Family Letters 1:60

John Adams to John Taylor, Apr. 1814, Works 6:469–72

12

Bicameralism

Introduction

When George Mason proclaimed in the Philadelphia Convention (no. 16) that "the mind of the people of America" was "well settled" in its attachment to the principle of having a legislature with more than one branch, he was not asserting that the matter was beyond contention. True, eleven states had a bicameral legislature. Yet the Continental Congress consisted of but one house, and even while speaking, Mason stood in the precincts of a unicameral state legislature that had existed since 1776 or (counting its colonial predecessor) since 1701. Not only was America not simply of one mind about the principle, but even those who adhered to the principle did so out of different considerations. Further, the singular features of the bicameralism finally adopted by the Philadelphia Convention perhaps owed as much to the suspicions, bordering on hostility, between the larger and smaller states of America as to the purely principled grounds for bicameralism. All this was known to Mason and his fellow delegates and colored their discussions as they moved freely between close theoretical reasoning and hard horse-trading.

Yet for all that, there was general acceptance of bicameralism by the Americans. Although one is tempted to trace much of that accord to their familiarity with the British model (see ch. 17, no. 9), there are grounds for arguing that bicameralism was generally accepted despite the British model. After all, the cumulative grievances that led to the declaration of American independence stemmed more than anything else from the policies passed in Westminster; in this respect Parliament's behavior constituted no strong case for bicameralism as a guard against shortsighted or passionate legislation. Moreover, the distinct social orders that underlay the separation of Lords and Commons in England were, in America, at most evanescent groupings. If, then, America did not yet have the makings of a permanent class of "well-born," what was the point in having a second or upper house?

Bicameralism and Security

Despite these counterindications, Britain's example and their own colonial experiences continued to commend bicameralism to the Americans. Their long-standing admiration for the British constitution (whether in its mythic uncorrupted form, or in spite of its flaws and abuses), and their vision of a truly balanced legislature, government, and society (see ch. 11, no. 2), lent special authority to the British model. Moreover, most of the colonies had already developed an upper legislative chamber out of their governor's council. Those councils typically represented the concentrated power of great landlords and wealthy merchants and brought them into confrontations with the more modest social and economic orders represented in the lower houses. If those experiences were not altogether happy, they nonetheless suggested to all the utility of having a chamber where one's most essential rights and dearest interests could be asserted and defended. Even in the absence of a permanent class of American lords, the principle of a chamber exercising analogous checks upon a covetous popular assembly or an aggrandizing executive was especially attractive to the owners of substantial property. But it was not only the rich who saw in bicameralism a potent means of reducing the risk that public trust would be betrayed—from whatever quarter.

The arguments offered for bicameralism thus suggest a quasi-aristocratic point of view and a profoundly republican point of view as well. In general, discussion of a second legislative chamber presumes that its membership would be smaller, hold a longer term of office, and be more select than the first. The two bodies would in that sense be visible physical representations of the few and the many. From there it is but a small further step to attribute the characteristic tempers of those groups to the two chambers and to find there the objects of one's particular fears and hopes. And as though to ensure the disparate characters of the two chambers, it was generally the case that the property qualifications for electing state senators and for holding the office itself were higher and more restrictive than for electors and members of the first house.

The first or lower chamber could then be viewed as an embodiment of the popular will of the day, an assemblage of representatives who come close to being reflexes of the people at large. Across the range of republican opinion, it was agreed that such a body was the necessary foundation of popular government resting on consent. But where the people at large can be arbitrary, tyrannical, and passionate, so too can their faithful mouthpieces (nos. 6, 8; see also ch. 15, no. 14). Or, partaking of the failings to which any unchecked body is exposed, a single assembly may be improperly influenced or self-serving or foolish with none to call it to its senses (no. 10). Such a people, such an assembly, require a check to save them from themselves. Alternatively one could argue that it is precisely in a regime grounded on popular sovereignty and devoid of any class vested with hereditary prerogatives that a second chamber, free to veto "the *united will* of the *whole community,* is not only *absurd* and *ridiculous,* but *highly dangerous*" (no. 9).

Proponents of a second chamber were not only wary of the many; some of these very same republicans were also concerned about the overbearing pretensions of the few and viewed the second chamber in that light. Thus Benjamin Rush in 1777 saw the isolation of rich men in a second chamber as the necessary condition for collecting the countervailing strength of "the men of middling fortunes" in the first house. Without such a concentration, the liberties of ordinary folk could not be safe from "that lust for dominion which is always connected with opulence." This isolation of men whose abilities and passions would prove "too much for simple honesty and plain sense" was, John Adams confessed, "to all honest and useful intents, an ostracism" (no. 14).

Bicameralism thus offered a double security against ambition or corruption and against betrayal of trust. All the more was this needed in a republican government where predominance of the legislature, and of the popular house within the legislature, might be taken for granted. So well understood was this, that Madison held it "more than superfluous" to enlarge upon the point (no. 22). Of course this security would be the greater, the more dissimilar the two houses were in their "genius," but all such differences had to fall within the limits set by "the genuine principles of republican government." With the single exception of the republican government imperative, one ought not to judge the qualifications and character of the two chambers by the same standard. "The perfect balance between liberty and power," Hamilton argued (no. 24), requires "the opposition and mutual controul" of distinctive bodies, the one "peculiarly endowed with sensibility," giving voice to popular feelings and concerns, the other marked by knowledge and firmness, enabling the government to pursue an energetic and consistent policy. Each house would then be disposed to keep the doings of the other under a close and suspicious watch. Here was a benefit of bicameralism that James Wilson (no. 26) held was available even where (as in Pennsylvania's new constitution of 1790) both houses were chosen by the same electorate and in the same manner, for it could be presumed that each chamber's "esprit du corps" would lead them to be "rivals in duty, rivals in fame, rivals for the good graces of their common constituents."

Wilson's reliance on a politically wholesome emulation between legislative houses had already been anticipated by the Federal Farmer (see ch. 11, no. 12). The representation and balance in the new system were by no means perfect, but the Federal Farmer had to admit that "in the present condition of the United States" not all that much could be done. The social basis was lacking for a genuine balance between differently constituted houses. The more common view, however, was that there was diversity enough in the two respects that matter most: ability and property (nos. 6, 8; see also ch. 15, no. 14). The second chamber was the proper place for those most distinguished in both. Where, as in Virginia's constitution of 1776, the two houses were not markedly distinctive, there was reason to doubt whether the benefits of bicameralism exceeded its costs. Jefferson's remedy was to heighten the difference (no. 11).

The Case for Unicameralism

The opposing argument is typically not so much a case for unicameralism as a case against bicameralism, and it suffers the fate of negative arguments. The principled case for unicameralism is the democratic one that the voice of the people is best heard and most effective in a plain, simple, uncomplicated system. The more common argument is that there is no special advantage in bicameralism. Francis Hopkinson thought that Pennsylvania was not doing all that badly hopping along "upon her *one leg*"; on the whole a single house took greater care when legislating (no. 12). The complications of a bicameral system made it more likely to malfunction, harder to repair, and at least "as likely to check a good bill as a bad one" (Republicus, no. 21)—a feature that the opponents of energetic government might have found endearing. At the very close of his life, Franklin echoed Hopkinson's sentiments, adding his own special grace notes. Viewed without sentimentality, English bicameralism was no product of political wisdom, but rather "the Effect of Necessity, arising from the preexisting Prevalence of an odious Feudal System" (no. 25). The creator of Poor Richard thought the political claims of private property to be excessive. Civil society was not like a business partnership where greater contributions entitled one to greater voting rights. The well-known distinction between persons and property in no way warranted devoting a legislative chamber to property as a distinct interest.

At the level of a national constitution, bicameralism looked beyond the social class and personal quality of the legislators to the issues of federalism and legislative function. While equality of state representation pointed in one direction, the abandonment of voting by states (as in the Continental Congress) pointed in another. Under the proposed Constitution the states clearly would have a more visible representation in the Senate than in the House of Representatives, and the state legislatures themselves would choose the Senators. (On this last point only a tiny handful in the Philadelphia Convention—Madison and Wilson among them—opposed any role for the states in the election of Senators, but they were unable to carry even their own delegations. Thus it was settled early and decisively that the states as such must have a voice in the national legislature.) Again, the requirement that all money bills originate in the house (Art. 1, sec. 7, cl. 1) bespeaks a difference in function closely connected to a difference in composition. Much the same can be said for the Senate's special role in advising and consenting with respect to treaties and appointments (Art. 2, sec. 2, cl. 2), and for the different roles marked out for the two legislative bodies in the impeachment process (Art. 1, sec. 2, cl. 5; Art. 1, sec. 3, cl. 6). A small continuing body, chosen indirectly for staggered terms longer than those of any other elected office in the government, would be better situated than most to take a long view.

Equality for Unequals

For the most part bicameralism was taken for granted and became part of the given background to the Philadelphia Convention's debate on the principle of representation in the upper house. It was here that old fears and resentments threatened to undo all. The question of what constituted a fair representation of states varying wildly in territory and numbers was as old as union itself. Arguments of justice and expediency had clashed for long, with no resolution (Continental Congress, nos. 3, 5). Compromises had come to nought. Protestations that the larger, that is, the presently or imminently most populous, states had no common interest in lording it over the smaller states fell upon deaf ears in states (such as Delaware) that were hemmed in and had no claims to trans-Appalachian lands (no. 13). Perhaps the only new argument (if it may be so dignified) raised in the convention was the threat voiced by Luther Martin of Maryland that "he had rather see partial Confederacies take place" than accede to a plan doing away with the equal voting strength enjoyed by the states under the Articles of Confederation (no. 18). Wilson of Pennsylvania argued that this jealousy stemmed from the private interest of state officials, not from the legitimate concern of individual citizens for their happiness, and as such deserved to be discounted (no. 17). Hamilton of New York argued that the smaller states' claim that a loss of equality entailed a loss of their liberty was altogether spurious. "The truth is it is a contest for power, not for liberty" (no. 18). But the truth of a rebuttal does not always make it more acceptable, and the smaller states persisted in what Madison called "their pertinacious adherence to an inadmissable plan" (no. 15). The compromise of 29 June gave the Federal Constitution's bicameralism its peculiar cast. After one final slap at the right of equal suffrage among the states as contradicting the "fundamental maxim of republican government" (see ch. 5, no. 23), all that the unreconciled opponents of equal suffrage in the Senate could do was to put the best face upon it that they could manage (no. 22; see also Hanson, Remarks on the Proposed Plan, 1788). It was not a case that Anti-Federalists from *large* states found persuasive (no. 23).

In the end Madison swallowed the equal representation of the states in the Senate as unavoidable. Making a virtue of necessity, he discovered some advantage in a legislative process that would elicit a dual majority, of people and states. In any event, the proposed Senate gave promise of being the locus of precisely those quasi-aristocratic virtues that republican principles would admit and republican government—if it were to endure—would require.

1

JAMES HARRINGTON, COMMONWEALTH OF OCEANA 56–61
1656

(See ch. 11, no. 2)

2

MONTESQUIEU, SPIRIT OF LAWS, BK. 11, CH. 6
1748

(See ch. 17, no. 9)

3

JOHN ADAMS, NOTES ON DEBATES IN CONGRESS
5–6 Sept. 1774
Diary 2:123–26

Mr. Duane then moved that a Committee should be appointed, to prepare Regulations for this Congress. Several Gentlemen objected. I then arose and asked Leave of the President to request of the Gentleman from New York, an Explanation, and that he would point out some particular Regulations which he had in his Mind. He mentioned particularly the Method of voting—whether it should be by Colonies, or by the Poll, or by Interests.

Mr. Henry then arose, and said this was the first general Congress which had ever happened—that no former Congress could be a Precedent—that We should have occasion for more general Congresses, and therefore that a precedent ought to be established now. That it would be great Injustice, if a little Colony should have the same Weight in the Councils of America, as a great one, and therefore he was for a Committee.

Major Sullivan observed that a little Colony had its All at Stake as well as a great one.

This is a Question of great Importance.—If We vote by Colonies, this Method will be liable to great Inequality and Injustice, for 5 small Colonies, with 100,000 People in each may outvote 4 large ones, each of which has 500,000 Inhabitants. If We vote by the Poll, some Colonies have more than their Proportion of Members, and others have less. If We vote by Interests, it will be attended with insuperable Difficulties, to ascertain the true Importance of each Colony.—Is the Weight of a Colony to be ascertained by the Number of Inhabitants merely—or by the Amount of their Trade, the Quantity of their Exports and Imports, or by any compound Ratio of both. This will lead us into such a Field of Controversy as will greatly perplex us. Besides I question whether it is possible to ascertain, at this Time, the Numbers of our People or the Value of our Trade. It will not do in such a Case, to take each other's Words. It ought to be ascertained by authentic Evidence, from Records.

. . . . .

Mr. Henry. Government is dissolved. Fleets and Armies and the present State of Things shew that Government is dissolved.—Where are your Land Marks? your Boundaries of Colonies.

We are in a State of Nature, Sir. I did propose that a Scale should be laid down. That Part of N. America which was once Mass. Bay, and that Part which was once Virginia, ought to be considered as having a Weight. Will not People complain, 10,000 Virginians have not outweighed 1000 others.

I will submit however. I am determined to submit if I am overruled.

A worthy Gentleman (Ego) near me, seemed to admit the Necessity of obtaining a more Adequate Representation.

I hope future Ages will quote our Proceedings with Applause. It is one of the great Duties of the democratical Part of the Constitution to keep itself pure. It is known in my Province, that some other Colonies are not so numerous or rich as they are. I am for giving all the Satisfaction in my Power.

The Distinctions between Virginians, Pensylvanians, New Yorkers and New Englanders, are no more.

I am not a Virginian, but an American.

Slaves are to be thrown out of the Question, and if the freemen can be represented according to their Numbers I am satisfyed.

Mr. Lynch. I differ in one Point from the Gentleman from Virginia, that is in thinking that Numbers only ought to determine the Weight of Colonies. I think that Property ought to be considered, and that it ought to be a compound of Numbers and Property, that should determine the Weight of the Colonies.

I think it cannot be now settled.

Mr. Rutledge. We have no legal Authority and Obedience to our Determinations will only follow the reasonableness, the apparent Utility, and Necessity of the Measures We adopt. We have no coercive or legislative Authority. Our Constituents are bound only in Honour, to observe our Determinations.

Govr. Ward. There are a great Number of Counties in Virginia, very unequal in Point of Wealth and Numbers, yet each has a Right to send 2 Members.

Mr. Lee. But one Reason, which prevails with me, and that is that we are not at this Time provided with proper Materials. I am afraid We are not.

Mr. Gadsden. I cant see any Way of voting but by Colonies.

Coll. Bland. I agree with the Gentleman (Ego) who spoke near me, that We are not at present provided with Materials to ascertain the Importance of each Colony. The Question is whether the Rights and Liberties of America shall be contended for, or given up to arbitrary Power.

Mr. Pendleton. If the Committee should find themselves unable to ascertain the Weight of the Colonies, by their

Numbers and Property, they will report this, and this will lay the Foundation for the Congress to take some other Steps to procure Evidence of Numbers and Property at some future Time.

Mr. Henry. I agree that authentic Accounts cannot be had—if by Authenticity is meant, attestations of officers of the Crown.

I go upon the Supposition, that Government is at an End. All Distinctions are thrown down. All America is all thrown into one Mass. We must aim at the Minutiae of Rectitude.

Mr. Jay. Could I suppose, that We came to frame an American Constitution, instead of indeavouring to correct the faults in an old one—I cant yet think that all Government is at an End. The Measure of arbitrary Power is not full, and I think it must run over, before We undertake to frame a new Constitution.

To the Virtue, Spirit, and Abilities of Virginia We owe much—I should always therefore from Inclination as well as Justice, be for giving Virginia its full Weight.

I am not clear that We ought not to be bound by a Majority tho ever so small, but I only mentioned it, as a Matter of Danger, worthy of Consideration.

4

DEMOCRATICUS, LOOSE THOUGHTS ON GOVERNMENT
7 June 1776
American Archives, 4th ser., 6:731–32

(See ch. 15, no. 14)

5

THOMAS JEFFERSON, NOTES ON DEBATES IN CONGRESS
30 July–1 Aug. 1776
Papers 1:323–27

The other article was in these words. "Art. XVII. In determining questions each colony shall have one vote."

July 30. 31. Aug. 1. present 41. members. Mr. Chase observed that this article was the most likely to divide us of any one proposed in the draught then under consideration. that the larger colonies had threatened they would not confederate at all if their weight in congress should not be equal to the numbers of people they added to the confederacy; while the smaller ones declared against an union if they did not retain an equal vote for the protection of their rights. that it was of the utmost consequence to bring the parties together, as should we sever from each other, either no foreign power will ally with us at all, or the different states will form different alliances, and thus increase the horrors of those scenes of civil war and bloodshed which in such a state of separation & independance would render us a miserable people. that our importance, our interests, our peace required that we should confederate, and that mutual sacrifices should be made to effect a compromise of this difficult question. he was of opinion the smaller colonies would lose their rights, if they were not in some instances allowed an equal vote; and therefore that a discrimination should take place among the questions which would come before Congress. that the smaller states should be secured in all questions concerning life or liberty & the greater ones in all respecting property. he therefore proposed that in votes relating to money, the voice of each colony should be proportioned to the number of it's inhabitants.

Dr. Franklin thought that the votes should be so proportioned in all cases. he took notice that the Delaware counties had bound up their Delegates to disagree to this article. he thought it a very extraordinary language to be held by any state, that they would not confederate with us unless we would let them dispose of our money. certainly if we vote equally we ought to pay equally: but the smaller states will hardly purchase the privilege at this price. that had he lived in a state where the representation, originally equal, had become unequal by time & accident he might have submitted rather than disturb government: but that we should be very wrong to set out in this practice when it is in our power to establish what is right. that at the time of the Union between England and Scotland the latter had made the objection which the smaller states now do. but experience had proved that no unfairness had ever been shewn them. that their advocates had prognosticated that it would again happen as in times of old that the whale would swallow Jonas, but he thought the prediction reversed in event and that Jonas had swallowed the whale, for the Scotch had in fact got possession of the government and gave laws to the English. he reprobated the original agreement of Congress to vote by colonies, and therefore was for their voting in all cases according to the number of taxables.

Dr. Witherspoon opposed every alteration of the article. all men admit that a confederacy is necessary. should the idea get abroad that there is likely to be no union among us, it will damp the minds of the people, diminish the glory of our struggle, & lessen it's importance, because it will open to our view future prospects of war & dissension among ourselves. if an equal vote be refused, the smaller states will become vassals to the larger; & all experience has shewn that the vassals & subjects of free states are the most enslaved. he instanced the Helots of Sparta & the provinces of Rome. he observed that foreign powers discovering this blemish would make it a handle for disengaging the smaller states from so unequal a confederacy. that the colonies should in fact be considered as individuals; and that as such in all disputes they should have an equal vote. that they are now collected as individuals making a bargain with each other, & of course had a right to vote as individuals. that in the East India company they voted by persons, & not by their proportion of stock. that the Belgic confederacy voted by provinces. that in questions of war the smaller states were as much interested as the larger, & therefore should vote equally; and indeed that the larger states were more likely to bring war on the confederacy, in proportion as their frontier was more extensive. he admitted that equality of representation was an excellent principle, but then it must be of things which are co-ordinate; that is, of things similar & of the same nature: that nothing relating to individuals could ever come before Congress; nothing but what would respect colonies. he distinguished between an incorporating & a federal union. the union of England was an incorporating one; yet Scotland had suffered by that union: for that it's inhabitants were drawn from it by the hopes of places & employments. nor was it an instance of equality of representation; because while Scotland was allowed nearly a thirteenth of representation, they were to pay only one fortieth of the land tax. he expressed his hopes that in the present enlightened state of men's minds we might expect a lasting confederacy, if it was founded on fair principles.

John Adams advocated the voting in proportion to numbers. he said that we stand here as the representatives of the people. that in some states the people are many, in others they are few; that therefore their vote here should be proportioned to the numbers from whom it comes. reason, justice, & equity never had weight enough on the face of the earth to govern the councils of men. it is interest alone which does it, and it is interest alone which can be trusted. that therefore the interests within doors should be the mathematical representatives of the interests without doors. that the individuality of the colonies is a mere sound. does the individuality of a colony increase it's wealth or numbers? if it does; pay equally. if it does not add weight in the scale of the confederacy, it cannot add to their rights, nor weight in argument. A. has £50. B. £500. C. £1000 in partnership. is it just they should equally dispose of the monies of the partnership? it has been said we are independant individuals making a bargain together. the question is not what we are now, but what we ought to be when our bargain shall be made. the confederacy is to make us one individual only; it is to form us, like separate parcels of metal, into one common mass. we shall no longer retain our separate individuality, but become a single individual as to all questions submitted to the Confederacy. therefore all those reasons which prove the justice & expediency of equal representation in other assemblies, hold good here. it has been objected that a proportional vote will endanger the smaller states. we answer that an equal vote will endanger the larger. Virginia, Pennsylvania, & Massachusets are the three greater colonies. consider their distance, their difference of produce, of interests, & of manners, & it is apparent they can never have an interest or inclination to combine for the oppression of the smaller. that the smaller will naturally divide on all questions with the larger. Rhodeisld. from it's relation, similarity & intercourse will generally pursue the same objects with Massachusets; Jersey, Delaware & Maryland with Pennsylvania.

Dr. Rush took notice that the decay of the liberties of the Dutch republic proceeded from three causes. 1. the perfect unanimity requisite on all occasions. 2. their obli-

gation to consult their constituents. 3. their voting by provinces. this last destroyed the equality of representation, and the liberties of Great Britain also are sinking from the same defect. that a part of our rights is deposited in the hands of Congress: why is it not equally necessary there should be an equal representation there? were it possible to collect the whole body of the people together, they would determine the questions submitted to them by their majority. why should not the same majority decide when voting here by their representatives? the larger colonies are so providentially divided in situation as to render every fear of their combining visionary. their interests are different, & their circumstances dissimilar. it is more probable they will become rivals & leave it in the power of the smaller states to give preponderance to any scale they please. the voting by the number of free inhabitants will have one excellent effect, that of inducing the colonies to discourage slavery & to encourage the increase of their free inhabitants.

Mr. Hopkins observed there were 4 larger, 4 smaller & 4 middlesized colonies. that the 4. largest would contain more than half the inhabitants of the Confederating states, & therefore would govern the others as they should please. that history affords no instance of such a thing as equal representation. the Germanic body votes by states. the Helvetic body does the same; & so does the Belgic confederacy. that too little is known of the antient confederations to say what was their practice.

Mr. Wilson thought that taxation should be in proportion to wealth, but that representation should accord with the number of freemen. that government is a collection or result of the wills of all. that if any government could speak the will of all it would be perfect; and that so far as it departs from this it becomes imperfect. it has been said that Congress is a representation of states; not of individuals. I say that the objects of it's care are all the individuals of the states. it is strange that annexing the name of 'State' to ten thousand men, should give them an equal right with forty thousand. this must be the effect of magic, not of reason. as to those matters which are referred to Congress, we are not so many states; we are one large state. we lay aside our individuality whenever we come here. the Germanic body is a burlesque on government: and their practice on any point is a sufficient authority & proof that it is wrong. the greatest imperfection in the constitution of the Belgic confederacy is their voting by provinces. the interest of the whole is constantly sacrificed to that of the small states. the history of the war in the reign of Q. Anne sufficiently proves this. it is asked Shall nine colonies put it into the power of four to govern them as they please? I invert the question and ask Shall two millions of people put it in the power of one million to govern them as they please? it is pretended too that the smaller colonies will be in danger from the greater. speak in honest language & say the minority will be in danger from the majority. and is there an assembly on earth where this danger may not be equally pretended? the truth is that our proceedings will then be consentaneous with the interests of the majority, and so they ought to be. the probability is much greater that the larger states will disagree than that they will combine. I defy the wit of man to invent a possible case or to suggest any one thing on earth which shall be for the interests of Virginia, Pennsylvania & Massachusets, and which will not also be for the interest of the other states.

the encroachments of their delegates, I am now convinced that a third branch of Legislation is at least unnecessary. But for the sake of Execution we must have a Magistrate solely executive, and with the aid of his Council (I mean a Privy Council) let him have such executive powers as may give energy to Government.

6

WILLIAM HOOPER TO THE CONGRESS OF THE
STATE OF NORTH CAROLINA
26 Oct. 1776
Colonial Records 10:867–68

The Constitution of Britain had for its object the union of the three grand qualities of virtue, wisdom and power as the characteristicks of perfect Government. From the people at large the first of these was most to be expected; the second from a selected few whom superiour Talents or better opportunities for Improvement had raised into a second Class, and the latter from some one whom variety of Circumstances may have placed in a singular and conspicuous point of view, and to whom Heaven had given talents to make him the choice of the people to entrust with powers for sudden and decisive execution. The middle class, like the hand which holds a pair of scales balancing between the *one* & the *many,* and impartially casting weight against the scale that preponderates in order to preserve that equality which is the essence of a mixed Monarchy, & is called the ballance of power. Might not this or something like this serve as a Model for us. A single branch of Legislation is a many headed Monster which without any check must soon defeat the very purposes for which it was created, and its members become a Tyranny dreadful in proportion to the numbers which compose it. And possessed of power uncontrolled, would soon exercise it to put themselves free from the restraint of those who made them, and to make their own political existence perpetual. The consultations of large bodies are likewise less correct and perfect than those where a few only are concerned. The people at large have generally just objects in their pursuit but often fall short in the means made use of to obtain them. A Warmth of Zeal may lead them into errors which a more cool, dispassionate enquiry may discover and rectify. This points out the necessity of another branch of legislation at least, which may be a refinement of the first choice of the people at large, selected for their Wisdom, remarkable Integrity, or that weight which arises from property and gives Independence and Impartiality to the human mind. For my own part I once thought it would be wise to adopt a double check as in the British Constitution, but from the Abuses which power in the hand of an Individual is liable to, & the unreasonableness that an individual should abrogate at pleasure the acts of the Representatives of the people, refined by a second body whom we may call for fashion's sake, Counsellors, & as they are a kind of barrier for the people's rights against

7

ONE OF THE PEOPLE
23 Nov. 1776
Pennsylvania Evening Post

But these wise patriots, that are (as they pretend) for no unnecessary alterations in our old form of government, have never in all their papers and proposals left their *favourite innovation* out of sight. A *Legislative Council* is their hobby horse. Something like a House of Lords they will have, where wisdom will forever reign. For in the fourth direction, the Representatives are instructed to use their endeavours to *divide the supreme legislative power* in such a manner as shall produce wise, just, and well digested counsels, and thus secure the state from the fatal influence of hasty, incorrect, passionate and prejudiced determinations. That is, let us have a Legislative Council for the *better sort*—an Upper and Lower House like some of our neighbours; that this wise Upper House, consisting of *choice spirits,* all *sons* of *Solon* and *Lycurgus,* may secure the state from the fatal influence of hasty, incorrect, passionate and prejudiced determinations, which is all we can reasonably expect from the Lower House, consisting chiefly of farmers and mechanics, while we in the other House will be famed for wise, prudent, just and well judged counsels.

But let it be remembered that we can expect no good, but tyranny and confusion from this Council.

Where could we more reasonably expect wise and well digested counsels than in the British House of Lords? There they have the dignitaries of the church, and the hereditary wisdom of all the nobility. With these Lords Spiritual and Temporal, the Judges of the kingdom are gravely seated on their wool packs, to contribute their share of jurisprudence and wisdom. Yet these demy gods were never counted wiser, nor more favorable to liberty than the House of Commons. Until that venerable body was ruined by bribery and corruption, they were the most respectable branch of that admired Constitution. They were brave, prudent and eloquent, they were the guardians of liberty, the glory of Britain, and an honor to mankind; the Upper House oft gave them trouble; but seldom prevented them from taking wrong measures; for it must be confessed that they were men, and have sometimes gone astray.

. . . . .

But if we had once got this Legislative Council established, which is to be famous for wisdom and well digested counsels, what struggles will be made to get a seat amongst them? For who would bear to sit in the Lower House, to share their ignominy, and to be teazed and harrassed with their hasty, incorrect, passionate, and prejudiced determinations? But may we not in time expect that these sons of wisdom will think it hard to submit to yearly elections by the ignorant vulgar? Will they not make a bold push to hold their seats for three or seven years, or even during life, as their wise predecessors in the House of Lords? And will they not make a push for places and pensions to support their dignity? If the Lower House opposes their measures, they will be reproached for their passion and prejudice, and be told that they were not chosen to check or dictate to them, but to be led and guided by their betters, the Upper House. If the Lower House can be brought to listen to the wisdom of their lordly masters, we have done with annual elections. They will be triennial or septennial, and every leader must have a place of honor, or profit, or an annuity for life for betraying the state. It may be said, that there is no danger of these evils. But we know that what has happened in Britain may happen in America. Power is encroaching, and deaf to the cries of humanity, and regardless of the rights of mankind.

8

BENJAMIN RUSH, OBSERVATIONS ON THE
GOVERNMENT OF PENNSYLVANIA
1777
Selected Writings 57–64, 67–69

I shall now proceed to say a few words upon particular parts of the Constitution.

In the second section, "the supreme legislature is vested in a *'single'* House of Representatives of the Freemen of the Commonwealth." By this section we find, that the supreme, absolute, and uncontrolled power of the whole State is lodged in the hands of *one body* of men. Had it been lodged in the hands of one man, it would have been less dangerous to the safety and liberties of the community. Absolute power should never be trusted to man. It has perverted the wisest heads, and corrupted the best hearts in the world. I should be afraid to commit my property, liberty and life to a body of angels for one whole year. The Supreme Being alone is qualified to possess supreme power over his creatures. It requires the wisdom and goodness of a Deity to control, and direct it properly.

In order to show the extreme danger of trusting all the legislative power of a State to a single representation, I shall beg leave to transcribe a few sentences from a letter, written by Mr. JOHN ADAMS, to one of his friends in North Carolina, who requested him to favour him with a plan of government for that State above a twelve-month ago. This illustrious Citizen, who is second to no man in America, in an inflexible attachment to the liberties of this country, and to republican forms of government, writes as follows,

"I think a people cannot be *long free,* nor *ever* happy,

whose government is in one Assembly. My reasons for this opinion are as follow,

1. "A single Assembly is liable to all the vices, follies and frailties of an individual,—subject to fits of humour,—starts of passions,* flights of enthusiasm,—partialities of prejudice, and consequently productive of hasty results and absurd judgments. All these errors ought to be corrected, and defects supplied by some controlling power.

2. "A single Assembly is apt to be avaricious, and in time will not scruple to exempt itself from burdens, which it will lay, without compunction, upon its constituents.

3. "A single Assembly is apt to grow ambitious, and after a time will not hestitate to vote itself perpetual. This was one fault of the Long Parliament, but more remarkably of Holland, whose Assembly first voted themselves from *annual* to *septennial,* then for *life,* and after a course of years, that all vacancies happening by death or otherwise, should be filled by *themselves,* without any application to constituents at all.

4. "Because a single Assembly possessed of all the powers of government would make arbitrary laws for their own interest, and adjudge all controversies in their own favor."†

If any thing could be necessary upon this subject, after such an authority, I might here add, that Montesquieu—Harrington—Milton—Addison—Price—Bolingbroke, and others, the wisest statesmen, and the greatest friends to Liberty in the world, have left testimonies upon record of the extreme folly and danger of a people's being governed by a single legislature. I shall content myself with the following extract from the last of those authors. The sentiments correspond exactly with those of our countryman before-mentioned.

"By simple forms of government, I mean such as lodge the whole supreme power, absolutely and without control, either in a single person, or in the principal persons of the community, or in the whole body of the people. Such governments are governments of arbitrary will, and therefore of all imaginable absurdities the most absurd. They stand in direct opposition to the sole motive of submission to any government whatsoever; for if men quit the State, and renounce the rights of nature, (one of which is, to be sure, that of being governed by their own will) they do this, that they may not remain exposed to the arbitrary will of other men, the weakest to that of the strongest, the few to that of the many. Now, in submitting to any single form of government whatever, they establish what they mean to avoid, and for fear of being exposed to arbitrary will sometimes,

---

*A Committee of the Convention, which formed the Constitution of Pennsylvania, published in the Pennsylvania Packet of October 15, 1776, as an apology for one of their Ordinances, that was thought to be arbitrary and unjust, that it was passed when "the minds of the Convention were agitated, and their passions inflamed."

†These reasons are given by our author for not lodging all power legislative, executive and judicial, in one body of men. This has been done, as will be shown hereafter in the Constitution of Pennsylvania: But, supposing it had been otherwise, our author adds, "shall the *whole* power of *legislation* rest in one Assembly? Most of the foregoing reasons (one is omitted) apply *equally* to prove, that the whole legislative power ought to be more *complex.*"

they choose to be governed by it always. These governments do not only degenerate into tyranny; they are tyranny in their very institution; and they who submit to them, are slaves, not subjects, however the supreme power may be exercised; for tyranny and slavery do not so properly consist in the stripes that are given and received, as in the power of giving them at pleasure, and the necessity of receiving them, whenever and for whatever they are inflicted."

I might go on further and show, that all the dissentions of Athens and Rome, so dreadful in their nature, and so fatal in their consequences, originated in single Assemblies possessing all the power of those commonwealths; but this would be the business of a volume, and not of a single essay.—I shall therefore pass on, to answer the various arguments that have been used in Pennsylvania, in support of a single legislature.

1. We are told, that the perfection of every thing consists in its simplicity,—that all mixtures in government are impurities, and that a single legislature is perfect, because it is simple.—To this I answer, that we should distinguish between simplicity in principles, and simplicity in the application of principles to practice. What can be more simple than the principles of mechanics, and yet into how many thousand forms have they been tortured by the ingenuity of man. A few simple elementary bodies compose all the matter of the universe, and yet how infinitely are they combined in the various forms and substances which they assume in the animal, vegetable, and mineral kingdoms. In like manner a few simple principles enter into the composition of all free governments. These principles are perfect security for property, liberty and life; but these principles admit of extensive combinations, when reduced to practice:—Nay more, they require them. A despotic government is the most simple government in the world, but instead of affording security to property, liberty or life, it obliges us to hold them all on the simple will of a capricious sovereign. I maintain therefore, that all governments are safe and free in proportion as they are compounded in a certain degree, and on the contrary, that all governments are dangerous and tyrannical in proportion as they approach to simplicity.

2. We are told by the friends of a single legislature, that there can be no danger of their becoming tyrannical, since they must partake of all the burdens they lay upon their constituents. Here we forget the changes that are made upon the head and heart by arbitrary power, and the cases that are recorded in history of *annual* Assemblies having refused to share with their constituents in the burdens which they had imposed upon them. If every elector in Pennsylvania is capable of being elected an assembly-man, then agreeably to the sixth section of the Constitution, it is possible for an Assembly to exist who do not possess a single foot of property in the State, and who can give no other evidence of a common interest in, or attachment to, the community than having paid "public taxes," which may mean poor-taxes. Should this be the case, (and there is no obstacle in the Constitution to prevent it) surely it will be in the power of such an Assembly to draw from the State the whole of its wealth in a few years, without contributing

any thing further towards it than their proportion of the trifling tax necessary to support the poor.—But I shall show in another place equal dangers from another class of men, becoming a majority in the Assembly.

3. We are told of instances of the House of Lords, in England, checking the most salutary laws, after they had passed the House of Commons, as a proof of the inconvenience of a compound legislature. I believed the fact to be true, but I deny its application in the present controversy. The House of Lords, in England, possess privileges and interests, which do not belong to the House of Commons. Moreover they derive their power from the crown and not from the people. No wonder therefore they consult their own interests, in preference to those of the People. In the State of Pennsylvania we wish for a council, with *no one* exclusive privilege, and we disclaim every idea of their possessing the smallest degree of power, but what is derived from the *annual* suffrages of the people. A body thus chosen could have no object in view but the happiness of their constituents. It is remarkable in Connecticut, that the legislative council of that State has in no one instance made amendments, or put a negative upon the acts of their Assembly, in the course of above one hundred years, in which both have not appeared to the people in a few months to have been calculated to promote their liberty and happiness.

4. We are told, that the Congress is a single legislature, therefore a single legislature is to be preferred to a compound one.—The objects of legislation in the Congress relate only to peace and war, alliances, trade, the Post-Office, and the government of the army and navy. They never touch the liberty, property, nor life of the individuals of any State in their resolutions, and even in their ordinary subjects of legislation, they are liable to be checked by *each* of the Thirteen States.

5. We have been told, that a legislative council or governor lays the foundation for aristocratical and monarchical power in a community. However ridiculous this objection to a compound legislature may appear, I have more than once heard it mentioned by the advocates for a single Assembly. Who would believe, that the same fountain of pure water should send forth, at the same time, wholesome and deadly streams? Are not the Council and Assembly both formed alike by the *annual* breath of the people? But I will suppose, that a legislative Council aspired after the honors of hereditary titles and power, would they not be *effectually* checked by the Assembly?

I cannot help commending the zeal that appears in my countrymen against the power of a King or a House of Lords. I concur with them in all their prejudices against hereditary titles, honour and power. History is little else than a recital of the follies and vices of kings and noblemen, and it is because I dread so much from them, that I wish to exclude them for ever from Pennsylvania, for notwithstanding our government has been called a simple democracy, I maintain, that a foundation is laid in it for the most complete aristocracy that ever existed in the world.

In order to prove this assertion, I shall premise two propositions, which have never been controverted: First, where there is wealth, there will be power; and, secondly, the rich have always been an over-match for the poor in all contests for power.

These truths being admitted, I desire to know what can prevent our single representation being filled, in the course of a few years, with a majority of rich men? Say not, the people will not choose such men to represent them. The influence of wealth at elections is irresistible. It has been seen and felt in Pennsylvania, and I am obliged in justice to my subject to say, that there are poor men among us as prepared to be influenced, as the rich are prepared to influence them. The fault must be laid in both cases upon human nature. The consequence of a majority of rich men getting into the legislature is plain. Their wealth will administer fuel to the love of arbitrary power that is common to all men. The present Assembly have furnished them with precedents for breaking the Constitution. Farewell now to annual elections! Public emergencies will sanctify the most daring measures. The clamours of their constituents will be silenced with offices, bribes or punishments. An aristocracy will be established, and Pennsylvania will be inhabited like most of the countries in Europe, with only two sorts of animals, tyrants and slaves.

It has often been said, that there is but one rank of men in America, and therefore, that there should be only one representation of them in a government. I agree, that we have no artificial distinctions of men into noblemen and commoners among us, but it ought to be remarked, that superior degrees of industry and capacity, and above all, commerce, have introduced inequality of property among us, and these have introduced natural distinctions of rank in Pennsylvania, as certain and general as the artificial distinctions of men in Europe. This will ever be the case while commerce exists in this country. The men of middling property and poor men can never be safe in a mixed representation with the men of over-grown property. Their liberties can only be secured by having exact bounds prescribed to their power, in the fundamental principles of the Constitution. By a representation of the men of middling fortunes in one house, their *whole* strength is collected against the influence of wealth. Without such a representation, the most violent efforts of individuals to oppose it would be divided and broken, and would want that system, which alone would enable them to check that lust for dominion which is always connected with opulence. The government of Pennsylvania therefore has been called most improperly a government for poor men. It carries in every part of it a poison to their liberties. It is impossible to form a government more suited to the passions and interests of rich men.

6. But says the advocate for a single legislature, if one of the advantages of having a Legislative Council arises from the Counsellors possessing more wisdom than the Assembly, why may not the members of the Council be thrown into the Assembly, in order to instruct and enlighten them? If sound reasoning always prevailed in popular Assemblies, this objection to a Legislative Council might have some weight. The danger in this case would be, that the Counsellors would partake of the passions and prejudices of the Assembly, by taking part in their debates; or, if they did not, that they would be so inconsiderable in point of numbers, that they would be constantly out-voted by the members of the Assembly.

. . . . .

Thus have I answered all the arguments that ever I have heard offered in favour of a single legislature, and I hope, silenced all the objections that have been made to a double representation of the people. I might here appeal further to the practice of our courts of law in favour of repeated deliberations and divisions. In a free government, the most inconsiderable portion of our liberty and property cannot be taken from us, without the judgment of two or three courts; but, by the Constitution of Pennsylvania, the whole of our liberty and property, and even our lives, may be taken from us, by the hasty and passionate decision of a single Assembly.

I shall conclude my observations upon this part of the Constitution, by summing up the advantages of a compound or double legislature.

1. There is the utmost *freedom* in a compound legislature. The decisions of two legislative bodies cannot fail of coinciding with the wills of a great majority of the community.

2. There is *safety* in such a government, in as much as each body possesses a free and independent power, so that they mutually check ambition and usurpation in each other.

3. There is the greatest *wisdom* in such a government. Every act being obliged to undergo the revision and amendments of two bodies of men, is necessarily strained of every mixture of folly, passion, and prejudice.*

4. There is the longest *duration* of freedom in such a government.†

5. There is the most *order* in such a government. By order, I mean obedience to laws, subordination to magistrates, civility and decency of behaviour, and the contrary of every thing like mobs and factions.

6. Compound governments are most agreeable to *human nature,* inasmuch as they afford the greatest scope for the expansion of the powers and virtues of the mind. Wisdom, learning, experience, with the most extensive benevolence, the most unshaken firmness, and the utmost elevation of soul, are all called into exercise by the opposite and different duties of the different representations of the people.

---

*The Militia Law of the Delaware State received twenty-four amendments from the Council after it had had three readings in the Assembly; all of which were adopted at once by the Assembly. I grant, the wisdom of men collected in any way that can be devised, cannot make a *perfect* law; but I am sure a Legislative Council would not have overlooked many inaccuracies in the laws passed in the last session of the present Assembly of Pennsylvania.

†Sparta, which possessed a compound legislature, preserved her liberties above five hundred years. The fatal dissentions of Athens and Rome ceased as soon as their Senates, which were filled only with rich men, were checked by another Representation of the people.

9

PENNSYLVANIA GAZETTE
26 March 1777

Sorry am I to see that rancourous contest concerning the Constitution of this State, revived with all the asperity it first commenced. The matter in debate seems a meer nothing: for when the sticklers for a Legislative Council urge the danger of having crude and inconsistent bills pass into laws, without a second digestion in another house, the fact is still admitted on the other side, and in several publications remedies for this evil have been proposed.

Philerene, whose calm and sensible performance does him much honour, goes, however, a little too far, in proposing that the people should instruct their representatives to vote a number of their own body a Council for revising the laws, and invest them with a negative power. Constituents should never trust Legislative Representatives with a power of altering the constitution; and to establish any power, which should be *able to controul* the immediate Representative of the whole people, would be an essential and fundamental alteration of the constitution. The wisdom of Pennsylvania collected in the late Convention concluded justly that the power of government really resided in the body of the people, and considering we have no hereditary King nor Lords, whose prerogatives entitle them to negatives in their own right, a negative, or power of controuling the *united will* of the *whole community,* is not only *absurd* and *ridiculous,* but *highly dangerous.* Consistent with their trust, the convention could not have established such a power, without special instructions for that purpose, neither had they a precedent for it in our former Constitution. Yet that there should be a power to revise, and most scrutinously to examine the Bills of the Assembly, will be allowed by every one who considers the necessity of having laws concordant with themselves and the Constitution, and adequate to the designs of their framers.

As the people, the *common people alone,* are the source of constituent power in this country, their immediate representatives are of course the *supreme delegate power.* This representative body may call to their assistance the advice of what bodies they judge necessary; but there is a material difference between calling in advice, and obliging ourselves to take it whether we approve of it or not. The republic of Holland has a great lawyer whom they call a Pensionary, whose business it is to examine all their bills, and point out every flaw or imperfection he can discover in them. The great lawyer, now set at the head of the judicial department, would undoubtedly take the same trouble, *without fee or reward,* were he applied to by the legislature for that purpose. We cannot suppose either the Council, or the Supreme Court, so mercenary as to deny a little extra service, when they are pretty generously gratified for what they do stately.

10

THE ESSEX RESULT
29 Apr. 1778
Handlin 343–44

But the legislative power must not be trusted with one assembly. A single assembly is frequently influenced by the vices, follies, passions, and prejudices of an individual. It is liable to be avaricious, and to exempt itself from the burdens it lays upon it's constituents. It is subject to ambition, and after a series of years, will be prompted to vote itself perpetual. The long parliament in England voted itself perpetual, and thereby, for a time, destroyed the political liberty of the subject. Holland was governed by one representative assembly annually elected. They afterwards voted themselves from annual to septennial; then for life; and finally exerted the power of filling up all vacancies, without application to their constituents. The government of Holland is now a tyranny *though a republic.*

The result of a single assembly will be hasty and indigested, and their judgments frequently absurd and inconsistent. There must be a second body to revise with coolness and wisdom, and to controul with firmness, independent upon the first, either for their creation, or existence. Yet the first must retain a right to a similar revision and controul over the second.

11

THOMAS JEFFERSON, NOTES ON THE STATE
OF VIRGINIA, QUERY 13, 118–20
1784

This constitution was formed when we were new and unexperienced in the science of government. It was the first too which was formed in the whole United States. No wonder then that time and trial have discovered very capital defects in it.

. . . . .

3. The senate is, by its constitution, too homogeneous with the house of delegates. Being chosen by the same electors, at the same time, and out of the same subjects, the choice falls of course on men of the same description. The purpose of establishing different houses of legislation is to introduce the influence of different interests or different principles. Thus in Great-Britain it is said their constitution relies on the house of commons for honesty, and the lords for wisdom; which would be a rational reliance if honesty were to be bought with money, and if wisdom were hereditary. In some of the American states the dele-

gates and senators are so chosen, as that the first represent the persons, and the second the property of the state. But with us, wealth and wisdom have equal chance for admission into both houses. We do not therefore derive from the separation of our legislature into two houses, those benefits which a proper complication of principles is capable of producing, and those which alone can compensate the evils which may be produced by their dissensions.

12

FRANCIS HOPKINSON TO JOHN JAY
11 Mar. 1786

Jay Correspondence 3:184

May I ask how you come on in your political family. Our *Law office* is at present open, and the debates and proceedings there afford ample room for amusement, speculation and observation. The two parties of our State are so nearly ballanced in the House of Assembly, that neither are sure of carrying a point. This situation excites the Orators and leading men of the House to the most vigorous exertions, and those who have leisure to attend the debates are sure to be highly gratified. When both parties unite in a measure, it is a thousand to one that it is a salutary and proper measure. Pennsylvania hops along upon her *one leg* better than I expected. I never liked our Constitution; yet the above metaphor suggests one advantage which I did not think of before: viz: That having but one branch of Legislature—or if you please, but one leg to support her, the old lady is obliged to be very attentive and circumspect in her positions and motions, lest she should fall and break her nose. Those who have two to depend upon, are apt to trip thro' carelessness. Your Constitution, I think hobbles on one leg and a stick. But enough of this nonsense.

13

GEORGE READ TO JOHN DICKINSON
17 Jan. 1787

Life 438–39

Finding that Virginia hath again taken the lead in the proposed convention at Philadelphia in May, as recommended in our report when at Annapolis, as by an act of their Assembly, passed the 22d of November last, and inserted in Dunlap's paper of the 15th of last month [appears], it occurred to me, as a prudent measure on the part of our State, that its Legislature should, in the act of appointment, so far restrain the powers of the commissioners, whom they shall name on this service, as that they may not extend to any alteration in that part of the fifth article of

the present Confederation, which gives each State *one vote* in determining questions in Congress, and the latter part of the thirteenth article, as to future alterations,—that is, that such clause shall be preserved or inserted, for the like purpose, in any revision that shall be made and agreed to in the proposed convention. I conceive our existence as a State will depend upon our preserving such rights, for I consider the acts of Congress hitherto, as to the ungranted lands in most of the larger States, as sacrificing the just claims of the smaller and bounded States to a proportional share therein, for the purpose of discharging the national debt incurred during the war; and such is my jealousy of most of the larger States, that I would trust nothing to their candor, generosity, or ideas of public justice in behalf of this State, from what has heretofore happened, and which, I presume, hath not escaped your notice. But as I am generally distrustful of my own judgment, and particularly in public matters of consequence, I wish your consideration of the prudence or propriety of the Legislature's adopting such a measure, and more particularly for that I do suppose you will be one of its commissioners. Persuaded I am, from what I have seen occasionally in the public prints and heard in private conversations, that the voice of the States will be one of the subjects of revision, and in a meeting where there will be so great an interested majority, I suspect the argument or oratory of the smaller State commissioners will avail little. In such circumstances I conceive it will relieve the commissioners of the State from disagreeable argumentation, as well as prevent the downfall of the State, which [without an equal vote] would at once become a cypher in the union, and have no chance of an accession of district, or even citizens; for, as we presently stand, our quota is increased upon us, in the requisition of this year, more than thirteen-eightieths since 1775, without any other reason that I can suggest than a promptness in the Legislature of this State to comply with all the Congress requisitions from time to time. This increase alone, without addition, would in the course of a few years banish many of its citizens and impoverish the remainder; therefore, clear I am that every guard that can be devised for this State's protection against future encroachment should be preserved or made. I wish your opinion on the subject as soon as convenient.

14

JOHN ADAMS, DEFENCE OF THE CONSTITUTIONS
OF GOVERNMENT OF THE UNITED STATES
1787

Works 4:290–91

The rich, the well-born, and the able, acquire an influence among the people that will soon be too much for simple honesty and plain sense, in a house of representatives. The most illustrious of them must, therefore, be separated from the mass, and placed by themselves in a senate; this is, to all honest and useful intents, an ostracism. A member of a senate, of immense wealth, the most respected birth, and transcendent abilities, has no influence in the nation, in comparison of what he would have in a single representative assembly. When a senate exists, the most powerful man in the state may be safely admitted into the house of representatives, because the people have it in their power to remove him into the senate as soon as his influence becomes dangerous. The senate becomes the great object of ambition; and the richest and the most sagacious wish to merit an advancement to it by services to the public in the house. When he has obtained the object of his wishes, you may still hope for the benefits of his exertions, without dreading his passions; for the executive power being in other hands, he has lost much of his influence with the people, and can govern very few votes more than his own among the senators.

15

JAMES MADISON, FEDERAL CONVENTION
19 June 1787
Farrand 1:319–22

---

7. He begged the smaller States which were most attached to Mr. Pattersons plan to consider the situation in which it would leave them. In the first place they would continue to bear the whole expense of maintaining their Delegates in Congress. It ought not to be said that if they were willing to bear this burden, no others had a right to complain. As far as it led the small States to forbear keeping up a representation, by which the public business was delayed, it was evidently a matter of common concern. An examination of the minutes of Congress would satisfy every one that the public business had been frequently delayed by this cause; and that the States most frequently unrepresented in Congs. were not the larger States. He reminded the convention of another consequence of leaving on a small State the burden of Maintaining a Representation in Congs. During a considerable period of the War, one of the Representatives of Delaware, in whom alone before the signing of the Confederation the entire vote of that State and after that event one half of its vote, frequently resided, was a Citizen & Resident of Pena. and held an office in his own State incompatible with an appointment from it to Congs. During another period, the same State was represented by three delegates two of whom were citizens of Penna.—and the third a Citizen of New Jersey. These expedients must have been intended to avoid the burden of supporting delegates from their own State. But whatever might have been ye. cause, was not in effect the vote of one State doubled, and the influence of another increased by it? In the 2d. place The coercion, on which the efficacy of the plan depends, can never be exerted but on themselves. The large States will be impregnable, the smaller only can feel the vengeance of it. He illustrated the

position by the history of the Amphyctionic Confederates: and the ban of the German Empire, It was the cobweb wch. could entangle the weak, but would be the sport of the strong.

8. He begged them to consider the situation in which they would remain in case their pertinacious adherence to an inadmissable plan, should prevent the adoption of any plan. The contemplation of such an event was painful; but it would be prudent to submit to the task of examining it at a distance, that the means of escaping it might be the more readily embraced. Let the union of the States be dissolved and one of two consequences must happen. Either the States must remain individually independent & sovereign; or two or more Confederacies must be formed among them. In the first event would the small States be more secure agst. the ambition & power of their larger neighbours, than they would be under a general Government pervading with equal energy every part of the Empire, and having an equal interest in protecting every part agst. every other part? In the second, can the smaller expect that their larger neighbours would confederate with them on the principle of the present confederacy, which gives to each member, an equal suffrage; or that they would exact less severe concessions from the smaller States, than are proposed in the scheme of Mr. Randolph?

The great difficulty lies in the affair of Representation; and if this could be adjusted, all others would be surmountable. It was admitted by both the gentlemen from N. Jersey, (Mr. Brearly and Mr. Patterson) that it would not be *just to allow Virga.* which was 16 times as large as Delaware an equal vote only. Their language was that it would not be *safe for Delaware* to allow Virga. 16 times as many votes. The expedient proposed by them was that all the States should be thrown into one mass and a new partition be made into 13 equal parts. Would such a scheme be practicable? The dissimelarities existing in the rules of property, as well as in the manners, habits and prejudices of the different States, amounted to a prohibition of the attempt. It had been found impossible for the power of one of the most absolute princes in Europe (K. of France) directed by the wisdom of one of the most enlightened and patriotic Ministers (Mr. Neckar) that any age has produced, to equalize in some points only the different usages & regulations of the different provinces. But admitting a general amalgamation and repartition of the States, to be practicable, and the danger apprehended by the smaller States from a proportional representation to be real; would not a particular and voluntary coalition of these with their neighbours, be less inconvenient to the whole community, and equally effectual for their own safety. If N. Jersey or Delaware conceive that an advantage would accrue to them from an equalization of the States, in which case they would necessaryly form a junction with their neighbors, why might not this end be attained by leaving them at liberty by the Constitution to form such a junction whenever they pleased? and why should they wish to obtrude a like arrangement on all the States, when it was, to say the least, extremely difficult, would be obnoxious to many of the States, and when neither the inconveniency, nor the benefit of the expedient to themselves, would be lessened, by confining it to themselves.—The prospect of many new States to the Westward was another consideration of importance. If they should come into the Union at all, they would come when they contained but but few inhabitants. If they shd. be entitled to vote according to their proportions of inhabitants, all would be right & safe. Let them have an equal vote, and a more objectionable minority than ever might give law to the whole.

16

GEORGE MASON, FEDERAL CONVENTION
20 June 1787
Farrand 1:339

Much has been said of the unsettled state of the mind of the people. he believed the mind of the people of America, as elsewhere, was unsettled as to some points; but settled as to others. In two points he was sure it was well settled. 1. in an attachment to Republican Government. 2. in an attachment to more than one branch in the Legislature. Their constitutions accord so generally in both these circumstances, that they seem almost to have been preconcerted. This must either have been a miracle, or have resulted from the genius of the people. The only exceptions to the establishmt. of two branches in the Legislatures are the State of Pa. & Congs. and the latter the only single one not chosen by the people themselves. What has been the consequence? The people have been constantly averse to giving that Body further powers—

17

JAMES WILSON, FEDERAL CONVENTION
20 June 1787
Farrand 1:343–44

Mr. Wilson, urged the necessity of two branches; observed that if a proper model was not to be found in other Confederacies it was not to be wondered at. The number of them was small & the duration of some at least short. The Amphyctionic & Achaean were formed in the infancy of political Science; and appear by their History & fate, to have contained radical defects, The Swiss & Belgic Confederacies were held together not by any vital principle of energy but by the incumbent pressure of formidable neighbouring nations: The German owed its continuance to the influence of the H. of Austria. He appealed to our own experience for the defects of our Confederacy. He had been 6 years in the 12 since the commencement of the Revolution, a member of Congress and had felt all its weaknesses. He appealed to the recollection of others

whether on many important occasions, the public interest had not been obstructed by the small members of the Union. The success of the Revolution was owing to other causes, than the Constitution of Congress. In many instances it went on even agst. the difficulties arising from Congs. themselves— He admitted that the large States did accede as had been stated, to the Confederation in its present form. But it was the effect of necessity not of choice. There are other instances of their yielding from the same motive to the unreasonable measures of the small States. The situation of things is now a little altered. He insisted that a jealousy would exist between the State Legislatures & the General Legislature: observing that the members of the former would have views & feelings very distinct in this respect from their constituents. A private citizen of a State is indifferent whether power be exercised by the Genl. or State Legislatures, provided it be exercised most for his happiness. His representative has an interest in its being exercised by the body to which he belongs. He will therefore view the National Legisl: with the eye of a jealous rival. He observed that the addresses of Congs. to the people at large, had always been better received & produced greater effect, than those made to the Legislatures.

18

RECORDS OF THE FEDERAL CONVENTION

[1:444; Madison, 28 June]

Mr. L. Martin resumed his discourse, contending that the Genl. Govt. ought to be formed for the States, not for individuals: that if the States were to have votes in proportion to their numbers of people, it would be the same thing whether their representatives were chosen by the Legislatures or the people; the smaller States would be equally enslaved; that if the large States have the same interest with the smaller as was urged, there could be no danger in giving them an equal vote; they would not injure themselves, and they could not injure the large ones on that supposition without injuring themselves and if the interests were not the same the inequality of suffrage wd— be dangerous to the smaller States.: that it will be in vain to propose any plan offensive to the rulers of the States, whose influence over the people will certainly prevent their adopting it: that the large States were weak at present in proportion to their extent: & could only be made formidable to the small ones, by the weight of their votes; that in case a dissolution of the Union should take place, the small States would have nothing to fear from their power; that if in such a case the three great States should league themselves together, the other ten could do so too: & that he had rather see partial Confederacies take place, than the plan on the table. This was the substance of the residue of his discourse which was delivered with much diffuseness & considerable vehemence.

. . . . .

Mr. Williamson. thought that if any political truth could be grounded on mathematical demonstration, it was that if the states were equally sovereign now, and parted with equal proportions of sovereignty, that they would remain equally sovereign. He could not comprehend how the smaller States would be injured in the case, and wished some gentleman would vouchsafe a solution of it. He observed that the small States, if they had a plurality of votes would have an interest in throwing the burdens off their own shoulders on those of the large ones. He begged that the expected addition of new States from the Westward might be kept in view. They would be small States, they would be poor States, they would be unable to pay in proportion to their numbers; their distance from market rendering the produce of their labour less valuable; they would consequently be tempted to combine for the purpose of laying burdens on commerce & consumption which would fall with greatest weight on the old States.

Mr. Madison sd. he was much disposed to concur in any expedient not inconsistent with fundamental principles, that could remove the difficulty concerning the rule of representation. But he could neither be convinced that the rule contended for was just, nor necessary for the safety of the small States agst. the large States. That it was not just, had been conceded by Mr. Breerly & Mr. Patterson themselves. The expedient proposed by them was a new partition of the territory of the U. States. The fallacy of the reasoning drawn from the equality of Sovereign States in the formation of compacts, lay in confounding mere Treaties, in which were specified certain duties to which the parties were to be bound, and certain rules by which their subjects were to be reciprocally governed in their intercourse, with a compact by which an authority was created paramount to the parties, & making laws for the government of them. If France, England & Spain were to enter into a Treaty for the regulation of commerce &c. with the Prince of Monacho & 4 or 5 other of the smallest sovereigns of Europe, they would not hesitate to treat as equals, and to make the regulations perfectly reciprocal. Wd. the case be the same if a Council were to be formed of deputies from each with authority and discretion, to raise money, levy troops, determine the value of coin &c? Would 30 or 40. million of people submit their fortunes into the hands, of a few thousands? If they did it would only prove that they expected more from the terror of their superior force, than they feared from the selfishness of their feeble associates Why are Counties of the same States represented in proportion to their numbers? Is it because the representatives are chosen by the people themselves? so will be the representatives in the Nationl. Legislature. Is it because, the larger have more at stake than the smaller? The case will be the same with the larger & smaller States. Is it because the laws are to operate immediately on their persons & properties? The same is the case in some degree as the articles of confederation stand; the same will be the case in a far greater degree under the plan proposed to be substituted. In the cases of captures, of piracies, and of offenses in a federal army, the property & persons of individuals depend on the laws of Congs. By the plan proposed a compleat power of taxation, the high-

est prerogative of supremacy is proposed to be vested in the National Govt. Many other powers are added which assimilate it to the Govt. of individual States. The negative on the State laws proposed, will make it an essential branch of the State Legislatures & of course will require that it should be exercised by a body established on like principles with the other branches of those Legislatures.— That it is not necessary to secure the small States agst. the large ones he conceived to be equally obvious: Was a combination of the large ones dreaded? this must arise either from some interest common to Va. Masts. & Pa. & distinguishing them from the other States or from the mere circumstance of similarity of size. Did any such common interest exist? In point of situation they could not have been more effectually separated from each other by the most jealous citizen of the most jealous State. In point of manners, Religion and the other circumstances, which sometimes beget affection between different communities, they were not more assimilated than the other States.—In point of the staple productions they were as dissimilar as any three other States in the Union.

The Staple of Masts. was *fish*, of Pa. *flower*, of Va. *Tobo.* Was a Combination to be apprehended from the mere circumstance of equality of size? Experience suggested no such danger. The journals of Congs. did not present any peculiar association of these States in the votes recorded. It had never been seen that different Counties in the same State, conformable in extent, but disagreeing in other circumstances, betrayed a propensity to such combinations. Experience rather taught a contrary lesson. Among individuals of superior eminence & weight in society, rivalships were much more frequent than coalitions. Among independent nations preeminent over their neighbours, the same remark was verified. Carthage & Rome tore one another to pieces instead of uniting their forces to devour the weaker nations of the Earth. The Houses of Austria & France were hostile as long as they remained the greatest powers of Europe. England & France have succeeded to the pre-eminence & to the enmity. To this principle we owe perhaps our liberty. A coalition between those powers would have been fatal to us. Among the principal members of antient & modern confederacies, we find the same effect from the same cause. The contintions, not the coalitions of Sparta, Athens & Thebes, proved fatal to the smaller members of the Amphyctionic Confederacy. The contentions, not the combinations of Prussia & Austria, have distracted & oppressed the Germanic empire. Were the large States formidable *singly* to their smaller neighbours? On this supposition the latter ought to wish for such a general Govt. as will operate with equal energy on the former as on themselves. The more lax the band, the more liberty the larger will have to avail themselves of their superior force. Here again Experience was an instructive monitor. What is ye situation of the weak compared with the strong in those stages of civilization in which the violence of individuals is least controuled by an efficient Government? The Heroic period of Antient Greece the feudal licentiousness of the middle ages of Europe, the existing condition of the American Savages, answer this question. What is the situation of the minor sovereigns in the great society of independent nations, in which the more powerful are under no controul but the nominal authority of the law of Nations? Is not the danger to the former exactly in proportion to their weakness. But there are cases still more in point. What was the condition of the weaker members of the Amphyctionic Confederacy. Plutarch (life of Themistocles) will inform us that it happened but too often that the strongest cities corrupted & awed the weaker, and that Judgment went in favor of the more powerful party. What is the condition of the lesser States in the German Confederacy? We all know that they are exceedingly trampled upon and that they owe their safety as far as they enjoy it, partly to their enlisting themselves, under the rival banners of the preeminent members, partly to alliances with neighbouring Princes which the Constitution of the Empire does not prohibit. What is the state of things in the lax system of the Dutch Confederacy? Holland contains about ½ the people, supplies about ½ of the money, and by her influence, silently & indirectly governs the whole Republic. In a word; the two extremes before us are a perfect separation & a perfect incorporation, of the 13 States. In the first case they would be independent nations subject to no law, but the law of nations. In the last, they would be mere counties of one entire republic, subject to one common law. In the first case the smaller states would have every thing to fear from the larger. In the last they would have nothing to fear. The true policy of the small States therefore lies in promoting those principles & that form of Govt. which will most approximate the States to the condition of Counties. Another consideration may be added. If the Genl. Govt. be feeble, the large States distrusting its continuance, and foreseeing that their importance & security may depend on their own size & strength, will never submit to a partition. Give to the Genl. Govt. sufficient energy & permanency, & you remove the objection. Gradual partitions of the large, & junctions of the small States will be facilitated, and time may effect that equalization, which is wished for by the small States, now, but can never be accomplished at once.

Mr. Wilson. The leading argument of those who contend for equality of votes among the States is that the States as such being equal, and being represented not as districts of individuals, but in their political & corporate capacities, are entitled to an equality of suffrage. According to this mode of reasoning the representation of the burroughs in Engld which has been allowed on all hands to be the rotten part of the Constitution, is perfectly right & proper. They are like the States represented in their corporate capacity like the States therefore they are entitled to equal voices, old Sarum to as many as London. And instead of the injury supposed hitherto to be done to London, the true ground of complaint lies with old Sarum; for London instead of two which is her proper share, sends four representatives to Parliament.

Mr. Sherman. The question is not what rights naturally belong to men; but how they may be most equally & effectually guarded in Society. And if some give up more than others in order to attain this end, there can be no room for complaint. To do otherwise, to require an equal

concession from all, if it would create danger to the rights of some, would be sacrificing the end to the means. The rich man who enters into Society along with the poor man, gives up more than the poor man. yet with an equal vote he is equally safe. Were he to have more votes than the poor man in proportion to his superior stake, the rights of the poor man would immediately cease to be secure. This consideration prevailed when the articles of confederation were formed.

[1:461; Madison, 29 June]

Doctr. Johnson. The controversy must be endless whilst Gentlemen differ in the grounds of their arguments; Those on one side considering the States as districts of people composing one political Society; those on the other considering them as so many political societies. The fact is that the States do exist as political Societies, and a Govt. is to be formed for them in their political capacity, as well as for the individuals composing them. Does it not seem to follow, that if the States as such are to exist they must be armed with some power of self-defence. This is the idea of (Col. Mason) who appears to have looked to the bottom of this matter. Besides the Aristocratic and other interests, which ought to have the means of defending themselves, the States have their interests as such, and are equally entitled to likes means. On the whole he thought that as in some respects the States are to be considered in their political capacity, and in others as districts of individual citizens, the two ideas embraced on different sides, instead of being opposed to each other, ought to be combined; that in *one* branch the *people*, ought to be represented; in the *other*, the *States*.

Mr. Ghorum. The States as now confederated have no doubt a right to refuse to be consolidated, or to be formed into any new system. But he wished the small States which seemed most ready to object, to consider which are to give up most, they or the larger ones. He conceived that a rupture of the Union wd. be an event unhappy for all, but surely the large States would be least unable to take care of themselves, and to make connections with one another. The weak therefore were most interested in establishing some general system for maintaining order. If among individuals, composed partly of weak, and partly of strong, the former most need the protection of law & Government, the case is exactly the same with weak & powerful States. What would be the situation of Delaware (for these things he found must be spoken out, & it might as well be done first as last) what wd. be the situation of Delaware in case of a separation of the States? Would she not lie at the mercy of Pennsylvania? would not her true interest lie in being consolidated with her, and ought she not now to wish for such a union with Pa. under one Govt. as will put it out of the power of Pena. to oppress her? Nothing can be more ideal than the danger apprehended by the States, from their being formed into one one nation. Massts. was originally three colonies, viz old Massts.—Plymouth—& the province of Mayne. These apprehensions existed then. An incorporation took place; all parties were safe & satisfied; and every distinction is now forgotten. The case was similar with Connecticut & Newhaven. The dread of Union was reciprocal; the consequence of it equally salutary and satisfactory. In like manner N. Jersey has been made one society out of two parts. Should a separation of the States take place, the fate of N. Jersey wd. be worst of all. She has no foreign commerce & can have but little. Pa. & N. York will continue to levy taxes on her consumption. If she consults her interest she wd. beg of all things to be annihilated. The apprehensions of the small States ought to be appeased by another reflection. Massts. will be divided. The province of Maine is already considered as approaching the term of its annexation to it; and Pa. will probably not increase, considering the present state of her population, & other events that may happen. On the whole he considered a Union of the States as necessary to their happiness, & a firm Genl. Govt. as necessary to their Union. He shd. consider it as his duty if his colleagues viewed the matter in the same light he did to stay here as long as any other State would remain with them, in order to agree on some plan that could with propriety be recommended to the people.

Mr. Elseworth, did not despair. He still trusted that some good plan of Govt. wd. be divised & adopted.

Mr. Read. He shd. have no objection to the system if it were truly national, but it has too much of a federal mixture in it. The little States he thought had not much to fear. He suspected that the large States felt their want of energy, & wished for a genl. Govt. to supply the defect. Massts. was evidently labouring under her weakness and he believed Delaware wd. not be in much danger if in her neighbourhood. Delaware had enjoyed tranquillity & he flattered himself wd. continue to do so. He was not however so selfish as not to wish for a good Genl. Govt. In order to obtain one the whole States must be incorporated. If the States remain, the representatives of the large ones will stick together, and carry every thing before them. The Executive also will be chosen under the influence of this partiality, and will betray it in his administration. These jealousies are inseparable from the scheme of leaving the States in Existence. They must be done away. The ungranted lands also which have been assumed by particular States must also be given up. He repeated his approbation of the plan of Mr. Hamilton, & wished it to be substituted in place of that on the table.

Mr. Madison agreed with Docr. Johnson, that the mixed nature of the Govt. ought to be kept in view; but thought too much stress was laid on the rank of the States as political societies. There was a gradation, he observed from the smallest corporation, with the most limited powers, to the largest empire with the most perfect sovereignty. He pointed out the limitations on the sovereignty of the States. as now confederated; their laws in relation to the paramount law of the Confederacy were analogous to that of bye laws to the supreme law, within a State. Under the proposed Govt. the powers of the States will be much farther reduced. According to the views of every member, the Genl. Govt. will have powers far beyond those exercised by the British Parliament when the States were part of the British Empire. It will in particular have the power, without the consent of the State Legislatures, to levy money directly on the people themselves; and therefore

not to divest such *unequal* portions of the people as composed the several States, of an *equal* voice, would subject the system to the reproaches & evils which have resulted from the vicious representation in G. B.

He entreated the gentlemen representing the small States to renounce a principle wch. was confessedly unjust, which cd. never be admitted, & if admitted must infuse mortality into a Constitution which we wished to last forever. He prayed them to ponder well the consequences of suffering the Confederacy to go to pieces. It had been sd. that the want of energy in the large states wd. be a security to the small. It was forgotten that this want of energy proceded from the supposed security of the States agst. all external danger. Let each State depend on itself for its security, & let apprehensions arise of danger from distant powers or from neighbouring States, & the languishing condition of all the States, large as well as small, wd. soon be transformed into vigorous & high toned Govts. His great fear was that their Govts. wd. then have too much energy, that these might not only be formidable in the large to the small States, but fatal to the internal liberty of all. The same causes which have rendered the old world the Theatre of incesssant wars, & have banished liberty from the face of it, wd. soon produce the same effects here. The weakness & jealousy of the small States wd. quickly introduce some regular military force agst. sudden danger from their powerful neighbours. The example wd. be followed by others, and wd. soon become universal. In time of actual war, great discretionary powers are constantly given to the Executive Magistrate. Constant apprehension of War, has the same tendency to render the head too large for the body. A standing military force, with an overgrown Executive will not long be safe companions to liberty. The means of defence agst. foreign danger, have been always the instruments of tyranny at home. Among the Romans it was a standing maxim to excite a war, whenever a revolt was apprehended. Throughout all Europe, the armies kept up under the pretext of defending, have enslaved the people. It is perhaps questionable, whether the best concerted system of absolute power in Europe cd. maintain itself, in a situation, where no alarms of external danger cd. tame the people to the domestic yoke. The insular situation of G. Britain was the principal cause of her being an exception to the general fate of Europe. It has rendered less defence necessary, and admitted a kind of defence wch. cd. not be used for the purpose of oppression.—These consequences he conceived ought to be apprehended whether the States should run into a total separation from each other, or shd. enter into partial confederacies. Either event wd. be truly deplorable; & those who might be accessary to either, could never be forgiven by their Country, nor by themselves.

Mr. Hamilton observed that individuals forming political Societies modify their rights differently, with regard to suffrage. Examples of it are found in all the States. In all of them some individuals are deprived of the right altogether, not having the requisite qualification of property. In some of the States the right of suffrage is allowed in some cases and refused in others. To vote for a member in one branch, a certain quantum of property, to vote for a member in another branch of the Legislature, a higher quantum of property is required. In like manner States may modify their right of suffrage differently, the larger exercising a larger, the smaller a smaller share of it. But as States are a collection of individual men which ought we to respect most, the rights of the people composing them, or of the artificial beings resulting from the composition. Nothing could be more preposterous or absurd than to sacrifice the former to the latter. It has been sd. that if the smaller States renounce their *equality*, they renounce at the same time their *liberty*. The truth is it is a contest for power, not for liberty. Will the men composing the small States be less free than those composing the larger. The State of Delaware having 40,000 souls will *lose power*, if she has ¹⁄₁₀ only of the votes allowed to Pa. having 400,000: but will the people of Del: *be less free*, if each citizen has an equal vote with each citizen of Pa. He admitted that common residence within the same State would produce a certain degree of attachment; and that this principle might have a certain influence in public affairs. He thought however that this might by some precautions be in a great measure excluded: and that no material inconvenience could result from it, as there could not be any ground for combination among the States whose influence was most dreaded. The only considerable distinction of interests, lay between the carrying & non-carrying States, which divide instead of uniting the largest States. No considerable inconvenience had been found from the division of the State of N. York into different districts, of different sizes.

Some of the consequences of a dissolution of the Union, and the establishment of partial confederacies, had been pointed out. He would add another of a most serious nature. Alliances will immediately be formed with different rival & hostile nations of Europes, who will foment disturbances among ourselves, and make us parties to all their own quarrels. Foreign nations having American dominions are & must be jealous of us. Their representatives betray the utmost anxiety for our fate, & for the result of this meeting, which must have an essential influence on it.—It had been said that respectability in the eyes of foreign Nations was not the object at which we aimed; that the proper object of republican Government was domestic tranquillity & happiness. This was an ideal distinction. No Governmt. could give us tranquillity & happiness at home, which did not possess sufficient stability and strength to make us respectable abroad. This was the critical moment for forming such a government. We should run every risk in trusting to future amendments. As yet we retain the habits of union. We are weak & sensible of our weakness. Henceforward the motives will become feebler, and the difficulties greater. It is a miracle that we were now here exercising our tranquil & free deliberations on the subject. It would be madness to trust to future miracles. A thousand causes must obstruct a reproduction of them.

Mr. Peirce considered the equality of votes under the Confederation as the great source of the public difficulties. The members of Congs. were advocates for local advantages. State distinctions must be sacrificed as far as the general good required: but without destroying the States.

Tho' from a small State he felt himself a Citizen of the U.S.

Mr. Gerry, urged that we never were independent States, were not such now, & never could be even on the principles of the Confederation. The States & the advocates for them were intoxicated with the idea of their *sovereignty*. He was a member of Congress at the time the federal articles were formed. The injustice of allowing each State an equal vote was long insisted on. He voted for it, but it was agst. his Judgment, and under the pressure of public danger, and the obstinacy of the lesser States. The present confederation he considered as dissolving. The fate of the Union will be decided by the Convention. If they do not agree on something, few delegates will probably be appointed to Congs. If they do Congs. will probably be kept up till the new System should be adopted—He lamented that instead of coming here like a band of brothers, belonging to the same family, we seemed to have brought with us the spirit of political negociators.

Mr. L. Martin. remarked that the language of the States being *Sovereign & independent,* was once familiar & understood; though it seemed now so strange & obscure. He read those passages in the articles of Confederation, which describe them in that language.

. . . . .

On the motion to agree to the clause as reported. "that the rule of suffrage in the 1st. branch ought not to be according to that established by the Articles of Confederation. Mass. ay. Cont. no N. Y. no. N. J. no. Pa. ay. Del. no. Md. divd. Va. ay. N. C. ay. S. C. ay. Geo. ay. [Ayes—6; noes—4; divided—1.]

Docr. Johnson & Mr. Elseworth moved to postpone the residue of the clause, and take up—ye 8—Resol: On question

Mass. no. Cont. ay. N. Y. ay. N. J. ay. Pa. ay. Del. no. Md. ay. Va. ay. N. C. ay. S. C. ay. Geo. ay. [Ayes—9; noes—2.]

Mr. Elseworth moved that the rule of suffrage in the 2d. branch be the same with that established by the articles of confederation". He was not sorry on the whole he said that the vote just passed, had determined against this rule in the first branch. He hoped it would become a ground of compromise with regard to the 2d. branch. We were partly national; partly federal. The proportional representation in the first branch was conformable to the national principle & would secure the large States agst. the small. An equality of voices was conformable to the federal principle and was necessary to secure the Small States agst. the large. He trusted that on this middle ground a compromise would take place. He did not see that it could on any other. And if no compromise should take place, our meeting would not only be in vain but worse than in vain. To the Eastward he was sure Massts. was the only State that would listen to a proposition for excluding the States as equal political Societies, from an equal voice in both branches. The others would risk every consequence rather than part with so dear a right. An attempt to deprive them of it, was at once cutting the body of America in two, and as he supposed would be the case, somewhere about this part of it. The large States he conceived would notwithstanding the equality of votes, have an influence that would maintain their superiority. Holland, as had been admitted (by Mr. Madison) had, notwithstanding a like equality in the Dutch Confederacy, a prevailing influence in the public measures. The power of self-defence was essential to the small States. Nature had given it to the smallest insect of the creation. He could never admit that there was no danger of combinations among the large States. They will like individuals find out and avail themselves of the advantage to be gained by it. It was true the danger would be greater, if they were contiguous and had a more immediate common interest. A defensive combination of the small States was rendered more difficult by their greater number. He would mention another consideration of great weight. The existing confederation was founded on the equality of the States in the article of suffrage: was it meant to pay no regard to this antecedent plighted faith. Let a strong Executive, a Judiciary & Legislative power be created; but Let not too much be attempted; by which all may be lost. He was not in general a half-way man, yet he preferred doing half the good we could, rather than do nothing at all. The other half may be added, when the necessity shall be more fully experienced.

19

ALEXANDER HAMILTON, FEDERALIST, NO. 22,
138–41
14 Dec. 1787

(See ch. 5, no. 23)

20

FEDERAL FARMER, NO. 11
10 Jan. 1788
Storing 2.8.145–46

(See ch. 11, no. 12)

21

REPUBLICUS
16 Feb. 1788
Storing 5.13.7

It has been disputed whether one house, or rather power of legislature be more eligible, or rather to be chosen than two. I shall hazard a few random thoughts on that subject. And first, if an institution answers all the ends designed by the institution, as well as any other institution, or plan could have done, or can do, there remain no possibility of its doing more; it is therefore perfect, if anything is added it becomes a redundancy, consequently an imperfection. I hope twill not be denied, that a single legislative body, is capable of making laws, the perfection of those laws depend on the wisdom, virtue, and integrity of the legislature, but does it appear, that more wisdom, virtue, and integrity, will, or can possibly be found in two houses than in one, provided they consist of the same number, but more particularly of the same identical person? No man will affirm this. But it may be said that a second house or senate, being generally fewer in number, do by their separation acquire an influence which would have been lost, had the whole been incorporated in one house. I answer, perhaps it might not have been lost; it would no doubt sometimes so happen, that they, in conjunction with the minority in the other house would be able to set aside some bills, which for want of their assistance there, have passed, this would have been a shorter, and easier way; and attended besides, with much less expence of time and money; and excepting in some such instances, all such influence ought to be lost; for in no instance ought the minority to govern the majority. Again, it is more simple: and it is a well known maxim that the simpler a machine is, it is the more perfect; the reason on which it is grounded is obvious: viz. because it is the less liable to disorder, the disorder more easily discovered, and when discovered, more easily repaired and in no instance is this maxim more applicable than in the great machine of government. But say they there ought to be two houses because there are two separate interests. I answer by denying that any community can possibly have any but one common public interest, that is, the greatest good of the whole and of every individual as a part of that whole: but if it be private interest that is meant, I confess that there are not only two, but twenty and it may be more private interests in every government, and the same argument would prove that there ought to be twenty or indeed five hundred houses of legislature in each government: and by proving too much falls to the ground. But the grand argument of all, is that by being separate they have a power of checking some bills which would otherwise pass into laws and might be detrimental to society. Had not this argument been produced on the other side, I should certainly have produced it in favour of one house: however I ask is a minority in one house, properly entitled to over rule a majority in the other? Are they not as likely to check a good bill as a bad one? and has it not in fact often happened? Is it not as probable that the second house lay some[?] of their checks on a good bill which perhaps they had little considered as that the first, should pass a bad one, where it had originated and perhaps[?] thoroughly considered? But let us turn the argument over and take a view of the other side of it. The inconsistencies that attend the idea of two houses are innumerable. Take one, supposing them both our representatives (tho it will be hard to prove them so) it makes their constituents to say in many instances by their representatives in one house, "this shall be a law," by their representatives in the other with respect to the same bill; "This shall not be a law." It impowers one body of men to enact statutes; and another to forbid their being carried into execution. It resembles a man putting forth his right hand to do some important business and then stretching forth his left hand to prevent it; but supposing them not our representatives at all, they have no business there, and all their mighty power of checking, is a mere farce.

22

JAMES MADISON, FEDERALIST, NO. 62, 416–19
27 Feb. 1788

III. The equality of representation in the senate is another point, which, being evidently the result of compromise between the opposite pretensions of the large and the small states, does not call for much discussion. If indeed it be right that among a people thoroughly incorporated into one nation, every district ought to have a *proportional* share in the government; and that among independent and sovereign states bound together by a simple league, the parties however unequal in size, ought to have an *equal* share in the common councils, it does not appear to be without some reason, that in a compound republic partaking both of the national and federal character, the government ought to be founded on a mixture of the principles of proportional and equal representation. But it is superfluous to try by the standards of theory, a part of the constitution which is allowed on all hands to be the result not of theory, but "of a spirit of amity, and that mutual deference and concession which the peculiarity of our political situation rendered indispensable." A common government with powers equal to its objects, is called for by the voice, and still more loudly by the political situation of America. A government founded on principles more consonant to the wishes of the larger states, is not likely to be obtained from the smaller states. The only option then for the former lies between the proposed government and a government still more objectionable. Under this alternative the advice of prudence must be, to embrace the lesser evil; and instead of indulging a fruitless anticipation of the possible mischiefs which may ensue, to contemplate rather the advantageous consequences which may qualify the sacrifice.

In this spirit it may be remarked, that the equal vote allowed to each state, is at once a constitutional recognition of the portion of sovereignty remaining in the individual states, and an instrument for preserving that residuary sovereignty. So far the quality ought to be no less acceptable to the large than to the small states; since they are not less solicitous to guard by every possible expedient against an improper consolidation of the states into one simple republic.

Another advantage accruing from this ingredient in the constitution of the senate, is the additional impediment it must prove against improper acts of legislation. No law or resolution can now be passed without the concurrence first of a majority of the people, and then of a majority of the states. It must be acknowledged that this complicated check on legislation may in some instances be injurious as well as beneficial; and that the peculiar defence which it involves in favour of the smaller states would be more rational, if any interests common to them, and distinct from those of the other states, would otherwise be exposed to peculiar danger. But as the larger states will always be able by their power over the supplies to defeat unreasonable exertions of this prerogative of the lesser states; and as the facility and excess of law-making seem to be the diseases to which our governments are most liable, it is not impossible that this part of the constitution may be more convenient in practice than it appears to many in contemplation.

IV. The number of senators and the duration of their appointment come next to be considered. In order to form an accurate judgment on both these points, it will be proper to enquire into the purposes which are to be answered by a senate; and in order to ascertain these it will be necessary to review the inconveniencies which a republic must suffer from the want of such an institution.

First. It is a misfortune incident to republican government, though in a less degree than to other governments, that those who administer it, may forget their obligations to their constituents, and prove unfaithful to their important trust. In this point of view, a senate, as a second branch of the legislative assembly, distinct from, and dividing the power with, a first, must be in all cases a salutary check on the government. It doubles the security to the people, by requiring the concurrence of two distinct bodies in schemes of usurpation or perfidy, where the ambition or corruption of one, would otherwise be sufficient. This is a precaution founded on such clear principles, and now so well understood in the United States, that it would be more than superfluous to enlarge on it. I will barely remark that as the improbability of sinister combinations will be in proportion to the dissimilarity in the genius of the two bodies; it must be politic to distinguish them from each other by every circumstance which will consist with a due harmony in all proper measures, and with the genuine principles of republican government.

Secondly. The necessity of a senate is not less indicated by the propensity of all single and numerous assemblies, to yield to the impulse of sudden and violent passions, and to be seduced by factious leaders, into intemperate and pernicious resolutions. Examples on this subject might be cited without number; and from proceedings within the United States, as well as from the history of other nations. But a position that will not be contradicted need not be proved. All that need be remarked is that a body which is to correct this infirmity ought itself be free from it, and consequently ought to be less numerous. It ought moreover to possess great firmness, and consequently ought to hold its authority by a tenure of considerable duration.

Thirdly. Another defect to be supplied by a senate lies in a want of due acquaintance with the objects and principles of legislation. It is not possible that an assembly of men called for the most part from pursuits of a private nature, continued in appointment for a short time, and led by no permanent motive to devote the intervals of public occupation to a study of the laws, the affairs and the comprehensive interests of their country, should, if left wholly to themselves, escape a variety of important errors in the exercise of their legislative trust. It may be affirmed, on the best grounds, that no small share of the present embarrassments of America is to be charged on the blunders of our governments; and that these have proceeded from the heads rather than the hearts of most of the authors of them. What indeed are all the repealing, explaining and amending laws, which fill and disgrace our voluminous codes, but so many monuments of deficient wisdom; so many impeachments exhibited by each succeeding against each preceding session; so many admonitions to the people of the value of those aids which may be expected from a well constituted senate?

A good government implies two things; first, fidelity to the object of government, which is the happiness of the people; secondly, a knowledge of the means by which that object can be best attained. Some governments are deficient in both these qualities: Most governments are deficient in the first. I scruple not to assert that in the American governments, too little attention has been paid to the last. The federal constitution avoids this error; and what merits particular notice, it provides for the last in a mode which increases the security for the first.

23

PATRICK HENRY, VIRGINIA
RATIFYING CONVENTION
12 June 1788
Storing 5.16.29

The Honorable Gentleman was pleased to say, that the representation of the people was the vital principle of this Government. I will readily agree that it ought to be so.—But I contend that this principle is only nominally, and not substantially to be found there. We contended with the British about representation; they offered us such a representation as Congress now does. They called it a virtual representation. If you look at that paper you will find it so there. Is there but a virtual representation in the upper House? The States are represented *as States*, by two Senators each. This is virtual, not actual. They encounter you with Rhode-Island and Delaware. This is not an actual representation. What does the term representation signify? It means that a certain district—a certain association of men should be represented in the Government for *certain ends*. These ends ought not to be impeded or obstructed in any manner. Here, Sir, this populous State has not an adequate share of legislative influence. The two petty States of Rhode-Island and Delaware, which together are infinitely inferior to this State, in extent and population, have double her weight, and can counteract her interest. I say, that the representation in the Senate, as ap-

plicable to States, is not actual. Representation is not therefore the vital principle of this Government—So far it is wrong.

24

ALEXANDER HAMILTON, NEW YORK
RATIFYING CONVENTION
25 June 1788
Papers 5:81

There are two objects in forming systems of government—Safety for the people, and energy in the administration. When these objects are united, the certain tendency of the system will be to the public welfare. If the latter object be neglected, the people's security will be as certainly sacrificed, as by disregarding the former. Good constitutions are formed upon a comparison of the liberty of the individual with the strength of government: If the tone of either be too high, the other will be weakened too much. It is the happiest possible mode of conciliating these objects, to institute one branch peculiarly endowed with sensibility, another with knowledge and firmness. Through the opposition and mutual controul of these bodies, the government will reach, in its regular operations, the perfect balance between liberty and power. The arguments of the gentlemen chiefly apply to the former branch—the house of representatives. If they will calmly consider the different nature of the two branches, they will see that the reasoning which justly applies to the representative house, will go to destroy the essential qualities of the senate. If the former is calculated perfectly upon the principles of caution, why should you impose the same principle upon the latter, which is designed for a different operation?

25

BENJAMIN FRANKLIN, QUERIES AND REMARKS
RESPECTING ALTERATIONS IN THE
CONSTITUTION OF PENNSYLVANIA
1789
Writings 10:55–60

III. On the Legislative Branch.

"*A plural Legislature is as necessary to good Government as a single Executive. It is not enough that your Legislature should be numerous; it should also be divided. Numbers alone are not a sufficient Barrier against the Impulses of Passion, the Combinations of Interest, the Intrigues of Faction, the Haste of Folly, or the Spirit of Encroachment. One Divison should watch over and controul the other, supply its Wants, correct its Blunders, and cross its Designs, should they [be] made up of the Portions of Sense and Knowledge which each Member brings to it.*"

On this it may be asked, May not the Wisdom brought to the Legislature by each Member be as effectual a Barrier against the Impulses of Passion, &c., when the Members are united in one Body, as when they are divided? If one Part of the Legislature may controul the Operations of the other, may not the Impulses of Passion, the Combinations of Interest, the Intrigues of Faction, the Haste of Folly, or the Spirit of Encroachment in one of those Bodies obstruct the good proposed by the other, and frustrate its Advantages to the Public? Have we not experienced in this Colony, when a Province under the Government of the Proprietors, the Mischiefs of a second Branch existing in the Proprietary Family, countenanced and aided by an Aristocratic Council? How many Delays and what great Expences were occasioned in carrying on the public Business; and what a Train of Mischiefs, even to the preventing of the Defence of the Province during several Years, when distressed by an Indian war, by the iniquitous Demand that the Proprietary Property should be exempt from Taxation! The Wisdom of a few Members in one single Legislative Body, may it not frequently stifle bad Motions in their Infancy, and so prevent their being adopted? whereas, if those wise Men, in case of a double Legislature, should happen to be in that Branch wherein the Motion did not arise, may it not, after being adopted by the other, occasion lengthy Disputes and Contentions between the two Bodies, expensive to the Public, obstructing the public Business, and promoting Factions among the People, many Tempers naturally adhering obstinately to Measures they have once publicly adopted? Have we not seen, in one of our neighbouring States, a bad Measure, adopted by one Branch of the Legislature, for Want of the Assistance of some more intelligent Members who had been packed into the other, occasion many Debates, conducted with much Asperity, which could not be settled but by an expensive general Appeal to the People? And have we not seen, in another neighbouring State, a similar Difference between the two Branches, occasioning long Debates and Contentions, whereby the State was prevented for many Months enjoying the Advantage of having Senators in the Congress of the United States? And has our present Legislative in one Assembly committed any Errors of Importance, which they have not remedied, or may not easily remedy; more easily, probably, than if divided into two Branches? And if the Wisdom brought by the Members to the Assembly is divided into two Branches, may it not be too weak in each to support a good Measure, or obstruct a bad one? The Division of the Legislature into two or three Branches in England, was it the Product of Wisdom, or the Effect of Necessity, arising from the preëxisting Prevalence of an odious Feudal System? which Government, notwithstanding this Division is now become in Fact an absolute Monarchy; since the King, by bribing the Representatives with the People's Money, carries, by his Ministers, all the Measures that please him; which is equivalent to governing without a Parliament, and renders the Machine of Government much more complex and expensive, and, from its being more complex, more easily put out of Order. Has not the famous political Fable of

the Snake, with two Heads and one Body, some useful Instruction contained in it? She was going to a Brook to drink, and in her Way was to pass thro' a Hedge, a Twig of which opposed her direct Course; one Head chose to go on the right side of the Twig, the other on the left; so that time was spent in the Contest, and, before the Decision was completed, the poor Snake died with thirst.

"Hence it is that the two Branches should be elected by Persons differently qualified; and in short, that, as far as possible, they should be made to represent different Interests. Under this Reasoning I would establish a Legislature of two Houses. The Upper should represent the Property; the Lower the Population of the State. The upper should be chosen by Freemen possessing in Lands and Houses one thousand Pounds; the Lower by all such as had resided four Years in the Country, and paid Taxes. The first should be chosen for four, the last for two years. They should in Authority be coequal."

Several Questions may arise upon this Proposition. 1st. What is the Proportion of Freemen possessing Lands and Houses of one thousand Pounds' value, compared to that of Freemen whose Possessions are inferior? Are they as one to ten? Are they even as one to twenty? I should doubt whether they are as one to fifty. If this minority is to chuse a Body expressly to controul that which is to be chosen by the great Majority of the Freemen, what have this great Majority done to forfeit so great a Portion of their Right in Elections? Why is this Power of Controul, contrary to the spirit of all Democracies, to be vested in a Minority, instead of a Majority? Then is it intended, or is it not, that the Rich should have a Vote in the Choice of Members for the lower House, while those of inferior Property are deprived of the Right of voting for Members of the upper House? And why should the upper House, chosen by a Minority, have equal Power with the lower chosen by a Majority? Is it supposed that Wisdom is the necessary concomitant of Riches, and that one Man worth a thousand Pounds must have as much Wisdom as Twenty who have each only 999; and why is Property to be represented at all? Suppose one of our Indian Nations should now agree to form a civil Society; each Individual would bring into the Stock of the Society little more Property than his Gun and his Blanket, for at present he has no other. We know, that, when one of them has attempted to keep a few Swine, he has not been able to maintain a Property in them, his neighbours thinking they have a Right to kill and eat them whenever they want Provision, it being one of their Maxims that hunting is free for all; the accumulation therefore of Property in such a Society, and its Security to Individuals in every Society, must be an Effect of the Protection afforded to it by the joint Strength of the Society, in the Execution of its Laws. Private Property therefore is a Creature of Society, and is subject to the Calls of that Society, whenever its Necessities shall require it, even to its last Farthing; its Contributions therefore to the public Exigencies are not to be considered as conferring a Benefit on the Publick, entitling the Contributors to the Distinctions of Honour and Power, but as the Return of an Obligation previously received, or the Payment of a just Debt. The Combinations of Civil Society are not like those of a

Set of Merchants, who club their Property in different Proportions for Building and Freighting a Ship, and may therefore have some Right to vote in the Disposition of the Voyage in a greater or less Degree according to their respective Contributions; but the important ends of Civil Society, and the personal Securities of Life and Liberty, these remain the same in every Member of the society; and the poorest continues to have an equal Claim to them with the most opulent, whatever Difference Time, Chance, or Industry may occasion in their Circumstances. On these Considerations, I am sorry to see the Signs this Paper I have been considering affords, of a Disposition among some of our People to commence an Aristocracy, by giving the Rich a predominancy in Government, a Choice peculiar to themselves in one half the Legislature to be proudly called the UPPER House, and the other Branch, chosen by the Majority of the People, degraded by the Denomination of the LOWER; and giving to this upper House a Permanency of four Years, and but two to the lower. I hope, therefore, that our Representatives in the Convention will not hastily go into these Innovations, but take the Advice of the Prophet, *"Stand in the old ways, view the ancient Paths, consider them well, and be not among those that are given to Change."*

26

JAMES WILSON, OF GOVERNMENT,
THE LEGISLATIVE DEPARTMENT,
LECTURES ON LAW
1791
Works 1:290–92, 414–15

The first remark, which I shall make on the structure of the legislative power, is, that it ought to be *divided*. In support of this position, which is, indeed, one of the most important in both the theory and the practice of government, many arguments may be advanced. Let me introduce one, by the declaration of an admired judge, whose manly candour must charm every generous mind. "It is the glory and happiness of our excellent constitution, that, to prevent any injustice, no man is concluded by the first judgment; but that, if he apprehends himself to be aggrieved, he has another court, to which he may resort for relief. For my part, I can say, that it is a consideration of great comfort to me, that, if I do err, my judgment is not conclusive to the party; but my mistake may be rectified, and so no injustice be done." Is less skill required—should less caution be observed—in making laws, than in explaining them? Are mistakes less likely to happen—are they less dangerous—is it less necessary to prevent or rectify them, in the former case, than in the latter? Which is most necessary? to preserve the streams, or to preserve the fountain from becoming turbid?

But the danger arising from mistakes and inaccuracies is not the only nor the greatest one, to be apprehended from a single body possessed of legislative power. It is impossible to restrain it in its operations. No other power in government can arrest the proceedings of that which makes the laws. Let us suppose, that this single body, in a lucky moment, should pass a law to restrain itself: in the next moment, an unlucky one, it might repeal the restraining law. Any mounds, which it might raise to confine itself, would still be within the sphere of its own motion; and whatever force should impel it, would necessarily impel those mounds along with it. To stop and to check, as well as to produce motion in this political globe, we must possess—what Archimedes wanted—another globe to stand upon.

A single legislature is calculated to unite in it all the pernicious qualities of the different extremes of bad government. It produces general weakness, inactivity, and confusion; and these are intermixed with sudden and violent fits of despotism, injustice, and cruelty.

But I will take the subject a little deeper: it is of the utmost consequence that it be fully discussed. In private life, how often and how fatally are we seduced, by our passions and by our prejudices, from those paths, which would lead us to our true interests? But are passions and prejudices less frequently to be found in publick bodies, than in individuals? Are they less powerful? Do they not become inflamed by mutual imitation and example? Will they not, if unrestrained, produce the most mischievous effects? Ye, who are versed in the science of human nature—ye, who have viewed it in the faithful mirrour of history—tell us, for you know, what answer should be given to these questions. Cannot you point out instances, in which the people have become the miserable victims of passions, operating upon their government without restraint? Cannot you point out other instances, in which the violence of one part of the government has been happily controlled by the constitutional interposition of another part?

There is not in the whole science of politicks a more solid or a more important maxim than this—that of all governments, those are the best, which, by the natural effect of their constitutions, are frequently renewed or drawn back to their first principles. When a single legislature is determined to depart from the principles of the constitution—and its incontrollable power may prompt the determination—there is no constitutional authority to arrest its progress. It may proceed, by long and hasty strides, in violating the constitution, till nothing but a revolution can stop its career. Far different will the case be, when the legislature consists of two branches. If one of them should depart, or attempt to depart from the principles of the constitution; it will be drawn back by the other. The very apprehension of the event will prevent the departure or the attempt.

In all the most celebrated governments both of ancient and of modern times, we find the legislatures composed of distinct bodies. Such was that formed at Athens by Solon. Such was that instituted at Sparta by Lycurgus. Such was that, which so long flourished at Rome. In our sister states, their legislatures consist of distinct bodies of men. Similar, upon this subject, is the constitution of the United States. And we can now happily say, that Pennsylvania no longer exhibits an instance to the contrary—that she no longer holds out to view a beacon to be avoided, instead of an example deserving imitation.

. . . . .

Between the senate of the United States, and that of Pennsylvania, there is one remarkable point of difference, of which it will be proper, in this place, to take particular notice. According to the constitution of the United States, two senators are chosen by the legislature of each state: while the members of the house of representatives are chosen by the people. According to the constitution of Pennsylvania, the senators are chosen by the citizens of the state, at the same time, in the same manner, and at the same place where they shall vote for representatives.

To choose the senators by the same persons, by whom the members of the house of representatives are chosen, is, we are told, to lose the material distinction, and, consequently, all the benefits which would result from the material distinction, between the two branches of the legislature.

If this, indeed, should be the necessary consequence of electing both branches by the same persons; the objection, it is confessed, would operate with a force irresistible. But many and strong reasons, we think, may be assigned, why all the advantages, to be expected from two branches of a legislature, may be gained and preserved, though those two branches derive their authority from precisely the same source.

A point of honour will arise between them. The esprit du corps will soon be introduced. The principle, and direction, and aim of this spirit will, we presume, be of the best and purest kind in the two houses. They will be rivals in duty, rivals in fame, rivals for the good graces of their common constituents.

Each house will be cautious, and careful, and circumspect, in those proceedings, which, they know, must undergo the strict and severe criticism of judges, whose inclination will lead them, and whose duty will enjoin them, not to leave a single blemish unnoticed or uncorrected. After all the caution, all the care, and all the circumspection, which can be employed, strict and severe criticism, led by inclination and enjoined by duty, will find something to notice and correct. Hence a double source of information, precision, and sagacity in planning, digesting, composing, comparing, and finishing the laws, both in form and substance. Every bill will, in some one or more steps of its progress, undergo the keenest scrutiny. Its relations, whether near or more remote, to the principles of freedom, jurisprudence, and the constitution will be accurately examined: and its effects upon the laws already existing will be maturely traced. In this manner, rash measures, violent innovations, crude projects, and partial contrivances will be stifled in the attempt to bring them forth. These effects of mutual watchfulness and mutual control between the two houses, will redound to the honour of each, and to the security and advantage of the state.

27

JOSEPH STORY, COMMENTARIES ON THE
CONSTITUTION 2:§§ 547–58
1833

§ 547. The utility of a subdivision of the legislative power into different branches, having a negative upon each other, is, perhaps, at the present time admitted by most persons of sound reflection. But it has not always found general approbation; and is, even now, sometimes disputed by men of speculative ingenuity, and recluse habits. It has been justly observed, that there is scarcely in the whole science of politics a more important maxim, and one, which bears with greater influence upon the practical operations of government. It has been already stated, that Pennsylvania, in her first constitution, adopted the scheme of a single body, as the depository of the legislative power, under the influence, as is understood, of a mind of a very high philosophical character. Georgia, also, is said in her first constituion, (since changed,) to have confided the whole legislative power to a single body. Vermont adopted the same course, giving, however, to the executive council a power of revision, and of proposing amendments, to which she yet adheres. We are also told by a distinguished statesman of great accuracy and learning, that at the first formation of our state constitutions, it was made a question of transcendant importance, and divided the opinions of our most eminent men. Legislation, being merely the expression of the will of the community, was thought to be an operation so simple in its nature, that inexperienced reason could not readily perceive the necessity of committing it to two bodies of men, each having a decisive check upon the action of the other. All the arguments derived from the analogy between the movements of political bodies, and the operations of physical nature; all the impulses of political parsimony; all the prejudices against a second co-ordinate legislative assembly stimulated by the exemplification of it in the British parliament, were against a division of the legislative power.

§ 548. It is also certain, that the notion, that the legislative power ought to be confided to a single body, has been, at various times, adopted by men eminent for their talents and virtues. Milton, Turgot, Franklin, are but a few among those, who have professedly entertained, and discussed the question. Sir James Mackintosh, in a work of a controversial character, written with the zeal and eloquence of youth, advocated the doctrine of a single legislative body. Perhaps his maturer life may have changed this early opinion. At all events, he can, in our day, count few followers. Against his opinion, thus uttered, there is the sad example of France itself, whose first constitution, in 1791, was formed on this basis, and whose proceedings the genius of this great man was employed to vindicate. She stands a monument of the folly and mischiefs of the scheme; and by her subsequent adoption of a division of the legislative power, she has secured to herself (as it is hoped) the permanent blessings of liberty. Against all visionary reasoning of this sort, Mr. Chancellor Kent has, in a few pages of pregnant sense and brevity, condensed a decisive argument. There is danger, however, that it may hereafter be revived; and indeed it is occasionally hinted by gifted minds, as a problem yet worthy of a fuller trial.

§ 549. It may not, therefore, be uninstructive to review some of the principal arguments, by which this division is vindicated. The first and most important ground is, that it forms a great check upon undue, hasty, and oppressive legislation. Public bodies, like private persons, are occasionally under the dominion of strong passions and excitements; impatient, irritable, and impetuous. The habit of acting together produces a strong tendency to what, for want of a better word, may be called the corporation spirit, or what is so happily expressed in a foreign phrase, *l'esprit du corps*. Certain popular leaders often acquire an extraordinary ascendency over the body, by their talents, their eloquence, their intrigues, or their cunning. Measures are often introduced in a hurry, and debated with little care, and examined with less caution. The very restlessness of many minds produces an utter impossibility of debating with much deliberation, when a measure has a plausible aspect, and enjoys a momentary favour. Nor is it infrequent, especially in cases of this sort, to overlook well-founded objections to a measure, not only because the advocates of it have little desire to bring them in review, but because the opponents are often seduced into a credulous silence. A legislative body is not ordinarily apt to mistrust its own powers, and far less the temperate exercise of those powers. As it prescribes its own rules for its own deliberations, it easily relaxes them, whenever any pressure is made for an immediate decision. If it feels no check but its own will, it rarely has the firmness to insist upon holding a question long enough under its own view, to see and mark it in all its bearings and relations on society.

§ 550. But it is not merely inconsiderate and rash legislation, which is to be guarded against, in the ordinary course of things. There is a strong propensity in public bodies to accumulate power in their own hands, to widen the extent of their own influence, and to absorb within their own circle the means, and the motives of patronage. If the whole legislative power is vested in a single body, there can be, practically, no restraint upon the fullest exercise of that power; and of any usurpation, which it may seek to excuse or justify, either from necessity or a superior regard to the public good. It has been often said, that necessity is the plea of tyrants; but it is equally true, that it is the plea of all public bodies invested with power, where no check exists upon its exercise. Mr. Hume has remarked with great sagacity, that men are generally more honest in their private, than in their public capacity; and will go greater lengths to serve a party, than when their own private interest is alone concerned. Honour is a great check upon mankind. But where a considerable body of men act together, this check is in a great measure removed, since a man is sure to be approved of by his own party, for what promotes the common interest; and he soon learns to despise the clamours of adversaries. This is by no means an

opinion peculiar to Mr. Hume. It will be found lying at the foundation of the political reasonings of many of the greatest men in all ages, as the result of a close survey of the passions, and infirmities, of the history, and experience of mankind. With a view, therefore, to preserve the rights and liberties of the people against unjust encroachments, and to secure the equal benefits of a free constitution, it is of vital importance to interpose some check against the undue exercise of the legislative power, which in every government is the predominating, and almost irresistible power.

§ 551. This subject is put in a very strong light by an eminent writer [John Adams], whose mode of reasoning can be best conveyed in his own words. "If," says he, "we should extend our candour so far, as to own, that the majority of mankind are generally under the dominion of benevolence and good intentions; yet it must be confessed, that a vast majority frequently transgress; and what is more decidedly in point, not only a majority, but almost all, confine their benevolence to their families, relations, personal friends, parish, village, city, county, province; and that very few indeed extend it impartially to the whole community. Now, grant but this truth, and the question is decided. If a majority are capable of preferring their own private interests, or that of their families, counties, and party, to that of the nation collectively, some provision must be made in the constitution in favour of justice, to compel all to respect the common right, the public good, the universal law in preference to all private and partial considerations." Again: "Of all possible forms of government, a sovereignty in one assembly, successively chosen by the people, is, perhaps, the best calculated to facilitate the gratification of self-love, and the pursuit of the private interests of a few individuals. A few eminent, conspicuous characters will be continued in their seats in the sovereign assembly from one election to another, whatever changes are made in the seats around them. By superior art, address, and opulence, by more splendid birth, reputations, and connexions, they will be able to intrigue with the people, and their leaders out of doors, until they worm out most of their opposers, and introduce their friends. To this end they will bestow all offices, contracts, privileges in commerce, and other emoluments on the latter, and their connexions, and throw every vexation and disappointment in the way of the former, until they establish such a system of hopes and fears throughout the whole state, as shall enable them to carry a majority in every fresh election of the house. The judges will be appointed by them and their party, and of consequence will be obsequious enough to their inclinations. The whole judicial authority, as well as the executive, will be employed, perverted, and prostituted, to the purposes of electioneering. No justice will be attainable; nor will innocence or virtue be safe in the judicial courts, but for the friends of the prevailing leaders. Legal prosecutions will be instituted, and carried on against opposers to their vexation and ruin. And as they have the public purse at command, as well as the executive and judicial power, the public money will be expended in the same way. No favours will be attainable, but by those, who will court the ruling demagogues of the house, by voting for their friends, and instruments; and pensions, and pecuniary rewards and gratifications, as well as honours, and offices of every kind, voted to friends and partisans, &c. &c. The press, that great barrier and bulwark of the rights of mankind, when it is protected by law, can no longer be free. If the authors, writers, and printers, will not accept of the hire, that will be offered them, they must submit to the ruin, that will be denounced against them. The presses, with much secrecy and concealment, will be made the vehicles of calumny against the minority, and of panegyric, and empirical applauses of the leaders of the majority, and no remedy can possibly be obtained. In one word, the whole system of affairs, and every conceivable motive of hope or fear, will be employed to promote the private interests of a few, and their obsequious majority; and there is no remedy but in arms. Accordingly we find in all the Italian republics, the minority always were driven to arms in despair."

§ 552. Another learned writer [James Wilson] has ventured on the bold declaration, that "a single legislature is calculated to unite in it all the pernicious qualities of the different extremes of bad government. It produces general weakness, inactivity, and confusion; and these are intermixed with sudden and violent fits of despotism, injustice and cruelty."

§ 553. Without conceding, that this language exhibits an unexaggerated picture of the results of the legislative power being vested in a single assembly, there is enough in it to satisfy the minds of considerate men, that there is great danger in such an exclusive deposit of it. Some check ought to be provided, to maintain the real balance intended by the constitution; and this check will be most effectually obtained by a co-ordinate branch of equal authority, and different organization, which shall have the same legislative power, and possess an independent negative upon the doings of the other branch. The value of the check will, indeed, in a great measure depend upon this difference of organization. If the term of office, the qualifications, the mode of election, the persons and interests represented by each branch, are exactly the same, the check will be less powerful, and the guard less perfect, than if some, or all of these ingredients differ, so as to bring into play all the various interests and influences, which belong to a free, honest, and enlightened society.

§ 554. The value, then, of a distribution of the legislative power, between two branches, each possessing a negative upon the other, may be summed up under the following heads. First: It operates directly as a security against hasty, rash, and dangerous legislation; and allows errors and mistakes to be corrected, before they have produced any public mischiefs. It interposes delay between the introduction, and final adoption of a measure; and thus furnishes time for reflection; and for the successive deliberations of different bodies, actuated by different motives, and organized upon different principles.

§ 555. In the next place, it operates indirectly as a preventive to attempts to carry private, personal, or party objects, not connected with the common good. The very circumstance, that there exists another body clothed with equal power, and jealous of its own rights, and indepen-

dent of the influence of the leaders, who favour a particular measure, by whom it must be scanned, and to whom it must be recommended upon its own merits, will have a silent tendency to discourage the efforts to carry it by surprise, or by intrigue, or by corrupt party combinations. It is far less easy to deceive, or corrupt, or persuade two bodies into a course, subversive of the general good, than it is one; especially if the elements, of which they are composed, are essentially different.

§ 556. In the next place, as legislation necessarily acts, or may act, upon the whole community, and involves interests of vast difficulty and complexity, and requires nice adjustments, and comprehensive enactments, it is of the greatest consequence to secure an independent review of it by different minds, acting under different, and sometimes opposite opinions and feelings; so, that it may be as perfect, as human wisdom can devise. An appellate jurisdiction, therefore, that acts, and is acted upon alternatively, in the exercise of an independent revisory authority, must have the means, and can scarcely fail to possess the will, to give it a full and satisfactory review. Every one knows, notwithstanding all the guards interposed to secure due deliberation, how imperfect all human legislation is; how much it embraces of doubtful principle, and of still more doubtful utility; how various, and yet how defective, are its provisions to protect rights, and to redress wrongs. Whatever, therefore, naturally and necessarily awakens doubt, solicits caution, attracts inquiry, or stimulates vigilance and industry, is of value to aid us against precipitancy in framing, or altering laws, as well as against yielding to the suggestions of indolence, the selfish projects of ambition, or the cunning devices of corrupt and hollow demagogues. For this purpose, no better expedient has, as yet, been found, than the creation of an independent branch of censors to revise the legislative enactments of others, and to alter, amend, or reject them at its pleasure, which, in return, its own are to pass through a like ordeal.

§ 557. In the next place, there can scarcely be any other adequate security against encroachments upon the constitutional rights and liberties of the people. Algernon Sidney has said with great force, that the legislative power is always arbitrary, and not to be trusted in the hands of any, who are not bound to obey the laws they make. But it is not less true, that it has a constant tendency to overleap its proper boundaries, from passion, from ambition, from inadvertence, from the prevalence of faction, or from the overwhelming influence of private interests. Under such circumstances, the only effectual barrier against oppression, accidental or intentional, is to separate its operations, to balance interest against interest, ambition against ambition, the combinations and spirit of dominion of one body against the like combinations and spirit of another. And it is obvious, that the more various the elements, which enter into the actual composition of each body, the greater the security will be. Mr. Justice Wilson has truly remarked, that, "when a single legislature is determined to depart from the principles of the constitution, *and its uncontrollable power may prompt the determination,* there is no constitutional authority to check its progress. It may proceed by long and hasty strides in violating the constitution, till nothing but a revolution can check its career. Far different will the case be, when the legislature consists of two branches. If one of them should depart, or attempt to depart, from the principles of the constitution, it will be drawn back by the other. The very apprehension of the event will prevent the departure, or the attempt."

§ 558. Such is an outline of the general reasoning, by which the system of a separation of the legislative power into two branches has been maintained. Experience has shown, that if in all cases it has not been found a complete check to inconsiderate or unconstitutional legislation; yet, that it has, upon many occasions, been found sufficient for the purpose. There is not probably at this moment a single state in the Union, which would consent to unite the two branches into one assembly; though there have not been wanting at all times minds of a high order, which have

been led by enthusiasm, or a love of simplicity, or a devotion to theory, to vindicate such a union with arguments, striking and plausible, if not convincing.

SEE ALSO:

Generally chs. 11, 17

Thomas Jefferson to John Adams, 16 May 1776, Papers 2:18–19

John Adams, Notes on Debates in Congress, 1 Aug. 1776, Diary 2:247–48

An Address of the Convention for Framing a New Constitution of Government for the State of Massachusetts-Bay to Their Constituents, Mar. 1780, Handlin 437

Alexander Contee Hanson, Aristides, Remarks on the Proposed Plan of a Federal Government, 1788, Pamphlets 223–24

Rev. John Leland, Objections to the Federal Constitution, Feb. 1788, Documentary History 4:527

Benjamin Rush to John Adams, 22 Jan. 1789, Letters 1:498–99

13

Representation

Introduction

None of the great constitutional themes is more complex and extensive than that of representation. It necessarily touches on popular consent, republicanism, constitutional limits, federalism, majority rule, minority rights, property, and equality. Furthermore, any investigation of the meaning of representation for the Founders is complicated by the fact that, for all or most, representative government was a foregone conclusion. To recover their reasonings about representation, one would need to consider how they were informed by a long experience with represen-

tative and not so representative institutions at home and in Britain. But beyond that one would need to reconsider the no longer argued case for the alternatives to representative government, alternatives that the Founders rejected outright. A statement of that case, however brief and oversimple, is indispensable to an understanding of their intention.

The Founders were driven, as it were, to representative government because the alternatives in their eyes were practically impossible, politically unacceptable, or both. On the one hand there was the simple direct democracy of an assembled citizenry. Whatever its merits at the level of a hamlet or township, it clearly was out of the question for a state or a large nation. On the other hand there was rule over the people. The representative government that the Americans pronounced good borrowed but a trace from the latter notion, a good deal from the notion of government by the people, but most of all concentrated on avoiding the errors and dangers associated with each. The result was something quite distinctive, truly a modern refinement of popular government.

The Modern Alternative

The modern notion of representation was developed in response to the ancient notion of rule. This distinction is evident in the fact that the heads of nontyrannical states are today called leaders, not rulers. Ruling rests on a claim by a part of a body politic to govern the whole according to that part's distinctive opinion of what is just. Each such opinion implies a comprehensive view of the good of the entire society. Thus each such claim to rule implies the fitness of that part to best serve the greater good of some political whole. According to this premodern notion every regime can be characterized by some such opinion, and every regime takes its distinctive character from its ruling part or parts, democratic, oligarchic, aristocratic, monarchic, or whatever. A change in rulers, so understood, is then indeed a revolutionary change. Even though the people remain so to speak the same (minus an indeterminate number of executed, exiles, and refugees), it is a different country, a different Athens, France, Russia, Cuba, Iran.

Except where the standard is that might makes right, the necessarily partisan claim to a right to rule presupposes some standard by which rival claims can be judged and rival notions of justice compared and weighed. Typically, however, partisans leave it at assertion; political life is not conducted as a seminar in political theory. Hence the claim to rule based on a superior (or the correct) notion of justice frequently is attended by intemperance both by the asserters of the claim and by those who find it unpersuasive. In practice, the unmitigated rule of the rich, the poor, the wise, the holy, or the pure has reduced the sum of human happiness. In practice, the properly mixed or balanced rule of partisans has seldom if ever appeared outside the pages of Aristotle. Whatever approximations to such a mixture existed among historical regimes were sure to command the close attention of men like Adams, Jefferson, and Madison.

Representative government seeks to reduce the risks of intemperate single-mindedness by changing the objects of political life. If the grander claim is also the riskier, a more modest political stance might conduce better to peace and prosperity. Rather than swing between mutually exclusive claims, society ought to address itself to adjusting the interests of men. Once people are disabused of, or denied the means to realize, their exclusive pretensions—to rule, to glory, to saintliness, to wisdom—they come to see their common vulnerability and their common concern for survival, well-being, and domestic tranquillity. Representation

is a mode of giving voice to their common concerns as refracted by their particular interests. Conflicting interests issue forth in conflicting opinions. Representation gives voice to those opinions—in assemblies rather than on barricades. While men still wish to have their way, they no longer insist upon it at all costs. They are content to have a say and a fair share of the benefits of government (at the price of a fair share of the burdens). Modern representatives are thus quite unlike premodern worthies who let the ruler know how they felt. Rather, they stand in relation to a constituency whose interests and opinions they express and seek to further. If "the regulation of these various and interfering interests forms the principal task of modern legislation" (see ch. 4, no. 19), it is noteworthy that, according to this same view, it is the representatives themselves who are to regulate those interests. This premise of modern representation is common (to some extent) to all of the eighteenth-century writers included here. Their debate is over how best to secure that objective.

The Purposes of Representation

The slogan "No taxation without representation" is a response to offended notions of rights, equity, and good sense: rights, because no part of any man's property can be taken without his or his representative's consent, or if taken without consent, only at the price of impoverishing the people and robbing men of an essential support of liberty (see ch. 17, no. 5); equity, because those who bear a burden ought to have a voice; good sense, because governors needlessly deprive themselves of a valuable source of information by excluding those who best know their situation (nos. 4, 8). Given this line of reasoning, why ought there to be representation at all? The obvious answer is that the people in a numerous and extensive commonwealth cannot conveniently assemble as a whole. To stand for the people, a representative body should then be a representation of the people or (more strictly) of the citizenry (no. 12; see also ch. 17, no. 9).

Beyond that there is the need for the people to have some control or check on their governors, and in that capacity representatives act as "attorneys" for the people, to be chosen, retained, or dismissed as the latter see fit (see ch. 17, no. 12). Burke (no. 6) put the point more dramatically: The singularity of the House of Commons lies not in its being the representative of the people, for this holds as well for King, Lords, Commons, and judges: "They all are trustees for the people." Rather, what makes the House of Commons singular is that it "was supposed originally to be *no part of the standing government*" of England. Far from being "a control upon the people," Burke argued, "it was designed as a control *for* the people." That it was not acting as such at the time John Adams and Burke wrote was for both authors a measure of that body's corruption.

Madison, writing as Publius, took a more guarded view in *Federalist*, nos. 10 and 63. Representation might indeed have a further advantage. By refining and enlarging the public views, representation might promote the public good better than would be the case were "the people themselves convened for the purpose. On the other hand, the effect may be inverted." It is not so much, then, the principle of representation that tempers popular prejudice and partiality, for the people may be flattered equally by representatives who would serve them ill as well. Rather, it is the principle of representation operating in an extended republic that makes all the difference (see ch. 4, nos. 19, 27). "For it cannot be believed that any form of representative government could have succeeded within the narrow limits occupied by the democracies of Greece." The expansive circumstances of the American republic would work equally and effectively against two forms of corruption: against representatives using their popularity to exploit and ultimately dominate the people, and against representatives becoming mere tools of those popular passions and immediate interests that might be intent on serving unjust objects, violating private rights, or defeating the permanent and aggregate interests of the community.

Whose Representative?

With different emphases on the purposes of representation, the several authors differed naturally enough in characterizing what was to be represented. James Burgh's short answer was: "the general sense of the people" (no. 8). A fuller and clearer answer was offered by the Federal Farmer (no. 20): "a full and equal representation is that in which the interests, feelings, opinions, and views of the people are collected, in such manner as they would be were the people all assembled." Only through such a representation of the citizenry as a whole could there be the desired sympathy and confidence between constituents and their representatives. Toward that end the Founders' Constitution would establish a lower house elected every two years directly by the people. Remarkably it would impose no restrictions of its own on the exercise of the ballot. Nor with regard to holding federal office does it set any property requirements (unlike many of the state constitutions of the time), or any religious test (unlike some of the state constitutions of the time), or any residence requirement beyond the representative's being an inhabitant of the state "when elected."

While no one denied the importance of sympathetic understanding, there was powerful resistance to what were perceived as parochial implications. Ought the several orders of men in the community to be guaranteed "a share in the business of legislation," as the Federal Farmer would have it, or should the emphasis be upon the nation as a whole and its broad overriding interests? Burke (no. 7) had no doubt that "Parliament is not a *congress* of ambassadors from different and hostile interests" but rather "a *deliberative* assembly of *one* nation, with *one interest, that of the whole.*" Though chosen by Bristol, he was "a member of parliament." Analogously, although each Senator is from a state and chosen by a state, none is a Senator *of* a state (no. 16; see also Webster, "On Government," 1788).

In his revolutionary ardor John Adams looked for a representative assembly that "should be in miniature an exact portrait of the people at large" (see ch. 4, no. 5); but he was concerned equally that the correct principle, "the

only moral foundation of government"—popular consent—not be pushed so far in practice as "to confound and destroy all distinctions, and prostrate all ranks to one common level" (no. 10). Adams held fast to the notion that "the perfection of the portrait consists in the likeness." But what was to be portrayed? "Numbers, or property, or both" (no., 17). The Essex Result (no. 12) was more emphatic. It too called for representatives who would be "an exact miniature of their constituents," but that process of miniaturization had to represent both numbers and property on the grounds that a law affecting both requires the consent of two majorities. Women were another matter (nos. 10, 11, 12).

One might presume a neat correspondence between the several views of what is to be represented and of who is to represent it. One might presume—rightly—that an Ames (no. 28), who held that "the representation of the people is something more than the people," would look askance at those who (in Hamilton's characterization of them) called for "an actual representation of all classes of the people by persons of each class." Similarly, those who wanted representatives to be "a true picture of the people," sympathizing "in all their distresses," able and disposed to "feel for the poor and middling class" (Smith, no. 37), would not find persuasive the argument of Hamilton in *Federalist*, no. 35 (no. 25), and take cold comfort indeed from his remark to the New York Ratifying Convention that the vices of the wealthy—those most likely to be prominent in government—"are probably more favorable to the prosperity of the state, than those of the indigent" (no. 38; see also no. 19). Yet it would be a mistake to assume that only the Federalists were hankering for representation by the natural *aristoi*, or that the Anti-Federalists believed simply that only one's own kind could be fully representative.

All could agree that a representative ought to sympathize with his constituents' situation, that he ought in all cases to prefer their interest to his own. Most could agree that the representative assembly ought to mirror the society as a whole. And even if some were willing to agree with John Adams that "the first necessary step [was] to depute power from the many to a few of the most wise and good," there was no consensus about where those *aristoi* were to be found (see ch. 4, no. 5). James Otis (no. 4) looked to "persons of the first reputation among their countrymen." Burke (no. 7) looked for assiduous men of fiercely independent judgment. Adams (no. 17) held that the people would choose whomever they thought knew more and were better disposed—"very often even than themselves." None of this explicitly located the likely social stratum of the representatives, whatever these men may have thought privately or have written elsewhere. The debate over the Constitution, however, brought this matter to the fore. Hamilton's day-long speech to the Philadelphia Convention made no secret of his dissatisfaction with both the Virginia and New Jersey plans in this respect as in others. He wished representation to be in the hands of "gentlemen of fortune and abilities," not in those of the "middling politician" (Yates's notes, no. 19). The more public argument of *Federalist*, no. 35, is largely a politic restatement of the same conclusion. "Discerning citizens" in the nonagricultural working class know that "their habits in life have not been such as to give them those acquired endowments, without which in a deliberative assembly the greatest natural abilities are for the most part useless."

Critics of the Constitution were prepared to grant part of this argument without (as Hamilton was very content to do) settling for a legislature composed of wealthy merchants, landlords, and men of the learned professions. In part, the Federal Farmer (no. 22) thought Hamilton's confidence was misplaced. "It is an observation, I believe, well founded, that the schools produce but few advocates for republican forms of government." But beyond that, something more was needed; he looked for "every order of men in the community . . . professional men, merchants, traders, farmers, mechanics, etc. to bring a just proportion of their best informed men respectively into the legislature." That in turn would require a much augmented representation to "let in a due proportion" of those numerous, valuable, but generally silent men, "the substantial and respectable part of the democracy." Here Anti-Federalists thought the Constitution's provision for periodic enlargement of the House of Representatives and for reapportionment among the states inadequate. Doubting that a sufficient augmentation could take place at the national level, George Mason saw no alternative but "to give power with a sparing hand to a Government thus imperfectly constructed" (no. 35).

Not only was Melancton Smith wary of the great powers authorized by the Constitution, but he would not concede the point of representation. "The knowledge necessary for the representation of a free people" went beyond what men of refined education could or would care to acquire: "acquaintance with the common concerns and occupations of the people, which men of the middling class of life are in general much better competent to, than those of a superior class." No representation of a free people would be adequate if it did not make room for "the substantial yeomanry of the country," men whose interests, tastes, and situation were not remote from those of the general public (no. 37). This impressive argument elicited a memorable response from Hamilton. Why, he wondered, should the people not elect "their most meritorious men"? But the question was ill put. It was not a case of the virtuous against the vicious. In time, the increasingly unequal distribution of wealth would lead inevitably to virtue's being "considered as only a graceful appendage of wealth." The choice would be between different kinds of vice, and the people presumably would prefer their interests to their prejudices (no. 38). Madison offered Virginians more hope. We ought not to rely on the virtue of rulers; depend rather on the "great republican principle, that the people will have [enough] virtue and intelligence to select men of virtue and wisdom" (no. 36). Like Montesquieu he held an irredeemably neglectful or corrupt people not fit for self-government. (See also ch. 18.)

Fair Representation

Various devices suggested themselves to those who pondered the question of how to achieve fair representation.

The scandal of Britain's notorious rotten boroughs made it a commonplace that a fair representation had in some sense to be an equal representation. For Locke (no. 2) the reluctance of a malapportioned legislature to reform itself could very properly be overcome by an executive prerogative guided "not by old custom, but true reason." James Burgh's vehemence in denouncing the mildness of Blackstone's strictures against what the former called "the monstrous irregularity of parliamentary representation" (no. 8) displays the frustration of waiting for what showed no signs of arriving. In its regulation of federal elections the Founders' Constitution requires decennial reapportionment of the House of Representatives among the states according to their populations (Art. 1, sec. 2, cl. 3); but beyond that the electoral details are left to the states unless Congress chooses to act on the matter (Art. 1, sec. 4, cl. 1).

What, however, was to be equal? Northampton's critique of the Massachusetts Constitution of 1780 (see ch. 15, no. 26) argued that representation should take account of "the principle of personal equality" as well as of "corporation equality." Both were matters of contention. In the Massachusetts historical context (and down into the nineteenth century), the representation of towns as such tended to be defended as a popular principle. On the other hand, the more conservative spokesmen for the larger towns and the more densely settled seaboard areas called for an apportionment weighted by population and/or property (treated as rough equivalents). Thus, curiously enough, places that were overrepresented by the population standard claimed to represent the people in their natural character as members of political communities. The perspective from which local township government is central to the development of American democracy might well consider the states in a similar way. In this sense the intense efforts of the delegates from small states at the Philadelphia Convention to secure the equal representation of states as political bodies (see ch. 12) may be viewed as a more democratic appeal than the representation of numbers alone (see Art. 1, sec. 3, cl. 1). (For the difficulties of trying to give every town, however small, some representation without ending up with an utterly ungainly assembly, see Handlin 42–46.)

The inequalities of representation in the Virginia Constitution of 1776 were, for Jefferson, among its "very capital defects" (no. 15). Generously, he traced the disproportion between the minority of enfranchised freeholders and the majority of those "who pay and fight," and the disproportion between land, fighting men, and representation in tidewater, piedmont, and backcountry, to the revolutionary Virginians' inexperience in the science of government. But now, some years later, there was no excuse for delaying remedy. Nor was there any excuse, Republicus thought (no. 31), for the Constitution's failure to provide that "every member of the union have a freedom of suffrage and that every equal number of people have an equal number of representatives." He only found it strange that anyone should contest "so plain a case."

Also open to question were the kinds of qualifications for electors that would best promote the purposes of representation. Jefferson saw no sense in Virginia's bicameralism given the homogeneity of the electorates for the two houses. His implied remedy was to vary the qualifications, not to abolish the senate (no. 15). Adams was inclined to let matters rest as they were, not opening a Pandora's box of endless controversy—and all the more so since "our people have never been very rigid in scrutinizing into the qualifications of voters" (no. 10). Others in Massachusetts were less accepting. The returns of Northampton (see ch. 15, no. 26) and Mansfield (6 June 1780) protested with somewhat rustic spelling, but well-schooled rhetoric and reasoning, against the injustice of excluding any "polls" (i.e., taxed adult males) from the electorate. For them, as for Paine (no. 40), a man without a vote was, in a manner of speaking, in slavery. Even so, the most democratic franchise proposals still included restrictions beyond sex and age. Extending suffrage to all taxpayers ruled out those who owned no taxable property. Residency requirements distinguished settled members of the community from "man" in the abstract. In one fashion or another the states sought to extend (and limit) the franchise to those giving evidence of their permanent attachment to the community. (George Mason would have had Virginia extend the right of suffrage "to every housekeeper who hath resided for one year last past in the country, and hath been the father of three children in this country." See Jefferson Papers 1:366.) The Founders' Constitution solved the question by leaving the franchise open-ended, in that it adopts as its own for the electors of the lower house the least restrictive requirements of the respective states. (See also ch. 16, no. 26; and Art. 1, sec. 2, cl. 1.)

Effective Representation

Eclipsing all these controversies and concerns was the issue of an adequate representation as expressed in the size of the proposed House of Representatives. (nos. 20, 22; see Art. 1, sec. 2, cl. 3.) The volume and intensity of criticism increased steadily through the deliberations of the Philadelphia Convention, the ratification debates, and beyond. "Scarce any article indeed in the whole constitution seems to be rendered more worthy of attention, by the weight of character and the apparent force of argument, with which it has been assailed." Madison's argument in *Federalist*, no. 55, deals less with Anti-Federalist notions of what is to be represented than with what it takes to have an effective representative assembly. His answer—large enough, but not too large—distills the understanding of one who had observed closely both "the cabals of a few" and "the confusion of a multitude" (see ch. 4, no. 19). No one knew better than Madison that enlargement beyond some optimal point may make "the countenance of the government . . . more democratic; but the soul that animates it will become more oligarchic" (no. 32).

A fair representation, once achieved, had still to be kept safe. An array of devices suggested themselves, of which the most controversial was the people's instructing their representatives. Adams saw this as a part of the check upon government that would help keep it popular (see ch. 17, no. 12). In this he perhaps had in mind the kind of instructions sent by Pittsfield (no. 13) to their delegates to the Massachusetts constitutional convention of 1779: de-

tailed statements of principles and preoccupations, ending with an injunction that the delegates use their heads, "any instructions herein contained to the contrary notwithstanding." Hamilton, surprisingly enough, seemed to assume an unqualified popular power of instruction (no. 38).

The classic attack on instructions was delivered by Burke in his postelection speech at Bristol (no. 7). The opinion of constituents ought to have great weight with a representative, but ought never to overwhelm "his unbiassed opinion, his mature judgment, his enlightened conscience." The sacrifice of these to popular opinion was, in Burke's eyes, nothing less than a dereliction of duty. Washington (no. 16), like Adams, took no exception to instructions on the local level; but if such instructions were to bind at the federal level, they would preclude any real deliberation in Congress and jeopardize the interests of the nation as a whole. Noah Webster ("On Government," 1788) traced most of the legislative ills of the times to this source. The assumed right to instruct representatives frequently amounted to "a right of doing infinite mischief, with the best intentions." It was in direct contradiction with the "design" of representation, which is to *collect the wisdom of the State*, not merely to mouth predetermined opinions.

Although *The Federalist* does not speak directly to the matter of instructions, the tendency of its argument is to oppose them strongly. Fundamental to Madison's judgment of political arrangements is the principle that "it is the reason of the public alone that ought to controul and regulate the government. The passions ought to be controuled and regulated by the government" (see ch. 2, no. 19). From this standpoint the very responsiveness of a legislative body may paradoxically diminish "a due responsibility in the government to the people." If a regard for long-term plans to serve long-term interests argues against annual elections and a numerous assembly, so too would it argue against binding instructions. And all the more if one is mindful that the people need "a defence against their own temporary errors and delusions," or (as Hamilton put it) if one realizes that there will always be occasions when "the interests of the people are at variance with their inclinations." (See Madison, ch. 4, no. 27; and Hamilton, ch. 2, no. 21.)

The issue was joined again in the First Congress (no. 39) during a discussion of what was to become the First Amendment. Once more those who thought instructions and representative government inseparable contended with those who thought them incompatible. The issue reemerged in the lame-duck session of a chastened Fourteenth Congress; see *Annals* 30:576–78, 585, 616–20, 625–35, 674–79 (1817).

Most but not all of the other safeguards were noncontroversial. The most powerful, of course, were the people's right to deny reelection (see ch. 17, no. 12) and the fact that representatives themselves would be subject to the laws they enacted (nos. 11, 25). The Founders' Constitution forbids the plural office-holding that had so offended the colonists as well as the cozy device of legislators voting themselves an office (Art. 1, sec. 6, cl. 2). But some thought more was needed. Republicus (no. 31) called for a rotation of officeholders enforced by "temporary intervals of ineligibility." The fear of a gulf between capital and hometown was present at the creation. (See Articles of Confederation, art. 5. For rotation in office as stipulated in state constitutions from 1776 to 1780 see the summary in W. P. Adams, *The First American Constitutions* 308–11 [1980].) In detailing what was missing in the provisions for the proposed Senate, Luther Martin (no. 27) indicated what he took to be necessary safeguards for a due dependency of representatives upon their constituents: frequent elections, popular recall, and no independent power to pay themselves. Although representation might be kept safe through the operations of bicameralism (no. 15) and federalism (no. 20), the relative homogeneity of those likely to succeed in political life continued to be troubling. Adams's early reliance on a broad distribution of landed property (no. 10) gave way to more elaborate and less sanguine proposals in later life (see Letter to John Taylor, Apr. 1814). Whether Melancton Smith's reliance on a "middling class" to check the excesses of the great and corrupt (no. 37) was a surer safeguard than Hamilton's reliance on shared interest (no. 38) was a continuing problem not amenable to a controlled experiment.

1

JOHN WINTHROP, THE HISTORY OF NEW ENGLAND
1:360–63; 2:277, 279–83
1639, 1645

[*22 May 1639*]

The court of elections was; at which time there was a small eclipse of the sun. Mr. Winthrop was chosen governour again, though some laboring had been, by some of the elders and others to have changed, not out of any dislike of him, (for they all loved and esteemed him,) but out of their fear lest it might make way for having a governour for life, which some had propounded as most agreeable to God's institution and the practice of all well ordered states. But neither the governour nor any other attempted the thing. . . . Another occasion of their jealousy was, the court, finding the number of deputies to be much increased by the addition of new plantations, thought fit, for the case both of the country and the court, to reduce all towns to two deputies. This occasioned some to fear, that the magistrates intended to make themselves stronger, and the deputies weaker, and so, in time, to bring all power into the hands of the magistrates; so as the people in some towns were much displeased with their deputies for yielding to such an order. Whereupon, at the next session, it was propounded to have the number of deputies restored; and allegations were made, that it was an infringement of their liberty; so as, after much debate, and such reasons given for diminishing the number of deputies, and clearly proved that their liberty consisted not in the number, but in the thing, divers of the deputies, who came with intent to reverse the last order, were, by force of reason, brought to uphold it; so that, when it was put to the vote, the last order for two deputies only was confirmed. Yet, the next day, a petition was brought to the court from the freemen of Roxbury, to have the third deputy restored. Whereupon the reasons of the court's proceedings were set down in writing, and all objections answered, and sent to such towns as were unsatisfied with this advice, that, if any could take away those reasons, or bring us better for what they did desire, we should be ready, at the next court, to repeal the said order.

The hands of some of the elders (learned and godly men) were to this petition, though suddenly drawn in, and without due consideration, for the lawfulness of it may well be questioned: for when the people have chosen men to be their rulers, and to make their laws, and bound themselves by oath to submit thereto, now to combine together (a lesser part of them) in a public petition to have any order repealed, which is not repugnant to the law of God, savors of resisting an ordinance of God; for the people, having deputed others, have no power to make or alter laws, but are to be subject; and if any such order seem unlawful or inconvenient, they were better prefer some reasons, etc., to the court, with manifestation of their desire to move them to a review, than peremptorily to petition to have it repealed, which amounts to a plain reproof of those whom God hath set over them, and putting dishonor upon them, against the tenor of the fifth commandment.

. . . . .

[*May 1645*]

Two of the magistrates and many of the deputies were of opinion that the magistrates exercised too much power, and that the people's liberty was thereby in danger; and other of the deputies (being about half) and all the rest of the magistrates were of a different judgment, and that authority was overmuch slighted, which, if not timely remedied, would endanger the commonwealth, and bring us to a mere democracy. By occasion of this difference, there was not so orderly carriage at the hearing, as was meet, each side striving unseasonably to enforce the evidence, and declaring their judgments thereupon, which should have been reserved to a more private debate, (as after it was,) so as the best part of two days was spent in this public agitation and examination of witnesses, etc. This being ended, a committee was chosen of magistrates and deputies, who stated the case, as it appeared upon the whole pleading and evidence, thought it cost much time, and with great difficulty did the committee come to accord upon it.

. . . . .

[*3 July 1645*]

. . . presently after the lecture the magistrates and deputies took their places in the meeting house, and the people being come together, and the deputy governour [John

Winthrop] placing himself within the bar, as at the time of the hearing, etc., the governour read the sentence of the court, without speaking any more, for the deputies had (by importunity) obtained a promise of silence from the magistrates. Then was the deputy governour desired by the court to go up and take his place again upon the bench, which he did accordingly, and the court being about to arise, he desired leave for a little speech, which was to this effect.

I suppose something may be expected from me, upon this charge that is befallen me, which moves me to speak now to you; yet I intend not to intermeddle in the proceedings of the court, or with any of the persons concerned therein. Only I bless God, that I see an issue of this troublesome business. I also acknowledge the justice of the court, and, for mine own part, I am well satisfied, I was publicly charged, and I am publicly and legally acquitted, which is all I did expect or desire. And though this be sufficient for my justification before men, yet not so before the God, who hath seen so much amiss in my dispensations (and even in this affair) as calls me to be humble. For to be publicly and criminally charged in this court, is matter of humiliation, (and I desire to make a right use of it,) notwithstanding I be thus acquitted. If her father had spit in her face, (saith the Lord concerning Miriam,) should she not have been ashamed seven days? Shame had lien upon her, whatever the occasion had been. I am unwilling to stay you from your urgent affairs, yet give me leave (upon this special occasion) to speak a little more to this assembly. It may be of some good use, to inform and rectify the judgments of some of the people, and may prevent such distempers as have arisen amongst us. The great questions that have troubled the country, are about the authority of the magistrates and the liberty of the people. It is yourselves who have called us to this office, and being called by you, we have our authority from God, in way of an ordinance, such as hath the image of God eminently stamped upon it, the contempt and violation whereof hath been vindicated with examples of divine vengeance. I entreat you to consider, that when you choose magistrates, you take them from among yourselves, men subject to like passions as you are. Therefore when you see infirmities in us, you should reflect upon your own, and that would make you bear the more with us, and not be severe censurers of the failings of your magistrates, when you have continual experience of the like infirmities in yourselves and others. We account him a good servant, who breaks not his covenant. The covenant between you and us is the oath you have taken of us, which is to this purpose, that we shall govern you and judge your causes by the rules of God's laws and our own, according to our best skill. When you agree with a workman to build you a ship or house, etc., he undertakes as well for his skill as for his faithfulness, for it is his profession, and you pay him for both. But when you call one to be a magistrate, he doth not profess nor undertake to have sufficient skill for that office, nor can you furnish him with gifts, etc., therefore you must run the hazard of his skill and ability. But if he fail in faithfulness, which by his oath he is bound unto, that

he must answer for. If it fall out that the case be clear to common apprehension, and the rule clear also, if he transgress here, the error is not in the skill, but in the evil of the will: it must be required of him. But if the case be doubtful, or the rule doubtful, to men of such understanding and parts as your magistrates are, if your magistrates should err here, yourselves must bear it.

For the other point concerning liberty, I observe a great mistake in the country about that. There is a twofold liberty, natural (I mean as our nature is now corrupt) and civil or federal. The first is common to man with beasts and other creatures. By this, man, as he stands in relation to man simply, hath liberty to do what he lists; it is a liberty to evil as well as to good. This liberty is incompatible and inconsistent with authority, and cannot endure the least restraint of the most just authority. The exercise and maintaining of this liberty makes men grow more evil, and in time to be worse than brute beasts: omnes sumus licentia deteriores. This is that great enemy of truth and peace, that wild beast, which all the ordinances of God are bent against, to restrain and subdue it. The other kind of liberty I call civil or federal, it may also be termed moral, in reference to the covenant between God and man, in the moral law, and the politic covenants and constitutions, amongst men themselves. This liberty is the proper end and object of authority, and cannot subsist without it; and it is a liberty to that only which is good, just, and honest. This liberty you are to stand for, with the hazard (not only of your goods, but) of your lives, if need be. Whatsoever crosseth this, is not authority, but a distemper thereof. This liberty is maintained and exercised in a way of subjection to authority; it is of the same kind of liberty wherewith Christ hath made us free. The woman's own choice makes such a man her husband; yet being so chosen, he is her lord, and she is to be subject to him, yet in a way of liberty, not of bondage; and a true wife accounts her subjection her honor and freedom, and would not think her condition safe and free, but in her subjection to her husband's authority. Such is the liberty of the church under the authority of Christ, her king and husband; his yoke is so easy and sweet to her as a bride's ornaments; and if through frowardness or wantonness, etc., she shake it off, at any time, she is at no rest in her spirit, until she take it up again; and whether her lord smiles upon her, and embraceth her in his arms, or whether he frowns, or rebukes, or smites her, she apprehends the sweetness of his love in all, and is refreshed, supported, and instructed by every such dispensation of his authority over her. On the other side, ye know who they are that complain of this yoke and say, let us break their bands, etc., we will not have this man to rule over us. Even so, brethren, it will be between you and your magistrates. If you stand for your natural corrupt liberties, and will do what is good in your own eyes, you will not endure the least weight of authority, but will murmur, and oppose, and be always striving to shake off that yoke; but if you will be satisfied to enjoy such civil and lawful liberties, such as Christ allows you, then will you quietly and cheerfully submit unto that authority which is set over you, in all the administrations of it, for your good.

Wherein, if we fail at any time, we hope we shall be willing (by God's assistance) to hearken to good advice from any of you, or in any other way of God; so shall your liberties be preserved, in upholding the honor and power of authority amongst you.

The deputy governour having ended his speech, the court arose, and the magistrates and deputies retired to attend their other affairs. Many things were observable in the agitation and proceedings about this case. It may be of use to leave a memorial of some of the most material, that our posterity and others may behold the workings of satan to ruin the colonies and churches of Christ in New England, and into what distempers a wise and godly people may fall in times of temptation; and when such have entertained some false and plausible principles, what deformed superstructures they will raise thereupon, and with what unreasonable obstinacy they will maintain them.

Some of the deputies had seriously conceived, that the magistrates affected an arbitrary government, and that they had (or sought to have) an unlimited power to do what they pleased without control, and that, for this end, they did strive so much to keep their negative power in the general court. This caused them to interpret all the magistrates' actions and speeches (not complying exactly with their own principles) as tending that way, by which occasions their fears and jealousies increased daily. For prevention whereof they judged it not unlawful to use even extrema remedia, as if salus populi had been now the transcendant rule to walk by, and that magistracy must be no other, in effect, than a ministerial office, and all authority, both legislative, consultative, and judicial, must be exercised by the people in their body representative. Hereupon they labored, equis et velis, to take away the negative vote. Failing of that, they pleaded that the magistrates had no power out of the general court, but what must be derived from the general court; and so they would have put upon them commissions, for what was to be done in the vacancy of the general court, and some of themselves to be joined with the magistrates, and some of the magistrates left out. This not being yielded unto, recourse was had to the elders for advice, and the case stated, with incredible wariness; but the elders casting the cause against them, (as is before declared,) they yet believed, (or at least would that others should,) that the elders' advice was as much for them in their sense as for the magistrates, (and if it were, they had no cause to shun the advice of the elders, as they have seemed to do ever since). This project not prevailing, the next is, for such a body of laws, with prescript penalties in all cases, as nothing might be left to the discretion of the magistrates, (while in the mean time there is no fear of any danger in reserving a liberty for their own discretion in every case,) many laws are agreed upon, some are not assented unto by the magistrates not finding them just. Then is it given out, that the magistrates would have no laws, etc.

2

JOHN LOCKE, SECOND TREATISE, §§ 157–58
1689

(See also §§ 134–42, in ch. 17, no. 5)

157. Things of this World are in so constant a Flux, that nothing remains long in the same State. Thus People, Riches, Trade, Power, change their Stations; flourishing mighty Cities come to ruine, and prove in time neglected desolate Corners, whilst other unfrequented places grow into populous Countries, fill'd with Wealth and Inhabitants. But things not always changing equally, and private interest often keeping up Customs and Priviledges, when the reasons of them are ceased, it often comes to pass, that in Governments, where part of the Legislative consists of *Representatives* chosen by the People, that in tract of time this *Representation* becomes very *unequal* and disproportionate to the reasons it was at first establish'd upon. To what gross absurdities the following of Custom, when Reason has left it, may lead, we may be satisfied when we see the bare Name of a Town, of which there remains not so much as the ruines, where scarce so much Housing as a Sheep-coat; or more inhabitants than a Shepherd is to be found, sends *as many Representatives* to the grand Assembly of Law-makers, as a whole County numerous in People, and powerful in riches. This Strangers stand amazed at, and every one must confess needs a remedy. Though most think it hard to find one, because the Constitution of the Legislative being the original and supream act of the Society, antecedent to all positive Laws in it, and depending wholly on the People, no inferiour Power can alter it. And therefore the *People*, when the *Legislative* is once Constituted, *having* in such a Government as we have been speaking of, *no Power* to act as long as the Government stands; this inconvenience is thought incapable of a remedy.

158. *Salus Populi Suprema Lex*, is certainly so just and fundamental a Rule, that he, who sincerely follows it, cannot dangerously err. If therefore the Executive, who has the power of Convoking the Legislative, observing rather the true proportion, than fashion of *Representation*, regulates, not by old custom, but true reason, the *number of Members,* in all places, that have a right to be distinctly represented, which no part of the People however incorporated can pretend to, but in proportion to the assistance, which it affords to the publick, it cannot be judg'd, to have set up a new Legislative, but to have restored the old and true one, and to have rectified the disorders, which succession of time had insensibly, as well as inevitably introduced. For it being the interest, as well as intention of the People, to have a fair and *equal Representative;* whoever brings it nearest to that, is an undoubted Friend, to, and Establisher of the Government, and cannot miss the Consent and Approbation of the Community. *Prerog-*

ative being nothing, but a Power in the hands of the Prince to provide for the publick good, in such Cases, which depending upon unforeseen and uncertain Occurrences, certain and unalterable Laws could not safely direct, whatsoever shall be done manifestly for the good of the People, and the establishing the Government upon its true Foundations, is, and always will be just *Prerogative.* The Power of Erecting new Corporations, and therewith *new Representatives,* carries with it a supposition, that in time the *measures of representation* might vary, and those places have a just right to be represented which before had none; and by the same reason, those cease to have a right, and be too inconsiderable for such a Priviledge, which before had it. 'Tis not a change from the present State, which perhaps Corruption, or decay has introduced, that makes an Inroad upon the Government, but the tendency of it to injure or oppress the People, and to set up one part, or Party, with a distinction from, and an unequal subjection of the rest. Whatsoever cannot but be acknowledged to be of advantage to the Society, and People in general, upon just and lasting measures, will always, when done, justifie it self; and whenever the People shall chuse their *Representatives upon* just and undeniably *equal measures* suitable to the original Frame of the Government, it cannot be doubted to be the will and act of the Society, whoever permitted, or caused them so to do.

3

MONTESQUIEU, SPIRIT OF LAWS, BK. 11, CH. 6
1748

(See ch. 17, no. 9)

4

JAMES OTIS, THE RIGHTS OF THE BRITISH
COLONIES ASSERTED AND PROVED
1764
Political Writings 326–27

The supreme national legislative cannot be altered justly 'till the commonwealth is dissolved, nor a subordinate legislative taken away without forfeiture or other good cause. Nor then can the subjects in the subordinate government be reduced to a state of slavery, and subject to the despotic rule of others. A state has no right to make slaves of the conquered. Even when the subordinate right of legislature is forfeited, and so declared, this cannot affect the natural persons either of those who were invested with it, or the inhabitants, so far as to deprive them of the rights of subjects and of men—The colonists will have an equitable right notwithstanding any such forfeiture of charter, to be represented in Parliament, or to have some new subordinate legislature

among themselves. It would be best if they had both. Deprived however of their common rights as subjects, they cannot lawfully be, while they remain such. A representation in Parliament from the several Colonies, since they are become so large and numerous, as to be called on not to maintain provincial government, civil and military among themselves, for this they have chearfully done, but to contribute towards the support of a national standing army, by reason of the heavy national debt, when they themselves owe a large one, contracted in the common cause, can't be tho't an unreasonable thing, nor if asked, could it be called an immodest request. *Qui sentis commodum sentire debet et onus,* has been tho't a maxim of equity. But that a man should bear a burthen for other people, as well as himself, without a return, never long found a place in any law-book or decrees, but those of the most despotic princes. Besides the equity of an American representation in parliament, a thousand advantages would result from it. It would be the most effectual means of giving those of both countries a thorough knowledge of each others interests; as well as that of the whole, which are inseparable.

Were this representation allowed; instead of the scandalous memorials and depositions that have been sometimes, in days of old, privately cooked up in an inquisitorial manner, by persons of bad minds and wicked views, and sent from America to the several boards, persons of the first reputation among their countrymen, might be on the spot, from the several colonies, truly to represent them. Future ministers need not, like some of their predecessors, have recourse for information in American affairs, to every vagabond stroller, that has run or rid post thro' America, from his creditors, or to people of no kind of reputation from the colonies; some of whom, at the time of administring their sage advice, have been as ignorant of the state of the country, as of the regions in Jupiter and Saturn.

No representation of the Colonies in parliament alone, would however be equivalent to a subordinate legislative among themselves; nor so well answer the ends of increasing their prosperity and the commerce of Great-Britain. It would be impossible for the parliament to judge so well, of their abilities to bear taxes, impositions on trade, and other duties and burthens, or of the local laws that might be really needful, as a legislative here.

5

JOHN ADAMS, CLARENDON, NO. 3
27 Jan. 1766
Papers 1:167–68

(See ch. 17, no. 12)

6

EDMUND BURKE, THOUGHTS ON THE CAUSE OF THE
PRESENT DISCONTENTS
1770
Works 1:347–49

The House of Commons was supposed originally to be *no part of the standing government of this country.* It was considered as a *control,* issuing *immediately* from the people, and speedily to be resolved into the mass from whence it arose. In this respect it was in the higher part of government what juries are in the lower. The capacity of a magistrate being transitory, and that of a citizen permanent, the latter capacity it was hoped would of course preponderate in all discussions, not only between the people and the standing authority of the crown, but between the people and the fleeting authority of the House of Commons itself. It was hoped that, being of a middle nature between subject and government, they would feel with a more tender and a nearer interest everything that concerned the people, than the other remoter and more permanent parts of legislature.

Whatever alterations time and the necessary accommodation of business may have introduced, this character can never be sustained, unless the House of Commons shall be made to bear some stamp of the actual disposition of the people at large. It would (among public misfortunes) be an evil more natural and tolerable, that the House of Commons should be infected with every epidemical phrensy of the people, as this would indicate some consanguinity, some sympathy of nature with their constituents, than that they should in all cases be wholly untouched by the opinions and feelings of the people out of doors. By this want of sympathy they would cease to be a House of Commons. For it is not the derivation of the power of that House from the people, which makes it in a distinct sense their representative. The king is the representative of the people; so are the lords; so are the judges. They all are trustees for the people, as well as the Commons; because no power is given for the sole sake of the holder; and although government certainly is an institution of Divine authority, yet its forms, and the persons who administer it, all originate from the people.

A popular origin cannot therefore be the characteristical distinction of a popular representative. This belongs equally to all parts of government, and in all forms. The virtue, spirit, and essence of a House of Commons consists in its being the express image of the feelings of the nation. It was not instituted to be a control *upon* the people, as of late it has been taught, by a doctrine of the most pernicious tendency. It was designed as a control *for* the people. Other institutions have been formed for the purpose of checking popular excesses; and they are, I apprehend, fully adequate to their object. If not, they ought to be made so. The House of Commons, as it was never in-tended for the support of peace and subordination, is miserably appointed for that service; having no stronger weapon than its mace, and no better officer than its sergeant at arms, which it can command of its own proper authority. A vigilant and jealous eye over executory and judicial magistracy; an anxious care of public money; an openness, approaching towards facility, to public complaint: these seem to be the true characteristics of a House of Commons. But an addressing House of Commons, and a petitioning nation; a House of Commons full of confidence, when the nation is plunged in despair; in the utmost harmony with ministers, whom the people regard with the utmost abhorrence; who vote thanks, when the public opinion calls upon them for impeachments; who are eager to grant, when the general voice demands account; who, in all disputes between the people and administration, presume against the people; who punish their disorders, but refuse even to inquire into the provocations to them; this is an unnatural, a monstrous state of things in this constitution. Such an assembly may be a great, wise, awful senate; but it is not, to any popular purpose, a House of Commons. This change from an immediate state of procuration and delegation to a course of acting as from original power, is the way in which all the popular magistracies in the world have been perverted from their purposes. It is indeed their greatest, and sometimes their incurable, corruption. For there is a material distinction between that corruption by which particular points are carried against reason, (this is a thing which cannot be prevented by human wisdom, and is of less consequence,) and the corruption of the principle itself. For then the evil is not accidental, but settled. The distemper becomes the natural habit.

7

EDMUND BURKE, SPEECH TO THE ELECTORS
OF BRISTOL
3 Nov. 1774
Works 1:446–48

I am sorry I cannot conclude without saying a word on a topic touched upon by my worthy colleague. I wish that topic had been passed by at a time when I have so little leisure to discuss it. But since he has thought proper to throw it out, I owe you a clear explanation of my poor sentiments on that subject.

He tells you that "the topic of instructions has occasioned much altercation and uneasiness in this city;" and he expresses himself (if I understand him rightly) in favour of the coercive authority of such instructions.

Certainly, gentlemen, it ought to be the happiness and glory of a representative to live in the strictest union, the closest correspondence, and the most unreserved communication with his constituents. Their wishes ought to have great weight with him; their opinion, high respect; their business, unremitted attention. It is his duty to sacrifice his repose, his pleasures, his satisfactions, to theirs; and above all, ever, and in all cases, to prefer their interest to his own. But his unbiassed opinion, his mature judgment, his enlightened conscience, he ought not to sacrifice to you, to any man, or to any set of men living. These he does not derive from your pleasure; no, nor from the law and the constitution. They are a trust from Providence, for the abuse of which he is deeply answerable. Your representative owes you, not his industry only, but his judgment; and he betrays, instead of serving you, if he sacrifices it to your opinion.

My worthy colleague says, his will ought to be subservient to yours. If that be all, the thing is innocent. If government were a matter of will upon any side, yours, without question, ought to be superior. But government and legislation are matters of reason and judgment, and not of inclination; and what sort of reason is that, in which the determination precedes the discussion; in which one set of men deliberate, and another decide; and where those who form the conclusion are perhaps three hundred miles distant from those who hear the arguments?

To deliver an opinion, is the right of all men; that of constituents is a weighty and respectable opinion, which a representative ought always to rejoice to hear; and which he ought always most seriously to consider. But *authoritative* instructions; *mandates* issued, which the member is bound blindly and implicitly to obey, to vote, and to argue for, though contrary to the clearest conviction of his judgment and conscience,—these are things utterly unknown to the laws of this land, and which arise from a fundamental mistake of the whole order and tenor of our constitution.

Parliament is not a *congress* of ambassadors from different and hostile interests; which interests each must maintain, as an agent and advocate, against other agents and advocates; but parliament is a *deliberative* assembly of *one* nation, with *one* interest, that of the whole; where, not local purposes, not local prejudices, ought to guide, but the general good, resulting from the general reason of the whole. You choose a member indeed; but when you have chosen him, he is not member of Bristol, but he is a member of *parliament*. If the local constituent should have an interest, or should form an hasty opinion, evidently opposite to the real good of the rest of the community, the member for that place ought to be as far, as any other, from any endeavour to give it effect. I beg pardon for saying so much on this subject. I have been unwillingly drawn into it; but I shall ever use a respectful frankness of communication with you. Your faithful friend, your devoted servant, I shall be to the end of my life: a flatterer you do not wish for.

8

JAMES BURGH, POLITICAL DISQUISITIONS
1:26–29, 36–38, 80–82
1774

Bk. II. Chap. II. Inadequate Representation, its Disadvantages.

To compare great things with small, could the *East India* company be said to be established on a proper foot, if 100 proprietors, whose stock amounted in all to 5,000 *l.* had the power of choosing the court of directors against the votes of 5000 proprietors, whose stock was worth 5,000,000 *l.* and if the court of directors, when chosen, possessed absolute power without appeal, and thought themselves responsible to no set of men upon earth? Or if a friendly society consisting of 100 members found that the whole power of the society was engrossed by 3 members; and that the others could obtain nothing they wanted, or in the manner they wished to have it; could this society be, with any shadow of propriety, called free? That parliamentary representation on its present foot, is as inconsistent with liberty, will appear but too clearly in the sequel.

That a *part* of the people, a *small* part of the people, and the most needy and *dependent* part of the people, should engross the power of electing legislators, and deprive the majority, and the independent part of the people of their right, which is, to choose legislators for themselves and the minority and dependent part of the people, is the grossest injustice that can be imagined.

Every government, to have a reasonable expectation of permanency, ought to be founded in *truth, justice,* and the *reason* of things. Our admirable constitution, the envy of *Europe,* is founded in *injustice.* Eight hundred individuals rule all, themselves accountable to none. Of these about 300 are *born* rulers, whether qualified or not. Of the others, a great many are *said* to be elected by a handful of beggars instead of the number and property, who have the right to be the electors. And of these pretended electors, the greatest part are *obliged* to choose the person nominated by some lord, or by the minister. Instead of the power's returning annually into the hands of the people, or, to speak properly of the boroughs, the lengthening of parliament to septenial, has deprived them of six parts in seven of their power; and if the power returned annually, as it ought, *all the people* would still have reason to complain, but the *handful,* who vote the members into the house.

In consequence of the inadequate state of representation, the sense of the people may be grosly misapprehended, or misrepresented, and it may turn out to be of very little consequence, that members were willing to obey the instructions of their constituents; because that would not be obeying the general sense of the people. For the people are not their constituents. The people of *England* are the innumerable multitude which fills, like one continued city, a great part of *Middlesex, Kent* and *Surry;* the countless inhabitants of the vast ridings of *Yorkshire,* the multitudes, who swarm in the cities and great towns of *Bristol, Liverpool, Manchester, Birmingham, Ely,* and others; some of which places have no representatives at all, and the rest are unequally represented. These places comprehend the greatest part of the people. Whereas the instructions would be sent from the hungry boroughs of *Cornwal, Devonshire,* &c. In short, the sense of the constituents would be, at best, only the sense of a few thousands; whereas it ought to be that of several hundreds of thousands, as will be very clearly made out by and by.

"Neither in *Scotland* nor *England* (says *Rapin*) are the resolutions of parliament to be always considered as the sense of the nation. It is a defect of the constitution of both houses, that the members of parliament receive no instructions from their electors. The moment they are met, they become masters and sovereigns of those by whom they are chosen, and palm upon the nation their own decisions for those of the public, though they are often contrary to the sentiments and interests of the people they represent. Instances are so frequent, that I need not stay to prove what I advance." "It must not be imagined (says he) that then," (in the times of *Henry* VIII.) "any more than at this day, whatever the parliament did was agreeable to the general opinion of the nation. The representative was chosen as a present, without any instruction concerning the points to be debated in parliament, nay without the people's knowing any thing of them. Thus the house of commons had, as I may say, an unlimited power to determine by a majority of votes, with the concurrence of the lords and assent of the king, what they deemed proper for the welfare of the kingdom." [In our times (the present always excepted) what they deem proper for the welfare of the junto.] "There was no necessity therefore, in order to obtain what the court desired, of having the consent of the people, but only the majority of voices in both houses. Hence it is easy to conceive, that the court used all imaginable means to cause such members to be elected, as were in their sentiments. This is now, and ever will be practiced, till some cure is found for this inconvenience. I call it an inconvenience, because it happens sometimes that the parliament passes acts contrary to the general opinion of the nation."

Under a whig ministry (says the same author) we see a whig parliament chosen, under a tory ministry a tory parliament. "It has frequently happened, that the resolutions of the lower house have been directly contrary to the sentiments of the people, whom they represented. So it is not the people, or commons of *England* that share the legislative power with the king and peers; but the representatives, who enjoy a privilege, which belongs only to the people in general, to whom however, they are not accountable for their conduct. All they can suffer, if they have acted in parliament contrary to the sense of their county, or borough, is not to be elected again."

Parliament under *Henry* VIII. confirmed the demolition of the papal power over *England,* and the dissolution of the religious houses; under *Edward* VI. demolished popery; under *Mary,* set it up again; under *Elizabeth,* over-

threw it a second time. So we have seen parliament stamp the *Americans,* then unstamp them, and then tax them in a new manner. Parliament has not, in these sudden doings and undoings, followed the sense of the people. The unsteady people are not so unsteady as this comes to. In former times, parliament was too much overawed by the authority of *kings:* in latter times, too much swayed by *ministerial* influence; and all this in consequence of its being in no respect a just and accountable representative of the people.

. . . . .

Bk. II. Chap. III. What would be adequate Parliamentary Representation.

Five millions, according to the estimate of my incomparable friend Dr. *Price,* and our best modern calculators, is nearest to the true number of the people of *England.* The males between 16 and 56 in 5 millions are 1,250,000, or a fourth part of the whole. As youth at 16 are of an age too immature to be capable of voting, so are many on the contrary capable of voting beyond the age of 56; and one may be supposed to make up for the other. It is commonly insisted on, that persons in servitude to others, and those who receive alms, ought not to be admitted to vote for members of parliament, because it is supposed, that their votes will be influenced by those, on whom they depend.

But the objection from influence would fall to the ground, if the state were on a right foot, and parliament free from court-influence. Supposing half the constitution in disorder, it is not easy to determine what would be best for the other half. My purpose is, to point out *all* the defects. And if the people will correct *all* I shall point out, I will then answer, that all shall go well; but not if they amend by *halves.*—To return,—

Every man has what may be called property, and unalienable property. Every man has a life, a personal liberty, a character, a right to his earnings, a right to a religious profession and worship according to his conscience, &c. and many men, who are in a state of dependence upon others, and who receive charity, have wives and children, in whom they have a right. Thus the poor are in danger of being injured by the government in a variety of ways. But, according to the commonly received doctrine, that servants, and those who receive alms, have no right to vote for members of parliament, an immense multitude of the people are utterly deprived of all power in determining who shall be the protectors of their lives, their personal liberty, their little property (which though singly considered is of small value, yet is upon the whole a very great object) and the chastity of their wives and daughters, &c. What is particularly hard upon the poor in this case is, that though they have no share in determining who shall be the lawgivers of their country, they have a very heavy share in raising the taxes which support government. The taxes on malt, on beer, leather, soap, candles, and other articles, which are paid chiefly by the poor, who are allowed *no votes* for members of parliament, amount to as much as a heavy land-tax. The landed interest would complain grievously, if they had no power of electing representatives.

And it is an established maxim in free states, that whoever contributes to the expenses of government ought to be satisfied concerning the application of the money contributed by them; consequently ought to have a share in electing those, who have the power of applying their money. Nor has the receiving of alms been always held a sufficient reason for refusing the privilege of voting, as appears by the following; "Resolved, *A.D.* 1690, That the free men of the port of *Sandwich,* inhabiting within the said borough, (although they receive *alms*) have a right to vote in electing barons to serve in parliament." Query, Whether there be not other instances of persons receiving alms, having a right to vote for members.

But, giving up the point, concerning the right of the poor to vote for members of parliament, the present state of parliamentary representation will still appear to be inadequate beyond all proportion. Of the 1,250,000, the whole number of males in *England,* we may well suppose that at least one third, or about 410,000 are housekeepers, and independent on alms. Divide this number by 513, the number of members for *England,* the quotient is 799 and a fraction, the round number is 800, which shews, that no member of parliament ought to carry his election against a competitor by fewer than 401 votes, that being a majority of 800, who have the right of voting, exclusive of the poor and dependent. It we allow *them* the right or privilege of choosing representatives, which I see no argument against, the number will be much greater, viz. about 1200, a majority of which is 601.

Bk. II. Chap. VII. Inadequate Representation universally complained of. Proposals by various Persons for redressing this Irregularity.

We see what light this grievance of inadequate parliamentary representation has been viewed in by the best politicians. If therefore judge *Blackstone* did, at the time he wrote the 172d page of the first vol. of his COMMENTARIES, recollect the miserable state of representation in our times, it is inconceivable how he could bring himself to write as he has done. "Only such are entirely excluded, from voting for members, says he, as can have no will of their own" [meaning poor and dependent people without property]. "There is hardly a free agent to be found, but what is entituled to a vote in some place or other in the kingdom." Did the learned judge consider, what he himself has observed, that the borough-members are four times as numerous, as the county members; that a few thousands of electors send in the majority of the house; that in many places a handful of beggars sends in as many members as the great and rich county of *York,* or city of *Bristol?* Did the learned judge consider these shocking absurdities, and monstrous disproportions, or did he consider the alarming influence the court has in parliament, when he wrote what follows, viz. "If any alteration might be wished, or suggested in the present frame of parliaments, it should be in favour of a more complete representation of the people." What! are we to put off with a cold If, in a case where our country lies bleeding to death? "If any alteration might be wished"—Let us go on then, and say, If the deliverance of

ourselves and our posterity from destruction might be wished; if any alteration of what must bring us to ruin might be wished—any alteration from a mockery rather than the reality of representation—any alteration from 300 placemen and pensioners sitting in the house of commons—any alteration from a corrupt court's commanding the majority of the elections into the house, and of the votes, when in it—any alteration from the parliament's becoming a mere outwork of the court—If it is, at last to be doubted, whether the saving of our country is to be wished, what must become of us? Had a hackneyed court-hireling written in this manner, it had been no matter of wonder. But if the most intelligent men in the nation are to endeavour to persuade the people that there is hardly room for a wish; that there is scarce any thing capable of alteration for the better, (the judge's four volumes are a continued panegyric) at the very time when there is hardly any thing in the condition, it ought to be in, at the time when we have upon us every symptom of a declining state, when we are sinking in a bottomless gulf of debt and corruption, the spirit of the constitution gone, the foundations of public security shaken, and the whole fabrick ready to come down in ruins upon our heads—if they who ought to be the watchmen of the public weal are thus to damp all proposals for redress of grievances—*Quo res summa loco?* In what condition is this once free and virtuous kingdom likely soon to be?

9

JOHN ADAMS, THOUGHTS ON GOVERNMENT
Apr. 1776
Papers 4:87–88

(See ch. 4, no. 5)

10

JOHN ADAMS TO JAMES SULLIVAN
26 May 1776
Papers 4:208–12

Your Favours of May 9th. and 17th. are now before me; and I consider them as the Commencement of a Correspondence, which will not only give me Pleasure, but may be of Service to the public, as, in my present Station I Stand in need of the best Intelligence, and the Advice of every Gentleman of Abilities and public Principles, in the Colony which has seen fit to place me here.

Our worthy Friend, Mr. Gerry has put into my Hand, a Letter from you, of the Sixth of May, in which you consider the Principles of Representation and Legislation, and give us Hints of Some Alterations, which you Seem to think necessary, in the Qualification of Voters.

I wish, Sir, I could possibly find Time, to accompany you, in your Investigation of the Principles upon which a Representative assembly Stands and ought to Stand, and in your Examination whether the Practice of our Colony, has been conformable to those Principles. But alass! Sir, my Time is So incessantly engrossed by the Business before me that I cannot Spare enough, to go through So large a Field: and as to Books, it is not easy to obtain them here, nor could I find a Moment to look into them, if I had them.

It is certain in Theory, that the only moral Foundation of Government is the Consent of the People. But to what an Extent Shall We carry this Principle? Shall We Say, that every Individual of the Community, old and young, male and female, as well as rich and poor, must consent, expressly to every Act of Legislation? No, you will Say. This is impossible. How then does the Right arise in the Majority to govern the Minority, against their Will? Whence arises the Right of the Men to govern Women, without their Consent? Whence the Right of the old to bind the Young, without theirs.

But let us first Suppose, that the whole Community of every Age, Rank, Sex, and Condition, has a Right to vote. This Community, is assembled—a Motion is made and carried by a Majority of one Voice. The Minority will not agree to this. Whence arises the Right of the Majority to govern, and the Obligation of the Minority to obey? from Necessity, you will Say, because there can be no other Rule. But why exclude Women? You will Say, because their Delicacy renders them unfit for Practice and Experience, in the great Business of Life, and the hardy Enterprizes of War, as well as the arduous Cares of State. Besides, their attention is So much engaged with the necessary Nurture of their Children, that Nature has made them fittest for domestic Cares. And Children have not Judgment or Will of their own. True. But will not these Reasons apply to others? Is it not equally true, that Men in general in every Society, who are wholly destitute of Property, are also too little acquainted with public Affairs to form a Right Judgment, and too dependent upon other Men to have a Will of their own? If this is a Fact, if you give to every Man, who has no Property, a Vote, will you not make a fine encouraging Provision for Corruption by your fundamental Law? Such is the Frailty of the human Heart, that very few Men, who have no Property, have any Judgment of their own. They talk and vote as they are directed by Some Man of Property, who has attached their Minds to his Interest.

Upon my Word, sir, I have long thought an Army, a Piece of Clock Work and to be governed only by Principles and Maxims, as fixed as any in Mechanicks, and by all that I have read in the History of Mankind, and in Authors, who have Speculated upon Society and Government, I am much inclined to think, a Government must manage a Society in the Same manner; and that this is Machinery too.

Harrington has Shewn that Power always follows Property. This I believe to be as infallible a Maxim, in Politicks, as, that Action and Re-action are equal, is in Mechanicks. Nay I believe We may advance one Step farther and affirm that the Ballance of Power in a Society, accompanies the Ballance of Property in Land. The only possible Way then of preserving the Ballance of Power on the side of equal Liberty and public Virtue, is to make the Acquisition of Land easy to every Member of Society: to make a Division of the Land into Small Quantities, So that the Multitude may be possessed of landed Estates. If the Multitude is possessed of the Ballance of real Estate, the Multitude will have the Ballance of Power, and in that Case the Multitude will take Care of the Liberty, Virtue, and Interest of the Multitude in all Acts of Government.

I believe these Principles have been felt, if not understood in the Massachusetts Bay, from the Beginning: And therefore I Should think that Wisdom and Policy would dictate in these Times, to be very cautious of making Alterations. Our people have never been very rigid in Scrutinizing into the Qualifications of Voters, and I presume they will not now begin to be so. But I would not advise them to make any alteration in the Laws, at present, respecting the Qualifications of Voters.

Your Idea, that those Laws, which affect the Lives and personal Liberty of all, or which inflict corporal Punishment, affect those, who are not qualified to vote, as well as those who are, is just. But, So they do Women, as well as Men, Children as well as Adults. What Reason Should there be, for excluding a Man of Twenty years, Eleven Months and twenty-seven days old, from a Vote when you admit one, who is twenty one? The Reason is, you must fix upon Some Period in Life, when the Understanding and Will of Men in general is fit to be trusted by the Public. Will not the Same Reason justify the State in fixing upon Some certain Quantity of Property, as a Qualification.

The Same Reasoning, which will induce you to admit all Men, who have no Property, to vote, with those who have, for those Laws, which affect the Person will prove that you ought to admit Women and Children: for generally Speaking, Women and Children, have as good Judgment, and as independent Minds as those Men who are wholly destitute of Property: these last being to all Intents and Purposes as much dependent upon others, who will please to feed, cloath, and employ them, as Women are upon their Husbands, or Children on their Parents.

As to your Idea, of proportioning the Votes of Men in Money Matters, to the Property they hold, it is utterly impracticable. There is no possible Way of Ascertaining, at any one Time, how much every Man in a Community, is worth; and if there was, So fluctuating is Trade and Property, that this State of it, would change in half an Hour. The Property of the whole Community, is Shifting every Hour, and no Record can be kept of the Changes.

Society can be governed only by general Rules. Government cannot accommodate itself to every particular Case, as it happens, nor to the Circumstances of particular Persons. It must establish general, comprehensive Regulations for Cases and Persons. The only Question is, which general Rule, will accommodate most Cases and most Persons.

Depend upon it, sir, it is dangerous to open So fruitfull a Source of Controversy and Altercation, as would be opened by attempting to alter the Qualifications of Voters. There will be no End of it. New Claims will arise. Women will demand a Vote. Lads from 12 to 21 will think their

Rights not enough attended to, and every Man, who has not a Farthing, will demand an equal Voice with any other in all Acts of State. It tends to confound and destroy all Distinctions, and prostrate all Ranks, to one common Levell.

11

RICHARD HENRY LEE TO MRS. HANNAH CORBIN
17 Mar. 1778
Letters 1:392–93

My Dear Sister,

Distressed as my mind is and has been by a variety of attentions, I am illy able by letter to give you the satisfaction I could wish on the several subjects of your letter. Reasonable as you are and friendly to the freedom and happiness of your country, I should have no doubt giving you perfect content in a few hours' conversation. You complain that widows are not represented, and that being temporary possessors of their estates ought not to be liable to the tax. The doctrine of representation is a large subject, and it is certain that it ought to be extended as far as wisdom and policy can allow; nor do I see that either of these forbid widows having property from voting, notwithstanding it has never been the practice either here or in England. Perhaps 'twas thought rather out of character for women to press into those tumultuous assemblages of men where the business of choosing representatives is conducted. And it might also have been considered as not so necessary, seeing that the representatives themselves, as their immediate constituents, must suffer the tax imposed in exact proportion as does all other property taxed, and that, therefore, it could not be supposed that taxes would be laid where the public good did not demand it. This, then, is the widow's security as well as that of the never married women, who have lands in their own right, for both of whom I have the highest respect, and would at any time give my consent to establish their right of voting. I am persuaded that it would not give them greater security, nor alter the mode of taxation you complain of; because the tax idea does not go to the consideration of perpetual property, but is accommodated to the high prices given for the annual profits. Thus no more than ½ per ct. is laid on the assessed value, although produce sells now 3 and 400 per cent above what it formerly did. Tobacco sold 5 or 6 years ago for 15s and 2d—now 'tis 50 and 55. A very considerable part of the property I hold is, like yours, temporary for my life only; yet I see the propriety of paying my proportion of the tax laid for the protection of property so long as that property remains in my possession and I derive use and profit from it. When we complained of British taxation we did so with much reason, and there is great difference between our case and that of the unrepresented in this country. The English Parliament nor their representatives would pay a farthing of the tax they im-

posed on us but quite otherwise. Their property would have been exonerated in exact proportion to the burthens they laid on ours. Oppressions, therefore, without end and taxes without reason or public necessity would have been our fate had we submitted to British usurpation. For my part I had much rather leave my children free than in possession of great nominal wealth, which would infallibly have been the case with all American possessions had our property been subject to the arbitrary taxation of a British Parliament.

12

THE ESSEX RESULT
29 Apr. 1778
Handlin 340–43

II. That in a free government, a law affecting the person and property of it's members, is not valid, unless it has the consent of a majority of the members, which majority should include those, who hold a major part of the property in the state.

It may be necessary to proceed further, and notice some particular principles, which should be attended to in forming the three several powers in a free republican government.

The first important branch that comes under our consideration, is the legislative body. Was the number of the people so small, that the whole could meet together without inconvenience, the opinion of the majority would be more easily known. But, besides the inconvenience of assembling such numbers, no great advantages could follow. Sixty thousand people could not discuss with candor, and determine with deliberation. Tumults, riots, and murder would be the result. But the impracticability of forming such an assembly, renders it needless to make any further observations. The opinions and consent of the majority must be collected from persons, delegated by every freeman of the state for that purpose. Every freeman, who hath sufficient discretion, should have a voice in the election of his legislators. To speak with precision, in every free state where the power of legislation is lodged in the hands of one or more bodies of representatives elected for that purpose, the person of every member of the state, and all the property in it, ought to be represented, because they are objects of legislation. All the members of the state are qualified to make the election, unless they have not sufficient discretion, or are so situated as to have no wills of their own. Persons not twenty one years old are deemed of the former class, from their want of years and experience. The municipal law of this country will not trust them with the disposition of their lands, and consigns them to the care of their parents or guardians. Women what age soever they are of, are also considered as not having a sufficient acquired discretion; not from a deficiency in their mental powers, but from the natural tenderness and delicacy of their minds, their retired mode of life, and various domestic duties. These concurring, prevent that promiscuous intercourse with the world, which is necessary to qualify them for electors. Slaves are of the latter class and have no wills. But are slaves members of a free government? We feel the absurdity, and would to God, the situation of America and the tempers of it's inhabitants were such, that the slave-holder could not be found in the land.

The rights of representation should be so equally and impartially distributed, that the representatives should have the same views, and interests with the people at large. They should think, feel, and act like them, and in fine, should be an exact miniature of their constituents. They should be (if we may use the expression) the whole body politic, with all it's property, rights, and priviledges, reduced to a smaller scale, every part being diminished in just proportion. To pursue the metaphor. If in adjusting the representation of freeman, any ten are reduced into one, all the other tens should be alike reduced: or if any hundred should be reduced to one, all the other hundreds should have just the same reduction. The representation ought also to be so adjusted, that it should be the interest of the representatives at all times, to do justice, therefore equal interest among the people, should have equal interest among the body of representatives. The majority of the representatives should also represent a majority of the people, and the legislative body should be so constructed, that every law affecting property, should have the consent of those who hold a majority of the property. The law would then be determined to be for the good of the whole by the proper judge, the majority, and the necessary consent thereto would be obtained: and all the members of the State would enjoy political liberty, and an equal degree of it. If the scale to which the body politic is to be reduced, is but a little smaller than the original, or, in other words, if a small number of freemen should be reduced to one, that is, send one representative, the number of representatives would be too large for the public good. The expences of government would be enormous. The body would be too unwieldy to deliberate with candor and coolness. The variety of opinions and oppositions would irritate the passions. Parties would be formed and factions engendered. The members would list under the banners of their respective leaders: address and intrigue would conduct the debates, and the result would tend only to promote the ambition or interest of a particular party. Such has always been in some degree, the course and event of debates instituted and managed by a large multitude.

For these reasons, some foreign politicians have laid it down as rule, that no body of men larger than an hundred, would transact business well: and Lord Chesterfield called the British house of commons a mere mob, because of the number of men which composed it.

Elections ought also to be free. No bribery, corruption, or undue influence should have place. They stifle the free voice of the people, corrupt their morals, and introduce a degeneracy of manners, a supineness of temper, and an inattention to their liberties, which pave the road for the approach of tyranny, in all it's frightful forms.

The man who buys an elector by his bribes, will see him again, and reap a profit from the bargain; and he thereby becomes a dangerous member of society. The legislative body will hold the purse strings, and men will struggle for a place in that body to acquire a share of the public wealth. It has always been the case. Bribery will be attempted, and the laws will not prevent it. All states have enacted severe laws against it, and they have been ineffectual. The defect was in the forms of government. They were not so contrived, as to prevent the practicability of it. If a small corporation can place a man in the legislative body, to bribe will be easy and cheap. To bribe a large corporation would be difficult and expensive, if practicable. In Great-Britain, the representatives of their counties and great cities are freely elected. To bribe the electors there, is impracticable: and their representatives are the most upright and able statesmen in parliament. The small boroughs are bought by the ministry and opulent men; and their representatives are the mere tools of administration or faction. Let us take warning.

A further check upon bribery is, when the corrupter of a people knows not the electors. If delegates were first appointed by a number of corporations, who at a short day were to elect their representatives, these bloodhounds in a state would be at fault. They would not scent their game. Besides, the representatives would probably be much better men—they would be double refined.

But it may be said, the virtuous American would blast with indignation the man, who should proffer him a bribe. Let it now be admitted as a fact. We ask, will that always be the case? The most virtuous states have become vicious. The morals of all people, in all ages, have been shockingly corrupted. The rigidly virtuous Spartans, who banished the use of gold and silver, who gloried in their poverty for centuries, at last fell a prey to luxury and corruption. The Romans, whose intense love to their country, astonishes a modern patriot, who fought the battles of the republic for three hundred years without pay, and who, as volunteers, extended her empire over Italy, were at last dissolved in luxury, courted the hand of bribery, and finally sold themselves as slaves, and prostrated their country to tryants the most ignominious and brutal. Shall we alone boast an exemption from the general fate of mankind? Are our private and political virtues to be transmitted untainted from generation to generation, through a course of ages? Have we not already degenerated from the pure morals and disinterested patriotism of our ancestors? And are not our manners becoming soft and luxurious, and have not our vices began to shoot? Would one venture to prophecy, that in a century from this period, we shall be a corrupt luxurious people, perhaps the close of that century would stamp this prophecy with the title of history.

The rights of representation should also be held sacred and inviolable, and for this purpose, representation should be fixed upon known and easy principles; and the constitution should make provision, that recourse should constantly be had to those principles within a very small period of years, to rectify the errors that will creep in through lapse of time, or alteration of situations. The want of fixed principles of government, and a stated regular recourse to them, have produced the dissolution of all states, whose constitutions have been transmitted to us by history.

13

INSTRUCTIONS OF PITTSFIELD, MASSACHUSETTS
1779
Taylor 117–19

Report of the Committee appointed by the Town to draw up Instructions for their Representatives in State Convention is as follows:—

To Col. Williams.

Sir,—As you have been duly elected by the town of Pittsfield their representative to meet in a convention of this State at Cambridge, the 1st of September next, for the purpose of forming a new Constitution for the people of this State, which we view as a matter of the greatest consequence to the present and future generations, it will doubtless be agreeable to you to understand their sentiments for the government of your deportment. You are therefore hereby instructed to unite with said convention in drawing up a Bill of Rights and in forming a new Constitution for the people of this State. We wish you to oppose all unnecessary delay in this great work, and to proceed in it with the utmost wisdom and caution.

In the Bill of Rights, you will endeavor that all those unalienable and important rights which are essential to true liberty, and form the basis of government in a free State, shall be inserted: particularly, that this people have a right to adopt that form of government which appears to us most eligible, and best calculated to promote the happiness of ourselves and posterity; that as all men by nature are free, and have no dominion one over another, and all power originates in the people, so, in a state of civil society, all power is founded in compact; that every man has an unalienable right to enjoy his own opinion in matters of religion, and to worship God in that manner that is agreeable to his own sentiments without any control whatsoever, and that no particular mode or sect of religion ought to be established, but that every one be protected in the peaceable enjoyment of his religious persuasion and way of worship; that no man can be deprived of liberty, and subjected to perpetual bondage and servitude, unless he has forfeited his liberty as a malefactor; that the people have a right peaceably to assemble, consider of their grievances, and petition for redress; that, as civil rulers derive their authority from the people, so they are accountable to them for the use of it; that elections ought to be free, equal, and annual; that, as all men are equal by nature, so, when they enter into a state of civil government, they are entitled precisely to the same rights and privileges, or to an equal degree of political happiness; that the right of trial by jury ought to be perpetual; that no man's property of right can be taken from him without his consent, given either in

person or by his representative; that no laws are obligatory on the people but those that have obtained a like consent, nor are such laws of any force, if, proceeding from a corrupt majority of the legislature, they are incompatible with the fundamental principles of government, and tend to subvert it; that the freedom of speech and debates and proceedings in the House of Representatives ought not to be questioned or impeached in any court, or place out of the General Court; that excessive bail shall not be required, nor excessive fines imposed, nor cruel and unjust punishments inflicted; that jurors ought to be duly impanelled and returned, and all jurors ought to be freeholders. These, and all other liberties which you find essential to true liberty, you will claim, demand, and insist upon, as the birthrights of this people.

In respect to the Constitution, you will use your best endeavors that the following things may be inserted in it amongst others: That the election of the representative body be annual; that no representative on any occasion shall absent himself from said House without leave first had from said body, but shall constantly attend on the business during the sessions. All taxes shall be levied with the utmost equality on polls, faculty, and property. You may consent to government by a Governor, Council, and House of Representatives. The Governor and Council shall have no negative voice upon the House of Representatives; but all disputed points shall be settled by the majority of the whole legislative body. The supreme judges of the executive courts shall be elected by the suffrages of the people at large, and be commissioned by the Governor. That all grants of money shall originate in the House of Representatives. The judges of the maritime courts, the attorney-general, and high sheriffs of each county, are to be appointed by the suffrages of people at large, and commissioned by the Governor. The justices of the Common Pleas and Quarter Sessions of the Peace in each county be elected by the suffrages of the people of said counties. That no person, unless of the Protestant religion, shall be Governor, Lieutenant-governor, or member of the Council or the House of Representatives.

The said Bill of Rights and Constitution you will move may be printed, and sent abroad for the approbation of the people of this State at large, and that each town be requested by said convention to show their approbation or disapprobation of every paragraph in said Bill of Rights and Constitution, and that it be not sent abroad for their approbation or disapprobation in the lump; and that the objectionable parts, if any such shall be, shall be pointed out by each town.

You are not to dissolve the convention, but to adjourn from time to time, as you shall find necessary, till said form of government is approved by the majority of the people.

On the whole, we empower you to act agreeable to the dictates of your own judgment after you have heard all the reasonings upon the various subjects of disquisition, having an invariable respect to the true liberty and real happiness of this State throughout all generations, any instructions herein contained to the contrary notwithstanding.

14

RETURN OF NORTHAMPTON, MASSACHUSETTS
22 May 1780
Handlin 557–85

(See ch. 15, no. 26)

15

THOMAS JEFFERSON, NOTES ON THE STATE OF
VIRGINIA, QUERY 13, 118–19
1784

This constitution was formed when we were new and unexperienced in the science of government. It was the first too which was formed in the whole United States. No wonder then that time and trial have discovered very capital defects in it.

1. The majority of the men in the state, who pay and fight for its support, are unrepresented in the legislature, the roll of freeholders intitled to vote, not including generally the half of those on the roll of the militia, or of the tax-gatherers.

2. Among those who share the representation, the shares are very unequal. Thus the county of Warwick, with only one hundred fighting men, has an equal representation with the county of Loudon, which has 1746. So that every man in Warwick has as much influence in the government as 17 men in Loudon. But lest it should be thought that an equal interspersion of small among large counties, through the whole state, may prevent any danger of injury to particular parts of it, we will divide it into districts, and shew the proportions of land, of fighting men, and of representation in each.

	Square miles	Fighting men	Dele-gates	Sena-tors
Between the sea-coast and falls of the rivers	11,205	19,012	71	12
Between the falls of the rivers and the Blue ridge of mountains	18,759	18,828	46	8
Between the Blue ridge and the Alleghaney	11,911	7,673	16	2
Between the Alleghaney and Ohio	79,650	4,458	16	2
Total	121,525	49,971	149	24

An inspection of this table will supply the place of commentaries on it. It will appear at once that nineteen thou-

sand men, living below the falls of the rivers, possess half the senate, and want four members only of possessing a majority of the house of delegates; a want more than supplied by the vicinity of their situation to the seat of government, and of course the greater degree of convenience and punctuality with which their members may and will attend in the legislature. These nineteen thousand, therefore, living in one part of the country, give law to upwards of thirty thousand, living in another, and appoint all their chief officers executive and judiciary. From the difference of their situation and circumstances, their interests will often be very different.

16

GEORGE WASHINGTON TO BUSHROD WASHINGTON
15 Nov. 1786
Writings 29:67

That representatives ought to be the mouth of their Constituents, I do not deny, nor do I mean to call in question the right of the latter to instruct them. It is to the embarrassment, into which they may be thrown by these instructions in *national matters* that my objections lie. In speaking of national matters I look to the foederal Government, which in my opinion it is the interest of every State to support; and to do this, as there are a variety of interests in the union, there must be a yielding of the parts to coalesce the whole. Now a County, a District, or even a State might decide on a measure, which, tho' apparently for the benefit of it in its unconnected state, may be repugnant to the interests of the nation, and eventually to the State itself as a part of the confederation. If then, members go instructed, to the Assembly, from certain Districts, the requisitions of Congress repugnant to the sense of them, and all the lights which they may receive from the communications of that body to the Legislature, must be unavailing; altho' the nature and necessity of them, when the reasons therefor are fully expounded; which can only be given by Congress to the Assembly thro' the Executive, and which come before them in their legislative capacity, are as clear as the sun. In local matters which concern the District; or things which respect the internal police of the State, there may be nothing amiss in instructions. In national matters also, the *sense*, but not the *Law* of the District may be given, leaving the Delegates to judge from the nature of the case and the evidence before them.

17

JOHN ADAMS, DEFENCE OF THE CONSTITUTIONS OF
GOVERNMENT OF THE UNITED STATES
1787

Works 4:284, 400–401

While it would be rash to say, that nothing further can be done to bring a free government, in all its parts, still nearer to perfection, the representations of the people are most obviously susceptible of improvement. The end to be aimed at, in the formation of a representative assembly, seems to be the sense of the people, the public voice. The perfection of the portrait consists in its likeness. Numbers, or property, or both, should be the rule; and the proportions of electors and members an affair of calculation. The duration should not be so long that the deputy should have time to forget the opinions of his constituents. Corruption in elections is the great enemy of freedom. Among the provisions to prevent it, more frequent elections, and a more general privilege of voting, are not all that might be devised. Dividing the districts, diminishing the distance of travel, and confining the choice to residents, would be great advances towards the annihilation of corruption.

. . . . .

A single assembly thus constituted, without any counterpoise, balance, or equilibrium, is to have all authority, legislative, executive, and judicial, concentrated in it. It is to make a constitution and laws by its own will, execute those laws at its own pleasure, and adjudge all controversies that arise concerning the meaning and application of them, at its own discretion. What is there to restrain it from making tyrannical laws, in order to execute them in a tyrannical manner? Will it be pretended, that the jealousy and vigilance of the people, and their power to discard them at the next election, will restrain them? Even this idea supposes a balance, an equilibrium, which M. Turgot holds in so much contempt; it supposes the people at large to be a check and control over the representative assembly. But this would be found a mere delusion. A jealousy between the electors and the elected neither ought to exist, nor is it possible to exist. It is a contradiction to suppose that a body of electors should have at one moment a warm affection and entire confidence in a man, so as to intrust him with authority, limited or unlimited, over their lives and fortunes; and the next moment after his election, to commence a suspicion of him, that shall prompt them to watch all his words, actions, and motions, and dispose them to renounce and punish him. They choose him, indeed, because they think he knows more, and is better disposed than the generality, and very often even than themselves. Indeed, the best use of a representative assembly, arises from the cordial affection and unreserved confidence which subsists between it and the collective body of the people. It is by such kind and candid intercourse alone, that the wants and desires of the people can be made known, on the one hand, or the necessities of the public communicated or reconciled to them, on the other. In

what did such a confidence in one assembly end, in Venice, Geneva, Biscay, Poland, but in an aristocracy and an oligarchy? There is no special providence for Americans, and their nature is the same with that of others.

18

JAMES WILSON, FEDERAL CONVENTION
6 June 1787

Farrand 1:132–33

Mr. Wilson. He wished for vigor in the Govt. but he wished that vigorous authority to flow immediately from the legitimate source of all authority. The Govt. ought to possess not only 1st. the *force* but 2ndly. the *mind or sense* of the people at large. The Legislature ought to be the most exact transcript of the whole Society. Representation is made necessary only because it is impossible for the people to act collectively. The opposition was to be expected he said from the *Governments,* not from the Citizens of the States. The latter had parted as was observed (by Mr. King) with all the necessary powers; and it was immaterial to them, by whom they were exercised, if well exercised. The State officers were to be losers of power. The people he supposed would be rather more attached to the national Govt. than to the State Govts. as being more important in itself, and more flattering to their pride. There is no danger of improper elections if made by *large* districts. Bad elections proceed from the smallness of the districts which give an opportunity to bad men to intrigue themselves into office.

19

ALEXANDER HAMILTON, FEDERAL CONVENTION
18 June 1787

Farrand 1:298–99

Such are the insuperable objections to both plans: and what is to be done on this occasion? I confess I am at a loss. I foresee the difficulty on a consolidated plan of drawing a representation from so extensive a continent to one place. What can be the inducements for gentlemen to come 600 miles to a national legislature? The expense would at least amount to £100,000. This however can be no conclusive objection if it eventuates in an extinction of state governments. The burthen of the latter would be saved, and the expense then would not be great. State distinctions would be found unnecessary, and yet I confess, to carry government to the extremities, the state governments reduced to corporations, and with very limited powers, might be necessary, and the expense of the national government become less burthensome.

Yet, I confess, I see great difficulty of drawing forth a

good representation. What, for example, will be the inducements for gentlemen of fortune and abilities to leave their houses and business to attend annually and long? It cannot be the wages; for these, I presume, must be small. Will not the power, therefore, be thrown into the hands of the demagogue or middling politician, who, for the sake of a small stipend and the hopes of advancement, will offer himself as a candidate, and the real men of weight and influence, by remaining at home, add strength to the state governments? I am at a loss to know what must be done—I despair that a republican form of government can remove the difficulties. Whatever may be my opinion, I would hold it however unwise to change that form of government.

20

FEDERAL FARMER, NO. 2
9 Oct. 1787
Storing 2.8.15

The essential parts of a free and good government are a full and equal representation of the people in the legislature, and the jury trial of the vicinage in the administration of justice—a full and equal representation, is that which possesses the same interests, feelings, opinions, and views the people themselves would were they all assembled—a fair representation, therefore, should be so regulated, that every order of men in the community, according to the common course of elections, can have a share in it—in order to allow professional men, merchants, traders, farmers, mechanics, etc. to bring a just proportion of their best informed men respectively into the legislature, the representation must be considerably numerous—We have about 200 state senators in the United States, and a less number than that of federal representatives cannot, clearly, be a full representation of this people, in the affairs of internal taxation and police, were there but one legislature for the whole union. The representation cannot be equal, or the situation of the people proper for one government only—if the extreme parts of the society cannot be represented as fully as the central—It is apparently impracticable that this should be the case in this extensive country—it would be impossible to collect a representation of the parts of the country five, six, and seven hundred miles from the seat of government.

21

JAMES MADISON, FEDERALIST, NO. 10, 62–63
22 Nov. 1787

(See ch. 4, no. 19)

22

FEDERAL FARMER, NO. 7
31 Dec. 1787
Storing 2.8.95–99

It being impracticable for the people to assemble to make laws, they must elect legislators, and assign men to the different departments of the government. In the representative branch we must expect chiefly to collect the confidence of the people, and in it to find almost entirely the force of persuasion. In forming this branch, therefore, several important considerations must be attended to. It must possess abilities to discern the situation of the people and of public affairs, a disposition to sympathize with the people, and a capacity and inclination to make laws congenial to their circumstances and condition: it must afford security against interested combinations, corruption and influence; it must possess the confidence, and have the voluntary support of the people.

I think these positions will not be controverted, nor the one I formerly advanced, that a fair and equal representation is that in which the interests, feelings, opinions and views of the people are collected, in such manner as they would be were the people all assembled. Having made these general observations, I shall proceed to consider further my principal position, viz. that there is no substantial representation of the people provided for in a government, in which the most essential powers, even as to the internal police of the country, are proposed to be lodged; and to propose certain amendments as to the representative branch: 1st, That there ought to be *an increase of the numbers of representatives:* And, 2dly, That the elections of them ought to be better secured.

1. The representation is unsubstantial and ought to be increased. In matters where there is much room for opinion, you will not expect me to establish my positions with mathematical certainty; you must only expect my observations to be candid, and such as are well founded in the mind of the writer. I am in a field where doctors disagree; and as to genuine representation, though no feature in government can be more important, perhaps, no one has been less understood, and no one that has received so imperfect a consideration by political writers. The ephori in Sparta, and the tribunes in Rome, were but the shadow; the representation in Great-Britain is unequal and insecure. In America we have done more in establishing this important branch on its true principles, than, perhaps, all the world besides: yet even here, I conceive, that very great improvements in representation may be made. In fixing this branch, the situation of the people must be surveyed and the number of representatives and forms of election apportioned to that situation. When we find a numerous people settled in a fertile and extensive country, possessing equality, and few or none of them oppressed with riches or wants, it ought to be the anxious care of the constitution and laws, to arrest them from national de-

pravity, and to preserve them in their happy condition. A virtuous people make just laws, and good laws tend to preserve unchanged a virtuous people. A virtuous and happy people by laws uncongenial to their characters, may easily be gradually changed into servile and depraved creatures. Where the people, or their representatives, make the laws, it is probable they will generally be fitted to the national character and circumstances, unless the representation be partial, and the imperfect substitute of the people. However, the people may be electors, if the representation be so formed as to give one or more of the natural classes of men in the society an undue ascendency over the others, it is imperfect; the former will gradually become masters, and the latter slaves. It is the first of all among the political balances, to preserve in its proper station each of these classes. We talk of balances in the legislature, and among the departments of government; we ought to carry them to the body of the people. Since I advanced the idea of balancing the several orders of men in a community, in forming a genuine representation, and seen that idea considered as chimerical, I have been sensibly struck with a sentence in the marquis Beccaria's treatise: this sentence was quoted by congress in 1774, and is as follows:—"In every society there is an effort continually tending to confer on one part the height of power and happiness, and to reduce the others to the extreme of weakness and misery; the intent of good laws is to oppose this effort, and to diffuse their influence universally and equally." Add to this Montesquieu's opinion, that "in a free state every man, who is supposed to be a free agent, ought to be concerned in his own government: therefore, the legislative should reside in the whole body of the people, or their representatives." It is extremely clear that these writers had in view the several orders of men in society, which we call aristocratical, democratical, merchantile, mechanic, &c. and perceived the efforts they are constantly, from interested and ambitious views, disposed to make to elevate themselves and oppress others. Each order must have a share in the business of legislation actually and efficiently. It is deceiving a people to tell them they are electors, and can chuse their legislators, if they cannot, in the nature of things, chuse men from among themselves, and genuinely like themselves. I wish you to take another idea along with you; we are not only to balance these natural efforts, but we are also to guard against accidental combinations; combinations founded in the connections of offices and private interests, both evils which are increased in proportion as the number of men, among which the elected must be, are decreased. To set this matter in a proper point of view, we must form some general ideas and descriptions of the different classes of men, as they may be divided by occupations and politically: the first class is the aristocratical. There are three kinds of aristocracy spoken of in this country—the first is a constitutional one, which does not exist in the United States in our common acceptation of the word. Montesquieu, it is true, observes, that where a part of the persons in a society, for want of property, age, or moral character, are excluded any share in the government, the others, who alone are the constitutional electors and elected, form this aristocracy; this, according to him,

exists in each of the United States, where a considerable number of persons, as all convicted of crimes, under age, or not possessed of certain property, are excluded any share in the government;—the second is an aristocratic faction: a junto of unprincipled men, often distinguished for their wealth or abilities, who combine together and make their object their private interests and aggrandizement; the existence of this description is merely accidental, but particularly to be guarded against. The third is the natural aristocracy; this term we use to designate a respectable order of men, the line between whom and the natural democracy is in some degree arbitrary; we may place men on one side of this line, which others may place on the other, and in all disputes between the few and the many, a considerable number are wavering and uncertain themselves on which side they are, or ought to be. In my idea of our natural aristocracy in the United States, I include about four or five thousand men; and among these I reckon those who have been placed in the offices of governors, of members of Congress, and state senators generally, in the principal officers of Congress, of the army and militia, the superior judges, the most eminent professional men, &c. and men of large property—the other persons and orders in the community form the natural democracy; this includes in general the yeomanry, the subordinate officers, civil and military, the fishermen, mechanics and traders, many of the merchants and professional men. It is easy to perceive that men of these two classes, the aristocratical, and democratical, with views equally honest, have sentiments widely different, especially respecting public and private expences, salaries, taxes, &c. Men of the first class associate more extensively, have a high sense of honor, possess abilities, ambition, and general knowledge; men of the second class are not so much used to combining great objects; they possess less ambition, and a larger share of honesty: their dependence is principally on middling and small estates, industrious pursuits, and hard labour, while that of the former is principally on the emoluments of large estates, and of the chief offices of government. Not only the efforts of these two great parties are to be balanced, but other interests and parties also, which do not always oppress each other merely for want of power, and for fear of the consequences; though they, in fact, mutually depend on each other; yet such are their general views, that the merchants alone would never fail to make laws favourable to themselves and oppressive to the farmers, &c. the farmers alone would act on like principles; the former would tax the land, the latter the trade. The manufacturers are often disposed to contend for monopolies, buyers make every exertion to lower prices, and sellers to raise them; men who live by fees and salaries endeavour to raise them, and the part of the people who pay them, endeavour to lower them; the public creditors to augment the taxes, and the people at large to lessen them. Thus, in every period of society, and in all the transactions of men, we see parties verifying the observation made by the Marquis; and those classes which have not their centinels in the government, in proportion to what they have to gain or lose, most infallibly be ruined.

Efforts among parties are not merely confined to property; they contend for rank and distinctions; all their passions in turn are enlisted in political controversies—Men, elevated in society, are often disgusted with the changeableness of the democracy, and the latter are often agitated with the passions of jealousy and envy: the yeomanry possess a large share of property and strength, are nervous and firm in their opinions and habits—the mechanics of towns are ardent and changeable, honest and credulous, they are inconsiderable for numbers, weight and strength, not always sufficiently stable for the supporting free governments: the fishing interest partakes partly of the strength and stability of the landed, and partly of the changeableness of the mechanic interest. As to merchants and traders, they are our agents in almost all money transactions; give activity to government, and possess a considerable share of influence in it. It has been observed by an able writer, that frugal industrious merchants are generally advocates for liberty. It is an observation, I believe, well founded, that the schools produce but few advocates for republican forms of government; gentlemen of the law, divinity, physic, &c. probably form about a fourth part of the people; yet their political influence, perhaps, is equal to that of all the other descriptions of men; if we may judge from the appointments to Congress, the legal characters will often, in a small representation, be the majority; but the more the representatives are encreased, the more of the farmers, merchants, &c. will be found to be brought into the government.

These general observations will enable you to discern what I intend by different classes, and the general scope of my ideas, when I contend for uniting and balancing their interests, feelings, opinions, and views in the legislature; we may not only so unite and balance these as to prevent a change in the government by the gradual exaltation of one part to the depression of others, but we may derive many other advantages from the combination and full representation; a small representation can never be well informed as to the circumstances of the people, the members of it must be too far removed from the people, in general, to sympathize with them, and too few to communicate with them: a representation must be extremely imperfect where the representatives are not circumstanced to make the proper communications to their constituents, and where the constituents in turn cannot, with tolerable convenience, make known their wants, circumstances, and opinions, to their representatives; where there is but one representative to 30,000 or 40,000 inhabitants, it appears to me, he can only mix, and be acquainted with a few respectable characters among his constituents, even double the federal representation, and then there must be a very great distance between the representatives and the people in general represented. On the proposed plan, the state of Delaware, the city of Philadelphia, the state of Rhode Island, the province of Main, the county of Suffolk in Massachusetts will have one representative each; there can be but little personal knowledge, or few communications, between him and the people at large of either of those districts. It has been observed, that mixing only with the respectable men, he will get the best information and ideas from them; he will also receive impressions favourable to their purposes particularly. Many plausible shifts have been made to divert the mind from dwelling on this defective representation, these I shall consider in another place.

23

FEDERAL FARMER, NO. 8
3 Jan. 1788
Storing 2.8.107–8

We may amuse ourselves with names; but the fact is, men will be governed by the motives and temptations that surround their situation. Political evils to be guarded against are in the human character, and not in the name of patrician or plebian. Had the people of Italy, in the early period of the republic, selected yearly, or biennially, four or five hundred of their best informed men, emphatically from among themselves, these representatives would have formed an honest respectable assembly, capable of combining in them the views and exertions of the people, and their respectability would have procured them honest and able leaders, and we should have seen equal liberty established. True liberty stands in need of a fostering hand; from the days of Adam she has found but one temple to dwell in securely; she has laid the foundation of one, perhaps her last, in America; whether this is to be compleated and have duration, is yet a question. Equal liberty never yet found many advocates among the great: it is a disagreeable truth, that power perverts men's views in a greater degree, than public employments inform their understandings—they become hardened in certain maxims, and more lost to fellow feelings. Men may always be too cautious to commit alarming and glaring iniquities; but they, as well as systems, are liable to be corrupted by slow degrees. Junius well observes, we are not only to guard against what men will do, but even against what they may do. Men in high public offices are in stations where they gradually lose sight of the people, and do not often think of attending to them, except when necessary to answer private purposes.

The body of the people must have this true representative security placed some where in the nation; and in the United States, or in any extended empire, I am fully persuaded can be placed no where, but in the forms of a federal republic, where we can divide and place it in several state or district legislatures, giving the people in these the means of opposing heavy internal taxes and oppressive measures in the proper stages. A great empire contains the amities and animosities of a world within itself. We are not like the people of England, one people compactly settled on a small island, with a great city filled with frugal merchants, serving as a common centre of liberty and union: we are dispersed, and it is impracticable for any but the few to assemble in one place: the few must be watched, checked, and often resisted—tyranny has ever shewn a prediliction to be in close amity with them, or the one man. Drive it from kings and it flies to senators, to dicemvirs, to dictators, to tribunes, to popular leaders, to military chiefs, &c.

24

FEDERAL FARMER, NO. 9
4 Jan. 1788
Storing 2.8.113–14, 125–26

But "the people must elect good men:"—Examine the system. Is it practicable for them to elect fit and proper representatives where the number is so small? "But the people may chuse whom they please." This is an observation, I believe, made without due attention to facts and the state of the community. To explain my meaning, I will consider the descriptions of men commonly presented to the people as candidates for the offices of representatives—we may rank them in three classes: 1. The men who form the natural aristocracy, as before defined. 2. Popular demagogues: these men also are often politically elevated, so as to be seen by the people through the extent of large districts; they often have some abilities, without principle, and rise into notice by their noise and arts. 3. The substantial and respectable part of the democracy: they are a numerous and valuable set of men, who discern and judge well, but from being generally silent in public assemblies are often overlooked: they are the most substantial and best informed men in the several towns, who occasionally fill the middle grades of offices, &c. who hold not a splendid, but a respectable rank in private concerns: these men are extensively diffused through all the counties, towns, and small districts in the union; even they, and their immediate connections, are raised above the majority of the people, and as representatives are only brought to a level with a more numerous part of the community, the middle orders, and a degree nearer the mass of the people. Hence it is that the best practical representation, even in a small state, must be several degrees more aristocratical than the body of the people. A representation so formed as to admit but few or none of the third class, is, in my opinion, not deserving of the name—even in armies, courts-martial are so formed as to admit subaltern officers into them. The true idea is, so to open and enlarge the representation as to let in due proportion of the third class with those of the first. Now, my opinion is, that the representation proposed is so small as that ordinarily very few or none of them can be elected; and, therefore, after all the parade of words and forms the government must possess the soul of aristocracy, or something worse, the spirit of popular leaders.

I observed in a former letter, that the state of Delaware[,] of Rhode-Island[,] the Province of Main, and each of the great counties in Massachusetts &c. would have one member, and rather more than one when the representatives shall be increased to one for each 30,000 inhabitants. In some districts the people are more dispersed and unequal than in others: In Delaware they are compact, in the Province of Main dispersed; how can the elections in either of those districts be regulated so as that a man of the third class can be elected?—Exactly the same principles and motives, the same uncontrolable circumstances, must govern the elections as in the choice of the governors. Call upon the people of either of those districts to chuse a governor, and it will, probably, never happen that they will not bestow a major part, or the greatest number, of their votes on some very conspicuous or very popular character. A man that is known among a few thousands of people, may be quite unknown among thirty or forty thousand. On the whole, it appears to me to be almost a self-evident position, that when we call on thirty or forty thousand inhabitants to unite in giving their votes for one man, it will be uniformly impracticable for them to unite in any men, except those few who have become eminent for their civil or military rank, or their popular legal abilities: it will be found totally impracticable for men in the private walks of life, except in the profession of the law, to become conspicuous enough to attract the notice of so many electors and have their suffrages.

. . . . .

We are not to expect even honest men rigidly to adhere to the line of strict impartiality, where the interest of themselves or friends is particularly concerned; if we do expect it, we shall deceive ourselves, and make a wrong estimate of human nature.

But it is asked how shall we remedy the evil, so as to complete and perpetuate the temple of equal laws and equal liberty? Perhaps we never can do it. Possibly we never may be able to do it in this immense country, under any one system of laws however modified; nevertheless, at present, I think the experiment worth a making. I feel an aversion to the disunion of the states, and to separate confederacies; the states have fought and bled in a common cause, and great dangers too may attend these confederacies. I think the system proposed capable of very considerable degrees of perfection, if we pursue first principles. I do not think that De Lolme, or any writer I have seen, has sufficiently pursued the proper inquiries and efficient means for making representation and balances in government more perfect; it is our task to do this in America. Our object is equal liberty, and equal laws diffusing their influence among all orders of men; to obtain this we must guard against the biass of interest and passions, against interested combinations, secret or open; we must aim at a balance of efforts and strength.

Clear it is, by increasing the representation we lessen the prospects of each member of congress being provided for in public offices: we proportionably lessen official influence and strengthen his prospects of becoming a private citizen, subject to the common burdens, without the compensation of the emoluments of office. By increasing the representation we make it more difficult to corrupt and influence the members; we diffuse them more extensively among the body of the people, perfect the balance, multiply information, strengthen the confidence of the people, and consequently support the laws on equal and free principles.

25

ALEXANDER HAMILTON, FEDERALIST, NO. 35, 218–22
5 Jan. 1788

One [objection] which if we may judge from the frequency of its repetition seems most to be relied on, is that the house of representatives is not sufficiently numerous for the reception of all the different classes of citizens; in order to combine the interests and feelings of every part of the community, and to produce a due sympathy between the representative body and its constituents. This argument presents itself under a very specious and seducing form; and is well calculated to lay hold of the prejudices of those to whom it is addressed. But when we come to dissect it with attention it will appear to be made up of nothing but fair sounding words. The object it seems to aim at is in the first place impracticable, and in the sense in which it is contended for is unnecessary. I reserve for another place the discussion of the question which relates to the sufficiency of the representative body in respect to numbers; and shall content myself with examining here the particular use which has been made of a contrary supposition in reference to the immediate subject of our inquiries.

The idea of an actual representation of all classes of the people by persons of each class is altogether visionary. Unless it were expressly provided in the Constitution that each different occupation should send one or more members the thing would never take place in practice. Mechanics and manufacturers will always be inclined with few exceptions to give their votes to merchants in preference to persons of their own professions or trades. Those discerning citizens are well aware that the mechanic and manufacturing arts furnish the materials of mercantile enterprise and industry. Many of them indeed are immediately connected with the operations of commerce. They know that the merchant is their natural patron and friend; and they are aware that however great the confidence they may justly feel in their own good sense, their interests can be more effectually promoted by the merchant than by themselves. They are sensible that their habits in life have not been such as to give them those acquired endowments, without which in a deliberative assembly the greatest natural abilities are for the most part useless; and that the influence and weight and superior acquirements of the merchants render them more equal to a contest with any spirit which might happen to infuse itself into the public councils unfriendly to the manufacturing and trading interests. These considerations and many others that might be mentioned prove, and experience confirms it, that artisans and manufacturers will commonly be disposed to bestow their votes upon merchants and those whom they recommend. We must therefore consider merchants as the natural representatives of all these classes of the community.

With regard to the learned professions, little need be observed; they truly form no distinct interest in society; and according to their situation and talents will be indiscriminately the objects of the confidence and choice of each other and of other parts of the community.

Nothing remains but the landed interest; and this in a political view and particulary in relation to taxes I take to be perfectly united from the wealthiest landlord to the poorest tenant. No tax can be laid on land which will not affect the proprietor of millions of acres as well as the proprietor of a single acre. Every land-holder will therefore have a common interest to keep the taxes on land as low as possible; and common interest may always be reckoned upon as the surest bond of sympathy. But if we even could suppose a distinction of interest between the opulent landholder and the middling farmer, what reason is there to conclude that the first would stand a better chance of being deputed to the national legislature than the last? If we take fact as our guide and look into our own senate and assembly we shall find that moderate proprietors of land prevail in both; nor is this less the case in the senate which consists of a smaller number than in the Assembly, which is composed of a greater number. Where the qualifications of the electors are the same, whether they have to choose a small or a large number their votes will fall upon those in whom they have most confidence; whether these happen to be men of large fortunes or of moderate property or of no property at all.

It is said to be necessary that all classes of citizens should have some of their own number in the representative body, in order that their feelings and interests may be the better understood and attended to. But we have seen that this will never happen under any arrangement that leaves the votes of the people free. Where this is the case, the representative body, with too few exceptions to have any influence on the spirit of the government, will be composed of land-holders, merchants, and men of the learned professions. But where is the danger that the interests and feelings of the different classes of citizens will not be understood or attended to by these three descriptions of men? Will not the land-holder know and feel whatever will promote or injure the interests of landed property? and will he not from his own interest in that species of property be sufficiently prone to resist every attempt to prejudice or incumber it? Will not the merchant understand and be disposed to cultivate as far as may be proper the interests of the mechanic and manufacturing arts to which his commerce is so nearly allied? Will not the man of the learned profession, who will feel a neutrality to the rivalships between the different branches of industry, be likely to prove an impartial arbiter between them, ready to promote either, so far as it shall appear to him conducive to the general interests of the society?

If we take into the account the momentary humors or dispositions which may happen to prevail in particular parts of the society, and to which a wise administration will never be inattentive, is the man whose situation leads to extensive inquiry and information less likely to be a competent judge of their nature, extent and foundation than one whose observation does not travel beyond the circle of his neighbours and acquaintances? Is it not natural that a man who is a candidate for the favour of the people and who is dependent on the suffrages of his fellow-citizens for the continuance of his public honors should take care to inform himself of their dispositions and inclinations and should be willing to allow them their proper degree of influence upon his conduct? This dependence, and the necessity of being bound himself and his posterity by the laws to which he gives his assent are the true, and they are the strong chords of sympathy between the representatives and the constituent.

There is no part of the administration of government that requires extensive information and a thorough knowledge of the principles of political economy so much as the business of taxation. The man who understands those principles best will be least likely to resort to oppressive expedients, or to sacrifice any particular class of citizens to the procurement of revenue. It might be demonstrated that the most productive system of finance will always be the least burthensome. There can be no doubt that in order to a judicious exercise of the power of taxation it is necessary that the person in whose hands it is should be acquainted with the general genius, habits and modes of thinking of the people at large and with the resources of the country. And this is all that can be reasonably meant by a knowledge of the interests and feelings of the people. In any other sense the proposition has either no meaning, or an absurd one. And in that sense let every considerate citizen judge for himself where the requisite qualification is most likely to be found.

26

ALEXANDER HAMILTON, FEDERALIST, NO. 36,
222–24
8 Jan. 1788

We have seen that the result of the observations, to which the foregoing number has been principally devoted, is that from the natural operation of the different interests and views of the various classes of the community, whether the representation of the people be more or less numerous, it will consist almost entirely of proprietors of land, of merchants and members of the learned professions, who will truly represent all those different interests and views. If it should be objected that we have seen other descriptions of men in the local Legislatures; I answer, that it is admitted there are exceptions to the rule, but not in sufficient number to influence the general complexion or character of the government. There are strong minds in every walk of life that will rise superior to the disadvantages of situation, and will command the tribute due to their merit, not only from the classes to which they particularly belong, but from the society in general. The door ought to be equally open to all; and I trust, for the credit of human nature, that we shall see examples of such vigorous plants flourishing in the soil of Foederal, as well as of State Legislation; but occasional instances of this sort, will not render the reasoning founded upon the general course of things less conclusive.

The subject might be placed in several other lights that would lead all to the same result; and in particular it might be asked, what greater affinity or relation of interest can be conceived between the carpenter and blacksmith, and the linen manufacturer or stocking weaver, than between the merchant and either of them? It is notorious, that there are often as great rivalships between different branches of the mechanic or manufacturing arts, as there are between any of the departments of labor and industry; so that unless the representative body were to be far more numerous than would be consistent with any idea of regularity or wisdom in its deliberations, it is impossible that what seems to be the spirit of the objection we have been considering, should ever be realised in practice. But I forbear to dwell any longer on a matter, which has hitherto worn too loose a garb to admit even of an accurate inspection of its real shape or tendency.

There is another objection of a somewhat more precise nature that claims our attention. It has been asserted that a power of internal taxation in the national Legislature could never be exercised with advantage, as well from the want of a sufficient knowledge of local circumstances as from an interference between the revenue laws of the Union and of the particular States. The supposition of a want of proper knowledge, seems to be entirely destitute of foundation. If any question is depending in a State Legislature respecting one of the counties which demands a knowledge of local details, how is it acquired? No doubt from the information of the members of the county. Cannot the like knowledge be obtained in the national Legislature from the representatives of each State. And is it not to be presumed that the men who will generally be sent there, will be possessed of the necessary degree of intelligence, to be able to communicate that information? Is the knowledge of local circumstances, as applied to taxation, a minute topographical acquaintance with all the mountains, rivers, streams, high-ways and bye-paths in each State, or is it a general acquaintance with its situation and resources—with the state of its agriculture, commerce, manufactures—with the nature of its products and consumptions—with the different degrees and kinds of its wealth, property and industry?

27

LUTHER MARTIN, GENUINE INFORMATION
1788

Storing 2.4.42

To prove *this*, and that the senate *as constituted* could not be a *security* for the *protection* and *preservation* of the *State* governments, and that the *senators* could not be justly considered the *representatives* of the *States* as *States*, it was observed, that upon *just principles of representation*, the *representative* ought to *speak* the sentiments of his *constituents*, and ought to *vote* in the *same manner* that his *constituents* would do (as far as he can judge) provided his constituents were acting in *person*, and had the same knowledge and information with himself; and therefore that the *representative* ought to be *dependant* on his *constituents*, and *answerable* to them; that the connexion between the *representative* and the *represented*, ought to be as *near* and as *close* as possible; according to these principles, Mr. Speaker, in this State it is provided by *its constitution*, that the representatives in Congress, shall be chosen *annually*, shall be *paid* by the *State*, and shall be subject to *recall* even within the year; so *cautiously* has our *constitution* guarded against an *abuse* of the trust reposed in our representatives in the federal government; whereas by the *third* and *sixth* sections of the *first* article of this new system, the senators are to be chosen for *six* years instead of being chosen *annually*; instead of being paid by their *States* who send them, *they* in conjunction with the other branch, are to *pay themselves* out of the treasury of the United States; and are not liable to be *recalled* during the period for which they are chosen: Thus, Sir, for *six years* the *senators* are rendered totally and absolutely *independent* of *their States*, of *whom* they ought to be the *representatives*, without any *bond* or *tie* between them: During that time they may join in measures *ruinous* and *destructive* to *their States*, even such as should *totally annihilate* their *State* governments, and their States *cannot recall them*, nor *exercise any controul over them*.

28

FISHER AMES, MASSACHUSETTS RATIFYING
CONVENTION
15 Jan. 1788

Elliot 2:8–9

Much has been said about the people divesting themselves of power, when they delegate it to representatives; and that all representation is to their disadvantage, because it is but an image, a copy; fainter and more imperfect than the original, the people, in whom the light of power is pri-

mary and unborrowed, which is only reflected by their delegates. I cannot agree to either of these opinions. The representation of the people is something more than the people. I know, sir, but one purpose which the people can effect without delegation, and that is to destroy a government. That they cannot erect a government, is evinced by our being thus assembled on their behalf. The people must govern by a majority, with whom all power resides. But how is the sense of this majority to be obtained? It has been said that a pure democracy is the best government for a small people who assemble in person. It is of small consequence to discuss it, as it would be inapplicable to the great country we inhabit. It may be of some use in this argument, however, to consider, that it would be very burdensome, subject to faction and violence; decisions would often be made by surprise, in the precipitancy of passion, by men who either understand nothing or care nothing about the subject; or by interested men, or those who vote for their own indemnity. It would be a government not by laws, but by men.

Such were the paltry democracies of Greece and Asia Minor, so much extolled, and so often proposed as a model for our imitation. I desire to be thankful that our people (said Mr. Ames) are not under any temptation to adopt the advice. I think it will not be denied that the people are gainers by the election of representatives. They may destroy, but they cannot exercise, the powers of government in person, but by their servants *they* govern: they do not renounce their power; they do not sacrifice their rights; they become the true sovereigns of the country when they delegate that power, which they cannot use themselves to their trustees.

29

JAMES MADISON, FEDERALIST, NO. 49, 340–43
2 Feb. 1788

(See ch. 2, no. 19)

30

JAMES MADISON, FEDERALIST, NO. 55, 372–74
13 Feb. 1788

The number of which the House of Representatives is to consist, forms another, and a very interesting point of view under which this branch of the federal legislature may be contemplated. Scarce any article indeed in the whole constitution seems to be rendered more worthy of attention, by the weight of character and the apparent force of argument, with which it has been assailed. The charges exhibited against it are, first, that so small a number of representatives will be an unsafe depositary of the public interests; secondly, that they will not possess a proper knowledge of the local circumstances of their numerous constituents; thirdly, that they will be taken from that class of citizens which will sympathize least with the feelings of the mass of the people, and be most likely to aim at a permanent elevation of the few on the depression of the many; fourthly, that defective as the number will be in the first instance, it will be more and more disproportionate, by the increase of the people, and the obstacles which will prevent a correspondent increase of the representatives.

In general it may be remarked on this subject, that no political problem is less susceptible of a precise solution, than that which relates to the number most convenient for a representative legislature: Nor is there any point on which the policy of the several states is more at variance; whether we compare their legislative assemblies directly with each other, or consider the proportions which they respectively bear to the number of their constituents. Passing over the difference between the smallest and largest states, as Delaware, whose most numerous branch consists of twenty-one representatives, and Massachusetts, where it amounts to between three and four hundred; a very considerable difference is observable among states nearly equal in population. The number of representatives in Pennsylvania is not more than one-fifth of that in the state last mentioned. New-York, whose population is to that of South-Carolina as six to five, has little more than one third of the number of representatives. As great a disparity prevails between the states of Georgia and Delaware, or Rhode-Island. In Pennsylvania the representatives do not bear a greater proportion to their constituents than of one for every four or five thousand. In Rhode-Island, they bear a proportion of at least one for every thousand. And according to the constitution of Georgia, the proportion may be carried to one for every ten electors; and must unavoidably far exceed the proportion in any of the other States.

Another general remark to be made is, that the ratio between the representatives and the people, ought not to be the same where the latter are very numerous, as where they are very few. Were the representatives in Virginia to be regulated by the standard in Rhode-Island, they would at this time amount to between four and five hundred; and twenty or thirty years hence, to a thousand. On the other hand, the ratio of Pennsylvania, if applied to the state of Delaware, would reduce the Representative assembly of the latter to seven or eight members. Nothing can be more fallacious than to found our political calculations on arithmetical principles. Sixty or seventy men, may be more properly trusted with a given degree of power than six or seven. But it does not follow, that six or seven hundred would be proportionally a better depositary. And if we carry on the supposition to six or seven thousand, the whole reasoning ought to be reversed. The truth is, that in all cases a certain number at least seems to be necessary to secure the benefits of free consultation and discussion, and to guard against too easy a combination for improper purposes: As on the other hand, the number ought at most to be kept within a certain limit, in order to avoid the confusion and intemperance of a multitude. In

all very numerous assemblies, of whatever characters composed, passion never fails to wrest the sceptre from reason. Had every Athenian citizen been a Socrates; every Athenian assembly would still have been a mob.

It is necessary also to recollect here the observations which were applied to the case of biennial elections. For the same reason that the limited powers of the Congress and the controul of the state legislatures, justify less frequent elections than the public safety might otherwise require; the members of the Congress need be less numerous than if they possessed the whole power of legislation, and were under no other than the ordinary restraints of other legislative bodies.

31

REPUBLICUS
16 Feb. 1788
Storing 5.13.3–4

And first the constitution should provide for a fair and equal representation. That is that every member of the union have a freedom of suffrage and that every equal number of people have an equal number of representatives; for if the preceding sentiments are just, no one deprived of suffrage, ought (unless he voluntarily adopt it at least implicitly) to be under the controul or direction of such constitution, or any law made in consequence of it: it is no law to him, he is in respect of it, still in a state of nature: and without equality of numbers it would be unjust; for it is incontestable that if every man has an equal natural right to governing power, he has an equal right to every thing that represents it; and if we suppose for instance one district to contain one hundred inhabitants, and another a thousand: each entitled to send two representatives; if we suppose the former to be only duly represented, then there will be nine hundred in the latter not represented at all; But this is so plain a case that it is only strange that it should ever have been controverted.

But again it should provide against their holding those trusts for long terms. This would call into public service a greater variety of estimable characters; would beget an emulation who should serve their country the most essentially; and make it perhaps as fashionable a virtue to serve the interest of the public, as it has been formerly a vice to serve the private interest of some favorite family or worthless dependent. Besides, this is a security which the people owe to themselves, for the fidelity of their servants; and perhaps the only good security they can have: add to this temporary intervals of ineligibility, that they may in a private capacity feel all the good and evil effects resulting from their administration; and be prevented from acquiring any influence, dangerous to the liberty of the community. Who ever doubts the utility of this provisionary measure let him just recur to the state of the British government under the triennial and septennial parliaments: and he will soon be satisfied.

32

JAMES MADISON, FEDERALIST, NO. 58, 395–96
20 Feb. 1788

One observation however I must be permitted, to add, on this subject, as claiming in my judgment a very serious attention. It is, that in all legislative assemblies, the greater the number composing them may be, the fewer will be the men who will in fact direct their proceedings. In the first place, the more numerous any assembly may be, of whatever characters composed, the greater is known to be the ascendancy of passion over reason. In the next place, the larger the number, the greater will be the proportion of members of limited information and of weak capacities. Now it is precisely on characters of this description that the eloquence and address of the few are known to act with all their force. In the antient republics, where the whole body of the people assembled in person, a single orator, or an artful statesman, was generally seen to rule with as compleat a sway, as if a sceptre had been placed in his single hands. On the same principle the more multitudinous a representative assembly may be rendered, the more it will partake of the infirmities incident to collective meetings of the people. Ignorance will be the dupe of cunning; and passion the slave of sophistry and declamation. The people can never err more than in supposing that by multiplying their representatives, beyond a certain limit, they strengthen the barrier against the government of a few. Experience will forever admonish them that on the contrary, *after securing a sufficient number for the purposes of safety, of local information, and of diffusive sympathy with the whole society,* they will counteract their own views by every addition to their representatives. The countenance of the government may become more democratic; but the soul that animates it will be more oligarchic. The machine will be enlarged, but the fewer and often, the more secret will be the springs by which its motions are directed.

33

JAMES MADISON, FEDERALIST, NO. 63, 427–28
1 Mar. 1788

(See ch. 4, no. 27)

34

ALEXANDER HAMILTON, FEDERALIST, NO. 71,
482–83
18 Mar. 1788

(See ch. 2, no. 21)

35

GEORGE MASON, VIRGINIA RATIFYING CONVENTION
4 June 1788
Storing 5.17.1

With respect to the representation so much applauded, I cannot think it such a full and free one as it is represented; but I must candidly acknowledge, that this defect results from the very nature of the Government. It would be impossible to have a full and adequate representation in the General Government; it would be too expensive and too unwieldy: We are then under the necessity of having this a very inadequate representation: Is this general representation to be compared with the real, actual, substantial representation of the State Legislatures? It cannot bear a comparison. To make representation real and actual, the number of Representatives ought to be adequate; they ought to mix with the people, think as they think, feel as they feel, ought to be perfectly amenable to them, and thoroughly acquainted with their interest and condition: Now these great ingredients are, either not at all, or in so small a degree, to be found in our Federal Representatives, that we have no real, actual, substantial representation; but I acknowledge it results from the nature of the Government: The necessity of this inconvenience may appear a sufficient reason not to argue against it: But, Sir, it clearly shews, that we ought to give power with a sparing hand to a Government thus imperfectly constructed. To a Government, which, in the nature of things, cannot but be defective, no powers ought to be given, but such as are absolutely necessary: There is one thing in it which I conceive to be extremely dangerous.

36

JAMES MADISON, VIRGINIA RATIFYING CONVENTION
20 June 1788
Papers 11:163

I have observed, that gentlemen suppose, that the general legislature will do every mischief they possibly can, and that they will omit to do every thing good which they are authorised to do. If this were a reasonable supposition, their objections would be good. I consider it reasonable to conclude, that they will as readily do their duty, as deviate from it: Nor do I go on the grounds mentioned by gentlemen on the other side—that we are to place unlimited confidence in them, and expect nothing but the most exalted integrity and sublime virtue. But I go on this great republican principle, that the people will have virtue and intelligence to select men of virtue and wisdom. Is there no virtue among us? If there be not, we are in a wretched situation. No theoretical checks—no form of government can render us secure. To suppose that any form of government will secure liberty or happiness without any virtue in the people, is a chimerical idea. If there be sufficient virtue and intelligence in the community, it will be exercised in the selection of these men. So that we do not depend on their virtue, or put confidence in our rulers, but in the people who are to choose them.

37

MELANCTON SMITH, NEW YORK RATIFYING CONVENTION
20–21 June 1788
Storing 6.12.9, 15–18

In Great Britain representation had been carried much farther than in any government we knew of, except our own; but in that country it now had only a name. America was the only country, in which the first fair opportunity had been offered. When we were Colonies, our representation was better than any that was then known: Since the revolution we had advanced still nearer to perfection. He considered it as an object, of all others the most important, to have it fixed on its true principle; yet he was convinced that it was impracticable to have such a representation in a consolidated government. However, said he, we may approach a great way towards perfection by encreasing the representation and limiting the powers of Congress. He considered that the great interests and liberties of the people could only be secured by the State Governments. He admitted, that if the new government was only confined to great national objects, it would be less exceptionable; but it extended to every thing dear to human nature. That this was the case could be proved without any long chain of reasoning:—for that power which had both the purse and the sword, had the government of the whole country, and might extend its powers to any and to every object. He had already observed, that by the true doctrine of representation, this principle was established—that the representative must be chosen by the free will of the majority of his constituents: It therefore followed that the representative should be chosen from small districts. This being admitted, he would ask, could 65 men, for 3,000,000, or 1 for 30,000, be chosen in this manner? Would they be possessed of the requisite information to make happy the great number of souls that were spread over this extensive country?—There was another objection to the clause: If great affairs of government were trusted to a few men, they would be more liable to corruption. Corruption, he knew, was unfashionable amongst us, but he supposed that Americans were like other men; and tho' they had hitherto displayed great virtues, still they were men; and therefore such steps should be taken as to prevent the possibility of corruption. We were now in that stage of society, in which we could deliberate with freedom;—how long it might

continue, God only knew! Twenty years hence, perhaps, these maxims might become unfashionable; we already hear, said he, in all parts of the country, gentlemen ridiculing that spirit of patriotism and love of liberty, which carried us through all our difficulties in times of danger.—When patriotism was already nearly hooted out of society, ought we not to take some precautions against the progress of corruption?

. . . . .

To determine whether the number of representatives proposed by this Constitution is sufficient, it is proper to examine the qualifications which this house ought to possess, in order to exercise their powers discreetly for the happiness of the people. The idea that naturally suggests itself to our minds, when we speak of representatives is, that they resemble those they represent; they should be a true picture of the people; possess the knowledge of their circumstances and their wants; sympathize in all their distresses, and be disposed to seek their true interests. The knowledge necessary for the representatives of a free people, not only comprehends extensive political and commercial information, such as is acquired by men of refined education, who have leisure to attain to high degrees of improvement, but it should also comprehend that kind of acquaintance with the common concerns and occupations of the people, which men of the middling class of life are in general much better competent to, than those of a superior class. To understand the true commercial interests of a country, not only requires just ideas of the general commerce of the world, but also, and principally, a knowledge of the productions of your own country and their value, what your soil is capable of producing, the nature of your manufactures, and the capacity of the country to increase both. To exercise the power of laying taxes, duties and excises with discretion, requires something more than acquaintance with the abstruse parts of the system of finance. It calls for a knowledge of the circumstances and ability of the people in general, a discernment how the burdens imposed will bear upon the different classes.

From these observations results this conclusion that the number of representatives should be so large, as that while it embraces men of the first class, it should admit those of the middling class of life. I am convinced that this Government is so constituted, that the representatives will generally be composed of the first class in the community, which I shall distinguish by the name of the natural aristocracy of the country. I do not mean to give offence by using this term. I am sensible this idea is treated by many gentlemen as chimerical. I shall be asked what is meant by the natural aristocracy—and told that no such distinction of classes of men exists among us. It is true it is our singular felicity that we have no legal or hereditary distinctions of this kind; but still there are real differences: Every society naturally divides itself into classes. The author of nature has bestowed on some greater capacities than on others— birth, education, talents and wealth, create distinctions among men as visible and of as much influence as titles, stars and garters. In every society, men of this class will command a superior degree of respect—and if the government is so constituted as to admit but few to exercise the powers of it, it will, according to the natural course of things, be in their hands. Men in the middling class, who are qualified as representatives, will not be so anxious to be chosen as those of the first. When the number is so small the office will be highly elevated and distinguished—the stile in which the members live will probably be high—circumstances of this kind, will render the place of a representative not a desirable one to sensible, substantial men, who have been used to walk in the plain and frugal paths of life.

Besides, the influence of the great will generally enable them to succeed in elections—it will be difficult to combine a district of country containing 30 or 40,000 inhabitants, frame your election laws as you please, in any one character; unless it be in one of conspicuous, military, popular, civil or legal talents. The great easily form associations; the poor and middling class form them with difficulty. If the elections be by plurality, as probably will be the case in this state, it is almost certain, none but the great will be chosen—for they easily unite their interest—The common people will divide, and their divisions will be promoted by the others. There will be scarcely a chance of their uniting, in any other but some great man, unless in some popular demagogue, who will probably be destitute of principle. A substantial yeoman of sense and discernment, will hardly ever be chosen. From these remarks it appears that the government will fall into the hands of the few and the great. This will be a government of oppression. I do not mean to declaim against the great, and charge them indiscriminately with want of principle and honesty.—The same passions and prejudices govern all men. The circumstances in which men are placed in a great measure give a cast to the human character. Those in middling circumstances, have less temptation—they are inclined by habit and the company with whom they associate, to set bounds to their passions and appetites—if this is not sufficient, the want of means to gratify them will be a restraint—they are obliged to employ their time in their respective callings—hence the substantial yeomanry of the country are more temperate, of better morals and less ambition than the great. The latter do not feel for the poor and middling class; the reasons are obvious—they are not obliged to use the pains and labour to procure property as the other.—They feel not the inconveniences arising from the payment of small sums. The great consider themselves above the common people—entitled to more respect—do not associate with them—they fancy themselves to have a right of pre-eminence in every thing. In short, they possess the same feelings, and are under the influence of the same motives, as an hereditary nobility. I know the idea that such a distinction exists in this country is ridiculed by some—But I am not the less apprehensive of danger from their influence on this account—Such distinctions exist all the world over—have been taken notice of by all writers on free government—and are founded in the nature of things. It has been the principal care of free governments to guard against the encroachments of the great. Common observation and experience prove the existence of such distinctions. Will any one say, that there does not exist in this country the pride of family, of wealth, of talents; and

that they do not command influence and respect among the common people? Congress, in their address to the inhabitants of the province of Quebec, in 1775, state this distinction in the following forcible words quoted from the Marquis Beccaria. "In every human society, there is an essay continually tending to confer on one part the height of power and happiness, and to reduce the other to the extreme of weakness and misery. The intent of good laws is to oppose this effort, and to diffuse their influence universally and equally." We ought to guard against the government being placed in the hands of this class—They cannot have that sympathy with their constituents which is necessary to connect them closely to their interest: Being in the habit of profuse living, they will be profuse in the public expences. They find no difficulty in paying their taxes, and therefore do not feel public burthens: Besides if they govern, they will enjoy the emoluments of the government. The middling class, from their frugal habits, and feeling themselves the public burdens, will be careful how they increase them.

But I may be asked, would you exclude the first class in the community, from any share in legislation? I answer by no means—they would be more dangerous out of power than in it—they would be factious—discontented and constantly disturbing the government—it would also be unjust—they have their liberties to protect as well as others—and the largest share of property. But my idea is, that the Constitution should be so framed as to admit this class, together with a sufficient number of the middling class to controul them. You will then combine the abilities and honesty of the community—a proper degree of information, and a disposition to pursue the public good. A representative body, composed principally of respectable yeomanry is the best possible security to liberty.—When the interest of this part of the community is pursued, the public good is pursued; because the body of every nation consists of this class. And because the interest of both the rich and the poor are involved in that of the middling class. No burden can be laid on the poor, but what will sensibly affect the middling class. Any law rendering property insecure, would be injurious to them.—When therefore this class in society pursue their own interest, they promote that of the public, for it is involved in it.

38

ALEXANDER HAMILTON, NEW YORK
RATIFYING CONVENTION
21 June 1788
Papers 5:36–37, 40–43

I agree that there should be a broad democratic branch in the national legislature. But this matter, Sir, depends on circumstances; It is impossible, in the first instance to be precise and exact with regard to the number; and it is equally impossible to determine to what point it may be proper in future to increase it. On this ground I am disposed to acquiesce. In my reasonings on the subject of government, I rely more on the interests and the opinions of men, than on any speculative parchment provisions whatever. I have found, that Constitutions are more or less excellent, as they are more or less agreeable to the natural operation of things: I am therefore disposed not to dwell long on curious speculations, or pay much attention to modes and forms; but to adopt a system, whose principles have been sanctioned by experience; adapt it to the real state of our country; and depend on probable reasonings for its operation and result. I contend that sixty-five and twenty-six in two bodies afford perfect security, in the present state of things; and that the regular progressive enlargement, which was in the contemplation of the General Convention, will leave not an apprehension of danger in the most timid and suspicious mind. It will be the interest of the large states to increase the representation: This will be the standing instruction to their delegates. But, say the gentlemen, the Members of Congress will be interested not to increase the number, as it will diminish their relative influence. In all their reasoning upon the subject, there seems to be this fallacy: They suppose that the representative will have no motive of action, on the one side, but a sense of duty; or on the other, but corruption: They do not reflect, that he is to return to the community; that he is dependent on the will of the people, and that it cannot be his interest to oppose their wishes. Sir, the general sense of the people will regulate the conduct of their representatives. I admit that there are exceptions to this rule: There are certain conjunctures, when it may be necessary and proper to disregard the opinions which the majority of the people have formed: But in the general course of things, the popular views and even prejudices will direct the actions of the rulers.

All governments, even the most despotic, depend, in a great degree, on opinion. In free republics, it is most peculiarly the case: In these, the will of the people makes the essential principle of the government; and the laws which control the community, receive their tone and spirit from the public wishes. It is the fortunate situation of our country, that the minds of the people are exceedingly enlightened and refined: Here then we may expect the laws to be proportionably agreeable to the standard of perfect policy; and the wisdom of public measures to consist with the most intimate conformity between the views of the representative and his constituent. If the general voice of the people be for an increase, it undoubtedly must take place: They have it in their power to instruct their representatives; and the State Legislatures, which appoint the Senators, may enjoin it also upon them.

. . . . .

It has been farther, by the gentlemen in opposition, observed, that a large representation is necessary to understand the interests of the people. This principle is by no means true in the extent to which the gentleman seems to carry it. I would ask, why may not a man understand the interests of thirty [thousand] as well as of twenty? The position appears to be made upon the unfounded presumption, that all the interests of all parts of the community

must be represented. No idea is more erroneous than this. Only such interests are proper to be represented, as are involved in the powers of the General Government. These interests come compleatly under the observation of one, or a few men; and the requisite information is by no means augmented in proportion to the increase of number. What are the objects of the Government? Commerce, taxation, &c. In order to comprehend the interests of commerce, is it necessary to know how wheat is raised, and in what proportion it is produced in one district and in another? By no means. Neither is this species of knowledge necessary in general calculations upon the subject of taxation. The information necessary for these purposes, is that which is open to every intelligent enquirer; and of which, five men may be as perfectly possessed as fifty. In royal governments, there are usually particular men to whom the business of taxation is committed. These men have the forming of systems of finance; and the regulation of the revenue. I do not mean to commend this practice. It proves however, this point; that a few individuals may be competent to these objects; and that large numbers are not necessary to perfection in the science of taxation. But granting, for a moment, that this minute and local knowledge of the gentlemen contend for, is necessary, let us see, if under the New Constitution, it will not probably be found in the representation. The natural and proper mode of holding elections, will be to divide the state into districts, in proportion to the number to be elected. This state will consequently be divided at first into six. One man from each district will probably possess all the knowledge the gentlemen can desire. Are the senators of this state more ignorant of the interests of the people, than the assembly? Have they not ever enjoyed their confidence as much? Yet, instead of six districts, they are elected in four; and the chance of their being collected from the smaller divisions of the state consequently diminished. Their number is but twenty-four; and their powers are co-extensive with those of the assembly, and reach objects, which are most dear to the people—life, liberty and property.

Sir, we hear constantly a great deal, which is rather calculated to awake our passions, and create prejudices, than to conduct us to truth, and teach us our real interests. I do not suppose this to be the design of the gentlemen. Why then are we told so often of an aristocracy? For my part, I hardly know the meaning of this word as it is applied. If all we hear be true, this government is really a very bad one. But who are the aristocracy among us? Where do we find men elevated to a perpetual rank above their fellow citizens; and possessing powers entirely independent of them? The arguments of the gentlemen only go to prove that there are men who are rich, men who are poor, some who are wise, and others who are not—. That indeed every distinguished man is an aristocrat. This reminds me of a description of the aristocrats, I have seen in a late publication, styled the Federal Farmer. The author reckons in the aristocracy, all governors of states, members of Congress, chief magistrates, and all officers of the militia. This description, I presume to say, is ridiculous. The image is a phantom. Does the new government render a rich man more eligible than a poor one? No. It requires no such qualification. It is bottomed on the broad and equal principle of your state constitution.

Sir, if the people have it in their option, to elect their most meritorious men; is this to be considered as an objection? Shall the constitution oppose their wishes, and abridge their most invaluable privilege? While property continues to be pretty equally divided, and a considerable share of information pervades the community; the tendency of the people's suffrages, will be to elevate merit even from obscurity. As riches increase and accumulate in few hands; as luxury prevails in society; virtue will be in a greater degree considered as only a graceful appendage of wealth, and the tendency of things will be to depart from the republican standard. This is the real disposition of human nature: It is what, neither the honorable member nor myself can correct. It is a common misfortune, that awaits our state constitution, as well as all others.

. . . . .

It is a harsh doctrine, that men grow wicked in proportion as they improve and enlighten their minds. Experience has by no means justified us in the supposition, that there is more virtue in one class of men than in another. Look through the rich and the poor of the community; the learned and the ignorant. Where does virtue predominate? The difference indeed consists, not in the quantity but kind of vices, which are incident to the various classes; and here the advantage of character belongs to the wealthy. Their vices are probably more favorable to the prosperity of the state, than those of the indigent; and partake less of moral depravity.

39

DEBATE IN HOUSE OF REPRESENTATIVES
15 Aug. 1789
Annals 1:733–45

Mr. TUCKER then moved to insert these words, "to instruct their Representatives" [in the language of the proposed amendment: "The freedom of speech and of the press, and the right of the people peaceably to assemble and consult for their common good, and to apply to the government for redress of grievances, shall not be infringed"].

Mr. HARTLEY wished the motion had not been made, for gentlemen acquainted with the circumstances of this country, and the history of the country from which we separated, differed exceedingly on this point. The members of the House of Representatives, said he, are chosen for two years, the members of the Senate for six.

According to the principles laid down in the Constitution, it is presumable that the persons elected know the interests and the circumstances of their constituents, and being checked in their determinations by a division of the Legislative power into two branches, there is little danger of error. At least it ought to be supposed that they have the confidence of the people during the period for which

they are elected; and if, by misconduct, they forfeit it, their constituents have the power of leaving them out at the expiration of that time—thus they are answerable for the part they have taken in measures that may be contrary to the general wish.

Representation is the principle of our Government; the people ought to have confidence in the honor and integrity of those they send forward to transact their business; their right to instruct them is a problematical subject. We have seen it attended with bad consequences, both in England and America. When the passions of the people are excited, instructions have been resorted to and obtained, to answer party purposes; and although the public opinion is generally respectable, yet at such moments it has been known to be often wrong; and happy is that Government composed of men of firmness and wisdom to discover, and resist popular error.

If, in a small community, where the interests, habits, and manners are neither so numerous or diversified, instructions bind not, what shall we say of instructions to this body? Can it be supposed that the inhabitants of a single district in a State, are better informed with respect to the general interests of the Union, than a select body assembled from every part? Can it be supposed that a part will be more desirous of promoting the good of the whole than the whole will of the part? I apprehend, sir, that Congress will be the best judges of proper measures, and that instructions will never be resorted to but for party purposes, when they will generally contain the prejudices and acrimony of the party, rather than the dictates of honest reason and sound policy.

In England, this question has been considerably agitated. The representatives of some towns in Parliament have acknowledged, and submitted to the binding force of instructions, while the majority have thrown off the shackles with disdain. I would not have this precedent influence our decision; but let the doctrine be tried upon its own merits, and stand or fall as it shall be found to deserve.

It appears to my mind, that the principle of representation is distinct from an agency, which may require written instructions. The great end of meeting is to consult for the common good; but can the common good be discerned without the object is reflected and shown in every light. A local or partial view does not necessarily enable any man to comprehend it clearly; this can only result from an inspection into the aggregate. Instructions viewed in this light will be found to embarrass the best and wisest men. And were all the members to take their seats in order to obey instructions, and those instructions were as various as it is probable they would be, what possibility would there exist of so accommodating each to the other as to produce any act whatever? Perhaps a majority of the whole might not be instructed to agree to any one point, and is it thus the people of the United States propose to form a more perfect union, provide for the common defence, and promote the general welfare?

Sir, I have known within my own time so many inconveniences and real evils arise from adopting the popular opinions on the moment, that although I respect them as much as any man, I hope this Government will particularly guard against them, at least that they will not bind themselves by a constitutional act, and by oath, to submit to their influence; if they do, the great object which this Government has been established to attain, will inevitably elude our grasp on the uncertain and veering winds of popular commotion.

Mr. PAGE.—The gentleman from Pennsylvania tells you, that in England this principle is doubted; how far this is consonant with the nature of the Government I will not pretend to say; but I am not astonished to find that the administrators of a monarchical Government are unassailable by the weak voice of the people; but under a democracy, whose great end is to form a code of laws congenial with the public sentiment, the popular opinion ought to be collected and attended to. Our present object is, I presume, to secure to our constituents and to posterity these inestimable rights. Our Government is derived from the people, of consequence the people have a right to consult for the common good; but to what end will this be done, if they have not the power of instructing their representatives? Instruction and representation in a republic appear to me to be inseparably connected; but were I the subject of a monarch, I should doubt whether the public good did not depend more upon the prince's will than the will of the people. I should dread a popular assembly consulting for the public good, because, under its influence, commotions and tumults might arise that would shake the foundation of the monarch's throne, and make the empire tremble in expectation. The people of England have submitted the crown to the Hanover family, and have rejected the Stuarts. If instructions upon such a revolution were considered binding, it is difficult to know what would have been the effects. It might be well, therefore, to have the doctrine exploded from that kingdom; but it will not be advanced as a substantial reason in favor of our treading in the same steps.

The honorable gentleman has said, that when once the people have chosen a representative, they must rely on his integrity and judgment during the period for which he is elected. I think, sir, to doubt the authority of the people to instruct their representatives, will give them just cause to be alarmed for their fate. I look upon it as a dangerous doctrine, subversive of the great end for which the United States have confederated. Every friend of mankind, every well-wisher of his country, will be desirous of obtaining the sense of the people on every occasion of magnitude; but how can this be so well expressed as in instructions to their representatives? I hope, therefore, that gentlemen will not oppose the insertion of it in this part of the report.

Mr. CLYMER.—I hope the amendment will not be adopted; but if our constituents choose to instruct us, that they may be left at liberty to do so. Do gentlemen foresee the extent of these words? If they have a constitutional right to instruct us, it infers that we are bound by those instructions; and as we ought not to decide constitutional questions by implication, I presume we shall be called upon to go further, and expressly declare the members of the Legislature bound by the instruction of their constituents. This is a most dangerous principle, utterly destruc-

tive of all ideas of an independent and deliberative body, which are essential requisites in the Legislatures of free Governments; they prevent men of abilities and experience from rendering those services to the community that are in their power, destroying the object contemplated by establishing an efficient General Government, and rendering Congress a mere passive machine.

Mr. SHERMAN.—It appears to me, that the words are calculated to mislead the people, by conveying an idea that they have a right to control the debates of the Legislature. This cannot be admitted to be just, because it would destroy the object of their meeting. I think, when the people have chosen a representative, it is his duty to meet others from the different parts of the Union, and consult, and agree with them to such acts as are for the general benefit of the whole community. If they were to be guided by instructions, there would be no use in deliberation; all that a man would have to do, would be to produce his instructions, and lay them on the table, and let them speak for him. From hence I think it may be fairly inferred, that the right of the people to consult for the common good can go no further than to petition the Legislature, or apply for a redress of grievances. It is the duty of a good representative to inquire what measures are most likely to promote the general welfare, and, after he has discovered them, to give them his support. Should his instructions, therefore, coincide with his ideas on any measure, they would be unnecessary; if they were contrary to the conviction of his own mind, he must be bound by every principle of justice to disregard them.

Mr. JACKSON was in favor of the right of the people to assemble and consult for the common good; it had been used in this country as one of the best checks on the British Legislature in their unjustifiable attempts to tax the colonies without their consent. America had no representatives in the British Parliament, therefore they could instruct none, yet they exercised the power of consultation to a good effect. He begged gentlemen to consider the dangerous tendency of establishing such a doctrine; it would necessarily drive the house into a number of factions. There might be different instructions from every State, and the representation from each State would be a faction to support its own measures.

If we establish this as a right, we shall be bound by those instructions; now, I am willing to leave both the people and representatives to their own discretion on this subject. Let the people consult and give their opinion; let the representative judge of it; and if it is just, let him govern himself by it as a good member ought to do; but if it is otherwise, let him have it in his power to reject their advice.

What may be the consequence of binding a man to vote in all cases according to the will of others? He is to decide upon a constitutional point, and on this question his conscience is bound by the obligation of a solemn oath; you now involve him in a serious dilemma. If he votes according to his conscience, he decides against his instructions; but in deciding against his instructions, he commits a breach of the constitution, by infringing the prerogative of the people, secured to them by this declaration. In short, it will give rise to such a variety of absurdities and inconsistencies, as no prudent Legislature would wish to involve themselves in.

Mr. GERRY.—By the checks provided in the constitution, we have good grounds to believe that the very framers of it conceived that the Government would be liable to maladministration, and I presume that the gentlemen of this House do not mean to arrogate to themselves more perfection than human nature has as yet been found to be capable of; if they do not, they will admit an additional check against abuses which this, like every other Government, is subject to. Instruction from the people will furnish this in a considerable degree.

It has been said that the amendment proposed by the honorable gentleman from South Carolina (Mr. TUCKER) determines this point, "that the people can bind their representatives to follow their instructions." I do not conceive that this necessarily follows. I think the representative, notwithstanding the insertion of these words, would be at liberty to act as he pleased; if he declined to pursue such measures as he was directed to attain, the people would have a right to refuse him their suffrages at a future election.

Now, though I do not believe the amendment would bind the representatives to obey the instructions, yet I think the people have a right both to instruct and bind them. Do gentlemen conceive that on any occasion instructions would be so general as to proceed from all our constituents? If they do, it is the sovereign will; for gentlemen will not contend that the sovereign will [resides] in the Legislature. The friends and patrons of this constitution have always declared that the sovereignty resides in the people, and that they do not part with it on any occasion; to say the sovereignty vests in the people, and that they have not a right to instruct and control their representatives, is absurd to the last degree. They must either give up their principle, or grant that the people have a right to exercise their sovereignty to control the whole Government, as well as this branch of it. But the amendment does not carry the principle to such an extent, it only declares the right of the people to send instructions; the representative will, if he thinks proper, communicate his instructions to the House, but how far they shall operate on his conduct, he will judge for himself.

The honorable gentleman from Georgia (Mr. JACKSON) supposes that instructions will tend to generate factions in this House; but he did not see how it could have that effect, any more than the freedom of debate had. If the representative entertains the same opinion with his constituents, he will decide with them in favor of the measure; if other gentlemen, who are not instructed on this point, are convinced by argument that the measure is proper, they will also vote with them; consequently, the influence of debate and of instruction is the same.

The gentleman says further, that the people have the right of instructing their representatives; if so, why not declare it? Does he mean that it shall lie dormant and never be exercised? If so, it will be a right of no utility. But much good may result from a declaration in the constitution that they possess this privilege; the people will be encouraged to come forward with their instructions, which will form a fund of useful information for the Legislature. We cannot, I apprehend, be too well informed of the true state, condition, and sentiment of our constituents, and perhaps this is the best mode in our power of obtaining information. I hope we shall never shut our ears against that information which is to be derived from the petitions and instructions of our constituents. I hope we shall never presume to think that all the wisdom of this country is concentred within the walls of this House. Men, unambitious of distinctions from their fellow-citizens, remain within their own domestic walk, unheard of and unseen, possessing all the advantages resulting from a watchful observance of public men and public measures, whose voice, if we would descend to listen to it, would give us knowledge superior to what could be acquired amidst the cares and bustles of a public life; let us then adopt the amendment, and encourage the diffident to enrich our stock of knowledge with the treasure of their remarks and observations.

Mr. MADISON.—I think the committee acted prudently in omitting to insert these words in the report they have brought forward; if, unfortunately, the attempt of proposing amendments should prove abortive, it will not arise from the want of a disposition in the friends of the constitution to do what is right with respect to securing the rights and privileges of the people of America, but from the difficulties arising from discussing and proposing abstract propositions, of which the judgment may not be convinced. I venture to say, that if we confine ourselves to an enumeration of simple, acknowledged principles, the ratification will meet with but little difficulty. Amendments of a doubtful nature will have a tendency to prejudice the whole system; the proposition now suggested partakes highly of this nature. It is doubted by many gentlemen here; it has been objected to in intelligent publications throughout the Union; it is doubted by many members of the State Legislatures. In one sense this declaration is true, in many others it is certainly not true; in the sense in which it is true, we have asserted the right sufficiently in what we have done; if we mean nothing more than this, that the people have a right to express and communicate their sentiments and wishes, we have provided for it already. The right of freedom of speech is secured; the liberty of the press is expressly declared to be beyond the reach of this Government; the people may therefore publicly address their representatives[,] may privately advise them, or declare their sentiments by petition to the whole body; in all these ways they may communicate their will. If gentlemen mean to go further, and to say that the people have a right to instruct their representatives in such a sense as that the delegates are obliged to conform to those instructions, the declaration is not true. Suppose they instruct a representative, by his vote, to violate the constitution; is he at liberty to obey such instructions? Suppose he is instructed to patronize certain measures, and from circumstances known to him, but not to his constituents, he is convinced that they will endanger the public good; is he obliged to sacrifice his own judgment to them? Is he absolutely bound to perform what he is instructed to do? Suppose he refuses, will his vote be the less valid, or the community be disengaged from that obedience which is due to the laws of the Union? If his vote must inevitably have the same effect, what sort of a right is this in the constitution, to instruct a representative who has a right to disregard the order, if he pleases? In this sense the right does not exist, in the other sense it does exist, and is provided largely for.

The honorable gentleman from Massachusetts asks if the sovereignty is not with the people at large. Does he infer that the people can, in detached bodies, contravene an act established by the whole people? My idea of the sovereignty of the people is, that the people can change the constitution if they please; but while the constitution exists, they must conform themselves to its dictates. But I do not believe that the inhabitants of any district can speak the voice of the people; so far from it, their ideas may contradict the sense of the whole people; hence the consequence that instructions are binding on the representative is of a doubtful, if not of a dangerous nature. I do not conceive, therefore, that it is necessary to agree in the proposition now made; so far as any real good is to arise from it, so far that real good is provided for; so far as it is of a doubtful nature, so far it obliges us to run the risk of losing the whole system.

Mr. SMITH, of South Carolina.—I am opposed to this motion, because I conceive it will operate as a partial inconvenience to the more distant States. If every member is to be bound by instructions how to vote, what are gentlemen from the extremities of the continent to do? Members from the neighboring States can obtain their instructions earlier than those from the Southern ones, and I presume that particular instructions will be necessary for particular measures; of consequence, we vote perhaps against instructions on their way to us, or we must decline voting at all. But what is the necessity of having a numerous representation? One member from a State can receive the instructions, and by his vote answer all the purposes of many, provided his vote is allowed to count for the proportion the State ought to send; in this way the business might be done at a less expense than having one or two hundred members in the House, which had been strongly contended for yesterday.

Mr. STONE.—I think the clause would change the Government entirely; instead of being a Government founded upon representation, it would be a democracy of singular properties.

I differ from the gentleman from Virginia, (Mr. MADISON,) if he thinks this clause would not bind the representative; in my opinion, it would bind him effectually, and I venture to assert, without diffidence, that any law passed by the Legislature would be of no force, if a majority of the members of this House were instructed to the contrary, provided the amendment became part of the constitution. What would follow from this? Instead of looking in the code of laws passed by Congress, your Judiciary would have to collect and examine the instructions from the various parts of the Union. It follows very clearly from hence, that the Government would be altered from a representative one to a democracy, wherein all laws are made immediately by the voice of the people.

This is a power not to be found in any part of the earth except among the Swiss cantons; there the body of the people vote upon the laws, and give instructions to their delegates. But here we have a different form of Government; the people at large are not authorized under it to vote upon the law, nor did I ever hear that any man required it. Why, then, are we called upon to propose amendments subversive of the principles of the constitution, which were never desired?

Several members now called for the question, and the Chairman being about to put the same:

Mr. GERRY.—Gentlemen seem in a great hurry to get this business through. I think, Mr. Chairman, it requires a further discussion; for my part, I had rather do less business and do it well, than precipitate measures before they are fully understood.

The honorable gentleman from Virginia (Mr. MADISON) stated, that if the proposed amendments are defeated, it will be by the delay attending the discussion of doubtful propositions; and he declares this to partake of that quality. It is natural, sir, for us to be fond of our own work. We do not like to see it disfigured by other hands. That honorable gentleman brought forward a string of propositions; among them was the clause now proposed to be amended: he is no doubt ready for the question, and determined not to admit what we think an improvement. The gentlemen who were on the committee, and brought in the report, have considered the subject, and are also ripe for a decision. But other gentlemen may crave a like indulgence. Is not the report before us for deliberation and discussion, and to obtain the sense of the House upon it; and will not gentlemen allow us a day or two for these purposes, after they have forced us to proceed upon them at this time? I appeal to their candor and good sense on the occasion, and am sure not to be refused; and I must inform them now, that they may not be surprised hereafter, that I wish all the amendments proposed by the respective States to be considered. Gentlemen say it is necessary to finish the subject, in order to reconcile a number of our fellow-citizens to the Government. If this is their principle, they ought to consider the wishes and intentions which the convention has expressed for them; if they do this, they will find that they expect and wish for the declaration proposed by the honorable gentleman over the way, (Mr. TUCKER,) and, of consequence, they ought to agree to it; and why it, with others recommended in the same way, were not reported, I cannot pretend to say; the committee know this best themselves.

The honorable gentleman near me (Mr. STONE) says, that the laws passed contrary to instruction will be nugatory. And other gentlemen ask, if their constituents instruct them to violate the constitution, whether they must do it. Sir, does not the constitution declare that all laws passed by Congress are paramount to the laws and constitutions of the several States; if our decrees are of such force as to set aside the State laws and constitutions, certainly they may be repugnant to any instructions whatever, without being injured thereby. But can we conceive that

our constituents would be so absurd as to instruct us to
violate our oath, and act directly contrary to the principles
of a Government ordained by themselves? We must look
upon them to be absolutely abandoned and false to their
own interests, to suppose them capable of giving such instructions.

If this amendment is introduced into the constitution, I
do not think we shall be much troubled with instructions;
a knowledge of the right will operate to check a spirit that
would render instruction necessary.

The honorable gentleman from Virginia asked, will not
the affirmative of a member who votes repugnant to his
instructions bind the community as much as the votes of
those who conform? There is no doubt, sir, but it will; but
does this tend to show that the constituent has no right to
instruct? Surely not. I admit, sir, that instructions contrary
to the constitution ought not to bind, though the sovereignty resides in the people. The honorable gentleman acknowledges that the sovereignty vests there; if so, it may
exercise its will in any case not inconsistent with a previous
contract. The same gentleman asks if we are to give the
power to the people in detached bodies to contravene the
Government while it exists. Certainly not; nor does the
proposed proposition extend to that point; it is only intended to open for them a convenient mode in which they
may convey their sense to their agents. The gentleman
therefore takes for granted what is inadmissible, that Congress will always be doing illegal things, and make it necessary for the sovereign to declare its pleasure.

He says the people have a right to alter the constitution,
but they have no right to oppose the Government. If,
while the Government exists, they have no right to control
it, it appears they have divested themselves of the sovereignty over the constitution. Therefore, our language,
with our principles, must change, and we ought to say that
the sovereignty existed in the people previous to the establishment of this Government. This will be ground for
alarm indeed, if it is true; but I trust, sir, too much to the
good sense of my fellow-citizens ever to believe that the
doctrine will generally obtain in this country of freedom.

Mr. VINING.—If, Mr. Chairman, there appears on one
side too great an urgency to despatch this business, there
appears on the other an unnecessary delay and procrasti-
nation equally improper and unpardonable. I think this
business has been already well considered by the House,
and every gentleman in it; however, I am not for an un-
seemly expedition.

The gentleman last up has insinuated a reflection upon
the committee for not reporting all the amendments proposed by some of the State conventions. I can assign a reason for this. The committee conceived some of them superfluous or dangerous, and found many of them so
contradictory that it was impossible to make any thing of
them; and this is a circumstance the gentleman cannot
pretend ignorance of.

Is it not inconsistent in that honorable member to complain of hurry, when he comes day after day reiterating
the same train of arguments, and demanding the attention
of this body by rising six or seven times on a question? I
wish, sir, this subject discussed coolly and dispassionately,

but hope we shall have no more reiterations or tedious
discussions; let gentlemen try to expedite public business,
and their arguments will be conducted in a laconic and
consistent manner. As to the business of instruction, I look
upon it inconsistent with the general good. Suppose our
constituents were to instruct us to make paper money; no
gentleman pretends to say it would be unconstitutional, yet
every honest mind must shudder at the thought. How can
we then assert that instructions ought to bind us in all
cases not contrary to the constitution?

Mr. LIVERMORE was not very anxious whether the words
were inserted or not, but he had a great deal of doubt on
the meaning of this whole amendment; it provides that the
people may meet and consult for the common good. Does
this mean a part of the people in a township or district, or
does it mean the representatives in the State Legislatures?
If it means the latter, there is no occasion for a provision
that the Legislature may instruct the members of this
body.

In some States the representatives are chosen by districts. In such case, perhaps, the instructions may be considered as coming from the district; but in other States,
each representative is chosen by the whole people. In New
Hampshire it is the case; the instructions of any particular
place would have but little weight, but a legislative instruction would have considerable influence upon each representative. If, therefore, the words mean that the Legislature may instruct, he presumed it would have considerable
effect, though he did not believe it binding. Indeed, he
was inclined to pay a deference to any information he
might receive from any number of gentlemen, even by a
private letter; but as for full binding force, no instructions
contained that quality. They could not, nor ought not to
have it, because different parties pursue different measures; and it might be expedient, nay, absolutely necessary,
to sacrifice them in mutual concessions.

The doctrine of instructions would hold better in England than here, because the boroughs and corporations
might have an interest to pursue totally immaterial to the
rest of the kingdom: in that case, it would be prudent to
instruct their members in Parliament.

Mr. GERRY wished the constitution amended without his
having any hand in it; but if he must interfere, he would
do his duty. The honorable gentleman from Delaware had
given him an example of moderation and laconic and consistent debate that he meant to follow; and would just observe to the worthy gentleman last up, that several States
had proposed the amendment, and among the rest New
Hampshire.

There was one remark which escaped him, when he was
up before. The gentleman from Maryland (Mr. STONE)
had said that the amendment would change the nature of
the Government, and make it a democracy. Now he had
always heard that it was a democracy; but perhaps he was
misled, and the honorable gentleman was right in distinguishing it by some other appellation; perhaps an aristocracy was a term better adapted to it.

Mr. SEDGWICK opposed the idea of the gentleman from
New Hampshire, that the State Legislature had the power
of instructing the members of this House; he looked upon

it as a subornation of the rights of the people to admit such an authority. We stand not here, said he, the representatives of the State Legislatures, as under the former Congress, but as the representatives of the great body of the people. The sovereignty, the independence, and the rights of the States are intended to be guarded by the Senate; if we are to be viewed in any other light, the greatest security the people have for their rights and privileges is destroyed.

But with respect to instructions, it is well worthy of consideration how they are to be procured. It is not the opinion of an individual that is to control my conduct; I consider myself as the representative of the whole Union. An individual may give me information, but his sentiments may be in opposition to the sense of the majority of the people. If instructions are to be of any efficacy, they must speak the sense of the majority of the people, at least of a State. In a State so large as Massachusetts it will behoove gentlemen to consider how the sense of the majority of the freemen is to be obtained and communicated. Let us take care to avoid the insertion of crude and indigested propositions, more likely to produce acrimony than that spirit of harmony which we ought to cultivate.

Mr. LIVERMORE said that he did not understand the honorable gentleman, or was not understood by him; he did not presume peremptorily to say what degree of influence the legislative instructions would have on a representative. He knew it was not the thing in contemplation here; and what he had said respected only the influence it would have on his private judgment.

Mr. AMES said there would be a very great inconvenience attending the establishment of the doctrine contended for by his colleague. Those states which had selected their members by districts would have no right to give them instructions, consequently the members ought to withdraw; in which case the House might be reduced below a majority, and not be able, according to the constitution, to do any business at all.

According to the doctrine of the gentleman from New Hampshire, one part of the Government would be annihilated; for of what avail is it that the people have the appointment of a representative, if he is to pay obedience to the dictates of another body?

Several members now rose, and called for the question.

Mr. PAGE was sorry to see gentlemen so impatient; the more so, as he saw there was very little attention paid to any thing that was said; but he would express his sentiments if he was only heard by the Chair. He discovered clearly, notwithstanding what had been observed by the most ingenious supporters of the opposition, that there was an absolute necessity for adopting the amendment. It was strictly compatible with the spirit and the nature of the Government; all power vests in the people of the United States; it is, therefore, a Government of the people, a democracy. If it were consistent with the peace and tranquillity of the inhabitants, every freeman would have a right to come and give his vote upon the law; but, inasmuch as this cannot be done, by reason of the extent of territory, and some other causes, the people have agreed that their representatives shall exercise a part of their authority. To pretend to refuse them the power of instructing their agents, appears to me to deny them a right. One gentleman asks how the instructions are to be collected. Many parts of this country have been in the practice of instructing their representatives; they found no difficulty in communicating their sense. Another gentleman asks if they were to instruct us to make paper money, what we would do. I would tell them, said he, it was unconstitutional; alter that, and we will consider on the point. Unless laws are made satisfactory to the people, they will lose their support, they will be abused or done away; this tends to destroy the efficiency of the Government.

It is the sense of several of the conventions that this amendment should take place; I think it my duty to support it, and fear it will spread an alarm among our constituents if we decline to do it.

Mr. WADSWORTH.—Instructions have frequently been given to the representatives of the United States; but the people did not claim as a right that they should have any obligation upon the representatives; it is not right that they should. In troublesome times, designing men have drawn the people to instruct the representatives to their harm; the representatives have, on such occasions, refused to comply with their instructions. I have known, myself, that they have been disobeyed, and yet the representative was not brought to account for it; on the contrary, he was caressed and reelected, while those who have obeyed them, contrary to their private sentiments, have ever after been despised for it. Now, if people considered it an inherent right in them to instruct their representatives, they would have undoubtedly punished the violation of them. I have no idea of instructions, unless they are obeyed; a discretional power is incompatible with them.

The honorable gentleman who was up last says, if he were instructed to make paper money, he would tell his constituents it was unconstitutional. I believe that is not the case, for this body would have a right to make paper money; but if my constituents were to instruct me to vote for such a measure, I would disobey them, let the consequence be what it would.

Mr. SUMTER.—The honorable gentlemen who are opposed to the motion of my colleague, do not treat it fairly. They suppose that it is meant to bind the representative to conform to his instructions. The mover of this question, I presume to say, has no such thing in idea. That they shall notice them and obey them, as far as is consistent and proper, may be very just; perhaps they ought to produce them to the House, and let them have as much influence as they deserve; nothing further, I believe, is contended for.

40

THOMAS PAINE, DISSERTATION ON THE FIRST
PRINCIPLES OF GOVERNMENT
1795

Life 5:221–25

The true and only true basis of representative government is equality of rights. Every man has a right to one vote, and no more in the choice of representatives. The rich have no more right to exclude the poor from the right of voting, or of electing and being elected, than the poor have to exclude the rich; and wherever it is attempted, or proposed, on either side, it is a question of force and not of right. Who is he that would exclude another? That other has a right to exclude him.

That which is now called aristocracy implies an inequality of rights; but who are the persons that have a right to establish this inequality? Will the rich exclude themselves? No. Will the poor exclude themselves? No. By what right then can any be excluded? It would be a question, if any man or class of men have a right to exclude themselves; but, be this as it may, they cannot have the right to exclude another. The poor will not delegate such a right to the rich, nor the rich to the poor, and to assume it is not only to assume arbitrary power, but to assume a right to commit robbery.

Personal rights, of which the right of voting for representatives is one, are a species of property of the most sacred kind: and he that would employ his pecuniary property, or presume upon the influence it gives him, to dispossess or rob another of his property or rights, uses that pecuniary property as he would use fire-arms, and merits to have it taken from him.

Inequality of rights is created by a combination in one part of the community to exclude another part from its rights. Whenever it be made an article of a constitution, or a law, that the right of voting, or of electing and being elected, shall appertain exclusively to persons possessing a certain quantity of property, be it little or much, it is a combination of the persons possessing that quantity to exclude those who do not possess the same quantity. It is investing themselves with powers as a self-created part of society, to the exclusion of the rest.

It is always to be taken for granted, that those who oppose an equality of rights never mean the exclusion should take place on themselves; and in this view of the case, pardoning the vanity of the thing, aristocracy is a subject of laughter. This self-soothing vanity is encouraged by another idea not less selfish, which is that the opposers conceive they are playing a safe game, in which there is a chance to gain and none to lose; that at any rate the doctrine of equality includes *them,* and that if they cannot get more rights than those whom they oppose and would exclude they shall not have less.

This opinion has already been fatal to thousands, who, not contented with *equal rights,* have sought more till they lost all, and experienced in themselves the degrading *inequality* they endeavored to fix upon others.

In any view of the case it is dangerous and impolitic, sometimes ridiculous, and always unjust to make property the criterion of the right of voting. If the sum or value of the property upon which the right is to take place be considerable it will exclude a majority of the people and unite them in a common interest against the government and against those who support it; and as the power is always with the majority, they can overturn such a government and its supporters whenever they please.

If, in order to avoid this danger, a small quantity of property be fixed, as the criterion of the right, it exhibits liberty in disgrace, by putting it in competition with accident and insignificance. When a broodmare shall fortunately produce a foal or a mule that, by being worth the sum in question, shall convey to its owner the right of voting, or by its death take it from him, in whom does the origin of such a right exist? Is it in the man, or in the mule? When we consider how many ways property may be acquired without merit, and lost without crime, we ought to spurn the idea of making it a criterion of rights.

But the offensive part of the case is that this exclusion from the right of voting implies a stigma on the moral character of the persons excluded; and this is what no part of the community has a right to pronounce upon another part. No external circumstance can justify it: wealth is no proof of moral character; nor poverty of the want of it.

On the contrary, wealth is often the presumptive evidence of dishonesty; and poverty the negative evidence of innocence. If therefore property, whether little or much, be made a criterion, the means by which that property has been acquired ought to be made a criterion also.

The only ground upon which exclusion from the right of voting is consistent with justice would be to inflict it as a punishment for a certain time upon those who should propose to take away that right from others. The right of voting for representatives is the primary right by which other rights are protected.

To take away this right is to reduce a man to slavery, for slavery consists in being subject to the will of another, and he that has not a vote in the election of representatives is in this case. The proposal therefore to disfranchise any class of men is as criminal as the proposal to take away property.

When we speak of right we ought always to unite with it the idea of duties; rights become duties by reciprocity. The right which I enjoy becomes my duty to guarantee it to another, and he to me; and those who violate the duty justly incur a forfeiture of the right.

In a political view of the case, the strength and permanent security of government is in proportion to the number of people interested in supporting it. The true policy therefore is to interest the whole by an equality of rights, for the danger arises from exclusions. It is possible to exclude men from the right of voting, but it is impossible to exclude them from the right of rebelling against that exclusion; and when all other rights are taken away the right of rebellion is made perfect.

41

ST. GEORGE TUCKER,
BLACKSTONE'S COMMENTARIES
1:APP. 193–94
1803

The representatives by this bill [the Virginia act of 1788 as amended by the act of 1792] are chosen immediately by the people, in a public manner, by the electors within an aggregate number of counties composing a district. The person chosen seems to be strictly the delegate of those by whom he is chosen, and bound by their instructions whenever they think proper to exercise the right. This principle has been denied by the British writers on their own government, and a deference to the maxims of that government probably prevented the decision of the question, when agitated in congress in the form of an article to a proposed bill of rights: but if the maxim be true, that all power is derived from the people; that magistrates are their trustees and servants, and at all times amenable to them for their conduct, it seems impossible to withhold our assent from the proposition, that in a popular government the representative is bound to speak the sense of his constituents upon every subject, where he is informed of it. The difficulty of collecting the sense of the people upon any question, forms no argument against their right to express that sense when they shall think proper so to do. Otherwise, by whatever denomination the government may be called, it is a confirmed aristocracy, in which the people have nothing more to do than to choose their rulers, over whose proceedings, however despotic, and repugnant to the nature and principles of the fundamental laws of the state, they have no control*. It will be an-

*"When we elect persons to represent us in parliament" (says a judicious writer) "we must not be supposed to depart from the smallest right which we have deposited with them. We make a lodgment, not a gift; we *entrust*, but *part with* nothing. And, were it possible that they should attempt to destroy that constitution which we had appointed them to maintain, they can no more be held in the rank of representatives than a factor turned pirate, can continue to be called the factor of those merchants whose goods he had plundered, and whose confidence he had betrayed. The men, whom we thus depute to parliament, are not the bare likeness or reflection of us their constituents; they actually contain our powers and privileges, and are, as it were, the very persons of the people they represent. We are the parliament in them? we speak and act by them. We have, therefore, a right to know what they are saying and doing. And should they contradict our sense, or swerve from our interests, we have a right to remonstrate in form, and direct them. By which means we become the regulators of our own conduct, and the institutors of our own laws, and nothing material can be done but by our authority and consent." Burgh's Political Disquisitions, Vol. 1 p. 202 . . . However inadmissible this doctrine may be in Great Britain, it seems perfectly adapted to the principles of our government.

swered, that the power of removing and punishing is not denied by this doctrine. I answer, that the power of preventing offences against the commonwealth, is to be preferred to that of punishing offenders: and if the government is virtually in the people, it ought to be so organized, that whenever they chuse to exercise the right of governing, they may do it without destroying it's existence. Corruption and mal-administration, unchecked, may drive them to a resumption of all the powers which they have entrusted to the government, and bring on tumults and disturbances which will end only with it's final dissolution: an event to be apprehended in all governments, but particularly in democracies, since dissatisfaction towards the administration may produce a desire of change in the constitution itself; and every change by which the government is in the smallest degree removed from its republican nature and principle, must be for the worse. This danger is effectually avoided by the principle here contended for. The aggregate of mankind understand their own interest and their own happiness better than any individual: they never can be supposed to have resigned the right of judging for themselves to any set of men whatsoever; it is a right which can never be voluntarily resigned, though it may be wrested from their hands by tyranny, or violated by the infidelity and perfidy of their servants.

42

JAMES MADISON, NOTE TO HIS SPEECH
ON THE RIGHT OF SUFFRAGE
1821
Documentary History 5:440–49

(See ch. 16, no. 26)

SEE ALSO:

Generally chs. 8, 12, 17; 1.2.1; 1.2.3; Amend. I (petition)

Address of the General Assembly of New York to Lieutenant Governor George Clarke, 7 Sept. 1737, Journal of the Votes and Proceedings of the General Assembly of the Colony of New-York 1:706–7 (1764)

Daniel Dulany, Considerations on the Propriety of Imposing Taxes in the British Colonies for the Purpose of Raising a Revenue, by Act of Parliament, 1765, Bailyn 1:608, 610–12, 614–16

Return of Mansfield, Massachusetts, 6 June 1780, Handlin 518–20

Noah Webster, An Examination into the Leading Principles of the Federal Constitution, 10 Oct. 1787, Pamphlets 39–41

Noah Webster, On Government, 1788, Collection 74–79

John Adams to John Taylor, Apr. 1814, Works 6:469–72

. . . and secure the Blessings of Liberty to ourselves and
our Posterity, . . .

14

Rights

Introduction

From the beginning, it seems, the language of America has been the language of rights. Whether conceived as the rights of "any naturall born subject of England" (no. 1), or as *the natural, inherent, divinely hereditary and indefeasible* rights" of British subjects (see ch. 3, no. 4), or as "those rights which god and the laws have given equally and independently to all" (no. 10), a statement of rights is a claim, not a request. The language of rights is not that of supplication.

That language, too, presupposes a particular kind of speaker and audience. Claimants must be mindful of what is due them; governors must be reminded that they govern a people who know what is due them. The public speech about rights, then, serves the double purpose of exhorting the bearers of those rights—"Let those flatter, who fear: it is not an American art" (Jefferson, no. 10)—and of warning the would-be transgressors of those rights. If the claim is writ bold and the threat subdued, it is nonetheless a claim coupled with a threat.

The dignity or urgency of the claim of those irreducible and inalienable rights is mirrored in the gravity and dreadfulness of the threat—a recourse to first principles, and beyond that an appeal to heaven, in short, revolution. Neither the claim nor the threat is to be taken lightly. A prudent people jealous of their rights, a prudent magistrate jealous of his office (or his head), would alike cherish that "great Charter of fundamentalls." They would equally welcome those solemn prescribed occasions when all members of the body politic are reminded of the distinctive prescriptions and prohibitions that define their collective life (no. 4). Much like the kings of Israel who were enjoined to write a copy of the Law and keep it by them that they might veer neither to the left nor to the right (Deut. 17:18–20), so too ought a free people to have their rights "Expressed in the fullest and most unequivocall terms" (no. 16). The conditions on which man agrees to enter into society ought to be marked out "with perspecuity and plainness . . . so as to admit of no Prevarication" (no. 17).

In this context the agitation over a bill of rights that distinguished many of the critical fights in the state ratifying conventions takes on a somewhat different appearance. However much the opponents of the Constitution may have used the issue of a bill of rights as a tactical device (hoping thereby to secure a second convention that might undo some of the more odious features of the proposed new government), they also intended something more. There is a deeper meaning to their discontent. The debate over the need for a bill of rights stirs fundamental questions of American constitutionalism, for much of that debate expresses the people's continuing and conflicting need for, and fear of, a government that could truly govern.

With the continuing influence of the English legal tradition and popular writings on the Englishman's liberties (nos. 3, 5), and with the spread and popularization of Locke's teaching by the readers of authors as diverse as John Trenchard, William Blackstone, and Samuel Adams

(see ch. 3), the language of rights became the common tongue. With the revolutionary productions of lawyer Jefferson's pen (no. 10; see also ch. 1, no. 5), the language of rights become eloquent. The right of a people was derived from the natural rights of individuals. Indeed, individuals had constituted themselves a people by acting on their own behalf: "For themselves they fought, for themselves they conquered, and for themselves alone they have right to hold." In this the ancestors of the Americans had acted as any might in exercising "a right, which nature has given to all men." But because their peoplehood is a consequence of this exercise of individual right, that people have a collective right to safeguard and "hold undisturbed the rights thus acquired at the hazard of their lives and loss of their fortunes." The burden of the Americans' grievance was not that their natural rights had been abridged—for example, "the exercise of a free trade with all parts of the world"—but that they had had no voice or hand in the matter. This was a situation inviting abuse and injury, the arbitrary sacrifice of American rights and interests to those of others. Jefferson was not being carried away by hyperbole when he denounced an act of 5 Geo. 2 forbidding an American subject from making "a hat for himself of the fur which he has taken perhaps on his own soil [as] An instance of despotism to which no parrallel can be produced in the most arbitrary ages of British history." In the face of such arbitrary high-handedness no individual rights could be secure. An individual's possession and free use of his head was hardly safer than that of his hat.

The Continental Congress put the matter as clearly as can be in its Declaration of Rights (see ch. 1, no. 1). The enjoyment of rights is inseparable from self-governance, and that means actual representation of those being governed. Those rights might be abridged or qualified in a number of ways, but the only legitimate manner of so doing would be to secure the consent of the holders of those rights. The notion that the people of America might be "virtually" represented by individuals neither chosen by nor accountable to themselves was altogether preposterous. Or, as Congress put it in its primer of rights produced for the enlightenment of the Quebecois (no. 12): "to live by the will of one man, or sett of men, is the production of misery to all men."

In defending their rights against British (and even their own) authorities, Americans could justify taking severe measures against the Tories. Along with Governor Jefferson (see ch. 3, no. 6), they recognized that securing one's own rights may necessitate denying rights to one's enemies. Yet even in the midst of revolutionary exertions against external threats, Americans were wary of internal threats to their rights. Behind a debate over the Continental Congress's power to arrange for the apprehension of army deserters lay questions of federalism, constitutionalism, and the security of the people's rights (no. 14). Those concerns peaked whenever the construction of new governmental forms came under discussion (no. 17; see also ch. 4, no. 8). Always implicit and usually explicit was the understanding that allegiance and protection are reciprocal. Thus it made sense to precede a frame of government with a declaration of rights (no. 16; see ch. 1, no. 6).

The Bill of Rights

It is customary to view the first ten amendments to the Constitution as the lasting legacy of the Anti-Federalist critics of 1787–88. After all, it was the Anti-Federalists who repeatedly remarked upon the absence from the proposed Constitution of a distinct list of guaranteed rights. It was they who clamored unceasingly for revision of the Constitution so as to remedy that omission. In comparison, the leading supporters of the Constitution, including Madison, appear as at best tardy and tepid proponents of a bill of rights.

Closer examination of the documents complicates this account considerably. For although it was indeed the critics who most visibly and audibly demanded a bill of rights, the amendments that finally were ratified were not of their making—nor most to their liking. It took Madison's persistence as floor manager in the House to get Congress to act on amendments as promptly as it did. And in the end it was not the critics' proposed amendments effecting structural changes or enshrining general republican maxims that were submitted to the states for ratification. Madison's successful strategy was to exclude these kinds of amendments (with the broad exception of the Tenth Amendment), while embracing the proposal of a "bill of rights." But even then it was not the critics' language that came before Congress for consideration but that of their most knowing and patient opponent. It is at least arguable that the voice of Patrick Henry and the pen of Richard Henry Lee finally were overcome by the parliamentary skills of James Madison.

The documents also invite some reflection on the passionate insistence of the Anti-Federalists and the dogged resistance (and occasional disdain) of the Federalists. What one regarded as having almost talismanic powers, the other viewed as mere surplusage or worse. From today's perspective each position seems strange, almost inexplicable. That sense of strangeness may bespeak a gulf between our understanding of the character and function of a bill of rights and theirs.

The urgent call for a bill of rights arose in the Philadelphia Convention only days before it brought its business to a close. Notwithstanding George Mason's insistence that the matter "might be prepared in a few hours," the weary delegates overwhelmingly rejected a motion so pregnant with difficulties and controversy (no. 20). The difficulties did not stem from a lack of models; eight state constitutions (plus that of not-yet-admitted Vermont) were prefaced by a declaration of rights. The difficulties had rather to do with need, effectiveness, and consequences. Did a government established by "We the people" and constituted as one of enumerated powers stand in need of a device that owed its origins to earlier struggles against monarchic pretensions? Were such prefatory declarations really part of a constitution or only admonitions that

would suffer the fate of other "parchment barriers"? And if indeed parts of a fundamental law, how and by whom were they to be enforced? Did the record of evasions and transgressions of the state constitutions' bills of rights recommend reliance on so slender a reed? Would a preoccupation with the limits of the exercise of power weaken popular support for a government of sufficient energy and decisiveness—sufficient, that is, to protect the enjoyment of those rights?

Here Federalist misgivings ran head-on into Anti-Federalist fears. "Universal experience" confirmed the necessity for "the most express declarations and reservations." Precisely because great powers had to be given, great restraints had to be placed on the exercise of those powers. How else "protect the just rights and liberty of Mankind from the silent powerful and ever active conspiracy of those who govern"? When Lee (no. 21) spoke of the urgent need for the proposed Constitution to be "bottomed upon a declaration, or Bill of Rights," he indeed had in view a foundation. Only on such bedrock could a people safely erect a framework of government allocating offices and powers. It was not enough to say, as did James Wilson (no. 23), that whatever was not given up was presumed to be retained. Indeed, the reach of the powers granted and the very generality of some of the Constitution's language argued decisively against such a presumption and for the most explicit affirmation of "that *Residuum* of natural rights, which is not intended to be given up to Society" (no. 22; see also no. 25; Impartial Examiner, no. 1, 20 Feb., 5 Mar. 1788). Moreover, on Wilson's premise, how was one to understand those few instances—as in Art. 1, sec. 9, and Art. 6, sec. 3—where the Constitution *does* impose limits, limits on power nowhere expressly granted? (Nos. 26, 44; but see no. 40.)

Wilson argued (no. 27) that a bill of rights was not only superfluous in a government of enumerated powers founded on popular sovereignty, but "preposterous and dangerous," "improper." Would not such a declaration be tantamount to an enumeration of reserved powers? And would not such an enumeration support the detested presumption that all that was not reserved was granted? Who would entrust the enjoyment of his liberties to some body's overweening claim to having made a complete enumeration? (See also no. 34.)

Logical and powerful as these arguments were, they could not dispose of the deep root of Anti-Federalist disquiet and declamation. A bill of rights was "a plain, strong, and accurate criterion by which the people might at once determine when, and in what instance their rights were violated." Without "a test of that kind" a people was disarmed before an aspiring tyranny that would have the effrontery and sophistication to face down any and all complaints (nos. 28, 29; see also Impartial Examiner, no. 1, 5 Mar. 1788). With so much at stake, Jefferson concluded (reaching for a universal): "a bill of rights is what the people are entitled to against every government on earth, general or particular, and what no just government should refuse, or rest on inference" (no. 30). The utility or danger of incomplete enumerations might be argued one way or the other, the Federal Farmer thought, but that did not dispose of the deep, continuous, and lasting value of a declaration of rights: establishing "in the minds of the people truths and principles which they might never otherwise have thought of, or soon forgot. If a nation means its systems, religious or political, shall have duration, it ought to recognize the leading principles of them in the front page of every family book." Freedom depended not on ancient concessions painfully extracted, not on legal documents confirming those concessions, but on each generation's "constantly keeping in view . . . the particular principles on which our freedom must always depend" (no. 32; see also Sentiments of Many, 18 June 1788; Edmund Randolph, 1809). In this respect, at least, the Anti-Federalist argument was unanswerable.

In the face of these persistent, if shifting, adverse arguments, some Federalists beat to windward and took a more favorable tack. Earlier arguments were not simply abandoned, but the stress was now on the sense in which "the whole Constitution is a declaration of rights" (James Bowdoin, 23 Jan. 1788). In the very Preamble of the Constitution was to be found "a better recognition of popular rights than volumes of those aphorisms which make the principal figure in several of our state bill of rights, and which would sound much better in a treatise of ethics than in a constitution of government" (Hamilton, no. 38). All in all, a government of limited enumerated powers, following policies determined and executed by popularly accountable "representatives and servants," was itself the best guarantor of individual rights. To ask for more was to mistake form for substance or, what was worse, to risk substance for the sake of form. (See also no. 45, and Benjamin Rush to David Ramsay, Spring 1788.)

James Iredell writing as "Marcus" (no. 36) was able to suggest how the enthusiasms of '76 had misled the framers of state constitutions into a hasty and ill-considered adoption of English safeguards against the abuses of royal prerogative. This was understandable—"the minds of men being so warmed with their exertions in the cause of liberty as to lean too much perhaps toward a jealousy of power to repose a proper confidence in their own government"—but it was for all that an error. Iredell could show not only that English precedents were inappropriate in an American republic, but that the typically admonitory or prohibitory language of a bill of rights could easily be sophisticated into mere babble. (See also no. 38.) Rather than rely on the magical properties of fine-sounding declarations, a sensible people would find its security in a properly constituted government and in a public opinion that kept that government to its charge.

The Politics of Ratification and Amendment

Yet the opposition obstinately kept up the cry for amendments to correct the excesses and supply the defects of the proposed Constitution. Massachusetts set a pattern for subsequent ratifications by appending a list of recommended "alterations and provisions" (no. 33). The Federalists' timely, if reluctant, acceptance of this form of ratification averted what they most dreaded: outright rejection

of the Constitution, or diversely conditional ratifications by the several states, or a reopening of the matter at a second constitutional convention. Equally important is that in publicly accepting the need for amendments, the Federalists put themselves in a position to manage the whole process. It was one thing, of course, for Virginia Baptists searching for "some one Caperble of the Task" of safeguarding religious liberty to turn to James Madison, Jr., of Orange County (Joseph Spencer, 28 Feb. 1788). His public credentials in this respect ran at least as far back as 1776 with his small but significant alteration of Mason's last article in the Virginia Declaration of Rights, and there could be no question of his adherence to the principle that made rights the end of government. But it was a far different thing to have in Madison's shaping and guiding hands such proposals as: Massachusetts' desire to reinstitute the Confederation's reservation to the several states of "all powers not expressly delegated" (cf. no. 33, Resolution no. 1, with Articles of Confederation, art. 2); or Jefferson's desire for unequivocal and unqualified prohibitions of standing armies, monopolies, and suspension of habeas corpus laws (no. 30); or Virginia's desire to have direct taxes raised by means of the state legislatures, or to require extraordinary legislative majorities in order to exercise the national commerce power (no. 43). No more inveterate opponent of such proposals could have been found in the United States.

Political necessity and cunning strategy thus recommended the same course: accede to the widespread popular call for a bill of rights. There was no denying an argument of this sort: "A Bill of Rights may be summed up in a few words. What do they tell us?—That our rights are reserved.—Why not say so? Is it because it will consume too much paper?" (Henry, no. 39; see also Mason, no. 42, and A Delegate Who Has Catched Cold, 25 June 1788.) If that was what was wanted, well and good. Iredell (North Carolina Ratifying Convention, 24 June 1788) could hardly object to "the most explicit declaration that all power depends upon the people; because, though it will not strengthen their rights, it may be the means of fixing them on a plainer foundation." But Iredell (no. 45) rejected as "a snare rather than a protection" anything purporting to be an exhaustive list of reserved rights, to say nothing of back-door efforts to reintroduce distinctive federal features of the Confederation. Thus the satisfaction some leading Federalists were prepared to give was guaranteed to be unsatisfying to those who had clamored loudest (no. 41). Nor was Madison's measured explanation of the sense in which he had "always been in favor of a bill of rights," while simultaneously never thinking its omission "a material defect" (no. 47), likely to have gratified his correspondent. For Jefferson (no. 46), like many critics of the Constitution, was intent on "guard[ing] the people against the federal government, as they are already guarded against their state governments in most instances." For Madison, however, the real danger, like "the real power," lay elsewhere.

Madison, to be sure, was not alone in seeing the dark side of majority rule. While his formulation of the problem remains a classic (see ch. 4, no. 19, and ch. 10, no. 16), the concern it bespeaks was hardly limited to Federalists. Nor was his solution the inevitable one. Thus the Anti-Federalist Agrippa in Massachusetts, starting from Madisonian ground, could make a case for a bill of rights as the proper remedy for majority misrule. It is precisely in "a government by ourselves" that additional bulwarks are needed against the wanton exercise of power. A bill of rights setting forth the purposes of the social compact would help "to secure the minority against the usurpation and tyranny of the majority" and help to defend "the sober and industrious part of the community . . . from the rapacity and violence of the vicious and idle" (no. 16, 5 Feb. 1788). Agrippa's fears and sentiments were echoed by A [Maryland] Farmer (no. 35). A proper governmental structure was indeed important (as James Wilson and others had argued), but insufficient. Given the frequent opposition between the rights of individuals and "the apparent interests of the majority," a democratic government especially stood in need of a bill of rights; "if these rights are not clearly and expressly ascertained, the individual must be lost."

If, then, Madison and Jefferson saw the great danger as coming from different quarters, it was (Madison tactfully suggested) because they were in a sense looking at different worlds (no. 47). Here and now, in post-Revolutionary America, the most likely source of oppression was "not from acts of Government contrary to the sense of its constituents, but from acts in which the Government is the mere instrument of the major number of the constituents. This is a truth of great importance, but not yet sufficiently attended to. . . ." A bill of rights would be of no use in countering "the tyrannical will" of a sovereign majority; it would be worse than foolish to place one's hopes on that. Madison was prepared to concede that a case could be made for adding a bill of rights, but only as a precaution. A solemn declaration might lead to its being viewed as fundamental and to its becoming "incorporated with the national sentiment." To that extent a bill of rights might "counteract the impulses of interest and passion." Here was an argument not far removed from the Federal Farmer. Furthermore, Madison granted, acts of governmental usurpation were hardly precluded by the republican form; to that extent, at least, Jefferson's fears and Jefferson's remedy were in point.

With the ratification of the Constitution assured, Madison could safely turn to the business of amendments. He was even obligated to do so, having been pushed, by the charges of opponents to his election to Congress, into making public promises to seek amendments of the right sort. And to ensure that the business would indeed be "pursued with a proper moderation and in a proper mode" (no. 48), he took charge of it himself. It is clear that from the outset he had resolved in his mind and to his own satisfaction all the whats, hows, and whys of amendment. As was the case in the Philadelphia Convention, so too in the House debates, the advantages of prior homework and calm reflection showed at every turn.

In raising and pressing the issue of amendment and in seeing the amendments through Congress, Madison kept two goals in the foreground of deliberation: "to satisfy the public mind that their liberties will be perpetual, and this without endangering any part of the constitution" (no. 50). He had to steer the proposed amendments between those who wanted no part of the business and those who had very different amendments in view. In this he fully succeeded.

He did not, however, succeed in incorporating the amendments in the body of the original Constitution. Here Madison had a double purpose in view. Drawing special attention to the amendments by mounting them as it were on the prow invited and reinforced the habit of considering a bill of rights and a constitution proper as very different things. It invited and reinforced the habit of easy and frequent recurrence to large, abstract first principles, a habit deeply at odds (Madison thought) with society's continuing need for regular, stable expectations. Tying the amendments onto the stern like a dinghy in tow might have an opposite bad effect, inviting people to consider the amendments as mere afterthoughts inferior in dignity to the great instrument itself. Blending the amendments into the body of the Constitution would avoid both dangers. Nor did Madison succeed in extending the reach of the Bill of Rights to the states, in keeping with his—as distinguished from the Anti-Federalists'—view of the main source of danger to rights. A decade later, however, as co-leader with Jefferson of the Republican opposition to the Alien and Sedition Acts, Madison found effective ways to use the Bill of Rights as a curb on the federal government, and in the process gave expanded meaning to its free speech provision. (See Report on the Virginia Resolutions, Jan. 1800.)

When, finally, "the nauseous project" (no. 53) was over, Madison had got more than he feared he might and less than he wished. But, most important, by his maneuverings he had seen to it that the continuing disgruntlement of some leading Anti-Federalists would no longer be mirrored in their followers. The general desire for a bill of rights had been satisfied, and the business of governing could proceed.

1

GENERAL ASSEMBLY OF MARYLAND, AN ACT FOR
THE LIBERTIES OF THE PEOPLE
1639

Maryland Archives 1:41

Be it Enacted By the Lord Proprietarie of this Province of and with the advice and approbation of the ffreemen of the same that all the Inhabitants of this Province being Christians (Slaves excepted[)] Shall have and enjoy all such rights liberties immunities priviledges and free customs within this Province as any naturall born subject of England hath or ought to have or enjoy in the Realm of England by force or vertue of the common law or Statute Law of England (saveing in such Cases as the same are or may be altered or changed by the Laws and ordinances of this Province)

And Shall not be imprisoned nor disseissed or dispossessed of their freehold goods or Chattels or be out Lawed Exiled or otherwise destroyed fore judged or punished then according to the Laws of this province saveing to the Lord proprietarie and his heirs all his rights and prerogatives by reason of his domination and Seigniory over this Province and the people of the same This Act to Continue till the end of the next Generall Assembly

2

THE BODY OF LIBERTIES OF THE MASSACHUSETS
COLLONIE IN NEW ENGLAND
1641

MHS Collections, 3d ser., 8:216–19

The free fruition of such liberties Immunities and priveledges as humanitie, Civilitie, and Christianitie call for as due to every man in his place and proportion without impeachment and Infringement hath ever bene and ever will be the tranquillitie and Stabilitie of Churches and Commonwealths. And the deniall or deprivall thereof, the disturbance if not the ruine of both.

We hould it therefore our dutie and safetie whilst we are about the further establishing of this Government to collect and expresse all such freedomes as for present we foresee may concerne us, and our posteritie after us, And to ratify them with our sollemne consent.

Wee doe therefore this day religiously and unanimously decree and confirme these following Rites, liberties and priveledges concerneing our Churches, and Civill State to be respectively impartiallie and inviolably enjoyed and observed throughout our Jurisdiction for ever.

1. No mans life shall be taken away, no mans honour or good name shall be stayned, no mans person shall be arested, restrayned, banished, dismembered, nor any wayes punished, no man shall be deprived of his wife or children, no mans goods or estaite shall be taken away from him, nor any way indammaged under colour of law or Countenance of Authoritie, unlesse it be by vertue or equitie of some expresse law of the Country waranting the same, established by a generall Court and sufficiently published, or in case of the defect of a law in any parteculer case by the word of God. And in Capitall cases, or in cases concerning dismembring or banishment according to that word to be judged by the Generall Court.

2. Every person within this Jurisdiction, whether Inhabitant or forreiner shall enjoy the same justice and law, that is generall for the plantation, which we constitute and execute one towards another without partialitie or delay.

3. No man shall be urged to take any oath or subscribe any articles, covenants or remonstrance, of a publique and Civill nature, but such as the Generall Court hath considered, allowed, and required.

4. No man shall be punished for not appearing at or before any Civill Assembly, Court, Councell, Magistrate, or Officer, nor for the omission of any office or service, if he shall be necessarily hindred by any apparent Act or providence of God, which he could neither foresee nor avoid. Provided that this law shall not prejudice any person of his just cost or damage, in any civill action.

5. No man shall be compelled to any publique worke or service unlesse the presse be grounded upon some act of the generall Court, and have reasonable allowance therefore.

6. No man shall be pressed in person to any office, worke, warres or other publique service, that is necessarily and suffiently exempted by any naturall or personall impediment, as by want of yeares, greatnes of age, defect of minde, fayling of sences, or impotencie of Lymbes.

7. No man shall be compelled to goe out of the limits of this plantation upon any offensive warres which this Commonwealth or any of our freinds or confederats shall volentarily undertake. But onely upon such vindictive and defensive warres in our owne behalfe or the behalfe of our freinds and confederats as shall be enterprized by the Counsell and consent of a Court generall, or by authority derived from the same.

8. No mans Cattel or goods of what kinde soever shall be pressed or taken for any publique use or service, unlesse it be by warrant grounded upon some act of the generall Court, nor without such reasonable prices and hire as the ordinairie rates of the Countrie do afford. And if his Cattle or goods shall perish or suffer damage in such service, the owner shall be suffiently recompenced.

9. No monopolies shall be granted or allowed amongst us, but of such new Inventions that are profitable to the Countrie, and that for a short time.

10. All our lands and heritages shall be free from all fines and licenses upon Alienations, and from all hariotts, wardships, Liveries, Primer-seisins, yeare day and wast, Escheates, and forfeitures, upon the deaths of parents or Ancestors, be they naturall, casuall or Juditiall.

11. All persons which are of the age of 21 yeares, and of right understanding and meamories, whether excom-

municate or condemned shall have full power and libertie to make there wills and testaments, and other lawfull alienations of theire lands and estates.

12. Every man whether Inhabitant or fforreiner, free or not free shall have libertie to come to any publique Court, Councel, or Towne meeting, and either by speech or writing to move any lawfull, seasonable, and materiall question, or to present any necessary motion, complaint, petition, Bill or information, whereof that meeting hath proper cognizance, so it be done in convenient time, due order, and respective manner.

13. No man shall be rated here for any estaite or revenue he hath in England, or in any forreine partes till it be transported hither.

14. Any Conveyance or Alienation of land or other estaite what so ever, made by any woman that is married, any childe under age, Ideott or distracted person, shall be good if it be passed and ratified by the consent of a generall Court.

15. All Covenous or fraudulent Alienations or Conveyances of lands, tenements, or any heriditaments, shall be of no validitie to defeate any man from due debts or legacies, or from any just title, clame or possession, of that which is so fraudulently conveyed.

16. Every Inhabitant that is an howse holder shall have free fishing and fowling in any great ponds and Bayes, Coves and Rivers, so farre as the sea ebbes and flowes within the presincts of the towne where they dwell, unlesse the free men of the same Towne or the Generall Court have otherwise appropriated them, provided that this shall not be extended to give leave to any man to come upon others proprietie without there leave.

17. Every man of or within this Jurisdiction shall have free libertie, notwithstanding any Civill power to remove both himselfe, and his familie at their pleasure out of the same, provided there be no legall impediment to the contrarie.

3

WILLIAM PENN, ENGLAND'S PRESENT INTEREST CONSIDERED, WITH HONOUR TO THE PRINCE, AND SAFETY TO THE PEOPLE
1675
Select Works 3:203–5

Chap I. Of English Rights.

There is no government in the world, but it must either stand upon *will* and *power,* or *condition* and *contract:* the one rules by men, the other by laws. And above all kingdoms under heaven, it is England's felicity to have her constitution so impartially just and free, that there cannot well be any thing more remote from arbitrariness, or more zealous of preserving the laws, by which its rights are maintained.

These laws are either fundamental, and so immutable;

or more superficial and temporary, and consequently alterable.

By *Superficial laws,* we understand such acts, laws, or statutes, as are suited to present occurrences, and emergencies of state; and which may as well be abrogated, as they were first made, for the good of the kingdom: for instance, those statutes that relate to victuals, clothes, times and places of trade, &c. which have ever stood, whilst the reason of them was in force; but when that benefit, which did once redound, fell by fresh accidents, they ended, according to that old maxim, *Cessante ratione legis, cessat lex.*

By *fundamental laws,* I do not only understand such as immediately spring from *synteresis* (that eternal principle of truth and sapience, more or less disseminated through mankind,) which are as the corner-stones of human structure, the basis of reasonable societies, without which all would run into heaps and confusion; to wit, *Honestè vivère, alterum non laedere, jus suum cuiq; tribuere,* that is, "To live honestly, not to hurt another, and to give every one their right," (excellent principles, and common to all nations) though that itself were sufficient to our present purpose; but those rights and privileges which I call *English,* and which are the proper birth-right of Englishmen, and may be reduced to these three.

I. An ownership, and undisturbed possession: that what they have is rightly theirs, and no body's else.

II. A voting of every law that is made, whereby that ownership or propriety may be maintained.

III. An influence upon, and a real share in, that judicatory power that must apply every such law; which is the ancient, necessary and laudable use of juries: if not found among the *Britons,* to be sure practised by the *Saxons,* and continued through the *Normans* to this very day.

That these have been the ancient and undoubted rights of Englishmen, as three great roots, under whose spacious branches the English People have been wont to shelter themselves against the storms of arbitrary government, I shall endeavour to prove.

4

THE CONCESSIONS AND AGREEMENTS OF THE PROPRIETORS, FREEHOLDERS, AND INHABITANTS OF THE PROVINCE OF WEST NEW-JERSEY
3 Mar. 1677
Boyd 83–89

The Charter or fundamentall Laws of West New Jersey agreed upon

Chapter 13

That these following concessions are the common Law or fundamentall Rights of the province of West New Jersey

That the common Law or fundamentall Rights and priviledges of West New Jersey are Individually agreed upon
by the Proprietors and freeholders thereof to be the foundation of the Government which is not to be altered by the
Legislative Authority or free Assembly hereafter mentioned and constituted But that the said Legislative Authority is constituted according to these fundamentalls to
make such Laws as agree with and maintaine the said fundamentalls and to make no Laws that in the least contradict differ or vary from the said fundamentalls under what
pretence or allegation soever.

Chapter 14

But if it so happen that any person or persons of the
said free Assembly shall therin designedly willfully and
Malitiously move or excite any to move any matter or
thing whatsoever that contradicts or any wayes subverts
any fundamentall of the said Laws in the constitution of
the Government of this province it being proved by seaven
honest and reputeable persons he or they shall be proceeded against as Traitors to the said Government.

Chapter 15

That these Concessions Law or great Charter of fundamentalls be recorded in a faire table in the assembly house
and that they be read at the beginning and disolveing of
every Generall free assembly And it is further agreed and
Ordained that the said Concessions Common Law or great
Charter of fundamentalls be writt in faire tables in every
Common Hall of Justice within this Province and that they
be read in sollemn manner foure times every yeare in the
presence of the People by the chiefe Magistrats of those
places.

Chapter 16

That no Men nor number of Men upon Eearth hath
power or Authority to rule over mens consciences in religious matters therefore it is consented agreed and ordained that no person or persons whatsoever within the
said Province at any time or times hereafter shall be any
waies upon any pretence whatsoever called in question or
in the least punished or hurt either in Person Estate or
Priveledge for the sake of his opinion Judgment faith or
worship towards God in matters of Religion but that all
and every such person and persons may from time to time
and at all times freely and fully have and enjoy his and
their Judgments and the exercise of their consciences in
matters of religious worship throughout all the said Province.

Chapter 17

That no proprietor Freeholder or Inhabitant of the said
Province of West New Jersey shall be deprived or condemned of Life limb Liberty estate Property or any wayes
hurt in his or their Priveledges Freedoms or Fra[n]chises
upon any account whatsoever without a due tryall and

Judgment passed by twelve good and Lawfull men of his
neighbourhood first had and that in all causes to be tried
and in all tryalls the person or persons araigned may except against any of the said Neighbourhood without any
reason Rendred (not exceeding thirty five) and in case of
any vallid reason alledged against every person nominated
for that service.

Chapter 18

And that no proprietor Freeholder free denison or Inhabitant in the said Province shall be attached arrested or
imprisoned for or by reason of any debt dutie or other
thing whatsoever (cases fellonious criminall and treasonable excepted) before he or she have personall summon or
summons left at his or her last dwelling place if in the said
Province by some legall Authorized Officer constituted
and appointed for that purpose to appeare in some Court
of Judicature for the said Province with a full and plaine
account of the cause or thing in demand as alsoe the name
or names of the person or persons at whose suite and the
Court where he is to appeare And that he hath at least
fourteen dayes time to appeare and answer the said suite
if he or she live or inhabitt within forty Miles English of
the said Court and if at further distance to have for every
twenty miles two dayes time more for his and their appeareance and so proportionably for a larger distance of
place.

That upon the recording of the summons and non appeareance of such person and persons a writt or attachment shall or may be issued out to arrest or attach the
person or persons of such defaulters to cause his or their
appeareance in such Court returnable at a day certaine to
answer the penalty or penalties in such suite or suites and
if he or they shall be Condemned by legal tryall and
Judgement the penalty or penalties shall be paid and satisfied out of his or their reall or personall Estate so Condemned or cause the person or persons soe condemned to
lie in execution till satisfaction of the debt and damages be
made Provided alwaies if such person or persons soe condemned shall pay and deliver such Estate Goods and Chattells which he or any other person hath for his or their use
and shall sollemnly declare and averr that he or they have
not any further Estate Goods or chattells wheresoever to
satisfie the person or persons (at whose suite he or they
are Condemned) their respective Judgments and shall alsoe bring and produce three other persons as Compurga-
tors who are Well knowne and of honest reputation and
approved of by the Commissioners of that division where
they dwell or inhabitt which shall in such open Court likewise sollemnly declare and averr that they believe in their
Consciences such person and persons soe Condemned hav
not wherewith further to pay the said condemnation or
Condemnations he or they shall be thence forthwith discharged from their said imprisonment any Law or custome to the contrary thereof heretofore in the said Province notwithstanding and upon such summons and default
of appeareance recorded as aforesaid and such person and
persons not appeareing within forty dayes after it shall
and may be lawfull for such Court of Judicature to pro-

ceed to tryall of twelve Lawfull men to Judgment against such defaulters and issue forth execution against his or their estate real and personall to satisfie such penalty or penalties to such debt and damages soe recorded as farr as it shall or may extend.

Chapter 19

That there shall be in every Court three Justices or Comissioners who shall sitt with the twelve men of the Neighbourhood with them to heare all causes and to assist the said twelve men of the neighbourhood in case of Law and that they the said Justices shall pronounce such Judgment as they shall receive from And be directed by the said twelve men in whom only the Judgment resides and not otherwise. And in case of their neglect and refusall that then one of the twelve by consent of the rest pronounce their owne Judgment as the Justices should have done. And if any Judgement shall be past in any case civill or Criminall by any other person or persons or any other way then according to this agreement and appointment it shall be held null and void and such person or persons soe presumeing to give Judgment shall be severely fined and upon complaint made to the generall Assembly by them be declared incapeable of any office or trust within this Province.

Chapter 20

That in all matters and causes civill and Criminall proofe is to be made by the sollemn and plaine averrment of at least two honest and reputeable persons And in case that any person or persons shall beare false witness and bring in his or their evidence contrary to the truth of the matter as shall be made plainly to Appeare that then every such person or persons shall in civill causes suffer the penalty which would be due to the person or persons he or they beare witness against. And in case any witness or witnesses on the behalfe of any person or persons indicted in a criminall cause shall be found to have borne false witness for feare gaine Mallice or favour and thereby hinder the due execution of the Law and deprive the suffering person or persons of their due satisfaction That then and in all other cases of false evidence such person or persons shall be first severely fined and next that he or they shall forever be disabled from being admitted in Evidence or into any publick office employment or service within this Province.

Chapter 21

That all and every person and persons whatsoever who shall prosecute or prefere any indictment or information against others for any personall injuries or matter Criminall or shall prosecute for any other Criminall cause (Treason Murther and Fellony only excepted) shall and may be Master of his owne process and have full power to forgive and remitt the person or persons offendeing against him or herselfe only as well before as after Judgment and Condemnation and pardon and remitt the sentence fine and punishment of the person or persons offending be it personnall or other whatsoever.

Chapter 22

That the tryalls of all Causes Civill and Criminall shall be heard and decided by the vardict or Judgment of twelve honest men of the neighbourhood only to be summoned and presented by the Sherriffe of that division or propriety where the fact or trespass is Committed and that no person or persons shall be compelled to fee any Attorney or Councellor to plead his cause but that all persons have free liberty to plead his owne cause if he please And that no person nor persons imprisoned upon any account whatever within this Province shall be obliged to pay any Fees to the officer or officers of the said prison either when committed or discharged.

Chapter 23

That in all public Courts of Justice for tryall of causes Civill or criminall any person or persons inhabitants of the said Province may freely come into and attend the said Courts and heare and be present at all or any Such tryalls as shal be there had or passed that Justice may not be done in a corner nor in any Covert manner (being intended and resolved by the help of the Lord and by these our Concessions and fundamentalls that all and every person and persons Inhabiting the said Province shall as farr as in us lies be free from oppression and slavery.

5

WILLIAM PENN, THE EXCELLENT PRIVILEDGE OF
LIBERTY AND PROPERTY BEING THE
BIRTH-RIGHT OF THE FREE-BORN
SUBJECTS OF ENGLAND
1687
Philobiblon Club ed. 3–12

To the Reader

It may reasonably be supposed that we shall find in this part of the world, many men, both old and young, that are strangers, in a great measure, to the true understanding of that inestimable inheritance that every Free-born Subject of England is heir unto by Birth-right, I mean that unparalleled privilege of *Liberty and Property,* beyond all the Nations in the world beside; and it is to be wished that all men did rightly understand their own happiness therein; in pursuance of which I do here present thee with that ancient Garland, the Fundamental Laws of England, bedecked with many precious privileges of *Liberty and Property,* by which every man that is a Subject to the Crown of England, may understand what is his right, and how to preserve it from unjust and unreasonable men: whereby appears the eminent care, wisdom and industry of our progenitors in providing for themselves and posterity so good a fortress that is able to repel the lust, pride and power of the Noble, as well as ignorance of the Ignoble; it being that excellent and discreet balance that gives every man his even proportion, which cannot be taken from him, nor be dispossessed of his life, liberty or estate, but by the trial and judgment of twelve of his equals, or Law of the Land, upon the penalty of the bitter curses of the whole people; so great was the zeal of our predecessors for the preservation of these Fundamental Liberties (contained in these Charters) from encroachment, that they employed all their policy and religious obligations to secure them entire and inviolable, albeit the contrary hath often been endeavoured, yet Providence hitherto hath preserved them as a blessing to the English Subjects.

The chief end of the publication hereof is for the information and understanding (what is their native right and inheritance) of such who may not have leisure from their Plantations to read large volumes; and beside, I know this Country is not furnished with Law-Books, and this being the root from whence all our wholesome English Laws spring, and indeed the line by which they must be squared, I have ventured to make it public, hoping it may be of use and service to many Freemen, Planters and Inhabitants in this Country, to whom it is sent and recommended, wishing it may raise up noble resolutions in all the Freeholders in these new Colonies, not to give away any thing of *Liberty and Property* that at present they do, (or of right as loyal English Subjects, ought to) enjoy, but take up the good example of our ancestors, and understand, that it is easy to part with or give away great privileges, but hard to be gained, if once lost. And therefore all depends upon our prudent care and actings to preserve and lay sure foundations for ourselves and the posterity of our loins.

PHILOPOLITES.

Introduction

In *France,* and other nations, the mere will of the Prince is Law, his word takes off any man's head, imposeth taxes, or seizes any man's estate, when, how and as often as he lists; and if one be accused, or but so much as suspected of any crime, he may either presently execute him, or banish, or imprison him at pleasure; or if he will be so gracious as to proceed by form of their laws, if any two villains will but swear against the poor party, his life is gone; nay, if there be no witness, yet he may be put on the rack, the tortures whereof make many an innocent person confess himself guilty, and then, with seeming justice, is executed. But,

In *England* the Law is both the measure and the bound of every Subject's duty and allegiance, each man having a fixed Fundamental Right born with him, as to freedom of his person and property in his estate, which he cannot be deprived of, but either by his consent, or some crime, for which the law has imposed such a penalty or forfeiture. For (1) all our Kings take a solemn oath at their Coronation to observe and cause the laws to be kept: (2) all our Judges take an oath wherein among other points they

swear, to do equal Law and Right to all the King's Subjects, rich and poor, and not to delay any person of Common Right for the Letters of the King, or of any other Person, or for any other cause: Therefore saith Fortescue, (who was first Chief Justice, and afterwards Lord Chancellor to King Henry the Sixth) in his Book *De Laudibus Legum Angliae,* cap. 9, *Non potest Rex Angliae,* etc. The King of England cannot alter nor change the laws of his realm at his pleasure; For why, he governeth his people by power not only royal, but also politic: If his power over them were only regal, then he might change the laws of his realm, and charge his Subjects with Tallage and other burthens, without their consent; but from this much differeth the power of a King whose government is politic; for he can neither change laws without the consent of his Subjects, nor yet charge them with impositions against their wills. With which accords Bracton, a learned Judge and Law-Author, in the Reign of King Henry the Third, saying, *Rex in Regno suo superiores habet Deum et Legem; i.e.,* The King in his Realm hath two superiors, God and the Law; for he is under the directive, though not coercive Power of the Law.

Tis true, the Law itself affirms, *the King can do no wrong,* which proceeds not only from a presumption, that so excellent a Person will do none, but also because he acts nothing but by Ministers, which (from the lowest to the highest) are answerable for their doings; so that if a King in passion should command A. to kill B. without process of law, A. may yet be prosecuted by Indictment or upon an Appeal (where no royal pardon is allowable) and must for the same be executed, such command notwithstanding.

This original happy Frame of Government is truly and properly called *an Englishman's Liberty,* a Privilege not exempt from the law, but to be freed in person and estate from arbitrary violence and oppression. A greater inheritance (saith Judge Coke) is derived to every one of us from our laws than from our parents. For without the former, what would the latter signify? And this Birth-right of Englishmen shines most conspicuously in two things:

1. PARLIAMENTS.
2. JURIES.

By the *First* the Subject has a share by his chosen Representatives in the Legislative (or law-making) Power; for no new laws bind the people of England, but such as are by common consent agreed on in that great Council.

By the *Second,* he has a share in the executive part of the law, no causes being tried, nor any man adjudged to lose life, member or estate, but upon the verdict of his Peers or Equals his neighbours, and of his own condition: These two grand pillars of English liberty, are the Fundamental Vital Privileges, whereby we have been, and are preserved more free and happy than any other people in the world, and (we trust) shall ever continue so: For whoever shall design to impair, pervert or undermine either of them, do strike at the very Constitution of our Government, and ought to be prosecuted and punished with the utmost zeal and rigour. To cut down the banks and let in the sea, or to poison all the springs and rivers in the kingdom, could not be a greater mischief; for this would only affect the present age, but the other will ruin and enslave all our posterity.

But beside these paramount privileges which the English are estated in by the original Constitution of their Government, there are others more particularly declared and expressed in divers Acts of Parliament too large to be inserted in this place.

6

BILL OF RIGHTS
1 W. & M., 2d sess., c. 2, 16 Dec. 1689

An act for declaring the rights and liberties of the subject, and settling the succession of the crown.

Whereas the lords spiritual and temporal, and commons assembled at *Westminster,* lawfully, fully, and freely representing all the estates of the people of this realm, did upon the thirteenth day of *February,* in the year of our Lord one thousand six hundred eighty eight, present unto their Majesties, then called and known by the names and stile of *William* and *Mary,* prince and princess of *Orange,* being present in their proper persons, a certain declaration in writing, made by the said lords and commons, in the words following; *viz.*

Whereas the late King *James* the Second, by the assistance of divers evil counsellors, judges, and ministers employed by him, did endeavour to subvert and extirpate the protestant religion, and the laws and liberties of this kingdom.

1. By assuming and exercising a power of dispensing with and suspending of laws, and the execution of laws, without consent of parliament.

2. By committing and prosecuting divers worthy prelates, for humbly petitioning to be excused from concurring to the said assumed power.

3. By issuing and causing to be executed a commission under the great seal for erecting a court called, *The court of commissioners for ecclesiastical causes.*

4. By levying money for and to the use of the crown, by pretence of prerogative, for other time, and in other manner, than the same was granted by parliament.

5. By raising and keeping a standing army within this kingdom in time of peace, without consent of parliament, and quartering soldiers contrary to law.

6. By causing several good subjects, being protestants, to be disarmed, at the same time when papists were both armed and employed, contrary to law.

7. By violating the freedom of election of members to serve in parliament.

8. By prosecutions in the court of King's bench, for matters and causes cognizable only in parliament; and by divers other arbitrary and illegal courses.

9. And whereas of late years, partial, corrupt, and unqualified persons have been returned and served on juries in trials, and particularly divers jurors in trials for high treason, which were not freeholders.

10. And excessive bail hath been required of persons committed in criminal cases, to elude the benefit of the laws made for the liberty of the subjects.

11. And excessive fines have been imposed; and illegal and cruel punishments inflicted.

12. And several grants and promises made of fines and forfeitures, before any conviction or judgment against the persons, upon whom the same same were to be levied.

All which are utterly and directly contrary to the known laws and statutes, and freedom of this realm.

And whereas the said late King *James* the Second having abdicated the government, and the throne being thereby vacant, his highness the prince of *Orange* (whom it hath pleased Almighty God to make the glorious instrument of delivering this kingdom from popery and arbitrary power) did (by the advice of the lords spiritual and temporal, and divers principal persons of the commons) cause letters to be written to the lords spiritual and temporal, being protestants; and other letters to the several counties, cities, universities, boroughs, and cinque-ports, for the choosing of such persons to represent them, as were of right to be sent to parliament, to meet and sit at *Westminster* upon the two and twentieth day of *January,* in this year one thousand six hundred eighty and eight, in order to such an establishment, as that their religion, laws, and liberties might not again be in danger of being subverted: upon which letters, elections have been accordingly made,

And thereupon the said lords spiritual and temporal, and commons, pursuant to their respective letters and elections, being now assembled in a full and free representative of this nation, taking into their most serious consideration the best means for attaining the ends aforesaid; do in the first place (as their ancestors in like case have usually done) for the vindicating and asserting their ancient rights and liberties, declare;

1. That the pretended power of suspending of laws, or the execution of laws, by regal authority, without consent of parliament, is illegal.

2. That the pretended power of dispensing with laws, or the execution of laws, by regal authority, as it hath been assumed and exercised of late, is illegal.

3. That the commission for erecting the late court of commissioners for ecclesiastical causes, and other commissions and courts of like nature are illegal and pernicious.

4. That levying money for or to the use of the crown, by pretence of prerogative, without grant of parliament, for longer time, or in other manner than the same is or shall be granted, is illegal.

5. That it is the right of the subjects to petition the King, and all committments and prosecutions for such petitioning are illegal.

6. That the raising or keeping a standing army within the kingdom in time of peace, unless it be with consent of parliament, is against law.

7. That the subjects which are protestants, may have arms for their defence suitable to their conditions, and as allowed by law.

8. That election of members of parliament ought to be free.

9. That the freedom of speech, and debates or proceed-

ings in parliament, ought not to be impeached or questioned in any court or place out of parliament.

10. That excessive bail ought not to be required, nor excessive fines imposed; nor cruel and unusual punishments inflicted.

11. That jurors ought to be duly impanelled and returned, and jurors which pass upon men in trials for high treason ought to be freeholders.

12. That all grants and promises of fines and forfeitures of particular persons before conviction, are illegal and void.

13. And that for redress of all grievances, and for the amending, strengthening, and preserving of the laws, parliaments ought to be held frequently.

And they do claim, demand, and insist upon all and singular the premises, as their undoubted rights and liberties; and that no declarations, judgments, doings or proceedings, to the prejudice of the people in any of the said premises, ought in any wise to be drawn hereafter into consequence or example.

To which demand of their rights they are particularly encouraged by the declaration of his highness the prince of *Orange*, as being the only means for obtaining a full redress and remedy therein.

Having therefore an entire confidence, That his said highness the prince of *Orange* will perfect the deliverance so far advanced by him, and will still preserve them from the violation of their rights, which they have here asserted, and from all other attempts upon their religion, rights, and liberties.

II. The said lords spiritual and temporal, and commons, assembled at *Westminster*, do resolve, that *William* and *Mary* prince and princess of *Orange* be, and be declared, King and Queen of *England, France* and *Ireland,* and the dominions thereunto belonging, to hold the crown and royal dignity of the said kingdoms and dominions to them the said prince and princess during their lives, and the life of the survivor of them; and that the sole and full exercise of the regal power be only in, and executed by the said prince of *Orange,* in the names of the said prince and princess, during their joint lives; and after their deceases, the said crown and royal dignity of the said kingdoms and dominions to be to the heirs of the body of the said princess; and for default of such issue to the princess *Anne* of *Denmark,* and the heirs of her body; and for default of such issue to the heirs of the body of the said prince of *Orange.* And the lords spiritual and temporal, and commons, do pray the said prince and princess to accept the same accordingly.

III. And that the oaths hereafter mentioned be taken by all persons of whom the oaths of allegiance and supremacy might be required by law, instead of them; and that the said oaths of allegiance and supremacy be abrogated.

I *A. B.* do sincerely promise and swear, That I will be faithful, and bear true allegiance, to their Majesties King *William* and Queen *Mary:*

So help me God.

I *A. B.* do swear, That I do from my heart abhor, detest, and abjure as impious and heretical, that damnable doc-

trine and position, *That princes excommunicated or deprived by the pope, or any authority of the see of* Rome, *may be deposed or murdered by their subjects, or any other whatsoever.* And I do declare, That no foreign prince, person, prelate, state, or potentate hath, or ought to have any jurisdiction, power, superiority, pre-eminence, or authority ecclesiastical or spiritual, within this realm:

So help me God.

IV. Upon which their said Majesties did accept the crown and royal dignity of the kingdoms of *England, France,* and *Ireland,* and the dominions thereunto belonging, according to the resolution and desire of the said lords and commons contained in the said declaration.

V. And thereupon their Majesties were pleased, That the said lords spiritual and temporal, and commons, being the two houses of parliament, should continue to sit, and with their Majesties royal concurrence make effectual provision for the settlement of the religion, laws and liberties of this kingdom, so that the same for the future might not be in danger again of being subverted; to which the said lords spiritual and temporal, and commons, did agree and proceed to act accordingly.

VI. *Now in pursuance of the premises, the said lords spiritual and temporal, and commons, in parliament assembled, for the ratifying, confirming and establishing the said declaration, and the articles, clauses, matters, and things therein contained, by the force of a law made in due form by authority of parliament, do pray that it may be declared and enacted, That all and singular the rights and liberties asserted and claimed in the said declaration, are the true, ancient, and indubitable rights and liberties of the people of this kingdom, and so shall be esteemed, allowed, adjudged, deemed, and taken to be, and that all and every the particulars aforesaid shall be firmly and strictly holden and observed, as they are expressed in the said declaration; and all officers and ministers whatsoever shall serve their Majesties and their successors according to the same in all times to come.*

7

MASSACHUSETTS HOUSE OF REPRESENTATIVES, CIRCULAR LETTER TO THE COLONIAL LEGISLATURES
11 Feb. 1768
S. Adams Writings 1:184–85

(See ch. 17, no. 13)

8

SAMUEL ADAMS, BOSTON GAZETTE
27 Feb. 1769
Writings 1:316–19

(See ch. 3, no. 4)

9

SLAVE PETITION TO THE GOVERNOR, COUNCIL, AND HOUSE OF REPRESENTATIVES OF THE PROVINCE OF MASSACHUSETTS
25 May 1774
MHS Collections, 5th ser., 3:432–33

The Petition of a Grate Number of Blackes of this Province who by divine permission are held in a state of Slavery within the bowels of a free and christian Country

Humbly Shewing

That your Petitioners apprehind we have in common with all other men a naturel right to our freedoms without Being depriv'd of them by our fellow men as we are a freeborn Pepel and have never forfeited this Blessing by aney compact or agreement whatever. But we were unjustly dragged by the cruel hand of power from our dearest frinds and sum of us stolen from the bosoms of our tender Parents and from a Populous Pleasant and plentiful country and Brought hither to be made slaves for Life in a Christian land. Thus are we deprived of every thing that hath a tendency to make life even tolerable, the endearing ties of husband and wife we are strangers to for we are no longer man and wife then our masters or mestreses thinkes proper marred or onmarred. Our children are also taken from us by force and sent maney miles from us wear we seldom or ever see them again there to be made slaves of for Life which sumtimes is vere short by Reson of Being dragged from their mothers Breest Thus our Lives are imbittered to us on these accounts By our deplorable situation we are rendered incapable of shewing our obedience to Almighty God how can a slave perform the duties of a husband to a wife or parent to his child How can a husband leave master and work and cleave to his wife How can the wife submit themselves to there husbands in all things. How can the child obey thear parents in all things. There is a grat number of us sencear . . . members of the Church of Christ how can the master and the slave be said to fulfil that command Live in love let Brotherly Love contuner and abound Beare yea onenothers Bordenes How can the master be said to Beare my Borden when he Beares me down whith the Have chanes of slavery and operson against my will and how can we fulfill our parte of duty to him whilst in this condition and as we cannot searve our God as we ought whilst in this situation Nither can we reap an equal benefet from the laws of the Land which doth not justifi but condemns Slavery or if there had bin aney Law to hold us in Bondege we are Humbely of the Opinon ther never was aney to inslave our children for life when Born in a free Countrey. We therefor Bage your Excellency and Honours will give this its deu weight and consideration and that you will accordingly cause an act of the legislative to be pessed that we may obtain our Natural right our freedoms and our children be set at lebety at the yeare of Twenty one for

whoues sekes more petequeley your Petitioners is in Duty ever to Pray.

10

THOMAS JEFFERSON, A SUMMARY VIEW OF THE RIGHTS OF BRITISH AMERICA
July 1774
Papers 1:121–35

Resolved that it be an instruction to the said deputies when assembled in General Congress with the deputies from the other states of British America to propose to the said Congress that an humble and dutiful address be presented to his majesty begging leave to lay before him as chief magistrate of the British empire the united complaints of his majesty's subjects in America; complaints which are excited by many unwarrantable incroachments and usurpations, attempted to be made by the legislature of one part of the empire, upon those rights which god and the laws have given equally and independently to all. To represent to his majesty that these his states have often individually made humble application to his imperial throne, to obtain thro' it's intervention some redress of their injured rights; to none of which was ever even an answer condescended. Humbly to hope that this their joint address, penned in the language of truth, and divested of those expressions of servility which would persuade his majesty that we are asking favors and not rights, shall obtain from his majesty a more respectful acceptance. And this his majesty will think we have reason to expect when he reflects that he is no more than the chief officer of the people, appointed by the laws, and circumscribed with definite powers, to assist in working the great machine of government erected for their use, and consequently subject to their superintendance. And in order that these our rights, as well as the invasions of them, may be laid more fully before his majesty, to take a view of them from the origin and first settlement of these countries.

To remind him that our ancestors, before their emigration to America, were the free inhabitants of the British dominions in Europe, and possessed a right, which nature has given to all men, of departing from the country in which chance, not choice has placed them, of going in quest of new habitations, and of there establishing new societies, under such laws and regulations as to them shall seem most likely to promote public happiness. That their Saxon ancestors had under this universal law, in like manner, left their native wilds and woods in the North of Europe, had possessed themselves of the island of Britain then less charged with inhabitants, and had established there that system of laws which has so long been the glory and protection of that country. Nor was ever any claim of superiority or dependance asserted over them by that mother country from which they had migrated: and were such a claim made it is beleived his majesty's subjects in

Great Britain have too firm a feeling of the rights derived to them from their ancestors to bow down the sovereignty of their state before such visionary pretensions. And it is thought that no circumstance has occurred to distinguish materially the British from the Saxon emigration. America was conquered, and her settlements made and firmly established, at the expence of individuals, and not of the British public. Their own blood was spilt in acquiring lands for their settlement, their own fortunes expended in making that settlement effectual. For themselves they fought, for themselves they conquered, and for themselves alone they have right to hold. No shilling was ever issued from the public treasures of his majesty or his ancestors for their assistance, till of very late times, after the colonies had become established on a firm and permanent footing. That then indeed, having become valuable to Great Britain for her commercial purposes, his parliament was pleased to lend them assistance against an enemy who would fain have drawn to herself the benefits of their commerce to the great aggrandisement of herself and danger of Great Britain. Such assistance, and in such circumstances, they had often before given to Portugal and other allied states, with whom they carry on a commercial intercourse. Yet these states never supposed that, by calling in her aid, they thereby submitted themselves to her sovereignty. Had such terms been proposed, they would have rejected them with disdain, and trusted for better to the moderation of their enemies, or to a vigorous exertion of their own force. We do not however mean to underrate those aids, which to us were doubtless valuable, on whatever principles granted: but we would shew that they cannot give a title to that authority which the British parliament would arrogate over us; and that they may amply be repaid, by our giving to the inhabitants of Great Britain such exclusive privileges in trade as may be advantageous to them, and at the same time not too restrictive to ourselves. That settlements having been thus effected in the wilds of America, the emigrants thought proper to adopt that system of laws under which they had hitherto lived in the mother country, and to continue their union with her by submitting themselves to the same common sovereign, who was thereby made the central link connecting the several parts of the empire thus newly multiplied.

But that not long were they permitted, however far they thought themselves removed from the hand of oppression, to hold undisturbed the rights thus acquired at the hazard of their lives and loss of their fortunes. A family of princes was then on the British throne, whose treasonable crimes against their people brought on them afterwards the exertion of those sacred and sovereign rights of punishment, reserved in the hands of the people for cases of extreme necessity, and judged by the constitution unsafe to be delegated to any other judicature. While every day brought forth some new and unjustifiable exertion of power over their subjects on that side the water, it was not to be expected that those here, much less able at that time to oppose the designs of despotism, should be exempted from injury. Accordingly that country which had been acquired by the lives, the labors and the fortunes of individual ad-

venturers, was by these princes at several times parted out and distributed among the favorites and followers of their fortunes; and by an assumed right of the crown alone were erected into distinct and independent governments; a measure which it is beleived his majesty's prudence and understanding would prevent him from imitating at this day; as no exercise of such a power of dividing and dismembering a country has ever occurred in his majesty's realm of England, tho' now of very antient standing; nor could it be justified or acquiesced under there or in any other part of his majesty's empire.

That the exercise of a free trade with all parts of the world, possessed by the American colonists as of natural right, and which no law of their own had taken away or abridged, was next the object of unjust incroachment. Some of the colonies having thought proper to continue the administration of their government in the name and under the authority of his majesty king Charles the first, whom notwithstanding his late deposition by the Common-wealth of England, they continued in the sovereignty of their state, the Parliament for the Common-wealth took the same in high offence, and assumed upon themselves the power of prohibiting their trade with all other parts of the world except the island of Great Britain. This arbitrary act however they soon recalled, and by solemn treaty entered into on the 12th. day of March 1651, between the said Commonwealth by their Commissioners and the colony of Virginia by their house of Burgesses, it was expressly stipulated by the 8th. article of the said treaty that they should have "free trade as the people of England do enjoy to all places and with all nations according to the laws of that Commonwealth." But that, upon the restoration of his majesty King Charles the second, their rights of free commerce fell once more a victim to arbitrary power: and by several acts of his reign as well as of some of his successors the trade of the colonies was laid under such restrictions as shew what hopes they might form from the justice of a British parliament were its uncontrouled power admitted over these states. History has informed us that bodies of men as well as individuals are susceptible of the spirit of tyranny. A view of these acts of parliament for regulation, as it has been affectedly called, of the American trade, if all other evidence were removed out of the case, would undeniably evince the truth of this observation. Besides the duties they impose on our articles of export and import, they prohibit our going to any Markets Northward of cape Finesterra in the kingdom of Spain for the sale of commodities which Great Britain will not take from us, and for the purchase of others with which she cannot supply us; and that for no other than the arbitrary purpose of purchasing for themselves by a sacrifice of our rights and interests, certain privileges in their commerce with an allied state, who, in confidence that their exclusive trade with America will be continued while the principles and power of the British parliament be the same, have induldged themselves in every exorbitance which their avarice could dictate, or our necessities extort: have raised their commodities called for in America to the double and treble of what they sold for before such exclusive privileges were given them, and of what better commodities of the same kind would cost us elsewhere; and at the same time give us much less for what we carry thither, than might be had at more convenient ports. That these acts prohibit us from carrying in quest of other purchasers the surplus of our tobaccoes remaining after the consumption of Great Britain is supplied: so that we must leave them with the British merchant for whatever he will please to allow us, to be by him reshipped to foreign markets, where he will reap the benefits of making sale of them for full value. That to heighten still the idea of parliamentary justice, and to shew with what moderation they are like to exercise power, where themselves are to feel no part of it's weight, we take leave to mention to his majesty certain other acts of British parliament, by which they would prohibit us from manufacturing for our own use the articles we raise on our own lands with our own labor. By an act passed in the 5th. year of the reign of his late majesty king George the second an American subject is forbidden to make a hat for himself of the fur which he has taken perhaps on his own soil. An instance of despotism to which no parrallel can be produced in the most arbitrary ages of British history. By one other act passed in the 23d. year of the same reign, the iron which we make we are forbidden to manufacture; and, heavy as that article is, and necessary in every branch of husbandry, besides commission and insurance, we are to pay freight for it to Great Britain, and freight for it back again, for the purpose of supporting, not men, but machines, in the island of Great Britain. In the same spirit of equal and impartial legislation is to be viewed the act of parliament passed in the 5th. year of the same reign, by which American lands are made subject to the demands of British creditors, while their own lands were still continued unanswerable for their debts; from which one of these conclusions must necessarily follow, either that justice is not the same thing in America as in Britain, or else that the British parliament pay less regard to it here than there. But that we do not point out to his majesty the injustice of these acts with intent to rest on that principle the cause of their nullity, but to shew that experience confirms the propriety of those political principles which exempt us from the jurisdiction of the British parliament. The true ground on which we declare these acts void is that the British parliament has no right to exercise authority over us.

That these exercises of usurped power have not been confined to instances alone in which themselves were interested; but they have also intermeddled with the regulation of the internal affairs of the colonies. The act of the 9th. of Anne for establishing a post office in America seems to have had little connection with British convenience, except that of accomodating his majesty's ministers and favorites with the sale of a lucrative and easy office.

That thus have we hastened thro' the reigns which preceded his majesty's, during which the violation of our rights were less alarming, because repeated at more distant intervals, than that rapid and bold succession of injuries which is likely to distinguish the present from all other periods of American story. Scarcely have our minds been

able to emerge from the astonishment into which one stroke of parliamentary thunder has involved us, before another more heavy and more alarming is fallen on us. Single acts of tyranny may be ascribed to the accidental opinion of a day; but a series of oppressions, begun at a distinguished period, and pursued unalterably thro' every change of ministers, too plainly prove a deliberate, systematical plan of reducing us to slavery.

That the act passed in the 4th. year of his majesty's reign intitled "an act [for granting certain duties"]
one other act passed in the 5th. year of his reign intitled
    "an act [for granting and applying certain stamp duties"]
one other act passed in the 6th. year of his reign intitled
    "an act [for the better securing the dependency of his
    majesty's dominions in America"]
and one other act passed in the 7th. year of his reign intitled "an act [for granting duties on paper, tea, etc."]
form that connected chain of parliamentary usurpation which has already been the subject of frequent applications to his majesty and the houses of Lords and Commons of Great Britain; and, no answers having yet been condescended to any of these, we shall not trouble his majesty with a repetition of the matters they contained.

But that one other act passed in the same 7th. year of his reign, having been a peculiar attempt, must ever require peculiar mention. It is intitled "an act [for suspending the legislature of New York."] One free and independent legislature hereby takes upon itself to suspend the powers of another, free and independent as itself, thus exhibiting a phaenomenon, unknown in nature, the creator and creature of it's own power. Not only the principles of common sense, but the common feelings of human nature must be surrendered up, before his majesty's subjects here can be persuaded to beleive that they hold their political existence at the will of a British parliament Shall these governments be dissolved, their property annihilated, and their people reduced to a state of nature, at the imperious breath of a body of men whom they never saw, in whom they never confided, and over whom they have no powers of punishment or removal, let their crimes against the American public be ever so great? Can any one reason be assigned why 160,000 electors in the island of Great Britain should give law to four millions in the states of America, every individual of whom is equal to every individual of them in virtue, in understanding, and in bodily strength? Were this to be admitted, instead of being a free people, as we have hitherto supposed, and mean to continue, ourselves, we should suddenly be found the slaves, not of one, but of 160,000 tyrants, distinguished too from all others by this singular circumstance that they are removed from the reach of fear, the only restraining motive which may hold the hand of a tyrant.

That by "an act to discontinue in such manner and for such time as are therein mentioned the landing and discharging lading or shipping of goods wares and merchandize at the town and within the harbor of Boston in the province of Massachusett's bay in North America" which was passed at the last session of British parliament, a large and populous town, whose trade was their sole subsistence, was deprived of that trade, and involved in utter ruin. Let us for a while suppose the question of right suspended, in order to examine this act on principles of justice. An act of parliament had been passed imposing duties on teas to be paid in America, against which act the Americans had protested as inauthoritative. The East India company, who till that time had never sent a pound of tea to America on their own account, step forth on that occasion the asserters of parliamentary right, and send hither many ship loads of that obnoxious commodity. The masters of their several vessels however, on their arrival in America, wisely attended to admonition, and returned with their cargoes. In the province of New England alone the remonstrances of the people were disregarded, and a compliance, after being many days waited for, was flatly refused. Whether in this the master of the vessel was governed by his obstinacy or his instructions, let those who know, say. There are extraordinary situations which require extraordinary interposition. An exasperated people, who feel that they possess power, are not easily restrained within limits strictly regular. A number of them assembled in the town of Boston, threw the tea into the ocean and dispersed without doing any other act of violence. If in this they did wrong, they were known, and were amenable to the laws of the land, against which it could not be objected that they had ever in any instance been obstructed or diverted from their regular course in favor of popular offenders. They should therefore not have been distrusted on this occasion. But that illfated colony had formerly been bold in their enmities against the house of Stuart, and were now devoted to ruin by that unseen hand which governs the momentous affairs of this great empire. On the partial representations of a few worthless ministerial dependants, whose constant office it has been to keep that government embroiled, and who by their treacheries hope to obtain the dignity of the British knighthood, without calling for a party accused, without asking a proof, without attempting a distinction between the guilty and the innocent, the whole of that antient and wealthy town is in a moment reduced from opulence to beggary. Men who had spent their lives in extending the British commerce, who had invested in that place the wealth their honest endeavors had merited, found themselves and their families thrown at once on the world for subsistence by it's charities. Not the hundredth part of the inhabitants of that town had been concerned in the act complained of; many of them were in Great Britain and in other parts beyond sea; yet all were involved in one indiscriminate ruin, by a new executive power unheard of till then, that of a British parliament. A property of the value of many millions of money was sacrifised to revenge, not repay, the loss of a few thousands. This is administering justice with a heavy hand indeed! And when is this tempest to be arrested in it's course? Two wharfs are to be opened again when his majesty shall think proper: the residue which lined the extensive shores of the bay of Boston are forever interdicted the exercise of commerce. This little exception seems to have been thrown in for no other purpose than that of setting a precedent for investing his majesty with legislative powers. If the pulse

of his people shall beat calmly under this experiment, another and another will be tried till the measure of despotism be filled up. It would be an insult on common sense to pretend that this exception was made in order to restore it's commerce to that great town. The trade which cannot be received at two wharfs alone, must of necessity be transferred to some other place; to which it will soon be followed by that of the two wharfs. Considered in this light it would be an insolent and cruel mockery at the annihilation of the town of Boston.

By the act for the suppression of riots and tumults in the town of Boston, passed also in the last session of parliament, a murder committed there is, if the governor pleases, to be tried in the court of King's bench in the island of Great Britain, by a jury of Middlesex. The witnesses too, on receipt of such a sum as the Governor shall think it reasonable for them to expend, are to enter into recognisance to appear at the trial. This is in other words taxing them to the amount of their recognisance; and that amount may be whatever a Governor pleases. For who does his majesty think can be prevailed on to cross the Atlantick for the sole purpose of bearing evidence to a fact? His expences are to be borne indeed as they shall be estimated by a Governor; but who are to feed the wife and children whom he leaves behind, and who have had no other subsistence but his daily labor? Those epidemical disorders too, so terrible in a foreign climate, is the cure of them to be estimated among the articles of expence, and their danger to be warded off by the almighty power of a parliament? And the wretched criminal, if he happen to have offended on the American side, stripped of his privilege of trial by peers, of his vicinage, removed from the place where alone full evidence could be obtained, without money, without counsel, without friends, without exculpatory proof, is tried before judges predetermined to condemn. The cowards who would suffer a countryman to be torn from the bowels of their society in order to be thus offered a sacrifice to parliamentary tyranny, would merit that everlasting infamy now fixed on the authors of the act! A clause for a similar purpose had been introduced into an act passed in the 12th. year of his majesty's reign entitled "an act for the better securing and preserving his majesty's dock-yards, magazines, ships, ammunition and stores," against which as meriting the same censures the several colonies have already protested.

That these are the acts of power assumed by a body of men foreign to our constitutions, and unacknowleged by our laws; against which we do, on behalf of the inhabitants of British America, enter this our solemn and determined protest. And we do earnestly intreat his majesty, as yet the only mediatory power between the several states of the British empire, to recommend to his parliament of Great Britain the total revocation of these acts, which however nugatory they be, may yet prove the cause of further discontents and jealousies among us.

That we next proceed to consider the conduct of his majesty, as holding the executive powers of the laws of these states, and mark out his deviations from the line of duty. By the constitution of Great Britain as well as of the several American states, his majesty possesses the power of refusing to pass into a law any bill which has already passed the other two branches of legislature. His majesty however and his ancestors, conscious of the impropriety of opposing their single opinion to the united wisdom of two houses of parliament, while their proceedings were unbiassed by interested principles, for several ages past have modestly declined the exercise of this power in that part of his empire called Great Britain. But by change of circumstances, other principles than those of justice simply have obtained an influence on their determinations. The addition of new states to the British empire has produced an addition of new, and sometimes opposite interests. It is now therefore the great office of his majesty to resume the exercise of his negative power, and to prevent the passage of laws by any one legislature of the empire which might bear injuriously on the rights and interests of another. Yet this will not excuse the wanton exercise of this power which we have seen his majesty practice on the laws of the American legislatures. For the most trifling reasons, and sometimes for no conceivable reason at all, his majesty has rejected laws of the most salutary tendency. The abolition of domestic slavery is the great object of desire in those colonies where it was unhappily introduced in their infant state. But previous to the infranchisement of the slaves we have, it is necessary to exclude all further importations from Africa. Yet our repeated attempts to effect this by prohibitions, and by imposing duties which might amount to a prohibition, have been hitherto defeated by his majesty's negative: thus preferring the immediate advantages of a few British corsairs to the lasting interests of the American states, and to the rights of human nature deeply wounded by this infamous practice. Nay the single interposition of an interested individual against a law was scarcely ever known to fail of success, tho' in the opposite scale were placed the interests of a whole country. That this is so shameful an abuse of a power trusted with his majesty for other purposes, as if not reformed would call for some legal restrictions.

With equal inattention to the necessities of his people here, has his majesty permitted our laws to lie neglected in England for years, neither confirming them by his assent, nor annulling them by his negative: so that such of them as have no suspending clause, we hold on the most precarious of all tenures, his majesty's will, and such of them as suspend themselves till his majesty's assent be obtained we have feared might be called into existence at some future and distant period, when time and change of circumstances shall have rendered them destructive to his people here. And to render this grievance still more oppressive, his majesty by his instructions has laid his governors under such restrictions that they can pass no law of any moment unless it have such suspending clause: so that, however immediate may be the call for legislative interposition, the law cannot be executed till it has twice crossed the Atlantic, by which time the evil may have spent it's whole force.

But in what terms reconcileable to majesty and at the same time to truth, shall we speak of a late instruction to his majesty's governor of the colony of Virginia, by which he is forbidden to assent to any law for the division of a county, unless the new county will consent to have no representative in assembly? That colony has as yet affixed no boundary to the Westward. Their Western counties therefore are of indefinite extent. Some of them are actually seated many hundred miles from their Eastern limits. Is it possible then that his majesty can have bestowed a single thought on the situation of those people, who, in order to obtain justice for injuries however great or small, must, by the laws of that colony, attend their county court at such a distance, with all their witnesses, monthly, till their litigation be determined? Or does his majesty seriously wish, and publish it to the world, that his subjects should give up the glorious right of representation, with all the benefits derived from that, and submit themselves the absolute slaves of his sovereign will? Or is it rather meant to confine the legislative body to their present numbers, that they may be the cheaper bargain whenever they shall become worth a purchase?

One of the articles of impeachment against Tresilian and the other judges of Westminster Hall in the reign of Richard the second, for which they suffered death as traitors to their country, was that they had advised the king that he might dissolve his parliament at any time: and succeeding kings have adopted the opinion of these unjust judges. Since the establishment however of the British constitution at the glorious* Revolution on it's free and antient principles, neither his majesty nor his ancestors have exercised such a power of dissolution in the island of Great Britain; and when his majesty was petitioned by the united voice of his people there to dissolve the present parliament, who had become obnoxious to them, his ministers were heard to declare in open parliament that his majesty possessed no such power by the constitution. But how different their language and his practice here! To declare as their duty required the known rights of their country, to oppose the usurpation of every foreign judicature, to disregard the imperious mandates of a minister or governor, have been the avowed causes of dissolving houses of representatives in America. But if such powers be really vested in his majesty, can he suppose they are there placed to awe the members from such purposes as these? When the representative body have lost the confidence of their constituents, when they have notoriously made sale of their most valuable rights, when they have assumed to themselves powers which the people never put into their hands, then indeed their continuing in office becomes dangerous to the state, and calls for an exercise of the power of dissolution. Such being the causes for which the representative body should and should not be dissolved, will it not appear strange to an unbiased observer that that of Great Britain was not dissolved, while those of the colonies have repeatedly incurred that sentence?

*On further enquiry I find two instances of dissolutions before the parl. would of itself have been at an end, viz. the parl. called to meet Aug. 24. 1698. was dissolved by K. Wm. Dec. 19. 1700. & a new one called to meet Feb. 6. 1701. which was also dissolved Nov. 11. 1701. & a new one met Dec. 30. 1701.

But your majesty or your Governors have carried this power beyond every limit known or provided for by the laws. After dissolving one house of representatives, they have refused to call another, so that for a great length of time the legislature provided by the laws has been out of existence. From the nature of things, every society must at all times possess within itself the sovereign powers of legislation. The feelings of human nature revolt against the supposition of a state so situated as that it may not in any emergency provide against dangers which perhaps threaten immediate ruin. While those bodies are in existence to whom the people have delegated the powers of legislation, they alone possess and may exercise those powers. But when they are dissolved by the lopping off one or more of their branches, the power reverts to the people, who may use it to unlimited extent, either assembling together in person, sending deputies, or in any other way they may think proper. We forbear to trace consequences further; the dangers are conspicuous with which this practice is replete.

That we shall at this time also take notice of an error in the nature of our landholdings, which crept in at a very early period of our settlement. The introduction of the Feudal tenures into the kingdom of England, though antient, is well enough understood to set this matter in a proper light. In the earlier ages of the Saxon settlement feudal holdings were certainly altogether unknown, and very few, if any, had been introduced at the time of the Norman conquest. Our Saxon ancestors held their lands, as they did their personal property, in absolute dominion, disencumbered with any superior, answering nearly to the nature of those possessions which the Feudalists term Allodial: William the Norman first introduced that system generally. The lands which had belonged to those who fell in the battle of Hastings, and in the subsequent insurrections of his reign, formed a considerable proportion of the lands of the whole kingdom. These he granted out, subject to feudal duties, as did he also those of a great number of his new subjects, who by persuasions or threats were induced to surrender them for that purpose. But still much was left in the hands of his Saxon subjects, held of no superior, and not subject to feudal conditions. These therefore by express laws, enacted to render uniform the system of military defence, were made liable to the same military duties as if they had been feuds: and the Norman lawyers soon found means to saddle them also with all the other feudal burthens. But still they had not been surrendered to the king, they were not derived from his grant, and therefore they were not holden of him. A general principle indeed was introduced that "all lands in England were held either mediately or immediately of the crown": but this was borrowed from those holdings which were truly feudal, and only applied to others for the purposes of illustration. Feudal holdings were therefore but exceptions out of the Saxon laws of possession, under which all lands were held in absolute right. These therefore still form the basis or groundwork of the Common law, to prevail wheresoever the exceptions have not taken place. America was not conquered by William the Norman, nor it's lands surrendered to him or any of his successors. Pos-

sessions there are undoubtedly of the Allodial nature. Our ancestors however, who migrated hither, were laborers, not lawyers. The fictitious principle that all lands belong originally to the king, they were early persuaded to beleive real, and accordingly took grants of their own lands from the crown. And while the crown continued to grant for small sums and on reasonable rents, there was no inducement to arrest the error and lay it open to public view. But his majesty has lately taken on him to advance the terms of purchase and of holding to the double of what they were, by which means the acquisition of lands being rendered difficult, the population of our country is likely to be checked. It is time therefore for us to lay this matter before his majesty, and to declare that he has no right to grant lands of himself. From the nature and purpose of civil institutions, all the lands within the limits which any particular society has circumscribed around itself, are assumed by that society, and subject to their allotment only. This may be done by themselves assembled collectively, or by their legislature to whom they may have delegated sovereign authority: and, if they are allotted in neither of these ways, each individual of the society may appropriate to himself such lands as he finds vacant, and occupancy will give him title.

That, in order to inforce the arbitrary measures before complained of, his majesty has from time to time sent among us large bodies of armed forces, not made up of the people here, nor raised by the authority of our laws. Did his majesty possess such a right as this, it might swallow up all our other rights whenever he should think proper. But his majesty has no right to land a single armed man on our shores; and those whom he sends here are liable to our laws for the suppression and punishment of Riots, Routs, and unlawful assemblies, or are hostile bodies invading us in defiance of law. When in the course of the late war it became expedient that a body of Hanoverian troops should be brought over for the defence of Great Britain, his majesty's grandfather, our late sovereign, did not pretend to introduce them under any authority he possessed. Such a measure would have given just alarm to his subjects in Great Britain, whose liberties would not be safe if armed men of another country, and of another spirit, might be brought into the realm at any time without the consent of their legislature. He therefore applied to parliament who passed an act for that purpose, limiting the number to be brought in and the time they were to continue. In like manner is his majesty restrained in every part of the empire. He possesses indeed the executive power of the laws in every state; but they are the laws of the particular state which he is to administer within that state, and not those of any one within the limits of another. Every state must judge for itself the number of armed men which they may safely trust among them, of whom they are to consist, and under what restrictions they are to be laid. To render these proceedings still more criminal against our laws, instead of subjecting the military to the civil power, his majesty has expressly made the civil subordinate to the military. But can his majesty thus put down all law under his feet? Can he erect a power superior to that which erected himself? He has done it indeed by force; but let him remember that force cannot give right.

That these are our grievances which we have thus laid before his majesty with that freedom of language and sentiment which becomes a free people, claiming their rights as derived from the laws of nature, and not as the gift of their chief magistrate. Let those flatter, who fear: it is not an American art. To give praise where it is not due, might be well from the venal, but would ill beseem those who are asserting the rights of human nature. They know, and will therefore say, that kings are the servants, not the proprietors of the people. Open your breast Sire, to liberal and expanded thought. Let not the name of George the third be a blot in the page of history. You are surrounded by British counsellors, but remember that they are parties. You have no ministers for American affairs, because you have none taken from among us, nor amenable to the laws on which they are to give you advice. It behoves you therefore to think and to act for yourself and your people. The great principles of right and wrong are legible to every reader: to pursue them requires not the aid of many counsellors. The whole art of government consists in the art of being honest. Only aim to do your duty, and mankind will give you credit where you fail. No longer persevere in sacrificing the rights of one part of the empire to the inordinate desires of another: but deal out to all equal and impartial right. Let no act be passed by any one legislature which may infringe on the rights and liberties of another. This is the important post in which fortune has placed you, holding the balance of a great, if a well poised empire. This, Sire, is the advice of your great American council, on the observance of which may perhaps depend your felicity and future fame, and the preservation of that harmony which alone can continue both to Great Britain and America the reciprocal advantages of their connection. It is neither our wish nor our interest to separate from her. We are willing on our part to sacrifice every thing which reason can ask to the restoration of that tranquility for which all must wish. On their part let them be ready to establish union on a generous plan. Let them name their terms, but let them be just. Accept of every commercial preference it is in our power to give for such things as we can raise for their use, or they make for ours. But let them not think to exclude us from going to other markets, to dispose of those commodities which they cannot use, nor to supply those wants which they cannot supply. Still less let it be proposed that our properties within our own territories shall be taxed or regulated by any power on earth but our own. The god who gave us life, gave us liberty at the same time: the hand of force may destroy, but cannot disjoin them. This, Sire, is our last, our determined resolution: and that you will be pleased to interpose with that efficacy which your earnest endeavors may insure to procure redress of these our great grievances, to quiet the minds of your subjects in British America against any apprehensions of future incroachment, to establish fraternal love and harmony thro' the whole empire, and that that may continue to the latest ages of time, is the fervent prayer of all British America.

11

CONTINENTAL CONGRESS, DECLARATION AND RESOLVES
14 Oct. 1774
Tansill 1–5

(See ch. 1, no. 1)

12

CONTINENTAL CONGRESS TO THE INHABITANTS OF THE PROVINCE OF QUEBEC
26 Oct. 1774
Journals 1:105–13

Friends and fellow-subjects,

We, the Delegates of the Colonies of New-Hampshire, Massachusetts-Bay, Rhode-Island and Providence Plantations, Connecticut, New-York, New-Jersey, Pennsylvania, the Counties of Newcastle Kent and Sussex on Delaware, Maryland, Virginia, North-Carolina and South-Carolina, deputed by the inhabitants of the said Colonies, to represent them in a General Congress at Philadelphia, in the province of Pennsylvania, to consult together concerning the best methods to obtain redress of our afflicting grievances, having accordingly assembled, and taken into our most serious consideration the state of public affairs on this continent, have thought proper to address your province, as a member therein deeply interested.

When the fortune of war, after a gallant and glorious resistance, had incorporated you with the body of English subjects, we rejoiced in the truly valuable addition, both on our own and your account; expecting, as courage and generosity are naturally united, our brave enemies would become our hearty friends, and that the Divine Being would bless to you the dispensations of his over-ruling providence, by securing to you and your latest posterity the inestimable advantages of a free English constitution of government, which it is the privilege of all English subjects to enjoy.

These hopes were confirmed by the King's proclamation, issued in the year 1763, plighting the public faith for your full enjoyment of those advantages.

Little did we imagine that any succeeding Ministers would so audaciously and cruelly abuse the royal authority, as to with-hold from you the fruition of the irrevocable rights, to which you were thus justly entitled.

But since we have lived to see the unexpected time, when Ministers of this flagitious temper, have dared to violate the most sacred compacts and obligations, and as you, educated under another form of government, have artfully been kept from discovering the unspeakable worth of *that* form you are now undoubtedly entitled to, we esteem it our duty, for the weighty reasons herein after mentioned, to explain to you some of its most important branches.

"In every human society," says the celebrated Marquis *Beccaria*, "there is an *effort, continually tending* to confer on one part the heighth of power and happiness, and to reduce the other to the extreme of weakness and misery. The intent of good laws is to *oppose this effort,* and to diffuse their influence *universally* and *equally.*"

Rulers stimulated by this pernicious "effort," and subjects animated by the just "intent of opposing good laws against it," have occasioned that vast variety of events, that fill the histories of so many nations. All these histories demonstrate the truth of this simple position, that to live by the will of one man, or sett of men, is the production of misery to all men.

On the solid foundation of this principle, Englishmen reared up the fabrick of their constitution with such a strength, as for ages to defy time, tyranny, treachery, internal and foreign wars: And, as an illustrious author of your nation, hereafter mentioned, observes,—"They gave the people of their Colonies, the form of their own government, and this government carrying prosperity along with it, they have grown great nations in the forests they were sent to inhabit."

In this form, the first grand right, is that of the people having a share in their own government by their representatives chosen by themselves, and, in consequence, of being ruled by *laws,* which they themselves approve, not by *edicts* of *men* over whom they have no controul. This is a bulwark surrounding and defending their property, which by their honest cares and labours they have acquired, so that no portions of it can legally be taken from them, but with their own full and free consent, when they in their judgment deem it just and necessary to give them for public service, and precisely direct the easiest, cheapest, and most equal methods, in which they shall be collected.

The influence of this right extends still farther. If money is wanted by Rulers, who have in any manner oppressed the people, they may retain it, until their grievances are redressed; and thus peaceably procure relief, without trusting to despised petitions, or disturbing the public tranquillity.

The next great right is that of trial by jury. This provides, that neither life, liberty nor property, can be taken from the possessor, until twelve of his unexceptionable countrymen and peers of his vicinage, who from that neighbourhood may reasonably be supposed to be acquainted with his character, and the characters of the witnesses, upon a fair trial, and full enquiry, face to face, in open Court, before as many of the people as chuse to attend, shall pass their sentence upon oath against him; a sentence that cannot injure him, without injuring their own reputation, and probably their interest also; as the question may turn on points, that, in some degree, concern the general welfare; and if it does not, their verdict may form a precedent, that, on a similar trial of their own, may militate against themselves.

Another right relates merely to the liberty of the person.

If a subject is seized and imprisoned, tho' by order of Government, he may, by virtue of this right, immediately obtain a writ, termed a Habeas Corpus, from a Judge, whose sworn duty it is to grant it, and thereupon procure any illegal restraint to be quickly enquired into and redressed.

A fourth right, is that of holding lands by the tenure of easy rents, and not by rigorous and oppressive services, frequently forcing the possessors from their families and their business, to perform what ought to be done, in all well regulated states, by men hired for the purpose.

The last right we shall mention, regards the freedom of the press. The importance of this consists, besides the advancement of truth, science, morality, and arts in general, in its diffusion of liberal sentiments on the administration of Government, its ready communication of thoughts between subjects, and its consequential promotion of union among them, whereby oppressive officers are shamed or intimidated, into more honourable and just modes of conducting affairs.

These are the invaluable rights, that form a considerable part of our mild system of government; that, sending its equitable energy through all ranks and classes of men, defends the poor from the rich, the weak from the powerful, the industrious from the rapacious, the peaceable from the violent, the tenants from the lords, and all from their superiors.

These are the rights, without which a people cannot be free and happy, and under the protecting and encouraging influence of which, these colonies have hitherto so amazingly flourished and increased. These are the rights, a profligate Ministry are now striving, by force of arms, to ravish from us, and which we are, with one mind, resolved never to resign but with our lives.

These are the rights *you* are entitled to and ought at this moment in perfection, to exercise. And what is offered to you by the late Act of Parliament in their place? Liberty of conscience in your religion? No. God gave it to you; and the temporal powers with which you have been and are connected, firmly stipulated for your enjoyment of it. If laws, divine and human, could secure it against the despotic caprices of wicked men, it was secured before. Are the French laws in *civil* cases restored? *It seems so.* But observe the cautious kindness of the Ministers, who pretend to be your benefactors. The words of the statute are—that those "laws shall be the rule, until they shall be *varied* or *altered* by any ordinances of the Governor and Council." Is the "certainty and lenity of the *criminal* law of England, and its benefits and advantages," commended in the said statute, and said to "have been sensibly felt by you," secured to you and your descendants? No. They too are subjected to arbitrary *"alterations"* by the Governor and Council; and a power is expressly reserved of appointing "such courts of *criminal, civil,* and *ecclesiastical* jurisdiction, as shall be thought proper." Such is the precarious tenure of mere *will,* by which you hold your lives and religion. The Crown and its Ministers are impowered, as far as they could be by Parliament, to establish even the *Inquisition* itself among you. Have you an Assembly composed of worthy men, elected by yourselves, and in whom you can confide, to make laws for you, to watch over your welfare, and to direct in what quantity, and in what manner, your money shall be taken from you? No. The power of making laws for you is lodged in the governor and council, all of them dependent upon, and removeable at, the *pleasure* of a Minister. Besides, another late statute, made without your consent, has subjected you to the impositions of *Excise*, the horror of all free states; thus wresting your property from you by the most odious of taxes, and laying open to insolent tax-gatherers, houses, the scenes of domestic peace and comfort, and called the castles of English subjects in the books of their law. And in the very act for altering your government, and intended to flatter you, you are not authorized to "assess, levy, or apply any *rates* and *taxes*, but for the inferior purposes of *making roads*, and erecting and repairing *public buildings*, or for other *local* conveniences, within your respective towns and districts." Why this degrading distinction? Ought not the property, honestly acquired by *Canadians*, to be held as sacred as that of *Englishmen*? Have not Canadians sense enough to attend to any other public affairs, than gathering stones from one place, and piling them up in another? Unhappy people! who are not only injured, but insulted. Nay more!—With such a superlative contempt of your understanding and spirit, has an insolent Ministry presumed to think of you, our respectable fellow-subjects, according to the information we have received, as firmly to perswade themselves that your gratitude, for the injuries and insults they have recently offered to you, will engage you to take up arms, and render yourselves the ridicule and detestation of the world, by becoming tools, in their hands, to assist them in taking that freedom from *us*, which they have treacherously denied to *you*; the unavoidable consequence of which attempt, if successful, would be the extinction of all hopes of you or your posterity being ever restored to freedom: For idiocy itself cannot believe, that, when their drudgery is performed, they will treat you with less cruelty than they have us, who are of the same blood with themselves.

What would your countryman, the immortal *Montesquieu*, have said to such a plan of domination, as has been framed for you? Hear his words, with an intenseness of thought suited to the importance of the subject.—"In a free state, every man, who is supposed a free agent, *ought to be concerned in his own government:* Therefore the *legislative* should reside in the whole body of the *people*, or their *representatives*."—"The political liberty of the subject is *a tranquillity of mind*, arising from the opinion each person has of his *safety*. In order to have this liberty, it is requisite the government be so constituted, as that one man need not be *afraid* of another. When the power of *making* laws, and the power of *executing* them, are *united* in the same person, or in the same body of Magistrates, *there can be no liberty;* because apprehensions may arise, lest the same *Monarch* or *Senate*, should *enact* tyrannical laws, to *execute* them in a tyrannical manner."

"The power of *judging* should be exercised by persons taken from the *body of the people*, at certain times of the year, and pursuant to a form and manner prescribed by law. *There is no liberty*, if the power of *judging* be not *separated* from the *legislative* and *executive* powers."

"Military men belong to a profession, which *may be* useful, but *is often* dangerous."—"The enjoyment of liberty, and even its support and preservation, consists in every man's being allowed to speak his thoughts, and lay open his sentiments."

Apply these decisive maxims, sanctified by the authority of a name which all Europe reveres, to your own state. You have a Governor, it may be urged, vested with the *executive* powers, or the powers of *administration:* In him, and in your Council, is lodged the power of *making laws.* You have *Judges*, who are to *decide* every cause affecting your lives, liberty or property. Here is, indeed, an appearance of the several powers being *separated* and *distributed* into *different* hands, for checks one upon another, the only effectual mode ever invented by the wit of men, to promote their freedom and prosperity. But scorning to be illuded by a tinsel'd outside, and exerting the natural sagacity of Frenchmen, *examine* the specious device, and you will find it, to use an expression of holy writ, "a whited sepulchre," for burying your lives, liberty and property.

Your *Judges*, and your *Legislative Council*, as it is called, are *dependant* on your *Governor*, and *he* is *dependant* on the servant of the Crown, in Great-Britain. The *legislative, executive* and *judging* powers are *all* moved by the nods of a Minister. Privileges and immunities last no longer than his smiles. When he frowns, their feeble forms dissolve. Such a treacherous ingenuity has been exerted in drawing up the code lately offered you, that every sentence, beginning with a benevolent pretension, concludes with a destructive power; and the substance of the whole, divested of its smooth words, is—that the Crown and its Ministers shall be as absolute throughout your extended province, as the despots of Asia or Africa. What can protect your property from taxing edicts, and the rapacity of necessitous and cruel masters? your persons from Letters de Cachet, gaols, dungeons, and oppressive services? your lives and general liberty from arbitrary and unfeeling rulers? We defy you, casting your view upon every side, to discover a single circumstance, promising from any quarter the faintest hope of liberty to you or your posterity, but from an entire adoption into the union of these Colonies.

What advice would the truly great man before-mentioned, that advocate of freedom and humanity, give you, was he now living, and knew that we, your numerous and powerful neighbours, animated by a just love of our invaded rights, and united by the indissoluble bands of affection and interest, called upon you, by every obligation of regard for yourselves and your children, as we now do, to join us in our righteous contest, to make common cause with us therein, and take a noble chance for emerging from a humiliating subjection under Governors, Intendants, and Military Tyrants, into the firm rank and condition of English freemen, whose custom it is, derived from their ancestors, to make those tremble, who dare to think of making them miserable?

Would not this be the purport of his address? "Seize the opportunity presented to you by Providence itself. You have been conquered into liberty, if you act as you ought. This work is not of man. You are a small people, compared to those who with open arms invite you into a fellowship. A moment's reflection should convince you which will be most for your interest and happiness, to have all the rest of North-America your unalterable friends, or your inveterate enemies. The injuries of Boston have roused and associated every colony, from Nova-Scotia to Georgia. Your province is the only link wanting, to compleat the bright and strong chain of union. Nature has joined your country to theirs. Do you join your political interests. For their own sakes, they never will desert or betray you. Be assured, that the happiness of a people inevitably depends on their liberty, and their spirit to assert it. The value and extent of the advantages tendered to you are immense. Heaven grant you may not discover them to be blessings after they have bid you an eternal adieu."

We are too well acquainted with the liberality of sentiment distinguishing your nation, to imagine, that difference of religion will prejudice you against a hearty amity with us. You know, that the transcendant nature of freedom elevates those, who unite in her cause, above all such low-minded infirmities. The Swiss Cantons furnish a memorable proof of this truth. Their union is composed of Roman Catholic and Protestant States, living in the utmost concord and peace with one another, and thereby enabled, ever since they bravely vindicated their freedom, to defy and defeat every tyrant that has invaded them.

Should there be any among you, as there generally are in all societies, who prefer the favours of Ministers, and their own private interests, to the welfare of their country, the temper of such selfish persons will render them incredibly active in opposing all public-spirited measures, from an expectation of being well rewarded for their sordid industry, by their superiors; but we doubt not you will be upon your guard against such men, and not sacrifice the liberty and happiness of the whole Canadian people and their posterity, to gratify the avarice and ambition of individuals.

We do not ask you, by this address, to commence acts of hostility against the government of our common Sovereign. We only invite you to consult your own glory and welfare, and not to suffer yourselves to be inveigled or intimidated by infamous ministers so far, as to become the instruments of their cruelty and despotism, but to unite with us in one social compact, formed on the generous principles of equal liberty, and cemented by such an exchange of beneficial and endearing offices as to render it perpetual. In order to complete this highly desirable union, we submit it to your consideration, whether it may not be expedient for you to meet together in your several towns and districts, and elect Deputies, who afterwards meeting in a provincial Congress, may chuse Delegates, to represent your province in the continental Congress to be held at Philadelphia on the tenth day of May, 1775.

In this present Congress, beginning on the fifth of the last month, and continued to this day, it has been, with universal pleasure and an unanimous vote, resolved, That we should consider the violation of your rights, by the act for altering the government of your province, as a violation of our own, and that you should be invited to accede to our confederation, which has no other objects than the perfect security of the natural and civil rights of all the constituent members, according to their respective circumstances, and the preservation of a happy and lasting connection with Great-Britain, on the salutary and constitutional principles herein before mentioned. For effecting these purposes, we have addressed an humble and loyal petition to his Majesty, praying relief of our and your grievances; and have associated to stop all importations from Great-Britain and Ireland, after the first day of December, and all exportations to those Kingdoms and the West-Indies, after the tenth day of next September, unless the said grievances are redressed.

That Almighty God may incline your minds to approve our equitable and necessary measures, to add yourselves to us, to put your fate, whenever you suffer injuries which you are determined to oppose, not on the small influence of your single province, but on the consolidated powers of North-America, and may grant to our joint exertions an event as happy as our cause is just, is the fervent prayer of us, your sincere and affectionate friends and fellow-subjects.

13

DECLARATION OF INDEPENDENCE
4 July 1776
Tansill 22–26

(See ch. 1, no. 5)

14

THOMAS BURKE, ABSTRACT OF DEBATES IN CONGRESS
25 Feb. 1777
Burnett 2:275–78

Feby 25th. The Question of Interest was again debated, and postponed A Report was taken up relative to Deserters. it stood Originally a recommendation of Congress to the several states to Enact Laws Empowering all Constables Ferry keepers and Freeholders to take up persons suspected of being Deserters and carry them before any Justice of the Peace. An Amendment was moved the purport of which was that the Power should go Immediately from Congress—without the Intervention of the states. many Gentlemen were inattentive and it passed. The Delegate from North Carolina desired to be informed if he might enter his Protest against it. he was informed by the chair that he could not. he then desired to have his dissent entered on the Journal. declaring he was not Apprehensive of any Injury from it in the state he represented because he knew it would never be there observed the People too well knowing the Maxims of their Government, but that as it was as much as his Life was worth to consent to the Congress exercising such a Power, he desired that he might be able to prove from the Journals that he did not. he said it appeared to him that Congress was herein assuming a Power to give authority from themselves to persons within the States to sieze and Imprison the persons of the citizens and thereby to endanger the personal Liberty of every man in America. A motion was now made for reconsidering. on the reconsideration the Debate lay chiefly between Mr. Wilson of Pensylvania, and the North Carolina Delegate Mr. Wilson argued that every object of Continental Concern was the subject of Continental Councils, that all Provisions made by the Continental Councils must be carried into execution by Continental authority. That the Army was certainly a Continental object, and preventing Desertion in it was certainly as Necessary an object as the raising of it, that nothing could be more Necessary to prevent Desertion than to take Effectual Measures for Apprehending Deserters, that this Power must Necessarily be in the Congress, and that they certainly had Power to authorise any persons in the states to put them in Execution. That the Power of taking up deserters was in every soldier and officers of the army, and that the Congress might make any Justice of Peace in any state such an Officer and thereby give him that Power, and if by making him an Officer they could give him that Power, they surely could without. that the officers and soldiers of the army were certainly not subject to the Laws of the states. That this was no more than what was every day done in appointing commissari[es] to purchase provisions and other things under the resolves of Congress. That the Congress had always directed their resolves to be put in Execution by Committess of Inspection and it was never denied that they had Power

The Delegate of North Carolina answered that he admitted Continental objects were subjects of Continental Councils but denied that the provisions made by Continental Councils were to be enforced by Continental authority. That it would be giving Congress a Power to prostrate all the Laws and Constitutions of the states because they might create a Power within each that must act entirely Independant of them, and might act directly contrary to them that they might by virtue of this Power render Ineffectual all the Bariers Provided in the states for the Security of the Rights of the Citizens for if they gave a Power to act coercively it must be against the subject of some State, and the subject of every state was entitled to the Protection of that particular state, and subject to the Laws of that alone, because to them alone did he give his consent, that he hoped the Gentleman would not Insist on this Principle which in its Nature was so very Extensive and alarming. That the states alone had Power to act coercively against their Citizens, and therefore were the only Power competent to carry into execution any Provisions whether Continental or Municipal. that he was well satisfied no Power on Earth would ever obtain authority to act coercively against any of the Citizens of the state he represented except under their own Legislature; unless it was obtained by Violence. that His fellow Citizens were struggling against unlawful exertions of Power, and they would submit to them from no authority. that he admitted the

army to be a proper object to be governed and directed by Continental Councils, and that it is proper the Congress should provide for punishing Desertion, and that Desertion was a very [great] evil, but that who is a Deserter or who is not is a Question that must be determined previous to any Punishment, and who ever can determin it has a Power over the Life and Liberty of the Citizens, for as much as any man may be accused of Desertion but every one accused may not be Guilty. that If the Congress has the Power to appoint any Person to decide this Question the Congress has Power unlimitted over the Lives and Liberties of all men in America and the Provisions so anxiously made by the respective States to Secure them, at once Vanish before this Tremendous Authority. however proper it might be for Congress to punish Desertion it was Necessary for the states to prevent arbitrary and unjust punishments and Imprisonments of their Citizens, and unless some mode were provided for trying the above Question every man was liable to be imprisoned at the Discretion of Officers and servants of the Congress no power could be competent to this but such as is created by the Legislature of each state, and if any Question releated to the Internal Polity of a state it certainly was this which Involved all the Rights of the Citizen's personal Freedom He would not speak for other states, but for his own he would declare that the Constitution had anxiously provided that no man should be Imprisoned or in any Degree Injured in his Person or Property but under the authority of the Laws of the state that it was a fundamental Maxim well understoo[d] there that no Magisterial authority could be given, but by the Legislature, and none could be exercised beyond what was expressly laid down in the Laws. The Congress certainly could not give a Power within any state to hear and Determin Offence or to sieze and Imprison the Persons of the Citizens. yet most assuredly the Power contended for was no less, unless every Deserter was branded in the Face so that it could be determined without [doubt] who was Deserter and who was not. he was sorry to hear the Gentleman say that the Officers and Soldiers of the Army were not subject to the Laws of the States, and hoped the Gentleman would retract it, for assuredly the army must always be in some State and might be in every State, and if they were not subject to the Laws of the respective States, it would follow that a powerful Body of men within any State might Violate with Impunity all the Rights of the Citizens and subject them to the worst of Oppressions. that being contrary to all the purposes for which men enter into Society, the admission of it must dissolve all Society and Government, and being peculiarly detested by the Americans who were struggling at the risque of Life and property against Oppression, it never could take place among them, until they lost all Common Sense, and all Love of Freedom That the Power of taking up deserters if it was in every officer and soldier it did not follow that every officer and soldier might call whom he pleased a deserter, and Imprison and punish him as such, that there must be a Power to determin whether deserter or not, and the Congress could give no such Power without giving authority to some Individuals within the states to exercise Magisterial Discretion and subject the citizens to that discretion. he could not conceive a state Independant if any Power could do this except their Internal Legislature who had their authority for that purpose from the People. he would declare firmly it could not be done in North Carolina by any other, if their Bill of Rights and Constitution were of any Effect, and not meer Waste paper. for they, provided that no free man within the state should be in any way or Degree restrained of his Liberty or damaged in his Property except under the Laws of the state to which h[is] consent must be given, because every freeman had a Voice [in the] Legislature. That in North Carolina no Military Officer could act in any civil department whatever, and he believed they could not in any state where Government was Established, yet if it were otherwise his civil authority must be derived from the state and not the Congress, and the rules and Limits whereby it was to be exercised must be expressly laid down by the state and could not be altered or extended by the Congress unless they had a Power over the Internal Laws of the states which Power never would be given, and no one pretended to.

15

THE ESSEX RESULT
29 Apr. 1778
Handlin 330–32

(See ch. 4, no. 8)

16

RETURN OF PLYMOUTH, MASSACHUSETTS
1 June 1778
Handlin 290–91

The Committee Appointed to take into Consideration the Constitution lately drawn up by the Convention of this State and to consider the Advantages and Disadvantages arriseing therefrom—Beg leave to report—That they have repeatedly perused said Constitution with great candor and deliberation and are of opinion, that many parts of it are bottomed on Principalls of Equal liberty, and calculated to secure the Governed, from the Encroachments of Ambition and the artifices of Designing rulers, such more Especially, is the Establishment, of Annual Elections in the Severall branches of the Legislature, Fundemental in Every free Government, and the best barrier against Corruption, and the restless passions of Mankind.

Your Committee would be happy,
if they could Speak with the Same applause, of Every Articall in the Constitution, but Justice to themselves and Posterity, Oblige them to point out Severall Things, which

they apprehend are Meterial Defects. . . . Your Committee are further of opinion, that a bill, Clearly Ascerting the rights of the people, as Men, Christians, and Subjects, aught to have Preceeded the Constitution, and these rights should be Expressed in the fullest and most unequivocall terms—Upon the whole as this Constitution, is in so many parts Defective, and as when once Established, it will probably remain unalterable, Except by Coercion and Violence, Your Committe think that it aught to be rejected—

17

RETURN OF BEVERLY, MASSACHUSETTS
1 June 1778
Handlin 295

These being the sentiments of the town, in conformity thereto, you are hereby instructed to oppose the ratification of the Plan proposed by the State Convention, and should it be voted in, when it appears a considerable part of the People are not in favor of it, to enter your Protest explicitly against it. But, should the same be set aside, we expect that some other Body, distinct from the General Court, be delegated from among the people for the sole and entire purpose of forming a Bill of Rights and Constitution of Government; the 1st of which, we conceive, ought to describe the Natural Rights of Man pure as he inherits them from the Great Parent of Nature, distinguishing those, the Controul of which he may part with to Society for Social Benefits, from those He cannot: and the 2nd Mark out, with perspicuity and plainness what portion of them, and on what Conditions, they are parted with, clearly defining all the Restrictions and Limitations of Government, so as to admit of no Prevarication. It should also contain a full and fixed assurance of the Equivalent to be received in return.

18

MASSACHUSETTS CONSTITUTION, A DECLARATION OF THE RIGHTS OF THE INHABITANTS OF THE COMMONWEALTH OF MASSACHUSETTS
2 Mar. 1780
Handlin 442–48

(See ch. 1, no. 6)

19

THOMAS JEFFERSON TO GARRET VAN METER
27 Apr. 1781
Papers 5:566

(See ch. 3, no. 6)

20

RECORDS OF THE FEDERAL CONVENTION

[2:340; Madison, 20 Aug.]

Mr. Pinkney submitted to the House, in order to be referred to the Committee of detail, the following propositions—"Each House shall be the Judge of its own privileges, and shall have authority to punish by imprisonment every person violating the same; or who, in the place where the Legislature may be sitting and during the time of its Session, shall threaten any of its members for any thing said or done in the House, or who shall assault any of them therefor—or who shall assault or arrest any witness or other person ordered to attend either of the Houses in his way going or returning; or who shall rescue any person arrested by their order."

"Each branch of the Legislature, as well as the Supreme Executive shall have authority to require the opinions of the supreme Judicial Court upon important questions of law, and upon solemn occasions"

"The privileges and benefit of the Writ of Habeas corpus shall be enjoyed in this Government in the most expeditious and ample manner; and shall not be suspended by the Legislature except upon the most urgent and pressing occasions, and for a limited time not exceeding months."

"The liberty of the Press shall be inviolably preserved"

"No troops shall be kept up in time of peace, but by consent of the Legislature"

"The military shall always be subordinate to the Civil power, and no grants of money shall be made by the Legislature for supporting military Land forces, for more than one year at a time"

"No soldier shall be quartered in any House in time of peace without consent of the owner."

"No person holding the office of President of the U.S., a Judge of their Supreme Court, Secretary for the department of Foreign Affairs, of Finance, of Marine, of War, or of   , shall be capable of holding at the same time any other office of Trust or Emolument under the U.S. or an individual State"

"No religious test or qualification shall ever be annexed to any oath of office under the authority of the U.S."

"The U.S. shall be for ever considered as one Body corporate and politic in law, and entitled to all the rights priv-ileges, and immunities, which to Bodies corporate do or ought to appertain"

"The Legislature of the U.S. shall have the power of making the great Seal which shall be kept by the President of the U.S. or in his absence by the President of the Senate, to be used by them as the occasion may require.—It shall be called the great Seal of the U.S. and shall be affixed to all laws."

"All Commissions and writs shall run in the name of the U.S."

"The Jurisdiction of the supreme Court shall be extended to all controversies between the U.S. and an individual State, or the U.S. and the Citizens of an individual State"

These propositions were referred to the Committee of detail without debate or consideration of them, by the House.

[2:587; Madison, 12 Sept.]

Mr. Williamson, observed to the House that no provision was yet made for juries in Civil cases and suggested the necessity of it.

Mr. Gorham. It is not possible to discriminate equity cases from those in which juries are proper. The Representatives of the people may be safely trusted in this matter.

Mr. Gerry urged the necessity of Juries to guard agst. corrupt Judges. He proposed that the Committee last appointed should be directed to provide a clause for securing the trial by Juries.

Col: Mason perceived the difficulty mentioned by Mr. Gorham. The jury cases cannot be specified. A general principle laid down on this and some other points would be sufficient. He wished the plan had been prefaced with a Bill of Rights, & would second a Motion if made for the purpose—It would give great quiet to the people; and with the aid of the State declarations, a bill might be prepared in a few hours.

Mr Gerry concurred in the idea & moved for a Committee to prepare a Bill of Rights. Col: Mason 2ded the motion.

Mr. Sherman. was for securing the rights of the people where requisite. The State Declarations of Rights are not repealed by this Constitution; and being in force are sufficient—There are many cases where juries are proper which cannot be discriminated. The Legislature may be safely trusted.

Col: Mason. The Laws of the U.S. are to be paramount to State Bills of Rights. On the question for a Come to prepare a Bill of Rights

N.H. no. Mas. abst. Ct no. N— J— no. Pa. no. Del— no. Md no. Va no. N— C. no. S— C— no— Geo— no. [Ayes— 0; noes—10; absent—1.]

21

RICHARD HENRY LEE TO GEORGE MASON
1 Oct. 1787
Mason Papers 3:997–98

It having been found from Universal experience that the most express declarations and reservations are necessary to protect the just rights and liberty of Mankind from the silent powerful and ever active conspiracy of those who govern—And it appearing to be the sense of the good people of America by the various Bills or Declarations of Rights whereon the Governments of the greater number of the States are founded; that such precautions are proper to restrain and regulate the exercise of the great powers necessarily given to Rulers—In conformity with these principles, and from respect for the public sentiment on this subject it is submitted

That the new Constitution proposed for the Government of the U. States be bottomed upon a declaration, or Bill of Rights, clearly and precisely stating the principles upon which this Social Compact is founded to wit, That the right of Conscience in matters of Religion shall not be violated—That the freedom of the Press shall be secured—That the trial by Jury in Criminal and Civil cases, and the modes prescribed by the Common Law for safety of Life in criminal prosecutions shall be held sacred—That standing Armies in times of peace are dangerous to liberty and ought not to be permitted unless assented to by two thirds of the Members composing each house of the Legislature under the new Constitution—That elections of the Members of the Legislature should be free and frequent—That the right administration of Justice should be secured by the freedom and independency of the Judges—That excessive Bail, excessive Fines, or cruel and unusual punishments should not be demanded or inflicted—That the right of the people to assemble peaceably for the purpose of petitioning the Legislature shall not be prevented. That the Citizens shall not be exposed to unreasonable searches, seizures of their persons, papers, houses, or property. And whereas it is necessary for the good of Society that the administration of government be conducted with all possible maturity of judgement; for which reason it hath been the practise of civilized nations, and so determined by every state in this Union, that a Council of State or Privy Council should be appointed to advise and assist in the arduous business assigned to the executive power—therefore, that the new Constitution be so amended as to admit the appointment of a Privy Council, to consist of eleven Members appointed by the President, but responsible for the advice they may give—for which purpose, the advice given shall be entered in a Council book, and signed by the Giver in all affairs of great concern. And that the Counsellors act under an oath of office.

22

RICHARD HENRY LEE TO SAMUEL ADAMS
5 Oct. 1787
Letters 2:444–45

Having long toiled with you my dear friend in the Vineyard of liberty, I do with great pleasure submit to your wisdom and patriotism, the objections that prevail in my mind against the new Constitution proposed for federal government—which objections I did propose to Congress in form of amendments to be discussed, and that such as were approved might be forwarded to the States with the Convention system. You will have been informed by other hands why these amendments were not considered and do not appear on the Journal, and the reasons that influenced a bare *tranmission* of the Convention plan, without a syllable of approbation or disapprobation on the part of Congress. I suppose my dear Sir, that the good people of the U. States in their late generous contest, contended for free government in the fullest, clearest, and strongest sense. That they had no idea of being brought under despotic rule under the notion of "Strong government," or in form of *elective despotism:* Chains being still Chains, whether made of gold or iron.

The corrupting nature of power, and its insatiable appetite for increase, hath proved the necessity, and procured the adoption of the strongest and most express declarations of that *Residuum* of natural rights, which is not intended to be given up to Society; and which indeed is not necessary to be given for any good social purpose. In a government therefore, when the power of judging what shall be for the *general welfare,* which goes to every object of human legislation; and where the laws of such Judges shall be the *supreme Law of the Land:* it seems to be of the last consequence to declare in most explicit terms the reservations above alluded to. So much for the propriety of a Bill of Rights as a necessary bottom to this new system—It is in vain to say that the defects in this new Constitution may be remedied by the Legislature created by it. The remedy, as it may, so it may not be applied—And if it should a subsequent Assembly may repeal the Acts of its predecessor for the parliamentary doctrine is "quod leges posteriores priores contrarias abrogant" 4 Inst. 43. Surely this is not a ground upon which a wise and good man would choose to rest the dearest rights of human nature.

23

JAMES WILSON, STATE HOUSE SPEECH
6 Oct. 1787
McMaster 143–44

When the people established the powers of legislation under their separate governments, they invested their representatives with every right and authority which they did
not in explicit terms reserve; and therefore upon every
question respecting the jurisdiction of the House of Assembly, if the frame of government is silent, the jurisdiction is efficient and complete. But in delegating federal
powers, another criterion was necessarily introduced, and
the congressional power is to be collected, not from tacit
implication, but from the positive grant expressed in the
instrument of the union. Hence, it is evident, that in the
former case everything which is not reserved is given; but
in the latter the reverse of the proposition prevails, and
everything which is not given is reserved.

This distinction being recognized, will furnish an answer
to those who think the omission of a bill of rights a defect
in the proposed constitution; for it would have been superfluous and absurd to have stipulated with a federal
body of our own creation, that we should enjoy those privileges of which we are not divested, either by the intention
or the act that has brought the body into existence. For
instance, the liberty of the press, which has been a copious
source of declamation and opposition—what control can
proceed from the Federal government to shackle or destroy that sacred palladium of national freedom? If, indeed, a power similar to that which has been granted for
the regulation of commerce had been granted to regulate
literary publications, it would have been as necessary to
stipulate that the liberty of the press should be preserved
inviolate, as that the impost should be general in its operation. With respect likewise to the particular district of ten
miles, which is to be made the seat of federal government,
it will undoubtedly be proper to observe this salutary precaution, as there the legis[la]tive power will be exclusively
lodged in the President, Senate, and House of Representatives of the United States. But this could not be an object
with the Convention, for it must naturally depend upon a
future compact, to which the citizens immediately interested will, and ought to be, parties; and there is no reason
to suspect that so popular a privilege will in that case be
neglected. In truth, then, the proposed system possesses
no influence whatever upon the press, and it would have
been merely nugatory to have introduced a formal declaration upon the subject—nay, that very declaration might
have been construed to imply that some degree of power
was given, since we undertook to define its extent.

24

FEDERAL FARMER, NO. 4
12 Oct. 1787
Storing 2.8.50–54

It is said, that when the people make a constitution, and
delegate powers that all powers not delegated by them to
those who govern is [*sic*] reserved in the people: and that
the people, in the present case, have reserved in themselves, and in their state governments, every right and
power not expressly given by the federal constitution to
those who shall administer the national government. It is
said on the other hand, that the people, when they make
a constitution, yield all power not expressly reserved to
themselves. The truth is, in either case, it is mere matter
of opinion and men usually take either side of the argument, as will best answer their purposes: But the general
presumption being, that men who govern, will, in doubtful
cases, construe laws and constitutions most favourably for
encreasing their own powers; all wise and prudent people,
in forming constitutions, have drawn the line, and carefully described the powers parted with and the powers reserved. By the state constitutions, certain rights have been
reserved in the people; or rather, they have been recognized and established in such a manner, that state legislatures are bound to respect them, and to make no laws infringing upon them. The state legislatures are obliged to
take notice of the bills of rights of their respective states.
The bills of rights, and the state constitutions, are fundamental compacts only between those who govern, and the
people of the same state.

In the year 1788 the people of the United States make
a federal constitution, which is a fundamental compact between them and their federal rulers; these rulers, in the
nature of things, cannot be bound to take notice of any
other compact. It would be absurd for them, in making
laws, to look over thirteen, fifteen, or twenty state constitutions, to see what rights are established as fundamental,
and must not be infringed upon, in making laws in the
society. It is true, they would be bound to do it if the people, in their federal compact, should refer to the state constitutions, recognize all parts not inconsistent with the federal constitution, and direct their federal rulers to take
notice of them accordingly; but this is not the case, as the
plan stands proposed at present; and it is absurd, to suppose so unnatural an idea is intended or implied. I think
my opinion is not only founded in reason, but I think it is
supported by the report of the convention itself. If there
are a number of rights established by the state constitutions, and which will remain sacred, and the general government is bound to take notice of them—it must take notice of one as well as another; and if unnecessary to
recognize or establish one by the federal constitution, it
would be unnecessary to recognize or establish another by

it. If the federal constitution is to be construed so far in connection with the state constitutions, as to leave the trial by jury in civil causes, for instance, secured; on the same principles it would have left the trial by jury in criminal causes, the benefits of the writ of habeas corpus, etc. secured; they all stand on the same footing; they are the common rights of Americans, and have been recognized by the state constitutions: But the convention found it necessary to recognize or re-establish the benefits of that writ, and the jury trial in criminal cases. As to *expost facto* laws, the convention has done the same in one case, and gone further in another. It is part of the compact between the people of each state and their rulers, that no *expost facto* laws shall be made. But the convention, by Art. I Sect. 10 have put a sanction upon this part even of the state compacts. In fact, the 9th and 10th Sections in Art. I. in the proposed constitution, are no more nor less, than a partial bill of rights; they establish certain principles as part of the compact upon which the federal legislators and officers can never infringe. It is here wisely stipulated, that the federal legislature shall never pass a bill of attainder, or *expost facto* law; that no tax shall be laid on articles exported, etc. The establishing of one right implies the necessity of establishing another and similar one.

On the whole, the position appears to me to be undeniable, that this bill of rights ought to be carried farther, and some other principles established, as a part of this fundamental compact between the people of the United States and their federal rulers.

It is true, we are not disposed to differ much, at present, about religion: but when we are making a constitution, it is to be hoped, for ages and millions yet unborn, why not establish the free exercise of religion, as a part of the national compact. There are other essential rights, which we have justly understood to be the rights of freemen; as freedom from hasty and unreasonable search warrants, warrants not founded on oath, and not issued with due caution, for searching and seizing men's papers, property, and persons. The trials by jury in civil causes, it is said, varies so much in the several states, that no words could be found for the uniform establishment of it. If so, the federal legislation will not be able to establish it by any general laws. I confess I am of opinion it may be established, but not in that beneficial manner in which we may enjoy it, for the reasons beforementioned. When I speak of the jury trial of the vicinage, or the trial of the fact in the neighbourhood—I do not lay so much stress upon the circumstance of our being tried by our neighbours: in this enlightened country men may be probably impartially tried by those who do not live very near them: but the trial of facts in the neighbourhood is of great importance in other respects. Nothing can be more essential than the cross examining witnesses, and generally before the triers of the facts in question. The common people can establish facts with much more ease with oral than written evidence; when trials of facts are removed to a distance from the homes of the parties and witnesses, oral evidence becomes intolerably expensive, and the parties must depend on written evidence, which to the common people is expensive and almost useless; it must be frequently taken ex

parte, and but very seldom leads to the proper discovery of truth.

The trial by jury is very important in another point of view. It is essential in every free country, that common people should have a part and share of influence, in the judicial as well as in the legislative department. To hold open to them the offices of senators, judges, and offices to fill which an expensive education is required, cannot answer any valuable purposes for them; they are not in a situation to be brought forward and to fill those offices; these, and most other offices of any considerable importance, will be occupied by the few. The few, the well born, etc. as Mr. Adams calls them, in judicial decisions as well as in legislation, are generally disposed, and very naturally too, to favour those of their own description.

25

A DEMOCRATIC FEDERALIST
17 Oct. 1787
Storing 3.5.1–4

The arguments of the Honorable Mr. Wilson, expressed in the speech he made at the state-house on the Saturday preceding the general election (as stated in the Pennsylvania Herald,) although extremely *ingenious* and the best that could be adduced in support of so bad a cause, are yet extremely *futile*, and will not stand the test of investigation.

In the first place, Mr. Wilson pretends to point out a leading discrimination between the State Constitutions, and the Constitution of the United States.—In the former, he says, every power which is not *reserved* is *given*, and in the latter, every power which is not *given* is *reserved:* And this may furnish an answer, he adds, to those who object, that a bill of rights has not been introduced in the proposed Federal Constitution. If this doctrine is true, and since it is the only security that we are to have for our natural rights, it ought at least to have been clearly expressed in the plan of government. The 2d. section of the present articles of confederation says: *Each State retains its sovereignty, freedom and independance,* AND EVERY POWER, JURISDICTION AND RIGHT WHICH IS NOT BY THIS CONFEDERATION EXPRESSLY DELEGATED TO THE UNITED STATES IN CONGRESS ASSEMBLED.—This declaration (for what purpose I know not) is entirely omitted in the proposed Constitution. And yet there is a material difference between this Constitution and the present confederation, for Congress in the latter are merely an executive body; it has no power to raise money, it has no *judicial jurisdiction*. In the other, on the contrary, the federal rulers are vested with each of the three essential powers of government—their laws are to be *paramount* to the laws of the different States, what then will there be to oppose to their encroachments? Should they ever pretend to tyrannize over the people, their *standing army*, will silence every popular effort, it will be theirs to explain the powers which have been granted to them; Mr. Wilson's distinction will be forgot, denied or explained away, and the liberty of the people will be no more.

It is said in the 2d. section of the 3d. article of the Federal Plan: "The judicial power shall extend to ALL CASES in *law* and *equity,* arising under this constitution." It is very clear that under this clause, the tribunal of the United States, may claim a right to the cognizance of all offences against the *general government,* and *libels* will not probably be excluded. Nay, those offences may be by them construed, or by law declared, *misprision of treason,* an offence which comes literally under their express jurisdiction.— Where is then the safety of our boasted liberty of the press? And in case of a *conflict of jurisdiction* between the courts of the United States, and those of the several Commonwealths, is it not easy to foresee which of the two will obtain the advantage?

Under the enormous power of the new confederation, which extends to the *individuals* as well as to the *States* of America, a thousand means may be devised to destroy effectually the liberty of the press—There is no knowing what corrupt and wicked judges may do in process of time, when they are not restrained by express laws. The case of *John Peter Zenger* of New-York, ought still to be present to our minds, to convince us how displeasing the liberty of the press is to men in high power—At any rate, I lay it down as a general rule, that wherever the powers of a government extend to the lives, the persons, and properties of the subject, all their rights ought to be clearly and expressly defined—otherwise they have but a poor security for their liberties.

26

BRUTUS, NO. 2
1 Nov. 1787
Storing 2.9.23–33

Though it should be admitted, that the argument[s] against reducing all the states into one consolidated government, are not sufficient fully to establish this point; yet they will, at least, justify this conclusion, that in forming a constitution for such a country, great care should be taken to limit and definite its powers, adjust its parts, and guard against an abuse of authority. How far attention has been paid to these objects, shall be the subject of future enquiry. When a building is to be erected which is intended to stand for ages, the foundation should be firmly laid. The constitution proposed to your acceptance, is designed not for yourselves alone, but for generations yet unborn. The principles, therefore, upon which the social compact is founded, ought to have been clearly and precisely stated, and the most express and full declaration of rights to have been made—But on this subject there is almost an entire silence.

If we may collect the sentiments of the people of Amer-

ica, from their own most solemn declarations, they hold this truth as self evident, that all men are by nature free. No one man, therefore, or any class of men, have a right, by the law of nature, or of God, to assume or exercise authority over their fellows. The origin of society then is to be sought, not in any natural right which one man has to exercise authority over another, but in the united consent of those who associate. The mutual wants of men, at first dictated the propriety of forming societies; and when they were established, protection and defence pointed out the necessity of instituting government. In a state of nature every individual pursues his own interest; in this pursuit it frequently happened, that the possessions or enjoyments of one were sacrificed to the views and designs of another; thus the weak were a prey to the strong, the simple and unwary were subject to impositions from those who were more crafty and designing. In this state of things, every individual was insecure; common interest therefore directed, that government should be established, in which the force of the whole community should be collected, and under such directions, as to protect and defend every one who composed it. The common good, therefore, is the end of civil government, and common consent, the foundation on which it is established. To effect this end, it was necessary that a certain portion of natural liberty should be surrendered, in order, that what remained should be preserved: how great a proportion of natural freedom is necessary to be yielded by individuals, when they submit to government, I shall not now enquire. So much, however, must be given up, as will be sufficient to enable those, to whom the administration of the government is committed, to establish laws for the promoting the happiness of the community, and to carry those laws into effect. But it is not necessary, for this purpose, that individuals should relinquish all their natural rights. Some are of such a nature that they cannot be surrendered. Of this kind are the rights of conscience, the right of enjoying and defending life, etc. Others are not necessary to be resigned, in order to attain the end for which government is instituted, these therefore ought not to be given up. To surrender them, would counteract the very end of government, to wit, the common good. From these observations it appears, that in forming a government on its true principles, the foundation should be laid in the manner I before stated, by expressly reserving to the people such of their essential natural rights, as are not necessary to be parted with. The same reasons which at first induced mankind to associate and institute government, will operate to influence them to observe this precaution. If they had been disposed to conform themselves to the rule of immutable righteousness, government would not have been requisite. It was because one part exercised fraud, oppression, and violence on the other, that men came together, and agreed that certain rules should be formed, to regulate the conduct of all, and the power of the whole community lodged in the hands of rulers to enforce an obedience to them. But rulers have the same propensities as other men; they are as likely to use the power with which they are vested for private purposes, and to the injury and oppression of those over whom they are placed, as individuals in a state of nature are to injure and oppress one another. It is therefore as proper that bounds should be set to their authority, as that government should have at first been instituted to restrain private injuries.

This principle, which seems so evidently founded in the reason and nature of things, is confirmed by universal experience. Those who have governed, have been found in all ages ever active to enlarge their powers and abridge the public liberty. This has induced the people in all countries, where any sense of freedom remained, to fix barriers against the encroachments of their rulers. The country from which we have derived our origin, is an eminent example of this. Their magna charta and bill of rights have long been the boast, as well as the security, of that nation. I need say no more, I presume, to an American, than, that this principle is a fundamental one, in all the constitutions of our own states; there is not one of them but what is either founded on a declaration or bill of rights, or has certain express reservation of rights interwoven in the body of them. From this it appears, that at a time when the pulse of liberty beat high and when an appeal was made to the people to form constitutions for the government of themselves, it was their universal sense, that such declarations should make a part of their frames of government. It is therefore the more astonishing, that this grand security, to the rights of the people, is not to be found in this constitution.

It has been said, in answer to this objection, that such declaration[s] of rights, however requisite they might be in the constitutions of the states, are not necessary in the general constitution, because, "in the former case, every thing which is not reserved is given, but in the latter the reverse of the proposition prevails, and every thing which is not given is reserved." It requires but little attention to discover, that this mode of reasoning is rather specious than solid. The powers, rights, and authority, granted to the general government by this constitution, are as complete, with respect to every object to which they extend, as that of any state government—It reaches to every thing which concerns human happiness—Life, liberty, and property, are under its controul. There is the same reason, therefore, that the exercise of power, in this case, should be restrained within proper limits, as in that of the state governments. To set this matter in a clear light, permit me to instance some of the articles of the bills of rights of the individuals states, and apply them to the case in question.

For the security of life, in criminal prosecutions, the bills of rights of most of the states have declared, that no man shall be held to answer for a crime until he is made fully acquainted with the charge brought against him; he shall not be compelled to accuse, or furnish evidence against himself—The witnesses against him shall be brought face to face, and he shall be fully heard by himself or counsel. That it is essential to the security of life and liberty, that trial of facts be in the vicinity where they happen. Are not provisions of this kind as necessary in the general government, as in that of a particular state? The powers vested in the new Congress extend in many cases to life; they are authorised to provide for the punishment of a variety of capital crimes, and no restraint is laid upon them in its

exercise, save only, that "the trial of all crimes, except in cases of impeachment, shall be by jury; and such trial shall be in the state where the said crimes shall have been committed." No man is secure of a trial in the county where he is charged to have committed a crime; he may be brought from Niagara to New-York, or carried from Kentucky to Richmond for trial for an offence, supposed to be committed. What security is there, that a man shall be furnished with a full and plain description of the charges against him? That he shall be allowed to produce all proof he can in his favor? That he shall see the witnesses against him face to face, or that he shall be fully heard in his own defence by himself or counsel?

For the security of liberty it has been declared, "that excessive bail should not be required, nor excessive fines imposed, nor cruel or unusual punishments inflicted—That all warrants, without oath or affirmation, to search suspected places, or seize any person, his papers or property, are grievous and oppressive."

These provisions are as necessary under the general government as under that of the individual states; for the power of the former is as complete to the purpose of requiring bail, imposing fines, inflicting punishments, granting search warrants, and seizing persons, papers, or property, in certain cases, as the other.

For the purpose of securing the property of the citizens, it is declared by all the states, "that in all controversies at law, respecting property, the ancient mode of trial by jury is one of the best securities of the rights of the people, and ought to remain sacred and inviolable."

Does not the same necessity exist of reserving this right, under this national compact, as in that of these states? Yet nothing is said respecting it. In the bills of rights of the states it is declared, that a well regulated militia is the proper and natural defence of a free government—That as standing armies in time of peace are dangerous, they are not to be kept up, and that the military should be kept under strict subordination to, and controuled by the civil power.

The same security is as necessary in this constitution, and much more so; for the general government will have the sole power to raise and to pay armies, and are under no controul in the exercise of it; yet nothing of this is to be found in this new system.

I might proceed to instance a number of other rights, which were as necessary to be reserved, such as, that elections should be free, that the liberty of the press should be held sacred; but the instances adduced, are sufficient to prove, that this argument is without foundation.—Besides, it is evident, that the reason here assigned was not the true one, why the framers of this constitution omitted a bill of rights; if it had been, they would not have made certain reservations, while they totally omitted others of more importance. We find they have, in the 9th section of the 1st article, declared, that the writ of habeas corpus shall not be suspended, unless in cases of rebellion—that no bill of attainder, or expost facto law, shall be passed—that no title of nobility shall be granted by the United States, &c. If every thing which is not given is reserved, what propriety is there in these exceptions? Does this constitution any where grant the power of suspending the habeas corpus, to make expost facto laws, pass bills of attainder, or grant titles of nobility? It certainly does not in express terms. The only answer that can be given is, that these are implied in the general powers granted. With equal truth it may be said, that all the powers, which the bills of right, guard against the abuse of, are contained or implied in the general ones granted by this constitution.

So far it is from being true, that a bill of rights is less necessary in the general constitution than in those of the states, the contrary is evidently the fact.—This system, if it is possible for the people of America to accede to it, will be an original compact; and being the last, will, in the nature of things, vacate every former agreement inconsistent with it. For it being a plan of government received and ratified by the whole people, all other forms, which are in existence at the time of its adoption, must yield to it. This is expressed in positive and unequivocal terms, in the 6th article, "That this constitution and the laws of the United States, which shall be made in pursuance thereof, and all treaties made, or which shall be made, under the authority of the United States, shall be the supreme law of the land; and the judges in every state shall be bound thereby, any thing in the *constitution*, or laws of any state, *to the contrary* notwithstanding.

"The senators and representatives before mentioned, and the members of the several state legislatures, and all executive and judicial officers, both of the United States, and of the several states, shall be bound, by oath or affirmation, to support this constitution."

It is therefore not only necessarily implied thereby, but positively expressed, that the different state constitutions are repealed and entirely done away, so far as they are inconsistent with this, with the laws which shall be made in pursuance thereof, or with treaties made, or which shall be made, under the authority of the United States; of what avail will the constitutions of the respective states be to preserve the rights of its citizens? should they be plead, the answer would be, the constitution of the United States, and the laws made in pursuance thereof, is the supreme law, and all legislatures and judicial officers, whether of the general or state governments, are bound by oath to support it. No priviledge, reserved by the bills of rights, or secured by the state government, can limit the power granted by this, or restrain any laws made in pursuance of it. It stands therefore on its own bottom, and must receive a construction by itself without any reference to any other—And hence it was of the highest importance, that the most precise and express declarations and reservations of rights should have been made.

This will appear the more necessary, when it is considered, that not only the constitution and laws made in pursuance thereof, but all treaties made, or which shall be made, under the authority of the United States, are the supreme law of the land, and supersede the constitutions of all the states. The power to make treaties, is vested in the president, by and with the advice and consent of two thirds of the senate. I do not find any limitation, or restriction, to the exercise of this power. The most important article in any constitution may therefore be repealed, even

without a legislative act. Ought not a government, vested with such extensive and indefinite authority, to have been restricted by a declaration of rights? It certainly ought.

So clear a point is this, that I cannot help suspecting, that persons who attempt to persuade people, that such reservations were less necessary under this constitution than under those of the states, are wilfully endeavouring to deceive, and to lead you into an absolute state of vassalage.

27

JAMES WILSON, PENNSYLVANIA RATIFYING
CONVENTION
28 Nov., 4 Dec. 1787
Elliot 2:434–37, 453–54

[*28 Nov.*]

This will be a proper time for making an observation or two on what may be called the preamble to this Constitution. I had occasion, on a former day, to mention that the leading principle in the politics, and that which pervades the American constitutions, is, that the supreme power resides in the people. This Constitution, Mr. President, opens with a solemn and practical recognition of that principle:—"We, the *people of the United States*, in order to form a more perfect union, establish justice, &c., *do* ordain and establish this Constitution for the United States of America." It is announced in *their* name—it receives its political existence from *their* authority: they ordain and establish. What is the necessary consequence? Those who ordain and establish have the power, if they think proper, to repeal and annul. A proper attention to this principle may, perhaps, give ease to the minds of some who have heard much concerning the necessity of a bill of rights.

Its establishment, I apprehend, has more force than a volume written on the subject. It renders this truth evident—that the people have a right to do what they please with regard to the government. I confess I feel a kind of pride in considering the striking difference between the foundation on which the liberties of this country are declared to stand in this Constitution, and the footing on which the liberties of England are said to be placed. The Magna Charta of England is an instrument of high value to the people of that country. But, Mr. President, from what source does that instrument derive the liberties of the inhabitants of that kingdom? Let it speak for itself. The king says, "*We* have *given* and *granted* to all archbishops, bishops, abbots, priors, earls, barons, and to all the freemen of this our realm, these liberties following, to be kept in our kingdom of England forever." When this was assumed as the leading principle of that government, it was no wonder that the people were anxious to obtain bills of rights, and to take every opportunity of enlarging and securing their liberties. But here, sir, the fee-simple remains in the people at large, and by this Constitution they do not part with it.

I am called upon to give a reason why the Convention omitted to add a bill of rights to the work before you. I confess, sir, I did think that, in point of propriety, the honorable gentleman ought first to have furnished some reasons to show such an addition to be necessary; it is natural to prove the affirmative of a proposition; and, if he had established the propriety of this addition, he might then have asked why it was not made.

I cannot say, Mr. President, what were the reasons of every member of that Convention for not adding a bill of rights. I believe the truth is, that such an idea never entered the mind of many of them. I do not recollect to have heard the subject mentioned till within about three days of the time of our rising; and even then, there was no direct motion offered for any thing of the kind. I may be mistaken in this; but as far as my memory serves me, I believe it was the case. A proposition to adopt a measure that would have supposed that we were throwing into the general government every power not expressly reserved by the people, would have been spurned at, in that house, with the greatest indignation. Even in a single government, if the powers of the people rest on the same establishment as is expressed in this Constitution, a bill of rights is by no means a necessary measure. In a government possessed of enumerated powers, such a measure would be not only unnecessary, but preposterous and dangerous. Whence comes this notion, that in the United States there is no security without a bill of rights? Have the citizens of South Carolina no security for their liberties? They have no bill of rights. Are the citizens on the eastern side of the Delaware less free, or less secured in their liberties, than those on the western side? The state of New Jersey has no bill of rights. The state of New York has no bill of rights. The states of Connecticut and Rhode Island have no bill of rights. I know not whether I have exactly enumerated the states who have not thought it necessary to add *a bill of rights* to their constitutions; but this enumeration, sir, will serve to show by experience, as well as principle, that, even in single governments, a bill of rights is not an essential or necessary measure. But in a government consisting of enumerated powers, such as is proposed for the United States, a bill of rights would not only be unnecessary, but, in my humble judgment, highly imprudent. In all societies, there are many powers and rights which cannot be particularly enumerated. A bill of rights annexed to a constitution is *an enumeration of the powers* reserved. If we attempt an enumeration, every thing that is not enumerated is presumed to be given. The consequence is, that an imperfect enumeration would throw all implied power into the scale of the government, and the rights of the people would be rendered incomplete. On the other hand, an imperfect enumeration of the powers of government reserves all implied power to the people; and by that means the constitution becomes incomplete. But of the two, it is much safer to run the risk on the side of the constitution; for an omission in the enumeration of the powers of government is neither so dangerous nor important as an omission in the enumeration of the rights of the people.

[*4 Dec.*]

A good deal has already been said concerning *a bill of rights*. I have stated, according to the best of my recollection, all that passed in Convention relating to that business. Since that time, I have spoken with a gentleman, who has not only his memory, but full notes that he had taken in that body, and he assures me that, upon this subject, no direct motion was ever made at all; and certainly, before we heard this so violently supported out of doors, some pains ought to have been taken to have tried its fate within; but the truth is, a bill of rights would, as I have mentioned already, have been not only unnecessary, but improper. In some governments, it may come within the gentleman's idea, when he says it can do no harm; but even in these governments, you find bills of rights do not uniformly obtain; and do those states complain who have them not? Is it a maxim in forming governments, that not only all the powers which are given, but also that all those which are reserved, should be enumerated? I apprehend that the powers given and reserved form the whole rights of the people, as men and as citizens. I consider that there are very few who understand the whole of these rights. All the political writers, from *Grotius* and *Puffendorf* down to *Vattel*, have treated on this subject; but in no one of those books, nor in the aggregate of them all, can you find a complete enumeration of rights appertaining to the people as men and as citizens.

There are two kinds of government—that where general power is intended to be given to the legislature, and that where the powers are particularly enumerated. In the last case, the implied result is, that nothing more is intended to be given than what is so enumerated, unless it results from the nature of the government itself. On the other hand, when general legislative powers are given, then the people part with their authority, and, on the gentleman's principle of government, retain nothing. But in a government like the proposed one, there can be no necessity for a bill of rights, for, on my principle, the people never part with their power. Enumerate all the rights of men! I am sure, sir, that no gentleman in the late Convention would have attempted such a thing. I believe the honorable speakers in opposition on this floor were members of the assembly which appointed delegates to that Convention; if it had been thought proper to have sent them into that body, how luminous would the dark conclave have been!— so the gentleman has been pleased to denominate that body. Aristocrats as they were, they pretended not to define the rights of those who sent them there. We ask, repeatedly, What harm could the addition of a bill of rights do? If it can do no good, I think that a sufficient reason to refuse having any thing to do with it. But to whom are we to report this bill of rights, if we should adopt it? Have we authority from those who sent us here to make one?

It is true, we may propose as well as any other private persons; but how shall we know the sentiments of the citizens of this state and of the other states? Are we certain that any one of them will agree with our definitions and enumerations?

28

JOHN SMILIE, PENNSYLVANIA RATIFYING
CONVENTION
28 Nov. 1787

McMaster 249–51, 254–56

I expected, Mr. President, that the honorable gentleman [James Wilson] would have proceeded to a full and explicit investigation of the proposed system, and that he would have made some attempts to prove that it was calculated to promote the happiness, power and general interests of the United States. I am sorry that I have been mistaken in this expectation, for surely the gentleman's talents and opportunities would have enabled him to furnish considerable information upon this important subject; but I shall proceed to make a few remarks upon those words in the preamble of this plan, which he has considered of so super-excellent a quality. Compare them, Sir, with the language used in forming the state constitution, and however superior they may be to the terms of the great charter of England; still, in common candor, they must yield to the more sterling expressions employed in this act. Let these speak for themselves:

"That all men are born equally free and independent, and have certain natural, inherent and unalienable rights, among which are the enjoying and defending life and liberty, acquiring possessing and protecting property, and pursuing and obtaining happiness and safety.

"That the people of this state have the sole, exclusive and inherent right of governing and regulating the internal police of the same.

"That all power being originally inherent in, and consequently derived from the people; therefore all officers of government, whether legislative or executive, are their trustees and servants, and at all times accountable to them.

"That government is, or ought to be, instituted for the common benefit, protection and security of the people, nation or community; and not for the particular emolument or advantage of any single man, family, or set of men, who are a part only of that community. And that the community hath an indubitable, unalienable, and indefeasible right to reform, alter or abolish government in such manner as shall be by that community judged most conducive to the public weal."

But the gentleman takes pride in the superiority of this short preamble when compared with Magna Charta—why, sir, I hope the rights of men are better understood at this day than at the framing of that deed, and we must be convinced that civil liberty is capable of still greater improvement and extension, than is known even in its present cultivated state. True, sir, the supreme authority naturally rests in the people, but does it follow, that therefore a declaration of rights would be superfluous? Because the peo-

ple have a right to alter and abolish government, can it therefore be inferred that every step taken to secure that right would be superfluous and nugatory? The truth is, that unless some criterion is established by which it could be easily and constitutionally ascertained how far our governors may proceed, and by which it might appear when they transgress their jurisdiction, this idea of altering and abolishing government is a mere sound without substance. Let us recur to the memorable declaration of the 4th of July, 1776. Here it is said:

"When in the course of human events, it becomes necessary for one people to dissolve the political bands which have connected them with another, and to assume among the powers of the earth the separate and equal station to which the laws [of nature and] of nature's God entitle them, a decent respect to the opinions of mankind requires that they should declare the causes which impel them to the separation.

"We hold these truths to be self-evident; that all men are created equal; that they are endowed by their Creator with certain unalienable rights; that among these are life, liberty, and the pursuit of happiness. That to secure these rights, governments are instituted among men, deriving their just powers from the consent of the governed; that when any form of government becomes destructive of these ends, it is the right of the people to alter or to abolish it, and to institute a new government, laying its foundation on such principles, and organizing its powers in such form, as to them shall seem most likely to effect their safety and happiness."

Now, Sir, if in the proposed plan, the gentleman can show any similar security for the civil rights of the people, I shall certainly be relieved from a weight of objection to its adoption, and I sincerely hope, that as he has gone so far, he will proceed to communicate some of the reasons (and undoubtedly they must have been powerful ones) which induced the late federal convention to omit a bill of rights, so essential in the opinion of many citizens to a perfect form of government.

. . . . .

The arguments which have been urged, Mr. President, have not, in my opinion, satisfactorily shown that a bill of rights would have been an improper, nay, that it is not a necessary appendage to the proposed system. As it has been denied that Virginia possesses a bill of rights, I shall on that subject only observe that Mr. Mason, a gentleman certainly of great information and integrity, has assured me that such a thing does exist, and I am persuaded I shall be able at a future period to lay it before the convention. But, Sir, the state of Delaware has a bill of rights, and I believe one of the honorable members (Mr. M'Kean) who now contests the necessity and propriety of that instrument, took a very conspicuous part in the formation of the Delaware government. It seems, however, that the members of the federal convention were themselves convinced, in some degree, of the expediency and propriety of a bill of rights, for we find them expressly declaring that the writ of habeas corpus and the trial by jury in criminal cases shall not be suspended or infringed. How does this indeed agree with the maxim that whatever is not given is reserved? Does it not rather appear from the reservation of these two articles that everything else, which is not specified, is included in the powers delegated to the government? This, Sir, must prove the necessity of a full and explicit declaration of rights; and when we further consider the extensive, the undefined powers vested in the administrators of this system, when we consider the system itself as a great political compact between the governors and the governed, a plain, strong, and accurate criterion by which the people might at once determine when, and in what instance their rights were violated, is a preliminary, without which, this plan ought not to be adopted. So loosely, so inaccurately are the powers which are enumerated in this constitution defined, that it will be impossible, without a test of that kind, to ascertain the limits of authority, and to declare when government has degenerated into oppression. In that event the contest will arise between the people and the rulers: "You have exceeded the powers of your office, you have oppressed us," will be the language of the suffering citizen. The answer of the government will be short—"We have not exceeded our power; you have no test by which you can prove it." Hence, Sir, it will be impracticable to stop the progress of tyranny, for there will be no check but the people, and their exertions must be futile and uncertain; since it will be difficult, indeed, to communicate to them the violation that has been committed, and their proceedings will be neither systematical nor unanimous. It is said, however, that the difficulty of framing a bill of rights was insurmountable; but, Mr. President, I cannot agree in this opinion. Our experience, and the numerous precedents before us, would have furnished a very sufficient guide. At present there is no security even for the rights of conscience, and under the sweeping force of the sixth article, every principle of a bill of rights, every stipulation for the most sacred and invaluable privileges of man, are left at the mercy of government.

29

ROBERT WHITEHILL, PENNSYLVANIA RATIFYING CONVENTION
28 Nov. 1787
McMaster 256, 261

I differ, Sir, from the honorable member from the city, [James Wilson] as to the impropriety or necessity of a bill of rights. If, indeed, the constitution itself so well defined the powers of the government that no mistake could arise, and, we were well assured that our governors would always act right, then we might be satisfied without an explicit reservation of those rights with which the people ought not, and mean not to part. But, Sir, we know that it is the nature of power to seek its own augmentation, and thus the loss of liberty is the necessary consequence of a loose or extravagant delegation of authority. National

freedom has been, and will be the sacrifice of ambition and power, and it is our duty to employ the present opportunity in stipulating such restrictions as are best calculated to protect us from oppression and slavery. Let us then, Mr. President, if other countries cannot supply an adequate example, let us proceed upon our own principles, and with the great end of government in view, the happiness of the people, it will be strange if we err. Government, we have been told, Sir, is yet in its infancy: we ought not therefore to submit to the shackles of foreign schools and opinions. In entering into the social compact, men ought not to leave their rulers at large, but erect a permanent landmark by which they may learn the extent of their authority, and the people be able to discover the first encroachments on their liberties.

. . . . .

A bill of rights, Mr. President, it has been said, would not only be unnecessary, but it would be dangerous, and for this special reason, that because it is not practicable to enumerate all the rights of the people, therefore it would be hazardous to secure such of the rights as we can enumerate! Truly, Sir, I will agree that a bill of rights may be a dangerous instrument, but it is to the views and projects of the aspiring ruler, and not the liberties of the citizen. Grant but this explicit criterion, and our governors will not venture to encroach; refuse it, and the people cannot venture to complain. From the formal language of magna charta we are next taught to consider a declaration of rights as superfluous; but, Sir, will the situation and conduct of Great Britain furnish a case parallel to that of America? It surely will not be contended that we are about to receive our liberties as a grant or concession from any power upon earth; so that if we learn anything from the English charter, it is this: that the people having negligently lost or submissively resigned their rights into the hands of the crown, they were glad to recover them upon any terms; their anxiety to secure the grant by the strongest evidence will be an argument to prove, at least, the expediency of the measure, and the result of the whole is a lesson instructing us to do by an easy precaution, what will hereafter be an arduous and perhaps insurmountable task.

30

THOMAS JEFFERSON TO JAMES MADISON
20 Dec. 1787
Papers 12:440

I will now add what I do not like. First the omission of a bill of rights providing clearly and without the aid of sophisms for freedom of religion, freedom of the press, protection against standing armies, restriction against monopolies, the eternal and unremitting force of the habeas corpus laws, and trials by jury in all matters of fact triable by the laws of the land and not by the law of Nations. To say, as Mr. Wilson does that a bill of rights was not necessary because all is reserved in the case of the general government which is not given, while in the particular ones all is given which is not reserved might do for the Audience to whom it was addressed, but is surely gratis dictum, opposed by strong inferences from the body of the instrument, as well as from the omission of the clause of our present confederation which had declared that in express terms. It was a hard conclusion to say because there has been no uniformity among the states as to the cases triable by jury, because some have been so incautious as to abandon this mode of trial, therefore the more prudent states shall be reduced to the same level of calamity. It would have been much more just and wise to have concluded the other way that as most of the states had judiciously preserved this palladium, those who had wandered should be brought back to it, and to have established general right instead of general wrong. Let me add that a bill of rights is what the people are entitled to against every government on earth, general or particular, and what no just government should refuse, or rest on inference.

31

FEDERAL FARMER, NO. 6
25 Dec. 1787
Storing 2.8.86

The following, I think, will be allowed to be unalienable or fundamental rights in the United States:—

No man, demeaning himself peaceably, shall be molested on account of his religion or mode of worship—The people have a right to hold and enjoy their property according to known standing laws, and which cannot be taken from them without their consent, or the consent of their representatives; and whenever taken in the pressing urgencies of government, they are to receive a reasonable compensation for it—Individual security consists in having free recourse to the laws—The people are subject to no laws or taxes not assented to by their representatives constitutionally assembled—They are at all times intitled to the benefits of the writ of habeas corpus, the trial by jury in criminal and civil causes—They have a right, when charged, to a speedy trial in the vicinage; to be heard by themselves or counsel, not to be compelled to furnish evidence against themselves, to have witnesses face to face, and to confront their adversaries before the judge—No man is held to answer a crime charged upon him till it be substantially described to him; and he is subject to no unreasonable searches or seizures of his person, papers or effects—The people have a right to assemble in an orderly manner, and petition the government for a redress of wrongs—The freedom of the press ought not to be restrained—No emoluments, except for actual service—No hereditary honors, or orders of nobility, ought to be allowed—The military ought to be subordinate to the civil authority, and no soldier be quartered on the citizens with-

out their consent—The militia ought always to be armed and disciplined, and the usual defence of the country—The supreme power is in the people, and power delegated ought to return to them at stated periods, and frequently—The legislative, executive, and judicial powers, ought always to be kept distinct—others perhaps might be added.

32

FEDERAL FARMER, NO. 16
20 Jan. 1788
Storing 2.8.196–203

Having gone through with the organization of the government, I shall now proceed to examine more particularly those clauses which respect its powers. I shall begin with those articles and stipulations which are necessary for accurately ascertaining the extent of powers, and what is given, and for guarding, limiting, and restraining them in their exercise. We often find, these articles and stipulations placed in bills of rights; but they may as well be incorporated in the body of the constitution, as selected and placed by themselves. The constitution, or whole social compact, is but one instrument, no more or less, than a certain number of articles or stipulations agreed to by the people, whether it consists of articles, sections, chapters, bills of rights, or parts of any other denomination, cannot be material. Many needless observations, and idle distinctions, in my opinion, have been made respecting a bill of rights. On the one hand, it seems to be considered as a necessary distinct limb of the constitution, and as containing a certain number of very valuable articles, which are applicable to all societies: and, on the other, as useless, especially in a federal government, possessing only enumerated power—nay, dangerous, as individual rights are numerous, and not easy to be enumerated in a bill or rights, and from articles, or stipulations, securing some of them, it may be inferred, that others not mentioned are surrendered. [These appear] to me to be general indefinite propositions without much meaning—and the man [James Wilson] who first advanced those of the latter description, in the present case, signed the federal constitution, which directly contradicts him. The supreme power is undoubtedly in the people, and it is a principle well established in my mind, that they reserve all powers not expressly delegated by them to those who govern; this is as true in forming a state as in forming a federal government. There is no possible distinction but this founded merely in the different modes of proceeding which take place in some cases. In forming a state constitution, under which to manage not only the great but the little concerns of a community: the powers to be possessed by the government are often too numerous to be enumerated; the people to adopt the shortest way often give general powers, indeed all powers, to the government, in some general words, and then, by a particular enumeration, take back, or rather say they however reserve certain rights as sacred, and which no laws shall be made to violate: hence the idea that all powers are given which are not reserved: but in forming a federal constitution, which *ex vi termine*, supposes state governments existing, and which is only to manage a few great national concerns, we often find it easier to enumerate particularly the powers to be delegated to the federal head, than to enumerate particularly the individual rights to be reserved; and the principle will operate in its full force, when we carefully adhere to it. When we particularly enumerate the powers given, we ought either carefully to enumerate the rights reserved, or be totally silent about them; we must either particularly enumerate both, or else suppose the particular enumeration of the powers given adequately draws the line between them and the rights reserved, particularly to enumerate the former and not the latter, I think most advisable: however, as men appear generally to have their doubts about these silent reservations, we might advantageously enumerate the powers given, and then in general words, according to the mode adopted in the 2d art. of the confederation, declare all powers, rights and privileges, are reserved, which are not explicitly and expressly given up. People, and very wisely too, like to be express and explicit about their essential rights, and not to be forced to claim them on the precarious and unascertained tenure of inferences and general principles, knowing that in any controversy between them and their rulers, concerning those rights, disputes may be endless, and nothing certain:—But admitting, on the general principle, that all rights are reserved of course, which are not expressly surrendered, the people could with sufficient certainty assert their rights on all occasions, and establish them with ease, still there are infinite advantages in particularly enumerating many of the most essential rights reserved in all cases: and as to the less important ones, we may declare in general terms, that all not expressly surrendered are reserved. We do not by declarations change the nature of things, or create new truths, but we give existence, or at least establish in the minds of the people truths and principles which they might never otherwise have thought of, or soon forgot. If a nation means its systems, religious or political, shall have duration, it ought to recognize the leading principles of them in the front page of every family book. What is the usefulness of a truth in theory, unless it exists constantly in the minds of the people, and has their assent:—we discern certain rights, as the freedom of the press, and the trial by jury, &c. which the people of England and of America of course believe to be sacred, and essential to their political happiness, and this belief in them is the result of ideas at first suggested to them by a few able men, and of subsequent experience; while the people of some other countries hear these rights mentioned with the utmost indifference; they think the privilege of existing at the will of a despot much preferable to them. Why this difference amongst beings every way formed alike. The reason of the difference is obvious—it is the effect of education, a series of notions impressed upon the minds of the people by examples, precepts and declarations. When the people of England got

together, at the time they formed Magna Charta, they did not consider it sufficient, that they were indisputably entitled to certain natural and unalienable rights[;] not depending on silent titles, they, by a declaratory act, expressly recognized them, and explicitly declared to all the world, that they were entitled to enjoy those rights; they made an instrument in writing, and enumerated those they then thought essential, or in danger, and this wise men saw was not sufficient: and therefore, that the people might not forget these rights, and gradually become prepared for arbitrary government, their discerning and honest leaders caused this instrument to be confirmed near forty times, and to be read twice a year in public places, not that it would lose its validity without such confirmations, but to fix the contents of it in the minds of the people, as they successively come upon the stage.—Men, in some countries do not remain free, merely because they are entitled to natural and unalienable rights; men in all countries are entitled to them, not because their ancestors once got together and enumerated them on paper, but because, by repeated negociations and declarations, all parties are brought to realize them, and of course to believe them to be sacred. Were it necessary, I might shew the wisdom of our past conduct, as a people in not merely comforting ourselves that we were entitled to freedom, but in constantly keeping in view, in addresses, bills of rights, in news-papers, &c. the particular principles on which our freedom must always depend.

It is not merely in this point of view, that I urge the engrafting in the constitution additional declaratory articles. The distinction, in itself just, that all powers not given are reserved, is in effect destroyed by this very constitution, as I shall particularly demonstrate—and even independent of this, the people, by adopting the constitution, give many general undefined powers to congress, in the constitutional exercise of which, the rights in question may be effected. Gentlemen who oppose a federal bill of rights, or further declaratory articles, seem to view the subject in a very narrow imperfect manner. These have for their objects, not only the enumeration of the rights reserved, but principally to explain the general powers delegated in certain material points, and to restrain those who exercise them by fixed known boundaries. Many explanations and restrictions necessary and useful, would be much less so, were the people at large all well and fully acquainted with the principles and affairs of government. There appears to be in the constitution, a studied brevity, and it may also be probable, that several explanatory articles were omitted from a circumstance very common. What we have long and early understood ourselves in the common concerns of the community, we are apt to suppose is understood by others, and need not be expressed; and it is not unnatural or uncommon for the ablest men most frequently to make this mistake. To make declaratory articles unnecessary in an instrument of government, two circumstances must exist; the rights reserved must be indisputably so, and in their nature defined; the powers delegated to the government, must be precisely defined by the words that convey them, and clearly be of such extent and nature as that, by no reasonable construction, they can be made to invade the rights and prerogatives intended to be left in the people.

The first point urged, is, that all power is reserved not expressly given, that particular enumerated powers only are given, that all others are not given, but reserved, and that it is needless to attempt to restrain congress in the exercise of powers they possess not. This reasoning is logical, but of very little importance in the common affairs of men; but the constitution does not appear to respect it even in any view. To prove this, I might cite several clauses in it. I shall only remark on two or three. By article 1, section 9, "No title of nobility shall be granted by congress" Was this clause omitted, what power would congress have to make titles of nobility? in what part of the constitution would they find it? The answer must be, that congress would have no such power—that the people, by adopting the constitution, will not part with it. Why then by a negative clause, restrain congress from doing what it would have no power to do? This clause, then, must have no meaning, or imply, that were it omitted, congress would have the power in question, either upon the principle that some general words in the constitution may be so construed as to give it, or on the principle that congress possess the powers not expressly reserved. But this clause was in the confederation, and is said to be introduced into the constitution from very great caution. Even a cautionary provision implies a doubt, at least, that it is necessary; and if so in this case, clearly it is also alike necessary in all similar ones. The fact appears to be, that the people in forming the confederation, and the convention, in this instance, acted, naturally, they did not leave the point to be settled by general principles and logical inferences; but they settle the point in a few words, and all who read them at once understand them.

The trial by jury in criminal as well as in civil causes, has long been considered as one of our fundamental rights, and has been repeatedly recognized and confirmed by most of the state conventions. But the constitution expressly establishes this trial in criminal, and wholly omits it in civil causes. The jury trial in criminal causes, and the benefit of the writ of habeas corpus, are already as effectually established as any of the fundamental or essential rights of the people in the United States. This being the case, why in adopting a federal constitution do we now establish these, and omit all others, or all others, at least with a few exceptions, such as again agreeing there shall be no ex post facto laws, no titles of nobility, &c. We must consider this constitution, when adopted, as the supreme act of the people, and in construing it hereafter, we and our posterity must strictly adhere to the letter and spirit of it, and in no instance depart from them: in construing the federal constitution, it will not be only impracticable, but improper to refer to the state constitutions. They are entirely distinct instruments and inferior acts: besides, by the people's now establishing certain fundamental rights, it is strongly implied, that they are of opinion, that they would not otherwise be secured as a part of the federal system, or be regarded in the federal administration as fundamental. Further, these same rights, being established by the state constitutions, and secured to the people, our recog-

nizing them now, implies, that the people thought them insecure by the state establishments, and extinguished or put afloat by the new arrangement of the social system, unless re-established.—Further, the people, thus establishing some few rights, and remaining totally silent about others similarly circumstanced, the implication indubitably is, that they mean to relinquish the latter, or at least feel indifferent about them. Rights, therefore, inferred from general principles of reason, being precarious and hardly ascertainable in the common affairs of society, and the people, in forming a federal constitution, explicitly shewing they conceive these rights to be thus circumstanced, and accordingly proceed to enumerate and establish some of them, the conclusion will be, that they have established all which they esteem valuable and sacred. On every principle, then, the people especially having began, ought to go through enumerating, and establish particularly all the rights of individuals, which can by any possibility come in question in making and executing federal laws. I have already observed upon the excellency and importance of the jury trial in civil as well as in criminal causes, instead of establishing it in criminal causes only; we ought to establish it generally;—instead of the clause of forty or fifty words relative to this subject, why not use the language that has always been used in this country, and say, "the people of the United States shall always be entitled to the trial by jury." This would shew the people still hold the right sacred, and enjoin it upon congress substantially to preserve the jury trial in all cases, according to the usage and custom of the country. I have observed before, that it is *the jury trial* we want; the little different appendages and modifications tacked to it in the different states, are no more than a drop in the ocean: the jury trial is a solid uniform feature in a free government; it is the substance we would save, not the little articles of form.

Security against expost facto laws, the trial by jury, and the benefits of the writ of habeas corpus, are but a part of those inestimable rights the people of the United States are entitled to, even in judicial proceedings, by the course of the common law. These may be secured in general words, as in New-York, the Western Territory, &c. by declaring the people of the United States shall always be entitled to judicial proceedings according to the course of the common law, as used and established in the said states. Perhaps it would be better to enumerate the particular essential rights the people are entitled to in these proceedings, as has been done in many of the states, and as has been done in England. In this case, the people may proceed to declare, that no man shall be held to answer to any offence, till the same be fully described to him; nor to furnish evidence against himself: that, except in the government of the army and navy, no person shall be tried for any offence, whereby he may incur loss of life, or an infamous punishment, until he be first indicted by a grand jury: that every person shall have a right to produce all proofs that may be favourable to him, and to meet the witnesses against him face to face: that every person shall be entitled to obtain right and justice freely and without delay; that all persons shall have a right to be secure from all unreasonable searches and seizures of their persons, houses, papers, or possessions; and that all warrants shall be deemed contrary to this right, if the foundation of them be not previously supported by oath, and there be not in them a special designation of persons or objects of search, arrest, or seizure: and that no person shall be exiled or molested in his person or effects, otherwise than by the judgment of his peers, or according to the law of the land. A celebrated writer observes upon this last article, that in itself it may be said to comprehend the whole end of political society. These rights are not necessarily reserved, they are established, or enjoyed but in few countries: they are stipulated rights, almost peculiar to British and American laws. In the execution of those laws, individuals, by long custom, by magna charta, bills of rights &c. have become entitled to them. A man, at first, by act of parliament, became entitled to the benefits of the writ of habeas corpus—men are entitled to these rights and benefits in the judicial proceedings of our state courts generally: but it will by no means follow, that they will be entitled to them in the federal courts, and have a right to assert them, unless secured and established by the constitution or federal laws. We certainly, in federal processes, might as well claim the benefits of the writ of habeas corpus, as to claim trial by a jury—the right to have council—to have witnesses face to face—to be secure against unreasonable search warrants, &c. was the constitution silent as to the whole of them:—but the establishment of the former, will evince that we could not claim them without it; and the omission of the latter, implies they are relinquished, or deemed of no importance. These are rights and benefits individuals acquire by compact; they must claim them under compacts, or immemorial usage—it is doubtful, at least, whether they can be claimed under immemorial usage in this country: and it is, therefore, we generally claim them under compacts, as charters and constitutions.

The people by adopting the federal constitution, give congress general powers to institute a distinct and new judiciary, new courts, and to regulate all proceedings in them, under the eight limitations mentioned in a former letter; and the further one, that the benefits of the habeas corpus act shall be enjoyed by individuals. Thus general powers being given to institute courts, and regulate their proceedings, with no provision for securing the rights principally in question, may not congress so exercise those powers, and constitutionally too, as to destroy those rights? clearly, in my opinion, they are not in any degree secured. But, admitting the case is only doubtful, would it not be prudent and wise to secure them and remove all doubts, since all agree the people ought to enjoy these valuable rights, a very few men excepted, who seem to be rather of opinion that there is little or nothing in them? Were it necessary I might add many observations to shew their value and political importance.

The constitution will give congress general powers to raise and support armies. General powers carry with them incidental ones, and the means necessary to the end. In the exercise of these powers, is there any provision in the constitution to prevent the quartering of soldiers on the inhabitants? you will answer, there is not. This may some-

times be deemed a necessary measure in the support of armies; on what principle can the people claim the right to be exempt from this burden? they will urge, perhaps, the practice of the country, and the provisions made in some of the state constitutions—they will be answered, that their claim thus to be exempt is not founded in nature, but only in custom and opinion, or at best, in stipulations in some of the state constitutions, which are local, and inferior in their operation, and can have no controul over the general government—that they had adopted a federal constitution—had noticed several rights, but had been totally silent about this exemption—that they had given general powers relative to the subject, which, in their operation, regularly destroyed the claim. Though it is not to be presumed, that we are in any immediate danger from this quarter, yet it is fit and proper to establish, beyond dispute, those rights which are particularly valuable to individuals, and essential to the permanency and duration of free government. An excellent writer observes, that the English, always in possession of their freedom, are frequently unmindful of the value of it: we, at this period, do not seem to be so well off, having, in some instances abused ours; many of us are quite disposed to barter it away for what we call energy, coercion, and some other terms we use as vaguely as that of liberty—There is often as great a rage for change and novelty in politics, as in amusements and fashions.

All parties apparently agree, that the freedom of the press is a fundamental right, and ought not to be restrained by any taxes, duties, or in any manner whatever. Why should not the people, in adopting a federal constitution, declare this, even if there are only doubts about it. But, say the advocates, all powers not given are reserved:—true; but the great question is, are not powers given, in the exercise of which this right may be destroyed? The people's or the printers claim to a free press, is founded on the fundamental laws, that is, compacts, and state constitutions, made by the people. The people, who can annihilate or alter those constitutions, can annihilate or limit this right. This may be done by giving general powers, as well as by using particular words. No right claimed under a state constitution, will avail against a law of the union, made in pursuance of the federal constitution: therefore the question is, what laws will congress have a right to make by the constitution of the union, and particularly touching the press? By art. 1. sect. 8. congress will have power to lay and collect taxes, duties, imposts and excise. By this congress will clearly have power to lay and collect all kind of taxes whatever—taxes on houses, lands, polls, industry, merchandize, &c.—taxes on deeds, bonds, and all written instruments—on writs, pleas, and all judicial proceedings, on licences, naval officers papers, &c. on newspapers, advertisements, &c. and to require bonds of the naval officers, clerks, printers, &c. to account for the taxes that may become due on papers that go through their hands. Printing, like all other business, must cease when taxed beyond its profits; and it appears to me, that a power to tax the press at discretion, is a power to destroy or restrain the freedom of it. There may be other powers given, in the exercise of which this freedom may be effected; and certainly it is of too much importance to be left thus liable to be taxed, and constantly to constructions and inferences. A free press is the channel of communication as to mercantile and public affairs; by means of it the people in large countries ascertain each others sentiments; are enabled to unite, and become formidable to those rulers who adopt improper measures. Newspapers may sometimes be the vehicles of abuse, and of many things not true; but these are but small inconveniencies, in my mind, among many advantages. A celebrated writer, I have several times quoted, speaking in high terms of the English liberties, says, "lastly the key stone was put to the arch, by the final establishment of the freedom of the press." I shall not dwell longer upon the fundamental rights, to some of which I have attended in this letter, for the same reasons that these I have mentioned, ought to be expressly secured, lest in the exercise of general powers given they may be invaded: it is pretty clear, that some other of less importance, or less in danger, might with propriety also be secured.

33

MASSACHUSETTS RATIFYING CONVENTION,
RATIFICATION AND PROPOSED AMENDMENTS
6 Feb. 1788
Elliot 2:176–78

The question being put, whether this Convention will accept of the report of the committee, as follows,—

Commonwealth of Massachusetts.
In Convention of the Delegates of the People of the Commonwealth of Massachusetts, 1788.

The Convention, having impartially discussed and fully considered the Constitution for the United States of America, reported to Congress by the Convention of delegates from the United States of America, and submitted to us by a resolution of the General Court of the said commonwealth, passed the twenty-fifth day of October last past; and acknowledging, with grateful hearts, the goodness of the Supreme Ruler of the universe in affording the people of the United States, in the course of his providence, an opportunity, deliberately and peaceably, without fraud or surprise, of entering into an explicit and solemn compact with each other, by assenting to and ratifying a new Constitution, in order to form a more perfect union, establish justice, insure domestic tranquillity, provide for the common defence, promote the general welfare, and secure the blessings of liberty to themselves and their posterity, DO, in the name and in behalf of the people of the commonwealth of Massachusetts, assent to and ratify the said Constitution for the United States of America.

And, as it is the opinion of this Convention, that certain amendments and alterations in the said Constitution would remove the fears and quiet the apprehensions of many of the good people of the commonwealth, and more effectually guard against an undue administration of the federal government, the Convention do therefore recommend that the following alterations and provisions be introduced into the said Constitution:—

First. That it be explicitly declared, that all powers not expressly delegated by the aforesaid Constitution are reserved to the several states, to be by them exercised.

Secondly. That there shall be one representative to every thirty thousand persons, according to the census mentioned in the Constitution, until the whole number of representatives amounts to two hundred.

Thirdly. That Congress do not exercise the powers vested in them by the 4th section of the 1st article, but in cases where a state shall neglect or refuse to make the regulations therein mentioned, or shall make regulations subversive of the rights of the people to a free and equal representation in Congress, agreeably to the Constitution.

Fourthly. That Congress do not lay direct taxes, but when the moneys arising from the impost and excise are insufficient for the public exigencies, nor then, until Congress shall have first made a requisition upon the states, to assess, levy, and pay their respective proportion of such requisitions, agreeably to the census fixed in the said Constitution, in such way and manner as the legislatures of the states shall think best, and, in such case, if any state shall neglect or refuse to pay its proportion, pursuant to such requisition, then Congress may assess and levy such state's proportion, together with interest thereon, at the rate of six per cent. per annum, from the time of payment prescribed in such requisitions.

Fifthly. That Congress erect no company with exclusive advantages of commerce.

Sixthly. That no person shall be tried for any crime, by which he may incur an infamous punishment, or loss of life, until he be first indicted by a grand jury, except in such cases as may arise in the government and regulation of the land and naval forces.

Seventhly. The Supreme Judicial Federal Court shall have no jurisdiction of causes between citizens of different states, unless the matter in dispute, whether it concern the realty or personalty, be of the value of three thousand dollars at the least; nor shall the federal judicial powers extend to any action between citizens of different states, where the matter in dispute, whether it concern the realty or personalty, is not of the value of fifteen hundred dollars at the least.

Eighthly. In civil actions between citizens of different states, every issue of fact, arising in actions at common law, shall be tried by a jury, if the parties, or either of them, request it.

Ninthly. Congress shall at no time consent that any person holding an office of trust or profit, under the United States, shall accept of a title of nobility, or any other title or office, from any king, prince, or foreign state.

461

And the Convention do, in the name and in the behalf of the people of this commonwealth, enjoin it upon their representatives in Congress, at all times, until the alterations and provisions aforesaid have been considered, agreeably to the 5th article of the said Constitution, to exert all their influence, and use all reasonable and legal methods, to obtain a ratification of the said alterations and provisions, in such manner as is provided in the said article.

And, that the United States, in Congress assembled, may have due notice of the assent and ratification of the said Constitution by this Convention, it is

Resolved, That the assent and ratification aforesaid be engrossed on parchment, together with the recommendation and injunction aforesaid, and with this resolution; and that his excellency, JOHN HANCOCK, President, and the Hon. WILLIAM CUSHING, Esq., Vice-President of this Convention, transmit the same, countersigned by the Secretary of the Convention, under their hands and seals, to the United States in Congress assembled.

34

ALEXANDER CONTEE HANSON, ARISTIDES, REMARKS ON THE PROPOSED PLAN OF A FEDERAL GOVERNMENT
1788
Pamphlets 241–43

I proceed to attack the whole body of anti-federalists in their strong hold. The proposed constitution contains no *bill of rights.*

Consider again the nature and intent of a federal republic. It consists of an assemblage of distinct states, each completely organized for the protection of its own citizens, and the whole consolidated, by express compact, under one head, for the general welfare and common defence.

Should the compact authorize the sovereign, or head to do all things it may think necessary and proper, then there is no limitation to its authority; and the liberty of each citizen in the union has no other security, than the sound policy, good faith, virtue, and perhaps proper interests, of the head.

When the compact confers the aforesaid general power, making nevertheless some special reservations and exceptions, then is the citizen protected further, so far as these reservations and exceptions shall extend.

But, when the compact ascertains and defines the power delegated to the federal head, then cannot this government, without manifest usurpation, exert any power not expressly, or by *necessary* implication, conferred by the compact.

This doctrine is so obvious and plain, that I am amazed any good man should deplore the omission of a bill of rights.

When we were told, that the celebrated Mr. Wilson had advanced this doctrine in effect, it was said, Mr. Wilson would not dare to speak thus to a CONSTITUTIONALIST. With talents inferior to that gentleman's, I will maintain the doctrine against any CONSTITUTIONALIST who will condescend to enter the lists, and behave like a gentleman.

It is, however, the idea of another most respectable character, that, as a bill of rights could do no harm, and might quiet the minds of many good people, the convention would have done well to indulge them. With all due deference, I apprehend, that a bill of rights might not be this innocent quieting instrument. Had the convention entered on the work, they must have comprehended within it everything, which the citizens of the United States claim as a natural or a civil right. An omission of a single article would have caused more discontent, than is either felt or pretended, on the present occasion. A multitude of articles might be the source of infinite controversy, by clashing with the powers intended to be given. To be full and certain, a bill of rights might have cost the convention more time, than was expended on their other work. The very appearance of it might raise more clamour than its omission,—I mean from those who study pretexts for condemning the whole fabric of the constitution.—"What! (might they say) did these exalted spirits imagine, that the natural rights of mankind depend on their gracious concession. If indeed they possessed that tyrannic sway, which, the kings of England had once usurped, we might humbly thank them for their *magna charta,* defective as it is. As that is not the case, we will not suffer it to be understood, that their *new-fangled* federal head shall domineer with the powers not excepted by their precious bill of rights. What! if the owner of 1,000 acres of land thinks proper to fell one half, is it necessary to take a release from the vendee of the other half? Just as necessary is it for the people to have a grant of their natural rights from a government which derives everything it has, from the grant of the people."

The restraints laid on the state legislatures will tend to secure domestic tranquility, more than all the bills, or declarations, of rights, which human policy could devise. It is very justly asserted, that the plan contains an avowal of many rights. It provides that no man, shall suffer by ex-post facto laws or bills of attainder. It declares, that gold and silver only shall be a tender for specie debts; and that no law shall impair the obligation of a contract.

35

A [MARYLAND] FARMER, NO. 1
15 Feb. 1788
Storing 5.1.4–16

To assert that bills of rights have always originated from, or been considered as grants of the King or Prince, and that the liberties which they secure are the gracious concessions of the sovereign, betrays an equal ignorance of history and of law, or what in effect amounts to the same thing a violent and precipitate zeal.

I believe no writer in the most venal age, has ever openly asserted this doctrine, but the prostituted, rotten Sir Robert Filmer, and Aristides—And the man who at this day would contend in England that their bill of rights is the grant of the King, would find the general contempt his only security—In saying this, I sincerely regret that the name of Aristides should be joined with that of Sir Robert Filmer, and I freely acknowledge that no contemptible degree of talents, and integrity render him who uses it, much more worthy of the very respectable association he has selected for himself—But the errors of such men alone are dangerous—the man who has too much activity of mind, or restlessness to be quiet, qualities to engage public and private esteem, talents to form and support an opinion, fortitude to avow it, and too much pride to be convinced, will at all times have weight in a free country, (especially where indolence is the general characteristic) though that weight he will always find impaired in proportion as he indulges levity, caprice and passion.

I will confine my inquiry to the English constitution—Example *there*, is in a great measure law *here*—and the authority of an American judge on a point of English law, should be digested with coolness and promulgated with caution, because it is frequently conclusory.

The celebrated and only bill of rights of Great-Britain, which is considered as the supreme law of the land, and not to be questioned or impeached in their courts, was the work of that convention of lords and commons in 1688, which declared that *King James 2d, had abdicated the crown, and that the throne had thereby become vacant,* and who after they had compleated and asserted this glorious declaration of the unalienable rights of their fellow citizens, pursuing the peculiar duty of a convention, conferred the crown of the three kingdoms on an alien and foreigner, William the 3d.

Can any man imagine that this convention could at that time, have considered these rights as the grant of a King, whom they previously declared to have abdicated the throne, or the gracious concessions of a Prince whom they were about to deprive forever of the crown? Or could they have considered this bill of rights as the concession of Prince William, at that time a foreigner and alien, not entitled to hold a foot of land, or any of the common rights of citizenship, and who could afterwards only derive his title to the crown from the same source, which gave authority and sanction to this fundamental and most inestimable law? or, could the British nation at that time, or ever since, have viewed this declaration, as the grant and concession of a King or Prince, when no King or Prince was at that time in existence?—But should there remain any minds yet unsatisfied, I refer such to the debates of that convention, which are preserved in Grey's debates in parliament, and there will be found in them, the principles of equal liberty, the inherent and unalienable rights of men, as amply and ably discussed, and as fully recognized by the authors of that blessing, the artists of that British

palladium, as ever they have since been by the animated patriots of America, or the present age.—I also refer them to an inestimable little treatise composed on this occasion by that accomplished lawyer and patriot, afterwards the Lord Somers—High Chancellor of Great-Britain—then a member of the convention, and chiefly instrumental in their great work—a pamphlet that should find a place in the library of every American judge at least—Whoever peruses these, will discover undeniable evidence, that the British convention, considered this their declaration, as the concession of no Prince, but the Prince of Heaven—whom alone they acknowledged as the author of their liberties—they will there find that a bill of rights, is an enumeration of those conditions on which the individuals of the empire agreed to confirm the social compact; and consequently that no power, which they thus conditionally delegated to the majority (in whatever form organized) should be so exercised as to infringe and impair these their natural rights—not vested in SOCIETY, but reserved to each member thereof.

This was not the doctrine of that period alone—It was the common law and constitution of England, so asserted and maintained by the ablest lawyers of every age of the empire.—The petition of right, which came forward in the reign of Charles 1st, said to have been originally penned by the celebrated Lord Coke—although in its title a contradiction in terms, is yet in substance equally strong and clear—asserting the rights of the people to be coeval with the government—We find this principle strenuously and ably maintained through all the works of this great man, and to this doctrine he finally, with the devotion of a freeman, and the fortitude of an Englishman, sacrificed his vanity, his ambition and his avarice—This last act of an aged and venerable judge, has obliterated the errors of a youthful courtier—it has made his peace with posterity, who with gratitude and indulgence has forgiven the conduct of a court lawyer, which she might have punished with detestation, although she could not correct.

Here I cannot but observe what strenuous bill of rights men, all the great luminaries of the English law have been: to Lord Coke and Lord Somers, I will add that [   ] of human nature, Sir Matthew Hale, in whom were united true Christian piety, Roman fortitude, and an understanding more than human.

This perfect man although firmly opposed to the violences of the mad fanatics of the age, stood up almost alone in that parliament which restored the regal government, in favor of a bill of rights—but the tide of popular rage, hastening to place the worthless Charles on the throne of his more worthless ancestors, was too strong, and the voice of that man could not be heard, who was the delight of his own and the admiration of succeeding ages.

It is true, that something like the doctrine of Aristides was frequently the language of courtiers and sycophants in the feeble reigns of the arbitrary Stuarts—times of impotent and impudent usurpation—and they grounded their assertions on the form of the statute of magna charta, a statute much estemed for the many valuable rights it ascertains—the enacting words of which imply it to be an act of the King—But Aristides must know that this was the frequent form of the ancient statutes, sometime it is the King alone enacts, sometime the King with advice and consent of the great men and Barons, and sometimes the three estates—Even at this day, the King uses these words in passing laws that bear the same implication; and we see even in America acts of authority issue under the name and signature of the Governor alone, who has not a voice unless the council are divided—But as to the legal and acknowledged authority of the King at the time of enacting magna charta, there can remain but little doubt. Henry Bracton a contemporary lawyer and judge, who has left us a compleat and able treatise on the laws of England, is thus clear and express—*Omnes quidem sub rege, ipse autem sub lege,* all are subject to the King, but the King is subject to the law—It will hardly then be imagined, that the supreme law and constitution were the grants and concessions of a Prince, who was thus in theory and practice, subject himself to ordinary acts of legislation—But all these things are so amply discussed and the authorities so accurately collected in the publication of my Lord Somers, that a reference must be much more satisfactory than a repetition.

If I understand Aristides, he says that it would have been considered as an arrogant usurpation of sovereign rights in the members of convention, to have affixed a bill of rights—Can he reconcile this position with another opinion in his remarks, where he maintains that in offering this constitution, they could only act as private individuals, any of whom have a right to propose a constitution to the Americans to adopt at their discretion—In this view they could only have proposed—it is certain they could not have enacted a bill of rights—Nor would there have been any usurpation in WE *the people, of the States of New Hampshire, Massachusetts, &c. securing to ourselves and our posterity the following unalienable rights, &c.* which is the stile of the new constitution—The convention have actually engrafted some of these natural rights, yet no one calls it an usurpation—nor can I believe that any of my fellow-citizens of the United States, would have discovered the least indignation, had they engrafted them all—The universal complaint has been that they have enumerated so few—But says Aristides, it would have been a work of great difficulty, if not impossible to have ascertained them—Are the fundamental rights of mankind at this day unknown? Are they so soon forgot? If they are not imprinted on our hearts, they are in several of the constitutions—Although various in form, they are certainly not contradictory in substance—It did not require the wisdom of a national convention to have reduced them into order, and such as would not have gained the suffrage of a majority, would never have been regretted by America—or, I will venture to assert, what I shall never believe, that the majority were very unworthy of the trust reposed in them—Nor yet can I believe, that the late convention were incompetent to a task that has never been undertaken in the separate States without success.

This constitution is to be the act of the individual members of the American empire—the highest source of

terrestrial power with us—As it is a subsequent act, it not only repeals all prior acts of the same authority where it interferes with them—But being a government of the people of all the States, I do not know what right the citizens of Maryland for instance, have to expect that the citizens of Connecticut or New-Jersey, will be governed by the laws or constitution of Maryland—or what benefit a citizen of Maryland could derive from his bill of rights in a court of the United States, which can only be governed by the constitution and laws of the United States—Nor will it help the question to say, what will certainly be denied, that the future Congress may provide by law for this,—that an ordinary law of the United States can make, is an admission that it can unmake, and to submit the bills of rights of the separate States to the power of every annual national parliament, is a very uncertain tenure indeed.

If a citizen of Maryland can have no benefit of his own bill of rights in the confederal courts, and there is no bill of rights of the United States—how could he take advantage of a natural right founded in reason, could he plead it and produce Locke, Sydney, or Montesquieu as authority? How could he take advantage of any of the common law rights, which have heretofore been considered as the birthright of Englishmen and their descendants, could he plead them and produce the authority of the English judges in his support? Unquestionably not, for the authority of the common law arises from the express adoption by the several States in their respective constitutions, and that in various degrees and under different modifications—If admitted at all, I do not see to what extent, and if admitted, it must be admitted as unalterable by ordinary acts of legislation, which would be impossible—and it could never be of use to an individual, but in combating some national law infringing natural right.—To render this more intelligible—suppose for instance, that an officer of the United States should force the house, the asylum of a citizen, by virtue of a general warrant, I would ask, are general warrants illegal by the constitution of the United States? Would a court, or even a jury, but juries are no longer to exist, punish a man who acted by express authority, upon the bare recollection of what once was law and right? I fear not, especially in those cases which may strongly interest the passions of government, and in such only have general warrants been used—Suppose a case that must and will frequently happen, for such happen almost daily in England—That an officer of the customs should break open the dwelling, and violate the sanctuary of a freeman, in search for smuggled goods—impost and revenue laws are and from necessity must be in their nature oppressive—in their execution they may and will become intolerable to a free people, no remedy has been yet found equal to the task of detering and curbing the insolence of office, but a jury—It has become an invariable maxim of English juries, to give ruinous damages whenever an officer has deviated from the rigid letter of the law, or been guilty of an unnecessary act of insolence or oppression—It is true these damages to the individual, are frequently paid by government, upon a certificate of the judge that there was probable cause of suspicion—But the same rea-

sons that would induce an English judge to give this certificate, would probably lead an American judge, who will be
judge and jury too, to spare the public purse, if not favour
a brother officer.

I could proceed with an enumeration of familiar [simi-
lar?] instances that must and will happen, that would be as
alarming as prolix: but it is not my intention to ring an
alarm bell—If I know myself I would rather conciliate
than divide—But says Aristides the government may establish [   ] for such cases, though not commanded; what
they will do I will not presume to say; but I can readily
and will hereafter prove if they do, they will violate the
constitution; and even admitting their power, it would be
but a slender thread to [   ] so great a stake upon.

Here I must meet a position that has been ingeniously
advanced—That all powers and rights not expressly given,
[   ] consequently reserved—If this is not downright political nonsense, it is at least, untrue in theory and impossible in practice—until man is gifted with one of the most
important attributes of the Deity—that of fore knowledge
and [   ] it will be impossible to limit *affirmatively* legislative [   ]. When a people part with the legislative power
to government they can no more say, you shall make such
and such [   ] than they can say, such and such events
shall happen—[   ] must be regulated by events—All the
precaution that [   ] to human wisdom, is the exertion of
a *negative* [   ] speaking thus in the language of a bill of
rights, no [   ] shall authorize, no plea of necessity shall
justify the legislature in making a law to abolish or infringe
the freedom of the press, or the liberty of conscience,
&c.—And even [   ] these bounds are expressly and
clearly affirmed, we [   ] lament that they do not always
prove an effectual safeguard against the power of government; but they are [   ] guard, and why shall we leave
our citizens totally [   ]. A gentleman, in the Pennsylvania convention, of [   ] reputation, said, that the form of
the constitution—the organization of power, is a bill of
rights—he had then a defensible, but unformed idea floating in his imagination [   ] however, expressed it inaccurately, and unfortunately [   ] on the wrong side of his
own question. A proper organization of power would most
probably prevent a violation [   ] bill of rights and prove
the best security of political [   ]. Such an organization is
nothing more than a good [   ] a mint or die, that will
make money in its proper form, [   ] the quantity of alloy must be regulated by law, or the people may be
cheated by a debased currency—The truth is, that the
rights of individuals are frequently opposed to the apparent interests of the majority—For this reason the greater
the portion of political freedom in a form of government
the greater the necessity of a bill of rights—often the natural rights of an individual are opposed to the presumed
interests or heated passions of a large majority of [   ]
democratic government; if these rights are not clearly and
expressly ascertained, the individual must be lost; and for
the truth of this I appeal to every man who has borne a
part in the legislative councils of America. In such government the tyranny of the legislature is most to be dreaded.—
In monarchical governments, the feelings of the majority

[   ] most frequently on the side of the individual from
the [   ] jealousy inseperably attendant on those forms
of government, where the tyranny of the executive prevails tyranny whether exercised in the garb of a despot, or
[   ] plain coat of a quaker, is equally detestable, and
should be guarded against.

If a bill of rights was that essential requisite to a [   ]
constitution, why was it omitted by a convention of the
ablest men in America, a large majority of whom were unquestionably well disposed? This has been a natural ineq-
uity [inquiry?], and perhaps the true reason yet remains to
be disclosed. I have been informed that the proposed constitution was carried through its several stages, in a very
inoffensive form to the last, and that it did not assume its
decided featues until days before the convention rose—the
changes then effected produced much difference of opinion—created some [   ] and their patience was too much
exhausted to make the necessary correspondent alterations
and additions. These [   ] may, I believe, be depended
on, but the inference is [   ] offered as conjecture—if
true, we may attribute the omission of a bill of rights, and
many other imperfections to [   ] rather than design.

36

JAMES IREDELL, MARCUS, ANSWERS TO
MR. MASON'S OBJECTIONS TO
THE NEW CONSTITUTION
1788
Pamphlets 335–36, 356, 359–60

I. Objection.

"There is no declaration of rights, and the laws of the
general government being paramount to the laws and constitutions of the several States, the declarations of rights in
the separate States are no security. Nor are the people secured even in the enjoyment of the benefit of the common
law, which stands here upon no other foundation than its
having been adopted by the respective acts forming the
Constitutions of the several States."

Answer.

I. As to the want of a declaration of rights. The introduction of these in England, from which the idea was originally taken, was in consequence of usurpations of the
Crown, contrary, as was conceived, to the principles of
their government. But there no original constitution is to
be found, and the only meaning of a declaration of rights
in that country is, that in certain particulars specified, the
Crown had no authority to act. Could this have been necessary had there been a constitution in being by which it
could have been clearly discerned whether the Crown had
such authority or not? Had the people, by a solemn instru-

ment, delegated particular powers to the Crown at the formation of their government, surely the Crown, which in that case could claim under that instrument only, could not have contended for more power than was conveyed by it. So it is in regard to the new Constitution here: the future government which may be formed under that authority certainly cannot act beyond the warrant of that authority. As well might they attempt to impose a King upon America, as go one step in any other respect beyond the terms of their institution. The question then only is, whether more power will be vested in the future government than is necessary for the general purposes of the union. This may occasion a ground of dispute—but after expressly defining the powers that are to be exercised, to say that they shall exercise no other powers (either by a general or particular enumeration) would seem to me both nugatory and ridiculous. As well might a Judge when he condemns a man to be hanged, give strong injunctions to the Sheriff that he should not be beheaded.*

. . . . .

VIII. Objection.

"Under their own construction of the general clause at the end of the enumerated powers, the Congress may grant monopolies in trade and commerce, constitute new crimes, inflict unusual and severe punishment, and extend their power as far as they shall think proper; so that the State Legislatures have no security for the powers now presumed to remain to them: or the people for their rights. There is no declaration of any kind for preserving the liberty of the press, the trial by jury in civil causes, nor against the danger of standing armies in time of peace."

. . . . .

As to the constituting of new crimes, and inflicting unusual and severe punishment, certainly the cases enumerated wherein the Congress are empowered either to define offences, or prescribe punishments, are such as are proper for the exercise of such authority in the general Legislature of the Union. They only relate to "counterfeiting the securities and current coin of the United States," to "piracies and felonies committed on the high seas, and offences against the law of nations," and to "treason against the United States." These are offences immediately affecting the security, the honor or the interest of the United States at large, and of course must come within the sphere of the Legislative authority which is intrusted with their protection. Beyond these authorities, Congress can exercise no other power of this kind, except in the enacting of penalties to enforce their acts of legislation in the cases where express authority is delegated to them, and if they could

not enforce such acts by the enacting of penalties those powers would be altogether useless, since a legislative regulation without some sanction would be an absurd thing indeed. The Congress having, for these reasons, a just right to authority in the above particulars, the question is, whether it is practicable and proper to prescribe limits to its exercise, for fear that they should inflict punishments unusual and severe. It may be observed, in the first place, that a declaration against "cruel and unusual punishments" formed part of an article in the Bill of Rights at the revolution in England in 1688. The prerogative of the Crown having been grossly abused in some preceding reigns, it was thought proper to notice every grievance they had endured, and those declarations went to an abuse of power in the Crown only, but were never intended to limit the authority of Parliament. Many of these articles of the Bill of Rights in England, without a due attention to the difference of the cases, were eagerly adopted when our constitutions were formed, the minds of men then being so warmed with their exertions in the cause of liberty as to lean too much perhaps towards a jealousy of power to repose a proper confidence in their own government. From these articles in the State constitutions many things were attempted to be transplanted into our new Constitution, which would either have been nugatory or improper. This is one of them. The expressions "unusual and severe" or "cruel and unusual" surely would have been too vague to have been of any consequence, since they admit of no clear and precise signification. If to guard against punishments being too severe, the Convention had enumerated a vast variety of cruel punishments, and prohibited the use of any of them, let the number have been ever so great, an inexhaustible fund must have been unmentioned, and if our government had been disposed to be cruel their invention would only have been put to a little more trouble. If to avoid this difficulty, they had determined, not negatively what punishments should not be exercised, but positively what punishments should, this must have led them into a labyrinth of detail which in the original constitution of a government would have appeared perfectly ridiculous, and not left a room for such changes, according to circumstances, as must be in the power of every Legislature that is rationally formed. Thus when we enter into particulars, we must be convinced that the proposition of such a restriction would have led to nothing useful, or to something dangerous, and therefore that its omission is not chargeable as a fault in the new Constitution. Let us also remember, that as those who are to make those laws must themselves be subject to them, their own interest and feelings will dictate to them not to make them unnecessarily severe; and that in the case of treason, which usually in every country exposes men most to the avarice and rapacity of government, care is taken that the innocent family of the offender shall not suffer for the treason of their relation. This is the crime with respect to which a jealousy is of the most importance, and accordingly it is defined with great plainness and accuracy, and the temptations to abusive prosecutions guarded against as much as possible.

---

*It appears to me a very just remark of Mr. Wilson's, in his celebrated speech, that a bill of rights would have been dangerous, as implying that without such a reservation the Congress would have had authority in the cases enumerated, so that if any had been omitted (and who would undertake to recite all the State and individual rights not relinquished by the new Constitution?) they might have been considered at the mercy of the general legislature.

37

BRUTUS, NO. 15
20 Mar. 1788
Storing 2.9.196

(See ch. 8, no. 34)

38

ALEXANDER HAMILTON, FEDERALIST, NO. 84, 575–81
28 May 1788

The most considerable of these remaining objections is, that the plan of the convention contains no bill of rights. Among other answers given to this, it has been upon different occasions remarked, that the constitutions of several of the states are in a similar predicament. I add, that New-York is of this number. And yet the opposers of the new system in this state, who profess an unlimited admiration for its constitution, are among the most intemperate partizans of a bill of rights. To justify their zeal in this matter, they alledge two things; one is, that though the constitution of New-York has no bill of rights prefixed to it, yet it contains in the body of it various provisions in favour of particular privileges and rights, which in substance amount to the same thing; the other is, that the constitution adopts in their full extent the common and statute law of Great-Britain, by which many other rights not expressed in it are equally secured.

To the first I answer, that the constitution proposed by the convention contains, as well as the constitution of this state, a number of such provisions.

Independent of those, which relate to the structure of the government, we find the following: Article I. section 3. clause 7. "Judgment in cases of impeachment shall not extend further than to removal from office, and disqualification to hold and enjoy any office of honour, trust or profit under the United States; but the party convicted shall nevertheless be liable and subject to indictment, trial, judgment and punishment, according to law." Section 9. of the same article, clause 2. "The privilege of the writ of *habeas corpus* shall not be suspended, unless when in cases of rebellion or invasion the public safety may require it." Clause 3. "No bill of attainder or *ex post facto* law shall be passed." Clause [8]. "No title of nobility shall be granted by the United States: And no person holding any office of profit or trust under them, shall, without the consent of the congress, accept of any present, emolument, office or title, of any kind whatever, from any king, prince or foreign state." Article III. section 2. clause 3. "The trial of all crimes, except in cases of impeachment, shall be by jury; and such trial shall be held in the state where the said crimes shall have been committed; but when not committed within any state, the trial shall be at such place or places as the congress may by law have directed." Section 3, of the same article, "Treason against the United States shall consist only in levying war against them, or in adhering to their enemies, giving them aid and comfort. No person shall be convicted of treason unless on the testimony of two witnesses to the same overt act, or on confession in open court." And clause [2], of the same section. "The congress shall have power to declare the punishment of treason, but no attainder of treason shall work corruption of blood, or forfeiture, except during the life of the person attainted."

It may well be a question whether these are not upon the whole, of equal importance with any which are to be found in the constitution of this state. The establishment of the writ of *habeas corpus*, the prohibition of *ex post facto* laws, and of TITLES OF NOBILITY, *to which we have no corresponding provisions in our constitution*, are perhaps greater securities to liberty and republicanism than any it contains. The creation of crimes after the commission of the fact, or in other words, the subjecting of men to punishment for things which, when they were done, were breaches of no law, and the practice of arbitrary imprisonments have been in all ages the favourite and most formidable instruments of tyranny. The observations of the judicious Blackstone in reference to the latter, are well worthy of recital. "To bereave a man of life (says he) or by violence to confiscate his estate, without accusation or trial, would be so gross and notorious an act of despotism, as must at once convey the alarm of tyranny throughout the whole nation; but confinement of the person by secretly hurrying him to goal, where his sufferings are unknown or forgotten, is a less public, a less striking, and therefore *a more dangerous engine* of arbitrary government." And as a remedy for this fatal evil, he is every where peculiarly emphatical in his encomiums on the *habeas corpus* act, which in one place he calls "the BULWARK of the British constitution."

Nothing need be said to illustrate the importance of the prohibition of titles of nobility. This may truly be denominated the corner stone of republican government; for so long as they are excluded, there can never be serious danger that the government will be any other than that of the people.

To the second, that is, to the pretended establishment of the common and statute law by the constitution, I answer, that they are expressly made subject "to such alterations and provisions as the legislature shall from time to time make concerning the same." They are therefore at any moment liable to repeal by the ordinary legislative power, and of course have no constitutional sanction. The only use of the declaration was to recognize the ancient law, and to remove doubts which might have been occasioned by the revolution. This consequently can be considered as no part of a declaration of rights, which under our constitutions must be intended as limitations of the power of the government itself.

It has been several times truly remarked, that bills of rights are in their origin, stipulations between kings and their subjects, abridgments of prerogative in favor of privilege, reservations of rights not surrendered to the prince. Such was MAGNA CHARTA, obtained by the Barons, sword in hand, from king John. Such were the subsequent confirmations of that charter by subsequent princes. Such was the *petition of right* assented to by Charles the First, in the beginning of his reign. Such also was the declaration of right presented by the lords and commons to the prince of Orange in 1688, and afterwards thrown into the form of an act of parliament, called the bill of rights. It is evident, therefore, that according to their primitive signification, they have no application to constitutions professedly founded upon the power of the people, and executed by their immediate representatives and servants. Here, in strictness, the people surrender nothing, and as they retain every thing, they have no need of particular reservations. "WE THE PEOPLE of the United States, to secure the blessings of liberty to ourselves and our posterity, do *ordain* and *establish* this constitution for the United States of America." Here is a better recognition of popular rights than volumes of those aphorisms which make the principal figure in several of our state bills of rights, and which would sound much better in a treatise of ethics than in a constitution of government.

But a minute detail of particular rights is certainly far less applicable to a constitution like that under consideration, which is merely intended to regulate the general political interests of the nation, than to a constitution which has the regulation of every species of personal and private concerns. If therefore the loud clamours against the plan of the convention on this score, are well founded, no epithets of reprobation will be too strong for the constitution of this state. But the truth is, that both of them contain all, which in relation to their objects, is reasonably to be desired.

I go further, and affirm that bills of rights, in the sense and in the extent in which they are contended for, are not only unnecessary in the proposed constitution, but would even be dangerous. They would contain various exceptions to powers which are not granted; and on this very account, would afford a colourable pretext to claim more than were granted. For why declare that things shall not be done which there is no power to do? Why for instance, should it be said, that the liberty of the press shall not be restrained, when no power is given by which restrictions may be imposed? I will not contend that such a provision would confer a regulating power; but it is evident that it would furnish, to men disposed to usurp, a plausible pretence for claiming that power. They might urge with a semblance of reason, that the constitution ought not to be charged with the absurdity of providing against the abuse of an authority, which was not given, and that the provision against restraining the liberty of the press afforded a clear implication, that a power to prescribe proper regulations concerning it, was intended to be vested in the national government. This may serve as a specimen of the numerous handles which would be given to the doctrine of constructive powers, by the indulgence of an injudicious zeal for bills of rights.

On the subject of the liberty of the press, as much has been said, I cannot forbear adding a remark or two: In the first place, I observe that there is not a syllable concerning it in the constitution of this state, and in the next, I contend that whatever has been said about it in that of any other state, amounts to nothing. What signifies a declaration that "the liberty of the press shall be inviolably preserved?" What is the liberty of the press? Who can give it any definition which would not leave the utmost latitude for evasion? I hold it to be impracticable; and from this, I infer, that its security, whatever fine declarations may be inserted in any constitution respecting it, must altogether depend on public opinion, and on the general spirit of the people and of the government.* And here, after all, as intimated upon another occasion, must we seek for the only solid basis of all our rights.

There remains but one other view of this matter to conclude the point. The truth is, after all the declamation we have heard, that the constitution is itself in every rational sense, and to every useful purpose, A BILL OF RIGHTS. The several bills of rights, in Great-Britain, form its constitution, and conversely the constitution of each state is its bill of rights. And the proposed constitution, if adopted, will be the bill of rights of the union. Is it one object of a bill of rights to declare and specify the political privileges of the citizens in the structure and administration of the government? This is done in the most ample and precise manner in the plan of the convention, comprehending various precautions for the public security, which are not to be found in any of the state constitutions. Is another object of a bill of rights to define certain immunities and modes of proceeding, which are relative to personal and private concerns? This we have seen has also been attended to, in a variety of cases, in the same plan. Adverting therefore to the substantial meaning of a bill of rights, it is absurd to allege that it is not to be found in the work of the convention. It may be said that it does not go far enough, though it will not be easy to make this appear; but it can with no propriety be contended that there is no such thing. It certainly must be immaterial what mode is observed as to the order of declaring the rights of the citizens, if they are to be found in any part of the instrument which establishes

---

*To show that there is a power in the constitution by which the liberty of the press may be affected, recourse has been had to the power of taxation. It is said that duties may be laid upon publications so high as to amount to a prohibition. I know not by what logic it could be maintained that the declarations in the state constitutions, in favour of the freedom of the press, would be a constitutional impediment to the imposition of duties upon publications by the state legislatures. It cannot certainly be pretended that any degree of duties, however low, would be an abrigement of the liberty of the press. We know that newspapers are taxed in Great-Britain, and yet it is notorious that the press no where enjoys greater liberty than in that country. And if duties of any kind may be laid without a violation of that liberty, it is evident that the extent must depend on legislative discretion, regulated by public opinion; so that after all, general declarations respecting the liberty of the press will give it no greater security than it will have without them. The same invasions of it may be effected under the state constitutions which contain those declarations through the means of taxation, as under the proposed constitution which has nothing of the kind. It would be quite as significant to declare that government ought to be free, that taxes ought not to be excessive, &c., as that the liberty of the press ought not to be restrained.

the government. And hence it must be apparent that much of what has been said on this subject rests merely on verbal and nominal distinctions, which are entirely foreign from the substance of the thing.

39

PATRICK HENRY, VIRGINIA RATIFYING CONVENTION
5–16 June 1788

Storing 5.16.2, 24, 36–37

[*5 June*]

A trifling minority may reject the most salutary amendments. Is this an easy mode of securing the public liberty? It is, Sir, a most fearful situation, when the most contemptible minority can prevent the alteration of the most oppressive Government; for it may in many respects prove to be such: Is this the spirit of republicanism? What, Sir, is the genius of democracy? Let me read that clause of the Bill of Rights of Virginia, which relates to this: 3d cl. "That Government is or ought to be instituted for the common benefit, protection, and security of the people, nation, or community: Of all the various modes and forms of Government, that is best which is capable of producing the greatest degree of happiness and safety, and is most effectually secured against the danger of mal-administration, and *that whenever any Government shall be found inadequate, or contrary to these purposes, a majority of the community hath, an undubitable, unalienable and indefeasible right to reform, alter, or abolish it, in such manner as shall be judged most conducive to the public weal.*" This, Sir, is the language of democracy; that a majority of the community have a right to alter their Government when found to be oppressive: But how different is the genius of your new Constitution from this? How different from the sentiments of freemen, that a contemptible minority can prevent the good of the majority? If then Gentlemen standing on this ground, are come to that point, that they are willing to bind themselves and their posterity to be oppressed, I am amazed and inexpressibly astonished.

[*12 June*]

We are told that all powers not given are reserved. I am sorry to bring forth hackneyed observations. But, Sir, important truths lose nothing of their validity or weight, by frequency of repetition. The English history is frequently recurred to by Gentlemen. Let us advert to the conduct of the people of that country. The people of England lived without a declaration of rights, till the war in the time of Charles 1st. That King made usurpations upon the rights of the people. Those rights were in a great measure before that time undefined. Power and privilege then depended on implication and logical discussion. Though the declaration of rights was obtained from that King, his usurpations cost him his life. The limits between the liberty of the people, and the prerogative of the King, were still not clearly defined. The rights of the people continued to be violated till the Steward family was banished in the year 1688. The people of England magnanimously defended their rights, banished the tyrant, and prescribed to William Prince of Orange, *by the Bill of Rights*, on what terms he should reign. And this Bill of Rights put an end to all construction and implication. Before this, Sir, the situation of the public liberty of England was dreadful. For upwards of a century the nation was involved in every kind of calamity, till the Bill of Rights put an end to all, by defining the rights of the people, and limiting the King's prerogative. Give me leave to add (if I can add any thing to so splendid an example) the conduct of the American people. They Sir, thought *a Bill of Rights* necessary. It is alledged that several States, in the formation of their governments, omitted a Bill of Rights. To this I answer, that they had the substance of a Bill of Rights contained in their Constitutions, which is the same thing. I believe that Connecticut has preserved by her Constitution her royal charter, which clearly defines and secures the great rights of mankind—Secure to us the great important rights of humanity, and I care not in what form it is done. Of what advantage is it to the American Congress to take away this great and general security? I ask of what advantage is it to the public or to Congress to drag an unhappy debtor, not for the sake of justice; but to gratify the malice of the plaintiff, with his witnesses to the Federal Court, from a great distance? What was the principle that actuated the Convention in proposing to put such dangerous powers in the hands of any one? Why is the trial by jury taken away? All the learned arguments that have been used on this occasion do not prove that it is secured. Even the advocates for the plan do not all concur in the certainty of its security. Wherefore is religious liberty not secured? One Honorable Gentleman who favors adoption, said that he had had his fears on the subject. If I can well recollect, he informed us that he was perfectly satisfied by the powers of reasoning (with which he is so happily endowed) that those fears were not well grounded. There is many a religious man who knows nothing of argumentative reasoning;— there are many of our most worthy citizens, who cannot go through all the labyrinths of syllogistic argumentative deductions, when they think that the rights of conscience are invaded. This sacred right ought not to depend on constructive logical reasoning. When we see men of such talents and learning, compelled to use their utmost abilities to convince themselves that there is no danger, is it not sufficient to make us tremble? Is it not sufficient to fill the minds of the ignorant part of men with fear? If Gentlemen believe that the apprehensions of men will be quieted, they are mistaken; since our best informed men are in doubt with respect to the security of our rights. Those who are not so well informed will spurn at the Government. When our common citizens, who are not possessed with such extensive knowledge and abilities, are called upon to change their Bill of Rights, (which in plain unequivocal terms, secures their most valuable rights and privileges) for construction and implication, will they implicitly acquiesce? Our Declaration of Rights tells us, "That all men are by nature free and independent, &c." (Here Mr. *Henry* read the Declaration of Rights.) Will they exchange these Rights for logical reasons? If you had a thousand acres of land, dependent on this, would you be satisfied with logical construction? Would you depend upon a title of so disputable a nature? The present opinions of individuals will be buried in entire oblivion when those rights will be thought of. That sacred and lovely thing Religion, ought not to rest on the ingenuity of logical deduction. Holy Religion, Sir, will be prostituted to the lowest purposes of human policy. What has been more productive of mischief among mankind than Religious disputes. Then here, Sir, is the foundation for such disputes, when it requires learning and logical deduction to perceive that religious liberty is secure.

[*16 June*]

I observed already, that the sense of the European nations, and particularly Great-Britain, is against the construction of rights being retained, which are not *expressly* relinquished. I repeat, that all nations have adopted this construction—That all rights not expressly and unequivocally reserved to the people, are impliedly and incidentally relinquished to rulers; as necessarily inseparable from the delegated powers. It is so in Great-Britain: For every possible right which is not reserved to the people by some express provision or compact, is within the King's prerogative. It is so in that country which is said to be in such full possession of freedom. It is so in Spain, Germany, and other parts of the world. Let us consider the sentiments which have been entertained by the people of America on this subject. At the revolution, it must be admitted, that it was their sense to put down those great rights which ought in all countries to be held inviolable and sacred. Virginia did so we all remember. She made a compact to reserve, expressly, certain rights. When fortified with full, adequate, and abundant representation, was she satisfied with that representation? No.—She most cautiously and guardedly reserved and secured those invaluable, inestimable rights and privileges, which no people, inspired with the least glow of the patriotic love of liberty, ever did, or ever can, abandon. She is called upon now to abandon them, and dissolve that compact which secured them to her. She is called upon to accede to another compact which most infallibly supercedes and annihilates her present one. Will she do it?—This is the question. If you intend to reserve your unalienable rights, you must have the most express stipulation. For if implication be allowed, you are ousted of those rights. If the people do not think it necessary to reserve them, they will be supposed to be given up. How were the Congressional rights defined when the people of America united by a confederacy to defend their liberties and rights against the tyrannical attempts of Great-Britain? The States were not then contented with implied reservation. No, Mr. Chairman. It was expressly declared in our Confederation that every right was retained by the States respectively, which was not given up to the Government of the United States. But there is no such thing here. You therefore by a natural and unavoidable implication, give up your rights to the General Government. Your own

example furnishes an argument against it. If you give up these powers, without a Bill of Rights, you will exhibit the most absurd thing to mankind that ever the world saw—A Government that has abandoned all its powers—The powers of direct taxation, the sword, and the purse. You have disposed of them to Congress, without a Bill of Rights—without check, limitation, or controul. And still you have checks and guards—still you keep barriers—pointed where? Pointed against your weakened, prostrated, enervated State Government! You have a Bill of Rights to defend you against the State Government, which is bereaved of all power; and yet you have none against Congress, though in full and exclusive possession of all power! You arm youselves against the weak and defenceless, and expose yourselves naked to the armed and powerful. Is not this a conduct of unexampled absurdity? What barriers have you to oppose to this most strong energetic Government? To that Government you have nothing to oppose. All your defence is given up. This is a real actual defect. . . .

And can any man think it troublesome, when we can by a small interference prevent our rights from being lost?— If you will, like the Virginian Government, give them knowledge of the extent of the rights retained by the people, and the powers themselves, they will, if they be honest men, thank you for it.—Will they not wish to go on sure grounds?—But if you leave them otherwise, they will not know how to proceed; and being in a state of uncertainty, they will assume rather than give up powers by implication. A Bill of Rights may be summed up in a few words. What do they tell us?—That our rights are reserved.— Why not say so? Is it because it will consume too much paper? Gentlemen's reasonings against a Bill of Rights, do not satisfy me. Without saying which has the right side, it remains doubtful. A Bill of Rights is a favourite thing with the Virginians, and the people of the other States likewise. It may be their prejudice, but the Government ought to suit their geniuses, otherwise its operation will be unhappy. A Bill of Rights, even if its necessity be doubtful, will exclude the possibility of dispute, and with great submission, I think the best way is to have no dispute. In the present Constitution, they are restrained from issuing general warrants to search suspected places, or seize persons not named, without evidence of the commission of the fact, &c. There was certainly some celestial influence governing those who deliberated on that Constitution:—For they have with the most cautious and enlightened circumspection, guarded those indefeasible rights, which ought ever to be held sacred. The officers of Congress may come upon you, fortified with all the terrors of paramount federal authority.—Excisemen may come in multitudes:—For the limitation of their numbers no man knows.—They may, unless the General Government be restrained by a Bill of Rights, or some similar restriction, go into your cellars and rooms, and search, ransack and measure, everything you eat, drink and wear. They ought to be restrained within proper bounds. With respect to the freedom of the press, I need say nothing; for it is hoped that the Gentlemen who shall compose Congress, will take care as little as possible, to infringe the rights of human nature.—This will result from their integrity. They should from prudence, abstain from violating the rights of their constituents. They are not however expressly restrained.— But whether they will intermeddle with that palladium of our liberties or not, I leave you to determine.

40

EDMUND RANDOLPH, VIRGINIA RATIFYING
CONVENTION
9, 17 June 1788
Elliot 3:191, 464–67

[*9 June*]

Our situation is radically different from that of the people of England. What have we to do with bills of rights? Six or seven states have none. Massachusetts has declared her bill of rights as no part of her Constitution. Virginia has a bill of rights, but it is no part of her Constitution. By not saying whether it is paramount to the Constitution or not, it has left us in confusion. Is the bill of rights consistent with the Constitution? Why, then, is it not inserted in the Constitution? Does it add any thing to the Constitution? Why is it not in the Constitution? Does it except any thing from the Constitution? Why not put the exceptions in the Constitution? Does it oppose the Constitution? This will produce mischief. The judges will dispute which is paramount. Some will say, the bill of rights is paramount: others will say, that the Constitution, being subsequent in point of time, must be paramount. A bill of rights, therefore, accurately speaking, is quite useless, if not dangerous to a republic.

[*17 June*]

If it would not fatigue the house too far, I would go back to the question of reserved rights. The gentleman supposes that complete and unlimited legislation is vested in the Congress of the United States. This supposition is founded on false reasoning. What is the present situation of this state? She has possession of all rights of sovereignty, except those given to the Confederation. She *must* delegate powers to the confederate government. It is necessary for her public happiness. Her weakness compels her to confederate with the twelve other governments. She trusts certain powers to the general government, in order to support, protect, and defend the Union. Now, is there not a demonstrable difference between the principle of the state government and of the general government? There is not a word said, in the state government, of the powers given to it, because they are general. But in the general Constitution, its powers are enumerated. Is it not, then, fairly deducible, that it has no power but what is expressly given it?—for if its powers were to be general, an enumeration would be needless.

But the insertion of the negative *restrictions* has given cause of triumph, it seems, to gentlemen. They suppose that it demonstrates that Congress are to have powers by implication. I will meet them on that ground. I persuade myself that every exception here mentioned is an exception, not from general powers, but from the particular powers therein vested. To what power in the general government is the exception made respecting the importation of negroes? Not from a general power, but from a particular power expressly enumerated. This is an exception from the power given them of regulating commerce. He asks, Where is the power to which the prohibition of suspending the *habeas corpus* is an exception? I contend that, by virtue of the power given to Congress to regulate courts, they could suspend the writ of *habeas corpus*. This is therefore an exception to that power.

The 3d restriction is, that no bill of attainder, or *ex post facto* law, shall be passed. This is a manifest exception to another power. We know well that attainders and *ex post facto* laws have always been the engines of criminal jurisprudence. This is, therefore, an exception to the criminal jurisdiction vested in that body.

. . . . .

On the subject of a bill of rights, the want of which has been complained of, I will observe that it has been sanctified by such reverend authority, that I feel some difficulty in going against it. I shall not, however, be deterred from giving my opinion on this occasion, let the consequence be what it may. At the beginning of the war, we had no certain bill of rights; for our charter cannot be considered as a bill of rights; it is nothing more than an investiture, in the hands of the Virginia citizens, of those rights which belonged to British subjects. When the British thought proper to infringe our rights, was it not necessary to mention, in our Constitution, those rights which ought to be paramount to the power of the legislature? Why is the bill of rights distinct from the Constitution? I consider bills of rights in this view—that the government should use them, when there is a departure from its fundamental principles, in order to restore them.

This is the true sense of a bill of rights. If it be consistent with the Constitution, or contain additional rights, why not put it in the Constitution? If it be repugnant to the Constitution, here will be a perpetual scene of warfare between them. The honorable gentleman has praised the bill of rights of Virginia, and called it his guardian angel, and vilified this Constitution for not having it. Give me leave to make a distinction between the representatives of the people of a particular country, who are appointed as the ordinary legislature, having no limitation to their powers, and another body arising from a compact, and with certain delineated powers. Were a bill of rights necessary in the former, it would not be in the latter; for the best security that can be in the latter is the express enumeration of its powers.

41

SAMUEL CHASE TO JOHN LAMB
13 June 1788
Leake 310

I was always averse from the adoption of the proposed Constitution, unless certain amendments, to declare and secure the great and essential rights of the people, could be previously obtained; because I thought, if they could not be procured before the ratification, they, very probably, could not be obtained afterwards; and the conduct of the advocates of the government confirm my opinion. I am convinced that the principal characters who support the government, will not agree to any amendments. A declaration of rights alone will be of no essential service. Some of the powers must be abridged, or public liberty will be endangered, and, in time, destroyed.

I have no hopes that any attempts will be made to obtain previous alterations, and I fear any attempt, after ratification, will be without effect. I consider the Constitution as radically defective in this essential; the bulk of the people can have nothing to say to it. The government is *not* a government of the people. It is *not* a government of representation. The people do *not* choose the House of Representatives. A right of election is declared, but it can not be exercised. It is a useless, nugatory right. By no mode of choice, by the people at large, or in districts, can they choose representatives. The right is immediate and given to all the people, but it is impracticable to be exercised by them.

I believe a very great majority of the people of this state are in favor of amendments, but they are depressed and inactive. They have lost all their former spirit and seem ready to submit to any master.

42

GEORGE MASON, VIRGINIA RATIFYING CONVENTION
16 June 1788
Papers 3:1084–85

MR. GEORGE MASON, still thought that there ought to be some express declaration in the constitution, asserting that rights not given to the general government, were retained by the states. He apprehended that unless this was done, many valuable and important rights would be concluded to be given up by implication. All governments were drawn from the people, though many were perverted to their oppression. The government of Virginia, he remarked, was drawn from the people; yet there were certain great and important rights, which the people by their bill of rights declared to be paramount to the power of the legislature. He asked, why should it not be so in this constitution? Was it because we were more substantially represented in it, than in the state government? If in the state government, where the people were substantially and fully represented, it was necessary that the great rights of human nature should be secure from the enc[r]oachments of the legislature; he asked, if it was not more necessary in this government, where they were but inadequately represented? He declared, that artful sophistry and evasions could not satisfy him. He could see no clear distinction between rights relinquished by a positive grant, and lost by implication. Unless there were a bill of rights, implication might swallow up all our rights.

43

VIRGINIA RATIFYING CONVENTION, PROPOSED AMENDMENTS TO THE CONSTITUTION
27 June 1788
Elliot 3:657–61

MR. WYTHE reported, from the committee appointed, such *amendments* to the proposed Constitution of government for the United States as were by them deemed necessary to be recommended to the consideration of the Congress which shall first assemble under the said Constitution, to be acted upon according to the mode prescribed in the 5th article thereof; and he read the same in his place, and afterwards delivered them in at the clerk's table, where the same were again read, and are as follows:—

"That there be a declaration or bill of rights asserting, and securing from encroachment, the essential and unalienable rights of the people, in some such manner as the following:—

"1st. That there are certain natural rights, of which men, when they form a social compact, cannot deprive or divest their posterity; among which are the enjoyment of life and liberty, with the means of acquiring, possessing, and protecting property, and pursuing and obtaining happiness and safety.

"2d. That all power is naturally invested in, and consequently derived from, the people; that magistrates therefore are their *trustees* and *agents*, at all times amenable to them.

"3d. That government ought to be instituted for the common benefit, protection, and security of the people; and that the doctrine of non-resistance against arbitrary power and oppression is absurd, slavish, and destructive to the good and happiness of mankind.

"4th. That no man or set of men are entitled to separate or exclusive public emoluments or privileges from the community, but in consideration of public services, which not being descendible, neither ought the offices of magistrate, legislator, or judge, or any other public office, to be hereditary.

"5th. That the legislative, executive, and judicial powers of government should be separate and distinct; and, that the members of the two first may be restrained from oppression by feeling and participating the public burdens, they should, at fixed periods, be reduced to a private station, return into the mass of the people, and the vacancies be supplied by certain and regular elections, in which all or any part of the former members to be eligible or ineligible, as the rules of the Constitution of government, and the laws, shall direct.

"6th. That the elections of representatives in the legislature ought to be free and frequent, and all men having sufficient evidence of permanent common interest with, and attachment to, the community, ought to have the right of suffrage; and no aid, charge, tax, or fee, can be set, rated, or levied, upon the people without their own consent, or that of their representatives, so elected; nor can they be bound by any law to which they have not, in like manner, assented, for the public good.

"7th. That all power of suspending laws, or the execution of laws, by any authority, without the consent of the representatives of the people in the legislature, is injurious to their rights, and ought not to be exercised.

"8th. That, in all criminal and capital prosecutions, a man hath a right to demand the cause and nature of his accusation, to be confronted with the accusers and witnesses, to call for evidence, and be allowed counsel in his favor, and to a fair and speedy trial by an impartial jury of his vicinage, without whose unanimous consent he cannot be found guilty, (except in the government of the land and naval forces;) nor can he be compelled to give evidence against himself.

"9th. That no freeman ought to be taken, imprisoned, or disseized of his freehold, liberties, privileges, or franchises, or outlawed, or exiled, or in any manner destroyed, or deprived of his life, liberty, or property, but by the law of the land.

"10th. That every freeman restrained of his liberty is entitled to a remedy, to inquire into the lawfulness thereof, and to remove the same, if unlawful, and that such remedy ought not to be denied nor delayed.

"11th. That, in controversies respecting property, and in suits between man and man, the ancient trial by jury is one of the greatest securities to the rights of the people, and to remain sacred and inviolable.

"12th. That every freeman ought to find a certain remedy, by recourse to the laws, for all injuries and wrongs he may receive in his person, property, or character. He ought to obtain right and justice freely, without sale, completely and without denial, promptly and without delay; and that all establishments or regulations contravening these rights are oppressive and unjust.

"13th. That excessive bail ought not to be required, nor excessive fines imposed, nor cruel and unusual punishments inflicted.

"14th. That every freeman has a right to be secure from all unreasonable searches and seizures of his person, his papers, and property; all warrants, therefore, to search suspected places, or seize any freeman, his papers, or property, without information on oath (or affirmation of a person religiously scrupulous of taking an oath) of legal and sufficient cause, are grievous and oppressive; and all general warrants to search suspected places, or to apprehend any suspected person, without specially naming or describing the place or person, are dangerous, and ought not to be granted.

"15th. That the people have a right peaceably to assemble together to consult for the common good, or to instruct their representatives; and that every freeman has a right to petition or apply to the legislature for redress of grievances.

"16th. That the people have a right to freedom of speech, and of writing and publishing their sentiments; that the freedom of the press is one of the greatest bulwarks of liberty, and ought not to be violated.

"17th. That the people have a right to keep and bear arms; that a well-regulated militia, composed of the body of the people trained to arms, is the proper, natural, and safe defence of a free state; that standing armies, in time of peace, are dangerous to liberty, and therefore ought to be avoided, as far as the circumstances and protection of the community will admit; and that, in all cases, the military should be under strict subordination to, and governed by, the civil power.

"18th. That no soldier in time of peace ought to be quartered in any house without the consent of the owner, and in time of war in such manner only as the law directs.

"19th. That any person religiously scrupulous of bearing arms ought to be exempted, upon payment of an equivalent to employ another to bear arms in his stead.

"20th. That religion, or the duty which we owe to our Creator, and the manner of discharging it, can be directed only by reason and conviction, not by force or violence; and therefore all men have an equal, natural, and unalienable right to the free exercise of religion, according to the dictates of conscience, and that no particular religious sect or society ought to be favored or established, by law, in preference to others."

Amendments to the Constitution.

"1st. That each state in the Union shall respectively retain every power, jurisdiction, and right, which is not by this Constitution delegated to the Congress of the United States, or to the departments of the federal government.

"2d. That there shall be one representative for every thirty thousand, according to the enumeration or census mentioned in the Constitution, until the whole number of representatives amounts to two hundred; after which, that number shall be continued or increased, as Congress shall direct, upon the principles fixed in the Constitution, by apportioning the representatives of each state to some greater number of people, from time to time, as population increases.

"3d. When the Congress shall lay direct taxes or excises, they shall immediately inform the executive power of each state, of the quota of such state, according to the census herein directed, which is proposed to be thereby raised; and if the legislature of any state shall pass a law which shall be effectual for raising such quota at the time required by Congress, the taxes and excises laid by Congress shall not be collected in such state.

"4th. That the members of the Senate and House of Representatives shall be ineligible to, and incapable of holding, any civil office under the authority of the United States, during the time for which they shall respectively be elected.

"5th. That the journals of the proceedings of the Senate and House of Representatives shall be published at least once in every year. except such parts thereof, relating to treaties, alliances, or military operations, as, in their judgment, require secrecy.

"6th. That a regular statement and account of the receipts and expenditures of public money shall be published at least once a year.

"7th. That no commercial treaty shall be ratified without the concurrence of two thirds of the whole number of the members of the Senate; and no treaty ceding, contracting, restraining, or suspending, the territorial rights or claims of the United States, or any of them, or their, or any of their rights or claims to fishing in the American seas, or navigating the American rivers, shall be made, but in cases of the most urgent and extreme necessity; nor shall any such treaty be ratified without the concurrence of three fourths of the whole number of the members of both houses respectively.

"8th. That no navigation law, or law regulating commerce, shall be passed without the consent of two thirds of the members present, in both houses.

"9th. That no standing army, or regular troops, shall be raised, or kept up, in time of peace, without the consent of two thirds of the members present, in both houses.

"10th. That no soldier shall be enlisted for any longer term than four years, except in time of war, and then for no longer term than the continuance of the war.

"11th. That each state respectively shall have the power to provide for organizing, arming, and disciplining its own militia, whensoever Congress shall omit or neglect to provide for the same. That the militia shall not be subject to martial law, except when in actual service, in time of war, invasion, or rebellion; and when not in the actual service of the United States, shall be subject only to such fines, penalties, and punishments, as shall be directed or inflicted by the laws of its own state.

"12th. That the exclusive power of legislation given to Congress over the federal town and its adjacent district, and other places, purchased or to be purchased by Congress of any of the states, shall extend only to such regulations as respect the police and good government thereof.

"13th. That no person shall be capable of being President of the United States for more than eight years in any term of sixteen years.

"14th. That the judicial power of the United States shall be vested in one Supreme Court, and in such courts of admiralty as Congress may from time to time ordain and establish in any of the different states. The judicial power shall extend to all cases in law and equity arising under treaties made, or which shall be made, under the authority of the United States; to all cases affecting ambassadors, other foreign ministers, and consuls; to all cases of admi-

ralty and maritime jurisdiction; to controversies to which the United States shall be a party; to controversies between two or more states, and between parties claiming lands under the grants of different states. In all cases affecting ambassadors, other foreign ministers, and consuls, and those in which a state shall be a party, the Supreme Court shall have original jurisdiction; in all other cases before mentioned, the Supreme Court shall have appellate jurisdiction, as to matters of law only, except in cases of equity, and of admiralty, and maritime jurisdiction, in which the Supreme Court shall have appellate jurisdiction both as to law and fact, with such exceptions and under such regulations as the Congress shall make: but the judicial power of the United States shall extend to no case where the cause of action shall have originated before the ratification of the Constitution, except in disputes between states about their territory, disputes between persons claiming lands under the grants of different states, and suits for debts due to the United States.

"15th. That, in criminal prosecutions, no man shall be restrained in the exercise of the usual and accustomed right of challenging or excepting to the jury.

"16th. That Congress shall not alter, modify, or interfere in the times, places, or manner of holding elections for senators and representatives, or either of them, except when the legislature of any state shall neglect, refuse, or be disabled, by invasion or rebellion, to prescribe the same.

"17th. That those clauses which declare that Congress shall not exercise certain powers, be not interpreted, in any manner whatsoever, to extend the powers of Congress; but that they be construed either as making exceptions to the specified powers where this shall be the case, or otherwise, as inserted merely for greater caution.

"18th. That the laws ascertaining the compensation of senators and representatives for their services, be postponed, in their operation, until after the election of representatives immediately succeeding the passing thereof; that excepted which shall first be passed on the subject.

"19th. That some tribunal other than the Senate be provided for trying impeachments of senators.

"20th. That the salary of a judge shall not be increased or diminished during his continuance in office, otherwise than by general regulations of salary, which may take place on a revision of the subject at stated periods of not less than seven years, to commence from the time such salaries shall be first ascertained by Congress."

44

THOMAS TREDWELL, NEW YORK RATIFYING
CONVENTION
2 July 1788
Elliot 2:398–400

The first and grand leading, or rather misleading, principle in this debate, and on which the advocates for this system of unrestricted powers must chiefly depend for its support, is that, in forming a constitution, whatever powers are not expressly granted or given the government, are reserved to the people, or that rulers cannot exercise any powers but those expressly given to them by the Constitution. Let me ask the gentlemen who advanced this principle, whether the commission of a Roman dictator, which was in these few words—to take care that the state received no harm—does not come up fully to their ideas of an energetic government; or whether an invitation from the people to one or more to come and rule over them, would not clothe the rulers with sufficient powers. If so, the principle they advance is a false one. Besides, the absurdity of this principle will evidently appear, when we consider the great variety of objects to which the powers of the government must necessarily extend, and that an express enumeration of them all would probably fill as many volumes as Pool's Synopsis of the Critics. But we may reason with sufficient certainty on the subject, from the sense of all the public bodies in the United States, who had occasion to form new constitutions. They have uniformly acted upon a direct and contrary principle, not only in forming the state constitutions and the old Confederation, but also in forming this very Constitution, for we do not find in every state constitution express resolutions made in favor of the people; and it is clear that the late Convention at Philadelphia, whatever might have been the sentiments of some of its members, did not adopt the principle, for they have made certain reservations and restrictions, which, upon that principle, would have been totally useless and unnecessary; and can it be supposed that that wise body, whose only apology for the great ambiguity of many parts of that performance, and the total omission of some things which many esteem essential to the security of liberty, was a great desire of brevity, should so far sacrifice that great and important object, as to insert a number of provisions which they esteemed totally useless? Why is it said that the privilege of the writ of *habeas corpus* shall not be suspended, unless, in cases of rebellion or invasion, the public safety may require it? What clause in the Constitution, except this very clause itself, gives the general government a power to deprive us of that great privilege, so sacredly secured to us by our state constitutions? Why is it provided that no bill of attainder shall be passed, or that no title of nobility shall be granted? Are there any clauses in the Constitution extending the powers of the general government to these objects? Some gentlemen say that these, though not necessary, were inserted for greater caution. I could have wished, sir, that a greater caution had been used to secure to us the freedom of election, a sufficient and responsible representation, the freedom of the press, and the trial by jury both in civil and criminal cases.

These, sir, are the rocks on which the Constitution should have rested; no other foundation can any man lay, which will secure the sacred temple of freedom against the power of the great, the undermining arts of ambition, and the blasts of profane scoffers—for such there will be in every age—who will tell us that all religion is in vain; that is, that our political creeds, which have been handed down to us by our forefathers as sacredly as our Bibles, and for which more of them have suffered martyrdom than for the creed of the apostles, are all nonsense; who will tell us that paper constitutions are mere paper, and that parchment is but parchment, that jealousy of our rulers is a sin, &c. I could have wished also that sufficient caution had been used to secure to us our religious liberties, and to have prevented the general government from tyrannizing over our consciences by a religious establishment—a tyranny of all others most dreadful, and which will assuredly be exercised whenever it shall be thought necessary for the promotion and support of their political measures. It is ardently to be wished, sir, that these and other invaluable rights of freemen had been as cautiously secured as some of the paltry local interests of some of the individual states. But it appears to me, that, in forming this Constitution, we have run into the same error which the lawyers and Pharisees of old were charged with; that is, while we have secured the tithes of mint, anise, and cumin, we have neglected the weightier matters of the law, judgment, mercy, and faith.

45

JAMES IREDELL, NORTH CAROLINA RATIFYING CONVENTION
28 July 1788
Elliot 4:148–49

With regard to a bill of rights, this is a notion originating in England, where no written constitution is to be found, and the authority of their government is derived from the most remote antiquity. Magna Charta itself is no constitution, but a solemn instrument ascertaining certain rights of individuals, by the legislature for the time being; and every article of which the legislature may at any time alter. This, and a bill of rights also, the invention of later times, were occasioned by great usurpations of the crown, contrary, as was conceived, to the principles of their government, about which there was a variety of opinions. But neither that instrument, nor any other instrument, ever attempted to abridge the authority of Parliament, which is supposed to be without any limitation whatever. Had their constitution been fixed and certain, a bill of rights would have been useless, for the constitution would have shown plainly the extent of that authority which they were disputing about. Of what use, therefore, can a bill of rights be in this Constitution, where the people expressly declare how much power they do give, and consequently retain all they do not? It is a declaration of particular powers by the people to their representatives, for particular purposes. It may be considered as a great power of attorney, under which no power can be exercised but what is expressly given. Did any man ever hear, before, that at the end of a power of attorney it was said that the attorney should not exercise more power than was there given him? Suppose, for instance, a man had lands in the counties of Anson and

Caswell, and he should give another a power of attorney to sell his lands in Anson, would the other have any authority to sell the lands in Caswell?—or could he, without absurdity, say, "'Tis true you have not expressly authorized me to sell the lands in Caswell; but as you had lands there, and did not say I should not, I thought I might as well sell those lands as the other." A bill of rights, as I conceive, would not only be incongruous, but dangerous. No man, let his ingenuity be what it will, could enumerate all the individual rights not relinquished by this Constitution. Suppose, therefore, an enumeration of a great many, but an omission of some, and that, long after all traces of our present disputes were at an end, any of the omitted rights should be invaded, and the invasion be complained of; what would be the plausible answer of the government to such a complaint? Would they not naturally say, "We live at a great distance from the time when this Constitution was established. We can judge of it much better by the ideas of it entertained at the time, than by any ideas of our own. The bill of rights, passed at that time, showed that the people did not think every power retained which was not given, else this bill of rights was not only useless, but absurd. But we are not at liberty to charge an absurdity upon our ancestors, who have given such strong proofs of their good sense, as well as their attachment to liberty. So long as the rights enumerated in the bill of rights remain unviolated, you have no reason to complain. This is not one of them." Thus a bill of rights might operate as a snare rather than a protection. If we had formed a general legislature, with undefined powers, a bill of rights would not only have been proper, but necessary; and it would have then operated as an exception to the legislative authority in such particulars. It has this effect in respect to some of the American constitutions, where the powers of legislation are general. But where they are powers of a particular nature, and expressly defined, as in the case of the Constitution before us, I think, for the reasons I have given, a bill of rights is not only unnecessary, but would be absurd and dangerous.

46

THOMAS JEFFERSON TO JAMES MADISON
31 July 1788
Papers 13:442–43

I sincerely rejoice at the acceptance of our new constitution by nine states. It is a good canvas, on which some strokes only want retouching. What these are, I think are sufficiently manifested by the general voice from North to South, which calls for a bill of rights. It seems pretty generally understood that this should go to Juries, Habeas corpus, Standing armies, Printing, Religion and Monopolies. I conceive there may be difficulty in finding general modification of these suited to the habits of all the states. But if such cannot be found then it is better to establish trials by jury, the right of Habeas corpus, freedom of the press and freedom of religion in all cases, and to abolish standing armies in time of peace, and Monopolies, in all cases, than not to do it in any. The few cases wherein these things may do evil, cannot be weighed against the multitude wherein the want of them will do evil. In disputes between a foreigner and a native, a trial by jury may be improper. But if this exception cannot be agreed to, the remedy will be to model the jury by giving the medietas linguae in civil as well as criminal cases. Why suspend the Hab. corp. in insurrections and rebellions? The parties who may be arrested may be charged instantly with a well defined crime. Of course the judge will remand them. If the publick safety requires that the government should have a man imprisoned on less probable testimony in those than in other emergencies; let him be taken and tried, retaken and retried, while the necessity continues, only giving him redress against the government for damages. Examine the history of England: see how few of the cases of the suspension of the Habeas corpus law have been worthy of that suspension. They have been either real treasons wherein the parties might as well have been charged at once, or sham-plots where it was shameful they should ever have been suspected. Yet for the few cases wherein the suspension of the hab. corp. has done real good, that operation is now become habitual, and the minds of the nation almost prepared to live under it's constant suspension. A declaration that the federal government will never restrain the presses from printing any thing they please, will not take away the liability of the printers for false facts printed. The declaration that religious faith shall be unpunished, does not give impunity to criminal acts dictated by religious error. The saying there shall be no monopolies lessens the incitements to ingenuity, which is spurred on by the hope of a monopoly for a limited time, as of 14. years; but the benefit even of limited monopolies is too doubtful to be opposed to that of their general suppression. If no check can be found to keep the number of standing troops within safe bounds, while they are tolerated as far as necessary, abandon them altogether, discipline well the militia, and guard the magazines with them. More than magazine-guards will be useless if few, and dangerous if many. No European nation can ever send against us such a regular army as we need fear, and it is hard if our militia are not equal to those of Canada or Florida. My idea then is, that tho' proper exceptions to these general rules are desirable and probably practicable, yet if the exceptions cannot be agreed on, the establishment of the rules in all cases will do ill in very few. I hope therefore a bill of rights will be formed to guard the people against the federal government, as they are already guarded against their state governments in most instances.

47

JAMES MADISON TO THOMAS JEFFERSON
17 Oct. 1788
Papers 11:297–300

The little pamphlet herewith inclosed will give you a collective view of the alterations which have been proposed for the new Constitution. Various and numerous as they appear they certainly omit many of the true grounds of opposition. The articles relating to Treaties—to paper money, and to contracts, created more enemies than all the errors in the System positive & negative put together. It is true nevertheless that not a few, particularly in Virginia have contended for the proposed alterations from the most honorable & patriotic motives; and that among the advocates for the Constitution, there are some who wish for further guards to public liberty & individual rights. As far as these may consist of a constitutional declaration of the most essential rights, it is probable they will be added; though there are many who think such addition unnecessary, and not a few who think it misplaced in such a Constitution. There is scarce any point on which the party in opposition is so much divided as to its importance and its propriety. My own opinion has always been in favor of a bill of rights; provided it be so framed as not to imply powers not meant to be included in the enumeration. At the same time I have never thought the omission a material defect, nor been anxious to supply it even by *subsequent* amendment, for any other reason than that it is anxiously desired by others. I have favored it because I supposed it might be of use, and if properly executed could not be of disservice. I have not viewed it in an important light 1. because I conceive that in a certain degree, though not in the extent argued by Mr. Wilson, the rights in question are reserved by the manner in which the federal powers are granted. 2 because there is great reason to fear that a positive declaration of some of the most essential rights could not be obtained in the requisite latitude. I am sure that the rights of Conscience in particular, if submitted to public definition would be narrowed much more than they are likely ever to be by an assumed power. One of the objections in New England was that the Constitution by prohibiting religious tests opened a door for Jews Turks & infidels. 3. because the limited powers of the federal Government and the jealousy of the subordinate Governments, afford a security which has not existed in the case of the State Governments, and exists in no other. 4 because experience proves the inefficacy of a bill of rights on those occasions when its controul is most needed. Repeated violations of these parchment barriers have been committed by overbearing majorities in every State. In Virginia I have seen the bill of rights violated in every instance where it has been opposed to a popular current. Notwithstanding the explicit provision contained in that instrument for the rights of Conscience it is well known

that a religious establishment wd. have taken place in that State, if the legislative majority had found as they expected, a majority of the people in favor of the measure; and I am persuaded that if a majority of the people were now of one sect, the measure would still take place and on narrower ground than was then proposed, notwithstanding the additional obstacle which the law has since created. Wherever the real power in a Government lies, there is the danger of oppression. In our Governments the real power lies in the majority of the Community, and the invasion of private rights is *cheifly* to be apprehended, not from acts of Government contrary to the sense of its constituents, but from acts in which the Government is the mere instrument of the major number of the constituents. This is a truth of great importance, but not yet sufficiently attended to: and is probably more strongly impressed on my mind by facts, and reflections suggested by them, than on yours which has contemplated abuses of power issuing from a very different quarter. Wherever there is an interest and power to do wrong, wrong will generally be done, and not less readily by a powerful & interested party than by a powerful and interested prince. The difference, so far as it relates to the superiority of republics over monarchies, lies in the less degree of probability that interest may prompt abuses of power in the former than in the latter; and in the security in the former agst. oppression of more than the smaller part of the society, whereas in the [latter] it may be extended in a manner to the whole. The difference so far as it relates to the point in question—the efficacy of a bill of rights in controuling abuses of power—lies in this, that in a monarchy the latent force of the nation is superior to that of the sovereign, and a solemn charter of popular rights must have a great effect, as a standard for trying the validity of public acts, and a signal for rousing & uniting the superior force of the community; whereas in a popular Government, the political and physical power may be considered as vested in the same hands, that is in a majority of the people, and consequently the tyrannical will of the sovereign is not [to] be controuled by the dread of an appeal to any other force within the community. What use then it may be asked can a bill of rights serve in popular Governments? I answer the two following which though less essential than in other Governments, sufficiently recommend the precaution. 1. The political truths declared in that solemn manner acquire by degrees the character of fundamental maxims of free Government, and as they become incorporated with the national sentiment, counteract the impulses of interest and passion. 2. Altho' it be generally true as above stated that the danger of oppression lies in the interested majorities of the people rather than in usurped acts of the Government, yet there may be occasions on which the evil may spring from the latter sources; and on such, a bill of rights will be a good ground for an appeal to the sense of the community. Perhaps too there may be a certain degree of danger, that a succession of artful and ambitious rulers, may by gradual & well-timed advances, finally erect an independent Government on the subversion of liberty. Should this danger exist at all, it is prudent to guard agst. it, especially when the precaution can do no injury. At the same time I must own that I see no tendency in our governments to danger on that side. It has been remarked that there is a tendency in all Governments to an augmentation of power at the expence of liberty. But the remark as usually understood does not appear to me well founded. Power when it has attained a certain degree of energy and independence goes on generally to further degrees. But when below that degree, the direct tendency is to further degrees of relaxation, until the abuses of liberty beget a sudden transition to an undue degree of power. With this explanation the remark may be true; and in the latter sense only is it in my opinion applicable to the Governments in America. It is a melancholy reflection that liberty should be equally exposed to danger whether the Government have too much or too little power, and that the line which divides these extremes should be so inaccurately defined by experience.

Supposing a bill of rights to be proper the articles which ought to compose it, admit of much discussion. I am inclined to think that *absolute* restrictions in cases that are doubtful, or where emergencies may overrule them, ought to be avoided. The restrictions however strongly marked on paper will never be regarded when opposed to the decided sense of the public; and after repeated violations in extraordinary cases, they will lose even their ordinary efficacy. Should a Rebellion or insurrection alarm the people as well as the Government, and a suspension of the Hab. Corp. be dictated by the alarm, no written prohibitions on earth would prevent the measure. Should an army in time of peace be gradually established in our neighbourhood by Britn: or Spain, declarations on paper would have as little effect in preventing a standing force for the public safety. The best security agst. these evils is to remove the pretext for them. With regard to monopolies they are justly classed among the greatest nusances in Government. But is it clear that as encouragements to literary works and ingenious discoveries, they are not too valuable to be wholly renounced? Would it not suffice to reserve in all cases a right to the Public to abolish the privilege at a price to be specified in the grant of it? Is there not also infinitely less danger of this abuse in our Governments, than in most others? Monopolies are sacrifices of the many to the few. Where the power is in the few it is natural for them to sacrifice the many to their own partialities and corruptions. Where the power, as with us, is in the many not in the few, the danger can not be very great that the few will be thus favored. It is much more to be dreaded that the few will be unnecessarily sacrificed to the many.

48

JAMES MADISON TO GEORGE EVE
2 Jan. 1789
Papers 11:404–5

Being informed that reports prevail not only that I am opposed to any amendments whatever to the new federal

Constitution; but that I have ceased to be a friend to the rights of Conscience; and inferring from a conversation with my brother William, that you are disposed to contradict such reports as far as your knowledge of my sentiments may justify, I am led to trouble you with this communication of them. As a private Citizen it could not be my wish that erroneous opinions should be entertained, with respect to either of those points, particularly, with respect to religious liberty. But having been induced to offer my services to this district as its representative in the federal Legislature, considerations of a public nature make it proper that, with respect to both, my principles and views should be rightly understood.

I freely own that I have never seen in the Constitution as it now stands those serious dangers which have alarmed many respectable Citizens. Accordingly whilst it remained unratified, and it was necessary to unite the States in some one plan, I opposed all previous alterations as calculated to throw the States into dangerous contentions, and to furnish the secret enemies of the Union with an opportunity of promoting its dissolution. Circumstances are now changed: The Constitution is established on the ratifications of eleven States and a very great majority of the people of America; and amendments, if pursued with a proper moderation and in a proper mode, will be not only safe, but may serve the double purpose of satisfying the minds of well meaning opponents, and of providing additional guards in favour of liberty. Under this change of circumstances, it is my sincere opinion that the Constitution ought to be revised, and that the first Congress meeting under it, ought to prepare and recommend to the States for ratification, the most satisfactory provisions for all essential rights, particularly the rights of Conscience in the fullest latitude, the freedom of the press, trials by jury, security against general warrants &c. I think it will be proper also to provide expressly in the Constitution, for the periodical increase of the number of Representatives until the amount shall be entirely satisfactory; and to put the judiciary department into such a form as will render vexatious appeals impossible. There are sundry other alterations which are either eligible in themselves, or being at least safe, are recommended by the respect due to such as wish for them.

I have intimated that the amendments ought to be proposed by the first Congress. I prefer this mode to that of a General Convention, 1st. because it is the most expeditious mode. A convention must be delayed, until ⅔ of the State Legislatures shall have applied for one; and afterwards the amendments must be submitted to the States; whereas if the business be undertaken by Congress the amendments may be prepared and submitted in March next. 2dly. because it is the most certain mode. There are not a few States who will absolutely reject the proposal of a Convention, and yet not be averse to amendments in the other mode. Lastly, it is the safest mode. The Congress, who will be appointed to execute as well as to amend the Government, will probably be careful not to destroy or endanger it. A convention, on the other hand, meeting in the present ferment of parties, and containing perhaps insidious characters from different parts of America, would at least spread a general alarm, and be but too likely to turn every thing into confusion and uncertainty. It is to be observed however that the question concerning a General Convention, will not belong to the federal Legislature. If ⅔ of the States apply for one, Congress can not refuse to call it: if not, the other mode of amendments must be pursued.

49

THOMAS JEFFERSON TO JAMES MADISON
15 Mar. 1789
Papers 14:659–61

Your thoughts on the subject of the Declaration of rights in the letter of Oct. 17. I have weighed with great satisfaction. Some of them had not occurred to me before, but were acknoleged just in the moment they were presented to my mind. In the arguments in favor of a declaration of rights, you omit one which has great weight with me, the legal check which it puts into the hands of the judiciary. This is a body, which if rendered independent, and kept strictly to their own department merits great confidence for their learning and integrity. In fact what degree of confidence would be too much for a body composed of such men as Wythe, Blair, and Pendleton? On characters like these the "civium ardor prava jubentium" would make no impression. I am happy to find that on the whole you are a friend to this amendment. The Declaration of rights is like all other human blessings alloyed with some inconveniences, and not accomplishing fully it's object. But the good in this instance vastly overweighs the evil. I cannot refrain from making short answers to the objections which your letter states to have been raised. 1. That the rights in question are reserved by the manner in which the federal powers are granted. Answer. A constitutive act may certainly be so formed as to need no declaration of rights. The act itself has the force of a declaration as far as it goes: and if it goes to all material points nothing more is wanting. In the draught of a constitution which I had once a thought of proposing in Virginia, and printed afterwards, I endeavored to reach all the great objects of public liberty, and did not mean to add a declaration of rights. Probably the object was imperfectly executed: but the deficiencies would have been supplied by others in the course of discussion. But in a constitutive act which leaves some precious articles unnoticed, and raises implications against others, a declaration of rights becomes necessary by way of supplement. This is the case of our new federal constitution. This instrument forms us into one state as to certain objects, and gives us a legislative and executive body for these objects. It should therefore guard us against their abuses of power within the feild submitted to them. 2. A positive declaration of some essential rights could not be obtained in the requisite latitude. Answer. Half a loaf is better than no bread. If we cannot secure all our rights,

let us secure what we can. 3. The limited powers of the federal government and jealousy of the subordinate governments afford a security which exists in no other instance. Answer. The first member of this seems resolvable into the 1st. objection before stated. The jealousy of the subordinate governments is a precious reliance. But observe that those governments are only agents. They must have principles furnished them whereon to found their opposition. The declaration of rights will be the text whereby they will try all the acts of the federal government. In this view it is necessary to the federal government also: as by the same text they may try the opposition of the subordinate governments. 4. Experience proves the inefficacy of a bill of rights. True. But tho it is not absolutely efficacious under all circumstances, it is of great potency always, and rarely inefficacious. A brace the more will often keep up the building which would have fallen with that brace the less. There is a remarkeable difference between the characters of the Inconveniencies which attend a Declaration of rights, and those which attend the want of it. The inconveniences of the Declaration are that it may cramp government in it's useful exertions. But the evil of this is shortlived, moderate, and reparable. The inconveniencies of the want of a Declaration are permanent, afflicting and irreparable: they are in constant progression from bad to worse. The executive in our governments is not the sole, it is scarcely the principal object of my jealousy. The tyranny of the legislatures is the most formidable dread at present, and will be for long years. That of the executive will come in it's turn, but it will be at a remote period. I know there are some among us who would now establish a monarchy. But they are inconsiderable in number and weight of character. The rising race are all republicans. We were educated in royalism: no wonder if some of us retain that idolatry still. Our young people are educated in republicanism. An apostacy from that to royalism is unprecedented and impossible. I am much pleased with the prospect that a declaration of rights will be added: and hope it will be done in that way which will not endanger the whole frame of the government, or any essential part of it.

50

JAMES MADISON, HOUSE OF REPRESENTATIVES
8 June 1789
Papers 12:196–209

When I first hinted to the house my intention of calling their deliberations to this object, I mentioned the pressure of other important subjects, and submitted the propriety of postponing this till the more urgent business was dispatched; but finding that business not dispatched, when the order of the day for considering amendments arrived, I thought it a good reason for a farther delay, I moved the postponement accordingly. I am sorry the same reason still exists in some degree; but operates with less force when it is considered, that it is not now proposed to enter into a full and minute discussion of every part of the subject, but merely to bring it before the house, that our constituents may see we pay a proper attention to a subject they have much at heart; and if it does not give that full gratification which is to be wished, they will discover that it proceeds from the urgency of business of a very important nature. But if we continue to postpone from time to time, and refuse to let the subject come into view, it may occasion suspicions, which, though not well founded, may tend to inflame or prejudice the public mind, against our decisions: they may think we are not sincere in our desire to incorporate such amendments in the constitution as will secure those rights, which they consider as not sufficiently guarded. The applications for amendments come from a very respectable number of our constituents, and it is certainly proper for congress to consider the subject, in order to quiet that anxiety which prevails in the public mind: Indeed I think it would have been of advantage to the government, if it had been practicable to have made some propositions for amendments the first business we entered upon; it would stifle the voice of complaint, and make friends of many who doubted its merits. Our future measures would then have been more universally agreeable and better supported; but the justifiable anxiety to put the government in operation prevented that; it therefore remains for us to take it up as soon as possible. I wish then to commence the consideration at the present moment; I hold it to be my duty to unfold my ideas, and explain myself to the house in some form or other without delay. I only wish to introduce the great work, and as I said before I do not expect it will be decided immediately; but if some step is taken in the business it will give reason to believe that we may come at a final result. This will inspire a reasonable hope in the advocates for amendments, that full justice will be done to the important subject; and I have reason to believe their expectation will not be defeated. I hope the house will not decline my motion for going into a committee.

. . . . .

I am sorry to be accessary to the loss of a single moment of time by the house. If I had been indulged in my motion, and we had gone into a committee of the whole, I think we might have rose, and resumed the consideration of other business before this time; that is, so far as it depended on what I proposed to bring forward. As that mode seems not to give satisfaction, I will withdraw the motion, and move you, sir, that a select committee be appointed to consider and report such amendments as are proper for Congress to propose to the legislatures of the several States, conformably to the 5th article of the constitution. I will state my reasons why I think it proper to propose amendments; and state the amendments themselves, so far as I think they ought to be proposed. If I thought I could fulfil the duty which I owe to myself and my constituents, to let the subject pass over in silence, I most certainly should not trespass upon the indulgence of this house. But I cannot do this; and am therefore compelled to beg a patient hearing to what I have to lay before you. And I do most sincerely believe that if congress will devote but one day to this subject, so far as to satisfy the public that we do not disregard their wishes, it will have a salutary influence on the public councils, and prepare the way for a favorable reception of our future measures. It appears to me that this house is bound by every motive of prudence, not to let the first session pass over without proposing to the state legislatures some things to be incorporated into the constitution, as will render it as acceptable to the whole people of the United States, as it has been found acceptable to a majority of them. I wish, among other reasons why something should be done, that those who have been friendly to the adoption of this constitution, may have the opportunity of proving to those who were opposed to it, that they were as sincerely devoted to liberty and a republican government, as those who charged them with wishing the adoption of this constitution in order to lay the foundation of an aristocracy or despotism. It will be a desirable thing to extinguish from the bosom of every member of the community any apprehensions, that there are those among his countrymen who wish to deprive them of the liberty for which they valiantly fought and honorably bled. And if there are amendments desired, of such a nature as will not injure the constitution, and they can be ingrafted so as to give satisfaction to the doubting part of our fellow citizens; the friends of the federal government will evince that spirit of deference and concession for which they have hitherto been distinguished.

It cannot be a secret to the gentlemen in this house, that, notwithstanding the ratification of this system of government by eleven of the thirteen United States, in some cases unanimously, in others by large majorities; yet still there is a great number of our constituents who are dissatisfied with it; among whom are many respectable for their talents, their patriotism, and respectable for the jealousy they have for their liberty, which, though mistaken in its object, is laudable in its motive. There is a great body of the people falling under this description, who at present feel much inclined to join their support to the cause of federalism, if they were satisfied in this one point: We ought not to disregard their inclination, but, on principles of amity and moderation, conform to their wishes, and expressly declare the great rights of mankind secured under this constitution. The acquiescence which our fellow citizens shew under the government, calls upon us for a like return of moderation. But perhaps there is a stronger motive than this for our going into a consideration of the subject; it is to provide those securities for liberty which are required by a part of the community. I allude in a particular manner to those two states who have not thought fit to throw themselves into the bosom of the confederacy: it is a desirable thing, on our part as well as theirs, that a re-union should take place as soon as possible. I have no doubt, if we proceed to take those steps which would be prudent and requisite at this juncture, that in a short time we should see that disposition prevailing in those states that are not come in, that we have seen prevailing [in] those states which are.

But I will candidly acknowledge, that, over and above all these considerations, I do conceive that the constitution may be amended; that is to say, if all power is subject to abuse, that then it is possible the abuse of the powers of the general government may be guarded against in a more secure manner than is now done, while no one advantage, arising from the exercise of that power, shall be damaged or endangered by it. We have in this way something to gain, and, if we proceed with caution, nothing to lose; and in this case it is necessary to proceed with caution; for while we feel all these inducements to go into a revisal of the constitution, we must feel for the constitution itself, and make that revisal a moderate one. I should be unwilling to see a door opened for a re-consideration of the whole structure of the government, for a re-consideration of the principles and the substance of the powers given; because I doubt, if such a door was opened, if we should be very likely to stop at that point which would be safe to the government itself: But I do wish to see a door opened to consider, so far as to incorporate those provisions for the security of rights, against which I believe no serious objection has been made by any class of our constituents, such as would be likely to meet with the concurrence of two-thirds of both houses, and the approbation of three-fourths of the state legislatures. I will not propose a single alteration which I do not wish to see take place, as intrinsically proper in itself, or proper because it is wished for by a respectable number of my fellow citizens; and therefore I shall not propose a single alteration but is likely to meet the concurrence required by the constitution.

There have been objections of various kinds made against the constitution: Some were levelled against its structure, because the president was without a council; because the senate, which is a legislative body, had judicial powers in trials on impeachments; and because the powers of that body were compounded in other respects, in a manner that did not correspond with a particular theory; because it grants more power than is supposed to be necessary for every good purpose; and controuls the ordinary powers of the state governments. I know some respectable characters who opposed this government on these grounds; but I believe that the great mass of the people who opposed it, disliked it because it did not contain effectual provision against encroachments on particular rights, and those safeguards which they have been long accustomed to have interposed between them and the magistrate who exercised the sovereign power: nor ought we to consider them safe, while a great number of our fellow citizens think these securities necessary.

It has been a fortunate thing that the objection to the government has been made on the ground I stated; because it will be practicable on that ground to obviate the objection, so far as to satisfy the public mind that their liberties will be perpetual, and this without endangering any part of the constitution, which is considered as essential to the existence of the government by those who promoted its adoption.

The amendments which have occurred to me, proper to be recommended by congress to the state legislatures, are these:

First. That there be prefixed to the constitution a declaration—That all power is originally vested in, and consequently derived from the people.

That government is instituted, and ought to be exercised for the benefit of the people; which consists in the enjoyment of life and liberty, with the right of acquiring and using property, and generally of pursuing and obtaining happiness and safety.

That the people have an indubitable, unalienable, and indefeasible right to reform or change their government, whenever it be found adverse or inadequate to the purposes of its institution.

. . . . .

Fourthly. That in article 1st, section 9, between clauses 3 and 4, be inserted these clauses, to wit, The civil rights of none shall be abridged on account of religious belief or worship, nor shall any national religion be established, nor shall the full and equal rights of conscience be in any manner, or on any pretext infringed.

The people shall not be deprived or abridged of their right to speak, to write, or to publish their sentiments; and the freedom of the press, as one of the great bulwarks of liberty, shall be inviolable.

The people shall not be restrained from peaceably assembling and consulting for their common good; nor from applying to the legislature by petitions, or remonstrances for redress of their grievances.

The right of the people to keep and bear arms shall not be infringed; a well armed, and well regulated militia being the best security of a free country: but no person religiously scrupulous of bearing arms, shall be compelled to render military service in person.

No soldier shall in time of peace be quartered in any house without the consent of the owner; nor at any time, but in a manner warranted by law.

No person shall be subject, except in cases of impeachment, to more than one punishment, or one trial for the same offence; nor shall be compelled to be a witness against himself; nor be deprived of life, liberty, or property without due process of law; nor be obliged to relinquish his property, where it may be necessary for public use, without a just compensation.

Excessive bail shall not be required, nor excessive fines imposed, nor cruel and unusual punishments inflicted.

The rights of the people to be secured in their persons, their houses, their papers, and their other property from all unreasonable searches and seizures, shall not be violated by warrants issued without probable cause, supported by oath or affirmation, or not particularly describing the places to be searched, or the persons or things to be seized.

In all criminal prosecutions, the accused shall enjoy the right to a speedy and public trial, to be informed of the cause and nature of the accusation, to be confronted with his accusers, and the witnesses against him; to have a compulsory process for obtaining witnesses in his favor; and to have the assistance of counsel for his defence.

The exceptions here or elsewhere in the constitution, made in favor of particular rights, shall not be so construed as to diminish the just importance of other rights retained by the people; or as to enlarge the powers delegated by the constitution; but either as actual limitations of such powers, or as inserted merely for greater caution.

Fifthly. That in article 1st, section 10, between clauses 1 and 2, be inserted this clause, to wit:

No state shall violate the equal rights of conscience, or the freedom of the press, or the trial by jury in criminal cases.

Sixthly. That article 3d, section 2, be annexed to the end of clause 2d, these words to wit: but no appeal to such court shall be allowed where the value in controversy shall not amount to   dollars: nor shall any fact triable by jury, according to the course of common law, be otherwise re-examinable than may consist with the principles of common law.

Seventhly. That in article 3d, section 2, the third clause be struck out, and in its place be inserted the clauses following, to wit:

The trial of all crimes (except in cases of impeachments, and cases arising in the land or naval forces, or the militia when on actual service in time of war or public danger) shall be by an impartial jury of freeholders of the vicinage, with the requisite of unanimity for conviction, of the right of challenge, and other accustomed requisites; and in all crimes punishable with loss of life or member, presentment or indictment by a grand jury, shall be an essential preliminary, provided that in cases of crimes committed within any county which may be in possession of an enemy, or in which a general insurrection may prevail, the trial may by law be authorised in some other county of the same state, as near as may be to the seat of the offence.

In cases of crimes committed not within any county, the trial may by law be in such county as the laws shall have prescribed. In suits at common law, between man and man, the trial by jury, as one of the best securities to the rights of the people, ought to remain inviolate.

Eighthly. That immediately after article 6th, be inserted, as article 7th, the clauses following, to wit:

The powers delegated by this constitution, are appropriated to the departments to which they are respectively distributed: so that the legislative department shall never exercise the powers vested in the executive or judicial; nor the executive exercise the powers vested in the legislative or judicial; nor the judicial exercise the powers vested in the legislative or executive departments.

The powers not delegated by this constitution, nor prohibited by it to the states, are reserved to the States respectively.

Ninthly. That article 7th, be numbered as article 8th.

The first of these amendments, relates to what may be called a bill of rights; I will own that I never considered this provision so essential to the federal constitution, as to make it improper to ratify it, until such an amendment was added; at the same time, I always conceived, that in a certain form and to a certain extent, such a provision was neither improper nor altogether useless. I am aware, that a great number of the most respectable friends to the government and champions for republican liberty, have thought such a provision, not only unnecessary, but even improper, nay, I believe some have gone so far as to think it even dangerous. Some policy has been made use of perhaps by gentlemen on both sides of the question: I acknowledge the ingenuity of those arguments which were drawn against the constitution, by a comparison with the policy of Great-Britain, in establishing a declaration of rights; but there is too great a difference in the case to warrant the comparison: therefore the arguments drawn from that source, were in a great measure inapplicable. In the declaration of rights which that country has established, the truth is, they have gone no farther, than to raise a barrier against the power of the crown; the power of the legislature is left altogether indefinite. Altho' I know whenever the great rights, the trial by jury, freedom of the press, or liberty of conscience, came in question in that body, the invasion of them is resisted by able advocates, yet their Magna Charta does not contain any one provision for the security of those rights, respecting which, the people of America are most alarmed. The freedom of the press and rights of conscience, those choicest privileges of the people, are unguarded in the British constitution.

But altho' the case may be widely different, and it may not be thought necessary to provide limits for the legislative power in that country, yet a different opinion prevails in the United States. The people of many states, have thought it necessary to raise barriers against power in all forms and departments of government, and I am inclined to believe, if once bills of rights are established in all the states as well as the federal constitution, we shall find that altho' some of them are rather unimportant, yet, upon the whole, they will have a salutary tendency.

It may be said, in some instances they do no more than state the perfect equality of mankind; this to be sure is an absolute truth, yet it is not absolutely necessary to be inserted at the head of a constitution.

In some instances they assert those rights which are exercised by the people in forming and establishing a plan of government. In other instances, they specify those rights which are retained when particular powers are given up to be exercised by the legislature. In other instances, they specify positive rights, which may seem to result from the nature of the compact. Trial by jury cannot be considered as a natural right, but a right resulting from the social compact which regulates the action of the community, but is as essential to secure the liberty of the people as any one of the pre-existent rights of nature. In other instances they lay down dogmatic maxims with respect to the construction of the government; declaring, that the legislative, executive, and judicial branches shall be kept separate and distinct: Perhaps the best way of securing this in practice is to provide such checks, as will prevent the encroachment of the one upon the other.

But whatever may be [the] form which the several states have adopted in making declarations in favor of particular rights, the great object in view is to limit and qualify the powers of government, by excepting out of the grant of power those cases in which the government ought not to act, or to act only in a particular mode. They point these exceptions sometimes against the abuse of the executive power, sometimes against the legislative, and, in some cases, against the community itself; or, in other words, against the majority in favor of the minority.

In our government it is, perhaps, less necessary to guard against the abuse in the executive department than any other; because it is not the stronger branch of the system, but the weaker: It therefore must be levelled against the legislative, for it is the most powerful, and most likely to be abused, because it is under the least controul; hence, so far as a declaration of rights can tend to prevent the exercise of undue power, it cannot be doubted but such declaration is proper. But I confess that I do conceive, that in a government modified like this of the United States, the great danger lies rather in the abuse of the community than in the legislative body. The prescriptions in favor of liberty, ought to be levelled against that quarter where the greatest danger lies, namely, that which possesses the highest prerogative of power: But this [is] not found in either the executive or legislative departments of government, but in the body of the people, operating by the majority against the minority.

It may be thought all paper barriers against the power of the community, are too weak to be worthy of attention. I am sensible they are not so strong as to satisfy gentlemen of every description who have seen and examined thoroughly the texture of such a defence; yet, as they have a tendency to impress some degree of respect for them, to establish the public opinion in their favor, and rouse the attention of the whole community, it may be one mean to controul the majority from those acts to which they might be otherwise inclined.

It has been said by way of objection to a bill of rights, by many respectable gentlemen out of doors, and I find opposition on the same principles likely to be made by gentlemen on this floor, that they are unnecessary articles of a republican government, upon the presumption that the people have those rights in their own hands, and that is the proper place for them to rest. It would be a sufficient answer to say that this objection lies against such provisions under the state governments as well as under the general government; and there are, I believe, but few gentlemen who are inclined to push their theory so far as to say that a declaration of rights in those cases is either ineffectual or improper. It has been said that in the federal government they are unnecessary, because the powers are enumerated, and it follows that all that are not granted by the constitution are retained: that the constitution is a bill of powers, the great residuum being the rights of the people; and therefore a bill of rights cannot be so necessary as if the residuum was thrown into the hands of the government. I admit that these arguments are not entirely without foundation; but they are not conclusive to the extent which has been supposed. It is true the powers of the general government are circumscribed; they are directed to particular objects; but even if government keeps within those limits, it has certain discretionary powers with respect to the means, which may admit of abuse to a certain extent, in the same manner as the powers of the state governments under their constitutions may to an indefinite

extent; because in the constitution of the United States there is a clause granting to Congress the power to make all laws which shall be necessary and proper for carrying into execution all the powers vested in the government of the United States, or in any department or officer thereof; this enables them to fulfil every purpose for which the government was established. Now, may not laws be considered necessary and proper by Congress, for it is them who are to judge of the necessity and propriety to accomplish those special purposes which they may have in contemplation, which laws in themselves are neither necessary or proper; as well as improper laws could be enacted by the state legislatures, for fulfilling the more extended objects of those governments. I will state an instance which I think in point, and proves that this might be the case. The general government has a right to pass all laws which shall be necessary to collect its revenue; the means for enforcing the collection are within the direction of the legislature: may not general warrants be considered necessary for this purpose, as well as for some purposes which it was supposed at the framing of their constitutions the state governments had in view. If there was reason for restraining the state governments from exercising this power, there is like reason for restraining the federal government.

It may be said, because it has been said, that a bill of rights is not necessary, because the establishment of this government has not repealed those declarations of rights which are added to the several state constitutions: that those rights of the people, which had been established by the most solemn act, could not be annihilated by a subsequent act of that people, who meant, and declared at the head of the instrument, that they ordained and established a new system, for the express purpose of securing to themselves and posterity the liberties they had gained by an arduous conflict.

I admit the force of this observation, but I do not look upon it to be conclusive. In the first place, it is too uncertain ground to leave this provision upon, if a provision is at all necessary to secure rights so important as many of those I have mentioned are conceived to be, by the public in general, as well as those in particular who opposed the adoption of this constitution. Beside some states have no bills of rights, there are others provided with very defective ones, and there are others whose bills of rights are not only defective, but absolutely improper; instead of securing some in the full extent which republican principles would require, they limit them too much to agree with the common ideas of liberty.

It has been objected also against a bill of rights, that, by enumerating particular exceptions to the grant of power, it would disparage those rights which were not placed in that enumeration, and it might follow by implication, that those rights which were not singled out, were intended to be assigned into the hands of the general government, and were consequently insecure. This is one of the most plausible arguments I have ever heard urged against the admission of a bill of rights into this system; but, I conceive, that may be guarded against. I have attempted it, as gentlemen may see by turning to the last clause of the 4th resolution.

It has been said, that it is unnecessary to load the constitution with this provision, because it was not found effectual in the constitution of the particular states. It is true, there are a few particular states in which some of the most valuable articles have not, at one time or other, been violated; but does it not follow but they may have, to a certain degree, a salutary effect against the abuse of power. If they are incorporated into the constitution, independent tribunals of justice will consider themselves in a peculiar manner the guardians of those rights; they will be an impenetrable bulwark against every assumption of power in the legislative or executive; they will be naturally led to resist every encroachment upon rights expressly stipulated for in the constitution by the declaration of rights. Beside this security, there is a great probability that such a declaration in the federal system would be inforced; because the state legislatures will jealously and closely watch the operations of this government, and be able to resist with more effect every assumption of power than any other power on earth can do; and the greatest opponents to a federal government admit the state legislatures to be sure guardians of the people's liberty. I conclude from this view of the subject, that it will be proper in itself, and highly politic, for the tranquility of the public mind, and the stability of the government, that we should offer something, in the form I have proposed, to be incorporated in the system of government, as a declaration of the rights of the people.

. . . . .

I wish also, in revising the constitution, we may throw into that section, which interdicts the abuse of certain powers in the state legislatures, some other provisions of equal if not greater importance than those already made. The words, "No state shall pass any bill of attainder, ex post facto law, &c." were wise and proper restrictions in the constitution. I think there is more danger of those powers being abused by the state governments than by the government of the United States. The same may be said of other powers which they possess, if not controuled by the general principle, that laws are unconstitutional which infringe the rights of the community. I should therefore wish to extend this interdiction, and add, as I have stated in the 5th resolution, that no state shall violate the equal right of conscience, freedom of the press, or trial by jury in criminal cases; because it is proper that every government should be disarmed of powers which trench upon those particular rights. I know in some of the state constitutions the power of the government is controuled by such a declaration, but others are not. I cannot see any reason against obtaining even a double security on those points; and nothing can give a more sincere proof of the attachment of those who opposed this constitution to these great and important rights, than to see them join in obtaining the security I have now proposed; because it must be admitted, on all hands, that the state governments are as liable to attack these invaluable privileges as the general government is, and therefore ought to be as cautiously guarded against.

I think it will be proper, with respect to the judiciary powers, to satisfy the public mind on those points which I have mentioned. Great inconvenience has been apprehended to suitors from the distance they would be dragged to obtain justice in the supreme court of the United States, upon an appeal on an action for a small debt. To remedy this, declare, that no appeal shall be made unless the matter in controversy amounts to a particular sum: This, with the regulations respecting jury trials in criminal cases, and suits at common law, it is to be hoped will quiet and reconcile the minds of the people to that part of the constitution.

I find, from looking into the amendments proposed by the state conventions, that several are particularly anxious that it should be declared in the constitution, that the powers not therein delegated, should be reserved to the several states. Perhaps words which may define this more precisely, than the whole of the instrument now does, may be considered as superfluous. I admit they may be deemed unnecessary; but there can be no harm in making such a declaration, if gentlemen will allow that the fact is as stated. I am sure I understand it so, and do therefore propose it.

These are the points on which I wish to see a revision of the constitution take place. How far they will accord with the sense of this body, I cannot take upon me absolutely to determine; but I believe every gentleman will readily admit that nothing is in contemplation, so far as I have mentioned, that can endanger the beauty of the government in any one important feature, even in the eyes of its most sanguine admirers. I have proposed nothing that does not appear to me as proper in itself, or eligible as patronised by a respectable number of our fellow citizens; and if we can make the constitution better in the opinion of those who are opposed to it, without weakening its frame, or abridging its usefulness, in the judgment of those who are attached to it, we act the part of wise and liberal men to make such alterations as shall produce that effect.

Having done what I conceived was my duty, in bringing before this house the subject of amendments, and also stated such as I wish for and approve, and offered the reasons which occurred to me in their support; I shall content myself for the present with moving, that a committee be appointed to consider of and report such amendments as ought to be proposed by congress to the legislatures of the states, to become, if ratified by three-fourths thereof, part of the constitution of the United States. By agreeing to this motion, the subject may be going on in the committee, while other important business is proceeding to a conclusion in the house. I should advocate greater dispatch in the business of amendments, if I was not convinced of the absolute necessity there is of pursuing the organization of the government; because I think we should obtain the confidence of our fellow citizens, in proportion as we fortify the rights of the people against the encroachments of the government.

51

HOUSE OF REPRESENTATIVES, REPORT OF THE
SELECT COMMITTEE ON AMENDMENTS
28 July 1789
Dumbauld 210–12

In the introductory paragraph before the words, *"We the people,"* add, "Government being intended for the benefit of the people, and the rightful establishment thereof being derived from their authority alone."

ART. I, SEC. 2, PAR. 3—Strike out all between the words, *"direct"* and *"and until such,"* and instead thereof insert, "After the first enumeration there shall be one representative for every thirty thousand until the number shall amount to one hundred; after which the proportion shall be so regulated by Congress that the number of Representatives shall never be less than one hundred, nor more than one hundred and seventy-five, but each State shall always have at least one Representative."

ART. 1, SEC. 6—Between the words *"United States,"* and *"shall in all cases,"* strike out *"they,"* and insert, "But no law varying the compensation shall take effect until an election of Representatives shall have intervened. The members."

ART. 1, SEC. 9—Between PAR. 2 and 3 insert, "No religion shall be established by law, nor shall the equal rights of conscience be infringed."

"The freedom of speech, and of the press, and the right of the people peaceably to assemble and consult for their common good, and to apply to the government for redress of grievances, shall not be infringed."

"A well regulated militia, composed of the body of the people, being the best security of a free State, the right of the people to keep and bear arms shall not be infringed, but no person religiously scrupulous shall be compelled to bear arms."

"No soldier shall in time of peace be quartered in any house without the consent of the owner, nor in time of war but in a manner to be prescribed by law."

"No person shall be subject, except in case of impeachment, to more than one trial or one punishment for the same offence, nor shall be compelled to be a witness against himself, nor be deprived of life, liberty, or property without due process of law; nor shall private property be taken for public use without just compensation."

"Excessive bail shall not be required, nor excessive fines imposed, nor cruel and unusual punishments inflicted."

"The right of the people to be secure in their person, houses, papers and effects, shall not be violated by warrants issuing, without probable cause supported by oath or affirmation, and not particularly describing the places to be searched, and the persons or things to be seized."

"The enumeration in this Constitution of certain rights shall not be construed to deny or disparage others retained by the people."

ART. 1, SEC. 10, between the 1st and 2d PAR. insert, "No State shall infringe the equal rights of conscience, nor the freedom of speech, or of the press, nor of the right of trial by jury in criminal cases."

ART. 3, SEC. 2, add to the 2d PAR. "But no appeal to such court shall be allowed, where the value in controversy shall not amount to one thousand dollars; nor shall any fact, triable by a Jury according to the course of the common law, be otherwise re-examinable than according to the rules of common law."

ART. 3, SEC. 2—Strike out the whole of the 3d paragraph, and insert—"In all criminal prosecutions the accused shall enjoy the right to a speedy and public trial, to be informed of the nature and cause of the accusation, to be confronted with the witnesses against him, to have compulsory process for obtaining witnesses in his favor, and to have the assistance of counsel for his defence."

"The trial of all crimes (except in cases of impeachment, and in cases arising in the land or naval forces, or in the militia, when in actual service in time of war or public danger) shall be by an impartial jury of freeholders of the vicinage, with the requisite of unanimity for conviction, the right of challenge and other accustomed requisites; and no person shall be held to answer for a capital, or otherwise infamous crime, unless on a presentment or indictment by a Grand Jury; but if a crime be committed in a place in the possession of an enemy, or in which an insurrection may prevail, the indictment and trial may by law be authorized in some other place within the same State; and if it be committed in a place not within a State, the indictment and trial may be at such place or places as the law may have directed."

"In suits at common law the right of trial by jury shall be preserved."

"Immediately after ART. 6, the following to be inserted as ART. 7."

"The powers delegated by this Constitution to the government of the United States, shall be exercised as therein appropriated, so that the Legislative shall never exercise the powers vested in the Executive or the Judicial; nor the Executive the powers vested in the Legislative or Judicial; nor the Judicial the powers vested in the Legislative or Executive."

"The powers not delegated by this Constitution, nor prohibited by it to the States, are reserved to the States respectively."

ART. 7 to be made ART. 8.

52

[1:707–10, 714–15, 717; 13 Aug.]

The House then resolved itself into a Committee of the Whole, Mr. BOUDINOT in the Chair, and took the amendments under consideration. The first article ran thus: "In the introductory paragraph of the Constitution, before the words 'We the people,' add 'Government being intended for the benefit of the people, and the rightful establishment thereof being derived from their authority alone.' "

Mr. SHERMAN.—I believe, Mr. Chairman, this is not the proper mode of amending the Constitution. We ought not to interweave our propositions into the work itself, because it will be destructive of the whole fabric. We might as well endeavor to mix brass, iron, and clay, as to incorporate such heterogeneous articles, the one contradictory to the other. Its absurdity will be discovered by comparing it with a law. Would any Legislature endeavor to introduce into a former act a subsequent amendment, and let them stand so connected? When an alteration is made in an act, it is done by way of supplement; the latter act always repealing the former in every specified case of difference.

Besides this, sir, it is questionable whether we have the right to propose amendments in this way. The Constitution is the act of the people, and ought to remain entire. But the amendments will be the act of the State Governments. Again, all the authority we possess is derived from that instrument; if we mean to destroy the whole, and establish a new Constitution, we remove the basis on which we mean to build. For these reasons, I will move to strike out that paragraph and substitute another.

The paragraph proposed was to the following effect:

> *Resolved, by the Senate and House of Representatives of the United States in Congress assembled,* That the following articles be proposed as amendments to the Constitution, and when ratified by three-fourths of the State Legislatures, shall become valid to all intents and purposes, as part of the same.

Under this title, the amendments might come in nearly as stated in the report, only varying the phraseology so as to accommodate them to a supplementary form.

Mr. MADISON.—Form, sir, is always of less importance than the substance; but on this occasion I admit that form is of some consequence, and it will be well for the House to pursue that which, upon reflection, shall appear to be the most eligible. Now it appears to me, that there is a neatness and propriety in incorporating the amendments into the Constitution itself; in that case, the system will remain uniform and entire; it will certainly be more simple when the amendments are interwoven into those parts to which they naturally belong, than it will if they consist of separate and distinct parts. We shall then be able to determine its meaning without references or comparison; whereas, if they are supplementary, its meaning can only be ascertained by a comparison of the two instruments, which will be a very considerable embarrassment. It will be difficult to ascertain to what parts of the instrument the amendments particularly refer; they will create unfavorable comparisons; whereas, if they are placed upon the footing here proposed, they will stand upon as good foundation as the original work. Nor is it so uncommon a thing as gentlemen suppose; systematic men frequently take up the whole law, and, with its amendments and alterations, reduce it into one act. I am not, however, very solicitous about the form, provided the business is but well completed.

Mr. SMITH did not think the amendment proposed by the honorable gentlemen from Connecticut was compatible with the Constitution, which declared, that the amendments recommended by Congress, and ratified by the Legislatures of three-fourths of the several States, should be part of this Constitution; in which case it would form one complete system; but according to the idea of the amendment, the instrument is to have five or six suits of improvements. Such a mode seems more calculated to embarrass the people than any thing else, while nothing in his opinion was a juster cause of complaint than the difficulties of knowing the law, arising from Legislative obscurities that might easily be avoided. He said, that it had certainly been the custom in several of the State Governments to amend their laws by way of supplement. But South Carolina had been an instance of the contrary practice, in revising the old code; instead of making acts in addition to acts, which is always attended with perplexity, she has incorporated them, and brought them forward as a complete system, repealing the old. This is what he understood was intended to be done by the committee; the present copy of the Constitution was to be done away, and a new one substituted in its stead.

. . . . .

Mr. LIVERMORE was clearly of opinion, that whatever amendments were made to the Constitution, they ought to stand separate from the original instrument. We have no right, said he, to alter a clause any otherwise than by a new proposition. We have well-established precedents for such a mode of procedure in the practice of the British Parliament and the State Legislatures throughout America. I do not mean, however, to assert that there has been no instance of a repeal of the whole law on enacting another; but this has generally taken place on account of the complexity of the original, with its supplements. Were we a mere Legislative body, no doubt it might be warrantable in us to pursue a similar method; but it is questionable whether it is possible for us, consistent with the oath we have taken, to attempt a repeal of the Constitution of the United States, by making a new one to substitute in its place; the reason of this is grounded on a very simple consideration. It is by virtue of the present Constitution, I presume, that we attempt to make another; now, if we proceed to the repeal of this, I cannot see upon what authority we shall erect another; if we destroy the base, the superstructure falls of course. At some future day it may be asked upon what authority we proceeded to raise and appropriate public moneys. We suppose we do it in virtue of the present Constitution; but it may be doubted whether we have a right to exercise any of its authorities while it is suspended, as it will certainly be from the time that two-thirds of both Houses have agreed to submit it to the State Legislatures; so that, unless we mean to destroy the whole Constitution, we ought to be careful how we attempt to amend it in the way proposed by the committee. From hence, I presume it will be more prudent to adopt the mode proposed by the gentleman from Connecticut, than it will be to risk the destruction of the whole by proposing amendments in the manner recommended by the committee.

Mr. VINING disliked a supplementary form, and said it was a bad reason to urge the practice of former ages, when there was a more convenient method of doing the business at hand. He had seen an act entitled an act to amend a supplement to an act entitled an act for altering part of an act entitled an act for certain purposes therein mentioned. If gentlemen were disposed to run into such jargon in amending and altering the Constitution, he could not help it; but he trusted they would adopt a plainness and simplicity of style on this and every other occasion, which should be easily understood. If the mode proposed by the gentleman from Connecticut was adopted, the system would be distorted, and like a careless written letter, have more attached to it in a postscript than was contained in the original composition.

The Constitution being a great and important work, ought all to be brought into one view, and made as intelligible as possible.

Mr. CLYMER was of opinion, with the gentleman from Connecticut, that the amendments ought not to be incorporated in the body of the work, which he hoped would remain a monument to justify those who made it; by a comparison, the world would discover the perfection of the original, and the superfluity of the amendments. He made this distinction, because he did not conceive any of the amendments essential, but as they were solicited by his fellow-citizens, and for that reason they were acquiesced in by others; he therefore wished the motion for throwing them into a supplementary form might be carried.

. . . . .

Mr. JACKSON.—I do not like to differ with gentlemen about form; but as so much has been said, I wish to give my opinion; it is this: that the original Constitution ought to remain inviolate, and not be patched up, from time to time, with various stuffs resembling Joseph's coat of many colors.

Some gentlemen talk of repealing the present Constitution and adopting an improved one. If we have this power, we may go on from year to year, making new ones; and in this way, we shall render the basis of the superstructure the most fluctuating thing imaginable, and the people will never know what the Constitution is. As for the alteration

proposed by the committee, to prefix before "We the people," certain dogmas, I cannot agree to it; the words, as they now stand, speak as much as it is possible to speak; it is a practical recognition of the right of the people to ordain and establish Governments, and is more expressive than any other mere paper declaration.

Mr. SHERMAN.—If I had looked upon this question as a mere matter of form, I should not have brought it forward, or troubled the committee with such a lengthy discussion. But, sir, I contend that amendments made in the way proposed by the committee are void. No gentleman ever knew an addition and alteration introduced into an existing law, and that any part of such law was left in force; but if it was improved or altered by a supplemental act, the original retained all its validity and importance, in every case where the two were not incompatible. But if these observations alone should be thought insufficient to support my motion, I would desire gentlemen to consider the authorities upon which the two Constitutions are to stand. The original was established by the people at large, by conventions chosen by them for the express purpose. The preamble to the Constitution declares the act; but will it be a truth in ratifying the next Constitution, which is to be done perhaps by the State Legislatures, and not conventions chosen for the purpose? Will gentlemen say it is "We the people" in this case? Certainly they cannot; for, by the present Constitution, we, nor all the Legislatures in the Union together, do not possess the power of repealing it. All that is granted us by the 5th article is, that whenever we shall think it necessary, we may propose amendments to the Constitution; not that we may propose to repeal the old, and substitute a new one.

Gentlemen say, it would be convenient to have it in one instrument, that people might see the whole at once; for my part, I view no difficulty on this point. The amendments reported are a declaration of rights; the people are secure in them, whether we declare them or not; the last amendment but one provides that the three branches of Government shall each exercise its own rights. This is well secured already; and, in short, I do not see that they lessen the force of any article in the Constitution; if so, there can be little more difficulty in comprehending them whether they are combined in one, or stand distinct instruments.

. . . . .

Mr. SHERMAN.—The gentlemen who oppose the motion say we contend for matter of form; they think it nothing more. Now we say we contend for substance, and therefore cannot agree to amendments in this way. If they are so desirous of having the business completed, they had better sacrifice what they consider but a matter of indifference to gentlemen, to go more unanimously along with them in altering the Constitution.

The question on Mr. SHERMAN's motion was now put and lost.

[1:717–19; 14 Aug.]

Mr. SMITH wished to transpose the words of the first amendment, as they did not satisfy his mind in the manner they stood.

Mr. GERRY said, they were not well expressed; we have

it here "government being intended for the benefit of the people;" this holds up an idea that all the Governments of the earth are intended for the benefit of the people. Now, I am so far from being of this opinion, that I do not believe that one out of fifty is intended for any such purpose. I believe the establishment of most Governments is to gratify the ambition of an individual, who, by fraud, force, or accident, had made himself master of the people. If we contemplate the history of nations, ancient or modern, we shall find they originated either in fraud or force, or both. If this is demonstrable, how can we pretend to say that Governments are intended for the benefit of those who are most oppressed by them. This maxim does not appear to me to be strictly true in fact, therefore I think we ought not to insert it in the Constitution. I shall therefore propose to amend the clause, by inserting "of right," then it will stand as it ought. I do not object to the principle, sir; it is a good one, but it does not generally hold in practice.

The question on inserting the words "of right" was put, and determined in the negative.

Mr. TUCKER.—I presume these propositions are brought forward under the idea of being amendments to the Constitution; but can this be esteemed an amendment of the Constitution? If I understand what is meant by the introductory paragraph, it is the preamble to the Constitution; but a preamble is no part of the Constitution. It is, to say the best, a useless amendment. For my part, I should as soon think of amending the concluding part, consisting of General Washington's letter to the President of Congress, as the preamble; but if the principle is of importance, it may be introduced into a bill of rights.

Mr. SMITH read the amendments on this head, proposed by the conventions of New York, Virginia, and North Carolina, from which it appeared that these States had expressed a desire to have an amendment of this kind.

Mr. TUCKER replied that the words "We the people do ordain and establish this Constitution for the United States of America," were a declaration of their action; this being performed, Congress have nothing to do with it. But if it was necessary to retain the principle, it might come in at some other place.

Mr. SUMTER thought this was not a proper place to introduce any general principle; perhaps, in going through with the amendments, something might be proposed subversive of what was there declared; wherefore he wished the committee would pass over the preamble until they had gone through all the amendments, and then, if alterations were necessary, they could be accommodated to what had taken place in the body of the Constitution.

Mr. LIVERMORE was not concerned about the preamble; he did not care what kind it was agreed to form in the committee; because when it got before the House, it would be undone if one member more than one-third of the whole opposed it.

Mr. PAGE thought the preamble no part of the Constitution; but if it was, it stood in no need of amendment; the words "We, the people," had the neatness and simplicity, while its expression was the most forcible of any he had ever seen prefixed to any Constitution. He did not

doubt the truth of the proposition brought forward by the committee, but he doubted its necessity in this place.

Mr. MADISON.—If it be a truth, and so self-evident that it cannot be denied—if it be recognised, as is the fact in many of the State Constitutions—and if it be desired by three important States to be added to this—I think they must collectively offer a strong inducement to the mind desirous of promoting harmony to acquiesce with the report; at least some strong arguments should be brought forward to show the reason why it is improper.

My worthy colleague says the original expression is neat and simple; that loading it with more words may destroy the beauty of the sentence; and others say it is unnecessary, as the paragraph is complete without it. Be it so in their opinion; yet still it appears important in the estimation of three States that this solemn truth should be inserted in the Constitution. For my part, sir, I do not think the association of ideas anywise unnatural; it reads very well in this place; so much so, that I think gentlemen, who admit it should come in somewhere else, will be puzzled to find a better place.

Mr. SHERMAN thought they ought not to come in in this place. The people of the United States have given their reasons for doing a certain act. Here we propose to come in and give them a right to do what they did on motives which appeared to them sufficient to warrant their determination; to let them know that they had a right to exercise a natural and inherent privilege, which they have asserted in a solemn ordination and establishment of the Constitution.

Now, if this right is indefeasible, and the people have recognised it in practice, the truth is better asserted than it can be by any words whatever. The words "We the people," in the original Constitution, are as copious and expressive as possible; any addition will only drag out the sentence without illuminating it; for these reasons it may be hoped the committee will reject the proposed amendment.

The question on the first paragraph of the report was put and carried in the affirmative, twenty-seven to twenty-three.

[1:745–47; 15 Aug.]

Mr. BURKE.—I do not mean to insist particularly upon this amendment [affirming the right of the people to give instructions to their representatives]; but I am very well satisfied that those that are reported and likely to be adopted by this House are very far from giving satisfaction to our constituents; they are not those solid and substantial amendments which the people expect; they are little better than whipsyllabub, frothy and full of wind, formed only to please the palate; or they are like a tub thrown out to a whale, to secure the freight of the ship and its peaceable voyage. In my judgment, the people will not be gratified by the mode we have pursued in bringing them forward. There was a committee of eleven appointed; and out of the number I think there were five who were members of the convention that formed the Constitution. Such gentlemen, having already given their opinion with respect to the perfection of the work, may be thought improper agents to bring forward amendments. Upon the whole, I think it will be found that we have done nothing but lose our time, and that it will be better to drop the subject now, and proceed to the organization of the Government.

. . . . .

Mr. MADISON was unwilling to take up any more of the time of the committee; but, on the other hand, he was not willing to be silent after the charges that had been brought against the committee, and the gentleman who introduced the amendments, by the honorable members on each side of him, (Messrs. SUMTER and BURKE.) Those gentlemen say that we are precipitating the business, and insinuate that we are not acting with candor. I appeal to the gentlemen who have heard the voice of their country, to those who have attended the debates of the State conventions, whether the amendments now proposed are not those most strenuously required by the opponents of the Constitution? It was wished that some security should be given for those great and essential rights which they have been taught to believe were in danger. I concurred, in the convention of Virginia, with those gentlemen, so far as to agree to a declaration of those rights which corresponded with my own judgment, and the other alterations which I had the honor to bring forward before the present Congress. I appeal to the gentlemen on this floor who are desirous of amending the Constitution, whether those proposed are not compatible with what are required by our constituents? Have not the people been told that the rights of conscience, the freedom of speech, the liberty of the press, and trial by jury, were in jeopardy? that they ought not to adopt the Constitution until those important rights were secured to them?

But while I approve of these amendments, I should oppose the consideration at this time of such as are likely to change the principles of the Government, or that are of a doubtful nature; because I apprehend there is little prospect of obtaining the consent of two-thirds of both Houses of Congress, and three-fourths of the State Legislatures, to ratify propositions of this kind; therefore, as a friend to what is attainable, I would limit it to the plain, simple, and important security that has been required. If I were inclined to make no alteration in the Constitution, I would bring forward such amendments as were of a dubious cast, in order to have the whole rejected.

Mr. BURKE never entertained an idea of charging gentlemen with the want of candor; but he would appeal to any man of sense and candor, whether the amendments contained in the report were any thing like the amendments required by the States of New York, Virginia, New Hampshire, and Carolina; and having these amendments in his hand, he turned to them to show the difference, concluding that all the important amendments were omitted in the report.

[1:773–76; 22 Aug.]

Mr. TUCKER moved the following as a proposition to be added to the same: "The Congress shall never impose direct taxes but where the moneys arising from the duties,

imposts, and excise, are insufficient for the public exigencies, nor then until Congress shall have made a requisition upon the States to assess, levy, and pay their respective proportions of such requisitions. And in case any State shall neglect or refuse to pay its proportion, pursuant to such requisition, then Congress may assess and levy such State's proportion, together with the interest thereon, at the rate of six per cent. per annum, from the time of payment prescribed by such requisition."

Mr. PAGE said, that he hoped every amendment to the Constitution would be considered separately in the manner this was proposed, but he wished them considered fully; it ought to have been referred to the committee of eleven, reported upon, and then to the Committee of the Whole. This was the manner in which the House had decided upon all those already agreed to; and this ought to be the manner in which this should be decided; he should be sorry to delay what was so nearly completed on any account. The House has but little time to sit, and the subject has to go before the Senate, therefore it requires of us all the expedition we can possibly give it. I would prefer putting a finishing hand to what has been already agreed to, and refer this to the Committee of eleven for their consideration.

Mr. TUCKER.—This proposition was referred to the committee, along with many others in the gross, but the Committee of eleven declined reporting upon it. I understood it to be in any gentleman's power to bring it forward when he thought proper, and it was under this influence that I proposed it, nor do I conceive it to be an improper time. The House is engaged in the discussion of amendments; they have made some progress, and I wish them to go on and complete what they have begun. This may be added without inconvenience, if it meet the sense of the House; but if it does not, I wish my constituents to be acquainted with our decision on the whole subject, and therefore hope it may be decided upon at this time.

Mr. JACKSON.—The gentleman has an undoubted right to bring forward the proposition; but I differ greatly with respect to its propriety. I hope, sir, the experience we have had will be sufficient to prevent us from ever agreeing to a relinquishment of such an essential power. The requisitions of the former Congress were ineffectual to obtain supplies; they remain to this day neglected by several States. If a sense of common danger, if war, and that a war of the noblest kind, a contest for liberty, were not sufficient to stimulate the States to a prompt compliance, when the means were abundant, by reason of the immense quantities of paper medium, can we ever expect an acquiescence to a requisition in future, when the only stimulus is honesty, to enable the Confederation to discharge the debts of the late war?

But suppose requisitions were likely to be, in some degree, complied with, (which, by the way, I never can admit.) in every case where a State had neglected or refused to furnish its quota, Congress must come in, assess, and collect it. Now, in every such case, I venture to affirm that jealousies would be excited, discontent would prevail, and civil wars break out. What less can gentlemen picture to themselves, when a Government has refused to perform its obligations, but that it will support its measures by the point of the bayonet?

Without the power of raising money to defray the expenses of Government, how are we to be secure against foreign invasion? What! can a Government exert itself, with its sinews torn from it? We can expect neither strength nor exertion; and without these are acquired and preserved, our union will not be lasting; we shall be rent asunder by intestine commotion, or exterior assault; and when that period arrives, we may bid adieu to all the blessings we have purchased at the price of our fortunes, and the blood of our worthiest heroes.

Mr. LIVERMORE thought this an amendment of more importance than any yet obtained; that it was recommended by five or six States, and therefore ought to engage their most serious consideration. It had been supposed that the United States would not attempt to levy direct taxes; but this was certainly a mistake. He believed nothing but the difficulty of managing the subject would deter them. The modes of levying and collecting taxes pursued by the several States are so various, that it is an insuperable obstacle to an attempt by the General Government.

He was sensible that the requisitions of the former Congress had not been fully complied with, and the defect of the Confederation was, that the Government had no powers to enforce a compliance. The proposition now under consideration obviated that difficulty. Suppose one or two States refused to comply, certainly the force of the others could compel them, and that is all that ought to be required; because it is not to be supposed that a majority of the States will refuse, as such an opposition must destroy the Union. He hoped the States would be left to furnish their quotas in a manner the most easy to themselves, as was requested by more than half of the present Union.

Unless something more effectual was done to improve the Constitution, he knew his constituents would be dissatisfied. As to the amendments already agreed to, they would not value them more than a pinch of snuff; they went to secure rights never in danger.

Mr. PAGE wished the proposition might be recommitted, for he was certain there was neither time nor inclination to add it to those already agreed upon.

He observed that the warmest friends to amendments differ in opinion on this subject; many of them have ceased urging it, while others have become strenuous advocates for the reverse. The most judicious and discerning men now declare that the Government ought never to part with this power. For his part, experience had convinced him that no reliance was to be had on requisitions, when the States had treated them with contempt in the hour of danger, and had abundant means of compliance. The public credit stood at this moment in the utmost need of support, and he could not consent to throw down one of its strongest props. He thought there was no danger of an abuse of this power, for the Government would not have recourse to it while the Treasury could be supplied from any other source; and when they did, they would be studious of adapting their law to the convenience of the States. He hoped, when the gentleman returned home to

New Hampshire, his constituents would give him credit for his exertions, and be better satisfied with the amendments than he now supposed them to be.

Mr. SUMTER felt himself so sensibly impressed with the importance of the subject, that if he apprehended the proposition would not have a fair discussion at this time, he would second the motion of commitment, and had not a doubt but the House would acquiesce in it.

Gentlemen had said that the States had this business much at heart. Yes, he would venture to say more, that if the power was not relinquished by the General Government, the State Governments would be annihilated. If every resource is taken from them, what remains in the power of the States for their support, or for the extinguishment of their domestic debt?

Mr. GERRY thought if the proposition was referred, that it ought to go to a Committee of the Whole, for he wished it to have a full and candid discussion. He would have something left in the power of every State to support itself, independent of the United States, and therefore was not satisfied with the amendment proposed. The Constitution, in its original state, gives to Congress the power of levying and collecting taxes, duties, imposts, and excise. The fault here is, that every thing is relinquished to the General Government. Now, the amendment gives the same power, with qualification, that there shall have been a previous requisition. This by no means came up to his idea; he thought that some particular revenue ought to be secured to the States, so as to enable them to support themselves.

He apprehended, when this clause in the Constitution was under the consideration of the several State conventions, they would not so readily have ratified it, if they had considered it more fully in the point of view in which he had now placed it; but if they had ratified it, it would have been under a conviction that Congress would admit such amendments as were necessary to the existence of the State Governments. At present, the States are divested of every means to support themselves. If they discover a new source of revenue, after Congress shall have diverted all the old ones into their treasury, the rapacity of the General Government can take that from them also. The States can have recourse to no tax, duty, impost, or excise, but what may be taken from them whenever the Congress shall be so disposed; and yet gentlemen must see that the annihilation of the State Governments will be followed by the ruin of this.

Now, what is the consequence of the amendment? Either the States will or will not comply with the requisitions. If they comply, they voluntarily surrender their means of support; if they refuse, the arms of Congress are raised to compel them, which, in all probability, may lay the foundation for civil war. What umbrage must it give every individual to have two sets of collectors and tax-gatherers surrounding his doors; the people then soured, and a direct refusal by the Legislature, will be the occasion of perpetual discord. He wished to alter this proposition in such a manner as to secure the support of the Federal Government and the State Governments likewise, and therefore wished the amendment referred to a Committee of the whole House.

53

JAMES MADISON TO RICHARD PETERS
19 Aug. 1789
Papers 12:346–48

The papers inclosed will shew that the nauseous project of amendments has not yet been either dismissed or despatched. We are so deep in them now, that right or wrong some thing must be done. I say this not by way of apology, for to be sincere I think no apology requisite. 1. because a constitutional provision in favr. of essential rights is a thing not improper in itself and was always viewed in that light by myself. It may be less necessary in a republic, than a Monarchy, & in a fedl. Govt. than the former, but it is in some degree rational in every Govt., since in every Govt. power may oppress, and declarations on paper, tho' not an effectual restraint, are not without some influence. 2. In many States the Constn. was adopted under a tacit compact in favr. of some subsequent provisions on this head. In Virga. It would have been *certainly* rejected, had no assurances been given by its advocates that such provisions would be pursued. As an honest man *I feel* my self bound by this consideration. 3. If the Candidates in Virga. for the House of Reps. had not taken this conciliary ground at the election, that State would have [been] represented almost wholly by disaffected characters, instead of the *federal* reps. now in Congs. 4. If amendts. had not been proposed from the federal side of the House, the proposition would have come *within three days*, from the adverse side. It is certainly best that they should appear to be the free gift of the friends of the Constitution rather than to be extorted by the address & weight of its enemies. 5. It will kill the opposition every where, and by putting an end to the disaffection to the Govt. itself, enable the administration to venture on measures not otherwise safe. Those who hate the Govt. will always join the party disaffected to measures of the admi[ni]s[tra]tion, and such a party will be created by every important measure. 6. If no amendts. be proposed the language of antifedl. leaders to the people, will be, we advised you not to adopt the Constn. witht. previous amendts—You listened to those who told you that subsequent securities for your rights would be most easily obtained—We urged you to insist on a Convention as the only effectual mode of obtaining these—You yielded to the assurances of those who told you that a Convention was unecessary, that Congs. wd. be the proper channel for getting what was wanted. &c &c. Here are fine texts for popular declaimers who wish to revive the antifedl. cause, and at the fall session of the Legislares. to blow the trumpet for a second Convention. In Virga. a majority of the Legislature last elected, is bitterly opposed to the Govt. and will be joined, if no amends. be proposed, by great nos. of the other side who will complain of being deceived. 7. Some amendts. are necssy for N. Carola. I am so informed by the best authorities in that State. I set out with

an apology for not writing sooner, I must conclude with one, for writing so much, & still more for writing so scurvily. Yrs truly

54

HOUSE OF REPRESENTATIVES, AMENDMENTS
24 Aug. 1789
Dumbauld 213–16

Article the First.

After the first enumeration, required by the first Article of the Constitution, there shall be one Representative for every thirty thousand, until the number shall amount to one hundred, after which the proportion shall be so regulated by Congress, that there shall be not less than one hundred Representatives, nor less than one Representative for every forty thousand persons, until the number of Representatives shall amount to two hundred, after which the proportion shall be so regulated by Congress, that there shall not be less than two hundred Representatives, nor less than one Representative for every fifty thousand persons.

Article the Second.

No law varying the compensation to the members of Congress, shall take effect, until an election of Representatives shall have intervened.

Article the Third.

Congress shall make no law establishing religion or prohibiting the free exercise thereof, nor shall the rights of Conscience be infringed.

Article the Fourth.

The Freedom of Speech, and of the Press, and the right of the People peaceably to assemble, and consult for their common good, and to apply to the Government for a redress of grievances, shall not be infringed.

Article the Fifth.

A well regulated militia, composed of the body of the People, being the best security of a free State, the right of the People to keep and bear arms, shall not be infringed, but no one religiously scrupulous of bearing arms, shall be compelled to render military service in person.

Article the Sixth.

No soldier shall, in time of peace, be quartered in any house without the consent of the owner, nor in time of war, but in a manner to be prescribed by law.

Article the Seventh.

The right of the People to be secure in their persons, houses, papers and effects, against unreasonable searches and seizures, shall not be violated, and no warrants shall issue, but upon probable cause supported by oath or affirmation, and particularly describing the place to be searched, and the persons or things to be seized.

Article the Eighth.

No person shall be subject, except in case of impeachment, to more than one trial, or one punishment for the same offence, nor shall be compelled in any criminal case, to be a witness against himself, nor be deprived of life, liberty or property, without due process of law; nor shall private property be taken for public use without just compensation.

Article the Ninth.

In all criminal prosecutions, the accused shall enjoy the right to a speedy and public trial, to be informed of the nature and cause of the accusation, to be confronted with the witnesses against him, to have compulsory process for obtaining witnesses in his favor, and to have the assistance of counsel for his defence.

Article the Tenth.

The trial of all crimes (except in cases of impeachment, and in cases arising in the land or naval forces, or in the militia when in actual service in time of War or public danger) shall be by an Impartial Jury of the Vicinage, with the requisite of unanimity for conviction, the right of challenge, and other accostomed requisites; and no person shall be held to answer for a capital, or otherways infamous crime, unless on a presentment or indictment by a Grand Jury; but if a crime be committed in a place in the possession of an enemy, or in which an insurrection may prevail, the indictment and trial may by law be authorised in some other place within the same State.

Article the Eleventh.

No appeal to the Supreme Court of the United States, shall be allowed, where the value in controversy shall not amount to one thousand dollars, nor shall any fact, triable by a Jury according to the course of the common law, be otherwise re-examinable, than according to the rules of common law.

Article the Twelfth.

In suits at common law, the right of trial by Jury shall be preserved.

Article the Thirteenth.

Excessive bail shall not be required, nor excessive fines imposed, nor cruel and unusual punishments inflicted.

Article the Fourteenth.

No State shall infringe the right of trial by Jury in criminal cases, nor the rights of conscience, nor the freedom of speech, or of the press.

Article the Fifteenth.

The enumeration in the Constitution of certain rights, shall not be construed to deny or disparage others retained by the people.

Article the Sixteenth.

The powers delegated by the Constitution to the government of the United States, shall be exercised as therein appropriated, so that the Legislative shall never exercise the powers vested in the Executive or Judicial; nor the Executive the powers vested in the Legislative or Judicial; nor the Judicial the powers vested in the Legislative or Executive.

Article the Seventeenth.

The powers not delegated by the Constitution, nor prohibited by it, to the States, are reserved to the States respectively.

55

SENATE, AMENDMENTS
9 Sept. 1789
Dumbauld 217–19

Article the First.

After the first enumeration, required by the first article of the Constitution, there shall be one Representative for every thirty thousand, until the number shall amount to one hundred; to which number one Representative shall be added for every subsequent increase of forty thousand, until the Representatives shall amount to two hundred, to which number one Representative shall be added for every subsequent increase of sixty thousand persons.

Article the Second.

No law, varying the compensation for the services of the Senators and Representatives, shall take effect, until an election of Representatives shall have intervened.

Article the Third.

Congress shall make no law establishing articles of faith, or a mode of worship, or prohibiting the free exercise of religion, or abridging the freedom of speech, or of the press, or the right of the people peaceably to assemble, and to petition to the government for a redress of grievances.

Article the Fourth.

A well regulated militia, being necessary to the security of a free State, the right of the people to keep and bear arms, shall not be infringed.

Article the Fifth.

No soldier shall, in time of peace, be quartered in any house, without the consent of the owner, nor in time of war, but in a manner to be prescribed by law.

Article the Sixth.

The right of the people to be secure in their persons, houses, papers, and effects, against unreasonable searches and seizures, shall not be violated, and no warrants shall issue, but upon probable cause, supported by oath or affirmation, and particularly describing the place to be searched, and the persons or things to be seized.

Article the Seventh.

No person shall be held to answer for a capital, or otherwise infamous crime, unless on a presentment or indictment of a Grand Jury, except in cases arising in the land or naval forces, or in the militia, when in actual service in time of war or public danger; nor shall any person be subject for the same offence to be twice put in jeopardy of life or limb; nor shall be compelled in any criminal case, to be a witness against himself, nor be deprived of life, liberty or property, without due process of law; nor shall private property be taken for public use without just compensation.

Article the Eighth.

In all criminal prosecutions, the accused shall enjoy the right to a speedy and public trial, to be informed of the nature and cause of the accusation, to be confronted with the witnesses against him, to have compulsory process for obtaining witnesses in his favour, and to have the assistance of counsel for his defence.

Article the Ninth.

In suits at common law, where the value in controversy shall exceed twenty dollars, the right of trial by Jury shall be preserved, and no fact, tried by a Jury, shall be otherwise re-examined in any court of the United States, than according to the rules of the common law.

Article the Tenth.

Excessive bail shall not be required, nor excessive fines imposed, nor cruel and unusual punishments inflicted.

Article the Eleventh.

The enumeration in the Constitution, of certain rights,

shall not be construed to deny or disparage others retained by the people.

Article the Twelfth.

The powers not delegated to the United States by the Constitution, nor prohibited by it to the States, are reserved to the States respectively, or to the people.

56

CONGRESS, AMENDMENTS AGREED TO AND PROPOSED TO THE STATES
25 Sept. 1789
Dumbauld 220–22

Article the first. After the first enumeration required by the first Article of the Constitution, there shall be one Representative for every thirty thousand, until the number shall amount to one hundred, after which, the proportion shall be so regulated by Congress, that there shall be not less than one hundred Representatives, nor less than one Representative for every forty thousand persons, until the number of Representatives shall amount to two hundred, after which the proportion shall be so regulated by Congress, that there shall not be less than two hundred Representatives, nor more than one Representative for every fifty thousand persons.

Article the second. No law, varying the compensation for the services of the Senators and Representatives, shall take effect, until an election of Representatives shall have intervened.

Article the third. Congress shall make no law respecting an establishment of religion, or prohibiting the free exercise thereof; or abridging the freedom of speech, or of the press, or the right of the people peaceably to assemble, and to petition the Government for a redress of grievances.

Article the fourth. A well regulated Militia, being necessary to the security of a free State, the right of the people to keep and bear Arms, shall not be infringed.

Article the fifth. No Soldier shall, in time of peace be quartered in any house, without the consent of the Owner, nor in time of war, but in a manner to be prescribed by law.

Article the sixth. The right of the people to be secure in their persons, houses, papers, and effects, against unreasonable searches and seizures, shall not be violated, and no Warrants shall issue, but upon probable cause, supported by Oath or affirmation, and particularly describing the place to be searched, and the persons or things to be seized.

Article the seventh. No person shall be held to answer for a capital, or otherwise infamous crime, unless on a presentment or indictment of a Grand Jury, except in cases arising in the land or naval forces, or in the Militia, when in actual service in time of War or public danger; nor shall any person be subject for the same offence to be twice put in jeopardy of life or limb, nor shall be compelled in any criminal case to be a witness against himself, nor be deprived of life, liberty, or property, without due process of law; nor shall private property be taken for public use without just compensation.

Article the eighth. In all criminal prosecutions, the accused shall enjoy the right to a speedy and public trial, by an impartial jury of the State and district wherein the crime shall have been committed, which district shall have been previously ascertained by law, and to be informed of the nature and cause of the accusation; to be confronted with the witnesses against him; to have compulsory process for obtaining witnesses in his favor, and to have the Assistance of Counsel for his defence.

Article the ninth. In suits at common law, where the value in controversy shall exceed twenty dollars, the right of trial by jury shall be preserved, and no fact tried by a jury shall be otherwise re-examined in any Court of the United States, than according to the rules of the common law.

Article the tenth. Excessive bail shall not be required, nor excessive fines imposed, nor cruel and unusual punishments inflicted.

Article the eleventh. The enumeration in the Constitution, of certain rights, shall not be construed to deny or disparage others retained by the people.

Article the twelfth. The powers not delegated to the United States by the Constitution, nor prohibited by it to the States, are reserved to the States respectively, or to the people.

SEE ALSO:

Generally ch. 3; Bill of Rights

Charter of Libertyes and Priviledges, 30 Oct. 1683, The Colonial Laws of New York from the Year 1664 to the Revolution (1894), 1:111–16

Act Declareing What Are the Rights and Priviledges of Their Majesties Subjects Inhabiting within Their Province of New York, 13 May 1691, The Colonial Laws of New York from the Year 1664 to the Revolution (1894), 1:244–48

Stamp Act Congress, Declaration of Rights, 19 Oct. 1765, Sources 270–71

Samuel Adams, The Rights of the Colonists, 20 Nov. 1772, Writings 2:350–59

Slave Petition to the Council and House of Representatives of the State of Massachusetts, 13 Jan. 1777, MHS Collections, 5th ser., 3:436–37

Oliver Ellsworth, Landholder, no. 6, 10 Dec. 1787, Essays 163

James Bowdoin, Massachusetts Ratifying Convention, 23 Jan. 1788, Elliot 2:87–88

Agrippa, no. 15, 29 Jan. 1788, Storing 4.6.67–71

Agrippa, no. 16, 5 Feb. 1788, Storing 4.6.73

Impartial Examiner, no. 1, 20 Feb., 5 Mar. 1788, Storing 5.14.5, 10, 14–15

Joseph Spencer to James Madison, 28 Feb. 1788, Documentary History 4:525–26

John Leland, Objections to the Federal Constitution, Feb. 1788, Documentary History 4:528

Noah Webster, Bills of Rights, 1788, Collection 45–48

Benjamin Rush to David Ramsay, Spring 1788, Letters 1:453

Sentiments of Many, 18 June 1788, Storing 5.20.1–2

A Delegate Who Has Catched Cold, 25 June 1788, Storing 5.19.13–18

Debate in North Carolina Ratifying Convention, 24 July 1788, Elliot 4:9–11

James Madison, Report on the Virginia Resolutions, Jan. 1800, Writings 6:385–401

Edmund Randolph, History of Virginia, 1809, 255

James Kent, Commentaries 2:1–8 (1827)

15

Equality

Introduction

Few features of the Constitution interest us today as much as equality. Although it is often the case that the questions the present poses to the past are largely an expression of contemporary concern—our questions rather than their questions—the issue of equality is an exception. For although the word "equality" appears nowhere in the document itself, our concern for equality is the direct consequence of the Founders' concern with equality. "The word fitly spoken" in 1776 (in Lincoln's memorable figure of speech) gave a special meaning and character to the Constitution, to the Union, and—by extension—to the people living their political lives in a regime defined by the Declaration, the Constitution, and the Union. To inquire closely into the Founders' understanding of equality is to scrutinize the very center of their political program—and ours.

Far, then, from being an alien category imposed upon a resistant matter, equality is a theme one encounters at almost every turn in the writings and arguments of the period. The difficulty lies not in want of evidence, but rather in our arbitrariness in singling out equality from the other great themes or problems with which it was connected. For it was not equality in the abstract that stirred men's passions so much as equality in the enjoyment of rights. What was to be the reach of that claim? There was much to argue over.

Many of the large issues that were to exercise Americans at the time of the establishment of the Constitution are already prefigured in the Putney Debates in England (no. 1). Here officers and men of the Puritans' New Model Army wrestled with the claim to which "the poorest he that is in England" was held to be entitled as much as "the greatest he." The immediate issue was equality in suffrage, but the implications—as the resistant officers were quick to point out—extended to representation, property, and the very elements of society itself. James Harrington, in his envisaged Oceana (no. 2), looked to the establishment in fact of an equal commonwealth, equal in both its foundation and its structure. An Agrarian Law would work against the concentration of landownership in the hands of the few and thereby prevent those few from overpowering the whole people. Concurrently a system of compulsory rotation of elected officials would forfend the creation of a magistracy separate from and hostile to the people at large. And yet for all this, Harrington's equal commonwealth would cherish the distinctions between men. In "a government of *laws* and not of *men*" individual superiority can be recognized without chagrin or resentment. Harrington expected a people enjoying a popular and equal suffrage to act on the understanding that "where men excel in virtue, the commonwealth is stupid and unjust if accordingly they do not excel in authority."

Thanks to John Locke's reformulation of Hobbes, the claim and implications of original equality became an American commonplace. (See ch. 2.) On the premise of original equality there is no natural subordination or ascendancy; everyone is as free as the next to order his acts or possessions or person as he sees fit. To say that all men

are by nature equal is to say that every man has an equal right to his natural freedom. As little as I can rightfully diminish your freedom without your consent can you diminish mine. The solidity of this claim is quite unshaken by the manifest inequalities among men, inequalities that may persuade some men to defer to others because of some acknowledged superiority. Although much of this original equality is superseded by the conventions of society and government, the foundation of civil society itself can only be the consent of free equals to submit to such an order. Finally, and in the most critical instance, the equal enjoyment of some rights persists—because unalienable.

By insisting upon the relatively even hand with which nature endows all men, Thomas Gordon, writing as Cato (no. 3), wished to impress upon his readers a healthy disdain for the trinkets and titles with which the few adorn themselves the better to gull the many. Confronted with the great inequalities of society, the many hasten to concoct or believe "a just Cause for Things that are not just." Reflections on men's natural equality should lead all to be more discriminating, to recognize the great role of "Contrivance or Chance" in countering the effects of nature. Instead of being dazzled or awed by blood, title, or place, instead of asking *who* the man is, we should inquire into *what* he is. The wanton, capricious, and often cruel effects of fortune may then be recognized for what they are. Cato did not say what a people should do on discovering that a titled ass or royal knave is, for all that, an ass or a knave. But on the other hand it is clear that he was not a crude environmentalist, ready on the instant to cry in extenuation that someone is depraved because he is deprived. If nature gives all her offspring heads and hands to provide for themselves, the expected consequences of natural equality will be inequality "according to the Use that they make of their Faculties, and of the Opportunities that they find." Here fortune can surely play cruel jokes, but in the most important respect, he thought, equality is still available to all. "To be great is not in every Man's Power; but to be good is in the Power of all: Thus far every Man may be [u]pon a Level with another, the Lowest with the Highest."

Montesquieu's discussion of equality in the context of the corruption or vulnerability of popular self-government struck an especially responsive note among the Americans. (See ch. 18, no. 3.) Equality was essential to democracy, but too much was as great a threat to that form of government as too little. So Montesquieu taught, and so a number of Founders were prepared to believe. There was no dearth of occasions for concern that there was not enough equality, or too much. Thus New Englanders could wonder and worry whether so comparatively unequal and divided a society as Virginia would be able to make a common cause against the British enemy (nos. 9, 10). Democraticus (no. 14) viewed the "principle of equality, this right," as a benchmark by which to judge a state's political liberty and, what is more, as the surest inducement to social cohesion and popular involvement. Yet that principle's hostility to "every species of subordination" did not extend to subordination arising from "the difference of capacity, disposition, and virtue." A Watchman (no. 15) did not feel compelled to raise that qualification as he mocked the pretensions of "some of our UNCOMMON PEOPLE" who were opposing the movement for what was to become the Pennsylvania constitution of 1776. These, not the leaders of the popular party, were the true vulgarians. Humble beginnings are not only an antidote to pride, but almost a source of pride in an egalitarian regime.

It was during those weeks of June and July 1776 that Virginia debated and passed its Declaration of Rights and that the Continental Congress laid hands on Jefferson's draft of a declaration of independence, giving witness to their sentiments (as he wryly noted), "not only by what they receive, but what they reject also." During that very period, however, a Citizen of New Jersey (no. 19) could complain of the aristocratical "ideas of government" prevailing among the common people as well as the rich. Such ideas had consequences: "The rich, having been used to govern, seem to think it is their right; and the poorer commonalty, having hitherto had little or no hand in government, seem to think it does not belong to them to have any."

Equal in Speech? Equal in Fact?

It is difficult to assess the truth of this characterization, not least because both pronouncements and recorded practices point in two directions. The letters of William Eddis (no. 6) depict a Maryland of great economic extremes, with a wretched underclass of servants and slaves and a vastly rich proprietary patronage, and yet notwithstanding all this, a prevalent sense of independence and equality even among "those who move in the humbler circles of life." Gouverneur Morris (no. 8) saw in the agitations of 1774 the end of the old order: "The mob begin to think and to reason. Poor reptiles!" Those very presuppositions that a Citizen of New Jersey was to attack as persistent atavisms here fill Morris with a sense of impending loss and regret.

The signals would be no less confusing or ambiguous if one tried to assess the relative equality of American society in revolt by looking at a handful of documents written within a half-dozen years of the Declaration of Independence. Jefferson's letter to David Rittenhouse on the inequality of talents (no. 23) makes an extraordinary gloss on the opening paragraph of the Declaration. His zeal as "a true Whig in science" led Jefferson to put politics in its place and, further, to be ready to put all men in their places: "we should dispose of and employ the geniuses of men according to their several orders and degrees." For Jefferson this was a matter of economy modeled on nature itself; true superiority was too rare a commodity to be misallocated or squandered or denied. Far from being in conflict with the Declaration's premise of the equality of rights, the rare talents of exceptional human beings (such as Rittenhouse) were the finest adornments of a regime where all were equally free to do their best. In the same spirit one might argue that the rare talents of exceptional human beings (such as Jefferson) were indispensable for securing the enjoyment of those equal rights. For all that, the premises of the Declaration were by no means truisms even to the Revolutionaries themselves. In the Return of Northampton, Massachusetts (no. 26), one is surprised less by the clear voice of Locke arising from the mists of the Connecticut River valley than by the perceived need to make a case for "personal equality." All taxpaying adult males have a right to give or withhold their consent; the case against taxation without representation apparently had still to be made in America as well as England.

It is hard to recognize in these several reflections on the inequality of talents and the unequal enjoyment of rights quite the American world depicted by Crèvecoeur or Franklin. Even discounting the deliberately idyllic tone of the first and the special rhetorical purposes of the second, we are left with an America that is the antithesis of all that Europe stands for: extremes of luxury and penury, pomp and wretchedness, dominion and domination. In the eyes of J. Hector St. John Crèvecoeur the American scene showed "a pleasing uniformity of decent competence," no palaces, no hovels. It was a happy people whose dictionary was luckily "short in words of dignity, and names of honour." Here laborers and men of the middling stations of life might long enjoy the gratifications of a "pleasing equality" (*Letters from an American Farmer*, Letter 3 [1782]). Franklin, too, stressed the "general happy Mediocrity" of fortune prevailing in America (no. 27). Europeans hoping to cash in on their real or fancied superiority to the Americans had best stay home; certainly birth, so highly valued in Europe, could hardly "be carried to a worse Market than that of America."

Given the ambiguities and contradictions in current (1780s) thought and actions, it is hardly to be expected that prophecies of the future course of equality in American society would speak with one voice. Jefferson's vivid encounter with the "enormous inequality" of the Old Regime, which had been productive of "so much misery to the bulk of mankind," confirmed his dedication to legislative policies that would augment and sustain the class of small landholders (no. 32). Therein lay the way for America to avoid Europe's distress. Madison granted readily enough "the comparative comfort of the Mass of people in the United States" (no. 33). But he was less certain than Jefferson—much less certain—that the Americans' superiority in this respect was sufficiently accounted for by the political advantages of a general freedom and of laws favoring the subdivision of property. When the United States too became "a Country fully peopled," Europe's puzzlement over the employment of the "great surplus of inhabitants" would become America's. It was a question whether republican society would manage better.

Meanwhile, however, statesmen framing a constitution for their posterity had to make some estimate of future probabilities. Those meeting at the Philadelphia Convention could do no less, and in the course of their labors showed strikingly different estimates of the future of equality in America. George Mason feared swinging from one of Montesquieu's extremes to the other; he saw the Convention as overreacting to earlier democratic excesses. In appealing for moderation he depicted an America where families rose and fell easily, and counseled those presently affluent and mighty to consider that "the course of a few years, not only might but certainly would, distribute their posterity throughout the lowest classes of Society." The pronounced inequalities of Mason's America bore little resemblance to Charles Pinckney's land of small differences and great openness. Like Jefferson, Pinckney saw strong forces at work in the situation of the Americans that would preserve and reinforce equality for a long time to come. Madison granted the undeniable features that set American society apart from states riven by hereditary distinctions and great inequality of wealth. But even now in 1787, he thought, America could not sensibly be regarded "as one homogeneous mass, in which every thing that affects a part will affect in the same manner the whole." As population grew, so too would "the proportion of those who will labour under all the hardships of life, and secretly sigh for a more equal distribution of its blessings." The future lay closer at hand than some suspected, "symptoms of a leveling spirit" already being discernible perhaps no farther away than western Massachusetts. To guard against this spirit and yet to do so in a manner compatible with republican principles was the great and urgent problem facing those "framing a system which we wish to last for ages."

A perceptive critic of the Constitution, the Federal Farmer (see ch. 13, no. 22), tried to judge the proposed institutional arrangements in the light of his own subtle taxonomy of America's contending interests. Among these the greatest were "the natural aristocracy"—officeholders, eminent professional men, men of large property—arrayed against "the natural democracy," the many others. The grounds of division were more complex than mere ownership of property; the effects of division were psychic as well as political. A concern for equality demanded a recognition of these inevitable nonegalitarian features of political life and a response to them. Hamilton, in contrast, saw the preponderant forces of equality in American society as something to be countered—within politically acceptable limits—for the sake of a respectable and effective government (no. 40).

Of all that generation of Founders, however, none compares to John Adams in his preoccupation with the problems of equality and inequality. Cranky, effusive, repetitive—and acute—his analysis testifies to a mind that was possessed by the "first principle" of the regime he helped shape. It was not for Adams a question of equality or no equality. He fully embraced the fundamental principles of equal natural rights and consent as taught by Locke and voiced by the Declaration. Rather it was a question of how to reckon with the actual inequalities in a constitution. How might one distinguish "not unuseful" inequalities—necessary results of nature's unequal distribution of understanding and activity—from "artificial inequalities," human contrivances that repeatedly and from time out of mind had subverted the very foundations of public decency and general liberty (no. 30)? Given that inequality is inevitable, the statesman's thoughts ought to be directed at neutralizing its worst effects and converting the "natural aristocracy" into "the greatest blessing of society." To do

so, however, required the most careful institutional arrangements, the most judicious management (no. 34). (See also ch. 11, no. 16.) Sober analysis had to precede sound policy: it was indispensable to recognize that the political problem was one of influence, not of rights. Whatever different bases men found for distinction, each could serve as a claim for privilege. In this sense anyone might be deemed an aristocrat who could command "one Vote in Addition to his own, by his Birth Fortune, Figure, Eloquence, Science, learning, Craft Cunning, or even his Character for good fellowship and a bon vivant" (no. 62). The attempt utterly to eradicate all privilege in the name of a mathematical equality was that terrifying amalgam of folly and fancy to which Napoleon had recently applied the term "Ideology"—a word (Adams confided to Jefferson) "which perfectly expresses my Opinion" (nos. 59, 63). Recognize instead that we are dealing with a part of "the Natural History of Man" (Letter to Jefferson, 14 Aug. 1813), a prejudice better accommodated than ignored or misunderstood. On the matter of accommodation Adams and Jefferson continued to differ, "as rational friends" and in fulfillment of their common belief "that we ought not to die before we have explained ourselves to each other" (Jefferson, no. 61).

An Equal Suffrage

Nothing displays so clearly the complexity (and the awareness of complexity) provoked by considerations of equality as those documents in which the discussion moved from high principle to high principle applied. A regard for circumstances tends to complicate rather than simplify issues, and so those discussions tend not to leave the reader with the satisfaction of an easy, pithy summary. What, for example, would be an equal suffrage under existing conditions? The Putney Debates (no. 1), Harrington (no. 2), Democraticus (no. 14), and John Adams (see ch. 13, no. 10) all spoke to the question, but with different voices, different emphases.

Adams was satisfied that it was better to wink at the generally free and easy interpretation of restrictive qualifications in Massachusetts than to stir the entire issue in an effort to bring principle and practice into harmony. For the principle, strictly interpreted and strictly applied, could hardly countenance the exclusion of women and minors and the propertyless; and those were exclusions for which Adams thought there were ample justifications. In one important respect John here spoke only for himself; Abigail had, and continued to have, her own view of what was owed women (nos. 9, 10, 12). Adams was, however, in the mainstream in rejecting mathematical equality, although not everyone would have adopted his language in opposing anything tending "to confound and destroy all Distinctions and prostrate all Ranks, to one common Levell." (Contrast no. 19.) Yet the people of Sutton, Massachusetts, even while vigorously criticizing the proposed (and later rejected) state constitution of 1778 for excluding free propertied "negroes, Indians and mulattoes" from voting, had no trouble accepting the exclusion of the propertyless or proposing a dilution of their vote (no. 22).

(These state arguments over suffrage would come to have a direct bearing on the government of the United States, since the Constitution of 1787 adopts the states' voting rules in determining the qualifications of electors of the United States House of Representatives.)

For the people of Northampton, Massachusetts, criticizing the proposed (and later accepted) state constitution of 1780 for failing to extend the suffrage to all adult taxpaying males, the call for "personal equality" was quite compatible with a recognized need for "corporation equality," the representation of town-corporations as such, regardless of their unequal size (no. 26). Far, then, from embodying the principle of equality, the maxim "one man, one vote" seemed rather to deny it. That at least appears to be the implicit conclusion of the Constitution of Massachusetts of 1780 (no. 25, ch. 1, sec. 3, art. 2). The very article that insists on an equal representation provides for a disproportionately large representation of the small incorporated towns scattered over the state. Luther Martin thought no less could be argued on behalf of the small states in the federal union (no. 37). (See also chs. 12 and 13.)

Property and Privilege

Equality considered in reference to property yielded similarly cautious conclusions. The record discloses no prominent movement of levelers, to say nothing of diggers, whatever the alarms set off by Shays and by Rhode Island (see, e.g., Farrand 2:332, 3:47–48). Yet these Founders were republicans, and most were sworn enemies to hereditary privileges and aristocratic pretensions, and to the seemingly unassailable battlements that European society had erected in defense of those privileges and pretensions. In this sense great inequality of property was not only suspect but a present danger (Adams, no. 10; Jefferson, no. 20; Madison, no. 50). For Benjamin Franklin it was even a question why property should be represented at all. Civil society was not like a partnership of merchant-adventurers whose voting rights were proportioned to their shares of investment (see ch. 12, no. 25). Other Founders, less enthusiastic or less financially secure, tried to address the main issue: how might the social and political effects of great wealth best be countered? To promote "equal Liberty," one needed to divide landownership into parcels small enough "to make the Acquisition of Land easy to every Member of Society" (Adams, see ch. 13, no. 10).

Equal possibilities were indispensable; equal holdings neither feasible nor desirable. A country of small wards or small republics, peopled and governed by men of small but adequate means, enjoying modest comforts and great independence: that was and continued to be Jefferson's vision of the government best suited "for the Man of these states." There need be no American analogue to "the Canaille of the cities of Europe," men so debased by the inequality of their societies as to pervert or endanger every public or private good (no. 61; see also no. 32). So, at least, it seemed to Jefferson looking at America and Europe from Paris or from atop Monticello. Closer to the scene,

Noah Webster agreed that popular government did indeed rest on a "fundamental law, favoring an equal or rather a general distribution of property" (no. 44). Anything hindering that distribution—be it perpetuities, primogeniture, entail, and the like—was counter to sound republican policy. But the ultimate effect of sound policy in this instance would be, paradoxically, evil consequences. Republican New England already showed what would be true for the entire United States: repeated subdivision led first to equality, then to impoverishment of the many, finally to enrichment of a few. Webster's fears were not shared by Justice Nathaniel Chipman of Vermont (no. 51), partly because he had greater faith in the very devices on which Webster relied to prevent great permanent accumulations. Whatever monopolized property or rendered it unalienable was indeed "a violation of the equal rights of man." But mere inequality of property was another matter; it was not necessarily "subversive of genuine liberty." Something like a law of nature would, if unimpeded, allow men to reap whatever they had sown, rising or sinking as the case might be. The Procrustean alternatives verged on tyranny. The author of the Declaration of Independence agreed (no. 64).

The Matter of Color

And then there was the matter of color. Whatever else might be said of the Founders' efforts to come to terms with the massive presence of black chattel slavery in the United States, obtuseness or indifference to the moral implications is not a charge that can stick. Their repeated references to the injustice of slavery were not limited to the secret discussions of the Philadelphia Convention. See Farrand 1:135 (Madison), 588 (G. Morris); 2:220 (Sherman), 221 (G. Morris), 364 (Martin), 370 (Mason), 371 (Ellsworth), 372 (Dickinson), 415 (Madison, Williamson), 417 (Madison). In public speech and in nonconfidential letters, the point was made again and again: slavery was deeply at odds with every principle that justified American resistance to British oppression. A people that literally had defined itself by reference to the principle of equality was in flagrant and profound contradiction with itself in holding other men slaves. The documents assembled here are only exemplary of some of the modes of expressing that deeply disquieting truth. Patrick Henry confessed outright to his Quaker correspondent that he was to be counted among those acting on "a Principle as repugnant to humanity as it is inconsistant with the Bible and destructive to Liberty." And why? "I am drawn along by ye. general inconvenience of living without them, I will not, I cannot justify it" (no. 7). Henry's candor was rare, not his reason (no. 41).

The inconsistency of a slave-trading and slave-owning America was given special point, of course, by the principled pronouncements of the Virginia Declaration of Rights and Declaration of Independence and the Massachusetts Declaration of Rights. The bearing of those pronouncements on the country's egregious inequality was lost on no one, neither at the moment nor after. See Randolph (no. 17), Jefferson (no. 18), Pickering (no. 29), Martin (no. 37). Yet noting the fact of incongruity and inconsistency was not enough. What was to be done? A master's having one slave to set free (Jay, Conditional Manumission, 21 Mar. 1784) bore little relation to a master's having hundreds to set free; the economic costs and social consequences were simply incomparable. It was important to recognize the difference, to admit the difficulty—not in order to excuse (no. 31), but in order to understand. The theory was plain; reducing it to practice, quite another matter (no. 39).

Here the massive fact was prejudice—again, not to be pleaded in extenuation (Franklin, no. 5), but no less real for all that. It lay on the surface, shaping public discourse (Hamilton, no. 24; Jay to Dongan, 27 Feb. 1792) and often preventing it (Madison, no. 45; Tucker to Belknap, 13 Aug. 1797). All proposals for change had to come to terms with that basic social datum: whites disdained and feared blacks (Jefferson, no. 28; Jay to Dongan, 27 Feb. 1792; Madison, no. 65). Under certain conditions the expression of those passions might account for emancipation—as in Massachusetts (no. 53). Regardless of whether the framers of the Massachusetts Constitution intended the result, that document's Declaration of Rights was in fact used in the state courts as a basis for attacking slavery. Here was an early but hardly unique instance of antislavery principles being bolstered by interest, passion, and prejudice.

Elsewhere, as in the parts of Virginia and South Carolina where blacks outnumbered whites, those passions pointed alternatively (or even simultaneously) to removal through colonization, or continued slavery for the indefinite future, or utter bewilderment. But the passion-inspired reasoning that commended colonization (nos. 28, 43) was questionable on two counts: the staggering costs and dedication necessary to bring about the wholesale removal of blacks (nos. 54, 55), and the resistance of enlightened folk to the notion that prejudice was invulnerable (nos. 47, 55). Yet even the most studiedly analytical proposals faltered in the entanglements of passion and could offer only the hope of hope (nos. 28, 56). Matters certainly were no better in the state and federal legislatures and courts. There the Founders' generation and their successors wrestled with the Constitution's provisions regarding the slave trade (Art. 1, sec. 9, cl. 1), the recovery of fugitive slaves (Art. 4, sec. 2, cl. 3), the three-fifths rule (Art. 1, sec. 2, cl. 3), and the complexities of excluding slavery from the territories and arranging for gradual emancipation in the northern states. Their struggles—and evasions—could not but shape the general understanding of equality.

But what if, as some few maintained, prejudice was indeed mutable? Would not then the full and equal incorporation of free blacks in American political and social life and in the land in which they had surely mixed their labor be a genuine if distant possibility? Northern abolitionist plans rested on this foundation. With the gradual education and moral improvement of freedmen, whites would come to extend and accept the blacks' enjoyment of political and civil liberty. This, of course, presumed that blacks had the capacity for such improvement (Franklin, no. 5; Hamilton, no. 24; Sullivan, no. 55)—and no less that whites had the capacity to alter their perceptions in the face of new facts. But if white prejudice was immutable and black resentment at their oppression implacable, then full equality was a will-o'-the-wisp. The available alternatives were bleak enough. Either slavery might continue as it was, or its rigors be mitigated into a form of "civil slavery" (no. 56), or the population of manumitted slaves be removed from American soil (no. 65). This, of course, presumed that black slaves had the capacity to learn to manage their own affairs—out of the reach of disdainful whites—whatever the final judgment might be of their native capacities (no. 28; see also Jefferson to Grégoire, 25 Feb. 1809). And it presumed no less what "A Freeman" (no. 47) denied—that whites had a "just right" to expel Africans who were as much Americans as the Europeans on this side of the Atlantic.

That white Americans had a right to make black slaves an offer they could not refuse—freedom on the condition of removal—was a point of which Jefferson, Tucker, and Madison seemed convinced. Although blacks were unquestionably the equals of whites in having the natural right to govern themselves, the profound differences in their common American past seemed to preclude the transformation of that natural right into a conventional right that blacks might enjoy under the Constitution. "Deep rooted prejudices entertained by the whites; ten thousand recollections, by the blacks, of the injuries they have sustained; new provocations; the real distinctions which nature has made"—Jefferson's litany went on and on. Blacks would need to be protected from their contemptuous former masters, who in turn would need to be protected from their vindictive former slaves. The new birth of black freedom could take place only in a new land of their own. It was a tragic irony to stagger the mind: A new nation, conceived in liberty and dedicated to the proposition that all men are created equal, erected in a land where "the mere distinction of colour [had been] made in the most enlightened period of time, a ground of the most oppressive dominion ever exercised by man over man" (Madison, Farrand 1:135). The agonies of the Founders and of their successors were as much a tribute to the power of that dedication to equality as a mark of its failure.

1

THE PUTNEY DEBATES
29 Oct. 1647
Woodhouse 52–76

(The paper called "An Agreement of the People" read. Afterwards the first article read by itself.)

["That the people of England, being at this day very unequally distributed by counties, cities, and boroughs, for the election of their deputies in Parliament, ought to be more indifferently proportioned, according to the number of the inhabitants: the circumstances whereof, for number, place, and manner, are to be set down before the end of this present Parliament."]

Ireton: The exception that lies in it is this. It is said, they are to be distributed according to the number of the inhabitants: "The people of England," &c. And this doth make me think that the meaning is, that every man that is an inhabitant is to be equally considered, and to have an equal voice in the election of those representers, the persons that are for the general Representative; and if that be the meaning, then I have something to say against it. But if it be only that those people that by the civil constitution of this kingdom, which is original and fundamental, and beyond which I am sure no memory of record does go—

[*Cowling, interrupting*]: Not before the Conquest.

[*Ireton*]: But before the Conquest it was so. If it be intended that those that by that constitution that was before the Conquest, that hath been beyond memory, such persons that have been before [by] that constitution [the electors], should be [still] the electors, I have no more to say against it.

. . . . .

Petty: We judge that all inhabitants that have not lost their birthright should have an equal voice in elections.

Rainborough: I desired that those that had engaged in it [might be included]. For really I think that the poorest he that is in England hath a life to live, as the greatest he; and therefore truly, sir, I think it's clear, that every man that is to live under a government ought first by his own consent to put himself under that government; and I do think that the poorest man in England is not at all bound in a strict sense to that government that he hath not had a voice to put himself under; and I am confident that, when I have heard the reasons against it, something will be said to answer those reasons, insomuch that I should doubt whether he was an Englishman or no, that should doubt of these things.

Ireton: That's [the meaning of] this, ["according to the number of the inhabitants"]?

Give me leave to tell you, that if you make this the rule I think you must fly for refuge to an absolute natural right, and you must deny all civil right; and I am sure it will come to that in the consequence. This, I perceive, is pressed as that which is so essential and due: the right of the people of this kingdom, and as they are the people of this kingdom, distinct and divided from other people, and that we must for this right lay aside all other considerations; this is so just, this is so due, this is so right to them. And that those that they do thus choose must have such a power of binding all, and loosing all, according to those limitations, this is pressed as so due, and so just, as [it] is argued, that it is an engagement paramount [to] all others: and you must for it lay aside all others; if you have engaged any otherwise, you must break it. [We must] so look upon these as thus held out to us; so it was held out by the gentleman that brought it yesterday. For my part, I think it is no right at all. I think that no person hath a right to an interest or share in the disposing of the affairs of the kingdom, and in determining or choosing those that shall determine what laws we shall be ruled by here—no person hath a right to this, that hath not a permanent fixed interest in this kingdom, and those persons together are properly the represented of this kingdom, and consequently are [also] to make up the representers of this kingdom, who taken together do comprehend whatsoever is of real or permanent interest in the kingdom. And I am sure otherwise I cannot tell what any man can say why a foreigner coming in amongst us—or as many as will coming in amongst us, or by force or otherwise settling themselves here, or at least by our permission having a being here—why they should not as well lay claim to it as any other. We talk of birthright. Truly [by] birthright there is thus much claim. Men may justly have by birthright, by their very being born in England, that we should not seclude them out of England, that we should not refuse to give them air and place and ground, and the freedom of the highways and other things, to live amongst us—not any man that is born here, though by his birth there come nothing at all (that is part of the permanent interest of this kingdom) to him. That I think is due to a man by birth. But that by a man's being born here he shall have a share in that power that shall dispose of the lands here, and of all things here, I do not think it a sufficient ground. I am sure if we look upon that which is the utmost (within [any] man's view) of what was originally the constitution of this kingdom, upon that which is most radical and fundamental, and which if you take away, there is no man hath any land, any goods, [or] any civil interest, that is this: that those that choose the representers for the making of laws by which this state and kingdom are to be governed, are the persons who, taken together, do comprehend the local interest of this kingdom; that is, the persons in whom all land lies, and those in corporations in whom all trading lies. This is the most fundamental constitution of this kingdom and [that] which if you do not allow, you allow none at all. This constitution hath limited and determined it that only those shall have voices in elections. It is true, as was said by a gentleman near me, the meanest man in England ought to have [a voice in the election of the government he lives under—but only if he has some local interest]. I say this: that those that have the meanest local interest—that man that hath but forty shillings a year, he *hath* as great voice in the election of a knight for the shire as he that hath ten thousand a year, or more if he had never so much; and therefore there is that regard had to it. But this [local interest], still the constitution of this government hath had an eye to (and what other government hath not an eye to this?). It doth not relate to the interest of the kingdom if it do not lay the foundation of the power that's given to the representers, in those who have a permanent and a local interest in the kingdom, and who taken all together do comprehend the whole [interest of the kingdom]. There is all the reason and justice that can be, [in this]: if I will come to live in a kingdom, being a foreigner to it, or live in a kingdom, having no permanent interest in it, [and] if I will desire as a stranger, or claim as one freeborn here, the air, the free passage of highways, the protection of laws, and all such things—if I will either desire them or claim them, [then] I (if I have no permanent interest in that kingdom) must submit to those laws and those rules [which they shall choose], who, taken together, do comprehend the whole interest of the kingdom. And if we shall go to take away this, we shall plainly go to take away all property and interest that any man hath either in land by inheritance, or in estate by possession, or anything else—[I say], if you take away this fundamental part of the civil constitution.

Rainborough: Truly, sir, I am of the same opinion I was, and am resolved to keep it till I know reason why I should not. I confess my memory is bad, and therefore I am fain to make use of my pen. I remember that, in a former speech [which] this gentleman brought before this [meeting], he was saying that in some cases he should not value whether [there were] a king or no king, whether lords or no lords, whether a property or no property. For my part I differ in that. I do very much care whether [there be] a king or no king, lords or no lords, property or no property; and I think, if we do not all take care, we shall all have none of these very shortly. But as to this present business. I do hear nothing at all that can convince me, why any man that is born in England ought not to have his voice in election of burgesses. It is said that if a man have not a permanent interest, he can have no claim; and [that] we must be no freer than the laws will let us be, and that there is no [law in any] chronicle will let us be freer than that we [now] enjoy. Something was said to this yesterday. I do think that the main cause why Almighty God gave men reason, it was that they should make use of that reason, and that they should improve it for that end and purpose that God gave it them. And truly, I think that half a loaf is better than none if a man be anhungry: [this gift of reason without other property may seem a small thing], yet I think there is nothing that God hath given a man that any [one] else can take from him. And therefore I say, that either it must be the Law of God or the law of man that must prohibit the meanest man in the kingdom to have this benefit as well as the greatest. I do not find anything in the Law of God, that a lord shall choose twenty burgesses, and a gentleman but two, or a poor man shall

choose none: I find no such thing in the Law of Nature, nor in the Law of Nations. But I do find that all Englishmen must be subject to English laws, and I do verily believe that there is no man but will say that the foundation of all law lies in the people, and if [it lie] in the people, I am to seek for this exemption.

And truly I have thought something [else]: in what a miserable distressed condition would many a man that hath fought for the Parliament in this quarrel, be! I will be bound to say that many a man whose zeal and affection to God and this kingdom hath carried him forth in this cause, hath so spent his estate that, in the way the state [and] the Army are going, he shall not hold up his head, if when his estate is lost, and not worth forty shillings a year, a man shall not have any interest. And there are many other ways by which [the] estates men have (if that be the rule which God in his providence does use) do fall to decay. A man, when he hath an estate, hath an interest in making laws, [but] when he hath none, he hath no power in it; so that a man cannot lose that which he hath for the maintenance of his family but he must [also] lose that which God and nature hath given him! And therefore I do [think], and am still of the same opinion, that every man born in England cannot, ought not, neither by the Law of God nor the Law of Nature, to be exempted from the choice of those who are to make laws for him to live under, and for him, for aught I know, to lose his life under. And therefore I think there can be no great stick in this.

Truly I think that there is not this day reigning in England a greater fruit or effect of tyranny than this very thing would produce. Truly I know nothing free but only the knight of the shire, nor do I know anything in a parliamentary way that is clear from the height and fulness of tyranny, but only [that]. As for this of corporations [which you also mentioned], it is as contrary to freedom as may be. For, sir, what is it? The King he grants a patent under the Broad Seal of England to such a corporation to send burgesses, he grants to [such] a city to send burgesses. When a poor base corporation from the King['s grant] shall send two burgesses, when five hundred men of estate shall not send one, when those that are to make their laws are called by the King, or cannot act [but] by such a call, truly I think that the people of England have little freedom.

Ireton: I think there was nothing that I said to give you occasion to think that I did contend for this, that such a corporation [as that] should have the electing of a man to the Parliament. I think I agreed to this matter, that all should be equally distributed. But the question is, whether it should be distributed to all persons, or whether the same persons that are the electors [now] should be the electors still, and it [be] equally distributed amongst *them.* . . .

All the main thing that I speak for, is because I would have an eye to property. I hope we do not come to contend for victory—but let every man consider with himself that he do not go that way to take away all property. For here is the case of the most fundamental part of the constitution of the kingdom, which if you take away, you take away all by that. Here men of this and this quality are determined to be the electors of men to the Parliament, and they are all those who have any permanent interest in the kingdom, and who, taken together, do comprehend the whole [permanent, local] interest of the kingdom. I mean by permanent [and] local, that [it] is not [able to be removed] anywhere else. As for instance, he that hath a freehold, and that freehold cannot be removed out of the kingdom; and so there's a [freeman of a] corporation, a place which hath the privilege of a market and trading, which if you should allow to all places equally, I do not see how you could preserve any peace in the kingdom, and that is the reason why in the constitution we have but some few market towns. Now those people [that have freeholds] and those [that] are the freemen of corporations, were looked upon by the former constitution to comprehend the permanent interest of the kingdom. For [first], he that hath his livelihood by his trade, and by his freedom of trading in such a corporation, which he cannot exercise in another, he is tied to that place, [for] his livelihood depends upon it. And secondly, that man hath an interest, hath a permanent interest there, upon which he may live, and live a freeman without dependence. These [things the] constitution [of] this kingdom hath looked at. Now I wish we may all consider of what rights you will challenge that all the people should have right to elections. Is it by the right of nature? If you will hold forth that as your ground, then I think you must deny all property too, and this is my reason. For thus: by that same right of nature (whatever it be) that you pretend, by which you can say, one man hath an equal right with another to the choosing of him that shall govern him—by the same right of nature, he hath the same [equal] right in any goods he sees—meat, drink, clothes—to take and use them for his sustenance. He hath a freedom to the land, [to take] the ground, to exercise it, till it; he hath the [same] freedom to anything that any one doth account himself to have any propriety in. Why now I say then, if you, against the most fundamental part of [the] civil constitution (which I have now declared), will plead the Law of Nature, that a man should (paramount [to] this, and contrary to this) have a power of choosing those men that shall determine what shall be law in this state, though he himself have no permanent interest in the state, [but] whatever interest he hath he may carry about with him—if this be allowed, [because by the right of nature] we are free, we are equal, one man must have as much voice as another, then show me what step or difference [there is], why [I may not] by the same right [take your property, though not] of necessity to sustain nature. It is for my better being, and [the better settlement of the kingdom]? Possibly not for it, neither: possibly I may not have so real a regard to the peace of the kingdom as that man who hath a permanent interest in it. He that is here to-day, and gone to-morrow, I do not see that he hath such a permanent interest. Since you cannot plead to it by anything but the Law of Nature, [or for anything] but for the end of better being, and [since] that better being is not certain, and [what is] more, destructive to another; upon these grounds, if you do, paramount [to] all constitutions, hold up this Law of Nature, I would fain have any man show me their bounds, where you will end, and [why you should not] take away all property.

Rainborough: I shall now be a little more free and open with you than I was before. I wish we were all true-hearted, and that we did all carry ourselves with integrity. If I did mistrust you I would [not] use such asseverations. I think it doth go on mistrust, and things are thought too [readily] matters of reflection, that were never intended. For my part, as I think, *you* forgot something that was in *my* speech, and you do not only yourselves believe that [some] men are inclining to anarchy, but you would make all men believe that. And, sir, to say because a man pleads that every man hath a voice [by right of nature], that therefore it destroys [by] the same [argument all property—this is to forget the Law of God]. That there's a property, the Law of God says it; else why [hath] God made that law, *Thou shalt not steal?* I am a poor man, therefore I must be [op]pressed: if I have no interest in the kingdom, I must suffer by all their laws be they right or wrong. Nay thus: a gentleman lives in a country and hath three or four lordships, as some men have (God knows how they got them); and when a Parliament is called he must be a Parliament-man; and it may be he sees some poor men, they live near this man, he can crush them—I have known an invasion to make sure he hath turned the poor men out of doors; and I would fain know whether the potency of [rich] men do not this, and so keep them under the greatest tyranny that was [ever] thought of in the world. And therefore I think that to that it is fully answered: God hath set down that thing as to propriety with this law of his, *Thou shalt not steal.* And for my part I am against any such thought, and, as for yourselves, I wish you would not make the world believe that we are for anarchy.

Cromwell: I know nothing but this, that they that are the most yielding have the greatest wisdom; but really, sir, this is not right as it should be. No man says that you have a mind to anarchy, but [that] the consequence of this rule tends to anarchy, must end in anarchy; for where is there any bound or limit set if you take away this [limit], that men that have no interest but the interest of breathing [shall have no voice in elections]? Therefore I am confident on 't, we should not be so hot one with another.

Rainborough: I know that some particular men we debate with [believe we] are for anarchy.

Ireton: . . . I have, with as much plainness and clearness of reason as I could, showed you how I did conceive the doing of this [that the paper advocates] takes away that which is the most original, the most fundamental civil constitution of this kingdom, and which is, above all, that constitution by which I have any property. If you will take away that and set up, as a thing paramount, whatever a man may claim by the law of Nature, though it be not a thing of necessity to him for the sustenance of nature; if you do make this your rule, I desire clearly to understand where then remains property.

Now then—I would misrepresent nothing—the answer which had anything of matter in it, the great and main answer upon which that which hath been said against this [objection] rests, seemed to be that it will not make a breach of property, [for this reason]: that there is a law, *Thou shalt not steal.* [But] the same law says, *Honour thy father and* [*thy*] *mother,* and that law doth likewise hold out that it doth extend to all that (in that place where we are in) are our governors; so that by that there is a forbidding of breaking a civil law when we may live quietly under it, and [that by] a divine law. Again it is said—indeed [was said] before—that there is no law, no divine law, that tells us that such a corporation must have the election of burgesses, such a shire [of knights], or the like. Divine law extends not to particular things. And so, on the other side, if a man were to demonstrate his [right to] property by divine law, it would be very remote. Our [right to] property descends from other things, as well as our right of sending burgesses. That divine law doth not determine particulars but generals in relation to man and man, and to property, and all things else: and we should be as far to seek if we should go to prove a property in [a thing by] divine law, as to prove that I have an interest in choosing burgesses of the Parliament by divine law. And truly, under favour, I refer it to all, whether there be anything of solution to that objection that I made, if it be understood—I submit it to any man's judgment.

Rainborough: To the thing itself—property [in the franchise]. I would fain know how it comes to be the property [of some men, and not of others]. As for estates and those kind of things, and other things that belong to men, it will be granted that they are property; but I deny that that is a property, to a lord, to a gentleman, to any man more than another in the kingdom of England. If it be a property, it is a property by a law—neither do I think that there is very little property in this thing by the law of the land, because I think that the law of the land in that thing is the most tyrannical law under heaven. And I would fain know what we have fought for. [For our laws and liberties?] And this is the old law of England—and that which enslaves the people of England—that they should be bound by laws in which they have no voice at all! [With respect to the divine law which says *Honour thy father and thy mother*] the great dispute is, who is a right father and a right mother? I am bound to know who is my father and mother; and—I take it in the same sense you do—I would have a distinction, a character whereby God commands me to honour [them]. And for my part I look upon the people of England so, that wherein they have not voices in the choosing of their [governors—their civil] fathers and mothers—they are not bound to that commandment.

Petty: I desire to add one word concerning the word *property.* It is for something that anarchy is so much talked of. For my own part I cannot believe in the least that it can be clearly derived from that paper. 'Tis true, that somewhat may be derived in the paper against the King, the power of the King, and somewhat against the power of the Lords; and the truth is when I shall see God going about to throw down King and Lords and property, then I shall be contented. But I hope that they may live to see the power of the King and the Lords thrown down, that

yet may live to see property preserved. And for this of changing the Representative of the nation, of changing those that choose the Representative, making of them more full, taking more into the number than formerly, I had verily thought we had all agreed in it that more should have chosen—all that had desired a more equal representation than we now have. For now those only choose who have forty shillings freehold. A man may have a lease for one hundred pounds a year, a man may have a lease for three lives, [but he has no voice]. But [as] for this [argument], that it destroys all right [to property] that every Englishman that is an inhabitant of England should choose and have a voice in the representatives, I suppose it is, [on the contrary], the only means to preserve all property. For I judge every man is naturally free; and I judge the reason why men [chose representatives] when they were in so great numbers that every man could not give his voice [directly], was that they who were chosen might preserve property [for all]; and therefore men agreed to come into some form of government that they might preserve property, and I would fain know, if we were to begin a government, [whether you would say], "You have not forty shillings a year, therefore you shall not have a voice." Whereas before there was a government every man had such a voice, and afterwards, and for this very cause, they did choose representatives, and put themselves into forms of government that they may preserve property, and therefore it is not to destroy it, [to give every man a voice].

Ireton: I think we shall not be so apt to come to a right understanding in this business, if one man, and another man, and another man do speak their several thoughts and conceptions to the same purpose, as if we do consider where the objection lies, and what the answer is which is made to it; and therefore I desire we may do so. To that which this gentleman spake last. The main thing that he seemed to answer was this: that he would make it appear that the going about to establish this government, [or] such a government, is not a destruction of property, nor does not tend to the destruction of property, because the people's falling into a government is for the preservation of property. What weight there [is in it] lies in this: since there is a falling into a government, and government is to preserve property, therefore this cannot be against property. The objection does not lie in that, the making of the representation more equal, but [in] the introducing of men into an equality of interest in this government, who have no property in this kingdom, or who have no local permanent interest in it. For if I had said that I would not wish at all that we should have any enlargement of the bounds of those that are to be the electors, then you might have excepted against it. But [what I said was] that I would not go to enlarge it beyond all bounds, so that upon the same ground you may admit of so many men from foreign states as would outvote you. The objection lies still in this. I do not mean that I would have it restrained to that proportion [that now obtains], but to restrain it still to men who have a local, a permanent interest in the kingdom, who have such an interest that they may live upon it as freeman, and who have such an interest as is fixed upon a place, and is not the same equally everywhere. If a man be an inhabitant upon a rack rent for a year, for two years, or twenty years, you cannot think that man hath any fixed or permanent interest. That man, if he pay the rent that his land is worth, and hath no advantage but what he hath by his land, is as good a man, may have as much interest, in another kingdom as here. I do not speak of not enlarging this [representation] at all, but of keeping this to the most fundamental constitution in this kingdom, that is, that no person that hath not a local and permanent interest in the kingdom should have an equal dependence in election [with those that have]. But if you go beyond this law, if you admit any man that hath a breath and being, I did show you how this will destroy property. It may come to destroy property thus. You may have such men chosen, or at least the major part of them, [as have no local and permanent interest]. Why may not those men vote against all property? [Again] you may admit strangers by this rule, if you admit them once to inhabit, and those that have interest in the land may be voted out of their land. It may destroy property that way. But here is the rule that you go by. You infer this to be the right of the people, of every inhabitant, because man hath such a right in nature, though it be not of necessity for the preserving of his being; [and] therefore you are to overthrow the most fundamental constitution for this. By the same rule, show me why you will not, by the same right of nature, make use of anything that any man hath, [though it be not] for the necessary sustenance of men. Show me what you will stop at; wherein you will fence any man in a property by this rule.

Rainborough: I desire to know how this comes to be a property in some men, and not in others.

Colonel [Nathaniel] Rich: I confess [there is weight in] that objection that the Commissary-General last insisted upon; for you have five to one in this kingdom that have no permanent interest. Some men [have] ten, some twenty servants, some more, some less. If the master and servant shall be equal electors, then clearly those that have no interest in the kingdom will make it their interest to choose those that have no interest. It may happen, that the majority may by law, not in a confusion, destroy property; there may be a law enacted, that there shall be an equality of goods and estate. I think that either of the extremes may be urged to inconveniency; that is, [that] men that have no interest as to estate should have no interest as to election [and that they should have an equal interest]. But there may be a more equitable division and distribution than that he that hath nothing should have an equal voice; and certainly there may be some other way thought of, that there may be a representative of the poor as well as the rich, and not to exclude all. I remember there were many workings and revolutions, as we have heard, in the Roman Senate; and there was never a confusion that did appear (and that indeed *was* come to) till the state came to know this kind of distribution of election. That is how the people's voices were bought and sold, and that by the poor; and thence it came that he was the richest man, and [a

man] of some considerable power among the soldiers, and one they resolved on, made himself a perpetual dictator. And if we strain too far to avoid monarchy in kings [let us take heed] that we do not call for emperors to deliver us from more than one tyrant.

Rainborough: I should not have spoken again. I think it is a fine gilded pill. But there is much danger, and it may seem to some that there is some kind of remedy [possible]. I think that we are better as we are [if it can be really proved] that the poor shall choose many [and] still the people be in the same case, be over-voted still. [But of this, and much else, I am unsatisfied], and therefore truly, sir, I should desire to go close to the business; and the [first] thing that I am unsatisfied in is how it comes about that there is such a propriety in some freeborn Englishmen, and not [in] others.

Cowling [demanded]: Whether the younger son have not as much right to the inheritance as the eldest.

Ireton: Will you decide it by the light of nature?
. . . . .

Wildman: Unless I be very much mistaken we are very much deviated from the first question. Instead of following the first proposition to inquire what is just, I conceive we look to prophecies, and look to what may be the event, and judge of the justness of a thing by the consequence. I desire we may recall [ourselves to the question] whether it be right or no. I conceive all that hath been said against it will be reduced to this [question of consequences], and [to] another reason—that it is against a fundamental law, that every person [choosing] ought to have a permanent interest, because it is not fit that those should choose Parliaments that have no lands to be disposed of by Parliament.

Ireton: If you will take it by the way, it is not fit that the representees should choose [as] the representers, or the persons who shall make the law in the kingdom, [those] who have not a permanent fixed interest in the kingdom. [The reason is the same in the two cases.]

Wildman: Sir, I do so take it; and I conceive that that is brought in for the same reason: that foreigners might [otherwise not only] come to have a voice in our elections as well as the native inhabitants, [but to be elected].

Ireton: That is upon supposition that these [foreigners] should be all inhabitants.

Wildman: I shall begin with the last first. The case is different with the native inhabitant and [the] foreigner. If a foreigner shall be admitted to be an inhabitant in the nation, so he will submit to that form of government as the natives do, he hath the same right as the natives but in this particular. Our case is to be considered thus, that we have been under slavery. That's acknowledged by all. Our very laws were made by our conquerors; and whereas it's spoken much of chronicles, I conceive there is no credit to be given to any of them; and the reason is because those that were our lords, and made us their vassals, would suffer nothing else to be chronicled. We are now engaged for our freedom. That's the end of Parliaments: not to constitute what is already [established, but to act] according to the just rules of government. Every person in England hath as clear a right to elect his representative as the greatest person in England. I conceive that's the undeniable maxim of government: that all government is in the free consent of the people. If [so], then upon that account there is no person that is under a just government, or hath justly his own, unless he by his own free consent be put under that government. This he cannot be unless he be consenting to it, and therefore, according to this maxim, there is never a person in England [but ought to have a voice in elections]. If [this], as that gentleman says, be true, there are no laws that in this strictness and rigour of justice [any man is bound to], that are not made by those who[m] he doth consent to. And therefore I should humbly move, that if the question be stated—which would soonest bring things to an issue—it might rather be thus: Whether any person can justly be bound by law, who doth not give his consent that such persons shall make laws for him?

Ireton: Let the question be so: Whether a man can be bound to any law that he doth not consent to? And I shall tell you, that he may and ought to be [bound to a law] that he doth not give a consent to, nor doth not choose any [to consent to]; and I will make it clear. If a foreigner come within this kingdom, if that stranger will have liberty [to dwell here] who hath no local interest here, he, as a man, it's true, hath air, [the passage of highways, the protection of laws, and all] that by nature; we must not expel [him] our coasts, give him no being amongst us, nor kill him because he comes upon our land, comes up our stream, arrives at our shore. It is a piece of hospitality, of humanity, to receive that man amongst us. But if that man be received to a being amongst us, I think that man may very well be content to submit himself to the law of the land; that is, the law that is made by those people that have a property, a fixed property, in the land. I think, if any man will receive protection from this people though [neither] he nor his ancestors, not any betwixt him and Adam, did ever give concurrence to this constitution, I think this man ought to be subject to those laws, and to be bound by those laws, so long as he continues amongst them. That is my opinion. A man ought to be subject to a law, that did not give his consent, but with this reservation, that if this man do think himself unsatisfied to be subject to this law he may go into another kingdom. And so the same reason doth extend, in my understanding, [to] that man that hath no permanent interest in the kingdom. If he hath money, his money is as good in another place as here; he hath nothing that doth locally fix him to this kingdom. If that man will live in this kingdom, or trade amongst us, that man ought to subject himself to the law made by the people who have the interest of this kingdom in them. And yet I do acknowledge that which you take to be so general a maxim, that in every kingdom, within every land, the original of power of making laws, of determining what shall be law in the land, does lie in the people—[but by the people is meant those] that are possessed of the permanent interest in the land. But whoever is extraneous to

this, that is, as good a man in another land, that man ought to give such a respect to the property of men that live in the land. They do not determine [that I shall live in this land]. Why should I have any interest in determining what shall be the law of this land?

Major [William] Rainborough: I think if it can be made to appear that it is a just and reasonable thing, and that it is for the preservation of all the [native] freeborn men, [that they should have an equal voice in election]—I think it ought to be made good unto them. And the reason is: that the chief end of this government is to preserve persons as well as estates, and if any law shall take hold of my person it is more dear than my estate.

. . . . .

Rainborough: For my part, I think we cannot engage one way or other in the Army if we do not think of the people's liberties. If we can agree where the liberty and freedom of the people lies, that will do all.

Ireton: I cannot consent so far. As I said before: when I see the hand of God destroying King, and Lords, and Commons too, [or] any foundation of human constitution, when I see God hath done it, I shall, I hope, comfortably acquiesce in it. But first, I cannot give my consent to it, because it is not good. And secondly, as I desire that this Army should have regard to engagements wherever they are lawful, so I would have them have regard to this [as well]: that they should not bring that scandal upon the name of God [and the Saints], that those that call themselves by that name, those whom God hath owned and appeared with—that we should represent ourselves to the world as men so far from being of that peaceable spirit which is suitable to the Gospel, as we should have bought peace of the world upon such terms—[as] we would not have peace in the world but upon such terms—as should destroy all property. If the principle upon which you move this alteration, or the ground upon which you press that we should make this alteration, do destroy all kind of property or whatsoever a man hath by human constitution, [I cannot consent to it]. The Law of God doth not give me property, nor the Law of Nature, but property is of human constitution. I have a property and this I shall enjoy. Constitution founds property. If either the thing itself that you press or the consequence [of] that you press [do destroy property], though I shall acquiesce in having no property, yet I cannot give my heart or hand to it; because it is a thing evil in itself and scandalous to the world, and I desire this Army may be free from both.

Sexby: I see that though liberty were our end, there is a degeneration from it. We have engaged in this kingdom and ventured our lives, and it was all for this: to recover our birthrights and privileges as Englishmen; and by the arguments urged there is none. There are many thousands of us soldiers that have ventured our lives; we have had little propriety in the kingdom as to our estates, yet we have had a birthright. But it seems now, except a man hath a fixed estate in this kingdom, he hath no right in this kingdom. I wonder we were so much deceived. If we had not a right to the kingdom, we were mere mercenary soldiers. There are many in my condition, that have as good a condition [as I have]; it may be little estate they have at present, and yet they have as much a [birth]right as those two who are their lawgivers, as any in this place. I shall tell you in a word my resolution. I am resolved to give my birthright to none. Whatsoever may come in the way, and [whatsoever may] be thought, I will give it to none. If this thing [be denied the poor], that with so much pressing after [they have sought, it will be the greatest scandal]. There was one thing spoken to this effect: that if the poor and those in low condition [were given their birthright it would be the destruction of this kingdom]. I think this was but a distrust of Providence. I do think the poor and meaner of this kingdom—I speak as in relation [to the condition of soldiers], in which we are—have been the means of the preservation of this kingdom. I say, in their stations, and really I think to their utmost possibility; and their lives have not been [held] dear for purchasing the good of the kingdom. [And now they demand the birthright for which they fought.] Those that act to this end are as free from anarchy or confusion as those that oppose it, and they have the Law of God and the law of their conscience [with them]. But truly I shall only sum up [in] this. I desire that we may not spend so much time upon these things. We must be plain. When men come to understand these things, they will not lose that which they have contended for. That which I shall beseech you is to come to a determination of this question.

Ireton: I am very sorry we are come to this point, that from reasoning one to another we should come to express our resolutions. I profess for my part, what I see is good for the kingdom, and becoming a Christian to contend for, I hope through God I shall have strength and resolution to do my part towards it. And yet I will profess direct contrary in some kind to what that gentleman said. For my part, rather than I will make a disturbance to a good constitution of a kingdom wherein I may live in godliness and honesty, and peace and quietness, I will part with a great deal of my birthright. I will part with my own property rather than I will be the man that shall make a disturbance in the kingdom for my property; and therefore if all the people in this kingdom, or [the] representative[s] of them all together, should meet and should give away my property I would submit to it, I would give it away. But that gentleman, and I think every Christian, ought to bear that spirit, to carry that in him, that he will not make a public disturbance upon a private prejudice.

Now let us consider where our difference lies. We all agree that you should have a Representative to govern, and this Representative to be as equal as you can [make it]. But the question is, whether this distribution can be made to all persons equally, or whether [only] amongst those equals that have the interest of England in them. That which I have declared [is] my opinion [still]. I think we ought to keep to that [constitution which we have now], both because it is a civil constitution—it is the most fundamental constitution that we have—and [because] there is so much justice and reason and prudence [in it]—as I dare confidently undertake to demonstrate—that there are

many more evils that will follow in case you do alter [it] than there can [be] in the standing of it. But I say but this in the general, that I do wish that they that talk of birth-rights—we any of us when we talk of birthrights—would consider what really our birthright is.

If a man mean by birthright, whatsoever I can challenge by the Law of Nature (suppose there were no constitution at all, no civil law and [no] civil constitution), [and] that *that* I am to contend for against constitution; [then] you leave no property, nor no foundation for any man to enjoy anything. But if you call that your birthright which is the most fundamental part of your constitution, then let him perish that goes about to hinder you or any man of the least part of your birthright, or will [desire to] do it. But if you will lay aside the most fundamental constitution, which is as good, for aught you can discern, as anything you can propose—at least it is a constitution, and I will give you consequence for consequence of good upon [that] constitution as you [can give] upon your birthright [without it]—and if you merely upon pretence of a birthright, of the right of nature, which is only true as for [your being, and not for] your better being; if you will upon that ground pretend that this constitution, the most fundamental constitution, the thing that hath reason and equity in it, shall not stand in your way, [it] is the same principle to me, say I, [as if] but for your better satisfaction you shall take hold of anything that a[nother] man calls his own.

Rainborough: Sir, I see that it is impossible to have liberty but all property must be taken away. If it be laid down for a rule, and if you will say it, it must be so. But I would fain know what the solider hath fought for all this while? He hath fought to enslave himself, to give power to men of riches, men of estates, to make him a perpetual slave. We do find in all presses that go forth none must be pressed that are freehold men. When these gentlemen fall out among themselves they shall press the poor scrubs to come and kill [one another for] them.

Ireton: . . . Give me leave [to say] but this one word. I [will] tell you what the soldier of the kingdom hath fought for. First, the danger that we stood in was that one man's will must be a law. The people of the kingdom must have this right at least, that they should not be concluded [but] by the Representative of those that had the interest of the kingdom. So[m]e men fought in this, because they were immediately concerned and engaged in it. Other men who had no other interest in the kingdom but this, that they should have the benefit of those laws made by the Representative, yet [fought] that they should have the benefit of this Representative. They thought it was better to be concluded by the common consent of those that were fixed men, and settled men, that had the interest of this kingdom [in them]. "And from that way," [said they], "I shall know a law and have a certainty." Every man that was born [in the country, that] is a denizen in it, that hath a freedom, he was capable of trading to get money, to get estates by; and therefore this man, I think, had a great deal of reason to build up such a foundation of interest to himself: that is, that the will of one man should not be a law, but that the law of this kingdom should be by a choice of persons to represent, and that choice to be made by, the generality of the kingdom. Here was a right that induced men to fight, and those men that had this interest, though this be not the utmost interest that other men have, yet they had *some* interest. Now [tell me] why we should go to plead whatsoever we can challenge by the right of nature against whatsoever any man can challenge by constitution. I do not see where that man will stop, as to point of property, [so] that he shall not use [against other property] that right he hath [claimed] by the Law of Nature against that constitution. I desire any man to show me where there is a difference. I have been answered, "Now we see liberty cannot stand without [destroying] property." Liberty may be had and property not be destroyed. First, the liberty of all those that have the permanent interest in the kingdom, *that* is provided for [by the constitution]. And [secondly, by an appeal to the Law of Nature] liberty cannot be provided for in a general sense, if property be preserved. For if property be preserved [by acknowledging a natural right in the possessor, so] that I am not to meddle with such a man's estate, his meat, his drink, his apparel, or other goods, then the right of nature destroys liberty. By the right of nature I am to have sustenance rather than perish; yet property destroys it for a man to have [this] by the right of nature, [even] suppose there be no human constitution.

Peter: I do say still, under favour, there is a way to cure all this debate. I will mind you of one thing: that upon the will of one man abusing us, [we reached agreement], and if the safety of the Army be in danger [so we may again]. I hope, it is not denied by any man that any wise, discreet man that hath preserved England [is worthy of a voice] in the government of it. So that, I profess to you, for my part I am clear the point of election should be amended [in that sense]. I think, they will desire no more liberty. If there were time to dispute it, I think they would be satisfied, and all *will* be satisfied.

Cromwell: I confess I was most dissatisfied with that I heard Mr. Sexby speak, of any man here, because it did savour so much of will. But I desire that all of us may decline that, and if we meet here really to agree to that which is for the safety of the kingdom, let us not spend so much time in such debates as these are, but let us apply ourselves to such things as are conclusive, and that shall be this. Everybody here would be willing that the Representative might be mended, that is, [that] it might be [made] better than it is. Perhaps it may be offered in that [other] paper [Heads of the Proposals] too lamely. If the thing [there] insisted upon be too limited, why perhaps there are a very considerable part of copyholders by inheritance that ought to have a voice; and there may be somewhat [in that paper] too [that] reflects upon the generality of the people [in denying them a voice]. I know our debates are endless if we think to bring it to an issue this way. If we may but resolve upon a committee, [things may be done]. If I cannot be satisfied to go so far as these gentlemen that bring this paper [An Agreement of the People], I say it again [and] I profess it, I shall freely and willingly withdraw myself, and I hope to do it in such a manner that the Army shall see that I shall by my with-

drawing satisfy the interest of the Army, the public interest of the kingdom, and those ends these men aim at. And I think if you do bring this to a result it were well.

Rainborough: If these men must be advanced, and other men set under foot, I am not satisfied. If their rules must be observed, and other men, that are [not] in authority, [be silenced, I] do not know how this can stand together [with the idea of a free debate]. I wonder how that should be thought wilfulness in one man that is reason in another; for I confess I have not heard anything that doth satisfy me, and though I have not so much wisdom, or [so many] notions in my head, I have so many [apprehensions] that I could tell an hundred [such] of the ruin of the people. I am not at all against a committee's meeting; and as you say—and I think every Christian ought to do the same— for my part I shall be ready, if I see the way that I am going, and the thing that I would insist on, will destroy the kingdom, I shall withdraw [from] it as soon as any. And therefore, till I see that, I shall use all the means [I can], and I think it is no fault in any man [to refuse] to sell that which is his birthright.

Sexby: I desire to speak a few words. I am sorry that my zeal to what I apprehend is good should be so ill resented. I am not sorry to see that which I apprehend is truth [disputed], but I am sorry the Lord hath darkened some so much as not to see it, and that is in short [this]. Do you [not] think it were a sad and miserable condition, that we have fought all this time for nothing? All here, both great and small, do think that we fought for something. I confess, many of us fought for those ends which, we since saw, were not those which caused us to go through difficulties and straits [and] to venture all in the ship with you. It had been good in you to have advertised us of it, and I believe you would have [had] fewer under your command to have commanded. But if this be the business, that an estate doth make men capable—it is no matter which way they get it, they are capable—to choose those that shall represent them, I think there are many that have not estates that in honesty have as much right in the freedom [of] their choice as any that have great estates. Truly, sir, [as for] your putting off this question and coming to some other, I dare say, and I dare appeal to all of them, that they cannot settle upon any other until this be done. It was the ground that we took up arms [on], and it is the ground which we shall maintain. Concerning my making rents and divisions in this way. As a particular, if I were but so, I could lie down and be trodden there; [but] truly I am sent by a regiment, [and] if I should not speak, guilt shall lie upon me, and I [should] think I were a covenant-breaker. I do not know how we have [been] answered in our arguments, and [as for our engagements], I conceive we shall not accomplish them to the kingdom when we deny them to ourselves. I shall be loath to make a rent and division, but, for my own part, unless I see this put to a question, I despair of an issue.

Clarke: The first thing that I should desire was, and is, this: that there might be a temperature and moderation of spirit within us; that we should speak with moderation, not with such reflection as was boulted one from another, but so speak and so hear as that which [is said] may be the droppings of love from one to another's hearts. Another word I have to say is [that] the grand question of all is, whether or no it be the property of every individual person in the kingdom to have a vote in election[s]; and the ground [on which it is claimed] is the Law of Nature, which, for my part, I think to be that law which is the ground of all constitutions. Yet really properties are the foundation of constitutions, [and not constitutions of property]. For if so be there were no constitutions, yet the Law of Nature does give a principle [for every man] to have a property of what he has, or may have, which is not another man's. This [natural right to] property is the ground of *meum* and *tuum*. Now there may be inconveniencies on both hands, but not so great freedom [on either as is supposed—not] the greater freedom, as I conceive, that all may have whatsoever [they have a mind to]. And if it come to pass that there be a difference, and that the one [claimant] doth oppose the other, then nothing can decide it but the sword, which is the wrath of God.

Audley: I see you have a long dispute [and] that you do intend to dispute here till the tenth of March. You have brought us into a fair pass, and the kingdom into a fair pass, for if your reasons are not satisfied, and we do not fetch all our waters from your wells, you threaten to withdraw yourselves. I could wish, according to our several protestations, we might sit down quietly, and there throw down ourselves where we see reason. I could wish we might all rise, and go to our duties, and set our work in hand. I see both [parties] at a stand; and if we dispute here, both are lost.

Cromwell: Really for my own part I must needs say, whilst we say we would not make reflections we do make reflections; and if I had not come hither with a free heart to do that that I was persuaded in my conscience is my duty, I should a thousand times rather have kept myself away. For I do think I had brought upon myself the greatest sin that I was [ever] guilty of, if I should have come to have stood before God in that former duty, and if [I did retreat from] that my saying—which I did say, and shall persevere to say—that I shall not, I cannot, against my conscience do anything. They that have stood so much for liberty of conscience, if they will not grant that liberty to every man, but say it is a deserting I know not what—if that [liberty] be denied me, I think there is not that equality that is professed to be amongst us. Though we should be satisfied in our consciences in what we do, we are told we purpose to leave the Army, or to leave our commands, as if we took upon us to do it as [a] matter of will. I did hear some gentlemen speak more of will than anything that was spoken this way, for more was spoken by way of will than of satisfaction, and if there be not more equality in our minds I can but grieve for it, I must do no more. I said this (and I say no more): that [if you would] make your businesses as well as you can, we might bring things to an understanding; [for] it was [in order] to be brought to a fair composure [that we met]. And when you have said [what you can for the paper and have heard our ob-jections], if [then] you should put this paper to the question without any qualifications, I doubt whether it would pass so freely. If we would have no difference we ought to put it [with due qualifications]. And let me speak clearly and freely—I have heard other gentlemen do the like: I have not heard the Commissary-General answered, not in one part, to my knowledge, not in a tittle. If, therefore, when I see there is an extremity of difference between you, [I move for a committee] to the end it may be brought nearer to a general satisfaction—if this [too] be thought a deserting of that interest, [I know not] if there can be anything more sharply said; I will not give it an ill word.

2

JAMES HARRINGTON, COMMONWEALTH OF OCEANA 70–75
1656

By what has been shown in *reason* and *experience* it may appear that, though commonwealths in general be governments of the senate proposing, the people resolving, and the magistracy executing, yet some are not so good at these orders as others, through some impediment or defect in the frame, balance, or capacity of them, according to which they are of divers kinds.

The first division of them is into such as are *single*, as Israel, Athens, Lacedaemon, etc., and such as are by *leagues*, as those of the Achaeans, Aetolians, Lyceans, Swiss, and Hollanders.

The second (being Machiavelli's) is into such as are for *preservation*, as Lacedaemon and Venice, and such as are for *increase*, as Athens and Rome, in which I can see no more than that the former take in no more citizens than are necessary for defense, and the latter so many as are capable of increase.

The third division (unseen hitherto) is into *equal* and *unequal*, and this is the main point especially as to domestic peace and tranquility. For to make a commonwealth unequal is to divide it into parties, which sets them at perpetual variance, the one party endeavoring to preserve their eminence and inequality, and the other to attain to equality. Whence the people of Rome derived their perpetual strife with the nobility or Senate. But in an *equal commonwealth* there can be no more strife than there can be overbalance in equal weights. Wherefore the commonwealth of Venice, being that which of all others is the most equal in the constitution, is that wherein there never happened any strife between the Senate and the people.

An equal commonwealth is such a one as is equal, both in the balance and foundation and in the superstructures; that is to say, in her Agrarian Law and in her rotation.

An *equal Agrarian* is a perpetual law establishing and preserving the balance of dominion by such a distribution that no one man or number of men within the compass of the few or aristocracy can come to overpower the whole people by their possessions in lands.

As the Agrarian answers to the foundation, so does rotation to the superstructures.

Equal rotation is equal vicissitude in government, or succession unto magistracy conferred for such convenient terms, enjoying equal vacations, as take in the whole body by parts succeeding others through the *free election* or suffrage of the people.

The contrary whereunto is prolongation of magistracy which, trashing the wheel of rotation, destroys the life or natural motion of a commonwealth.

The election or suffrage of the people is freest where it is made or given in such a manner that it can neither oblige *(qui beneficium accepit libertatem vendidit)* ["Who accepts a gift sells liberty"] nor disoblige another or, through fear of an enemy or bashfulness toward a friend, impair a man's liberty.

Wherefore says Cicero, *"Grata populo est tabella quae frontes aperit hominum, mentes tegit, datque eam libertatem ut quod velint faciant,"* ["For if the people cherishes its privilege of voting by ballot, which allows a man to wear a smooth brow while it cloaks the secrets of his heart, and which leaves him free to act as he chooses, while he gives any promise he may be asked to give, why do you insist that the courts should determine what a vote cannot?"] the tablet (or ballot of the people of Rome, who gave their votes by throwing tablets or little pieces of wood secretly into urns marked for the negative or affirmative) was a welcome constitution to the people, as that which, not impairing the assurance of their brows, increased the freedom of their judgment. I have not stood upon a more particular description of this ballot because that of Venice, exemplified in the Model, is of all others the most perfect.

An equal commonwealth (by that which has been said) *is a government established upon an equal Agrarian, arising into the superstructures or three orders: the senate debating and proposing, the people resolving, and the magistracy executing by an equal rotation through the suffrage of the people given by the ballot.* For though rotation may be without the ballot, and the ballot without rotation, yet the ballot not only as to the ensuing Model includes both, but is by far the most equal way; for which cause under the name of the ballot I shall hereafter understand both that and rotation too.

Now having reasoned the principles of an equal commonwealth, I should come to give an instance of such a one in experience if I could find it. But if this work be of any value, it lies in that it is the first example of a commonwealth that is perfectly equal. For Venice, though she come the nearest, yet is a commonwealth for preservation, and such a one, considering the paucity of citizens taken in and the number not taken in, is externally unequal. And though every commonwealth that holds provinces must in that regard be such, yet not to that degree. Nevertheless, Venice internally and for her capacity is by far the most equal, though she has not in my judgment arrived at the full perfection of equality, both because her laws supplying the defect of an Agrarian are not so clear nor effectual at the foundation, nor her superstructures by the virtue of her ballot or rotation exactly librated, in regard that, through the paucity of her citizens, her greater magistracies are continually wheeled through a few hands.

As is confessed by Gianotti where he says that if a gentleman come once to be *Savio di terra ferma*, it seldom happens that he fails from thenceforth to be adorned with some one of the greater magistracies, as *Savi di mare*, *Savi di terra ferma*, *Savi Grandi*, Counselors, those of the decemvirate or dictatorian council, the *Aurogatori* or censors which require no vacation or interval. Wherefore, if this in Venice or that in Lacedaemon, where the kings were hereditary and the senators (though elected by the people) for life, cause no inequality (which is hard to be conceived) in a commonwealth for preservation or such a one as consists of a few citizens, yet is it manifest that it would cause a very great one in a commonwealth for increase or consisting of the many, which by the engrossing [of] the magistracies in a few hands would be obstructed in their rotation.

But there be [those] that say (and think it a strong objection), let a commonwealth be as equal as you can imagine, two or three men when all is done will govern it; and there is that in it which, notwithstanding the pretended sufficiency of a popular state, amounts to a plain confession of the imbecility of that policy and of the prerogative of monarchy, for as much as popular governments in difficult cases have had recourse to dictatorian power as in Rome.

To which I answer, that as truth is a spark whereunto objections are like bellows, so in this our commonwealth shines. For the eminence acquired by suffrage of the people in a commonwealth, especially if it be *popular* and *equal*, can be ascended by no other steps than the universal acknowledgment of virtue; and where men excel in virtue, the commonwealth is stupid and unjust if accordingly they do not excel in authority. Wherefore this is both the advantage of virtue, which has her due encouragement, and the commonwealth, which has her due services. These are the philosophers which Plato would have to be princes, the princes which Solomon would have to be mounted, and their steeds are those of *authority*, not *empire*. Or, if they be buckled to the chariot of empire, as that of the dictatorian power, like the chariot of the sun it is glorious for terms and vacations or intervals. And as a commonwealth is a government of *laws* and not of *men*, so is this the principality of the virtue and not of the man. If that fail or set in one, it rises in another, which is created his immediate successor.

> . . . *Uno avulso non deficit alter,*
> *Aureus, et simili frondescit virga metallo.*

> ["And when [a bough] is torn away,
> another gold one grows in its place
> with leaves of the same metal."]

And this takes away that vanity from under the sun which is an error proceeding more or less from all other rulers under heaven but an equal commonwealth.

These things considered, it will be convenient in this place to speak a word to such as go about to insinuate to the nobility or gentry a fear of the people, or into the people a fear of the nobility or gentry, as if their interests were each destructive to [the] other, when in truth an army may as well consist of soldiers without officers or of officers without soldiers, as a commonwealth, especially such a one as is capable of greatness, of a people without a gentry or of a gentry without a people. Wherefore this (though not always so intended, as may appear by Machiavelli who else would be guilty) is a pernicious error. There is something first in the making of a commonwealth, then in the governing of her, and last of all in the leading of her armies, which, though there be great divines, great lawyers, great men in all professions, seems to be peculiar to the genius of a gentleman. For so it is in the universal series of [history], that if any man have founded a commonwealth, he was first a gentleman. Moses had his education by the daughter of Pharaoh; Theseus and Solon, of noble birth, were held by the Athenians worthy to be kings; Lycurgus was of the blood-royal; Romulus and Numa princes; Brutus and Publicola patricians; the Gracchi that lost their lives for the people of Rome and the restitution of that commonwealth were the sons of a father adorned with two Triumphs, and of Cornelia, the daughter of Scipio, who being sought in marriage by King Ptolemy, disdained to be the queen of Egypt. And the most renowned Olphaus Megaletor [Oliver Cromwell], sole Legislator (as you will see) of the Commonwealth of Oceana, was derived from a noble family. Nor will it be any occasion of scruple in this case that Hobbes affirms the politics to be no ancienter than his book *De cive*. Such also as have gotten any fame in the civil government of a commonwealth, or by the leading of her armies, have been gentlemen. For so in all other respects were those plebeian magistrates elected by the people of Rome, being of known descents and of equal virtues, save only that they were excluded from the name by the usurpation of the patricians. Holland, through this defect at home, has borrowed princes for her generals and gentlemen for her commanders, of divers nations. And Switzerland, if she have defect in this kind, rather lends her people to the colors of other princes than makes that noble use of them herself which should assert the liberty of mankind. For where there is not a nobility to bolt out the people, they are slothful, regardless of the world and the public interest of liberty, as even that of Rome had been without her gentry. Wherefore let the people embrace the gentry in peace as the light of their eyes and in war as the trophy of their arms. And if Cornelia disdained to be Queen of Egypt, if a Roman consul looked down from his tribunal upon the greatest king, let the nobility love and cherish the people that afford them a throne so much higher in a commonwealth, and in the acknowledgment of their virtue, than the crowns of monarchs.

3

Thomas Gordon, Cato's Letters, no. 45
16 Sept. 1721
Jacobson 101–6

Men are naturally equal, and none ever rose above the rest but by Force or Consent: No Man was ever born above all the rest, nor below them all; and therefore there never was any Man in the World so good or so bad, so high or so low, but he had his Fellow. Nature is a kind and benevolent Parent; she constitutes no particular Favourites with Endowments and Privileges above the rest; but for the most part sends all her Offspring into the World furnished with the Elements of Understanding and Strength, to provide for themselves: She gives them Heads to consult their own Security, and Hands to execute their own Counsels; and according to the Use that they make of their Faculties, and of the Opportunities that they find, Degrees of Power and Names of Distinction grow amongst them, and their natural Equality is lost.

Thus Nature, who is their Parent, deals with Men: But Fortune, who is their Nurse, is not so benevolent and impartial; she acts wantonly and capriciously, often cruelly; and counterplotting Justice as well as Nature, frequently sets the Fool above the wise Man, and the Best below the Worst.

And from hence it is, that the most Part of the World, attending much more to the noisy Conduct and glaring Effects of Fortune, than to the quiet and regular Proceedings of Nature, are misled in their Judgment upon this Subject: They confound Fortune with Nature, and too often ascribe to natural Merit and Excellency the Works of Contrivance or Chance. This however, shews that Reason and Equity run in our Heads, while we endeavour to find a just Cause for Things that are not just; and this is the Source of the Reverence which we pay to Men whom Fortune sometimes lifts on high, though Nature had placed them below. The Populace rarely see any Creature rise, but they find a Reason for it in his Parts; when probably the true one will be found in his own Baseness, or another Man's Folly.

From the same Reasoning may be seen why it is, that, let who will be at the Head of a Party, he is always extolled by his Party as superior to the rest of Mankind; and let who will be the first Man of his Country, he will never fail being complimented by many as the first of his Species. But the Issue and their own Behaviour constantly shew, that the highest are upon a Level with the rest, and often with the lowest. Men that are high are almost ever seen in a false Light; the most Part see them at a great Distance, and through a magnifying Medium; some are dazzled with their Splendor, many are awed by their Power. Whatever appears shining or terrible, appears great, and is magnified by the Eye and the Imagination.

That Nature has made Men equal, we know and feel; and when People come to think otherwise, there is no Excess of Folly and Superstition which they may not be brought to practise. Thus they have made Gods of dead Men, and paid divine Honours to many while they were yet living: They saw them to be but Men, yet they worshipped them as Gods. And even they who have not gone quite so far, have yet, by their wild Notions of Inequality, done as much Mischief; they have made Men, and often wicked Men, to be Vice-Gods; and then made God's Power (falsely so called) as irresistible in the Hands of Men as in his own, and much more frightful.

It is evident to common Sense, that there ought to be no

Inequality in Society, but for the Sake of Society; but these Men have made one Man's Power and Will the Cause of all Men's Misery. They gave him as far as they could the Power of God, without obliging him to practise the Mercy and Goodness of God.

Those that think themselves furthest above the rest, are generally by their Education below them all. They are debased by a Conceit of their Greatness: They trust to their Blood; which, speaking naturally, gives them no Advantage; and neglect their Mind, which alone, by proper Improvements, sets one Man above another. It is not Blood or Nature, but Art or Accident, which makes one Man excel others. *Aristotle,* therefore, must either have been in Jest, when he said, that he, who naturally excelled all others, ought to govern all; or said it to flatter his Pupil and Prince, *Alexander* the Great. It is certain, that such a Man never yet was found in the World, and never will be found till the End of it. *Alexander* himself, notwithstanding the Greatness of his Spirit, and his Conquests, had in his own Army, and perhaps among the common Soldiers, Men naturally as great and brave as himself, and many more wise.

Whoever pretends to be naturally superior to other Men, claims from Nature what she never gave to any Man. He sets up for being more than a Man; a Character with which Nature has nothing to do. She has thrown her Gifts in common amongst us; and as the highest Offices of Nature fall to the Share of the Mean as well as of the Great, her vilest Offices are performed by the Great as well as by the Mean: Death and Diseases are the Portion of Kings as well as of Clowns; and the Corpse of a Monarch is no more exempted from Stench and Putrefaction, than the Corpse of a Slave.

Mors aequo pulsat pede.

[Pale Death with foot impartial knocks at poor men's hovels and princes' citadels.]

All the Arts and Endowments of Men to acquire Preeminence and Advantages over one another, are so many Proofs and Confessions that they have not such Pre-eminence and Advantages from Nature; and all their Pomp, Titles, and Wealth, are Means and Devices to make the World think that they who possess them are superior in Merit to those that want them. But it is not much to the Glory of the upper Part of Mankind, that their boasted and superior Merit is often the Work of Heralds, Artificers, and Money; and that many derive their whole Stock of Fame from Ancestors, who lived an Age or many Ages ago.

The first Founders of great Families were not always Men of Virtue or Parts; and where they were so, those that came after them did frequently, and almost generally, by trusting to their Blood, disgrace their Name. Such is the Folly of the World, and the Inconvenience of Society, to allow Men to be great by Proxy! An Evil that can scarce ever be cured. The Race of *French* Kings, called by their Historians in Contempt, *Les Rois faineants* and the Succession of the *Roman Caesars,* (in both which, for one good

Prince they had ten that were intolerable, either for Folly, or Cruelty, and often for both) might be mentioned as known Proofs of the above Truth; and every Reader will find in his own Memory many more.

I have been told of a Prince, who, while yet under Age, being reproved by his Governor for doing Things ill or indecent, used to answer, *Je suis Roy; I am King;* as if his Quality had altered the Nature of Things, and he himself had been better than other Men, while he acted worse. But he spoke from that Spirit which had been instilled into him from his Cradle. *I am King!* What then, Sir? The Office of a King is not to do Evil, but to prevent it. You have Royal Blood in your Veins: But the Blood of your Page is, without being Royal, as good as yours; or, if you doubt, try the Difference in a Couple of Porringers next Time you are ill; and learn from this Consideration and Experiment, that by Nature you are no better than your People, though subject from your Fortune to be worse, as many of your Ancestors have been.

If my Father got an Estate and Title by Law or the Sword, I may by Virtue of his Will or his Patent enjoy his Acquisition; but if I understand neither Law nor the Sword, I can derive Honour from neither: My Honour therefore is, in the Reason of Things purely nominal; and I am still by Nature a *Plebeian,* as all Men are.

There is nothing moral in Blood, or in Title, or in Place: Actions only, and the Causes that produce them, are moral. He therefore is best that does best. Noble Blood prevents neither Folly, nor Lunacy, nor Crimes: but frequently begets or promotes them: And Noblemen, who act infamously, derive no Honour from virtuous Ancestors, whom they dishonour. A Man who does base Things, is not noble; nor great, if he do little Things: A sober Villager is a better Man than a debauched Lord; an honest Mechanick than a Knavish Courtier.

. . . *Nobilitas sola est atque unica virtus.*

. . . .

Prima mihi debes animi bona; sanctus haberi
Justitiacque tenax factis, dictisque mereris?

Juv. Sat. 8.

[Virtue is the only and sole real nobility. . . .
You owe first the virtues of the mind—
do you deserve to be accounted honest, and
tenacious of justice, in word and deed?]

We cannot bring more natural Advantages into the World than other Men do; but we can acquire more Virtue in it than we generally acquire. To be great is not in every Man's Power; but to be good is in the Power of all: Thus far every Man may be [u]pon a Level with another, the Lowest with the Highest: and Men might thus come to be morally as well as naturally equal.

4

MONTESQUIEU, SPIRIT OF LAWS,
BK. 15, CHS. 1, 4–8
1748

(See also bk. 8, chs. 2–3, in ch. 18, no. 3)

1.—Of civil Slavery

Slavery, properly so called, is the establishment of a right which gives to one man such a power over another as renders him absolute master of his life and fortune. The state of slavery is in its own nature bad. It is neither useful to the master nor to the slave; not to the slave, because he can do nothing through a motive of virtue; nor to the master, because by having an unlimited authority over his slaves he insensibly accustoms himself to the want of all moral virtues, and thence becomes fierce, hasty, severe, choleric, voluptuous, and cruel.

In despotic countries, where they are already in a state of political servitude, civil slavery is more tolerable than in other governments. Every one ought to be satisfied in those countries with necessaries and life. Hence the condition of a slave is hardly more burdensome than that of a subject.

But in a monarchical government, where it is of the utmost importance that human nature should not be debased or dispirited, there ought to be no slavery. In democracies, where they are all upon equality; and in aristocracies, where the laws ought to use their utmost endeavors to procure as great an equality as the nature of the government will permit, slavery is contrary to the spirit of the constitution: it only contributes to give a power and luxury to the citizens which they ought not to have.

4.—Another Origin of the Right of Slavery

I would as soon say that religion gives its professors a right to enslave those who dissent from it, in order to render its propagation more easy.

This was the notion that encouraged the ravagers of America in their iniquity. Under the influence of this idea they founded their right of enslaving so many nations; for these robbers, who would absolutely be both robbers and Christians, were superlatively devout.

Louis XIII was extremely uneasy at a law by which all the negroes of his colonies were to be made slaves; but it being strongly urged to him as the readiest means for their conversion, he acquiesced without further scruple.

5.—Of the Slavery of the Negroes

Were I to vindicate our right to make slaves of the negroes, these should be my arguments:—

The Europeans, having extirpated the Americans, were obliged to make slaves of the Africans, for clearing such vast tracts of land.

Sugar would be too dear if the plants which produce it were cultivated by any other than slaves.

These creatures are all over black, and with such a flat nose that they can scarcely be pitied.

It is hardly to be believed that God, who is a wise Being, should place a soul, especially a good soul, in such a black ugly body.

It is so natural to look upon color as the criterion of human nature, that the Asiatics, among whom eunuchs are employed, always deprive the blacks of their resemblance to us by a more opprobrious distinction.

The color of the skin may be determined by that of the hair, which, among the Egyptians, the best philosophers in the world, was of such importance that they put to death all the red-haired men who fell into their hands.

The negroes prefer a glass necklace to that gold which polite nations so highly value. Can there be a greater proof of their wanting common sense?

It is impossible for us to suppose these creatures to be men, because, allowing them to be men, a suspicion would follow that we ourselves are not Christians.

Weak minds exaggerate too much the wrong done to the Africans. For were the case as they state it, would the European powers, who make so many needless conventions among themselves, have failed to enter into a general one, in behalf of humanity and compassion?

6.—The true Origin of the Right of Slavery

It is time to inquire into the true origin of the right of slavery. It ought to be founded on the nature of things; let us see if there be any cases where it can be derived thence.

In all despotic governments people make no difficulty in selling themselves; the political slavery in some measure annihilates the civil liberty.

According to Mr. Perry, the Muscovites sell themselves very readily: their reason for it is evident—their liberty is not worth keeping.

At Achim every one is for selling himself. Some of the chief lords have not less than a thousand slaves, all principal merchants, who have a great number of slaves themselves, and these also are not without their slaves. Their masters are their heirs, and put them into trade. In those states, the freemen being overpowered by the government, have no better resource than that of making themselves slaves to the tyrants in office.

This is the true and rational origin of that mild law of slavery which obtains in some countries: and mild it ought to be, as founded on the free choice a man makes of a master, for his own benefit; which forms a mutual convention between the two parties.

7.—Another Origin of the Right of Slavery

There is another origin of the right of slavery, and even of the most cruel slavery which is to be seen among men.

There are countries where the excess of heat enervates the body, and renders men so slothful and dispirited that nothing but the fear of chastisement can oblige them to perform any laborious duty: slavery is there more reconcilable to reason; and the master being as lazy with respect to his sovereign as his slave is with regard to him, this adds a political to a civil slavery.

Aristotle endeavors to prove that there are natural slaves; but what he says is far from proving it. If there be any such, I believe they are those of whom I have been speaking.

But as all men are born equal, slavery must be accounted unnatural, though in some countries it be founded on natural reason; and a wide difference ought to be made between such countries, and those in which even natural reason rejects it, as in Europe, where it has been so happily abolished.

Plutarch, in the "Life of Numa," says that in Saturn's time there was neither slave nor master. Christianity has restored that age in our climates.

8.—Inutility of Slavery among us

Natural slavery, then, is to be limited to some particular parts of the world. In all other countries, even the most servile drudgeries may be performed by freemen.

Experience verifies my assertion. Before Christianity had abolished civil slavery in Europe, working in the mines was judged too toilsome for any but slaves or malefactors: at present there are men employed in them who are known to live comfortably. The magistrates have, by some small privileges, encouraged this profession: to an increase of labor they have joined an increase of gain; and have gone so far as to make those people better pleased with their condition than with any other which they could have embraced.

No labor is so heavy but it may be brought to a level with the workman's strength, when regulated by equity, and not by avarice. The violent fatigues which slaves are made to undergo in other parts may be supplied by a skilful use of ingenious machines. The Turkish mines in the Bannat of Temeswaer, though richer than those of Hungary, did not yield so much; because the working of them depended entirely on the strength of their slaves.

I know not whether this article be dictated by my understanding or by my heart. Possibly there is not that climate upon earth where the most laborious services might not with proper encouragement be performed by freemen. Bad laws having made lazy men, they have been reduced to slavery because of their laziness.

5

BENJAMIN FRANKLIN TO JOHN WARING
17 Dec. 1763
Papers 10:395–96

Being but just return'd home from a Tour thro' the north-

ern Colonies, that has employ'd the whole Summer, my Time at present is so taken up that I cannot now write fully in answer to the Letters I have receiv'd from you, but purpose to do it shortly. This is chiefly to acquaint you, that I have visited the Negro School here in Company with the Revd. Mr. Sturgeon and some others; and had the Children thoroughly examin'd. They appear'd all to have made considerable Progress in Reading for the Time they had respectively been in the School, and most of them answer'd readily and well the Questions of the Catechism; they behav'd very orderly, showd a proper Respect and ready Obedience to the Mistress, and seem'd very attentive to, and a good deal affected by, a serious Exhortation with which Mr. Sturgeon concluded our Visit. I was on the whole much pleas'd, and from what I then saw, have conceiv'd a higher Opinion of the natural Capacities of the black Race, than I had ever before entertained. Their Apprehension seems as quick, their Memory as strong, and their Docility in every Respect equal to that of white Children. You will wonder perhaps that I should ever doubt it, and I will not undertake to justify all my Prejudices, nor to account for them.

6

WILLIAM EDDIS, LETTERS FROM AMERICA
20 Sept. 1770, 17 Feb. 1772
Land 35–41, 63–65

Your information relative to the situation of servants in this country is far from being well founded. I have now been upwards of twelve months resident in Maryland, and am thereby enabled to convey to you a tolerable idea on this subject.

Persons in a state of servitude are under four distinct denominations: negroes, who are the entire property of their respective owners; convicts, who are transported from the mother country for a limited term; indented servants, who are engaged for five years previous to their leaving England; and free-willers, who are supposed, from their situation, to possess superior advantages.

The negroes in this province are, in general, natives of the country, very few in proportion being imported from the coast of Africa. They are better clothed, better fed, and better treated, than their unfortunate brethren, whom a more rigid fate hath subjected to slavery in our West India islands; neither are their employments so laborious, nor the acts of the legislature so partially oppressive against them. The further we proceed to the northward, the less number of people are to be found of this complexion. In the New England government, negroes are almost as scarce as on your side of the Atlantic, and but few are under actual slavery; but as we advance to the south, their multitudes astonishingly increase, and in the Carolinas they considerably exceed the number of white inhabitants.*

Maryland is the only province into which convicts may be freely imported. The Virginians have inflicted very severe penalties on any masters of vessels, or others, who may attempt to introduce persons under this description into their colony. They have been influenced in this measure by an apprehension that, from the admission of such inmates into their families, the prevalence of bad example might tend to universal depravity, in spite of every regulation and restraining law.

Persons convicted of felony and in consequence transported to this continent, if they are able to pay the expense of passage, are free to pursue their fortune agreeably to their inclinations or abilities. Few, however, have means to avail themselves of this advantage. These unhappy beings are, generally, consigned to an agent, who classes them suitably to their real or supposed qualifications; advertises them for sale, and disposes of them, for seven years, to planters, to mechanics, and to such as choose to retain them for domestic service. Those who survive the term of servitude seldom establish their residence in this country: the stamp of infamy is too strong upon them to be easily erased; they either return to Europe and renew their former practices; or, if they have fortunately imbibed habits of honesty and industry, they remove to a distant situation, where they may hope to remain unknown, and be enabled to pursue with credit every possible method of becoming useful members of society.

In your frequent excursions about the great metropolis, you cannot but observe numerous advertisements offering the most seducing encouragement to adventurers under every possible description; to those who are disgusted with the frowns of fortune in their native land; and to those of an enterprising disposition, who are tempted to court her smiles in a distant region. These persons are referred to agents, or crimps, who represent the advantages to be obtained in America in colors so alluring that it is almost impossible to resist their artifices. Unwary persons are accordingly induced to enter into articles, by which they engage to become servants, agreeable to their respective qualifications, for the term of five years; every necessary accommodation being found them during the voyage; and

*Notwithstanding the climate of North America is less favorable to the constitution of negroes than the European settlements in the torrid zone, they nevertheless increase rapidly in almost every part of that extensive continent. The last importation of slaves into Maryland was, as I am credibly informed, in the year 1769; and though great losses have been sustained in consequence of the war, and desertions to the British standard, their numbers are at least doubled since that time, without any foreign supply. To account for a circumstance apparently so improbable, it must be observed that on the American continent the planters generally adopted a more liberal mode in their African intercourse than has been pursued in the islands. They did not import slaves for the supply of foreign settlements, but purchased for their own immediate use, without any particular preference to either sex. The consequence is obvious: they have multiplied in a due proportion, and notwithstanding the occasional severity of the climate and the recent calamities of war, their numbers are fully sufficient for their respective occupations.

every method taken that they may be treated with tenderness and humanity during the period of servitude; at the expiration of which they are taught to expect that opportunities will assuredly offer to secure to the honest and industrious a competent provision for the remainder of their days.

The generality of the inhabitants in this province are very little acquainted with those fallacious pretenses, by which numbers are continually induced to embark for this continent. On the contrary, they too generally conceive an opinion that the difference is merely nominal between the indented servant and the convicted felon; nor will they readily believe that people who had the least experience in life, and whose characters were unexceptionable, would abandon their friends and families and their ancient connections, for a servile situation in a remote appendage to the British empire. From this persuasion they rather consider the convict as the more profitable servant, his term being for seven, the latter only for five years; and, I am sorry to observe, that there are but few instances wherein they experience different treatment. Negroes being a property for life, the death of slaves, in the prime of youth or strength, is a material loss to the proprietor; they are, therefore, almost in every instance, under more comfortable circumstances than the miserable European, over whom the rigid planter exercises an inflexible severity. They are strained to the utmost to perform their allotted labor; and, from a prepossession in many cases too justly founded, they are supposed to be receiving only the just reward which is due to repeated offenses. There are doubtless many exceptions to this observation, yet, generally speaking, they groan beneath a worse than Egyptian bondage. By attempting to lighten the intolerable burthen, they often render it more insupportable. For real or imaginary causes, these frequently attempt to escape, but very few are successful; the country being intersected with rivers, and the utmost vigilance observed in detecting persons under suspicious circumstances who, when apprehended, are committed to close confinement, advertised, and delivered to their respective masters; the party who detects the vagrant being entitled to a reward. Other incidental charges arise. The unhappy culprit is doomed to a severe chastisement; and a prolongation of servitude is decreed in full proportion to expenses incurred and supposed inconveniences resulting from a desertion of duty.

The situation of the free-willer is, in almost every instance, more to be lamented than either that of the convict or the indented servant, the deception which is practiced on those of this description being attended with circumstances of greater duplicity and cruelty. Persons under this denomination are received under express conditions that on their arrival in America they are to be allowed a stipulated number of days to dispose of themselves to the greatest advantage. They are told that their services will be eagerly solicited in proportion to their abilities; that their reward will be adequate to the hazard they encounter by courting fortune in a distant region; and that the parties with whom they engage will readily advance the sum agreed on for their passage; which, being averaged at about nine pounds sterling, they will speedily be enabled to repay, and to enjoy, in a state of liberty, a comparative situation of ease and affluence.

With these pleasing ideas they support with cheerfulness the hardships to which they are subjected during the voyage; and, with the most anxious sensations of delight, approach the land which they consider as the scene of future prosperity. But scarce have they contemplated the diversified objects which naturally attract attention; scarce have they yielded to the pleasing reflection that every danger, every difficulty, is happily surmounted, before their fond hopes are cruelly blasted, and they find themselves involved in all the complicated miseries of a tedious, laborious, and unprofitable servitude.

Persons resident in America, being accustomed to procure servants for a very trifling consideration, under absolute terms for a limited period, are not often disposed to hire adventurers, who expect to be gratified in full proportion to their acknowledged qualifications; but, as they support authority with a rigid hand, they little regard the former situation of their unhappy dependants.

This disposition, which is almost universally prevalent, is well known to the parties who on your side of the Atlantic engage in this iniquitous and cruel commerce. It is therefore an article of agreement with these deluded victims that if they are not successful in obtaining situations on their own terms within a certain number of days after their arrival in the country, they are then to be sold, in order to defray the charges of passage, at the discretion of the master of the vessel or the agent to whom he is consigned in the province.

You are also to observe that servants imported, even under this favorable description, are rarely permitted to set their feet on shore until they have absolutely formed their respective engagements. As soon as the ship is stationed in her berth, planters, mechanics, and others, repair on board; the adventurers of both sexes are exposed to view, and very few are happy enough to make their own stipulations, some very extraordinary qualifications being absolutely requisite to obtain this distinction; and even when this is obtained, the advantages are by no means equivalent to their sanguine expectations. The residue, stung with disappointment and vexation, meet with horror the moment which dooms them, under an appearance of equity, to a limited term of slavery. Character is of little importance; their abilities not being found of a superior nature, they are sold as soon as their term of election is expired, apparel and provision being their only compensation; till, on the expiration of five tedious laborious years, they are restored to a dearly purchased freedom.

From this detail, I am persuaded you will not longer imagine that the servants in this country are in a better situation than those in Britain. You have heard of convicts who rather chose to undergo the severest penalties of the law than endure the hardships which are annexed to their situation during a state of servitude on this side the Atlantic. Indolence, accompanied with a train of vicious habits, has doubtless great influence on the determination of such unhappy wretches; but it is surely to be lamented that men whose characters are unblemished, whose views are founded on honest and industrious principles, should fall a sacrifice to avarice and delusion, and indiscriminately be blended with the most profligate and abandoned of mankind.

It seems astonishing that a circumstance so well known, particularly in this province, should not have been generally circulated through every part of the British empire. Were the particulars of this iniquitous traffic universally divulged, those who have established offices in London and in the principal seaports for the regular conduct of this business would be pointed out to obloquy, and their punishment would serve as a beacon to deter the ignorant and unwary from becoming victims to the insidious practices of avarice and deceit.

I am ready to admit there is every appearance of candor on the part of the agents and their accomplices. Previous to the embarkation of any person under the respective agreements, the parties regularly comply with the requisitions of a law wisely calculated to prevent clandestine transportation; they appear before a magistrate and give their voluntary assent to the obligations they have mutually entered into. But are not such adventurers induced to this measure in consequence of ignorance and misrepresentation? Assuredly they are. They are industriously taught to expect advantages infinitely superior to their most sanguine views in Britain. Every lucrative incentive is delineated in the most flattering colors; and they fondly expect to acquire that independence in the revolution of a few years which the longest life could not promise with the exertion of their best abilities in the bosom of their native country.

. . . . .

The annual revenue of the proprietary arising from the sale of lands and the yearly quit rent, after deducting all the various charges of government, averages at twelve thousand five hundred pounds *per annum*. All offices excepting those in the service of the customs are in his gift, or in the gift of his representative for the time being. This patronage includes a very extensive range of lucrative and respectable stations, and consequently throws great weight and influence into the scale of government.

This influence is considered by many as inimical to the essential interests of the people; a spirit of party is consequently excited, and every idea of encroachment is resisted by the popular faction with all the warmth of patriotic enthusiasm.

I have before observed that elections in this province are triennial. The delegates returned are generally persons of the greatest consequence in their different counties; and many of them are perfectly acquainted with the political and commercial interest of their constituents. I have frequently heard subjects debated with great powers of eloquence and force of reason; and the utmost regularity and propriety distinguish the whole of their proceedings.

. . . . .

A litigious spirit is very apparent in this country. The assizes are held twice in the year in the city of Annapolis, and the number of causes then brought forward is really incredible. Though few of the gentlemen who practice in the courts have been regularly called to the bar, there are several who are confessedly eminent in their profession; and those who are possessed of superior abilities have full employment for the exertion of their talents, and are paid in due proportion by their respective clients.

The natives of these provinces, even those who move in the humbler circles of life, discover a shrewdness and penetration not generally observable in the mother country. On many occasions they are inquisitive even beyond the bounds of propriety; they discriminate characters with the greatest accuracy, and there are few who do not seem perfectly conversant with the general and particular interests of the community. An idea of equality also seems generally to prevail, and the inferior order of people pay but little external respect to those who occupy superior stations.

7

PATRICK HENRY TO ROBERT PLEASANTS
18 Jan. 1773
Meade 299–300

I take this oppo. to acknowledge the receipt of A Benezets Book against the Slave Trade. I thank you for it. It is not a little surprising that Christianity, whose chief excellence consists in softning the human heart, in cherishing & improving its finer Feelings, should encourage a Practice so totally repugnant to the first Impression of right & wrong. What adds to the wonder is that this Abominable Practice has been introduced in ye. most enlightened Ages, Times that seem to have pretentions to boast of high Improvements in the Arts, Sciences, & refined Morality, h[ave] brought into general use, & guarded by many Laws, a Species of Violence & Tyranny, which our more rude & barbarous, but more honest Ancestors detested. Is it not amazing, that at a time, when ye. Rights of Humanity are defined & understood with precision, in a Country above all others fond of Liberty, that in such an Age, & such a Country we find Men, professing a Religion ye. most humane, mild, meek, gentle & generous; adopting a Principle as repugnant to humanity as it is inconsistant with the Bible and destructive to Liberty.

Every thinking honest Man rejects it in Speculation, how few in Practice from conscienscious Motives? The World in general has denied ye. People a share of its honours, but the Wise will ascribe to ye. a just Tribute of virtuous Praise, for ye. Practice of a train of Virtues among which yr. disagreement to Slavery will be principally ranked.—I cannot but wish well to a people whose System imitates ye. Example of him whose Life was perfect.—And believe m[e], I shall honour the Quakers for their noble Effort to abolish Slavery. It is equally calculated to promote moral & political Good.

Would any one believe that I am Master of Slaves of my own purchase! I am drawn along by ye. general inconvenience of living without them, I will not, I cannot justify it. However culpable my Conduct, I will so far pay my de-

voir to Virtue, as to own the excellence & rectitude of her Precepts, & to lament my want of conforming to them.—

I believe a time will come when an oppo. will be offered to abolish this lamentable Evil.—Every thing we can do is to improve it, if it happens in our day, if not, let us transmit to our descendants together with our Slaves, a pity for their unhappy Lot, & an abhorrence for Slavery. If we cannot reduce this wished for Reformation to practice, let us treat the unhappy victims with lenity, it is ye. furthest advance we can make toward Justice [We owe to the] purity of our Religion to shew that it is at variance with that Law which warrants Slavery.—

Here is an instance that silent Meetings (ye. scoff of reverd. Doctrs.) have done yt. wch. learned & elaborate Preaching could not effect, so much preferable are the genuine dictates of Conscience & a steady attention to its feelings above ye. teachings of those Men who pretend to have found a better Guide. I exhort you to persevere in so worthy a resolution, Some of your People disagree, or at least are lukewarm in the abolition of Slavery. Many treat ye. Resolution of your Meeting with redicule, & among those who throw Contempt on it, are Clergymen, whose surest Guard against both Redicule & Contempt is a certain Act of Assembly.—

I know not where to stop, I could say many things on this Subject; a serious review of which gives a gloomy perspective to future times.

8

GOUVERNEUR MORRIS TO JOHN PENN
20 May 1774
American Archives, 4th ser., 1:342–43

You have heard, and you will hear, a great deal about politics, and in the heap of chaff *you* may find some grains of good sense. Believe me, sir, freedom and religion are only watchwords. We have appointed a Committee, or rather we have nominated one. Let me give you the history of it. It is needless to premise, that the lower orders of mankind are more easily led by specious appearances than those of a more exalted station. This, and many similar propositions, you know better than your humble servant.

The troubles in *America,* during *Grenville's* administration, put our gentry upon this finesse. They stimulated some daring coxcombs to rouse the mob into an attack upon the bounds of order and decency. These fellows became the *Jack Cades* of the day, the leaders in all the riots, the belwethers of the flock. The reason of the manoeuvre in those who wished to keep fair with the Government, and at the same time to receive the incense of popular applause, you will readily perceive. On the whole, the shepherds were not much to blame in a politic point of view. The belwethers jingled merrily, and roared out liberty, and property, and religion, and a multitude of cant terms, which every one thought he understood, and was egregiously mistaken. For you must know the shepherds kept the dictionary of the day, and, like the mysteries of the ancient mythology, it was not for profane eyes or ears. This answered many purposes; the simple flock put themselves entirely under the protection of these most excellent shepherds. By and bye behold a great metamorphosis, without the help of *Ovid* or his divinities, but entirely effectuated by two modern Genii, the god of Ambition and the goddess of Faction. The first of these prompted the shepherds to shear some of their flock, and then, in conjunction with the other, converted the belwethers into shepherds. That we have been in hot water with the *British* Parliament ever since every body knows. Consequently these new shepherds had their hands full of employment. The old ones kept themselves least in sight, and a want of confidence in each other was not the least evil which followed. The port of *Boston* has been shut up. These sheep, simple as they are, cannot be gulled as heretofore. In short, there is no ruling them; and now, to leave the metaphor, the heads of the mobility grow dangerous to the gentry, and how to keep them down is the question. While they correspond with the other Colonies, call and dismiss popular assemblies, make resolves to bind the consciences of the rest of mankind, bully poor printers, and exert with full force all their other tribunitial powers, it is impossible to curb them.

But art sometimes goes farther than force, and, therefore, to trick them handsomely a Committee of patricians was to be nominated, and into their hands was to be committed the majesty of the people, and the highest trust was to be reposed in them by a mandate that they should take care, *quod respublica non capiat injuriam*. The tribunes, through the want of good legerdemain in the senatorial order, perceived the finesse; and yesterday I was present at a grand division of the city, and there I beheld my fellow-citizens very accurately counting all their chickens, not only before any of them were hatched, but before above one half of the eggs were laid. In short, they fairly contended about the future forms of our Government, whether it should be founded upon aristocratic or democratic principles.

I stood in the balcony, and on my right hand were ranged all the people of property, with some few poor dependants, and on the other all the tradesmen, &c., who thought it worth their while to leave daily labour for the good of the country. The spirit of the *English* Constitution has yet a little influence left, and bu[t] a little. The remains of it, however, will give the wealthy people a superiority this time, but would they secure it they must banish all schoolmasters and confine all knowledge to themselves. This cannot be. The mob begin to think and to reason. Poor reptiles! it is with them a vernal morning; they are struggling to cast off their winter's slough, they bask in the sunshine, and ere noon they will bite, depend upon it. The gentry begin to fear this. Their Committee will be appointed, they will deceive the people, and again forfeit a share of their confidence. And if these instances of what with one side is policy, with the other perfidy, shall continue to increase, and become more frequent, farewell aristocracy. I see, and I see it with fear and trembling, that

if the disputes with *Great Britain* continue, we shall be under the worst of all possible dominions; we shall be under the domination of a riotous mob.

9

ABIGAIL ADAMS TO JOHN ADAMS
31 Mar. 1776
Butterfield 120–21

I wish you would ever write me a Letter half as long as I write you; and tell me if you may where your Fleet are gone? What sort of Defence Virginia can make against our common Enemy? Whether it is so situated as to make an able Defence? Are not the Gentery Lords and the common people vassals, are they not like the uncivilized Natives Brittain represents us to be? I hope their Riffel Men who have shewen themselves very savage and even Blood thirsty; are not a specimen of the Generality of the people.

I am willing to allow the Colony great merit for having produced a Washington but they have been shamefully duped by a Dunmore.

I have sometimes been ready to think that the passion for Liberty cannot be Eaquelly Strong in the Breasts of those who have been accustomed to deprive their fellow Creatures of theirs. Of this I am certain that it is not founded upon that generous and christian principal of doing to others as we would that others should do unto us.

. . . . .

I long to hear that you have declared an independancy—and by the way in the new Code of Laws which I suppose it will be necessary for you to make I desire you would Remember the Ladies, and be more generous and favourable to them than your ancestors. Do not put such unlimited power into the hands of the Husbands. Remember all Men would be tyrants if they could. If perticuliar care and attention is not paid to the Laidies we are determined to foment a Rebelion, and will not hold ourselves bound by any Laws in which we have no voice, or Representation.

That your Sex are Naturally Tyrannical is a Truth so thoroughly established as to admit of no dispute, but such of you as wish to be happy willingly give up the harsh title of Master for the more tender and endearing one of Friend. Why then, not put it out of the power of the vicious and the Lawless to use us with cruelty and indignity with impunity. Men of Sense in all Ages abhor those customs which treat us only as the vassals of your Sex. Regard us then as Beings placed by providence under your protection and in immitation of the Supreem Being make use of that power only for our happiness.

10

JOHN ADAMS TO ABIGAIL ADAMS
14 Apr. 1776
Butterfield 121–23

You ask where the Fleet is. The inclosed Papers will inform you. You ask what Sort of Defence Virginia can make. I believe they will make an able Defence. Their Militia and minute Men have been some time employed in training them selves, and they have Nine Battallions of regulars as they call them, maintained among them, under good Officers, at the Continental Expence. They have set up a Number of Manufactories of Fire Arms, which are busily employed. They are tolerably supplied with Powder, and are successfull and assiduous, in making Salt Petre. Their neighbouring Sister or rather Daughter Colony of North Carolina, which is a warlike Colony, and has several Battallions at the Continental Expence, as well as a pretty good Militia, are ready to assist them, and they are in very good Spirits, and seem determined to make a brave Resistance.—The Gentry are very rich, and the common People very poor. This Inequality of Property, gives an Aristocratical Turn to all their Proceedings, and occasions a strong Aversion in their Patricians, to Common Sense. But the Spirit of these Barons, is coming down, and it must submit.

. . . . .

As to your extraordinary Code of Laws, I cannot but laugh. We have been told that our Struggle has loosened the bands of Government every where. That Children and Apprentices were disobedient—that schools and Colledges were grown turbulent—that Indians slighted their Guardians and Negroes grew insolent to their Masters. But your Letter was the first Intimation that another Tribe more numerous and powerfull than all the rest were grown discontented.—This is rather too coarse a Compliment but you are so saucy, I wont blot it out.

Depend upon it, We know better than to repeal our Masculine systems. Altho they are in full Force, you know they are little more than Theory. We dare not exert our Power in its full Latitude. We are obliged to go fair, and softly, and in Practice you know We are the subjects. We have only the Name of Masters, and rather than give up this, which would compleatly subject Us to the Despotism of the Peticoat, I hope General Washington, and all our brave Heroes would fight. I am sure every good Politician would plot, as long as he would against Despotism, Empire, Monarchy, Aristocracy, Oligarchy, or Ochlocracy.— A fine Story indeed. I begin to think the Ministry as deep as they are wicked. After stirring up Tories, Landjobbers, Trimmers, Bigots, Canadians, Indians, Negroes, Hanoverians, Hessians, Russians, Irish Roman Catholicks, Scotch Renegadoes, at last they have stimulated the to demand new Priviledges and threaten to rebell.

11

PENNSYLVANIA EVENING POST
27 Apr. 1776

The essence of liberty consists in our having it in our power to choose our own rulers, and so far as we exercise this power we are truly free, and no farther. Many advantages flow from such a plan of government. The following two have rarely been attended to, but every one will perceive them as soon as mentioned.

A poor man has rarely the honor of speaking to a gentleman on any terms, and never with familiarity but for a few weeks before the election. How many poor men, common men, and mechanics have been made happy within this fortnight by a shake of the hand, a pleasing smile and a little familiar chat with gentlemen, who have not for these seven years past condescended to look at them. Blessed state which brings all so nearly on a level! What a clever man is Mr. _____ says my neighbour, how agreeable and familiar! He has no pride at all! He talked as freely to me for half an hour as if he were my neighbour _____ there! I wish it were election time always! Thursday next he will lose all knowledge of _____, and pass me in the streets as if he never knew me.

How kind and clever is the man who proposes to be Sheriff, for two months before the election; he knows every body, smiles upon and salutes every body, until the election is over; but then to the end of the year, he has no time to speak to you, he is so engaged in seizing your property by writ of venditioni exponas, and selling your goods at vendue.

Thus the right of annual elections will ever oblige gentlemen to speak to you once a year, who would despise you forever were it not that you can bestow something upon them.

Lying is so vulgar a failing that no gentleman would have any thing to say to it but at elections. Then indeed the greatest gentleman in the city will condescend to lye with the least of us. This year their humility is amazing; for they have stooped to the drudgery of going from house to house to circulate election lyes about division of property. I cannot commend their policy herein, for such poor rascals as I am with [wish?] nothing more. However it shews their willingness to come to a pin, which is such a favor that we ought to be truly thankful for it.

In a word, electioneering and aristocratical pride are incompatible, and if we would have gentlemen ever to come down to our level, we must guard our right of election effectually, and not let the Assembly take it out of our hands. Do you think ever Mr. J___ _____ would ever speak to you, if it were not for the May election? Be freemen then, and you will be companions for gentlemen annually.

12

ABIGAIL ADAMS TO JOHN ADAMS
7 May 1776
Butterfield 127

A Government of more Stability is much wanted in this colony, and they are ready to receive it from the Hands of the Congress, and since I have begun with Maxims of State I will add an other viz. that a people may let a king fall, yet still remain a people, but if a king let his people slip from him, he is no longer a king. And as this is most certainly our case, why not proclaim to the World in decisive terms your own importance?

Shall we not be dispiced by foreign powers for hesitateing so long at a word?

I can not say I think you very generous to the Ladies, for whilst you are proclaiming peace and good will to Men, Emancipating all Nations, you insist upon retaining an absolute power over Wives. But you must remember that Arbitary power is like most other things which are very hard, very liable to be broken—and notwithstanding all your wise Laws and Maxims we have it in our power not only to free ourselves but to subdue our Masters, and without voilence throw both your natural and legal authority at our feet—

"Charm by accepting, by submitting sway
Yet have our Humour most when we obey."

13

JOHN ADAMS TO JAMES SULLIVAN
26 May 1776
Papers 4:208–12

(See ch. 13, no. 10)

14

DEMOCRATICUS, LOOSE THOUGHTS
ON GOVERNMENT
7 June 1776
American Archives, 4th ser., 6:730–32

In whatever situation we take a view of man, whether ranging the forests in the rude state of his primeval existence, or in the smooth situation of polished society; wheresoever we place him—on the burning sands of *Africa,* the freezing coasts of *Labrador,* or the more congenial climes of the temperate zones—we shall everywhere find him the same complex being, a slave to his passions, and tossed and agitated by a thousand disagreeing virtues and discordant vices.

To correct this freedom and versatility of his nature, to put a stop to the violences which must take place from this disordered state of his reign, and to separate his virtues from his vices, and call them forth into action, men find it necessary either to submit to the casual rule of superior abilities, or, by arranging themselves into societies, to establish forms and regulations for the good of the whole. These forms and regulations admit of a very great variety; but whether they be derived from the casual subordination, or the positive institutions of men, this is still a leading principle in them all, "That the people have at all times a right, from the sacred and unalienable Charter of the Almighty, to change or alter the Government under which they live, where those changes and alterations tend to the general good of the community, and the happiness of its members."

But where is this general good, this national felicity, to be found? It is more than probable that it will be found, in the greatest proportion, in that society which best secures the observance of justice, which inspires and preserves the virtue of its members, and which actually engages them in the exercise of their best talents and happiest dispositions.

The security to justice is the political liberty of the State, promulgated by its laws, which relates to the supreme power and the subject, and is the object of political law; or from the subject to one another, and is the object of civil and criminal law. This political liberty will always be most perfect where the laws have derogated least from the original right of men—the right to equality, which is adverse to every species of subordination beside that which arises from the difference of capacity, disposition, and virtue. It is this sense of equality which gives to every man a right to frame and execute his own laws, which alone can secure the observance of justice, and diffuse equal and substantial liberty to the people; for those laws must necessarily be the most perfect which are dictated or corrected by the sense of parties in one capacity, to whom they are to be applied in another. Hence that fundamental maxim in all just Governments, that the law-makers must never be above the law; and hence arises the horrour of that idolatrous paramount superiority of Kings, which is the government of force, and the subversion of all law. It is this principle of equality, this right, which is inherent in every member of the community, to give his own consent to the laws by which he is to be bound, which alone can inspire and preserve the virtue of its members, by placing them in a relation to the publick and to their fellow-citizens, which has a tendency to engage the heart and affections to both. Men love the community in which they are treated with justice, and in which they meet with considerations proportioned to the proofs they give of ability and good intentions. They love those with whom they live on terms of equality, and under a sense of common interests. It engages them in the exercise of their best talents and happiest dispositions, for the Government and defence of their country are the best and noblest occupations of men. They lead to the exercise of the greatest virtues and most respectable talents, which is the greatest blessing that any institution can bestow. Thrice happy is that people where the members at large may be entrusted with their own Government and defence; but, alas! such are the limited powers of men that this equal and perfect system of legislation is seldom to be found in the world, and can only take place in small communities; for whenever the society becomes numerous or extensive, the privilege of legislation in a collective capacity, from the impracticability of convening, must unavoidably and necessarily cease.

To remedy this evil, a method has been embraced of deputing Representatives from the people at large. Several requisites, however, are necessary to render this representation adequate to the trust. It ought to be full, equal, free; and as it is, at best, but a species of aristocracy, it is indispensably necessary to guard against the evils which are attendant on this form of Government. And its power should be purely legislative.

A full representation is necessary to render the influence of bribery and art more difficult. The propriety of an equal representation must occur to every one who does not wish to give an undue influence to some parts of the community over others. This may be obtained in either of two ways, by the number of freeholders, or by the quantity of land; but as in countries that are rapidly increasing in population, the number of freeholders must be perpetually varying, the method by the number of acres must be the easiest and most permanent; and as our lands become divided into more hands, every year will increase the perfection of this kind of representation, especially, too, if we put an end to proprietaries, entails, and other monopolies of lands, those remains of ancient tyranny, which will always be incompatible with the spirit of equality and right Government. The freedom of election is necessary for the well-being of the laws and the liberties of the State, which would otherwise fall a sacrifice to the altars of bribery and corruption and party spirit. To this end, the Representatives should be the unbiased choice of the people, by ballot, in which no man should make interest, either directly or indirectly, for himself or his friend, under the penalty of a heavy fine, and an exclusion from the House of Representatives forever; for it is generally found that the people will choose right if left to themselves. To check the aristocratick principle, which always inclines to tyranny, it will be necessary to keep the Representatives dependant on the people by annual elections; and perhaps it may be thought a further improvement to establish a limited kind of rotation, as a sure and certain means of diffusing the Government into more hands, and training up a greater number of able statesmen.

But as even under these restrictions an overgrown popularity may be dangerous to the safety of the State, or an arbitrary representative body may find means of imposing partial temporary laws on the people, it will be expedient to erect a second legislative power, independent of the first, or House of Representatives, consisting of a small number of the ablest men in the nation, whose right it shall be to have a negative on the lower House. These may consist of twelve, elected by a Committee of twenty-

one in each County, chosen by the people for that purpose. This mode of election will obviate the inconveniences of a choice by the people at large, and remove the absurdity of leaving it to the House of Representatives; for as they would be the mere creatures of that body, they must necessarily be subservient to their will and pleasure.

A third power must also be established, unconnected with legislation, and independent of either of the two branches, whose business shall be wholly executive of the political laws of the State. This power should be lodged in one person only, for the advantage of despatch and execution of business, chosen out of the upper House of the Legislature by a majority of votes from the Committees, to be aided and assisted by the upper House in all cases of emergencies not sufficiently provided for by the laws. This office should be unconnected with the powers of legislation, for it is a solecism in politicks to invest the different powers of legislation and the execution of the laws in the same hands; and as this power will be a trust of the first importance, and the most dangerous to liberty, it will be indispensably prudent to fill it up in rotation.

To all these different departments of Government, as well as to all others, such moderate salaries ought to be affixed as to place the sense of publick virtue higher in the estimation of the people than the thirst of gain; and lastly, an independent Court of Judicature should be established for civil and criminal matters, to whom every member in the State ought to be subject, even unto death.

Such an arrangement of the powers of Government will erect different orders of men, who, like parties in the State, will mutually watch and restrain the partialities to which any particular party or interest may incline, and thus establish a Government which is most likely to inspire, preserve, and exercise the virtues of its members, and enforce a strict obedience to the laws, which is the foundation of all political liberty and national felicity; and thus, too, will all government be ultimately in the hands of the people, whose right it is.

15

A WATCHMAN, PENNSYLVANIA PACKET
10 June 1776

It is now high time, my dear Countrymen, to emancipate yourselves from the delusions of such artful men. You have been told that you are unfit to have any share in the formation of a new government, and yet you are acknowledged at the same time to compose nine-tenths of the people of Pennsylvania. Strange that the majority should yield to the minority in a matter of so much consequence! But your LEADERS, it is said, are men of no fortune. I deny the charge. In the first place you have no leaders—you all act from the impulses of public and not party spirit, and in the second place you have nine-tenths of the property of

Pennsylvania on your side [of] the question. But you are told that you are all aiming at offices and power—Suppose this were true, you are *just* in your aims, for all offices and power belong solely to you, and are in your gift.

Here I cannot help making a digression from my subject. It was a custom among the Jews on certain occasions, to acknowledge the origin of their families as an antidote to pride. "A Syrian ready to perish was my father," was the confession with which they approached the temple. Suppose the same acknowledgement was demanded from some of our UNCOMMON PEOPLE. I believe the answer should be, a poor tradesman, a day-labourer, or a vagrant, "ready to perish was my father."—Talk not, ye pretenders to rank and gentility, of your elevated stations.—They are derived from those very people whom you treat with so much contempt. Talk not of their *vulgar* countenances and behaviour. Their vulgarity is seated only in their MANNERS. It occupies a higher place among yourselves. It is seated in your MINDS. This the profane, obscene, and trifling conversation so peculiar to high life abundantly witnesses. Had you concurred in the present virtuous and necessary measure of instituting a new government, you would have probably continued to occupy your posts and offices, with that additional lustre which they would have received from being the unbiassed gifts of freemen, but you have now forfeited the confidence of the people, by despising their authority, and you have furnished them with a suspicion that in taking up arms you yielded only to the violence of the times, or that you meant to fight for your offices, and not for your country.

16

VIRGINIA DECLARATION OF RIGHTS
12 June 1776
Mason Papers 1:287–89

(See ch. 1, no. 3)

17

EDMUND RANDOLPH, HISTORY OF VIRGINIA 253
ca. 1809

The bill of rights and the constitution [of Virginia] are monuments which deserve the attention of every republican, as containing some things which we may wish to be retrenched and others which cannot be too much admired.

The declaration in the first article of the bill of rights that all men are by nature equally free and independent was opposed by Robert Carter Nicholas, as being the forerunner or pretext of civil convulsion. It was answered, perhaps with too great an indifference to futurity, and not

without inconsistency, that with arms in our hands, asserting the general rights of man, we ought not to be too nice and too much restricted in the delineation of them; but that slaves, not being constituent members of our society, could never pretend to any benefit from such a maxim.

18

THOMAS JEFFERSON, NOTES ON DEBATES IN CONGRESS
2–4 July 1776
Papers 1:314–19

Congress proceeded the same day [July 2] to consider the declaration of Independence, which had been reported & laid on the table the Friday preceding, and on Monday referred to a commee. of the whole. the pusillanimous idea that we had friends in England worth keeping terms with, still haunted the minds of many. for this reason those passages which conveyed censures on the people of England were struck out, lest they should give them offence. the clause too, reprobating the enslaving the inhabitants of Africa, was struck out in complaisance to South Carolina & Georgia, who had never attempted to restrain the importation of slaves, and who on the contrary still wished to continue it. our Northern brethren also I believe felt a little tender under those censures; for tho' their people have very few slaves themselves yet they had been pretty considerable carriers of them to others. the debates having taken up the greater parts of the 2d. 3d. & 4th. days of July were, in the evening of the last closed. the declaration was reported by the commee., agreed to by the house, and signed by every member present except Mr. Dickinson. As the sentiments of men are known not only by what they receive, but what they reject also, I will state the form of the declaration as originally reported. the parts struck out by Congress shall be distinguished by a black line drawn under them; & those inserted by them shall be placed in the margin or in a concurrent column.*

A Declaration by the representatives of the United States of America, in [General] Congress assembled

When in the course of human events it becomes necessary for one people to dissolve the political bands which have connected them with another, and to assume among the powers of the earth the separate & equal station to which the laws of nature and of nature's god entitle them, a decent respect to the opinions of mankind requires that they should declare the causes which impel them to the separation.

We hold these truths to be self evident: that all men are created equal; that they are endowed by their creator with

---

*[EDITORS' NOTE.—In this text Congress's insertions are set in bold face.]

certain [inherent and] inalienable rights; that among these are life, liberty & the pursuit of happiness: that to secure these rights, governments are instituted among men, deriving their just powers from the consent of the governed; that whenever any form of government becomes destructive of these ends, it is the right of the people to alter or to abolish it, & to institute new government, laying it's foundation on such principles, & organising it's powers in such form, as to them shall seem most likely to effect their safety & happiness. prudence indeed will dictate that governments long established should not be changed for light & transient causes; and accordingly all experience hath shewn that mankind are more disposed to suffer while evils are sufferable than to right themselves by abolishing the forms to which they are accustomed. but when a long train of abuses & usurpations [begun at a distinguished period and] pursuing invariably the same object, evinces a design to reduce them under absolute despotism it is their right, it is their duty to throw off such government, & to provide new guards for their future security. such has been the patient sufferance of these colonies; & such is now the necessity which constrains them to **alter** [expunge] their former systems of government. the history of the present king of Great Britain is a history of **repeated** [unremitting] injuries & usurpations, [among which appears no solitary fact to contradict the uniform tenor of the rest but all have] **all having** in direct object the establishment of an absolute tyranny over these states. to prove this let facts be submitted to a candid world [for the truth of which we pledge a faith yet unsullied by falsehood.]

he has refused his assent to laws the most wholsome & necessary for the public good.

he has forbidden his governors to pass laws of immediate & pressing importance, unless suspended in their operation till his assent should be obtained; & when so suspended, he has utterly neglected to attend to them.

he has refused to pass other laws for the accomodation of large districts of people, unless those people would relinquish the right of representation in the legislature, a right inestimable to them, & formidable to tyrants only.

he has called together legislative bodies at places unusual, uncomfortable, and distant from the depository of their public records, for the sole purpose of fatiguing them into compliance with his measures.

he has dissolved representative houses repeatedly [& continually] for opposing with manly firmness his invasions on the rights of the people.

he has refused for a long time after such dissolutions to cause others to be elected, whereby the legislative powers, incapable of annihilation, have returned to the people at large for their exercise, the state remaining in the mean time exposed to all the dangers of invasion from without & convulsions within.

he has endeavored to prevent the population of these states; for that purpose obstructing the laws for naturalization of foreigners, refusing to pass others to encourage their migrations hither, & raising the conditions of new appropriations of lands.

he has **obstructed** [suffered] the administration of jus-

tice [totally to cease in some of these states] **by** refusing his assent to laws for establishing judiciary powers.

he has made [our] judges dependant on his will alone, for the tenure of their offices, & the amount & paiment of their salaries.

he has erected a multitude of new offices [by a self assumed power] and sent hither swarms of new officers to harrass our people and eat out their substance.

he has kept among us in times of peace standing armies [and ships of war] without the consent of our legislatures.

he has affected to render the military independant of, & superior to the civil power.

he has combined with others to subject us to a jurisdiction foreign to our constitutions & unacknoleged by our laws, giving his assent to their acts of pretended legislation for quartering large bodies of armed troops among us; for protecting them by a mocktrial from punishment for any murders which they should commit on the inhabitants of these states; for cutting off our trade with all parts of the world; for imposing taxes on us without our consent; for depriving us **in many cases** of the benefits of trial by jury; for transporting us beyond seas to be tried for pretended offences; for abolishing the free system of English laws in a neighboring province, establishing therein an arbitrary government, and enlarging it's boundaries, so as to render it at once an example and fit instrument for introducing the same absolute rule into these **colonies** [states]; for taking away our charters, abolishing our most valuable laws, and altering fundamentally the forms of our governments; for suspending our own legislatures, & declaring themselves invested with power to legislate for us in all cases whatsoever.

he has abdicated government here **by declaring us out of his protection & waging war against us.** [withdrawing his governors, and declaring us out of his allegiance & protection]

he has plundered our seas, ravaged our coasts, burnt our towns, & destroyed the lives of our people.

he is at this time transporting large armies of foreign mercenaries to compleat the works of death, desolation & tyranny already begun with circumstances of cruelty and perfidy **scarcely paralleled in the most barbarous ages, & totally** unworthy the head of a civilized nation.

he has constrained our fellow citizens taken captive on the high seas to bear arms against their country, to become the executioners of their friends & brethren, or to fall themselves by their hands.

he has **excited domestic insurrections amongst us, & has** endeavored to bring on the inhabitants of our frontiers the merciless Indian savages, whose known rule of warfare is an undistinguished destruction of all ages, sexes, & conditions [of existence.]

[he has incited treasonable insurrections of our fellow-citizens, with the allurements of forfeiture & confiscation of our property.

he has waged cruel war against human nature itself, violating it's most sacred rights of life and liberty in the persons of a distant people who never offended him, captivating & carrying them into slavery in another hemisphere or to incur miserable death in their transportation thither. this piratical warfare, the opprobrium of *infidel* powers, is the warfare of the *Christian* king of Great Britain. determined to keep open a market where *Men* should be bought & sold, he has prostituted his negative for suppressing every legislative attempt to prohibit or to restrain this execrable commerce. and that this assemblage of horrors might want no fact of distinguished die, he is now exciting those very people to rise in arms among us, and to purchase that liberty of which he has deprived them, by murdering the people on whom he also obtruded them: thus paying off former crimes committed against the *Liberties* of one people, with crimes which he urges them to commit against the *lives* of another.]

In every stage of these oppressions we have petitioned for redress in the most humble terms: our repeated petitions have been answered only by repeated injuries. a prince whose character is thus marked by every act which may define a tyrant is unfit to be the ruler of a **free** people [who mean to be free. future ages will scarcely believe that the hardiness of one man adventured, within the short compass of twelve years only, to lay a foundation so broad & so undisguised for tyranny over a people fostered & fixed in principles of freedom.]

Nor have we been wanting in attentions to our British brethren. we have warned them from time to time of attempts by their legislature to extend **an unwarrantable** [a] jurisdiction over **us** [these our states.] we have reminded them of the circumstances of our emigration & settlement here, [no one of which could warrant so strange a pretension: that these were effected at the expence of our own blood & treasure, unassisted by the wealth or the strength of Great Britain: that in constituting indeed our several forms of government, we had adopted one common king, thereby laying a foundation for perpetual league & amity with them: but that submission to their parliament was no part of our constitution, nor ever in idea, if history may be credited: and,] we **have** appealed to their native justice and magnanimity **and we have conjured them by** [as well as to] the ties of our common kindred to disavow these usurpations which **would inevitably** [were likely to] interrupt our connection and correspondence. they too have been deaf to the voice of justice & of consanguinity, [and when occasions have been given them, by the regular course of their laws, of removing from their councils the disturbers of our harmony, they have, by their free election, re-established them in power. at this very time too they are permitting their chief magistrate to send over not only souldiers of our common blood, but Scotch & foreign mercenaries to invade & destroy us. these facts have given the last stab to agonizing affection, and manly spirit bids us to renounce for ever these unfeeling brethren. we must endeavor to forget our former love for them, and to hold them as we hold the rest of mankind enemies in war, in peace friends. we might have been a free and a great people together; but a communication of grandeur & of freedom it seems is below their dignity. be it so, since they will have it. the road to happiness & to glory is open to us too. we will tread it apart from them, and] **we must therefore** acquiesce in the necessity which denounces our [eternal]

separation **and hold them as we hold the rest of mankind, enemies in war, in peace friends.[!]***

We therefore the representatives of the United states of America in General Congress assembled do in the name, & by the authority of the good people of these [states reject & renounce all allegiance & subjection to the kings of Great Britain & all others who may hereafter claim by, through or under them: we utterly dissolve all political connection which may heretofore have subsisted between us & the people or parliament of Great Britain: & finally we do assert & declare these colonies to be free & independant states,] & that as free & independant states, they have full power to levy war, conclude peace, contract alliances, establish commerce, & to do all other acts & things which independant states may of right do. and for the support of this declaration we mutually pledge to each other our lives, our fortunes & our sacred honour.

We therefore the representatives of the United states of America in General Congress assembled, appealing to the supreme judge of the world for the rectitude of our intentions, do in the name, & by the authority of the good people of these colonies, solemnly publish & declare that these United colonies are & of right ought to be free & independant states; that they are absolved from all allegiance to the British crown, and that all political connection between them & the state of Great Britain is, & ought to be, totally dissolved; & that as free & independant states they have full power to levy war, conclude peace, contract alliances, establish commerce & to do all other acts & things which independant states may of right do.

and for the support of this declaration, with a firm reliance on the protection of divine providence we mutually pledge to each other our lives, our fortunes & our sacred honour.

*[EDITORS' NOTE.—The following paragraphs appeared in two unequal columns in Jefferson Papers. A space here shows where the first column ended and the second began.]

19

A CITIZEN OF NEW JERSEY, PENNSYLVANIA
EVENING POST
30 July 1776

Although it be granted, on all hands, that all power originates from the people; yet it is plain, that in those colonies where the government has, from the beginning, been in the hands of a very few rich men, the ideas of government both in the minds of those rich men, and of the common people, are rather aristocratical than popular. The rich, having been used to govern, seem to think it is their right; and the poorer commonalty, having hitherto had little or no hand in government, seem to think it does not belong to them to have any.

From this cause, I imagine, it came to pass that the New-Jersey Convention, in their charter, made it a qualification for a member of their Lower House of Assembly, that he be possessed of an estate of five hundred pounds, and of a Member of their Council, that he have an estate of one thousand pound. This I esteem a hurtful remnant of the feudal constitution. Why should these be made qualifications? Are not many, who have not these qualifications, as fit to serve their country in either of these capacities, as any that are worth the money? This I think cannot be denied. The only reason that occurs to my mind, which can be pleaded in justification of this regulation, is that it renders the legislators independant. But according to my observation, many who are not worth so much, are of more independant spirits, and will not be so soon biassed by the prospect of gain, as those in general who are much richer than themselves.

Besides, why should not the same qualification be insisted on for a Judge in any Court, and for any considerable officer, whether civil or military? The necessity of independant men in all these cases is much the same. By these means the government, in every part, would be in the hands of the rich only, and therefore in all reason ought to be exercised *over* the rich only, and the poor, and those in moderate circumstances, ought to be entirely excused from bearing any part of the burden of a government, from the honors of which they are wholly excluded.

In short, I cannot see but that our maxim in this government is perfectly right, and that the experience of more than a century confirms the propriety of it, that any elector hath a right to be elected into any office of state.

20

THOMAS JEFFERSON, AUTOBIOGRAPHY
1821
Works 1:57–59

Our delegation [to the Continental Congress] had been renewed for the ensuing year commencing Aug. 11. [1776] but the new government [of Virginia] was now organized, a meeting of the legislature was to be held in Oct. and I had been elected a member by my county. I knew that our legislation under the regal government had many very vicious points which urgently required reformation, and I thought I could be of more use in forwarding that work. I therefore retired from my seat in Congress on the 2d. of Sep. resigned it, and took my place in the legislature of my state, on the 7th. of October.

. . . . .

On the 12th. I obtained leave to bring in a bill declaring tenants in tail to hold their lands in fee simple. In the earlier times of the colony when lands were to be obtained for little or nothing, some provident individuals procured large grants, and, desirous of founding great families for themselves, settled them on their descendants in fee-tail.

The transmission of this property from generation to generation in the same name raised up a distinct set of families who, being privileged by law in the perpetuation of their wealth were thus formed into a Patrician order, distinguished by the splendor and luxury of their establishments. From this order too the king habitually selected his Counsellors of State, the hope of which distinction devoted the whole corps to the interests & will of the crown. To annul this privilege, and instead of an aristocracy of wealth, of more harm and danger, than benefit, to society, to make an opening for the aristocracy of virtue and talent, which nature has wisely provided for the direction of the interests of society, & scattered with equal hand through all it's conditions, was deemed essential to a well ordered republic. To effect it no violence was necessary, no deprivation of natural right, but rather an enlargement of it by a repeal of the law. For this would authorize the present holder to divide the property among his children equally, as his affections were divided; and would place them, by natural generation on the level of their fellow citizens. But this repeal was strongly opposed by Mr. Pendleton, who was zealously attached to ancient establishments; and who, taken all in all, was the ablest man in debate I have ever met with. He had not indeed the poetical fancy of Mr. Henry, his sublime imagination, his lofty and overwhelming diction; but he was cool, smooth and persuasive; his language flowing, chaste & embellished, his conceptions quick, acute and full of resource; never vanquished; for if he lost the main battle, he returned upon you, and regained so much of it as to make it a drawn one, by dexterous manoeuvres, skirmishes in detail, and the recovery of small advantages which, little singly, were important altogether. You never knew when you were clear of him, but were harassed by his perseverance until the patience was worn down of all who had less of it than himself. Add to this that he was one of the most virtuous & benevolent of men, the kindest friend, the most amiable & pleasant of companions, which ensured a favorable reception to whatever came from him. Finding that the general principles of entails could not be maintained, he took his stand on an amendment which he proposed, instead of an absolute abolition, to permit the tenant in tail to convey in fee simple, if he chose it: and he was within a few votes of saving so much of the old law. But the bill passed finally for entire abolition.

21

REJECTED CONSTITUTION FOR MASSACHUSETTS
1778
Handlin 192–93

V.—Every male inhabitant of any town in this State, being free and twenty one years of age, excepting negroes, Indians and mulattoes, shall be entitled to vote for a Representative or Representatives, as the case may be, in the town, where he is resident; provided he has paid taxes in said town (unless by law excused from taxes) and been resident therein one full year, immediately preceding such voting, or that such town has been his known and usual place of abode for that time, or that he is considered as an inhabitant thereof; and every such inhabitant qualified as above, and worth sixty pounds, clear of all charges thereon, shall be entitled to put in his vote for Governor, Lieutenant Governor and Senators or Representatives, shall be by ballot, and not otherwise.

22

RETURN OF SUTTON, MASSACHUSETTS
18 May 1778
Handlin 231–32

The four first Articles we don't object against.

But the V Article appears to us to wear a very gross complexion of slavery; and is diametrically repugnant to the grand and Fundamental maxim of Humane Rights; viz. *"That Law to bound all must be assented to by all."* which this Article by no means admits of, when it excludes free men, and men of property from a voice in the Elections of Representatives; Negroes etc. are excluded even tho they are free and men of property. This is manifestly ading to the already acumulated Load of guilt lying upon the Land in supporting the slave trade when the poor innocent Affricans who never hurt or offered any Injury or Insult to this country have been so unjustly assaulted inhumanely Murdered many of them; to make way for stealing others, and then cruelly brought from their native Land, and sold here like Beasts and yet now by this constitution, if by any good Providence they or any of their Posterity, obtain their Freedom and a handsome estate yet they must excluded the Privileges of Men! this must be the *bringing or incurring more Wrath upon us.* And it must be thought more insulting tho not so cruel, to deprive the original Natives of the Land the Privileges of Men. We also cant but observe that by this Article the Convention had in contemplation of having many more slaves beside the Poor Africans, when they say of others beside; being *Free* and 21 years old

We therefore think that we ought to have an Article expressive of what the State is to consist of. And to say in express Terms that every person within the State 21 years of Age shall have a sole absolute Property in himself and all his earnings having an exclusive Right to make all manner contracts, and shall so Remain until they are rendered *non compos Mentis* by lawful Authority, or have forfeited their Freedom by misdemeanour and so adjudged by Authority proper to try the same; or their service legally disposed of for the discharge of some Debt Damage or Trespass. And then that every Male Inhabitant free as afforesaid etc. Provided that Men who lie a Burden upon the publick or have little or no Property ought not to have

a full or equal Vote with those that have an estate, in voting for a Representative, for then a Representative may be chosen without any property, and as the proposed Constitution stands there is all the chance that could be wished, for designing mischevious Men to purchase themselves seats in the House; for poor, shiftless spendthrifty men and inconsiderate youngsters that have no property are cheap bought (that is) their votes easily procured Choose a Representative to go to court, to vote away the Money of those that have Estates; and the Representative with all his constitutents or Voters not pay so much Taxes as one poor *Negro, Indian or Molatto* that is not allowed to put in a single vote. Perhaps if all under what used to be voters for Representatives; were reconed each Vote equal to half one of the old voters it might be about a just and proper Medium. It is farther to be observed that this Article is grossly inconsistant with the XIV which provides that all Money Bills or Acts for levying and granting Money shall originate solely in the House and not be subject to any amendment, by the Senate; when the Representatives are chosen by Persons of no Property, and there must be sixty Pounds clear Estate to vote for a Governor or Senator. If men of no Property might vote for any part of the Legislature and not the whole; it ought to be that part of the Legislature which are under the greatest Restraints as to Money Bills Acts or Resolves.

23

THOMAS JEFFERSON TO DAVID RITTENHOUSE
19 July 1778
Papers 2:202–3

Writing to a philosopher, I may hope to be pardoned for intruding some thoughts of my own, tho' they relate to him personally. Your time for two years past has, I beleive, been principally employed in the civil government of your country. Tho' I have been aware of the authority our cause would acquire with the world from it's being known that yourself and Doctr. Franklin were zealous friends to it, and am myself duly impressed with a sense of the arduousness of government, and the obligation those are under who are able to conduct it, yet I am also satisfied there is an order of geniusses above that obligation, and therefore exempted from it. No body can conceive that nature ever intended to throw away a Newton upon the occupations of a crown. It would have been a prodigality for which even the conduct of providence might have been arraigned, had he been by birth annexed to what was so far below him. Cooperating with nature in her ordinary oeconomy, we should dispose of and employ the geniusses of men according to their several orders and degrees. I doubt not there are in your country many persons equal to the task of conducting government: but you should consider that the world has but one Ryttenhouse, and that it never had one before. The amazing mechanical representation of the solar system which you conceived and executed, has never been surpassed by any but the work of which it is a copy. Are those powers then, which being intended for the erudition of the world, like air and light, the world's common property, to be taken from their proper pursuit to do the commonplace drudgery of governing a single state, a work which may be executed by men of an ordinary stature, such as are always and every where to be found? Without having ascended mount Sina for inspiration, I can pronounce that the precept, in the decalogue of the vulgar, that they shall not make to themselves "the likeness of any thing that is in the heavens above" is reversed for you, and that you will fulfill the highest purposes of your creation by employing yourself in the perpetual breach of that inhibition. For my own country in particular you must remember something like a promise that it should be adorned with one of them. The taking of your city by the enemy has hitherto prevented the proposition from being made and approved by our legislature. The zeal of a true Whig in science must excuse the hazarding these free thoughts, which flow from a desire of promoting the diffusion of knowledge and of your fame, and from one who can assure you truly that he is with much sincerity & esteem Your most obedt. & most humble servt.

24

ALEXANDER HAMILTON TO JOHN JAY
14 Mar. 1779
Papers 2:17–18

Col Laurens, who will have the honor of delivering you this letter, is on his way to South Carolina, on a project, which I think, in the present situation of affairs there, is a very good one and deserves every kind of support and encouragement. This is to raise two three or four batalions of negroes; with the assistance of the government of that state, by contributions from the owners in proportion to the number they possess. If you should think proper to enter upon the subject with him, he will give you a detail of his plan. He wishes to have it recommended by Congress to the state; and, as an inducement, that they would engage to take those batalions into Continental pay.

It appears to me, that an expedient of this kind, in the present state of Southern affairs, is the most rational, that can be adopted, and promises very important advantages. Indeed, I hardly see how a sufficient force can be collected in that quarter without it; and the enemy's operations there are growing infinitely serious and formidable. I have not the least doubt, that the negroes will make very excellent soldiers, with proper management; and I will venture to pronounce, that they cannot be put in better hands than those of Mr. Laurens. He has all the zeal, intelligence, enterprise, and every other qualification requisite to succeed in such an undertaking. It is a maxim with some great military judges, that with sensible officers soldiers can hardly be too stupid; and on this principle it is thought that the Russians would make the best troops in the world, if they were under other officers than their own. The King of Prussia is among the number who maintain this doctrine and has a very emphatical saying on the occasion, which I do not exactly recollect. I mention this, because I frequently hear it objected to the scheme of embodying negroes that they are too stupid to make soldiers. This is so far from appearing to me a valid objection that I think their want of cultivation (for their natural faculties are probably as good as ours) joined to that habit of subordination which they acquire from a life of servitude, will make them sooner bec[o]me soldiers than our White inhabitants. Let officers be men of sense and sentiment, and the nearer the soldiers approach to machines perhaps the better.

I foresee that this project will have to combat much opposition from prejudice and self-interest. The contempt we have been taught to entertain for the blacks, makes us fancy many things that are founded neither in reason nor experience; and an unwillingness to part with property of so valuable a kind will furnish a thousand arguments to show the impracticability or pernicious tendency of a scheme which requires such a sacrifice. But it should be considered, that if we do not make use of them in this way, the enemy probably will; and that the best way to counteract the temptations they will hold out will be to offer them ourselves. An essential part of the plan is to give them their freedom with their muskets. This will secure their fidelity, animate their courage, and I believe will have a good influence upon those who remain, by opening a door to their emancipation. This circumstance, I confess, has no small weight in inducing me to wish the success of the project; for the dictates of humanity and true policy equally interest me in favour of this unfortunate class of men.

25

MASSACHUSETTS CONSTITUTION
OF 1780
Handlin 454–55

Chapter I.

Section III. House of Representatives.

ART. I.—There shall be in the Legislature of this Commonwealth, a representation of the people, annually elected, and founded upon the principle of equality.

II.—And in order to provide for a representation of the citizens of this Commonwealth, founded upon the principle of equality, every corporate town, containing one hundred and fifty rateable polls, may elect one Representative: Every corporate town, containing three hundred and seventy-five rateable polls, may elect two Representatives: Every corporate town, containing six hundred rateable polls, may elect three Representatives; and proceeding in that manner, making two hundred and twenty-five rateable polls the mean increasing number for every additional Representative.

Provided nevertheless, that each town now incorporated, not having one hundred and fifty rateable polls, may elect one Representative: but no place shall hereafter be incorporated with the privilege of electing a Representative, unless there are within the same one hundred and fifty rateable polls.

. . . . .

IV.—Every male person, being twenty-one years of age, and resident in any particular town in this Commonwealth for the space of one year next preceding, having a freehold estate within the same town, of the annual income of three pounds, or any estate of the value of sixty pounds, shall have a right to vote in the choice of a Representative or Representatives for the said town.

26

RETURN OF NORTHAMPTON, MASSACHUSETTS
22 May 1780
Handlin 577–85

Also we greatly disapprove of the fourth article of the third section of the first chapter, intitled house of Representatives, as materially defective, and as rescinding the natural, essential, and unalienable rights of many persons, inhabitants of this Commonwealth, to vote in the choice of a Representative or Representatives, for the town in which they are or may be inhabitants; and we beg leave to propose that the following addition should be made to the said fourth article, to wit, and also every rateable poll being twenty one years of age, and who shall have been resident in this Commonwealth for the space of three years next preceeding, and who shall be willing to take such oath of allegiance to the Commonwealth as the Laws for the time being shall prescribe.

In order to make the first article of this chapter, expressly conformable to your elegant address to your countrymen, and also to make it consistent with the principle of personal equality (which we conceive ought to be attended to, as well as the principle of corporation equality) ' it ought to run thus, viz. There shall be in the legislature of this Commonwealth, a representative of the persons of the people annually elected; and in order to provide for a representation of the Citizens of this Commonwealth founded upon the said principle of personal equality, the said fourth article ought to contain the above proposed addition or something tantamount. We are obliged, Gentlemen, to believe that all along in settling the bill of rights, and constructing the frame of Government, the convention had it full in their intention, that the house of representatives should be chosen, and appointed, in such manner as that they should be as properly, and, truly, a representative of the persons as the Senate of the property of the Commonwealth. We say that we are constrained to such a belief, because the convention themselves have plainly declared the same to have been their intention. And it is impossible for us to admit so black a thought as to imagine that the convention had an intention, by their address, to beguile their constituents into a supposition, that provision was made in the frame of Government, for a representative of the persons, as well as for the property of the Commonwealth, when really at the same time they were conscious that it was not so in fact; and that in truth there was not in all the frame of Government, any ground for such distinction, as is supposed in the address; for however justly and exactly the number of Senators in the frame of Government may be apportioned according to the property of each district, and provision made that they should continue forever hereafter to be so apportioned, yet that can never afford any foundation for the distinction of a representative of the persons, and a representative of the property of the Commonwealth: for altho such a provision will truly determine the share or particular part of any given whole number which every district into which the whole State may be divided, shall elect and depute; yet nothing can be more clear than that the ground of distinction between a personal and property representation, must wholly depend on the qualifications of the electors, and that if there shall be no difference made between the qualifications of the voters for the members of the house of Representatives, and for the members of the Senate, but each member of both houses shall be chosen by the same identical persons, as they must necessarily be if the voters for the members of both houses are all to have precisely the like qualifications and no part of the number of persons, having the like qualifications are to be excluded, then the distinction abovesaid is wholly out of doors and becomes an absolute nullity. Who would ever imagine that if all the male persons in this State of the age of twenty one years and of no property should by the constitution have as good a right to give their votes for the Senators, as the men in the State of the best property, and the votes of all the voters should have an equal estimation in determining the election. We say, into whose head could it ever enter to denominate a body so elected, a representative of the property of the Commonwealth however exactly and minutely the number or share of the whole Senate, which each district should be intitled to elect, might be adjusted to the property of each district, in relation to the property of the whole Commonwealth? but the case is so evident that it would be affrontive to dwell any longer upon it. We must therefore judge that this default of providing for a personal representative in the legislature, proceeded from inadvertency and forgetfulness, an infirmity which human nature is universally liable to. And we are further obliged to account for this omission, in the Constitution, in the way abovesaid, by an attention to several matters in the declaration of rights, which, when carefully reviewed, and considered by the Convention, we persuade ourselves will appear, not to harmonize with the omission which we are observing upon.

But that we may come home to the enquiry, concerning the justice of excluding such individuals, inhabitants of this State, from voting, not to say from a right to vote in the choice of a representative (for that is impossible) as come within the description of the proposed addition to the said fourth article; we beg that a recurrence may be had to the second paragraph of the preamble to the declaration of rights. There we find it declared, "that the body politick" (perhaps it might have been more properly said the constitution of the body politick) "is formed by a voluntary association of individuals, it is a social compact by" "which the whole people covenants with each citizen, and each citizen with the whole people that all shall be governed by certain Laws for the common good: it is the duty of the people therefore, in framing a constitution of Government, to provide for an equitable mode of making laws, as well" etc. Now can any one say, that the citizens of the State, who are included in the description of the proposed addition, and who do not answer the description of the said fourth article, as it now stands, have ever covenanted, consented, and agreed, or will ever covenant, consent, and agree, with the rest of the people, to be governed by Laws founded on an article of a constitution, which totally excludes them from any share or voice in appointing the legislature for the State; or will such persons ever consent, and agree, to be governed by laws, which shall be enacted by a legislature, appointed wholly without their participation; or can a constitution so framed be said to provide for an equitable mode of making laws, etc. Will any one stand forth and say, that persons who have been born within the state, and have always lived in it, till they have arrived to the age of twenty one years, perhaps much above that age, and who have always paid their poll tax, ever since they were sixteen years old, and are still rateable, and are rated and pay for their polls, the sum set on each poll, in every rate that is made for defraying either the continental State, or town charges, be the same higher or lower; we say, will any one affirm, that such persons are not citizens of the Commonwealth? Is not the consequence then, if the said paragraph is true, that an association of many individuals, of the State, which without consent totally excludes many such adult male persons, from any participation in the appointment of the legislature, is in fact no constitution, and does not make a body politick? yea, is it not absolutely a void business? As to what may be replied, by way of answer in behalf of infants, that is, persons under the age of twenty one years, we ask leave to refer to what Mr. Locke has most judiciously said, on that head, in the sixth chapter of the second book of his treatise of Government, intitled paternal power; which is much too lengthy to be recited on this occasion, but well deserving to be resorted to. And as to the case of women, of whatever age or condition they may be, we ask leave to refer to what is very sensibly, as well as genteelly said on the Subject, in the twenty ninth page of the Essex result. We also humbly conceive that the exclusion which we

complain of, directly militates and is absolutely repugnant to the genuine sense of the first article of the declaration of Rights; unless it be true that a majority of any State have a right without any forfeiture of the minority to deprive them of what the said first article declares are the natural, essential, and unalienable rights of all men. By that article all men are declared "to be born free and equal;" this is true only with respect to the right of dominion, and jurisdiction over one another. The right of enjoying that equality, freedom, and liberty, is, in the same article, declared unalienable, Very strange it would be, if others should have a right by their superior strength, to take away a right from any individual, which he himself could not alienate by his own consent and agreement; but this will truly be the case, or the exclusion which we except to, is directly repugnant to this first article.

If it is true that all men are naturally equal with respect to a right of dominion, government, and jurisdiction, over each other, that is to say, no one has any degree or spark of such right over another, then it will follow that any given number of such equals, will, if they should all live on the earth for thirty years, and no one of them within that time should be guilty of any crime or fault whereby he should forfeit his native equality and freedom; and no one of them should consent to come under the power and dominion of one or more of the rest, or alienate his native equality and freedom, (and by the way the article declares that he has no right to alienate it,) we suppose that at the end of the thirty years, they will all be as equal and free, as they were at the first moment of their existence. We further suppose that if one hundred of such equal freemen should be at once on the earth together, of what age soever they were, and some one of the hundred, should happen to have an hundred times as much brutal strength, as all the other individuals taken singly, or, perhaps, what is an equivalent thereto, an hundred times as much natural cunning, as any individual of the rest, he would not have any rights against the will of any one of his bretheren, to assume the exercise of dominion and jurisdiction over him, however easy it might be for him to do it; and if no one of the hundred would have a right to do so, we suppose that no ten together would have any right to it, and if not ten, then ninety nine of the hundred would not have any right to domination over the remaining hundreth man; for nought to nought gives but nought; the inevitable consequence then is, that if the ninety nine should endeavour to subjugate, and exercise government, over the hundredth man, without his consent, he would have a good right to resist, and in case the ninety nine should overcome and subdue him, the hundredth man would have a good right, at any time, when any lucky moment presented, to do any thing that should be necessary, to regain his natural liberty and freedom, whereof he had been thus wrongfully deprived; full as good a right against the ninety nine as he would have had against any single one of the hundred, who by his superior brutal strength, had usurped upon him. Now Gentlemen in case the form of Government which you have sent out to the people, shall be affirmed and established, is it not intended that every rateable poll of this state, of the age of twenty one years, shall be obliged to submit, and be subject to such a legislative body, as is therein projected and described? is it not intended that all such persons shall be the subjects of their legislation? and that their persons shall be controlable by the laws of that legislature whether they ever were or shall be the owners of a freehold estate within this state of the annual income of three pounds, or of any estate of the value of sixty pounds or not? Is it not intended that they shall be obliged to contribute to the subsidies, taxes, imposts, or duties, which shall be established, fixed, and laid by such a legislative, and be liable to be restrained of their liberty by the acts of such a legislative, for such causes as they shall judge they ought to be, whether they ever were or shall be qualified, as is expressed in the said fourth article of the third section of chapter first, intitled "house of representatives" or not? then will not such persons be in a state of absolute slavery to such a legislative, while they shall continue without the quantum of property prescribed in the said article? If they are to be subject to the jurisdiction and legislation of your legislature, with regard to life, liberty, and their day wages, or whatever small property they may acquire, and yet have no voice in the appointment of that legislature, what is the difference of their condition from that of the hundredth man who without his consent had jurisdiction usurped over him, by the other ninety nine or any single one of the above mentioned hundred of superior animal strength or natural cunning? But perhaps it will be said that this subjugation of these persons unqualified to vote, and consequently excluded by the Said fourth article, is done by their own consent, as it is done by the convention in whose choice they have, or might have had, a vote; and that Mr. Locke tells us, "that the liberty of a man in society is to be under no other legislative power, but such as is established by his consent;" and that the said legislative body, to be from time to time established without their participation, will be by their consent, as it has been done by the convention, the appointment of which body they had a voice, and consequently they were their agents; and, as their agents have consented to it, it is become the act of the constituents: We answer, that the objection supposes what is not true in fact, to wit, that the convention have been impowered and authorized to agree upon and establish a model of Government for this state, it is certain that the convention have never had such a power given to them, as is evident, if we consider the proposals upon which they were elected, which were that delegates should be chosen by the several towns in this State, for the sole purpose of devising and agreeing upon a constitution or frame of Government to be communicated and laid before the people; which, if two thirds of the people capable of acting, to wit, the freemen of the state, of the age of twenty one years, should accept and affirm, it should then, and not till then, be the constitution of this state, and binding on the whole. And the same is further evident, to wit, that the Convention have no power to establish a Constitution for the State, if they themselves understand their own powers; for they themselves by clear implication acknowledge that they have no such power, in their second resolve of the second

of March last, whereby they ask the people that such a power may be given them; not expressly and directly indeed, but implicitly and indirectly: And wherefore do they ask it, if they had it given them by their original appointment? So that if the people should now affirm the frame of Government which the convention have communicated to them, containing the said fourth article, whereby many adult rateable persons who are inhabitants and citizens of this state, and have never done any thing to forfeit their natural and most important rights, are excluded from voting for a representative or representatives for the towns where they dwell; it will be precisely a like case, with that above put, to wit, where the ninety nine of an hundred free and equal men conclude to usurp dominion and jurisdiction over the hundredth man against his will, that is, to deprive him of his natural liberty, which is no other than to enslave him when he has been guilty of nothing, whereby he had forfeited that natural liberty and equality. It is certain that the said section, intitled "house of representatives," supposes that the polls in the State whether they shall be owners of property or not, will always be taxed; witness the second article of the said section, and we know that they always have been the subjects of legislation in this state and have had many heavy burdens and services set on them by the legislature, expecially in time of war, and that will, no doubt, continue to be the case (though probably not in so great a degree) even if they should have a voice in the appointment of representatives.

Dont we know that whenever any mention is made of a tax act, or proposal in the legislature of taxation, it is always spoken of as a tax on polls and estates; that whenever a list is ordered for the purpose of a new valuation, an exact account is directed to be taken of the number of polls above the age of sixteen years in the several towns in this state: and that when the house or their Comittee are settling a valuation, the first business always is to fix the proportion of a single poll to a thousand pound; and dont we know that the owners of a large property, generally, upon such occasions, strive to get the polls share as high as they can; for they are fully sensible, that it is their interest, that the polls share should not be low, for the higher that is, the less will remain on the estates; and they conduct in the case accordingly. Now do we hear from these poor polls, a single objection against the persons who are owners of large property, their voting for the members of the house of representatives? they consider that such property-holders have personal interests and concerns as well as the poor day laborer; further, do they object a word against the owners of the property chusing one entire branch of the legislature, exclusive of themselves, to be guardians of such property? they feel and own the force of the argument for property's having great weight in the legislature, because property ever was, and ever will be, the subject of legislation and taxation. But pray Gentlemen, shall not the polls, the persons of the state, have some weight also, who will always be the subjects of legislation and taxation? Are life, members, and liberty of no value or consideration? Indeed Gentlemen we are shocked at the thought, that the persons of adult men should, like live stock and dead chattels, be brought to account to augment the capital whereon to draw representatives for particular towns, in the same manner as such chattels are to be brought into the property capitals to augment the number of Senators, and when they have been improved and made the most of that may be for that purpose, they should be wholly sunk and discarded not to say like villains but absolutely like brute beasts. Shall these poor adult persons who are always to be taxed as high as our men of property shall prevail to have them set, and their low pittances of day wages, be taken to lighten the burden on property, shall these poor polls who have gone for us into the greatest perils, and undergone infinite fatigues in the present war to rescue us from slavery, and had a great hand, under God, in working out the great salvation in our land, which is, in a great degree wrought out, some of them leaving at home their poor families, to endure the sufferings of hunger and nakedness, shall they now be treated by us like villains and African slaves? God forbid. What have they done to forfeit this right of participating in the choice of one branch of the two branches which are to constitute our legislative, when they are willing that your men of property should enjoy the exclusive right of chusing the first branch? have they forfeited it in the exercise which they have made of this right of participating in the choice of you Gentlemen to your important, very important trust? we hope not, and we hope that you will on further consideration verify it, that they have not, by giving them a voice in the choice and appointment of that very branch of the legislative, which you yourselves tell us is by you intended, to be the representative of the persons of the Commonwealth, and thereby remove all cause for them to regret their choice of you.

Gentlemen, we cannot yet dismiss this very affecting subject. Shall we treat these polls precisely as Britain intended and resolved to treat all the sons of America? that is to say, to bind us in all cases whatsoever, without a single vote for the legislature who were to bind and legislate for us: at which all Americans who deserved freedom, had the highest indignation, and that most justly. We say, who deserved freedom; for he who is willing to enslave his brother, is, if possible, less deserving of liberty, than he who is content to be enslaved. Shall we who hold property, when God shall have fully secured it to us, be content to see our brethren, who have done their full share in procuring that security, shall we be content and satisfied, we say, to see these our deserving brethren on election days, standing aloof, and sneaking into corners, and ashamed to show their heads, in the meetings of freemen, because, by the constitution of the land, they are doomed intruders, if they should appear at such meetings? the thought is abhorrent to justice and too afflictive to good minds to be endured.

27

BENJAMIN FRANKLIN, INFORMATION TO THOSE
WHO WOULD REMOVE TO AMERICA
Sept. 1782
Writings 8:603–14

Many Persons in Europe, having directly or by Letters, express'd to the Writer of this, who is well acquainted with North America, their Desire of transporting and establishing themselves in that Country; but who appear to have formed, thro' Ignorance, mistaken Ideas and Expectations of what is to be obtained there; he thinks it may be useful, and prevent inconvenient, expensive, and fruitless Removals and Voyages of improper Persons, if he gives some clearer and truer Notions of that part of the World, than appear to have hitherto prevailed.

He finds it is imagined by Numbers, that the Inhabitants of North America are rich, capable of rewarding, and dispos'd to reward, all sorts of Ingenuity; that they are at the same time ignorant of all the Sciences, and, consequently, that Strangers, possessing Talents in the Belles-Lettres, fine Arts, &c., must be highly esteemed, and so well paid, as to become easily rich themselves; that there are also abundance of profitable Offices to be disposed of, which the Natives are not qualified to fill; and that, having few Persons of Family among them, Strangers of Birth must be greatly respected, and of course easily obtain the best of those Offices, which will make all their Fortunes; that the Governments too, to encourage Emigrations from Europe, not only pay the Expence of personal Transportation, but give Lands gratis to Strangers, with Negroes to work for them, Utensils of Husbandry, and Stocks of Cattle. These are all wild Imaginations; and those who go to America with Expectations founded upon them will surely find themselves disappointed.

The Truth is, that though there are in that Country few People so miserable as the Poor of Europe, there are also very few that in Europe would be called rich; it is rather a general happy Mediocrity that prevails. There are few great Proprietors of the Soil, and few Tenants; most People cultivate their own Lands, or follow some Handicraft or Merchandise; very few rich enough to live idly upon their Rents or Incomes, or to pay the high Prices given in Europe for Paintings, Statues, Architecture, and the other Works of Art, that are more curious than useful. Hence the natural Geniuses, that have arisen in America with such Talents, have uniformly quitted that Country for Europe, where they can be more suitably rewarded. It is true, that Letters and Mathematical Knowledge are in Esteem there, but they are at the same time more common than is apprehended; there being already existing nine Colleges or Universities, viz. four in New England, and one in each of the Provinces of New York, New Jersey, Pensilvania, Maryland, and Virginia, all furnish'd with learned Professors; besides a number of smaller Academies; these educate many of their Youth in the Languages, and those Sciences that qualify men for the Professions of Divinity, Law, or Physick. Strangers indeed are by no means excluded from exercising those Professions; and the quick Increase of Inhabitants everywhere gives them a Chance of Employ, which they have in common with the Natives. Of civil Offices, or Employments, there are few; no superfluous Ones, as in Europe; and it is a Rule establish'd in some of the States, that no Office should be so profitable as to make it desirable. The 36th Article of the Constitution of Pennsilvania, runs expressly in these Words; "As every Freeman, to preserve his Independence, (if he has not a sufficient Estate) ought to have some Profession, Calling, Trade, or Farm, whereby he may honestly subsist, there can be no Necessity for, nor Use in, establishing Offices of Profit; the usual Effects of which are Dependance and Servility, unbecoming Freemen, in the Possessors and Expectants; Faction, Contention, Corruption, and Disorder among the People. Wherefore, whenever an Office, thro' Increase of Fees or otherwise, becomes so profitable, as to occasion many to apply for it, the Profits ought to be lessened by the Lagislature."

These Ideas prevailing more or less in all the United States, it cannot be worth any Man's while, who has a means of Living at home, to expatriate himself, in hopes of obtaining a profitable civil Office in America; and, as to military Offices, they are at an End with the War, the Armies being disbanded. Much less is it adviseable for a Person to go thither, who has no other Quality to recommend him but his Birth. In Europe it has indeed its Value; but it is a Commodity that cannot be carried to a worse Market than that of America, where people do not inquire concerning a Stranger, *What is he?* but, *What can he do?* If he has any useful Art, he is welcome; and if he exercises it, and behaves well, he will be respected by all that know him; but a mere Man of Quality, who, on that Account, wants to live upon the Public, by some Office or Salary, will be despis'd and disregarded. The Husbandman is in honor there, and even the Mechanic, because their Employments are useful. The People have a saying, that God Almighty is himself a Mechanic, the greatest in the Univers; and he is respected and admired more for the Variety, Ingenuity, and Utility of his Handyworks, than for the Antiquity of his Family. They are pleas'd with the Observation of a Negro, and frequently mention it, that *Boccarorra* (meaning the White men) *make de black man workee, make de Horse workee, make de Ox workee, make ebery ting workee; only de Hog. He, de hog, no workee; he eat, he drink, he walk about, he go to sleep when he please, he libb like a Gentleman.* According to these Opinions of the Americans, one of them would think himself more oblig'd to a Genealogist, who could prove for him that his Ancestors and Relations for ten Generations had been Ploughmen, Smiths, Carpenters, Turners, Weavers, Tanners, or even Shoemakers, and consequently that they were useful Members of Society; than if he could only prove that they were Gentlemen, doing nothing of Value, but living idly on the Labour of others, mere *fruges consumere nati*,[1] and

[1]". . . born / Merely to eat up the corn."—WATTS.

otherwise *good for nothing*, till by their Death their Estates, like the Carcass of the Negro's Gentleman-Hog, come to be *cut up.*

With regard to Encouragements for Strangers from Government, they are really only what are derived from good Laws and Liberty. Strangers are welcome, because there is room enough for them all, and therefore the old Inhabitants are not jealous of them; the Laws protect them sufficiently, so that they have no need of the Patronage of Great Men; and every one will enjoy securely the Profits of his Industry. But, if he does not bring a Fortune with him, he must work and be industrious to live. One or two Years' residence gives him all the Rights of a Citizen; but the government does not at present, whatever it may have done in former times, hire People to become Settlers, by Paying their Passages, giving Land, Negroes, Utensils, Stock, or any other kind of Emolument whatsoever. In short, America is the Land of Labour, and by no means what the English call *Lubberland*, and the French *Pays de Cocagne*, where the streets are said to be pav'd with half-peck Loaves, the Houses til'd with Pancakes, and where the Fowls fly about ready roasted, crying, *Come eat me!*

Who then are the kind of Persons to whom an Emigration to America may be advantageous? And what are the Advantages they may reasonably expect?

Land being cheap in that Country, from the vast Forests still void of Inhabitants, and not likely to be occupied in an Age to come, insomuch that the Propriety of an hundred Acres of fertile Soil full of Wood may be obtained near the Frontiers, in many Places, for Eight or Ten Guineas, hearty young Labouring Men, who understand the Husbandry of Corn and Cattle, which is nearly the same in that Country as in Europe, may easily establish themselves there. A little Money sav'd of the good Wages they receive there, while they work for others, enables them to buy the Land and begin their Plantation, in which they are assisted by the Good-Will of their Neighbours, and some Credit. Multitudes of poor People from England, Ireland, Scotland, and Germany, have by this means in a few years become wealthy Farmers, who, in their own Countries, where all the Lands are fully occupied, and the Wages of Labour low, could never have emerged from the poor Condition wherein they were born.

From the salubrity of the Air, the healthiness of the Climate, the plenty of good Provisions, and the Encouragement to early Marriages by the certainty of Subsistence in cultivating the Earth, the Increase of Inhabitants by natural Generation is very rapid in America, and becomes still more so by the Accession of Strangers; hence there is a continual Demand for more Artisans of all the necessary and useful kinds, to supply those Cultivators of the Earth with Houses, and with Furniture and Utensils of the grosser sorts, which cannot so well be brought from Europe. Tolerably good Workmen in any of those mechanic Arts are sure to find Employ, and to be well paid for their Work, there being no Restraints preventing Strangers from exercising any Art they understand, nor any Permission necessary. If they are poor, they begin first as Servants or Journeymen; and if they are sober, industrious, and frugal, they soon become Masters, establish themselves in Business, marry, raise Families, and become respectable Citizens.

Also, Persons of moderate Fortunes and Capitals, who, having a Number of Children to provide for, are desirous of bringing them up to Industry, and to secure Estates for their Posterity, have Opportunities of doing it in America, which Europe does not afford. There they may be taught and practise profitable mechanic Arts, without incurring Disgrace on that Account, but on the contrary acquiring Respect by such Abilities. There small Capitals laid out in Lands, which daily become more valuable by the Increase of People, afford a solid Prospect of ample Fortunes thereafter for those Children. The Writer of this has known several Instances of large Tracts of Land, bought, on what was then the Frontier of Pensilvania, for Ten Pounds per hundred Acres, which after 20 years, when the Settlements had been extended far beyond them, sold readily, without any Improvement made upon them, for three Pounds per Acre. The Acre in America is the same with the English Acre, or the Acre of Normandy.

Those, who desire to understand the State of Government in America, would do well to read the Constitutions of the several States, and the Articles of Confederation that bind the whole together for general Purposes, under the Direction of one Assembly, called the Congress. These Constitutions have been printed, by order of Congress, in America; two Editions of them have also been printed in London; and a good Translation of them into French has lately been published at Paris.

Several of the Princes of Europe having of late years, from an Opinion of Advantage to arise by producing all Commodities and Manufactures within their own Dominions, so as to diminish or render useless their Importations, have endeavoured to entice Workmen from other Countries by high Salaries, Privileges, &c. Many Persons, pretending to be skilled in various great Manufactures, imagining that America must be in Want of them, and that the Congress would probably be dispos'd to imitate the Princes above mentioned, have proposed to go over, on Condition of having their Passages paid, Lands given, Salaries appointed, exclusive Privileges for Terms of years, &c. Such Persons, on reading the Articles of Confederation, will find, that the Congress have no Power committed to them, or Money put into their Hands, for such purposes; and that if any such Encouragement is given, it must be by the Government of some separate State. This, however, has rarely been done in America; and, when it has been done, it has rarely succeeded, so as to establish a Manufacture, which the Country was not yet so ripe for as to encourage private Persons to set it up; Labour being generally too dear there, and Hands difficult to be kept together, every one desiring to be a Master, and the Cheapness of Lands inclining many to leave Trades for Agriculture. Some indeed have met with Success, and are carried on to Advantage; but they are generally such as require only a few Hands, or wherein great Part of the Work is performed by Machines. Things that are bulky, and of so small Value as not well to bear the Expence of Freight, may often be made cheaper in the Country than they can be imported; and the Manufacture of such

Things will be profitable wherever there is a sufficient Demand. The Farmers in America produce indeed a good deal of Wool and Flax; and none is exported, it is all work'd up; but it is in the Way of domestic Manufacture, for the Use of the Family. The buying up Quantities of Wool and Flax, with the Design to employ Spinners, Weavers, &c., and form great Establishments, producing Quantities of Linen and Woollen Goods for Sale, has been several times attempted in different Provinces; but those Projects have generally failed, goods of equal Value being imported cheaper. And when the Governments have been solicited to support such Schemes by Encouragements, in Money, or by imposing Duties on Importation of such Goods, it has been generally refused, on this Principle, that, if the Country is ripe for the Manufacture, it may be carried on by private Persons to Advantage; and if not, it is a Folly to think of forcing Nature. Great Establishments of Manufacture require great Numbers of Poor to do the Work for small Wages; these Poor are to be found in Europe, but will not be found in America, till the Lands are all taken up and cultivated, and the Excess of People, who cannot get Land, want Employment. The Manufacture of Silk, they say, is natural in France, as that of Cloth in England, because each Country produces in Plenty the first Material; but if England will have a Manufacture of Silk as well as that of Cloth, and France one of Cloth as well as that of Silk, these unnatural Operations must be supported by mutual Prohibitions, or high Duties on the Importation of each other's Goods; by which means the Workmen are enabled to tax the home Consumer by greater Prices, while the higher Wages they receive makes them neither happier nor richer, since they only drink more and work less. Therefore the Governments in America do nothing to encourage such Projects. The People, by this Means, are not impos'd on, either by the Merchant or Mechanic. If the Merchant demands too much Profit on imported Shoes, they buy of the Shoemaker; and if he asks too high a Price, they take them of the Merchant; thus the two Professions are checks on each other. The Shoemaker, however, has, on the whole, a considerable Profit upon his Labour in America, beyond what he had in Europe, as he can add to his Price a Sum nearly equal to all the Expences of Freight and Commission, Risque or Insurance, &c., necessarily charged by the Merchant. And the Case is the same with the Workmen in every other Mechanic Art. Hence it is, that Artisans generally live better and more easily in America than in Europe; and such as are good Oeconomists make a comfortable Provision for Age, and for their Children. Such may, therefore, remove with Advantage to America.

In the long-settled Countries of Europe, all Arts, Trades, Professions, Farms, &c., are so full, that it is difficult for a poor Man, who has Children, to place them where they may gain, or learn to gain, a decent Livelihood. The Artisans, who fear creating future Rivals in Business, refuse to take Apprentices, but upon Conditions of Money, Maintenance, or the like, which the Parents are unable to comply with. Hence the Youth are dragg'd up in Ignorance of every gainful Art, and oblig'd to become Soldiers, or Servants, or Thieves, for a Subsistence. In

America, the rapid Increase of Inhabitants takes away that Fear of Rivalship, and Artisans willingly receive Apprentices from the hope of Profit by their Labour, during the Remainder of the Time stipulated, after they shall be instructed. Hence it is easy for poor Families to get their Children instructed; for the Artisans are so desirous of Apprentices, that many of them will even give Money to the Parents, to have Boys from Ten to Fifteen Years of Age bound Apprentices to them till the Age of Twenty-one; and many poor Parents have, by that means, on their Arrival in the Country, raised Money enough to buy Land sufficient to establish themselves, and to subsist the rest of their Family by Agriculture. These Contracts for Apprentices are made before a Magistrate, who regulates the Agreement according to Reason and Justice, and, having in view the Formation of a future useful Citizen, obliges the Master to engage by a written Indenture, not only that, during the time of Service stipulated, the Apprentice shall be duly provided with Meat, Drink, Apparel, washing, and Lodging, and, at its Expiration, with a compleat new Suit of Cloaths, but also that he shall be taught to read, write, and cast Accompts; and that he shall be well instructed in the Art or Profession of his Master, or some other, by which he may afterwards gain a Livelihood, and be able in his turn to raise a Family. A Copy of this Indenture is given to the Apprentice or his Friends, and the Magistrate keeps a Record of it, to which recourse may be had, in case of Failure by the Master in any Point of Performance. This desire among the Masters, to have more Hands employ'd in working for them, induces them to pay the Passages of young Persons, of both Sexes, who, on their Arrival, agree to serve them one, two, three, or four Years; those, who have already learnt a Trade, agreeing for a shorter Term, in proportion to their Skill, and the consequent immediate Value of their Service; and those, who have none, agreeing for a longer Term, in consideration of being taught an Art their Poverty would not permit them to acquire in their own Country.

The almost general Mediocrity of Fortune that prevails in America obliging its People to follow some Business for subsistence, those Vices, that arise usually from Idleness, are in a great measure prevented. Industry and constant Employment are great preservatives of the Morals and Virtue of a Nation. Hence bad Examples to Youth are more rare in America, which must be a comfortable Consideration to Parents. To this may be truly added, that serious Religion, under its various Denominations, is not only tolerated, but respected and practised. Atheism is unknown there; Infidelity rare and secret; so that persons may live to a great Age in that Country, without having their Piety shocked by meeting with either an Atheist or an Infidel. And the Divine Being seems to have manifested his Approbation of the mutual Forbearance and Kindness with which the different Sects treat each other, by the remarkable Prosperity with which He has been pleased to favour the whole Country.

28

THOMAS JEFFERSON, NOTES ON THE STATE OF VIRGINIA, QUERIES 14 AND 18, 137–43, 162–63 1784

To emancipate all slaves born after passing the act. The bill reported by the revisors does not itself contain this proposition; but an amendment containing it was prepared, to be offered to the legislature whenever the bill should be taken up, and further directing, that they should continue with their parents to a certain age, then be brought up, at the public expence, to tillage, arts or sciences, according to their geniusses, till the females should be eighteen, and the males twenty-one years of age, when they should be colonized to such place as the circumstances of the time should render most proper, sending them out with arms, implements of houshold and of the handicraft arts, seeds, pairs of the useful domestic animals, &c. to declare them a free and independant people, and extend to them our alliance and protection, till they shall have acquired strength; and to send vessels at the same time to other parts of the world for an equal number of white inhabitants; to induce whom to migrate hither, proper encouragements were to be proposed. It will probably be asked, Why not retain and incorporate the blacks into the state, and thus save the expence of supplying, by importation of white settlers, the vacancies they will leave? Deep rooted prejudices entertained by the whites; ten thousand recollections, by the blacks, of the injuries they have sustained; new provocations; the real distinctions which nature has made; and many other circumstances, will divide us into parties, and produce convulsions which will probably never end but in the extermination of the one or the other race.—To these objections, which are political, may be added others, which are physical and moral. The first difference which strikes us is that of colour. Whether the black of the negro resides in the reticular membrane between the skin and scarf-skin, or in the scarf-skin itself; whether it proceeds from the colour of the blood, the colour of the bile, or from that of some other secretion, the difference is fixed in nature, and is as real as if its seat and cause were better known to us. And is this difference of no importance? Is it not the foundation of a greater or less share of beauty in the two races? Are not the fine mixtures of red and white, the expressions of every passion by greater or less suffusions of colour in the one, preferable to that eternal monotony, which reigns in the countenances, that immoveable veil of black which covers all the emotions of the other race? Add to these, flowing hair, a more elegant symmetry of form, their own judgment in favour of the whites, declared by their preference of them, as uniformly as is the preference of the Oran-ootan for the black women over those of his own species. The circumstance of superior beauty, is thought worthy attention in the propagation of our horses, dogs, and other domestic animals; why not in that of man? Besides those of colour, figure, and hair, there are other physical distinctions proving a difference of race. They have less hair on the face and body. They secrete less by the kidnies, and more by the glands of the skin, which gives them a very strong and disagreeable odour. This greater degree of transpiration renders them more tolerant of heat, and less so of cold, than the whites. Perhaps too a difference of structure in the pulmonary apparatus, which a late ingenious experimentalist has discovered to be the principal regulator of animal heat, may have disabled them from extricating, in the act of inspiration, so much of that fluid from the outer air, or obliged them in expiration, to part with more of it. They seem to require less sleep. A black, after hard labour through the day, will be induced by the slightest amusements to sit up till midnight, or later, though knowing he must be out with the first dawn of the morning. They are at least as brave, and more adventuresome. But this may perhaps proceed from a want of forethought, which prevents their seeing a danger till it be present. When present, they do not go through it with more coolness or steadiness than the whites. They are more ardent after their female: but love seems with them to be more an eager desire, than a tender delicate mixture of sentiment and sensation. Their griefs are transient. Those numberless afflictions, which render it doubtful whether heaven has given life to us in mercy or in wrath, are less felt, and sooner forgotten with them. In general, their existence appears to participate more of sensation than reflection. To this must be ascribed their disposition to sleep when abstracted from their diversions, and unemployed in labour. An animal whose body is at rest, and who does not reflect, must be disposed to sleep of course. Comparing them by their faculties of memory, reason, and imagination, it appears to me, that in memory they are equal to the whites; in reason much inferior, as I think one could scarcely be found capable of tracing and comprehending the investigations of Euclid; and that in imagination they are dull, tasteless, and anomalous. It would be unfair to follow them to Africa for this investigation. We will consider them here, on the same stage with the whites, and where the facts are not apocryphal on which a judgment is to be formed. It will be right to make great allowances for the difference of condition, of education, of conversation, of the sphere in which they move. Many millions of them have been brought to, and born in America. Most of them indeed have been confined to tillage, to their own homes, and their own society: yet many have been so situated, that they might have availed themselves of the conversation of their masters; many have been brought up to the handicraft arts, and from that circumstance have always been associated with the whites. Some have been liberally educated, and all have lived in countries where the arts and sciences are cultivated to a considerable degree, and have had before their eyes samples of the best works from abroad. The Indians, with no advantages of this kind, will often carve figures on their pipes not destitute of design and merit. They will crayon out an animal, a plant, or a country, so as to prove the existence of a germ in their minds which only wants cultivation. They astonish you with strokes of the most sublime oratory;

such as prove their reason and sentiment strong, their imagination glowing and elevated. But never yet could I find that a black had uttered a thought above the level of plain narration; never see even an elementary trait of painting or sculpture. In music they are more generally gifted than the whites with accurate ears for tune and time, and they have been found capable of imagining a small catch. Whether they will be equal to the composition of a more extensive run of melody, or of complicated harmony, is yet to be proved. Misery is often the parent of the most affecting touches in poetry.—Among the blacks is misery enough, God knows, but no poetry. Love is the peculiar oestrum of the poet. Their love is ardent, but it kindles the senses only, not the imagination. Religion indeed has produced a Phyllis Whately; but it could not produce a poet. The compositions published under her name are below the dignity of criticism. The heroes of the Dunciad are to her, as Hercules to the author of that poem. Ignatius Sancho has approached nearer to merit in composition; yet his letters do more honour to the heart than the head. They breathe the purest effusions of friendship and general philanthropy, and shew how great a degree of the latter may be compounded with strong religious zeal. He is often happy in the turn of his compliments, and his stile is easy and familiar, except when he affects a Shandean fabrication of words. But his imagination is wild and extravagant, escapes incessantly from every restraint of reason and taste, and, in the course of its vagaries, leaves a tract of thought as incoherent and eccentric, as is the course of a meteor through the sky. His subjects should often have led him to a process of sober reasoning: yet we find him always substituting sentiment for demonstration. Upon the whole, though we admit him to the first place among those of his own colour who have presented themselves to the public judgment, yet when we compare him with the writers of the race among whom he lived, and particularly with the epistolary class, in which he has taken his own stand, we are compelled to enroll him at the bottom of the column. This criticism supposes the letters published under his name to be genuine, and to have received amendment from no other hand; points which would not be of easy investigation. The improvement of the blacks in body and mind, in the first instance of their mixture with the whites, has been observed by every one, and proves that their inferiority is not the effect merely of their condition of life. We know that among the Romans, about the Augustan age especially, the condition of their slaves was much more deplorable than that of the blacks on the continent of America. The two sexes were confined in separate apartments, because to raise a child cost the master more than to buy one. Cato, for a very restricted indulgence to his slaves in this particular, took from them a certain price. But in this country the slaves multiply as fast as the free inhabitants. Their situation and manners place the commerce between the two sexes almost without restraint.—The same Cato, on a principle of oeconomy, always sold his sick and superannuated slaves. He gives it as a standing precept to a master visiting his farm, to sell his old oxen, old waggons, old tools, old and diseased servants, and every thing else become useless. "Vendat boves vetulos, plaustrum vetus, ferramenta, vetera, servum senem, servum morbosum, & si quid aliud supersit vendat." The American slaves cannot enumerate this among the injuries and insults they receive. It was the common practice to expose in the island of Aesculapius, in the Tyber, diseased slaves, whose cure was like to become tedious. The Emperor Claudius, by an edict, gave freedom to such of them as should recover, and first declared, that if any person chose to kill rather than to expose them, it should be deemed homicide. The exposing them is a crime of which no instance has existed with us; and were it to be followed by death, it would be punished capitally. We are told of a certain Vedius Pollio, who, in the presence of Augustus, would have given a slave as food to his fish, for having broken a glass. With the Romans, the regular method of taking the evidence of their slaves was under torture. Here it has been thought better never to resort to their evidence. When a master was murdered, all his slaves, in the same house, or within hearing, were condemned to death. Here punishment falls on the guilty only, and as precise proof is required against him as against a freeman. Yet notwithstanding these and other discouraging circumstances among the Romans, their slaves were often their rarest artists. They excelled too in science, insomuch as to be usually employed as tutors to their master's children. Epictetus, Diogenes, Phaedon, Terence, and Phaedrus, were slaves. But they were of the race of whites. It is not their condition then, but nature, which has produced the distinction.—Whether further observation will or will not verify the conjecture, that nature has been less bountiful to them in the endowments of the head, I believe that in those of the heart she will be found to have done them justice. That disposition to theft with which they have been branded, must be ascribed to their situation, and not to any depravity of the moral sense. The man, in whose favour no laws of property exist, probably feels himself less bound to respect those made in favour of others. When arguing for ourselves, we lay it down as a fundamental, that laws, to be just, must give a reciprocation of right: that, without this, they are mere arbitrary rules of conduct, founded in force, and not in conscience: and it is a problem which I give to the master to solve, whether the religious precepts against the violation of property were not framed for him as well as his slave? And whether the slave may not as justifiably take a little from one, who has taken all from him, as he may slay one who would slay him? That a change in the relations in which a man is placed should change his ideas of moral right and wrong, is neither new, nor peculiar to the colour of the blacks. Homer tells us it was so 2600 years ago.

ἥμισυ γάρ τ᾽ ἀρετῆς ἀποαίνυται εὐρύοπα Ζεὺς
ἀνέρος, εὖτ᾽ ἄν μιν κατὰ δούλιον ἦμαρ ἕλησιν·

(Od. 17. 323.)

Jove fix'd it certain, that whatever day
Makes man a slave, takes half his worth away.

But the slaves of which Homer speaks were whites. Notwithstanding these considerations which must weaken their respect for the laws of property, we find among them numerous instances of the most rigid integrity, and as many as among their better instructed masters, of benevolence, gratitude, and unshaken fidelity.—The opinion, that they are inferior in the faculties of reason and imagination, must be hazarded with great diffidence. To justify a general conclusion, requires many observations, even where the subject may be submitted to the Anatomical knife, to Optical glasses, to analysis by fire, or by solvents. How much more then where it is a faculty, not a substance, we are examining; where it eludes the research of all the senses; where the conditions of its existence are various and variously combined; where the effects of those which are present or absent bid defiance to calculation; let me add too, as a circumstance of great tenderness, where our conclusion would degrade a whole race of men from the rank in the scale of beings which their Creator may perhaps have given them. To our reproach it must be said, that though for a century and a half we have had under our eyes the races of black and of red men, they have never yet been viewed by us as subjects of natural history. I advance it therefore as a suspicion only, that the blacks, whether originally a distinct race, or made distinct by time and circumstances, are inferior to the whites in the endowments both of body and mind. It is not against experience to suppose, that different species of the same genus, or varieties of the same species, may possess different qualifications. Will not a lover of natural history then, one who views the gradations in all the races of animals with the eye of philosophy, excuse an effort to keep those in the department of man as distinct as nature has formed them? This unfortunate difference of colour, and perhaps of faculty, is a powerful obstacle to the emancipation of these people. Many of their advocates, while they wish to vindicate the liberty of human nature, are anxious also to preserve its dignity and beauty. Some of these, embarrassed by the question "What further is to be done with them?" join themselves in opposition with those who are actuated by sordid avarice only. Among the Romans emancipation required but one effort. The slave, when made free, might mix with, without staining the blood of his master. But with us a second is necessary, unknown to history. When freed, he is to be removed beyond the reach of mixture.

· · · · ·

It is difficult to determine on the standard by which the manners of a nation may be tried, whether *catholic*, or *particular*. It is more difficult for a native to bring to that standard the manners of his own nation, familiarized to him by habit. There must doubtless be an unhappy influence on the manners of our people produced by the existence of slavery among us. The whole commerce between master and slave is a perpetual exercise of the most boisterous passions, the most unremitting despotism on the one part, and degrading submissions on the other. Our children see this, and learn to imitate it; for man is an imitative animal. This quality is the germ of all education in him. From his cradle to his grave he is learning to do what he sees others do. If a parent could find no motive either in his philanthropy or his self-love, for restraining the intemperance of passion towards his slave, it should always be a sufficient one that his child is present. But generally it is not sufficient. The parent storms, the child looks on, catches the lineaments of wrath, puts on the same airs in the circle of smaller slaves, gives a loose to his worst of passions, and thus nursed, educated, and daily exercised in tyranny, cannot but be stamped by it with odious peculiarities. The man must be a prodigy who can retain his manners and morals undepraved by such circumstances. And with what execration should the statesman be loaded, who permitting one half the citizens thus to trample on the rights of the other, transforms those into despots, and these into enemies, destroys the morals of the one part, and the amor patriae of the other. For if a slave can have a country in this world, it must be any other in preference to that in which he is born to live and labour for another: in which he must lock up the faculties of his nature, contribute as far as depends on his individual endeavours to the evanishment of the human race, or entail his own miserable condition on the endless generations proceeding from him. With the morals of the people, their industry also is destroyed. For in a warm climate, no man will labour for himself who can make another labour for him. This is so true, that of the proprietors of slaves a very small proportion indeed are ever seen to labour. And can the liberties of a nation be thought secure when we have removed their only firm basis, a conviction in the minds of the people that these liberties are of the gift of God? That they are not to be violated but with his wrath? Indeed I tremble for my country when I reflect that God is just: that his justice cannot sleep for ever: that considering numbers, nature and natural means only, a revolution of the wheel of fortune, an exchange of situation, is among possible events: that it may become probable by supernatural interference! The Almighty has no attribute which can take side with us in such a contest.—But it is impossible to be temperate and to pursue this subject through the various considerations of policy, of morals, of history natural and civil. We must be contented to hope they will force their way into every one's mind. I think a change already perceptible, since the origin of the present revolution. The spirit of the master is abating, that of the slave rising from the dust, his condition mollifying, the way I hope preparing, under the auspices of heaven, for a total emancipation, and that this is disposed, in the order of events, to be with the consent of the masters, rather than by their extirpation.

29

TIMOTHY PICKERING TO RUFUS KING
6 Mar. 1785
King Life 1:45–46

In looking over the Act of Congress of the 23d of April 1784 (Mr. Jefferson's act) and the present report of an ordinance relative to these lands, I observe no provision is made for ministers of the Gospel, nor even for schools and academies. The latter might have been brought into view; tho' after the admission of *Slavery,* it was right to say noth-

ing of *Christianity.* Yet so glaring an inconsistency could not have occasioned much surprise. It is easy to be inconsistent. Congress made this important declaration "that all men are created equal; that they are endowed by their Creator with certain inalienable rights, and that among these are *life, liberty* and the *pursuit* of happiness," and these truths were held to be self evident. These great truths are echoed through the U.S., nevertheless a proposition for preventing a violation of these truths in a country yet unsettled and from which such violence might easily have been excluded, did not obtain! What pretence (argument there could be none) could be offered for its rejection? I should indeed have objected to the period proposed (the year 1800) for the exclusion of slavery, for the admission of it for a day or an hour ought to have been forbidden. It will be infinitely easier to prevent the Evil at first, than to eradicate or check it at any future time. How would Congress wish the new states to be settled, by slaves or by freemen? Take any given period, say 50 years—Will those States in that time have more acres of improved land by the admission than by the exclusion of slaves? In respect to population and improvement, compare Pennsylvania with Maryland and Virginia, particularly the latter. But why do I expostulate with you who already see all the reasons on this subject in points of view more striking than I can place them? Forgive me if my solicitude to prevent the greatest of evils has rendered me prolix. To suffer the continuance of slaves until they can gradually be emancipated in States already overrun with them may be pardonable, because unavoidable without hazarding greater evils; but to introduce them into countries where none now exist, countries which have been talked of—which we have boasted of—as an asylum to the oppressed of the Earth—can never be forgiven. For God's sake, then, let one more effort be made to prevent so terrible a calamity. The fundamental constitutions of the States are yet liable to alterations, and this is probably the only time when the evil can certainly be prevented.

30

JOHN ADAMS TO ELBRIDGE GERRY
25 Apr. 1785
Gerry Life 1:427–31

What is to be done with the Cincinnati? Is that order of chivalry, that inroad upon our first principle, equality, to be connived at? It is the deepest piece of cunning yet attempted. It is sowing the seeds of all that European courts wish to grow up among us, viz. of vanity, ambition, corruption, discord and sedition. Are we so dim-sighted as not to see, that the taking away the hereditary descent of it will not prevent its baneful influence? Who will think of preventing the son from wearing a ribbon and a bit of gold that his father wore? Mankind love to see one child at least of every beloved and respected father possessed of his estate, his office, &c. after his decease. Besides, when once the people begin to think these marks rewards, these marks are soon considered as the only proofs of merit. Such marks should not be adopted in any country where there is virtue, love of country, love of labour. When virtue is lost ambition succeeds. Then indeed ribbons and garters become necessary, but never till then. Then indeed these should be public rewards conferred by the state, the civil sovereign, not private men or bodies. I have been asked, why I have not written against it? Can it be necessary for me to write upon such a thing? I wrote twenty years ago some papers which have been called an essay on the feudal law, in which my sentiments and the sentiments of our ancestors are sufficiently expressed concerning all such distinctions and all orders of chivalry and nobility. But, sir, while reputations are so indiscreetly puffed, while thanks and statues are so childishly awarded, and the greatest real services are so coldly received, I had almost said censured, we are in the high road to have no virtues left, and nothing but ambition to reward. Ribbons are not the only reward of ambition. Wealth and power must keep them company. My countrymen give reputations to individuals that are real tyrannies. No man dare resist or oppose them. No wonder then that such reputations introduce chivalry, &c. without opposition, though without authority. The cry of gratitude, gratitude, is animal magnetism; it bewitches all mankind, and has established every tyranny, imposture and usurpation that ever existed upon earth; so true are those words of Machiavel, "Not ingratitude, but too much love, is the constant fault of the people." This is a subject that requires a volume; and you see I am in haste. I could not have believed, if I had not seen it, that our officers could have adopted such a scheme, or the people, the legislatures or congress have submitted to it one moment. I don't wonder at a marquis de la Fayette or a baron Steuben: they were born and bred to such decorations and the taste for them. From the moment that captain Jones had his cross of merit bestowed by the king and consented to by congress, I suspected that some such project was in contemplation. Awful, my friend, is the task of the intelligent advocate for liberty. The military spirit, the ecclesiastical spirit, the commercial spirit, and innumerable other evil spirits are eternally devising mischief to his cause and disturbing his repose. It is a constant warfare from the cradle to the grave without comfort, thanks, or rewards, and is always overcome at last.

Is not this institution against our confederation? Is it not against the declarations of rights in several of the states? Is it not an act of sovereignty disposing and creating of public rewards presumptuously enterprized by private gentlemen? Is the assembly a lawful assembly? Is it not cruel to call this a club for private friendship, or a society for charity for officers' widows and children? Would even such a society be lawful without the permission of the legislature? Is it not substituting honour for virtue in the infancy of a republic? Must it not introduce and perpetuate contests and dissentions, pernicious in all governments but especially in ours? Is it not an effectual subversion of our equality? Inequalities of riches cannot be avoided as long as nature gives inequality of understanding and activity.

And these inequalities are not unuseful. But artificial inequalities of decorations, birth and title not accompanying public truth, are those very inequalities which have exterminated virtue and liberty, and substituted ambition and slavery in all ages and countries. I don't wonder that the word, republican, is odious and unpopular throughout the world. I don't wonder that so few, even of the great writers, have admired this form of government. Plato himself, I am fully persuaded from his writings, was not a republican. It is the best of governments while the people are republicans, i. e. virtuous, simple and of independent spirit. But when the people are avaricious, ambitious and vain, instead of being virtuous, poor and proud, it is not. A republican is an equivocal title; a Dutchman, a Genoese, a Venetian, a Swiss, a Genevan and an Englishman are all called republicans. Among all these shades you will scarcely find the true colour. Our countrymen may be the nearest; but there is so much wealth among them and such an universal rage of avarice, that I often fear they will only make their real republicans miserable for a few years, and then become like the rest of the world. If this appears to be their determination, it is not worth the while of you and me to die martyrs to singular notions. You are young and may turn fine gentleman yet. I am too old, and therefore will retire to Pen's Hill,

The world forgetting, by the world forgot.

31

JOHN JAY TO RICHARD PRICE
27 Sept. 1785
MS Columbia Univ.

The Cause of Liberty like most other good Causes, will have its Difficulties and sometimes its Persecutions to struggle with. It has advanced more rapidly in this than other Countries, but all its objects are not yet attained and I much doubt whether they ever will be in this or any other terrestrial State. That Men should pray and fight for their own Freedom and yet keep others in Slavery is certainly acting a very inconsistent as well as unjust and perhaps impious part, but the History of Mankind is filled with Instances of human Improprieties. The wise and the good never form the Majority of any large Society and it seldom happens that their Measures are uniformly adopted or that they can always prevent being overborne themselves by the strong and almost never ceasing union of the wicked and the weak. These Circumstances tell us to be patient and moderate those Sanguine Expectations, which warm and good Hearts often mislead even wise Heads to entertain on these Subjects. All that the best Men can do is to persevere in doing their Duty to their Country, and leave the Consequences to him who made it their Duty; being neither elated by success however great nor discouraged by Disappointments however frequent or mortifying.

32

THOMAS JEFFERSON TO JAMES MADISON
28 Oct. 1785
Papers 8:681–82

Seven o'clock, and retired to my fireside, I have determined to enter into conversation with you; this [Fontainebleau] is a village of about 5,000 inhabitants when the court is not here and 20,000 when they are, occupying a valley thro' which runs a brook, and on each side of it a ridge of small mountains most of which are naked rock. The king comes here in the fall always, to hunt. His court attend him, as do also the foreign diplomatic corps. But as this is not indispensably required, and my finances do not admit the expence of a continued residence here, I propose to come occasionally to attend the king's levees, returning again to Paris, distant 40 miles. This being the first trip, I set out yesterday morning to take a view of the place. For this purpose I shaped my course towards the highest of the mountains in sight, to the top of which was about a league. As soon as I had got clear of the town I fell in with a poor woman walking at the same rate with myself and going the same course. Wishing to know the condition of the labouring poor I entered into conversation with her, which I began by enquiries for the path which would lead me into the mountain: and thence proceeded to enquiries into her vocation, condition and circumstance. She told me she was a day labourer, at 8. sous or 4 d. sterling the day; that she had two children to maintain, and to pay a rent of 30 livres for her house (which would consume the hire of 75 days), that often she could get no emploiment, and of course was without bread. As we had walked together near a mile and she had so far served me as a guide, I gave her, on parting 24 sous. She burst into tears of a gratitude which I could perceive was unfeigned, because she was unable to utter a word. She had probably never before received so great an aid. This little attendrissement, with the solitude of my walk led me into a train of reflections on that unequal division of property which occasions the numberless instances of wretchedness which I had observed in this country and is to be observed all over Europe. The property of this country is absolutely concentered in a very few hands, having revenues of from half a million of guineas a year downwards. These employ the flower of the country as servants, some of them having as many as 200 domestics, not labouring. They employ also a great number of manufacturers, and tradesmen, and lastly the class of labouring husbandmen. But after all these comes the most numerous of all the classes, that is, the poor who cannot find work. I asked myself what could be the reason that so many should be permitted to beg who are willing to work, in a country where there is a very considerable proportion of uncultivated lands? These lands are kept idle mostly for the sake of game. It should seem then that it must be because of

the enormous wealth of the proprietors which places them above attention to the increase of their revenues by permitting these lands to be laboured. I am conscious that an equal division of property is impracticable. But the consequences of this enormous inequality producing so much misery to the bulk of mankind, legislators cannot invent too many devices for subdividing property, only taking care to let their subdivisions go hand in hand with the natural affections of the human mind. The descent of property of every kind therefore to all the children, or to all the brothers and sisters, or other relations in equal degree is a politic measure, and a practicable one. Another means of silently lessening the inequality of property is to exempt all from taxation below a certain point, and to tax the higher portions of property in geometrical progression as they rise. Whenever there is in any country, uncultivated lands and unemployed poor, it is clear that the laws of property have been so far extended as to violate natural right. The earth is given as a common stock for man to labour and live on. If, for the encouragement of industry we allow it to be appropriated, we must take care that other employment be furnished to those excluded from the appropriation. If we do not the fundamental right to labour the earth returns to the unemployed. It is too soon yet in our country to say that every man who cannot find employment but who can find uncultivated land, shall be at liberty to cultivate it, paying a moderate rent. But it is not too soon to provide by every possible means that as few as possible shall be without a little portion of land. The small landholders are the most precious part of a state.

33

JAMES MADISON TO THOMAS JEFFERSON
19 June 1786
Papers 9:76–77

Since my last which was of the 18th. of May I have recd. your very agreeable favor of the 28th. of Octobr. I began to fear it had miscarried. Your reflections on the idle poor of Europe, form a valuable lesson to the Legislators of every Country, and particularly of a new one. I hope you will enable yourself before you return to America to compare with this description of people in France the Condition of the indigent part of other communities in Europe where the like causes of wretchedness exist in a less degree. I have no doubt that the misery of the lower classes will be found to abate wherever the Government assumes a freer aspect, & the laws favor a subdivision of property. Yet I suspect that the difference will not fully account for the comparative comfort of the Mass of people in the United States. Our limited population has probably as large a share in producing this effect as the political advantages which distinguish us. A certain degree of misery seems inseparable from a high degree of populousness. If the lands in Europe which are now dedicated to the amusement of the idle rich, were parcelled out among the idle poor, I readily conceive the happy revolution which would be experienced by a certain proportion of the latter. But still would there not remain a great proportion unrelieved? No problem in political Oeconomy has appeared to me more puzzling than that which relates to the most proper distribution of the inhabitants of a Country fully peopled. Let the lands be shared among them ever so wisely, & let them be supplied with labourers ever so plentifully; as there must be a great surplus of subsistence, there will also remain a great surplus of inhabitants, a greater by far than will be employed in cloathing both themselves & those who feed them, and in administering to both, every other necessary & even comfort of life. What is to be done with this surplus? Hitherto we have seen them distributed into Manufacturers of superfluities, idle proprietors of productive funds, domestics, soldiers, merchants, mariners, and a few other less numerous classes. All these classes notwithstanding have been found insufficient to absorb the redundant members of a populous society; and yet a reduction of most of those classes enters into the very reform which appears so necessary & desireable. From a more equal partition of property, must result a greater simplicity of manners, consequently a less consumption of manufactured superfluities, and a less proportion of idle proprietors & domestics. From a juster Government must result less need of soldiers either for defence agst. dangers from without or disturbances from within. The number of merchants must be inconsiderable under any modification of Society; and that of Mariners will depend more on geographical position, than on the plan of legislation. But I forget that I am writing a letter not a dissertation.

34

JOHN ADAMS, DEFENCE OF THE CONSTITUTIONS
OF GOVERNMENT OF THE UNITED STATES
1787
Works 4:381–82, 391–98, 413–15; 5:488

Wherever we have seen a territory somewhat larger, arts and sciences more cultivated, commerce flourishing, or even agriculture improved to any great degree, an aristocracy has risen up in a course of time, consisting of a few rich and honorable families, who have united with each other against both the people and the first magistrate; who have wrested from the former, by art and by force, all their participation in the government; and have even inspired them with so mean an esteem of themselves, and so deep a veneration and strong attachment to their rulers, as to believe and confess them a superior order of beings.

We have seen these noble families, although necessitated to have a head, extremely jealous of his influence, anxious to reduce his power, and to constrain him to as near a level as possible with themselves; always endeavoring to establish a rotation, by which they may all equally be entitled in turn to the preëminence, and likewise anxious to preserve to themselves as large a share as possible of power in the executive and judicial, as well as the legislative departments of the state.

These patrician families have also appeared in every instance to be equally jealous of each other, and to have contrived, by blending lot and choice, by mixing various bodies in the elections to the same offices, and even by a resort to the horrors of an inquisition, to guard against the sin that so easily besets them, of being wholly influenced and governed by a junto or oligarchy of a few among themselves.

We have seen no one government in which is a distinct separation of the legislative from the executive power, and of the judicial from both, or in which any attempt has been made to balance these powers with one another, or to form an equilibrium between the one, the few, and the many, for the purpose of enacting and executing equal laws, by common consent, for the general interest, excepting in England.

Shall we conclude, from these melancholy observations, that human nature is incapable of liberty, that no honest equality can be preserved in society, and that such forcible causes are always at work as must reduce all men to a submission to despotism, monarchy, oligarchy, or aristocracy?

By no means. We have seen one of the first nations in Europe, possessed of ample and fertile territories at home and extensive dominions abroad, of a commerce with the whole world, immense wealth, and the greatest naval power which ever belonged to any nation, which has still preserved the power of the people by the equilibrium we are contending for, by the trial by jury, and by constantly refusing a standing army. The people of England alone, by preserving their share in the legislature, at the expense of the blood of heroes and patriots, have enabled their king to curb the nobility, without giving him a standing army.

After all, let us compare every constitution we have seen with those of the United States of America, and we shall have no reason to blush for our country. On the contrary, we shall feel the strongest motives to fall upon our knees, in gratitude to heaven for having been graciously pleased to give us birth and education in that country, and for having destined us to live under her laws! We shall have reason to exult, if we make our comparison with England and the English constitution. Our people are undoubtedly sovereign; all the landed and other property is in the hands of the citizens; not only their representatives, but their senators and governors, are annually chosen; there are no hereditary titles, honors, offices, or distinctions; the legislative, executive, and judicial powers are carefully separated from each other; the powers of the one, the few, and the many are nicely balanced in the legislatures; trials by jury are preserved in all their glory, and there is no standing army; the *habeas corpus* is in full force; the press is the most free in the world. Where all these circumstances take place, it is unnecessary to add that the laws alone can govern.

. . . . .

540

Let us now return to M. Turgot's idea of a government consisting in a single assembly. He tells us our republics are "founded on the equality of all the citizens, and, therefore, 'orders' and 'equilibriums' are unnecessary, and occasion disputes." But what are we to understand here by equality? Are the citizens to be all of the same age, sex, size, strength, stature, activity, courage, hardiness, industry, patience, ingenuity, wealth, knowledge, fame, wit, temperance, constancy, and wisdom? Was there, or will there ever be, a nation, whose individuals were all equal, in natural and acquired qualities, in virtues, talents, and riches? The answer of all mankind must be in the negative. It must then be acknowledged, that in every state, in the Massachusetts, for example, there are inequalities which God and nature have planted there, and which no human legislator ever can eradicate. I should have chosen to have mentioned Virginia, as the most ancient state, or indeed any other in the union, rather than the one that gave me birth, if I were not afraid of putting suppositions which may give offence, a liberty which my neighbors will pardon. Yet I shall say nothing that is not applicable to all the other twelve.

In this society of Massachusettensians then, there is, it is true, a moral and political equality of rights and duties among all the individuals, and as yet no appearance of artificial inequalities of condition, such as hereditary dignities, titles, magistracies, or legal distinctions; and no established marks, as stars, garters, crosses, or ribbons; there are, nevertheless, inequalities of great moment in the consideration of a legislator, because they have a natural and inevitable influence in society. Let us enumerate some of them:—1. There is an inequality of wealth; some individuals, whether by descent from their ancestors, or from greater skill, industry, and success in business, have estates both in lands and goods of great value; others have no property at all; and of all the rest of society, much the greater number are possessed of wealth, in all the variety of degrees between these extremes; it will easily be conceived that all the rich men will have many of the poor, in the various trades, manufactures, and other occupations in life, dependent upon them for their daily bread; many of smaller fortunes will be in their debt, and in many ways under obligations to them; others, in better circumstances, neither dependent nor in debt, men of letters, men of the learned professions, and others, from acquaintance, conversation, and civilities, will be connected with them and attached to them. Nay, farther, it will not be denied, that among the wisest people that live, there is a degree of admiration, abstracted from all dependence, obligation, expectation, or even acquaintance, which accompanies splendid wealth, insures some respect, and bestows some influence. 2. Birth. Let no man be surprised that this species of inequality is introduced here. Let the page in history be quoted, where any nation, ancient or modern, civilized or savage, is mentioned, among whom no difference was made between the citizens, on account of their extraction. The truth is, that more influence is allowed to this advantage in free republics than in despotic governments, or than would be allowed to it in simple monarchies, if severe laws had not been made from age to age to secure

it. The children of illustrious families have generally greater advantages of education, and earlier opportunities to be acquainted with public characters, and informed of public affairs, than those of meaner ones, or even than those in middle life; and what is more than all, an habitual national veneration for their names, and the characters of their ancestors described in history, or coming down by tradition, removes them farther from vulgar jealousy and popular envy, and secures them in some degree the favor, the affection, and respect of the public. Will any man pretend that the name of Andros, and that of Winthrop, are heard with the same sensations in any village of New England? Is not gratitude the sentiment that attends the latter, and disgust the feeling excited by the former? In the Massachusetts, then, there are persons descended from some of their ancient governors, counsellors, judges, whose fathers, grandfathers, and great-grandfathers, are remembered with esteem by many living, and who are mentioned in history with applause, as benefactors to the country, while there are others who have no such advantage. May we go a step farther,—Know thyself, is as useful a precept to nations as to men. Go into every village in New England, and you will find that the office of justice of the peace, and even the place of representative, which has ever depended only on the freest election of the people, have generally descended from generation to generation, in three or four families at most. The present subject is one of those which all men respect, and all men deride. It may be said of this part of our nature, as Pope said of the whole:—

"Of human nature, wit her worst may write,
We all revere it in our own despite."

If, as Harrington says, the ten commandments were voted by the people of Israel, and have been enacted as laws by all other nations; and if we should presume to say, that nations had a civil right to repeal them, no nation would think proper to repeal the fifth, which enjoins honor to parents. If there is a difference between right and wrong; if any thing can be sacred; if there is one idea of moral obligation; the decree of nature must force upon every thinking being and upon every feeling heart the conviction that honor, affection, and gratitude are due from children to those who gave them birth, nurture, and education. The sentiments and affections which naturally arise from reflecting on the love, the cares, and the blessings of parents, abstracted from the consideration of duty, are some of the most forcible and most universal. When religion, law, morals, affection, and even fashion, thus conspire to fill every mind with attachment to parents, and to stamp deep upon the heart their impressions, is it to be expected that men should reverence their parents while they live, and begin to despise or neglect their memories as soon as they are dead? This is in nature impossible. On the contrary, every little unkindness and severity is forgotten, and nothing but endearments remembered with pleasure.

The son of a wise and virtuous father finds the world about him sometimes as much disposed as he himself is, to honor the memory of his father; to congratulate him as the successor to his estate; and frequently to compliment him with elections to the offices he held. A sense of duty, his passions and his interest, thus conspiring to prevail upon him to avail himself of this advantage, he finds a few others in similar circumstances with himself; they naturally associate together, and aid each other. This is a faint sketch of the source and rise of the family spirit; very often the disposition to favor the family is as strong in the town, county, province, or kingdom, as it is in the house itself. The enthusiasm is indeed sometimes wilder, and carries away, like a torrent, all before it.

These observations are not peculiar to any age; we have seen the effects of them in San Marino, Biscay, and the Grisons, as well as in Poland and all other countries. Not to mention any notable examples which have lately happened near us, it is not many months since I was witness to a conversation between some citizens of Massachusetts. One was haranguing on the jealousy which a free people ought to entertain of their liberties, and was heard by all the company with pleasure. In less than ten minutes, the conversation turned upon their governor; and the jealous republican was very angry at the opposition to him. "The present governor," says he, "has done us such services, that he ought to rule us, he and his posterity after him, for ever and ever." "Where is your jealousy of liberty?" demanded the other. "Upon my honor," replies the orator, "I had forgot that; you have caught me in an inconsistency; for I cannot know whether a child of five years old will be a son of liberty or a tyrant." His jealousy was the dictate of his understanding. His confidence and enthusiasm the impulse of his heart.

The pompous trumpery of ensigns, armorials, and escutcheons are not, indeed, far advanced in America. Yet there is a more general anxiety to know their originals, in proportion to their numbers, than in any nation of Europe; arising from the easier circumstances and higher spirit of the common people. And there are certain families in every state equally attentive to all the proud frivolities of heraldry. That kind of pride, which looks down on commerce and manufactures as degrading, may, indeed, in many countries of Europe, be a useful and necessary quality in the nobility. It may prevent, in some degree, the whole nation from being entirely delivered up to the spirit of avarice. It may be the cause why honor is preferred by some to money. It may prevent the nobility from becoming too rich, and acquiring too large a proportion of the landed property. In America, it would not only be mischievous, but would expose the highest pretensions of the kind to universal ridicule and contempt. Those other hauteurs, of keeping the commons at a distance, and disdaining to converse with any but a few of a certain race, may in Europe be a favor to the people, by relieving them from a multitude of assiduous attentions and humiliating compliances, which would be troublesome. It may prevent the nobles from caballing with the people, and gaining too much influence with them in elections and otherwise. In America, it would justly excite universal indignation; the vainest of all must be of the people, or be nothing. While every office is equally open to every competitor, and the people must decide upon every pretension to a place in

the legislature, that of governor and senator, as well as representative, no such airs will ever be endured. At the same time, it must be acknowledged, that some men must take more pains to deserve and acquire an office than others, and must behave better in it, or they will not hold it.

We cannot presume that a man is good or bad, merely because his father was one or the other; and we should always inform ourselves first, whether the virtues and talents are inherited, before we yield our confidence. Wise men beget fools, and honest men knaves; but these instances, although they may be frequent, are not general. If there is often a likeness in feature and figure, there is generally more in mind and heart, because education contributes to the formation of these as well as nature. The influence of example is very great, and almost universal, especially that of parents over their children. In all countries it has been observed, that vices, as well as virtues, very often run down in families from age to age. Any man may go over in his thoughts the circle of his acquaintance, and he will probably recollect instances of a disposition to mischief, malice, and revenge, descending in certain breeds from grandfather to father and son. A young woman was lately convicted at Paris of a trifling theft, barely within the law which decreed a capital punishment. There were circumstances, too, which greatly alleviated her fault; some things in her behavior that seemed innocent and modest; every spectator, as well as the judges, was affected at the scene, and she was advised to petition for a pardon, as there was no doubt it would be granted. "No," says she; "my grandfather, father, and brother were all hanged for stealing; it runs in the blood of our family to steal, and be hanged. If I am pardoned now, I shall steal again in a few months more inexcusably; and, therefore, I will be hanged now." An hereditary passion for the halter is a strong instance, to be sure, and cannot be very common; but something like it too often descends in certain breeds, from generation to generation.

If vice and infamy are thus rendered less odious, by being familiar in a family, by the example of parents and by education, it would be as unhappy as unaccountable, if virtue and honor were not recommended and rendered more amiable to children by the same means.

There are, and always have been, in every state, numbers possessed of some degree of family pride, who have been invariably encouraged, if not flattered in it, by the people. These have most acquaintance, esteem, and friendship with each other, and mutually aid each other's schemes of interest, convenience, and ambition. Fortune, it is true, has more influence than birth. A rich man, of an ordinary family and common decorum of conduct, may have greater weight than any family merit commonly confers without it.

It will be readily admitted, there are great inequalities of merit, or talents, virtues, services, and what is of more moment, very often of reputation. Some, in a long course of service in an army, have devoted their time, health, and fortunes, signalized their courage and address, exposed themselves to hardships and dangers, lost their limbs, and shed their blood, for the people. Others have displayed their wisdom, learning, and eloquence in council, and in various other ways acquired the confidence and affection of their fellow-citizens to such a degree, that the public have settled into a kind of habit of following their example and taking their advice.

There are a few, in whom all these advantages of birth, fortune, and fame are united.

These sources of inequality, which are common to every people, and can never be altered by any, because they are founded in the constitution of nature; this natural aristocracy among mankind, has been dilated on, because it is a fact essential to be considered in the institution of a government. It forms a body of men which contains the greatest collection of virtues and abilities in a free government, is the brightest ornament and glory of the nation, and may always be made the greatest blessing of society, if it be judiciously managed in the constitution. But if this be not done, it is always the most dangerous; nay, it may be added, it never fails to be the destruction of the commonwealth.

What shall be done to guard against it? Shall they be all massacred? This experiment has been more than once attempted, and once at least executed. Guy Faux attempted it in England; and a king of Denmark, aided by a popular party, effected it once in Sweden; but it answered no good end. The moment they were dead another aristocracy instantly arose, with equal art and influence, with less delicacy and discretion, if not principle, and behaved more intolerably than the former. The country, for centuries, never recovered from the ruinous consequences of a deed so horrible, that one would think it only to be met with in the history of the kingdom of darkness.

There is but one expedient yet discovered, to avail the society of all the benefits from this body of men, which they are capable of affording, and at the same time, to prevent them from undermining or invading the public liberty; and that is, to throw them all, or at least the most remarkable of them, into one assembly together, in the legislature; to keep all the executive power entirely out of their hands as a body; to erect a first magistrate over them, invested with the whole executive authority; to make them dependent on that executive magistrate for all public executive employments; to give that first magistrate a negative on the legislature, by which he may defend both himself and the people from all their enterprises in the legislature; and to erect on the other side an impregnable barrier against them, in a house of commons, fairly, fully, and adequately representing the people, who shall have the power both of negativing all their attempts at encroachment in the legislature, and of withholding from them and from the crown all supplies, by which they may be paid for their services in executive offices, or even the public service may be carried on to the detriment of the nation.

We have seen, both by reasoning and in experience, what kind of equality is to be found or expected in the simplest people in the world. There is not a city nor a village, any more than a kingdom or a commonwealth, in Europe or America; not a horde, clan, or tribe, among the negroes of Africa, or the savages of North or South America; nor a private club in the world, in which inequalities are not more or less visible. There is, then, a certain degree of weight, which property, family, and merit, will have in the public opinion and deliberations. If M. Turgot had discovered a mode of ascertaining the quantity which they ought to have, and had revealed it to mankind, so that it might be known to every citizen, he would have deserved more of gratitude than is due to all the inventions of philosophers. But, as long as human nature shall have passions and imagination, there is too much reason to fear that these advantages, in many instances, will have more influence than reason and equity can justify.

. . . . .

Upon these principles, and to establish a method of enacting laws that must of necessity be wise and equal, the people of most of the United States of America agreed upon that division of the legislative power into two houses, the house of representatives and the senate, which have given so much disgust to M. Turgot. Harrington will show us equally well the propriety and necessity of the other branch, the governor. But, before we proceed to that, it may be worth while to observe the similitude between this passage and some of those sentiments and expressions of Swift, which were quoted in a former letter; and there is in the *Idea of a Patriot King,* written by his friend, Lord Bolingbroke, a passage to the same purpose, so nobly expressed, that I cannot forbear the pleasure of transcribing it. "It seems to me that, in order to maintain the moral system of the universe at a certain point, far below that of ideal perfection, (for we are made capable of conceiving what we are not capable of attaining,) it has pleased the Author of Nature to mingle, from time to time, among the societies of men a few, and but a few of those on whom he has been graciously pleased to confer a larger proportion of the ethereal spirit, than in the ordinary course of his providence he bestows on the sons of men. These are they who engross almost the whole reason of the species. Born to direct, to guide, and to preserve, if they retire from the world their splendor accompanies them, and enlightens even the darkness of their retreat. If they take a part in public life, the effect is never indifferent. They either appear the instruments of Divine vengeance, and their course through the world is marked by desolation and oppression, by poverty and servitude; or they are the guardian angels of the country they inhabit, studious to avert the most distant evil, and to procure peace, plenty, and the greatest of human blessings, liberty."

If there is, then, in society such a natural aristocracy as these great writers pretend, and as all history and experience demonstrate, formed partly by genius, partly by birth, and partly by riches, how shall the legislator avail himself of their influence for the equal benefit of the public? and how, on the other hand, shall he prevent them from disturbing the public happiness? I answer, by arranging them all, or at least the most conspicuous of them, together in one assembly, by the name of a senate; by separating them from all pretensions to the executive power, and by controlling in the legislative their ambition and avarice, by an assembly of representatives on one side, and by the executive authority on the other. Thus you will have the benefit of their wisdom, without fear of their pas-

543

sions. If among them there are some of Lord Boling-broke's guardian angels, there will be some of his instruments of Divine vengeance too. The latter will be here restrained by a threefold tie,—by the executive power, by the representative assembly, and by their peers in the senate. But if these were all admitted into a single popular assembly, the worst of them might in time obtain the ascendency of all the rest. In such a single assembly, as has been observed before, almost the whole of this aristocracy will make its appearance, being returned members of it by the election of the people. These will be one class. There will be another set of members, of middling rank and circumstances, who will justly value themselves upon their independence, their integrity, and unbiased affection to their country, and will pique themselves upon being under no obligation. But there will be a third class, every one of whom will have his leader among the members of the first class, whose character he will celebrate, and whose voice he will follow; and this party, after a course of time, will be the most numerous. The question then will be, whether this aristocracy in the house will unite or divide? and it is too obvious, that destruction to freedom must be the consequence equally of their union or of their division. If they unite generally in all things, as much as they certainly will in respecting each other's wealth, birth, and parts, and conduct themselves with prudence, they will strengthen themselves by insensible degrees, by playing into each other's hands more wealth and popularity, until they become able to govern elections as they please, and rule the people at discretion. An independent member will be their aversion; all their artifices will be employed to destroy his popularity among his constituents, and bring in a disciple of their own in his place.

But if they divide, each party will, in a course of time, have the whole house, and consequently the whole state, divided into two factions, which will struggle in words, in writing, and at last in arms, until Caesar or Pompey must be emperor, and entail an endless line of tyrants on the nation. But long before this catastrophe, and indeed through every scene of the drama, the laws, instead of being permanent, and affording constant protection to the lives, liberties, and properties of the citizens, will be alternately the sport of contending factions, and the mere vibrations of a pendulum. From the beginning to the end it will be a government of men, now of one set, and then of another; but never a government of laws.

. . . . .

Perhaps it may be said, that in America we have no distinctions of ranks, and therefore shall not be liable to those divisions and discords which spring from them; but have we not laborers, yeomen, gentlemen, esquires, honorable gentlemen, and excellent gentlemen? and are not these distinctions established by law? have they not been established by our ancestors from the first plantation of the country? and are not those distinctions as earnestly desired and sought, as titles, garters, and ribbons are in any nation of Europe? We may look as wise, and moralize as gravely as we will; we may call this desire of distinction childish and silly; but we cannot alter the nature of men; human nature is thus childish and silly; and its Author has made

it so, undoubtedly for wise purposes; and it is setting ourselves up to be wiser than nature, and more philosophical than Providence, to censure it. All that we can say in America is, that legal distinctions, titles, powers, and privileges, are not hereditary; but that the disposition to artificial distinctions, to titles, and ribbons, and to the hereditary descent of them, is ardent in America, we may see by the institution of the Cincinnati. There is not a more remarkable phenomenon in universal history, nor in universal human nature, than this order. The officers of an army, who had voluntarily engaged in a service under the authority of the people, whose creation and preservation was upon the principle that the body of the people were the only fountain of power and of honor; officers, too, as enlightened and as virtuous as ever served in any army; the moment they had answered the end of their creation, instituted titles and ribbons, and hereditary descents, by their own authority only, without the consent or knowledge of the people, or their representatives or legislatures.

35

RECORDS OF THE FEDERAL CONVENTION

[1:48; Madison, 31 May]

Mr. Gerry. The evils we experience flow from the excess of democracy. The people do not want virtue; but are the dupes of pretended patriots. In Massts. it has been fully confirmed by experience that they are daily misled into the most baneful measures and opinions by the false reports circulated by designing men, and which no one on the spot can refute. One principal evil arises from the want of due provision for those employed in the administration of Governnt. It would seem to be a maxim of democracy to starve the public servants. He mentioned the popular clamour in Massts. for the reduction of salaries and the attack made on that of the Govr. though secured by the spirit of the Constitution itself. He had he said been too republican heretofore: he was still however republican, but had been taught by experience the danger of the levilling spirit.

Mr. Mason. argued strongly for an election of the larger branch by the people. It was to be the grand depository of the democratic principle of the Govt. It was, so to speak, to be our House of Commons—It ought to know & sympathise with every part of the community; and ought therefore to be taken not only from different parts of the whole republic, but also from different districts of the larger members of it, which had in several instances particularly in Virga., different interests and views arising from difference of produce, of habits &c &. He admitted that we had been too democratic but was afraid we sd. incautiously run into the opposite extreme. We ought to attend to the rights of every class of the people. He had often wondered at the indifference of the superior classes of society to this dictate of humanity & policy, considering that however affluent their circumstances, or elevated their situations, might be, the course of a few years, not only might but certainly would, distribute their posterity throughout the lowest classes of Society. Every selfish motive therefore, every family attachment, ought to recommend such a system of policy as would provide no less carefully for the rights—and happiness of the lowest than of the highest orders of Citizens.

[1:397, 400; Madison, 25 June]

Mr. Pinkney spoke as follows.—The efficacy of the System will depend on this article [relating to the composition of the upper house]. In order to form a right judgmt. in the case it will be proper to examine the situation of this Country more accurately than it has yet been done. The people of the U. States are perhaps the most singular of any we are acquainted with. Among them there are fewer distinctions of fortune & less of rank, than among the inhabitants of any other nation. Every freeman has a right to the same protection & security; and a very moderate share of property entitles them to the possession of all the honors and privileges the public can bestow: hence arises a greater equality, than is to be found among the people of any other country, and an equality which is more likely to continue—I say this equality is likely to continue, because in a new Country, possessing immense tracts of uncultivated lands, where every temptation is offered to emigration & where industry must be rewarded with competency, there will be few poor, and few dependent— Every member of the Society almost, will enjoy an equal power of arriving at the supreme offices & consequently of directing the strength & sentiments of the whole Community. None will be excluded by birth, & few by fortune, from voting for proper persons to fill the offices of Government—the whole community will enjoy in the fullest sense that kind of political liberty which consists in the power the members of the State reserve to themselves, of arriving at the public offices, or at least, of having votes in the nomination of those who fill them.

If this State of things is true & the prospect of its continuing probable, it is perhaps not politic to endeavour too close an imitation of a Government calculated for a people whose situation is, & whose views ought to be extremely different

. . . . .

I have said that such a body [analogous to the British House of Lords] cannot exist in this Country for ages, and that untill the situation of our people is exceedingly changed no necessity will exist for so permanent a part of the Legislature. To illustrate this I have remarked that the people of the United States are more equal in their circumstances than the people of any other Country—that they have very few rich men among them,—by rich men I mean those whose riches may have a dangerous influence, or such as are esteemed rich in Europe—perhaps there are not one hundred such on the Continent: that it is not probable this number will be greatly increased: that the genius of the people, their mediocrity of situation & the prospects which are afforded their industry in a country

which must be a new one for centuries are unfavorable to the rapid distinction of ranks. The destruction of the right of primogeniture & the equal division of the property of Intestates will also have an effect to preserve this mediocrity: for laws invariably affect the manners of a people. On the other hand that vast extent of unpeopled territory which opens to the frugal & industrious a sure road to competency & independence will effectually prevent for a considerable time the increase of the poor or discontented, and be the means of preserving that equality of condition which so eminently distinguishes us.

If equality is as I contend the leading feature of the U. States, where then are the riches & wealth whose representation & protection is the peculiar province of this permanent body. Are they in the hands of the few who may be called rich; in the possession of less than a hundred citizens? certainly not. They are in the great body of the people, among whom there are no men of wealth, and very few of real poverty.—Is it probable that a change will be created, and that a new order of men will arise? If under the British Government, for a century no such change was probable, I think it may be fairly concluded it will not take place while even the semblance of Republicanism remains. How is this change to be effected? Where are the sources from whence it is to flow? From the landed interest? No. That is too unproductive & too much divided in most of the States. From the Monied interest? If such exists at present, little is to be apprehended from that source. Is it to spring from commerce? I believe it would be the first instance in which a nobility sprang from merchants. Besides, Sir, I apprehend that on this point the policy of the U. States has been much mistakem. We have unwisely considered ourselves as the inhabitants of an old instead of a new country. We have adopted the maxims of a State full of people & manufactures & established in credit. We have deserted our true interest, and instead of applying closely to those improvements in domestic policy which would have ensured the future importance of our commerce, we have rashly & prematurely engaged in schemes as extensive as they are imprudent. This however is an error which daily corrects itself & I have no doubt that a few more severe trials will convince us, that very different commercial principles ought to govern the conduct of these States.

The people of this country are not only very different from the inhabitants of any State we are acquainted with in the modern world; but I assert that their situation is distinct from either the people of Greece or Rome, or of any State we are acquainted with among the antients.— Can the orders introduced by the institution of Solon, can they be found in the United States? Can the military habits & manners of Sparta be resembled to our habits & manners? Are the distinctions of Patrician & Plebeian known among us? Can the Helvetic or Belgic confederacies, or can the unwieldly, unmeaning body called the Germanic Empire, can they be said to possess either the same or a situation like ours? I apprehend not.—They are perfectly different, in their distinctions of rank, their Constitutions, their manners & their policy.

Our true situation appears to me to be this.—a new extensive Country containing within itself the materials for forming a Government capable of extending to its citizens all the blessings of civil & religious liberty—capable of making them happy at home. This is the great end of Republican Establishments. We mistake the object of our government, if we hope or wish that it is to make us respectable abroad. Conquest or superiority among other powers is not or ought not ever to be the object of republican systems. If they are sufficiently active & energetic to rescue us from contempt & preserve our domestic happiness & security, it is all we can expect from them,—it is more than almost any other Government ensures to its citizens.

I believe this observation will be found generally true: that no two people are so exactly alike in their situation or circumstances as to admit the exercise of the same Government with equal benefit: that a system must be suited to the habits & genius of the People it is to govern, and must grow out of them.

The people of the U.S. may be divided into three classes—*Professional men* who must from their particular pursuits always have a considerable weight in the Government while it remains popular—*Commercial men,* who may or may not have weight as a wise or injudicious commercial policy is pursued.—If that commercial policy is pursued which I conceive to be the true one, the merchants of this Country will not or ought not for a considerable time to have much weight in the political scale.—The third is the *landed interest,* the owners and cultivators of the soil, who are and ought ever to be the governing spring in the system.—These three classes, however distinct in their pursuits are individually equal in the political scale, and may be easily proved to have but one interest. The dependence of each on the other is mutual. The merchant depends on the planter. Both must in private as well as public affairs be connected with the professional men; who in their turn must in some measure depend on them. Hence it is clear from this manifest connection, & the equality which I before stated exists, & must for the reasons then assigned, continue, that after all there is one, but one great & equal body of citizens composing the inhabitants of this Country among whom there are no distinctions of rank, and very few or none of fortune.

For a people thus circumstanced are we then to form a Government & the question is what kind of Government is best suited to them.

Will it be the British Govt.? No. Why? Because G. Britain contains three orders of people distinct in their situation, their possessions & their principles.—These orders combined form the great body of the Nation, And as in national expences the wealth of the whole community must contribute, so ought each component part to be properly & duly represented.—No other combination of power could form this due representation, but the one that exists.—Neither the peers or the people could represent the royalty, nor could the Royalty & the people form a proper representation for the Peers.—Each therefore must of necessity be represented by itself, or the sign of itself; and this accidental mixture has certainly formed a Government admirably well balanced.

But the U. States contain but one order that can be assimilated to the British Nation.—this is the order of Commons. They will not surely then attempt to form a Government consisting of three branches, two of which shall have nothing to represent. They will not have an Executive & Senate (hereditary) because the King &˙Lords of England are so. The same reasons do not exist and therefore the same provisions are not necessary.

We must as has been observed suit our Governmt. to the people it is to direct.

[1:422; Madison, 26 June]

[Mr. Madison.] In all civilized Countries the people fall into different classes havg. a real or supposed difference of interests. There will be creditors & debtors, farmers, merchts. & manufacturers. There will be particularly the distinction of rich & poor. It was true as had been observd. (by Mr Pinkney) we had not among us those hereditary distinctions, of rank which were a great source of the contests in the ancient Govts. as well as the modern States of Europe, nor those extremes of wealth or poverty which characterize the latter. We cannot however be regarded even at this time, as one homogeneous mass, in which every thing that affects a part will affect in the same manner the whole. In framing a system which we wish to last for ages, we shd. not lose sight of the changes which ages will produce. An increase of population will of necessity increase the proportion of those who will labour under all the hardships of life, & secretly sigh for a more equal distribution of its blessings. These may in time outnumber those who are placed above the feelings of indigence. According to the equal laws of suffrage, the power will slide into the hands of the former. No agrarian attempts have yet been made in this Country, but symptoms of a leveling spirit, as we have understood, have sufficiently appeared in a certain quarters to give notice of the future danger. How is this danger to be guarded agst. on republican principles? How is the danger in all cases of interested coalitions to oppress the minority to be guarded agst.?

. . . . .

Mr. Hamilton. He did not mean to enter particularly into the subject. He concurred with Mr. Madison in thinking we were now to decide for ever the fate of Republican Government; and that if we did not give to that form due stability and wisdom, it would be disgraced & lost among ourselves, disgraced & lost to mankind for ever. He acknowledged himself not to think favorably of Republican Government; but addressed his remarks to those who did think favorably of it, in order to prevail on them to tone their Government as high as possible. He professed himself to be as zealous an advocate for liberty as any man whatever, and trusted he should be as willing a martyr to it though he differed as to the form in which it was most eligible.—He concurred also in the general observations of (Mr. Madison) on the subject, which might be supported by others if it were necessary. It was certainly true that nothing like an equality of property existed: that an inequality would exist as long as liberty existed, and that it would unavoidably result from that very liberty itself. This inequality of property constituted the great & fundamental distinction in Society. When the Tribunitial power had levelled the boundary between the *patricians & plebeians* what followed? The distinction between rich & poor was substituted. He meant not however to enlarge on the subject.

36

FEDERAL FARMER, NO. 7
31 Dec. 1787
Storing 2.8.97–98

(See ch. 13, no. 22)

37

LUTHER MARTIN, GENUINE INFORMATION
1788
Storing 2.4.28–29, 63–71

The Jersey propositions being thus rejected, the convention took up those reported by the committee, and proceeded to debate them by paragraphs: it was now that they who disapproved the report found it necessary to make a *warm* and *decided opposition*, which took place upon the discussion of the seventh resolution, which related to the *inequality* of representation in the *first* branch. Those who advocated this inequality, urged, that when the articles of confederation were formed, it was *only* from *necessity* and *expediency* that the States were admitted *each* to have an *equal vote;* but that our situation was *now altered,* and therefore those States who considered it contrary to their interest, would *no longer abide* by it. They said no State ought to wish to have influence in government, except in proportion to what it contributes to it; that if it contributes but little, it ought to have but a small vote; that taxation and representation ought always to go together; that if one State had *sixteen times as many inhabitants* as another, or was *sixteen times as wealthy,* it ought to have *sixteen times as many votes;* that an inhabitant of Pennsylvania ought to have as much weight and consequence as an inhabitant of Jersey or Delaware; that it was contrary to the feelings of the human mind; what the *large States* would *never* submit to; that the *large States* would have *great objects* in view, in which they would never permit the *smaller States* to thwart them; that *equality of suffrage* was the rotten part of the constitution, and that this was a happy time to get clear of it. In fine, that it was the poison which contaminated our whole system, and the source of all the evils we experienced.

This, Sir, is the substance of the arguments, if arguments they may be called, which were used in favour of *inequality of suffrage.*—Those who advocated the *equality of suffrage,* took the matter up on the original principles of government; they urged, that all men considered in a state of nature, before any government formed, are equally free and independent, no one having any right or authority to exercise power over another, and this *without any regard to difference in personal strength, understanding, or wealth*— That when such individuals enter into government, they have *each a right* to an *equal voice* in its first formation, and afterwards have *each* a right to an *equal vote* in every matter which relates to their government—That if it could be done conveniently, they have a right to exercise it in person—Where it cannot be done in person but for convenience, representatives are appointed to act for them, *every person* has a *right* to an *equal vote,* in choosing that representative who is entrusted to do for the whole, that which the whole, if they could assemble, might do in person, and in the transacting of which each would have an equal voice—That if we were to admit, because a man was *more wise, more strong,* or *more wealthy,* he should be entitled to *more votes* than another, it would be *inconsistent with the freedom and liberty of that other,* and would reduce him to *slavery*—Suppose, for instance, ten individuals in a state of nature, about to enter into government, *nine* of whom are *equally wise, equally strong, and equally wealthy,* the *tenth* is *ten times as wise, ten times as strong,* or *ten times as rich:* if for this reason he is to have *ten votes* for *each vote of either of the others,* the *nine* might as well *have no vote at all,* since though the *whole nine* might assent to a measure, yet the *vote* of the *tenth* would *countervail,* and *set aside all their votes*—If this *tenth* approved of what *they* wished to adopt, it would be well, but if he disapproved, he could prevent it, and in the same manner he could carry into execution *any measure he wished, contrary to the opinion of all the others,* he having *ten votes,* and the *other* altogether but *nine*—It is evident that on these principles, the *nine* would have *no will nor discretion of their own,* but must be *totally dependent* on the *will* and *discretion* of the *tenth,* to *him* they would be as *absolutely slaves* as any negro is to his *master*—If *he* did not attempt to carry into execution any measures injurious to the *other nine,* it could only be said that they had a *good master,* they would not be the *less slaves,* because they would be *totally dependent* on the *will of another,* and not on *their own will*—They might not *feel their chains,* but they would notwithstanding *wear them,* and whenever their *master* pleased he might draw them so tight as to gall them to the bone. Hence it was urged the *inequality of representation,* or giving to one man more votes than another on account of his wealth, etc. was *altogether inconsistent with the principles of liberty,* and in the *same proportion as it should be adopted,* in favour of *one or more,* in *that proportion are the others inslaved*—It was urged, that though every individual should have an equal voice in the government, yet, even the superior wealth, strength, or understanding, would give great and undue advantages to those who possessed them. That wealth attracts respect and attention; superior strength would cause the weaker and more feeble to be cautious how they offended, and to put up with small injuries rather than to engage in an unequal contest—In like manner superior understanding would give its possessor many opportunities of profiting at the expence of the more ignorant. Having thus established these principles with respect to the *rights* of *individuals* in a *state of nature,* and what is due to *each* on entering into government, principles established by every writer on liberty, they proceeded to shew that *States,* when *once formed,* are considered *with respect* to *each other* as *individuals* in a state of nature; that, like individuals each *State* is considered *equally free* and *equally independent,* the *one* having no right to exercise authority over the *other,* though *more strong, more wealthy,* or *abounding with more inhabitants*—That when a number of *States* unite themselves under a *federal government,* the *same principles apply* to *them* as when a *number of individual men* unite themselves under a *State government*—That every argument which shews *one man* ought not to have *more votes* than *another,* because he is *wiser, stronger* or *wealthier,* proves that *one State* ought not to have *more votes* than *another,* because it is *stronger, richer,* or more *populous*—And that by *giving one State,* or *one or two States more votes* than the *others,* the *others* thereby are *enslaved to such State or States,* having the *greater number of votes,* in the *same manner* as in the case before put of *individuals* where *one* has *more votes than the others*—That the reason why each individual man in forming a State government should have an equal vote is, because each individual before he enters into government is *equally free* and *independent*—So *each State,* when *States enter* into a *federal government,* are entitled to an *equal vote,* because before they entered into such federal government, *each State* was *equally free* and *equally independent*—That *adequate* representation of *men formed into a State government,* consists in *each man* having an *equal voice,* either personally, or if by representatives, that he should have an equal voice in choosing the representative—So adequate representation of *States* in a *federal government,* consists in *each State* having an *equal voice* either in person or by its representative in every thing which relates to the federal government—That this *adequacy of representation* is *more important* in a *federal,* than in a *State* government, because the members of a State government, the *district* of which is *not very large,* have generally such a *common interest,* that laws can scarcely be made by *one* part *oppressive* to the *others,* without *their suffering in common:* but the *different States* composing an *extensive federal empire,* widely distant *one* from the *other,* may have *interests so totally distinct,* that the *one* part might be be greatly *benefited* by what would be *destructive* to the *other.*

. . . . .

By the *ninth* section of this article, the importation of such persons as any of the States now existing, shall think proper to admit, shall not be prohibited prior to the year one thousand eight hundred and eight, but a duty may be imposed on such importation not exceeding ten dollars for each person.

The design of this clause is to prevent the general government from prohibiting the importation of slaves, but the same reasons which caused them to strike out the word "*national,*" and not admit the word "*stamps,*" influenced them here to guard against the word "*slaves,*" they anxiously sought to avoid the admission of expressions which might be odious in the ears of Americans, although they were willing to admit into their system those *things* which the *expressions* signified: And hence it is, that the clause is

so worded, as really to authorise the general government to impose a duty of ten dollars on every foreigner who comes into a State to become a citizen, whether he comes *absolutely free,* or *qualifiedly* so as a servant; although this is contrary to the design of the framers, and the duty was only meant to extend to the importation of *slaves.*

This clause was the subject of a great diversity of sentiment in the convention:—as the system was reported by the committee of detail, the provision was general, that such importation should not be prohibited, without confining it to any particular period. This was rejected by eight States—Georgia, South-Carolina, and I think North-Carolina voting for it.

We were then told by the delegates of the two first of those States, that their States would never agree to a system which put it in the power of the general government to prevent the importation of slaves, and that they, as delegates from those States, must withhold their assent from such a system.

A committee of one member from each State was chosen by ballot, to take this part of the system under their consideration, and to endeavour to agree upon some report, which should reconcile those States; to this committee also was referred the following proposition, which had been reported by the committee of detail, to wit, "No *navigation act* shall be passed without the assent of *two thirds* of the members present in each house;" a proposition which the *staple* and *commercial* States were solicitous to *retain,* lest their *commerce* should be placed too much under the power of the *eastern* States, but which these last States were as anxious to *reject.*—This committee, of which also I had the honour to be a member, met and took under their consideration the subjects committed to them; I found the *eastern* States, notwithstanding their *aversion to slavery,* were very willing to indulge the southern States, at least with a temporary liberty to prosecute the *slave trade,* provided the southern States would in their turn gratify them, by laying no *restriction* on *navigation acts;* and after a very little time, the committee by a great majority, agreed on a report, by which the general government was to be prohibited from preventing the importation of slaves for a limited time, and the restrictive clause relative to navigation acts was to be omitted.

This report was adopted by a majority of the convention, but not without considerable opposition.—It was said, that we had but just assumed a place among independent nations, in consequence of our opposition to the attempts of Great-Britain to *enslave us;* that this opposition was grounded upon the *preservation* of *those rights,* to which God and Nature had entitled *us,* not in *particular,* but in *common* with *all the rest of mankind*—That we had *appealed* to the *Supreme being* for his *assistance,* as the *God of freedom,* who could not but *approve* our efforts to preserve the *rights* which he had thus *imparted to his creatures;* that now, when we scarcely had risen from our *knees,* from *supplicating* his *aid* and *protection*—in *forming our government* over *a free people,* a government formed pretendedly on the *principles* of *liberty* and for *its preservation,*—in *that* government to have a provision, not only putting it out *of its power* to restrain and *prevent* the *slave trade,* but *even encouraging that most infamous traffic,* by giving the *States power* and *influence* in the *union, in proportion* as they *cruelly and wantonly sport with the rights of their fellow creatures,* ought to be considered as a *solemn mockery of,* and *insult to, that God* whose protection we had then implored, and could not fail to hold us up in *detestation,* and render us *contemptible* to every *true friend* of liberty in the world. It was said, it ought to be considered that *national* crimes can *only be,* and *frequently are, punished* in this world by *national punishments,* and that the *continuance* of the slave trade, and thus giving it a *national sanction* and *encouragement,* ought to be considered as *justly exposing* us to the *displeasure* and *vengeance* of *Him,* who is equal Lord of all, and who views with equal eye, the poor *African slave* and his *American master!*

It was urged, that by this system, we were giving the general government full and absolute power to regulate commerce, under which general power it would have a right to *restrain, or totally prohibit* the *slave trade:* it must therefore, appear to the world absurd and disgraceful to the last degree, that we should *except* from the exercise of that power, the *only branch* of *commerce* which is *unjustifiable in its nature,* and *contrary* to the *rights* of *mankind*—That on the contrary, we ought *rather to prohibit expressly* in our *constitution,* the *further importation* of *slaves;* and to *authorise* the general government from time to time, to make such regulations as should be thought most advantageous for the *gradual abolition* of *slavery,* and the *emancipation* of the *slaves* which are already in the States.

That *slavery* is *inconsistent* with the *genius of republicanism,* and has a tendency to *destroy* those *principles* on which it is *supported,* as it *lessens the sense* of the *equal rights* of *mankind,* and habituates us to *tyranny* and *oppression.* It was further urged, that by this system of government, every State is to be protected both from *foreign invasion* and from *domestic insurrections;* that from this consideration, it was of the *utmost importance* it should have a power to restrain the importation of slaves, since in proportion as the number of slaves were increased in any State, in the same proportion the State is *weakened* and *exposed* to foreign invasion, or domestic insurrection, and by *so much the less* will it be able to protect itself against *either;* and therefore will by so much the more, want aid from, and be a burthen to, the union. It was further said, that as in this system we were giving the general government a power under the idea of national character, or national interest, to regulate even our *weights* and *measures,* and have prohibited all possibility of *emitting paper money,* and *passing instalment laws, &c.* It must appear still more extraordinary, that we should prohibit the government from interfering with the slave trade, than which *nothing* could so *materially affect* both our *national honour* and *interest.*—These reasons influenced me both on the committee and in convention, most decidedly to oppose and vote against the clause, as it now makes a part of the system.

You will perceive, Sir, not only that the general government is prohibited from interfering in the slave trade *before* the year eighteen hundred and eight, but that there is no provision in the constitution that it shall *afterwards* be prohibited, nor any security that such prohibition will ever take place; and I think there is great reason to believe, that

if the importation of slaves is permitted until the year eighteen hundred and eight, it will not be prohibited afterwards: At *this time* we do not generally hold this commerce in so *great* abhorrence as we have done—When our liberties were at stake, we *warmly* felt for the *common rights of men*—The danger being thought to be past, which threatened ourselves, we are daily growing *more insensible* to those rights—In those States who have restrained or prohibited the importation of slaves, it is only done by legislative acts which may be repealed—When those States find that they must in their *national character* and *connexion* suffer in the *disgrace,* and share in the *inconveniencies* attendant upon that detestable and iniquitous traffic, they may be desirous also to share in the *benefits* arising from it, and the odium attending it will be greatly effaced by the sanction which is given to it in the general government.

38

YEOMANRY OF MASSACHUSETTS
25 Jan. 1788
Storing 4.19.2–3

When we see the adherents to this constitution chiefly made up of civil and ecclesiastical gown men, and their dependents, the expedient they have hit upon is not likely to have the intended effect. There are many men destitute of eloquence, yet they can see and hear—They can think and judge, and are therefore not likely to be wheedled out of their senses by the sophistical reasonings of all the advocates for this new constitution in the country combined. We know this is not true; and as we well know the design of such representations, we would have those gentlemen know, that it will not take. They must pull upon some other string, or they must fail. Another thing they tell us, that the constitution must be good, from the characters which composed the Convention that framed it. It is graced with the names of a Washington and a Franklin. Illustrious names, we allow—worthy characters in civil society. Yet we cannot suppose them, to be infallible guides, neither yet that a man must necessarily incur guilt to himself merely by dissenting from them in opinion.

We cannot think the noble general, has the same ideas with ourselves, with regard to the rules of right and wrong. We cannot think, he acts a very consistent part, or did through the whole of the contest with Great Britain: who, notwithstanding he wielded the sword in defence of American liberty, yet at the same time was, and is to this day, living upon the labours of several hundreds of miserable Africans, as free born as himself; and some of them very likely descended from parents who, in point of property and dignity in their own country, might cope with any man in America. We do not conceive we are to be overborne by the weight of any names, however revered. "ALL MEN ARE BORN FREE AND EQUAL;" if so, every man hath a natural and unalienable right to his own opinion, and, for asserting this right, ought not to be stigmatized with the epithets of tenacious and dogmatical.

39

JOHN JAY TO THE PRESIDENT OF THE [ENGLISH] SOCIETY FOR PROMOTING THE MANUMISSION OF SLAVES
June 1788
Correspondence 3:340–44

Our society has been favoured with your letter of the 1st of May last, and are happy that efforts so honourable to the nation are making in your country to promote the cause of justice and humanity relative to the Africans. That they who know the value of liberty, and are blessed with the enjoyment of it, ought not to subject others to slavery, is, like most other moral precepts, more generally admitted in theory than observed in practice. This will continue to be too much the case while men are impelled to action by their passions rather than their reason, and while they are more solicitous to acquire wealth than to do as they would be done by. Hence it is that India and Africa experience unmerited oppression from nations which have been long distinguished by their attachment to their civil and religious liberties, but who have expended not much less blood and treasure in violating the rights of others than in defending their own. The United States are far from being irreproachable in this respect. It undoubtedly is very inconsistent with their declarations on the subject of human rights to permit a single slave to be found within their jurisdiction, and we confess the justice of your strictures on that head.

Permit us, however, to observe, that although consequences ought not to deter us from doing what is right, yet that it is not easy to persuade men in general to act on that magnanimous and disinterested principle. It is well known that errors, either in opinion or practice, long entertained or indulged, are difficult to eradicate, and particularly so when they have become, as it were, incorporated in the civil institutions and domestic economy of a whole people.

Prior to the great revolution, the great majority or rather the great body of our people had been so long accustomed to the practice and convenience of having slaves, that very few among them even doubted the propriety and rectitude of it. Some liberal and conscientious men had, indeed, by their conduct and writings, drawn the lawfulness of slavery into question, and they made converts to that opinion; but the number of those converts compared with the people at large was then very inconsiderable. Their doctrines prevailed by almost insensible degrees, and was like the little lump of leaven which was put into three measures of meal: even at this day, the whole mass is far from being leavened, though we have good reason to hope and to believe that if the natural operations of

truth are constantly watched and assisted, but not forced and precipitated, that end we all aim at will finally be attained in this country.

The Convention which formed and recommended the new Constitution had an arduous task to perform, especially as local interests, and in some measure local prejudices, were to be accommodated. Several of the States conceived that restraints on slavery might be too rapid to consist with their particular circumstances; and the importance of union rendered it necessary that their wishes on that head should, in some degree, be gratified.

It gives us pleasure to inform you, that a disposition favourable to our views and wishes prevails more and more, and that it has already had an influence on our laws. When it is considered how many of the legislators in the different States are proprietors of slaves, and what opinions and prejudices they have imbibed on the subject from their infancy, a sudden and total stop to this species of oppression is not to be expected.

We will cheerfully co-operate with you in endeavouring to procure advocates for the same cause in other countries, and perfectly approve and commend your establishing a correspondence in France. It appears to have produced the desired effect; for Mons. De Varville, the secretary of a society for the like benevolent purpose at Paris, is now here, and comes instructed to establish a correspondence with us, and to collect such information as may promote our common views. He delivered to our society an extract from the minutes of your proceedings, dated 8th of April last, recommending him to our attention, and upon that occasion they passed the resolutions of which the enclosed are copies.

We are much obliged by the pamphlets enclosed with your letter, and shall constantly make such communications to you as may appear to us interesting.

By a report of the committee for superintending the school we have established in this city for the education of negro children, we find that proper attention is paid to it, and that ———— scholars are now taught in it. By the laws of this State, masters may now liberate healthy slaves of a proper age without giving security that they shall not become a parish charge; and the exportation as well as importation of them is prohibited. The State has also manumitted such as became its property by confiscation; and we have reason to expect that the maxim, that every man, of whatever colour, is to be presumed to be free until the contrary be shown, will prevail in our courts of justice. Manumissions daily become more common among us; and the treatment which slaves in general meet with in this State is very little different from that of other servants.

40

ALEXANDER HAMILTON TO GEORGE WASHINGTON
5 May 1789
Papers 5:335–37

In conformity to the intimation you were pleased to honor me with on   evening last I have reflected on the etiquette proper to be observed by the President and now submit the ideas which have occurred to me on the subject.

The public good requires as a primary object that the dignity of the office should be supported. Whatever is essential to this ought to be pursued though at the risk of partial or momentary dissatisfaction. But care will be necessary to avoid extensive disgust or discontent. Men's minds are prepared for a pretty high tone in the demeanour of the Executive; but I doubt whether for so high a tone as in the abstract might be desireable. The notions of equality are yet in my opinion too general and too strong to admit of such a distance being placed between the President and other branches of the government as might even be consistent with a due proportion. The following plan will I think steer clear of extremes and involve no very material inconveniences.

I The President to have a levee day once a week for receiving visits. An hour to be fixed at which it shall be understood that he will appear and consequently that the visitors are previously to be assembled. The President to remain half an hour, in which time he may converse cursorily on indifferent subjects with such persons as shall strike his attention, and at the end of that half hour disappear. Some regulation will be hereafter necessary to designate those who may visit. A mode of introduction through particular officers will be indispensable. No visits to be returned.

II The President to accept no invitations: and to give formal entertainments only twice or four times a year on the anniversaries of important events in the revolution. If twice, the day of the declaration of Independence, and that of the inauguration of the President, which completed the organization of the Constitution, to be preferred; if four times, the day of the treaty of alliance with france & that of the definitive treaty with Britain to be added. The members of the two houses of the legislature Principal officers of the Government Foreign ministers and other distinguished strangers only to be invited. The numbers form in my mind an objection—But there may be separate tables in separate rooms. This is practiced in some European Courts. I see no other method in which foreign Ministers can with propriety be included in any attentions of the table which the President may think fit to pay.

III The President on the levée days either by himself or some Gentleman of his household to give informal invitations to family dinners on the days of invitation. Not more than six or eight to be invited at a time & the matter to be confined essentially to members of the legislature and other official characters. The President never to remain long at table.

I think it probable that the last article will not correspond with the ideas of most of those with whom Your Excellency may converse but on pretty mature reflection I believe it will be necessary to remove the idea of too immense an inequality, which I fear would excite dissatisfaction and cabal. The thing may be so managed as neither to occasion much waste of time, nor to infringe on dignity.

It is an important point to consider what persons may have access to Your Excellency on business. The heads of departments will of course have this privilege. Foreign Ministers of some descriptions will also be intitled to it. In Europe I am informed ambassadors only have direct access to the Chief Magistrate. Something very *near* what prevails there would in my opinion be right. The distinction of rank between diplomatic characters requires attention and the door of access ought not to be too wide to that class of persons. I have thought that the members of the Senate should also have a right of *individual* access on matters relative to the *public administration*. In England & France Peers of the realm have this right. We have none such in this Country, but I believe that it will be satisfactory to the people to know that there is some body of men in the state who have a right of continual communication with the President. It will be considered as a safeguard against secret combinations to deceive him.

I have asked myself—will not the representatives expect the same privilege and be offended if they are not allowed to participate with the Senate? There is sufficient danger of this, to merit consideration. But there is a reason for the distinction in the constitution. The Senate are coupled with the President in certain executive functions; treaties and appointments. This makes them in a degree his constitutional counsellors and gives them a *peculiar* claim to the right of access. On the whole, I think the discrimination will be proper & may be hazarded.

I have chosen this method of communication, because I understood Your Excellency, that it would be most convenient to you. The unstudied and unceremonious manner of it will I hope not render it the less acceptable. And if in the execution of your commands at any time I consult frankness and simplicity more than ceremony or profession, I flatter myself you will not on that account distrust the sincerity of the assurance I now give of my cordial wishes for your personal happiness and the success of your administration.

41

EDMUND RANDOLPH TO JAMES MADISON
19 May 1789
Madison Papers 12:168–69

I wish, that by communicating with a friend, I could forget the situation of my wife. She suspects and I fear truly, that she has a cancer in her mouth. She supposes, that she feels all the acknowledged symptoms of that cruel ulcer, and that it has advanced most rapidly for a month past. In this country [Virginia] real aid is unattainable; nay even that species of aid, which can merely flatter, is unattainable. I have resolved, if the alarm should prove decidedly true, to carry her to Europe or Philadelphia. The former holds out the best source of hope; but I see no chance of converting property into sterling money. The latter would be visited with more ease. But as I should be obliged almost to become a resident there, should I go upon such an errand, pecuniary difficulties would be equally great. An effort, however, must be made, even at the risque of my whole fortune. Indeed I have sometimes seriously thought of attempting something professional, should I be compelled to visit Philadelphia without being able to raise money from my estate. In that case, a new revolution would take place with me. For if I found that I could live there, I should emancipate my slaves, and thus end my days, without undergoing any anxiety about the injustice of holding them. But I really do not know, why I have troubled you with this detail, unless I am imperceptibly led to unbosom myself to you without reserve; being always Yrs. mo. sincerely & afftely.

42

BENJAMIN FRANKLIN, QUERIES AND REMARKS RESPECTING ALTERATIONS IN THE CONSTITUTION OF PENNSYLVANIA
1789

Writings 10:58–60

(See ch. 12, no. 25)

43

JAMES MADISON, MEMORANDUM ON AN AFRICAN COLONY FOR FREED SLAVES
ca. 20 Oct. 1789

Papers 12:437–38

Without enquiring into the practicability or the most proper means of establishing a Settlement of freed blacks on the Coast of Africa, it may be remarked as one motive to the benevolent experiment that if such an asylum was provided, it might prove a great encouragement to manumission in the Southern parts of the U. S. and even afford the best hope yet presented of putting an end to the slavery in which not less than 600,000 unhappy negroes are now involved.

In all the Southern States of N. America, the laws permit masters, under certain precautions to manumit their slaves. But the continuance of such a permission in some of the States is rendered precarious by the ill effects suffered from freedmen who retain the vices and habits of slaves. The same consideration becomes an objection with many humane masters agst. an exertion of their legal right of freeing their slaves. It is found in fact that neither the good of the Society, nor the happiness of the individuals restored to freedom is promoted by such a change in their condition.

In order to render this change eligible as well to the Society as to the Slaves, it would be necessary that a compleat incorporation of the latter into the former should result from the act of manumission. This is rendered impossible by the prejudices of the Whites, prejudices which proceeding principally from the difference of colour must be considered as permanent and insuperable.

It only remains then that some proper external receptacle be provided for the slaves who obtain their liberty. The interior wilderness of America, and the Coast of Africa seem to present the most obvious alternative. The former is liable to great if not invincible objections. If the settlement were attempted at a considerable distance from the White frontier, it would be destroyed by the Savages who have a peculiar antipathy to the blacks: If the attempt were made in the neighbourhood of the White Settlements, peace would not long be expected to remain between Societies, distinguished by such characteristic marks, and retaining the feelings inspired by their former relation of oppressors & oppressed. The result then is that an experiment for providing such an external establishment for the blacks as might induce the humanity of Masters, and by degrees both the humanity & policy of the Governments, to forward the abolition of slavery in America, ought to be pursued on the Coast of Africa or in some other foreign situation.

44

NOAH WEBSTER, MISCELLANEOUS REMARKS ON DIVIZIONS OF PROPERTY . . . IN THE UNITED STATES
Feb. 1790

Collection 326–32

In attending to the principles of government, the leeding idea that strikes the mind, iz, that political power depends mostly on property; consequently guvernment will take its complection from the divisions of property in the state.

In despotic states, the subjects must not possess property in fee; for an exclusiv possession of lands inspires ideas of independence, fatal to despotism. To support such guvernments, it iz necessary that the laws should giv the prince a sovereign control over the property az wel az the lives of hiz subjects. There are however very few countries, where the guvernment iz so purely arbitrary, that the peeple can be deprived of life and estate, without some legal formalities. Even when the first possession waz the voluntary gift of the prince, grants or concessions, sanctioned by prescription, haz often established rights in the subject, of which he cannot be deprived without a judicial process.

In Europe the feudal system of tenures haz given rise to a singular species of guvernment. Most of the countries are said to be guverned by *monarkies;* but many of the guvernments might, with propriety, be called *aristocratic republics.* The barons, who possess the lands, hav most of the power in their own hands. Formerly the kings were but lords of a superior rank, *primi inter pares;* and they were originally electiv. This iz stil the case in Poland, which continues to be what other states in Europe were, an *aristocratic republic.* But from the twelfth to the sixteenth century, the princes, in many countries, were struggling to circumscribe the power of the barons, and their attempts, which often desolated their dominions, were attended with various success. What they could not accomplish by force, they sometimes obtained by stratagem. In some countries the commons were called in to support the royal prerogativs, and thus obtained a share in legislation, which haz since been augmented by vast accessions of power and influence, from a distribution and encreese of welth. This haz been the case in England. In other countries, the prince haz combined with the barons to depress the peeple. Where the prince holds the privilege of disposing of civil, military and ecclesiastical offices, it haz been eezy to attach the nobility to hiz interest, and by this coalition, peece haz often been secured in a kingdom; but the peeple hav been kept in vassalage. Thus by the laws of the feudal system, most of the commons in Europe are kept in a state of dependence on the great landholders.

But commerce haz been favorable to mankind. Az the rules of succession to estates, every where established in Europe, are calculated to aggrandize the *few* at the expense of the *many,* commerce, by creating and accumulating personal estate, haz introduced a new species of power to ballance the influence of the landed property. Commerce found its way from Italy and the eest, to Germany and England, diffusing in its progress freedom, knowledge and independence. Commerce iz favorable to freedom; it flurishes most in republics; indeed a free intercourse by trade iz almost fatal to despotism; for which reezon, some princes lay it under severe restrictions: In other countries it iz discuraged by public opinion, which renders trade disreputable. This iz more fatal to it, than the edicts of tyrants.

The basis of a democratic and a republican form of guvernment, iz, a fundamental law, favoring an equal or rather a general distribution of property. It iz not necessary nor possible that every citizen should hav exactly an equal portion of land and goods, but the laws of such a state should require an equal distribution of intestate estates, and bar all perpetuities. Such laws occasion constant revolutions of property, and thus hold out to all men equal motivs to vigilance and industry. They excite emulation, by giving every citizen an equal change of being rich and respectable.

In no one particular do the American states differ from European nations more widely, than in the rules which regulate the tenure and distribution of lands. This circumstance alone wil, for ages at leest, prezerve a government in the united states, very different from any which now exists or can arize in Europe.

In New England, intestate estates desend to all the children or other heirs in equal portions, except to the oldest son, who haz two shares. This exception in favor of the oldest son, waz copied from the levitical code, which waz made the basis of the first New England institutions. The legislature of Massachusetts, at their May session, 1789, abolished that absurd exception; and nothing but inveterate habit keeps it alive in the other states.*

In consequence of theze laws, the peeple of New England enjoy an equality of condition, unknown in any other part of the world. To the same cause may be ascribed the rapid population of theze states; for estates by division are kept small, by which meens every man iz obliged to labor, and labor iz the direct cause of population. For the same reezon, the peeple of theze states, feel and exert the pride of independence. Their equality makes them mild and condesending, capable of being convinced and guverned by persuasion; but their independence renders them irritable and obstinate in resisting force and oppression. A man by associating familiarly with them, may eezily coax them into hiz views, but if he assumes any airs of superiority, he iz treeted with az little respect az a servant. The principal inconvenience arizing from theze dispositions iz, that a man who happens to be a little distinguished for hiz property or superior education iz ever exposed to their envy, and the tung of slander iz bizzy in backbiting him. In this manner, they oppoze distinctions of rank, with great success. This however iz a private inconvenience; but there iz an evil, arising from this jealousy, which deeply affects their guvernment. Averse to distinctions, and reddy to humble superiority, they become the dupes of a set of artful men, who, with small talents for business and no regard for the public interest, are always familiar with every class of peeple, slyly hinting something to the disadvantage of great and honest men, and pretending to be frends to the public welfare. The peeple are thus guverned at times by the most unqualified men among them. If a man wil shake hands with every one he meets, attend church constantly, and assume a goodly countenance; if he wil not swear or play cards, he may arrive to the first offices in the government, without one single talent for the proper discharge of hiz duty; he may even defraud the public revenu and be accused of it on the most indubitable evidence, yet by laying hiz hand on hiz brest, casting hiz eyes to heaven, and calling God to witness hiz innocence, he may wipe away the popular suspicions, and be a fairer candidate for preferment than be-

---

*Lands in Connecticut desend to the heirs in the following manner: First to children, and if none, then to brothers and sisters or their legal representativs of the whole blud; then to parents; then to brothers and sisters of the half blud; then to next of kin, the whole blud taking the preference when of equal degree with the half blud.

fore hiz accusation. So far az the harts of the peeple are concerned, the disposition here mentioned iz a high recommendation, for it proves them mild, unsuspecting and humane: But government suffers a material injury from this turn of mind; and were it not for a few men who are boldly honest, and indefatigable in detecting impositions on the public, the government of theze states would always be, az it often iz, in the hands of the weekest, or wickedest of the citizens.

. . . . .

Altho the principle iz tru that a general distribution of lands iz the basis of a republican form of government, yet there iz an evil arising out of this distribution, which the New England states now feel, and which wil increase with the population of the country. The tracts of land first taken up by the settlers, were not very considerable; and theze having been repeetedly divided among a number of heirs, hav left the present proprietors almost without subsistence for their families. Vast numbers of men do not possess more than thirty or forty akers eech, and many not half the quantity. It iz with difficulty that such men can support families and pay taxes. Indeed most of them are unable to do it; they involve themselves in det; the creditors take the little land they possess, and the peeple are driven, poor and helpless, into an uncultivated wilderness. Such are the effects of an equal division of lands among heirs; and such the causes of emigration to the western territories. Emigration indeed iz a present remedy for the evil; but when settlements hav raized the valu of the western lands neerly to that on the Atlantic coast, emigrations wil mostly ceese. They wil not entirely ceese, until the continent iz peepled to the Pacific ocean; and that period iz distant; but whenever they ceese, our republican inhabitants, unable to subsist on the small portions of land, assigned them by the laws of division, must hav recourse to manufactures. The holders of land wil be fewer in number, because monied men wil hav the advantage of purchasing lands very low of the necessitous inhabitants, who wil be multiplied by the very laws of the state, respecting landed property. Other laws however could not be tolerated in theze states. In Europe, provision iz made for younger sons, in the army, the church, the navy, or in the numerous manufactures of the countries. But in America, such provision cannot be made; and therefore our laws eezely provide for all the children, where they are not provided for by the parents.

By extending our views to futurity, we see considerable changes in the condition of theze republican states. The laws, by barring entailments, prevent the establishment of families in permanent affluence; we are therefore in little danger of a hereditary aristocracy. But the same laws, by dividing inheritances, tho their first effect iz to create equality, ultimately tend to impoverish a great number of citizens, and thus giv a few men, who commanded money, an advantage in procuring lands at less than their real valu. The evil iz increased in a state, where there iz a scarcity of cash, occasioned by the course of trade, or by laws limiting the interest on money loaned: Such iz the case in Connecticut. A man who haz money may purchase wel cultivated farms in that state for seventy, and sometimes

for fifty per cent. of the real valu. Such a situation iz favorable to the accumulation of great estates, and the creation of distinctions; but while alienations of real estates are rendered necessary by the laws, the genius of the guvernment will not be materially changed.

The causes which destroyed the ancient republics were numerous; but in Rome, one principal cause waz, the vast inequality of fortunes, occasioned partly by the strategems of the patricians and partly by the spoils of their enemies, or the exactions of tribute in their conquered provinces. Rome, with the *name* of a republic, waz several ages loozing the *spirit* and *principle*. The Gracchi endevored to check the growing evil by an agrarian law; but were not successful. In Cesar's time, the Romans were ripened for a change of guvernment; the *spirit* of a commonwelth waz lost, and Cesar waz but an instrument of altering the *form,* when it could no longer exist. Cesar iz execrated az the tyrant of hiz country; and Brutus, who stabbed him, iz applauded az a *Roman*. But such waz the state of things in Rome, that Cesar waz a better ruler than Brutus would hav been; for when the spirit of a government iz lost, the form must change.

Brutus would hav been a tyrannical demagogue, or hiz zeel to restore the commonwelth would hav protracted the civil war and factions which raged in Rome and which finally must hav subsided in monarky. Cesar waz absolute, but hiz guvernment waz moderate, and hiz name waz sufficient to repress faction and prezerve tranquillity. The zeel of Brutus waz intemperate and rash; for when abuses hav acquired a certain degree of strength; when they are interwoven with every part of government, it iz prudence to suffer many evils, rather than risk the application of a violent remedy.

How far the Roman history furnishes the data, on which the politicians of America may calculate the future changes in our form of government, iz left to every man's own opinion. Our citizens now hold lands in fee; this renders them bold in independence: They all labor, and therefore make hardy soldiers; they all reed, and of course understand their rights; they rove uncontrolled in the forest; therefore they know the use of arms. But wil not poor peeple multiply, and the possessions of real estates be diminished in number, and increased in size? Must not a great proportion of our citizens becum manufacturers and thus looz the bodies and the spirit of soldiers? While the mass of knowlege wil be increased by discuveries and experience, wil it not be confined to fewer men? In short, wil not our forests be levelled, or confined to a few proprietors? and when our peeple ceese to hunt, will not the body of them neglect the use of arms? Theze are questions of magnitude; but the present generation can answer them only in prospect and speculation. At any rate, the genius of every guvernment must addapt itself to the peculiar state and spirit of the peeple who compose the state, and when the Americans looz the *principles* of a free guvernment, it follows that they will speedily looz the *form.* Such a change would, az in Rome, be ascribed to *bad* men; but it is more rational to ascribe it to an imperceptible progress of corruption, or thoze insensible changes which steel into the best constitutions of government.

45

JAMES MADISON TO BENJAMIN RUSH
20 Mar. 1790

Papers 13:109

The Petitions on the subject of Slavery have employed more than a week, and are still before a Committee of the whole. The Gentlemen from S. Carolina & Georgia are intemperate beyond all example and even all decorum. They are not content with palliating slavery as a deeprooted abuse, but plead for the lawfulness of the African trade itself—nor with protesting agst. the object of the Memorials, but lavish the most virulent language on the authors of them. If this folly did not reproach the public councils, it ought to excite no regret in the patrons of Humanity & freedom. Nothing could hasten more the progress of those reflections & sentiments which are secretly undermining the institution which this mistaken zeal is laboring to secure agst. the most distant approach of danger.

46

JOHN ADAMS TO SAMUEL ADAMS
18 Oct. 1790

Works 6:416–20

(See ch. 11, no. 16)

47

A FREEMAN, MARYLAND GAZETTE
30 Dec. 1790

Let me, without any appearance of prejudice, to or against features, hair or colour, ask, what kind of freedom [for the manumitted slave] would it be, and what right have we to bring it about *"on exportation?"* We have no just right to export [or] banish any man, unless he previously violates some law, which inflicts transportation as a just punishment for his crime.—A different sentiment cannot correspond with the idea, that *"all men are born equally free, and in point of human rights to liberty, stand on equal ground."* But where would you export them to? They are as much *Americans* now as we, and we as much *Europeans* as they are *Africans.*—Nothing but a mind influenced by prejudice or partiality can countermand or contemn this idea or argument.

48

JAMES WILSON, OF MAN, AS A MEMBER OF
SOCIETY, LECTURES ON LAW
1791

Works 1:240–41

In civil society, previously to the institution of civil government, all men are equal. Of one blood all nations are made; from one source the whole human race has sprung.

When we say, that all men are equal; we mean not to apply this equality to their virtues, their talents, their dispositions, or their acquirements. In all these respects, there is, and it is fit for the great purposes of society that there should be, great inequality among men. In the moral and political as well as in the natural world, diversity forms an important part of beauty; and as of beauty, so of utility likewise. That social happiness, which arises from the friendly intercourse of good offices, could not be enjoyed, unless men were so framed and so disposed, as mutually to afford and to stand in need of service and assistance. Hence the necessity not only of great variety, but even of great inequality in the talents of men, bodily as well as mental. Society supposes mutual dependence: mutual dependence supposes mutual wants: all the social exercises and enjoyments may be reduced to two heads—that of giving, and that of receiving: but these imply different aptitudes to give and to receive.

Many are the degrees, many are the varieties of human genius, human dispositions, and human characters. One man has a turn for mechanicks; another, for architecture; one paints; a second makes poems; this excels in the arts of a military; the other, in those of civil life. To account for these varieties of taste and character, is not easy; is, perhaps, impossible. But though their efficient cause it may be difficult to explain; their final cause, that is, the intention of Providence in appointing them, we can see and admire. These varieties of taste and character induce different persons to choose different professions and employments in life: these varieties render mankind mutually beneficial to each other, and prevent too violent oppositions of interest in the same pursuit. Hence we enjoy a variety of conveniences; hence the numerous arts and sciences have been invented and improved; hence the sources of commerce and friendly intercourse between different nations have been opened; hence the circulation of truth has been quickened and promoted; hence the operations of social virtue have been multiplied and enlarged.

> Heaven, forming each on other to depend,
> Bids each on other for assistance call,
> 'Till one man's weakness grows the strength of all.
> Wants, frailties, passions closer still ally
> The common interest, or endear the tie:
> To these we owe true friendship, love sincere,
> Each home-felt joy, that life inherits here.
>
> [Pope, *Essay on Man*]

How insipidly uniform would human life and manners be, without the beautiful variety of colours, reflected upon them by different tastes, different tempers, and different characters!

But however great the variety and inequality of men may be with regard to virtue, talents, taste, and acquirements; there is still one aspect, in which all men in society, previous to civil government, are equal. With regard to all, there is an equality in rights and in obligations; there is that "jus aequum," that equal law, in which the Romans placed true freedom. The natural rights and duties of man belong equally to all. Each forms a part of that great system, whose greatest interest and happiness are intended by all the laws of God and nature. These laws prohibit the wisest and the most powerful from inflicting misery on the meanest and most ignorant; and from depriving them of their rights or just acquisitions. By these laws, rights, natural or acquired, are confirmed, in the same manner, to all; to the weak and artless, their small acquisitions, as well as to the strong and artful, their large ones. If much labour employed entitles the active to great possessions, the indolent have a right, equally sacred, to the little possessions, which they occupy and improve.

As in civil society, previous to civil government, all men are equal; so, in the same state, all men are free. In such a state, no one can claim, in preference to another, superiour right: in the same state, no one can claim over another superiour authority.

49

THOMAS JEFFERSON, NOTES OF A CONVERSATION WITH ALEXANDER HAMILTON
13 Aug. 1791
Hamilton Papers 9:33–34

Th: J. mentioned to him a lre recd. from J. A. [John Adams] disavowing Publicola, & denying that he ever entertd. a wish to bring this country under a hereditary executive, or introduce an hereditary branch of legislature &c. See his lre. A. H. condemning mr A's writings & most particularly Davila, as having a tendency to weaken the present govmt declared in substance as follows. "I own it is my own opn, tho' I do not publish it in Dan & Bersheba, that the present govmt is not that which will answer the ends of society by giving stability & protection to it's rights, and that it will probably be found expedient to go into the British form. However, since we have undertaken the experiment, I am for giving it a fair course, whatever my expectns may be. The success indeed so far is greater than I had expected, & therefore at present success seems more possible than it had done heretofore, & there are still other & other stages of improvemt which, if the present does not succeed, may be tried & ought to be tried before we give up the republican form altogether for that mind

must be really depraved which would not prefer the equality of political rights which is the foundn of pure republicanism, if it can be obtained consistently with order. Therefore whoever by his writings disturbs the present order of things, is really blameable, however pure his intentns may be, & he was sure mr Adams's were pure." This is the substance of a declaration made in much more lengthy terms, & which seemed to be more formal than usual for a private conversn. between two, & as if intended to qualify some less guarded expressions which had been dropped on former occasions. Th: J. has committed it to writing in the moment of A.H.'s leaving the room.

50

JAMES MADISON, PARTIES
23 Jan. 1792
Papers 14:197–98

In every political society, parties are unavoidable. A difference of interests, real or supposed, is the most natural and fruitful source of them. The great object should be to combat the evil: 1. By establishing a political equality among all. 2. By withholding *unnecessary* opportunities from a few, to increase the inequality of property, by an immoderate, and especially an unmerited, accumulation of riches. 3. By the silent operation of laws, which, without violating the rights of property, reduce extreme wealth towards a state of mediocrity, and raise extreme indigence towards a state of comfort. 4. By abstaining from measures which operate differently on different interests, and particularly such as favor one interest at the expence of another. 5. By making one party a check on the other, so far as the existence of parties cannot be prevented, nor their views accommodated. If this is not the language of reason, it is that of republicanism.

In all political societies, different interests and parties arise out of the nature of things, and the great art of politicians lies in making them checks and balances to each other. Let us then increase these *natural distinctions* by favoring an inequality of property; and let us add to them *artificial distinctions,* by establishing *kings,* and *nobles,* and *plebeians.* We shall then have the more checks to oppose to each other: we shall then have the more scales and the more weights to perfect and maintain the equilibrium. This is as little the voice of reason, as it is that of republicanism.

From the expediency, in politics, of making natural parties, mutual checks on each other, to infer the propriety of creating artificial parties, in order to form them into mutual checks, is not less absurd than it would be in ethics, to say, that new vices ought to be promoted, where they would counteract each other, because this use may be made of existing vices.

51

NATHANIEL CHIPMAN, SKETCHES OF THE
PRINCIPLES OF GOVERNMENT 177–82
1793

Of the Nature of Equality in Republics.

Some of the most eminent writers on government, have supposed an equality of property, as well as of rights to be necessary in a republic. They have, therefore, prescribed limits to individual acquisition. The Reason given is, that riches give power to those who possess them, and that those who possess power, will always abuse it to the oppression of others. If this be a good reason for limiting the acquisition of riches, there is equal reason for limiting the improvement of bodily strength and mental abilities. Such a step would be an abridgement of the primary rights of man, and counteract almost all the laws of his nature. It would, perhaps, could it be reduced to practice, place the whole human race in a state of fearless quietude; but it would be a state of tasteless enjoyment, of stupid inactivity, not to be envied by the lowest tribes of the animal creation.

If such be the principles of a republican government, it is a government out of nature. Those have made a wiser choice, who have submitted to the less tyrannical principles of absolute monarchy. These are not the principles of a republic. They are the principles of anarchy, and of popular tyranny.

We have just now enquired into the nature of equality among men, and have seen in what it consists; a free and equal enjoyment of the primary rights, which are, the intellectual rights, and the right which men have of using their powers and faculties, under certain reciprocal modifications, for their own convenience and happiness. The equality necessary in a republic, requires nothing more, than this equality of primary rights. I shall here instance in the right of acquisition only, as being sufficient for my present purpose.

To the security of this right, certain regulations, as to the modes and conditions of enjoying the secondary rights, or in other words, of holding property, are necessary. Not, indeed, as to the quantity, but the freedom of acquisition, use, and disposal. To give to any individual, or class of men, a monopoly, an exclusive right of acquisition in those things, which nature has made the subjects of property, to perpetuate, and render them unalienable in their hands, is an exclusion of the rights of others. It is a violation of the equal rights of man. Of this nature are all exclusive privileges; all perpetuities of riches and honor, and all the pretended rights of primogeniture. Inequality of property, in the possession of individuals, is not directly, nor by inevitable consequence, subversive of genuine liberty. Those laws are, indeed, subversive of liberty, which, by establishing perpetuities, deprive the owner of a right of disposal, and others, so far as they extend, of the right of acquisition; which annex privileges to property, and by making it a qualification in government, create a powerful aristocracy.

Riches are the fruit of industry. Honor the fruit of merit. Both ought, as to their continuance, and the influence which attends them, to be left to the conduct of the possessor. If a man, who, by industry and economy, has acquired riches, become indolent, or profligate, let him sink into poverty. Let those who are still industrious and economical, succeed to his enjoyments, as to their just reward. If a man, who, by noble and virtuous actions, has acquired honor, the esteem of mankind, will behave infamously, let him sink into contempt. To exclude the meritorious from riches and honors, and to perpetuate either to the undeserving, are equally injurious to the rights of man in society. In both it is to counteract the laws of nature, which have, by the connection of cause and effect, annexed the proper rewards and punishments to the actions of men. Wealth, or at least, a competency, is the reward, provided by the laws of nature, for prudent industry; want, the punishment of idleness and profligacy.

If we make equality of property necessary in a society, we must employ force, against both the industrious and the indolent. On the one hand, the industrious must be restrained, from every exertion, which may exceed the power, or inclination of common capacities; on the other hand, the indolent must be forcibly stimulated to common exertions. This would be acting the fable of Procrustes, who, by stretching, or lopping to his iron bedstead, would reduce every man to his own standard length.

If this method should be deemed ineligible, the only alternative will be, either by open violence, or the secret fraud of the law, to turn a certain portion of the well-earned acquisitions of the vigilant and industrious, to the use of the indolent and neglectful.

Let us not, in a Republic, attempt the extreme of equality: It verges on the extreme of tyranny. Guarantee to every man, the full enjoyment of his natural rights. Banish all exclusive privileges; all perpetuities of riches and honors. Leave free the acquisition and disposal of property to supply the occasions of the owner, and to answer all claims of right, both of the society, and of individuals. To give a stimulus to industry, to provide solace and assistance, in the last helpless stages of life, and a reward for the attentions of humanity, confirm to the owner the power of directing, who shall succeed to his right of property after his death; but let it be without any limitation, or restraint upon the future use, or disposal. Divert not the consequences of actions, as to the individual actors, from their proper course. Let no preference be given to any one in government, but what his conduct can secure, from the sentiments of his fellow citizens. Of property, left to the disposal of the law, let a descent from parents to children, in equal portions, be held a sacred principle of the constitution. Secure but these, and every thing will flow in the channel intended by nature. The operation of the equal laws of nature, tend to exclude, or correct every dangerous excess.

Thus industry will be excited; arts will flourish, and virtuous conduct meet its just reward, the esteem and confidence of mankind. Am I deceived? or are these the true principles of equality in a democratic republic? Principles, which will secure its prosperity, and, if any thing in this stage of existence can be durable, its perpetual duration.

52

ST. GEORGE TUCKER TO JEREMY BELKNAP
24 Jan. 1795

MHS Collections, 5th ser., 3:379–81

Having never visited the Eastern States, it has been my misfortune never to have had the pleasure of a personal acquaintance with any of those eminent literary characters which that part of the United States has produced, and, if I may credit Fame, abounds with, more than any other part of our common country; a circumstance probably not more mortifying to myself than of real disadvantage to this part of the United States, since a more frequent intercourse and intimate acquaintance between the several parts of the Union would probably contribute more to remove local prejudices and cement the bond of union than any other project, unsupported by such a foundation. To supply, as far as respects myself, this inconvenience in some measure, I have prevailed on my friend, the Rev. Mr. Hust, to favor me with a letter of introduction, which I take the liberty to enclose, and to request your pardon for thus intruding my correspondence upon you; a liberty which private considerations alone could scarcely justify on any account, and which, I fear, you will think fully commensurate to the occasion which prompts it.

The introduction of slavery into this country is at this day considered among its greatest misfortunes by a very great majority of those who are reproached for an evil which the present generation could no more have avoided than an hereditary gout or leprosy. The malady has proceeded so far as to render it doubtful whether any specific can be found to eradicate, or even to palliate, the disease. Having, in my official character as professor of law in the college at this place [Williamsburg], had occasion to notice the several acts of the legislature on the subject, I find that, even before the commencement of the present century, an attempt was made to check the importation of slaves, by imposing a duty on them. The act was indeed only temporary, but was renewed as often as the influence of the African Company in England would permit. At length the duty was made payable by the buyers; but the acts imposing it were still temporary, though constantly renewed whenever an extraordinary supply of money was required, and was gradually increased from five to twenty per cent, ad valorem. As soon as the Revolution took place, the legislature passed an act prohibiting the importation of slaves, under the severest penalties; and permitting, what had hitherto been prohibited, the voluntary emancipation of them by their masters. The question of a general emancipation has not, that I know, been brought on the carpet in the legislature; but I am fully persuaded that circumstance is altogether owing to the difficulties which present themselves to every reflecting mind. To assist in removing them is the object of this letter; for having observed, with much pleasure, that slavery has been wholly exterminated from the Massachusetts, and being impressed with an idea that it once had existence there, I have cherished a hope that we may, from the example of our sister State, learn what methods are most likely to succeed in removing the same evil from among ourselves. With this view, I have taken the liberty to enclose a few queries, which, if your leisure will permit you to answer, you will confer on me a favor which I shall always consider as an obligation; and if, in the pursuits in which you are engaged, any subject should occur in which you may be disposed to obtain information from this quarter, I will not promise to afford it you, but I assure you that I will most faithfully endeavour to do it.

Queries respecting the Introduction, Progress, and Abolition of Slavery in Massachusetts.

1st. The first introduction of negroes or other slaves in Massachusetts?

2d. Whether the African trade was carried on thither? at what period it commenced? to what extent it was carried on? when it began to decline? and when it was wholly discontinued?

3d. Whether it was carried on by European or American adventurers? by what means its declension first began? whether from legislative discouragement or other causes? and to what causes its abolition is to be ascribed?

4th. The state of slavery in the Massachusetts when slaves were most numerous? their number when most numerous? their proportion to the number of white persons at that period?

5th. The mode by which slavery hath been abolished there? whether by a general and simultaneous emancipation? or at different periods? or whether by declaring all persons born after a particular period free?

6th. At what period slavery was wholly abolished? what were their numbers and proportion to the whites at that period?

7th. What is the condition of emancipated negroes? is any, and what, provision made for their education and maintenance during infancy, or in a state of decrepitude, age, or insanity?

8th. What are their political rights or disabilities? if there be any discrimination between them and white persons?

9th. Is there any perceptible difference between the general moral or social conduct of emancipated persons, or their descendants, and others?

10th. Are intermarriages frequent between blacks and whites? if so, are such alliances more frequent between black men and white women, or the contrary?

11th. Does harmony in general prevail between the blacks and white citizens? do they associate freely together? or is there a pre-eminence claimed by the one, and either avowedly or tacitly admitted by the other?

53

JOHN ADAMS TO JEREMY BELKNAP
21 Mar. 1795

MHS Collections, 5th ser., 3:401–2

I have read the queries concerning the rise and progress of slavery; but, as it is a subject to which I have never given any very particular attention, I may not be able to give you so much information as many others. I was concerned in several causes in which negroes sued for their freedom, before the Revolution. The arguments in favour of their liberty were much the same as have been urged since in pamphlets and newspapers, in debates in Parliament, &c., arising from the rights of mankind, which was the fashionable word at that time. Since that time, they have dropped the "kind."

Argument might have some weight in the abolition of slavery in the Massachusetts, but the real cause was the multiplication of labouring white people, who would no longer suffer the rich to employ these sable rivals so much to their injury. This principle has kept negro slavery out of France, England, and other parts of Europe. The common people would not suffer the labour, by which alone they could obtain a subsistence, to be done by slaves. If the gentlemen had been permitted by law to hold slaves, the common white people would have. put the negroes to death, and their masters too, perhaps.

I never knew a jury, by a verdict, to determine a negro to be a slave. They always found them free. As I was not in the General Court in 1773, I have no particular remembrance of the petition for the liberation of all the blacks, and know not how it was supported or treated.

The common white people, or rather the labouring people, were the cause of rendering negroes unprofitable servants. Their scoffs and insults, their continual insinuations, filled the negroes with discontent, made them lazy, idle, proud, vicious, and at length wholly useless to their masters, to such a degree that the abolition of slavery became a measure of oeconomy.

54

ST. GEORGE TUCKER TO JEREMY BELKNAP
29 June 1795

MHS Collections, 5th ser., 3:407–10

Whatever disposition the first settlers in Virginia or their immediate descendants might have had to encourage slavery, the present generation are, I am persuaded, more liberal; and a large majority of slave-holders among us would cheerfully concur in any feasible plan for the abolition of it. The objections to the measure are drawn from the deeprooted prejudices in the minds of the whites against the blacks, the general opinion of their mental inferiority, and an aversion to their corporeal distinctions from us, both which considerations militate against a general incorporation of them with us; the danger of granting them a practical admission to the rights of citizens; the possibility of their becoming idle, dissipated, and finally a numerous banditti, instead of turning their attention to industry and labour; the injury to agriculture in a large part of the State, where they are almost the only labourers, should they withdraw themselves from the culture of the earth; and the impracticability, and perhaps the dangerous policy, of an attempt to colonize them within the limits of the United States, or elsewhere. Mr. Jefferson seems to hint at this expedient; but surely he could not have weighed the difficulties and expence of an attempt to colonize 300,000 persons. If the attempt were made within the United States, it would probably include a provision for the slaves in the other States, amounting, on the whole, to 800,000. Could the funds of the United States support such a colony? If an army of 3 or 4 thousand men in the Western country is supported at such expence as that a bushel of corn has sometimes cost $10 before it reached the camp, what would be the expence of colonizing such an host? If even 20,000 colonists were yearly sent out, how enormous would be the expence, and how great the undertaking. Yet, with 20,000 colonists only sent out yearly, the numbers of those which remain would continually encrease, if the same causes which have hitherto contributed to their multiplication should be continued. Besides, what hardships, what destruction, would not the wretched colonists be exposed to? If humanity plead for their emancipation, it pleads more strongly against colonization; for, having stated the impracticability of it within the United States, I pass over the scheme of sending them back to their native country, to effectuate which, without the most cruel oppression, would require the utmost exertion of all the maritime powers in Europe, united with those of America, and a territory of ten times the extent that all the powers of Europe possess in Africa. One of three courses, then, must inevitably be pursued: either to *incorporate them with us*, to *grant them freedom without any participation of civil rights*, or to *retain them in slavery*. If it be true that either nature or long habit have depraved their faculties so as to render them, in their present state, an inferior order of beings, may not an attempt to elevate them depress those who mingle and incorporate with them? May not such an attempt be frustrated by prejudices too deeply rooted to be eradicated? The numbers being so nearly equal in Virginia, may not such prejudices generate a civil war, and end in the extermination of one party or the other? especially as Nature herself has fixed the characters by which those parties would be discriminated, so long as either existed. To the second measure, it has been objected that, by granting freedom only, without civil rights, you will stimulate them to procure by force what you have refused to grant them, which must lay the foundation of all the evils to be apprehended from a full incorporation of them amongst us. And to both measures it is further objected, that agriculture will languish as soon as they who are now compelled to till the ground are left at liberty to work or be idle, as most agreeable to them; that experience among us has shewn that emancipated blacks rarely are industrious; that, if so great a proportion of the inhabitants of the country should become idle, they will soon owe their subsistence to plunder alone; that those who wish for their emancipation equally wish for their total removal from the limits of the State; that, having been long accustomed to strict restraint in small bodies, they will not easily be restrained by general laws, which they have never been in the habit of regarding as having any relation to them. Those who argue thus contend that their present condition (the rigors of slavery having been much softened among us within these few years) is infinitely preferable to that degraded freedom they would enjoy, if emancipated. They insist that they are better clothed, lodged, and fed, than if it depended upon themselves to provide their own food, raiment, and houses; that the restraint upon them prevents their falling into vicious habits, which emancipated blacks appear too prone to contract. It may be observed, indeed, that, although the number of slaves is to the free blacks as 24 to 1, yet there are many more of the latter brought to answer for their crimes in courts of judicature than of the former. One reason for this undoubtedly is that slaves are punished by their masters for petty larcenies, for which a free man can only be punished by due course of law. But, even of capital crimes, more are committed by free blacks than by slaves. And, if I may judge by my own experience in courts which I have attended, the proportion of free black criminals to whites is nearly as one to three, though the proportion of free blacks to whites is not more than one for thirty-six. It is, however, but just to observe that I do not recollect more than one instance of murder committed by a free black, and in that instance he was an accomplice with a white man, who was the principal in the murder. Among slaves, murder is not very uncommon; and not unfrequently their victims have been their overseers, and sometimes, though very rarely, their own masters or mistresses, by means of poison. In most of these cases, the most humane persons have been the sufferers. They occur, however, so very seldom, that I am inclined to believe as many cases happen in England of masters or mistresses murdered by their servants, as in Virginia.

I have taken the liberty of troubling you with these remarks, wishing, if your leisure will permit, to learn your sentiments on a subject of such importance to humanity, which is, unhappily, involved in a labyrinth of political difficulties. I feel myself sometimes prompted to exclaim, "Fiat justitia ruat coelum"! but the scene now passing in the West Indies prompts me to suspend my opinion, and to doubt whether it will not be wiser to set about *amending the condition of the slave* than to make him a miserable free man. Your communications on this subject, whenever your leisure will permit, without interrupting your other pursuits, will be most gratefully received.

55

JAMES SULLIVAN TO JEREMY BELKNAP
30 July 1795

MHS Collections, 5th ser., 3:412–15

I have read, with great pleasure, the letter you were so obliging as to put into my hands from your very valuable correspondent, Mr. Tucker. I admire the goodness of his heart, and the elegance and patriotism of his sentiments; but he, like other good men, has to enjoy by anticipation that which can never be accomplished in his day. The subject which is so near his heart, and appears to employ so great a part of his public contemplations, is not new to me. I have had Governor Jefferson's ideas upon it some years ago, and gave him my opinion, which I will presently give to you, in one word. The objections stated by Mr. Tucker to three measures proposed for emancipating the black people of United America are all well maintained by his unanswerable arguments; while the pain he evidently feels to find a fourth, to which no insurmountable objection could be made, does great honour to his character as a man, and in some degree attones for the violation of human rights which his fellow-citizens have been guilty of. The freedom of the blacks, without allowing them to participate of civil privileges, appears to me the most eligible of the three measures which he has contemplated. But I am clearly of opinion that this would be nothing more than to throw 300,000 of the human race, idle, profligate, and miserable, on the bosom of the earth. These, urged by extreme hunger, and encouraged by combinations of aggravated complaints, supported by an idea of justice from their former sufferings, would take by force what the white people should procure by agriculture; and thus, unless overpowered and destroyed by military coercion, would spread famine and pestilence through the country. An idea that they would, on such an emancipation, or on one of any other kind, become industrious and regular, will, in my opinion, prove clearly fallacious. Besides this, if they should be inclined to labour, where would they be supplied with lands? or who would furnish them with the means for beginning their new mode of life? To let them have the full liberty of free citizens would be worse still; for the necessity of civil government proves that mankind are corrupt and wicked, and we should find these people holding their suffrages at auction, without holding property worthy of their attention, or a sense of civil liberty worthy of one moment's anxiety. This measure would involve the Southern States in calamity and distress, if not in ruin. The scheme of colonizing them has all the objections that your learned and ingenious correspondent has stated. The expence of carrying them to their new plantation, and furnishing them there with as much support as is generally claimed by the most industrious white people who go into a new country, is more than the Treasury of the United

States could possibly bear, even if there were no other expences of government.

Should the 300,000 blacks of Virginia emigrate, under an idea of colonizing, those of the three Southern States would of course be united with them: this would exhibit a multitude of half a million of people, at the least. On their way to their new world, and while they were beginning their settlements, some kind of civil government would be necessary. We have in history but one picture of such an enterprize; and there we see it was necessary, not only to open the sea, by a miracle, for them to pass, but more necessary to close it again, in order to prevent their return. Promises of the most luxuriant kind, assured by a constant and obvious chain of miracles, could hardly restrain them from rebellions and insurrections. Even then, though a spontaneous supply of bread from Heaven supported the camp, and every measure was adopted which could affect the human heart with a proper sense of a necessity for a good and regular government, yet so incapable were the men, who had been bred in a state of slavery, either to submit to or maintain a system of state policy, that it was necessary to waste them all in the wilderness. Should half a million of people, who had been bred in a state of slavery, find themselves in a country where they were free from a legal restraint, excepting what they should provide for themselves, they could never reduce their individual members to a state of civil society. The emigrants from Europe to America had been always under a government where civil liberty was much contemplated, and as fully enjoyed as it could be in a monarchy; but there never was, or ever can be, a migration of a multitude of slaves to a country of freedom.

The negroes, if they were to colonize, would at once, in separate and independent bodies, commit depredations on their neighbours, and bring the other States into a necessity of reducing them by the sword. From the difficulties suggested by Mr. Tucker, it would seem as if the case was without remedy, and that a state of slavery is entailed for ever on some part of the inhabitants of free America. But there is, in my mind, this resource; and I am obliged to think that it is the only one in the case, and that a very slow one. As there is no way to eradicate the prejudice which education has fixed in the minds of the white against the black people, otherwise than by raising the blacks, by means of mental improvements, nearly to the same grade with the whites, the emancipation of the slaves in United America must be slow in its progress, and ages must be employed in the business. The time necessary to effect this purpose must be as extensive, at least, as that in which slavery has been endured here. The children of the slaves must, at the public expence, be educated in the same manner as the children of their masters; being at the same schools, &c., with the rising generation, that prejudice, which has been so long and inveterate against them on account of their situation and colour, will be lessened within thirty or forty years. There is an objection to this, which embraces all my feelings; that is, that it will tend to a mixture of blood, which I now abhor; but yet, as I feel, I fear that I am not a pure Republican, delighting in the

equal rights of all the human race. This mode of education will fit the rising progeny of the black people either to participate with the whites in a free government, or to colonize, and have one of their own. The negroes born after a certain future day may be considered as free at 40 years, those after another at 30, and those after another at 21 years of age. This will, in the course of time, emancipate all the slaves. To induce them to be industrious members of the community, a certain portion of property ought to be considered as necessary to their holding civil offices, or enjoying civil privileges, in common with other citizens. This process, I know, is too slow for the warm and philanthropic feelings of your elegant correspondent; and carries with it the idea of a curse being entailed in the Southern States from the fathers to the children, to the third and fourth generation. Be that as it may, I think the best way is to make haste slowly, and to bear for a time an evil with patience, rather than to aggravate its miseries, and render future attempts discouraging. There have been few instances indeed, in history, where a man educated as a slave has been capable of enjoying freedom. In the most despotic governments, there have appeared champions for liberty; but the event has generally evinced to the world that the greater part of these had acted only from a spirit of ambitious heroism, because they have generally been tyrants as soon as they had established their own power to rule.

There is no doubt a great disparity in the natural abilities of mankind, and we have great reason to believe that the organization of the Affricans is such as prevents their receiving the more fine and sublime impressions equally with the white people; and yet we do not know but that, giving them the same prospects, placing them under the force of the same motives, and conferring upon them the same advantages for the space of time in which 3 or 4 generations shall rise and fall, will so mend the race, and so increase their powers of perception, and so strengthen their faculty for comparing ideas, and understanding the nature and connexion of the external things with which man is surrounded on this globe, as that they may exceed the white people.

56

ST. GEORGE TUCKER, A DISSERTATION ON SLAVERY, IN BLACKSTONE'S COMMENTARIES 2:APP. 31–32, 35–43, 54–55, 68–69, 74–81 (1803)
1796

In the preceding inquiry into the absolute rights of the citizens of united America, we must not be understood as if those rights were equally and universally the privilege of all the inhabitants of the United States, or even of all those, who may challenge this land of freedom as their native country. Among the blessings which the Almighty hath showered down on these states, there is a large portion of the bitterest draught that ever flowed from the cup of affliction. Whilst America hath been the land of promise to Europeans, and their descendants, it hath been the vale of death to millions of the wretched sons of Africa. The genial light of liberty, which hath here shone with unrivalled lustre on the former, hath yielded no comfort to the latter, but to them hath proved a pillar of darkness, whilst it hath conducted the former to the most enviable state of human existence. Whilst we were offering up vows at the shrine of liberty, and sacrificing hecatombs upon her altars; whilst we swore irreconcileable hostility to her enemies, and hurled defiance in their faces; whilst we adjured the God of Hosts to witness our resolution to live free, or die, and imprecated curses on their heads who refused to unite with us in establishing the empire of freedom; we were imposing upon our fellow men; who differ in complexion from us, a *slavery*, ten thousand times more cruel than the utmost extremity of those grievances and oppressions, of which we complained. Such are the inconsistencies of human nature; such the blindness of those who pluck not the beam out of their own eyes, whilst they can espy a moat, in the eyes of their brother; such that partial system of morality which confines rights and injuries, to particular complexions; such the effect of that self-love which justifies, or condemns, not according to principle, but to the agent. Had we turned our eyes inwardly when we supplicated the Father of Mercies to aid the injured and oppressed; when we invoked the Author of Righteousness to attest the purity of our motives, and the justice of our cause*; and implored the God of Battles to aid our exertions in it's defence, should we not have stood more self convicted than the contrite publican! Should we not have left our gift upon the altar, that we might be first reconciled to our brethren whom we held in bondage? should we not have loosed their chains, and broken their fetters? Or if the difficulties and dangers of such an experiment prohibited the attempt during the convulsions of a revolution, is it not our duty to embrace the first moment of constitutional health and vigour, to effectuate so desirable an object, and to remove from us a stigma, with which our enemies will never fail to upbraid us, nor our consciences to reproach us? To form a just estimate of this obligation, to demonstrate the incompatability of a state of slavery with the principles of our government, and of that revolution upon which it is founded, and to elucidate the practicability of it's total, though gradual abolition, it will be proper to consider the nature of slavery, its properties, attendants, and consequences in general; it's rise, progress, and present state, not only in this commonwealth, but in such of our sister states as have either perfected, or commenced the great work of it's extirpation; with the means they have adopted to effect it, and those which the circum-

stances and situation of our country may render it most expedient for us to pursue, for the attainment of the same noble and important end†.

. . . . .

I. When a nation is, from any external cause, deprived of the right of being governed by it's own laws, only, such a nation may be considered as in a state of *political slavery*. Such is the state of conquered countries, and, generally, of colonies, and other dependant governments. Such was the state of united America before the revolution. In this case the personal rights of the subject may be so far secured by wholesome laws, as that the individual may be esteemed free, whilst the state is subject to a higher power: this subjection of one nation, or people, to the will of another, constitutes the first species of slavery, which, in order to distinguish it from the other two, I have called political; inasmuch as it exists only in respect to the governments, and not to the individuals of the two countries. Of this it is not our business to speak, at present.

II. Civil liberty, according to judge Blackstone, being no other than natural liberty so far restrained by human laws, and no farther, as is necessary and expedient for the general advantage of the public, whenever that liberty is, by the laws of the state, further restrained than is necessary and expedient for the general advantage, a state of *civil slavery* commences immediately: this may affect the whole society, and every description of persons in it, and yet the constitution of the state be perfectly free. And this happens whenever the laws of a state respect the form, or energy of the government, more than the happiness of the citizen; as in Venice, where the most oppressive species of civil slavery exists; extending to every individual in the state, from the poorest gondolier to the members of the senate, and the doge himself.

This species of slavery also exists whenever there is an inequality of rights, or privileges, between the subjects or citizens of the same state, except such as necessarily results from the exercise of a public office; for the pre-eminence of one class of men must be founded and erected upon the depression of another; and the measure of exaltation in the former, is that of the slavery of the latter. In all governments, however constituted, or by what description soever denominated, wherever the distinction of rank prevails, or is admitted by the constitution, this species of slavery exists. It existed in every nation, and in every government in Europe before the French revolution. It existed in the American colonies before they became independent states; and notwithstanding the maxims of equality which have been adopted in their several constitutions, it exists in most, if not all, of them, at this day, in the persons of our *free* negroes and mulattoes; whose civil incapacities are almost as numerous as the civil rights of our free citizens.

---

*The American standard, at the commencement of those hostilities which terminated in the revolution, had these words upon it. . . . AN APPEAL TO HEAVEN!

†The Editor [Tucker] here takes the liberty of making his acknowledgments to the reverend Jeremiah Belknap, D. D. of Boston, and to Zephaniah Swift, Esq. representative in Congress from Connecticut, for their obliging communications; he hath occasionally made use of them in several parts of this Lecture, where he may have omitted referring to them.

A brief enumeration of them, may not be improper before we proceed to the third head.

Free negroes and mulattoes are by our constitution excluded from the right of suffrage, and by consequence, I apprehend, from office too: they were formerly incapable of serving in the militia, except as drummers or pioneers, but of late years I presume they were enrolled in the lists of those that bear arms*, though formerly punishable for presuming to appear at a musterfield. During the revolutionary war many of them were enlisted as soldiers in the regular army. Even slaves were not rejected from military service at that period, and such as served faithfully during the period of their enlistment, were emancipated by an act passed after the conclusion of the war. An act of justice to which they were entitled upon every principle. All but housekeepers, and persons residing upon the frontiers, are prohibited from keeping, or carrying any gun, powder, shot, club, or other weapon offensive or defensive: Resistance to a white person, in any case, was, formerly, and now, in any case, except a wanton assault on the negroe or mulattoe, is punishable by whipping. No negroe or mulattoe can be a witness in any prosecution, or civil suit in which a white person is a party. Free negroes, together with slaves, were formerly denied the benefit of clergy in cases where it was allowed to white persons; but they are now upon an equal footing as to the allowance of clergy. Emancipated negroes may be sold to pay the debts of their former master contracted before their emancipation; and they may be hired out to satisfy their taxes where no sufficient distress can be had. Their children are to be bound out apprentices by the overseers of the poor. Free negroes have all the advantages in capital cases, which white men are entitled to, except a trial by a jury of their own complexion: and a slave suing for his freedom shall have the same privilege. Free negroes residing, or employed to labour in any town, must be registered; the same thing is required of such as go at large in any county. The penalty in both cases is a fine upon the person employing, or harbouring them, and imprisonment of the negroe. The migration of free negroes or mulattoes to this state is also prohibited; and those who do migrate hither may be sent back to the place from whence they came. Any person, not being a negroe, having one-fourth or more negroe blood in him, is deemed a mulattoe. The law formerly made no other distinction between negroes and mulattoes, whether slaves or freemen. But now the act of 1796, c. 2, which abolishes the punishment of death, except in case of murder, in all cases where any free person may be convicted, creates a most important distinction in their favour; slaves not being entitled to the same benefit. These incapacities and disabilities are evidently the fruit of the third species of slavery, of which it remains to speak; or, rather, they are scions from the same common stock: which is,

---

*This was the case under the laws of the state; but the act of 2 Cong. c. 33, for establishing an uniform militia throughout the United States, seems to have excluded all but free white men from bearing arms in the militia.

III. That condition in which one man is subject to be directed by another in all his actions, and this constitutes a state of *domestic slavery;* to which state all the incapacities and disabilities of civil slavery are incident, with the weight of other numerous calamities superadded thereto. And here it may be proper to make a short inquiry into the origin and foundation of domestic slavery in other countries, previous to it's fatal introduction into this.

Slaves, says Justinian, are either born such or become so. They are born slaves when they are children of bond women; and they become slaves, either by the law of nations, that is, by captivity; for it is the practice of our generals to sell their captives, being accustomed to preserve, and not to destroy them: or by the civil law, which happens when a free person, above the age of twenty, suffers himself to be sold for the sake of sharing the price given for him. The author of the Commentaries on the Laws of England thus combats the reasonableness of all these grounds: "The conqueror," says he, "according to the civilians, had a right to the life of his captive; and having spared that, has a right to deal with him as he pleases. But it is an untrue position, when taken generally, that by the law of nature or nations, a man may kill his enemy: he has a right to kill him only in particular cases; in cases of absolute necessity for self-defence; and it is plain that this absolute necessity did not subsist, since the victor did not actually kill him, but made him prisoner. War itself is justifiable only on principles of self-preservation; and therefore it gives no other right over prisoners but merely to disable them from doing harm to us, by confining their persons: much less can it give a right to kill, torture, abuse, plunder, or even to enslave, an enemy, when the war is over. Since, therefore, the right of *making* slaves by captivity, depends on a supposed right of slaughter, that foundation failing, the consequence drawn from it must fail likewise. But, secondly, it is said slavery may begin *jure civili;* when one man sells himself to another. This, if only meant of contracts to serve, or work for, another, is very just: but when applied to strict slavery, in the sense of the laws of old Rome or modern Barbary, is also impossible. Every sale implies a price, a *quid pro quo,* an equivalent given to the seller, in lieu of what he transfers to the buyer; but what equivalent can be given for life and liberty, both of which, in absolute slavery, are held to be in the master's disposal? His property, also, the very price he seems to receive, devolves, *ipso facto,* to his master, the instant he becomes a slave. In this case, therefore, the buyer gives nothing, and the seller receives nothing: of what validity then can a sale be, which destroys the very principles upon which all sales are founded? Lastly we are told, that besides these two ways by which slaves are acquired, they may also be hereditary; 'servi nascuntur;' the children of acquired slaves are, 'jure naturae,' by a negative kind of birthright, slaves also. . . . But *this, being built on the two former rights,* must *fall* together with them. If neither captivity, nor the sale of one's self, can by the law of nature and reason reduce the parent to slavery, *much less* can they reduce the offspring." Thus by the most clear, manly, and convincing reasoning does this excellent author refute every claim, upon which the practice of slavery is founded, or by which it has been supposed to be justified, at least, in modern times*. But were we even to admit, that a captive taken in a *just war,* might by his conqueror be reduced to a state of slavery, this could not justify the claim of Europeans to reduce the natives of Africa to that state: it is a melancholy, though well-known fact, that in order to furnish supplies of these unhappy people for the purposes of the slave trade, the Europeans have constantly, by the most insidious (I had almost said infernal) arts, fomented a kind of perpetual warfare among the ignorant and miserable people of Africa; and instances have not been wanting, where, by the most shameful breach of faith, they have trepanned and made slaves of the *sellers* as well as the *sold.* That such horrid practices have been sanctioned by a civilized nation; that a nation ardent in the cause of liberty, and enjoying it's blessings in the fullest extent, can continue to vindicate a right established upon such a foundation; that a people who have declared, "That *all men* are by nature *equally free* and *independent,*" and have made this declaration the first article in the foundation of their government, should in defiance of so sacred a truth, recognized by themselves in so solemn a manner, and on so important an occasion, tolerate a practice incompatible therewith, is such an evidence of the weakness and inconsistency of human nature, as every man who hath a spark of patriotic fire in his bosom must wish to see removed from his own country. If ever there was a cause, if ever an occasion, in which all hearts should be united, every nerve strained, and every power exerted, surely the restoration of human nature to it's unalienable right, is such. Whatever obstacles, therefore, may hitherto have retarded the attempt, he that can appreciate the honour and happiness of his country, will think it time that we should attempt to surmount them.

. . . . .

Civil, or rather social rights, we may remember, are reducible to three primary heads; the right of personal security; the right of personal liberty; and the right of private property. In a state of slavery the two last are wholly abolished, the person of the slave being at the absolute disposal of his master; and property, what he is incapable, in that state, either of acquiring, or holding, to his own use. Hence it will appear how perfectly irreconcilable a state of slavery is to the principles of a democracy, which, form the *basis* and *foundation* of our government. For our bill of rights, declares, "that all men are, by nature *equally free,* and independent, and have certain rights of which they cannot deprive or divest their posterity . . . namely, the enjoyment of life and *liberty,* with the means of *acquiring* and *possessing property.*" This is, indeed, no more than a recognition of the first principles of the law of nature, which teaches us this equality, and enjoins every man, whatever advantages he may possess over another, as to the various qualities or endowments of body or mind, to

*These arguments are, in fact, borrowed from the Spirit of Laws. Lib. xv. c. 2.

practise the precepts of the law of nature to those who are in these respects his *inferiors,* no less than it enjoins his *inferiors* to practise them towards *him.* Since he has no more right to insult *them,* than they have to injure him. Nor does the *bare unkindness of nature,* or of fortune condemn a man to a *worse* condition than others, as to the enjoyment of common privileges. It would be hard to reconcile reducing the negroes to a state of slavery to these principles, unless we first degrade them below the rank of human beings, not only politically, but also physically and morally. . . . The Roman lawyers look upon those only properly as *persons,* who are *free,* putting *slaves* into the rank of *goods* and *chattels;* and the policy of our legislature, as well as the practise of slave-holders in America in general, seems conformable to that idea: but surely it is time we should admit the evidence of moral truth, and learn to regard them as our fellow men, and equals, except in those particulars where accident, or possibly nature, may have given us some advantage; a recompence, for which they, perhaps, enjoy in other respects.

. . . . .

The extirpation of slavery from the United States, is a task equally arduous and momentous. To restore the blessings of liberty to near a million of oppressed individuals, who have groaned under the yoke of bondage, and to their descendants, is an object, which those who trust in Providence, will be convinced would not be unaided by the Divine Author of our being, should we invoke his blessing upon our endeavours. Yet human prudence forbids that we should precipitately engage in a work of such hazard as a general and simultaneous emancipation. The mind of a man must in some measure be formed for his future condition. The early impressions of obedience and submission, which slaves have received among us, and the no less habitual arrogance and assumption of superiority, among the whites, contribute, equally, to unfit the former for *freedom,* and the latter for *equality.*

. . . . .

"But why not retain and *"incorporate the blacks into the state?"* This question has been well answered by Mr. Jefferson, and who is there so free from prejudices among us, as candidly to declare that he has none against such a measure? The recent scenes transacted in the French colonies in the West Indies are enough to make one shudder with the apprehension of realizing similar calamities in this country. Such probably would be the event of an attempt to smother those prejudices which have been cherished for a period of almost two centuries. Many persons who regret domestic slavery, contend that in abolishing it, we must also abolish that scion from it, which I have denominated *civil* slavery. That there must be no distinction of rights; that the descendants of Africans, as men, have an equal claim to all civil rights, as the descendants of Europeans; and upon being delivered from the yoke of bondage have a right to be admitted to all the privileges of a citizen. . . . But have not men when they enter into a state of society, a right to admit, or exclude any description of persons, as they think proper? If it be true, as Mr. Jefferson seems to suppose, that the Africans are really an inferior race of mankind*, will not sound policy advise their exclusion from a society in which they have not yet been admitted to participate in civil rights; and even to guard against such admission, at any future period, since it may eventually depreciate the whole national character? And if prejudices have taken such deep root in our minds, as to render it impossible to eradicate this opinion, ought not so general an error, if it be one, to be respected? Shall we not relieve the necessities of the naked diseased beggar, unless we will invite him to a seat at our table; nor afford him shelter from the inclemencies of the night air, unless we admit him also to share our bed! To deny that we ought to abolish slavery, without incorporating the Negroes into the state, and admitting them to a full participation of all our civil and social rights, appears to me to rest upon a similar foundation. The experiment so far as it has been already made among us, proves that the emancipated blacks are not ambitious of civil rights. To prevent the generation of such an ambition, appears to comport with sound policy; for if it should ever rear its head, its partizans, as well as its opponents, will be enlisted by nature herself, and always ranged in formidable array against each other. We must therefore endeavour to find some middle course, between the tyrannical and iniquitous policy which holds so many human creatures in a state of grievous bondage, and that which would turn loose a numerous, starving, and enraged banditti, upon the innocent descendants of their former oppressors. *Nature, time* and *sound policy* must cooperate with each other to produce such a change: if either be neglected, the work will be incomplete, dangerous, and not improbably destructive.

The plan therefore which I would presume to propose for the consideration of my countrymen is such, as the number of slaves, the difference of their nature, and habits, and the state of agriculture, among us, might render it *expedient*, rather than *desirable* to adopt: and would partake partly of that proposed by Mr. Jefferson, and adopted in other states; and partly of such cautionary restrictions, as a due regard to situation and circumstances, and even to *general* prejudices, might recommend to those, who engage in so arduous, and perhaps unprecedented an undertaking.

1. Let every female born after the adoption of the plan, be free, and transmit freedom to all the descendants, both male and female.

2. As a compensation to those persons, in whose families such females, or their descendants may be born, for the expence and trouble of their maintenance during infancy, let them serve such persons until the age of twenty-eight years: let them then receive twenty dollars in money, two suits of clothes, suited to the season, a hat, a pair of shoes, and two blankets. If these things be not voluntarily

done, let the county courts enforce the performance, upon complaint.

3. Let all negroe children be registered with the clerk of the county or corporation court, where born, within one month after their birth: let the person in whose family they are born, take a copy of the register, and deliver it to the mother, or if she die, to the child, before it is of the age of twenty-one years. Let any negro claiming to be free, and above the age of puberity, be considered as of the age of twenty-eight years, if he or she be not registered as required.

4. Let all the negro servants be put on the same footing as white servants and apprentices now are, in respect to food, raiment, correction, and the assignment of their service from one to another.

5. Let the children of negroes and mulattoes, born in the families of their parents, be bound to service by the overseers of the poor, until they shall attain the age of twenty-one years. Let all above that age, who are not house-keepers, nor have voluntarily bound themselves to service for a year before the first day of February annually, be then bound for the remainder of the year by the overseers of the poor. To stimulate the overseers of the poor to perform their duty, let them receive fifteen per cent. of their wages, from the person hiring them, as a compensation for their trouble, and ten per cent. per annum out of the wages of such as they may bind apprentices.

6. If at the age of twenty-seven years, the master of a negro or mulattoe servant be unwilling to pay his freedom dues, above mentioned, at the expiration of the succeeding year, let him bring him into the county court, clad and furnished with necessaries as before directed, and pay into court five dollars, for the servant, and thereupon let the court direct him to be hired by the overseers of the poor for the succeeding year, in the manner before directed.

7. Let no negro or mulatto be capable of taking, holding, or exercising, any public office, freehold, franchise, or privilege†, or any estate in lands or tenements, other than a lease not exceeding twenty-one years. . . . Nor of keeping, or bearing arms‡, unless authorised so to do by some act of the general assembly, whose duration shall be limited to three years. Nor of contracting matrimony with any other than a negroe or mulattoe; nor be an attorney; nor be a juror; nor a witness in any court of judicature, except against, or between negroes and mulattoes. Nor be an executor or administrator; nor capable of making any will or testament; nor maintain any real action; nor be a trustee of lands or tenements himself, nor any other person to be a trustee to him or to his use.

8. Let all persons born after the passing of the act, be considered as entitled to the same mode of trial in criminal cases, as free negroes and mulattoes are now entitled to.

The restrictions in this plan may appear to savour strongly of prejudice: whoever proposes any plan for the

---

*The celebrated David Hume, in his Essay on National Character, advances the same opinion; Doctor Beattie, in his Essay on Truth, controverts it with many powerful arguments. Early prejudices, had we more satisfactory information than we can possibly possess on the subject at present, would render an inhabitant of a country where negroe slavery prevails, an improper umpire between them.

†The Romans, before the time of Justinian, adopted a similar policy, in respect to their freed-men. Gibbon, vol. 1, 58.

‡See Spirit of Laws, 12, 15, 1. Blackst. Com. 417.

abolition of slavery must either encounter, or accommodate himself, to prejudice. . . . I have preferred the latter; not that I pretend to be wholly exempt from it, but that I might avoid as many obstacles as possible to the completion of so desirable a work, as the abolition of slavery*. Though I am opposed to the banishment of the negroes, I wish not to encourage their future residence among us. By denying them the most valuable privileges which civil government affords, I wish to render it their inclination and their interest to seek those privileges in some other climate. There is an immense unsettled territory on this continent† more congenial to their natural constitutions than ours, where they may perhaps be received upon more favourable terms than we can permit them to remain with us. Emigrating in small numbers, they will be able to effect settlements more easily than in large numbers; and without the expence or danger of numerous colonies. By releasing them from the yoke of bondage, and enabling them to seek happiness wherever they can hope to find it, we surely confer a benefit, which no one can sufficiently appreciate, who has not tasted of the bitter curse of compulsory servitude. By excluding them from offices, we may hope that the seeds of ambition would be buried too deep, ever to germinate: by disarming them, we may calm our apprehensions of their resentments arising from past sufferings; by incapacitating them from holding lands, we should add one inducement more to emigration, and effectually remove the foundation of ambition, and party-struggles. Their personal rights, and their property, though limited, would, whilst they remain among us, be under the protection of the laws; and their condition not at all inferior to that of the *labouring* poor in most other countries. Under such an arrangement we might reasonably hope, that time would either remove from us a race of men, whom we wish not to incorporate with us, or obliterate those prejudices, which now form an obstacle to such incorporation.

But it is not from the want of liberality to the emancipated race of blacks that I apprehend the most serious objections to the plan I have ventured to suggest. . . . Those slave holders (whose numbers I trust are few) who have been in the habit of considering their fellow creatures as no more than cattle, and the rest of the brute creation, will exclaim that they are to be deprived of their *property*, without compensation. Men who will shut their ears against this moral truth, that all men are by nature *free*, and *equal*, will not even be convinced that they do not possess

*If, upon experiment, it should appear advisable to hasten the operation of this plan, or to enlarge the privileges of free negroes, it will be both easier, and safer so to do, than to retrench any privilege once granted, or to retard the operation of the original plan, after it has been adopted, and in part carried into execution.

†The immense territory of Louisiana, which extends as far south as the lat. 25° and the two Floridas, would probably afford a ready asylum for such as might choose to become Spanish subjects. How far their political rights might be enlarged in these countries, is, however, questionable: but the climate is undoubtedly more favourable to the African constitution, than ours, and from this cause it is not improbable that emigrations from these states would in time be very considerable.

a *property* in an *unborn* child: they will not distinguish between allowing to *unborn* generations the absolute and unalienable rights of human nature, and taking away that which they *now possess;* they will shut their ears against truth, should you tell them, the loss of the mother's labour for nine months, and the maintenance of a child for a dozen or fourteen years, is amply compensated by the service of that child for as many years more, as he has been an expence to them. But if the voice of reason, justice, and humanity, be not stifled by sordid avarice, or unfeeling tyranny, it would be easy to convince even those who have entertained such erroneous notions, that the right of one man over another is neither founded in nature, nor in sound policy. That it cannot extend to those *not in being;* that no man can in reality be *deprived* of what he doth not possess: that fourteen years labour by a young person in the prime of life, is an ample compensation for a few months of labour lost by the mother, and for the maintenance of a child, in that coarse homely manner that negroes are brought up: and lastly, that a state of slavery is not only perfectly incompatible with the principles of government, but with the safety and security of their masters. History evinces this. At this moment we have the most awful demonstrations of it. Shall we then neglect a duty, which every consideration, moral, religious, political, or *selfish,* recommends? Those who wish to postpone the measure, do not reflect that every day renders the task more arduous to be performed. We have now 300,000 slaves among us. Thirty years hence we shall have double the number. In sixty years we shall have 1,200,000: and in less than another century from this day, even that enormous number will be doubled. Milo acquired strength enough to carry an ox, by beginning with the ox while he was yet a calf. If we complain that the calf is too heavy for our shoulders, what will the ox be?

57

JOHN ADAMS TO GEORGE CHURCHMAN
AND JACOB LINDLEY
24 Jan. 1801
Works 9:92–93

Although I have never sought popularity by any animated speeches or inflammatory publications against the slavery of the blacks, my opinion against it has always been known, and my practice has been so conformable to my sentiments that I have always employed freemen, both as domestics and laborers, and never in my life did I own a slave. The abolition of slavery must be gradual, and accomplished with much caution and circumspection. Violent means and measures would produce greater violations of justice and humanity than the continuance of the practice. Neither Mr. Mifflin nor yourselves, I presume, would be willing to venture on exertions which would probably excite insurrections among the blacks to rise against their masters, and imbue their hands in innocent blood.

There are many other evils in our country which are growing (whereas the practice of slavery is fast diminishing), and threaten to bring punishment on our land more immediately than the oppression of the blacks. That sacred regard to truth in which you and I were educated, and which is certainly taught and enjoined from on high, seems to be vanishing from among us. A general relaxation of education and government, a general debauchery as well as dissipation, produced by pestilential philosophical principles of Epicurus, infinitely more than by shows and theatrical entertainments; these are, in my opinion, more serious and threatening evils than even the slavery of the blacks, hateful as that is. I might even add that I have been informed that the condition of the common sort of white people in some of the Southern States, particularly Virginia, is more oppressed, degraded, and miserable, than that of the negroes. These vices and these miseries deserve the serious and compassionate consideration of friends, as well as the slave trade and the degraded state of the blacks. I wish you success in your benevolent endeavors to relieve the distresses of our fellow creatures, and shall always be ready to coöperate with you as far as my means and opportunities can reasonably be expected to extend.

58

JOHN ADAMS TO THOMAS JEFFERSON
9 July 1813
Cappon 2:352

Your "ἄριστοι" [aristocrats] are the most difficult Animals to manage, of anything in the whole Theory and practice of Government. They will not suffer themselves to be governed. They not only exert all their own Subtilty Industry and courage, but they employ the Commonalty, to knock to pieces every Plan and Model that the most honest Architects in Legislation can invent to keep them within bounds. Both Patricians and Plebeians are as furious as the Workmen in England to demolish labour-saving Machinery.

But who are these "ἄριστοι"? Who shall judge? Who shall select these choice Spirits from the rest of the Congregation? Themselves? We must first find out and determine who themselves are. Shall the congregation choose? Ask Xenophon. Perhaps hereafter I may quote you Greek. Too much in a hurry at present, english must suffice. Xenophon says that the ecclesia, always chooses the worst Men they can find, because none others will do their dirty work. This wicked Motive is worse than Birth or Wealth. Here I want to quote Greek again. But the day before I received your Letter of June 27. I gave the Book to George Washington Adams going to the Accadamy at Hingham. The

Title is ΗΘΙΚΗ ΠΟΙΗΣΙΣ a Collection of Moral Sentences from all the most Ancien[t] Greek Poets. In one of the oldest of them I read in greek that I cannot repeat, a couplet the Sense of which was

"Nobility in Men is worth as much as it is in Horses Asses or Rams: but the meanest blooded Puppy, in the World, if he gets a little money, is as good a man as the best of them." Yet Birth and Wealth together have prevailed over Virtue and Talents in all ages. The Many, will acknowledge no other "ἄριστοι". Your Experience of This Truth, will not much differ from that of your old Friend

59

JOHN ADAMS TO THOMAS JEFFERSON
13 July 1813
Cappon 2:354–55

The first time, that you and I differed in Opinion on any material Question; was after your Arrival from Europe; and that point was the french Revolution.

You was well persuaded in your own mind that the Nation would succeed in establishing a free Republican Government: I was as well persuaded, in mine, that a project of such a Government, over five and twenty millions people, when four and twenty millions and five hundred thousands of them could neither write nor read: was as unnatural irrational and impracticable; as it would be over the Elephants Lions Tigers Panthers Wolves and Bears in the Royal Menagerie, at Versailles. Napoleon has lately invented a Word, which perfectly expresses my Opinion at that time and ever since. He calls the Project Ideology. And John Randolph, tho he was 14 years ago, as wild an Enthusiast for Equality and Fraternity, as any of them; appears to be now a regenerated Proselite to Napoleons Opinion and mine, that it was all madness.

The Greeks in their Allegorical Style said that the two Ladies Αριστοκρατια [Aristocracy] and δημοκ[ρ]ατια [democracy], always in a quarrel, disturbed every neighbourhood with their brawls. It is a fine Observation of yours that "Whig and Torey belong to Natural History." Inequalities of Mind and Body are so established by God Almighty in his constitution of Human Nature that no Art or policy can ever plain them down to a Level. I have never read Reasoning more absurd, Sophistry more gross, in proof of the Athanasian Creed, or Transubstantiation, than the subtle labours of Helvetius and Rousseau to demonstrate the natural Equality of Mankind. Jus cuique [Justice for everyone]; the golden rule; do as you would be done by; is all the Equality that can be supported or defended by reason, or reconciled to common Sense.

60

JOHN ADAMS TO THOMAS JEFFERSON
2 Sept. 1813
Cappon 2:371–72

Now, my Friend, who are the ἄριστοι [aristocrats]? Philosophy may Answer "The Wise and Good." But the World, Mankind, have by their practice always answered, "the rich the beautiful and well born." And Philosophers themselves in marrying their Children prefer the rich the handsome and the well descended to the wise and good.

What chance have Talents and Virtues in competition, with Wealth and Birth? and Beauty?

> Haud facile emergunt, quorum Virtutibus obstant [i.e., obstat] Res Angusta Domi.

> One truth is clear,; by all the World confess'd
> Slow rises worth, by Poverty oppress'd.

The five Pillars of Aristocracy, are Beauty Wealth, Birth, Genius and Virtues. Any one of the three first, can at any time over bear any one or both of the two last.

Let me ask again, what a Wave of publick Opinion, in favour of Birth has been spread over the Globe, by Abraham, by Hercules, by Mahomet, by Guelphs, Ghibellines, Bourbons, and a miserable Scottish Chief Steuart? By Zingis by, by, by, a million others? And what a Wave will be spread by Napoleon and by Washington? Their remotest Cousins will be sought and will be proud, and will avail themselves of their descent. Call this Principle, Prejudice, Folly Ignorance, Baseness, Slavery, Stupidity, Adulation, Superstition or what you will. I will not contradict you. But the Fact, in natural, moral, political and domestic History I cannot deny or dispute or question.

And is this great Fact in the natural History of Man? This unalterable Principle of Morals, Philosophy, Policy domestic felicity, and dayly Experience from the Creation; to be overlooked, forgotten neglected, or hypocritically waived out of Sight; by a Legislator? By a professed Writer upon civil Government, and upon Constitutions of civil Government?

. . . . .

You may laugh at the introduction of Beauty, among the Pillars of Aristocracy. But Madame Barry says Le veritable Royauté est la B[e]autee [true royalty is beauty], and there is not a more certain Truth. Beauty, Grace, Figure, Attitude, Movement, have in innumerable Instances prevailed over Wealth, Birth, Talents Virtues and every thing else, in Men of the highest rank, greatest Power, and sometimes, the most exalted Genius, greatest Fame, and highest Merit.

61

THOMAS JEFFERSON TO JOHN ADAMS
28 Oct. 1813
Cappon 2:387–92

According to the reservation between us, of taking up one of the subjects of our correspondence at a time, I turn to your letters of Aug. 16. and Sep. 2.

The passage you quote from Theognis, I think has an Ethical, rather than a political object. The whole piece is a moral *exhortation*, παραίνεσις, and this passage particularly seems to be a reproof to man, who, while with his domestic animals he is curious to improve the race by employing always the finest male, pays no attention to the improvement of his own race, but intermarries with the vicious, the ugly, or the old, for considerations of wealth or ambition. It is in conformity with the principle adopted afterwards by the Pythagoreans, and expressed by Ocellus in another form. Περι δε τῆς ἐκ τῶν αλληλων ανθρωπων γενεσεως etc.—ουχ ἡδονης ἑνεκα ἡ μιξις. Which, as literally as intelligibility will admit, may be thus translated. "Concerning the interprocreation of men, how, and of whom it shall be, in a perfect manner, and according to the laws of modesty and sanctity, conjointly, this is what I think right. First to lay it down that we do not commix for the sake of pleasure, but of the procreation of children. For the powers, the organs and desires for coition have not been given by god to man for the sake of pleasure, but for the procreation of the race. For as it were incongruous for a mortal born to partake of divine life, the immortality of the race being taken away, god fulfilled the purpose by making the generations uninterrupted and continuous. This therefore we are especially to lay down as a principle, that coition is not for the sake of pleasure." But Nature, not trusting to this moral and abstract motive, seems to have provided more securely for the perpetuation of the species by making it the effect of the oestrum implanted in the constitution of both sexes. And not only has the commerce of love been indulged on this unhallowed impulse, but made subservient also to wealth and ambition by marriages without regard to the beauty, the healthiness, the understanding, or virtue of the subject from which we are to breed. The selecting the best male for a Haram of well chosen females also, which Theognis seems to recommend from the example of our sheep and asses, would doubtless improve the human, as it does the brute animal, and produce a race of veritable αριστοι [aristocrats]. For experience proves that the moral and physical qualities of man, whether good or evil, are transmissible in a certain degree from father to son. But I suspect that the equal rights of men will rise up against this privileged Solomon, and oblige us to continue acquiescence under the Ἀμαυρωσις γενεος ἀστων [the degeneration of the race of men] which Theognis complains of, and to content ourselves with the accidental aristoi produced by the fortuitous concourse of breeders. For I agree with you that there is a natural aristocracy among men. The grounds of this are virtue and talents. Formerly bodily powers gave place among the aristoi. But since the invention of gunpowder has armed the weak as well as the strong with missile death, bodily strength, like beauty, good humor, politeness and other accomplishments, has become but an auxiliary ground of distinction. There is also an artificial aristocracy founded on wealth and birth, without either virtue or talents; for with these it would belong to the first class. The natural aristocracy I consider as the most precious gift of nature for the instruction, the trusts, and government of society. And indeed it would have been inconsistent in creation to have formed man for the social state, and not to have provided virtue and wisdom enough to manage the concerns of the society. May we not even say that that form of government is the best which provides the most effectually for a pure selection of these natural aristoi into the offices of government? The artificial aristocracy is a mischievous ingredient in government, and provision should be made to prevent it's ascendancy. On the question, What is the best provision, you and I differ; but we differ as rational friends, using the free exercise of our own reason, and mutually indulging it's errors. *You* think it best to put the Pseudo-aristoi into a separate chamber of legislation where they may be hindered from doing mischief by their coordinate branches, and where also they may be a protection to wealth against the Agrarian and plundering enterprises of the Majority of the people. I think that to give them power in order to prevent them from doing mischief, is arming them for it, and increasing instead of remedying the evil. For if the coordinate branches can arrest their action, so may they that of the coordinates. Mischief may be done negatively as well as positively. Of this a cabal in the Senate of the U. S. has furnished many proofs. Nor do I believe them necessary to protect the wealthy; because enough of these will find their way into every branch of the legislation to protect themselves. From 15. to 20. legislatures of our own, in action for 30. years past, have proved that no fears of an equalisation of property are to be apprehended from them.

I think the best remedy is exactly that provided by all our constitutions, to leave to the citizens the free election and separation of the aristoi from the pseudo-aristoi, of the wheat from the chaff. In general they will elect the real good and wise. In some instances, wealth may corrupt, and birth blind them; but not in sufficient degree to endanger the society.

It is probable that our difference of opinion may in some measure be produced by a difference of character in those among whom we live. From what I have seen of Massachusets and Connecticut myself, and still more from what I have heard, and the character given of the former by yourself, who know them so much better, there seems to be in those two states a traditionary reverence for certain families, which has rendered the offices of the government nearly hereditary in those families. I presume that from an early period of your history, members of these families happening to possess virtue and talents, have hon-

estly exercised them for the good of the people, and by their services have endeared their names to them.

In coupling Connecticut with you, I mean it politically only, not morally. For having made the Bible the Common law of their land they seem to have modelled their morality on the story of Jacob and Laban. But altho' this hereditary succession to office with you may in some degree be founded in real family merit, yet in a much higher degree it has proceeded from your strict alliance of church and state. These families are canonised in the eyes of the people on the common principle "you tickle me, and I will tickle you." In Virginia we have nothing of this. Our clergy, before the revolution, having been secured against rivalship by fixed salaries, did not give themselves the trouble of acquiring influence over the people. Of wealth, there were great accumulations in particular families, handed down from generation to generation under the English law of entails. But the only object of ambition for the wealthy was a seat in the king's council. All their court then was paid to the crown and it's creatures; and they Philipised in all collisions between the king and people. Hence they were unpopular; and that unpopularity continues attached to their names. A Randolph, a Carter, or a Burwell must have great personal superiority over a common competitor to be elected by the people, even at this day.

At the first session of our legislature after the Declaration of Independence, we passed a law abolishing entails. And this was followed by one abolishing the privilege of Primogeniture, and dividing the lands of intestates equally among all their children, or other representatives. These laws, drawn by myself, laid the axe to the root of Pseudo-aristocracy. And had another which I prepared been adopted by the legislature, our work would have been compleat. It was a Bill for the more general diffusion of learning. This proposed to divide every county into wards of 5. or 6. miles square, like your townships; to establish in each ward a free school for reading, writing and common arithmetic; to provide for the annual selection of the best subjects from these schools who might receive at the public expense a higher degree of education at a district school; and from these district schools to select a certain number of the most promising subjects to be compleated at an University, where all the useful sciences should be taught. Worth and genius would thus have been sought out from every condition of life, and compleatly prepared by education for defeating the competition of wealth and birth for public trusts.

My proposition had for a further object to impart to these wards those portions of self-government for which they are best qualified, by confiding to them the care of their poor, their roads, police, elections, the nomination of jurors, administration of justice in small cases, elementary exercises of militia, in short, to have made them little republics, with a Warden at the head of each, for all those concerns which, being under their eye, they would better manage than the larger republics of the county or state. A general call of ward-meetings by their Wardens on the same day thro' the state would at any time produce the genuine sense of the people on any required point, and would enable the state to act in mass, as your people have so often done, and with so much effect, by their town meetings. The law for religious freedom, which made a part of this system, having put down the aristocracy of the clergy, and restored to the citizen the freedom of the mind, and those of entails and descents nurturing an equality of condition among them, this on Education would have raised the mass of the people to the high ground of moral respectability necessary to their own safety, and to orderly government; and would have compleated the great object of qualifying them to select the veritable aristoi, for the trusts of government, to the exclusion of the Pseudalists: and the same Theognis who has furnished the epigraphs of your two letters assures us that "ουδεμιαν πω, Κυρν' αγαθοι πολιν ωλεσαν ανδρες" ["Curnis, good men have never harmed any city"]. Altho' this law has not yet been acted on but in a small and inefficient degree, it is still considered as before the legislature, with other bills of the revised code, not yet taken up, and I have great hope that some patriotic spirit will, at a favorable moment, call it up, and make it the key-stone of the arch of our government.

With respect to Aristocracy, we should further consider that, before the establishment of the American states, nothing was known to History but the Man of the old world, crouded within limits either small or overcharged, and steeped in the vices which that situation generates. A government adapted to such men would be one thing; but a very different one that for the Man of these states. Here every one may have land to labor for himself if he chuses; or, preferring the exercise of any other industry, may exact for it such compensation as not only to afford a comfortable subsistence, but wherewith to provide for a cessation from labor in old age. Every one, by his property, or by his satisfactory situation, is interested in the support of law and order. And such men may safely and advantageously reserve to themselves a wholsome controul over their public affairs, and a degree of freedom, which in the hands of the Canaille of the cities of Europe, would be instantly perverted to the demolition and destruction of every thing public and private. The history of the last 25. years of France, and of the last 40. years in America, nay of it's last 200. years, proves the truth of both parts of this observation.

But even in Europe a change has sensibly taken place in the mind of Man. Science had liberated the ideas of those who read and reflect, and the American example had kindled feelings of right in the people. An insurrection has consequently begun, of science, talents and courage against rank and birth, which have fallen into contempt. It has failed in it's first effort, because the mobs of the cities, the instrument used for it's accomplishment, debased by ignorance, poverty and vice, could not be restrained to rational action. But the world will recover from the panic of this first catastrophe. Science is progressive, and talents and enterprize on the alert. Resort may be had to the people of the country, a more governable power from their principles and subordination; and rank, and birth, and tinsel-aristocracy will finally shrink into insignificance,

even there. This however we have no right to meddle with. It suffices for us, if the moral and physical condition of our own citizens qualifies them to select the able and good for the direction of their government, with a recurrence of elections at such short periods as will enable them to displace an unfaithful servant before the mischief he meditates may be irremediable.

I have thus stated my opinion on a point on which we differ, not with a view to controversy, for we are both too old to change opinions which are the result of a long life of inquiry and reflection; but on the suggestion of a former letter of yours, that we ought not to die before we have explained ourselves to each other. We acted in perfect harmony thro' a long and perilous contest for our liberty and independance. A constitution has been acquired which, tho neither of us think perfect, yet both consider as competent to render our fellow-citizens the happiest and the securest on whom the sun has ever shone. If we do not think exactly alike as to it's imperfections, it matters little to our country which, after devoting to it long lives of disinterested labor, we have delivered over to our successors in life, who will be able to take care of it, and of themselves.

62

John Adams to Thomas Jefferson
15 Nov. 1813
Cappon 2:397–402

We are now explicitly agreed, in one important point, vizt. That "there is a natural Aristocracy among men; the grounds of which are Virtue and Talents."

You very justly indulge a little merriment upon this solemn subject of Aristocracy. I often laugh at it too, for there is nothing in this laughable world more ridiculous than the management of it by almost all the nations of the Earth. But while We smile, Mankind have reason to say to Us, as the froggs said to the Boys, What is Sport to you is Wounds and death to Us. When I consider the weakness, the folly, the Pride, the Vanity, the Selfishness, the Artifice, the low craft and meaning cunning, the want of Principle, the Avarice the unbounded Ambition, the unfeeling Cruelty of a majority of those (in all Nations) who are allowed an aristocratical influence; and on the other hand, the Stupidity with which the more numerous multitude, not only become their Dupes, but even love to be Taken in by their Tricks: I feel a stronger disposition to weep at their destiny, than to laugh at their Folly.

But tho' We have agreed in one point, in Words, it is not yet certain that We are perfectly agreed in Sense. Fashion has introduced an indeterminate Use of the Word "Talents." Education, Wealth, Strength, Beauty, Stature, Birth, Marriage, graceful Attitudes and Motions, Gait, Air, Complexion, Physiognomy, are Talents, as well as Genius and Science and learning. Any one of these Talents, that in fact commands or influences true Votes in Society, gives to the Man who possesses it, the Character of an Aristocrat, in my Sense of the Word.

Pick up, the first 100 men you meet, and make a Republick. Every Man will have an equal Vote. But when deliberations and discussions are opened it will be found that 25, by their Talents, Virtues being equal, will be able to carry 50 Votes. Every one of these 25, is an Aristocrat, in my Sense of the Word; whether he obtains his one Vote in Addition to his own, by his Birth Fortune, Figure, Eloquence, Science, learning, Craft Cunning, or even his Character for good fellowship and a bon vivant.

What gave Sir William Wallace his amazing Aristocratical Superiority? His Strength. What gave Mrs. Clark, her Aristocratical Influence to create Generals Admirals and Bishops? her Beauty. What gave Pompadour and Du Barry the Power of making Cardinals and Popes? their Beauty. You have seen the Palaces of Pompadour and Du Barry: and I have lived for years in the Hotel de Velentinois, with Franklin who had as many Virtues as any of them. In the investigation of the meaning of the Word "Talents" I could write 630 Pages, as pertinent as John Taylors of Hazelwood. But I will select a single Example: for female Aristocrats are nearly as formidable in Society as male.

A daughter of a green Grocer, walks the Streets in London dayly with a baskett of Cabbage, Sprouts, Dandlions and Spinage on her head. She is observed by the Painters to have a beautiful Face, an elegant figure, a graceful Step and a debonair. They hire her to Sitt. She complies, and is painted by forty Artists in a Circle around her. The scientific Sir William Hamilton outbids the Painters, sends her to Schools for a genteel Education and Marries her. This Lady not only causes the Tryumphs of the Nile of Copinhagen and Trafalgar, but separates Naples from France and finally banishes the King and Queen from Sicilly. Such is the Aristocracy of the natural Talent of Beauty. Millions of Examples might be quoted from History sacred and profane, from Eve, Hannah, Deborah Susanna Abigail, Judith, Ruth, down to Hellen Madame de Maintenon and Mrs. Fitcherbert. For mercy's sake do not compell me to look to our chaste States and Territories, to find Women, one of whom lett go, would, in the Words of Holopherne's Guards "deceive the whole Earth."

The Proverbs of Theognis, like those of Solomon, are Observations on human nature, ordinary life, and civil Society, with moral reflections on the facts. I quoted him as a Witness of the Fact, that there was as much difference in the races of Men as in the breeds of Sheep; and as a sharp reprover and censurer of the sordid mercenary practice of disgracing Birth by preferring gold to it. Surely no authority can be more expressly in point to prove the existence of Inequalities, not of rights, but of moral intellectual and physical inqualities in Families, descents and Generations. If a descent from, pious, virtuous, wealthy litterary or scientific Ancestors is a letter of recommendation, or introduction in a Mans his favour, and enables him to influence only one vote in Addition to his own, he is an Aristocrat, for a democrat can have but one Vote.

Aaron Burr had 100,000 Votes from the single Circumstance of his descent from President Burr and President Edwards.

Your commentary on the Proverbs of Theognis reminded me of two solemn Charactors, the one resembling John Bunyan, the other Scarron. The one John Torrey: the other Ben. Franklin. Torrey a Poet, an Enthusiast, a superstitious Bigot, once very gravely asked my Brother Cranch, "whether it would not be better for Mankind, if Children were always begotten from religious motives only"? Would not religion, in this sad case, have as little efficacy in encouraging procreation, as it has now in discouraging it? I should apprehend a decrease of population even in our Country where it increases so rapidly. In 1775 Franklin made a morning Visit, at Mrs. Yards to Sam. Adams and John. He was unusually loquacious. "Man, a rational Creature"! said Franklin. "Come, Let Us suppose a rational Man. Strip him of all his Appetites, especially of his hunger and thirst. He is in his Chamber, engaged in making Experiments, or in pursuing some Problem. He is highly entertained. At this moment a Servant Knocks, "Sir dinner is on Table." "Dinner! Pox! Pough! But what have you for dinner?" Ham and Chickens. "Ham"! "And must I break the chain of my thoughts, to go down and knaw a morsel of damn'd Hogs Arse"? "Put aside your Ham." "I will dine tomorrow."

Take away Appetite and the present generation would not live a month and no future generation would ever exist. Thus the exalted dignity of human Nature would be annihilated and lost. And in my opinion, the whole loss would be of no more importance, than putting out a Candle, quenching a Torch, or crushing a Firefly, *if in this world only We have hope.*

Your distinction between natural and artificial Aristocracy does not appear to me well founded. Birth and Wealth are conferred on some Men, as imperiously by Nature, as Genius, Strength or Beauty. The Heir is honours and Riches, and power has often no more merit in procuring these Advantages, than he has in obtaining an handsome face or an elegant figure. When Aristocracies, are established by human Laws and honour Wealth and Power are made hereditary by municipal Laws and political Institutions, then I acknowledge artificial Aristocracy to commence: but this never commences, till Corruption in Elections becomes dominant and uncontroulable. But this artificial Aristocracy can never last. The everlasting Envys, Jealousies, Rivalries and quarrells among them, their cruel rapacities upon the poor ignorant People their followers, compell these to sett up Caesar, a Demagogue to be a Monarch and Master, pour mettre chacun a sa place [to put each one in his place]. Here you have the origin of all artificial Aristocracy, which is the origin of all Monarchy. And both artificial Aristocracy, and Monarchy, and civil, military, political and hierarchical Despotism, have all grown out of the natural Aristocracy of "Virtues and Talents." We, to be sure, are far remote from this. Many hundred years must roll away before We shall be corrupted. Our pure, virtuous, public spirited federative Republick will last for ever, govern the Globe and introduce the perfection of Man, his perfectability being already proved by Price Priestly, Condorcet Rousseau Diderot and Godwin.

"Mischief has been done by the Senate of U.S." I have known and felt more of this mischief, than Washington, Jefferson and Madison altoge[the]r. But this has been all caused by the constitutional Power of the Senate in Executive Business, which ought to be immediately, totally and eternally abolished.

Your distinction between the aristoi and pseudo aristoi, will not help the matter. I would trust one as soon as the other with unlimited Power. The Law wisely refuses an Oath as a witness in his own cause to the Saint as well as to the Sinner.

No Romance would be more amusing, than the History of your Virginian and our new England Aristocratical Families. Yet even in Rhode Island, where there has been no Clergy, no Church, and I had almost said, no State, and some People say no religion, there has been a constant respect for certain old Families. 57 or 58 years ago, in company with Col. Counsellor, Judge, John Chandler, whom I have quoted before, a Newspaper was brought in. The old Sage asked me to look for the News from Rhode Island and see how the Elections had gone there. I read the List of Wantons, Watsons, Greens, Whipples, Malbones etc. "I expected as much" said the aged Gentleman, "for I have always been of Opinion, that in the most popular Governments, the Elections will generally go in favour of the most ancient families." To this day when any of these Tribes and We may Add Ellerys, Channings Champlins etc are pleased to fall in with the popular current, they are sure to carry all before them.

You suppose a difference of Opinion between You and me, on the Subject of Aristocracy. I can find none. I dislike and detest hereditary honours, Offices Emoluments established by Law. So do you. I am for ex[c]luding legal hereditary distinctions from the U.S. as long as possible. So are you. I only say that Mankind have not yet discovered any remedy against irresistable Corruption in Elections to Offices of great Power and Profit, but making them hereditary.

But will you say our Elections are pure? Be it so; upon the whole. But do you recollect in history, a more Corrupt Election than that of Aaron Burr to be President, or that of De Witt Clinton last year. By corruption, here I mean a sacrifice of every national Interest and honour, to private and party Objects.

I see the same Spirit in Virginia, that you and I see in Rhode Island and the rest of New England. In New York it is a struggle of Family Feuds. A fewdal Aristocracy. Pensylvania is a contest between German, Irish and old English Families. When Germans and Irish Unite, they give 30,000 majorities. There is virtually a White Rose and a Red Rose a Caesar and a Pompey in every State in this Union and Contests and dissentions will be as lasting. The Rivalry of Bourbons and Noailleses produced the French Revolution, and a similar Competition for Consideration and Influence, exists and prevails in every Village in the World.

Where will terminate the Rabies Agri [madness for land]? The Continent will be scattered over with Manors, much larger than Livingstons, Van Ranselaers or Philips's. Even our Deacon Strong will have a Principality among you Southern Folk. What Inequality of Talents will be produced by these Land Jobbers?

Where tends the Mania for Banks? At my Table in Philadelphia, I once proposed to you to unite in endeavours to obtain an Amendment of the Constitution, prohibiting to the separate States the Power of creating Banks; but giving Congress Authority to establish one Bank, with a branch in each State; the whole limited to Ten Millions of dollars. Whether this Project was wise or unwise, I know not, for I had deliberated little on it then and have never thought it worth thinking much of since. But you spurned the Proposition from you with disdain.

This System of Banks begotten, hatched and brooded by Duer, Robert and Governeur Morris, Hamilton and Washington, I have always considered as a System of national Injustice. A Sacrifice of public and private Interest to a few Aristocratical Friends and Favourites. My scheme could have had no such Effect.

Verres plundered Temples and robbed a few rich Men; but he never made such ravages among private property in general, nor swindled so much out of the pocketts of the poor and the middle Class of People as these Banks have done. No people but this would have borne the Imposition so long. The People of Ireland would not bear Woods half pence. What Inequalities of Talent, have been introduced into this Country by these Aristocratical Banks!

Our Winthrops, Winslows, Bradfords, Saltonstalls, Quincys, Chandlers, Leonards Hutchinsons Olivers, Sewalls etc are precisely in the Situation of your Randolphs, Carters and Burwells, and Harrisons. Some of them unpopular for the part they took in the late revolution, but all respected for their names and connections and whenever they fall in with the popular Sentiments, are preferred, cetoris paribus to all others. When I was young, the Summum Bonum in Massachusetts, was to be worth ten thousand pounds Sterling, ride in a Chariot, be Colonel of a Regiment of Militia and hold a seat in his Majesty's Council. No Mans Imagination aspired to any thing higher beneath the Skies. But these Plumbs, Chariots, Colonelships and counsellorships are recorded and will never be forgotten. No great Accumulations of Land were made by our early Settlers. Mr. Bausoin a French Refugee, made the first great Purchases and your General Dearborne, born under a fortunate Starr is now enjoying a large Portion of the Aristocratical sweets of them.

As I have no Amanuenses but females, and there is so much about generation in this letter that I dare not ask any one of them to copy it, and I cannot copy it myself I must beg of you to return it to me, your old Friend

63

JOHN ADAMS TO THOMAS JEFFERSON
16 July 1814

Cappon 2:437–38

After all; as long as Property exists, it will accumulate in Individuals and Families. As long as Marriage exists, Knowledge, Property and Influence will accumulate in Families. Your and our equal Partition of intestate Estates, instead of preventing will in time augment the Evil, if it is one.

The French Revolutionists saw this, and were so far consistent. When they burned Pedigrees and genealogical Trees, they anni[hi]lated, as far as they could, Marriages, knowing that Marriage, among a thousand other things was an infallible Source of Aristocracy. I repeat it, so sure as the Idea and the existence of PROPERTY is admitted and established in Society, Accumulations of it will be made, the Snow ball will grow as it rolls.

64

THOMAS JEFFERSON TO JOSEPH MILLIGAN
6 Apr. 1816

Writings 14:466

Whether property alone, and the whole of what each citizen possesses, shall be subject to contribution, or only its surplus after satisfying his first wants, or whether the faculties of body and mind shall contribute also from their annual earnings, is a question to be decided. But, when decided, and the principle settled, it is to be equally and fairly applied to all. To take from one, because it is thought that his own industry and that of his fathers has acquired too much, in order to spare to others, who, or whose fathers have not exercised equal industry and skill, is to violate arbitrarily the first principle of association, "the *guarantee* to every one of a free exercise of his industry, and the fruits acquired by it." If the overgrown wealth of an individual be deemed dangerous to the State, the best corrective is the law of equal inheritance to all in equal degree; and the better, as this enforces a law of nature, while extra-taxation violates it.

65

JAMES MADISON TO ROBERT J. EVANS
15 June 1819

Writings 8:439–47

I have recd. your letter of the 3d instant, requesting such hints as may have occurred to me on the subject of an eventual extinguishment of slavery in the U. S.

Not doubting the purity of your views, and relying on the discretion by which they will be regulated, I cannot refuse such a compliance as will at least manifest my respect for the object of your undertaking.

A general emancipation of slaves ought to be 1. gradual. 2. equitable & satisfactory to the individuals immediately concerned. 3. consistent with the existing & durable prejudices of the nation.

That it ought, like remedies for other deeprooted and wide-spread evils, to be gradual, is so obvious that there seems to be no difference of opinion on that point.

To be equitable & satisfactory, the consent of both the Master & the slave should be obtained. That of the Master will require a provision in the plan for compensating a loss of what he held as property guarantied by the laws, and recognised by the Constitution. That of the slave, requires that his condition in a state of freedom, be preferable in his own estimation, to his actual one in a state of bondage.

To be consistent with existing and probably unalterable prejudices in the U. S. the freed blacks ought to be permanently removed beyond the region occupied by or allotted to a White population. The objections to a thorough incorporation of the two people are, with most of the Whites insuperable; and are admitted by all of them to be very powerful. If the blacks, strongly marked as they are by Physical & lasting peculiarities, be retained amid the Whites, under the degrading privation of equal rights political or social, they must be always dissatisfied with their condition as a change only from one to another species of oppression; always secretly confederated agst. the ruling & privileged class; and always uncontrouled by some of the most cogent motives to moral and respectable conduct. The character of the free blacks, even where their legal condition is least affected by their colour, seems to put these truths beyond question. It is material also that the removal of the blacks be to a distance precluding the jealousies & hostilities to be apprehended from a neighboring people stimulated by the contempt known to be entertained for their peculiar features; to say nothing of their vindictive recollections, or the predatory propensities which their State of Society might foster. Nor is it fair, in estimating the danger of Collisions with the Whites, to charge it wholly on the side of the Blacks. There would be reciprocal antipathies doubling the danger.

The colonizing plan on foot, has as far as it extends, a due regard to these requisites; with the additional object of bestowing new blessings civil & religious on the quarter of the Globe most in need of them. The Society proposes to transport to the African Coast all free & freed blacks who may be willing to remove thither; to provide by fair means, &, it is understood with a prospect of success, a suitable territory for their reception; and to initiate them into such an establishment as may gradually and indefinitely expand itself.

The experiment, under this view of it, merits encouragement from all who regard slavery as an evil, who wish to see it diminished and abolished by peaceable & just means; and who have themselves no better mode to propose. Those who have most doubted the success of the experiment must at least have wished to find themselves in an error.

But the views of the Society are limited to the case of blacks already free, or who may be *gratuitously* emancipated. To provide a commensurate remedy for the evil, the plan must be extended to the great Mass of blacks, and must embrace a fund sufficient to induce the Master as well as the slave to concur in it. Without the concurrence of the Master, the benefit will be very limited as it relates to the Negroes; and essentially defective, as it relates to the U. States; and the concurrence of Masters, must, for the most part, be obtained by purchase.

Can it be hoped that voluntary contributions, however adequate to an auspicious commencement, will supply the sums necessary to such an enlargement of the remedy? May not another question be asked? Would it be reasonable to throw so great a burden on the individuals distinguished by their philanthropy and patriotism?

The object to be obtained, as an object of humanity, appeals alike to all; as a National object, it claims the interposition of the nation. It is the nation which is to reap the benefit. The nation therefore ought to bear the burden.

Must then the enormous sums required to pay for, to transport, and to establish in a foreign land all the slaves in the U. S. as their Masters may be willg. to part with them, be taxed on the good people of the U. S. or be obtained by loans swelling the public debt to a size pregnant with evils next in degree to those of slavery itself?

Happily it is not necessary to answer this question by remarking that if slavery as a national evil is to be abolished, and it be just that it be done at the national expence, the amount of the expence is not a paramount consideration. It is the peculiar fortune, or, rather a providential blessing of the U. S. to possess a resource commensurate to this great object, without taxes on the people, or even an increase of the public debt.

I allude to the vacant territory the extent of which is so vast, and the vendible value of which is so well ascertained.

Supposing the number of slaves to be 1,500,000, and their price to average 400 drs, the cost of the whole would be 600 millions of dollrs. These estimates are probably beyond the fact; and from the no. of slaves should be deducted 1. those whom their Masters would not part with. 2. those who may be gratuitously set free by their Masters. 3. those acquiring freedom under emancipating regulations of the States. 4. those preferring slavery where they are, to freedom in an African settlement. On the other hand, it is to be noted that the expence of removal & set-

tlement is not included in the estimated sum; and that an increase of the slaves will be going on during the period required for the execution of the plan.

On the whole the aggregate sum needed may be stated at about 600 Mils. of dollars.

This will require 200 mils. of Acres at 3 dolrs. per Acre; or 300 mils. at 2 dollrs. per Acre a quantity which tho' great in itself, is perhaps not a third part of the disposable territory belonging to the U. S. And to what object so good so great & so glorious, could that peculiar fund of wealth be appropriated? Whilst the sale of territory would, on one hand be planting one desert with a free & civilized people, it would on the other, be giving freedom to another people, and filling with them another desert. And if in any instances, wrong has been done by our forefathers to people of one colour, by dispossessing them of their soil, what better atonement is now in our power than that of making what is rightfully acquired a source of justice & of blessings to a people of another colour?

As the revolution to be produced in the condition of the negroes must be gradual, it will suffice if the sale of territory keep pace with its progress. For a time at least the proceeds wd. be in advance. In this case it might be best, after deducting the expence incident to the surveys & sales, to place the surplus in a situation where its increase might correspond with the natural increase of the unpurchased slaves. Should the proceeds at any time fall short of the calls for their application, anticipations might be made by temporary loans to be discharged as the land should find a Market.

But it is probable that for a considerable period, the sales would exceed the calls. Masters would not be willing to strip their plantations & farms of their laborers too rapidly. The slaves themselves, connected as they generally are by tender ties with others under other Masters, would be kept from the list of emigrants by the want of the multiplied consents to be obtained. It is probable indeed that for a long time a certain portion of the proceeds might safely continue applicable to the discharge of the debts or to other purposes of the Nation. Or it might be most convenient, in the outset, to appropriate a certain proportion only of the income from sales, to the object in view, leaving the residue otherwise applicable.

Should any plan similar to that I have sketched, be deemed eligible in itself no particular difficulty is foreseen from that portion of the nation which with a common interest in the vacant territory has no interest in slave property. They are too just to wish that a partial sacrifice shd. be made for the general good; and too well aware that whatever may be the intrinsic character of that description of property, it is one known to the constitution, and, as such could not be constitutionally taken away without just compensation. That part of the Nation has indeed shewn a meritorious alacrity in promoting, by pecuniary contributions, the limited scheme for colonizing the Blacks, & freeing the nation from the unfortunate stain on it, which justifies the belief that any enlargement of the scheme, if founded on just principles would find among them its earliest & warmest patrons. It ought to have great weight that the vacant lands in question have for the most part been derived from grants of the States holding the slaves to be redeemed & removed by the sale of them.

It is evident however that in effectuating a general emancipation of slaves, in the mode which has been hinted, difficulties of other sorts would be encountered. The provision for ascertaining the joint consent of the masters & slaves; for guarding agst. unreasonable valuations of the latter; and for the discrimination of those not proper to be conveyed to a foreign residence, or who ought to remain a charge on Masters in whose service they had been disabled or worn out and for the annual transportation of such numbers, would Require the mature deliberations of the National Councils. The measure implies also the practicability of procuring in Africa, an enlargement of the district or districts, for receiving the exiles, sufficient for so great an augmentation of their numbers.

Perhaps the Legislative provision best adapted to the case would be an incorporation of the Colonizing Society or the establishment of a similar one, with proper powers, under the appointment & superintendence of the National Executive.

In estimating the difficulties however incident to any plan of general emancipation, they ought to be brought into comparison with those inseparable from other plans, and be yielded to or not according to the result of the comparison.

One difficulty presents itself which will probably attend every plan which is to go into effect under the Legislative provisions of the National Govt. But whatever may be the defect of existing powers of Congress, the Constitution has pointed out the way in which it can be supplied. And it can hardly be doubted that the requisite powers might readily be procured for attaining the great object in question, in any mode whatever approved by the Nation.

If these thoughts can be of any aid in your search of a remedy for the great evil under which the nation labors, you are very welcome to them. You will allow me however to add that it will be most agreeable to me, not to be publickly referred to in any use you may make of them.

66

THOMAS JEFFERSON TO JOHN HOLMES
22 Apr. 1820
Works 12:158–60

I thank you, dear Sir, for the copy you have been so kind as to send me of the letter to your constituents on the Missouri question. It is a perfect justification to them. I had for a long time ceased to read newspapers, or pay any attention to public affairs, confident they were in good hands, and content to be a passenger in our bark to the shore from which I am not distant. But this momentous question, like a fire bell in the night, awakened and filled me with terror. I considered it at once as the knell of the Union. It is hushed, indeed, for the moment. But this is a reprieve only, not a final sentence. A geographical line,

coinciding with a marked principle, moral and political, once conceived and held up to the angry passions of men, will never be obliterated; and every new irritation will mark it deeper and deeper. I can say, with conscious truth, that there is not a man on earth who would sacrifice more than I would to relieve us from this heavy reproach, in any *practicable* way. The cession of that kind of property, for so it is misnamed, is a bagatelle which would not cost me a second thought, if, in that way, a general emancipation and *expatriation* could be effected; and gradually, and with due sacrifices, I think it might be. But as it is, we have the wolf by the ears, and we can neither hold him, nor safely let him go. Justice is in one scale, and self-preservation in the other. Of one thing I am certain, that as the passage of slaves from one State to another, would not make a slave of a single human being who would not be so without it, so their diffusion over a greater surface would make them individually happier, and proportionally facilitate the accomplishment of their emancipation, by dividing the burthen on a greater number of coadjutors. An abstinence too, from this act of power, would remove the jealousy excited by the undertaking of Congress to regulate the condition of the different descriptions of men composing a State. This certainly is the exclusive right of every State, which nothing in the constitution has taken from them and given to the General Government. Could Congress, for example, say, that the non-freemen of Connecticut shall be freemen, or that they shall not emigrate into any other State?

I regret that I am now to die in the belief, that the useless sacrifice of themselves by the generation of 1776, to acquire self-government and happiness to their country, is to be thrown away by the unwise and unworthy passions of their sons, and that my only consolation is to be, that I live not to weep over it. If they would but dispassionately weigh the blessings they will throw away, against an abstract principle more likely to be effected by union than by scission, they would pause before they would perpetrate this act of suicide on themselves, and of treason against the hopes of the world. To yourself, as the faithful advocate of the Union, I tender the offering of my high esteem and respect.

67

THOMAS JEFFERSON TO WILLIAM JOHNSON
12 June 1823
Writings 15:439–42

Our opponents are far ahead of us in preparations for placing their cause favorably before posterity. Yet I hope even from some of them the escape of precious truths, in angry explosions or effusions of vanity, which will betray the genuine monarchism of their principles. They do not themselves believe what they endeavor to inculcate, that we were an opposition party, not on principle, but merely seeking for office. The fact is, that at the formation of our government, many had formed their political opinions on European writings and practices, believing the experience of old countries, and especially of England, abusive as it was, to be a safer guide than mere theory. The doctrines of Europe were, that men in numerous associations cannot be restrained within the limits of order and justice, but by forces physical and moral, wielded over them by authorities independent of their will. Hence their organization of kings, hereditary nobles, and priests. Still further to constrain the brute force of the people, they deem it necessary to keep them down by hard labor, poverty and ignorance, and to take from them, as from bees, so much of their earnings, as that unremitting labor shall be necessary to obtain a sufficient surplus barely to sustain a scanty and miserable life. And these earnings they apply to maintain their privileged orders in splendor and idleness, to fascinate the eyes of the people, and excite in them an humble adoration and submission, as to an order of superior beings. Although few among us had gone all these lengths of opinion, yet many had advanced, some more, some less, on the way. And in the convention which formed our government, they endeavored to draw the cords of power as tight as they could obtain them, to lessen the dependence of the general functionaries on their constituents, to subject to them those of the States, and to weaken their means of maintaining the steady equilibrium which the majority of the convention had deemed salutary for both branches, general and local. To recover, therefore, in practice the powers which the nation had refused, and to warp to their own wishes those actually given, was the steady object of the federal party. Ours, on the contrary, was to maintain the will of the majority of the convention, and of the people themselves. We believed, with them, that man was a rational animal, endowed by nature with rights, and with an innate sense of justice; and that he could be restrained from wrong and protected in right, by moderate powers, confided to persons of his own choice, and held to their duties by dependence on his own will. We believed that the complicated organization of kings, nobles, and priests, was not the wisest nor best to effect the happiness of associated man; that wisdom and virtue were not hereditary; that the trappings of such a machinery, consumed by their ex-

pense, those earnings of industry, they were meant to protect, and, by the inequalities they produced, exposed liberty to sufferance. We believed that men, enjoying in ease and security the full fruits of their own industry, enlisted by all their interests on the side of law and order, habituated to think for themselves, and to follow their reason as their guide, would be more easily and safely governed, than with minds nourished in error, and vitiated and debased, as in Europe, by ignorance, indigence and oppression. The cherishment of the people then was our principle, the fear and distrust of them, that of the other party. Composed, as we were, of the landed and laboring interests of the country, we could not be less anxious for a government of law and order than were the inhabitants of the cities, the strongholds of federalism. And whether our efforts to save the principles and form of our Constitution have not been salutary, let the present republican freedom, order and prosperity of our country determine.

SEE ALSO:

Generally chs. 12, 13, 18; 1.2.3; 1.8.3 (Indians); 1.9.1; 1.10.1; 4.2.3

J. Hector St. John Crèvecoeur, Letters from an American Farmer, Letter 3 (1782), 48–51, 52–56, 72–80 (1925)

David Cooper, A Serious Address to the Rulers of America, On the Inconsistency of Their Conduct respecting Slavery 7–15, 17–19 (1783)

John Jay, Conditional Manumission of Benoit, 21 Mar. 1784, Unpublished Papers 2:705–6

Aristocrotis, 1788, Storing 3.16.3, 5

John Adams to Benjamin Rush, 18 Apr. 1790, Old Family Letters 1:60

John Jay to J. C. Dongan, 27 Feb. 1792, Correspondence 3:414–15

St. George Tucker to Jeremy Belknap, 13 Aug. 1797, MHS Collections, 5th ser., 3:427–28 (1877)

St. George Tucker, Blackstone's Commentaries 1:App. 28–29, 216–22 (1803)

Thomas Jefferson to Henri Grégoire, 25 Feb. 1809, Works 11:99–100

John Adams to Thomas Jefferson, 14 Aug. 1813, Cappon 2:365–66

John Adams to John Taylor, post 26 Dec. 1814, Works 6:493–97, 500–504

16

Property

Introduction

The bald opposition between human rights and property rights is asserted commonly enough today but would have been largely unintelligible to the Founders. John Adams, for instance, thought "Property is surely a right of mankind as really as liberty" (no. 15). Similarly, Alexander Hamilton's promise at the beginning of *The Federalist Papers* that they would show how adoption of the Constitution would provide additional security to the preservation of republican government, "to liberty and to property," treated this triad as complementary goods, not as incompatibles. Of course the Founders were keenly aware of the persistent problem posed for political life by the opposition between those with and those without property. Not the least of the considerations that led Hamilton to pronounce "energy in the executive . . . a leading character in the definition of good government" was its essential role in protecting property "against those irregular and high handed combinations, which sometimes interrupt the ordinary course of justice" (see ch. 9, no. 10). Like thinkers at least as far back as Plato and Aristotle, the Founders saw this opposition as a two-sided problem stemming from both the overbearing rich and the resentful poor. All thinking about property had to begin with that pre-Marxian commonplace.

Although the term "property" is conspicuously missing from the original Constitution (it does not appear until Amendment V), that hardly bespeaks indifference. Taxes, duties, imposts, excises, lands, commerce, bankruptcies, bills of credit, the exclusive rights of authors and inventors, contracts, debts, and engagements—all matters of explicit Constitutional provision (see, e.g., Art. 1, sec. 8, cls. 1–4, 8; Art. 1, sec. 10; Art. 4, sec. 2, cl. 3)—manifestly pertain to property. Less clear is what the Constitution's signers and ratifiers meant by property, indeed, even whether it was viewed as a means or as an end in itself. That property rights form a buffer protecting the individual from governmental abuse was assumed but not dwelt on.

The texts collected here testify to shifting meanings. Shifting political implications also therefore were inevitable, for property has broad connections with suffrage, the purposes of representation, institutional arrangements, economic policy, and the like. Generally speaking, the authors and political actors agreed: proprietorship is a condition for entry and full participation in political life, a prerequisite for the necessary independence that would guard the citizenry from becoming the mere instruments of the powerful and ambitious, a token of the seriousness of one's commitment to stability and order, and a claim to a full voice in the disposition of the community's affairs, especially as those bear on the enjoyment of one's own. They did not, however, agree on what constituted politically relevant proprietorship, on what it should take to establish that one had a stake in the country's public life.

All in all, then, property was seen as a good, albeit a problematic good. Not all kinds or all amounts were simply praiseworthy. In considering the problems and arriving at their several judgments, these men (unlike their Puritan contemporaries or predecessors) viewed the matter from an emphatically political perspective. Political economy was too important to be left to economists or theologians.

First place in the discussion of these matters rightly belongs to John Locke, whose analysis (no. 3) profoundly shaped the language and thinking of those who followed. His emphasis on the distinct bases of property (before and after the establishment of civil society) had the effect of joining a primordial, presocial claim with conventionally established terms for the exercise of that claim. The social utility of a man's laboring to satisfy his wants (variously rated at 90 percent, 99 percent, and over 99.9 percent of the value of things), is a powerful inducement for a ruler to secure the conditions under which each man might enjoy his own. In the state of nature, where men are equal—and equally vulnerable—each discovers that "the enjoyment of the property he has in this state is very unsafe, very unsecure." Sensibly enough, men join "for the mutual *Preservation* of their Lives, liberties and Estates, which I call by the general Name, Property." In this comprehensive sense of "property," a man's liberties are his possession as much as his possessions are a function of his liberties. Political society is to be guided by its charge to preserve property so understood, and it is to be judged by its effectiveness in so doing. Furthermore, if the preservation of property (thus broadly defined) is indeed the chief end of society and government, whatever "invades the *Fundamental Law of Property* . . . subverts the end of Government." The far-reaching implications of all this—at once revolutionary and conservative—were perceived and elaborated by Locke's successors.

Blackstone's account (no. 5) repeats, while absolutizing, Locke's insistence on the fundamental triad of rights or liberties. "Every man of rank or property" ought to understand thoroughly the foundations of all that he cherishes lest his ignorance "hurry him into faction and licentiousness on the one hand, or a pusillanimous indifference and criminal submission on the other." These were lessons to take to heart, and of all Blackstone's readers none did so more avidly than the litigious Americans (see ch. 1, no. 2). Two documents stemming from two different controversies serve to illustrate the point. The first bears the mark of Samuel Adams's powerful argumentation during the

crisis rekindled by the arrival in Boston of customs commissioners to enforce the Townshend Acts (no. 6). The other is the town of Sutton's response to the proposed constitution for Massachusetts of 1778; nothing about that critique is crude other than its orthography (see ch. 15, no. 22).

It was clear that the establishment of popular government carried many implications for the tenure of property. Gouverneur Morris put the difficulty plainly in a set of unpublished ruminations (no. 8). The progressive development of a commercial society enhanced civil liberty by requiring the security of property, good faith, and the like. All these operated as so many restraints on the political liberty of the ruling part (be it prince or popular majority). Though civil liberty required political liberty for its defence, an unrestricted governmental authority would "sacrifice the End to the Means." At bottom lay a continuing and necessary struggle between opposing forces.

Jefferson's persistent battle to expunge entail and primogeniture from the revised laws of revolutionary Virginia was rightly viewed by him at the time and in his autobiographical recollections forty-five years later as part of "a system by which every fibre would be eradicated of antient or future aristocracy, and a foundation laid for a government truly republican." (See ch. 15, no. 20 and ch. 4, no. 7.) But if the new modes and orders required changes in the character of property holdings, no less might the security of property require some adjustments in popular government. John Adams (no. 15), like Hamilton, Madison, and other Founders, rejected outright the notion that popular liberty neither would nor could endanger the holdings of what necessarily would be a minority. Special safeguards were accordingly in order. (See also Essex Result, in ch. 4, no. 8.)

The claims of society upon private property—touched by Locke and treated summarily by Blackstone—were examined more fully by Franklin and Jefferson. Their arguments raise and assess the claim of natural right and its implications for a just social policy. Franklin insisted that all property beyond that required for the "Conservation of the Individual and the Propagation of the Species" could be enjoyed only on terms that the public might set through its laws (no. 12; see also ch. 12, no. 25). Jefferson, too, maintained that holders of property, who owed all of its safe enjoyment and much of its title to "social law" rather than nature, could not raise absolute claims that denied society what its welfare required (no. 25). Nor could the claims of natural right "to labor the earth" be ignored while there remained uncultivated land and needy men (see ch. 15, no. 32).

Property figured large in the Constitutional Convention's attempts to fix the proper basis of representation (no. 16). Gouverneur Morris's objections to numbers as the sole basis appear to rest on both a fear of the poor and a fear of the rich: both envy and ambition threaten a free, civilized society. In this view of things, limiting suffrage to those owning land would help secure "the main object of Society" and avert the danger of an aristocracy installed with the purchased votes of the propertyless. Mason challenged Morris's statement of the problem as well as his solution as viewing "things too much through a British Medium." In settling the criteria for suffrage one ought to look for "evidence of attachment to & permanent common interest with the Society." Such evidence could not sensibly be limited to ownership of land. "Ought the merchant, the monied man, the parent of a number of children whose fortunes are to be pursued in their own Country, to be viewed as suspicious characters, and unworthy to be trusted with the common rights of their fellow Citizens[?]" Would it make sense, Franklin argued further, to give this mark of disesteem to honorable and public-spirited common people? Madison, too, viewed the matter as a prudential question, but came down on the other side. "Viewing the subject in its merits alone, the freeholders of the Country would be the safest depositories of Republican liberty." If the issue of "conflicting feelings of the Class with, and the Class without property" was not yet acute, that was owing to the singularly fortunate circumstances of the United States at the time. But times and circumstances would change. Madison was to have various occasions to rethink and reformulate his notions of a prudential accommodation between those who feared to lose and others who hoped to gain: while advising founders contemplating a new constitution for Kentucky (see ch. 17, no. 25), while editing his notes of the Philadelphia Convention (no. 26), and while considering the issue in the context of the Virginia Constitutional Convention of 1829–30 (no. 27).

In the end the Philadelphia Convention would leave the thorny matter of voter qualifications to the states by accepting their least restrictive standards (for electors of the lower houses of the state legislatures), and by imposing no additional federal requirements of its own (see ch. 13). The House of Representatives would thus be as popular or democratic a body as the states severally chose for it to be. The rule of numbers in the legislature would be mitigated by the indirect election of Senators and the equal weight of unequal states in the upper chamber, and by the three-fifths rule for counting slaves when reckoning state populations to be represented in the lower chamber. And, unlike a number of state constitutions of the time, the Founders' Constitution would set no property requirements of a particular kind or level in order to hold any federal office.

The problems raised for property and by property seemed inescapable and seemed inseparable from its unequal distribution. Given that "*property* is the basis of *power*," Noah Webster (no. 17) thought that only "*a general and tolerably equal distribution of landed property*" would secure republican liberty. Given the same premise, Melancton Smith (no. 20) thought that the number of representatives should be numerous enough to make it likely that "a sufficient number of the middling class" would be elected—sufficient, that is, to control the extremes of the great and the poor. Like Smith, Madison entertained no notion of a distribution of property equal enough to avert the turmoils of domestic faction (see ch. 4, no. 19). America was not fit for a Harringtonian Agrarian (see ch. 15, no. 2). Reliance would be placed on other devices: not removing the causes of faction, but rather controlling its effects.

The range of meanings attached to property persisted. Madison's essay for the party press (no. 23) stated a conclusion with highly partisan implications, but the statement itself in its generality would have raised few eyebrows among the Americans: "as a man is said to have a right to his property, he may be equally said to have a property in his rights." In this "larger and juster meaning," a threat to one form of property was a threat to the whole of it. William Paterson's discussion (no. 24)—this time not as Founder, but as Supreme Court Justice riding circuit—recurs to the language of the Declaration of Independence and beyond that to Locke's *Second Treatise*. The government's treatment of property—ringed as it was with constitutional safeguards—was itself a test of the possibility of constitutional government. This was an issue in which literally everyone had a stake.

1

WILLIAM BRADFORD, OF PLYMOUTH
PLANTATION 120–21
1623

All this while no supply was heard of, neither knew they when they might expect any. So they began to think how they might raise as much corn as they could, and obtain a better crop than they had done, that they might not still thus languish in misery. At length, after much debate of things, the Governor (with the advice of the chiefest amongst them) gave way that they should set corn every man for his own particular, and in that regard trust to themselves; in all other things to go on in the general way as before. And so assigned to every family a parcel of land, according to the proportion of their number, for that end, only for present use (but made no division for inheritance) and ranged all boys and youth under some family. This had very good success, for it made all hands very industrious, so as much more corn was planted than otherwise would have been by any means the Governor or any other could use, and saved him a great deal of trouble, and gave far better content. The women now went willingly into the field, and took their little ones with them to set corn; which before would allege weakness and inability; whom to have compelled would have been thought great tyranny and oppression.

The experience that was had in this common course and condition, tried sundry years and that amongst godly and sober men, may well evince the vanity of that conceit of Plato's and other ancients applauded by some of later times; that the taking away of property and bringing in community into a commonwealth would make them happy and flourishing; as if they were wiser than God. For this community (so far as it was) was found to breed much confusion and discontent and retard much employment that would have been to their benefit and comfort. For the young men, that were most able and fit for labour and service, did repine that they should spend their time and strength to work for other men's wives and children without any recompense. The strong, or man of parts, had no more in division of victuals and clothes than he that was weak and not able to do a quarter the other could; this was thought injustice. The aged and graver men to be ranked and equalized in labours and victuals, clothes, etc., with the meaner and younger sort, thought it some indignity and disrespect unto them. And for men's wives to be commanded to do service for other men, as dressing their meat, washing their clothes, etc., they deemed it a kind of slavery, neither could many husbands well brook it. Upon the point all being to have alike, and all to do alike, they thought themselves in the like condition, and one as good as another; and so, if it did not cut off those relations that God hath set amongst men, yet it did at least much diminish and take off the mutual respects that should be preserved amongst them. And would have been worse if they had been men of another condition. Let none object this is men's corruption, and nothing to the course itself. I answer, seeing all men have this corruption in them, God in His wisdom saw another course fitter for them.

2

JAMES HARRINGTON, COMMONWEALTH
OF OCEANA 70–72
1656

(See ch. 15, no. 2)

3

JOHN LOCKE, SECOND TREATISE,
§§ 25–51, 123–26
1689

(See also §§ 138–40, in ch. 17, no. 5)

Chap. V. Of Property.

25. Whether we consider natural *Reason*, which tells us, that Men, being once born, have a right to their Preservation, and consequently to Meat and Drink, and such other things, as Nature affords for their Subsistence: Or *Revelation*, which gives us an account of those Grants God made of the World to *Adam*, and to *Noah*, and his Sons, 'tis very clear, that God, as King *David* says, *Psal.* CXV. xvi. *has given the Earth to the Children of Men*, given it to Mankind in common. But this being supposed, it seems to some a very great difficulty, how any one should ever come to have a *Property* in any thing: I will not content my self to answer, That if it be difficult to make out *Property*, upon a supposition, that God gave the World to *Adam* and his Posterity in common; it is impossible that any Man, but one universal Monarch, should have any *Property*, upon a supposition, that God gave the World to *Adam*, and his Heirs in Succession, exclusive of all the rest of his Posterity. But I shall endeavour to shew, how Men might come to have a *property* in several parts of that which God gave to Mankind in common, and that without any express Compact of all the Commoners.

26. God, who hath given the World to Men in common, hath also given them reason to make use of it to the best advantage of Life, and convenience. The Earth, and all that is therein, is given to Men for the Support and Comfort of their being. And though all the Fruits it naturally produces, and Beasts it feeds, belong to Mankind in common, as they are produced by the spontaneous hand of Nature; and no body has originally a private Dominion, exclusive of the rest of Mankind, in any of them, as they are thus in their natural state: yet being given for the use of Men, there must of necessity be a means *to appropriate* them some way or other before they can be of any use, or at all beneficial to any particular Man. The Fruit, or Venison, which nourishes the wild *Indian*, who knows no Inclosure, and is still a Tenant in common, must be his and so his, *i.e.* a part of him, that another can no longer have any right to it, before it can do him any good for the support of his Life.

27. Though the Earth, and all inferior Creatures be common to all Men, yet every Man has a *Property* in his own *Person*. This no Body has any Right to but himself. The *Labour* of his Body, and the *Work* of his Hands, we may say, are properly his. Whatsoever then he removes out of the State that Nature hath provided, and left it in, he hath mixed his *Labour* with, and joyned to it something that is his own, and thereby makes it his *Property*. It being by him removed from the common state Nature placed it in, hath by this *labour* something annexed to it, that excludes the common right of other Men. For this *Labour* being the unquestionable Property of the Labourer, no man but he can have a right to what that is once joyned to, at least where there is enough, and as good left in common for others.

28. He that is nourished by the Acorns he pickt up under an Oak, or the Apples he gathered from the Trees in the Wood, has certainly appropriated them to himself. No Body can deny but the nourishment is his. I ask then, When did they begin to be his? When he digested? Or when he eat? Or when he boiled? Or when he brought them home? Or when he pickt them up? And 'tis plain, if the first gathering made them not his, nothing else could. That *labour* put a distinction between them and common. That added something to them more than Nature, the common Mother of all, had done; and so they became his private right. And will any one say he had no right to those Acorns or Apples he thus appropriated, because he had not the consent of all Mankind to make them his? Was it a Robbery thus to assume to himself what belonged to all in Common? If such a consent as that was necessary, Man had starved, notwithstanding the Plenty God had

given him. We see in *Commons*, which remain so by Compact, that 'tis the taking any part of what is common, and removing it out of the state Nature leaves it in, which *begins the Property;* without which the Common is of no use. And the taking of this or that part, does not depend on the express consent of all the Commoners. Thus the Grass my Horse has bit; the Turfs my Servant has cut; and the Ore I have digg'd in any place where I have a right to them in common with others, become my *Property,* without the assignation or consent of any body. The *labour* that was mine, removing them out of that common state they were in, hath *fixed* my *Property* in them.

29. By making an explicit consent of every Commoner, necessary to any ones appropriating to himself any part of what is given in common, Children or Servants could not cut the Meat which their Father or Master had provided for them in common, without assigning to every one his peculiar part. Though the Water running in the Fountain be every ones, yet who can doubt, but that in the Pitcher is his only who drew it out? His *labour* hath taken it out of the hands of Nature, where it was common, and belong'd equally to all her Children, and *hath* thereby *appropriated* it to himself.

30. Thus this Law of reason makes the Deer, that *Indian's* who hath killed it; 'tis allowed to be his goods who hath bestowed his labour upon it, though before, it was the common right of every one. And amongst those who are counted the Civiliz'd part of Mankind, who have made and multiplied positive Laws to determine Property, this original Law of Nature for the *beginning of Property,* in what was before common, still takes place; and by vertue thereof, what Fish any one catches in the Ocean, that great and still remaining Common of Mankind; or what Ambergriese any one takes up here, is *by* the *Labour* that removes it out of that common state Nature left it in, *made* his *Property* who takes that pains about it. And even amongst us the Hare that any one is Hunting, is thought his who pursues her during the Chase. For being a Beast that is still looked upon as common, and no Man's private Possession; whoever has imploy'd so much *labour* about any of that kind, as to find and pursue her, has thereby removed her from the state of Nature, wherein she was common, and hath *begun a Property.*

31. It will perhaps be objected to this, That if gathering the Acorns, or other Fruits of the Earth, *&c.* makes a right to them, then any one may *ingross* as much as he will. To which I Answer, Not so. The same Law of Nature, that does by this means give us Property, does also *bound that Property too. God has given us all things richly,* 1 Tim. vi. 17. is the Voice of Reason confirmed by Inspiration. But how far has he given it us? *To enjoy.* As much as any one can make use of to any advantage of life before it spoils; so much he may by his labour fix a Property in. Whatever is beyond this, is more than his share, and belongs to others. Nothing was made by God for Man to spoil or destroy. And thus considering the plenty of natural Provisions there was a long time in the World, and the few spenders, and to how small a part of that provision the industry of one Man could extend it self, and ingross it to the preju-

dice of others; especially keeping within the *bounds,* set by reason of what might serve for his *use;* there could be then little room for Quarrels or Contentions about Property so establish'd.

32. But the *chief matter of Property* being now not the Fruits of the Earth, and the Beasts that subsist on it, but the *Earth it self;* as that which takes in and carries with it all the rest: I think it is plain, that *Property* in that too is acquired as the former. *As much Land* as a Man Tills, Plants, Improves, Cultivates, and can use the Product of, so much is his *Property.* He by his Labour does, as it were, inclose it from the Common. Nor will it invalidate his right to say, Every body else has an equal Title to it; and therefore he cannot appropriate, he cannot inclose, without the Consent of all his Fellow-Commoners, all Mankind. God, when he gave the World in common to all Mankind, commanded Man also to labour, and the penury of his Condition required it of him. God and his Reason commanded him to subdue the Earth, *i.e.* improve it for the benefit of Life, and therein lay out something upon it that was his own, his labour. He that in Obedience to this Command of God, subdued, tilled and sowed any part of it, thereby annexed to it something that was his *Property,* which another had no Title to, nor could without injury take from him.

33. Nor was this *appropriation* of any parcel of *Land,* by improving it, any prejudice to any other Man, since there was still enough, and as good left; and more than the yet unprovided could use. So that in effect, there was never the less left for others because of his inclosure for himself. For he that leaves as much as another can make use of, does as good as take nothing at all. No Body could think himself injur'd by the drinking of another Man, though he took a good Draught, who had a whole River of the same Water left him to quench his thirst. And the Case of Land and Water, where there is enough of both, is perfectly the same.

34. God gave the World to Men in Common; but since he gave it them for their benefit, and the greatest Conveniencies of Life they were capable to draw from it, it cannot be supposed he meant it should always remain common and uncultivated. He gave it to the use of the Industrious and Rational, (and *Labour* was to be *his Title* to it;) not to the Fancy or Covetousness of the Quarrelsom and Contentious. He that had as good left for his Improvement, as was already taken up, needed not complain, ought not to meddle with what was already improved by another's Labour: If he did, 'tis plain he desired the benefit of another's Pains, which he had no right to, and not the Ground which God had given him in common with others to labour on, and whereof there was as good left, as that already possessed, and more than he knew what to do with, or his Industry could reach to.

35. 'Tis true, in *Land* that is *common* in *England,* or any other Country, where there is Plenty of People under Government, who have Money and Commerce, no one can inclose or appropriate any part, without the consent of all his Fellow-Commoners: Because this is left common by Compact, *i.e.* by the Law of the Land, which is not to be

violated. And though it be Common, in respect of some Men, it is not so to all Mankind; but is the joint property of this Countrey, or this Parish. Besides, the remainder, after such inclosure, would not be as good to the rest of the Commoners as the whole was, when they could all make use of the whole: whereas in the beginning and first peopling of the great Common of the World, it was quite otherwise. The Law Man was under, was rather for *appropriating*. God Commanded, and his Wants forced him to *labour*. That was his *Property* which could not be taken from him where-ever he had fixed it. And hence subduing or cultivating the Earth, and having Dominion, we see are joyned together. The one gave Title to the other. So that God, by commanding to subdue, gave Authority so far to *appropriate*. And the Condition of Humane Life, which requires Labour and Materials to work on, necessarily introduces *private Possessions*.

36. The measure of Property, Nature has well set, by the Extent of Mens *Labour, and the Conveniency of Life:* No Mans Labour could subdue, or appropriate all: nor could his Enjoyment consume more than a small part; so that it was impossible for any Man, this way, to intrench upon the right of another, or acquire, to himself, a Property, to the Prejudice of his Neighbour, who would still have room, for as good, and as large a Possession (after the other had taken out his) as before it was appropriated. This *measure* did confine every Man's *Possession*, to a very moderate Proportion, and such as he might appropriate to himself, without Injury to any Body in the first Ages of the World, when Men were more in danger to be lost, by wandering from their Company, in the then vast Wilderness of the Earth, than to be straitned for want of room to plant in. And the same *measure* may be allowed still, without prejudice to any Body, as full as the World seems. For supposing a Man, or Family, in the state they were, at first peopling of the World by the Children of *Adam*, or *Noah;* let him plant in some in-land, vacant places of *America*, we shall find that the *Possessions* he could make himself upon the *measures* we have given, would not be very large, nor, even to this day, prejudice the rest of Mankind, or give them reason to complain, or think themselves injured by this Man's Incroachment, though the Race of Men have now spread themselves to all the corners of the World, and do infinitely exceed the small number [which] was at the beginning. Nay, the extent of *Ground* is of so little value, *without labour,* that I have heard it affirmed, that in *Spain* it self, a Man may be permitted to plough, sow, and reap, without being disturbed, upon Land he has no other Title to, but only his making use of it. But, on the contrary, the Inhabitants think themselves beholden to him, who, by his Industry on neglected, and consequently waste Land, has increased the stock of Corn, which they wanted. But be this as it will, which I lay no stress on; This I dare boldly affirm, That the same *Rule of Propriety, (viz.)* that every Man should have as much as he could make use of, would hold still in the World, without straitning any body, since there is Land enough in the World to suffice double the Inhabitants had not the *Invention of Money*, and the tacit Agreement of Men to put a value on it, introduced (by

Consent) larger Possessions, and a Right to them; which, how it has done, I shall, by and by, shew more at large.

37. This is certain, That in the beginning, before the desire of having more than Men needed, had altered the intrinsick value of things, which depends only on their usefulness to the Life of Man; or [Men] had *agreed, that a little piece of yellow Metal,* which would keep without wasting or decay, should be worth a great piece of Flesh, or a whole heap of Corn; though Men had a Right to appropriate, by their Labour, each one to himself, as much of the things of Nature, as he could use: Yet this could not be much, nor to the Prejudice of others, where the same plenty was still left, to those who would use the same Industry. To which let me add, that he who appropriates land to himself by his labour, does not lessen but increase the common stock of mankind. For the provisions serving to the support of humane life, produced by one acre of inclosed and cultivated land, are (to speak much within compasse) ten times more, than those, which are yeilded by an acre of Land, of an equal richnesse, lyeing wast in common. And therefor he, that incloses Land and has a greater plenty of the conveniencys of life from ten acres, than he could have from an hundred left to Nature, may truly be said, to give ninety acres to Mankind. For his labour now supplys him with provisions out of ten acres, which were but the product of an hundred lying in common. I have here rated the improved land very low in making its product but as ten to one, when it is much nearer an hundred to one. For I aske whether in the wild woods and uncultivated wast of America left to Nature, without any improvement, tillage or husbandry, a thousand acres will yeild the needy and wretched inhabitants as many conveniencies of life as ten acres of equally fertile land doe in Devonshire where they are well cultivated?

Before the Appropriation of Land, he who gathered as much of the wild Fruit, killed, caught, or tamed, as many of the Beasts as he could; he that so employed his Pains about any of the spontaneous Products of Nature, as any way to alter them, from the state which Nature put them in, *by* placing any of his *Labour* on them, did thereby *acquire a Property in them:* But if they perished, in his Possession, without their due use; if the Fruits rotted, or the Venison putrified, before he could spend it, he offended against the common Law of Nature, and was liable to be punished; he invaded his Neighbour's share, for he had *no Right, farther than his Use* called for any of them, and they might serve to afford him Conveniencies of Life.

38. The same *measures* governed the *Possession of Land* too: Whatsoever he tilled and reaped, laid up and made use of, before it spoiled, that was his peculiar Right; whatsoever he enclosed, and could feed, and make use of, the Cattle and Product was also his. But if either the Grass of his Inclosure rotted on the Ground, or the Fruit of his planting perished without gathering, and laying up, this part of the Earth, notwithstanding his Inclosure, was still to be looked on as Waste, and might be the Possession of any other. Thus, at the beginning, *Cain* might take as much Ground as he could till, and make it his own Land, and yet leave enough to *Abel*'s Sheep to feed on; a few

Acres would serve for both their Possessions. But as Families increased, and Industry inlarged their Stocks, their *Possessions inlarged* with the need of them; but yet it was commonly *without any fixed property in the ground* they made use of, till they incorporated, settled themselves together, and built Cities, and then, by consent, they came in time, to set out the *bounds of their distinct Territories,* and agree on limits between them and their Neighbours, and by Laws within themselves, settled the *Properties* of those of the same Society. For we see, that in that part of the World which was first inhabited, and therefore like to be best peopled, even as low down as *Abraham's* time, they wandred with their Flocks, and their Herds, which was their substance, freely up and down; and this *Abraham* did, in a Country where he was a Stranger. Whence it is plain, that at least, a great part of the *Land lay in common;* that the Inhabitants valued it not, nor claimed Property in any more than they made use of. But when there was not room enough in the same place, for their Herds to feed together, they, by consent, as *Abraham* and *Lot* did, *Gen.* xiii. 5. separated and inlarged their pasture, where it best liked them. And for the same Reason *Esau* went from his Father, and his Brother, and planted in *Mount Seir,* Gen. xxxvi. 6.

39. And thus, without supposing any private Dominion, and property in *Adam,* over all the World, exclusive of all other Men, which can no way be proved, nor any ones Property be made out from it; but supposing the *World* given as it was to the Children of Men *in common,* we see how *labour* could make Men distinct titles to several parcels of it, for their private uses; wherein there could be no doubt of Right, no room for quarrel.

40. Nor is it so strange, as perhaps before consideration it may appear, that the *Property of labour* should be able to over-ballance the Community of Land. For 'tis *Labour* indeed that *puts the difference of value* on every thing; and let any one consider, what the difference is between an Acre of Land planted with Tobacco, or Sugar, sown with Wheat or Barley; and an Acre of the same Land lying in common, without any Husbandry upon it, and he will find, that the improvement of *labour makes* the far greater part of *the value.* I think it will be but a very modest Computation to say, that of the *Products* of the Earth useful to the Life of man 9/10 are the *effects of labour:* nay, if we will rightly estimate things as they come to our use, and cast up the several Expenses about them, what in them is purely owing to *Nature,* and what to *labour,* we shall find, that in most of them 99/100 are wholly to be put on the account of *labour.*

41. There cannot be a clearer demonstration of any thing, than several Nations of the *Americans* are of this, who are rich in Land, and poor in all the Comforts of Life; whom Nature having furnished as liberally as any other people, with the materials of Plenty, *i.e.* a fruitful Soil, apt to produce in abundance, what might serve for food, rayment, and delight; yet for want of improving it by labour, have not one hundredth part of the Conveniencies we enjoy: And a King of a large fruitful Territory there feeds, lodges, and is clad worse than a day Labourer in *England.*

42. To make this a little clearer, let us but trace some of the ordinary provisions of Life, through their several progresses, before they come to our use, and see how much they receive of their *value from Humane Industry.* Bread, Wine and Cloth, are things of daily use, and great plenty, yet notwithstanding, Acorns, Water, and Leaves, or Skins, must be our Bread, Drink and Clothing, did not *labour* furnish us with these more useful Commodities. For whatever *Bread* is more worth than Acorns, *Wine* than Water, and *Cloth* or *Silk* than Leaves, Skins, or Moss, that is wholly *owing to labour* and industry. The one of these being the Food and Rayment which unassisted Nature furnishes us with; the other provisions which our industry and pains prepare for us, which how much they exceed the other in value, when any one hath computed, he will then see, how much *labour makes the far greatest part of the value* of things, we enjoy in this World: And the ground which produces the materials, is scarce to be reckon'd in, as any, or at most, but a very small, part of it; So little, that even amongst us, Land that is left wholly to Nature, that hath no improvement of Pasturage, Tillage, or Planting, is called, as indeed it is, *wast;* and we shall find the benefit of it amount to little more than nothing. This shews, how much numbers of men are to be preferd to largenesse of dominions, and that the increase of lands and the right imploying of them is the great art of government. And that Prince who shall be so wise and godlike as by established laws of liberty to secure protection and incouragement to the honest industry of Mankind against the oppression of power and narrownesse of Party will quickly be too hard for his neighbours. But this bye the bye. To return to the argument in hand.

43. An Acre of Land that bears here Twenty Bushels of Wheat, and another in *America,* which, with the same Husbandry, would do the like, are without doubt, of the same natural, intrinsick Value. But yet the Benefit Mankind receïves from the one, in a Year, is worth 5 *l.* and from the other possibly not worth a Penny, if all the Profit an *Indian* received from it were to be valued, and sold here; at least, I may truly say, not 1/1000. 'Tis *Labour* then which *puts the greatest part of Value upon Land,* without which it would scarcely be worth any thing: 'tis to that we owe the greatest part of all its useful Products; for all that the Straw, Bran, Bread, of that Acre of Wheat, is more worth than the Product of an Acre of as good Land, which lies wast, is all the Effect of Labour. For 'tis not barely the Plough-man's Pains, the Reaper's and Thresher's Toil, and the Bakers Sweat, is to be counted into the *Bread* we eat; the Labour of those who broke the Oxen, who digged and wrought the Iron and Stones, who felled and framed the Timber imployed about the Plough, Mill, Oven, or any other Utensils, which are a vast Number, requisite to this Corn, from its being seed to be sown to its being made Bread, must all be *charged on* the account of *Labour,* and received as an effect of that; Nature and the Earth furnished only the almost worthless Materials, as in themselves. 'Twould be a strange *Catalogue of things, that Industry provided and made use of, about every Loaf of Bread,* before it came to our use, if we could trace them; Iron, Wood, Leather, Bark,

Timber, Stone, Bricks, Coals, Lime, Cloth, Dying-Drugs, Pitch, Tar, Masts, Ropes, and all the Materials made use of in the Ship, that brought any of the Commodities made use of by any of the Workmen, to any part of the Work, all which, 'twould be almost impossible, at least too long, to reckon up.

44. From all which it is evident, that though the things of Nature are given in common, yet Man (by being Master of himself, and *Proprietor of his own Person,* and the actions or *Labour* of it) had still in himself *the great Foundation of Property;* and that which made up the great part of what he applied to the Support or Comfort of his being, when Invention and Arts had improved the conveniencies of Life, was perfectly his own, and did not belong in common to others.

45. Thus *Labour,* in the Beginning, *gave a Right of Property,* where-ever any one was pleased to imploy it, upon what was common, which remained, a long while, the far greater part, and is yet more than Mankind makes use of. Men, at first, for the most part, contented themselves with what un-assisted Nature Offered to their Necessities: and though afterwards, in some parts of the World, (where the Increase of People and Stock, with the *Use of Money*) had made Land scarce, and so of some Value, the several *Communities* settled the Bounds of their distinct Territories, and by Laws within themselves, regulated the Properties of the private Men of their Society, and so, *by Compact* and Agreement, *settled the Property* which Labour and Industry began; and the Leagues that have been made between several States and Kingdoms, either expressly or tacitly disowning all Claim and Right to the Land in the others Possession, have, by common Consent, given up their Pretences to their natural common Right, which originally they had to those Countries, and so have, by *positive agreement, settled a Property* amongst themselves, in distinct Parts and parcels of the Earth: yet there are still *great Tracts of Ground* to be found, which (the Inhabitants thereof not having joyned with the rest of Mankind, in the consent of the Use of their common Money) *lie waste,* and are more than the People, who dwell on it, do, or can make use of, and so still lie in common. Tho' this can scarce happen amongst that part of Mankind, that have consented to the use of Money.

46. The greatest part of *things really useful* to the Life of Man, and such as the necessity of subsisting made the first Commoners of the World look after, as it doth the *Americans* now, are generally things *of short duration;* such as, if they are not consumed by use, will decay and perish of themselves: Gold, Silver, and Diamonds, are things, that Fancy or Agreement hath put the Value on, more then real Use, and the necessary Support of Life. Now of those good things which Nature hath provided in common, every one had a Right (as hath been said) to as much as he could use, and had a Property in all that he could affect with his Labour: all that his Industry could extend to, to alter from the State Nature had put it in, was his. He that *gathered* a Hundred Bushels of Acorns or Apples, had thereby a *Property* in them; they were his Goods as soon as gathered. He was only to look that he used them before

they spoiled; else he took more than his share, and robb'd others. And indeed it was a foolish thing, as well as dishonest, to hoard up more than he could make use of. If he gave away a part to any body else, so that it perished not uselesly in his Possession, these he also made use of. And if he also bartered away Plumbs that would have rotted in a Week, for Nuts that would last good for his eating a whole Year, he did no injury; he wasted not the common Stock; destroyed no part of the portion of Goods that belonged to others, so long as nothing perished uselesly in his hands. Again, if he would give us Nuts for a piece of Metal, pleased with its colour; or exchanged his Sheep for Shells, or Wool for a sparkling Pebble or a Diamond, and keep those by him all his Life, he invaded not the Right of others, he might heap up as much of these durable things as he pleased; the *exceeding of the bounds of his* just *Property* not lying in the largeness of his Possession, but the perishing of any thing uselesly in it.

47. And thus *came in the use of Money,* some lasting thing that Men might keep without spoiling, and that by mutual consent Men would take in exchange for the truly useful, but perishable Supports of Life.

48. And as different degrees of Industry were apt to give Men Possessions in different Proportions, so this *Invention of Money* gave them the opportunity to continue to enlarge them. For supposing an Island, separated from all possible Commerce with the rest of the World, wherein there were but a hundred Families, but there were Sheep, Horses and Cows, with other useful Animals, wholsome Fruits, and Land enough for Corn for a hundred thousand times as many, but nothing in the Island, either because of its Commonness, or Perishableness, fit to supply the place of *Money:* What reason could any one have there to enlarge his Possessions beyond the use of his Family, and a plentiful supply to its Consumption, either in what their own Industry produced, or they could barter for like perishable, useful Commodities, with others? Where there is not something both lasting and scarce, and so valuable to be hoarded up, there Men will not be apt to enlarge their *Possessions of Land,* were it never so rich, never so free for them to take. For I ask, What would a Man value Ten Thousand, or an Hundred Thousand Acres of excellent *Land,* ready cultivated, and well stocked too with Cattle, in the middle of the in-land Parts of *America,* where he had no hopes of Commerce with other Parts of the World, to draw *Money* to him by the Sale of the Product? It would not be worth the inclosing, and we should see him give up again to the wild Common of Nature, whatever was more than would supply the Conveniencies of Life to be had there for him and his Family.

49. Thus in the beginning all the World was *America,* and more so than that is now; for no such thing as *Money* was any where known. Find out something that hath the *Use and Value of Money* amongst his Neighbours, you shall see the same Man will begin presently to *enlarge* his *Possessions.*

50. But since Gold and Silver, being little useful to the Life of Man in proportion to Food, Rayment, and Car-

riage, has its *value* only from the consent of Men, whereof Labour yet makes, in great part, *the measure,* it is plain, that Men have agreed to disproportionate and unequal Possession of the Earth, they having by a tacit and voluntary consent found out a way, how a man may fairly possess more land than he himself can use the product of, by receiving in exchange for the overplus, Gold and Silver, which may be hoarded up without injury to any one, these metalls not spoileing or decaying in the hands of the possessor. This partage of things, in an inequality of private possessions, men have made practicable out of the bounds of Societie, and without compact, only by putting a value on gold and silver and tacitly agreeing in the use of Money. For in Governments the Laws regulate the right of property, and the possession of land is determined by positive constitutions.

51. And thus, I think, it is very easie to conceive without any difficulty, *how Labour could at first begin a title of Property* in the common things of Nature, and how the spending it upon our uses bounded it. So that there could then be no reason of quarrelling about Title, nor any doubt about the largeness of Possession it gave. Right and conveniency went together; for as a Man had a Right to all he could imploy his Labour upon, so he had no temptation to labour for more than he could make use of. This left no room for Controversie about the Title, nor for Incroachment on the Right of others; what Portion a Man carved to himself, was easily seen; and it was useless as well as dishonest to carve himself too much, or take more than he needed.

Chap. IX. Of the Ends of Political Society and Government.

123. If Man in the State of Nature be so free, as has been said; If he be absolute Lord of his own Person and Possessions, equal to the greatest, and subject to no Body, why will he part with his Freedom? Why will he give up this Empire, and subject himself to the Dominion and Controul of any other Power? To which 'tis obvious to Answer, that though in the state of Nature he hath such a right, yet the Enjoyment of it is very uncertain, and constantly exposed to the Invasion of others. For all being Kings as much as he, every Man his Equal, and the greater part no strict Observers of Equity and Justice, the enjoyment of the property he has in this state is very unsafe, very unsecure. This makes him willing to quit a Condition, which however free, is full of fears and continual dangers: And 'tis not without reason, that he seeks out, and is willing to joyn in Society with others who are already united, or have a mind to unite for the mutual *Preservation* of their Lives, Liberties and Estates, which I call by the general Name, *Property.*

124. The great and *chief end* therefore, of Mens uniting into Commonwealths, and putting themselves under Government, *is the Preservation of their Property.* To which in the state of Nature there are many things wanting.

First, There wants an *establish'd,* settled, known *Law,* received and allowed by common consent to be the Standard of Right and Wrong, and the common measure to decide all Controversies between them. For though the Law of Nature be plain and intelligible to all rational Creatures; yet Men being biassed by their Interest, as well as ignorant for want of study of it, are not apt to allow of it as a Law binding to them in the application of it to their particular Cases.

125. *Secondly,* In the State of Nature there wants a *known and indifferent Judge,* with Authority to determine all differences according to the established Law. For every one in that state being both Judge and Executioner of the Law of Nature, Men being partial to themselves, Passion and Revenge is very apt to carry them too far, and with too much heat, in their own Cases; as well as negligence, and unconcernedness, to make them too remiss, in other Mens.

126. *Thirdly,* In the state of Nature there often wants *Power* to back and support the Sentence when right, and to *give* it due *Execution.* They who by any Injustice offended, will seldom fail, where they are able, by force to make good their Injustice: such resistance many times makes the punishment dangerous, and frequently destructive, to those who attempt it.

4

JOHN TRENCHARD, CATO'S LETTERS, NO. 68
3 Mar. 1721
Jacobson 177–78

To live securely, happily, and independently, is the End and Effect of Liberty; and it is the Ambition of all Men to live agreeably to their own Humours and Discretion. Nor did ever any Man that could live satisfactorily without a Master, desire to live under one; and real or fancied Necessity alone makes Men the Servants, Followers, and Creatures of one another. And therefore all Men are animated by the Passion of acquiring and defending Property, because Property is the best Support of that Independency, so passionately desired by all Men. Even Men the most dependent have it constantly in their Heads and their Wishes, to become independent one Time or other; and the Property which they are acquiring, or mean to acquire by that Dependency, is intended to bring them out of it, and to procure them an agreeable Independency. And as Happiness is the Effect of Independency, and Independency the Effect of Property; so certain Property is the Effect of Liberty alone, and can only be secured by the Laws of Liberty; Laws which are made by Consent, and cannot be repealed without it.

All these Blessings, therefore, are only the Gifts and Consequences of Liberty, and only to be found in free Countries, where Power is fixed on one Side, and Property secured on the other; where the one cannot break Bounds without Check, Penalties or Forfeiture, nor the other suffer Diminution without Redress; where the People have no Masters but the Laws, and such as the Laws appoint;

where both Laws and Magistracy are formed by the People or their Deputies; and no Demands are made upon them, but what are made by the Law, and they know to a Penny what to pay before it is asked; where they that exact from them more than the Law allows, are punishable by the Law; and where the Legislators are equally bound by their own Acts, equally involved in the Consequences.

5

WILLIAM BLACKSTONE, COMMENTARIES
1:134–35, 140–41
1765

III. The third absolute right, inherent in every Englishman, is that of property: which consists in the free use, enjoyment, and disposal of all his acquisitions, without any control or diminution, save only by the laws of the land. The original of private property is probably founded in nature, as will be more fully explained in the second book of the ensuing commentaries: but certainly the modifications under which we at present find it, the method of conserving it in the present owner, and of translating it from man to man, are entirely derived from society; and are some of those civil advantages, in exchange for which every individual has resigned a part of his natural liberty. The laws of England are therefore, in point of honor and justice, extremely watchful in ascertaining and protecting this right. Upon this principle the great charter has declared that no freeman shall be disseised, or divested, of his freehold, or of his liberties, or free customs, but by the judgment of his peers, or by the law of the land. And by a variety of antient statutes it is enacted, that no man's lands or goods shall be seised into the king's hands, against the great charter, and the law of the land; and that no man shall be disinherited, nor put out of his franchises or freehold, unless he be duly brought to answer, and be forejudged by course of law; and if any thing be done to the contrary, it shall be redressed, and holden for none.

So great moreover is the regard of the law for private property, that it will not authorize the least violation of it; no, not even for the general good of the whole community. If a new road, for instance, were to be made through the grounds of a private person, it might perhaps be extensively beneficial to the public; but the law permits no man, or set of men, to do this without consent of the owner of the land. In vain may it be urged, that the good of the individual ought to yield to that of the community; for it would be dangerous to allow any private man, or even any public tribunal, to be the judge of this common good, and to decide whether it be expedient or no. Besides, the public good is in nothing more essentially interested, than in the protection of every individual's private rights, as modelled by the municipal law. In this, and similar cases the legislature alone can, and indeed frequently does, interpose, and compel the individual to acquiesce.

But how does it interpose and compel? Not by absolutely stripping the subject of his property in an arbitrary manner; but by giving him a full indemnification and equivalent for the injury thereby sustained. The public is now considered as an individual, treating with an individual for an exchange. All that the legislature does is to oblige the owner to alienate his possessions for a reasonable price; and even this is an exertion of power, which the legislature indulges with caution, and which nothing but the legislature can perform.

Nor is this the only instance in which the law of the land has postponed even public necessity to the sacred and inviolable rights of private property. For no subject of England can be constrained to pay any aids or taxes, even for the defence of the realm or the support of government, but such as are imposed by his own consent, or that of his representatives in parliament.

. . . . .

In these several articles consist the rights, or, as they are frequently termed, the liberties of Englishmen: liberties more generally talked of, than thoroughly understood; and yet highly necessary to be perfectly known and considered by every man of rank or property, lest his ignorance of the points whereon it is founded should hurry him into faction and licentiousness on the one hand, or a pusillanimous indifference and criminal submission on the other. And we have seen that these rights consist, primarily, in the free enjoyment of personal security, of personal liberty, and of private property. So long as these remain inviolate, the subject is perfectly free; for every species of compulsive tyranny and oppression must act in opposition to one or other of these rights, having no other object upon which it can possibly be employed. To preserve these from violation, it is necessary that the constitution of parliaments be supported in it's full vigor; and limits certainly known, be set to the royal prerogative. And, lastly, to vindicate these rights, when actually violated or attacked, the subjects of England are entitled, in the first place, to the regular administration and free course of justice in the courts of law; next to the right of petitioning the king and parliament for redress of grievances; and lastly to the right of having and using arms for self-preservation and defense. And all these rights and liberties it is our birthright to enjoy entire; unless where the laws of our country have laid them under necessary restraints. Restraints in themselves so gentle and moderate, as will appear upon farther enquiry, that no man of sense or probity would wish to see them slackened. For all of us have it in our choice to do every thing that a good man would desire to do; and are restrained from nothing, but what would be pernicious either to ourselves or our fellow citizens. So that this review of our situation may fully justify the observation of a learned French author, who indeed generally both thought and wrote in the spirit of genuine freedom; and who hath not scrupled to profess, even in the very bosom of his native country, that the English is the only nation in the world, where political or civil liberty is the direct end of it's constitution. Recommending therefore to the student in our laws a farther and more accurate search into this extensive and important title, I shall close my remarks upon it with the expiring wish of the famous father Paul to his country, "ESTO PERPETUA!"

6

HOUSE OF REPRESENTATIVES OF MASSACHUSETTS TO DENNYS DE BERDT
12 Jan. 1768

S. Adams Writings 1:137–39

It is observable that though many have disregarded life, and contemned liberty, yet there are few men who do not agree that property is a valuable acquisition, which ought to be held sacred. Many have fought, and bled, and died for this, who have been insensible to all other obligations. Those who ridicule the ideas of right and justice, faith and truth among men, will put a high value upon money. Property is admitted to have an existence, even in the savage state of nature. The bow, the arrow, and the tomahawk; the hunting and the fishing ground, are species of property, as important to an American savage, as pearls, rubies, and diamonds are to the Mogul, or a Nabob in the East, or the lands, tenements, hereditaments, messuages, gold and silver of the Europeans. And if property is necessary for the support of savage life, it is by no means less so in civil society. The Utopian schemes of levelling, and a community of goods, are as visionary and impracticable, as those which vest all property in the Crown, are arbitrary, despotic, and in our government unconstitutional. Now, what property can the colonists be conceived to have, if their money may be granted away by others, without their consent? This most certainly is the present case; for they were in no sense represented in Parliament, when this act for raising a revenue in America was made. The stamp act was grievously complained of by all the colonies; and is there any real difference between this act and the stamp act? They were both designed to raise a revenue in America, and in the same manner, viz. by duties on certain commodities. The payment of the duties imposed by the stamp act, might have been eluded by a total disuse of the stamped paper; and so may the payment of these duties, by the total disuse of the articles on which they are laid; but in neither case, without difficulty. Therefore, the subjects here, are reduced to the hard alternative, either of being obliged totally to disuse articles of the greatest necessity, in common life, or to pay a tax without their consent.

The security of right and property, is the great end of government. Surely, then, such measures as tend to render right and property precarious, tend to destroy both property and government; for these must stand and fall together. It would be difficult, if possible, to show, that the present plan of taxing the colonies is more favorable to them, than that put in use here, before the revolution. It seems, by the event, that our ancestors were, in one respect, not in so melancholy a situation, as we, their posterity, are. In those times, the Crown, and the ministers of the Crown, without the intervention of Parliament, demolished charters, and levied taxes on the colonies, at pleasure. Governor Andross, in the time of James II. declared, that wherever an Englishman sets his foot, all he hath is the King's; and Dudley declared, at the Council Board, and even on the sacred seat of justice, that the privilege of Englishmen, not to be taxed without their consent, and the laws of England, would not follow them to the ends of the earth. It was, also, in those days, declared in Council, that the King's subjects in New England did not differ much from slaves; and that the only difference was, that they were not bought and sold. But there was, even in those times an excellent Attorney General, Sir William Jones, who was of another mind; and told King James, that he could no more grant a commission to levy money on his subjects in Jamaica, though a conquered island, without their consent, by an Assembly, than they could discharge themselves from their allegiance to the English Crown. But the misfortune of the colonists at present is, that they are taxed by Parliament, without their consent. This, while the Parliament continues to tax us, will ever render our case, in one respect, more deplorable and remediless, under the best of Kings, than that of our ancestors was, under the worst. They found relief by the interposition of Parliament. But by the intervention of that very power, we are taxed, and can appeal for relief, from their final decision, to no power on earth; for there is no power on earth above them.

7

EDMUND BURKE, SPEECH ON CONCILIATION WITH THE COLONIES
22 Mar. 1775

Works 1:464–65, 467–68

(See ch. 1, no. 2)

8

GOUVERNEUR MORRIS, POLITICAL ENQUIRIES
1776

Amerikastudien 21:329–31 (1976)

Of Society

Of these three Things Life Liberty Property the first can be enjoyed as well without the aid of Society as with it. The second better. We must therefore seek in the third for the Cause of Society. Without Society Property in Goods is extremely precarious. There is not even the Idea of Property in Lands. Conventions to defend each others Goods naturally apply to the Defense of those places where the Goods are deposited. The Object of such Conventions must be to preserve for each his own Share. It follows therefore that Property is the principal Cause & Object of Society.

Of the Progress of Society

Property in Goods is the first Step in Progression from a State of Nature to that of Society. Till Property in Lands be admitted Society continues rude and barbarous. After the Lands are divided a long Space intervenes before perfect Civilization is effected. The Progress will be accelerated or retarded in Proportion as the Administration of Justice is more or less exact. Here then are three distinct Kinds of Society: Rude and which must continue so. 2 progressive towards Civilization. 3 Civilized. For Instances of each take 1. The Tartar Hordes & American Savages, 2^d The History of any European Kingdom before the sixteenth Century and the present State of Poland, 3^{ly} the actual Circumstances of France and England. If the foregoing Reflections be just, this Conclusion results that the State of Society is perfected in Proportion as the Rights of Property are secured.

Of Natural Liberty

Natural Liberty absolutely excludes the Idea of political Liberty since it implies in every man the Right to do what he pleases. So long, therefore, as it exists Society cannot be established. And when Society is established natural Liberty must cease. It must be restricted. But Liberty restricted is no longer the same. He who wishes to enjoy natural Rights must establish himself where natural Rights are admitted. He must live alone.

If he prefers Society the utmost Liberty he can enjoy is political. Is there a Society in which this political Liberty is perfect? Shall it be said that Poland is that Society? It must first be admitted that nine tenths of the Nation (the Serfs) are not Men. But dignify the Nobles with an exclusive Title to the Rank of Humanity and then examine their Liberum Veto. By this it is in the Power of a single Dissent to prevent a Resolution. Unanimity therefore being required no Man is bound but by his own Consent, at least no nobleman. If it be the Question to enact a Law this is well. But suppose the Reverse or suppose the public Defence at Stake. In both Cases the Majority are bound by the Minority or even by one—this then is not political Liberty.

Progress of Society. The Effect on political Liberty

We find then that perfect political Liberty is a Contradiction in terms. Its Limitation is essential to its Existence. Like natural Liberty it is a theory. *A* has the natural Right to do as he pleases. So has *B*. *A* in Consequence of his natural Right binds *B* to an oak. If it be said that Each is to use his Right so not to injure that of another we come at once within the Pale of civil or social Right.

That Degree of political Liberty essential to one State of Society is incompatible with another. The Mohawks or Oneidas may assemble together & decide by the Majority of Votes. The six Nations must decide by a Majority of

Sachems.—In a numerous Society Representation must be substituted to a general assemblage. But Arts produce a Change as essential as Population. In order that Government decide properly it must understand the Subject. The Objects of Legislation are in a rude Society simple, in a more advanced State complex. Of two Things therefore one. Either Society must stop in its Progression for the Purpose of preserving political Liberty or the latter must be checked that the former may proceed.

Where political Liberty is in Excess Property must be insecure and where Property is not secured Society cannot advance. Suppose a State governed by Representatives equally & annually chosen of which the Majority to govern. Either the Laws would be so arbitrary & fluctuating as to destroy Property or Property would so influence the Legislature as to destroy Liberty. Between these two extremes Anarchy.

Of Commerce

The most rapid advances in the State of Society are produced by Commerce. Is it a Blessing or a Curse? Before this question be decided let the present and former State of commercial Countries be compared. Commerce once begun is from its own Nature progressive. It may be crippled[?] or destroyed not fixed. It requires not only the perfect Security of Property but perfect good faith. Hence its Effects are to encrease civil and to diminish political Liberty. If the public be in Debt to an Individual political Liberty enables a Majority to cancel the obligation, but the Spirit of Commerce exacts punctual Payment. In a Despotism everything must bend to the Prince. He can seize the Property of his Subject but the Spirit of Commerce requires that Property be sacred. It requires also that every Citizen have the Right freely to use his Property.

Now as Society is in itself Progressive, as Commerce gives a mighty spring to that progressive Force, as the Effects of both joint & separate are to diminish political Liberty, and as Commerce cannot be stationary the Society without it may. It follows that political Liberty must be restrained or Commerce prohibited. If a medium be sought it will occasion a Contest between the Spirit of Commerce and that of the Government till Commerce is ruined or Liberty destroyed, perhaps both. These Reflections are justified by the different Italian Republics.

Civil Liberty in Connection with political

Political Liberty considered separately from civil Liberty can have no other Effect than to gratify Pride. That Society governs itself is a pleasing Reflection to Members at their Ease but will it console him whose Property is confiscated by an unjust Law? A Majority influenced by the Heat of Party Spirit banishes a virtuous Man and takes his Effects. Is Poverty or is Exile less bitter decreed by a thousand than inflicted by one? Examine that Majority. In the Madness of Victory are they free from Apprehension? What happens this Day to the Victim of their Rage may it not happen tomorrow to his Persecutors?

If we consider political in Connection with civil Liberty we place the former as the Guard and Security to the latter. But if the latter be given up for the former we sacrifice the End to the Means. We have seen that the Progress of Society tends to Encrease civil and diminish political Liberty. We shall find on Reflection that civil Liberty itself restricts political. Every Right of the Subject with Respect to the Government must derogate from its Authority or be thereby destroyed. The Authority of Magistrates is taken from that Mass of Power which in rude Societies and un-ballanced Democracies is wielded by the Majority. Every Separation of the Executive and judicial Authority from the Legislature is a Diminution of political and Encrease of civil Liberty. Every Check and Ballance of that Legislature has a like Effect. And yet by these Means alone can political Liberty itself be secured. Its Excess becomes Destruction.

In looking back we shall be struck with the following Progression. Happiness the Object of Government. Virtue the Source of Happiness. Civil Liberty the Guardian of Virtue, political Liberty the Defence of civil, Restrictions on political Liberty the only Means of preserving it.

9

THOMAS JEFFERSON, AUTOBIOGRAPHY
1821

Works 1:57–59, 68–69, 77–78

(See ch. 15, no. 20, and ch. 4, no. 7)

10

THE ESSEX RESULT
29 Apr. 1778

Handlin 335–36

(See ch. 4, no. 8)

11

RETURN OF SUTTON, MASSACHUSETTS
18 May 1778

Handlin 231–32

(See ch. 15, no. 22)

12

BENJAMIN FRANKLIN TO ROBERT MORRIS
25 Dec. 1783

Writings 9:138

The Remissness of our People in Paying Taxes is highly blameable; the Unwillingness to pay them is still more so. I see, in some Resolutions of Town Meetings, a Remonstrance against giving Congress a Power to take, as they call it, the People's Money out of their Pockets, tho' only to pay the Interest and Principal of Debts duly contracted. They seem to mistake the Point. Money, justly due from the People, is their Creditors' Money, and no longer the Money of the People, who, if they withold it, should be compell'd to pay by some Law.

All Property, indeed, except the Savage's temporary Cabin, his Bow, his Matchcoat, and other little Acquisitions, absolutely necessary for his Subsistence, seems to me to be the Creature of public Convention. Hence the Public has the Right of Regulating Descents, and all other Conveyances of Property, and even of limiting the Quantity and the Uses of it. All the Property that is necessary to a Man, for the Conservation of the Individual and the Propagation of the Species, is his natural Right, which none can justly deprive him of: But all Property superfluous to such purposes is the Property of the Publick, who, by their Laws, have created it, and who may therefore by other Laws dispose of it, whenever the Welfare of the Publick shall demand such Disposition. He that does not like civil Society on these Terms, let him retire and live among Savages. He can have no right to the benefits of Society, who will not pay his Club towards the Support of it.

13

THOMAS JEFFERSON TO JAMES MADISON
28 Oct. 1785

Papers 8:681–82

(See ch. 15, no. 32)

14

REMONSTRANCE AND PETITION OF THE FREE INHABITANTS OF LUNENBERG COUNTY, VIRGINIA
29 Nov. 1785

W. & M. Q., 3d ser., 30:140–43 (1973)

To the Honorable the General Assembly of Virginia, The Remonstrance and Petition of the free Inhabitants of the County of Lunenberg,

Gentlemen,

When the british Parliament usurp'd a right to Dispose of our Property, it was not the Matter, but the Manner adopted for that purpose, that alarm'd us; as it tended to establish a principle which might one day prove fatal to our rights of Property: In order therefore to fix a Tenure in our property on a Basis of Security not to be shaken in future, we dissolved our union with our parent Country, and by a selferected power bravely and wisely establish'd a Constitution and form of Government, grounded on a full and clear Declaration of such rights as naturally pertain to Men born free and determined to be respectfully and absolutely so as human Institutions can make them: This we effected by our representatives, to whom we delegated our power, in General Convention; Whose Wisdom, Integrity, Fortitude, and patriotic Zeal will ever reflect Glory on them and honor on their Constituents. In support of this happy Establishment, with its attendant Blessings we have chearfully sacrificed our Ease, Lives and fortunes, and waded thro' Deluges of civil Blood to that unequivocal Liberty, which alone characterises the free independent Citizen, and distinguishes him from the subjugated Vassal of despotic Rule.

Thus happily possess'd of all the rational rights of freedom, this Country might have stood the Envy of admiring Nations, to the end of the Time, had the same Wisdom fidelity and patriotic Zeal, which gave Being to this Glorious Work, continued to guide the public Councils of the State: But how far this has, or had not, been our happy Lot, let past Violations of our sacred rights of property, and the recent Invasions of them from such Examples, testify to the World. And here we could wish not to call to Mind, particulars: Suffice it therefore only to *Mention* the Act for funding our Paper Money, which not only involved Thousands of our most valuable Citizens in irretriev'ble ruin, but stabb'd the very Vitals of public Faith. But it was said to be expedient; And we acquiesced in it; But never did, nor ever will, admit it as a ruling Precedent [in] the Wanton Disposal of our property, of any kind, whenever the chimerical Flights of a fanatic Spirit, or the venal Views of a corrupted heart shall prompt to the rash attempt—No! we have seald with our Blood, a Title to the full, free, and absolute Enjoyment of every species of our Property, whensoever, or howsoever legally acquired; a Purchase of too great Value to be sacrificed to the Caprice, or Interest of any rank or Description of Men, however dignified, or distinguished, either by the confidential Suffrages of their fellow-Citizens, or otherwise.

To this free, and we trust, inoffensive, as well as necessary Communication of our Sentiments, on the most important Subject that ever arrested the attention of a free People, we are enforced by a daring attempt now on foot in several Counties in this State by Petitions warmly advocated by some Men of considerable weight to wreste from us, by an Act of the Legislature, the most valuable and indispensable Article of our Property, our Slaves, by a general Emancipation of them: An Attempt that involves in it not only a flagrant Contempt of the constituent Powers of the Commonwealth, in which it's Majesty resides and which we are sorry to have occasion to observe seem

to be forgotten by too many, and a daring attack on that sacred Constitution thereby establishd; but also, Want, Poverty, Distress and ruin to the free Citizen; the Horrors of all the rapes, Robberies, Murders, and Outrages, which an innumerable Host of unprincipled, unpropertied, vindictive, and remorseless Banditti are capable of perpetrating; Neglect, famine and Death to the abandoned black Infant, and superannuated Parent; inevitable Bankruptcy to the revenue; Desparation and revolt to the disappointed, oppressed Citizen; and sure and final ruin to this once happy, free, and flourishing Country: And all this [*illeg.*] to answer no one civil, religious, or national Purpose, whatever. Such a Scheme indeed consists very well with the principles and Designs of a *Bute*, or a *North*, whose Finger is sufficiently visible in it; nor should we have wonder'd to see the despicable Cabal of an expiring Faction rearing its batterd Front on any occasion that might minister to the Disturbance of Governmente: But when we see those very Men who have been honor'd with the fullest Confidence of their fellow Citizens inviting Great Britain, by their Apostasy, to effect that Tyranny over us which we have taught her to feel is not in her Arms to compass; when we see such Men, If such there are, prostituting their [views] by uniting them with a proscribed Coke an imperious Asb[ur]y and other contemptible Emissaries and Hirelings of Britain in promoting and advocating a Measure which they know must involve their fellow Citizens in Distress and Desparation, not to be described, or thought of, without Horror; and their Country in inevitable ruin. No Language can express our Indignation, Contempt and Destestation of the apostate Wretches: For tho' we admit it to be the indisputable right of the Citizen to apply to the Legislature by Petition on any or otherwise Subject within the Cognizance of their constitutional Powers; yet we positively deny a right in any Man or Description of Men, even to move the Legislature in any Manner, to violate the smallest Article of our Constitution, as it is not only a contempt of that, but strongly implies a Want of Wisdom, Integrity, or Spirit in our representatives, to discharge the high Trust [so] found in them, want of either of which would render them very unfit Objects of the Confidence of their Constituents, and of course, dangerous and contemptible. It therefore cannot be admitted that any Man has a right, to petition or otherwise press the Legislature to divest us of our known rights of Property, which are so clearly defined; so fully acknowledged; and so solemnly ratified and confirmd, by our Bill of rights, as not to admit of an equivocal Construction, nor of the smallest Alteration or Diminution, by any Power, but that which originally authorised its Establishment. To an unequivocal Construction therefore of this Bill of rights we now appeal, and claim the utmost Benefits of it; not doubting the hearty Concurrence of our faithful representatives in what ever may tend to promote our mutual Interests; preserve our rights inviolate; secure to us all the Blessings of a free, undisturbd, independent Government; and So, an indiscriminate Diffusion of Peace, Wealth, and happiness among the free Citizens of this Commonwealth. And as the lasting Welfare of our Country, and the happiness of its Citizens depend [*illeg.*]

invariable Adherence to our Constitution, we most solemnly adjure, and humbly pray, that you, Gentlemen, to whom we have committed the Guardianship of our rights of Property, will in no Instance, permit them to be call'd in Question; Particularly, that you will discountenance, and utterly reject every Motion and Proposal for emancipating our Slaves; That you will immediately, and totally repeal the Act for permitting Owners of Slaves to emancipate them; That you will provide effectually for the good Government, and due restraint of those already set free, whose disorderly Conduct, and thefts and outrages, are so generally the just Subject of Complaint; but particularly whose Insolences, and Violences so freequently of late committed to and on our respectable Maids and Matrons, which are a Disgrace to Government.

And We shall ever Pray/etc etc etc etc

15

JOHN ADAMS, DEFENCE OF THE CONSTITUTIONS OF GOVERNMENT OF THE UNITED STATES 1787

Works 6:8–9

Suppose a nation, rich and poor, high and low, ten millions in number, all assembled together; not more than one or two millions will have lands, houses, or any personal property; if we take into the account the women and children, or even if we leave them out of the question, a great majority of every nation is wholly destitute of property, except a small quantity of clothes, and a few trifles of other movables. Would Mr. Nedham be responsible that, if all were to be decided by a vote of the majority, the eight or nine millions who have no property, would not think of usurping over the rights of the one or two millions who have? Property is surely a right of mankind as really as liberty. Perhaps, at first, prejudice, habit, shame or fear, principle or religion, would restrain the poor from attacking the rich, and the idle from usurping on the industrious; but the time would not be long before courage and enterprise would come, and pretexts be invented by degrees, to countenance the majority in dividing all the property among them, or at least, in sharing it equally with its present possessors. Debts would be abolished first; taxes laid heavy on the rich, and not at all on the others; and at last a downright equal division of every thing be demanded, and voted. What would be the consequence of this? The idle, the vicious, the intemperate, would rush into the utmost extravagance of debauchery, sell and spend all their share, and then demand a new division of those who purchased from them. The moment the idea is admitted into society, that property is not as sacred as the laws of God, and that there is not a force of law and public justice to protect it, anarchy and tyranny commence. If "THOU SHALT NOT COVET," and "THOU SHALT NOT STEAL," were not commandments of Heaven, they must be made

inviolable precepts in every society, before it can be civilized or made free.

16

RECORDS OF THE FEDERAL CONVENTION

[1:533; Madison, 5 July]

The 1st. proposition in the Report for fixing the representation in the 1st. branch, one member for every 40,000 inhabitants, being taken up.

Mr. Govr. Morris objected to that scale of apportionment. He thought property ought to be taken into the estimate as well as the number of inhabitants. Life and liberty were generally said to be of more value, then property. An accurate view of the matter would nevertheless prove that property was the main object of Society. The savage State was more favorable to liberty than the Civilized; and sufficiently so to life. It was preferred by all men who had not acquired a taste for property; it was only renounced for the sake of property which could only be secured by the restraints of regular Government. These ideas might appear to some new, but they were nevertheless just. If property then was the main object of Govt. certainly it ought to be one measure of the influence due to those who were to be affected by the Governmt. He looked forward also to that range of New States which wd. soon be formed in the west. He thought the rule of representation ought to be so fixed as to secure to the Atlantic States a prevalence in the National Councils. The new States will know less of the public interest than these, will have an interest in many respects different, in particular will be little scrupulous of involving the Community in wars the burdens & operations of which would fall chiefly on the maritime States. Provision ought therefore to be made to prevent the maritime States from being hereafter outvoted by them. He thought this might be easily done by irrevocably fixing the number of representatives which the Atlantic States should respectively have, and the number which each new State will have. This wd. not be unjust, as the western settlers wd. previously know the conditions on which they were to possess their lands. It would be politic as it would recommend the plan to the present as well as future interest of the States which must decide the fate of it.

Mr. Rutledge. The gentleman last up had spoken some of his sentiments precisely. Property was certainly the principal object of Society. If numbers should be made the rule of representation, the Atlantic States will be subjected to the Western. He moved that the first proposition in the report be postponed in order to take up the following viz. "that the suffrages of the several States be regulated and proportioned according to the sums to be paid towards the general revenue by the inhabitants of each State respectively; that an apportionment of suffrages, according to the ratio aforesaid shall be made and regulated at the end of   years from the 1st. meeting of the Legislature of the U. S. and at the end of every   years but that for the present, and until the period above mentioned, the suffrages shall be for N. Hampshire   Massachts.   &c—

Col. Mason said the case of new States was not unnoticed in the Committee; but it was thought and he was himself decidedly of opinion that if they made a part of the Union, they ought to be subject to no unfavorable discriminations. Obvious considerations required it.

Mr. Radolph concurred with Col. Mason.

On question on Mr. Rutlidges motion.

Masts. no. Cont. no. N. Y. no. N. J. no. Pa. no. Del. no. Maryd. no. Va. no. N. C. no. S. C. ay. Geo. not on floor [Ayes—1; noes—9; absent—1.]

[1:540; Madison, 6 July]

Mr. Govr. Morris moved to commit so much of the Report as relates to "1 member for every 40,000 inhabitants" His view was that they might absolutely fix the number for each State in the first instance; leaving the Legislature at liberty to provide for changes in the relative importance of the States, and for the case of new States.

Mr. Wilson 2ded. the motion; but with a view of leaving the Committee under no implied shackles.

. . . . .

Mr. King wished the clause to be committed chiefly in order to detach it from the Report with which it had no connection. He thought also that the Ratio of Representation proposed could not be safely fixed, since in a century & a half our computed increase of population would carry the number of representatives to an enormous excess; that ye. number of inhabitants was not the proper index of ability & wealth; that property was the primary object of Society; and that in fixing a ratio this ought not to be excluded from the estimate. With regard to New States, he observed that there was something peculiar in the business which had not been noticed. The U.S. were now admitted to be proprietors of the Country, N. West of the Ohio. Congs. by one of their ordinances have impoliticly laid it out into ten States, and have made it a fundamental article of compact with those who may become settlers, that as soon as the number in any one State shall equal that of the smallest of the 13 original States, it may claim admission into the Union. Delaware does not contain it is computed more than 35,000 souls, and for obvious reasons will not increase much for a considerable time. It is possible then that if this plan be persisted in by Congs. 10 new votes may be added, without a greater addition of inhabitants than are represented by the single vote of Pena. The plan as it respects one of the new States is already irrevocable, the sale of the lands having commenced, and the purchasers & settlers will immediately become entitled to all the privileges of the compact.

Mr. Butler agreed to the Commitment if the Committee were to be left at liberty. He was persuaded that the more the subject was examined, the less it would appear that the number of inhabitants would be a proper rule of proportion. If there were no other objection the changeableness of the standard would be sufficient. He concurred with

those who thought some balance was necessary between the old & New States. He contended strenuously that property was the only just measure of representation. This was the great object of Governt: the great cause of war, the great means of carrying it on.

Mr. Pinkney saw no good reason for committing. The value of land had been found on full investigation to be an impracticable rule. The contributions of revenue including imports & exports, must be too changeable in their amount; too difficult to be adjusted; and too injurious to the non-commercial States. The number of inhabitants appeared to. him the only just & practicable rule. He thought the blacks ought to stand on an equality with whites: But wd.—agree to the ratio settled by Congs. He contended that Congs. had no right under the articles of Confederation to authorize the admission of new States; no such case having been provided for.

Mr. Davy, was for committing the clause in order to get at the merits of the question arising on the Report. He seemed to think that wealth or property ought to be represented in the 2d. branch; and numbers in the 1st. branch.

On the motion for committing as made by Mr. Govr. Morris.

Masts. ay—Cont. ay. N. Y. no N. J. no. Pa ay. Del. no. Md. divd. Va. ay. N. C. ay. S. C. ay. Geo. ay. [Ayes—7; noes—3; divided—1.]

[2:121; Madison, 26 July]

Mr Mason moved "that the Committee of detail be instructed to receive a clause requiring certain qualifications of landed property & citizenship [of the U. States] in members of the Legislature, and disqualifying persons having unsettled Accts. with or being indebted to the U.S. [from being members of the Natl. Legislature"]—He observed that persons of the latter descriptions had frequently got into the State Legislatures, in order to promote laws that might shelter their delinquencies; and that this evil had crept into Congs. if Report was to be regarded.

Mr. Pinckney seconded the motion

Mr Govr. Morris. If qualifications are proper, he wd. prefer them in the electors rather than the elected. As to debtors of the U.S. they are but few. As to persons having unsettled accounts he believed them to be pretty many. He thought however that such a discrimination would be both odious & useless. and in many instances unjust & cruel. The delay of settlemt. had been more the fault of the public than of the individuals. What will be done with those patriotic Citizens who have lent money, or services or property to their Country, without having been yet able to obtain a liquidation of their claims? Are they to be excluded?

Mr. Ghorum was for leaving to the Legislature, the providing agst such abuses as had been mentioned.

Col. Mason mentioned the parliamentary qualifications adopted in the Reign of Queen Anne, which he said had met with universal approbation.

Mr. Madison had witnessed the zeal of men having accts. with the public, to get into the Legislatures for sinister purposes. He thought however that if any precaution were to be taken for excluding them, the one proposed by Col. Mason ought to be new modelled. It might be well to limit the exclusion to persons who had recd money from the public, and had not accounted for it.

Mr Govr. Morris—It was a precept of great antiquity as well as of high authority that we should not be righteous overmuch. He thought we ought to be equally on our guard agst. being wise over much. The proposed regulation would enable the Govent. to exclude particular persons from office as long as they pleased. He mentioned the case of the Commander in chief's presenting his account for secret services, which he said was so moderate that every one was astonished at it; and so simple that no doubt could arise on it. Yet had the Auditor been disposed to delay the settlement, how easily might he have affected it, and how cruel wd. it be in such a case to keep a distinguished & meritorious Citizen under a temporary disability & disfranchisement. He mentioned this case merely to illustrate the objectionable nature of the proposition. He was opposed to such minutious regulations in a Constitution. The parliamentary qualifications quoted by Col. Mason, had been disregarded in practice; and was but a scheme of the landed agst the monied interest.

Mr Pinckney & Genl. Pinckney moved to insert by way of amendmt. the words Judiciary & Executive so as to extend the qualifications to those departments which was agreed to nem con

Mr. Gerry thought the inconveniency of excluding a few worthy individuals who might be public debtors or have unsettled accts ought not to be put in the Scale agst the public advantages of the regulation, and that the motion did not go far enough.

Mr. King observed that there might be great danger in requiring landed property as a qualification since it would exclude the monied interest, whose aids may be essential in particular emergencies to the public safety.

Mr. Dickenson. was agst. any recital of qualifications in the Constitution. It was impossible to make a compleat one, and a partial one would by implication tie up the hands of the Legislature from supplying the omissions, The best defence lay in the freeholders who were to elect the Legislature. Whilst this Source should remain pure, the public interest would be safe. If it ever should be corrupt, no little expedients would repel the danger. He doubted the policy of interweaving into a Republican constitution a veneration for wealth. He had always understood that a veneration for poverty & virtue, were the objects of republican encouragement. It seemed improper that any man of merit should be subjected to disabilities in a Republic where merit was understood to form the great title to public trust, honors & rewards.

Mr Gerry if property be one object of Government, provisions for securing it can not be improper.

Mr. Madison moved to strike out the word *landed*, before the word, "qualifications". If the proposition sd. be agreed to he wished the Committee to be at liberty to report the best criterion they could devise. Landed possessions were no certain evidence of real wealth. Many enjoyed them to a great extent who were more in debt than they were worth. The unjust laws of the States had proceeded more from this class of men, than any others. It had often happened that men who had acquired landed property on credit, got into the Legislatures with a view of promoting an unjust protection agst. their Creditors. In the next place, if a small quantity of land should be made the standard. it would be no security.—if a large one, it would exclude the proper representatives of those classes of Citizens who were not landholders. It was politic as well as just that the interests & rights of every class should be duly represented & understood in the public Councils. It was a provision every where established that the Country should be divided into districts & representatives taken from each, in order that the Legislative Assembly might equally understand & sympathise, with the rights of the people in every part of the Community. It was not less proper that every class of Citizens should have an opportunity of making their rights be felt & understood in the public Councils. The three principle classes into which our citizens were divisible, were the landed the commercial, & the manufacturing. The 2d. & 3rd. class, bear as yet a small proportion to the first. The proportion however will daily increase. We see in the populous Countries in Europe now, what we shall be hereafter. These classes understand much less of each others interests & affairs, than men of the same class inhabiting different districts. It is particularly requisite therefore that the interests of one or two of them should not be left entirely to the care, or the impartiality of the third. This must be the case if landed qualifications should be required; few of the mercantile, and scarcely any of the manufacturing class, chusing whilst they continue in business to turn any part of their Stock into landed property. For these reasons he wished if it were possible that some other criterion than the mere possession of land should be devised. He concurred with Mr. Govr. Morris in thinking that qualifications in the Electors would be much more effectual than in the elected. The former would discriminate between real & ostensible property in the latter; But he was aware of the difficulty of forming any uniform standard that would suit the different circumstances & opinions prevailing in the different States.

Mr. Govr Morris 2ded. the motion.

On the Question for striking out "landed"

N. H. ay. Mas. ay. Ct. ay N. J. ay. Pa. ay. Del. ay. Md. no Va. ay. N. C. ay. S. C. ay. Geo. ay. [Ayes—10; noes—1.]

On Question on 1st. part of Col. Masons proposition as to qualification of property & citizenship" as so amended N. H. ay. Masts. ay. Ct. no. N. J. ay. Pa. no. Del. no. Md. ay. Va. ay. N. C. ay. S. C. ay. Geo. ay. [Ayes—8; noes—3.]

"The 2d. part, for disqualifying debtors, and persons having unsettled accounts", being under consideration

Mr. Carrol moved to strike out "having unsettled accounts"

Mr. Ghorum seconded the motion; observing that it would put the commercial & manufacturing part of the people on a worse footing than others as they would be most likely to have dealings with the public.

Mr. L— Martin. if these words should be struck out, and the remaining words concerning debtors retained, it will be the interest of the latter class to keep their accounts unsettled as long as possible.

Mr. Wilson was for striking them out. They put too much power in the hands of the Auditors, who might combine with rivals in delaying settlements in order to prolong the disqualifications of particular men. We should consider that we are providing a Constitution for future generations, and not merely for the peculiar circumstances of the moment. The time has been, and will again be when the public safety may depend on the voluntary aids of individuals which will necessarily open accts. with the public, and when such accts. will be a characteristic of patriotism. Besides a partial enumeration of cases will disable the Legislature from disqualifying odious & dangerous characters.

Mr. Langdon was for striking out the whole clause for the reasons given by Mr Wilson. So many Exclusions he thought too would render the system unacceptable to the people.

Mr. Gerry. If the argumts. used to day were to prevail, we might have a Legislature composed of public debtors, pensioners, placemen & contractors. He thought the proposed qualifications would be pleasing to the people. They will be considered as a security agst unnecessary or undue burdens being imposed on them He moved to add "pensioners" to the disqualified characters which was negatived.

N. H. no Mas. ay. Con. no. N. J. no. Pa. no. Del no Maryd. ay. Va. no. N. C. divided. S. C. no. Geo. ay. [Ayes—3; noes—7; divided—1.]

Mr. Govr. Morris The last clause, relating to public debtors will exclude every importing merchant. Revenue will be drawn it is foreseen as much as possible, from trade. Duties of course will be bonded. and the Merchts. will remain debtors to the public. He repeated that it had not been so much the fault of individuals as of the public that transactions between them had not been more generally liquidated & adjusted. At all events to draw from our short & scanty experience rules that are to operate through succeeding ages, does not savour much of real wisdom.

On question for striking out "persons having unsettled accounts with the U. States."

N. H. ay. Mas. ay. Ct. ay. N. J. no. Pa. ay. Del. ay. Md. ay. Va. ay. N. C. ay. S. C. ay. Geo. no. [Ayes—9; noes—2.]

Mr. Elseworth was for disagreeing to the remainder of the clause disqualifying public debtors; and for leaving to the wisdom of the Legislature and the virtue of the Citizens, the task of providing agst. such evils. Is the smallest as well largest debtor to be excluded? Then every arrear of taxes will disqualify. Besides how is it to be known to the people when they elect who are or are not public debtors. The exclusion of pensioners & placemen in Engd is founded on a consideration not existing here. As persons of that sort are dependent on the Crown, they tend to increase its influence.

Mr. Pinkney sd. he was at first a friend to the proposition, for the sake of the clause relating to qualifications of property; but he disliked the exclusion of public debtors; it went too far. It wd. exclude persons who had purchased confiscated property or should purchase Western territory of the public, and might be some obstacle to the sale of the latter.

On the question for agreeing to the clause disqualifying public debtors

N. H. no. Mas- no. Ct. no. N- J. no. Pa. no. Del. no. Md. no. Va. no. N. C. ay. S. C. no. Geo. ay. [Ayes—2; noes—9.]

[2:202; Madison, 7 Aug.]

Mr. Elseworth. How shall the freehold be defined? Ought not every man who pays a tax to vote for the representative who is to levy & dispose of his money? Shall the wealthy merchants and manufacturers, who will bear a full share of the public burdens be not allowed a voice in the imposition of them—taxation and representation ought to go together.

Mr. Govr. Morris. He had long learned not to be the dupe of words. The sound of Aristocracy therefore, had no effect on him. It was the thing, not the name, to which he was opposed, and one of his principal objections to the Constitution as it is now before us, is that it threatens this Country with an Aristocracy. The aristocracy will grow out of the House of Representatives. Give the votes to people who have no property, and they will sell them to the rich who will be able to buy them. We should not confine our attention to the present moment. The time is not distant when this Country will abound with mechanics & manufacturers who will receive their bread from their employers. Will such men be the secure & faithful Guardians of liberty? Will they be the impregnable barrier agst. aristocracy?—He was as little duped by the association of the words, "taxation & Representation"—The man who does not give his vote freely is not represented. It is the man who dictates the vote. Children do not vote. Why? because they want prudence. because they have no will of their own. The ignorant & the dependent can be as little trusted with the public interest. He did not conceive the difficulty of defining "freeholders" to be insuperable. Still less that the restriction could be unpopular. 9/10 of the people are at present freeholders and these will certainly be pleased with it. As to Merchts. &c. if they have wealth & value the right they can acquire it. If not they don't deserve it.

Col. Mason. We all feel too strongly the remains of antient prejudices, and view things too much through a British Medium. A Freehold is the qualification in England, & hence it is imagined to be the only proper one. The true idea in his opinion was that every man having evidence of attachment to & permanent common interest with the Society ought to share in all its rights & privileges. Was this qualification restrained to freeholders? Does no other kind of property but land evidence a common interest in the proprietor? does nothing besides property mark a permanent attachment. Ought the merchant, the monied man, the parent of a number of children whose fortunes are to be pursued in their own Country, to be viewed as suspicious characters, and unworthy to be trusted with the common rights of their fellow Citizens

Mr. Madison. the right of suffrage is certainly one of the fundamental articles of republican Government, and ought not to be left to be regulated by the Legislature. A gradual abridgment of this right has been the mode in which Aristocracies have been built on the ruins of popular forms. Whether the Constitutional qualification ought to be a freehold, would with him depend much on the probable reception such a change would meet with in States where the right was now exercised by every description of people. In several of the States a freehold was now the qualification. Viewing the subject in its merits alone, the freeholders of the Country would be the safest depositories of Republican liberty. In future times a great majority of the people will not only be without landed, but any other sort of, property. These will either combine under the influence of their common situation; in which case, the rights of property & the public liberty, will not be secure in their hands: or which is more probable, they will become the tools of opulence & ambition, in which case there will be equal danger on another side. The example of England has been misconceived by Col Mason. A very small proportion of the Representatives are there chosen by freeholders. The greatest part are chosen by the Cities & boroughs, in many of which the qualification of suffrage is as low as it is in any one of the U. S. and it was in the boroughs & Cities rather than the Counties, that bribery most prevailed, & the influence of the Crown on elections was most dangerously exerted.[1]

Docr. Franklin. It is of great consequence that we shd. not depress the virtue & public spirit of our common people; of which they displayed a great deal during the war, and which contributed principally to the favorable issue of it. He related the honorable refusal of the American seamen who were carried in great numbers into the British Prisons during the war, to redeem themselves from misery or to seek their fortunes, by entering on board the Ships of the Enemies to their Country; contrasting their patriotism with a contemporary instance in which the British seamen made prisoners by the Americans, readily entered

[1]Note to Speech of J. Madison of August 7th, 1787.

As appointments for the General Government here contemplated will, in part, be made by the State Governments: all the Citizens in States where the right of suffrage is not limited to the holders of property, will have an indirect share of representation in the General Government. But this does not satisfy the fundamental principle that men cannot be justly bound by laws in making of which they have no part. Persons and property being both essential objects of Government, the most that either can claim, is such a structure of it as will leave a reasonable security for the other. And the most obvious provision of this double character, seems to be that of confining to the holders of property, the object deemed least secure in popular Governments, the right of suffrage for one of the two Legislative branches. This is not without example among us, as well as other Constitutional modifications, favoring the influence of property in the Government. But the United States have not reached the stage of Society in which conflicting feelings of the Class with, and the Class without property, have the operation natural to them in Countries fully peopled. The most difficult of all political arrangements is that of so adjusting the claims of the two Classes as to give security to each, and to promote the welfare of all. The federal principle, which enlarges the sphere of power without departing from the elective basis of it, and controls in various ways the propensity in small republics to rash measures and the facility of forming and executing them, will be found the best expedient yet tried for solving the problem.

on the ships of the latter on being promised a share of the prizes that might be made out of their own Country. This proceeded he said, from the different manner in which the common people were treated in America & G. Britain. He did not think that the elected had any right in any case to narrow the privileges of the electors. He quoted as arbitrary the British Statute setting forth the danger of tumultuous meetings, and under that pretext, narrowing the right of suffrage to persons having freeholds of a certain value; observing that this Statute was soon followed by another under the succeeding Parliamt. subjecting the people who had no votes to peculiar labors & hardships. He was persuaded also that such a restriction as was proposed would give great uneasiness in the populous States. The sons of a substantial farmer, not being themselves freeholders, would not be pleased at being disfranchised, and there are a great many persons of that description.

Mr. Mercer. The Constitution is objectionable in many points, but in none more than the present. He objected to the footing on which the qualification was put, but particularly to the *mode of election* by the people. The people can not know & judge of the characters of Candidates. The worse possible choice will be made. He quoted the case of the Senate in Virga. as an example in point- The people in Towns can unite their votes in favor of one favorite; & by that means always prevail over the people of the Country, who being dispersed will scatter their votes among a variety of candidates.

Mr. Rutledge thought the idea of restraining the right of suffrage to the freeholders a very unadvised one. It would create division among the people & make enemies of all those who should be excluded.

[2:248; Madison, 10 Aug.]

Art. VI. sect. 2. taken up. ["The Legislature of the United States shall have authority to establish such uniform qualifications of the members of each House, with regard to property, as to the said Legislature shall seem expedient."]

Mr. Pinkney—The Committee as he had conceived were instructed to report the proper qualifications of property for the members of the Natl. Legislature; instead of which they have referred the task to the Natl. Legislature itself. Should it be left on this footing, the first Legislature will meet without any particular qualifications of property; and if it should happen to consist of rich men they might fix such such qualifications as may be too favorable to the rich; if of poor men, an opposite extreme might be run into. He was opposed to the establishment of an undue aristocratic influence in the Constitution but he thought it essential that the members of the Legislature, the Executive, and the Judges—should be possessed of competent property to make them independent & respectable. It was prudent when such great powers were to be trusted to connect the tie of property with that of reputation in securing a faithful administration. The Legislature would have the fate of the Nation put into their hands. The President would also have a very great influence on it. The Judges would have not only important causes between Citizen & Citizen but also where foreigners are concerned. They will even be the Umpires between the U. States and individual States as well as between one State & another. Were he to fix the quantum of property which should be required, he should not think of less than one hundred thousand dollars for the President, half of that sum for each of the Judges, and in like proportion for the members of the Natl. Legislature. He would however leave the sums blank. His motion was that the President of the U. S. the Judges, and members of the Legislature should be required to swear that they were respectively possessed of a clear unincumbered Estate to the amount of———in the case of the President, &c &c—

Mr. Rutlidge seconded the motion; observing, that the Committee had reported no qualifications because they could not agree on any among themselves, being embarrassed by the danger on one side of displeasing the people by making them high, and on the other of rendering them nugatory by making them low.

Mr. Elseworth. The different circumstances of different parts of the U. S. and the probable difference between the present and future circumstances of the whole, render it improper to have either *uniform* or *fixed* qualifications. Make them so high as to be useful in the S. States, and they will be inapplicable to the E. States. Suit them to the latter, and they will serve no purpose in the former. In like manner what may be accommodated to the existing State of things among us, may be very inconvenient in some future state of them. He thought for these reasons that it was better to leave this matter to the Legislative discretion than to attempt a provision for it in the Constitution.

Doctr Franklin expressed his dislike of every thing that tended to debase the spirit of the common people. If honesty was often the companion of wealth, and if poverty was exposed to peculiar temptation, it was not less true that the possession of property increased the desire of more property—Some of the greatest rogues he was ever acquainted with, were the richest rogues. We should remember the character which the Scripture requires in Rulers, that they should be men hating covetousness—This Constitution will be much read and attended to in Europe, and if it should betray a great partiality to the rich—will not only hurt us in the esteem of the most liberal and enlightened men there, but discourage the common people from removing to this Country.

The Motion of Mr. Pinkney was rejected by so general a *no*, that the States were not called.

Mr Madison was opposed to the Section as vesting an improper & dangerous power in the Legislature. The qualifications of electors and elected were fundamental articles in a Republican Govt. and ought to be fixed by the Constitution. If the Legislature could regulate those of either, it can by degrees subvert the Constitution. A Republic may be converted into an aristocracy or oligarchy as well by limiting the number capable of being elected, as the number authorised to elect. In all cases where the representatives of the people will have a personal interest distinct from that of their Constituents, there was the same reason for being jealous of them, as there was for relying on them with full confidence, when they had a common interest. This was one of the former cases. It was as improper as to allow them to fix their own wages, or their own privileges. It was a power also, which might be made subservient to the views of one faction agst. another. Qualifications founded on artificial distinctions may be devised, by the stronger in order to keep out partizans of a weaker faction.

Mr. Elseworth, admitted that the power was not unexceptionable; but he could not view it as dangerous. Such a power with regard to the electors would be dangerous because it would be much more liable to abuse.

Mr. Govr. Morris moved to strike out "with regard to property" in order to leave the Legislature entirely at large.

Mr. Williamson. This could surely never be admitted. Should a majority of the Legislature be composed of any particular description of men, of lawyers for example, which is no improbable supposition, the future elections might be secured to their own body.

Mr. Madison observed that the British Parliamt. possessed the power of regulating the qualifications both of the electors, and the elected; and the abuse they had made of it was a lesson worthy of our attention. They had made the changes in both cases subservient to their own views, or to the views of political or Religious parties.

Question on the motion to strike out with regard to property

N. H. no. Mas. no. Ct. ay. N. J. ay. Pa. ay. Del. no. Md. no. Va. no. N. C. no. S. C. no. Geo- ay. [Ayes—4; noes—7.]

Mr Rutlidge was opposed to leaving the power to the Legislature—He proposed that the qualifications should be the same as for members of the State Legislatures.

Mr. Wilson thought it would be best on the whole to let the Section go out. A uniform rule would probably be never fixed by the Legislature. and this particular power would constructively exclude every other power of regulating qualifications-

On the question for agreeing to Art—VI—sect—2d

N. H. ay. Mas. ay. Ct. no. N. J. no. Pa. no. Md. no. Va. no. N. C. no S. C. no. Geo. ay—[Ayes—3; noes—7.]

17

Noah Webster, An Examination into the Leading Principles of the Federal Constitution
10 Oct. 1787
Pamphlets 58–61

In America, we begin our empire with more popular privileges than the Romans ever enjoyed. We have not to struggle against a monarch or an aristocracy—power is lodged in the mass of the people.

On reviewing the English history, we observe a progress similar to that in Rome—an incessant struggle for liberty from the date of Magna Charta, in John's reign, to the revolution. The struggle has been successful, by abridging the enormous power of the nobility. But we observe that the power of the people has increased in an exact proportion to their acquisitions of property. Wherever the right of primogeniture is established, property must accumulate and remain in families. Thus the landed property in England will never be sufficiently distributed, to give the powers of government wholly into the hands of the people. But to assist the struggle for liberty, commerce has interposed, and in conjunction with manufacturers, thrown a vast weight of property into the democratic scale. Wherever we cast our eyes, we see this truth, that *property* is the basis of *power;* and this, being established as a cardinal point, directs us to the means of preserving our freedom. Make laws, irrevocable laws in every state, destroying and barring entailments; leave real estates to revolve from hand to hand, as time and accident may direct; and no family influence can be acquired and established for a series of generations—no man can obtain dominion over a large territory—the laborious and saving, who are generally the best citizens, will possess each his share of property and power, and thus the balance of wealth and power will continue where it is, in the *body of the people.*

A general and tolerably equal distribution of landed property is the whole basis of national freedom: The system of the great Montesquieu will ever be erroneous, till the words *property or lands in fee simple* are substituted for *virtue,* throughout his *Spirit of Laws.*

Virtue, patriotism, or love of country, never was and never will be, till mens' natures are changed, a fixed, permanent principle and support of government. But in an agricultural country, a general possession of land in fee simple, may be rendered perpetual, and the inequalities introduced by commerce, are too fluctuating to endanger government. An equality of property, with a necessity of alienation, constantly operating to destroy combinations of powerful families, is the very *soul of a republic*—While this continues, the people will inevitably possess both *power* and *freedom;* when this is lost, power departs, liberty expires, and a commonwealth will inevitably assume some other form.

The liberty of the press, trial by jury, the Habeas Corpus writ, even Magna Charta itself, although justly deemed the palladia of freedom, are all inferior considerations, when compared with a general distribution of real property among every class of people.* The power of entailing estates is more dangerous to liberty and republican government, than all the constitutions that can be written on paper, or even than a standing army. Let the people have

*Montesquieu supposed *virtue* to be the principle of a republic. He derived his notions of this form of government, from the astonishing firmness, courage and patriotism which distinguished the republics of Greece and Rome. But this *virtue* consisted in pride, contempt of strangers and a martial enthusiasm which sometimes displayed itself in defence of their country. These principles are never permanent—they decay with refinement, intercourse with other nations and increase of wealth. No wonder then that these republics declined, for they were not founded on fixed principles; and hence authors imagine that republics cannot be durable. None of the celebrated writers on government seems

property, and they *will* have power—a power that will for ever be exerted to prevent a restriction of the press, and abolition of trial by jury, or the abridgement of any other privilege. The liberties of America, therefore, and her forms of government, stand on the broadest basis. Removed from the fears of a foreign invasion and conquest, they are not exposed to the convulsions that shake other governments; and the principles of freedom are so general and energetic, as to exclude the possibility of a change in our republican constitutions.

But while *property* is considered as the *basis* of the freedom of the American yeomanry, there are other auxiliary supports; among which is the *information of the people.* In no country, is education so general—in no country, have the body of the people such a knowledge of the rights of men and the principles of government. This knowledge, joined with a keen sense of liberty and a watchful jealousy, will guard our constitutions, and awaken the people to an instantaneous resistance of encroachments.

---

to have laid sufficient stress on a general possession of real property in fee-simple. Even the author of the *Political Sketches,* in the *Museum* for the month of September, seems to have passed it over in silence; although he combats Montesquieu's system, and to prove it false, enumerates some of the principles which distinguish our governments from others, and which he supposes constitutes the support of republics.

The English writers on law and government consider Magna Charta, trial by juries, the Habeas Corpus act, and the liberty of the press, as the bulwarks of freedom. All this is well. But in no government of consequence in Europe, is freedom established on its true and immoveable foundation. The property is too much accumulated, and the accumulations too well guarded, to admit the *true principle of republics.* But few centuries have elapsed, since the body of the people were vassals. To such men, the smallest extension of popular privileges, was deemed an invaluable blessing. Hence the encomiums upon trial by juries, and the articles just mentioned. But these people have never been able to mount to the source of *liberty, estates in fee,* or at least but partially; they are yet obliged to drink at the streams. Hence the English jealousy of certain rights, which are guaranteed by acts of parliament. But in America, and here alone, we have gone at once to the *fountain of liberty,* and raised the people to their true dignity. Let the lands be possessed by the people in fee-simple, let the fountain be kept pure, and the streams will be pure of course. Our jealousy of *trial by jury, the liberty of the press,* &c., is totally groundless. Such rights are inseparably connected with the *power* and *dignity* of the people, which rest on their *property.* They cannot be abridged. All *other* [free] nations have wrested *property* and *freedom* from *barons* and *tyrants; we* begin our empire with full possession of property and all its attending rights.

18

JAMES MADISON, FEDERALIST, NO. 10, 58–65
22 Nov. 1787

(See ch. 4, no. 19)

19

ALEXANDER HAMILTON, FEDERALIST, NO. 70, 471–72
15 Mar. 1788

(See ch. 9, no. 10)

20

MELANCTON SMITH, NEW YORK
RATIFYING CONVENTION
21 June 1788

Storing 6.12.15–18

(See ch. 13, no. 37)

21

JAMES MADISON, OBSERVATIONS ON JEFFERSON'S
DRAFT OF A CONSTITUTION FOR VIRGINIA
15 Oct. 1788

Papers 11:287–88

(See ch. 17, no. 25)

22

BENJAMIN FRANKLIN, QUERIES AND REMARKS
RESPECTING ALTERATIONS IN THE
CONSTITUTION OF PENNSYLVANIA
1789

Writings 10:58–60

(See ch. 12, no. 25)

23

JAMES MADISON, PROPERTY
29 Mar. 1792

Papers 14:266–68

This term in its particular application means "that dominion which one man claims and exercises over the external things of the world, in exclusion of every other individual."

In its larger and juster meaning, it embraces every thing to which a man may attach a value and have a right; and *which leaves to every one else the like advantage.*

In the former sense, a man's land, or merchandize, or money is called his property.

In the latter sense, a man has a property in his opinions and the free communication of them.

He has a property of peculiar value in his religious opinions, and in the profession and practice dictated by them.

He has a property very dear to him in the safety and liberty of his person.

He has an equal property in the free use of his faculties and free choice of the objects on which to employ them.

In a word, as a man is said to have a right to his property, he may be equally said to have a property in his rights.

Where an excess of power prevails, property of no sort is duly respected. No man is safe in his opinions, his person, his faculties, or his possessions.

Where there is an excess of liberty, the effect is the same, tho' from an opposite cause.

Government is instituted to protect property of every sort; as well that which lies in the various rights of individuals, as that which the term particularly expresses. This being the end of government, that alone is a *just* government, which *impartially* secures to every man, whatever is his *own*.

According to this standard of merit, the praise of affording a just securing to property, should be sparingly bestowed on a government which, however scrupulously guarding the possessions of individuals, does not protect them in the enjoyment and communication of their opinions, in which they have an equal, and in the estimation of some, a more valuable property.

More sparingly should this praise be allowed to a government, where a man's religious rights are violated by penalties, or fettered by tests, or taxed by a hierarchy. Conscience is the most sacred of all property; other property depending in part on positive law, the exercise of that, being a natural and unalienable right. To guard a man's house as his castle, to pay public and enforce private debts with the most exact faith, can give no title to invade a man's conscience which is more sacred than his castle, or to withhold from it that debt of protection, for which the public faith is pledged, by the very nature and original conditions of the social pact.

That is not a just government, nor is property secure under it, where the property which a man has in his personal safety and personal liberty, is violated by arbitrary seizures of one class of citizens for the service of the rest. A magistrate issuing his warrants to a press gang, would be in his proper functions in Turkey or Indostan, under appellations proverbial of the most compleat despotism.

That is not a just government, nor is property secure under it, where arbitrary restrictions, exemptions, and monopolies deny to part of its citizens that free use of their faculties, and free choice of their occupations, which not only constitute their property in the general sense of the word; but are the means of acquiring property strictly so called. What must be the spirit of legislation where a manufacturer of linen cloth is forbidden to bury his own child in a linen shroud, in order to favour his neighbour who manufactures woolen cloth; where the manufacturer and wearer of woolen cloth are again forbidden the oeconomical use of buttons of that material, in favor of the manufacturer of buttons of other materials!

A just security to property is not afforded by that government, under which unequal taxes oppress one species of property and reward another species: where arbitrary taxes invade the domestic sanctuaries of the rich, and excessive taxes grind the faces of the poor; where the keenness and competitions of want are deemed an insufficient spur to labor, and taxes are again applied, by an unfeeling policy, as another spur; in violation of that sacred property, which Heaven, in decreeing man to earn his bread by the sweat of his brow, kindly reserved to him, in the small repose that could be spared from the supply of his necessities.

If there be a government then which prides itself in maintaining the inviolability of property; which provides that none shall be taken *directly* even for public use without indemnification to the owner, and yet *directly* violates the property which individuals have in their opinions, their religion, their persons, and their faculties; nay more, which *indirectly* violates their property, in their actual possessions, in the labor that acquires their daily subsistence, and in the hallowed remnant of time which ought to relieve their fatigues and soothe their cares, the influence [inference?] will have been anticipated, that such a government is not a pattern for the United States.

If the United States mean to obtain or deserve the full praise due to wise and just governments, they will equally respect the rights of property, and the property in rights: they will rival the government that most sacredly guards the former; and by repelling its example in violating the latter, will make themselves a pattern to that and all other governments.

24

VANHORNE'S LESSEE V. DORRANCE
2 Dall. 304, 310–13 (1795)

[Paterson, J.] Having made these preliminary observations, we shall proceed to contemplate the quieting and confirming act, and to bring its validity to the test of the Constitution.

In the course of argument, the counsel on both sides relied upon certain parts of the late Bill of Rights and Constitution of *Pennsylvania*, which I shall now read, and then refer to them occasionally in the sequel of the charge.

(The Judge then read the 1st. 8th. and 11th articles of the Declaration of Rights; and the 9th. and 46th sections of the Constitution of *Pennsylvania*. See 1 *Vol. Dall. Edit. Penn. Laws p. 55. 6. 60. in the Appendix.*)

From these passages it is evident; that the right of acquiring and possessing property, and having it protected, is one of the natural, inherent, and unalienable rights of man. Men have a sense of property: Property is necessary to their subsistence, and correspondent to their natural wants and desires; its security was one of the objects, that induced them to unite in society. No man would become a member of a community, in which he could not enjoy the fruits of his honest labour and industry. The preservation of property then is a primary object of the social compact, and, by the late Constitution of *Pennsylvania*, was made a fundamental law. Every person ought to contribute his proportion for public purposes and public exigencies; but no one can be called upon to surrender or sacrifice his whole property, real and personal, for the good of the community, without receiving a recompence in value. This would be laying a burden upon an individual, which ought to be sustained by the society at large. The *English* history does not furnish an instance of the kind; the Parliament, with all their boasted omnipotence, never committed such an outrage on private property; and if they had, it would have served only to display the dangerous nature of unlimited authority; it would have been an exercise of power and not of right. Such an act would be a monster in legislation, and shock all mankind. The legislature, therefore, had no authority to make an act divesting one citizen of his freehold, and vesting it in another, without a just compensation. It is inconsistent with the principles of reason, justice, and moral rectitude; it is incompatible with the comfort, peace, and happiness of mankind; it is contrary to the principles of social alliance in every free government; and lastly, it is contrary both to the letter and spirit of the Constitution. In short, it is what every one would think unreasonable and unjust in his own case. The next step in the line of progression is, whether the Legislature had authority to make an act, divesting one citizen of his freehold and vesting it in another, even with compensation. That the Legislature, on certain emergencies, had authority to exercise this high power, has been urged from the nature of the social compact, and from the words of the Constitution, which says, that the House of Representatives shall have all other powers necessary for the Legislature of a free state or commonwealth; but they shall have no power to add to, alter, abolish, or infringe any part of this Constitution. The course of reasoning, on the part of the defendant, may be comprized in a few words. The despotic power, as it is aptly called by some writers, of taking private property, when state necessity requires, exists in every government; the existence of such power is necessary; government could not subsist without it; and if this be the case, it cannot be lodged any where with so much safety as with the Legislature. The presumption is, that they will not call it into exercise except in urgent cases, or cases of the first necessity. There is force in this reasoning. It is, however, difficult to form a case, in which the necessity of a state can be of such a nature, as to authorize or excuse the seizing of landed property belonging to one citizen, and giving it to another citizen. It is immaterial to the state, in which of its citizens the land is vested; but it is of primary importance, that, when vested, it should be secured, and the proprietor protected in the enjoyment of it. The constitution encircles, and renders it an holy thing. We must, gentlemen, bear constantly in mind, that the present is a case of landed property; vested by law in one set of citizens, attempted to be divested, for the purpose of vesting the same property in another set of citizens. It cannot be assimilated to the case of personal property taken or used in time of war or famine, or other extreme necessity; it cannot be assimilated to the temporary possession of land itself, on a pressing public emergency, or the spur of the occasion. In the latter case there is no change of property, no divestment of right; the title remains, and the proprietor, though out of possession for a while, is still proprietor and lord of the soil. The possession grew out of the occasion and ceases with it: Then the right of necessity is satisfied and at an end; it does not affect the title, is temporary in its nature, and cannot exist forever. The constitution expressly declares, that the right of acquiring, possessing, and protecting property is natural, inherent, and unalienable. It is a right not *ex gratia* from the legislature, but *ex debito* from the constitution. It is sacred; for, it is further declared, that the legislature shall have no power to add to, alter, abolish, or infringe any part of, the constitution. The constitution is the origin and measure of legislative authority. It says to legislators, thus far ye shall go and no further. Not a particle of it should be shaken; not a pebble of it should be removed. Innovation is dangerous. One incroachment leads to another; precedent gives birth to precedent; what has been done may be done again; thus radical principles are generally broken in upon, and the constitution eventually destroyed. Where is the security, where the inviolability of property, if the legislature, by a private act, affecting particular persons only, can take land from one citizen, who acquired it legally, and vest it in another? The rights of private property are regulated, protected, and governed by general, known, and established laws; and decided upon, by general, known, and established tribunals; laws and tribunals not made and created on an instant exigency, on an urgent emergency, to serve a present turn, or the interest of a moment. Their operation and influence are equal and universal; they press alike on all. Hence security and safety, tranquillity and peace. One man is not afraid of another, and no man afraid of the legislature. It is infinitely wiser and safer to risk some possible mischiefs, than to vest in the legislature so unnecessary, dangerous, and enormous a power as that which has been exercised on the present occasion; a power, that, according to the full extent of the argument, is boundless and omnipotent: For, the legislature judged of the necessity of the case, and also of the nature and value of the equivalent.

Such a case of necessity, and judging too of the compensation, can never occur in any nation. Singular, indeed, and untoward must be the state of things, that would induce the Legislature, supposing they had the power, to divest one individual of his landed estate merely for the purpose of vesting it in another, even upon full indemnification; unless that indemnification be ascertained in the manner which I shall mention hereafter.

But admitting, that the Legislature can take the real estate of A. and give it to B. on making compensation, the principle and reasoning upon it go no further than to shew, that the Legislature are the sole and exclusive judges of the necessity of the case, in which this despotic power should be called into action. It cannot, on the principles of the social alliance, or of the Constitution, be extended beyond the point of judging upon every existing case of necessity. The Legislature declare and enact, that such are the public exigencies, or necessities of the State, as to authorise them to take the land of A. and give it to B.; the dictates of reason and the eternal principles of justice, as well as the sacred principles of the social contract, and the Constitution, direct, and they accordingly declare and ordain, that A. shall receive compensation for the land. But here the Legislature must stop; they have run the full length of their authority, and can go no further: they cannot constitutionally determine upon the amount of the compensation, or value of the land. Public exigencies do not require, necessity does not demand, that the Legislature should, of themselves, without the participation of the proprietor, or intervention of a jury, assess the value of the thing, or ascertain the amount of the compensation to be paid for it.

25

THOMAS JEFFERSON TO ISAAC MCPHERSON
13 Aug. 1813
Writings 13:333–34

It has been pretended by some, (and in England especially,) that inventors have a natural and exclusive right to their inventions, and not merely for their own lives, but inheritable to their heirs. But while it is a moot question whether the origin of any kind of property is derived from nature at all, it would be singular to admit a natural and even an hereditary right to inventors. It is agreed by those who have seriously considered the subject, that no individual has, of natural right, a separate property in an acre of land, for instance. By an universal law, indeed, whatever, whether fixed or movable, belongs to all men equally and in common, is the property for the moment of him who occupies it, but when he relinquishes the occupation, the property goes with it. Stable ownership is the gift of social law, and is given late in the progress of society. It would be curious then, if an idea, the fugitive fermentation of an individual brain, could, of natural right, be claimed in exclusive and stable property. If nature has made any one thing less susceptible than all others of exclusive property, it is the action of the thinking power called an idea, which an individual may exclusively possess as long as he keeps it to himself; but the moment it is divulged, it forces itself into the possession of every one, and the receiver cannot dispossess himself of it. Its peculiar character, too, is that no one possesses the less, because every other possesses the whole of it. He who receives an idea from me, receives instruction himself without lessening mine; as he who lights his taper at mine, receives light without darkening me. That ideas should freely spread from one to another over the globe, for the moral and mutual instruction of man, and improvement of his condition, seems to have been peculiarly and benevolently designed by nature, when she made them, like fire, expansible over all space, without lessening their density in any point, and like the air in which we breathe, move, and have our physical being, incapable of confinement or exclusive appropriation. Inventions then cannot, in nature, be a subject of property. Society may give an exclusive right to the profits arising from them, as an encouragement to men to pursue ideas which may produce utility, but this may or may not be done, according to the will and convenience of the society, without claim or complaint from anybody. Accordingly, it is a fact, as far as I am informed, that England was, until we copied her, the only country on earth which ever, by a general law, gave a legal right to the exclusive use of an idea. In some other countries it is sometimes done, in a great case, and by a special and personal act, but, generally speaking, other nations have thought that these monopolies produce more embarrassment than advantage to society; and it may be observed that the nations which refuse monopolies of invention, are as fruitful as England in new and useful devices.

26

JAMES MADISON, NOTE TO HIS SPEECH ON THE
RIGHT OF SUFFRAGE
1821

Documentary History 5:440–49

These observations (in the Speech of J. M. See debates in the Convention of 1787. on the [7th] day of [August]) do not convey the speaker's more full & matured view of the subject, which is subjoined. He felt too much at the time the example of Virginia

The right of suffrage is a fundamental Article in Republican Constitutions. The regulation of it is, at the same time, a task of peculiar delicacy. Allow the right exclusively to property, and the rights of persons may be oppressed. The feudal polity alone sufficiently proves it. Extend it equally to all, and the rights of property or the claims of justice may be overruled by a majority without property, or interested in measures of injustice. Of this abundant proof is afforded by other popular Govts. and is not without examples in our own, particularly in the laws impairing the obligation of contracts.

In civilized communities, property as well as personal rights is an essential object of the laws, which encourage industry by securing the enjoyment of its fruits: that industry from which property results, & that enjoyment which consists not merely in its immediate use, but in its posthumous destination to objects of choice and of kindred affection.

In a just & a free, Government, therefore, the rights both of property & of persons ought to be effectually guarded. Will the former be so in case of a universal &

equal suffrage? Will the latter be so in case of a suffrage confined to the holders of property?

As the holders of property have at stake all the other rights common to those without property, they may be the more restrained from infringing, as well as the less tempted to infringe the rights of the latter. It is nevertheless certain, that there are various ways in which the rich may oppress the poor; in which property may oppress liberty; and that the world is filled with examples. It is necessary that the poor should have a defence against the danger.

On the other hand, the danger to the holders of property can not be disguised, if they be undefended against a majority without property. Bodies of men are not less swayed by interest than individuals, and are less controlled by the dread of reproach and the other motives felt by individuals. Hence the liability of the rights of property, and of the impartiality of laws affecting it, to be violated by Legislative majorities having an interest real or supposed in the injustice: Hence agrarian laws, and other leveling schemes: Hence the cancelling or evading of debts, and other violations of contracts. We must not shut our eyes to the nature of man, nor to the light of experience. Who would rely on a fair decision from three individuals if two had an interest in the case opposed to the rights of the third? Make the number as great as you please, the impartiality will not be increased, nor any further security against injustice be obtained, than what may result from the greater difficulty of uniting the wills of a greater number.

In all Govts. there is a power which is capable of oppressive exercise. In Monarchies and Aristocracies oppression proceeds from a want of sympathy & responsibility in the Govt. towards the people. In popular Governments the danger lies in an undue sympathy among individuals composing a majority, and a want of responsibility in the majority to the minority. The characteristic excellence of the political System of the U. S. arises from a distribution and organization of its powers, which at the same time that they secure the dependence of the Govt. on the will of the nation, provides better guards than are found in any other popular Govt. against interested combinations of a Majority against the rights of a Minority.

The U. States have a precious advantage also in the actual distribution of property particularly the landed property; and in the universal hope of acquiring property. This latter peculiarity is among the happiest contrasts in their situation to that of the old world, where no anticipated change in this respect, can generally inspire a like sympathy with the rights of property. There may be at present, a Majority of the Nation, who are even freeholders, or the heirs, or aspirants to Freeholds. And the day may not be very near when such will cease to make up a Majority of the community. But they cannot always so continue. With every admissible subdivision of the Arable lands, a populousness not greater than that of England or France, will reduce the holders to a Minority. And whenever the Majority shall be without landed or other equivalent property and without the means or hope of acquiring it, what is to secure the rights of property agst. the danger from an equality & universality of suffrage, vesting compleat power

601

over property in hands without a share in it: not to speak of a danger in the mean time from a dependence of an increasing number on the wealth of a few? In other Countries this dependence results in some from the relations between Landlords & Tenants in other both from that source, & from the relations between wealthy capitalists & indigent labourers. In the U. S. the occurrence must happen from the last source; from the connection between the great Capitalists in Manufactures & Commerce and the members employed by them. Nor will accumulations of Capital for a certain time be precluded by our laws of descent & of distribution; such being the enterprize inspired by free Institutions, that great wealth in the hands of individuals and associations, may not be unfrequent. But it may be observed, that the opportunities, may be diminished, and the permanency defeated by the equalizing tendency of the laws.

No free Country has ever been without parties, which are a natural offspring of Freedom. An obvious and permanent division of every people is into the owners of the Soil, and the other inhabitants. In a certain sense the Country may be said to belong to the former. If each landholder has an exclusive property in his share, the Body of Landholders have an exclusive property in the whole. As the Soil becomes subdivided, and actually cultivated by the owners, this view of the subject derives force from the principle of natural law, which vests in individuals an exclusive right to the portions of ground with which he has incorporated his labour & improvements. Whatever may be the rights of others derived from their birth in the Country, from their interest in the high ways & other parcels left open for common use as well, as in the national Edifices and monuments; from their share in the public defence, and from their concurrent support of the Govt., it would seem unreasonable to extend the right so far as to give them when become the majority, a power of Legislation over the landed property without the consent of the proprietors. Some barrier agst the invasion of their rights would not be out of place in a just & provident System of Govt. The principle of such an arrangement has prevailed in all Govts. where peculiar privileges or interests held by a part were to be secured agst. violation, and in the various associations where pecuniary or other property forms the stake. In the former case a defensive right has been allowed; and if the arrangement be wrong, it is not in the defense, but in the kind of privilege to be defended. In the latter case, the shares of suffrage allotted to individuals, have been with acknowledged justice apportioned more or less to their respective interests in the Common Stock.

These reflections suggest the expediency of such a modification of Govt. as would give security to the part of the Society having most at stake and being most exposed to danger. Three modifications present themselves.

1. *Confining* the right of suffrage to freeholders, & to such as hold an equivalent property, convertible of course into freeholds. The objection to this regulation is obvious. It violates the vital principle of free Govt. that those who are to be bound by laws, ought to have a voice in making them. And the violation wd. be more strikingly unjust as the lawmakers become the minority: The regulation would be as unpropitious also as it would be unjust. It would engage the numerical & physical force in a constant struggle agst. the public authority; unless kept down by a standing army fatal to all parties.

2. Confining the right of suffrage for one Branch to the holders of property, and for the other Branch to those without property. This arrangement which wd. give a mutual defence, where there might be mutual danger of encroachment, has an aspect of equality & fairness. But it wd. not be in fact either equal or fair, because the rights to be defended would be unequal, being on one side those of property as well as of persons, and on the other those of persons only. The temptation also to encroach tho' in a certain degree mutual, wd. be felt more strongly on one side than on the other; It wd. be more likely to beget an abuse of the Legislative Negative in extorting concessions at the expence of property, than the reverse. The division of the State into the two Classes, with distinct & independt. Organs of power, and without any intermingled Agency whatever, might lead to contests & antipathies not dissimilar to those between the Patricians & Plebeians at Rome.

3. Confining the right of electing one Branch of the Legislature to freeholders, and admitting all others to a common right with holders of property, in electing the other Branch. This wd. give a defensive power to holders of property, and to the class also without property when becoming a majority of electors, without depriving them in the mean time of a participation in the public Councils. If the holders of property would thus have a twofold share of representation, they wd. have at the same time a twofold stake in it, the rights of property as well as of persons the twofold object of political Institutions. And if no exact & safe equilibrium can be introduced, it is more reasonable that a preponderating weight shd. be allowed to the greater interest than to the lesser. Experience alone can decide how far the practice in this case would correspond with the Theory. Such a distribution of the right of suffrage was tried in N. York and has been abandoned whether from experienced evils, or party calculations, may possibly be a question. It is still on trial in N. Carolina, with what practical indications is not known. It is certain that the trial, to be satisfactory ought to be continued for no inconsiderable period; untill in fact the non freeholders should be the majority.

4. Should Experience or public opinion require an equal & universal suffrage for each branch of the Govt., such as prevails generally in the U. S., a resource favorable to the rights of landed & other property, when its possessors become the Minority, may be found in an enlargement of the Election Districts for one branch of the Legislature, and an extension of its period of service. Large districts are manifestly favorable to the election of persons of general respectability, and of probable attachment to the rights of property, over competitors depending on the personal solicitations practicable on a contracted theatre. And altho' an ambitious candidate, of personal distinction, might occasionally recommend himself to popular choice by espousing a popular though unjust object, it might rarely happen to many districts at the same time. The tendency

of a longer period of service would be, to render the Body more stable in its policy, and more capable of stemming popular currents taking a wrong direction, till reason & justice could regain their ascendancy.

5. Should even such a modification as the last be deemed inadmissible, and universal suffrage and very short periods of elections within contracted spheres be required for each branch of the Govt., the security for the holders of property when the minority, can only be derived from the ordinary influence possessed by property, & the superior information incident to its holders; from the popular sense of justice enlightened & enlarged by a diffusive education; and from the difficulty of combining & effectuating unjust purposes throughout an extensive country; a difficulty essentially distinguishing the U. S. and even most of the individual States, from the small communities where a mistaken interest or contagious passion, could readily unite a majority of the whole under a factious leader, in trampling on the rights of the Minor party.

Under every view of the subject, it seems indispensable that the Mass of Citizens should not be without a voice, in making the laws which they are to obey, & in chusing the Magistrates, who are to administer them, and if the only alternative be between an equal & universal right of suffrage for each branch of the Govt. and a confinement of the *entire* right to a part of the Citizens, it is better that those having the greater interest at stake namely that of property & persons both, should be deprived of half their share in the Govt.; than, that those having the lesser interest, that of personal rights only, should be deprived of the whole.

27

JAMES MADISON, NOTE ON SUFFRAGE
1829
Letters 4:28–30

The right of suffrage being of vital importance, and approving an extension of it to housekeepers and heads of families, I will suggest a few considerations which govern my judgment on the subject.

Were the Constitution on hand to be adapted to the present circumstances of our country, without taking into view the changes which time is rapidly producing, an unlimited extension of the right would probably vary little the character of our public councils or measures. But as we are to prepare a system of government for a period which it is hoped will be a long one, we must look to the prospective changes in the condition and composition of the society on which it is to act.

It is a law of nature, now well understood, that the earth under a civilized cultivation is capable of yielding subsistence for a large surplus of consumers beyond those having an immediate interest in the soil; a surplus which must increase with the increasing improvements in agriculture,

and the labour-saving arts applied to it. And it is a lot of humanity, that of this surplus a large proportion is necessarily reduced by a competition for employment to wages which afford them the bare necessaries of life. The proportion being without property, or the hope of acquiring it, cannot be expected to sympathize sufficiently with its rights to be safe depositories of power over them.

What is to be done with this unfavoured class of the community? If it be, on one hand, unsafe to admit them to a full share of political power, it must be recollected, on the other, that it cannot be expedient to rest a republican government on a portion of the society having a numerical and physical force excluded from, and liable to be turned against it, and which would lead to a standing military force, dangerous to all parties and to liberty itself. This view of the subject makes it proper to embrace in the partnership of power every description of citizens having a sufficient stake in the public order and the stable administration of the laws, and particularly the housekeepers and heads of families, most of whom, "having given hostages to fortune," will have given them to their country also.

This portion of the community, added to those who, although not possessed of a share of the soil, are deeply interested in other species of property, and both of them added to the territorial proprietors, who in a certain sense may be regarded as the owners of the country itself, form the safest basis of free government. To the security for such a government, afforded by these combined members, may be farther added the political and moral influence emanating from the actual possession of authority, and a just and beneficial exercise of it.

It would be happy if a state of society could be found or framed in which an equal voice in making the laws might be allowed to every individual bound to obey them. But this is a theory which, like most theories, confessedly requires limitations and modifications. And the only question to be decided in this, as in other cases, turns on the particular degree of departure in practice required by the essence and object of the theory itself.

It must not be supposed that a crowded state of population, of which we have no example here, and which we know only by the image reflected from examples elsewhere, is too remote to claim attention.

The ratio of increase in the United States [makes it probable] that the present

12 millions	will in	25 years be	24 millions.
24 "		50 "	48 "
48 "		75 "	96 "
96 "		100 "	192 "

There may be a gradual decrease of the ratio of increase, but it will be small as long as the agriculture shall yield its abundance. Great Britain has doubled her population in the last fifty years, notwithstanding its amount in proportion to its territory at the commencement of that period; and Ireland is a much stronger proof of the effect of an increasing product of food in multiplying the consumers.

How far this view of the subject will be affected by the republican laws of descent and distribution, in equalizing the property of the citizens and in reducing to the minimum mutual surpluses for mutual supplies, cannot be inferred from any direct and adequate experiment. One result would seem to be a deficiency of the capital for the expensive establishments which facilitate labour and cheapen its products on one hand; and on the other, of the capacity to purchase the costly and ornamental articles consumed by the wealthy alone, who must cease to be idlers and become labourers. Another, the increased mass of labourers added to the production of necessaries by the withdrawal for this object, of a part of those now employed in producing luxuries, and the addition to the labourers from the class of present consumers of luxuries. To the effect of these changes, intellectual, moral, and social, the institutions and laws of the country must be adapted; and it will require for the task all the wisdom of the wisest patriots.

Supposing the estimate of the growing population of the United States to be nearly correct, and the extent of their territory to be eight or nine hundred millions of acres, and one-fourth of it to consist of arable surface, there will, in a century or a little more, be nearly as crowded a population in the United States as in Great Britain or France; and if the present Constitution, (of Virginia,) with all its flaws, has lasted more than half a century, it is not an unreasonable hope that an amended one will last more than a century.

If these observations be just, every mind will be able to develop and apply them.

SEE ALSO:

Generally chs. 12, 13
Cotton Mather, Durable Riches 1–20 (1695)

. . . do ordain and establish this Constitution for the
United States of America.

17

Constitutional Government

Introduction

For authors, proponents, and critics of the Constitution alike, no principle was more fundamental than that such an instrument was indispensable for those hoping to live safe and happy lives. It has been said that the Age of Enlightenment might more properly be called the Age of Constitutions. But that age's thinkers came to their definitions of a constitution only gradually and haltingly and without ever reaching consensus. Indeed, for all their preoccupation with the making of constitutions, they did not speak of "constitutionalism." We, by contrast, can hardly do without the term or the distinction it implies. Today, every nation-state hardy enough to issue its own postage stamps sports a constitution. Rarely does one not lay claim to being governed according to the rule of law; and more rare is the tyrant who cannot point to his shiny little constitution. Today, accordingly, we are obliged to ask whether what purports to be a constitution does in fact embody and secure the main features of constitutionalism.

In the eighteenth century the hypocrisy of tyrants led them in other directions, and the question could be put more simply. It was not whether a nation had a living constitution or only the appearance of one, but, did it have a constitution at all? Men could ask that question even of England, where legislative supremacy included the power to extend the duration of a sitting Parliament. In the eyes of the Americans of the Revolutionary era, only a scant fraction of mankind then enjoyed (or ever had enjoyed) the benefits of constitutional government. No small part of their revolutionary fervor turned on the belief that American practice and its success would have worldwide significance in precisely this regard. "It has been frequently remarked, that it seems to have been reserved to the people of this country, by their conduct and example, to decide the important question, whether societies of men are really capable or not, of establishing good government from reflection and choice, or whether they are forever destined to depend, for their political constitutions, on accident and force. If there be any truth in the remark, the crisis, at which we are arrived, may with propriety be regarded as the era in which that decision is to be made; and a wrong election of the part we shall act, may, in this view, deserve to be considered as the general misfortune of mankind" (Hamilton, *Federalist*, no. 1).

Though Americans may have taken it for granted by 1787 that their experiments in constitutional government would be decisive, they did not arrive at their understanding of the term in quite the same self-confident manner. Ancient as the word was, "constitution" continued to carry a range of primary and derivative meanings. When William Penn called his a "frame of government" (no. 4), he was emphasizing the primary need served by a constitution: establishing a structure on which to arrange the powers and offices of governance. Structures, however, are to be understood in terms of their ends, and Penn's ends were shaped in part, if only in part, by his theology of sin. That is, believing that man's fall from grace necessitated external law and coercion "to terrify evil doers," he believed no less that government should go beyond the business of correction: it ought, he thought, "to cherish those who do well." In so doing it might become "durable," achieving the kind of stability that would postpone inevitable decline. A constitution is indispensable for establishing what he called the conditions of "evenness"—governance without abuse, the simultaneous enjoyment of liberty and performance of duty. At bottom, though, what matters most is not the frame but the quality of the men within it: "That, therefore, which makes a good constitution, must keep it."

A Fence against Oppression

John Locke's analysis (no. 5) addresses itself to what Penn called "the coarsest part" of governance. Guiding himself principally by the original condition, "those inconveniences of the State of Nature" that impelled men to associate in the first place, Locke was able to derive a definition of, and standard for, civil society out of the original contractual intention, which is in turn inferable from the original danger. The transaction by which each individual gave up his unqualified right to be judge in his own case, and authorized the society to establish a common judge over him and his fellows, makes sense only as a means of enhancing each one's safety and security or (alternatively expressed) as a means of better preserving his property. It is literally absurd, literally self-contradictory, to imagine men contracting to submit to an absolute, arbitrary power. Such a power, strictly speaking, has no subjects, only slaves; arbitrary government, strictly speaking, is no government at all. No one ought to think that even uninstructed "Men are so foolish that they take care to avoid what Mischiefs may be done them by *Pole-cats*, or *Foxes*, but are content, nay think it Safety, to be devoured by *Lions*." Any move toward arbitrary power, toward power which cannot be called to account, betrays the great end of civil society.

The better to secure their natural rights individuals first freely contracted with one another to form a civil society. They also agreed to be bound henceforth by their major voice. That majority, acting in the name of the entire people, "alone can appoint the form of the Commonwealth, which is by Constituting the Legislative, and appointing in whose hands that shall be." That act is the fundamental positive law of the commonwealth, its original constitution. All powers of the government stem from that original act of limited delegation from the people. It is this understanding of "the *Bounds* which the trust that is put in them by the Society, and the Law of God and Nature, have *set to the Legislative* Power of every Commonwealth, in all Forms of Government" that issues forth as constitutionalism. (See also no. 23.)

Some of the institutional implications of Locke's argument are expressed with pungency and clarity by the Eng-

lishmen John Trenchard and Thomas Gordon in *Cato's Letters* (nos. 6, 7, 8), whose polemics enjoyed wide circulation and frequent reprinting in the colonies. Constitutional checks and safeguards, limited government, is of the essence. The great art—"the only Secret"—in forming a free government is "to make the Interests of the Governors and of the Governed the same, as far as human Policy can contrive." If, as both Locke and Cato contended, liberty or the protection of natural rights is the end in view, what is needed is not simplicity (or as we might say, efficiency), but complexity. Some variations on this theme were developed by Montesquieu in a work especially cherished by republicans, *The Spirit of Laws* (no. 9). He portrayed an English constitution dedicated above all to political liberty, a constitution whose complications built each man's confidence that he need not fear another. Montesquieu's England was a model because its constitution of limited and mutually checking powers moderated governors. It was a proof, he suggested, that "a government may be so constituted, as no man shall be compelled to do things to which the law does not oblige him, nor forced to abstain from things which the law permits." Montesquieu's exemplar of constitutionalism is the constitution of a modern liberal state.

Americans viewing the British constitution found much to praise, but emphases differed significantly. During the agitation over the Sugar Act (and soon, the Stamp Act), Richard Henry Lee (no. 10) stressed that the intention of the British constitution could not be fulfilled without securing popular consent to taxation. The House of Representatives of Massachusetts (no. 11) spoke of the inherent and inalienable rights of all men, said to be confirmed—not created—by Magna Charta, and of the "constitutional rights of the subjects of this Province." Aggrieved colonists were ever mindful of their charter rights and of their rights as Englishmen. John Adams, writing as Clarendon (no. 12), characterized the British constitution not by parliamentary practice or legislation or custom, but by the end of the government thereby constituted. All government professed to aim at the public good. The British constitution was distinctive because "liberty is its end, its use, its designation, drift, and scope, as much as grinding corn is the use of a mill, . . . or life and health the designation of the human body." Its peculiar mixture of forms and powers was addressed to that end.

With the escalation of hostilities attending passage of the Townshend Acts, the House of Representatives of Massachusetts (no. 13) was prompted to emphasize the feature of fixed limits in a free state's constitution. A constitution "ascertains and limits both sovereignty and allegiance." Parliament could not "overleap" its bounds without destroying its legitimacy. Carolinians were similarly reminded that the King and his ministers had no discretionary power "to make ordinances to supply any defect which they may imagine in the constitution" (see Iredell to *North-Carolina Gazette*, 10 Sept. 1773). In Virginia the Fairfax County Resolves (no. 14) reaffirmed the continuity in America of "the Civil-Constitution and Form of Government" of Great Britain and identified the vital principle of that constitution: that the people shall be governed only by laws to which they have consented through freely chosen, similarly situated, and popularly accountable representatives.

The People's Higher Law

The separate and higher status of the people in their constitutive capacity, as distinguished from the representatives of the people in their ordinary legislative capacity, became a more prominent and insistent theme as the formal break between Britain and her colonies drew near (see ch. 2). The widely read English Whig James Burgh (no. 15) used the distinction to attack Blackstone's notions of unlimited parliamentary power and privilege. Like Alexander Hamilton (no. 16), Burgh warned against so full a preoccupation with the threat of monarchic despotism as would leave men blind to the risk of parliamentary encroachments and arbitrariness. Americans chafing under parliamentary high-handedness were confirmed in their belief that explicit constitutional defenses were essential if their liberties were to be preserved, even from representatives of their own choosing. Precisely because of its special and close connection to the ultimate source of political authority, a constitution could rightly claim to be more weighty, more fundamental than any act of ordinary legislation. In developing their case for this position, two of the Founders produced classic statements of constitutionalism. One was Jefferson's critique (in *Notes on the State of Virginia*), of the Virginia Constitution of 1776 as a legislative act "transcendant to the powers" of that or any other legislature. No fixed bulwark for the people's rights could be erected on so unsteady a foundation (no. 20). The other was Hamilton's masterly exposition of the Constitution as the higher law, the expression of the settled intention of the people, and hence of "superior obligation and validity" to statutory law, the expression of the intention of the mere agents of the people (no. 24).

So it was that arguments advanced as grounds of protest and resistance became arguments used directly as grounds for creating new republics. In the language of the Pittsfield Petitions (no. 17), it is "the Approbation of the Majority of the people" that gives "Life and being" to a constitution. Nothing lacking that special authorization is entitled to be treated as a foundation. Thinking likewise, the Concord town meeting (no. 18) rejected outright any pretensions of "the Supreme Legislative" to form and prescribe a constitution for the inhabitants of Massachusetts. If the great work of founding were to be done in the right way and with the right results no such shortcuts were permissible. In fact, Massachusetts delayed adopting a new constitution for four years into the Revolution and in the process provided others with a model of founding by special convention and ratification by the people.

By this general line of reasoning Britain would be no model at all. Indeed, the anonymous author of *Four Letters on Interesting Subjects* (no. 19) could deny that the English, given their "absolute legislative powers," had anything that might properly be called a constitution. Further, he insisted on fixing "all the great rights which man never mean, nor ever ought, to lose" through constitutional guarantees; nothing less would offer adequate security. Similarly, any alterations that might be prompted by periodic examination of a constitution should require approval by "a clear majority of all the inhabitants."

A Self-denying Ordinance

Against these constitutional restraints would arise a host of pressing claims—of convenience, of alleged necessity, of unprecedented circumstances, of a presumed "contrary sense of the people." Hamilton and Madison, in sharply reasoned statements that precede the writing of the Constitution, took arms against these claims. Writing as Phocion (no. 21), Hamilton insisted on treating a constitution as prescribing the scope of governmental discretion and binding governors and governed alike until it was "dissolved with the same solemnity and certainty with which it was made." Madison, writing as an advisor to those contemplating a constitution for the as yet unformed state of Kentucky, took a similar hard line against "temporary deviations from fundamental principles." While he was loath to define the "indefinite"—for Madison, no less than for Hamilton, a government had to have the power to govern—"it is very practicable . . . to enumerate the essential exceptions" to legislative power. Both the people and their agents must be restrained from doing just anything they took a fancy to. (See Madison to Caleb Wallace, 23 Aug. 1785.)

Here, then, was a test to which any proposed or existing constitution had to be put. Would it, in fact, render government both popular and safe—responsive and accountable to the people's will yet no mere unthinking reflex of that will? For Madison the immediate and pressing question was whether the newly proposed Constitution would indeed make for safe government. There were, he confessed to Jefferson (no. 22), reasons to fault the plan. Though it represented an advance over the Articles of Confederation—"a Confederacy of independent States"—it still was not more than "a feudal system of republics." As such it was not adequate to secure the federal government against the encroachments of the states nor "to prevent instability and injustice in the legislation of the States." The remedy for Madison lay in a congressional power to veto state laws, a proposal he had steadfastly fought for in the Philadelphia Convention but to no avail. "It may be asked how private rights will be more secure under the Guardianship of the General Government than under the State Governments, since they are both founded on the republican principle which refers the ultimate decision to the will of the majority. . . ." Madison found the answer to that question in the very extent of the republic: its sheer size and heterogeneity made possible the benign application of that "reprobated axiom of tyranny," divide and rule. But if a large republic made it difficult for "oppressive combinations" to form, so too did it make it difficult for "a defensive concert" against administrative tyranny. Here the Constitution ought to be scrutinized to see whether the government it established is "sufficiently controuled itself, from setting up an interest adverse to that of the entire Society." Further detailed evidence of what

Madison took to be the ingredients of a sufficiently controlled government may be gathered from his close critique of Jefferson's draft of a constitution for Virginia, observations written for the would-be founding fathers of Kentucky (no. 25).

In both these instances, as Madison got down to cases, his writing testifies amply to the reciprocal influence of practice and theory in the formation of constitutional government in America. Long experience (stretching back to life under the earliest colonial charters) informed the Founders' reasoning, even while their study of the approved authorities on government led them to new directions.

1

MAYFLOWER COMPACT
11 Nov. 1620
Bradford 75–76

I shall a little return back, and begin with a combination made by them before they came ashore; being the first foundation of their government in this place. Occasioned partly by the discontented and mutinous speeches that some of the strangers amongst them had let fall from them in the ship: That when they came ashore they would use their own liberty, for none had power to command them, the patent they had being for Virginia and not for New England, which belonged to another government, with which the Virginia Company had nothing to do. And partly that such an act by them done, this their condition considered, might be as firm as any patent, and in some respects more sure.

The form was as followeth:

IN THE NAME OF GOD, AMEN.

We whose names are underwritten, the loyal subjects of our dread Sovereign Lord King James, by the Grace of God of Great Britain, France, and Ireland King, Defender of the Faith, etc.

Having undertaken, for the Glory of God and advancement of the Christian Faith and Honour of our King and Country, a Voyage to plant the First Colony in the Northern Parts of Virginia, do by these presents solemnly and mutually in the presence of God and one of another, Covenant and Combine ourselves together into a Civil Body Politic, for our better ordering and preservation and furtherance of the ends aforesaid; and by virtue hereof to enact, constitute and frame such just and equal Laws, Ordinances, Acts, Constitutions and Offices, from time to time, as shall be thought most meet and convenient for the general good of the Colony, unto which we promise all due submission and obedience. In witness whereof we have hereunder subscribed our names at Cape Cod, the 11th of November, in the year of the reign of our Sovereign Lord King James, of England, France and Ireland the eighteenth, and of Scotland the fifty-fourth. Anno Domini 1620.

2

ORDINANCE AND CONSTITUTION FOR COUNCIL AND ASSEMBLY IN VIRGINIA
24 July 1621
Jamestown 126–28

To all people to whom these presents shall come, bee seen or heard, the Treasuror, Council and Company of Adventurers and Planters of the City of London for the First Collony in Virginia send greeting: knowe yee that wee, the said Treasuror, Counsell and Company, takeing into our carefull consideracion the present state of the said Colony in Virginia, and intending by the Devine assistance to settle such a forme of government ther as may bee to the greatest benifitt and comfort of the people and wherby all injustice, grevance and oppression may bee prevented and kept of as much as is possible from the said Colony, have thought fitt to make our entrance by ordaining & establishing such supreame Counsells as may not only bee assisting to the Governor for the time being in administracion of justice and the executing of other duties to his office belonging, but also by ther vigilent care & prudence may provide as well for remedy of all inconveniencies groweing from time to time as also for the advancing of encrease, strength, stabillitie and prosperitie of the said Colony:

Wee therefore, the said Treasuror, Counsell and Company, by authoritie directed to us from His Majestie under his Great Seale, upon mature deliberacion doe hereby order & declare that from hence forward ther bee towe supreame Counsells in Virginia for the better government of the said Colony as aforesaid: the one of which Counsells to bee called the Counsell of State and whose office shall chiefflie bee assisting, wth ther care, advise & circomspection, to the said Governor; shall be chosen, nominated, placed and displaced from time to time by us, the said Treasurer, Counsell & Company and our successors; which Counsell of State shall consiste for the present onlie of those persons whose names are here inserted, vizt.: Sir Francis Wyatt, Governor of Virginia; Captaine Francis West; Sir George Yeardley, Knight; Sir William Newce, Knight, Marshall of Virginia; Mr. George Sandys, Tresuror; Mr. George Thorpe, Deputy of the Colledge; Captaine Thomas Newce, Deputy for the Company; Mr. Christopher Davison, Secretarie; Doctor Potts, Phesition to the Company; Mr. Paulet; Mr. Leech; Captaine Nathaniell Powell; Mr. Roger Smith; Mr. John Berkley; Mr. John Rolfe; Mr. Ralfe Hamer; Mr. John Pountus; Mr. Michael Lapworth; Mr. Harwood; [and] Mr. Samuel Macocke. Which said Counsellors and Counsell wee earnestlie pray & desier, and in His Majesties name strictlie charge and command, that all factious parcialties and sinister respects laid aside, they bend ther care and endeavors to assist the said Governor first and principallie in advancement of the honor and service of Almightie God and the enlargement of His kingdome amongste those heathen people; and next in the erecting of the said Colonie in one obedience to His Majestie and all lawful authoritie from His Majestis dirived; and lastlie in maitaining the said people in justice and Christian conversation among themselves and in strength and habillitie to wth stand ther ennimies. And this Counsell is to bee alwaies, or for the most part, residing about or neere the said Governor. The other Counsell, more generall, to bee called by the Governor, and yeerly, of course, & no oftner but for very extreuordinaire & important occasions, shall consist for present of the aid Counsell of State and of tow burgesses out of every towne, hunder [hundred] and other particuler plantacion to bee respetialy chosen by the inhabitants. Which Counsell shalbee called the Generall Assemblie, wherein as also in the said Counsell of State, all matters shall be decided, determined & ordered by the greater part of the voices then present, reserveing alwaies to the Governor a negative voice. And this Generall Assembly shall have free power to treat, consult & conclude as well of all emergent occasions concerning the pupliqe weale of the said Colony and evrie parte therof as also to make, ordeine & enact such generall lawes & orders for the behoof of the said Colony and the good govermt therof as shall time to time appeare necessarie or requisite. Wherin as in all other things wee requier the said Gennerall Assembly, as also the said Counsell of State, to imitate and followe the policy of the forme of goverment, lawes, custome, manners of loyall and other administracion of justice used in the realme of England, as neere as may bee even as ourselves by His Majesties lettres patents are required; provided that noe lawes or ordinance made in the said Generall Assembly shalbe and continew in force and validitie, unlese the same shalbe sollemlie ratified and confirmed in a generall greater court of the said court here in England and so ratified and returned to them under our seale. It being our intent to affoord the like measure also unto the said Colony that after the government of the [said Colony, shall once have been well framed & settled accordingly, which is to be done by us as by authoritie derived from] his Majestie and the sa[me shall] have bene soe by us declared, no orders of our court afterwarde shall binde [the said] Colony unles they bee ratified in like manner in ther Generall Assembly.

In wittnes wherof wee have hereunto sett our common seale the 24th day of [July] 1621, and in the yeare of the raigne of our governoure, Lord James by the . . . of God of England, Scotland, France & Ireland, King, Defendor of the . . . vizt., of England, France and Scotland the nineteenth and of Scotland the fower and fiftieth.

3

ROYAL COMMISSION FOR REGULATING PLANTATIONS
28 Apr. 1634
Bradford 422–25

CHARLES by the grace of GOD King of England, Scotland, France, and Ireland, Defender of the Faith, ETC.

To the most Reverend father in Christ, our well beloved and faithful counsellor William, by divine Providence Archbishop of Canterbury, of all England Primate and Metropolitan; Thomas Lord Coventry, Keeper of our Great Seal of England; the most Reverent father in Christ our well beloved and most faithful counselor, Richard, by divine Providence Archbishop of York, Primate and Metropolitan; our well beloved and most faithful cousins and counselors, Richard Earl of Portland, our High Treasurer of England; Henry Earl of Manchester, Keeper of our Privy Seal; Thomas, Earl of Arundel and Surrey, Earl Marshal of England; Edward Earl of Dorset, Chamberlain of our most dear consort the Queen; and our beloved and faithful councillors, Francis Lord Cottington, Councillor and Undertreasurer of our Exchequer; Sir Thomas Edmonds knight, Treasurer of our household; Sir Henry Vane knight, comptroller of the same household; Sir John Cook knight, one of our Privy Secretaries, And Francis Windebank knight, another of our Privy Secretaries, Greeting.

Whereas very many of our subjects and of our late father's of beloved memory, our sovereign lord James, late King of England, by means of license royal, not only with desire of enlarging the territories of our empire but chiefly out of a pious and religious affection, and desire of propagating the gospel of our Lord Jesus Christ, with great industry and expenses have caused to be planted large colonies of the English nation in divers parts of the world altogether unmanured and void of inhabitants, or occupied of the barbarous people that have no knowledge of divine worship. We being willing to provide a remedy for the tranquility and quietness of those people, and being very confident of your faith and wisdom, justice and provident circumspection, have constituted you, the aforesaid Archbishop of Canterbury, Lord Keeper of the Great Seal of England, the Archbishop of York, etc. and any five or more of you, our Commissioners. And to you and any five or more of you, we do give and commit power for the government and safety of the said colonies drawn, or which out of the English nation into those parts hereafter shall be drawn, to make laws, constitutions and ordinances pertaining either to the public state of these colonies or the private profit of them. And concerning the lands, goods, debts and succession in those parts, and how they shall demean themselves towards foreign princes and their people, or how they shall bear themselves towards us and our subjects, as well in any foreign parts whatsoever or on the seas in those parts or in their return sailing home or which may pertain to the clergy government, or to the cure of souls among the people there living, and exercising trade in those parts, by designing out congruent portions arising in tithes, oblations and other things there, according to your sound discretions in political and civil causes, and by having the advice of two or three bishops for the settling, making and ordering of the business for the designing of necessary ecclesiastical and clergy portions, which you shall cause to be called and taken to you. And to make provision against the violation of those laws, constitutions and ordinances, by imposing penalties and mulcts, imprisonment if there be cause and that the quality of the offense do require it, by deprivation of member or life, to be inflicted. With power also (our assent being had) to remove and displace the governors or rulers of those colonies for causes which to you shall seem lawful and others in their stead to constitute. And require an account of their rule and government, and whom you shall find culpable, either by deprivation from their place or by imposition of a mulct upon the goods of them in those parts to be levied, or banishment from those provinces in which they have been governor or otherwise to cashier according to the quantity of the offense. And to constitute judges and magistrates political and civil, for civil causes and under the power and form which to you, five or more of you, shall seem expedient. And judges and magistrates and dignities to causes ecclesiastical, and under the power and form which to you, five or more of you, with the bishops vicegerents (provided by the Archbishop of Canterbury for the time being) shall seem expedient; and to ordain courts, pretorian and tribunal, as well ecclesiastical as civil, of judgments; to determine the forms and manner of proceedings in the same, and of appealing from them in matters and causes as well criminal as civil, personal, real and mixed, and to their seats of justice, what may be equal and well ordered and what crimes, faults or excesses of contracts or injuries ought to belong to the ecclesiastical court, and what to the civil court and seat of justice.

Provided, nevertheless, that the laws, ordinances and constitutions of this kind, shall not be put in execution before our assent be had thereunto in writing under our signet, signed at least; and this assent being had and the same publicly proclaimed in the provinces in which they are to be executed, we will and command that those laws, ordinances, and constitutions, more fully to obtain strength and be observed, and shall be inviolably of all men whom they shall concern.

Notwithstanding, it shall be for you, or any five or more of you, (as is aforesaid) although those laws, constitutions and ordinances shall be proclaimed with our royal assent, to change, revoke and abrogate them and other new ones, in form aforesaid, from time to time frame and make as aforesaid; and to new evils arising, or new dangers, to apply new remedies as is fitting, so often as to you it shall seem expedient.

Furthermore, you shall understand that we have constituted you, and every five or more of you, the aforesaid Archbishop of Canterbury; Thomas Lord Coventry,

Keeper of the Great Seal of England; Richard Bishop of York, Richard Earl of Portland, Henry Earl of Manchester, Thomas Earl of Arundel and Surrey, Edward Earl of Dorset, Francis Lord Cottington, Sir Thomas Edmonds knight, Sir Henry Vane knight, Sir Francis Windebank knight, our Commissioners to hear and determine according to your sound discretions all manner of complaints either against those colonies or their rulers or governors, at the instance of the parties grieved, or at their accusation brought concerning injuries from hence or from thence between them and their members to be moved and to call the parties before you. And to the parties or to their procurators from hence or from thence being heard, the full complement of justice to be exhibited. Giving unto you or any five or more of you power that if you shall find any of the colonies aforesaid or any of the chief rulers upon the jurisdictions of others by unjust possession or usurpation or one against another making grievance or in rebellion against us, or withdrawing from our allegiance, or our commandments not obeying, consultation first with us in that case had, to cause those colonies or the rulers of them for the causes aforesaid, or for other just causes, either to return to England or to command them to other places designed, even as according to your sound discretions it shall seem to stand with equity and justice or necessity. Moreover, we do give unto you and any five or more of you power and special command over all the charters, letters patents and rescripts royal of the regions, provinces, islands or lands in foreign parts, granted for rising colonies, to cause them to be brought before you. And the same being received, if anything surreptitiously or unduly have been obtained, or that by the same privileges, liberties and prerogatives hurtful to us or to our crown or to foreign princes, have been prejudicially suffered or granted, the same being better made known unto you, five or more of you, to command them according to the laws and customs of England to be revoked, and to do such other things which to the profit and safeguard of the aforesaid colonies and of our subjects resident in the same, shall be necessary. And therefore we do command you that about the premises at days and times which for these things you shall make provision, that you be diligent in attendance as it becometh you; giving in precept also and firmly enjoining we do give command to all and singular chief rulers of provinces into which the colonies aforesaid have been drawn, or shall be drawn, and concerning the colonies themselves, and concerning others that have been interest therein, that they give attendance upon you and be observant and obedient unto your warrants in those affairs, as often as and even as in our name they shall be required, at their peril.

In testimony whereof we have caused these our letters to be made patent.

Witness ourself at Westminster the 28th day of April, in the tenth year of our reign.

By writ from the Privy Seal,

Anno Domini 1634   WILLIES

4

WILLIAM PENN, PREFACE TO THE FRAME OF
GOVERNMENT
1682

American Colonial Documents 175–77

When the great and wise God had made the world, of all his creatures it pleased him to choose man his deputy to rule it, and to fit him for so great a charge and trust he did not only qualify him with skill and power, but with integrity to use them justly. This native goodness was equally his honour and his happiness, and whilst he stood here, all went well; there was no need of coercive or compulsive means; the precept of divine love and truth in his bosom was the guide and keeper of his innocency. But lust prevailing against duty, made a lamentable breach upon it, and the law that before had no power over him, took place upon him and his disobedient posterity, that such as would not live conformable to the holy law within, should fall under the reproof and correction of the just law without, in a judicial administration.

This the apostle teaches us in divers of his epistles. The law (says he) was added because of transgression; in another place, knowing that the law was not made for the righteous man but for the disobedient and ungodly, for sinners, for unholy and profane, for murderers, for whoremongers, for them that defile themselves with mankind, and for menstealers, for liars, for perjured persons, etc. But this is not all. He opens and carries the matter of government a little further: let every soul be subject to the higher powers for there is no power but of God. The powers that be are ordained of God: whosoever therefore resisteth the power, resisteth the ordinance of God. For rulers are not a terror to good works, but to evil; wilt thou then not be afraid of the power? Do that which is good, and thou shalt have praise of the same. He is the minister of God to thee for good. Wherefore ye must needs be subject, not only for wrath, but for conscience' sake.

This settles the divine right of government beyond exception, and that for two ends: first, to terrify evil-doers; secondly, to cherish those that do well, which gives government a life beyond corruption and makes it as durable in the world as good men shall be. So that government seems to me a part of religion itself, a thing sacred in its institution and end. For if it does not directly remove the cause, it crushes the effects of evil, and is as such (though a lower yet) an emanation of the same Divine Power that is both author and object of pure religion; the difference lying here, that the one is more free and mental, the other more corporal and compulsive in its operations, but that is only to evil-doers; government itself being otherwise as capable of kindness, goodness and charity as a more private society. They weakly err that think there is no other use of government than correction, which is the coarsest part of it; daily experience tells us that the care and regulation of

many other affairs more soft and daily necessary make up much the greatest part of government and which must have followed the peopling of the world had Adam never fell, and will continue among men on earth under the highest attainments they may arrive at, by the coming of the blessed second Adam, the Lord from heaven. Thus much of government in general, as to its rise and end.

For particular frames and models it will become me to say little, and comparatively I will say nothing. My reasons are: first, that the age is too nice and difficult for it, there being nothing the wits of men are more busy and divided upon. 'Tis true, they seem to agree in the end, to wit, happiness, but in the means they differ as to divine, so to this human felicity, and the cause is much the same, not always want of light and knowledge, but want of using them rightly. Men side with their passions against their reason, and their sinister interests have so strong a bias upon their minds that they lean to them against the good of the things they know.

Secondly, I do not find a model in the world that time, place, and some singular emergences have not necessarily altered; nor is it easy to frame a civil government that shall serve all places alike.

Thirdly, I know what is said by the several admirers of monarchy, aristocracy and democracy, which are the rule of one, a few, and many, and are the three common ideas of government, when men discourse on that subject. But I choose to solve the controversy with this small distinction, and it belongs to all three: any government is free to the people under it (whatever be the frame) where the laws rule, and the people are a party to those laws, and more than this is tyranny, oligarchy, and confusion.

But lastly, when all is said, there is hardly one frame of government in the world so ill designed by its first founders that in good hands would not do well enough, and story tells us the best in ill ones can do nothing that is great or good; witness the Jewish and Roman states. Governments, like clocks, go from the motion men give them, and as governments are made and moved by men, so by them they are ruined too. Wherefore governments rather depend upon men than men upon governments. Let men be good, and the government cannot be bad; if it be ill, they will cure it. But if men be bad, let the government be never so good, they will endeavour to warp and spoil to their turn.

I know some say, let us have good laws and no matter for the men that execute them. But let them consider that though good laws do well, good men do better; for good laws may want good men, and be abolished or invaded by ill men; but good men will never want good laws, nor suffer ill ones. 'Tis true, good laws have some awe upon ill ministers, but that is where they have not power to escape or abolish them, and the people are generally wise and good; but a loose and depraved people (which is to the question) love laws and an administration like themselves. That, therefore, which makes a good constitution, must keep it; viz., men of wisdom and virtue, qualities that because they descend not with worldly inheritances, must be carefully propagated by a virtuous education of youth, for which after ages will owe more to the care and prudence of founders, and the successive magistracy, than to their parents for their private patrimonies.

These considerations of the weight of government, and the nice and various opinions about it, made it uneasy to me to think of publishing the ensuing frame and conditional laws, foreseeing both the censures they will meet with from men of differing humours and engagements, and the occasion they may give of discourse beyond my design.

But next to the power of necessity (which is a solicitor that will take no denial) this induced me to a compliance that we have (with reverence to God and good conscience to men) to the best of our skill, contrived and composed the FRAME and LAWS of this government to the great end of all government, viz., to support power in reverence with the people and to secure the people from the abuse of power, that they may be free by their just obedience, and the magistrates honourable for their just administration; for liberty without obedience is confusion, and obedience without liberty is slavery. To carry this evenness is partly owing to the constitution, and partly to the magistracy; where either of these fail, government will be subject to convulsions; but where both are wanting, it must be totally subverted: then where both meet, the government is like to endure. Which I humbly pray and hope God will please to make the lot of this of Pennsylvania.

5

JOHN LOCKE, SECOND TREATISE,
§§ 89–94, 134–42, 212
1689

89. Where-ever therefore any number of Men are so united into one Society, as to quit every one his Executive Power of the Law of Nature, and to resign it to the publick, there and there only is a *Political, or Civil Society*. And this is done where-ever any number of Men, in the state of Nature, enter into Society to make one People, one Body Politick under one Supreme Government, or else when any one joyns himself to, and incorporates with any Government already made. For hereby he authorizes the Society, or which is all one, the Legislative thereof to make Laws for him as the publick good of the Society shall require; to the Execution whereof, his own assistance (as to his own Decrees) is due. And this *puts Men* out of a State of Nature *into* that of a *Commonwealth*, by setting up a Judge on Earth, with Authority to determine all the Controversies, and redress the Injuries, that may happen to any Member of the Commonwealth; which Judge is the Legislative, or Magistrates appointed by it. And where-ever there are any number of Men, however associated, that have no such decisive power to appeal to, there they are still *in the state of Nature*.

90. Hence it is evident, that *Absolute Monarchy*, which by

some Men is counted the only Government in the World, is indeed *inconsistent with Civil Society*, and so can be no Form of Civil Government at all. For the *end of Civil Society*, being to avoid, and remedy those inconveniencies of the State of Nature, which necessarily follow from every Man's being Judge in his own Case, by setting up a known Authority, to which every one of that Society may Appeal upon any Injury received, or Controversie that may arise, and which every one of the Society ought to obey; where-ever any persons are, who have not such an Authority to Appeal to, for the decision of any difference between them, there those persons are still *in the state of Nature*. And so is every *Absolute Prince* in respect of those who are under his *Dominion*.

91. For he being suppos'd to have all, both Legislative and Executive Power in himself alone, there is no Judge to be found, no Appeal lies open to any one, who may fairly, and indifferently, and with Authority decide, and from whose decision relief and redress may be expected of any Injury or Inconveniency, that may be suffered from the Prince or by his Order: So that such a Man, however intitled, *Czar*, or *Grand Signior*, or how you please, is as much *in the state of Nature*, with all under his Dominion, as he is with the rest of Mankind. For where-ever any two Men are, who have no standing Rule, and common Judge to Appeal to on Earth for the determination of Controversies of Right betwixt them, there they are still *in the state of Nature*, and under all the inconveniencies of it,* with only this woful difference to the Subject, or rather Slave of an Absolute Prince: That whereas, in the ordinary State of Nature, he has a liberty to judge of his Right, and according to the best of his Power, to maintain it; now whenever his Property is invaded by the Will and Order of his Monarch, he has not only no Appeal, as those in Society ought to have, but as if he were degraded from the common state of Rational Creatures, is denied a liberty to judge of, or to defend his Right, and so is exposed to all the Misery and Inconveniencies that a Man can fear from one, who being in the unrestrained state of Nature, is yet corrupted with Flattery, and armed with Power.

92. For he that thinks *absolute Power purifies Mens Bloods*, and corrects the baseness of Humane Nature, need read but the History of this, or any other Age to be convinced

*To take away all such mutual Grievances, Injuries and Wrongs, i.e. such as attend Men in the State of Nature. There was no way but only by growing into Composition and Agreement amongst themselves, by ordaining some kind of Government publick, and by yielding themselves subject thereunto, that unto whom they granted Authority to Rule and Govern, by them the Peace, Tranquility, and happy Estate of the rest might be procured. Men always knew that where Force and Injury was offered, they might be Defenders of themselves; they knew that however Men may seek their own Commodity; yet if this were done with Injury unto others, it was not to be suffered, but by all Men, and all good Means to be withstood. Finally, they knew that no Man might in reason take upon him to determine his own Right, and according to his own Determination proceed in maintenance thereof, in as much as every Man is towards himself, and them whom he greatly affects, partial; and therefore that Strifes and Troubles should be endless, except they gave their common Consent, all to be ordered by some, whom they should agree upon, without which Consent there would be no reason that any Man should take upon him to be Lord or Judge over another. Hooker's Eccl. Pol. I. 1. Sect. 10.

of the contrary. He that would have been insolent and in-jurious in the Woods of *America,* would not probably be much better in a Throne; where perhaps Learning and Religion shall be found out to justifie all, that he shall do to his Subjects, and the Sword presently silence all those that dare question it. For what the *Protection of Absolute Monarchy* is, what kind of Fathers of their Countries it makes Princes to be, and to what a degree of Happiness and Security it carries Civil Society where this sort of Government is grown to perfection, he that will look into the late Relation of *Ceylon,* may easily see.

93. *In Absolute Monarchies* indeed, as well as other Governments of the World, the Subjects have an Appeal to the Law, and Judges to decide any Controversies, and restrain any Violence that may happen betwixt the Subjects themselves, one amongst another. This every one thinks necessary, and believes he deserves to be thought a declared Enemy to Society and Mankind, who should go about to take it away. But whether this be from a true Love of Mankind and Society, and such a Charity as we owe all one to another, there is reason to doubt. For this is no more, than what every Man who loves his own Power, Profit, or Greatness, may, and naturally must do, keep those Animals from hurting or destroying one another who labour and drudge only for his Pleasure and Advantage, and so are taken care of, not out of any Love the Master has for them, but Love of himself, and the Profit they bring him. For if it be asked, what Security, *what Fence* is there in such a State, *against the Violence and Oppression of this Absolute Ruler?* The very Question can scarce be born. They are ready to tell you, that it deserves Death only to ask after Safety. Betwixt Subject and Subject, they will grant, there must be Measures, Laws, and Judges, for their mutual Peace and Security: But as for the *Ruler,* he ought to be *Absolute,* and is above all such Circumstances: because he has Power to do more hurt and wrong, 'tis right when he does it. To ask how you may be guarded from harm, or injury on that side where the strongest hand is to do it, is presently the Voice of Faction and Rebellion. As if when Men quitting the State of Nature entered into Society, they agreed that all of them but one, should be under the restraint of Laws, but that he should still retain all the Liberty of the State of Nature, increased with Power, and made licentious by Impunity. This is to think that Men are so foolish that they take care to avoid what Mischiefs may be done them by *Pole-Cats,* or *Foxes,* but are content, nay think it Safety, to be devoured by *Lions.*

94. But whatever Flatterers may talk to amuze Peoples Understandings, it hinders not Men, from feeling: and when they perceive, that any Man, in what Station soever, is out of the Bounds of the Civil Society which they are of; and that they have no Appeal on Earth against any harm they may receive from him, they are apt to think themselves in the state of Nature, in respect of him, whom they find to be so; and to take care as soon as they can, to have that *Safety and Security in Civil Society,* for which it was first instituted, and for which only they entered into it. And therefore, though perhaps at first, (as shall be shewed more at large hereafter in the following part of this Dis-

course) some one good and excellent Man, having got a Preheminency amongst the rest, had this Deference paid to his Goodness and Vertue, as to a kind of Natural Authority, that the chief Rule, with Arbitration of their differences, by a tacit Consent devolved into his hands, without any other caution, but the assurance they had of his Uprightness and Wisdom: yet when time, giving Authority, and (as some Men would perswade us) Sacredness to Customs, which the negligent, and unforeseeing Innocence of the first Ages began, had brought in Successors of another Stamp, the People finding their Properties not secure under the Government, as then it was, (whereas Government has no other end but the preservation of Property) could never be safe nor at rest, *nor think themselves in Civil Society,* till the Legislature was placed in collective Bodies of Men, call them Senate, Parliament, or what you please.* By which means every single person became subject, equally with other the meanest Men, to those Laws, which he himself, as part of the Legislative had established: nor could any one, by his own Authority, avoid the force of the Law, when once made, nor by any pretence of Superiority, plead exemption, thereby to License his own, or the Miscarriages of any of his Dependants. *No Man in Civil Society can be exempted from the Laws of it.* For if any Man may do, what he thinks fit, and there be no Appeal on Earth, for Redress or Security against any harm he shall do; I ask, Whether he be not perfectly still in the State of Nature, and so can be *no part or Member of that Civil Society:* unless any one will say, the State of Nature and Civil Society are one and the same thing, which I have never yet found any one so great a Patron of Anarchy as to affirm.

Chap. XI. Of the Extent of the Legislative Power.

134. The great end of Mens entring into Society, being the enjoyment of their Properties in Peace and Safety, and the great instrument and means of that being the Laws establish'd in that Society; the *first and fundamental positive Law* of all Commonwealths, *is the establishing of the Legislative Power;* as the *first and fundamental natural Law,* which is to govern even the Legislative it self, is *the preservation of the Society,* and (as far as will consist with the publick good) of every person in it. This *Legislative* is not only *the supream power* of the Commonwealth, but sacred and unalterable in the hands where the Community have once placed it; nor can any Edict of any Body else, in what Form soever conceived, or by what Power soever backed, have the force and obligation of a *Law,* which has not its *Sanction from that Legislative,* which the publick has chosen and appointed. For without this the Law could not have that,

---

**At the first, when some certain kind of Regiment was once appointed, it may be that nothing was then farther thought upon for the manner of governing, but all permitted unto their Wisdom and Discretion, which were to Rule, till by experience they found this for all parts very inconvenient, so as the thing which they had devised for a Remedy, did indeed but increase the Sore, which it should have cured. They saw, that to live by one Man's Will, became the cause of all Mens misery. This constrained them to come unto Laws wherein all Men might see their Duty beforehand, and know the Penalties of transgressing them.* Hooker's Eccl. Pol. I. 1. Sect. 10.

which is absolutely necessary to its being a *Law, the consent of the Society,* over whom no Body can have a power to make Laws, but by their own consent,* and by Authority received from them; and therefore all the *Obedience,* which by the most solemn Ties any one can be obliged to pay, ultimately terminates in this *Supream Power,* and is directed by those Laws which it enacts: nor can any Oaths to any Foreign Power whatsoever, or any Domestick Subordinate Power, discharge any Member of the Society from his *Obedience to the Legislative,* acting pursuant to their trust, nor oblige him to any Obedience contrary to the Laws so enacted, or farther than they do allow; it being ridiculous to imagine one can be tied ultimately to *obey* any *Power* in the Society, which is not *the Supream.*

135. Though the *Legislative,* whether placed in one or more, whether it be always in being, or only by intervals, tho' it be the *Supream* Power in every Common-wealth; yet,

First, It is *not,* nor can possibly be absolutely *Arbitrary* over the Lives and Fortunes of the People. For it being but the joynt power of every Member of the Society given up to that Person, or Assembly, which is Legislator, it can be no more than those persons had in a State of Nature before they enter'd into Society, and gave up to the Community. For no Body can transfer to another more power than he has in himself; and no Body has an absolute Arbitrary Power over himself, or over any other, to destroy his own Life, or take away the Life or Property of another. A Man, as has been proved, cannot subject himself to the Arbitrary Power of another; and having in the State of Nature no Arbitrary Power over the Life, Liberty, or Possession of another, but only so much as the Law of Nature gave him for the preservation of himself, and the rest of Mankind; this is all he doth, or can give up to the Common-wealth, and by it to the *Legislative Power,* so that the Legislative can have no more than this. Their Power in the utmost Bounds of it, is *limited to the publick good* of the Society. It is a Power, that hath no other end but preservation, and therefore can never have a right to destroy, enslave, or designedly to impoverish the Subjects.† The

Obligations of the Law of Nature, cease not in Society but only in many Cases are drawn closer, and have by Humane Laws known Penalties annexed to them, to inforce their observation. Thus the Law of Nature stands as an Eternal Rule to all Men, *Legislators* as well as others. The *Rules* that they make for other Mens Actions, must, as well as their own and other Mens Actions, be conformable to the Law of Nature, *i.e.* to the Will of God, of which that is a Declaration, and the *fundamental Law of Nature* being *the preservation of Mankind,* no Humane Sanction can be good, or valid against it.

136. *Secondly,* The *Legislative,* or Supream Authority, cannot assume to its self a power to Rule by extempory Arbitrary Decrees,‡ but *is bound to dispense Justice,* and decide the Rights of the Subject *by promulgated standing Laws, and known Authoris'd Judges.* For the Law of Nature being unwritten, and so no where to be found but in the minds of Men, they who through Passion or Interest shall miscite, or misapply it, cannot so easily be convinced of their mistake where there is no establish'd Judge: And so it serves not, as it ought, to determine the Rights, and fence the Properties of those that live under it, especially where every one is Judge, Interpreter, and Executioner of it too, and that in his own Case: And he that has right on his side, having ordinarily but his own single strength, hath not force enough to defend himself from Injuries, or to punish Delinquents. To avoid these Inconveniencies which disorder Mens Properties in the state of Nature, Men unite into Societies, that they may have the united strength of the whole Society to secure and defend their Properties, and may have *standing Rules* to bound it, by which every one may know what is his. To this end it is that Men give up all their Natural Power to the Society which they enter into, and the Community put the Legislative Power into such hands as they think fit, with this trust, that they shall be govern'd by *declared Laws,* or else their Peace, Quiet, and Property will still be at the same uncertainty, as it was in the state of Nature.

137. Absolute Arbitrary Power, or Governing without *settled standing Laws,* can neither of them consist with the ends of Society and Government, which Men would not quit the freedom of the state of Nature for, and tie themselves up under, were it not to preserve their Lives, Liberties and Fortunes; and by *stated Rules* of Right and Property to secure their Peace and Quiet. It cannot be

---

The lawful Power of making Laws to Command whole Politick Societies of Men belonging so properly unto the same intire Societies, that for any Prince or Potentate of what kind soever upon Earth, to exercise the same of himself, and not by express Commission immediately and personally received from God, or else by Authority derived at the first from their consent, upon whose persons they impose Laws, it is no better than meer Tyranny. Laws they are not therefore which publick Approbation hath not made so. Hooker's Eccl. Pol. l. 1. Sect. 10. Of this point therefore we are to note, that sith Men naturally have no full and perfect Power to Command whole Politick Multitudes of Men, therefore utterly without our Consent, we could in such sort be at no Mans Commandment living. And to be commanded we do consent when that Society, whereof we be a part, hath at any time before consented, without revoking the same after by the like universal agreement.

Laws therefore humane, of what kind soever, are available by consent. Ibid.

†*Two Foundations there are which bear up publick Societies, the one a natural inclination, whereby all Men desire sociable Life and Fellowship; the other an Order, expressly or secretly agreed upon, touching the manner of their union in living together; the latter is that which we call the Law of a Common-weal, the very Soul of a Politick Body, the parts whereof are by Law animated, held together, and set on work in such actions as the common good requireth. Laws politick, ordain'd for external*

order and regiment amongst Men, are never framed as they should be, unless presuming the will of Man to be inwardly obstinate, rebellious, and averse from all Obedience to the sacred Laws of his Nature; in a word, unless presuming Man to be in regard of his depraved Mind, little better than a wild Beast, they do accordingly provide notwithstanding, so to frame his outward Actions, that they be no hindrance unto the common good, for which Societies are instituted. Unless they do this they are not perfect. Hooker's Eccl. Pol. l. 1. Sect. 10.*

‡*Humane Laws are measures in respect of Men, whose actions they must direct, howbeit such measures they are as have also their higher Rules to be measured by, which Rules are two, the Law of God, and the Law of Nature; so that Laws Humane must be made according to the general Laws of Nature, and without contradiction to any positive Law of Scripture, otherwise they are ill made, Ibid. l. 3. Sect. 9.*

To constrain Men to any thing inconvenient doth seem unreasonable. Ibid. l. 1. Sect. 10.

supposed that they should intend, had they a power so to do, to give to any one, or more, an *absolute Arbitrary Power* over their Persons and Estates, and put a force into the Magistrates hand to execute his unlimited Will arbitrarily upon them: This were to put themselves into a worse condition than the state of Nature, wherein they had a Liberty to defend their Right against the Injuries of others, and were upon equal terms of force to maintain it, whether invaded by a single Man, or many in Combination. Whereas by supposing they have given up themselves to the *absolute Arbitrary Power* and will of a Legislator, they have disarmed themselves, and armed him, to make a prey of them when he pleases. He being in a much worse condition who is exposed to the Arbitrary Power of one Man, who has the Command of 100000. than he that is expos'd to the Arbitrary Power of 100000. single Men: no Body being secure, that his Will, who has such a Command, is better, than that of other Men, though his Force be 100000. times stronger. And therefore whatever Form the Common-wealth is under, the Ruling Power ought to govern by *declared* and *received Laws*, and not by extemporary Dictates and undetermined Resolutions. For then Mankind will be in a far worse condition, than in the State of Nature, if they shall have armed one or a few Men with the joynt power of a Multitude, to force them to obey at pleasure the exorbitant and unlimited Decrees of their sudden thoughts, or unrestrain'd, and till that moment unknown Wills without having any measures set down which may guide and justifie their actions. For all the power the Government has, being only for the good of the Society, as it ought not to be *Arbitrary* and at Pleasure, so it ought to be exercised by *established and promulgated Laws:* that both the People may know their Duty, and be safe and secure within the limits of the Law, and the Rulers too kept within their due bounds, and not to be tempted, by the Power they have in their hands, to imploy it to such purposes, and by such measures, as they would not have known, and own not willingly.

138. *Thirdly,* The *Supream Power cannot take* from any Man any part of his *Property* without his own consent. For the preservation of Property being the end of Government, and that for which Men enter into Society, it necessarily supposes and requires, that the People should *have Property,* without which they must be suppos'd to lose that by entring into Society, which was the end for which they entered into it, too gross an absurdity for any Man to own. *Men* therefore *in Society having Property,* they have such a right to the goods, which by the Law of the Community are theirs, that no Body hath a right to take their substance, or any part of it from them, without their own consent; without this, they have no *Property* at all. For I have truly no *Property* in that, which another can by right take from me, when he pleases, against my consent. Hence it is a mistake to think, that the Supream or *Legislative Power* of any Commonwealth, can do what it will, and dispose of the Estates of the Subject *arbitrarily,* or take any part of them at pleasure. This is not much to be fear'd in Governments where the *Legislative* consists, wholly or in part, in Assemblies which are variable, whose Members upon the Disso-

lution of the Assembly, are Subjects under the common Laws of their Country, equally with the rest. But in Governments, where the *Legislative* is in one lasting Assembly always in being, or in one Man, as in Absolute Monarchies, there is danger still, that they will think themselves to have a distinct interest, from the rest of the Community; and so will be apt to increase their own Riches and Power, by taking, what they think fit, from the People. For a Man's *Property* is not at all secure, though there be good and equitable Laws to set the bounds of it, between him and his Fellow Subjects, if he who commands those Subjects, have Power to take from any private Man, what part he pleases of his *Property,* and use and dispose of it as he thinks good.

139. But *Government* into whatsoever hands it is put, being as I have before shew'd, intrusted with this condition, and *for this end,* that Men might have and secure *their Properties,* the Prince or Senate, however it may have power to make Laws for the regulating of *Property* between the Subjects one amongst another, yet can never have a Power to take to themselves the whole or any part of the Subjects *Property,* without their own consent. For this would be in effect to leave them no *Property* at all. And to let us see, that even *absolute Power,* where it is necessary, is *not Arbitrary* by being absolute, but is still limited by that reason, and confined to those ends, which required it in some Cases to be absolute, we need look no farther than the common practice of Martial Discipline. For the Preservation of the Army, and in it of the whole Commonwealth, requires an *absolute Obedience* to the Command of every Superiour Officer, and it is justly Death to disobey or dispute the most dangerous or unreasonable of them: but yet we see, that neither the Serjeant, that could command a Souldier to march up to the mouth of a Cannon, or stand in a Breach, where he is almost sure to perish, can command that Soldier to give him one penny of his Money; nor the *General,* that can condemn him to Death for deserting his Post, or for not obeying the most desperate Orders, can yet with all his absolute Power of Life and Death, dispose of one Farthing of that Soldiers Estate, or seize one jot of his Goods; whom yet he can command any thing, and hang for the least Disobedience. Because such a blind Obedience is necessary to that end for which the Commander has his Power, *viz.* the preservation of the rest; but the disposing of his Goods has nothing to do with it.

140. 'Tis true, Governments cannot be supported without great Charge, and 'tis fit every one who enjoys his share of the Protection, should pay out of his Estate his proportion for the maintenance of it. But still it must be with his own Consent, *i.e.* the Consent of the Majority, giving it either by themselves, or their Representatives chosen by them. For if any one shall claim a *Power to lay* and levy *Taxes* on the People, by his own Authority, and without such consent of the People, he thereby invades the *Fundamental Law of Property,* and subverts the end of Government. For what property have I in that which another may by right take, when he pleases to himself?

141. *Fourthly,* The *Legislative cannot transfer the Power of*

Making Laws to any other hands. For it being but a delegated Power from the People, they, who have it, cannot pass it over to others. The People alone can appoint the Form of the Commonwealth, which is by Constituting the Legislative, and appointing in whose hands that shall be. And when the People have said, We will submit to rules, and be govern'd by *Laws* made by such Men, and in such Forms, no Body else can say other Men shall make *Laws* for them; nor can the people be bound by any *Laws* but such as are Enacted by those, whom they have Chosen, and Authorised to make *Laws* for them. The power of the *Legislative* being derived from the People by a positive voluntary Grant and Institution, can be no other, than what that positive Grant conveyed, which being only to make *Laws*, and not to make *Legislators*, the *Legislative* can have no power to transfer their Authority of making Laws, and place it in other hands.

142. These are the *Bounds* which the trust that is put in them by Society, and the Law of God and Nature, have *set to the Legislative* Power of every Commonwealth, in all Forms of Government.

First, They are to govern by *promulgated establish'd Laws,* not to be varied in particular Cases, but to have one Rule for Rich and Poor, for the Favourite at Court, and the Country Man at Plough.

Secondly, These *Laws* also ought to be designed *for* no other end ultimately but *the good of the People.*

Thirdly, they must *not raise Taxes* on the Property of the People, *without the Consent of the People,* given by themselves, or their Deputies. And this properly concerns only such Governments where the *Legislative* is always in being, or at least where the People have not reserv'd any part of the Legislative to Deputies, to be from time to time chosen by themselves.

Fourthly, The *Legislative* neither must *nor can transfer the Power of making Laws* to any Body else, or place it any where but where the People have.

· · · · ·

212. Besides this over-turning from without, *Governments are dissolved from within.*

First, When the *Legislative is altered.* Civil Society being a State of Peace, amongst those who are of it, from whom the State of War is excluded by the Umpirage, which they have provided in their Legislative, for the ending all Differences, that may arise amongst any of them, 'tis in their *Legislative,* that the Members of a Commonwealth are united, and combined together into one coherent living Body. This *is the Soul that gives Form, Life, and Unity* to the Commonwealth: From hence the several Members have their mutual Influence, Sympathy, and Connexion: And therefore when the *Legislative* is broken, or *dissolved,* Dissolution and Death follows. For the *Essence and Union of the Society* consisting in having one Will, the Legislative, when once established by the Majority, has the declaring, and as it were keeping of that Will. The *Constitution of the Legislative* is the first and fundamental Act of Society, whereby provision is made for the *Continuation of their Union,* under the Direction of Persons, and Bonds of Laws made by persons authorized thereunto, by the Consent and Appointment of the People, without which no one Man, or number of Men, amongst them, can have Authority of making Laws, that shall be binding to the rest. When any one, or more, shall take upon them to make Laws, whom the People have not appointed so to do, they make Laws without Authority, which the People are not therefore bound to obey; by which means they come again to be out of subjection, and may constitute to themselves a *new Legislative,* as they think best, being in full liberty to resist the force of those, who without Authority would impose any thing upon them. Every one is at the disposure of his own Will, when those who had by the delegation of the Society, the declaring of the publick Will, are excluded from it, and others usurp the place who have no such Authority or Delegation.

6

John Trenchard, Cato's Letters, no. 60
6 Jan. 1721
Jacobson 116–23

All Government proved to be instituted by Men, and only to intend the general Good of Men.

There is no Government now upon Earth, which owes its Formation or Beginning to the immediate Revelation of God, or can derive its Existence from such Revelation: It is certain, on the contrary, that the Rise and Institution or Variation of Government, from Time to Time, is within the Memory of Men or of Histories; and that every Government, which we know at this Day in the World, was established by the Wisdom and Force of mere Men, and by the Concurrence of Means and Causes evidently human. Government therefore can have no Power, but such as Men can give, and such as they actually did give, or permit for their own 'Sakes: Nor can any Government be in Fact framed but by Consent, if not'of every Subject, yet of as many as can compel the rest; since no Man, or Council of Men, can have personal Strength enough to govern Multitudes by Force, or can claim to themselves and their Families any Superiority, or natural Sovereignty over their Fellow-Creatures naturally as good as them. Such Strength, therefore where-ever it is, is civil and accumulative Strength, derived from the Laws and Constitutions of the Society, of which the Governors themselves are but Members.

So that to know the Jurisdiction of Governors, and its Limits, we must have Recourse to the Institution of Government, and ascertain those Limits by the Measure of Power, which Men in the State of Nature have over themselves and one another: And as no Man can take from many, who are stronger than him, what they have no Mind to give him; and he who has not Consent must have Force, which is itself the Consent of the Stronger; so no Man can give to another either what is none of his own, or what in its own Nature is inseparable from himself; as his Religion particularly is.

Every Man's Religion is his own; nor can the Religion of any Man, of what Nature or Figure soever, be the Religion of another Man, unless he also chooses it; which Action utterly excludes all Force, Power, or Government. Religion can never come without Conviction, nor can Conviction come from Civil Authority; Religion, which is the Fear of God, cannot be subject to Power, which is the Fear of Man. It is a Relation between God and our own Souls only, and consists in a Disposition of Mind to obey the Will of our great Creator, in the Manner which we think most acceptable to him. It is independent upon all human Directions, and superior to them; and consequently uncontroulable by external Force, which cannot reach the free Faculties of the Mind, or inform the Understanding, much less convince it. Religion therefore, which can never be subject to the Jurisdiction of another, can never be alienated to another, or put in his Power.

Nor has any Man in the State of Nature Power over his own Life, or to take away the Life of another, unless to defend his own, or what is as much his own, namely, his Property. This Power therefore, which no Man has, no Man can transfer to another.

Nor could any Man in the State of Nature, have a Right to violate the Property of another; that is, what another had acquired by his Act or Labour; or to interrupt him in his Industry and Enjoyments, as long as he himself was not injured by that Industry and those Enjoyments. No Man therefore could transfer to the Magistrate that Right which he had not himself.

No Man in his Senses was ever so wild as to give an unlimited Power to another to take away his Life, or the Means of Living, according to the Caprice, Passion, and unreasonable Pleasure of that other: But if any Man restrained himself from any Part of his Pleasures, or parted with any Portion of his Acquisitions, he did it with the honest Purpose of enjoying the rest with the greater Security, and always in Subserviency to his own Happiness, which no Man will or can willingly and intentionally give away to any other whatsoever.

And if any one, through his own Inadvertence, or by the Fraud or Violence of another, can be drawn into so foolish a Contract, he is relievable by the eternal Laws of God and Reason. No Engagement that is wicked and unjust can be executed without Injustice and Wickedness: This is so true, that I question whether there be a Constitution in the World which does not afford, or pretend to afford, a Remedy for relieving ignorant, distressed, and unwary Men, trepanned into such Engagements by artful Knaves, or frightened into them by imperious ones. So that here the Laws of Nature and general Reason supersede the municipal and positive Laws of Nations; and no where oftner than in *England.* What else was the Design, and ought to be the Business, of our Courts of Equity? And I hope whole Countries and Societies are no more exempted from the Privileges and Protection of Reason and Equity, than are private Particulars.

Here then is the natural Limitation of the Magistrate's Authority: He ought not to take what no Man ought to give; nor exact what no Man ought to perform: All he has is given him, and those that gave it must judge of the Application. In Government there is no such Relation as Lord and Slave, lawless Will and blind Submission; nor ought to be amongst Men: But the only Relation is that of Father and Children, Patron and Client, Protection and Allegiance, Benefaction and Gratitude, mutual Affection and mutual Assistance.

So that the Nature of Government does not alter the natural Right of Men to Liberty, which in all political Societies is alike their Due: But some Governments provide better than others for the Security and impartial Distribution of that Right. There has been always such a constant and certain Fund of Corruption and Malignity in human Nature, that it has been rare to find that Man, whose Views and Happiness did not center in the Gratification of his Appetites, and worst Appetites, his Luxury, his Pride, his Avarice, and Lust of Power; and who considered any publick Trust reposed in him, with any other View, than as the Means to satiate such unruly and dangerous Desires! And this has been most eminently true of Great Men, and those who aspired to Dominion. They were first made Great for the Sake of the Publick, and afterwards at its Expence. And if they had been content to have been moderate Traytors, Mankind would have been still moderately happy; but their Ambition and Treason observing no Degrees, there was no Degree of Vileness and Misery which the poor People did not often feel.

The Appetites therefore of Men, especially of Great Men, are carefully to be observed and stayed, or else they will never stay themselves. The Experience of every Age convinces us, that we must not judge of Men by what they ought to do, but by what they will do; and all History affords but few Instances of Men trusted with great Power without abusing it, when with Security they could. The Servants of Society, that is to say, its Magistrates, did almost universally serve it by seizing it, selling it, or plundering it; especially when they were left by the Society unlimited as to their Duty and Wages. In that Case these faithful Stewards generally took all; and, being Servants, made Slaves of their Masters.

For these Reasons, and convinced by woful and eternal Experience, Societies found it necessary to lay Restraints upon their Magistrates or publick Servants, and to put Checks upon those who would otherwise put Chains upon them; and therefore these Societies set themselves to model and form national Constitutions with such Wisdom and Art, that the publick Interest should be consulted and carried at the same Time, when those entrusted with the Administration of it were consulting and pursuing their own.

Hence grew the Distinction between Arbitrary and Free Governments: Not that more or less Power was vested in the one than in the other; nor that either of them lay under less or more Obligations, in Justice, to protect their Subjects, and study their Ease, Prosperity, and Security, and to watch for the same. But the Power and Sovereignty of Magistrates in free Countries was so qualified, and so divided into different Channels, and committed to the Direction of so many different Men, with different Interests

619

and Views, that the Majority of them could seldom or never find their Account in betraying their Trust in fundamental Instances. Their Emulation, Envy, Fear, or Interest, always made them Spies and Checks upon one another. By all which Means the People have often come at the Heads of those who forfeited their Heads, by betraying the People.

In despotick Governments Things went far otherwise, those Governments having been framed otherwise; if the same could be called Governments, where the Rules of publick Power were dictated by private and lawless Lust; where Folly and Madness often swayed the Scepter, and blind Rage weilded the Sword. The whole Wea[l]th of the State, with its Civil or Military Power, being in the Prince, the People could have no Remedy but Death and Patience, while he oppressed them by the Lump, and butchered them by Thousands: Unless perhaps the Ambition or personal Resentments of some of the Instruments of his Tyranny procured a Revolt, which rarely mended their Condition.

The only Secret therefore in forming a Free Government, is to make the Interests of the Governors and of the Governed the same, as far as human Policy can contrive. Liberty cannot be preserved any other Way. Men have long found, from the Weakness and Depravity of themselves and one another, that most Men will act for Interest against Duty, as often as they dare. So that to engage them to their Duty, Interest must be linked to the Observance of it, and Danger to the Breach of it. Personal Advantages and Security, must be the rewards of Duty and Obedience; and Disgrace, Torture, and Death, the Punishment of Treachery and Corruption.

Human Wisdom has yet found out but one certain Expedient to effect this; and that is, to have the Concerns of all directed by all, as far as possibly can be: And where the Persons interested are too numerous, or live too distant to meet together on all Emergencies, they must moderate Necessity by Prudence, and act by Deputies, whose Interest is the same with their own, and whose Property is so intermingled with theirs, and so engaged upon the same Bottom, that Principals and Deputies must stand and fall together. When the Deputies thus act for their own Interest, by acting for the Interest of their Principals; when they can make no Law but what they themselves, and their Posterity, must be subject to; when they can give no Money, but what they must pay their Share of; when they can do no Mischief, but what must fall upon their own Heads in common with their Countrymen; their Principals may then expect good Laws, little Mischief, and much Frugality.

Here therefore lies the great Point of Nicety and Care in forming the Constitution, that the Persons entrusted and representing, shall either never have any Interest detached from the Persons entrusting and represented, or never the Means to pursue it. Now to compass this great Point effectually, no other Way is left, but one of these two, or rather both; namely, to make the Deputies so numerous, that there may be no Possibility of corrupting the Majority; or, by changing them so often, that there is no sufficient Time to corrupt them, and to carry the Ends of that Corruption. The People may be very sure, that the major Part of their Deputies being honest, will keep the rest so; and that they will all be honest, when they have no Temptations to be Knaves.

We have some Sketch of this Policy in the Constitution of our several great Companies, where the General Court, composed of all its Members, constitutes the Legislature, and the Consent of that Court is the Sanction of their Laws; and where the Administration of their Affairs is put under the Conduct of a certain Number chosen by the Whole. Here every Man con[c]erned saw the Necessity of securing Part of their Property, by putting the Persons entrusted under proper Regulations; however remiss they may be in takeing Care of the Whole. And if Provision had been made, That, as a Third Part of the Directors are to go out every Year, so none should stay in above Three, (as I am told was as first promised) all Juggling with Courtiers, and raising great Estates by Confederacy, at the Expence of the Company, had, in a great Measure, been prevented; though there were still wanting other Limitations, which might have effectually obviated all those Evils.

This was the ancient Constitution of *England:* Our Kings had neither Revenues large enough, nor Offices gainful and numerous enough in their Disposal, to corrupt any considerable Number of Members; nor any Force to frighten them. Besides, the same Parliament seldom or never met twice: For, the serving in it being found an Office of Burthen, and not of Profit, it was thought reasonable that all Men qualified should, in their Turns, leave their Families and domestick Concerns, to serve the Publick; and their Borough bore their Charges. The only Grievance then was, that they were not called together often enough, to redress the Grievances which the People suffered from the Court during their Intermission: And therefore a Law was made in *Edward* the IIId's Time, That Parliaments should be holden once a Year.

But this Law, like the late Queen's Peace, did not execute itself; and therefore the Court seldom convened them, but when they wanted Money, or had other Purposes of their own to serve; and sometimes raised Money without them: Which arbitrary proceeding brought upon the Publick numerous Mischiefs; and, in the Reign of King *Charles* the Ist, a long and bloody Civil War. In that Reign an Act was Passed, That they should meet of themselves, if they were not called according to the Direction of that Law; which was worthily repealed upon the Restoration of King *Charles* the IId: And in the same kind Fit, a great Revenue was given him for Life, and continued to his Brother. By which Means these Princes were enabled to keep standing Troops, to corrupt Parliaments, or to live without them; and to commit such Acts of Power as brought about, and indeed forced the People upon the late happy *Revolution.* Soon after which a new Act was passed, That Parliaments should be rechosen once in three Years: Which Law was also repealed, upon his Majesty's Accession to the Throne, that the present Parliament might have Time to rectify those Abuses which we labour under, and to make Regulations proper to prevent them *All* for the future. *All* which has since been happily effected; and, I bless God, we are told, that the People will have the Opportunity to thank them, in another Election, for their great Services to their Country. I shall be always ready, on my Part, to do them Honour, and pay them my Acknowledgments, in the most effectual Manner in my Power.—But more of this in the succeeding Papers.

7

JOHN TRENCHARD, CATO'S LETTERS, NO. 61
13 Jan. 1721
Jacobson 123–27

How free Governments are to be framed so as to last, and how they differ from such as are arbitrary.

The most reasonable Meaning that can be put upon this Apothegm, that *Virtue is its own Reward,* is, that it seldom meets with any other. God himself, who having made us, best knows our Natures, does not trust to the intrinsick Excellence and native Beauty of Holiness alone, to engage us in its Interests and Pursuits, but recommends it to us by the stronger and more affecting Motives of Rewards and Punishments. No wise Man, therefore, will in any Instance of Moment trust to the mere Integrity of another. The Experience of all Ages may convince us, that Men, when they are above Fear, grow for the most part above Honesty and Shame: And this is particularly and certainly true of Societies of Men, when they are numerous enough to keep one another in Countenance; for when the Weight of Infamy is divided amongst many, no one sinks under his own Burthen.

Great Bodies of Men have seldom judged what they ought to do, by any other Rule than what they could do. What Nation is there that has not oppressed any other, when the same could be done with Advantage and Security? What Party has ever had Regard to the Principles which they professed, or ever reformed the Errors which they condemned? What Company, or particular Society of Merchants or Tradesmen, has ever acted for the Interest of general Trade, though it always filled their Mouths in private Conversation?

And yet Men, thus formed and qualified, are the Materials for Government. For the Sake of Men it is instituted, by the Prudence of Men it must be conducted; and the Art of political Mechanism is, to erect a firm Building with such crazy and corrupt Materials. The strongest Cables are made out of loose Hemp and Flax; the World itself may, with the Help of proper Machines, be moved by the Force of a single Hair; and so may the Government of the World, as well as the World itself. But whatever Discourses I shall hereafter make upon this great and useful Subject, I shall confine myself in this Letter to free monarchical Constitutions alone, and to the Application of some of the Principles laid down in my last.

It is there said, that when the Society consists of too many, or when they live too far apart to be able to meet together, to take Care of their own Affairs, they can no otherwise preserve their Liberties, than by choosing Deputies to represent them, and to act for them; and that these Deputies must be either so numerous, that there can be no Means of corrupting the Majority; or so often changed, that there shall be no Time to do it so as to answer any End by doing it. Without one of these Regulations, or both, I lay it down as a certain Maxim in Politicks, that it is impossible to preserve a free Government long.

I think I may with great Modesty affirm, that in former Reigns the People of *England* found no sufficient Security in the Number of their Representatives. What with the Crowd of Offices in the Gift of the Crown, which were possessed by Men of no other Merit, nor held by any other Tenure, but merely a Capacity to get into the House of Commons, and the Disservice which they could and would do their Country there: What with the Promises and Expectations given to others, who by Court-Influence, and often by Court-Money, carried their Elections: What by artful Caresses, and the familiar and deceitful Addresses of great Men to weak Men: What with luxurious Dinners, and Rivers of *Burgundy, Champaign,* and *Tokay,* thrown down the Throats of Gluttons; and what with Pensions, and other personal Gratifications, bestowed where Wind and Smoke would not pass for current Coin: What with Party Watch-Words and imaginary Terrors, spread amongst the drunken 'Squires, and the deluded and enthusiastick Bigots, of dreadful Designs in *Embrio,* to blow up the Church, and the Protestant Interest; and sometimes with the Dread of mighty Invasions just ready to break upon us from the Man in the Moon: I say, by all these corrupt Arts, the Representatives of the *English* People, in former Reigns, have been brought to betray the People, and to join with their Oppressors. So much are Men governed by artful Applications to their private Passions and Interest. And it is evident to me, that if ever we have a weak or an ambitious Prince, with a Ministry like him, we must find out some other Resources, or acquiesce in the Loss of our Liberties. The Course and Transiency of human Affairs will not suffer us to live always under the present righteous Administration.

So that I can see no Means in human Policy to preserve the publick Liberty and a monarchical Form of Government together, but by the frequent fresh Elections of the People's Deputies: This is what the Writers in Politicks call Rotation of Magistracy. Men, when they first enter into Magistracy, have often their former Condition before their Eyes: They remember what they themselves suffered, with their Fellow-Subjects, from the Abuse of Power, and how much they blamed it; and so their first Purposes are to be humble, modest, and just; and probably, for some Time, they continue so. But the Possession of Power soon alters and viciates their Hearts, which are at the same time sure to be leavened, and puffed up to an unnatural Size, by the deceitful Incense of false Friends, and by the prostrate Submission of Parasites. First, they grow indifferent to all their good Designs, then drop them: Next, they lose their Moderation; afterwards, they renounce all Measures with their old Acquaintance and old Principles; and seeing themselves in magnifying Glasses, grow, in Conceit, a different Species from their Fellow-Subjects; and so by too

sudden Degrees become insolent, rapacious and tyrannical, ready to catch at all Means, often the vilest and most
oppressive, to raise their Fortunes as high as their imaginary Greatness. So that the only Way to put them in mind
of their former Condition, and consequently of the Condition of other People, is often to reduce them to it; and
to let others of equal Capacities share of Power in their
Turn: This also is the only Way to qualify Men, and make
them equally fit for Dominion and Subjection.

A Rotation therefore, in Power and Magistracy, is essentially necessary to a free Government: It is indeed the
Thing itself; and constitutes, animates, and informs it, as
much as the Soul constitutes the Man. It is a Thing sacred
and inviolable, where-ever Liberty is thought sacred; nor
can it ever be committed to the Disposal of those who are
trusted with the Preservation of National Constitutions:
For though they may have the Power to model it for the
publick Advantage, and for the more effectual Security of
that Right; yet they can have none to give it up, or, which
is the same Thing, to make it useless.

The Constitution of a limited Monarchy, is the joint
Concurrence of the Crown and of the Nobles (without
whom it cannot subsist) and of the Body of the People, to
make Laws for the common Benefit of the Subject; and
where the People, through Number or Distance, cannot
meet, they must send Deputies to speak in their Names,
and to attend upon their Interest: These Deputies therefore act by, under, and in Subserviency to the Constitution, and have not a Power above it and over it.

8

JOHN TRENCHARD, CATO'S LETTERS, NO. 62
20 Jan. 1721
Jacobson 127–31

*An Enquiry into the Nature and Extent of Liberty;
with its Loveliness and Advantages, and the vile
Effects of Slavery.*

I Have shewn, in a late Paper, wherein consists the Difference between Free and Arbitrary Governments, as to
their frame and Constitution; and in this and the following
I shall show their different Spirit and Effects. But first I
shall shew wherein Liberty itself consists.

By Liberty, I understand the Power which every Man
has over his own Actions, and his Right to enjoy the Fruit
of his Labour, Art, and Industry, as far as by it he hurts
not the Society, or any Members of it, by taking from any
Member, or by hindering him from enjoying what he himself enjoys. The Fruits of a Man's honest Industry are the
just Rewards of it, ascertained to him by natural and eternal Equity, as is his Title to use them in the Manner which
he thinks fit: And thus, with the above Limitations, every
Man is sole Lord and Arbiter of his own private Actions
and Property.—A Character of which no Man living can
divest him but by Usurpation, or his own Consent.

The entering into political Society, is so far from a Departure from his natural Right, that to preserve it was the
sole Reason why Men did so; and mutual Protection and
Assistance is the only reasonable Purpose of all reasonable
Societies. To make such Protection practicable, Magistracy
was formed, with Power to defend the Innocent from Violence, and to punish those that offered it; nor can there
be any other Pretence for Magistracy in the world. In order to this good End, the Magistrate is intrusted with conducting and applying the united Force of the Community;
and with exacting such a Share of every Man's Property,
as is necessary to preserve the Whole, and to defend every
Man and his Property from foreign and domestick Injuries. These are the Boundaries of the Power of the Magistrate, who deserts his Function whenever he breaks
them. By the Laws of Society, he is more limited and restrained than any Man amongst them; since, while they are
absolutely free in all their Actions, which purely concern
themselves; all his Actions, as a publick Person, being for
the Sake of Society, must refer to it, and answer the Ends
of it.

It is a mistaken Notion in Government, that the Interest
of the Majority is only to be consulted, since in Society
every Man has a Right to every Man's Assistance in the
Enjoyment and Defence of his private Property; otherwise
the greater Number may sell the lesser, and divide their
Estates amongst themselves; and so, instead of a Society,
where all peaceable Men are protected, become a Conspiracy of the Many against the Minority. With as much Equity
may one Man wantonly dispose of all, and Violence may
be sanctified by mere Power.

And it is as foolish to say, that Government is concerned
to meddle with the private Thoughts and Actions of Men,
while they injure neither the Society, nor any of its Members. Every Man is, in Nature and Reason, the Judge and
Disposer of his own domestick Affairs; and, according to
the Rules of Religion and Equity, every Man must carry
his own Conscience. So that neither has the Magistrate a
Right to direct the private Behaviour of men; nor has the
Magistrate, or any body else, any manner of Power to
model People's Speculations, no more than their Dreams.
Government being intended to protect Men from the Injuries of one another, and not to direct them in their own
Affairs, in which no one is interested but themselves; it is
plain, that their Thoughts and domestick Concerns are exempted intirely from its Jurisdiction: In Truth, Mens
Thoughts are not subject to their own Jurisdiction.

Idiots and Lunaticks indeed, who cannot take Care of
themselves, must be taken Care of by others: But whilst
Men have their five Senses, I cannot see what the Magistrate has to do with Actions by which the Society cannot
be affected; and where he meddles with such, he meddles
impertinently or tyrannically. Must the Magistrate tie up
every Man's Legs, because some Men fall into Ditches? Or,
must he put out their Eyes, because with them they see
lying Vanities? Or, would it become the Wisdom and Care
of Governors to establish a travelling Society, to prevent
People, by a proper Confinement, from throwing themselves into Wells, or over Precipices; Or to endow a Fraternity of Physicians and Surgeons all over the Nation, to take

Care of their Subjects Health, without being consulted; and to vomit, bleed, purge, and scarify them at Pleasure, whether they would or no, just as these established Judges of Health should think fit? If this were the Case, what a Stir and Hubbub should we soon see kept about the established Potions and Lancets? Every Man, Woman, or Child, though ever so healthy, must be a Patient, or woe be to them! The best Diet and Medicines would soon grow pernicious from any other Hand; and their Pills alone, however ridiculous, insufficient, or distasteful, would be attended with a Blessing.

Let People alone, and they will take Care of themselves, and do it best; and if they do not, a sufficient Punishment will follow their Neglect, without the Magistrate's Interposition and Penalties. It is plain, that such busy Care and officious Intrusion into the personal Affairs, or private Actions, Thoughts, and Imaginations of Men, has in it more Craft than Kindness; and is only a Device to mislead People, and pick their Pockets, under the false Pretence of the publick and their private Go[o]d. To quarrel with any Man for his Opinions, Humours, or the Fashion of his Clothes, is an Offence taken without being given. What is it to a Magistrate how I wash my Hands, or cut my Corns; what Fashion or Colours I wear, or what Notions I entertain, or what Gestures I use, or what Words I pronounce, when they please me, and do him and my Neighbour no Hurt? As well may he determine the Colour of my Hair, and controul my Shape and Features.

True and impartial Liberty is therefore the Right of every Man to pursue the natural, reasonable, and religious Dictates of his own Mind; to think what he will, and act as he thinks, provided he acts not to the Prejudice of another; to spend his own Money himself, and lay out the Produce of his Labour his own Way; and to labour for his own Pleasure and Profit, and not for others who are idle, and would live and riot by pillaging and oppressing him, and those that are like him.

So that Civil Government is only a partial Restraint put by the Laws of Agreement and Society upon natural and absolute Liberty, which might otherwise grow licentious: And Tyranny is an unlimited Restraint put upon natural Liberty, by the Will of one or a few. Magistracy, amongst a free People, is the Exercise of Power for the Sake of the People; and Tyrants abuse the People, for the Sake of Power. Free Government is the protecting the People in their Liberties by stated Rules: Tyranny is a brutish Struggle for unlimited Liberty to one or a few, who would rob all others of their Liberty, and act by no Rule but lawless Lust.

9

MONTESQUIEU, SPIRIT OF LAWS, BK. 6, CH. 2; BK. 11, CHS. 1–7, 20
1748

[Book 6]

2.—Of the Simplicity of Criminal Laws in different Governments

We hear it generally said that justice ought to be administered with us as in Turkey. Is it possible, then, that the most ignorant of all nations should be the most clearsighted on a point which it most behooves mankind to know?

If we examine the set forms of justice with respect to the trouble the subject undergoes in recovering his property or in obtaining satisfaction for an injury or affront, we shall find them doubtless too numerous: but if we consider them in the relation they bear to the liberty and security of every individual, we shall often find them too few; and be convinced that the trouble, expense, delays, and even the very dangers of our judiciary proceedings are the price that each subject pays for his liberty.

In Turkey, where little regard is shown to the honor, life, or estate of the subject, all causes are speedily decided. The method of determining them is a matter of indifference, provided they be determined. The pasha, after a quick hearing, orders which party he pleases to be bastinadoed, and then sends them about their business.

Here it would be dangerous to be of a litigious disposition; this supposes a strong desire of obtaining justice, a settled aversion, an active mind, and a steadiness in pursuing one's point. All this should be avoided in a government where fear ought to be the only prevailing sentiment, and in which popular disturbances are frequently attended with sudden and unforeseen revolutions. Here every man ought to know that the magistrate must not hear his name mentioned, and that his security depends entirely on his being reduced to a kind of annihilation.

But in moderate governments, where the life of the meanest subject is deemed precious, no man is stripped of his honor or property until after a long inquiry; and no man is bereft of life till his very country has attacked him—an attack that is never made without leaving him all possible means of making his defence.

Hence it is that when a person renders himself absolute, he immediately thinks of reducing the number of laws. In a government thus constituted they are more affected with particular inconveniences than with the liberty of the subject, which is very little minded.

In republics, it is plain that as many formalities at least are necessary as in monarchies. In both governments they increase in proportion to the value which is set on the honor, fortune, liberty, and life of the subject.

In republican governments, men are all equal; equal

they are also in despotic governments: in the former, because they are everything; in the latter, because they are nothing.

[Book 11]

1.—A general Idea

I make a distinction between the laws that establish political liberty as it relates to the constitution, and those by which it is established as it relates to the citizen. The former shall be the subject of this book; the latter I shall examine in the next.

2.—Different Significations of the word Liberty

There is no word that admits of more various significations, and has made more varied impressions on the human mind, than that of liberty. Some have taken it as a means of deposing a person on whom they had conferred a tyrannical authority; others for the power of choosing a superior whom they are obliged to obey; others for the right of bearing arms, and of being thereby enabled to use violence; others, in fine, for the privilege of being governed by a native of their own country, or by their own laws. A certain nation for a long time thought liberty consisted in the privilege of wearing a long beard. Some have annexed this name to one form of government exclusive of others: those who had a republican taste applied it to this species of polity; those who liked a monarchical state gave it to monarchy. Thus they have all applied the name of liberty to the government most suitable to their own customs and inclinations: and as in republics the people have not so constant and so present a view of the causes of their misery, and as the magistrates seem to act only in conformity to the laws, hence liberty is generally said to reside in republics, and to be banished from monarchies. In fine, as in democracies the people seem to act almost as they please, this sort of government has been deemed the most free, and the power of the people has been confounded with their liberty.

3.—In what Liberty consists

It is true that in democracies the people seem to act as they please; but political liberty does not consist in an unlimited freedom. In governments, that is, in societies directed by laws, liberty can consist only in the power of doing what we ought to will, and in not being constrained to do what we ought not to will.

We must have continually present to our minds the difference between independence and liberty. Liberty is a right of doing whatever the laws permit, and if a citizen could do what they forbid he would be no longer possessed of liberty, because all his fellow-citizens would have the same power.

4.—The same Subject continued

Democratic and aristocratic states are not in their own nature free. Political liberty is to be found only in moderate governments; and even in these it is not always found. It is there only when there is no abuse of power. But constant experience shows us that every man invested with power is apt to abuse it, and to carry his authority as far as it will go. Is it not strange, though true, to say that virtue itself has need of limits?

To prevent this abuse, it is necessary from the very nature of things that power should be a check to power. A government may be so constituted, as no man shall be compelled to do things to which the law does not oblige him, nor forced to abstain from things which the law permits.

5.—Of the End or View of different Governments

Though all governments have the same general end, which is that of preservation, yet each has another particular object. Increase of dominion was the object of Rome; war, that of Sparta; religion, that of the Jewish laws; commerce, that of Marseilles; public tranquility, that of the laws of China: navigation, that of the laws of Rhodes; natural liberty, that of the policy of the Savages; in general, the pleasures of the prince, that of despotic states; that of monarchies, the prince's and the kingdom's glory; the independence of individuals is the end aimed at by the laws of Poland, thence results the oppression of the whole.

One nation there is also in the world that has for the direct end of its constitution political liberty. We shall presently examine the principles on which this liberty is founded; if they are sound, liberty will appear in its highest perfection.

To discover political liberty in a constitution, no great labor is requisite. If we are capable of seeing it where it exists, it is soon found, and we need not go far in search of it.

6.—Of the Constitution of England

In every government there are three sorts of power: the legislative; the executive in respect to things dependent on the law of nations; and the executive in regard to matters that depend on the civil law.

By virtue of the first, the prince or magistrate enacts temporary or perpetual laws, and amends or abrogates those that have been already enacted. By the second, he makes peace or war, sends or receives embassies, establishes the public security, and provides against invasions. By the third, he punishes criminals, or determines the disputes that arise between individuals. The latter we shall call the judiciary power, and the other simply the executive power of the state.

The political liberty of the subject is a tranquillity of mind arising from the opinion each person has of his safety. In order to have this liberty, it is requisite the government be so constituted as one man need not be afraid of another.

When the legislative and executive powers are united in the same person, or in the same body of magistrates, there can be no liberty; because apprehensions may arise, lest the same monarch or senate should enact tyrannical laws, to execute them in a tyrannical manner.

Again, there is no liberty, if the judiciary power be not separated from the legislative and executive. Were it joined with the legislative, the life and liberty of the subject would be exposed to arbitrary control; for the judge would be then the legislator. Were it joined to the executive power, the judge might behave with violence and oppression.

There would be an end of everything, were the same man or the same body, whether of the nobles or of the people, to exercise those three powers, that of enacting laws, that of executing the public resolutions, and of trying the causes of individuals.

Most kingdoms in Europe enjoy a moderate government because the prince who is invested with the two first powers leaves the third to his subjects. In Turkey, where these three powers are united in the Sultan's person, the subjects groan under the most dreadful oppression.

In the republics of Italy, where these three powers are united, there is less liberty than in our monarchies. Hence their government is obliged to have recourse to as violent methods for its support as even that of the Turks; witness the state inquisitors, and the lion's mouth into which every informer may at all hours throw his written accusations.

In what a situation must the poor subject be in those republics! The same body of magistrates are possessed, as executors of the laws, of the whole power they have given themselves in quality of legislators. They may plunder the state by their general determinations; and as they have likewise the judiciary power in their hands, every private citizen may be ruined by their particular decisions.

The whole power is here united in one body; and though there is no external pomp that indicates a despotic sway, yet the people feel the effects of it every moment.

Hence it is that many of the princes of Europe, whose aim has been levelled at arbitrary power, have constantly set out with uniting in their own persons all the branches of magistracy, and all the great offices of state.

I allow indeed that the mere hereditary aristocracy of the Italian republics does not exactly answer to the despotic power of the Eastern princes. The number of magistrates sometimes moderate the power of the magistracy; the whole body of the nobles do not always concur in the same design; and different tribunals are erected, that temper each other. Thus at Venice the legislative power is in the council, the executive in the *pregadi,* and the judiciary in the *quarantia.* But the mischief is, that these different tribunals are composed of magistrates all belonging to the same body; which constitutes almost one and the same power.

The judiciary power ought not to be given to a standing senate; it should be exercised by persons taken from the body of the people at certain times of the year, and consistently with a form and manner prescribed by law, in order to erect a tribunal that should last only so long as necessity requires.

By this method the judicial power, so terrible to mankind, not being annexed to any particular state or profession, becomes, as it were, invisible. People have not then the judges continually present to their view; they fear the office, but not the magistrate.

In accusations of a deep and criminal nature, it is proper the person accused should have the privilege of choosing, in some measure, his judges, in concurrence with the law; or at least he should have a right to except against so great a number that the remaining part may be deemed his own choice.

The other two powers may be given rather to magistrates or permanent bodies, because they are not exercised on any private subject; one being no more than the general will of the state, and the other the execution of that general will.

But though the tribunals ought not to be fixed, the judgments ought; and to such a degree as to be ever conformable to the letter of the law. Were they to be the private opinion of the judge, people would then live in society, without exactly knowing the nature of their obligations.

The judges ought likewise to be of the same rank as the accused, or, in other words, his peers; to the end that he may not imagine he is fallen into the hands of persons inclined to treat him with rigor.

If the legislature leaves the executive power in possession of a right to imprison those subjects who can give security for their good behavior, there is an end of liberty; unless they are taken up, in order to answer without delay to a capital crime, in which case they are really free, being subject only to the power of the law.

But should the legislature think itself in danger by some secret conspiracy against the state, or by a correspondence with a foreign enemy, it might authorize the executive power, for a short and limited time, to imprison suspected persons, who in that case would lose their liberty only for a while, to preserve it forever.

And this is the only reasonable method that can be substituted to the tyrannical magistracy of the Ephori, and to the state inquisitors of Venice, who are also despotic.

As in a country of liberty, every man who is supposed a free agent ought to be his own governor; the legislative power should reside in the whole body of the people. But since this is impossible in large states, and in small ones is subject to many inconveniences, it is fit the people should transact by their representatives what they cannot transact by themselves.

The inhabitants of a particular town are much better acquainted with its wants and interests than with those of other places; and are better judges of the capacity of their neighbors than of that of the rest of their countrymen. The members, therefore, of the legislature should not be chosen from the general body of the nation; but it is proper that in every considerable place a representative should be elected by the inhabitants.

The great advantage of representatives is, their capacity of discussing public affairs. For this the people collectively are extremely unfit, which is one of the chief inconveniences of a democracy.

It is not at all necessary that the representatives who have received a general instruction from their constituents should wait to be directed on each particular affair, as is practised in the diets of Germany. True it is that by this way of proceeding the speeches of the deputies might with greater propriety be called the voice of the nation; but, on the other hand, this would occasion infinite delays; would give each deputy a power of controlling the assembly; and, on the most urgent and pressing occasions, the wheels of government might be stopped by the caprice of a single person.

When the deputies, as Mr. Sidney well observes, represent a body of people, as in Holland, they ought to be accountable to their constituents; but it is a different thing in England, where they are deputed by boroughs.

All the inhabitants of the several districts ought to have a right of voting at the election of a representative, except such as are in so mean a situation as to be deemed to have no will of their own.

One great fault there was in most of the ancient republics, that the people had a right to active resolutions, such as require some execution, a thing of which they are absolutely incapable. They ought to have no share in the government but for the choosing of representatives, which is within their reach. For though few can tell the exact degree of men's capacities, yet there are none but are capable of knowing in general whether the person they choose is better qualified than most of his neighbors.

Neither ought the representative body to be chosen for the executive part of government, for which it is not so fit; but for the enacting of laws, or to see whether the laws in being are duly executed, a thing suited to their abilities, and which none indeed but themselves can properly perform.

In such a state there are always persons distinguished by their birth, riches, or honors; but were they to be confounded with the common people, and to have only the weight of a single vote like the rest, the common liberty would be their slavery, and they would have no interest in supporting it, as most of the popular resolutions would be against them. The share they have, therefore, in the legislature ought to be proportioned to their other advantages in the state; which happens only when they form a body that has a right to check the licentiousness of the people, as the people have a right to oppose any encroachment of theirs.

The legislative power is therefore committed to the body of the nobles, and to that which represents the people, each having their assemblies and deliberations apart, each their separate views and interests.

Of the three powers above mentioned, the judiciary is in some measure next to nothing: there remain, therefore, only two; and as these have need of a regulating power to moderate them, the part of the legislative body composed of the nobility is extremely proper for this purpose.

The body of the nobility ought to be hereditary. In the first place it is so in its own nature; and in the next there must be a considerable interest to preserve its privileges— privileges that in themselves are obnoxious to popular envy, and of course in a free state are always in danger.

But as a hereditary power might be tempted to pursue its own particular interests, and forget those of the people, it is proper that where a singular advantage may be gained by corrupting the nobility, as in the laws relating to the supplies, they should have no other share in the legislation than the power of rejecting, and not that of resolving.

By the power of resolving I mean the right of ordaining by their own authority, or of amending what has been ordained by others. By the power of rejecting I would be understood to mean the right of annulling a resolution taken by another; which was the power of the tribunes at Rome. And though the person possessed of the privilege of rejecting may likewise have the right of approving, yet this approbation passes for no more than a declaration, that he intends to make no use of his privilege of rejecting, and is derived from that very privilege.

The executive power ought to be in the hands of a monarch, because this branch of government, having need of despatch, is better administered by one than by many: on the other hand, whatever depends on the legislative power is oftentimes better regulated by many than by a single person.

But if there were no monarch, and the executive power should be committed to a certain number of persons selected from the legislative body, there would be an end then of liberty; by reason the two powers would be united, as the same persons would sometimes possess, and would be always able to possess, a share in both.

Were the legislative body to be a considerable time without meeting, this would likewise put an end to liberty. For of two things one would naturally follow: either that there would be no longer any legislative resolutions, and then the state would fall into anarchy; or that these resolutions would be taken by the executive power, which would render it absolute.

It would be needless for the legislative body to continue always assembled. This would be troublesome to the representatives, and, moreover, would cut out too much work for the executive power, so as to take off its attention to its office, and oblige it to think only of defending its own prerogatives, and the right it has to execute.

Again, were the legislative body to be always assembled, it might happen to be kept up only by filling the places of the deceased members with new representatives; and in that case, if the legislative body were once corrupted, the evil would be past all remedy. When different legislative bodies succeed one another, the people who have a bad opinion of that which is actually sitting may reasonably entertain some hopes of the next: but were it to be always the same body, the people upon seeing it once corrupted would no longer expect any good from its laws; and of course they would either become desperate or fall into a state of indolence.

The legislative body should not meet of itself. For a body is supposed to have no will but when it is met; and besides, were it not to meet unanimously, it would be impossible to determine which was really the legislative body; the part assembled, or the other. And if it had a right to prorogue itself, it might happen never to be prorogued; which would be extremely dangerous, in case it should ever attempt to encroach on the executive power. Besides, there are seasons, some more proper than others, for assembling the legislative body: it is fit, therefore, that the executive power should regulate the time of meeting, as well as the duration of those assemblies, according to the circumstances and exigencies of a state known to itself.

Were the executive power not to have a right of restraining the encroachments of the legislative body, the latter would become despotic; for as it might arrogate to itself what authority it pleased, it would soon destroy all the other powers.

But it is not proper, on the other hand, that the legislative power should have a right to stay the executive. For as the execution has its natural limits, it is useless to confine it; besides, the executive power is generally employed in momentary operations. The power, therefore, of the Roman tribunes was faulty, as it put a stop not only to the legislation, but likewise to the executive part of government; which was attended with infinite mischief.

But if the legislative power in a free state has no right to stay the executive, it has a right and ought to have the means of examining in what manner its laws have been executed; an advantage which this government has over that of Crete and Sparta, where the Cosmi and the Ephori gave no account of their administration.

But whatever may be the issue of that examination, the legislative body ought not to have a power of arraigning the person, nor, of course, the conduct, of him who is intrusted with the executive power. His person should be sacred, because as it is necessary for the good of the state to prevent the legislative body from rendering themselves arbitrary, the moment he is accused or tried there is an end of liberty.

In this case the state would be no longer a monarchy, but a kind of republic, though not a free government. But as the person intrusted with the executive power cannot abuse it without bad counsellors, and such as have the laws as ministers, though the laws protect them as subjects, these men may be examined and punished—an advantage which this government has over that of Gnidus, where the law allowed of no such thing as calling the Amymones to an account, even after their administration; and therefore the people could never obtain any satisfaction for the injuries done them.

Though, in general, the judiciary power ought not to be united with any part of the legislative, yet this is liable to three exceptions, founded on the particular interest of the party accused.

The great are always obnoxious to popular envy; and were they to be judged by the people, they might be in danger from their judges, and would, moreover, be deprived of the privilege which the meanest subject is possessed of in a free state, of being tried by his peers. The nobility, for this reason, ought not to be cited before the ordinary courts of judicature, but before that part of the legislature which is composed of their own body.

It is possible that the law, which is clear sighted in one sense, and blind in another, might, in some cases, be too severe. But as we have already observed, the national judges are no more than the mouth that pronounces the words of the law, mere passive beings, incapable of moderating either its force or rigor. That part, therefore, of

the legislative body, which we have just now observed to be a necessary tribunal on another occasion, also is a necessary tribunal in this; it belongs to its supreme authority to moderate the law in favor of the law itself, by mitigating the sentence.

It might also happen that a subject intrusted with the administration of public affairs may infringe the rights of the people, and be guilty of crimes which the ordinary magistrates either could not or would not punish. But, in general, the legislative power cannot try causes: and much less can it try this particular case, where it represents the party aggrieved, which is the people. It can only, therefore, impeach. But before what court shall it bring its impeachment? Must it go and demean itself before the ordinary tribunals, which are its inferiors, and, being composed, moreover, of men who are chosen from the people as well as itself, will naturally be swayed by the authority of so powerful an accuser? No: in order to preserve the dignity of the people and the security of the subject, the legislative part which represents the people must bring in its charge before the legislative part which represents the nobility, who have neither the same interests nor the same passions.

Here is an advantage which this government has over most of the ancient republics, where this abuse prevailed, that the people were at the same time both judge and accuser.

The executive power, pursuant of what has been already said, ought to have a share in the legislature by the power of rejecting; otherwise it would soon be stripped of its prerogative. But should the legislative power usurp a share of the executive, the latter would be equally undone.

If the prince were to have a part in the legislature by the power of resolving, liberty would be lost. But as it is necessary he should have a share in the legislature for the support of his own prerogative, this share must consist in the power of rejecting.

The change of government at Rome was owing to this, that neither the senate, who had one part of the executive power, nor the magistrates, who were intrusted with the other, had the right of rejecting, which was entirely lodged in the people.

Here, then, is the fundamental constitution of the government we are treating of. The legislative body being composed of two parts, they check one another by the mutual privilege of rejecting. They are both restrained by the executive power, as the executive is by the legislative.

These three powers should naturally form a state of repose or inaction. But as there is a necessity for movement in the course of human affairs, they are forced to move, but still in concert.

As the executive power has no other part in the legislative than the privilege of rejecting, it can have no share in the public debates. It is not even necessary that it should propose, because as it may always disapprove of the resolutions that shall be taken, it may likewise reject the decisions on those proposals which were made against its will.

In some ancient commonwealths, where public debates were carried on by the people in a body, it was natural for the executive power to propose and debate in conjunction with the people, otherwise their resolutions must have been attended with a strange confusion.

Were the executive power to determine the raising of public money, otherwise than by giving its consent, liberty would be at an end; because it would become legislative in the most important point of legislation.

If the legislative power was to settle the subsidies, not from year to year, but forever, it would run the risk of losing its liberty, because the executive power would be no longer dependent; and when once it was possessed of such a perpetual right, it would be a matter of indifference whether it held it of itself or of another. The same may be said if it should come to a resolution of intrusting, not an annual, but a perpetual command of the fleets and armies to the executive power.

To prevent the executive power from being able to oppress, it is requisite that the armies with which it is intrusted should consist of the people, and have the same spirit as the people, as was the case at Rome till the time of Marius. To obtain this end, there are only two ways, either that the persons employed in the army should have sufficient property to answer for their conduct to their fellow-subjects, and be enlisted only for a year, as was customary at Rome; or if there should be a standing army, composed chiefly of the most despicable part of the nation, the legislative power should have a right to disband them as soon as it pleased; the soldiers should live in common with the rest of the people; and no separate camp, barracks, or fortress should be suffered.

When once an army is established, it ought not to depend immediately on the legislative, but on the executive power; and this from the very nature of the thing, its business consisting more in action than in deliberation.

It is natural for mankind to set a higher value upon courage than timidity, on activity than prudence, on strength than counsel. Hence the army will ever despise a senate, and respect their own officers. They will naturally slight the orders sent them by a body of men whom they look upon as cowards, and therefore unworthy to command them. So that as soon as the troops depend entirely on the legislative body, it becomes a military government; and if the contrary has ever happened, it has been owing to some extraordinary circumstances. It is because the army was always kept divided; it is because it was composed of several bodies that depended each on a particular province: it is because the capital towns were strong places, defended by their natural situation, and not garrisoned with regular troops. Holland, for instance, is still safer than Venice; she might drown or starve the revolted troops; for as they are not quartered in towns capable of furnishing them with necessary subsistence, this subsistence is of course precarious.

In perusing the admirable treatise of Tacitus "On the Manners of the Germans," we find it is from that nation the English have borrowed the idea of their political government. This beautiful system was invented first in the woods.

As all humans things have an end, the state we are speaking of will lose its liberty, will perish. Have not Rome, Sparta, and Carthage perished? It will perish when the legislative power shall be more corrupt than the executive.

It is not my business to examine whether the English actually enjoy this liberty or not. Sufficient it is for my purpose to observe that it is established by their laws; and I inquire no further.

Neither do I pretend by this to undervalue other governments, nor to say that this extreme political liberty ought to give uneasiness to those who have only a moderate share of it. How should I have any such design, I who think that even the highest refinement of reason is not always desirable, and that mankind generally find their account better in mediums than in extremes?

Harrington, in his "Oceana," has also inquired into the utmost degree of liberty to which the constitution of a state may be carried. But of him, indeed, it may be said that for want of knowing the nature of real liberty he busied himself in pursuit of an imaginary one; and that he built a Chalcedon, though he had a Byzantium before his eyes.

7.—Of the Monarchies we are acquainted with

The monarchies we are acquainted with have not, like that we have been speaking of, liberty for their direct view: the only aim is the glory of the subject, of the state, and of the sovereign. But hence there results a spirit of liberty, which in those states is capable of achieving as great things, and of contributing as much, perhaps, to happiness, as liberty itself.

Here the three powers are not distributed and founded on the model of the constitution above mentioned; they have each a particular distribution, according to which they border more or less on political liberty; and if they did not border upon it, monarchy would degenerate into despotic government.

20.—The End of this Book

I should be glad to inquire into the distribution of the three powers, in all the moderate governments we are acquainted with, in order to calculate the degrees of liberty which each may enjoy. But we must not always exhaust a subject, so as to leave no work at all for the reader. My business is not to make people read, but to make them think.

10

RICHARD HENRY LEE TO ———
31 May 1764
Letters 1:5–7

Many late determinations of the great, on your side of the water, seem to prove a resolution, to oppress North America with the iron hand of power, unrestrained by any sentiment, drawn from reason, the liberty of mankind, or the genius of their own government. 'Tis said the House of

Commons readily resolved, that it had "a right to tax the subject here, without the consent of his representative;" and that, in consequence of this, they had proceeded to levy on us a considerable annual sum, for the support of a body of troops to be kept up in this quarter. Can it be supposed that those brave adventurous Britons, who originally conquered and settled these countries, through great dangers to themselves and benefit to the mother country, meant thereby to deprive themselves of the blessings of that free government of which they were members, and to which they had an unquestionable right? or can it be imagined that those they left behind them in Britain, regarded those worthy adventurers, by whose distress and enterprise they saw their country so much enlarged in territory, and increased in wealth, as aliens to their society, and meriting to be enslaved by their superior power? No, my dear sir, neither one nor the other of these can be true, because reason, justice, and the particular nature of the British constitution, nay, of all government, cry out against such opinions! Surely no reasonable being would, at the apparent hazard of his life, quit liberty for slavery; nor could it be just in the benefited, to repay their benefactors with chains instead of the most grateful acknowledgments. And as certain it is, that "the free possession of property, the right to be governed by laws made by our representatives, and the illegality of taxation without consent," are such essential principles of the British constitution, that it is a matter of wonder how men, who have almost imbibed them in their mother's milk, whose very atmosphere is charged with them, should be of opinion that the people of America were to be taxed without consulting their representatives! It will not avail to say that these restrictions on the right of taxation, are meant to restrain only the sovereign, and not Parliament. The intention of the constitution is apparent, to prevent unreasonable impositions on the people; and no method is so likely to do that, as making their own consent necessary, for the establishment of such impositions. But if no such consent is allowed in our case, it will still be an aggravation of our misfortune to be the slaves of five hundred masters instead of one. It would seem, indeed, to be unquestionably true, that before a part of any community can be justly deprived of the rights and privileges, to which they are entitled by the constitution and laws, there must have been some great and palpable injury offered by them to the society of which they are a part. But did this happen in the case of the first settlers of America? or did they, by any treasonable combination against, or by any violation offered to, the laws of their country, make it proper, in their country, to deprive them of their birth right? It remains, therefore, that we cannot be deprived of English liberty, though it may appear expedient that we should be despoiled of it.

Whereas the just rights of his Majesty's subjects of this Province, derived to them from the British Constitution, as well as the royal charter, have been lately drawn into question: in order to ascertain the same, this House do unanimously come into the following resolves:—

1. *Resolved,* That there are certain essential rights of the British Constitution of government, which are founded in the law of God and nature, and are the common rights of mankind;—therefore,

2. *Resolved,* That the inhabitants of this Province are unalienably entitled to those essential rights in common with all men: and that no law of society can, consistent with the law of God and nature, divest them of those rights.

3. *Resolved,* That no man can justly take the property of another without his consent; and that upon this original principle, the right of representation in the same body which exercises the power of making laws for levying taxes, which is one of the main pillars of the British Constitution, is evidently founded.

4. *Resolved,* That this inherent right, together with all other essential rights, liberties, privileges, and immunities of the people of Great Britain, have been fully confirmed to them by Magna Charta, and by former and by later acts of Parliament.

5. *Resolved,* That his Majesty's subjects in America are, in reason and common sense, entitled to the same extent of liberty with his Majesty's subjects in Britain.

6. *Resolved,* That by the declaration of the royal charter of this Province, the inhabitants are entitled to all the rights, liberties, and immunities of free and natural subjects of Great Britain to all intents, purposes, and constructions whatever.

7. *Resolved,* That the inhabitants of this Province appear to be entitled to all the rights aforementioned by an act of Parliament, 13th of Geo. II.

8. *Resolved,* That those rights do belong to the inhabitants of this Province upon the principle of common justice; their ancestors having settled this country at their sole expense, and their posterity having approved themselves most loyal and faithful subjects of Great Britain.

9. *Resolved,* That every individual in the Colonies is as advantageous to Great Britain as if he were in Great Britain and held to pay his full proportion of taxes there; and as the inhabitants of this Province pay their full proportion of taxes for the support of his Majesty's government here, it is unreasonable for them to be called upon to pay any part of the charges of the government there.

10. *Resolved,* That the inhabitants of this Province are not, and never have been, represented in the Parliament

of Great Britain; and that such a representation there as the subjects in Britain do actually and rightfully enjoy *is impracticable* for the subjects in America;—and further, that in the opinion of this House, the several subordinate powers of legislation in America were constituted upon the apprehensions of this *impracticability.*

11. *Resolved,* That the only method whereby the constitutional rights of the subjects of this Province can be secure, consistent with a subordination to the supreme power of Great Britain, is by the continued exercise of such powers of government as are granted in the royal charter, and a firm adherence to the privileges of the same.

12. *Resolved,*—as a just conclusion from some of the foregoing resolves,—That all acts made by any power whatever, other than the General Assembly of this Province, imposing taxes on the inhabitants, are infringements of our inherent and unalienable rights as men and British subjects, and render void the most valuable declarations of our charter.

13. *Resolved,* That the extension of the powers of the Court of Admiralty within this Province is a most violent infraction of the right of trials by juries,—a right which this House, upon the principles of their British ancestors, hold most dear and sacred; it being the only security of the lives, liberties, and properties of his Majesty's subjects here.

14. *Resolved,* That this House owe the strictest allegiance to his most sacred Majesty King George the Third; that they have the greatest veneration for the Parliament; and that they will, after the example of all their predecessors from the settlement of this country, exert themselves to their utmost in supporting his Majesty's authority in the Province, in promoting the true happiness of his subjects, and in enlarging the extent of his dominion.

Ordered, That all the foregoing resolves be kept in the records of this House, that a just sense of liberty and the firm sentiments of loyalty be transmitted to posterity.

12

JOHN ADAMS, CLARENDON, NO. 3
27 Jan. 1766
Papers 1:164–70

You are pleased to charge the Colonists with ignorance of the British constitution—But let me tell you there is not even a *Son of Liberty* among them who has not manifested a deeper knowledge of it, and a warmer attachment to it, than appears in any of your late writings. They know the true constitution and all the resources of liberty in it, as well as in the law of nature which is one principal foundation of it, and in the temper and character of the people, much better than you, if we judge by your late most impudent pieces, or than your patron and master, if we judge by his late conduct.

The people in America have discovered the most accurate judgment about the real constitution, I say, by their whole behaviour, excepting the excesses of a few, who took advantage of the general enthusiasm, to perpetrate their ill designs: tho' there has been great enquiry, and some apparent puzzle among them about a formal, logical, technical definition of it. Some have defined it to [be] the practice of parliament; others, the judgments and precedents of the King's courts; but either of these definitions would make it a constitution of wind and weather, because, the parliaments have sometimes voted the King absolute and the judges have sometimes adjudg'd him to be so. Some have call'd it custom, but this is as fluctuating and variable as the other. Some have call'd it the most perfect combination of human powers in society, which finite wisdom has yet contrived and reduced to practice, for the preservation of liberty and the production of happiness. This is rather a character of the constitution, and a just observation concerning it, than a regular definition of it; and leaves us still to dispute what it is. Some have said that the whole body of the laws; others that King, Lords, and Commons, make the constitution. There has also been much inquiry and dispute about the essentials and fundamentals of the constitution, and many definitions and descriptions have been attempted: But there seems to be nothing satisfactory to a rational mind, in any of these definitions: Yet I cannot say, that I am at any loss about any man's meaning when he speaks of the British constitution, or of the essentials and fundamentals of it.

What do we mean when we talk of the constitution of the human body? What by a strong and robust, or a weak and feeble constitution? Do we not mean certain contextures of the nerves, fibres, and muscles, or certain qualities of the blood and juices, as fizy, or watery, phlegmatic or fiery, acid or alkaline? We can never judge of any constitution without considering the *end* of it; and no judgment can be formed of the human constitution, without considering it as productive of *life* or *health* or *strength*. The physician shall tell one man that certain kinds of exercise, or diet, or medicine, are not adapted to his constitution, that is, not compatible with his *health,* which he would readily agree are the most productive of *health* in another. The patient's habit abounds with acid, and acrimonious juices: Will the doctor order vinegar, lemmon juice, barberries and cramberries, to work a cure? These would be unconstitutional remedies; calculated to increase the evil, which arose from the want of a balance, between the acid and alkaline ingredients, in his composition. If the patient's nerves are overbraced, will the doctor advise to jesuits bark? There is a certain quantity of exercise, diet, and medicine, best adapted to every man's constitution, will keep him in the best health and spirits, and contribute the most to the prolongation of his life. These determinate quantities are not perhaps known to him, or any other person: but here lies the proper province of the physician to study his constitution and give him the best advice what and how much he may eat and drink; when and how long he shall sleep; how far he may walk or ride in a day; what air and weather he may improve for this purpose; when he shall take physick, and of what sort it shall be; in order to preserve and perfect his *health,* and prolong his *life.* But there are certain other parts of the body, which the *physician* can in no case have any *authority* to *destroy* or *deprave;* which may properly be called *stamina vitae,* or *essentials* and *fundamentals of the constitution.* Parts, without which life itself cannot be preserved a moment. Annihilate the heart, lungs, brain, animal spirits, blood; any one of these, and life will depart at once. These may be strictly called fundamentals, of the human constitution: Tho' the limbs may be all amputated, the eyes put out, and many other mutilations practiced to impair the strength, activity and other attributes of the man; and yet the essentials to life may remain, unimpaired many years.

Similar observations may be made with equal propriety concerning every kind of machinery. A clock has also a constitution, that is a certain combination of weights, wheels and levers, calculated for a certain use and end, the mensuration of time. Now the constitution of a clock, does not imply such a perfect constructure of movement as shall never go too fast or too slow, as shall never gain nor lose a second of time, in a year or century. This is the proper business of Quare, Tomlinson, and Graham, to execute the workmanship like artists, and come as near to perfection, i.e. as near to a perfect mensuration of time, as the human eye and finger will allow. But yet there are certain parts of a clock, without which, it will not go at all, and you can have from it no better account of the time of day, than from the ore of gold, silver brass and iron, out of which it was wrought. These parts therefore are the essentials and fundamentals of a clock.

Let us now enquire whether the same reasoning is not applicable in all its parts to government. For government is a frame, a scheme, a system, a combination of powers, for a certain end, viz the good of the whole community. The public good, the salus populi is the professed end of all government, the most despotic, as well as the most free. I shall enter into no examination which kind of government, whether either of the forms of the schools, or any mixture of them is the best calculated for this end. This is the proper inquiry of the founders of Empires. I shall take for granted, what I am sure no Briton will controvert, viz. that Liberty is essential to the public good, the salus populi. And here lies the difference between the British constitution, and other forms of government, viz. that Liberty is its end, its use, its designation, drift and scope, as much as grinding corn is the use of a mill, the transportation of burdens the end of a ship, the mensuration of time the scope of a watch, or life and health the designation of the human body.

Were I to define the British constitution, therefore, I should say, it is a limited monarchy, or a mixture of the three forms of government commonly known in the schools, reserving as much of the monarchial splendor, the aristocratical independency, and the democratical freedom, as are necessary, that each of these powers may have a controul both in legislation and execution, over the other two, for the preservation of the subjects liberty.

According to this definition, the first grand division of constitutional powers is, into those of legislation and those of execution. In the power of legislation, the King, Lords, Commons, and People, are to be considered as essential and fundamental parts of the constitution. I distinguish between the house of commons, and the people who depute them, because there is in nature and fact a real difference; and these last have as important a department in the constitution as the former, I mean the power of election. The constitution is not grounded on "the enormous faith of millions made for one." It stands not on the supposition that kings are the favourites of heaven; that their power is more divine than the power of the people, and unlimited but by their own will and discretion. It is not built on the doctrine that a few nobles or rich commons have a right to inherit the earth, and all the blessings and pleasures of it: and that the multitude, the million, the populace, the vulgar, the mob, the herd and the rabble, as the great always delight to call them, have no rights at all, and were made only for their use, to be robbed and butchered at their pleasure. No, it stands upon this principle, that the meanest and lowest of the people, are, by the unalterable indefeasible laws of God and nature, as well intitled to the benefit of the air to breathe, light to see, food to eat, and clothes to wear, as the nobles or the king. All men are born equal: and the drift of the British constitution is to preserve as much of this equality, as is compatible with the people's security against foreign invasions and domestic usurpation. It is upon these fundamental principles, that popular power was placed as essential in the constitution of the legislature; and the constitution would be as compleat without a kingly as without a popular power. This popular power however, when the numbers grew large, became impracticable to be exercised by the universal and immediate suffrage of the people: and this impracticability has introduced from the feudal system, an expedient which we call a representation. This expedient is only an equivalent for the suffrage of the whole people, in the common management of public concerns. It is in reality nothing more than this, the people chuse attornies to vote for them in the great council of the nation, reserving always the fundamentals of the government, reserving also a right to give their attornies instructions how to vote, and a right, at certain stated intervals of choosing a new, discarding an old attorney, and choosing a wiser and a better. And it is this reservation, of fundamentals, of the right of giving instructions, and of new elections, which creates a popular check, upon the whole government which alone secures the constitution from becoming an aristocracy, or a mixture of monarchy and aristocracy only.

The other grand division of power, is that of execution. And here the King is by the constitution, supreme executor of the laws, and is always present in person or by his judges, in his courts, distributing justice among the people. But the executive branch of the constitution, as far as respects the administration of justice, has in it a mixture of popular power too. The judges answer to questions of law: but no further. Were they to answer to questions of fact as well as law, being few they might be easily corrupted; being commonly rich and great, they might learn to despise the common people, and forget the feelings of humanity: and then the subjects liberty and security would be lost. But by the British constitution, *ad questionem facti respondent juratores,* the jurors answer to the question of fact. In this manner the subject is guarded, in the execution of the laws. The people choose a grand jury to make enquiry and presentment of crimes. Twelve of these must agree in finding the Bill. And the petit jury must try the same fact over again, and find the person guilty before he can be punished. Innocence therefore, is so well protected in this wise constitution, that no man can be punished till twenty four of his Neighbours have said upon oath, that he is guilty. So it is also in the tryal of causes between party and party: No man's property or liberty can be taken from him, till twelve men in his Neighbourhood, have said upon oath, that by laws of his own making it ought to be taken away, i.e. that the facts are such as to fall within such laws.

Thus it seems to appear that two branches of popular power, voting for members of the house of commons, and tryals by juries, the one in the legislative and the other in the executive part of the constitution are as essential and fundamental, to the great end of it, the preservation of the subject's liberty, to preserve the balance and mixture of the government, and to prevent its running into an oligarchy or aristocracy; as the lords and commons are to prevent its becoming an absolute monarchy. These two popular powers therefore are the heart and lungs, the main spring, and the center wheel, and without them, the body must die; the watch must run down; the government must become arbitrary, and this our law books have settled to be the death of the laws and constitution. In these two powers consist wholly, the liberty and security of the people: They have no other fortification against wanton, cruel power: no other indemnification against being ridden like horses, fleeced like sheep, worked like cattle, and fed and cloathed like swine and hounds: No other defence against fines, imprisonments, whipping posts, gibbets, bastenadoes and racks. This is that constitution which has prevailed in Britain from an immense antiquity: It prevailed, and the House of Commons and tryals by juries made a part of it, in Saxon times, as may be abundantly proved by many monuments still remaining in the Saxon language: That constitution which had been for so long a time the envy and admiration of surrounding nations: which has been, no less than five and fifty times, since the Norman conquest, attacked in parliament, and attempted to be altered, but without success; which has been so often defended by the people of England, at the expence of oceans of their blood, and which, co operating with the invincible spirit of liberty, inspired by it into the people, has never yet failed to work the ruin of the authors of all settled attempts to destroy it.

What a fine reflection and consolation is it for a man to reflect that he can be subjected to no laws, which he does not make himself, or constitute some of his friends to make for him: his father, brother, neighbour, friend, a man of his own rank, nearly of his own education, fortune, habits, passions, prejudices, one whose life and fortune and liberty are to be affected like those of his constituents, by the laws he shall consent to for himself and them. What a satisfaction is it to reflect, that he can lie under the imputation of no guilt, be subjected to no punishment, lose none of his property, or the necessaries, conveniencies or

ornaments of life, which indulgent providence has showered around him: but by the judgment of his peers, his equals, his neighbours, men who know him, and to whom he is known; who have no end to serve by punishing him; who wish to find him innocent, if charged with a crime; and are indifferent, on which side the truth lies, if he disputes with his neighbour.

Your writings, Mr. Pym, have lately furnished abundant Proofs, that the infernal regions, have taken from you, all your shame, sense, conscience and humanity: otherwise I would appeal to them who has discovered the most ignorance of the British constitution; you who are for exploding the whole system of popular power, with regard to the Americans, or they who are determined to stand by it, in both its branches, with their lives and fortunes?

13

MASSACHUSETTS HOUSE OF REPRESENTATIVES, CIRCULAR LETTER TO THE COLONIAL LEGISLATURES
11 Feb. 1768
S. Adams Writings 1:184–86

The House of Representatives of this Province have taken into their serious Consideration, the great difficultys that must accrue to themselves & their Constituents, by the operation of several acts of Parliament imposing Duties & Taxes on the American Colonys.

As it is a Subject in which every Colony is deeply interested they have no reason to doubt but your Assembly is deeply impressd with its Importance & that such constitutional measures will be come into as are proper. It seems to be necessary, that all possible Care should be taken, that the Representations of the several Assembly upon so delicate a point, should harmonize with each other: The House therefore hope that this letter will be candidly considerd in no other Light, than as expressing a Disposition freely to communicate their mind to a Sister Colony, upon a common Concern in the same manner as they would be glad to receive the Sentiments of your or any other House of Assembly on the Continent.

The House have humbly represented to the ministry, their own Sentiments that His Majestys high Court of Parliament is the supreme legislative Power over the whole Empire: That in all free States the Constitution is fixd; & as the supreme Legislative derives its Power & Authority from the Constitution, it cannot overleap the Bounds of it without destroying its own foundation: That the Constitution ascertains & limits both Sovereignty & allegiance, & therefore, his Majestys American Subjects who acknowlege themselves bound by the Ties of Allegiance, have an equitable Claim to the full enjoymt of the fundamental Rules of the British Constitution. That it is an essential unalterable Right in nature, ingrafted into the British Constitution, as a fundamental Law & ever held sacred & irrevocable by the Subjects within the Realm, that what a man has honestly acquir'd is absolutely his own, which he may freely give, but cannot be taken from him without his consent: That the American Subjects may therefore exclusive of any Consideration of Charter Rights, with a decent firmness adapted to the Character of free men & Subjects assert this natural and constitutional Right.

It is moreover their humble opinion, which they express with the greatest Deferrence to the Wisdom of the Parliament that the Acts made there imposing Duties on the People of this province with the sole & express purpose of raising a Revenue, are Infringments of their natural & constitutional Rights because as they are not represented in the British Parliamt His Majestys Commons in Britain by those Acts grant their Property without their consent.

This House further are of Opinion that their Constituents considering their local Circumstances cannot by any possibility be represented in the Parliament, & that it will forever be impracticable that they should be equally represented there & consequently not at all; being seperated by an Ocean of a thousand leagues: and that his Majestys Royal Predecessors for this reason were graciously pleas'd to form a subordinate legislature here that their subjects might enjoy the unalienable Right of a Representation. Also that considering the utter Impracticability of their ever being fully & equally represented in parliamt, & the great Expence that must unavoidably attend even a partial representation there, this House think that a taxation of their Constituents, even without their Consent, grievous as it is, would be preferable to any Representation that could be admitted for them there.

14

FAIRFAX COUNTY RESOLVES
18 July 1774
Mason Papers 1:201–3

At a general Meeting of the Freeholders and Inhabitants of the County of Fairfax on Monday the 18th day of July 1774, at the Court House, George Washington Esquire Chairman, and Robert Harrison Gent. Clerk of the said Meeting—

1. RESOLVED that this Colony and Dominion of Virginia can not be considered as a conquered Country; and if it was, that the present Inhabitants are the Descendants not of the Conquered, but of the Conquerors.

That the same was not setled at the national Expence of England, but at the private Expence of the Adventurers, our Ancestors, by solemn Compact with, and under the Auspices and Protection of the British Crown; upon which we are in every Respect as dependant, as the People of Great Britain, and in the same Manner subject to all his Majesty's just, legal, and constitutional Prerogatives. That our Ancestors, when they left their native Land, and setled in America, brought with them (even if the same had not been confirmed by Charters) the Civil-Constitution and Form of Government of the Country they came from; and were by the Laws of Nature and Nations, entitled to all it's Privileges, Immunities and Advantages; which have descended to us their Posterity, and ought of Right to be as fully enjoyed, as if we had still continued within the Realm of England.

2. RESOLVED that the most important and valuable Part of the British Constitution, upon which it's very Existence depends, is the fundamental Principle of the People's being governed by no Laws, to which they have not given their Consent, by Representatives freely chosen by themselves; who are affected by the Laws they enact equally with their Constituents; to whom they are accountable, and whose Burthens they share; in which consists the Safety and Happiness of the Community: for if this Part of the Constitution was taken away, or materially altered, the Government must degenerate either into an absolute and despotic Monarchy, or a tyrannical Aristocracy, and the Freedom of the People be annihilated.

3. RESOLVED therefore, as the Inhabitants of the american Colonies are not, and from their Situation can not be represented in the British Parliament, that the legislative Power here can of Right be exercised only by our own Provincial Assemblys or Parliaments, subject to the Assent or Negative of the British Crown, to be declared within some proper limited Time. But as it was thought just and reasonable that the People of Great Britain shou'd reap Advantages from these Colonies adequate to the Protection they afforded them, the British Parliament have claimed and exercised the Power of regulating our Trade and Commerce, so as to restrain our importing from foreign Countrys, such Articles as they cou'd furnish us with, of their own Growth or Manufacture, or exporting to foreign Countrys such Articles and Portions of our Produce, as Great Britain stood in Need of, for her own Consumption or Manufactures. Such a Power directed with Wisdom and Moderation, seems necessary for the general Good of that great Body-politic of which we are a Part; altho' in some Degree repugnant to the Principles of the Constitution. Under this Idea our Ancestors submitted to *it:* the Experience of more than a Century, during the Government of his Majesty's Royal Predecessors, hath proved it's Utility, and the reciprocal Benefits flowing from it produced mutual uninterrupted Harmony and Good-Will, between the Inhabitants of Great Britain and her Colonies; who during that long Period, always considered themselves as one and the same People: and tho' such a Power is capable of Abuse, and in some Instances hath been stretched beyond the original Design and Institution. Yet to avoid Strife and Contention with our fellow-Subjects, and strongly impressed with the Experience of mutual Benefits, we always Chearfully acquiesced in it, while the entire Regulation of our internal Policy, and giving and granting our own Money were preserved to our own provincial Legislatures.

4. RESOLVED that it is the Duty of these Colonies, on all Emergencies, to contribute, in Proportion to their Abilities, Situation and Circumstances, to the necessary Charge of supporting and defending the British Empire, of which

they are Part; that while we are treated upon an equal Footing with our fellow Subjects, the Motives of Self-Interest and Preservation will be a sufficient Obligation; as was evident thro' the Course of the last War; and that no Argument can be fairly applyed to the British Parliament's taxing us, upon a Presumption that we shou'd refuse a just and reasonable Contribution, but will equally operate in Justification of the Executive-Power taxing the People of England, upon a Supposition of their Representatives refusing to grant the necessary Supplies.

5. RESOLVED that the Claim lately assumed and exercised by the British Parliament, of making all such Laws as they think fit, to govern the people of these Colonies, and to extort from us our Money with out our Consent, is not only diametrically contrary to the first Principles of the Constitution, and the original Compacts by which we are dependant upon the British Crown and Government; but is totally incompatible with the Privileges of a free People, and the natural Rights of Mankind; will render our own Legislatures merely nominal and nugatory, and is calculated to reduce us from a State of Freedom and Happiness to Slavery and Misery.

6. RESOLVED that Taxation and Representation are in their Nature inseperable; that the Right of withholding, or of giving and granting their own Money is the only effectual Security to a free People, against the Incroachments of Despotism and Tyranny; and that whenever they yield the One, they must quickly fall a Prey to the other.

7. RESOLVED that the Powers over the People of America now claimed by the British House of Commons, in whose Election we have no Share, on whose Determinations we can have no Influence, whose Information must be always defective and often false, who in many Instances may have a seperate, and in some an opposite Interest to ours, and who are removed from those Impressions of tenderness and compassion arising from personal Intercourse and Connections, which soften the Rigours of the most despotic Governments, must if continued, establish the most grievous and intollerable Species of Tyranny and Oppression, that ever was inflicted upon Mankind.

15

JAMES BURGH, POLITICAL DISQUISITIONS
1:221–23, 226–27
1774

No set of men empowered *only* to make *laws,* can, without an express commission from the people, *alter the constitution,* because it is only upon the *principles* of the *constitution,* that they had their power entrusted to them; and the principles of the constitution will never bear them out in *overthrowing* the constitution. The *people,* whose original and inherent power established the constitution, *may change* the constitution, or empower a set of men to change it.

Writers, on the side of this assumed boundless parliamentary privilege, by accustoming themselves to think of the house of commons as the *representative* of the people, fall into the mistake, that whatever is right for the *one* is right for the *other* likewise, and that whatever the *people's* power reaches to, is likewise within the reach of the assembly of *representatives.* And this is, generally speaking, true. But there is a distinction to be made. The people have certain *incommunicable* powers, which their representatives can upon no occasion challenge to themselves. The people alone can *elect* representatives. The whole body of representatives have not in themselves the power to *take into,* to *exclude,* or to *expel* from their house one single member, otherwise than according to notorious and stated *laws* made by the *whole* legislative power, and assented to by the *people.* This may be explained by comparing it with the king's power of commissioning embassadors for foreign courts; which power is *incommunicably* inherent in him, in such manner, that all the embassadors employed by the king cannot by any power of their own send an embassador to, or dismiss, or expel one from the most inconsiderable court. Yet every embassador, when furnished with his credentials, has the power of representing the king his master's person at the court to which he is sent, in all those matters and things which enter into the function of an embassador. Again, the people alone have the power of determining for how long a *period* they will continue their representatives in office. The assembly of representatives have not power to continue their own authority one day beyond the time, for which they were elected. If they have, they may, at any time, erect themselves into *peers,* and insist on keeping their seats for life. Again, an assembly of representatives have no power to assume to themselves any unprecedented *privilege;* but the people have power to confer on their representatives what privileges they please, to limit them as they please, and even to new-model the whole government.

In the case of a court of directors, established by a trading company, it is universally understood, that the directors, when once established by the *proprietors,* have power to do whatever the proprietors could do for the common advantage of the company, this power being still left to the explication and limitation of the proprietors. But, when a director dies, or resigns, the court of directors cannot put *another* in his place. This is the incommunicable privilege of the proprietors. Nor can the directors lengthen, beyond the intention of their *constituents,* the *time* for which they were appointed. Nor can they assume to themselves any one power or *privilege,* different from those given them by the proprietors. Nor can they *refuse* a duly elected director, nor take in one of their *own* chusing, nor *expel* one chosen by the proprietors, otherwise than according to the laws of the company, and the powers originally reposed in them. Nor can they *alter* any thing *fundamental* in the constitution of the company; but the *proprietors* can; so far as to the total *dissolution* of the incorporate body. Therefore, when Mr. *Prynne* was threatened by Sir *H. Vane,* and Sir *A. Haselrig,* to be voted out of the house of commons, *A. D.* 1659, he answered, "He knew of no one in the house who had a *right* to vote him out, being equally *entrusted* with themselves for the whole nation, and those he represented."

. . . . .

Judge *Blackstone,* in his account of the unknown and *unlimited* power and privileges of parliament, seems to forget, that the safety of the people *limits* all free governments. It is true that the people of *England,* not being accustomed, till lately, to apprehend danger from any quarter, but the *throne* (tyranny having been an old trick among kings from *Nimrod's* time down) have all along encouraged and supported their *parliaments* in extending their power, as the only sure bulwark against regal encroachments. But latter ages have taught us the necessity of looking out for security against *parliamentary* encroachments. And, the method is not by lessening the power of *parliament,* but by lessening the power of the *court* over the parliament. For a parliament is not (as a king) *naturally* hostile to liberty. If ever a parliament comes to oppose, or injure the people, it must be in consequence of an *unnatural* influence acting in it. Therefore our modern male-contents seem to be in a wrong pursuit. To retrench the power of their *representatives,* would be lessening their *own* power. To break through the corrupt influence of the *court* over their representatives, would be making them *truly* their representatives. Take away court-influence, and the 558 will of course pursue the interest of their country, as any other set of gentlemen would do, because their *own* will be involved in it, when they have no places or pensions to indemnify them. At the same time it cannot be denied, that for a house of commons, though ever so incorrupt and uninfluenced by the court, to be ever grasping at new privileges, and assuming new powers, descending from the dignity of representatives of the majesty of the people of *Britain,* taking upon themselves the office of the justices, prosecuting, imprisoning, and fining, a set of printers and booksellers, depriving the subject of his trial by jury, and employing their time in hunting out small offenders, while they should be battling the gigantic enemies of liberty and virtue, and planning measures for making unborn millions happy; it cannot be denied, I say, that such proceedings as these are infinitely *beneath* the attention of a house of commons, though it should be granted, that the *power* of the house of commons, being the power of the *people,* ought not to be *limited.* All things are *lawful* for them; but all things are not *expedient.* The truth of the matter is, That if our houses of commons had kept to their proper sphere, we should never have seen any *libels* against them, nor any *occasion* for prosecuting, imprisoning, and fining; or if there had, the *courts* of king's bench and common pleas were open.

16

ALEXANDER HAMILTON, THE FARMER REFUTED
23 Feb. 1775

Papers 1:100–101

You are mistaken, when you confine arbitrary government to a monarchy. It is not the supreme power being placed in one, instead of many, that discriminates an arbitrary from a free government. When any people are ruled by laws, in framing which, they have no part, that are to bind them, to all intents and purposes, without, in the same manner, binding the legislators themselves, they are in the strictest sense slaves, and the government with respect to them, is despotic. Great-Britain is itself a free country; but it is only so because its inhabitants have a share in the legislature: If they were once divested of that, they would cease to be free. So that, if its jurisdiction be extended over other countries that have no actual share in its legislature, it becomes arbitary to them; because they are destitute of those checks and controuls which constitute that *moral* security which is the very essence of civil liberty.

I will go farther, and assert, that the authority of the British Parliament over America, would, in all probability, be a more intolerable and excessive species of despotism than an absolute monarchy.* The power of an absolute prince is not temporary, but perpetual. He is under no temptation to purchase the favour of one part of his dominions, at the expence of another; but, it is his interest to treat them all, upon the same footing. Very different is the case with regard to the Parliament: The Lords and Commons both, have a private and separate interest to pursue. They must be, wonderfully, disinterested, if they would not make us bear a very disproportional part of the public burthens, to avoid them as much as possible themselves. The people of Britain must, *in reality,* be an order of superior beings, not cast in the same mould, with the common degenerate race of mortals, if the sacrifice of our interest and ease to theirs be not, extremely, welcome and alluring. But should experience teach us, that they are only mere mortals, fonder of themselves than their neighbours, the philanthropy and integrity of their representatives will be of a transcendent and matchless nature,

*Mr. Hume, in enumerating those political maxims, which will be eternally true, speaks thus: "It may easily be observed, that though free governments have been commonly the most happy, for those who partake of their freedom, yet are they the most ruinous and oppressive to *their provinces.*" He goes on to give many solid reasons for this, and among other things, observes, that "a free state necessarily makes a great distinction (between herself and the provinces) and must continue to do so, 'till men learn to love their neighbours as well as themselves." He confirms his reflections by many historical facts and concludes them thus: "Compare the *pais conquis* of France with Ireland, and you will be convinced of this truth; though this latter kingdom being in a good measure peopled from England, possesses so many rights and privileges, as should naturally make it challenge better treatment."

should they not gratify the natural propensities of their constituents, in order to ingratiate themselves, and enhance their popularity.

17

PITTSFIELD PETITIONS
29 May 1776
Handlin 90–93

We further beg leave to represent that we were deeply affected at the Misrepresentations that have been made of us and the County in general, as Men deeply in Debt, dishonest, ungovernable, heady untractable, without principle and good Conduct and ever ready to oppose lawful Authority, as Mobbes disturbers of peace order and Union, unwilling to submit to any Government, or ever to pay our Debts, so that we have been told a former House of Representatives had it in actual Contemplation to send an armed force to effect that by violence which reason only ought to effect at the present Day.

We beg leave to lay before your Honors our Principles real Views and Designs in what we have hitherto done and what Object we are reaching after, with this Assurance if we have erred it is thro' Ignorance and not bad Intention.—

We beg leave therefore to represent that we have always been persuaded that the people are the fountain of power.

That since the Dissolution of the power of Great Britain over these Colonies they have fallen into a state of Nature.

That the first step to be taken by a people in such a state for the Enjoyment or Restoration of Civil Government amongst them, is the formation of a fundamental Constitution as the Basis and ground work of Legislation.

That the Approbation of the Majority of the people of this fundamental Constitution is absolutely necessary to give Life and being to it. That then and not 'till then is the foundation laid for Legislation. We often hear of the fundamental Constitution of Great Britain, which all political Writers (except ministerial ones) set above the King, Lords, and Commons, which they cannot change, nothing short of the great rational Majority of the people being sufficient for this.

That a Representative Body may form, but cannot impose said fundamental Constitution upon a people. They being but servants of the people cannot be greater than their Masters, and must be responsible to them. If this fundamental Constitution is above the whole Legislature, the Legislature cannot certainly make it, it must be the Approbation of the Majority which gives Life and being to it.—

That said fundamental Constitution has not been formed for this Province the Corner stone is not yet laid and whatever Building is reared without a foundation must fall into Ruins.

That this can be instantly effected with the Approbation of the Continental Congress and Law subordination and good government flow in better than their antient Channels in a few Months Time.—That till this is done we are but beating the Air and doing what will and must be undone afterwards, and all our labour is lost and on divers Accounts much worse than lost.

That a Doctrine lately broached in this County by several of the Justices newly created without the Voice of the People, that the Representatives of the People may form Just what fundamental Constitution they please and impose it upon the people and however obnoxious to them they can obtain no relief from it but by a New Election, and if our Representatives should never see fit to give the people one that pleases them there is no help for it appears to us to be the rankest kind of Toryism, the self same Monster we are now fighting against.

These are some of the Truths we firmly believe and are countenanced in believing them by the most respectable political Writers of the last and present Century, especially by Mr. Burgh in his political Disquisitions for the publication of which one half of the Continental Congress were subscribers.

We beg leave further to represent that we by no means object to the most speedy Institution of Legal Government thro' this province and that we are as earnestly desirous as any others of this great Blessing.

That knowing the strong Byass of human Nature to Tyranny and Despotism we have Nothing else in View but to provide for Posterity against the wanton Exercise of power which cannot otherwise be done than by the formation of a fundamental Constitution. What is the fundamental Constitution of this province, what are the unalienable Rights of the people the power of the Rulers, how often to be elected by the people etc. have any of these Things been as yet ascertained. Let it not be said by future posterity that in this great this noble this glorious Contest we made no provision against Tyranny amongst ourselves.

We beg leave to assure your Honors that the purest and most disinterested Love of posterity and a fervent desire of transmitting to them a fundamental Constitution securing their sacred Rights and Immunities against all Tyrants that may spring up after us has moved us in what we have done. We have not been influenced by hope of Gain or Expectation of Preferment and Honor. We are no discontented faction we have no fellowship with Tories, we are the staunch friends of the Union of these Colonies and will support and maintain your Honors in opposing Great Britain with our Lives and Treasure.

But if Commissions should be recalled and the Kings Name struck out of them, if the Fee Table be reduced never so low, and multitudes of other things be done to still the people all is to us as Nothing whilst the foundation is unfixed the Corner stone of Government unlaid. We have heard much of Governments being founded in Compact. What Compact has been formed as the foundation of Government in this province?—We beg leave further to represent that we have undergone many grievous oppressions in this County and that now we wish a Barrier might be set up against such oppressions, against which we can have no security long till the foundation of Government be well established.—

We beg leave further to represent these as the Sentiments of by far the Majority of the people in this County as far as we can Judge and being so agreeable to Reason Scripture and Common Sence, as soon as the Attention of people in this province is awakened we doubt not but the Majority will be with us.

We beg leave further to observe that if this Honourable Body shall find that we have embraced Errors dangerous to the safety of these Colonies it is our Petition that our Errors may be detected and you shall be put to no further Trouble from us but without an Alteration in our Judgment the Terrors of this World will not daunt us we are determined to resist Great Britain to the last Extremity and all others who may claim a similar Power over us. Yet we hold not to an Imperium in Imperio we will be determined by the Majority.—

Your Petitioners beg leave therefore to Request that this Honourable Body would form a fundamental Constitution for this province after leave is asked and obtained from the Honourable Continental Congress and that said Constitution be sent abroad for the Approbation of the Majority of the people in this Colony that in this way we may emerge from a state of Nature and enjoy again the Blessing of Civil Government in this way the Rights and Liberties of future Generations will be secured and the Glory of the present Revolution remain untarnished and future Posterity rise up and call this Honourable Council and house of Representatives blessed

and as in Duty bound will ever pray

18

CONCORD TOWN MEETING RESOLUTIONS
21 Oct. 1776
Handlin 152–53

At a meeting of the Inhabitants of the Town of Concord being free and twenty one years of age and upward, met by adjournment on the twenty first Day of October 1776 to take into Consideration a Resolve of the Honorable House of Representatives of this State on the 17th of September Last, the Town Resolved as followes——

Resolve 1st. That this State being at Present destitute of a Properly established form of Goverment, it is absolutely necesary that one should be emmediatly formed and established——

Resolved 2 That the Supreme Legislative, either in their Proper Capacity, or in Joint Committee, are by no means a Body proper to form and Establish a Constitution, or form of Government; for Reasons following.

first Because we Conceive that a Constitution in its Proper Idea intends a System of Principles Established to Secure

the Subject in the Possession and enjoyment of their Rights and Priviliges, against any Encroachments of the Governing Part——

2d Because the Same Body that forms a Constitution have of Consequence a power to alter it. 3d—Because a Constitution alterable by the Supreme Legislative is no Security at all to the Subject against any Encroachment of the Governing part on any, or on all of their Rights and priviliges.

Resolve 3d. That it appears to this Town highly necesary and Expedient that a Convention, or Congress be immediately Chosen, to form and establish a Constitution, by the Inhabitants of the Respective Towns in this State, being free and of twenty one years of age, and upwards, in Proportion as the Representatives of this State formerly ware Chosen; the Convention or Congress not to Consist of a greater number then the House of assembly of this State heretofore might Consist of, Except that each Town and District shall have Liberty to Send one Representative or otherwise as Shall appear meet to the Inhabitents of this State in General

Resolve 4th. that when the Convention, or Congress have formed a Constitution they adjourn for a Short time, and Publish their Proposed Constitution for the Inspection and Remarks of the Inhabitents of this State.

Resolved 5ly. That the Honorable House of assembly of this State be Desired to Recommend it to the Inhabitants of the State to Proceed to Chuse a Convention or Congress for the Purpas abovesaid as soon as Possable.

19

FOUR LETTERS ON INTERESTING SUBJECTS
18–24
1776

Among the many publications which have appeared on the subject of political Constitutions, none, that I have seen, have properly defined what is meant by *a Constitution,* that word having been bandied about without any determinate sense being affixed thereto. A Constitution, and a form of government, are frequently confounded together, and spoken of as synonimous things; whereas they are not only different, but are established for different purposes: All countries have some form of government, but few, or perhaps none, have truly a Constitution. The form of government in England is by a king, lords and commons; but if you ask an Englishman what he means when he speaks of the English Constitution, he is unable to give you any answer. The truth is, the English have no fixed Constitution. The prerogative of the crown, it is true, is under several restrictions; but the legislative power, which includes king, lords and commons, is under none; and whatever acts *they* pass, are laws, be they ever so oppressive or arbitrary. England is likewise defective in Constitution in three other material points, viz. The crown, by virtue of a patent from itself, can increase the number of the lords (one of the legislative branches) at his pleasure. Queen Ann created six in one day, for the purpose of making a majority for carrying a bill then passing, who were afterwards distinguished by the name of the six occasional lords. Lord Bathurst, the father of the present chancellor, is the only surviving one. The crown can likewise, by a patent, incorporate any town or village, small or great, and empower it to send members to the house of commons, and fix what the precise number of the electors shall be. And an act of the legislative power, that is, an act of king, lords, and commons, can again diminish the house of commons to what number they please, by disfranchising any county, city or town.

It is easy to perceive that individuals by agreeing to erect forms of government, (for the better security of themselves) must give up some part of their liberty for that purpose; and it is the particular business of a Constitution to mark out *how much* they shall give up. In this sense it is easy to see that the English have no Constitution, because they have given up every thing; their legislative power being unlimited without either condition or controul, except in the single instance of trial by Juries. No country can be called *free* which is governed by an absolute power; and it matters not whether it be an absolute royal power or an absolute legislative power, as the consequences will be the same to the people. That England is governed by the latter, no man can deny, there being, as is said before, no Constitution in that country which says to the legislative powers, "Thus far shalt thou go, and no farther." There is nothing to prevent them passing a law which shall exempt themselves from the payment of taxes, or which shall give the house of commons power to sit for life, or to fill up the vacancies by appointing others, like the Corporation of Philadelphia. In short, an act of parliament, to use a court phrase, can do any thing but make a man a woman.

A Constitution, when completed, resolves the two following questions: First, What shall the form of government be? And secondly, What shall be its power? And the last of these two is far more material than the first. The Constitution ought likewise to make provision in those cases where it does not empower the legislature to act.

The forms of government are numerous, and perhaps the simplest is the best. The notion of checking by having different houses, has but little weight in it, when inquired into, and in all cases it tends to embarrass and prolong business; besides, what kind of checking is it that one house is to receive from another? or which is the house that is most to be trusted to? They may fall out about forms and precedence, and check one another's honour and tempers, and thereby produce petulances and ill-will, which a more simple form of government would have prevented. That some kind of convenience might now and then arise from having two houses, is granted, and the same may be said of twenty houses; but the question is, whether such a mode would not produce more hurt than good. The more houses the more parties; and perhaps the ill consequence to this country would be, that the landed interest would get into one house, and the commercial interest into the other; and by that means a perpetual and dangerous opposition would be kept up, and no business be got through: Whereas, were there a large, equal and annual representation in one house *only*, the different parties, by being thus blended together, would hear each others arguments, which advantage they cannot have if they sit in different houses. To say, there ought to be two houses, because there are two sorts of interest, is the very reason why there ought to be but one, and *that one* to consist of every sort. The lords and commons in England formerly made but one house; and it is evident, that by separating men you lessen the quantity of knowledge, and increase the difficulties of business. However, let the form of government be what it may, in this, or other provinces, so long as it answers the purpose of the people, and they approve it, they will be happy under it. That which suits one part of the Continent may not in every thing suit another; and when each is pleased, however variously, the matter is ended. No man is a true republican, or worthy of the name, that will not give up his single voice to that of the public: his private opinion he may retain; it is obedience only that is his duty.

The chief convenience arising from two houses is, that the second may sometimes amend small imperfections which would otherwise pass; yet, there is nearly as much chance of their making alterations for the worse as the better; and the supposition that a single house may become arbitrary, can with more reason be said of two; because their strength is greater. Besides, when all the supposed advantages arising from two houses are put together, they do not appear to balance the disadvantage. A division in one house will not retard business, but serves rather to illustrate; but a difference between two houses may produce serious consequences. In queen Ann's reign a quarrel arose between the upper and lower house, which was carried to such a pitch that the nation was under very terrifying apprehensions, and the house of commons was dissolved to prevent worse mischief. A like instance was nearly happening about six years ago, when the members of each house very affrontingly turned one another by force out of doors: The two best bills in the last sessions in England were entirely lost by having two houses: the bill for encreasing liberty of conscience, by taking off the necessity of subscription to the thirty-nine articles, Athanasian creed, &c. after passing the lower house by a very great majority, was thrown out by the upper one; and at the time that the nation was starving with the high price of corn, the bill for regulating the importation and exportation of grain, after passing the lower house, was lost by a *difference* between the two, and when returned from the upper one was thrown on the floor by the commons, and indignantly trampled under foot.—Perhaps most of the Colonies will have two houses, and it will probably be of benefit to have some little difference in the forms of government, as those which do not like one, may r[es]ide in another, and by trying different experiments, the best form will the sooner be found out, as the preference at present rests on conjecture.

Government is generally distinguished into three parts, Executive, Legislative and Judicial; but this is more a distinction of words than things. Every king or governor in giving his assent to laws acts legislatively, and not executively: The house of lords in England is both a legislative and judicial body. In short, the distinction is perplexing, and however we may refine and define, there is no more than two powers in any government, viz. the power to make laws, and the power to execute them; for the judical power is only a branch of the executive, the CHIEF of every country being the first magistrate.

A Constitution should lay down some permanent ratio, by which the representation should afterwards encrease or decrease with the number of inhabitants; for the right of representation, which is a natural one, ought not to depend upon the will and pleasure of future legislatures. And for the same reason perfect liberty of conscience; security of person against unjust imprisonments, similar to what is called the Habeas Corpus act; the mode of trial in all law and criminal cases; in short, all the great rights which man never mean, nor ever ought, to lose, should be *guaranteed,* not *granted,* by the Constitution; for at the forming a Constitution we ought to have in mind, that whatever is left to be secured by law only, may be altered by another law. That Juries ought to be judges of law, as well as fact, should be clearly described; for though in some instances Juries may err, it is generally from tenderness, and on the right side. A man cannot be *guilty* of a *good* action, yet if the fact only is to be proved (which is Lord Mansfield's doctrine) and the Jury not empowered to determine in their own minds, whether the fact proved to be done is a crime or not, a man may hereafter be found guilty of going to church or meeting.

· · · · ·

It is the part of a Constitution to fix the manner in which the officers of government shall be chosen, and determine the principal outlines of their power, their time of duration, manner of commissioning them, &c. The line, so far as respects their election, seems easy, which is, by the representatives of the people; provincial officers can be chosen no other way, because the whole province cannot be convened, any more than the whole of the Associators could be convened for choosing generals. Civil officers for towns and countries may easily be chosen by election. The mode of choosing delegates for Congress deserves consideration, as they are not officers but legislators. Positive provincial instructions have a tendency to disunion, and, if admitted, will one day or other rend the Continent of America. A continental Constitution, when fixed, will be the best boundaries of Congressional power, and in matters for the general good, they ought to be as free as assemblies. The notion, which some have, of excluding the military from the legislature is unwise, because it has a tendency to make them form a distinct party of their own. Annual elections, strengthened by some kind of periodical exclusion, seem the best guard against the encroachments of power; suppose the exclusion was triennial, that is, that no person should be returned a member of assembly for more than three succeeding years, nor be capable of being returned again till he had been absent three years. Such a mode would greatly encrease the circle of knowledge, make men cautious how they acted, and prevent the disagreeableness of giving offence, by removing some, to make room for others of equal, or perhaps superior, merit. Something of the same kind may be practised respecting Presidents or Governors, not to be eligible after a certain number of returns; and as no person, after filling that rank, can, consistent with character, descend to any other office or employment; and as it may not always happen that the most wealthy are the most capable, some decent provision therefore should be made for them in their retirement from the world. Whoever reflects on this, will see many good advantages arising from it.

Modest and decent honorary titles, so as they be neither hereditary, nor convey legislative authority, are of use in a state; they are, when properly conferred, the badges of merit. The love of the public is the chief reward which a generous man seeks; and, surely! if *that* be an honour, the mode of conferring it must be so likewise.

Next to the forming a good Constitution, is the means of p[re]serving it. If once the legislative power breaks in upon it, the effect will be the same as if a kingly power did it. The Constitution, in either case, will receive its death wound, and "the outward and visible sign," or mere form of government only will remain. "I wish," says Lord Camden, "that the maxim of Machiavel was followed, that of examining a Constitution, at certain periods, according to its first principles; this would correct abuses, and supply defects." The means here pointed out for preserving a Constitution are easy, and some article in the Constitution may provide, that at the expiration of every seven or any other number of years a *Provincial Jury* shall be elected, to enquire if any inroads have been made in the Constitution, and to have power to remove them; but not to make alterations, unless a clear majority of all the inhabitants shall so direct.

Farther observations were intended to have been offered in these letters, but the sudden turn of military affairs hath prevented them; I shall therefore conclude with remarking, that perfection in government, like perfection in all other earthly things, is not to be hoped for. A single house, or a duplication of them, will alike have their evils; and the defect is incurable, being founded in the nature of man, and the instability of things.

20

THOMAS JEFFERSON, NOTES ON THE STATE OF
VIRGINIA, QUERY 13, 121–29
1784

---

5. That the ordinary legislature may alter the constitution itself. On the discontinuance of assemblies, it became necessary to substitute in their place some other body, competent to the ordinary business of government, and to the calling forth the powers of the state for the maintenance of our opposition to Great-Britain. Conventions were therefore introduced, consisting of two delegates from each county, meeting together and forming one house, on

the plan of the former house of Burgesses, to whose places they succeeded. These were at first chosen anew for every particular session. But in March 1775, they recommended to the people to chuse a convention, which should continue in office a year. This was done accordingly in April 1775, and in the July following that convention passed an ordinance for the election of delegates in the month of April annually. It is well known, that in July 1775, a separation from Great-Britain and establishment of Republican government had never yet entered into any person's mind. A convention therefore, chosen under that ordinance, cannot be said to have been chosen for purposes which certainly did not exist in the minds of those who passed it. Under this ordinance, at the annual election in April 1776, a convention for the year was chosen. Independance, and the establishment of a new form of government, were not even yet the objects of the people at large. One extract from the pamphlet called Common Sense had appeared in the Virginia papers in February, and copies of the pamphlet itself had got into a few hands. But the idea had not been opened to the mass of the people in April, much less can it be said that they had made up their minds in its favor. So that the electors of April 1776, no more than the legislators of July 1775, not thinking of independance and a permanent republic, could not mean to vest in these delegates powers of establishing them, or any authorities other than those of the ordinary legislature. So far as a temporary organization of government was necessary to render our opposition energetic, so far their organization was valid. But they received in their creation no powers but what were given to every legislature before and since. They could not therefore pass an act transcendant to the powers of other legislatures. If the present assembly pass any act, and declare it shall be irrevocable by subsequent assemblies, the declaration is merely void, and the act repealable, as other acts are. So far, and no farther authorized, they organized the government by the ordinance entitled a Constitution or Form of government. It pretends to no higher authority than the other ordinances of the same session; it does not say, that it shall be perpetual; that it shall be unalterable by other legislatures; that it shall be transcendant above the powers of those, who they knew would have equal power with themselves. Not only the silence of the instrument is a proof they thought it would be alterable, but their own practice also: for this very convention, meeting as a House of Delegates in General Assembly with the new Senate in the autumn of that year, passed acts of assembly in contradiction to their ordinance of government; and every assembly from that time to this has done the same. I am safe therefore in the position, that the constitution itself is alterable by the ordinary legislature. Though this opinion seems founded on the first elements of common sense, yet is the contrary maintained by some persons. 1. Because, say they, the conventions were vested with every power necessary to make effectual opposition to Great-Britain. But to complete this argument, they must go on, and say further, that effectual opposition could not be made to Great-Britain, without establishing a form of government perpetual and unalterable by the legislature; which is not true. An opposition

which at some time or other was to come to an end, could not need a perpetual institution to carry it on: and a government, amendable as its defects should be discovered, was as likely to make effectual resistance, as one which should be unalterably wrong. Besides, the assemblies were as much vested with all powers requisite for resistance as the conventions were. If therefore these powers included that of modelling the form of government in the one case, they did so in the other. The assemblies then as well as the conventions may model the government; that is, they may alter the ordinance of government. 2. They urge, that if the convention had meant that this instrument should be alterable, as their other ordinances were, they would have called it an ordinance: but they have called it a *constitution,* which *by force of the term* means "an act above the power of the ordinary legislature." I answer, that *constitutio, constitutum, statutum, lex,* are convertible terms. "A *constitution* is called that which is made by the ruler. An *ordinance,* that which is rewritten by emperors or ordained. A *statute* is called the same as law." *Constitution* and *statute* were originally terms of the civil law, and from thence introduced by Ecclesiastics into the English law. Thus in the statute 25. Hen. 8. c. 19. §1. *"Constitutions and ordinances"* are used as synonimous. The term *constitution* has many other significations in physics and in politics; but in Jurisprudence, whenever it is applied to any act of the legislature, it invariably means a statute, law, or ordinance, which is the present case. No inference then of a different meaning can be drawn from the adoption of this title: on the contrary, we might conclude, that, by their affixing to it a term synonimous with ordinance, or statute, they meant it to be an ordinance or statute. But of what consequence is their meaning, where their power is denied? If they meant to do more than they had power to do, did this give them power? It is not the name, but the authority which renders an act obligatory. Lord Coke says, "an article of the statute 11 R. 2. c. 5. that no person should attempt to revoke any ordinance then made, is repealed, for that such restraint is against the jurisdiction and power of the parliament." 4. inst. 42. and again, "though divers parliaments have attempted to restrain subsequent parliaments, yet could they never effect it; for the latter parliament hath ever power to abrogate, suspend, qualify, explain, or make void the former in the whole or in any part thereof, notwithstanding any words of restraint, prohibition, or penalty, in the former: for it is a maxim in the laws of the parliament, *"because subsequent laws nullify earlier laws which are contrary."* 4. inst. 43.—To get rid of the magic supposed to be in the word *constitution,* let us translate it into its definition as given by those who think it above the power of the law; and let us suppose the convention instead of saying, "We, the ordinary legislature, establish a *constitution,*" had said, "We, the ordinary legislature, establish an act *above the power of the ordinary legislature.*" Does not this expose the absurdity of the attempt? 3. But, say they, the people have acquiesced, and this has given it an authority superior to the laws. It is true, that the people did not rebel against it: and was that a time for the people to rise in rebellion? Should a prudent acquiescence, at a critical time, be construed into a confirmation of every illegal thing done during that period? Besides, why should they rebel? At an annual election, they had chosen delegates for the year, to exercise the ordinary powers of legislation, and to manage the great contest in which they were engaged. These delegates thought the contest would be best managed by an organized government. They therefore, among others, passed an ordinance of government. They did not presume to call it perpetual and unalterable. They well knew they had no power to make it so; that our choice of them had been for no such purpose, and at a time when we could have no such purpose in contemplation. Had an unalterable form of government been meditated, perhaps we should have chosen a different set of people. There was no cause then for the people to rise in rebellion. But to what dangerous lengths will this argument lead? Did the acquiescence of the colonies under the various acts of power exercised by Great-Britain in our infant state, confirm these acts, and so far invest them with the authority of the people as to render them unalterable, and our present resistance wrong? On every unauthoritative exercise of power by the legislature, must the people rise in rebellion, or their silence be construed into a surrender of that power to them? If so, how many rebellions should we have had already? One certainly for every session of assembly. The other states in the Union have been of opinion, that to render a form of government unalterable by ordinary acts of assembly, the people must delegate persons with special powers. They have accordingly chosen special conventions to form and fix their governments. The individuals then who maintain the contrary opinion in this country, should have the modesty to suppose it possible that they may be wrong and the rest of America right. But if there be only a possibility of their being wrong, if only a plausible doubt remains of the validity of the ordinance of government, is it not better to remove that doubt, by placing it on a bottom which none will dispute? If they be right, we shall only have the unnecessary trouble of meeting once in convention. If they be wrong, they expose us to the hazard of having no fundamental rights at all. True it is, this is no time for deliberating on forms of government. While an enemy is within our bowels, the first object is to expel him. But when this shall be done, when peace shall be established, and leisure given us for intrenching within good forms, the rights for which we have bled, let no man be found indolent enough to decline a little more trouble for placing them beyond the reach of question. If any thing more be requisite to produce a conviction of the expediency of calling a convention, at a proper season, to fix our form of government, let it be the reflection,

6. That the assembly exercises a power of determining the Quorum of their own body which may legislate for us. After the establishment of the new form they adhered to the *Law of the majority*, founded in common law as well as common right. It is the natural law of every assembly of men, whose numbers are not fixed by any other law. They continued for some time to require the presence of a majority of their whole number, to pass an act. But the British parliament fixes its own quorum: our former assemblies fixed their own quorum: and one precedent in favour of power is stronger than an hundred against it. The

house of delegates therefore have lately voted that, during the present dangerous invasion, forty members shall be a house to proceed to business. They have been moved to this by the fear of not being able to collect a house. But this danger could not authorize them to call that a house which was none: and if they may fix it at one number, they may at another, till it loses its fundamental character of being a representative body. As this vote expires with the present invasion, it is probable the former rule will be permitted to revive: because at present no ill is meant. The power however of fixing their own quorum has been avowed, and a precedent set. From forty it may be reduced to four, and from four to one: from a house to a committee, from a committee to a chairman or speaker, and thus an oligarchy or monarchy be substituted under forms supposed to be regular. "All bad examples are derived from good ones; but when power comes to the ignorant or the less good, the new example is transferred from the worthy and fit to the unworthy and unfit." When therefore it is considered, that there is no legal obstacle to the assumption by the assembly of all the powers legislative, executive, and judiciary, and that these may come to the hands of the smallest rag of delegation, surely the people will say, and their representatives, while yet they have honest representatives, will advise them to say, that they will not acknowledge as laws any acts not considered and assented to by the major part of their delegates.

In enumerating the defects of the constitution, it would be wrong to count among them what is only the error of particular persons. In December 1776, our circumstances being much distressed, it was proposed in the house of delegates to create a *dictator,* invested with every power legislative, executive and judiciary, civil and military, of life and of death, over our persons and over our properties: and in June 1781, again under calamity, the same proposition was repeated, and wanted a few votes only of being passed.—One who entered into this contest from a pure love of liberty, and a sense of injured rights, who determined to make every sacrifice, and to meet every danger, for the re-establishment of those rights on a firm basis, who did not mean to expend his blood and substance for the wretched purpose of changing this master for that, but to place the powers of governing him in a plurality of hands of his own choice, so that the corrupt will of no one man might in future oppress him, must stand confounded and dismayed when he is told, that a considerable portion of that plurality had meditated the surrender of them into a single hand, and, in lieu of a limited monarch, to deliver him over to a despotic one! How must we find his efforts and sacrifices abused and baffled, if he may still by a single vote be laid prostrate at the feet of one man! In God's name, from whence have they derived this power? Is it from our ancient laws? None such can be produced. Is it from any principle in our new constitution, expressed or implied? Every lineament of that expressed or implied, is in full opposition to it. Its fundamental principle is, that the state shall be governed as a commonwealth. It provides a republican organization, proscribes under the name of *prerogative* the exercise of all powers undefined by the laws; places on this basis the whole system of our laws; and, by consolidating them together, chuses that they shall be left to stand or fall together, never providing for any circumstances, nor admitting that such could arise, wherein either should be suspended, no, not for a moment. Our antient laws expressly declare, that those who are but delegates themselves shall not delegate to others powers which require judgment and integrity in their exercise.—Or was this proposition moved on a supposed right in the movers of abandoning their posts in a moment of distress? The same laws forbid the abandonment of that post, even on ordinary occasions; and much more a transfer of their powers into other hands and other forms, without consulting the people. They never admit the idea that these, like sheep or cattle, may be given from hand to hand without an appeal to their own will.—Was it from the necessity of the case? Necessities which dissolve a government, do not convey its authority to an oligarchy or a monarchy. They throw back, into the hands of the people, the powers they had delegated, and leave them as individuals to shift for themselves. A leader may offer, but not impose himself, nor be imposed on them. Much less can their necks be submitted to his sword, their breath be held at his will or caprice. The necessity which should operate these tremendous effects should at least be palpable and irresistible. Yet in both instances, where it was feared, or pretended with us, it was belied by the event. It was belied too by the preceding experience of our sister states, several of whom had grappled through greater difficulties without abandoning their forms of government. When the proposition was first made, Massachusets had found even the government of committees sufficient to carry them through an invasion. But we at the time of that proposition were under no invasion. When the second was made, there had been added to this example those of Rhode-Island, New-York, New-Jersey, and Pennsylvania, in all of which the republican form had been found equal to the task of carrying them through the severest trials. In this state alone did there exist so little virtue, that fear was to be fixed in the hearts of the people, and to become the motive of their exertions and the principle of their government? The very thought alone was treason against the people; was treason against mankind in general; as rivetting for ever the chains which bow down their necks, by giving to their oppressors a proof, which they would have trumpeted through the universe, of the imbecility of republican government, in times of pressing danger, to shield them from harm. Those who assume the right of giving away the reins of government in any case, must be sure that the herd, whom they hand on to the rods and hatchet of the dictator, will lay their necks on the block when he shall nod to them. But if our assemblies supposed such a resignation in the people, I hope they mistook their character. I am of opinion, that the government, instead of being braced and invigorated for greater exertions under their difficulties, would have been thrown back upon the bungling machinery of county committees for administration, till a convention could have been called, and its wheels again set into regular motion. What a cruel moment was this for creating such an embarrassment, for putting to the proof the attachment of our countrymen to republican government! Those who meant well, of the advocates for this measure, (and most of them meant well, for I know them personally, had been their fellow-labourers in the common cause, and had often proved the purity of their principles), had been seduced in their judgment by the example of an ancient republic, whose constitution and circumstances were fundamentally different. They had sought this precedent in the history of Rome, where alone it was to be found, and where at length too it had proved fatal. They had taken it from a republic, rent by the most bitter factions and tumults, where the government was of a heavy-handed unfeeling aristocracy, over a people ferocious, and rendered desperate by poverty and wretchedness; tumults which could not be allayed under the most trying circumstances, but by the omnipotent hand of a single despot. Their constitution therefore allowed a temporary tyrant to be erected, under the name of a Dictator; and that temporary tyrant, after a few examples, became perpetual. They misapplied this precedent to a people, mild in their dispositions, patient under their trial, united for the public liberty, and affectionate to their leaders. But if from the constitution of the Roman government there resulted to their Senate a power of submitting all their rights to the will of one man, does it follow, that the assembly of Virginia have the same authority? What clause in our constitution has substituted that of Rome, by way of residuary provision, for all cases not otherwise provided for? Or if they may step ad libitum into any other form of government for precedents to rule us by, for what oppression may not a precedent be found in this world of the *war of all people against all things?*—Searching for the foundations of this proposition, I can find none which may pretend a colour of right or reason, but the defect before developed, that there being no barrier between the legislative, executive, and judiciary departments, the legislature may seize the whole: that having seized it, and possessing a right to fix their own quorum, they may reduce that quorum to one, whom they may call a chairman, speaker, dictator, or by any other name they please.—Our situation is indeed perilous, and I hope my countrymen will be sensible of it, and will apply, at a proper season, the proper remedy; which is a convention to fix the constitution, to amend its defects, to bind up the several branches of government by certain laws, which when they transgress their acts shall become nullities; to render unnecessary an appeal to the people, or in other words a rebellion, on every infraction of their rights, on the peril that their acquiescence shall be construed into an intention to surrender those rights.

21

ALEXANDER HAMILTON, A SECOND LETTER FROM PHOCION
Apr. 1784

Papers 3:548–51

In the first formation of a government the society may multiply its precautions as much, and annex as many conditions to the enjoyment of its rights, as it shall judge expedient; but when it has once adopted a constitution, that constitution must be the measure of its discretion, in providing for its own safety, and in prescribing the conditions upon which its privileges are to be enjoyed. If the constitution declares that persons possessing certain qualifications shall be entitled to certain rights, while that constitution remains in force, the government which is the mere creature of the constitution, can divest no citizen, who has the requisite qualifications, of his corresponding rights. It may indeed enact laws and annex to the breach of them the penalty of forfeiture; but before that penalty can operate, the existence of the fact, upon which it is to take place, must be ascertained in that mode which the constitution and the fundamental laws have provided. If trial by jury is the mode known and established by that constitution and those laws, the persons who administer the government in deviating from that course will be guilty of usurpation. If the constitution declares that the legislative power of the state shall be vested in one set of men and the judiciary power in another; and those who are appointed to act in a legislative capacity undertake the office of judges, if, instead of confining themselves to passing laws, with proper sanctions to enforce their observance, they go out of their province to decide who are the violators of those laws, they subvert the constitution and erect a tyranny. If the constitution were even silent on particular points those who are intrusted with its power, would be bound in exercising their discretion to consult and pursue its spirit, and to conform to the dictates of reason and equity; if, instead of this, they should undertake to declare whole classes of citizens disfranchised and excluded from the common rights of the society, without hearing, trial, examination or proof; if, instead of waiting to take away the rights of citizenship from individuals, till the state has convicted them of crimes, by which they are to lose them, before the ordinary and regular tribunal, they institute an inquisition into mens consciences, and oblige them to give up their privileges, or undertake to interpret the law at the hazard of perjury; they expose themselves to the imputation of injustice and oppression.

The right of a government to prescribe the conditions on which its privileges shall be enjoyed, is bounded with respect to those who are already included in the compact, by its original conditions; in admitting strangers it may add new ones; but it cannot without a breach of the social compact deprive those, who have been once admitted of their rights, unless for some declared cause of forfeiture authenticated with the solemnities required by the subsisting compact.

The rights too of a republican government are to be modified and regulated by the principles of such a government. These principles dictate, that no man shall lose his rights without a hearing and conviction, before the proper tribunal; that previous to his disfranchisement, he shall have the full benefit of the laws to make his defence; and that his innocence shall be presumed till his guilt has been proved. These with many other maxims, never to be forgotten in any but tyrannical governments, oppose the aims of those who quarrel with the principles of Phocion.

Cases indeed of extreme necessity are exceptions to all general rules; but these only exist, when it is manifest the safety of the community is in imminent danger. Speculations of possible danger never can be justifying causes of departures from principles on which in the ordinary course of things all private security depends—from principles which constitute the essential distinction between free and arbitrary governments.

When the advocates for legislature discriminations are driven from one subterfuge to another, their last resting place is—that this is a new case, the case of a revolution. Your principles are all right say they, in the ordinary course of society, but they do not apply to a situation like ours. This is opening a wilderness, through all the labyrinths of which, it is impossible to pursue them: The answer to this must be, that there are principles eternally true and which apply to all situations; such as those that have been already enumerated—that we are not now in the midst of a revolution but have happily brought it to a successful issue—that we have a constitution formed as a rule of conduct—that the frame of our government is determined and the general principle of it is settled—that we have taken our station among nations have claimed the benefit of the laws which regulate them, and must in our turn be bound by the same laws—that those eternal principles of social justice forbid the inflicting punishment upon citizens, by an abridgement of rights, or in any other manner, without conviction of some specific offence by regular trial and condemnation—that the constitution we have formed makes the trial by jury the only proper mode of ascertaining the delinquences of individuals—that legislative discriminations, to supersede the necessity of inquiry and proof, would be an usurpation on the judiciary powers of the government, and a renunciation of all the maxims of civil liberty—that by the laws of nations and the rules of justice, we are bound to observe the engagements entered into on our behalf, by that power which is invested with the constitutional prerogative of treaty—and that the treaty we have made in its genuine sense, ties up the hands of government from any species of future prosecution or punishment, on account of the part taken by individuals in the war.

Among the extravagancies with which these prolific times abound, we hear it often said that the constitution being the creature of the people, their sense with respect to any measure, if it even stand in opposition to the constitution, will sanctify and make it right.

Happily, for us, in this country, the position is not to be controverted; that the constitution is the creature of the people; but it does not follow that they are not bound by it, while they suffer it to continue in force; nor does it follow, that the legislature, which is, on the other hand, a creature of the constitution, can depart from it, on any presumption of the contrary sense of the people.

The constitution is the compact made between the society at large and each individual. The society therefore, cannot without breach of faith and injustice, refuse to any individual, a single advantage which he derives under that compact, no more than one man can refuse to perform his agreement with another. If the community have good reasons for abrogating the old compact, and establishing a new one, it undoubtedly has a right to do it; but until the compact is dissolved with the same solemnity and certainty with which it was made, the society, as well as individuals, are bound by it.

All the authority of the legislature is delegated to them under the constitution; their rights and powers are there defined; if they exceed them, 'tis a treasonable usurpation upon the power and majesty of the people; and by the same rule that they may take away from a single individual the rights he claims under the constitution, they may erect themselves into perpetual dictators. The sense of the people, if urged in justification of the measure, must be considered as a mere pretext; for that sense cannot appear to them in a form so explicit and authoritative, as the constitution under which they act; and if it could appear with equal authenticity, it could only bind, when it had been preceded by a declared change in the form of government.

The contrary doctrine serves to undermine all those rules, by which individuals can know their duties and their rights, and to convert the government into a government of *will* not of *laws*.

22

JAMES MADISON TO THOMAS JEFFERSON
24 Oct. 1787
Papers 10:207–15

You will herewith receive the result of the Convention, which continued its Session till the 17th. of September. I take the liberty of making some observations on the subject which will help to make up a letter, if they should answer no other purpose.

It appeared to be the sincere and unanimous wish of the Convention to cherish and preserve the Union of the States. No proposition was made, no suggestion was thrown out, in favor of a partition of the Empire into two or more Confederacies.

It was generally agreed that the objects of the Union could not be secured by any system founded on the principle of a confederation of sovereign States. A *voluntary*

observance of the federal law by all the members, could never be hoped for. A *compulsive* one could evidently never be reduced to practice, and if it could, involved equal calamities to the innocent & the guilty, the necessity of a military force both obnoxious & dangerous, and in general, a scene resembling much more a civil war, than the administration of a regular Government.

Hence was embraced the alternative of a Government which instead of operating, on the States, should operate without their intervention on the individuals composing them; and hence the change in the principle and proportion of representation.

This ground-work being laid, the great objects which presented themselves were 1. to unite a proper energy in the Executive and a proper stability in the Legislative departments, with the essential characters of Republican Government. 2. to draw a line of demarkation which would give to the General Government every power requisite for general purposes, and leave to the States every power which might be most beneficially administered by them. 3. to provide for the different interests of different parts of the Union. 4. to adjust the clashing pretensions of the large and small States. Each of these objects was pregnant with difficulties. The whole of them together formed a task more difficult than can be well concieved by those who were not concerned in the execution of it. Adding to these considerations the natural diversity of human opinions on all new and complicated subjects, it is impossible to consider the degree of concord which ultimately prevailed as less than a miracle.

The first of these objects as it respects the Executive, was peculiarly embarrassing. On the question whether it should consist of a single person, or a plurality of co-ordinate members, on the mode of appointment, on the duration in office, on the degree of power, on the re-eligibility, tedious and reiterated discussions took place. The plurality of co-ordinate members had finally but few advocates. Governour Randolph was at the head of them. The modes of appointment proposed were various, as by the people at large—by electors chosen by the people—by the Executives of the States—by the Congress, some preferring a joint ballot of the two Houses—some a separate concurrent ballot allowing to each a negative on the other house—some a nomination of several canditates by one House, out of whom a choice should be made by the other. Several other modifications were started. The expedient at length adopted seemed to give pretty general satisfaction to the members. As to the duration in office, a few would have preferred a tenure during good behaviour—a considerable number would have done so, in case an easy & effectual removal by impeachment could be settled. It was much agitated whether a long term, seven years for example, with a subsequent & perpetual ineligibility, or a short term with a capacity to be re-elected, should be fixed. In favor of the first opinion were urged the danger of a gradual degeneracy of re-elections from time to time, into first a life and then a heriditary tenure, and the favorable effect of an incapacity to be reappointed, on the independent exercise of the Executive authority. On the other side it was contended that the prospect of necessary degradation, would discourage the most dignified characters from aspiring to the office, would take away the principal motive to the faithful discharge of its duties—the hope of being rewarded with a reappointment, would stimulate ambition to violent efforts for holding over the constitutional term—and instead of producing an independent administration, and a firmer defence of the constitutional rights of the department, would render the officer more indifferent to the importance of a place which he would soon be obliged to quit for ever, and more ready to yield to the incroachmts. of the Legislature of which he might again be a member. The questions concerning the degree of power turned chiefly on the appointment to offices, and the controul on the Legislature. An *absolute* appointment to all offices—to some offices—to no offices, formed the scale of opinions on the first point. On the second, some contended for an absolute negative, as the only possible mean of reducing to practice, the theory of a free Government which forbids a mixture of the Legislative & Executive powers. Others would be content with a revisionary power to be overruled by three fourths of both Houses. It was warmly urged that the judiciary department should be associated in the revision. The idea of some was that a separate revision should be given to the two departments— that if either objected two thirds; if both three fourths, should be necessary to overrule.

In forming the Senate, the great anchor of the Government, the questions as they came within the first object turned mostly on the mode of appointment, and the duration of it. The different modes proposed were, 1. by the House of Representatives 2. by the Executive, 3. by electors chosen by the people for the purpose. 4. by the State Legislatures. On the point of duration, the propositions descended from good-behavior to four years, through the intermediate terms of nine, seven, six, & five years. The election of the other branch was first determined to be triennial, and afterwards reduced to biennial.

The second object, the due partition of power, between the General & local Governments, was perhaps of all, the most nice and difficult. A few contended for an entire abolition of the States; some for indefinite power of Legislation in the Congress, with a negative on the laws of the States: some for such a power without a negative: some for a limited power of legislation, with such a negative: the majority finally for a limited power without the negative. The question with regard to the Negative underwent repeated discussions, and was finally rejected by a bare majority. As I formerly intimated to you my opinion in favor of this ingredient, I will take this occasion of explaining myself on the subject. Such a check on the States appears to me necessary 1. to prevent encroachments on the General authority. 2. to prevent instability and injustice in the legislation of the States.

1. Without such a check in the whole over the parts, our system involves the evil of imperia in imperio. If a compleat supremacy some where is not necessary in every Society, a controuling power at least is so, by which the general authority may be defended against encroachments of the subordinate authorities, and by which the latter may be restrained from encroachments on each other. If the

supremacy of the British Parliament is not necessary as has been contended, for the harmony of that Empire; it is evident I think that without the royal negative or some equivalent controul, the unity of the system would be destroyed. The want of some such provision seems to have been mortal to the antient Confederacies, and to be the disease of the modern. Of the Lycian Confederacy little is known. That of the Amphyctions is well known to have been rendered of little use whilst it lasted, and in the end to have been destroyed by the predominance of the local over the federal authority. The same observation may be made, on the authority of Polybius, with regard to the Achaean League. The Helvetic System scarcely amounts to a Confederacy, and is distinguished by too many peculiarities, to be a ground of comparison. The case of the United Netherlands is in point. The authority of a Statholder, the influence of a Standing army, the common interest in the conquered possessions, the pressure of surrounding danger, the guarantee of foreign powers, are not sufficient to secure the authority and interests of the generality, agst. the antifederal tendency of the provincial sovereignties. The German Empire is another example. A Hereditary chief with vast independent resources of wealth and power, a federal Diet, with ample parchment authority, a regular Judiciary establishment, the influence of the neighbourhood of great & formidable Nations, have been found unable either to maintain the subordination of the members, or to prevent their mutual contests & encroachments. Still more to the purpose is our own experience both during the war and since the peace. Encroachments of the States on the general authority, sacrifices of national to local interests, interferences of the measures of different States, form a great part of the history of our political system. It may be said that the new Constitution is founded on different principles, and will have a different operation. I admit the difference to be material. It presents the aspect rather of a feudal system of republics, if such a phrase may be used, than of a Confederacy of independent States. And what has been the progress and event of the feudal Constitutions? In all of them a continual struggle between the head and the inferior members, until a final victory has been gained in some instances by one, in others, by the other of them. In one respect indeed there is a remarkable variance between the two cases. In the feudal system the sovereign, though limited, was independent; and having no particular sympathy of interests with the great Barons, his ambition had as full play as theirs in the mutual projects of usurpation. In the American Constitution The general authority will be derived entirely from the subordinate authorities. The Senate will represent the States in their political capacity; the other House will represent the people of the States in their individual capac[it]y. The former will be accountable to their constituents at moderate, the latter at short periods. The President also derives his appointment from the States, and is periodically accountable to them. This dependence of the General, on the local authorities, seems effectually to guard the latter against any dangerous encroachments of the former: Whilst the latter, within their respective limits, will be continually sensible of the abridgment of their power, and be stimulated by ambition to resume the surrendered portion of it. We find the representatives of Counties and corporations in the Legislatures of the States, much more disposed to sacrifice the aggregate interest, and even authority, to the local views of their Constituents: than the latter to the former. I mean not by these remarks to insinuate that an esprit de corps will not exist in the national Goverment or that opportunities may not occur, of extending its jurisdiction in some points. I mean only that the danger of encroachments is much greater from the other side, and that the impossibility of dividing powers of legislation, in such a manner, as to be free from different constructions by different interests, or even from ambiguity in the judgment of the impartial, requires some such expedient as I contend for. Many illustrations might be given of this impossibility. How long has it taken to fix, and how imperfectly is yet fixed the legislative power of corporations, though that power is subordinate in the most compleat manner? The line of distinction between the power of regulating trade and that of drawing revenue from it, which was once considered as the barrier of our liberties, was found on fair discussion, to be absolutely undefinable. No distinction seems to be more obvious than that between spiritual and temporal matters. Yet wherever they have been made objects of Legislation, they have clashed and contended with each other, till one or the other has gained the supremacy. Even the Boundaries between the Executive, Legislative & Judiciary powers, though in general so strongly marked in themselves, consist in many instances of mere shades of difference. It may be said that the Judicial authority under our new system will keep the States within their proper limits, and supply the place of a negative on their laws. The answer is, that it is more convenient to prevent the passage of a law, than to declare it void after it is passed; that this will be particularly the case, where the law aggrieves individuals, who may be unable to support an appeal agst. a State to the supreme Judiciary; that a State which would violate the Legislative rights of the Union, would not be very ready to obey a Judicial decree in support of them, and that a recurrence to force, which in the event of disobedience would be necessary, is an evil which the new Constitution meant to exclude as far as possible.

2. A constitutional negative on the laws of the States seems equally necessary to secure individuals agst. encroachments on their rights. The mutability of the laws of the States is found to be a serious evil. The injustice of them has been so frequent and so flagrant as to alarm the most stedfast friends of Republicanism. I am persuaded I do not err in saying that the evils issuing from these sources contributed more to that uneasiness which produced the Convention, and prepared the public mind for a general reform, than those which accrued to our national character and interest from the inadequacy of the Confederation to its immediate objects. A reform therefore which does not make provision for private rights, must be materially defective. The restraints agst. paper emissions, and violations of contracts are not sufficient. Supposing them to be effectual as far as they go, they are short of the mark. Injustice may be effected by such an infinitude of legislative expedients, that where the disposition exists it can only be controuled by some provision which reaches all cases whatsoever. The partial provision made, supposes the disposition which will evade it. It may be asked how private rights will be more secure under the Guardianship of the General Government than under the State Governments, since they are both founded on the republican principle which refers the ultimate decision to the will of the majority, and are distinguished rather by the extent within which they will operate, than by any material difference in their structure. A full discussion of this question would, if I mistake not, unfold the true principles of Republican Government, and prove in contradiction to the concurrent opinions of theoretical writers, that this form of Goverment, in order to effect its purposes, must operate not within a small but an extensive sphere. I will state some of the ideas which have occurred to me on this subject. Those who contend for a simple Democracy, or a pure republic, actuated by the sense of the majority, and operating within narrow limits, assume or suppose a case which is altogether fictitious. They found their reasoning on the idea, that the people composing the Society, enjoy not only an equality of political rights; but that they have all precisely the same interests, and the same feelings in every respect. Were this in reality the case, their reasoning would be conclusive. The interest of the majority would be that of the minority also; the decisions could only turn on mere opinion concerning the good of the whole, of which the major voice would be the safest criterion; and within a small sphere, this voice could be most easily collected, and the public affairs most accurately managed. We know however that no Society ever did or can consist of so homogeneous a mass of Citizens. In the savage State indeed, an approach is made towards it; but in that State little or no Government is necessary. In all civilized Societies, distinctions are various and unavoidable. A distinction of property results from that very protection which a free Government gives to unequal faculties of acquiring it. There will be rich and poor; creditors and debtors; a landed interest, a monied interest, a mercantile interest, a manufacturing interest. These classes may again be subdivided according to the different productions of different situations & soils, & according to different branches of commerce, and of manufactures. In addition to these natural distinctions, artificial ones will be founded, on accidental differences in political, religious or other opinions, or an attachment to the persons of leading individuals. However erroneous or ridiculous these grounds of dissention and faction, may appear to the enlightened Statesman, or the benevolent philosopher, the bulk of mankind who are neither Statesmen nor Philosophers, will continue to view them in a different light. It remains then to be enquired whether a majority having any common interest, or feeling any common passion, will find sufficient motives to restrain them from oppressing the minority. An individual is never allowed to be a judge or even a witness in his own cause. If two individuals are under the biass of interest or enmity agst. a third, the rights of the latter could never be safely referred to the majority of the three. Will two thousand individuals be less apt to oppress one

thousand, or two hundred thousand, one hundred thousand? Three motives only can restrain in such cases. 1. a prudent regard to private or partial good, as essentially involved in the general and permanent good of the whole. This ought no doubt to be sufficient of itself. Experience however shews that it has little effect on individuals, and perhaps still less on a collection of individuals, and least of all on a majority with the public authority in their hands. If the former are ready to forget that honesty is the best policy; the last do more. They often proceed on the converse of the maxim: that whatever is politic is honest. 2. respect for character. This motive is not found sufficient to restrain individuals from injustice, and loses its efficacy in proportion to the number which is to divide the praise or the blame. Besides as it has reference to public opinion, which is that of the majority, the Standard is fixed by those whose conduct is to be measured by it. 3. Religion. The inefficacy of this restraint on individuals is well known. The conduct of every popular Assembly, acting on oath, the strongest of religious ties, shews that individuals join without remorse in acts agst. which their consciences would revolt, if proposed to them separately in their closets. When Indeed Religion is kindled into enthusiasm, its force like that of other passions is increased by the sympathy of a multitude. But enthusiasm is only a temporary state of Religion, and whilst it lasts will hardly be seen with pleasure at the helm. Even in its coolest state, it has been much oftener a motive to oppression than a restraint from it. If then there must be different interests and parties in Society; and a majority when united by a common interest or passion can not be restrained from oppressing the minority, what remedy can be found in a republican Government, where the majority must ultimately decide, but that of giving such an extent to its sphere, that no common interest or passion will be likely to unite a majority of the whole number in an unjust pursuit. In a large Society, the people are broken into so many interests and parties, that a common sentiment is less likely to be felt, and the requisite concert less likely to be formed, by a majority of the whole. The same security seems requisite for the civil as for the religious rights of individuals. If the same sect form a majority and have the power, other sects will be sure to be depressed. Divide et impera, the reprobated axiom of tyranny, is under certain qualifications, the only policy, by which a republic can be administered on just principles. It must be observed however that this doctrine can only hold within a sphere of a mean extent. As in too small a sphere oppressive combinations may be too easily formed agst. the weaker party; so in too extensive a one, a defensive concert may be rendered too difficult against the oppression of those entrusted with the administration. The great desideratum in Government is, so to modify the sovereignty as that it may be sufficiently neutral between different parts of the Society to controul one part from invading the rights of another, and at the same time sufficiently controuled itself, from setting up an interest adverse to that of the entire Society. In absolute monarchies, the Prince may be tolerably neutral towards different classes of his subjects, but may sacrifice the happiness of all to his personal ambition or avarice. In small republics,

the sovereign will is controuled from such a sacrifice of the entire Society, but is not sufficiently neutral towards the parts composing it. In the extended Republic of the United States, The General Government would hold a pretty even balance between the parties of particular States, and be at the same time sufficiently restrained by its dependence on the community, from betraying its general interests.

Begging pardon for this immoderate digression I return to the third object abovementioned, the adjustment of the different interests of different parts of the Continent. Some contended for an unlimited power over trade including exports as well as imports, and over slaves as well as other imports; some for such a power, provided the concurrence of two thirds of both House were required; Some for such a qualification of the power, with an exemption of exports and slaves, others for an exemption of exports only. The result is seen in the Constitution. S. Carolina & Georgia were inflexible on the point of the slaves.

The remaining object created more embarrassment, and a greater alarm for the issue of the Convention than all the rest put together. The little States insisted on retaining their equality in both branches, unless a compleat abolition of the State Governments should take place; and made an equality in the Senate a sine qua non. The large States on the other hand urged that as the new Government was to be drawn principally from the people immediately and was to operate directly on them, not on the States; and consequently as the States wd. lose that importance which is now proportioned to the importance of their voluntary compliances with the requisitions of Congress, it was necessary that the representation in both Houses should be in proportion to their size. It ended in the compromise which you will see, but very much to the dissatisfaction of several members from the large States.

23

IMPARTIAL EXAMINER, NO. 1
20 Feb. 1788
Storing 5.14.2

In pursuing this address I beg leave to premise that the only true point of distinction between arbitrary and free governments seems to be, that in the former the governors are invested with powers of acting according to their own wills, without any other limits than what they themselves may understand to be necessary for the general good; whereas in the latter they are intrusted with no such unlimited authority, but are restrained in their operations to conform to certain fundamental principles, the preservation whereof is expressly stipulated for in the *civil compact:* and whatever is not so stipulated for is virtually and impliedly given up. Societies so constituted invest their supreme governors with ample powers of exerting themselves according to their own judgment in every thing not inconsistent with or derogatory to those principles; and so long as they adhere to such restrictions, their deeds ought not to be rescinded or controuled by any other power whatsoever. Those principles are certain inherent rights pertaining to all mankind in a state of natural liberty, which through the weakness, imperfection, and depravity of human nature cannot be secured in that state. Men, therefore, agree to enter into society, that by the united force of *many* the rights of *each* individual may be protected and secured. These are in all just governments laid down as a foundation to the *civil compact,* which contains a *covenant* between *each* with *all,* that they shall enter into one society to be governed by the same powers; establishes for that purpose the *frame* of government; and consequently creates a *Convention* between *every* member, binding those, who shall at any time be intrusted with power, to a faithful administration of their trust according to the form of the *civil policy,* which they have so constituted, and obliging all to a due obedience therein. There can be no other just origin of civil power, but some such mutual contract of all the people: and although their great object in forming society is an intention to secure their natural rights; yet the relations arising from this *political union* create certain duties and obligations to the state, which require a sacrifice of some portion of those rights and of that exuberance of liberty, which obtains in a state of nature.— This, however, being compensated by certain other adventitious rights and privileges, which are acquired by the social connection; it follows that the advantages derived from a government are to be estimated by the *strength* of the *security,* which is attended at once with the *least sacrifice* and the *greatest acquired benefits.* That government, therefore, which is best adapted for promoting these three *great ends,* must certainly be the best constituted scheme of *civil policy.* Here, then, it may not be improper to remark that persons forming a social community cannot take too much precaution when they are about to establish the plan of their government. They ought to construct it in such a manner as to procure the best possible security for their rights;—in doing this they ought to give up no greater share than what is understood to be absolutely necessary:—and they should endeavor so to organize, arrange and connect it's several branches, that when duly exercised it may tend to promote the *common good* of all, and contribute as many advantages, as the civil institution is capable of. It has been before observed that the only just origin of civil power is a contract entered into by all the people for that purpose.—If this position be true (and, I dare presume, it is not controverted, at least in this country) right reason will always suggest the expediency of adhering to the essential requisites in forming that contract upon true principles. A cautious people will consider all the inducements to enter into the *social state,* from the most important object down to the minutest prospect of advantage. Every motive with them will have its due weight. They will not pay a curious attention to trifles and overlook matters of great consequence:—and in pursuing these steps they will provide for the attainment of *each* point in view with a care—with an earnestness proportionate to its dignity, and according as it involves a *greater* or a *lesser* interest. It is

evident, therefore that they should attend most diligently to those sacred rights, which they have received with their birth, and which can neither be retained to themselves, nor transmitted to ther posterity, unless they are *expressly reserved:* for it is a maxim, I dare say, universally acknowledged, that when men establish a system of government, in granting the powers therein they are always understood to surrender whatever they do not so expressly reserve. This is obvious from the very design of the civil institution, which is adopted in lieu of the state of natural liberty, wherein each individual, being equally intitled to the enjoyment of all natural rights, and having equally a just authority to exercise full powers of acting, with relation to other individuals, in any manner not injurious to their rights, must, when he enters into society, be presumed to give up all those powers into the hands of the state by submitting his whole conduct to the direction thereof. This being done by every member, it follows, as a regular conclusion, that all such powers, whereof the whole were possessed, so far as they related to each other individually, are of course given up by the mere act of union. If this surrender be made without any reservation, the conclusion is equally plain and regular, that *each* and *all* have given up not only those powers, which relate to others, but likewise every claim, which pertained to themselves, as individuals. For the universality of the grant in this case must necessarily include every *power* of acting, and every *claim* of possessing or obtaining any thing—except according to the regulations of the state. Now a right being properly defined, "a power or claim established by law, to act, or to possess, or to obtain something from others," every natural right is such *power* or *claim* established by the law of nature. Thus, it is manifest, that in a society constituted after this manner, every right whatsoever will be under the power and controul of the civil jurisdiction. This is the leading characteristic of an arbitrary government, and whenever any people establish a system like this, they subject themselves to one, which has not a single property of a free constitution. Hence results the necessity of an *express stipulation* for all such rights as are intended to be exempted from the civil authority.

24

ALEXANDER HAMILTON, FEDERALIST, NO. 78,
524–25
28 May 1788

Some perplexity respecting the right of the courts to pronounce legislative acts void, because contrary to the constitution, has arisen from an imagination that the doctrine would imply a superiority of the judiciary to the legislative power. It is urged that the authority which can declare the acts of another void, must necessarily be superior to the one whose acts may be declared void. As this doctrine is of great importance in all the American constitutions, a brief discussion of the grounds on which it rests cannot be un-acceptable.

There is no position which depends on clearer princi-ples, than that every act of a delegated authority, contrary to the tenor of the commission under which it is exercised, is void. No legislative act therefore contrary to the consti-tution can be valid. To deny this would be to affirm that the deputy is greater than his principal; that the servant is above his master; that the representatives of the people are superior to the people themselves; that men acting by virtue of powers may do not only what their powers do not authorise, but what they forbid.

If it be said that the legislative body are themselves the constitutional judges of their own powers, and that the construction they put upon them is conclusive upon the other departments, it may be answered, that this cannot be the natural presumption, where it is not to be collected from any particular provisions in the constitution. It is not otherwise to be supposed that the constitution could in-tend to enable the representatives of the people to substi-tute their *will* to that of their constituents. It is far more rational to suppose that the courts were designed to be an intermediate body between the people and the legislature, in order, among other things, to keep the latter within the limits assigned to their authority. The interpretation of the laws is the proper and peculiar province of the courts. A constitution is in fact, and must be, regarded by the judges as a fundamental law. It therefore belongs to them to as-certain its meaning as well as the meaning of any particu-lar act proceeding from the legislative body. If there should happen to be an irreconcileable variance between the two, that which has the superior obligation and validity ought of course to be preferred; or in other words, the constitution ought to be preferred to the statute, the inten-tion of the people to the intention of their agents.

Nor does this conclusion by any means suppose a supe-riority of the judicial to the legislative power. It only sup-poses that the power of the people is superior to both; and that where the will of the legislature declared in its stat-utes, stands in opposition to that of the people declared in the constitution, the judges ought to be governed by the latter, rather than the former. They ought to regulate their decisions by the fundamental laws, rather than by those which are not fundamental.

25

JAMES MADISON, OBSERVATIONS ON JEFFERSON'S DRAFT OF A CONSTITUTION FOR VIRGINIA
15 Oct. 1788
Papers 11:285–93

Senate. The term of two years is too short. Six years are not more than sufficient. A Senate is to withstand the oc-casional impetuosities of the more numerous branch. The members ought therefore to derive a firmness from the tenure of their places. It ought to supply the defect of knowledge and experience incident to the other branch, there ought to be time given therefore for attaining the qualifications necessary for that purpose. It ought finally to maintain that system and steadiness in public affairs without which no Government can prosper or be respect-able. This cannot be done by a body undergoing a fre-quent change of its members. A Senate for six years will not be dangerous to liberty. On the contrary it will be one of its best guardians. By correcting the infirmities of pop-ular Government, it will prevent that disgust agst. that form which may otherwise produce a sudden transition to some very different one. It is no secret to any attentive & dispassionate observer of the pol: Situation of the U.S. that the real danger to republican liberty has lurked in that cause.

The appointment of Senators by districts seems to be objectionable. A spirit of *locality* is inseparable from that mode. The evil is fully displayed in the County represen-tations; the members of which are every where observed to lose sight of the aggregate interests of the Community, and even to sacrifice them to the interests or prejudices of their respective constituents. In general these local inter-ests are miscalculated. But it is not impossible for a mea-sure to be accomodated to the particular interests of every County or district, when considered by itself, and not so, when considered in relation to each other and to the whole State; in the same manner as the interests of individuals may be very different in a State of nature and in a Political Union. The most effectual remedy for the local biass is to impress on the minds of the Senators an attention to the interest of the whole Society by making them the choice of the whole Society, each citizen voting for every Senator. The objection here is that the fittest characters would not be sufficiently known to the people at large. But in free Governments, merit and notoriety of character are rarely separated, and such a regulation would connect them more and more together. Should this mode of election be on the whole not approved, that established in Maryland presents a valuable alternative. The latter affords perhaps a greater security for the selection of merit. The inconve-niences chargeable on it are two: first that the Council of electors favors cabal. Against this the shortness of its exis-tence is a good antidote. Secondly that in a large State the meeting of the Electors must be expensive if they be paid, or badly attended if the service be onerous. To this it may be answered that in a case of such vast importance, the expence which could not be great, ought to be disre-garded. Whichever of these modes may be preferred, it cannot be amiss so far to admit the plan of districts as to restrain the choice to persons residing in different parts of the State. Such a regulation will produce a diffusive con-fidence in the Body, which is not less necessary than the other means of rendering it useful. In a State having large towns which can easily unite their votes the precaution would be essential to an immediate choice by the people at large. In Maryland no regard is paid to residence. And what is remarkable vacancies are filled by the Senate itself. This last is an obnoxious expedient and cannot in any point of view have much effect. It was probably meant to obviate the trouble of occasional meetings of the Electors. But the purpose might have been otherwise answered by allowing the unsuccessful candidates to supply vacancies according to the order of their standing on the list of votes, or by requiring provisional appointments to be made along with the positive ones. If an election by districts be unavoidable and the ideas here suggested be sound, the evil will be diminished in proportion to the extent given to the districts, taking two or more Senators from each district.

Electors. The first question arising here is how far property ought to be made a qualification. There is a middle way to be taken which corresponds at once with the Theory of free government and the lessons of experience. A freehold or equivalent of a certain value may be annexed to the right of vot[in]g for Senators, & the right left more at large in the election of the other House. Examples of this distinction may be found in the Constitutions of several States, particularly if I mistake not, of North Carolina & N. York. This middle mode reconciles and secures the two cardinal objects of Government, the rights of persons, and the rights of property. The former will be sufficiently guarded by one branch, the latter more particularly by the other. Give all power to property; and the indigent [will] be oppressed. Give it to the latter and the effect may be transposed. Give a defensive share to each and each will be secure. The necessity of thus guarding the rights of property was for obvious reasons unattended to in the commencement of the Revolution. In all the Governments which were considered as beacons to republican patriots & lawgivers, the rights of persons were subjected to those of property. The poor were sacrificed to the rich. In the existing state of American population, & American property [,] the two classes of rights were so little discriminated that a provision for the rights of persons was supposed to include of itself those of property, and it was natural to infer from the tendency of republican laws, that these different interests would be more and more identified. Experience and investigation have however produced more correct ideas on this subject. It is now observed that in all populous countries, the smaller part only can be interested in preserving the rights of property. It must be foreseen that America, and Kentucky itself will by degrees arrive at this State of Society; that in some parts of the Union a very great advance is already made towards it. It is well understood that interest leads to injustice as well when the opportunity is presented to bodies of men, as to individuals; to an interested majority in a republic, as to the interested minority of any other form of Government. The time to guard agst. this danger is at the first forming of the Constitution, and in the present state of population when the bulk of the people have a sufficient interest in possession or in prospect to be attached to the rights of property, without being insufficiently attached to the rights of persons. Liberty not less than justice pleads for the policy here recommended. If all power be suffered to slide into hands not interested in the rights of property which must be the case whenever a majority fall under that description, one of two things cannot fail to happen; either they will unite against the other description and become the dupes & in-

struments of ambition, or their poverty & independence will render them the mercenary instruments of wealth. In either case liberty will be subverted; in the first by a despotism growing out of anarchy, in the second, by an oligarchy founded on corruption.

The second question under this head is whether the ballot be not a better mode than that of voting viva voce. The comparative experience of the States pursuing the different modes is in favor of the first. It is found less difficult to guard against fraud in that, than against bribery in the other.

Exclusions. Does not the exclusion of Ministers of the Gospel as such violate a fundamental principle of liberty by punishing a religious profession with the privation of a civil right? Does it not violate another article of the plan itself which exempts religion from the cognizance of Civil power? Does it not violate justice by at once taking away a right and prohibiting a compensation for it. And does it not in fine violate impartiality by shutting the door agst the Ministers of one religion and leaving it open for those of every other.

The re-eligibility of members after accepting offices of profit is so much opposed to the present way of thinking in America that any discussion of the subject would probably be a waste of time.

Limits of power. It is at least questionable whether death ought to be confined to "Treason and murder." It would not therefore be prudent to tie the hands of Government in the manner here proposed. The prohibition of pardon, however specious in theory would have practical consequences, which render it inadmissible. A single instance is a sufficient proof. The crime of treason is generally shared by a number, and often a very great number. It would be politically if not morally wrong to take away the lives of all, even if every individual were equally guilty. What name would be given to a severity which made no distinction between the legal & the moral offence—between the deluded multitude, and their wicked leaders. A second trial would not avoid the difficulty; because the oaths of the jury would not permit them to hearken to any voice but the inexorable voice of the law.

The power of the Legislature to appoint any other than their own officers departs too far from the Theory which requires a separation of the great Depts of Government. One of the best securities against the creation of unnecessary offices or tyrannical powers, is an exclusion of the authors from all share in filling the one, or influence in the execution of the others. The proper mode of appointing to offices will fall under another head.

Executive Governour. An election by the Legislature is liable to insuperable objections. It not only tends to faction intrigue and corruption, but leaves the Executive under the influence of an improper obligation to that department. An election by the people at large, as in this & several other States—or by Electors as in the appointment of the Senate in Maryland, or indeed by the people through any other channel than their legislative representatives, seems to be far preferable. The ineligibility a second time, though not perhaps without advantages, is also liable to a variety of strong objections. It takes away one powerful motive to a faithful & useful administration, the desire of acquiring that title to a re-appointment. By rendering a periodical change of men necessary, it discourages beneficial undertakings which require perseverance and system, or, as frequently happened in the Roman Consulate, either precipitates or prevents the execution of them. It may inspire desperate enterprizes for the attainment of what is not attainable by legitimate means. It fetters the judgment and inclination of the Community; and in critical moments would either produce a violation of the Constitution, or exclude a choice which might be essential to the public safety. Add to the whole, that by putting the Executive Magistrate in the situation of the tenant of an unrenewable lease, it would tempt him to neglect the constitutional rights of his department, and to connive at usurpations by the Legislative department, with which he may connect his future ambition or interest.

The clause restraining the first Magistrate from the immediate command of the military force would be made better by excepting cases in which he should receive the sanction of the two branches of the Legislature.

Council of State. The following variations are suggested. 1. The election to be made by the people immediately, or thro' some other medium than the Legislature. 2. A distributive choice should perhaps be secured as in the case of the Senate. 3 instead of an ineligibility a second time, a rotation as in the federal Senate, with an abrdgmt. of the term to be substituted.

The appointment to offices is, of all the functions of Republican & perhaps every other form of Government, the most difficult to guard against abuse. Give it to a numerous body, and you at once destroy all responsibility, and create a perpetual source of faction and corruption. Give it to the Executive wholly, and it may be made an engine of improper influence and favoritism. Suppose the power were divided thus: let the Executive alone make all the subordinate appointments; and the Govr. and Senate as in the Fedl. Constn:, those of the superior order. It seems particularly fit that the Judges, who are to form a distinct department should owe their offices partly to each of the other departments rather than wholly to either.

Judiciary. Much detail ought to [be] avoided in the constitutional regulation of this department, that there may be room for changes which may be demanded by the progressive changes in the state of our population. It is at least doubtful whether the number of Courts, the number of Judges, or even the boundaries of Jurisdiction ought to be made unalterable but by a revisal of the Constitution. The precaution seems no otherwise necessary than as it may prevent sudden modifications of the establishment, or addition of obsequious Judges, for the purpose of evadg. the checks of the Constn. & giv[in]g effect to some sinister policy of the Legisre. But might not the same object be otherwise attained? By prohibiting, for example, any innovations in those particulars without the consent of that department: or without the annual sanction of two or three successive assemblies; over & above the other prerequisites to the passage of a law.

The model here proposed for a Court of Appeals is not recommended by experience. It is found as might well be presumed that the members are always warped in their appellate decisions by an attachment to the principles and jurisdiction of their respective Courts & still more so by the previous decision on the case removed by appeal. The only effectual cure for the evil, is to form a Court of Appeals, of distinct and select Judges. The expence ought not be admitted as an objection. 1. because the proper administration of Justice is of too essential a nature to be sacrificed to that consideration. 2. The number of inferior Judges might in that case be lessened. 3. The whole department may be made to support itself by a judicious tax on law proceedings.

The excuse for non-attendance would be a more proper subject of enquiry some where else than in the Court to which the party belonged. Delicacy, mutual connivance &c. would soon reduce the regulation to mere form; or if not, it might become a disagreeable source of little irritations among the members. A certificate from the local Court or some other local authority where the party might reside or happen to be detained from his duty, expressing the cause of absence as well as that it was judged to be satisfactory, might be safely substituted. Few Judges would improperly claim their wages, if such a formality stood in the way. These observations are applicable to the Council of State.

A Court of Impeachments is among the most puzzling articles of a republican Constitution; and it is far more easy to point out defects in any plan, than to supply a cure for them. The diversified expedients adopted in the Constitutions of the several States prove how much the compilers were embarrassed on this subject. The plan here proposed varies from all of them; and is perhaps not less than any a proof of the difficulties which pressed the ingenuity of its author. The remarks arising on it are 1. that it seems not to square with reason, that the right to impeach should be united to that of trying the impeachment, & consequently in a proportional degree, to that of sharing in the appointment of, or influence on the Tribunal to which the trial may belong. 2. As the Executive & Judiciary would form a majority of the Court, and either have a right to impeach, too much might depend on a combination of these departments. This objection would be still stronger, if the members of the Assembly were capable as proposed of holding offices, and were amenable in that capacity to the Court. 3. The H. of Delegates and either of those departments could appt. a majority of the Court. Here is another danger of combination, and the more to be apprehended as that branch of the Legisl: wd. also have the right to impeach, a right in their hands of itself sufficiently weighty; and as the power of the Court wd. extend to the head of the Ex. by whose independence the constitutil. rights of that department are to be secured agst. Legislative usurpations. 4. The dangers in the two last cases would be still more formidable; as the power extends not only to deprivation; but to future incapacity of office. In the case of all officers of sufficient importance to be objects of factious persecution, the latter branch of power is in every view of a delicate nature. In that of the Cheif Magistrate, it seems inadmissible, if he be chosen by the Legislature; and much more so, if immediately by the people themselves. A temporary incapacitation is the most that cd. be properly authorised.

The 2 great desiderata in a Court of impeachts. are 1. impartiality. 2. respectability—the first in order to a right—the second in order to a satisfactory decision. These characteristics are arrived at in the following modification—Let the Senate be denied the right to impeach. Let ⅓ of the members be struck out, by alternate nominations of the prosecutors & party impeached; the remaining ⅔ to be the *Stamen* of the Court. When the H: of Del: impeach, let the Judges or a certain proportion of them—and the Council of State be associated in the trial. When the Govr. or Council impeaches, let the Judges only be associated: When the Judges impeach let the Council only be associated. But if the party impeached by the H. of Dels. be a member of the Ex. or Judicy. let that of which he is a member not be associated. If the party impeached belong to one & be impeached by the other of these branches, let neither of them be associated, the decision being in this case left with the Senate alone or if that be thought exceptionable, a few members might be added by the H. of Ds. ⅔ of the Court should in all cases be necessary to a conviction, & the cheif Magistrate *at least* should be exempt from a sentence of perpetual if not of temporary incapacity. It is extremely probable that a critical discussion of this outline may discover objections which do not occur. Some do occur; but appear not to be greater than are incident to any different modification of the Tribunal.

The establishment of trials by Jury & viva voce testimony in *all* cases and in *all* Courts, is to say the least a delicate experiment; and would most probably be either violated, or be found inconvenient.

Council of Revision. A revisionary power is meant as a check to precipitate, to unjust, and to unconstitutional laws. These important ends would it is conceived be more effectually secured, without disarming the Legislature of its requisite authority, by requiring bills to be separately communicated to the Exec: & Judicy. depts. If either of these object, let ⅔, if both ¾ of each House be necessary to overrule the objection; and if either or both protest agst. a bill as violating the Constitution, let it moreover be suspended, notwithstanding the overruling proportion of the Assembly, until there shall have been a subsequent election of the H. of Ds. and a repassage of the bill by ⅔ or ¾ of both Houses, as the case may be. It sd. not be allowed the Judges or the Ex to pronounce a law thus enacted, unconstitul. & invalid.

In the State Constitutions & indeed in the Fedl. one also, no provision is made for the case of a disagreement in expounding them; and as the Courts are generally the last in making their decision, it results to them, by refusing or not refusing to execute a law, to stamp it with its final character. This makes the Judiciary Dept paramount in fact to the Legislature, which was never intended, and can never be proper:

The extension of the Habs. Corps. to the cases in which it has been usually suspended, merits consideration at least. If there be emergences which call for such a suspension, it can have no effect to prohibit it, because the prohibition will assuredly give way to the impulse of the moment; or rather it will have the bad effect of facilitating other violations that may be less necessary. The Exemption of the press from liability in every case for *true facts*, is also an innovation and as such ought to be well considered. This essential branch of liberty is perhaps in more danger of being interrupted by local tumults, or the silent awe of a predominant party, than by any direct attacks of Power.

SEE ALSO:

Generally ch. 2

Charter of the Massachusetts Bay Company, 4 Mar. 1629, American Colonial Documents 72, 75–84

Jean Jacques Burlamaqui, The Principles of Politic Law, ch. 7, §§ 1–50 (1751), 2:44–62 (3d ed. 1784)

Emmerich de Vattel, The Law of Nations, or, Principles of the Law of Nature, bk. 1, ch. 3, §§ 26–37 (1758)

James Iredell, Letter to the North-Carolina Gazette, 10 Sept. 1773, Papers 1:165

Pennsylvania Constitution of 1776, Thorpe 5:3081–92

Thomas Jefferson, Draught of a Fundamental Constitution for the Commonwealth of Virginia, May–June 1783, Papers 6:294–305

James Madison to Caleb Wallace, 23 Aug. 1785, Papers 8:350–56

Noah Webster, On Government, 1788, Collection 59–71

Thomas Jefferson to Noah Webster, Jr., 4 Dec. 1790, Papers 18:131–33

18

Epilogue: Securing the Republic

Introduction

To found a republic was one thing; to have and to hold it, yet another. When Dr. Franklin replied to the lady eager to be the first to learn what the Philadelphia Convention had wrought in secrecy, his answer was as revealing of the problem as it was expressive of his peculiar turn of mind. "Well, Doctor, what have we got—a republic or a monarchy?" "A republic—if you can keep it."

One need hardly say that the Founders were concerned with more than the act of founding, however pressing and difficult that great effort was to be. As men of affairs they thought of the problems of the morrow as well. A proper founding implied a proper regard for the principles of preservation. To be sure, the future could not simply be foreseen or foreclosed; the care and thoughtfulness of the past could not render superfluous the care and thoughtfulness of each succeeding living generation. And yet it would be trifling with matters of vast concern to propose a form of government without giving heed to how it might best be preserved against the most likely sources of internal corruption and external danger.

The whole elaborated system of federalism, separation of powers, checks and balances, enumerated powers, secured rights, periodic accountability of officials to the electorate, and the other arrangements that were to give American constitutionalism its special character were so many barriers against the persistent and predictable forces that might make popular government a hollow or cruel mockery. But governmental institutions could go only so far. While a constitution and its institutions might elicit and shape certain kinds of conduct, it also was true that a corrupt or slavish people could ruin even a very good constitution. What really mattered, in the last analysis, was the kind of people who would make up the American public. Their strengths, their limits, were the outer boundaries of what was possible.

The civic character of that public was neither a given, fixed beyond the power of statesmen to alter or redirect, nor an infinitely malleable substance to be shaped by institutions at will or whim. It was, after all, for *this* people in *this* land that a government was to be founded. American circumstances offered expanded possibilities, to be sure. Thus Americans could aim at a fuller measure of liberty and self-government than others had achieved. But like Solon, the American founders also knew that circumstances were a powerful restraint on plans and dreams; it was their business to propose not the best that they could imagine, but the best that their people would accept. See Farrand 1:125 (Butler), 491 (Bedford); *Federalist*, no. 38 (Madison). Within those limits much—but not everything—could be done.

From our vantage point the preoccupation of that founding generation with what they called "manners" seems extraordinary. Their concern was less with the fine points of etiquette (though that too was within their purview), than with the habits and moral tastes of a people who were about to take a new turn in their career of self-government.* This also used to be called "civility." If we have any terms in current speech corresponding to "manners" they might be "values" or "opinions" or even "philosophy" (in the sense in which a television interviewer may ask a professional athlete or the manager of an election campaign what his "philosophy" is). Those manners were the matrix as it were of public life; but they might also be guided or reinforced or restrained by the institutions and workings of a particular governmental system. Given the right manners, Americans might long enjoy the benefits projected in the Preamble. In the absence of those manners, or with those manners present only in a weak and attenuated form, the government would stand only till external or internal shocks reduced the whole to rubble. That possibility seemed neither remote nor unlikely if the history of earlier efforts at self-governance were any indication. To be concerned about the chances of political decay or even ruin was a sign of practical sense informed by long experience, not the flutterings of a paranoid imagination.

The Character of a Self-governing People

What kind of a people, then, did a republic require? How were they to be distinguished from those who were fit only to be ruled by others placed permanently above them? What might be expected of a self-governing people in the way of maintaining their fitness for self-government? At least this much was certain: nothing was easy or automatic. Free air or free soil did not assure the continuing succession of free citizens. Liberty, as Algernon Sidney had argued, might indeed be the precondition for the desired kinds of excellence, but it would be a mistake to rank good republicans among the promiscuous productions of nature. Yet what precisely were the desired kinds of excellence? Very much turned on how one answered that question.

The thinker to whom political writers regularly recurred in these matters was Montesquieu. His *Spirit of Laws* (no. 3) had proposed a taxonomy of regimes based on their several principles—the spring or activating passion that constituted and sustained a particular regime. Popular or republican government depended on virtue, but virtue understood in a special sense. Montesquieu took pains to make it clear that he was speaking of political virtue, the virtue not of the Christian but of "the political honest man," the man who loves the laws and is moved by that love. "Now, a government is like every thing else: to preserve it we must love it." Was such love possible in a world preoccupied with private wants and private pleasures, with manufactures, commerce, and luxury? Was such love possible in a world where people are all too well instructed in contradictory duties, where what we learn from our parents and teachers is "effaced" by what we learn from the world? Nowhere was "the whole power of education" more surely needed than in a republic, for nowhere did more depend on the presence of a public-spirited citizenry. Without such a citizenry—one able to preserve "the spirit of equality" without falling victim to the corruption of extreme democracy—no self-government was possible.

Republican writers such as Samuel Adams (no. 6) came to view such an education as the fundamental task of statesmanship. Manners made certain laws possible or effective, but laws might also be used by magistrates to form the manners of a people. Whatever else they might tolerate or accept, republicans could not afford to brook a spirit of public indifference and private corruption. It was to those evils that public policy ought to be addressed. But how? The high-toned admonitory language of the Proclamation of the General Court of the Colony of Massachusetts-Bay (23 Jan. 1776) could not be used everywhere nor for very long even in Massachusetts. And yet it seemed evident to John Adams that a low-toned citizenry could retain neither a republic nor its liberty (nos. 7, 9).

There were those who argued against simplistic readings (or misreadings) of Montesquieu. The collapsing of public and private virtue into one another was preposterous, and resting one's political expectations on a general, widespread "disinterested attachment to the public good" was no less preposterous. So at least thought Carter Braxton (no. 10) in a pamphlet opposing John Adams's *Thoughts on Government* and in which Braxton argued for continued adherence to what he saw as the uncorrupted principles of the English Constitution. To speak of agrarian and sumptuary laws in any but naturally sterile lands was to be

*"By Manners, I mean not here, Decency of behaviour; as how one man should salute another, or how a man should wash his mouth, or pick his teeth before company, and such other points of the *Small Moralls;* But those qualities of mankind, that concern their living together in Peace, and Unity." Hobbes, *Leviathan,* Pt. 1, ch. 11, beginning (1651).

blinded by theory. A republic that required those means to preserve itself from decay was no fit form for a people living in a bountiful land. Whatever theory might prescribe, such people "will always claim a right of using and enjoying the fruits of their honest industry, unrestrained by any ideal principles of government, and will gather estates for themselves and children without regarding the whimsical impropriety of being richer than their neighbours." Hamilton agreed: the model for Americans could not be early Sparta or Rome, and crying up to the heavens the necessity of disinterestedness would not make Americans into what they were not (no. 15).

Although John Adams might agree with Braxton and Hamilton in this respect—that Americans never were nor ought to be Spartans (Letter to James Warren, 4 July 1786)—he was not quite as ready as they to let matters rest there. Republican government presupposed a degree of popular enlightenment: popular understanding and morals had in some way to be improved; "vulgar prejudices and popular superstitions" had in some way to be dissipated where these opposed themselves to good government. Republican virtue was then the order of the day, but it could not be classical or Christian or even Montesquieuan virtue (if by that one means an absence of ambition and avarice). As a general rule men could not be expected to love the whole better than their particular selves, or to prefer the public to the private. Only a system of well-digested laws could embody that degree of public-spiritedness. What could be expected of ordinary folk was a degree of "reverence and obedience to the laws" that would bend the actions of self-regarding men in public-regarding directions (no. 17). (See also J. Adams to S. Adams, 18 Oct. 1790, in ch. 11, no. 16.)

For many Anti-Federalists this was not enough. The Virginian author of a Proposal for Reviving Christian Conviction (no. 19) argued that it is especially republican government that requires a support for moral rectitude. A desire for popularity would commend a lax enforcement of the laws; "the allurements of self-interest and self-gratification" would prove irresistible, whatever the cost in public welfare and happiness. To hold men to their duty something more than self-interest was needed: it was "necessary to call in the aid of religion."

Fears and Hopes

Federalist responses to the problem of republican manners were quite diverse. Some, like Madison (see ch. 4, no. 19), thought it futile to expect that religious exhortation would suffice to restrain injustice. However valuable it would be to have a people sharing enlightened faith and morals, these alone would not secure the conditions of self-government. The intricacies of institutional arrangements, the variety of modes of working and living in a large country, the gradual enlistment of enlightened self-interest in support of a government that met general expectations of fairness and security, the transmutation of politically ruinous passions into civilly acceptable levels of competition: all these would work more surely and quietly to preserve republic and republicans. Others, like Noah Webster, were less hopeful. Ultimately, corruption was the

destiny of every people possessed by possessiveness; wealth and vices would flourish in tandem. That destiny might be retarded, or at least not accelerated, by a careful regard to a revolution in manners that ought to complement the act of political revolution. America had yet to declare its independence of European manners, European corruption. (See Remarks on the Manners . . . of the United States, 1787.) Still others, like Hamilton (see ch. 13, no. 38), thought the agitation over republican virtue mistaken and misleading. In time, growing economic inequality would strip the problem of any practical significance. "As riches increase and accumulate in few hands; as luxury prevails in society; virtue will be in a greater degree considered as only a graceful appendage of wealth, and the tendency of things will be to depart from the republican standard." There was no point in viewing the political problem as one of virtue and vice contending for preeminence, still less in terms of an especially virtuous class of men struggling against the wicked. In actuality there were different kinds of vice, and here sound policy dictated favoring those kinds that were most likely to promote "the prosperity of the state."

Hamilton's calm acceptance of the ultimate (and not far distant) corruption of the republic was in several respects singular. Most republicans did not view the prospect with comparable equanimity or resignation. Following Harrington and Montesquieu, they tried to discriminate among the probable moral causes of ruin and sought to forfend, counter, or mitigate those causes wherever possible. It was not only revolutionary ardor that led John Adams to proclaim that "a positive Passion for the public good, the public Interest, Honour, Power and Glory [must be] established in the Minds of the People," and that "this public Passion must be Superiour to all private Passions" (no. 9). For in almost the next breath Adams feared that even in most-favored New England "Selfishness and Littleness" were common, the insinuating "Spirit of Commerce . . . rampant," and the whole project of building a republic doubtful.

Their often-remarked preoccupation with corruption testifies to the Founders' keen awareness of the gap between aspirations and the matter at hand. The founding of a durable republic in America was to be the preeminent act of philanthropy. Their grand dreams of setting a universal example and their desperate efforts to cope with a host of difficulties and embarrassments, petty and large, colored their views of today and tomorrow. They searched for means of bringing low circumstance up to the level of high hope. Richard Henry Lee (no. 12) was ready to purge the Continental Congress of its scoffing Mandevilles "who laugh at virtue, and with vain ostentatious display of words will deduce from vice, public good!" Samuel Adams dreaded the new Massachusetts government's easy slide into "Pomp & Parade," seductive invitations from on high to a more general dedication to "Idleness Dissipation & Extravagancy" (no. 14). By 1786 it was clear to James Warren that Massachusetts was "verging to confusion and anarchy," a predictable consequence of the manifest "total Change in principles and Manners" that had taken place during John Adams's absence abroad (30 Apr. 1786). John

Adams was not as gloomy, if only because he could not recall so resplendent a past as Warren had imagined (4 July 1786). Even when events supplied Warren with what he took to be his trump card bearing the face of Capt. Daniel Shays (22 Oct. 1786), Adams still would not fold. Going back to 1760, 1755, even 1745, "You will be very sensible that our Countrymen have never merited the Character of very exalted Virtue. It is not to be expected that they should have grown much better. I find myself very much averse to believe they are grown much worse" (9 Jan. 1787).

Yet it was arguable that the proposed Constitution would establish a government and encourage policies entailing dangers beyond those hitherto known and feared in American political life. Here was indeed a government well mounted, affording a wealth of temptations and opportunities to the ambitious and unscrupulous (see Impartial Examiner, no. 1, 5 Mar. 1788). Patrick Henry saw a "perilous cession of powers," unchecked by any body within the government that might be moved to act for the public good by the "powerful irresistible stimulus of self-love" (see ch. 11, no. 13). Was everything, then, to depend on "fair distinterested patriotism"—on so slender a reed? Madison, as always, drew back from rigid dualism (see ch. 13, no. 36). All was not being ventured on the assumption that one should "expect nothing [in the Congress] but the most exalted integrity and sublime virtue." But then neither should one assume that the electorate would be lacking in "sufficient virtue and intelligence" to choose soberly and well. If it were in fact the case that such discretion was beyond the people's capacity, then Americans would indeed be in a wretched situation and quite plainly unfit for any form of self-government (no. 22).

Securing the republic would demand the attention and care of statesmen and legislators at all levels, as well as of the general community from which they would be drawn. Readers of Burgh, Trenchard and Gordon, Sidney, Harrington, and Machiavelli knew that frequent recurrence to fundamentals, the formative principles of constitutions, was indispensable for safety and preservation. This was as true at the level of a small military unit (no. 5) as it was for the society as a whole (see Virginia Declaration of Rights, art. 15, in ch. 1, no. 3). Then, too, the objects of ambition could be redirected by judicious laws and institutional arrangements, and the pursuit of fopperies or domination replaced by the "sober, industrious and frugal" civility, the "conscious dignity, becoming Freemen" (no. 8). None of this presumed a radical transformation of human nature; projects premised on the sufficiency of high motives were doomed. Patriotism, to be sure, existed and had done much, but on its own could not support the conduct of a great and lasting war; "it will not endure unassisted by Interest" (Washington to Banister, 21 Apr. 1778). From all these devices—the resort to first principles, the taming of ambition, and the unsentimental reliance on self-interest—much good had been achieved and could yet be expected. But most promising of all, at least according to some of the most prominent Founders, was a properly constituted system of education.

The Education of a Self-governing People

Our present-day awareness of propaganda, indoctrination, and even brainwashing trying to pass muster as education complicates the task of recovering the Founders' intentions. The very notion of the political uses of education conjures up visions of Nazi schools for barbarians or heavy-handed re-education camps for slow learners of Marxist truths. But if we resist that easy ellipsis and refrain from reading twentieth-century refinements into eighteenth-century proposals, it is possible to recognize an honorable attempt to deal with a continuing problem. What if the Massachusetts Constitution of 1780 were correct in asserting (no. 13) that "wisdom, and knowledge, as well as virtue, diffused generally among the body of the people [are] necessary for the preservation of their rights and liberties"? Would it then not be a high duty of legislators and magistrates to consider appropriate means of encouraging that diffusion with a view to promoting "sincerity, good humor, and all social affections, and generous sentiments among the people"?

Of course the means of pursuing that great good might take many forms. One critic of the Constitution thought it made better sense to "render the people more capable of being *a law to themselves*"—through an education in Christian piety and morals—than to resort to ever higher toned constitutions in an effort to restrain "turbulent vice and injustice in society." (See Charles Turner, Massachusetts Ratifying Convention, 6 Feb. 1788.) Mercy Warren in her *History of the Rise, Progress and Termination of the American Revolution* (1805) suggested countering the postrevolutionary "relaxation of manners" by catering to individuals' natural desire for distinction. Acts of disinterested greatness were the preserve of only a few; but might not more people be induced to make great exertions for the public good if their ambition to be noticed could be satisfied thereby? It was at least a question to be considered, "how far honorary rewards are consistent with the principles of republicanism." In any event rulers and people alike had to be weaned from unwholesome principles and unwholesome tastes.

This was a subject to which Dr. Benjamin Rush warmed. A properly republican education was vastly more economical than society's time- and money-wasting preoccupation with punishment. And in this task of setting young minds aright, nothing was more useful than religion, the principles of Christianity, and especially the Bible. Since Rush believed that "a Christian cannot fail of being a republican," he was eager to blend "religion, liberty and learning." These would "mutually assist in correcting the abuses, and in improving the good effects of each other." His scheme of enlightened patriotism for Pennsylvania would not eschew the "reinforcement of prejudice," the memories of shared experiences that through "one general, and uniform system of education, will render the mass of the people more homogeneous" and more tractable. A republic depending on the wills of the people must see to it that those wills are themselves republican. With the right mode of education it would be possible "to convert men into republican machines" fit to perform their parts "in the great machine of the government of the state" (no. 30). Rush's plan for a federal university, proposed hot on the heels of the adoption of the Constitution (29 Oct. 1788), reflected his own sense of priorities. Here was one of the more urgent tasks facing the new Congress. "We shall never restore public credit, regulate our militia, build a navy, or revive our commerce until we remove the ignorance and prejudices and change the habits of our citizens"; and to do that the people needed to be inspired with "federal principles." That inspiration would take place in a mode already marked out by Hobbes (*Leviathan*, "Review and Conclusion," end). The true doctrine imbibed by young men during their two or three years' association in a national university would afterwards be disseminated by them "through every county, township, and village of the United States."

Washington himself made a major effort to disseminate federal principles through his Farewell Address (no. 29). It was an argument that took for granted the Americans' love of liberty; what required argument and elaboration was rather the means of securing the blessings of liberty. It is in this context that union is cherished, faction condemned, the spirit of innovation viewed askance, and religion and morality pronounced "indispensable supports," "great Pillars of human happiness." If indeed "virtue or morality is a necessary spring of popular government," then it follows for Washington that institutions for the general diffusion of knowledge must be "an object of primary importance." While Washington's (and Madison's) repeated efforts to establish a national university came to nought (see Farrand 2:321, 616), there were others at work proposing a model of education that might be adopted in all of the states. Among these, Noah Webster and Thomas Jefferson were preeminent.

In Webster's emendation of Montesquieu (see ch. 16, no. 17), not virtue but "a general and tolerably equal distribution of landed property" was the basis of national freedom. Nonetheless, education remained an "auxiliary support," a means whereby the people might remain informed of the rights of men and the principles of government and watchfully jealous of those who sought their support. A closer look at the subject (no. 26) disclosed that a distinctively American education was needed—American history, American principles, learning directed to the kind of lives and habits befitting a republican yeomanry. This ought to be made available to all through a system of universal public education. Webster's speller, reader, dictionary, and even his grammar might fairly be regarded as his practical contribution to that political project.

Jefferson's involvement with public education extended over a half-century, but perhaps he never put the matter more pithily than in his preamble to a Bill for the More General Diffusion of Knowledge (no. 11). All the major ingredients of his educational system are there: the great political end to be sought, the distinct practical means to be used, the enlistment of human inequality in the struggle to safeguard the equal enjoyment of rights, the unwavering dedication to utility. All that followed (and in Jeffer-

son's case it was a great deal), was commentary. His elaborate restatement of the principles of the Bill in *Notes on the State of Virginia* (no. 16) shows in detail Jefferson's understanding of the maxim, "from each according to his abilities, to each according to his needs." Under his pyramidal scheme there would be an annual raking of "the best geniusses . . . from the rubbish" for further education at public expense. That which the rich could buy, the poor could deserve. The largest part of Jefferson's discussion is directed to what *all* would learn, for "of all the views of this law none is more important, none more legitimate, than that of rendering the people the safe, as they are the ultimate, guardians of their own liberty."

Jefferson's later preoccupation with higher education in no way eclipsed his concern for the education of the general population. The snippy self-sufficiency of "our postrevolutionary youth" made more vivid the impoverished state of education in America (no. 32). But while the protracted efforts to found the University of Virginia were Jefferson's response to that social need, the context of higher education, too, remained political and expressed (with appropriate transformations) the urgent civic objectives of primary education (no. 33).

Madison's lifelong partnership with Jefferson never precluded his own gentle glosses to the senior man's orthodoxies, or quiet demurrers to his enthusiastic excesses. To the end, Madison's voice and hands remained his own. His thought about the preservation of the republic was no exception. In his party press essay on the optimal republican distribution of occupations (no. 28), Madison introduced his attempt at "a perfect theory on this subject" with an immediate denial that the theory could conceivably be legislated into practice or that it "ought to be attempted by violence on the will or property of individuals." Yet the political and social benefits of a largely agrarian (though not necessarily noncommercial) life were worth bearing in mind—by "public authority" tempted to "empirical experiments by power" (a nod toward the Secretary of the Treasury) and by ordinary folk choosing freely among alternative occupations. For occupations were ways of life and did not conform equally well to the preconditions of self-government. (This was a truth Madison could have gleaned from Adam Smith's *Wealth of Nations* as readily as from Thomas Jefferson's *Notes on the State of Virginia*.) Sound policy, then, would not force or foster the growth of that sector of the economy least likely to produce good republicans. But, if Madison's silence is meaningful, neither would sound policy try to thwart the growth of such occupations. Over the long run the preservation of free institutions could not depend on the preponderance of farmers and cottage industry. Nor could preservation depend on the support of religion. In truth, any sort of alliance or coalition between government and religion only worked to corrupt both. Because of "a strong bias towards the old error" in some parts of America, public opinion ought to be instructed and confirmed in the truth—verified by the experiences of Virginia and others—that "religion & Govt. will both exist in greater purity, the less they are mixed together" (no. 34).

Like Gouverneur Morris (no. 31), Madison looked for the source of American greatness in the same quarter where he looked for American survival. Perhaps both Founders indicated thereby their belief that what was at issue was not mere survival but the preservation of something especially fine and rare. Morris located that source in something he called national spirit—"a high haughty generous and noble Spirit." In revulsion at one extreme— a hypothetical "Herd of piddling huchstering" wretches— Morris held forth the other extreme, "the brave Band at Thermopylae." America would find itself somewhere on that continuum, but where? Morris's tone is high, the speech is of inflexible will, the resonance is of Greece and Rome.

Madison, in contrast, placed his reliance upon a general system of education, for "popular Government, without popular information, or the means of acquiring it, is but a Prologue to a Farce or a Tragedy; or, perhaps both" (no. 35). Here lay "the best security against crafty & dangerous encroachments on the public liberty." A publicly supported system would counter the monopoly of superior information otherwise enjoyed by the rich and hence reduce their disproportionate influence. But the political benefits accruing from such public support, Madison thought, clearly transcended class interests. For in the last analysis it was here, in the spectacle of "Liberty & Learning, each leaning on the other for their mutual & surest support" that America would establish "its truest and most durable celebrity."

1

JAMES MCHENRY, ANECDOTE
18—
Farrand 3:85

A lady asked Dr. Franklin Well Doctor what have we got a republic or a monarchy—A republic replied the Doctor if you can keep it.

2

JAMES HARRINGTON, COMMONWEALTH OF OCEANA 37–38, 103
1656

But the tillage bringing up a good soldiery brings up a good commonwealth which [Bacon], in the praise of Panurgus, did not [understand], nor Panurgus in deserving that praise. For where the owner of the plough comes to have the sword, too, he will use it in defense of his own; whence it has happened that the people of Oceana, in proportion to their property, have been always free. And the genius of this nation has ever had some resemblance with that of ancient Italy, which was wholly addicted to commonwealths, and where Rome came to make the greatest account of her rustic tribes and to call her consuls from the plough. For, in the way of parliaments, which was the government of this realm, men of country lives have been still entrusted with the greatest affairs, and the people have constantly had an aversion from the ways of the court; ambition, loving to be gay and to fawn, has been a gallantry looked upon as having something in it of the livery and husbandry or the country way of life, though of a grosser spinning, as the best stuff of a commonwealth according to Aristotle (*Agricolarum democratica respublica op-*

tima), such a one being the most obstinate assertress of her liberty and the least subject to innovation or turbulency. Wherefore till the foundations (as will be hereafter shown) were removed, this people was observed to be the least subject to shakings and turbulency of any. Whereas commonwealths upon which the city life has had the stronger influence, as Athens, have seldom or never been quiet, but at best are found to have injured their own business by overdoing it. Whence the urban tribes of Rome consisting of the *turba forensis*, libertines that had received their freedom by manumission, were of no reputation in comparison of the rustics. It is true that with Venice it may seem to be otherwise, in regard the gentlemen (for so are all such called as have right unto that government) are wholly addicted to the city life; but then the *turba forensis*, the secretaries, *cittadini*, with the rest of the populace, are wholly excluded. Otherwise a commonwealth, consisting but of one city, would doubtless be stormy, in regard that ambition would be every man's trade; but where it consists of a country, the plough in the hands of the owner finds him a better calling and produces the most innocent and steady genius of a commonwealth, such as is that of Oceana.

. . . . .

A people (says Machiavelli) that is corrupt is not capable of a commonwealth. But in showing what a corrupt people is, he has either involved himself or me, nor can I otherwise come out of the labyrinth than by saying that, the balance altering, a people as to the foregoing government must of necessity be corrupt. But corruption in this sense signifies no more than that the *corruption of one government* (as in natural bodies) *is the generation of another.* Wherefore, if the balance alter from monarchy, the corruption of the people in this case is that which makes them capable of a commonwealth. But whereas I am not ignorant that the corruption which he means is in manners, this also is from the balance. For the balance swaying from monarchical into popular abates the luxury of the nobility and, enriching the people, brings the government from a more private to a more public interest, which coming nearer, as has been shown, to justice and right reason, the people upon a like alteration is so far from such corruption of manners as should render them incapable of a commonwealth, that of necessity they must thereby contract such reformation of manners as will bear no other kind of government. On the other side, where the balance changes from popular to oligarchical or monarchical, the public interest with the reason and justice included in the same becomes more private, luxury is introduced in the place of temperance, and servitude in that of freedom. Which causes such a corruption of manners both in the nobility and the people as, by the example of Rome in the time of the triumvirate, is more at large discovered by the author to have been altogether incapable of a commonwealth.

3

MONTESQUIEU, SPIRIT OF LAWS, NOTES; BK. 3,
CHS. 1–9; BK. 4, CHS. 4–5; BK. 5, CHS. 1–7;
BK. 7, CHS. 1–2; BK. 8, CHS. 1–3
1748

Author's Explanatory Notes

1. For the better understanding of the first four books of this work, it is to be observed that what I distinguish by the name of virtue, in a republic, is the love of one's country, that is, the love of equality. It is not a moral, nor a Christian, but a political virtue; and it is the spring which sets the republican government in motion, as honor is the spring which gives motion to monarchy. Hence it is that I have distinguished the love of one's country, and of equality, by the appellation of political virtue. My ideas are new, and therefore I have been obliged to find new words, or to give new acceptations to old terms, in order to convey my meaning. They, who are unacquainted with this particular, have made me say most strange absurdities, such as would be shocking in any part of the world, because in all countries and governments morality is requisite.

2. The reader is also to notice that there is a vast difference between saying that a certain quality, modification of the mind, or virtue, is not the spring by which government is actuated, and affirming that it is not to be found in that government. Were I to say such a wheel or such a pinion is not the spring which sets the watch going, can you infer thence that it is not to be found in the watch? So far is it from being true that the moral and Christian virtues are excluded from monarchy, that even political virtue is not excluded. In a word, honor is found in a republic, though its spring be political virtue; and political virtue is found in a monarchical government, though it be actuated by honor.

To conclude, the honest man of whom we treat in the third book, chapter 5, is not the Christian, but the political honest man, who is possessed of the political virtue there mentioned. He is the man who loves the laws of his country, and who is actuated by the love of those laws. I have set these matters in a clearer light in the present edition by giving a more precise meaning to my expression: and in most places where I have made use of the word virtue I have taken care to add the term political.

[Book 3]

1.—Difference between the Nature and Principle of Government

Having examined the laws in relation to the nature of each government, we must investigate those which relate to its principle.

There is this difference between the nature and principle* of government, that the former is that by which it is constituted, the latter that by which it is made to act. One is its particular structure, and the other the human passions which set it in motion.

Now, laws ought no less to relate to the principle than to the nature of each government. We must, therefore, inquire into this principle, which shall be the subject of this third book.

2.—Of the Principle of different Governments

I have already observed that it is the nature of a republican government, that either the collective body of the people, or particular families, should be possessed of the supreme power; of a monarchy that the prince should have this power, but in the execution of it should be directed by established laws; of a despotic government, that a single person should rule according to his own will and caprice. This enables me to discover their three principles; which are thence naturally derived. I shall begin with a republican government, and in particular with that of democracy.

3.—Of the Principle of Democracy

There is no great share of probity necessary to support a monarchical or despotic government. The force of laws in one, and the prince's arm in the other, are sufficient to direct and maintain the whole. But in a popular state, one spring more is necessary, namely, virtue.

What I have here advanced is confirmed by the unanimous testimony of historians, and is extremely agreeable to the nature of things. For it is clear that in a monarchy, where he who commands the execution of the laws generally thinks himself above them, there is less need of virtue than in a popular government, where the person intrusted with the execution of the laws is sensible of his being subject to their direction.

Clear is it also that a monarch who, through bad advice or indolence, ceases to enforce the execution of the laws, may easily repair the evil; he has only to follow other advice, or to shake off this indolence. But when, in a popular government, there is a suspension of the laws, as this can proceed only from the corruption of the republic, the state is certainly undone.

A very droll spectacle it was in the last century to behold the impotent efforts of the English towards the establishment of democracy. As they who had a share in the direction of public affairs were void of virtue; as their ambition

---

*This is a very important distinction, whence I shall draw many consequences; for it is the key of an infinite number of laws.

was inflamed by the success of the most daring of their members; as the prevailing parties were successively animated by the spirit of faction, the government was continually changing: the people, amazed at so many revolutions, in vain attempted to erect a commonwealth. At length, when the country had undergone the most violent shocks, they were obliged to have recourse to the very government which they had so wantonly proscribed.

When Sylla thought of restoring Rome to her liberty, this unhappy city was incapable of receiving that blessing. She had only the feeble remains of virtue, which were continually diminishing. Instead of being roused from her lethargy by Caesar, Tiberius, Caius Claudius, Nero, and Domitian, she riveted every day her chains; if she struck some blows, her aim was at the tyrant, not at the tyranny.

The politic Greeks, who lived under a popular government, knew no other support than virtue. The modern inhabitants of that country are entirely taken up with manufacture, commerce, finances, opulence, and luxury.

When virtue is banished, ambition invades the minds of those who are disposed to receive it, and avarice possesses the whole community. The objects of their desires are changed; what they were fond of before has become indifferent; they were free while under the restraint of laws, but they would fain now be free to act against law; and as each citizen is like a slave who has run away from his master, that which was a maxim of equity he calls rigor; that which was a rule of action he styles constraint; and to precaution he gives the name of fear. Frugality, and not the thirst of gain, now passes for avarice. Formerly the wealth of individuals constituted the public treasure; but now this has become the patrimony of private persons. The members of the commonwealth riot on the public spoils, and its strength is only the power of a few, and the license of many.

Athens was possessed of the same number of forces when she triumphed so gloriously as when with such infamy she was enslaved. She had twenty thousand citizens, when she defended the Greeks against the Persians, when she contended for empire with Sparta, and invaded Sicily. She had twenty thousand when Demetrius Phalereus numbered them, as slaves are told by the head in a market place. When Philip attempted to lord it over Greece, and appeared at the gates of Athens, she had even then lost nothing but time. We may see in Demosthenes how difficult it was to awaken her; she dreaded Philip, not as the enemy of her liberty, but of her pleasures. This famous city, which had withstood so many defeats, and having been so often destroyed had as often risen out of her ashes, was overthrown at Chaeronea, and at one blow deprived of all hopes of resource. What does it avail her that Philip sends back her prisoners, if he does not return her men? It was ever after as easy to triumph over the forces of Athens as it had been difficult to subdue her virtue.

How was it possible for Carthage to maintain her ground? When Hannibal, upon his being made praetor, endeavored to hinder the magistrates from plundering the republic, did not they complain of him to the Romans? Wretches, who would fain be citizens without a city, and be beholden for their riches to their very destroyers! Rome

soon insisted upon having three hundred of their principal citizens as hostages; she obliged them next to surrender their arms and ships; and then she declared war. From the desperate efforts of this defenceless city, one may judge of what she might have performed in her full vigor, and assisted by virtue.

4.—Of the Principle of Aristocracy

As virtue is necessary in a popular government, it is requisite also in an aristocracy. True it is that in the latter it is not so absolutely requisite.

The people, who in respect to the nobility are the same as the subjects with regard to a monarch, are restrained by their laws. They have, therefore, less occasion for virtue than the people in a democracy. But how are the nobility to be restrained? They who are to execute the laws against their colleagues will immediately perceive that they are acting against themselves. Virtue is therefore necessary in this body, from the very nature of the constitution.

An aristocratic government has an inherent vigor, unknown to democracy. The nobles form a body, who by their prerogative, and for their own particular interest, restrain the people; it is sufficient that there are laws in being to see them executed.

But easy as it may be for the body of the nobles to restrain the people, it is difficult to restrain themselves. Such is the nature of this constitution, that it seems to subject the very same persons to the power of the laws, and at the same time to exempt them.

Now such a body as this can restrain itself only in two ways; either by a very eminent virtue, which puts the nobility in some measure on a level with the people, and may be the means of forming a great republic; or by an inferior virtue, which puts them at least upon a level with one another, and upon this their preservation depends.

Moderation is therefore the very soul of this government; a moderation, I mean, founded on virtue, not that which proceeds from indolence and pusillanimity.

5.—That Virtue is not the Principle of a Monarchical Government

In monarchies policy effects great things with as little virtue as possible. Thus in the nicest machines, art has reduced the number of movements, springs, and wheels.

The state subsists independently of the love of our country, of the thirst of true glory, of self-denial, of the sacrifice of our dearest interests, and of all those heroic virtues which we admire in the ancients, and to us are known only by tradition.

The laws supply here the place of those virtues; they are by no means wanted, and the state dispenses with them: an action performed here in secret is in some measure of no consequence.

Though all crimes be in their own nature public, yet there is a distinction between crimes really public and those that are private, which are so called because they are more injurious to individuals than to the community.

Now in republics private crimes are more public, that is, they attack the constitution more than they do individuals;

and in monarchies, public crimes are more private, that is, they are more prejudicial to private people than to the constitution.

I beg that no one will be offended with what I have been saying; my observations are founded on the unanimous testimony of historians. I am not ignorant that virtuous princes are so very rare; but I venture to affirm, that in a monarchy it is extremely difficult for the people to be virtuous.*

Let us compare what the historians of all ages have asserted concerning the courts of monarchs; let us recollect the conversations and sentiments of people of all countries, in respect to the wretched character of courtiers, and we shall find that these are not airy speculations, but truths confirmed by a sad and melancholy experience.

Ambition in idleness; meanness mixed with pride; a desire of riches without industry; aversion to truth; flattery, perfidy, violation of engagements, contempt of civil duties, fear of the prince's virtue, hope from his weakness, but, above all, a perpetual ridicule cast upon virtue, are, I think, the characteristics by which most courtiers in all ages and countries have been constantly distinguished. Now, it is exceedingly difficult for the leading men of the nation to be knaves, and the inferior sort to be honest; for the former to be cheats, and the latter to rest satisfied with being only dupes.

But if there should chance to be some unlucky honest man among the people, Cardinal Richelieu, in his political testament, seems to hint that a prince should take care not to employ him. So true is it that virtue is not the spring of this government! It is not indeed excluded, but it is not the spring of government.

6.—In what Manner Virtue is Supplied in a Monarchical Government

But it is high time for me to have done with this subject, lest I should be suspected of writing a satire against monarchical government. Far be it from me; if monarchy wants one spring, it is provided with another. Honor, that is, the prejudice of every person and rank, supplies the place of the political virtue of which I have been speaking, and is everywhere her representative: here it is capable of inspiring the most glorious actions, and, joined with the force of laws, may lead us to the end of government as well as virtue itself.

Hence, in well-regulated monarchies, they are almost all good subjects, and very few good men; for to be a good man, a good intention is necessary, and we should love our country, not so much on our own account, as out of regard to the community.

7.—Of the Principle of Monarchy

A monarchical government supposes, as we have already observed, pre-eminences and ranks, as likewise a noble descent. Now, since it is the nature of honor to aspire to pre-

*I speak here of political virtue, which is also moral virtue as it is directed to the public good; very little of private moral virtue, and not at all of that virtue which relates to revealed truths. This will appear better, book V., chap. 2.

ferments and titles, it is properly placed in this government.

Ambition is pernicious in a republic. But in a monarchy it has some good effects; it gives life to the government, and is attended with this advantage, that it is in no way dangerous, because it may be continually checked.

It is with this kind of government as with the system of the universe, in which there is a power that constantly repels all bodies from the centre, and a power of gravitation that attracts them to it. Honor sets all the parts of the body politic in motion, and by its very action connects them; thus each individual advances the public good, while he only thinks of promoting his own interest.

True it is, that philosophically speaking it is a false honor which moves all the parts of the government; but even this false honor is as useful to the public as true honor could possibly be to private persons.

Is it not very exacting to oblige men to perform the most difficult actions, such as require an extraordinary exertion of fortitude and resolution, without other recompense than that of glory and applause?

8.—That Honor is not the Principle of Despotic Government

Honor is far from being the principle of despotic government: mankind being here all upon a level, no one person can prefer himself to another; and as on the other hand they are all slaves, they can give themselves no sort of preference.

Besides, as honor has its laws and rules; as it knows not how to submit; as it depends in a great measure on a man's own caprice, and not on that of another person: it can be found only in countries in which the constitution is fixed, and where they are governed by settled laws.

How can despotism abide with honor? The one glories in the contempt of life; and the other is founded on the power of taking it away. How can honor, on the other hand, bear with despotism? The former has its fixed rules, and peculiar caprices; but the latter is directed by no rule, and its own caprices are subversive of all others.

Honor, therefore, a thing unknown in arbitrary governments, some of which have not even a proper word to express it, is the prevailing principle in monarchies; here it gives life to the whole body politic, to the laws, and even to the virtues themselves.

9.—Of the Principle of Despotic Government

As virtue is necessary in a republic, and in a monarchy honor, so fear is necessary in a despotic government: with regard to virtue, there is no occasion for it, and honor would be extremely dangerous.

Here the immense power of the prince devolves entirely upon those whom he is pleased to intrust with the administration. Persons capable of setting a value upon themselves would be likely to create disturbances. Fear must therefore depress their spirits, and extinguish even the least sense of ambition.

A moderate government may, whenever it pleases, and without the least danger, relax its springs. It supports itself by the laws, and by its own internal strength. But when a despotic prince ceases for one single moment to uplift his arm, when he cannot instantly demolish those whom he has intrusted with the first employments, all is over: for as fear, the spring of this government, no longer subsists, the people are left without a protector.

It is probably in this sense the Cadis maintained that the Grand Seignior was not obliged to keep his word or oath, when he limited thereby his authority.

It is necessary that the people should be judged by laws, and the great men by the caprice of the prince, that the lives of the lowest subject should be safe, and the pasha's head ever in danger. We cannot mention these monstrous governments without horror. The Sophi of Persia, dethroned in our days by Mahomet, the son of Miriveis, saw the constitution subverted before this resolution, because he had been too sparing of blood.

History informs us that the horrid cruelties of Domitian struck such a terror into the governors, that the people recovered themselves a little during his reign. Thus a torrent overflows one side of a country, and on the other leaves fields untouched, where the eye is refreshed by the prospect of fine meadows.

[Book 4]

4.—Difference between the Effects of Ancient and Modern Education

Most of the ancients lived under governments that had virtue for their principle; and when this was in full vigor they performed actions unusual in our times, and at which our narrow minds are astonished.

Another advantage their education possessed over ours was that it never could be effaced by contrary impressions. Epaminondas, the last year of his life, said, heard, beheld, and performed the very same things as at the age in which he received the first principles of his education.

In our days we receive three different or contrary educations, namely, of our parents, of our masters, and of the world. What we learn in the latter effaces all the ideas of the former. This, in some measure, arises from the contrast we experience between our religious and worldly engagements, a thing unknown to the ancients.

5.—Of Education in a Republican Government

It is in a republican government that the whole power of education is required. The fear of despotic governments naturally arises of itself amidst threats and punishments; the honor of monarchies is favored by the passions, and favors them in its turn; but virtue is a self-renunciation, which is ever arduous and painful.

This virtue may be defined as the love of the laws and of our country. As such love requires a constant preference of public to private interest, it is the source of all private virtues; for they are nothing more than this very preference itself.

This love is peculiar to democracies. In these alone the government is intrusted to private citizens. Now, a government is like every thing else: to preserve it we must love it.

Has it ever been known that kings were not fond of monarchy, or that despotic princes hated arbitrary power?

Every thing, therefore, depends on establishing this love in a republic; and to inspire it ought to be the principal business of education: but the surest way of instilling it into children is for parents to set them an example.

People have it generally in their power to communicate their ideas to their children; but they are still better able to transfuse their passions.

If it happens otherwise, it is because the impressions made at home are effaced by those they have received abroad.

It is not the young people that degenerate; they are not spoiled till those of maturer age are already sunk into corruption.

[Book 5]

1.—Idea of this Book

That the laws of education should relate to the principle of each government has been shown in the preceding book. Now the same may be said of those which the legislator gives to the whole society. The relation of laws to this principle strengthens the several springs of government; and this principle derives thence, in its turn, a new degree of vigor. And thus it is in mechanics, that action is always followed by reaction.

Our design is, to examine this relation in each government, beginning with the republican state, the principle of which is virtue.

2.—What is meant by Virtue in a political State

Virtue in a republic is a most simple thing; it is a love of the republic; it is a sensation, and not a consequence of acquired knowledge, a sensation that may be felt by the meanest as well as by the highest person in the state. When the common people adopt good maxims, they adhere to them more steadily than those whom we call gentlemen. It is very rarely that corruption commences with the former: nay, they frequently derive from their imperfect light a stronger attachment to the established laws and customs.

The love of our country is conducive to a purity of morals, and the latter is again conducive to the former. The less we are able to satisfy our private passions, the more we abandon ourselves to those of a general nature. How comes it that monks are so fond of their order? It is owing to the very cause that renders the order insupportable. Their rule debars them from all those things by which the ordinary passions are fed; there remains therefore only this passion for the very rule that torments them. The more austere it is, that is, the more it curbs their inclinations, the more force it gives to the only passion left them.

3.—What is meant by a Love of the Republic in a Democracy

A love of the republic in a democracy is a love of the democracy; as the latter is that of equality.

A love of the democracy is likewise that of frugality.

Since every individual ought here to enjoy the same happiness and the same advantages, they should consequently taste the same pleasures and form the same hopes, which cannot be expected but from a general frugality.

The love of equality in a democracy limits ambition to the sole desire, to the sole happiness, of doing greater services to our country than the rest of our fellow-citizens. They cannot all render her equal services, but they all ought to serve her with equal alacrity. At our coming into the world, we contract an immense debt to our country, which we can never discharge.

Hence distinctions here arise from the principle of equality, even when it seems to be removed by signal services or superior abilities.

The love of frugality limits the desire of having to the study of procuring necessaries to our family, and superfluities to our country. Riches give a power which a citizen cannot use for himself, for then he would be no longer equal. They likewise procure pleasures which he ought not to enjoy, because these would be also repugnant to the equality.

Thus well-regulated democracies, by establishing domestic frugality, made way at the same time for public expenses, as was the case at Rome and Athens, when magnificence and profusion arose from the very fund of frugality. And as religion commands us to have pure and unspotted hands when we make our offerings to the gods, the laws required a frugality of life to enable them to be liberal to our country.

The good sense and happiness of individuals depend greatly upon the mediocrity of their abilities and fortunes. Therefore, as a republic, where the laws have placed many in a middling station, is composed of wise men, it will be wisely governed; as it is composed of happy men, it will be extremely happy.

4.—In what Manner the Love of Equality and Frugality is inspired

The love of equality and of a frugal economy is greatly excited by equality and frugality themselves, in societies where both these virtues are established by law.

In monarchies and despotic governments, nobody aims at equality; this does not so much as enter their thoughts; they all aspire to superiority. People of the very lowest condition desire to emerge from their obscurity, only to lord it over their fellow-subjects.

It is the same with respect to frugality. To love it, we must practise and enjoy it. It is not those who are enervated by pleasure that are fond of a frugal life; were this natural and common, Alcibiades would never have been the admiration of the universe. Neither is it those who envy or admire the luxury of the great; people that have present to their view none but rich men, or men miserable like themselves, detest their wretched condition, without loving or knowing the real term or point of misery.

A true maxim it is, therefore, that in order to love equality and frugality in a republic, these virtues must have been previously established by law.

5.—In what Manner the Laws establish Equality in a Democracy

Some ancient legislators, as Lycurgus and Romulus, made an equal division of lands. A settlement of this kind can never take place except upon the foundation of a new republic; or when the old one is so corrupt, and the minds of the people are so disposed, that the poor think themselves obliged to demand, and the rich obliged to consent to, a remedy of this nature.

If the legislator, in making a division of this kind, does not enact laws at the same time to support it, he forms only a temporary constitution; inequality will break in where the laws have not precluded it, and the republic will be utterly undone.

Hence for the preservation of this equality it is absolutely necessary there should be some regulation in respect to women's dowries donations, successions, testamentary settlements, and all other forms of contracting. For were we once allowed to dispose of our property to whom and how we pleased, the will of each individual would disturb the order of the fundamental law.

. . . . .

Though real equality be the very soul of a democracy, it is so difficult to establish, that an extreme exactness in this respect would not be always convenient. Sufficient is it to establish a census, which shall reduce or fix the differences to a certain point: it is afterwards the business of particular laws to level, as it were, the inequalities, by the duties laid upon the rich, and by the ease afforded to the poor. It is moderate riches alone that can give or suffer this sort of compensation; for as to men of overgrown estates, everything which does not contribute to advance their power and honor is considered by them as an injury.

All inequality in democracies ought to be derived from the nature of the government, and even from the principle of equality. For example, it may be apprehended that people who are obliged to live by their labor would be too much impoverished by a public employment, or neglect the duties attending it; that artisans would grow insolent, and that too great a number of freemen would overpower the ancient citizens. In this case the equality in a democracy may be suppressed for the good of the state. But this is only an apparent equality; for a man ruined by a public employment would be in a worse condition than his fellow-citizens; and this same man, being obliged to neglect his duty, would reduce the rest to a worse condition than himself, and so on.

6.—In what Manner the Laws ought to maintain Frugality in a Democracy

It is not sufficient in a well-regulated democracy that the divisions of land be equal; they ought also to be small, as was customary among the Romans. "God forbid," said Curius to his soldiers, "that a citizen should look upon that as a small piece of land which is sufficient to maintain him."

As equality of fortunes supports frugality, so the latter

maintains the former. These things, though in themselves different, are of such a nature as to be unable to subsist separately; they reciprocally act upon each other; if one withdraws itself from a democracy, the other surely follows it.

True is it that when a democracy is founded on commerce, private people may acquire vast riches without a corruption of morals. This is because the spirit of commerce is naturally attended with that of frugality, economy, moderation, labor, prudence, tranquillity, order, and rule. So long as this spirit subsists, the riches it produces have no bad effect. The mischief is, when excessive wealth destroys the spirit of commerce, then it is that the inconveniences of inequality begin to be felt.

In order to support this spirit, commerce should be carried on by the principal citizens; this should be their sole aim and study; this the chief object of the laws: and these very laws, by dividing the estates of individuals in proportion to the increase of commerce, should set every poor citizen so far at his ease as to be able to work like the rest, and every wealthy citizen in such a mediocrity as to be obliged to take some pains either in preserving or acquiring a fortune.

It is an excellent law in a trading republic to make an equal division of the paternal estate among the children. The consequence of this is, that how great soever a fortune the father has made, his children, being not so rich as he, are induced to avoid luxury, and to work as he has done. I speak here only of trading republics; as to those that have no commerce, the legislator must pursue quite different measures.

In Greece there were two sorts of republics: the one military, like Sparta; the other commercial, as Athens. In the former, the citizens were obliged to be idle; in the latter, endeavors were used to inspire them with the love of industry and labor. Solon made idleness a crime, and insisted that each citizen should give an account of his manner of getting a livelihood. And, indeed, in a well-regulated democracy, where people's expenses should extend only to what is necessary, every one ought to have it; for how should their wants be otherwise supplied?

7.—Other Methods of favoring the Principle of Democracy

An equal division of lands cannot be established in all democracies. There are some circumstances in which a regulation of this nature would be impracticable, dangerous, and even subversive of the constitution. We are not always obliged to proceed to extremes. If it appears that this division of lands, which was designed to preserve the people's morals, does not suit the democracy, recourse must be had to other methods.

If a permanent body be established to serve as a rule and pattern of manners; a senate, to which years, virtue, gravity, and eminent services procure admittance; the senators, by being exposed to public view like the statues of the gods, must naturally inspire every family with sentiments of virtue.

Above all, this senate must steadily adhere to the ancient institutions, and mind that the people and the magistrates never swerve from them.

The preservation of the ancient customs is a very considerable point in respect to manners. Since a corrupt people seldom perform any memorable actions, seldom establish societies, build cities, or enact laws; on the contrary, since most institutions are derived from people whose manners are plain and simple, to keep up the ancient customs is the way to preserve the original purity of morals.

Besides, if by some revolution the state has happened to assume a new form, this seldom can be effected without infinite pains and labor, and hardly ever by idle and debauched persons. Even those who had been the instruments of the revolution were desirous it should be relished, which is difficult to compass without good laws. Hence it is that ancient institutions generally tend to reform the people's manners, and those of modern date to corrupt them. In the course of a long administration, the descent to vice is insensible; but there is no reascending to virtue without making the most generous efforts.

It has been questioned whether the members of the senate we are speaking of ought to be for life or only chosen for a time. Doubtless they ought to be for life, as was the custom at Rome, at Sparta, and even at Athens. For we must not confound the senate at Athens, which was a body that changed every three months, with the Areopagus, whose members, as standing patterns, were established for life.

Let this be, therefore, a general maxim; that in a senate designed to be a rule, and the depository, as it were, of manners, the members ought to be chosen for life: in a senate intended for the administration of affairs, the members may be changed.

The spirit, said Aristotle, waxes old as well as the body. This reflection holds good only in regard to a single magistrate, but cannot be applied to a senatorial assembly.

At Athens, besides the Areopagus, there were guardians of the public morals, as well as of the laws. At Sparta, all the old men were censors. At Rome, the censorship was committed to two particular magistrates. As the senate watched over the people, the censors were to have an eye over the people and the senate. Their office was, to reform the corruptions of the republic, to stigmatize indolence, to censure neglects, and to correct mistakes; as to flagrant crimes, these were left to the punishment of the laws.

That Roman law which required the accusations in cases of adultery to be public was admirably well calculated for preserving the purity of morals; it intimidated married women, as well as those who were to watch over their conduct.

Nothing contributes more to the preservation of morals than an extreme subordination of the young to the old. Thus they are both restrained, the former by their respect for those of advanced age, and the latter by their regard for themselves.

Nothing gives a greater force to the laws than a perfect subordination between the citizens and the magistrate. "The great difference which Lycurgus established between Sparta and the other cities," says Xenophon, "consists chiefly in the obedience the citizens show to their laws;

they run when the magistrate calls them. But at Athens a rich man would be highly displeased to be thought dependent on the magistrate."

Paternal authority is likewise of great use towards the preservation of morals. We have already observed, that in a republic there is not so coercive a force as in other governments. The laws must, therefore, endeavor to supply this defect by some means or other; and this is done by paternal authority.

Fathers at Rome had the power of life and death over their children. At Sparta, every father had a right to correct another man's child.

Paternal authority ended at Rome together with the republic. In monarchies, where such a purity of morals is not required, they are controlled by no other authority than that of the magistrates.

The Roman laws, which accustomed young people to dependence, established a long minority. Perhaps we are mistaken in conforming to this custom; there is no necessity for so much constraint in monarchies.

This very subordination in a republic might make it necessary for the father to continue in the possession of his children's fortune during life, as was the custom at Rome. But this is not agreeable to the spirit of monarchy.

[Book 7]

1.—Of Luxury

Luxury is ever in proportion to the inequality of fortunes. If the riches of a state are equally divided there will be no luxury; for it is founded merely on the conveniences acquired by the labor of others.

In order to have this equal distribution of riches, the law ought to give to each man only what is necessary for nature. If they exceed these bounds, some will spend, and others will acquire, by which means an inequality will be established.

Supposing what is necessary for the support of nature to be equal to a given sum, the luxury of those who have only what is barely necessary will be equal to a cipher: if a person happens to have double that sum, his luxury will be equal to one; he that has double the latter's substance will have a luxury equal to three; if this be still doubled, there will be a luxury equal to seven; so that the property of the subsequent individual being always supposed double to that of the preceding, the luxury will increase double, and a unit be always added, in this progression, 0, 1, 3, 7, 15, 31, 63, 127.

In Plato's republic, luxury might have been exactly calculated. There were four sorts of censuses or rates of estates. The first was exactly the term beyond poverty, the second was double, the third triple, the fourth quadruple to the first. In the first census, luxury was equal to a cipher; in the second to one, in the third to two, in the fourth to three: and thus it followed in an arithmetical proportion.

Considering the luxury of different nations with respect to one another, it is in each state a compound proportion to the inequality of fortunes among the subjects, and to the inequality of wealth in different states. In Poland, for example, there is an extreme inequality of fortunes, but the poverty of the whole hinders them from having so much luxury as in a more opulent government.

Luxury is also in proportion to the populousness of the towns, and especially of the capital; so that it is in a compound proportion to the riches of the state, to the inequality of private fortunes, and to the number of people settled in particular places.

In proportion to the populousness of towns, the inhabitants are filled with notions of vanity and actuated by an ambition of distinguishing themselves by trifles.* If they are very numerous, and most of them strangers to one another, their vanity redoubles, because there are greater hopes of success. As luxury inspires these hopes, each man assumes the marks of a superior condition. But by endeavoring thus at distinction, every one becomes equal, and distinction ceases; as all are desirous of respect, nobody is regarded.

Hence arises a general inconvenience. Those who excel in a profession set what value they please on their labor; this example is followed by people of inferior abilities, and then there is an end of all proportion between our wants and the means of satisfying them. When I am forced to go to law, I must be able to fee counsel; when I am sick, I must have it in my power to fee a physician.

It is the opinion of several, that the assemblage of so great a multitude of people in capital cities is an obstruction to commerce, because the inhabitants are no longer at a proper distance from each other. But I cannot think so; for men have more desires, more wants, more fancies, when they live together.

2.—Of sumptuary Laws in a Democracy

We have observed that in a republic, where riches are equally divided, there can be no such thing as luxury; and as we have shown in Book V., that this equal distribution constitutes the excellence of a republican government; hence it follows, that the less luxury there is in a republic, the more it is perfect. There was none among the old Romans, none among the Lacedaemonians; and in republics where this equality is not quite lost, the spirit of commerce, industry, and virtue renders every man able and willing to live on his own property, and consequently prevents the growth of luxury.

The laws concerning the new division of lands, insisted upon so eagerly in some republics, were of the most salutary nature. They are dangerous, only as they are sudden. By reducing instantly the wealth of some, and increasing that of others, they form a revolution in each family, and must produce a general one in the state.

In proportion as luxury gains ground in a republic, the minds of the people are turned towards their particular interests. Those who are allowed only what is necessary

---

*"In large and populous cities," says the author of the "Fable of the Bees," tom. i. p. 133, "they wear clothes above their rank, and, consequently, have the pleasure of being esteemed by a vast majority, not as what they are, but what they appear to be.—They have the satisfaction of imagining that they appear what they would be: which, to weak minds, is a pleasure almost as substantial as they could reap from the very accomplishment of their wishes."

have nothing but their own reputation and their country's glory in view. But a soul depraved by luxury has many other desires, and soon becomes an enemy to the laws that confine it. The luxury in which the garrison of Rhegium began to live was the cause of their massacring the inhabitants.

No sooner were the Romans corrupted than their desires became boundless and immense. Of this we may judge by the price they set on things. A pitcher of Falernian wine was sold for a hundred Roman denarii; a barrel of salt meat from the kingdom of Pontus cost four hundred; a good cook four talents; and for boys, no price was reckoned too great. When the whole world, impelled by the force of corruption, is immersed in voluptuousness what must then become of virtue?

[Book 8]

1.—General Idea of this Book

The corruption of every government generally begins with that of its principles.

2.—Of the Corruption of the Principles of Democracy

The principle of democracy is corrupted not only when the spirit of equality is extinct, but likewise when they fall into a spirit of extreme equality, and when each citizen would fain be upon a level with those whom he has chosen to command him. Then the people, incapable of bearing the very power they have delegated, want to manage everything themselves, to debate for the senate, to execute for the magistrate, and to decide for the judges.

When this is the case, virtue can no longer subsist in the republic. The people are desirous of exercising the functions of the magistrates, who cease to be revered. The deliberations of the senate are slighted; all respect is then laid aside for the senators, and consequently for old age. If there is no more respect for old age, there will be none presently for parents; deference to husbands will be likewise thrown off, and submission to masters. This license will soon become general, and the trouble of command be as fatiguing as that of obedience. Wives, children, slaves will shake off all subjection. No longer will there be any such thing as manners, order, or virtue.

We find in Xenophon's Banquet a very lively description of a republic in which the people abused their equality. Each guest gives in his turn the reason why he is satisfied. "Content I am," says Chamides, "because of my poverty. When I was rich, I was obliged to pay my court to informers, knowing I was more liable to be hurt by them than capable of doing them harm. The republic constantly demanded some new tax of me; and I could not decline paying. Since I have grown poor, I have acquired authority; nobody threatens me; I rather threaten others. I can go or stay where I please. The rich already rise from their seats and give me the way. I am a king, I was before a slave: I paid taxes to the republic, now it maintains me: I am no longer afraid of losing: but I hope to acquire."

The people fall into this misfortune, when those in whom they confide, desirous of concealing their own corruption, endeavor to corrupt them. To disguise their own ambition, they speak to them only of the grandeur of the state; to conceal their own avarice, they incessantly flatter theirs.

The corruption will increase among the corruptors, and likewise among those who are already corrupted. The people will divide the public money among themselves, and, having added the administration of affairs to their indolence, will be for blending their poverty with the amusements of luxury. But with their indolence and luxury, nothing but the public treasure will be able to satisfy their demands.

We must not be surprised to see their suffrages given for money. It is impossible to make great largesses to the people without great extortion: and to compass this, the state must be subverted. The greater the advantages they seem to derive from their liberty, the nearer they approach towards the critical moment of losing it. Petty tyrants arise who have all the vices of a single tyrant. The small remains of liberty soon become insupportable; a single tyrant starts up, and the people are stripped of every thing, even of the profits of their corruption.

Democracy has, therefore, two excesses to avoid—the spirit of inequality, which leads to aristocracy or monarchy, and the spirit of extreme equality, which leads to despotic power, as the latter is completed by conquest.

True it is, that those who corrupted the Greek republics did not always become tyrants. This was because they had a greater passion for eloquence than for the military art. Besides there reigned an implacable hatred in the breasts of the Greeks against those who subverted a republican government; and for this reason anarchy degenerated into annihilation, instead of being changed into tyranny.

But Syracuse being situated in the midst of a great number of petty states, whose government had been changed from oligarchy to tyranny, and being governed by a senate scarcely ever mentioned in history, underwent such miseries as are the consequence of a more than ordinary corruption. This city, ever a prey to licentiousness, or oppression, equally laboring under the sudden and alternate succession of liberty and servitude, and notwithstanding her external strength, constantly determined to a revolution by the least foreign power—this city, I say, had in her bosom an immense multitude of people, whose fate it was to have always this cruel alternative, either of choosing a tyrant to govern them, or of acting the tyrant themselves.

3.—Of the Spirit of extreme Equality

As distant as heaven is from earth, so is the true spirit of equality from that of extreme equality. The former does not imply that everybody should command, or that no one should be commanded, but that we obey or command our equals. It endeavors not to shake off the authority of a master, but that its masters should be none but its equals.

In the state of nature, indeed, all men are born equal, but they cannot continue in this equality. Society makes them lose it, and they recover it only by the protection of the laws.

Such is the difference between a well-regulated democracy and one that is not so, that in the former men are equal only as citizens, but in the latter they are equal also as magistrates, as senators, as judges, as fathers, as husbands, or as masters.

The natural place of virtue is near to liberty; but it is not nearer to excessive liberty than to servitude.

4

EDMUND BURKE, SPEECH ON CONCILIATION WITH THE COLONIES
22 Mar. 1775
Works 1:464–71

(See ch. 1, no. 2)

5

GEORGE MASON, REMARKS ON ANNUAL ELECTIONS FOR THE FAIRFAX INDEPENDENT COMPANY
Apr. 1775
Papers 1:229–32

A moment's reflection upon the principles on which this company was first instituted, and the purposes for which it was formed, will evince the propriety of the gentleman's motion; for it has been wisely observed by the deepest politician who ever put pen to paper, that no institution can be long preserved, but by frequent recurrence to those maxims on which it was formed.

This company is essentially different from a common collection of mercenary soldiers. It was formed upon the liberal sentiments of public good, for the great and useful purposes of defending our country, and preserving those inestimable rights which we inherit from our ancestors; it was intended in these times of extreme danger, when we are threatened with the ruin of that constitution under which we were born, and the destruction of all that is dear to us, to rouse the attention of the public, to introduce the use of arms and discipline, to infuse a martial spirit of emulation, and to provide a fund of officers; that in case of absolute necessity, the people might be the better enabled to act in defence of their invaded liberty. Upon this generous and public-spirited plan, gentlemen of the first fortune and character among us have become members of the Fairfax Independent Company, have submitted to stand in the ranks as common soldiers, and to pay due obedience to the officers of their own choice. This part of the country has the glory of setting so laudable an example: let us not tarnish it by any little dirty views of party, of mean self-interest or of low ambition.

We came equals into this world, and equals shall we go out of it. All men are by nature born equally free and independent. To protect the weaker from the injuries and insults of the stronger were societies first formed; when men entered into compacts to give up some of their natural rights, that by union and mutual assistance they might secure the rest; but they gave up no more than the nature of the thing required. Every society, all government, and every kind of civil compact therefore, is or ought to be, calculated for the general good and safety of the community. Every power, every authority vested in particular men is, or ought to be, ultimately directed to this sole end; and whenever any power or authority whatever extends further, or is of longer duration than is in its nature necessary for these purposes, it may be called government, but it is in fact oppression.

Upon these natural just and simple positions were civil laws and obligations framed, and from this source do even the most arbitrary and despotic powers this day upon earth derive their origin. Strange indeed that such superstructures should be raised upon such a foundation! But when we reflect upon the insidious arts of wicked and designing men, the various and plausible pretences for continuing and increasing authority, the incautious nature of the many, and the inordinate lust of power in the few, we shall no longer be surprised that free-born man hath been enslaved, and that those very means which were contrived for his preservation have been perverted to his ruin; or, to borrow a metaphor from Holy Writ, that the kid hath been seethed in his mother's milk.

To prevent these fatal effects, and to restore mankind to its native rights hath been the study of some of the best men that this world ever produced; and the most effectual means that human wisdom hath ever been able to devise, is frequently appealing to the body of the people, to those constituent members from whom authority originated, for their approbation or dissent. Whenever this is neglected or evaded, or the free voice of the people is suppressed or corrupted; or whenever any military establishment or authority is not, by some certain mode of rotation, dissolved into and blended with that mass from which it was taken, inevitable destruction to the state follows.

> "Then down the precipice of time it goes,
> And sinks in moments, which in ages rose."

The history of all nations who have had liberty and lost it, puts these facts beyond doubt. We have great cause to fear that this crisis is approaching in our mother country. Her constitution has strong symptoms of decay. It is our duty by every means in our power to prevent the like here.

If it be objected to the intended regulation that there may be inconvenience in changing officers who, by having served as such, have acquired a superior degree of military knowledge, the example and experience of the most warlike and victorious people that ever existed is directly against such a suggestion.

While the Roman Commonwealth preserved its vigour, new consuls were annually elected, new levies made, and new officers appointed; a general was often recalled from the head of a victorious army, in the midst of a dangerous and important war, and a successor sent to finish the expedition which he had begun. A long and almost constant series of success proved the wisdom and utility of measures which carried victory through the world, and at the same time secured the public safety and liberty at home; for by these means the people had always an inexhaustible fund of experienced officers, upon every emergency, untainted with the dangerous impressions which continued command naturally makes. But when by degrees these essential maxims of the state were undermined, and pretences were found to continue commanders beyond the stated times, their army no longer considered themselves the soldiers of the Republic, but as the troops of Marius or of Sylla, of Pompey or of Ceasar, of Marc Antony or of Octavius. The dissolution of that once glorious and happy commonwealth was the natural consequence, and has afforded a useful lesson to succeeding generations.

It has been lately observed by a learned and revered writer, that North America is the only great nursery of freemen now left upon the face of the earth. Let us cherish the sacred deposit. Let us strive to merit this greatest encomium that ever was bestowed upon any country. In all our associations; in all our agreements let us never lose sight of this fundamental maxim—that all power was originally lodged in, and consequently is derived from, the people. We should wear it as a breastplate, and buckle it on as our armour.

The application of these general principles to the subject before us is too obvious to need a minute illustration. By investing our officers with a power for life, or for an unlimited time, we are acting diametrically contrary to the principles of that liberty for which we profess to contend, and establishing a precedent which may prove fatal. By the purport of the proposed regulation every objection is obviated, every inconvenience removed; and the design of the institution strictly adhered to. It is calculated to prevent the abuse of authority, and the insolence of office on the one hand, and create a proper spirit of emulation on the other; and by an annual rotation, will in a few years breed a number of officers. The proposed interval of a year will defeat undue influence or cabals; and the capacity of being rechosen afterwards, opens a door to the return of officers of approved merit, and will always be a means of excluding unworthy men, whom an absolute rotation would of necessity introduce. The exception made in favor of the gentleman who by the unanimous voice of the company now commands it, is a very proper one, justly due to his public merit and experience; it is peculiarly suited to our circumstances, and was dictated, not by compliment, but conviction.

In a company thus constituted, no young man will think himself degraded by doing duty in the ranks, which he may in his turn command, or has commanded. For these reasons I very cordially give my assent to the gentleman's motion, and hope it will have the unanimous approbation of this company. If any of the members continue to think that the choice of the officers ought to be confined to this town, they can introduce it by way of amendment to the motion, and the merits of the proposition may be freely discussed.

6

SAMUEL ADAMS TO JAMES WARREN
4 Nov. 1775
Writings 3:235–37

Let me talk with you a little about the Affairs of our own Colony. I perswade my self, my dear Friend, that the greatest Care and Circumspection will be used to conduct its internal Police with Wisdom and Integrity. The Eyes of Mankind will be upon you to see whether the Government, which is now more popular than it has been for many years past, will be productive of more Virtue moral and political. We may look up to Armies for our Defence, but Virtue is our best Security. It is not possible that any State shd long remain free, where Virtue is not supremely honord. This is as seasonably as it is justly said by one of the most celebrated Writers of the present time. Perhaps the Form of Governmt now adopted & set up in the Colony may be permanent. Should it be only temporary the golden opportunity of recovering the Virtue & reforming the Manners of our Country should be industriously improvd. Our Ancestors in the most early Times laid an excellent Foundation for the security of Liberty by setting up in a few years after their Arrival a publick Seminary of Learning; and by their Laws they obligd every Town consisting of a certain Number of Families to keep and maintain a Grammar School. I shall be very sorry, if it be true as I have been informd, that some of our Towns have dismissd their Schoolmasters, alledging that the extraordinary Expence of defending the Country renders them unable to support them. I hope this Inattention to the Principles of our Forefathers does not prevail. If there should be any Danger of it, would not the leading Gentlemen do eminent Service to the Publick, by impressing upon the Minds of the People, the Necessity & Importance of encouraging that System of Education, which in my opinion is so well calculated to diffuse among the Individuals of the Community the Principles of Morality, so essentially necessary to the Preservation of publick Liberty.

There are Virtues & vices which are properly called *political*. "Corruption, Dishonesty to ones Country Luxury and Extravagance tend to the Ruin of States." The opposite Virtues tend to their Establishment. But "there is a Connection between Vices as well as Virtues and one opens the Door for the Entrance of another." Therefore "Wise and able Politicians will guard against other Vices," and be attentive to promote every Virtue. He who is void of virtuous Attachments in private Life, is, or very soon will be void of all Regard for his Country. There is seldom an Instance of a Man guilty of betraying his Country, who had not before lost the Feeling of moral Obligations in his private Connections. Before [Dr. Benjamin Church, Jr.] was detected of holding a criminal Correspondence with the Enemies of his Country, his Infidelity to his Wife had been notorious. Since private and publick Vices, are in

Reality, though not always apparently, so nearly connected, of how much Importance, how necessary is it, that the utmost Pains be taken by the Publick, to have the Principles of Virtue early inculcated on the Minds even of Children, and the moral Sense kept alive, and that the wise Institutions of our Ancestors for these great Purposes be encouragd by the Government. For no People will tamely surrender their Liberties, nor can any be easily subdued, when Knowledge is diffusd and Virtue is preservd. On the Contrary, when People are universally ignorant, and debauchd in their Manners, they will sink under their own Weight without the Aid of foreign Invaders.

7

JOHN ADAMS TO MERCY WARREN
8 Jan. 1776
Warren-Adams Letters 1:201–2

Pray Madam, are you for an American Monarchy or Republic? Monarchy is the genteelest and most fashionable Government, and I dont know why the Ladies ought not to consult Elegance and the Fashion as well in Government as Gowns, Bureaus or Chariots.

For my own part I am so tasteless as to prefer a Republic, if We must erect an independent Government in America, which you know is utterly against my Inclination. But a Republic, altho it will infallibly beggar me and my Children, will produce Strength, Hardiness Activity, Courage, Fortitude and Enterprise; the manly noble and Sublime Qualities in human Nature, in Abundance. A Monarchy would probably, somehow or other make me rich, but it would produce so much Taste and Politeness so much Elegance in Dress, Furniture, Equipage, so much Musick and Dancing, so much Fencing and Skaiting, so much Cards and Backgammon; so much Horse Racing and Cockfighting, so many Balls and Assemblies, so many Plays and Concerts that the very Imagination of them makes me feel vain, light, frivolous and insignificant.

It is the Form of Government which gives the decisive Colour to the Manners of the People, more than any other Thing. Under a well regulated Commonwealth, the People must be wise virtuous and cannot be otherwise. Under a Monarchy they may be as vicious and foolish as they please, nay, they cannot but be vicious and foolish. As Politicks therefore is the Science of human Happiness and human Happiness is clearly best promoted by Virtue, what thorough Politician can hesitate who has a new Government to build whether to prefer a Commonwealth or a Monarchy?

But, Madam, there is one Difficulty which I know not how to get over.

Virtue and Simplicity of Manners are indispensably necessary in a Republic among all orders and Degrees of Men. But there is so much Rascallity, so much Venality and Corruption, so much Avarice and Ambition such a Rage for Profit and Commerce among all Ranks and Degrees of Men even in America, that I sometimes doubt whether there is public Virtue enough to Support a Republic. There are two Vices most detestably predominant in every Part of America that I have yet seen which are as incompatible with the Spirit of a Commonwealth, as Light is with Darkness; I mean Servility and Flattery. A genuine Republican can no more fawn and cringe than he can domineer. Shew me the American who cannot do all. I know two or Three, I think, and very few more. However, it is the Part of a great Politician to make the Character of his People, to extinguish among them the Follies and Vices that he sees, and to create in them the Virtues and Abilities which he sees wanting. I wish I was sure that America has one such Politician but I fear she has not.

8

JOHN ADAMS, THOUGHTS ON GOVERNMENT
Apr. 1776
Papers 4:91–92

Laws for the liberal education of youth, especially of the lower class of people, are so extremely wise and useful, that to a humane and generous mind, no expence for this purpose would be thought extravagant.

The very mention of sumptuary laws will excite a smile. Whether our countrymen have wisdom and virtue enough to submit to them I know not. But the happiness of the people might be greatly promoted by them, and a revenue saved sufficient to carry on this war forever. Frugality is a great revenue, besides curing us of vanities, levities and fopperies which are real antidotes to all great, manly and warlike virtues.

. . . . .

A Constitution, founded on these principles, introduces knowledge among the People, and inspires them with a conscious dignity, becoming Freemen. A general emulation takes place, which causes good humour, sociability, good manners, and good morals to be general. That elevation of sentiment, inspired by such a government, makes the common people brave and enterprizing. That ambition which is inspired by it makes them sober, industrious and frugal. You will find among them some elegance, perhaps, but more solidity; a little pleasure, but a great deal of business—some politeness, but more civility. If you compare such a country with the regions of domination, whether Monarchial or Aristocratical, you will fancy yourself in Arcadia or Elisium.

9

JOHN ADAMS TO MERCY WARREN
16 Apr. 1776
Warren-Adams Letters 1:222–23

The Form of Government, which you admire, when its Principles are pure is admirable, indeed, it is productive of every Thing, which is great and excellent among Men. But its Principles are as easily destroyed, as human Nature is corrupted. Such a Government is only to be supported by pure Religion or Austere Morals. Public Virtue cannot exist in a Nation without private, and public Virtue is the only Foundation of Republics. There must be a positive Passion for the public good, the public Interest, Honour, Power and Glory, established in the Minds of the People, or there can be no Republican Government, nor any real Liberty: and this public Passion must be Superiour to all private Passions. Men must be ready, they must pride themselves, and be happy to sacrifice their private Pleasures, Passions and Interests, nay, their private Friendships and dearest Connections, when they stand in Competition with the Rights of Society.

Is there in the World a Nation, which deserves this Character? There have been several, but they are no more. Our dear Americans perhaps have as much of it as any Nation now existing, and New England perhaps has more than the rest of America. But I have seen all along my Life Such Selfishness and Littleness even in New England, that I sometimes tremble to think that, altho We are engaged in the best Cause that ever employed the Human Heart yet the Prospect of success is doubtful not for Want of Power or of Wisdom but of Virtue.

The Spirit of Commerce, Madam, which even insinuates itself into Families, and influences holy Matrimony, and thereby corrupts the morals of families as well as destroys their Happiness, it is much to be feared is incompatible with that purity of Heart and Greatness of soul which is necessary for an happy Republic.

This Same Spirit of Commerce is as rampant in New England as in any Part of the World. Trade is as well understood and as passionately loved there as any where.

Even the Farmers and Tradesmen are addicted to Commerce; and it is too true that Property is generally the standard of Respect there as much as anywhere. While this is the Case there is great Danger that a Republican Government would be very factious and turbulent there. Divisions in Elections are much to be dreaded. Every man must seriously set himself to root out his Passions, Prejudices and Attachments, and to get the better of his private Interest. The only reputable Principle and Doctrine must be that all Things must give Way to the public.

10

CARTER BRAXTON, AN ADDRESS TO THE CONVENTION OF THE COLONY AND ANCIENT DOMINION OF VIRGINIA; ON THE SUBJECT OF GOVERNMENT IN GENERAL, AND RECOMMENDING A PARTICULAR FORM TO THEIR CONSIDERATION
May 1776
Scribner 518, 520–23

When despotism had displayed her banners, and with unremitting ardor and fury, scattered her engines of oppression through this wide extended continent; the virtuous opposition of the people to its progress, relaxed the tone of government in almost every colony, and occasioned in many instances a total suspension of law.

These inconveniences however were natural; and the mode readily submitted to, as there was then reason to hope, that justice would be done to our injured country; the same laws, executed under the same authority, soon regain their former use and lustre; and peace, raised on a permanent foundation, bless this our native land.

But since these hopes have hitherto proved delusive; and time instead of bringing us relief, daily brings forth new proofs of British tyranny, and thereby separates us further from that reconciliation we so ardently wished; does it not become the duty of your and every other Convention, to assume the reins of government, and no longer suffer the people to live without the benefit of law, and order the protection it affords? Anarchy and riot will follow a continuance of its suspension, and render the enjoyment of our liberties and future quiet, at least very precarious.

Presuming that this object will, e're long, engage your attention, and fully persuaded that when it does, it will be considered with all the candor and deliberation due to its importance; I have ventured to collect my sentiments on the subject, and in a friendly manner offer them to your consideration. Should they suggest any hints that may tend to improve or embellish the fabrick you are about to erect; I shall deem myself happy in having contributed my mite to the benefit of a people I esteem, and country to which I owe every obligation.

Taking for granted therefore the necessity of instituting a government capable of affording all the blessings, of which, the most cruel attempts have been made to deprive us; the first enquiry will be, which of the various forms is best adapted to our situation, and will in every respect most probably answer our purpose.

Various are the opinions of men on this subject, and different are the plans proposed for your adoption. Prudence will direct you to examine them with jealous eye, and weigh the pretensions of each with care as well as impartiality. Your, and your children's welfare depends upon the choice. Let it therefore neither be marked by a blind attachment to ancient prejudices, on the one hand; or a restless spirit of innovation, on the other.

. . . . .

Men are prone to condemn the whole, because a part is objectionable, but certainly it would in the present case be more wise to consider, whether if the constitution was brought back to its original state, and its present imperfections remedied, it would not afford more happiness than any other.

If the independence of the Commons could be secured, and the dignity of the Lords preserved, how can a government be better formed for the preservation of freedom? And is there any thing more easy than this? If placemen and pensioners were excluded a seat in either house, and elections made triennial, what danger could be apprehended from prerogative. I have the best authority for asserting, that with these improvements, added to the suppression of boroughs and giving the people an equal and adequate representation, England would have remained a land of liberty to the latest ages.

Judge of the *principle* of this constitution by the great effects it has produced. Their code of laws, the boast of Englishmen and of freedom; the rapid progress they have made in trade, in arts and sciences, the respect they command from their neighbours, then gaining the empire of the sea, are all powerful arguments of the wisdom of that constitution and government which raised the people of that island to their late degree of greatness. But though I admire their perfections I must mourn their faults, and though I would guard against and cast off their oppression, yet would I retain all their wise maxims, and derive advantage from their mistakes and misfortunes.

The testimony of the learned Montesquieu in favour of the English constitution is very respectable. "There is (says he) one nation in the world, that has for the direct end of its constitution political liberty." Again he says, "it is not my business to examine whether the English actually enjoy this liberty or not, sufficient it is for my purpose to observe, that it is established by their laws, and I inquire no farther."

This constitution and these laws have also been those of Virginia, and let it be remembered that under them she flourished and was happy. The same principles which led the English to greatness, animates us. To that principle our laws, our customs, and our manners are adapted, and it would be perverting all order, to oblige us, by a novel government, to give up our laws, our customs, and our manners.

However necessary it may be to shake off the authority of arbitrary British dictators, we ought nevertheless to adopt and perfect that system, which England has suffered to be so grossly abused, and the experience of ages has taught us to venerate. This, like almost every thing else, is perhaps liable to objections; and probably the difficulty of adapting a limited monarchy will be largely insisted on. Admit this objection to have weight, and that we cannot in every instance assimilate a government to that, yet no good reason can be assigned, why the same *principle* or spirit may not in great measure be preserved.

But honorable as this spirit is, we daily see it calumniated by advocates for popular governments; and rendered obnoxious to all whom their artifices can influence or delude. The systems recommended to the Colonies, seem to accord with the temper of the times, and are fraught with all the tumult and riot incident to simple democracy. Systems which many think in their interest to support, and without doubt will be industriously propagated among you. The best of these systems exist only in theory, and were never confirmed by the experience, even of those who recommend them. I flatter myself therefore that you will not quit a substance actually enjoyed, for a shadow or phantom, by which, instead of being benefited many have been misled or perplexed.

Let us examine the principles they assign to their government, and try its merits by the unerring standard of truth. In a late pamphlet it is thus stated. The happiness of man as well as his dignity consists in Virtue, *if there be a form of government, then whose principle is virtue, will not every sober man acknowledge it better calculated to promote the general happiness of society than any other form.* Virtue is the principle of a republic, therefore a republic is the best form of government. The author, with what design I know not, seems to have cautiously blended *private* and *public* virtue, as if for the purpose of confounding the two, and thereby recommending his plan under the amiable appearance of courting *virtue.*

It is well known that *private* and *public* virtue are materially different. The happiness and dignity of man I admit consists in the practice of *private* virtues, and to this he is stimulated by the rewards promised to such conduct. In this he acts for himself, and with a view of promoting his own particular welfare.

Public virtue, on the other hand, means a disinterested attachment to the public good, exclusive and independent of all private and selfish interest, and which, though sometimes possessed by a few individuals, never characterised the mass of the people in any state. And this is said to be the principle of democratical governments, and to influence every subject of it to pursue such measures as conduce to the prosperity of the whole. A man therefore, to qualify himself for a member of such a community, must divest himself of all interested motives, and engage in no pursuits which do not ultimately redound to the benefit of society. He must not through ambition desire to be great, because it would destroy that equality on which the security of the government depends, nor ought he to be rich, lest he be tempted to indulge himself in those luxuries which though lawful are not expedient, and might occasion envy and emulation. Should a person deserve the esteem of his fellow citizens and become popular, he must be neglected, if not banished, lest his growing influence disturb the equilibrium. It is remarkable that neither the justice of Aristides or the bravery of Themistocles could shield men from the darts of envy and jealousy.—nor are modern times without examples of the same kind.

To this species of government every thing that looks like elegance and refinement, is inimical however necessary to the introduction of manufacturers, and the cultivation of arts and sciences. Hence in some ancient republics, flowed those numberless sumptuary laws, which restrained men to plainness and similarity in dress and diet; and all the mischiefs which attend Agrarian laws and unjust attempts to maintain their idol equality by an equal division of property.

Schemes like these may be practicable in countries so steril by nature as to afford a scanty supply of the necessaries and none of the conveniences, of life: But they can never meet with a favourable reception from people who inhabit a country to which providence has been more bountiful. They will always claim a right of using and enjoying the fruits of their honest industry, unrestrained by any ideal principles of government, and will gather estates for themselves and children without regarding the whimsical impropriety of being richer than their neighbours. These are rights which freemen will never consent to relinquish, and after fighting for deliverance from one species of tyranny, it would be unreasonable to expect they should tamely acquiesce under another.

The truth is that men will not be poor from choice or compulsion, and these governments can exist only in countries where the people are so from necessity. In all others they have ceased almost as soon as erected, and in many instances been succeeded by despotism, and the arbitrary sway of some usurper, who had before perhaps gained the confidence of the people, by eulogiums on liberty, and possessing no property of his own, by most disinterestedly opposing depredations on that of his neighbours.

11

THOMAS JEFFERSON, PREAMBLE TO A BILL FOR THE MORE GENERAL DIFFUSION OF KNOWLEDGE
Fall 1778

Papers 2:526–27

Whereas it appeareth that however certain forms of government are better calculated than others to protect individuals in the free exercise of their natural rights, and are at the same time themselves better guarded against degeneracy, yet experience hath shewn, that even under the best forms, those entrusted with power have, in time, and by slow operations, perverted it into tyranny; and it is believed that the most effectual means of preventing this would be, to illuminate, as far as practicable, the minds of the people at large, and more especially to give them knowledge of those facts, which history exhibiteth, that, possessed thereby of the experience of other ages and countries, they may be enabled to know ambition under all its shapes, and prompt to exert their natural powers to defeat its purposes; And whereas it is generally true that that people will be happiest whose laws are best, and are best administered, and that laws will be wisely formed, and

honestly administered, in proportion as those who form and administer them are wise and honest; whence it becomes expedient for promoting the publick happiness that those persons, whom nature hath endowed with genius and virtue, should be rendered by liberal education worthy to receive, and able to guard the sacred deposit of the rights and liberties of their fellow citizens, and that they should be called to that charge without regard to wealth, birth or other accidental condition or circumstance; but the indigence of the greater number disabling them from so educating, at their own expence, those of their children whom nature hath fitly formed and disposed to become useful instruments for the public, it is better that such should be sought for and educated at the common expence of all, than that the happiness of all should be confided to the weak or wicked: . . .

12

RICHARD HENRY LEE TO HENRY LAURENS
6 June 1779

Letters 2:62–63

However, after all that has happened I cannot help yet hoping, that a majority will be found among the representatives of young Republics who will support able and honest servants, whilst they properly censure and discountenance the knavish abusers of public trust. Methinks our Congress should direct to be written in large characters and placed in the most visible part of their Session Hall the following just sentiment of the excellent Montesquieu "There is no great share of probity necessary to support a Monarchical or Despotic government. The force of laws in one, and the Princes arm in the other, are sufficient to direct and maintain the whole. But in a popular state, one spring more is *necessary,* namely *Virtue.*" If he had added Vigilance his fabric would have been complete. I know there are Mandevilles among you who laugh at virtue, and with vain ostentatious display of words will deduce from vice, public good! But such men are much fitter to be Slaves in the corrupt, rotten despotisms of Europe, than to remain citizens of young and rising republics. The Committee of Philadelphia have my free consent to send all such within the enemies lines. I think this useful Committee would have no difficulty in saying with certainty Thou, & Thou, & Thou, & Thou, & Thou, & Thou, & Thou art the man. Tho not perfectly pure after this selection, such a Load would be removed, that a young and vigorous constitution might soon work itself clean and perfect health take place.

13

MASSACHUSETTS CONSTITUTION OF 1780
Handlin 467

Chapter V.

Section II. The Encouragement of Literature, etc.

Wisdom, and knowledge, as well as virtue, diffused generally among the body of the people, being necessary for the preservation of their rights and liberties; and as these depend on spreading the opportunities and advantages of education in the various parts of the country, and among the different orders of the people, it shall be the duty of legislators and magistrates, in all future periods of this Commonwealth, to cherish the interests of literature and the sciences, and all seminaries of them; especially the university at Cambridge, public schools, and grammar schools in the towns; to encourage private societies and public institutions, rewards and immunities, for the promotion of agriculture, arts, sciences, commerce, trades, manufactures, and a natural history of the country; to countenance and inculcate the principles of humanity and general benevolence, public and private charity, industry and frugality, honesty and punctuality in their dealings; sincerity, good humour, and all social affections, and generous sentiments among the people.

14

SAMUEL ADAMS TO JOHN SCOLLAY
30 Dec. 1780
Writings 4:236–38

Our Government, I perceive, is organizd on the Basis of the new Constitution. I am affraid there is more Pomp & Parade than is consistent with those sober Republican Principles, upon which the Framers of it thought they had founded it. Why should this new Oera be introducd with Entertainments expensive & tending to dissipate the Minds of the People? Does it become us to lead the People to such publick Diversions as promote Superfluity of Dress & Ornament, when it is as much as they can bear to support the Expense of cloathing a naked Army? Will Vanity & Levity ever be the Stability of Government, either in States, in Cities, or what, let me hint to you is of the last Importance, in *Families?* Of what Kind are those Manners, by which, as we are truly informd in a late Speech, "not only the freedom but the very Existence of Republicks is greatly affected?" How fruitless is it, to recommend "the adapting the Laws in the most perfect Manner possible, to the Suppression of Idleness Dissipation & Extravagancy," if such Recommendations are counteracted by the Exam-

ple of Men of Religion, Influence & publick Station? I meant to consider this Subject in the View of the mere Citizen.

. . . . .

Our Bradfords, Winslows & Winthrops would have revolted at the Idea of opening Scenes of Dissipation & Folly; knowing them to be inconsistent with their great Design, in transplanting themselves into what they called this "Outside of the World." But I fear I shall say too much. I love the People of Boston. I once thought, that City would be the *Christian* Sparta. But Alas! Will men never be free! They will be free no longer than while they remain virtuous. Sidney tells us, there are times when People are not worth saving. Meaning, when they have lost their Virtue. I pray God, this may never be truly said of my beloved Town.

15

ALEXANDER HAMILTON, CONTINENTALIST, NO. 6
4 July 1782
Papers 3:103

We may preach till we are tired of the theme, the necessity of disinterestedness in republics, without making a single proselyte. The virtuous declaimer will neither persuade himself nor any other person to be content with a double mess of porridge, instead of a reasonable stipend for his services. We might as soon reconcile ourselves to the Spartan community of goods and wives, to their iron coin, their long beards, or their black broth. There is a total dissimulation in the circumstances, as well as the manners, of society among us; and it is as ridiculous to seek for models in the simple ages of Greece and Rome, as it would be to go in quest of them among the Hottentots and Laplanders.

16

THOMAS JEFFERSON, NOTES ON THE STATE OF
VIRGINIA, QUERIES 14 AND 19,
146–49, 164–65
1784

Another object of the revisal is, to diffuse knowledge more generally through the mass of the people. This bill proposes to lay off every county into small districts of five or six miles square, called hundreds, and in each of them to establish a school for teaching reading, writing, and arithmetic. The tutor to be supported by the hundred, and every person in it entitled to send their children three years gratis, and as much longer as they please, paying for it. These schools to be under a visitor, who is annually to chuse the boy, of best genius in the school, of those whose parents are too poor to give them further education, and to send him forward to one of the grammar schools, of which twenty are proposed to be erected in different parts of the country, for teaching Greek, Latin, geography, and the higher branches of numerical arithmetic. Of the boys thus sent in any one year, trial is to be made at the grammar schools one or two years, and the best genius of the whole selected, and continued six years, and the residue dismissed. By this means twenty of the best geniusses will be raked from the rubbish annually, and be instructed, at the public expence, so far as the grammar schools go. At the end of six years instruction, one half are to be discontinued (from among whom the grammar schools will probably be supplied with future masters); and the other half, who are to be chosen for the superiority of their parts and disposition, are to be sent and continued three years in the study of such sciences as they shall chuse, at William and Mary college, the plan of which is proposed to be enlarged, as will be hereafter explained, and extended to all the useful sciences. The ultimate result of the whole scheme of education would be the teaching all children of the state reading, writing, and common arithmetic: turning out ten annually of superior genius, well taught in Greek, Latin, geography, and the higher branches of arithmetic: turning out ten others annually, of still superior parts, who, to those branches of learning, shall have added such of the sciences as their genius shall have led them to: the furnishing to the wealthier part of the people convenient schools, at which their children may be educated, at their own expence.—The general objects of this law are to provide an education adapted to the years, to the capacity, and the condition of every one, and directed to their freedom and happiness. Specific details were not proper for the law. These must be the business of the visitors entrusted with its execution. The first stage of this education being the schools of the hundreds, wherein the great mass of the people will receive their instruction, the principal foundations of future order will be laid here. Instead therefore of putting the Bible and Testament into the hands of the children, at an age when their judgments are not sufficiently matured for religious enquiries, their memories may here be stored with the most useful facts from Grecian, Roman, European and American history. The first elements of morality too may be instilled into their minds; such as, when further developed as their judgments advance in strength, may teach them how to work out their own greatest happiness, by shewing them that it does not depend on the condition of life in which chance has placed them, but is always the result of a good conscience, good health, occupation, and freedom in all just pursuits.—Those whom either the wealth of their parents or the adoption of the state shall destine to higher degrees of learning, will go on to the grammar schools, which constitute the next stage, there to be instructed in the languages. The learning Greek and Latin, I am told, is going into disuse in Europe. I know not what their manners and occupations may call for: but it would be very ill-judged in us to follow their example in this instance. There is a certain period of life, say from eight to fifteen or sixteen years of age, when the mind, like the body, is

not yet firm enough for laborious and close operations. If applied to such, it falls an early victim to premature exertion; exhibiting indeed at first, in these young and tender subjects, the flattering appearance of their being men while they are yet children, but ending in reducing them to be children when they should be men. The memory is then most susceptible and tenacious of impressions; and the learning of languages being chiefly a work of memory, it seems precisely fitted to the powers of this period, which is long enough too for acquiring the most useful languages antient and modern. I do not pretend that language is science. It is only an instrument for the attainment of science. But that time is not lost which is employed in providing tools for future operation: more especially as in this case the books put into the hands of the youth for this purpose may be such as will at the same time impress their minds with useful facts and good principles. If this period be suffered to pass in idleness, the mind becomes lethargic and impotent, as would the body it inhabits if unexercised during the same time. The sympathy between body and mind during their rise, progress and decline, is too strict and obvious to endanger our being misled while we reason from the one to the other.—As soon as they are of sufficient age, it is supposed they will be sent on from the grammar schools to the university, which constitutes our third and last stage, there to study those sciences which may be adapted to their views.—By that part of our plan which prescribes the selection of the youths of genius from among the classes of the poor, we hope to avail the state of those talents which nature has sown as liberally among the poor as the rich, but which perish without use, if not sought for and cultivated.—But of all the views of this law none is more important, none more legitimate, than that of rendering the people the safe, as they are the ultimate, guardians of their own liberty. For this purpose the reading in the first stage, where *they* will receive their whole education, is proposed, as has been said, to be chiefly historical. History by apprising them of the past will enable them to judge of the future; it will avail them of the experience of other times and other nations; it will qualify them as judges of the actions and designs of men; it will enable them to know ambition under every disguise it may assume; and knowing it, to defeat its views. In every government on earth is some trace of human weakness, some germ of corruption and degeneracy, which cunning will discover, and wickedness insensibly open, cultivate, and improve. Every government degenerates when trusted to the rulers of the people alone. The people themselves therefore are its only safe depositories. And to render even them safe their minds must be improved to a certain degree. This indeed is not all that is necessary, though it be essentially necessary. An amendment of our constitution must here come in aid of the public education. The influence over government must be shared among all the people. If every individual which composes their mass participates of the ultimate authority, the government will be safe; because the corrupting the whole mass will exceed any private resources of wealth: and public ones cannot be provided but by levies on the people. In this case every man would have to pay his own price. The government of

Great-Britain has been corrupted, because but one man in ten has a right to vote for members of parliament. The sellers of the government therefore get nine-tenths of their price clear. It has been thought that corruption is restrained by confining the right of suffrage to a few of the wealthier of the people: but it would be more effectually restrained by an extension of that right to such numbers as would bid defiance to the means of corruption.

Lastly, it is proposed, by a bill in this revisal, to begin a public library and gallery, by laying out a certain sum annually in books, paintings, and statues.

. . . . .

We never had an interior trade of any importance. Our exterior commerce has suffered very much from the beginning of the present contest. During this time we have manufactured within our families the most necessary articles of cloathing. Those of cotton will bear some comparison with the same kinds of manufacture in Europe; but those of wool, flax and hemp are very coarse, unsightly, and unpleasant: and such is our attachment to agriculture, and such our preference for foreign manufactures, that be it wise or unwise, our people will certainly return as soon as they can, to the raising raw materials, and exchanging them for finer manufactures than they are able to execute themselves.

The political oeconomists of Europe have established it as a principle that every state should endeavour to manufacture for itself: and this principle, like many others, we transfer to America, without calculating the difference of circumstance which should often produce a difference of result. In Europe the lands are either cultivated, or locked up against the cultivator. Manufacture must therefore be resorted to of necessity not of choice, to support the surplus of their people. But we have an immensity of land courting the industry of the husbandman. Is it best then that all our citizens should be employed in its improvement, or that one half should be called off from that to exercise manufactures and handicraft arts for the other? Those who labour in the earth are the chosen people of God, if ever he had a chosen people, whose breasts he has made his peculiar deposit for substantial and genuine virtue. It is the focus in which he keeps alive that sacred fire, which otherwise might escape from the face of the earth. Corruption of morals in the mass of cultivators is a phaenomenon of which no age nor nation has furnished an example. It is the mark set on those, who not looking up to heaven, to their own soil and industry, as does the husbandman, for their subsistance, depend for it on the casualties and caprice of customers. Dependance begets subservience and venality, suffocates the germ of virtue, and prepares fit tools for the designs of ambition. This, the natural progress and consequence of the arts, has sometimes perhaps been retarded by accidental circumstances: but, generally speaking, the proportion which the aggregate of the other classes of citizens bears in any state to that of its husbandmen, is the proportion of its unsound to its healthy parts, and is a good-enough barometer whereby to measure its degree of corruption. While we have land to labour then, let us never wish to see our citizens occupied at a work-bench, or twirling a distaff. Carpenters, masons, smiths, are wanting in husbandry: but, for the general operations of manufacture, let our workshops remain in Europe. It is better to carry provisions and materials to workmen there, than bring them to the provisions and materials, and with them their manners and principles. The loss by the transportation of commodities across the Atlantic will be made up in happiness and permanence of government. The mobs of great cities add just so much to the support of pure government, as sores do to the strength of the human body. It is the manners and spirit of a people which preserve a republic in vigour. A degeneracy in these is a canker which soon eats to the heart of its laws and constitution.

17

JOHN ADAMS, DEFENCE OF THE CONSTITUTIONS OF GOVERNMENT OF THE UNITED STATES
1787
Works 6:130–31, 206–8

The right of a nation to kill a tyrant, in cases of necessity, can no more be doubted, than that to hang a robber, or kill a flea. But killing one tyrant only makes way for a worse, unless the people have sense, spirit, and honesty enough to establish and support a constitution guarded at all points against tyranny; against the tyranny of the one, the few, and the many. Let it be the study, therefore, of lawgivers and philosophers, to enlighten the people's understandings and improve their morals, by good and general education; to enable them to comprehend the scheme of government, and to know upon what points their liberties depend; to dissipate those vulgar prejudices and popular superstitions that oppose themselves to good government; and to teach them that obedience to the laws is as indispensable in them as in lords and kings.

. . . . .

But not to enlarge on this, let us proceed to the inquiry, what is virtue? It is not that classical virtue which we see personified in the choice of Hercules, and which the ancient philosophers summed up in four words,—prudence, justice, temperance, and fortitude. It is not Christian virtue, so much more sublime, which is summarily comprehended in universal benevolence. What is it then? According to Montesquieu, it should seem to be merely a negative quality; the absence only of ambition and avarice; and he thinks that what he thus advances is confirmed by the unanimous testimony of historians. But is this matter well considered? Look over the history of any republic, and can you find a period in it, in which ambition and avarice do not appear in very strong characters, and in which ambitious men were not the most popular? In Athens, Pisistratus and his successors were more popular, as well as ambitious, than Solon, Themistocles than Aristides, &c. In Rome, under the kings, the eternal plots of the nobles against the lives of the kings, to usurp their thrones, are proofs of an ardent and unbridled ambition. Nay, if we attentively examine the most virtuous characters, we shall find unequivocal marks of an ardent ambition. The elder Brutus, Camillus, Regulus, Curius, Aemilius, Cato, all discover an ambition, a thirst of glory, as strong as that of Caesar; an honorable ambition, an ambition governed by justice, if you will; but an ambition still. But there is not a period in Athenian or Roman annals, when great characters did not appear actuated by ambition of another kind; an unjust and dishonorable ambition; such as Pisistratus, Themistocles, Appius Claudius, &c.; and these characters were always more popular than the others, and were supported chiefly by plebeians, not senates and patricians. If the absence of avarice is necessary to republican virtue, can you find any age or country in which republican virtue has existed? That single characters, or a few among the patricians, have existed, who were exempt from avarice, has been already admitted; but that a moment ever existed, in any country, where property was enjoyed, when the body of the people were universally or even generally exempted from avarice, is not easy to prove. Every page of the history of Rome appears equally marked with ambition and avarice; and the only difference appears in the means and objects. In some periods the nation was extremely poor, in others immensely rich; but the passions existed in all; and the Roman soldiers and common people were forever quarrelling with their most virtuous generals, for refusing to indulge their avarice, by distributing the spoils among them, and for loving the public too well, by putting the booty into the public treasury.

Shall we say then that republican virtue is nothing but simple poverty; and that poverty alone can support such a government? But Montesquieu tells us, virtue in a republic, is a love of the republic; virtue in a democracy, is a love of the democracy; and why might he not have said, that virtue in a monarchy is a love of the monarchy; in a despotism, of the despot; in a mixed government, of the mixture? Men in general love their country and its government. Can it be proved that Athenians loved Athens, or Romans, Rome, more than Frenchmen love France, or Englishmen their island?

There are two principal causes of discrimination; the first is, the greatness or smallness of the state. A citizen of a small republic, who knows every man and every house in it, appears generally to have the strongest attachment to it, because nothing can happen in it that does not interest and affect his feelings; but in a great nation, like France or England, a man is, as it were, lost in the crowd; there are very few persons that he knows, and few events that will much affect him; yet you will find him as much attached to his circle of friends and knowledge as the inhabitant of the small state. The second is, the goodness or badness of the constitution, the climate, soil, &c. Other things being equal, that constitution, whose blessings are the most felt, will be most beloved; and accordingly we find, that governments the best ordered and balanced have been most beloved, as Sparta, Athens, Carthage, Rome, and England, and we might add Holland, for there has been, in practice and effect, a balance of three powers

in that country, though not sufficiently defined by law. Moral and Christian, and political virtue, cannot be too much beloved, practised, or rewarded; but to place liberty on that foundation only would not be safe; but it may be well questioned, whether love of the body politic is precisely moral or Christian virtue, which requires justice and benevolence to enemies as well as friends, and to other nations as well as our own. It is not true, in fact, that any people ever existed who loved the public better than themselves, their private friends, neighbors, &c., and therefore this kind of virtue, this sort of love, is as precarious a foundation for liberty as honor or fear; it is the laws alone that really love the country, the public, the whole better than any part; and that form of government which unites all the virtue, honor, and fear of the citizens, in a reverence and obedience to the laws, is the only one in which liberty can be secure, and all orders, and ranks, and parties, compelled to prefer the public good before their own; that is the government for which we plead.

18

NOAH WEBSTER, AN EXAMINATION INTO THE LEADING PRINCIPLES OF THE FEDERAL CONSTITUTION
10 Oct. 1787

Pamphlets 58–61

(See ch. 16, no. 17)

19

A PROPOSAL FOR REVIVING CHRISTIAN CONVICTION
11 Oct. 1787

Storing 5.8.1–4

The unpromising situation of national affairs has of late, induced many well meaning people to submit to the public their sentiments, however unpolished, respecting the proper means of effecting a reform. Several have, and very justly, pointed out the want of virtue, public and private, as one principal source of our distresses, and have recommended the practice thereof with the most plausible arguments. To such writers the community is certainly much indebted for their well meant endeavours. But alas! the experience of every age evinces that arguments drawn from the native charms of moral rectitude, and its necessary connection with the happiness and welfare of states, are too feeble to ensure the requisite practice of virtue when opposed to the allurements of self-interest and self-gratification.

While mankind consider the obligations to the exercise of virtue as derived from no higher source than the advantages accruing therefrom to society, it is no difficult matter for every individual to satisfy himself, that, provided he can persuade others to the disinterested practice, his dispensing with it in his own case will be a thing of little moment. Hence declamations on the advantages and necessity of public and private virtue fall from the lips of every one, while their lives are stained with the most sordid and selfish practices. Though the different states into which mankind are formed, have, generally speaking, enacted laws to restrain and punish enormities, to countenance virtue and discourage vice; yet the most approved and wisest legislators in all ages, in order to give efficacy to their civil institutions, have found it necessary to call in the aid of religion; and in no form of government whatever has the influence of religious principles been found so requisite as in that of a republic. It requires but a slight degree of observation to be convinced that mankind require the awe of some power to confine them within the line of their duty. The dread of a rapacious tyrant ready to take advantage of the smallest misdemeanor (in order to fill his coffers or gratify a cruel disposition) may preserve quiet and order among the subjects, or rather slaves, of a despotic prince. Even in limited monarchies the security of the sovereign as well as the privileges of the people, depending on a strict attention to the laws, in a great measure, secures their being duly administered. But what is there to correct the injustice and irregularities of the member of a republic, even where the most salutary laws exist, while he can associate numbers in his interest; or supposing the administration of the laws in the hands of such as have a fellow-feeling, or are unwilling to risk their popularity by punctually enforcing them.

Whatever influence speculative vanity may ascribe to the indefinite principle termed honor, or political refinement, to an artful collusion of interests, sound reason as well as experience proves that a due sense of responsibility to the Deity, as the author of those moral laws, an observance of which constitutes the happiness and welfare of societies as well as individuals, is the mean most likely to give a right direction to the conduct of mankind. The man who carries his prospects forward to futurity, and considers himself a candidate for the favor of omnipotence, will be actuated, in the general tenor of his life, by motives that elevate him above the little interests and passions which disturb the peace of society, and will discharge the relative duties of his station, unawed by the fear of man, with a consistence and steadiness correspondent to the principle from which he acts.

It has been the misfortune of our infant legislature that in the multiplicity of business which has come before them, they have not had leisure to attend sufficiently to the importance of religious concerns to the welfare of the state. In consequence of this a cold indifference towards religion has crept upon the minds of the elderly; our illiterate youth have been raised in almost total ignorance thereof; and those of liberal education, forming their opinions of it from the absurd notions and practices of a few ignorant and presumptuous enthusiasts, have contracted a hearty contempt for every thing sacred.

20

JAMES MADISON, FEDERALIST, NO. 10, 56–65
22 Nov. 1787

(See ch. 4, no. 19)

21

THOMAS JEFFERSON TO JAMES MADISON
20 Dec. 1787
Papers 12:442

I own I am not a friend to a very energetic government. It is always oppressive. The late rebellion in Massachusets has given more alarm than I think it should have done. Calculate that one rebellion in 13 states in the course of 11 years, is but one for each state in a century and a half. No country should be so long without one. Nor will any degree of power in the hands of government prevent insurrections. France with all it's despotism, and two or three hundred thousand men always in arms has had three insurrections in the three years I have been here in every one of which greater numbers were engaged than in Massachusets and a great deal more blood was spilt. In Turkey, which Montesquieu supposes more despotic, insurrections are the events of every day. In England, where the hand of power is lighter than here, but heavier than with us they happen every half dozen years. Compare again the ferocious depredations of their insurgents with the order, the moderation and the almost self extinguishment of ours.—After all, it is my principle that the will of the Majority should always prevail. If they approve the proposed Convention in all it's parts, I shall concur in it chearfully, in hopes that they will amend it whenever they shall find it work wrong. I think our governments will remain virtuous for many centuries; as long as they are chiefly agricultural; and this will be as long as there shall be vacant lands in any part of America. When they get piled upon one another in large cities, as in Europe, they will become corrupt as in Europe. Above all things I hope the education of the common people will be attended to; convinced that on their good sense we may rely with the most security for the preservation of a due degree of liberty.

22

JAMES MADISON, FEDERALIST, NO. 55, 375–78
13 Feb. 1788

The true question to be decided then is whether the smallness of the number [of the House of Representatives], as a temporary regulation, be dangerous to the public liberty: Whether sixty five members for a few years, and a hundred or two hundred for a few more, be a safe depositary for a limited and well guarded power of legislating for the United States? I must own that I could not give a negative answer to this question, without first obliterating every impression which I have received with regard to the present genius of the people of America, the spirit, which actuates the state legislatures, and the principles which are incorporated with the political character of every class of citizens. I am unable to conceive that the people of America in their present temper, or under any circumstances which can speedily happen, will chuse, and every second year repeat the choice of sixty-five or an hundred men, who would be disposed to form and pursue a scheme of tyranny or treachery. I am unable to conceive that the state legislatures which must feel so many motives to watch, and which possess so many means of counteracting the federal legislature, would fail either to detect or to defeat a conspiracy of the latter against the liberties of their common constituents. I am equally unable to conceive that there are at this time, or can be in any short time, in the United States any sixty-five or an hundred men capable of recommending themselves to the choice of the people at large, who would either desire or dare within the short space of two years, to betray the solemn trust committed to them. What change of circumstances time and a fuller population of our country may produce, requires a prophetic spirit to declare, which makes no part of my pretensions. But judging from the circumstances now before us, and from the probable state of them within a moderate period of time, I must pronounce that the liberties of America can not be unsafe in the number of hands proposed by the federal constitution.

From what quarter can the danger proceed? Are we afraid of foreign gold? If foreign gold could so easily corrupt our federal rulers, and enable them to ensnare and betray their constituents, how has it happened that we are at this time a free and independent nation? The Congress which conducted us through the revolution were a less numerous body than their successors will be; they were not chosen by nor responsible to their fellow citizens at large; though appointed from year to year, and recallable at pleasure, they were generally continued for three years; and prior to the ratification of the federal articles, for a still longer term; they held their consultations always under the veil of secrecy; they had the sole transaction of our affairs with foreign nations; through the whole course of the war, they had the fate of their country more in their hands, than it is to be hoped will ever be the case with our future representatives; and from the greatness of the prize at stake and the eagerness of the party which lost it, it may well be supposed, that the use of other means than force would not have been scrupled; yet we know by happy experience that the public trust was not betrayed; nor has the purity of our public councils in this particular ever suffered even from the whispers of calumny.

Is the danger apprehended from the other branches of the federal government? But where are the means to be found by the President or the Senate, or both? Their emoluments of office it is to be presumed will not, and without a previous corruption of the house of representatives cannot, more than suffice for very different purposes: Their private fortunes, as they must all be American citizens, cannot possibly be sources of danger. The only means then which they can possess, will be in the dispensation of appointments. Is it here that suspicion rests her charge? Sometimes we are told that this fund of corruption is to be exhausted by the President in subduing the virtue of the Senate. Now the fidelity of the other house is to be the victim. The improbability of such a mercenary and perfidious combination of the several members of government standing on as different foundations as republican principles will well admit, and at the same time accountable to the society over which they are placed, ought alone to quiet this apprehension. But fortunately the constitution has provided a still further safeguard. The members of the Congress are rendered ineligible to any civil offices that may be created or of which the emoluments may be increased, during the term of their election. No offices therefore can be dealt out to the existing members, but such as may become vacant by ordinary casualties; and to suppose that these would be sufficient to purchase the guardians of the people, selected by the people themselves, is to renounce every rule by which events ought to be calculated, and to substitute an indiscriminate and unbounded jealousy, with which all reasoning must be vain. The sincere friends of liberty who give themselves up to the extravagancies of this passion are not aware of the injury they do their own cause. As there is a degree of depravity in mankind which requires a certain degree of circumspection and distrust: So there are other qualities in human nature, which justify a certain portion of esteem and confidence. Republican government presupposes the existence of these qualities in a higher degree than any other form. Were the pictures which have been drawn by the political jealousy of some among us, faithful likenesses of the human character, the inference would be that there is not sufficient virtue among men for self-government; and that nothing less than the chains of despotism can restrain them from destroying and devouring one another.

23

PATRICK HENRY, VIRGINIA
RATIFYING CONVENTION
9 June 1788
Storing 5.16.14

(See ch. 11, no. 13)

24

JAMES MADISON, VIRGINIA
RATIFYING CONVENTION
20 June 1788

Papers 11:163

(See ch. 13, no. 36)

25

ALEXANDER HAMILTON, NEW YORK
RATIFYING CONVENTION
21 June 1788

Papers 5:42–43

(See ch. 13, no. 38)

26

NOAH WEBSTER, ON THE EDUCATION OF YOUTH
IN AMERICA
1788

Collection 23–26

Another defect in our schools, which, since the revolution, is become inexcuseable, is the want of proper books. The collections which are now used consist of essays that respect foreign and ancient nations. The minds of youth are perpetually led to the history of Greece and Rome or to Great Britain; boys are constantly repeating the declamations of Demosthenes and Cicero, or debates upon some political question in the British Parliment. These are excellent specimens of good sense, polished stile and perfect oratory; but they are not interesting to children. They cannot be very useful, except to young gentlemen who want them as models of reasoning and eloquence, in the pulpit or at the bar.

But every child in America should be acquainted with his own country. He should read books that furnish him with ideas that will be useful to him in life and practice. As soon as he opens his lips, he should rehearse the history of his own country; he should lisp the praise of liberty, and of those illustrious heroes and statesmen, who have wrought a revolution in her favor.

A selection of essays, respecting the settlement and geography of America; the history of the late revolution and of the most remarkable characters and events that distinguished it, and a compendium of the principles of the federal and provincial governments, should be the principal school book in the United States. These are interesting objects to every man; they call home the minds of youth and fix them upon the interests of their own country, and they

assist in forming attachments to it, as well as in enlarging the understanding.

"It is observed by the great Montesquieu, that the laws of education ought to be relative to the principles of the government."

In despotic governments, the people should have little or no education, except what tends to inspire them with a servile fear. Information is fatal to despotism.

In monarchies, education should be partial, and adapted to the rank of each class of citizens. But "in a republican government," says the same writer, "the whole power of education is required." Here every class of people should *know* and *love* the laws. This knowlege should be diffused by means of schools and newspapers; and an attachment to the laws may be formed by early impressions upon the mind.

Two regulations are essential to the continuance of republican goverments: 1. Such a distribution of lands and such principles of descent and alienation, as shall give every citizen a power of acquiring what his industry merits.* 2. Such a system of education as gives every citizen an opportunity of acquiring knowlege and fitting himself for places of trust. These are fundamental articles; the *sine qua non* of the existence of the American republics.

Hence the absurdity of our copying the manners and adopting the institutions of Monarchies.

In several States, we find laws passed, establishing provision for colleges and academies, where people of property may educate their sons; but no provision is made for instructing the poorer rank of people, even in reading and writing. Yet in these same States, every citizen who is worth a few shillings annually, is entitled to vote for legislators.† This appears to me a most glaring solecism in government. The constitutions are *republican*, and the laws of education are *monarchical*. The *former* extend civil rights to every honest industrious man; the *latter* deprive a large proportion of the citizens of a most valuable privilege.

In our American republics, where [government] is in the hands of the people, knowlege should be universally diffused by means of public schools. Of such consequence is it to society, that the people who make laws, should be well informed, that I conceive no Legislature can be justified in neglecting proper establishments for this purpose.

When I speak of a diffusion of knowlege, I do not mean merely a knowlege of spelling books, and the New Testament. An acquaintance with ethics, and with the general principles of law, commerce, money and government, is necessary for the yeomanry of a republican state. This acquaintance they might obtain by means of books calculated for schools, and read by the children, during the winter months, and by the circulation of public papers.

"In Rome it was the common exercise of boys at school, to learn the laws of the twelve tables by heart, as they did their poets and classic authors." What an excellent practice this in a free government!

*The power of entailing real estates is repugnant to the spirit of our American governments.
†I have known instructions from the inhabitants of a county, two thirds of whom could not write their names. How competent must such men be to decide an important point in legislation!

It is said, indeed by many, that our common people are already too well informed. Strange paradox! The truth is, they have too much knowlege and spirit to resign their share in government, and are not sufficiently informed to govern themselves in all cases of difficulty.

There are some acts of the American legislatures which astonish men of information; and blunders in legislation are frequently ascribed to bad intentions. But if we examin the men who compose these legislatures, we shall find that wrong measures generally proceed from ignorance either in the men themselves, or in their constituents. They often mistake their own interest, because they do not foresee the remote consequences of a measure.

It may be true that all men cannot be legislators; but the more generally knowlege is diffused among the substantial yeomanry, the more perfect will be the laws of a republican state.

Every small district should be furnished with a school, at least four months in a year; when boys are not otherwise employed. This school should be kept by the most reputable and well informed man in the district. Here children should be taught the usual branches of learning; submission to superiors and to laws; the moral or social duties; the history and transactions of their own country; the principles of liberty and government. Here the rough manners of the wilderness should be softened, and the principles of virtue and good behaviour inculcated. The *virtues* of men are of more consequence to society than their *abilities;* and for this reason, the *heart* should be cultivated with more assiduity than the *head.*

Such a general system of education is neither impracticable nor difficult; and excepting the formation of a federal government that shall be efficient and permanent, it demands the first attention of American patriots. Until such a system shall be adopted and pursued; until the Statesman and Divine shall unite their efforts in *forming* the human mind, rather than in loping its excrescences, after it has been neglected; until Legislators discover that the only way to make good citizens and subjects, is to nourish them from infancy; and until parents shall be convinced that the *worst* of men are not the proper teachers to make the *best;* mankind cannot know to what a degree of perfection society and government may be carried. America affords the fairest opportunities for making the experiment, and opens the most encouraging prospect of success.

27

JOHN ADAMS TO SAMUEL ADAMS
18 Oct. 1790
Works 6:416–20

(See ch. 11, no. 16)

28

JAMES MADISON, REPUBLICAN DISTRIBUTION
OF CITIZENS
5 Mar. 1792
Papers 14:244–46

A perfect theory on this subject would be useful, not because it could be reduced to practice by any plan of legislation, or ought to be attempted by violence on the will or property of individuals: but because it would be a monition against empirical experiments by power, and a model to which the free choice of occupations by the people, might gradually approximate the order of society.

The best distribution is that which would most favor *health, virtue, intelligence* and *competency* in the *greatest number* of citizens. It is needless to add to these objects, *liberty* and *safety.* The first is presupposed by them. The last must result from them.

The life of the husbandman is pre-eminently suited to the comfort and happiness of the individual. *Health,* the first of blessings, is an appurtenance of his property and his employment. *Virtue,* the health of the soul, is another part of his patrimony, and no less favored by his situation. *Intelligence* may be cultivated in this as well as in any other walk of life. If the mind be less susceptible of polish in retirement than in a crowd, it is more capable of profound and comprehensive efforts. Is it more ignorant of some things? It has a compensation in its ignorance of others. *Competency* is more universally the lot of those who dwell in the country, when liberty is at the same time their lot. The extremes both of want and of waste have other abodes. 'Tis not the country that peoples either the Bridewells or the Bedlams. These mansions of wretchedness are tenanted from the distresses and vices of overgrown cities.

The condition, to which the blessings of life are most denied is that of the sailor. His health is continually assailed and his span shortened by the stormy element to which he belongs. His virtue, at no time aided, is occasionally exposed to every scene that can poison it. His mind, like his body, is imprisoned within the bark that transports him. Though traversing and circumnavigating the globe, he sees nothing but the same vague objects of nature, the same monotonous occurrences in ports and docks; and at home in his vessel, what new ideas can shoot from the unvaried use of the ropes and the rudder, or from the society of comrades as ignorant as himself. In the supply of his wants he often feels a scarcity, seldom more than a bare sustenance; and if his ultimate prospects do not embitter the present moment, it is because he never looks beyond it. How unfortunate, that in the intercourse, by which nations are enlightened and refined, and their means of safety extended, the immediate agents should be distinguished by the hardest condition of humanity.

The great interval between the two extremes, is, with a few exceptions, filled by those who work the materials furnished by the earth in its natural or cultivated state.

It is fortunate in general, and particularly for this country, that so much of the ordinary and most essential consumption, takes place in fabrics which can be prepared in every family, and which constitute indeed the natural ally of agriculture. The former is the work within doors, as the latter is without; and each being done by hands or at times, that can be spared from the other, the most is made of every thing.

The class of citizens who provide at once their own food and their own raiment, may be viewed as the most truly independent and happy. They are more: they are the best basis of public liberty, and the strongest bulwark of public safety. It follows, that the greater the proportion of this class to the whole society, the more free, the more independent, and the more happy must be the society itself.

In appreciating the regular branches of manufacturing and mechanical industry, their tendency must be compared with the principles laid down, and their merits graduated accordingly. Whatever is least favorable to vigor of body, to the faculties of the mind, or to the virtues or the utilities of life, instead of being forced or fostered by public authority, ought to be seen with regret as long as occupations more friendly to human happiness, lie vacant.

The several professions of more elevated pretensions, the merchant, the lawyer, the physician, the philosopher, the divine, form a certain proportion of every civilized society, and readily adjust their numbers to its demands, and its circumstances.

29

GEORGE WASHINGTON, FAREWELL ADDRESS
19 Sept. 1796
Writings 35:217–36

In looking forward to the moment, which is intended to terminate the career of my public life, my feelings do not permit me to suspend the deep acknowledgment of that debt of gratitude wch. I owe to my beloved country, for the many honors it has conferred upon me; still more for the stedfast confidence with which it has supported me; and for the opportunities I have thence enjoyed of manifesting my inviolable attachment, by services faithful and persevering, though in usefulness unequal to my zeal. If benefits have resulted to our country from these services, let it always be remembered to your praise, and as an instructive example in our annals, that, under circumstances in which the Passions agitated in every direction were liable to mislead, amidst appearances sometimes dubious, viscissitudes of fortune often discouraging, in situations in which not unfrequently want of Success has countenanced the spirit of criticism, the constancy of your support was the essential prop of the efforts, and a guarantee of the plans by which they were effected. Profoundly penetrated with this idea, I shall carry it with me to my grave, as a strong incitement to unceasing vows that Heaven may continue to you the choicest tokens of its beneficence; that your Union and brotherly affection may be perpetual; that the free constitution, which is the work of your hands, may be sacredly maintained; that its Administration in every department may be stamped with wisdom and Virtue; that, in fine, the happiness of the people of these States, under the auspices of liberty, may be made complete, by so careful a preservation and so prudent a use of this blessing as will acquire to them the glory of recommending it to the applause, the affection, and adoption of every nation which is yet a stranger to it.

Here, perhaps, I ought to stop. But a solicitude for your welfare, which cannot end but with my life, and the apprehension of danger, natural to that solicitude, urge me on an occasion like the present, to offer to your solemn contemplation, and to recommend to your frequent review, some sentiments; which are the result of much reflection, of no inconsiderable observation, and which appear to me all important to the permanency of your felicity as a People. These will be offered to you with the more freedom, as you can only see in them the disinterested warnings of a parting friend, who can possibly have no personal motive to biass his counsel. Nor can I forget, as an encouragement to it, your endulgent reception of my sentiments on a former and not dissimilar occasion.

Interwoven as is the love of liberty with every ligament of your hearts, no recommendation of mine is necessary to fortify or confirm the attachment.

The Unity of Government which constitutes you one people is also now dear to you. It is justly so; for it is a main Pillar in the Edifice of your real independence, the support of your tranquility at home; your peace abroad; of your safety; of your prosperity; of that very Liberty which you so highly prize. But as it is easy to foresee, that from different causes and from different quarters, much pains will be taken, many artifices employed, to weaken in your minds the conviction of this truth; as this is the point in your political fortress against which the batteries of internal and external enemies will be most constantly and actively (though often covertly and insidiously) directed, it is of infinite moment, that you should properly estimate the immense value of your national Union to your collective and individual happiness; that you should cherish a cordial, habitual and immoveable attachment to it; accustoming yourselves to think and speak of it as of the Palladium of your political safety and prosperity; watching for its preservation with jealous anxiety; discountenancing whatever may suggest even a suspicion that it can in any event be abandoned, and indignantly frowning upon the first dawning of every attempt to alienate any portion of our Country from the rest, or to enfeeble the sacred ties which now link together the various parts.

For this you have every inducement of sympathy and interest. Citizens by birth or choice, of a common country, that country has a right to concentrate your affections. The name of AMERICAN, which belongs to you, in your national capacity, must always exalt the just pride of Patriotism, more than any appellation derived from local discriminations. With slight shades of difference, you have the same Religeon, Manners, Habits and political Principles. You have in a common cause fought and triumphed together. The independence and liberty you possess are the work of joint councils, and joint efforts; of common dangers, sufferings and successes.

But these considerations, however powerfully they address themselves to your sensibility are greatly outweighed by those which apply more immediately to your Interest. Here every portion of our country finds the most commanding motives for carefully guarding and preserving the Union of the whole.

The *North*, in an unrestrained intercourse with the *South*, protected by the equal Laws of a common government, finds in the productions of the latter, great additional resources of Maratime and commercial enterprise and precious materials of manufacturing industry. The *South* in the same Intercourse, benefitting by the Agency of the *North*, sees its agriculture grow and its commerce expand. Turning partly into its own channels the seamen of the *North*, it finds its particular navigation envigorated; and while it contributes, in different ways, to nourish and increase the general mass of the National navigation, it looks forward to the protection of a Maratime strength, to which itself is unequally adapted. The *East*, in a like intercourse with the *West*, already finds, and in the progressive improvement of interior communications, by land and water, will more and more find a valuable vent for the commodities which it brings from abroad, or manufactures at home. The *West* derives from the *East* supplies requisite to its growth and comfort, and what is perhaps of still greater consequence, it must of necessity owe the *secure* enjoyment of indispensable *outlets* for its own productions to the weight, influence, and the future Maratime strength of the Atlantic side of the Union, directed by an indissoluble community of Interest as *one Nation*. Any other tenure by which the *West* can hold this essential advantage, whether derived from its own seperate strength, or from an apostate and unnatural connection with any foreign Power, must be intrinsically precarious.

While then every part of our country thus feels an immediate and particular Interest in Union, all the parts combined cannot fail to find in the united mass of means and efforts greater strength, greater resource, proportionably greater security from external danger, a less frequent interruption of their Peace by foreign Nations; and, what is of inestimable value! they must derive from Union an exemption from those broils and Wars between themselves, which so frequently afflict neighbouring countries, not tied together by the same government; which their own rivalships alone would be sufficient to produce, but which opposite foreign alliances, attachments and intrigues would stimulate and imbitter. Hence likewise they will avoid the necessity of those overgrown Military establishments, which under any form of Government are inauspicious to liberty, and which are to be regarded as particularly hostile to Republican Liberty: In this sense it is, that your Union ought to be considered as a main prop of your liberty, and that the love of the one ought to endear to you the preservation of the other.

These considerations speak a persuasive language to every reflecting and virtuous mind, and exhibit the contin-

uance of the UNION as a primary object of Patriotic desire. Is there a doubt, whether a common government can embrace so large a sphere? Let experience solve it. To listen to mere speculation in such a case were criminal. We are authorized to hope that a proper organization of the whole, with the auxiliary agency of governments for the respective Sub divisions, will afford a happy issue to the experiment. 'Tis well worth a fair and full experiment With such powerful and obvious motives to Union, affecting all parts of our country, while experience shall not have demonstrated its impracticability, there will always be reason, to distrust the patriotism of those, who in any quarter may endeavor to weaken its bands.

In contemplating the causes wch. may disturb our Union, it occurs as matter of serious concern, that any ground should have been furnished for characterizing parties by *Geographical* discriminations: *Northern* and *Southern; Atlantic* and *Western;* whence designing men may endeavour to excite a belief that there is a real difference of local interests and views. One of the expedients of Party to acquire influence, within particular districts, is to misrepresent the opinions and aims of other Districts. You cannot shield yourselves too much against the jealousies and heart burnings which spring from these misrepresentations. They tend to render Alien to each other those who ought to be bound together by fraternal affection. The Inhabitants of our Western country have lately had a useful lesson on this head. They have seen, in the Negociation by the Executive, and in the unanimous ratification by the Senate, of the Treaty with Spain, and in the universal satisfaction at that event, throughout the United States, a decisive proof how unfounded were the suspicions propagated among them of a policy in the General Government and in the Atlantic States unfriendly to their Interests in regard to the MISSISSIPPI. They have been witnesses to the formation of two Treaties, that with G: Britain and that with Spain, which secure to them every thing they could desire, in respect to our Foreign relations, towards confirming their prosperity. Will it not be their wisdom to rely for the preservation of these advantages on the UNION by wch. they were procured? Will they not henceforth be deaf to those advisers, if such there are, who would sever them from their Brethren and connect them with Aliens?

To the efficacy and permanency of Your Union, a Government for the whole is indispensable. No Alliances however strict between the parts can be an adequate substitute. They must inevitably experience the infractions and interruptions which all Alliances in all times have experienced. Sensible of this momentous truth, you have improved upon your first essay, by the adoption of a Constitution of Government, better calculated than your former for an intimate Union, and for the efficacious management of your common concerns. This government, the offspring of our own choice uninfluenced and unawed, adopted upon full investigation and mature deliberation, completely free in its principles, in the distribution of its powers, uniting security with energy, and containing within itself a provision for its own amendment, has a just claim to your confidence and your support. Respect for its authority, compliance with its Laws, acquiescence in its measures, are duties enjoined by the fundamental maxims of true Liberty. The basis of our political systems is the right of the people to make and to alter their Constitutions of Government. But the Constitution which at any time exists, 'till changed by an explicit and authentic act of the whole People, is sacredly obligatory upon all. The very idea of the power and the right of the People to establish Government presupposes the duty of every Individual to obey the established Government.

All obstructions to the execution of the Laws, all combinations and Associations, under whatever plausible character, with the real design to direct, controul counteract, or awe the regular deliberation and action of the Constituted authorities are distructive of this fundamental principle and of fatal tendency. They serve to organize faction, to give it an artificial and extraordinary force; to put in the place of the delegated will of the Nation, the will of a party; often a small but artful and enterprizing minority of the Community; and, according to the alternate triumphs of different parties, to make the public administration the Mirror of the ill concerted and incongruous projects of faction, rather than the organ of consistent and wholesome plans digested by common councils and modefied by mutual interests. However combinations or Associations of the above description may now and then answer popular ends, they are likely, in the course of time and things, to become potent engines, by which cunning, ambitious and unprincipled men will be enabled to subvert the Power of the People, and to usurp for themselves the reins of Government; destroying afterwards the very engines which have lifted them to unjust dominion.

Towards the preservation of your Government and the permanency of your present happy state, it is requisite, not only that you steadily discountenance irregular oppositions to its acknowledged authority, but also that you resist with care the spirit of innovation upon its principles however specious the pretexts. one method of assault may be to effect, in the forms of the Constitution, alterations which will impair the energy of the system, and thus to undermine what cannot be directly overthrown. In all the changes to which you may be invited, remember that time and habit are at least as necessary to fix the true character of Governments, as of other human institutions; that experience is the surest standard, by which to test the real tendency of the existing Constitution of a country; that facility in changes upon the credit of mere hypotheses and opinion exposes to perpetual change, from the endless variety of hypotheses and opinion: and remember, especially, that for the efficient management of your common interests, in a country so extensive as ours, a Government of as much vigour as is consistent with the perfect security of Liberty is indispensable. Liberty itself will find in such a Government, with powers properly distributed and adjusted, its surest Guardian. It is indeed little else than a name, where the Government is too feeble to withstand the enterprises of faction, to confine each member of the Society within the limits prescribed by the laws and to maintain all in the secure and tranquil enjoyment of the rights of person and property.

I have already intimated to you the danger of Parties in the State, with particular reference to the founding of them on Geographical discriminations. Let me now take a more comprehensive view, and warn you in the most solemn manner against the baneful effects of the Spirit of Party, generally

This spirit, unfortunately, is inseperable from our nature, having its root in the strongest passions of the human Mind. It exists under different shapes in all Governments, more or less stifled, controuled, or repressed; but, in those of the popular form it is seen in its greatest rankness and is truly their worst enemy.

The alternate domination of one faction over another, sharpened by the spirit of revenge natural to party dissention, which in different ages and countries has perpetrated the most horrid enormities, is itself a frightful despotism. But this leads at length to a more formal and permanent despotism. The disorders and miseries, which result, gradually incline the minds of men to seek security and repose in the absolute power of an Individual: and sooner or later the chief of some prevailing faction more able or more fortunate than his competitors, turns this disposition to the purposes of his own elevation, on the ruins of Public Liberty.

Without looking forward to an extremity of this kind (which nevertheless ought not to be entirely out of sight) the common and continual mischiefs of the spirit of Party are sufficient to make it the interest and the duty of a wise People to discourage and restrain it.

It serves always to distract the Public Councils and enfeeble the Public administration. It agitates the Community with ill founded jealousies and false alarms, kindles the animosity of one part against another, foments occasionally riot and insurrection. It opens the door to foreign influence and corruption, which find a facilitated access to the government itself through the channels of party passions. Thus the policy and the will of one country, are subjected to the policy and will of another.

There is an opinion that parties in free countries are useful checks upon the Administration of the Government and serve to keep alive the spirit of Liberty. This within certain limits is probably true, and in Governments of a Monarchical cast Patriotism may look with endulgence, if not with favour, upon the spirit of party. But in those of the popular character, in Governments purely elective, it is a spirit not to be encouraged. From their natural tendency, it is certain there will always be enough of that spirit for every salutary purpose. And there being constant danger of excess, the effort ought to be, by force of public opinion, to mitigate and assuage it. A fire not to be quenched; it demands a uniform vigilance to prevent its bursting into a flame, lest instead of warming it should consume.

It is important, likewise, that the habits of thinking in a free Country should inspire caution in those entrusted with its administration, to confine themselves within their respective Constitutional spheres; avoiding in the exercise of the Powers of one department to encroach upon another. The spirit of encroachment tends to consolidate the powers of all the departments in one, and thus to create whatever the form of government, a real despotism. A just estimate of that love of power, and proneness to abuse it, which predominates in the human heart is sufficient to satisfy us of the truth of this position. The necessity of reciprocal checks in the exercise of political power; by dividing and distributing it into different depositories, and constituting each the Guardian of the Public Weal against invasions by the others, has been evinced by experiments ancient and modern; some of them in our country and under our own eyes. To preserve them must be as necessary as to institute them. If in the opinion of the People, the distribution or modification of the Constitutional powers be in any particular wrong, let it be corrected by an amendment in the way which the Constitution designates. But let there be no change by usurpation; for though this, in one instance, may be the instrument of good, it is the customary weapon by which free governments are destroyed. The precedent must always greatly overbalance in permanent evil any partial or transient benefit which the use can at any time yield.

Of all the dispositions and habits which lead to political prosperity, Religion and morality are indispensable supports. In vain would that man claim the tribute of Patriotism, who should labour to subvert these great Pillars of human happiness, these firmest props of the duties of Men and citizens. The mere Politician, equally with the pious man ought to respect and to cherish them. A volume could not trace all their connections with private and public felicity. Let it simply be asked where is the security for property, for reputation, for life, if the sense of religious obligation *desert* the oaths, which are the instruments of investigation in Courts of Justice? And let us with caution indulge the supposition, that morality can be maintained without religion. Whatever may be conceded to the influence of refined education on minds of peculiar structure, reason and experience both forbid us to expect that National morality can prevail in exclusion of religious principle.

'Tis substantially true, that virtue or morality is a necessary spring of popular government. The rule indeed extends with more or less force to every species of free Government. Who that is a sincere friend to it, can look with indifference upon attempts to shake the foundation of the fabric

Promote then as an object of primary importance, Institutions for the general diffusion of knowledge. In proportion as the structure of a government gives force to public opinion, it is essential that public opinion should be enlightened

As a very important source of strength and security, cherish public credit. One method of preserving it is to use it as sparingly as possible: avoiding occasions of expence by cultivating peace, but remembering also that timely disbursements to prepare for danger frequently prevent much greater disbursements to repel it; avoiding likewise the accumulation of debt, not only by shunning occasions of expence, but by vigorous exertions in time of Peace to discharge the Debts which unavoidable wars may have occasioned, not ungenerously throwing upon posterity the burthen which we ourselves ought to bear. The execution

of these maxims belongs to your Representatives, but it is necessary that public opinion should cooperate. To facilitate to them the performance of their duty, it is essential that you should practically bear in mind, that towards the payment of debts there must be Revenue; that to have Revenue there must be taxes; that no taxes can be devised which are not more or less inconvenient and unpleasant; that the intrinsic embarrassment inseperable from the selection of the proper objects (which is always a choice of difficulties) ought to be a decisive motive for a candid construction of the Conduct of the Government in making it, and for a spirit of acquiescence in the measures for obtaining Revenue which the public exigencies may at any time dictate.

Observe good faith and justice towds. all Nations. Cultivate peace and harmony with all. Religion and morality enjoin this conduct; and can it be that good policy does not equally enjoin it? It will be worthy of a free, enlightened, and, at no distant period, a great Nation, to give to mankind the magnanimous and too novel example of a People always guided by an exalted justice and benevolence. Who can doubt that in the course of time and things the fruits of such a plan would richly repay any temporary advantages wch. might be lost by a steady adherence to it? Can it be, that Providence has not connected the permanent felicity of a Nation with its virtue? The experiment, at least, is recommended by every sentiment which ennobles human Nature. Alas! is it rendered impossible by its vices?

In the execution of such a plan nothing is more essential than that permanent, inveterate antipathies against particular Nations and passionate attachments for others should be excluded; and that in place of them just and amicable feelings towards all should be cultivated. The Nation, which indulges towards another an habitual hatred, or an habitual fondness, is in some degree a slave. It is a slave to its animosity or to its affection, either of which is sufficient to lead it astray from its duty and its interest. Antipathy in one Nation against another, disposes each more readily to offer insult and injury, to lay hold of slight causes of umbrage, and to be haughty and intractable, when accidental or trifling occasions of dispute occur. Hence frequent collisions, obstinate envenomed and bloody contests. The Nation, prompted by illwill and resentment sometimes impels to War the Government, contrary to the best calculations of policy. The Government sometimes participates in the national propensity, and adopts through passion what reason would reject; at other times, it makes the animosity of the Nation subservient to projects of hostility instigated by pride, ambition and other sinister and pernicious motives. The peace often, sometimes perhaps the Liberty, of Nations has been the victim.

So likewise, a passionate attachment of one Nation for another produces a variety of evils. Sympathy for the favourite nation, facilitating the illusion of an imaginary common interest, in cases where no real common interest exists, and infusing into one the enmities of the other, betrays the former into a participation in the quarrels and Wars of the latter, without adequate inducement or justification: It leads also to concessions to the favourite Nation of priviledges denied to others, which is apt doubly to injure the Nation making the concessions; by unnecessarily parting with what ought to have been retained; and by exciting jealousy, ill will, and a disposition to retaliate, in the parties from whom eql. priviledges are withheld: And it gives to ambitious, corrupted, or deluded citizens (who devote themselves to the favourite Nation) facility to betray, or sacrifice the interests of their own country, without odium, sometimes even with popularity; gilding with the appearances of a virtuous sense of obligation a commendable deference for public opinion, or a laudable zeal for public good, the base or foolish compliances of ambition corruption or infatuation.

As avenues to foreign influence in innumerable ways, such attachments are particularly alarming to the truly enlightened and independent Patriot. How many opportunities do they afford to tamper with domestic factions, to practice the arts of seduction, to mislead public opinion, to influence or awe the public Councils! Such an attachment of a small or weak, towards a great and powerful Nation, dooms the former to be the satellite of the latter.

Against the insidious wiles of foreign influence, (I conjure you to believe me fellow citizens) the jealousy of a free people ought to be *constantly* awake; since history and experience prove that foreign influence is one of the most baneful foes of Republican Government. But that jealousy to be useful must be impartial; else it becomes the instrument of the very influence to be avoided, instead of a defence against it. Excessive partiality for one foreign nation and excessive dislike of another, cause those whom they actuate to see danger only on one side, and serve to veil and even second the arts of influence on the other. Real Patriots, who may resist the intriegues of the favourite, are liable to become suspected and odious; while its tools and dupes usurp the applause and confidence of the people, to surrender their interests.

The Great rule of conduct for us, in regard to foreign Nations is in extending our commercial relations to have with them as little *political* connection as possible. So far as we have already formed engagements let them be fulfilled, with perfect good faith. Here let us stop.

Europe has a set of primary interests, which to us have none, or a very remote relation. Hence she must be engaged in frequent controversies, the causes of which are essentially foreign to our concerns. Hence therefore it must be unwise in us to implicate ourselves, by artificial ties, in the ordinary vicissitudes of her politics, or the ordinary combinations and collisions of her friendships, or enmities:

Our detached and distant situation invites and enables us to pursue a different course. If we remain one People, under an efficient government, the period is not far off, when we may defy material injury from external annoyance; when we may take such an attitude as will cause the neutrality we may at any time resolve upon to be scrupulously respected; when belligerent nations, under the impossibility of making acquisitions upon us, will not lightly hazard the giving us provocation; when we may choose peace or war, as our interest guided by our justice shall Counsel.

Why forego the advantages of so peculiar a situation? Why quit our own to stand upon foreign ground? Why, by interweaving our destiny with that of any part of Europe, entangle our peace and prosperity in the toils of European Ambition, Rivalship, Interest, Humour or Caprice?

'Tis our true policy to steer clear of permanent Alliances, with any portion of the foreign world. So far, I mean, as we are now at liberty to do it, for let me not be understood as capable of patronising infidility to existing engagements (I hold the maxim no less applicable to public than to private affairs, that honesty is always the best policy). I repeat it therefore, let those engagements be observed in their genuine sense. But in my opinion, it is unnecessary and would be unwise to extend them.

Taking care always to keep ourselves, by suitable establishments, on a respectably defensive posture, we may safely trust to temporary alliances for extraordinary emergencies.

Harmony, liberal intercourse with all Nations, are recommended by policy, humanity and interest. But even our Commercial policy should hold an equal and impartial hand: neither seeking nor granting exclusive favours or preferences; consulting the natural course of things; diffusing and deversifying by gentle means the streams of Commerce, but forcing nothing; establishing with Powers so disposed; in order to give to trade a stable course, to define the rights of our Merchants, and to enable the Government to support them; conventional rules of intercourse, the best that present circumstances and mutual opinion will permit, but temporary, and liable to be from time to time abandoned or varied, as experience and circumstances shall dictate; constantly keeping in view, that 'tis folly in one Nation to look for disinterested favors from another; that it must pay with a portion of its Independence for whatever it may accept under that character; that by such acceptance, it may place itself in the condition of having given equivalents for nominal favours and yet of being reproached with ingratitude for not giving more. There can be no greater error than to expect, or calculate upon real favours from Nation to Nation. 'Tis an illusion which experience must cure, which a just pride ought to discard.

In offering to you, my Countrymen these counsels of an old and affectionate friend, I dare not hope they will make the strong and lasting impression, I could wish; that they will controul the usual current of the passions, or prevent our Nation from running the course which has hitherto marked the Destiny of Nations: But if I may even flatter myself, that they may be productive of some partial benefit, some occasional good; that they may now and then recur to moderate the fury of party spirit, to warn against the mischiefs of foreign Intriegue, to guard against the Impostures of pretended patriotism; this hope will be a full recompence for the solicitude for your welfare, by which they have been dictated.

30

BENJAMIN RUSH, OF THE MODE OF EDUCATION
PROPER IN A REPUBLIC
1798

Selected Writings 87–89, 92, 94–96

The business of education has acquired a new complexion by the independence of our country. The form of government we have assumed, has created a new class of duties to every American. It becomes us, therefore, to examine our former habits upon this subject, and in laying the foundations for nurseries of wise and good men, to adapt our modes of teaching to the peculiar form of our government.

The first remark that I shall make upon this subject is, that an education in our own, is to be preferred to an education in a foreign country. The principle of patriotism stands in need of the reinforcement of prejudice, and it is well known that our strongest prejudices in favour of our country are formed in the first one and twenty years of our lives. The policy of the Lacedemonians is well worthy of our imitation. When Antipater demanded fifty of their children as hostages for the fulfillment of a distant engagement, those wise republicans refused to comply with his demand, but readily offered him double the number of their adult citizens, whose habits and prejudices could not be shaken by residing in a foreign country. Passing by, in this place, the advantages to the community from the early attachment of youth to the laws and constitution of their country, I shall only remark, that young men who have trodden the paths of science together, or have joined in the same sports, whether of swimming, skating, fishing, or hunting, generally feel, thro' life, such ties to each other, as add greatly to the obligations of mutual benevolence.

I conceive the education of our youth in this country to be peculiarly necessary in Pennsylvania, while our citizens are composed of the natives of so many different kingdoms in Europe. Our schools of learning, by producing one general, and uniform system of education, will render the mass of the people more homogeneous, and thereby fit them more easily for uniform and peaceable government.

I proceed in the next place, to enquire, what mode of education we shall adopt so as to secure to the state all the advantages that are to be derived from the proper instruction of youth; and here I beg leave to remark, that the only foundation for a useful education in a republic is to be laid in Religion. Without this there can be no virtue, and without virtue there can be no liberty, and liberty is the object and life of all republican governments.

Such is my veneration for every religion that reveals the attributes of the Deity, or a future state of rewards and punishments, that I had rather see the opinions of Confucius or Mahomed inculcated upon our youth, than see them grow up wholly devoid of a system of religious principles. But the religion I mean to recommend in this place, is that of the New Testament.

It is foreign to my purpose to hint at the arguments which establish the truth of the Christian revelation. My only business is to declare, that all its doctrines and precepts are calculated to promote the happiness of society, and the safety and well being of civil government. A Christian cannot fail of being a republican. The history of the creation of man, and of the relation of our species to each other by birth, which is recorded in the Old Testament, is the best refutation that can be given to the divine right of kings, and the strongest argument that can be used in favor of the original and natural equality of all mankind. A Christian, I say again, cannot fail of being a republican, for every precept of the Gospel inculcates those degrees of humility, self-denial, and brotherly kindness, which are directly opposed to the pride of monarchy and the pageantry of a court. A Christian cannot fail of being useful to the republic, for his religion teacheth him, that no man "liveth to himself." And lastly, a Christian cannot fail of being wholly inoffensive, for his religion teacheth him, in all things to do to others what he would wish, in like circumstances, they should do to him.

. . . . .

From the observations that have been made it is plain, that I consider it is possible to convert men into republican machines. This must be done, if we expect them to perform their parts properly, in the great machine of the government of the state. That republic is sophisticated with monarchy or aristocracy that does not revolve upon the wills of the people, and these must be fitted to each other by means of education before they can be made to produce regularity and unison in government.

. . . . .

With the usual arts and sciences that are taught in our American colleges, I wish to see a regular course of lectures given upon History and Chronology. The science of government, whether it relates to constitutions or laws, can only be advanced by a careful selection of facts, and these are to be found chiefly in history. Above all, let our youth be instructed in the history of the ancient republics, and the progress of liberty and tyranny in the different states of Europe. I wish likewise to see the numerous facts that relate to the origin and present state of commerce, together with the nature and principles of money, reduced to such a system, as to be intelligible and agreeable to a young man. If we consider the commerce of our metropolis only as the avenue of the wealth of the state, the study of it merits a place in a young man's education; but, I consider commerce in a much higher light when I recommend the study of it in republican seminaries. I view it as the best security against the influence of hereditary monopolies of land, and, therefore, the surest protection against aristocracy. I consider its effects as next to those of religion in humanizing mankind, and lastly, I view it as the means of uniting the different nations of the world together by the ties of mutual wants and obligations.

. . . . .

I beg pardon for having delayed so long to say any thing of the separate and peculiar mode of education proper for women in a republic. I am sensible that they must concur in all our plans of education for young men, or no laws will ever render them effectual. To qualify our women for this purpose, they should not only be instructed in the usual branches of female education, but they should be taught the principles of liberty and government; and the obligations of patriotism should be inculcated upon them. The opinions and conduct of men are often regulated by the women in the most arduous enterprizes of life; and their approbation is frequently the principal reward of the hero's dangers, and the patriot's toils. Besides, the first impressions upon the minds of children are generally derived from the women. Of how much consequence, therefore, is it in a republic, that they should think justly upon the great subject of liberty and government!

The complaints that have been made against religion, liberty and learning, have been, against each of them in a separate state. Perhaps like certain liquors, they should only be used in a state of mixture. They mutually assist in correcting the abuses, and in improving the good effects of each other. From the combined and reciprocal influence of religion, liberty and learning upon the morals, manners and knowledge of individuals, of these, upon government, and of government, upon individuals, it is impossible to measure the degrees of happiness and perfection to which mankind may be raised. For my part, I can form no ideas of the golden age, so much celebrated by the poets, more delightful, than the contemplation of that happiness which it is now in the power of the legislature of Pennsylvania to confer upon her citizens, by establishing proper modes and places of education in every part of the state.

31

GOUVERNEUR MORRIS, NATIONAL GREATNESS
ca. 1800
Amerikastudien 21:332–34 (1976)

Had it been permitted to consult my Wishes on this Day I should have selected a Theme more suited to my Talents or rather have shrouded their Weakness in the Veil of Silence. For I feel but too well that in venturing to discuss the Subject of national Greatness I must fall short of the Ideas in your Minds and disappoint your expectations. Instead of irradiating with the Light of Genius I must take the more humble Course of Investigation and begin by Enquiring what is national Greatness. Does it consist in Numbers Wealth or Extent of Territory? Certainly not. Swollen with the Pride inspired by such Circumstances the Persians addressed their Master as the Great King but Darius felt in repeated Discomfiture the Superiority of a great Nation led by Alexander. We see in our Day a Prince who may boast that the Sun never sets on his Domaine yet his Authority superseded in his Ports and insulted in his Capital, it would seem as if his Territory were extended

around the Globe only to display before all the World his ignominious Condition. Such is the State of that proud Monarchy which once menaced the Liberties of Europe. But who trembles now at the Name of Spain? There is none so abject. Nay should there exist a Government in which fear is the incurable Disease no Paroxism would be excited by the Menace of Spain. To the Wise a Word is sufficient and therefore it will be needless before this Audience to prove that a nation small like Greece may rise to the Heights of national Greatness while Littleness shall mark every public Act of a numerous People. And equally needless must it be to express what you cannot but feel: that in Proportion to the high Esteem Respect & Admiration with which we View the Splendor of Greece in the Day of her Glory is our profound Contempt for those who presiding over a powerful People shall tamely submit to the multiplied Repetition of Indignities from all who thro Interest or for Sport may plunder & insult them. These are Feelings so natural that to disguise them would be vain, to suppress them impossible. I could indeed, were I to indulge a licentious Imagination suppose a Number of Men who without national Spirit or Sentiment shall presume to call themselves a Nation—I can suppose a Herd of piddling huchstering Individuals base and insensible except to Blows who in the Stroke of a Cudgel estimate only the Smart and comparing it with the Labor and Expence of Resistance submit Resentment to the Rules of Calculation[;] I can suppose such Wretches streched over a wilde Surface which they call their Country but which they hold as Tenants at Will to the first Invader. Nay I can suppose them to be governed by wretches still more vile who derive their Power from the meanest Propensity who sacrifice on the Alter of Avarice to get the means of indulging Malice and render a beggarly Account of the Saving of Doits while national Honor national Dignity and national Glory are wholly forgotten.

All this I say may be figured by a fancy which should disdain the Confine of Reason and Truth. But from such a Picture the ingenuous Mind must turn loathing away with Contempt and Detestation. We feel that if the disgusting Image could be realized, a Horde so selfish would soon be swept away or reduced to their proper Condition of Slaves. We are consoled therefore by the Reflection that whenever Providence may permit the Existence of such a political Monster it will be only that speedy and compleat Ruin may deter other Nations from a Conduct so mean so base so vile.

Let us pause. Perhaps there never was a Society of Men so compleatly void of virtue. But between them and the brave Band at Thermopylae Gradations are infinite.

Perhaps it may be asked if Genius & Excellence in the Arts constitute national Greatness? To this Question the Answer must be given with Caution and not without some Modification. The Ages of Pericles of Augustus & of Louis the fourteenth were indeed Ages of Splendor. They were unquestionably the Evidence but I must venture to believe they were the Result not the Cause of national Greatness. A Nation truly great cannot but excel in Arts as well as in Arms. And as a Great Mind stamps with its own Impression the most common Arts so national Greatness will show itself alike in the Councils of Policy, in the Works of Genius, in Monuments of Magnificence and Deeds of Glory. All these are the fruits but they are not the Tree.

Here I anticipate the general and the generous Question: Does it not consist in Liberty? That Liberty is a kind and fostering Nurse of Greatness will be cheerfully and cordially admitted but as we have seen National Greatness where there was no Freedom, so we have seen free Nations where Baseness rather than Greatness constituted the national Character. The Intrepidity of the Swiss Troops is generally known and acknowledged. In a Contest for freedom with the Duke of Burgundy the Nation was great and covered itself with Glory but Alas how changed, how fallen when distributing stipendiary Aid to hostile Hosts. Their Valor was arrayed against itself and Brothers fell by the Swords of Brothers. They became at length the proverbial Examples of mercenary Disposition. And then neither Liberty no[r] Discipline nor Courage rescued Helvetian Fame from the Charge of Baseness.

Thus then We have seen that a People may be numerous powerful wealthy free brave and inured to War without being Great, and by reflecting on the Reason why a Combination of those Qualities and Circumstances will not alone suffice. We are close to the true Source and Principle of national Greatness. It is in the national Spirit. It is in that high, haughty, generous and noble Spirit which prizes Glory more than wealth and holds Honor dearer than Life. It is that Spirit, the inspiring Soul of Heroes which raises Men above the Level of Humanity. It is present with us when we read the Story of antient Rome. It [s]wells our Bosoms at the View of her gigantic Deeds and makes us feel that we must ever be irresistible while human Nature shall remain unchanged. I have called it a high haughty generous and noble Spirit. It is high—Elevated above all low and vulgar Considerations. It is haughty—Despising whatever is little and mean whether in Character Council or Conduct. It is generous—granting freely to the weak and to the Indigent Protection and Support. It is noble—Dreading Shame and Dishonor as the greatest Evil, esteeming Fame and Glory beyond all Things human.

When this Spirit prevails the Government, whatever it's Form, will be wise and energetic because such Government alone will be borne by such Men. And such a Government seeking the true Interest of those over whom they preside will find it in the Establishment of a national Character becoming the Spirit by which the Nation is inspired. Foreign Powers will then know that to withhold a due Respect and Deference is dangerous. That Wrongs may be forgiven but that Insults will be avenged. As a necessary Result every Member of the Society bears with him every where full Protection & when he appears his firm and manly Port mark him of a superior Order in the Race of Man. The Dignity of Sentiment which he has inhaled with his native Air gives to his Manner an Ease superior to the Politeness of Courts and a Grace unrivalled by the Majesty of Kings.

These are Blessings which march in the train of national Greatness and come on the Pinions of youthful Hope. I anticipate the Day when to command Respect in the re-motest Regions it will be sufficient to say I am an American. Our Flag shall then wave in Glory over the Ocean and our Commerce feel no Restraint but what our own Government may impose. Happy thrice happy Day. Thank God, to reach this envied State we need only to Will. Yes my countrymen. Our Destiny depends on our Will. But if we would stand high on the Record of Time that Will must be inflexible.

32

THOMAS JEFFERSON TO JOHN ADAMS
5 July 1814
Cappon 2:434

But why am I dosing you with these Ante-diluvian topics? Because I am glad to have some one to whom they are familiar, and who will not recieve them as if dropped from the moon. Our post-revolutionary youth are born under happier stars than you and I were. They acquire all learning in their mothers' womb, and bring it into the world ready-made. The information of books is no longer necessary; and all knolege which is not innate, is in contempt, or neglect at least. Every folly must run it's round; and so, I suppose, must that of self-learning, and self sufficiency; of rejecting the knolege acquired in past ages, and starting on the new ground of intuition. When sobered by experience I hope our successors will turn their attention to the advantages of education. I mean of education on the broad scale, and not that of the petty *academies*, as they call themselves, which are starting up in every neighborhood, and where one or two men, possessing Latin, and sometimes Greek, a knolege of the globes, and the first six books of Euclid, imagine and communicate this as the sum of science. They commit their pupils to the theatre of the world with just taste enough of learning to be alienated from industrious pursuits, and not enough to do service in the ranks of science. We have some exceptions indeed. I presented one to you lately, and we have some others. But the terms I use are general truths. I hope the necessity will at length be seen of establishing institutions, here as in Europe, where every branch of science, useful at this day, may be taught in it's highest degrees. Have you ever turned your thoughts to the plan of such an institution? I mean to a specification of the particular sciences of real use in human affairs, and how they might be so grouped as to require so many professors only as might bring them within the views of a just but enlightened economy? I should be happy in a communication of your ideas on this problem, either loose or digested.

33

[THOMAS JEFFERSON, JAMES MADISON, ET AL.,]
REPORT OF THE COMMISSIONERS APPOINTED TO
FIX THE SITE OF THE UNIVERSITY OF VIRGINIA
4 Aug. 1818
Early History 434–35

3, 4. In proceeding to the third and fourth duties prescribed by the Legislature, of reporting "the branches of learning, which should be taught in the University, and the number and description of the professorships they will require," the Commissioners were first to consider at what point it was understood that university education should commence? Certainly not with the alphabet, for reasons of expediency and impracticability, as well from the obvious sense of the Legislature, who, in the same act, make other provision for the primary instruction of the poor children, expecting, doubtless, that in other cases it would be provided by the parent, or become, perhaps, subject of future and further attention of the Legislature. The objects of this primary education determine its character and limits. These objects would be,

To give to every citizen the information he needs for the transaction of his own business;

To enable him to calculate for himself, and to express and preserve his ideas, his contracts and accounts, in writing;

To improve, by reading, his morals and faculties;

To understand his duties to his neighbors and country, and to discharge with competence the functions confided to him by either;

To know his rights; to exercise with order and justice those he retains; to choose with discretion the fiduciary of those he delegates; and to notice their conduct with diligence, with candor, and judgment;

And, in general, to observe with intelligence and faithfulness all the social relations under which he shall be placed.

To instruct the mass of our citizens in these, their rights, interests and duties, as men and citizens, being then the objects of education in the primary schools, whether private or public, in them should be taught reading, writing and numerical arithmetic, the elements of mensuration, (useful in so many callings,) and the outlines of geography and history. And this brings us to the point at which are to commence the higher branches of education, of which the Legislature require the development; those, for example, which are,

To form the statesmen, legislators and judges, on whom public prosperity and individual happiness are so much to depend;

To expound the principles and structure of government, the laws which regulate the intercourse of nations, those formed municipally for our own government, and a sound spirit of legislation, which, banishing all arbitrary and unnecessary restraint on individual action, shall leave us free to do whatever does not violate the equal rights of another;

To harmonize and promote the interests of agriculture, manufactures and commerce, and by well informed views of political economy to give a free scope to the public industry;

To develop the reasoning faculties of our youth, enlarge their minds, cultivate their morals, and instill into them the precepts of virtue and order;

To enlighten them with mathematical and physical sciences, which advance the arts, and administer to the health, the subsistence, and comforts of human life;

And, generally, to form them to habits of reflection and correct action, rendering them examples of virtue to others, and of happiness within themselves.

These are the objects of that higher grade of education, the benefits and blessings of which the Legislature now propose to provide for the good and ornament of their country, the gratification and happiness of their fellow-citizens, of the parent especially, and his progeny, on which all his affections are concentrated.

34

JAMES MADISON TO EDWARD LIVINGSTON
10 July 1822
Writings 9:101–3

Notwithstanding the general progress made within the two last centuries in favour of this branch of liberty, & the full establishment of it, in some parts of our Country, there remains in others a strong bias towards the old error, that without some sort of alliance or coalition between Govt. & Religion neither can be duly supported. Such indeed is the tendency to such a coalition, and such its corrupting influence on both the parties, that the danger cannot be too carefully guarded agst. And in a Govt. of opinion, like ours, the only effectual guard must be found in the soundness and stability of the general opinion on the subject. Every new & successful example therefore of a perfect separation between ecclesiastical and civil matters, is of importance. And I have no doubt that every new example, will succeed, as every past one has done, in shewing that religion & Govt. will both exist in greater purity, the less they are mixed together. It was the belief of all sects at one time that the establishment of Religion by law, was right & necessary; that the true religion ought to be established in exclusion of every other; And that the only question to be decided was which was the true religion. The example of Holland proved that a toleration of sects, dissenting from the established sect, was safe & even useful. The example of the Colonies, now States, which rejected religious establishments altogether, proved that all Sects might be safely & advantageously put on a footing of equal

& entire freedom; and a continuance of their example since the declaration of Independence, has shewn that its success in Colonies was not to be ascribed to their connection with the parent Country. If a further confirmation of the truth could be wanted, it is to be found in the examples furnished by the States, which have abolished their religious establishments. I cannot speak particularly of any of the cases excepting that of Virga. where it is impossible to deny that Religion prevails with more zeal, and a more exemplary priesthood than it ever did when established and patronised by Public authority. We are teaching the world the great truth that Govts. do better without Kings & Nobles than with them. The merit will be doubled by the other lesson that Religion flourishes in greater purity, without than with the aid of Govt.

35

JAMES MADISON TO W. T. BARRY
4 Aug. 1822
Writings 9:103–9

The liberal appropriations made by the Legislature of Kentucky for a general system of Education cannot be too much applauded. A popular Government, without popular information, or the means of acquiring it, is but a Prologue to a Farce or a Tragedy; or, perhaps both. Knowledge will forever govern ignorance: And a people who mean to be their own Governors, must arm themselves with the power which knowledge gives.

I have always felt a more than ordinary interest in the destinies of Kentucky. Among her earliest settlers were some of my particular friends and Neighbors. And I was myself among the foremost advocates for submitting to the Will of the "District" the question and the time of its becoming a separate member of the American family. Its rapid growth & signal prosperity in this character have afforded me much pleasure; which is not a little enhanced by the enlightened patriotism which is now providing for the State a Plan of Education embracing every class of Citizens, and every grade & department of Knowledge. No error is more certain than the one proceeding from a hasty & superficial view of the subject: that the people at large have no interest in the establishment of Academies, Colleges, and Universities, where a few only, and those not of the poorer classes can obtain for their sons the advantages of superior education. It is thought to be unjust that all should be taxed for the benefit of a part, and that too the part least needing it.

If provision were not made at the same time for every part, the objection would be a natural one. But, besides the consideration when the higher Seminaries belong to a plan of general education, that it is better for the poorer classes to have the aid of the richer by a general tax on property, than that every parent should provide at his own expence for the education of his children, it is certain that every Class is interested in establishments which give to the human mind its highest improvements, and to every Country its truest and most durable celebrity.

Learned Institutions ought to be favorite objects with every free people. They throw that light over the public mind which is the best security against crafty & dangerous encroachments on the public liberty. They are the nurseries of skilful Teachers for the schools distributed throughout the Community. They are themselves schools for the particular talents required for some of the Public Trusts, on the able execution of which the welfare of the people depends. They multiply the educated individuals from among whom the people may elect a due portion of their public Agents of every description; more especially of those who are to frame the laws; by the perspicuity, the consistency, and the stability, as well as by the just & equal spirit of which the great social purposes are to be answered.

Without such Institutions, the more costly of which can scarcely be provided by individual means, none but the few whose wealth enables them to support their sons abroad can give them the fullest education; and in proportion as this is done, the influence is monopolized which superior information every where possesses. At cheaper & nearer seats of Learning parents with slender incomes may place their sons in a course of education putting them on a level with the sons of the Richest. Whilst those who are without property, or with but little, must be peculiarly interested in a System which unites with the more Learned Institutions, a provision for diffusing through the entire Society the education needed for the common purposes of life. A system comprizing the Learned Institutions may be still further recommended to the more indigent class of Citizens by such an arrangement as was reported to the General Assembly of Virginia, in the year 1779, by a Committee[1] appointed to revise laws in order to adapt them to the genius of Republican Government. It made part of a "Bill for the more general diffusion of knowledge" that wherever a youth was ascertained to possess talents meriting an education which his parents could not afford, he should be carried forward at the public expence, from seminary to seminary, to the completion of his studies at the highest.

But why should it be necessary in this case, to distinguish the Society into classes according to their property? When it is considered that the establishment and endowment of Academies, Colleges, and Universities are a provision, not merely for the existing generation, but for succeeding ones also; that in Governments like ours a constant rotation of property results from the free scope to industry, and from the laws of inheritance, and when it is considered moreover, how much of the exertions and privations of all are meant not for themselves, but for their posterity, there can be little ground for objections from any class, to plans of which every class must have its turn of benefits. The rich man, when contributing to a permanent plan for the education of the poor, ought to reflect

---

[1] The report was made by Mr. Jefferson, Mr. Pendleton, and Mr. Wythe.

that he is providing for that of his own descendants; and the poor man who concurs in a provision for those who are not poor that at no distant day it may be enjoyed by descendants from himself. It does not require a long life to witness these vicissitudes of fortune.

It is among the happy peculiarities of our Union, that the States composing it derive from their relation to each other and to the whole, a salutary emulation, without the enmity involved in competitions among States alien to each other. This emulation, we may perceive, is not without its influence in several important respects; and in none ought it to be more felt than in the merit of diffusing the light and the advantages of Public Instruction. In the example therefore which Kentucky is presenting, she not only consults her own welfare, but is giving an impulse to any of her sisters who may be behind her in the noble career.

Throughout the Civilized World, nations are courting the praise of fostering Science and the useful Arts, and are opening their eyes to the principles and the blessings of Representative Government. The American people owe it to themselves, and to the cause of free Government, to prove by their establishments for the advancement and diffusion of Knowledge, that their political Institutions, which are attracting observation from every quarter, and are respected as Models, by the new-born States in our own Hemisphere, are as favorable to the intellectual and moral improvement of Man as they are conformable to his individual & social Rights. What spectacle can be more edifying or more seasonable, than that of Liberty & Learning, each leaning on the other for their mutual & surest support?

The Committee, of which your name is the first, have taken a very judicious course in endeavouring to avail Kentucky of the experience of elder States, in modifying her Schools. I enclose extracts from the laws of Virginia on that subject; though I presume they will give little aid; the less as they have as yet been imperfectly carried into execution. The States where such systems have been long in operation will furnish much better answers to many of the enquiries stated in your Circular. But after all, such is the diversity of local circumstances, more particularly as the population varies in density & sparseness, that the details suited to some may be little so to others. As the population however, is becoming less & less sparse, and it will be well in laying the foundation of a Good System, to have a view to this progressive change, much attention seems due to examples in the Eastern States, where the people are most compact, & where there has been the longest experience in plans of popular education.

I know not that I can offer on the occasion any suggestions not likely to occur to the Committee. Were I to hazard one, it would be in favour of adding to Reading, Writing, & Arithmetic, to which the instruction of the poor, is commonly limited, some knowledge of Geography; such as can easily be conveyed by a Globe & Maps, and a concise Geographical Grammar. And how easily & quickly might a general idea even, be conveyed of the Solar System, by the aid of a Planatarium of the Cheapest construction. No information seems better calculated to expand the mind and gratify curiosity than what would thus be imparted.

This is especially the case, with what relates to the Globe we inhabit, the Nations among which it is divided, and the characters and customs which distinguish them. An acquaintance with foreign Countries in this mode, has a kindred effect with that of seeing them as travellers, which never fails, in uncorrupted minds, to weaken local prejudices, and enlarge the sphere of benevolent feelings. A knowledge of the Globe & its various inhabitants, however slight, might moreover, create a taste for Books of Travels and Voyages; out of which might grow a general taste for History, an inexhaustible fund of entertainment & instruction. Any reading not of a vicious species must be a good substitute for the amusements too apt to fill up the leisure of the labouring classes.

36

JAMES MADISON TO THOMAS JEFFERSON
8 Feb. 1825
Writings 9:218–20

I have looked with attention over your intended proposal of a text book for the Law School. It is certainly very material that the true doctrines of liberty, as exemplified in our Political System, should be inculcated on those who are to sustain and may administer it. It is, at the same time, not easy to find standard books that will be both guides & guards for the purpose. Sidney & Locke are admirably calculated to impress on young minds the right of Nations to establish their own Governments, and to inspire a love of free ones; but afford no aid in guarding our Republican Charters against constructive violations. The Declaration of Independence, tho' rich in fundamental principles, and saying every thing that could be said in the same number of words, falls nearly under a like observation. The "Federalist" may fairly enough be regarded as the most authentic exposition of the text of the federal Constitution, as understood by the Body which prepared & the Authority which accepted it. Yet it did not foresee all the misconstructions which have occurred; nor prevent some that it did foresee. And what equally deserves remark, neither of the great rival Parties have acquiesced in all its comments. It may nevertheless be admissible as a School book, if any will be that goes so much into detail. It has been actually admitted into two Universities, if not more—those of Harvard and Rh: Island; but probably at the choice of the Professors, without any injunction from the superior authority. With repect to the Virginia Document of 1799, there may be more room for hesitation. Tho' corresponding with the predominant sense of the Nation; being of local origin & having reference to a state of Parties not yet extinct, an absolute prescription of it, might excite prejudices against the University as under Party Banners, and induce the more bigoted to withhold from it their sons, even when destined for other than the studies of the Law School. It may be added that the Document is not on every point satisfactory to all who belong to the same Party. Are we sure that to our brethren of the Board it is so? In framing a political creed, a like difficulty occurs as in the case of religion tho' the public right be very different in the two cases. If the Articles be in very general terms, they do not answer the purpose; if in very particular terms, they divide & exclude where meant to unite & fortify. The best that can be done in our case seems to be, to avoid the two extremes, by referring to selected Standards without requiring an unqualified conformity to them, which indeed might not in every instance be possible. The selection would give them authority with the Students, and might controul or counteract deviations of the Professor. I have, for your consideration, sketched a modification of the operative passage in your draught, with a view to relax the absoluteness of its injunction, and added to your list of Documents the Inaugural Speech and the Farewell Address of President Washington. They may help down what might be less readily swallowed, and contain nothing which is not good; unless it be the laudatory reference in the Address to the Treaty of 1795 with G. B. which ought not to weigh against the sound sentiments characterizing it.

After all, the most effectual safeguard against heretical intrusions into the School of Politics, will be an Able & Orthodox Professor, whose course of instruction will be an example to his successors, and may carry with it a sanction from the Visitors.

SEE ALSO:

Algernon Sidney, Discourses concerning Government (published posthumously 1698), Works 233–37 (1772)

James Burgh, Political Disquisitions 3:1–6, 30–31, 85–88, 90, 202–4, 419–21, 423–25 (1775)

Proclamation of the General Court of the Colony of Massachusetts-Bay, 23 Jan. 1776, Handlin 65–68

George Washington to John Banister, 21 Apr. 1778, Writings 11:286

James Warren to John Adams, 30 Apr. 1786, Warren-Adams Letters 2:272–73

John Adams to James Warren, 4 July 1786, Warren-Adams Letters 2:277

James Warren to John Adams, 22 Oct. 1786, Warren-Adams Letters 2:278–79

John Adams to James Warren, 9 Jan. 1787, Warren-Adams Letters 2:280–81

Noah Webster, Remarks on the Manners, Government, and Debt of the United States, 1787, Collection 81–87

Charles Turner, Massachusetts Ratifying Convention, 6 Feb. 1788, Storing 4.18.2

Impartial Examiner, no. 1, 5 Mar. 1788, Storing 5.14.14–15

Benjamin Rush, A Plan for a Federal University, 29 Oct. 1788, Letters 1:491–95

Benjamin Rush, The Bible as a School Book, 1791, Selected Writings 130

Mercy Warren, History of the Rise, Progress and Termination of the American Revolution, 1805, Storing 6.14.150–55

James Madison, Second Annual Message, 5 Dec. 1810, Richardson 1:485

New York Commission Report on a System for the Organization and Establishment of Common Schools, 14 Feb. 1812, T. E. Finegan, Free Schools: A Documentary History of the Free School Movement in New York State 37–39 (1921)

James Madison, Seventh Annual Message, 5 Dec. 1815, Richardson 1:568

James Madison to Peter S. DuPonceau, May 1821, Writings 9:63–64

Short Titles Used

Documentary citations given in short-title forms as "Life," "Papers," "Works," etc., are to be understood as referring to editions of the author of that particular document. Exceptions are clearly noted.

John Adams, Diary *Diary and Autobiography of John Adams.* Edited by L. H. Butterfield et al. 4 vols. Cambridge: Belknap Press of Harvard University Press, 1961.

John Adams, Papers *Papers of John Adams.* Edited by Robert J. Taylor et al. Cambridge: Belknap Press of Harvard University Press, 1977–.

John Adams, Works *The Works of John Adams.* Edited by Charles Francis Adams. 10 vols. Boston: Little, Brown & Co., 1850–56.
See also: Butterfield; Cappon; Warren-Adams Letters

J. Q. Adams, Writings *Writings of John Quincy Adams.* Edited by Worthington Chauncey Ford. 7 vols. New York: Macmillan Co., 1913–17.

Samuel Adams, Writings *The Writings of Samuel Adams.* Edited by Harry Alonzo Cushing. 4 vols. New York: G. P. Putnam's Sons, 1904–8.

American Archives *American Archives.* Edited by M. St. Clair Clarke and Peter Force. 4th ser., 6 vols. Washington, D.C., 1837–46. 5th ser., 3 vols. Washington, D.C., 1848–53.

American Colonial Documents Jensen, Merrill, ed. *American Colonial Documents to 1776.* English Historical Documents, edited by David C. Douglas, vol. 9. New York: Oxford University Press, 1969.

Annals *Annals of Congress. The Debates and Proceedings in the Congress of the United States.* "History of Congress." 42 vols. Washington, D.C.: Gales & Seaton, 1834–56.

Bailyn Bailyn, Bernard, ed. *Pamphlets of the American Revolution, 1750–1776.* Vol. 1, *1750–1765.* Cambridge: Belknap Press of Harvard University Press, 1965.

Blackstone, Commentaries Blackstone, William. *Commentaries on the Laws of England: A Facsimile of the First Edition of 1765–1769.* Chicago: University of Chicago Press, 1979.

Boyd Boyd, Julian P., ed. *Fundamental Laws and Constitutions of New Jersey, 1664–1964.* New Jersey Historical Series, vol. 17. Princeton: D. Van Nostrand Co., Inc., 1964.

Bradford, Of Plymouth Plantation Bradford, William. *Of Plymouth Plantation, 1620–1647.* Edited by Samuel Eliot Morison. New York: Modern Library, 1967.

Burgh [Burgh, James.] *Political Disquisitions: or, An Enquiry into Public Errors, Defects, and Abuses. . . .* 3 vols. London, 1774–75.

Burke, Works *The Works of the Right Honourable Edmund Burke.* 6 vols. London: Henry G. Bohn, 1854–56.

Burnett Burnett, Edmund C., ed. *Letters of Members of the Continental Congress.* 8 vols. Washington: Carnegie Institution of Washington, 1921–36.

Butterfield Adams, Abigail Smith. *The Book of Abigail and John: Selected Letters of the Adams Family, 1762–1784.* Edited by L. H. Butterfield et al. Cambridge: Harvard University Press, 1975.

Cannon *The Letters of Junius.* Edited by John Cannon. Oxford: At the Clarendon Press, 1978.

Cappon *The Adams-Jefferson Letters: The Complete Correspondence between Thomas Jefferson and Abigail and John Adams.* Edited by Lester J. Cappon. 2 vols. Chapel Hill: University of North Carolina Press for the Institute of Early American History and Culture, Williamsburg, Virginia, 1959.

Chase Chase, Frederick. *A History of Dartmouth College and the Town of Hanover New Hampshire.* Edited by John K. Lord. 2 vols. Cambridge: John Wilson & Son, 1891.

Colonial Records *The Colonial Records of North Carolina.* Edited by William L. Saunders. 10 vols. Raleigh: Josephus Daniels, 1886–90.

Crèvecoeur Crèvecoeur, J. Hector St. John. *Letters from an American Farmer.* New York: Albert & Charles Boni, 1925.

Documentary History *Documentary History of the Constitution of the United States of America, 1786–1870.* 5 vols. Washington, D.C.: Department of State, 1901–5.

Dumbauld Dumbauld, Edward. *The Bill of Rights and What It Means Today.* Norman: University of Oklahoma Press, 1957.

Early History *Early History of the University of Virginia, as Contained in the Letters of Thomas Jefferson and Joseph C. Cabell, Hitherto Unpublished. . . .* Richmond: J. W. Randolph, 1856.

Elliot Elliot, Jonathan, ed. *The Debates in the Several State Conventions on the Adoption of the Federal Constitution as Recommended by the General Convention at Philadelphia in 1787. . . .* 5 vols. 2d ed. 1888. Reprint. New York: Burt Franklin, n.d.

Emlyn Hale, Sir Matthew. *Historia Placitorum Coronae. The History of the Pleas of the Crown.* Edited by Sollom Emlyn. 2 vols. London, 1736. Reprint. Classical English Law Texts. London: Professional Books, Ltd., 1971.

Essays Ford, Paul Leicester, ed. *Essays on the Constitution of the United States, Published during Its Discussion by the People, 1787–1788.* Brooklyn: Historical Printing Club, 1892.

Farrand Farrand, Max, ed. *The Records of the Federal Convention of 1787.* Rev. ed. 4 vols. New Haven and London: Yale University Press, 1937.

Federalist Hamilton, Alexander; Madison, James; and Jay, John. *The Federalist.* Edited by Jacob E. Cooke. Middletown, Conn.: Wesleyan University Press, 1961.

Foster Foster, Sir Michael. *A Report of Some Proceedings on the Commission . . . for the Trial of the Rebels in the Year 1746 . . . , and of Other Crown Cases.* London, 1762. Reprint. Classical English Law Texts. Abingdon, England: Professional Books, Ltd., 1982.

Four Letters on Interesting Subjects *Four Letters on Interesting Subjects.* Philadelphia: 1776. Evans 14759.

Franklin, Papers *The Papers of Benjamin Franklin.* Edited by Leonard W. Labaree et al. New Haven: Yale University Press, 1959–.

Franklin, Writings *The Writings of Benjamin Franklin.* Edited by Albert Henry Smyth. 10 vols. New York: Macmillan Co., 1905–7.

Gerry, Life Austin, James T. *The Life of Elbridge Gerry. With Contemporary Letters.* 2 vols. Boston, 1828–29.

Gray Hale, Sir Matthew. *The History of the Common Law of England.* Edited by Charles M. Gray. Classics of British Historical Literature. Chicago: University of Chicago Press, 1971.

Gwyn Gwyn, W. B. *The Meaning of the Separation of Powers: An Analysis of the Doctrine from Its Origin to the Adoption of the United States Constitution.* Tulane Studies in Political Science, vol. 9. New Orleans: Tulane University, 1965.

Hamilton, Papers *The Papers of Alexander Hamilton.* Edited by Harold C. Syrett et al. 26 vols. New York and London: Columbia University Press, 1961–79.

See also: Federalist

Handlin Handlin, Oscar, and Handlin, Mary, eds. *The Popular Sources of Political Authority: Documents on the Massachusetts Constitution of 1780.* Cambridge: Belknap Press of Harvard University Press, 1966.

Harrington *The Political Writings of James Harrington: Representative Selections.* Edited by Charles Blitzer. New York: Liberal Arts Press, 1955.

History of Congress *History of Congress; Exhibiting a Classification of the Proceedings of the Senate, and the House of Representatives, from March 4, 1789, to March 3, 1793. . . . Philadelphia: Lea & Blanchard, 1843.*

Hume Hume, David. *Essays Moral, Political and Literary.* 1742, 1752.

Hurst Hurst, James Willard. *The Law of Treason in the United States: Collected Essays.* Westport, Conn.: Greenwood Publishing Corp., 1971.

Iredell, Life *Life and Correspondence of James Iredell.* Edited by Griffith J. McRee. 2 vols. New York: D. Appleton & Co., 1857.

Iredell, Papers *The Papers of James Iredell.* Edited by Don Higginbotham. Raleigh: North Carolina Division of Archives and History, 1976–.

Jacobson Trenchard, John, and Gordon, Thomas. *Cato's Letters.* In *The English Libertarian Heritage,* edited by David L. Jacobson. American Heritage Series. Indianapolis: Bobbs-Merrill, 1965.

Jamestown, The Three Charters of the Virginia Company of London *The Three Charters of the Virginia Company of London.* Jamestown 350th Anniversary Historical Booklet, no. 4. 1957

Jay, Correspondence *The Correspondence and Public Papers of John Jay.* Edited by Henry P. Johnston. 4 vols. New York and London: G. P. Putnam's Sons, 1890–93.

Jay, Unpublished Papers *John Jay: Unpublished Papers.* Edited by Richard B. Morris et al. New York: Harper & Row, 1975–.

See also: Federalist

Jefferson, Notes on the State of Virginia Jefferson, Thomas. *Notes on the State of Virginia.* Edited by William Peden. Chapel Hill: University of North Carolina Press for the Institute of Early American History and Culture, Williamsburg, Virginia, 1954.

Jefferson, Papers *The Papers of Thomas Jefferson.* Edited by Julian P. Boyd et al. Princeton: Princeton University Press, 1950–.

Jefferson, Works *The Works of Thomas Jefferson.* Collected and edited by Paul Leicester Ford. Federal Edition. 12 vols. New York and London: G. P. Putnam's Sons, 1904–5.

Jefferson, Writings *The Writings of Thomas Jefferson.* Edited by Andrew A. Lipscomb and Albert Ellery Bergh. 20 vols. Washington: Thomas Jefferson Memorial Association, 1905.

Jensen *The Documentary History of the Ratification of the Constitution.* Edited by Merrill Jensen et al. Madison: State Historical Society of Wisconsin, 1976–.

Journals *Journals of the Continental Congress, 1774–1789.* Edited by Worthington C. Ford et al. 34 vols. Washington, D.C.: Government Printing Office, 1904–37.

Kent Kent, James. *Commentaries on American Law.* 4 vols. New York, 1826–30.

King, Life *The Life and Correspondence of Rufus King.* Edited by Charles R. King. 6 vols. New York: G. P. Putnam's Sons, 1894–1900.

Land Eddis, William. *Letters from America.* Edited by Aubrey C. Land. Cambridge: Belknap Press of Harvard University Press, 1969.

Leake Leake, Isaac Q. *Memoir of the Life and Times of General John Lamb.* Albany, N.Y., 1857.

Lee, Letters *The Letters of Richard Henry Lee.* Edited by James Curtis Ballagh. 2 vols. New York: Macmillan Co., 1911–14.

Lincoln, Collected Works *The Collected Works of Abraham Lincoln.* Edited by Roy P. Basler et al. 8 vols. New Brunswick, N.J.: Rutgers University Press, 1953.

Locke, Second Treatise Locke, John. *Two Treatises of Government.* Edited by Peter Laslett. New York: Mentor Books, New American Library, 1965.

See also: Montuori

Machiavelli Machiavelli, Niccolò. *Discourses on the First Ten Books of Titus Livius.* Translated by Christian E. Detmold. New York: Modern Library, 1940.

McMaster McMaster, John Bach, and Stone, Frederick D., eds. *Pennsylvania and the Federal Constitution, 1787–1788.* Lancaster: Published for the Subscribers by the Historical Society of Pennsylvania, 1888.

Madison, Letters *Letters and Other Writings of James Madison.* Published by order of Congress. 4 vols. Philadelphia: J. B. Lippincott & Co., 1865.

Madison, Papers *The Papers of James Madison.* Edited by William T. Hutchinson et al. Chicago and London: University of Chicago Press, 1962–77 (vols. 1–10); Charlottesville: University Press of Virginia, 1977– (vols. 11–).

Madison, W. & M. Q. Fleet, Elizabeth. "Madison's 'Detached Memoranda.' " *William and Mary Quarterly*, 3d ser., 3 (1946): 534–68.

Madison, Writings *The Writings of James Madison.* Edited by Gaillard Hunt. 9 vols. New York: G. P. Putnam's Sons, 1900–1910.

See also: Federalist

Marshall, Life Beveridge, Albert J. *The Life of John Marshall.* 4 vols. Boston: Houghton Mifflin Co., 1916–19.

Marshall, Papers *The Papers of John Marshall.* Edited by Herbert A. Johnson et al. Chapel Hill: University of North Carolina Press, in association with the Institute of Early American History and Culture, Williamsburg, Virginia, 1974–.

Maryland Archives *Archives of Maryland: Proceedings and Acts of the General Assembly of Maryland.* Edited by William Hand Browne. Vol. 1. Baltimore: Maryland Historical Society, 1883.

Mason, Papers *The Papers of George Mason, 1725–1792.* Edited by Robert A. Rutland. 3 vols. Chapel Hill: University of North Carolina Press, 1970.

Meade Meade, Robert Douthat. *Patrick Henry: Patriot in the Making.* Philadelphia: J. B. Lippincott Co., 1957.

MHS Collections *Collections of the Massachusetts Historical Society.*

Monroe, Writings *The Writings of James Monroe.* Edited by Stanislaus Murray Hamilton. 7 vols. New York and London: G. P. Putnam's Sons, 1898–1903.

Montesquieu *The Spirit of Laws.* 1748. Translated by Thomas Nugent, 1750.

Montuori Locke, John. *A Letter concerning Toleration.* Latin and English texts revised and edited by Mario Montuori. The Hague: Martinus Nijhoff, 1963.

Gouverneur Morris, Amerikastudien Adams, Willi Paul. " 'The Spirit of Commerce Requires that Property be Sacred': Gouverneur Morris and the American Revolution." *Amerikastudien* 21 (1976): 309–31.

Gouverneur Morris, Life *The Life of Gouverneur Morris, with Selections from His Correspondence and Miscellaneous Papers.* Edited by Jared Sparks. 3 vols. Boston, 1832.

Robert Morris, Papers *The Papers of Robert Morris, 1781–1784.* Edited by E. James Ferguson et al. Pittsburgh: University of Pittsburgh Press, 1973–.

New England Federalism Adams, Henry, ed. *Documents Relating to New-England Federalism.* Boston: Little, Brown & Co., 1877.

Niles Niles, Hezekiah, *Principles and Acts of the Revolution in America.* Centennial Offering. New York: A. S. Barnes & Co., 1876.

Old Family Letters Biddle, Alexander. *Old Family Letters.* Ser. A. Philadelphia: J. B. Lippincott Co., 1892.

Otis, Political Writings "Some Political Writings of James Otis." Collected by Charles F. Mullett. *University of Missouri Studies* 4 (1929): 257–432.

Paine, Life *The Life and Works of Thomas Paine.* Edited by William M. Van der Weyde. Patriots' Edition. 10 vols. New Rochelle, N.Y.: Thomas Paine National Historical Association, 1925.

Pamphlets Ford, Paul Leicester, ed. *Pamphlets on the Constitution of the United States, Published during Its Discussion by the People, 1787–1788.* Brooklyn, 1888. Reprint. New York: De Capo Press, 1968.

Penn, Select Works *The Select Works of William Penn.* 5 vols. 3d ed. London, 1782.

Pickering, Life Upham, Charles W. *The Life of Timothy Pickering.* 2 vols. Boston: Little, Brown & Co., 1873.

Pinkney Wheaton, Henry. *Some Account of the Life, Writings, and Speeches of William Pinkney.* Baltimore: E. J. Coale, 1826.

Randolph, History of Virginia Randolph, Edmund. *History of Virginia.* Edited by Arthur H. Shaffer. Charlottesville: University Press of Virginia for the Virginia Historical Society, 1970.

Rawle Rawle, William. *A View of the Constitution of the United States of America.* 2d ed. Philadelphia, 1829. Reprint. New York: Da Capo Press, 1970.

Read, Life Read, William Thompson. *Life and Correspondence of George Read.* Philadelphia: J. B. Lippincott & Co., 1870.

Records of the Federal Convention. *See* Farrand

Remonstrance and Petition, W. & M. Q. Schmidt, F. T., and Wilhelm, B. R. "Early Proslavery Petitions in Virginia." *William and Mary Quarterly*, 3d ser., 30 (1973): 133–46.

Richardson Richardson, James D., comp. *A Compilation of the Messages and Papers of the Presidents, 1789–1897.* 10 vols. Washington, D.C.: Government Printing Office, 1896–99.

Robertson Robertson, C. Grant, ed. *Select Statutes, Cases and Documents to Illustrate English Constitutional History, 1660–1832.* 4th ed., rev. London: Methuen & Co., Ltd., 1923.

Rush, Letters *Letters of Benjamin Rush.* Edited by L. H. Butterfield. 2 vols. Memoirs of the American Philosophical Society, vol. 30, parts 1 and 2. Princeton: Princeton University Press, for the American Philosophical Society, 1951.

Rush, Selected Writings *The Selected Writings of Benjamin Rush.* Edited by Dagobert D. Runes. New York: Philosophical Library, 1947.

Scribner *Revolutionary Virginia: The Road to Independence.* Vol 6, *The Time for Decision, 1776: A Documentary Record*, edited by Robert L. Scribner and Brent Tarter. Charlottesville: University Press of Virginia for the Virginia Independence Bicentennial Commission, 1981.

Sidney, Works *The Works of Algernon Sydney. A New Edition.* London, 1772.

Sources *Sources of Our Liberties.* Edited by Richard L. Perry under the general supervision of John C. Cooper. [Chicago:] American Bar Foundation, 1952.

State Trials *State Trials of the United States during the Administrations of Washington and Adams.* Edited by Francis Wharton. Philadelphia: Carey & Hart, 1849.

Stokes Stokes, Anton Phelps, ed. *Church and State in the United States.* 3 vols. New York: Harper & Bros., 1950.

Storing Storing, Herbert J., ed. *The Complete Anti-Federalist.* 7 vols. Chicago: University of Chicago Press, 1981.

Story Story, Joseph. *Commentaries on the Constitution of the United States.* 3 vols. Boston, 1833.

Tansill *Documents Illustrative of the Formation of the Union of the American States.* Edited by Charles C. Tansill. 69th Cong., 1st sess. House Doc. No. 398. Washington, D.C.: Government Printing Office, 1927.

Taylor Taylor, Robert J., ed. *Massachusetts, Colony to Commonwealth: Documents on the Formation of Its Constitution, 1775–1780.* Chapel Hill: University of North Carolina Press for the Institute of Early American History and Culture, Williamsburg, Virginia, 1961.

Thorpe Thorpe, Francis Newton, ed. *The Federal and State Constitutions, Colonial Charters, and Other Organic Laws of the States, Territories, and Colonies Now or Heretofore Forming the United States of America.* 7 vols. Washington, D.C.: Government Printing Office, 1909.

Tucker, Blackstone's Commentaries Tucker, St. George. *Blackstone's Commentaries: With Notes of Reference to the Constitution and Laws of the Federal Government of the United States and of the Commonwealth of Virginia.* 5 vols. Philadelphia, 1803. Reprint. South Hackensack, N.J.: Rothman Reprints, 1969.

Walker, U. Pa. L. Rev. Radin, Max. "The Doctrine of the Separation of Powers in Seventeenth Century Controversies." *University of Pennsylvania Law Review* 86 (1938): 842–66.

Warren, Life Frothingham, Richard. *Life and Times of Joseph Warren.* Boston: Little, Brown & Co., 1865.

Warren-Adams Letters *Warren-Adams Letters, Being Chiefly a Correspondence among John Adams, Samuel Adams, and James Warren.* Vol. 2, 1778–1814. Collections of the Massachusetts Historical Society, vol. 73. [Boston:] Massachusetts Historical Society, 1925.

Washington, Writings *The Writings of George Washington from the Original Manuscript Sources, 1745–1799.* Edited by John C. Fitzpatrick. 39 vols. Washington, D.C.: Government Printing Office, 1931–44.

Webster, Collection Webster, Noah. *A Collection of Essays and Fugitiv Writings on Moral, Historical, Political and Literary Subjects.* Boston, 1790. Reprint. Delmar, N.Y.: Scholars' Facsimiles & Reprints, 1977.

Webster, Political Papers Webster, Noah. *A Collection of Papers on Political, Literary and Moral Subjects.* New York, 1843. Reprint. New York: Burt Franklin, 1968.

Wharton Wharton, Francis, ed. *The Revolutionary Diplomatic Correspondence of the United States.* 6 vols. Washington, D.C.: Government Printing Office, 1889.

Wilson, Works *The Works of James Wilson.* Edited by Robert Green McCloskey. 2 vols. Cambridge: Belknap Press of Harvard University Press, 1967.

Winthrop Winthrop, John. *The History of New England from 1630 to 1649.* Edited by James Savage. 2 vols. Boston: Little, Brown & Co., 1853.

Woodhouse Woodhouse, A. S. P., ed. *Puritanism and Liberty, Being the Army Debates (1647–9) from the Clarke Manuscripts with Supplementary Documents.* 2d ed. London: J. M. Dent & Sons Ltd., 1951.

Index of Constitutional Provisions

Table of Cases

State v. ——, 1 Hayw. 28 (N.C. 1794), Amend. V (due process), no. 16

—— v. *Edwards,* 2 Nott & McC. 376 (S.C. 1819), Amends. V–VI, no. 39

—— v. *Garrigues,* 1 Hayw. 241 (N.C. 1795), Amends. V–VI, no. 28

—— v. *Howell,* R. M. Charlton 120 (Ga. 1821), 4.2.2, no. 7; Amend. VIII, no. 17

—— v. *Mitchell,* 3 Ind. 229 (1833), Amend. II, no. 11

—— v. *Randall,* 2 Aiken 89 (Vt. 1827), 1.8.6, no. 3

—— v. *Squires,* 1 Tyler 147 (Vt. 1801), Amends. V–VI, no. 30

—— v. *Tutt,* 2 Bailey 44 (S.C. 1830), 1.8.6, no. 4

Strawbridge v. *Curtiss,* 3 Cranch 267 (1806), 3.2.1, no. 49

Stuart v. *Laird,* 1 Cranch 299 (1803), 3.1, no. 27

Sturges v. *Crowninshield,* 4 Wheat. 122 (1819), 1.8.4 (bankruptcy), no. 10

Taylor v. *Briden,* 8 Johns. R. 172 (N.Y. 1811), 4.1, no. 9

The Thomas & Henry, 1 Marshall's C.C. 367 (C.C.D.Va. 1818), Amend. V (due process), no. 21

Titus Oates, Case of, 10 How. St. Tr. 1079, 1316 (K.B. 1685), Amend. VIII, no. 1

Treasurer v. *Moore,* 3 Brev. 550 (S.C. 1815), Amend. IV, no. 19

Turner v. *Bank of North America,* 4 Dall. 8 (1799), 3.2.1, no. 43

United States v. *Bailey,* 24 Fed. Cas. 937, no. 14,495 (C.C.D.Tenn. 1834), 1.8.3 (Indians), no. 12

—— v. *Benner,* 24 Fed. Cas. 1084, no. 14,568 (C.C.E.D.Pa. 1830), 2.2.2–3, no. 33

—— v. *Bevans,* 3 Wheat. 336 (1818), 3.2.1, no. 71

—— v. *Burr,* 25 Fed. Cas. 25, no. 14,692b (C.C.D.Va. 1807), Amends. V–VI, no. 33

—— v. *Burr,* 25 Fed. Cas. 30, no. 14,692d (C.C.D.Va. 1807), 2.1.1, no. 19

—— v. *Burr,* 25 Fed. Cas. 38, no. 14,692e (C.C.D.Va. 1807), Amends. V–VI, no. 34

—— v. *Burr,* 25 Fed. Cas. 49, no. 14,692g (C.C.D.Va. 1807), Amends. V–VI, no. 35

—— v. *Burr,* 25 Fed. Cas. 55, no. 14,693 (C.C.D.Va. 1807), 3.3.1–2, no. 22

—— v. *Charles,* 25 Fed. Cas. 409, no. 14,786 (C.C.D.C. 1813), Amends. V–VI, no. 36

—— v. *Cisna,* 25 Fed. Cas. 422, no. 14,795 (C.C.D.Ohio 1835), 1.8.3 (Indians), no. 13

—— v. *Coolidge,* 1 Wheat. 415 (1816), 3.2.1, no. 66

—— v. *Cooper,* 25 Fed. Cas. 631, no. 14,865 (C.C.D.Pa. 1800), Amend. I (speech), no. 25

—— v. *Cornell,* 25 Fed. Cas. 646, no. 14,867 (C.C.D.R.I. 1819), 1.8.17, no. 16

—— v. *Fisher,* 2 Cranch 358 (1805), 1.8.4 (bankruptcy), no. 4

—— v. *Gilbert,* 25 Fed. Cas. 1287, no. 15,204 (C.C.D.Mass. 1834), Amends. V–VI, no. 53

—— v. *Gillies,* 25 Fed. Cas. 1321, no. 15,206 (C.C.D.Pa. 1815), 1.8.4 (citizenship), no. 18

—— v. *Gooding,* 12 Wheat. 460 (1827), Amends. V–VI, no. 45

—— v. *Hart,* 26 Fed. Cas. 193, no. 15,316 (C.C.D.Pa. 1817), 6.2, no. 33

—— v. *Hoar,* 26 Fed. Cas. 329, no. 15,373 (C.C.D.Mass. 1821), 6.2, no. 36

—— v. *Hoxie,* 26 Fed. Cas. 397, no. 15,407 (C.C.D.Vt. 1808), 3.3.1–2, no. 23

—— v. *Hudson & Goodwin,* 7 Cranch 32 (1812), 3.2.1, no. 56

—— v. *Insurgents,* 26 Fed. Cas. 499, no. 15,443 (C.C.D.Pa. 1795), Amends. V–VI, no. 27

—— v. *Jacobson,* 26 Fed. Cas. 567, no. 15,461 (C.C.D.N.Y. 1817), 3.1, no. 33

—— v. *Marchant,* 12 Wheat. 480 (1827), Amends. V–VI, no. 46

—— v. *Maurice,* 2 Marshall's C.C. 96 (C.C.D.Va. 1823), 2.2.2–3, no. 55

—— v. *Miller,* 26 Fed. Cas. 1254, no. 15,772 (C.C.D.C. 1821), Amends. V–VI, no. 41

—— v. *More,* 3 Cranch 159 (1805), 3.2.2, no. 8

—— v. *Ortega,* 11 Wheat. 467 (1826), 3.2.1, no. 81

—— v. *Perez,* 9 Wheat. 579 (1824), Amends. V–VI, no. 43

—— v. *Peters,* 5 Cranch 115 (1809), 3.2.1, no. 51

—— v. *Rathbone,* 27 Fed. Cas. 711, no. 16,121 (C.C.S.D.N.Y. 1828), Amend. VII, no. 19

—— v. *Ravara,* 27 Fed. Cas. 713, nos. 16,122, 16,122a (C.C.D.Pa. 1793, 1794), 3.2.1, no. 36

—— v. *Robins,* 27 Fed. Cas. 825, no. 16,175 (D.S.C. 1799), 6.2, no. 25

—— v. *Rose,* 2 Cranch C.C. 567 (C.C.D.C. 1825), Amend. VII, no. 18

—— v. *Saline Bank,* 1 Pet. 100 (1828), Amends. V–VI, no. 47

—— v. *Schooner Little Charles,* 1 Marshall's C.C. 380 (C.C.D.Va. 1819), 3.2.1, no. 73

—— v. *Schooner Peggy,* 1 Cranch 103 (1801), 6.2, no. 27

—— v. *Shive,* 27 Fed. Cas. 1065, no. 16,278 (C.C.E.D.Pa. 1832), 3.2.3, no. 18; Amends. V–VI, no. 51

—— v. *Smith,* 5 Wheat. 153 (1820), 1.8.10, no. 9

—— v. *The William,* 28 Fed. Cas. 614, no. 16,700 (D.Mass. 1808), 1.8.3 (commerce), no. 12

—— v. *Wilson,* 7 Pet. 150 (1833), 2.2.1, no. 29

—— v. *Worrall,* 2 Dall. 384 (C.C.D.Pa. 1798), 3.2.1, no. 40

—— v. *Yale Todd* (1794), in *United States* v. *Ferreira,* 13 How. 40 (1851), 3.2.1, no. 37

University of North Carolina v. *Fox,* 1 Mur. 58 (N.C. 1805), Amend. V (due process), no. 19

Updegraph v. *Commonwealth,* 11 Serg. & Rawle 394 (Pa. 1824), Amend. I (speech), no. 30

Vanderheyden v. *Young,* 11 Johns. R. 150 (N.Y. 1814), 1.8.16, no. 14

Vanhorne's Lessee v. *Dorrance,* 2 Dall. 304 (C.C.D.Pa. 1795), vol. 1, ch. 16, no. 24; Amend. V (due process), no. 17

Ware v. *Hylton,* 3 Dall. 199 (1796), 6.2, no. 21

Wayman v. *Southard,* 10 Wheat. 1 (1825), 1.1, no. 8

Wellington, et al., Petitioners, 16 Pick. 87 (Mass. 1834), Amend. V (due process), no. 27

Wetherbee v. *Johnson,* 14 Mass. 412 (1817), 3.2.1, no. 69

Wharton v. *Morris,* 1 Dall. 125 (Pa. 1785), 1.8.5, no. 4

Wheaton v. *Peters,* 8 Pet. 591 (1834), 1.8.8, no. 15

Wilkes v. *Wood,* 98 Eng. Rep. 489 (C.P. 1763), Amend. IV, no. 4

Willson v. *Blackbird Creek Marsh Co.,* 2 Pet. 245 (1829), 1.8.3 (commerce), no. 20

Wiscart v. *D'Auchy,* 3 Dall. 321 (1796), 3.2.2, no. 7

Wright v. *Deacon,* 5 Serg. & Rawle 62 (Pa. 1819), 4.2.3, no. 11

Yates v. *Lansing,* 5 Johns. R. 282 (N.Y. 1810), 3.1, no. 30

Index of Authors and Documents

References are to chapter or to constitutional section, and to document number. References to volume 1 are by chapter and document number (e.g., ch. 15, no. 23); references to constitutional provisions in volumes 2–4 are by article, section, clause, and document number (e.g., 1.8.8, no. 12); and references to volume 5 are by Amendment and document number (e.g., Amend. I [religion], no. 66). In the case of documents whose several clauses are ranged under a large number of headings (e.g., the Bill of Rights of 1689, the Massachusetts Constitution of 1780, and the like), reference is made only to appearances of the complete text.